Code of Federal Regulations

Title 12
Banks and Banking

Parts 600 to 899

Revised as of January 1, 2012

Containing a codification of documents
of general applicability and future effect

As of January 1, 2012

Published by the Office of the Federal Register
National Archives and Records Administration
as a Special Edition of the Federal Register

Table of Contents

	Page
Explanation	v

Title 12:

    Chapter VI—Farm Credit Administration 3

    Chapter VII—National Credit Union Administration 351

    Chapter VIII—Federal Financing Bank 1009

Finding Aids:

    Table of CFR Titles and Chapters 1019

    Alphabetical List of Agencies Appearing in the CFR 1039

    List of CFR Sections Affected 1049

Cite this Code: CFR

To cite the regulations in this volume use title, part and section number. Thus, 12 CFR 600.1 *refers to title 12, part 600, section 1.*

Explanation

The Code of Federal Regulations is a codification of the general and permanent rules published in the Federal Register by the Executive departments and agencies of the Federal Government. The Code is divided into 50 titles which represent broad areas subject to Federal regulation. Each title is divided into chapters which usually bear the name of the issuing agency. Each chapter is further subdivided into parts covering specific regulatory areas.

Each volume of the Code is revised at least once each calendar year and issued on a quarterly basis approximately as follows:

Title 1 through Title 16..as of January 1
Title 17 through Title 27..as of April 1
Title 28 through Title 41..as of July 1
Title 42 through Title 50..as of October 1

The appropriate revision date is printed on the cover of each volume.

LEGAL STATUS

The contents of the Federal Register are required to be judicially noticed (44 U.S.C. 1507). The Code of Federal Regulations is prima facie evidence of the text of the original documents (44 U.S.C. 1510).

HOW TO USE THE CODE OF FEDERAL REGULATIONS

The Code of Federal Regulations is kept up to date by the individual issues of the Federal Register. These two publications must be used together to determine the latest version of any given rule.

To determine whether a Code volume has been amended since its revision date (in this case, January 1, 2012), consult the "List of CFR Sections Affected (LSA)," which is issued monthly, and the "Cumulative List of Parts Affected," which appears in the Reader Aids section of the daily Federal Register. These two lists will identify the Federal Register page number of the latest amendment of any given rule.

EFFECTIVE AND EXPIRATION DATES

Each volume of the Code contains amendments published in the Federal Register since the last revision of that volume of the Code. Source citations for the regulations are referred to by volume number and page number of the Federal Register and date of publication. Publication dates and effective dates are usually not the same and care must be exercised by the user in determining the actual effective date. In instances where the effective date is beyond the cut-off date for the Code a note has been inserted to reflect the future effective date. In those instances where a regulation published in the Federal Register states a date certain for expiration, an appropriate note will be inserted following the text.

OMB CONTROL NUMBERS

The Paperwork Reduction Act of 1980 (Pub. L. 96-511) requires Federal agencies to display an OMB control number with their information collection request.

Many agencies have begun publishing numerous OMB control numbers as amendments to existing regulations in the CFR. These OMB numbers are placed as close as possible to the applicable recordkeeping or reporting requirements.

OBSOLETE PROVISIONS

Provisions that become obsolete before the revision date stated on the cover of each volume are not carried. Code users may find the text of provisions in effect on a given date in the past by using the appropriate numerical list of sections affected. For the period before April 1, 2001, consult either the List of CFR Sections Affected, 1949–1963, 1964–1972, 1973–1985, or 1986–2000, published in eleven separate volumes. For the period beginning April 1, 2001, a "List of CFR Sections Affected" is published at the end of each CFR volume.

"[RESERVED]" TERMINOLOGY

The term "[Reserved]" is used as a place holder within the Code of Federal Regulations. An agency may add regulatory information at a "[Reserved]" location at any time. Occasionally "[Reserved]" is used editorially to indicate that a portion of the CFR was left vacant and not accidentally dropped due to a printing or computer error.

INCORPORATION BY REFERENCE

What is incorporation by reference? Incorporation by reference was established by statute and allows Federal agencies to meet the requirement to publish regulations in the Federal Register by referring to materials already published elsewhere. For an incorporation to be valid, the Director of the Federal Register must approve it. The legal effect of incorporation by reference is that the material is treated as if it were published in full in the Federal Register (5 U.S.C. 552(a)). This material, like any other properly issued regulation, has the force of law.

What is a proper incorporation by reference? The Director of the Federal Register will approve an incorporation by reference only when the requirements of 1 CFR part 51 are met. Some of the elements on which approval is based are:

(a) The incorporation will substantially reduce the volume of material published in the Federal Register.

(b) The matter incorporated is in fact available to the extent necessary to afford fairness and uniformity in the administrative process.

(c) The incorporating document is drafted and submitted for publication in accordance with 1 CFR part 51.

What if the material incorporated by reference cannot be found? If you have any problem locating or obtaining a copy of material listed as an approved incorporation by reference, please contact the agency that issued the regulation containing that incorporation. If, after contacting the agency, you find the material is not available, please notify the Director of the Federal Register, National Archives and Records Administration, 8601 Adelphi Road, College Park, MD 20740-6001, or call 202-741-6010.

CFR INDEXES AND TABULAR GUIDES

A subject index to the Code of Federal Regulations is contained in a separate volume, revised annually as of January 1, entitled CFR INDEX AND FINDING AIDS. This volume contains the Parallel Table of Authorities and Rules. A list of CFR titles, chapters, subchapters, and parts and an alphabetical list of agencies publishing in the CFR are also included in this volume.

An index to the text of "Title 3—The President" is carried within that volume.

The Federal Register Index is issued monthly in cumulative form. This index is based on a consolidation of the "Contents" entries in the daily Federal Register.

A List of CFR Sections Affected (LSA) is published monthly, keyed to the revision dates of the 50 CFR titles.

REPUBLICATION OF MATERIAL

There are no restrictions on the republication of material appearing in the Code of Federal Regulations.

INQUIRIES

For a legal interpretation or explanation of any regulation in this volume, contact the issuing agency. The issuing agency's name appears at the top of odd-numbered pages.

For inquiries concerning CFR reference assistance, call 202–741–6000 or write to the Director, Office of the Federal Register, National Archives and Records Administration, 8601 Adelphi Road, College Park, MD 20740-6001 or e-mail fedreg.info@nara.gov.

THIS TITLE

Title 12—BANKS AND BANKING is composed of eight volumes. The parts in these volumes are arranged in the following order: Parts 1–199, 200–219, 220–229, 230–299, 300–499, 500–599, part 600–899, and 900–end. The first volume containing parts 1–199 is comprised of chapter I—Comptroller of the Currency, Department of the Treasury. The second, third and fourth volumes containing parts 200–299 are comprised of chapter II—Federal Reserve System. The fifth volume containing parts 300–499 is comprised of chapter III—Federal Deposit Insurance Corporation and chapter IV—Export-Import Bank of the United States. The sixth volume containing parts 500–599 is comprised of chapter V—Office of Thrift Supervision, Department of the Treasury. The seventh volume containing parts 600–899 is comprised of chapter VI—Farm Credit Administration, chapter VII—National Credit Union Administration, chapter VIII—Federal Financing Bank. The eighth volume containing part 900–end is comprised of chapter IX—Federal Housing Finance Board, chapter XI—Federal Financial Institutions Examination Council, chapter XIV—Farm Credit System Insurance Corporation, chapter XV—Department of the Treasury, chapter XVII—Office of Federal Housing Enterprise Oversight, Department of Housing and Urban Development and chapter XVIII—Community Development Financial Institutions Fund, Department of the Treasury. The contents of these volumes represent all of the current regulations codified under this title of the CFR as of January 1, 2012.

For this volume, Jonn V. Lilyea was Chief Editor. The Code of Federal Regulations publication program is under the direction of Michael L. White, assisted by Ann Worley.

Title 12—Banks and Banking

(This book contains part 600 to 899)

	Part
CHAPTER VI—Farm Credit Administration	600
CHAPTER VII—National Credit Union Administration	700
CHAPTER VIII—Federal Financing Bank	810

CHAPTER VI—FARM CREDIT ADMINISTRATION

SUBCHAPTER A—ADMINISTRATIVE PROVISIONS

Part		Page
600	Organization and functions	5
601	Employee responsibilities and conduct	6
602	Releasing information	7
603	Privacy Act regulations	14
604	Farm Credit Administration Board meetings	18
605	Information	21
606	Enforcement of nondiscrimination on the basis of handicap in programs or activities conducted by the Farm Credit Administration	23
607	Assessment and apportionment of administrative expenses	29
608	Collection of claims owed the United States	34

SUBCHAPTER B—FARM CREDIT SYSTEM

609	Electronic commerce	47
610	Registration of mortgage loan originators	50
611	Organization	56
612	Standards of conduct and referral of known or suspected criminal violations	97
613	Eligibility and scope of financing	106
614	Loan policies and operations	113
615	Funding and fiscal affairs, loan policies and operations, and funding operations	158
616	Leasing	209
617	Borrower rights	211
618	General provisions	225
619	Definitions	234
620	Disclosure to shareholders	237
621	Accounting and reporting requirements	254
622	Rules of practice and procedure	261
623	Practice before the Farm Credit Administration	275
624	[Reserved]	
625	Application for award of fees and other expenses under the Equal Access to Justice Act	279
626	Nondiscrimination in lending	285

Part		Page
627	Title IV conservators, receivers, and voluntary liquidations	288
630	Disclosure to investors in systemwide and consolidated bank debt obligations of the Farm Credit System	298
650	Federal Agricultural Mortgage Corporation general provisions	313
651	Federal Agricultural Mortgage Corporation governance	318
652	Federal Agricultural Mortgage Corporation funding and fiscal affairs	320
653–654	[Reserved]	
655	Federal Agricultural Mortgage Corporation disclosure and reporting requirements	349

SUBCHAPTER A—ADMINISTRATIVE PROVISIONS

PART 600—ORGANIZATION AND FUNCTIONS

Subpart A—Farm Credit Administration

Sec.
600.1 The Farm Credit Act.
600.2 Farm Credit Administration.
600.3 Farm Credit Administration Board.
600.4 Organization of the Farm Credit Administration.

Subpart B—Rules and Procedures for Service Upon the Farm Credit Administration

600.10 Service of Process.

AUTHORITY: Secs. 5.7, 5.8, 5.9, 5.10, 5.11, 5.17, 8.11 of the Farm Credit Act (12 U.S.C. 2241, 2242, 2243, 2244, 2245, 2252, 2279aa–11).

SOURCE: 53 FR 16693, May 11, 1988, unless otherwise noted.

Subpart A—Farm Credit Administration

SOURCE: 70 FR 69645, Nov. 17, 2005, unless otherwise noted.

§ 600.1 The Farm Credit Act.

The Farm Credit Act of 1971, Public Law 92–181 recodified and replaced the prior laws under which the Farm Credit Administration (FCA) and the institutions of the Farm Credit System (System or FCS) were organized and operated. The prior laws, which were repealed and superseded by the Act, are identified in section 5.40(a) of the Act. Subsequent amendments to the Act and enactment dates are as follows: Public Law 94–184, December 31, 1975; Public Law 95–443, October 10, 1978; Public Law 96–592, December 24, 1980; Public Law 99–190, December 19, 1985; Public Law 99–198, December 23, 1985; Public Law 99–205, December 23, 1985; Public Law 99–509, October 21, 1986; Public Law 100–233, January 6, 1988; Public Law 100–399, August 17, 1988; Public Law 100–460, October 1, 1988; Public Law 101–73, August 9, 1989; Public Law 101–220, December 12, 1989; Public Law 101–624, November 28, 1990; Public Law 102–237, December 13, 1991; Public Law 102–552, October 28, 1992; Public Law 103–376, October 19, 1994; Public Law 104–105, February 10, 1996; Public Law 104–316, October 19, 1996; Public Law 107–171, May 13, 2002. The law is codified at 12 U.S.C. 2000, *et seq.*

§ 600.2 Farm Credit Administration.

(a) *Background.* The Farm Credit Administration is an independent, non-appropriated fund agency in the executive branch of the Federal Government. The FCA Board and employees carry out the FCA's functions, powers, and duties.

(b) *Locations.* FCA's headquarters address is 1501 Farm Credit Drive, McLean, Virginia 22102–5090. The FCA has the following field offices:

1501 Farm Credit Drive, McLean, VA 22102–5090.
2051 Killebrew Drive, Suite 610, Bloomington, Minnesota 55425–1899.
511 East Carpenter Freeway, Suite 650, Irving, TX 75062–3930.
3131 South Vaughn Way, Suite 250, Aurora, CO 80014–3507.
2180 Harvard Street, Suite 300, Sacramento, California 95815–3323.

§ 600.3 Farm Credit Administration Board.

(a) *FCA Board.* The President appoints the three full-time Board members with the advice and consent of the Senate. The Board manages, administers, and establishes policies for FCA. The Board promulgates the rules and regulations implementing the Farm Credit Act of 1971, as amended, and provides for the examination of Farm Credit System institutions.

(b) *Chairman of the FCA Board.* The Chairman of the Board is FCA's Chief Executive Officer. The Chairman directs the implementation of the policies and regulations adopted by the Board and, after consulting the Board, the execution of the administrative functions and duties of FCA. In carrying out the Board's policies, the Chairman acts as the spokesperson for the Board and represents the Board and FCA in their official relations within the Federal Government.

§ 600.4 Organization of the Farm Credit Administration.

(a) *Offices and functions.* The primary offices of the FCA are:

(1) *Office of Congressional and Public Affairs.* The Office of Congressional and Public Affairs performs Congressional liaison duties and coordinates and disseminates Agency communications.

(2) *Office of Examination.* The Office of Examination evaluates the safety and soundness of FCS institutions and their compliance with law and regulations and manages FCA's enforcement and supervision functions.

(3) *Office of General Counsel.* The Office of General Counsel provides legal advice and services to the FCA Chairman, the FCA Board, and Agency staff.

(4) *Office of Inspector General.* The Office of Inspector General conducts independent audits, inspections, and investigations of Agency programs and operations and reviews proposed legislation and regulations.

(5) *Office of Regulatory Policy.* The Office of Regulatory Policy develops policies and regulations for the FCA Board's consideration; evaluates regulatory and statutory prior approvals; manages the Agency's chartering activities; and analyzes policy and strategic risks to the System.

(6) *Office of Management Services.* The Office of Management Services provides financial management services. It administers the Agency's information resources management program; human resources management program; and contracts, procurement, mail services, and payroll.

(7) *Office of Secondary Market Oversight.* The Office of Secondary Market Oversight regulates and examines the Federal Agricultural Mortgage Corporation for safety and soundness and compliance with law and regulations.

(8) *Secretary to the Board.* The Secretary to the Board serves as the parliamentarian for the Board and keeps permanent and complete records and minutes of the acts and proceedings of the Board.

(b) *Additional Information.* You may obtain more information on the FCA's organization by visiting our Web site at *http://www.fca.gov*. You may also contact the Office of Congressional and Public Affairs:

(1) In writing at FCA, 1501 Farm Credit Drive, McLean, Virginia 22102–5090;

(2) By e-mail at *info-line@fca.gov;* or

(3) By telephone at (703) 883–4056.

Subpart B—Rules and Procedures for Service Upon the Farm Credit Administration

§ 600.10 Service of Process.

(a) Except as otherwise provided in the Farm Credit Administration regulations, the Federal Rules of Civil Procedure or by order of a court with jurisdiction over the Farm Credit Administration, any legal process upon the Farm Credit Administration shall be duly issued and served upon the Secretary to the Farm Credit Administration Board, 1501 Farm Credit Drive, McLean, Virginia 22102–5090.

(b) Service of process upon the Secretary to the Farm Credit Administration Board may be effected by personally delivering a copy of the documents to the Secretary or by sending a copy of the documents to the Secretary by registered or certified mail.

(c) The Secretary shall promptly forward a copy of all documents to the General Counsel and to any Farm Credit Administration personnel named in the caption of the documents.

[54 FR 50736, Dec. 11, 1989, as amended at 59 FR 21642, Apr. 26, 1994]

PART 601—EMPLOYEE RESPONSIBILITIES AND CONDUCT

AUTHORITY: 5 U.S.C. 7301; 12 U.S.C. 2243, 2252.

§ 601.100 Cross-references to employee ethical conduct standards and financial disclosure regulations.

Board members, officers, and other employees of the Farm Credit Administration are subject to the Standards of Ethical Conduct for Employees of the Executive Branch at 5 CFR part 2635, the Farm Credit Administration regulation at 5 CFR part 4101, which supplements the Executive Branch-wide Standards, and the executive branch-

Farm Credit Administration

§ 602.2

wide financial disclosure regulations at 5 CFR part 2634.

[60 FR 30782, June 12, 1995]

PART 602—RELEASING INFORMATION

Subpart A—Information and Records Generally

Sec.
602.1 Purpose and scope.
602.2 Disclosing reports of examination.

Subpart B—Availability of Records of the Farm Credit Administration

602.3 Definitions.
602.4 How to make a request.
602.5 FCA response to requests for records.
602.6 FOIA exemptions.
602.7 Confidential business information.
602.8 Appeals.
602.9 Current FOIA index.

Subpart C—FOIA Fees

602.10 Definitions.
602.11 Fees by type of requester.
602.12 Fees.
602.13 Fee waiver.
602.14 Advance payments—notice.
602.15 Interest on unpaid fees.
602.16 Combining requests.

Subpart D—Testimony and Production of Documents in Legal Proceedings in Which FCA is Not a Named Party

602.17 Policy.
602.18 Definitions.
602.19 Request for testimony or production of documents.
602.20 Testimony of FCA employees.
602.21 Production of FCA documents.
602.22 Fees.
602.23 Responses to demands served on FCA employees.
602.24 Responses to demands served on non-FCA employees or entities.

Subpart E—Release of Records in Public Rulemaking Files

602.25 General.

AUTHORITY: Secs. 5.9, 5.17; 12 U.S.C. 2243, 2252; 5 U.S.C. 301, 552; 52 FR 10012; E.O. 12600, 52 FR 23781, 3 CFR 1987, p. 235.

SOURCE: 64 FR 41770, Aug. 2, 1999, unless otherwise noted.

Subpart A—Information and Records Generally

§ 602.1 Purpose and scope.

This part contains FCA's rules for disclosing our records or information; processing requests for records under the Freedom of Information Act (5 U.S.C. 552, as amended)(FOIA); FOIA fees; disclosing otherwise exempt information in litigation when FCA is not a party; and getting documents in public rulemaking files. Part 603 of this chapter tells you how to get records about yourself under the Privacy Act of 1974, 5 U.S.C. 552a.

§ 602.2 Disclosing reports of examination.

(a) *Disclosure by FCA.* Reports of examination are FCA property. We prepare them for our confidential use and the use of the institution examined. We do not give reports of examination to the public. Except as provided in this section, only the Chairman or the Chairman's designee may consent to disclosing reports of examination of Farm Credit System institutions and other institutions subject to our examination. You may send a written request to our General Counsel that explains why we should give permission.

(b) *Disclosure by Farm Credit System institutions.* An institution that we have examined may disclose its report of examination to its officers, directors, and agents, such as its attorney or accountant, if they agree to keep the report confidential. In addition, banks may disclose their reports of examination to their affiliated associations, associations may disclose their reports to their supervisory bank, and service corporations may disclose their reports of examination to the institutions that own them. An institution may not disclose these institutions' reports of examination to any other person without our written permission.

(c) *Disclosure to governmental entities.* Without waiving any privilege, we will disclose reports of examination to other Federal government entities:

(1) In response to a Federal court order;

(2) In response to a request of either House or a Committee or Subcommittee of Congress; or

§ 602.3

(3) When requested for confidential use in an official investigation by authorized representatives of other Federal agencies.

Subpart B—Availability of Records of the Farm Credit Administration

§ 602.3 Definitions.

Appeal means a request under the FOIA asking for the reversal of a decision.

Business information means trade secrets or other commercial or financial information that is privileged or confidential.

Business submitter means any person or entity that gives business information to the Government.

FOIA request means a written request for FCA records, made by any person or entity that either directly or indirectly invokes the FOIA or this part.

Record means all documentary materials, such as books, papers, maps, photographs, and machine-readable materials, regardless of physical form or characteristics (for example, electronic format) in our possession and control when we receive your FOIA request.

§ 602.4 How to make a request.

(a) *How to make and address a request.* Your request for records must be in writing and addressed to the FOIA Officer, Farm Credit Administration. You may send it:

(1) By mail to 1501 Farm Credit Drive, McLean, Virginia 22102–5090;

(2) By facsimile to (703) 790–0052; or

(3) By E-mail to *foiaofficer@fca.gov*.

(b) *Description of requested records.* You must describe the requested records in enough detail to let us find them with a reasonable effort. If the description is inadequate, we will ask you to provide more information and the 20-day response period under § 602.5(a) will not begin until we receive your reply.

(c) *Faster response.* You may ask for a faster response to your FOIA request by giving us a statement, certified to be true, that you have a "compelling need." The FOIA Officer will tell you within 10 calendar days after receiving the request whether we will respond to it faster. If so, we will respond to your request as soon as we can. A *compelling need* means:

(1) Someone's life or physical safety may be in danger if we do not respond to the request faster; or

(2) You urgently need to tell the public about Federal government activity as a representative of the news media.

(d) *Request for personal information.* If you or your representative requests your personal information, we may require you to give us a notarized request, identify yourself under penalty of perjury, or provide other proof of your identity.

(e) *Fees.* When making a request, you must tell us the most you are willing to pay. Our charges are in the fee tables in §§ 602.11 and 602.12. You may also want to tell us the purpose of your request so we can classify your request for fee purposes.

(f) *Other requests.* To ensure the public has timely information about our activities, the Office of Congressional and Public Affairs will make available copies of public documents, such as the FCA annual report and media advisories.

§ 602.5 FCA response to requests for records.

(a) *Response time.* Within 20 business days of receiving your request, the FOIA Officer will tell you whether we have granted or denied it. If you send your request to the wrong address, the 20-day response time will not begin until the FOIA Officer receives your request.

(b) *Extension of response time.* In "unusual circumstances," the FOIA Officer may extend the 20-day response time for up to 10 more business days by telling you in writing why we need more time and the date we will mail you our response. As used in this subpart, "unusual circumstances" means our need to:

(1) Search for and get the requested records from field offices or other locations;

(2) Search for, get, and review many records identified in a single request;

(3) Consult with another Federal agency having a substantial interest in the request; or

Farm Credit Administration § 602.8

(4) Consult with two or more FCA offices having a substantial interest in the request.

(c) *Referrals.* If you ask for records we have that another Federal agency originated, we will refer the request to the originating agency and tell you about the referral. If you should have sent your request to another Federal agency, we will refer the request to that agency and so advise you.

§ 602.6 FOIA exemptions.

The FOIA allows agencies to withhold documents in certain categories. For instance, we do not have to give you documents that relate to our examination of institutions or that would violate the personal privacy of an individual. If we do not give you a document because the FOIA does not require us to, we will tell you which FOIA exemption applies to our decision.

§ 602.7 Confidential business information.

(a) *FCA disclosure.* FCA may disclose business information from a business submitter only under this section. This section will not apply if:

(1) We decide the business submitter has no valid basis to object to disclosure;

(2) The information has been published lawfully or made available to the public; or

(3) Law (other than the FOIA) requires disclosure of the information.

(b) *Notice by FCA.* When we receive a request for confidential business information, the FOIA Officer will promptly tell the requester and the business submitter in writing that the responsive records may be free from disclosure under the FOIA. We will give the business submitter a reasonable time to object to the proposed disclosure of the responsive records and tell the requester whenever:

(1) The business submitter has in good faith labeled the information a trade secret or commercial or financial information that is privileged or confidential. We will provide such notice for 10 years after receiving the information unless the business submitter justifies the need for a longer period; or

(2) We believe that disclosing the information may result in commercial or financial injury to the business submitter.

(c) *Objection to release.* A business submitter who objects to our releasing the requested information should tell us in writing why the information is a trade secret or commercial or financial information that is privileged or confidential.

(d) *FCA response.* (1) We will consider carefully a business submitter's objections. If we decide to disclose business information over the submitter's objection, the FOIA Officer will explain to the submitter in writing why we disagreed with the submitter's objection and describe the business information to be disclosed.

(2) We will tell the requester and the submitter the proposed disclosure date at the same time.

(3) If a submitter sues to prevent release, we will promptly tell the requester and will not disclose the business information until after the court's decision.

(4) If a requester sues to compel disclosure, we will promptly tell the business submitter.

§ 602.8 Appeals.

(a) *How to appeal.* You may appeal a total or partial denial of your FOIA request within 30 calendar days of the date of the denial letter. Your appeal must be in writing and addressed to the Director, Office of Management Services (OMS), Farm Credit Administration. You may send it:

(1) By mail to 1501 Farm Credit Drive, McLean, Virginia 22102–5090;

(2) By facsimile to (703) 893–2608; or

(3) By E-mail to *foiaappeal@fca.gov*.

(b) *FCA action on appeal.* Within 20 business days of receiving your appeal, the OMS Director will tell you, in writing, whether we have granted or denied it. If you send your appeal to the wrong address, the 20-day response time will not begin until the OMS Director receives your appeal.

(c) *Unusual circumstances.* In unusual circumstances, the OMS Director may extend the 20-day response time by telling you in writing why we need more time and the date we will mail

§ 602.9

you our response. All extensions, including any extension of the response time for the first request, may not total more than 10 business days.

[64 FR 41770, Aug. 2, 1999, as amended at 70 FR 69645, Nov. 17, 2005]

§ 602.9 Current FOIA index.

FCA will make a current index available for public inspection and copying, as required by the FOIA. We will give you an index for the cost of copying it. Because we rarely receive requests for an index, we have not published one in the FEDERAL REGISTER.

Subpart C—FOIA Fees

§ 602.10 Definitions.

Commercial use request means an information request by an individual or entity seeking information for a use or purpose that furthers the commercial, trade, or profit interests of that individual or entity.

Direct costs means the costs FCA incurs in searching for and reproducing documents to respond to a FOIA request. For a commercial use request, it also means the costs we incur in reviewing documents to respond to the request. Direct costs include the pro rated cost of the salary of the employee performing the work (based on the basic rate of pay plus 16 percent to cover benefits) and the cost of operating reproduction equipment. They do not include overhead expenses.

Educational institution means a preschool, a public or private elementary or secondary school, an institution of undergraduate or graduate higher education, an institution of professional education, or an institution of vocational education that runs a program of scholarly research.

Noncommercial scientific institution means a nonprofit institution that conducts scientific research that is not intended to promote any particular product or industry.

Pages mean 8–1/2 × 11 inch or 11 × 14 inch paper copies.

Representative of the news media means any person actively gathering news for an entity that publishes or broadcasts news to the public. *News* means information about current events or of current interest to the public.

Reproduce (or reproduction) means copying a record.

Review means looking at documents found in response to a FOIA request to decide whether any portion should be withheld. It does not include the time spent resolving legal or policy issues.

Search means all time spent looking for material responsive to a FOIA request, including page-by-page or line-by-line identification of material within documents.

§ 602.11 Fees by type of requester.

Depending on your identity and the purpose of your request, the FCA may charge you the direct costs of searching for responsive records, reviewing the records, and reproducing them. If necessary, we will seek clarification before classifying the request.

(a) *Educational institutions and noncommercial scientific institutions.* We charge fees for reproduction costs only. The first 100 pages are free. You must show that the request is sanctioned by an educational or noncommercial scientific institution and that you seek the records for scholarly or scientific research, not for a commercial use.

(b) *Representatives of the news media.* We charge fees for reproduction costs only. The first 100 pages are free. You must be a representative of the news media, and the request must not be made for a commercial use. A request for records supporting news distribution is not a request for a commercial use.

(c) *Commercial use.* We charge the direct cost for search, review, and reproduction. Commercial use requesters are not entitled to free search time or free reproduction. We will charge you even if we do not disclose any records.

(d) *All others.* The first 2 hours of search time and the first 100 pages of reproduction are free. After that, we will charge you for search and reproduction costs. We will charge you for a search even if we do not disclose any records.

(e) *Fee table.* The fee information in paragraphs (a) through (d) of this section is presented in the table to this paragraph. You may apply for a waiver if your request is not mostly in your

Farm Credit Administration § 602.14

commercial interest and the disclosure is in the public interest. See § 602.13.

FEE TABLE

Type of requester	Charges for Search time	Charges for Review time	Reproduction
•Educational •Noncommercial scientific users •News media	No Charge	No charge	First 100 pages free, $ 0.15 a page after that.
Commercial Users [1]	All direct costs	All direct costs	$0.15 a page.
All others [1]	First 2 hours free, all direct costs after that.	No charge	First 100 pages free, $0.15 a page after that.

[1] You are responsible for fees even if we do not disclose any records.

[64 FR 41770, Aug. 2, 1999; 64 FR 45589, Aug. 20, 1999]

§ 602.12 Fees.

(a) FCA may charge:

(1) For manual searches for records and for review, the pro rated cost of the salary of the employee doing the work.

(2) For computer searches for records, the direct costs of computer search time and supply or material costs.

(3) For each page made by photocopy or similar method, fifteen cents a page, and for other forms of copying, the direct costs.

(4) The direct costs of elective services, such as certifying records as true copies or sending records by special methods.

(b) We will not charge fees when total assessed fees are less than $15.00.

(c) You must pay by personal check, bank draft drawn on a United States bank, or postal money order made payable to the Treasury of the United States.

(d) We treat a request about yourself under Privacy Act fee rules.

(e) The information in paragraphs (a) and (b) of this section is presented in the table to this paragraph. Direct costs means the costs FCA incurs in searching for, reviewing, and reproducing documents to respond to a request. Direct costs include pro rated salary and reproduction costs. We will not charge fees when they total less than $15.00.

FEE AMOUNTS TABLE

Type of fee	Amount of fee
Manual Search and Review	Pro rated Salary Costs.
Computer Search	Direct Costs.
Photocopy	$0.15 a page.
Other Reproduction Costs	Direct Costs.
Elective Services	Direct Costs.

§ 602.13 Fee waiver.

We may waive or reduce fees if disclosure is not mostly in your commercial interest but, instead, is in the public interest because it will advance public understanding of the Federal government's operations or activities.

§ 602.14 Advance payments—notice.

(a) If fees will be more than $25.00 and you have not told us in advance that you will pay estimated fees, we will tell you the estimated amount and ask that you agree to pay it. Except as noted in this section, we will begin processing the FOIA request when we receive your agreement to pay.

(b) If estimated fees exceed $250.00 and you have a history of promptly paying fees charged for information requests, we may respond to your request based on your agreement to pay.

(c) If estimated fees exceed $250.00 and you have no history of paying fees, we may require you to pay in advance.

(d) If you have previously failed to pay fees for information requests or paid them late, you must pay any fees still owed, plus interest calculated under § 602.15, and the estimated fees before we will respond to a new or a pending request.

§ 602.15

(e) If we require advance payment or an advance agreement to pay, we will not consider your request to be received and will not respond to it until you meet the requirement.

§ 602.15 Interest on unpaid fees.

If you fail to pay fees on time, FCA may charge you interest starting on the 31st calendar day following the date we bill you. We will charge you interest at the rate allowed by law (31 U.S.C. 3717) on the billing date.

§ 602.16 Combining requests.

You may not avoid paying fees by filing multiple requests at the same time. When FCA reasonably believes that you, alone or with others, are breaking down a request into a series of requests to avoid fees, we will combine the requests and charge accordingly. We will assume that multiple requests within a 30-day period have been made to avoid fees.

Subpart D—Testimony and Production of Documents in Legal Proceedings in Which FCA is Not a Named Party

§ 602.17 Policy.

(a) The rules in this subpart preserve the confidentiality of FCA's documents and information, conserve employees' time for official duties, uphold fairness in litigation, and help the Chairman decide when to allow testimony and to produce documents. This subpart does not affect access to documents under the FOIA or the Privacy Act. See subpart B of this part and part 603 of this chapter.

(b) Generally, we will not produce documents voluntarily and employees will not appear as witnesses voluntarily in any legal proceeding. However, in limited circumstances, the Chairman may allow the production of documents or testimony when the Chairman decides it would be in the best interest of FCA or the public. All privileged documents produced under this subpart remain our property. Any employee having information or privileged documents may disclose them only as allowed by the Chairman.

§ 602.18 Definitions.

Court means any entity conducting a legal proceeding.

Demand means any order, subpoena, or other legal process for testimony or documents.

Direct costs means FCA's costs to search for, review, and reproduce documents to respond to a request. Direct costs include the pro rated cost of the salary of the employee performing the work (based on the basic rate of pay plus 16 percent to cover benefits) and the cost of operating reproduction equipment.

Document means any record or other documentary materials, such as books, papers, maps, photographs, and machine-readable materials, regardless of physical form or characteristics (for example, electronic format) in our possession and control when we receive the request.

Employee means any present or former FCA employee, any present or former FCA Board member, any former Federal Farm Credit Board member, any present or former FCA-appointed receiver or conservator, and any present or former agent or contractor.

FCA Counsel means the General Counsel, a Department of Justice attorney, or counsel authorized by FCA to act for the FCA or an employee.

General Counsel means the FCA's General Counsel or designee.

Legal proceeding means any administrative, civil, or criminal proceeding, including a discovery proceeding, before a court when FCA is not a named party and has not instituted the legal proceeding.

§ 602.19 Request for testimony or production of documents.

(a) *How to make and address a request.* Your request for an employee's testimony about official matters or the production of documents must be in writing and addressed to the General Counsel, 1501 Farm Credit Drive, McLean, Virginia 22102–5090.

(b) Your request must contain the following:

(1) Title of the case;
(2) Forum;
(3) Your interest in the case;
(4) Summary of the litigation issues;
(5) Reasons for the request;

(6) Why the confidential information is important; and

(7) An explanation of why the testimony or document you want is not reasonably available from another source. If you want testimony, you must also state how you intend to use the testimony, provide a subject matter summary of the requested testimony, and explain why a document could not be used instead.

(c) The General Counsel may ask you to limit your request to make it less burdensome or to give us information to help us decide if providing documents or testimony is in the public interest.

§ 602.20 Testimony of FCA employees.

(a) An employee may testify only as the Chairman approves in writing. Generally, an employee may testify only by deposition or written interrogatory. An employee may give only factual testimony and may not give opinion testimony.

(b) If, in response to your request, the Chairman decides that an employee may testify, you must serve the employee with a subpoena under applicable Federal or State rules of procedure and at the same time send a copy of the subpoena by registered mail to the General Counsel.

(c) Normally, depositions will be taken at the employee's office, at a time convenient to the employee and the FCA. FCA counsel may represent FCA's interests at the deposition.

(d) If you request the deposition, you must give the General Counsel a copy of the deposition transcript at no charge.

§ 602.21 Production of FCA documents.

(a) An FCA employee may produce documents only as the Chairman allows.

(b) Before we will release any documents, the requesting party must get an acceptable protective order from the court before which the action is pending that will preserve the confidentiality of the documents to be released.

(c) On request, we may provide certified or authenticated copies of documents.

§ 602.22 Fees.

(a) For documents released under this subpart, FCA will charge:

(1) The direct costs of searching for responsive records, including the use of a computer, reviewing the records, and reproducing them. We also will charge for the direct costs of any other services and materials that we provide at your request.

(2) Fifteen cents a copy for each page made by photocopy or similar process.

(3) The direct costs for each certification or authentication of documents.

(b) You must pay by personal check, bank draft drawn on a United States bank, or postal money order made payable to FCA. We will waive fees of $15.00 or less. We will send the documents after we receive your payment.

§ 602.23 Responses to demands served on FCA employees.

(a) An employee served with a demand or a subpoena in a legal proceeding must immediately tell the General Counsel of such service, the testimony or documents described in the demand, and all relevant facts.

(b) When the Chairman does not allow testimony or production of documents, FCA Counsel will provide the regulations in this subpart to the party or court issuing the demand and explain that the employee may not testify or produce documents without the Chairman's prior approval.

(c) If the court rules the employee must comply with the demand regardless of the Chairman's instructions not to do so, the employee must respectfully refuse to comply.

(d) FCA's decision under this subpart to comply or not to comply with any demand is not a waiver, an assertion of privilege, or an objection based on relevance, technical deficiency, or any other ground. We may oppose any demand on any legal ground.

§ 602.24 Responses to demands served on non-FCA employees or entities.

If you are not an employee and are served with a demand or a subpoena in a legal proceeding directing you to produce or testify about an FCA report of examination, other document created or adopted by FCA, or any related

§ 602.25

document, you must object and immediately tell the General Counsel of such service, the testimony or documents described in the demand, and all relevant facts. You also must object to the production of any documents on the basis that they are FCA's property and cannot be released without FCA's consent. You should tell the requester the production of documents or testimony must follow the procedures in this part.

Subpart E—Release of Records in Public Rulemaking Files

§ 602.25 General.

FCA has a public rulemaking file for each regulation. You may get copies of documents in the public rulemaking file by sending a written request to the Director, Regulation and Policy Division, Office of Policy and Analysis, Farm Credit Administration, 1501 Farm Credit Drive, McLean, Virginia 22102–5090. We will charge fifteen cents a copy for each page. We will waive fees of $15.00 or less.

PART 603—PRIVACY ACT REGULATIONS

Sec.
603.300 Purpose and scope.
603.305 Definitions.
603.310 Procedures for requests pertaining to individual records in a record system.
603.315 Times, places, and requirements for identification of individuals making requests.
603.320 Disclosure of requested information to individuals.
603.325 Special procedures for medical records.
603.330 Request for amendment to record.
603.335 Agency review of request for amendment of record.
603.340 Appeal of an initial adverse determination of a request to amend a record.
603.345 Fees for providing copies of records.
603.350 Criminal penalties.
603.355 Exemptions.

AUTHORITY: Secs. 5.9, 5.17 of the Farm Credit Act (12 U.S.C. 2243, 2252); 5 U.S.C. app. 3, 5 U.S.C. 552a (j)(2) and (k)(2).

SOURCE: 40 FR 40454, Sept. 2, 1975, unless otherwise noted.

§ 603.300 Purpose and scope.

(a) This part is published by the Farm Credit Administration pursuant to the Privacy Act of 1974 (Pub. L. 93–579, 5 U.S.C. 552a) which requires each Federal agency to promulgate rules to establish procedures for notification and disclosure to an individual of agency records pertaining to that person, and for review of such records.

(b) The records covered by this part include:

(1) Personnel and employment records maintained by the Farm Credit Administration which are not covered by §§ 293.101 through 293.108 of the regulations of the Office of Personnel Management (5 CFR 293.101 through 293.108), and

(2) Other records contained in record systems maintained by the Farm Credit Administration.

[40 FR 40454, Sept. 2, 1975, as amended at 51 FR 41941, Nov. 20, 1986]

§ 603.305 Definitions.

For the purposes of this part:

(a) *Agency* means the Farm Credit Administration.

(b) *Individual* means a citizen of the United States or an alien lawfully admitted for permanent residence;

(c) *Maintain* includes maintain, collect, use, or disseminate;

(d) *Record* means any item, collection, or grouping of information about an individual that is maintained by an agency including, but not limited to, that person's education, financial transactions, medical history, and criminal or employment history, and that contains that person's name, or the identifying number, symbol, or other identifying particular assigned to the individual, such as a finger or voice print or photograph;

(e) *Routine use* means, with respect to the disclosure of a record, the use of such record for a purpose that is compatible with the purpose for which it was collected;

(f) *Statistical record* means a record in a system of records maintained for statistical research or reporting purposes only and not used in whole or in part in making any determination about an identifiable individual, except as provided by 13 U.S.C. 8;

Farm Credit Administration

§ 603.320

(g) *System of records* means a group of any records under the control of any agency from which information is retrieved by the name of an individual or by some identifying number, symbol, or other identifying particular assigned to the individual.

[51 FR 41941, Nov. 20, 1986]

§ 603.310 Procedures for requests pertaining to individual records in a record system.

(a) Any present or former employee of the Farm Credit Administration seeking access to that person's official civil service records maintained by the Farm Credit Administration shall submit a request in such manner as is prescribed by the Office of Personnel Management.

(b) Individuals shall submit their requests in writing to the Privacy Act Officer, Office of General Counsel, Farm Credit Administration, McLean, Virginia 22102–5090, when seeking to obtain from the Farm Credit Administration:

(1) Notification of whether the agency maintains a record pertaining to that person in a system of records;

(2) Notification of whether the agency has disclosed a record for which an accounting of disclosure is required to be maintained and made available to that person;

(3) A copy of a record pertaining to that person or the accounting of its disclosure;

(4) The review of a record pertaining to that person or the accounting of its disclosure. The request shall state the full name and address of the individual, and identify the system or systems of records believed to contain the information or record sought.

[51 FR 41941, Nov. 20, 1986, as amended at 61 FR 67185, Dec. 20, 1996]

§ 603.315 Times, places, and requirements for identification of individuals making requests.

The individual making written requests for information or records ordinarily will not be required to verify that person's identity. The signature upon such requests shall be deemed to be a certification by the requester that he or she is the individual to whom the record pertains, or the parent of a minor, or the duly appointed legal guardian of the individual to whom the record pertains. The Privacy Act Officer, however, may require such additional verification of identity in any instance in which the Privacy Act Officer deems it advisable.

[51 FR 41941, Nov. 20, 1986]

§ 603.320 Disclosure of requested information to individuals.

(a) The Privacy Act Officer shall, within a reasonable period of time after the date of receipt of a request for information of records:

(1) Determine whether or not such request shall be granted,

(2) Notify the requester of the determination and, if the request is denied, of the reasons therefor, and

(3) Notify the requester that fees for reproducing copies of records may be charged as provided in § 603.345 of this part.

(b) If access to a record is denied because the information therein has been compiled by the Farm Credit Administration in reasonable anticipation of a civil or criminal action proceeding, the Privacy Act Officer shall notify the requester of that person's right to judicial appeal under 5 U.S.C. 552a(g).

(c)(1) If access to a record is granted, the requester shall notify the Officer whether the requested record is to be copied and mailed to the requester or whether the record is to be made available for personal inspection.

(2) A requester who is an individual may be accompanied by an individual selected by the requester when the record is disclosed, in which case the requester may be required to furnish a written statement authorizing the discussion of the record in the presence of the accompanying person.

(d) If the record is to be made available for personal inspection, the requester shall arrange with the Privacy Act Officer a mutually agreeable time in the offices of the Farm Credit Administration for inspection of the record.

[40 FR 40454, Sept. 2, 1975, as amended at 51 FR 41941, Nov. 20, 1986]

§ 603.325 Special procedures for medical records.

Medical records in the custody of the Farm Credit Administration which are not subject to Office of Personnel Management regulations shall be disclosed either to the individual to whom they pertain or that person's authorized or legal representative or to a licensed physician named by the individual.

[51 FR 41942, Nov. 20, 1986]

§ 603.330 Request for amendment to record.

(a) If, after disclosure of the requested information, an individual believes that the record is not accurate, relevant, timely, or complete, that person may request in writing that the record be amended. Such a request shall be submitted to the Privacy Act Officer and shall contain identification of the system of records and the record or information therein, a brief description of the material requested to be changed, the requested change or changes, and the reason for such change or changes.

(b) The Privacy Act Officer shall acknowledge receipt of the request within 10 days (excluding Saturdays, Sundays, and legal holidays) and, if a determination has not been made, advise the individual when that person may expect to be advised of action taken on the request. The acknowledgment may contain a request for additional information needed to make a determination.

[51 FR 41942, Nov. 20, 1986]

§ 603.335 Agency review of request for amendment of record.

Upon receipt of a request for amendment of a record, the Privacy Act Officer shall:

(a) Correct any portion of a record which the individual making the request believes is not accurate, relevant, timely, or complete and thereafter inform the individual in writing of such correction, or

(b) Inform the individual in writing of refusal to amend the record and of the reasons therefor, and advise that the individual may appeal such determination as provided in § 603.340 of this part.

[40 FR 40454, Sept. 2, 1975, as amended at 51 FR 41942, Nov. 20, 1986]

§ 603.340 Appeal of an initial adverse determination of a request to amend a record.

(a) Not more than 10 days (excluding Saturdays, Sundays, and legal holidays) after receipt by an individual of an adverse determination on the individual's request to amend a record or otherwise, the individual may appeal to the Director, Office of Management Services.

(b) The appeal shall be by letter, mailed or delivered to the Director, Office of Management Services, Farm Credit Administration, McLean, Virginia 22102–5090. The letter shall identify the records involved in the same manner they were identified to the Privacy Act Officer, shall specify the dates of the request and adverse determination, and shall indicate the expressed basis for that determination. Also, the letter shall state briefly and succinctly the reasons why the adverse determination should be reversed.

(c) The review shall be completed and a final determination made by the Director not later than 30 days (excluding Saturdays, Sundays, and legal holidays) from receipt of the request for such review, unless the Director extends such 30-day period for good cause. If the 30-day period is extended, the individual shall be notified of the reasons therefor.

(d) If the Director refuses to amend the record in accordance with the request, the individual shall be notified of the right to file a concise statement setting forth that person's disagreement with the final determination and that person's right under 5 U.S.C. 552a(g)(1)(A) to a judicial review of the final determination.

(e) If an amendment of a record as requested upon review is refused, there shall be included in the disputed portion of the record a copy of the concise statement filed by the individual together with a concise statement of the reasons for not amending the record as requested. Such statements will be included when disclosure of the disputed

Farm Credit Administration §603.355

record is made to persons and agencies as authorized under 5 U.S.C. 552a.

[40 FR 40454, Sept. 2, 1975, as amended at 51 FR 41942, Nov. 20, 1986; 56 FR 2673, Jan. 24, 1991; 70 FR 69645, Nov. 17, 2005]

§603.345 Fees for providing copies of records.

Fees for providing copies of records shall be charged in accordance with §§602.11 and 602.12 of this chapter.

[40 FR 40454, Sept. 2, 1975, as amended at 56 FR 28479, June 21, 1991; 71 FR 54900, Sept. 20, 2006]

§603.350 Criminal penalties.

Section 552a (*l*) (3) of the Privacy Act (5 U.S.C. 552a(i)(3)) makes it a misdemeanor, subject to a maximum fine of $5,000, to knowingly and willfully request or obtain any record concerning any individual from an agency under false pretenses. Sections 552a (i) (1) and (2) of the Act (5 U.S.C. 552a (i) (1), (2)) provide penalties for violation by agency employees of the Act or regulations established thereunder.

[40 FR 40454, Sept. 2, 1975, as amended at 71 FR 54900, Sept. 20, 2006]

§603.355 Exemptions.

(a) *Specific.* Pursuant to 5 U.S.C. 552a(k)(2), the investigatory material compiled for law enforcement purposes in the following systems of records is exempt from subsections (c)(3), (d), (e)(1), (e)(4) (G), (H), and (I) and (f) of 5 U.S.C. 552a and from the provisions of this part:

Farm Credit Bank loans—FCA.
Production Credit Association loans—FCA.
Agricultural Credit Association loans—FCA.
Federal Land Credit Association loans—FCA.
Agricultural Credit Bank loans—FCA.
Office of Inspector General Investigative Files—FCA.

(b) *General.* (1) In addition, pursuant to 5 U.S.C. 552a (j)(2), investigatory materials compiled for criminal law enforcement in the system of records described in (b)(2) are exempt from all subsections of 5 U.S.C. 552a, except (b), (c) (1) and (2), (e)(4) (A) through (F), (e) (6), (7), (9), (10), and (11), and (i). Exemptions from the particular subsections are justified for the following reasons:

(i) From subsection (c)(3) because making available to a record subject the accounting of disclosures from records concerning him/her would reveal investigative interest on the part of the OIG. This would enable record subjects to impede the investigation by, for example, destroying evidence, intimidating potential witnesses, or fleeing the area to avoid inquiries or apprehension by law enforcement personnel.

(ii) From subsection (c)(4) because this system is exempt from the access provisions of subsection (d) pursuant to subsection (j)(2) of the Privacy Act.

(iii) From subsection (d) because the records contained in this system relate to official Federal investigations. Individual access to those records might compromise ongoing investigations, reveal confidential informants or constitute unwarranted invasions of the personal privacy of third parties who are involved in a certain investigation. Amendment of the records would interfere with ongoing criminal law enforcement proceedings and impose an impossible administrative burden by requiring criminal investigations to be continuously reinvestigated.

(iv) From subsections (e) (1) and (5) because in the course of law enforcement investigations, information may occasionally be obtained or introduced the accuracy of which is unclear or which is not strictly relevant or necessary to a specific investigation. In the interests of effective law enforcement, it is appropriate to retain all information that may aid in establishing patterns of criminal activity. Moreover, it would impede the specific investigative process if it were necessary to assure the relevance, accuracy, timeliness and completeness of all information obtained.

(v) From subsection (e)(2) because in a law enforcement investigation the requirement that information be collected to the greatest extent possible from the subject individual would present a serious impediment to law enforcement in that the subject of the investigation would be informed of the existence of the investigation and would therefore be able to avoid detection, apprehension, or legal obligations or duties.

(vi) From subsection (e)(3) because to comply with the requirements of this subsection during the course of an investigation could impede the information gathering process, thus hampering the investigation.

(vii) From subsections (e)(4) (G), and (H), and (I), (e)(8), (f), (g) and (h) because this system is exempt from the access provisions of subsection (d) pursuant to subsection (j) of the Privacy Act.

(2) Office of Inspector General Investigative Files—FCA.

[56 FR 2673, Jan. 24, 1991, as amended at 57 FR 32421, July 22, 1992]

PART 604—FARM CREDIT ADMINISTRATION BOARD MEETINGS

Sec.
604.400 Definitions.
604.405 Notice of public observation.
604.410 Scope of application.
604.415 Open meetings.
604.420 Exemptive provisions.
604.425 Announcement of meetings.
604.430 Closure of meetings.
604.435 Record of closed meetings or closed portion of a meeting.
604.440 Requests for information.

AUTHORITY: Secs. 5.9, 5.17 of the Farm Credit Act; 12 U.S.C. 2243, 2252.

§ 604.400 Definitions.

For purposes of this part:

(a) *Agency* means the Farm Credit Administration.

(b) *Board* means the Farm Credit Administration Board.

(c) *Exempt meeting* and *exempt portion of a meeting* mean, respectively, a meeting or that part of a meeting designated as provided in § 604.430 of this part as closed to the public by reason of one or more of the exemptive provisions listed in § 604.420 of this part.

(d) *Meeting* means the deliberations of at least two (quorum) members of the Board where such deliberations determine or result in joint conduct or disposition of official Farm Credit Administration business.

(e) *Member* means any one of the members of the Board.

(f) *Open meeting* means a meeting or portion of a meeting which is not an exempt meeting or an exempt portion of a meeting.

(g) *Public observation* means the right of any member of the public to attend and observe, but not participate or interfere in any way in, an open meeting of the Board, within the limits of reasonable and comfortable accommodations made available for such purpose by the Farm Credit Administration.

[51 FR 41942, Nov. 20, 1986]

§ 604.405 Notice of public observation.

(a) A member of the public is not required to give advance notice to the Farm Credit Administration of an intention to exercise the right of public observation of an open meeting of the Board. However, in order to permit the Farm Credit Administration to determine the amount of space and number of seats which must be made available to accommodate individuals who desire to exercise the right of public observation, such individuals are requested to give notice to the Farm Credit Administration at least two business days before the start of the open meeting of the intention to exercise such right.

(b) Notice of intention to exercise the right of public observation may be given in writing, in person, or by telephone to the official designated in § 604.440 of this part.

(c) Individuals who have not given advance notice of intention to exercise the right of public observation will not be permitted to attend and observe the open meeting of the Board if the available space and seating are necessary to accommodate individuals who gave advance notice of such intention to the Farm Credit Administration.

[42 FR 12161, Mar. 3, 1977. Redesignated and amended at 51 FR 41942, Nov. 20, 1986]

§ 604.410 Scope of application.

The provisions of this part apply to meetings of the Board, and do not apply to conferences or other gatherings of employees of the Farm Credit Administration who meet or join with others, except at meetings of the Board, to deliberate official agency business.

[51 FR 41942, Nov. 20, 1986]

Farm Credit Administration

§ 604.415 Open meetings.

Every meeting and portion of a meeting of the Board shall be open to public observation unless the Board determines that such meeting or portion of a meeting will involve the discussion of matters which are within one or more of the exemptive provisions listed in § 604.420 of this part, and that the public interest is not served by the discussion of such matters in an open meeting.

[51 FR 41943, Nov. 20, 1986]

§ 604.420 Exemptive provisions.

Except in a case where the Board determines that the public interest requires otherwise, a meeting or portion of a meeting may be closed to public observation where the Board determines that the meeting or portion of the meeting is likely to:

(a) Disclose matters that are:

(1) Specifically authorized under criteria established by an Executive order to be kept secret in the interests of national defense or foreign policy, and

(2) In fact properly classified pursuant to such Executive order;

(b) Relate solely to the internal personnel rules and practices of the Farm Credit Administration;

(c) Disclose matters specifically exempted from disclosure by statute (other than 5 U.S.C. 552): *Provided*, That such statute:

(1) Requires that the matters be withheld from the public in such a manner as to leave no discretion on the issue, or

(2) Establishes particular types of matters to be withheld;

(d) Disclose trade secrets and privileged or confidential commercial or financial information obtained from a person;

(e) Involve accusing any person of a crime, or formally censuring any person;

(f) Disclose information of a personal nature where disclosure would constitute a clearly unwarranted invasion of personal privacy;

(g) Disclose investigator records compiled for law enforcement purposes, or information which if written would be contained in such records, but only to the extent that the production of such records or information would:

(1) Interfere with enforcement proceedings;

(2) Deprive a person of a right to a fair trial or an impartial adjudication;

(3) Constitute an unwarranted invasion of personal privacy;

(4) Disclose the identity of a confidential source and, in the case of a record compiled by a criminal law enforcement authority in the course of a criminal investigation, or by an agency conducting a lawful national security intelligence investigation, confidential information furnished only by the confidential source;

(5) Disclose investigative techniques and procedures; or

(6) Endanger the life or physical safety of law enforcement personnel;

(h) Disclose information contained in or related to examination, supervision, operating, or condition reports prepared by, on behalf of, or for the use of the Farm Credit Administration;

(i) Disclose information the premature disclosure of which would:

(1) Significantly endanger the stability of any Farm Credit System institution, including banks, associations, service organizations, or the Funding Corporation; or

(2) Be likely to significantly frustrate implementation of a proposed action of the Farm Credit Administration: *Provided*, said Administration has not already disclosed to the public the content or nature of its proposed action, or is not required by law to make such disclosure on its own initiative prior to taking final action on such proposal; or

(j) Specifically concern participation by the Farm Credit Administration in a civil action or proceeding otherwise involving a determination on the record before an opportunity for a hearing.

[51 FR 41943, Nov. 20, 1986, as amended at 56 FR 2673, Jan. 24, 1991; 75 FR 35967, June 24, 2010]

§ 604.425 Announcement of meetings.

(a) The Board meets in the offices of the Farm Credit Administration, McLean, Virginia 22102–5090, on the second Thursday of each month, unless the Board fixes a different time and/or place for a meeting and follows the requirements of paragraph (b) of this section.

(b)(1) The Farm Credit Administration shall make available for public inspection the time, place, and subject matter of the meeting, and whether it is to be open or closed, by posting notice on its public notice board or on its public Web site except to the extent that such information is exempt from disclosure under the provisions of § 604.420 of this part. The public announcement must be made at least 1 week before the meeting, unless a majority of the FCA Board determines by a recorded vote that agency business requires that a meeting be called on lesser notice, in which case the announcement shall be made at the earliest practicable time.

(2) Once a meeting has been announced, the time, place, and subject matter of the meeting and whether it is open or closed to the public may be changed following the requirements of the Government in the Sunshine Act, 5 U.S.C. 552b.

[74 FR 44727, Aug. 31, 2009]

§ 604.430 Closure of meetings.

(a) A majority of the meetings or portions of a majority of the meetings of the board are exempt by reason of § 604.420 (d), (h), (i)(1), or (j) of this part. An exempt meeting or an exempt portion of a meeting shall be closed to the public when at least two members of the Board vote by a recorded vote of the Board at the beginning of the exempt meeting or exempt portion of a meeting to close such meeting or such exempt portion, and the General Counsel, Farm Credit Administration, publicly certifies that, in his or her opinion, the meeting or portion of the meeting may be closed to the public stating each relevant exemptive provision listed in § 604.420 of this part.

(b) A copy of the vote of the Board to close a meeting or an exempt portion thereof reflecting the vote of each member on the question, and a copy of the certification of General Counsel, shall be made available for public inspection in the offices of the Farm Credit Administration, or pursuant to telephonic or written requests.

(c) A copy of the certification of the General Counsel, together with a statement from the presiding officer of the meeting setting forth the time and place of an exempt meeting or an exempt portion of a meeting which was closed and the persons present, shall be retained by the Farm Credit Administration for a period of at least 2 years after the date of such closed meeting or closed portion of a meeting.

[42 FR 12161, Mar. 3, 1977. Redesignated and amended at 51 FR 41943, Nov. 20, 1986]

§ 604.435 Record of closed meetings or closed portion of a meeting.

(a) The Farm Credit Administration shall maintain a complete transcript or electronic recording adequate to record fully the proceedings of each closed meeting or closed portion of a meeting, except that in the case of a meeting or portion of a meeting closed to the public pursuant to § 604.420 (d), (h), (i)(1), or (j) of this part, the Farm Credit Administration shall maintain either such transcript, recording, or a set of minutes.

(b) Any minutes so maintained shall fully and clearly describe all matters discussed and shall provide a full and accurate summary of any actions taken, and the reasons therefor, including a description of each of the views expressed on any item and the record of any roll call vote. All documents considered in connection with any action shall be identified in the minutes.

(c) The Farm Credit Administration shall promptly make available to the public, in its offices, the transcript, electronic recording, or minutes, of the discussion of any item on the agenda of a closed meeting, or closed portion of a meeting, except for such item or items of discussion which the Farm Credit Administration determines to contain information which may be withheld under § 604.420 of this part. Copies of such transcript or minutes, or a transcription of such recording disclosing the identity of each speaker, shall be furnished to any person at the actual cost of duplication or transcription.

(d) The Farm Credit Administration shall maintain a complete verbatim copy of the transcript, a complete copy of the minutes, or a complete electronic recording of each closed meeting

Farm Credit Administration

§ 605.501

or closed portion of a meeting for a period of 2 years after the date of such closed meeting or closed portion of a meeting.

(e) All actions required or permitted by this section to be undertaken by the Farm Credit Administration shall be by or under the authority of the Secretary to the Board.

[42 FR 12161, Mar. 3, 1977. Redesignated and amended at 51 FR 41943, Nov. 20, 1986; 56 FR 2673, Jan. 24, 1991; 70 FR 69645, Nov. 17, 2005]

§ 604.440 Requests for information.

Requests to the Farm Credit Administration for information about the time, place, and subject matter of a meeting, whether it or any portion thereof is closed to the public, and any requests for copies of the transcript or minutes, or of a transcript of an electronic recording of a closed meeting, or closed portion of a meeting, to the extent not exempt from disclosure by the provisions of § 604.420 of this part, shall be addressed to the Secretary to the Board, Farm Credit Administration, McLean, Virginia 22102-5090.

[51 FR 41944, Nov. 20, 1986, as amended at 59 FR 21642, Apr. 26, 1994]

PART 605—INFORMATION

Sec.
605.500 Policy.
605.501 Information Security Officer.
605.502 Program and procedures.

AUTHORITY: Secs. 5.9, 5.12, 5.17 of the Farm Credit Act; 12 U.S.C. 2243, 2246, 2252.

§ 605.500 Policy.

It is the policy of the Farm Credit Administration to act in matters relating to national security information in accordance with Executive Order 13292 and directives issued thereunder by the Information Security Oversight Office (ISOO).

[49 FR 9859, Mar. 16, 1984, as amended at 71 FR 54900, Sept. 20, 2006]

§ 605.501 Information Security Officer.

(a) The Information Security Officer of the Farm Credit Administration shall be responsible for implementation and oversight of the information security program and procedures adopted by the Agency pursuant to the Executive order. This officer shall be the recipient of questions, suggestions, and complaints regarding all elements of this program and shall be solely responsible for changes to it and for the assurance that it is at all times consistent with the Executive order and ISOO directive.

(b) The Information Security Officer shall be the Farm Credit Administration's official contact for requests for declassification of materials submitted under the Executive order, regardless of the point of origin of such requests, and shall assure that such requests for records in the Farm Credit Administration's possession that were originated by another agency shall be forwarded to the originating agency. The Farm Credit Administration shall include a copy of the records requested together with its recommendation for action. Upon receipt, the originating agency shall process the request in accordance with 32 CFR 2001.33(a)(2)(i). Upon request, the originating agency shall communicate its declassification determination to the Farm Credit Administration. The Farm Credit Administration shall inform the requester of the determination within 1 year from the date of receipt, except in unusual circumstances. If an appeal is made on a denial of a mandatory declassification review request, the originating agency's appellate authority shall normally make a determination within 30 working days following the receipt of an appeal. If additional time is required to make a determination, the originating appellate authority shall notify the requester of the additional time needed and provide the requester with the reason for extension. The originating agency's appellate authority shall notify the requester in writing of the final determination and of the reasons for any denial. Such officer shall also assure that requests for declassification submitted under the Freedom of Information Act are handled in accordance with that Act.

[49 FR 9859, Mar. 16, 1984, as amended at 71 FR 54900, Sept. 20, 2006]

§ 605.502 Program and procedures.

(a) The Farm Credit Administration has no authority for the original classification of information for national security purposes. Only those agencies described in the Executive order may so classify information.

(b) *Derivative classification.* "Derivative classification" means the incorporating, paraphrasing, restating or generating in new form information that is already classified, and marking the newly developed material consistent with the classification markings that apply to the source information. Derivative classification includes the classification of information based on classification guidance. The duplication or reproduction of existing classified information is not derivative classification.

(c) *Mandatory declassification review.* "Mandatory declassification review" means the review for declassification of classified information in response to a request for declassification that meets the requirements under section 3.5 of the Executive order. All requests for review for declassification under the mandatory review provisions of the Executive order shall be handled by the Information Security Officer or his/her designee.

(d) *Handling of classified documents.* All documents bearing the terms "Top Secret," "Secret," and "Confidential" shall be delivered to the Information Security Officer or his/her designee immediately upon receipt. All potential recipients of such documents shall be advised of the names of such designees. In the event that the Information Security Officer or his/her designee is not available to receive such documents, they shall be sent to the FCA mailroom and stored in the combination safe and secured unopened until the Information Security Officer is available. Under no cirumstances shall classified materials that cannot be delivered be stored other than in the designated safe. All materials not immediately deliverable or able to be secured in the designated safe shall be returned to the sender, under appropriate cover, for redelivery to the FCA at the next earliest opportunity.

(e) *Reproduction.* Reproduction of classified materials shall take place only in accordance with section 4.2(g) of the Executive order and any limitations imposed by the originator. Should copies be made, they shall be subject to the same controls as the original document. Records showing the number and distribution of copies shall be maintained by the Information Security Officer or his/her designee, and the log stored with the original documents. These measures shall not restrict reproduction for the purposes of Mandatory Review.

(f) *Storage.* In accordance with 32 CFR 2001.43, all classified documents shall be stored in combination safes located at the primary headquarters and/or a Field Office, Office of Examination, Farm Credit Administration. The combinations shall be changed as required by directives issued by ISOO. The combinations shall be known only to the Information Security Officer and his/her designees who have appropriate security clearances.

(g) *Employee education.* All employees who have been granted a security clearance and who have occasion to handle classified materials shall be advised of handling, reproduction, and storage procedures and shall be required to review the Executive order and appropriate ISOO directives.

(h) *Agency terminology.* No official of the Farm Credit Administration shall use the terms "Top Secret", "Secret", or "Confidential" except in relation to materials classified for national security purposes. As a Federal regulatory agency, the Farm Credit Administration maintains certain internal documents that relate to its examination and supervision of the institutions of the Farm Credit System. Such documents are limited in use and distribution. Material that is of a sensitive nature to the Farm Credit Administration may be designated "Executive Document."

(i) *Nondisclosure agreement.* In accordance with 32 CFR 2003.20, the Farm Credit Administration requires that any person whose position requires access to classified information must execute a nondisclosure agreement on Standard Form 312—Classified Information Nondisclosure Agreement. Persons not executing such nondisclosure agreements are subject to sanctions of

Farm Credit Administration § 606.602

Executive Order 13292. It is the policy of the Farm Credit Administration that any employee authorized access to classified information holds a personal responsibility for safeguarding against unlawful disclosures, and such employees are prohibited from disclosure without consent of the FCA Information Security Officer. Any such unauthorized disclosure will be reported to the Information Security Oversight Office, the Department of Justice, the Department of State, the Federal Emergency Management Agency, and to any other Federal agency for which the Farm Credit Administration has access to classified information, as such reportings are subject to interpretation as required by statute and Executive order. Any employee who knowingly disclosed classified information or who refuses to cooperate with an investigation may be subject to mandatory administrative sanctions, including as a minimum, denial of further access to classified information. Further sanctions could include demotion or dismissal depending on the circumstances of a particular case.

(j) *Freedom of Information request.* All inquiries regarding requests for classified information under the Freedom of Information Act (5 U.S.C. 552), including those from the news media, shall be referred to the FCA FOI Officer, Office of Congressional and Public Affairs, Farm Credit Administration, and shall be handled in accordance with provisions of that statute and applicable regulations.

[49 FR 9859, Mar. 16, 1984, as amended at 52 FR 18200, May 14, 1987; 59 FR 21643, Apr. 26, 1994; 71 FR 54900, Sept. 20, 2006]

PART 606—ENFORCEMENT OF NONDISCRIMINATION ON THE BASIS OF HANDICAP IN PROGRAMS OR ACTIVITIES CONDUCTED BY THE FARM CREDIT ADMINISTRATION

Sec.
606.601 Purpose.
606.602 Application.
606.603 Definitions.
606.604–606.609 [Reserved]
606.610 Self-evaluation.
606.611 Notice.
606.612–606.629 [Reserved]
606.630 General prohibitions against discrimination.
606.631–606.639 [Reserved]
606.640 Employment.
606.641–606.648 [Reserved]
606.649 Program accessibility: Discrimination prohibited.
606.650 Program accessibility: Existing facilities.
606.651 Program accessibility: New construction and alterations.
606.652–606.659 [Reserved]
606.660 Communications.
606.661–606.669 [Reserved]
606.670 Compliance procedures.
606.671–606.999 [Reserved]

AUTHORITY: 29 U.S.C. 794.

SOURCE: 53 FR 19889, June 1, 1988, unless otherwise noted.

§ 606.601 Purpose.

The purpose of this part is to effectuate section 119 of the Rehabilitation Comprehensive Services, and Developmental Disabilities Amendments of 1978, which amended section 504 of the Rehabilitation Act of 1973 to prohibit discrimination on the basis of handicap in programs or activities conducted by Executive agencies or the United States Postal Service.

§ 606.602 Application.

(a) This part applies to all programs or activities conducted by the agency. For example, members of the public may participate in the following "programs and activities" of the FCA:

(1) Attending open meetings of the Farm Credit Board.

(2) Making inquiries or filing complaints.

(3) Using the FCA library in McLean, Virginia.

(4) Seeking employment with FCA.

(5) Attending any meeting, conference, seminar, or other program open to the public.

This list is illustrative only and failure to include an activity does not necessarily mean that it is not covered by this regulation.

(b) This regulation does not apply to the institutions that are regulated or examined by the FCA. However, this regulation governs the conduct of FCA personnel, in their interaction with employees of such institutions and employees of other Federal agencies,

§ 606.603

while discharging their official FCA duties.

§ 606.603 Definitions.

For purposes of this part, the term:

(a) *Agency* means the Farm Credit Administration.

(b) *Assistant Attorney General* means the Assistant Attorney General, Civil Rights Division, United States Department of Justice.

(c) *Auxiliary aids* means services or devices that enable persons with impaired sensory, manual, or speaking skills to have an equal opportunity to participate in, and enjoy the benefits of, programs or activities conducted by the agency. For example, auxiliary aids useful for persons with impaired vision include readers, Brailled materials, audio recordings, and other similar services and devices. Auxiliary aids useful for persons with impaired hearing include telephone handset amplifiers, telephones compatible with hearing aids, telecommunication devices for deaf persons (TDDs), interpreters, note-takers, written materials, and other similar services and devices.

(d) *Complete complaint* means a written statement that contains the complainant's name and address and describes the agency's alleged discriminatory action in sufficient detail to inform the agency of the nature and date of the alleged violation of section 504. It shall be signed by the complainant or by someone authorized to do so on his or her behalf. Complaints filed on behalf of classes or third parties shall describe or identify (by name, if possible) the alleged victims of discrimination.

(e) *Facility* means all or any portion of buildings, structures, equipment, roads, walks, parking lots, rolling stock or other conveyances, or other real or personal property.

(f) *Individual with handicaps* means any person who has a physical or mental impairment that substantially limits one or more major life activities, has a record of such an impairment, or is regarded as having such an impairment. As used in this definition, the phrase:

(1) *Physical or mental impairment* includes:

(i) Any physiological disorder or condition, cosmetic disfigurement, or anatomical loss affecting one or more of the following body systems: Neurological; musculoskeletal; special sense organs; respiratory, including speech organs; cardiovascular; reproductive; digestive; genitourinary; hemic and lymphatic; skin; and endocrine; or

(ii) Any mental or psychological disorder, such as mental retardation, organic brain syndrome, emotional or mental illness, and specific learning disabilities. The term *physical or mental impairment* includes, but is not limited to, such diseases and conditions as orthopedic, visual, speech, and hearing impairments, cerebral palsy, epilepsy, muscular dystrophy, multiple sclerosis, cancer, heart disease, diabetes, mental retardation, emotional illness, and drug addiction and alcoholism.

(2) *Major life activities* includes functions such as caring for oneself, performing manual tasks, walking, seeing, hearing, speaking, breathing, learning, and working.

(3) *Has a record of such an impairment* means has a history of, or has been misclassified as having, a mental or physical impairment that substantially limits one more major life activities.

(4) *Is regarded as having an impairment* means:

(i) Has a physical or mental impairment that does not substantially limit major life activities but is treated by the agency as constituting such a limitation;

(ii) Has a physical or mental impairment that substantially limits major life activities only as a result of the attitudes of others toward such impairment; or

(iii) Has none of the impairments defined in paragraph (f)(1) of this definition but is treated by the agency as having such an impairment.

(g) *Qualified individual with handicaps* means an individual with handicaps who meets the essential eligibility requirements for participation in the program or activity conducted by the agency. With respect to employment, a qualified individual with handicaps is one who meets the definition of *qualified handicapped person* set forth in 29 CFR 1613.702(f), which is made applicable to this part by § 606.640 of this rule.

Farm Credit Administration

§ 606.630

(h) *Section 504* means section 504 of the Rehabilitation Act of 1973 (Pub. L. 93–112, 87 Stat. 394 (29 U.S.C. 794)), as amended by the Rehabilitation Act Amendments of 1974 (Pub. L. 93–516, 88 Stat. 1617); the Rehabilitation, Comprehensive Services, and Developmental Disabilities Amendments of 1978 (Pub. L. 95–602, 92 Stat. 2955); and the Rehabilitation Act Amendments of 1986 (Pub. L. 99–506, 100 Stat. 1810).

§§ 606.604–606.609 [Reserved]

§ 606.610 Self-evaluation.

(a) The agency shall, within one year of the effective date of this part, evaluate its current policies and practices, and the effects thereof, that do not or may not meet the requirements of this part, and, to the extent modification of any such policies and practices is required, the agency shall proceed to make the necessary modifications.

(b) The agency shall provide an opportunity to interested persons, including individuals with handicaps or organizations representing individuals with handicaps, to participate in the self-evaluation process by submitting comments (both oral and written).

(c) The agency shall, for at least three years following completion of the evaluation required under paragraph (a) of this section, maintain on file and make available for public inspection:

(1) A list of the interested persons who commented, with copies of comments received;

(2) A description of areas examined and any problems identified; and

(3) A description of any modifications made.

§ 606.611 Notice.

The agency shall make available to employees, applicants, participants, beneficiaries, and other interested persons such information regarding the provisions of this part and its applicability to the programs or activities conducted by the agency, and make such information available to them in such manner as the agency head finds necessary to apprise such persons of the protections against discrimination assured them by section 504 and this regulation.

§§ 606.612–606.629 [Reserved]

§ 606.630 General prohibitions against discrimination.

(a) No qualified individual with handicaps, on the basis of handicap, shall be excluded from participation in, be denied the benefits of, or otherwise be subjected to discrimination under any program or activity of the agency.

(b)(1) The agency, in providing any aid, benefit, or service, may not, directly or through contractual or other arrangements, on the basis of handicap:

(i) Deny a qualified individual with handicaps the oportunity to participate in or benefit from the activity, aid, benefit, or service;

(ii) Afford a qualified individual with handicaps an opportunity to participate in or benefit from the aid, benefit, or service that is not equal to that afforded others;

(iii) Provide a qualified individual with handicaps with an aid, benefit, or service that is not as effective in affording equal opportunity to obtain the same result, to gain the same benefit, or to reach the same level of achievement as that provided to others;

(iv) Provide different or separate aid, benefits, or services to individuals with handicaps or to any class of individuals with handicaps than is provided to others unless such action is necessary to provide qualified individuals with handicaps with aid, benefits, or services that are as effective as those provided to others;

(v) Deny a qualified individual with handicaps the opportunity to participate as a member of planning or advisory boards;

(vi) Otherwise limit a qualified individual with handicaps in the enjoyment of any right, privilege, advantage, or opportunity enjoyed by others receiving the aid, benefit, or service.

(2) The agency may not deny a qualified individual with handicaps the opportunity to participate in programs or activities that are not separate or different, despite the existence of permissibly separate or different programs or activities.

(3) The agency may not, directly or through contractual or other arrangements, utilize criteria or methods of

administration the purpose or effect of which would:

(i) Subject qualified individuals with handicaps to discrimination on the basis of handicap; or

(ii) Defeat or substantially impair accomplishment of the objectives of a program or activity with respect to individuals with handicaps.

(4) The agency may not, in determining the site or location of a facility, make selections the purpose or effect of which would:

(i) Exclude individuals with handicaps from, deny them the benefits of, or otherwise subject them to discrimination under any program or activity conducted by the agency; or

(ii) Defeat or substantially impair the accomplishment of the objectives of a program or activity with respect to individuals with handicaps.

(5) The agency, in the selection of procurement contractors, may not use criteria that subject qualified individuals with handicaps to discrimination on the basis of handicap.

(c) The exclusion of nonhandicapped persons from the benefits of a program limited by Federal statute or Executive order to individuals with handicaps or the exclusion of a specific class of individuals with handicaps from a program limited by Federal statute or Executive order to a different class of individuals with handicaps is not prohibited by this part.

(d) The agency shall administer programs and activities in the most integrated setting appropriate to the needs of qualified individuals with handicaps.

§§ 606.631–606.639 [Reserved]

§ 606.640 Employment.

No qualified individual with handicaps shall, on the basis of handicap, be subjected to discrimination in employment under any program or activity conducted by the agency. The definitions, requirements, and procedures of section 501 of the Rehabilitation Act of 1973 (29 U.S.C. 791), as established by the Equal Employment Opportunity Commission in 29 CFR part 1613, shall apply to employment in the agency.

§§ 606.641–606.648 [Reserved]

§ 606.649 Program accessibility: Discrimination prohibited.

Except as otherwise provided in § 606.650, no qualified individual with handicaps shall, because the agency's facilities are inaccessible to or unusable by individuals with handicaps, be denied the benefits of, be excluded from participation in, or otherwise be subjected to discrimination under any program or activity conducted by the agency.

§ 606.650 Program accessibility: Existing facilities.

(a) *General.* The agency shall operate each program or activity so that the program or activity, when viewed in its entirety, is readily accessible to and usable by individuals with handicaps. This paragraph does not:

(1) Necessarily require the agency to make each of its existing facilities accessible to and usable by individuals with handicaps;

(2) Require the agency to take any action that it can demonstrate would result in a fundamental alteration in the nature of a program or activity or in undue financial and administrative burdens. In those circumstances where agency personnel believe that the proposed action would fundamentally alter the program or activity or would result in undue financial and administrative burdens, the agency has the burden of proving that compliance with paragraph (a) of this section would result in such alteration or burdens. The decision that compliance would result in such alteration or burdens must be made by the agency head or his or her designee after considering all agency resources available for use in the funding and operation of the conducted program or activity, and must be accompanied by a written statement of the reasons for reaching that conclusion. In preparing the report, the agency shall make reasonable efforts to ensure that the person(s) to be accommodated has an opportunity to provide relevant information. If an action would result in such an alteration or such burdens, the agency shall take any other action

Farm Credit Administration § 606.660

that would not result in such an alteration or such burdens but would nevertheless ensure that individuals with handicaps receive the benefits and services of the program or activity.

(b) *Methods.* The agency may comply with the requirements of this section through such means as redesign of equipment, reassignment of services to accessible buildings, assignment of aides to beneficiaries, home visits, delivery of services at alternate accessible sites, alteration of existing facilities and construction of new facilities, or any other methods that result in making its programs or activities readily accessible to and usable by individuals with handicaps. The agency is not required to make structural changes in existing facilities where other methods are effective in achieving compliance with this section. The agency, in making alterations to existing buildings, shall meet accessibility requirements to the extent compelled by the Architectural Barriers Act of 1968, as amended (42 U.S.C. 4151 through 4157), and any regulations implementing it. In choosing among available methods for meeting the requirements of this section, the agency shall give priority to those methods that offer programs and activities to qualified individuals with handicaps in the most integrated setting appropriate.

(c) *Time period for compliance.* The agency shall comply with the obligations established under this section within sixty days of the effective date of this part except that where structural changes in facilities are undertaken, such changes shall be made within three years of the effective date of this part, but in any event as expeditiously as possible.

(d) *Transition plan.* In the event that structural changes to facilities will be undertaken to achieve accessibility, the agency shall develop, within six months of the effective date of this part, a transition plan setting forth the steps necessary to complete such changes. The agency shall provide an opportunity to interested persons, including individuals with handicaps or organizations representing individuals with handicaps, to participate in the development of the transition plan by submitting comments (both oral and written). A copy of the transition plan shall be made available for public inspection. The plan shall, at a minimum:

(1) Identify physical obstacles in the agency's facilities that limit the accessibility of its programs or activities to individuals with handicaps;

(2) Describe in detail the methods that will be used to make the facilities accessible;

(3) Specify the schedule for taking the steps necessary to achieve compliance with this section, and if the time period of the transition plan is longer than one year, identify steps that will be taken during each year of the transition period;

(4) Indicate the official responsible for implementation of the plan; and

(5) Identify the persons or groups who commented on the plan.

§ 606.651 **Program accessibility: New construction and alterations.**

Each building or part of a building that is constructed or altered by, on behalf of, or for the use of the agency shall be designed, constructed, or altered so as to be readily accessible to and usable by individuals with handicaps. The definitions, requirements, and standards of the Architectural Barriers Act (42 U.S.C. 4151 through 4157), as established in 41 CFR 101–19.600 to 101–19.607, apply to buildings covered by this section.

§§ 606.652–606.659 [Reserved]

§ 606.660 **Communications.**

(a) The agency shall take appropriate steps to ensure effective communication with applicants, participants, personnel of other Federal entities, and members of the public.

(1) The agency shall furnish appropriate auxiliary aids where necessary to afford an individual with handicaps an equal opportunity to participate in and enjoy the benefits of a program or activity conducted by the agency.

(i) In determining what type of auxiliary aid is necessary, the agency shall give primary consideration to the requests of the individual with handicaps.

(ii) The agency need not provide individually prescribed devices, readers for personal use or study, or other devices of a personal nature.

(2) Where the agency communicates with applicants and beneficiaries by telephone, telecommunication devices for deaf persons (TDDs) or equally effective telecommunication systems shall be used.

(b) The agency shall ensure that interested persons, including persons with impaired vision or hearing, can obtain information as to the existence and location of accessible services, activities, and facilities.

(c) The agency shall provide signage at a primary entrance to each of its inaccessible facilities directing users to a location at which they can obtain information about accessible facilities. The international symbol for accessibility shall be used at each primary entrance of an accessible facility.

(d) This section does not require the agency to take any action that it can demonstrate would result in a fundamental alteration in the nature of a program or activity or in undue financial and administrative burdens. In those circumstances where agency personnel believe that the proposed action would fundamentally alter the program or activity or would result in undue financial and administrative burdens, the agency has the burden of proving that compliance with this section would result in such alteration or burdens. The decision that compliance would result in such alteration or burdens must be made by the agency head or his or her designee after considering all agency resources available for use in the funding and operation of the conducted program or activity, and must be accompanied by a written statement of the reasons for reaching that conclusion. In preparing the report, the agency shall make reasonable efforts to ensure that the person(s) to be accommodated has an opportunity to provide relevant information. If an action required to comply with this section would result in such an alteration or such burdens, the agency shall take any other action that would not result in such an alteration or such burdens but would nevertheless ensure that, to the maximum extent possible, individuals with handicaps receive the benefits and services of the program or activity.

§§ 606.661–606.669 [Reserved]

§ 606.670 Compliance procedures.

(a) Except as provided in paragraph (b) of this section, this section applies to all allegations of discrimination on the basis of handicap in programs and activities conducted by the agency.

(b) The agency shall process complaints alleging violations of section 504 with respect to employment according to the procedures established by the Equal Employment Opportunity Commission in 29 CFR part 1613 pursuant to section 501 of the Rehabilitation Act of 1973 (29 U.S.C. 791).

(c) Responsibility for implementation and operation of this section shall be vested in the Director, Office of Management Services, Farm Credit Administration, 1501 Farm Credit Drive, McLean, VA 22102–5090.

(d) The agency shall accept and investigate all complete complaints for which it has jurisdiction. All complete complaints must be filed within 180 days of the alleged act of discrimination. The agency may extend this time period for good cause.

(e) If the agency receives a complaint over which it does not have jurisdiction, it shall promptly notify the complainant and shall make reasonable efforts to refer the complaint to the appropriate Government entity.

(f) The agency shall notify the Architectural and Transportation Barriers Compliance Board upon receipt of any complaint alleging that a building or facility that is subject to the Architectural Barriers Act of 1968, as amended (42 U.S.C. 4151 through 4157), is not readily accessible to and usable by individuals with handicaps.

(g) Within 180 days of the receipt of a complete complaint for which it has jurisdiction, the agency shall notify the complainant of the results of the investigation in a letter containing:

(1) Findings of fact and conclusions of law;

(2) A description of a remedy for each violation found; and

(3) A notice of the right to appeal.

(h) Appeals of the findings of fact and conclusions of law or remedies must be filed by the complainant within 90 days of receipt from the agency of the letter required by this paragraph. The agency may extend this time for good cause.

(i) Timely appeals shall be accepted and processed by the Director, Equal Employment Opportunity, or his/her designee, Farm Credit Administration, 1501 Farm Credit Drive, McLean, VA 22102–5090.

(j) The head of the agency shall notify the complainant of the results of the appeal within 60 days of the receipt of the request. If the head of the agency determines that additional information is needed from the complainant, he or she shall have 60 days from the date of receipt of the additional information to make his or her determination on the appeal.

(k) The time limits cited in paragraphs (g) and (j) of this section may be extended with the permission of the Assistant Attorney General.

(l) The agency may delegate its authority for conducting complaint investigations to other Federal agencies, except that the authority for making the final determination may not be delegated to another agency.

[53 FR 19889, June 1, 1988, as amended at 56 FR 2674, Jan. 24, 1991; 70 FR 69645, Nov. 17, 2005]

§§ 606.671–606.999 [Reserved]

PART 607—ASSESSMENT AND APPORTIONMENT OF ADMINISTRATIVE EXPENSES

Sec.
607.1 Purpose and scope.
607.2 Definitions.
607.3 Assessment of banks, associations, and designated other System entities.
607.4 Assessment of other System entities.
607.5 Notice of assessment.
607.6 Payment of assessment.
607.7 Late-payment charges on assessments.
607.8 Reimbursements for services to non-System entities.
607.9 Reimbursable billings.
607.10 Adjustments for overpayment or underpayment of assessments.
607.11 Report of assessments and expenses.

AUTHORITY: Secs. 5.15, 5.17 of the Farm Credit Act (12 U.S.C. 2250, 2252) and 12 U.S.C. 3025.

SOURCE: 58 FR 10942, Feb. 23, 1993, unless otherwise noted.

§ 607.1 Purpose and scope.

The regulations in part 607 implement the provisions of section 5.15 of the Farm Credit Act of 1971, 12 U.S.C. 2001 *et seq.* (Act) relating to Farm Credit Administration (FCA) assessments. The regulations prescribe the procedures for the equitable apportionment of FCA annual administrative expenses and necessary reserves among Farm Credit System (System) institutions. Pursuant to section 5.15(a) of the Act, the regulations also provide for the separate assessment of the FCA's costs of supervising and examining the Federal Agricultural Mortgage Corporation (FAMC). The regulations further provide for the reimbursement of expenses incurred in performing statutorily required examinations of non-System entities.

§ 607.2 Definitions.

For the purpose of this part, the following definitions shall apply:

(a) *Assessment* means the annual amount to be paid by each System institution to the Farm Credit Administration in accordance with section 5.15 of the Act.

(b) *Average risk-adjusted asset base* means the average of the risk-adjusted asset base (as determined in accordance with § 615.5210 of this chapter) of banks, associations, and designated other System entities, calculated as follows:

(1) For banks, associations, and designated other System entities with four quarters of risk-adjusted assets as of June 30 of each year, the sum of the average daily risk-adjusted assets as of the last day of the quarter as reported on each quarterly Call Report Schedule RC-G to the FCA for the most recent four quarters immediately preceding each September 15, divided by four;

(2) Except as provided in paragraphs (b)(3) and (b)(4) of this section, for banks, associations, and designated other System entities with less than four quarters of risk-adjusted assets as of June 30 of each year, the sum of the average daily risk-adjusted assets as of the last day of the quarter reported on each quarterly Call Report Schedule RC-G to the FCA for the quarters in which it was in existence immediately preceding September 15, divided by the

§ 607.3

number of quarters for which the Call Report Schedule RC-G was received;

(3) For banks, associations, and designated other System entities that were formed through mergers, consolidations, or transfers of direct lending authority, and have less than four quarters of risk-adjusted assets as of June 30, the sum of the average daily risk-adjusted assets as of the last day of the quarter for the most recent four quarters immediately preceding September 15 as reported on each quarterly Call Report Schedule RC-G filed by the newly chartered institution and the institutions that were merged or consolidated or that received direct lending authority, divided by four;

(4) For banks, associations, and designated other System entities chartered during the period July 1 through September 30 of each year that were not formed by the merger or consolidation of existing System institutions or the transfer of direct lending authority from another System institution, the total of the average daily risk-adjusted assets as of the last day of the quarter as reported on Call Report Schedule RC-G for the quarter ending September 30.

(c) *Composite Financial Institution Rating System (FIRS) rating* means the composite numerical assessment of the financial condition of an institution assigned to the institution by the FCA based on its most recent examination of the institution. The FIRS factors are generally considered to be important indicators of an institution's financial health. Institutions are rated on each of the factors during an examination. The composite FIRS rating ranges from 1 to 5, with a lower number indicating a better financial condition than a higher number.

(d) *Delinquent amount* means an amount owed to the FCA that has not been paid by the date specified in the FCA's Notice of Assessment or billing.

(e) *Designated other System entities* means other System entities designated by the FCA in § 607.3(c) to be assessed on the same basis as banks and associations under § 607.3.

(f) *Direct expenses* means the expenses of the FCA attributable to the performance of examinations.

(g) *Indirect expenses* means all FCA expenses that are not attributable to the performance of examinations.

(h) *Non-System entities* means the National Consumer Cooperative Bank, the National Cooperative Bank Development Corporation, and any other entity that is required to be examined, supervised, or otherwise regulated by the FCA that is not a System institution.

(i) *Notice of Assessment* means a written notice to each System institution showing the total amount assessed and owing, the fiscal year covered by the assessment, the amounts of installment payments, and the due dates for such payments. For banks, associations, and designated other System entities, the Notice of Assessment shall also include an individualized assessment table showing the assessment under § 607.3(b)(2), where applicable.

(j) *Other System entities* means any service corporation chartered under section 4.25 of the Act, the FAMC, the Federal Farm Credit Banks Funding Corporation, the Farm Credit Finance Corporation of Puerto Rico, and any other entity statutorily designated as a System institution that is not a bank or association.

(k) *System institutions* means banks, associations, and other System entities.

[58 FR 10942, Feb. 23, 1993, as amended at 59 FR 37403, July 22, 1994; 63 FR 34268, June 24, 1998; 70 FR 35348, June 17, 2005; 75 FR 35968, June 24, 2010]

§ 607.3 Assessment of banks, associations, and designated other System entities.

(a) Banks, associations, and other System entities designated in paragraph (c) of this section will be assessed annually pursuant to this section for funds to cover a portion of the FCA's administrative expenses and for such funds as may be required to maintain a necessary reserve. The total amount of the annual assessment of banks, associations, and designated other System entities shall be based on the FCA budget for each fiscal year plus such amount as may be required to maintain a necessary reserve, excluding amounts to be assessed against

Farm Credit Administration § 607.3

other System entities and reimbursements received from non-System entities.

(b) The assessment shall be apportioned among the banks, associations, and designated other System entities as follows:

(1) Thirty (30) percent of the assessment under this section shall be apportioned to each bank, association, and designated other System entity on the basis of each institution's pro rata share of the total average risk-adjusted asset base.

(2) Seventy (70) percent of the assessment under this section shall be apportioned to each bank, association, and designated other System entity based upon the amounts of the institution's average risk-adjusted assets that fall within the graduated risk-adjusted asset tiers contained in the following table. An institution's total assessment under this paragraph is the sum of the amounts assessed for risk-adjusted assets falling into each applicable tier, subject to adjustment for its FIRS rating as required in paragraphs (b)(2)(i) and (b)(2)(ii) of this section. The same assessment rate (designated as X_1 or a declining percentage of X_1 in the following table) will be applied to each dollar value of risk-adjusted assets falling within each tier, increased where applicable, by the amounts prescribed in paragraphs (b)(2)(i) and (b)(2)(ii) of this section. The actual assessment rate under this paragraph shall be determined annually based on relative average risk-adjusted asset bases, the FIRS ratings of individual institutions, and the FCA budget as adjusted pursuant to paragraph (a) of this section, but the relationship between the rates applied to each tier shall remain constant as set forth in the following table.

Average risk-adjusted asset size range (in millions)		Assessment rate
Over	To	
$0	$25	X_1
25	50	$.85X_1$
50	100	$.75X_1$
100	500	$.60X_1$
500	1,000	$.50X_1$
1,000	7,000	$.35X_1$
7,000	10,000	$.20X_1$
10,000		$.10X_1$

Example: XYZ association has a FIRS rating of 2 and average risk-adjusted assets of $500.4 million. The value of X_1 has been determined to be .000917, based on an FCA budget of $40.29 million.

X_1=.000917 therefore
$25,000,000×.0917% .... = $22,925
$.85X_1$=.000780 therefore
$25,000,000×.0780% .... = 19,500
$.75X_1$=.000688 therefore
$50,000,000×.0688% .... = 34,400
$.60X_1$=.000550 therefore
$400,000,000×.0550% .... = 220,000
$.50X_1$=.000458 therefore
$400,000×.0458% .... = 183

Total Assessment
under § 607.3(b)(2) ...... = 297,008

(i) If the FCA assigns a bank, association, or designated other System entity a composite FIRS rating of 3 following its most recent examination of the institution prior to the date of assessment, the assessment provided for in paragraph (b)(2) of this section shall be increased by 20 percent.

(ii) If the FCA assigns a bank, association, or designated other System entity a composite FIRS rating of 4 or 5 following its most recent examination of the institution prior to the date of assessment, the assessment provided for in paragraph (b)(2) of this section shall be increased by 40 percent.

(iii) Banks, associations, and designated other System entities that were formed through mergers or consolidations and have not been examined before their initial assessment under this section shall be deemed to have a composite FIRS rating equivalent to the best composite FIRS rating assigned to the merged or consolidated institutions in the FCA's most recent examination of the individual institutions prior to the date of merger or consolidation. Newly chartered institutions not formed through mergers or consolidations that have not been examined before their initial assessment under this section shall be deemed to have a composite FIRS rating of 2.

(3) Each bank, association, and designated other System entity shall pay a minimum assessment of $20,000 regardless of the result of the application of the assessment formula established by paragraphs (b)(1) and (b)(2) of this section. If such a minimum assessment

§ 607.4

is apportioned to an institution, that institution's average risk-adjusted asset base shall be deducted from the total average risk-adjusted asset base, and $20,000 shall be deducted from the total assessment amount for purposes of determining the assessments of banks, associations, and designated other System entities paying more than the $20,000 minimum assessment.

(c) Other System entities designated to be assessed in accordance with this section are:

The Farm Credit Services Leasing Corporation.

(d) Assessments may be adjusted periodically to reflect:

(1) Changes in the FCA budget and necessary reserve; and

(2) Any overpayment or underpayment by a bank, association, or designated other System entity in the prior fiscal year.

[58 FR 10942, Feb. 23, 1993, as amended at 63 FR 34268, June 24, 1998]

§ 607.4 Assessment of other System entities.

(a)(1) Unless otherwise designated to be assessed under § 607.3, and with the exception of FAMC as provided in paragraph (b) of this section, other System entities will be assessed for estimated direct expenses plus an allocated portion of FCA indirect expenses and such amount as may be required to maintain a necessary reserve. The estimate for direct expenses shall take into account the direct expenses incurred in the most recent examination of the entity preceding each September 15 and expected increases or decreases in examination work for the next fiscal year. A proportional amount of FCA indirect expenses will be allocated to each entity based on the estimated direct expenses related to the particular entity as a percentage of the total budgeted direct expenses of the agency (excluding direct expenses under paragraph (b) of this section) for the fiscal year covered by the assessment.

(2) Assessments of other System entities under paragraph (a)(1) of this section may be adjusted periodically to reflect:

(i) Changes in the FCA budget and necessary reserve; and

(ii) Any overpayment or underpayment by such other System entity in the prior fiscal year.

(b) *Assessment of Federal Agricultural Mortgage Corporation.* The FCA shall assess FAMC for the estimated cost of FCA's regulation, supervision, and examination of FAMC, including reasonably related administrative and overhead expenses. FAMC's assessment may be adjusted periodically to reflect changes in the FCA budget and to reconcile differences between FAMC's assessment and FCA's actual expenditures for regulation of FAMC in the prior fiscal year.

§ 607.5 Notice of assessment.

(a) Except as provided in paragraph (b) of this section, prior to September 15 of each year, the FCA shall determine the amount of assessment to be collected from each System institution for the next fiscal year under §§ 607.3 and 607.4 and shall provide each System institution with a Notice of Assessment. The total amount assessed each System institution in the Notice of Assessment shall be an obligation of each institution on October 1 of each fiscal year. The total amount assessed each System institution shall be payable not less often than quarterly in equal installments during each fiscal year, subject to adjustment pursuant to §§ 607.3(d), 607.4(a)(2), 607.4(b), and 607.10.

(b) For banks, associations and designated other System entities chartered during the period July 1 through September 30 of each year, the FCA shall, prior to December 15, determine the amount of assessment to be collected from each such institution for the remainder of the fiscal year and provide the institution with a Notice of Assessment. The total amount of the assessment becomes an obligation of the institution on January 1 and shall be payable in equal installments, subject to adjustment pursuant to §§ 607.3(d) and 607.10, not less often than quarterly for the remainder of the fiscal year. The first installment shall be due on January 1. This paragraph shall not apply to banks, associations, and designated other System entities formed by merger, consolidation, or transfer of direct lending authority.

(c) In the event of the proposed cancellation of the charter of a System institution, the unpaid installments of the total amount of the institution's assessment shall be provided for prior to the cancellation of the charter.

§ 607.6 Payment of assessment.

(a) System institutions shall pay the amounts due as scheduled in the FCA Notice of Assessment. Payment shall be made by electronic funds transfer (EFT) for credit to the FCA's account in the Department of the Treasury, by check to the FCA for deposit, or by such other means as the FCA may authorize.

(b) Payments made by EFT that are not received by the close of business on the due date shall be considered delinquent in accordance with § 607.7.

(c) Payments made by check that are not received by the FCA before the close of business on the third workday preceding the due date shall be considered delinquent in accordance with § 607.7.

§ 607.7 Late-payment charges on assessments.

(a) If any portion of a scheduled installment of a System institution's total assessment or the reimbursement billed to a non-System entity is not paid by the due date, the overdue amount shall be considered delinquent.

(b) Delinquent amounts shall be charged late-payment interest at the United States Treasury Department's current value of funds rate published in the FEDERAL REGISTER. Late payment interest shall be expressed as an annual rate of interest and shall accrue on a daily basis starting on the due date of the delinquent amount and continuing through the date payment is received by the FCA.

(c) The FCA shall waive the collection of interest on the delinquent amounts if such amounts are paid within 30 days of the date interest begins to accrue. The FCA may waive interest due on delinquent amounts upon finding no fault with the performance of the remitter.

(d) The FCA shall charge an amount necessary to cover the administrative costs incurred as a result of collection of any delinquent amount.

(e) The FCA shall charge a penalty of 6 percent per annum on any portion of a delinquent amount that is more than 90 days past due. Such penalty shall accrue from the date the amount became delinquent.

§ 607.8 Reimbursements for services to non-System entities.

Non-System entities shall be assessed for direct expenses plus an amount for FCA indirect expenses reasonably related to the services rendered to the non-System entity. Such related indirect expenses shall be calculated as a percentage of the FCA's overall indirect expenses based on the extent of FCA activities with respect to the non-System entity during the period since the entity's most recent assessment.

§ 607.9 Reimbursable billings.

The FCA shall bill the amounts due for services to non-System entities each year subsequent to the issuance of their respective Reports of Examination. Amounts billed are due in full within 30 days from the date billed. If the billed amount or any portion thereof remains unpaid at close of business on the due date, such amount or portion shall be considered delinquent in accordance with § 607.7.

§ 607.10 Adjustments for overpayment or underpayment of assessments.

Where adjustments for overpayment or underpayment of assessments are made pursuant to §§ 607.3(d), 607.4(a)(2), and 607.4(b), credits for overpayments or charges for underpayments shall be based on FCA administrative operating expenses incurred in the applicable fiscal year and on funds required to be maintained pursuant to section 5.15 of the Act. Such credits or charges shall be applied to the next applicable assessment payment due during the current or subsequent fiscal year. Where such adjustments are made, the FCA shall provide the institution with a statement of adjustment at least 15 days prior to the date when the institution's next assessment payment is due. Adjustments in assessments shall be made in principal amount only. Overdue amounts under § 607.7 are not underpayments for assessment adjustment purposes.

§ 607.11 Report of assessments and expenses.

By January 15 of each calendar year, the FCA shall provide each assessed System institution with a report of assessments and expenses for the preceding fiscal year showing total assessments and other income received as applied to expenses incurred by major budget category and amounts set aside for a necessary reserve.

PART 608—COLLECTION OF CLAIMS OWED THE UNITED STATES

Subpart A—Administrative Collection of Claims

Sec.
608.801 Authority.
608.802 Applicability.
608.803 Definitions.
608.804 Delegation of authority.
608.805 Responsibility for collection.
608.806 Demand for payment.
608.807 Right to inspect and copy records.
608.808 Right to offer to repay claim.
608.809 Right to agency review.
608.810 Review procedures.
608.811 Special review.
608.812 Charges for interest, administrative costs, and penalties.
608.813 Contracting for collection services.
608.814 Reporting of credit information.
608.815 Credit report.

Subpart B—Administrative Offset

608.820 Applicability.
608.821 Collection by offset.
608.822 Notice requirements before offset.
608.823 Right to review of claim.
608.824 Waiver of procedural requirements.
608.825 Coordinating offset with other Federal agencies.
608.826 Stay of offset.
608.827 Offset against amounts payable from Civil Service Retirement and Disability Fund.

Subpart C—Offset Against Salary

608.835 Purpose.
608.836 Applicability of regulations.
608.837 Definitions.
608.838 Waiver requests and claims to the General Accounting Office.
608.839 Procedures for salary offset.
608.840 Refunds.
608.841 Requesting current paying agency to offset salary.
608.842 Responsibility of the FCA as the paying agency.
608.843 Nonwaiver of rights by payments.

AUTHORITY: Sec. 5.17 of the Farm Credit Act; 12 U.S.C. 2252; 31 U.S.C. 3701–3719; 5 U.S.C. 5514; 4 CFR parts 101–105; 5 CFR part 550.

SOURCE: 59 FR 13187, Mar. 21, 1994, unless otherwise noted.

Subpart A—Administrative Collection of Claims

§ 608.801 Authority.

The regulations of this part are issued under the Federal Claims Collection Act of 1966, as amended by the Debt Collection Act of 1982, 31 U.S.C. 3701–3719 and 5 U.S.C. 5514, and in conformity with the joint regulations issued under that Act by the General Accounting Office and the Department of Justice (joint regulations) prescribing standards for administrative collection, compromise, suspension, and termination of agency collection actions, and referral to the General Accounting Office and to the Department of Justice for litigation of civil claims for money or property owed to the United States (4 CFR parts 101–105).

§ 608.802 Applicability.

This part applies to all claims of indebtedness due and owing to the United States and collectible under procedures authorized by the Federal Claims Collection Act of 1966, as amended by the Debt Collection Act of 1982. The joint regulations and this part do not apply to conduct in violation of antitrust laws, tax claims, claims between Federal agencies, or to any claim which appears to involve fraud, presentation of a false claim, or misrepresentation on the part of the debtor or any other party having an interest in the claim, unless the Justice Department authorizes the Farm Credit Administration, pursuant to 4 CFR 101.3, to handle the claim in accordance with the provisions of 4 CFR parts 101–105. Additionally, this part does not apply to Farm Credit Administration assessments under part 607 of this chapter.

§ 608.803 Definitions.

In this part (except where the term is defined elsewhere in this part), the following definitions shall apply:

(a) *Administrative offset* or *offset*, as defined in 31 U.S.C. 3701(a)(1), means

Farm Credit Administration

§ 608.805

withholding money payable by the United States Government to, or held by the Government for, a person to satisfy a debt the person owes the Government.

(b) *Agency* means a department, agency, or instrumentality in the executive or legislative branch of the Government.

(c) *Claim* or *debt* means money or property owed by a person or entity to an agency of the Federal Government. A "claim" or "debt" includes amounts due the Government from loans insured by or guaranteed by the United States and all other amounts due from fees, leases, rents, royalties, services, sales of real or personal property, overpayment, penalties, damages, interest, and fines.

(d) *Claim certification* means a creditor agency's written request to a paying agency to effect an administrative offset.

(e) *Creditor agency* means an agency to which a claim or debt is owed.

(f) *Debtor* means the person or entity owing money to the Federal Government.

(g) *FCA* means the Farm Credit Administration.

(h) *Hearing official* means an individual who is responsible for reviewing a claim under § 608.810 of this part.

(i) *Paying agency* means an agency of the Federal Government owing money to a debtor against which an administrative or salary offset can be effected.

(j) *Salary offset* means an administrative offset to collect a debt under 5 U.S.C. 5514 by deductions at one or more officially established pay intervals from the current pay account of a debtor.

§ 608.804 Delegation of authority.

The FCA official(s) designated by the Chairman of the Farm Credit Administration are authorized to perform all duties which the Chairman is authorized to perform under these regulations, the Federal Claims Collection Act of 1966, as amended, and the joint regulations issued under that Act.

§ 608.805 Responsibility for collection.

(a) The collection of claims shall be aggressively pursued in accordance with the provisions of the Federal Claims Collection Act of 1966, as amended, the joint regulations issued under that Act, and these regulations. Debts owed to the United States, together with charges for interest, penalties, and administrative costs, should be collected in one lump sum unless otherwise provided by law. If a debtor requests installment payments, the debtor, as requested by the FCA, shall provide sufficient information to demonstrate that the debtor is unable to pay the debt in one lump sum. When appropriate, the FCA shall arrange an installment payment schedule. Claims which cannot be collected directly or by administrative offset shall be either written off as administratively uncollectible or referred to the General Counsel for further consideration.

(b) The Chairman, or designee of the Chairman, may compromise claims for money or property arising out of the activities of the FCA, where the claim (exclusive of charges for interest, penalties, and administrative costs) does not exceed $100,000. When the claim exceeds $100,000 (exclusive of charges for interest, penalties, and administrative costs), the authority to accept a compromise rests solely with the Department of Justice. The standards governing the compromise of claims are set forth in 4 CFR part 103.

(c) The Chairman, or designee of the Chairman, may suspend or terminate the collection of claims which do not exceed $100,000 (exclusive of charges for interest, penalties, and administrative costs) after deducting the amount of any partial payments or collections. If, after deducting the amount of any partial payments or collections, a claim exceeds $100,000 (exclusive of charges for interest, penalties, and administrative costs), the authority to suspend or terminate rests solely with the Department of Justice. The standards governing the suspension or termination of claim collections are set forth in 4 CFR part 104.

(d) The FCA shall refer claims to the Department of Justice for litigation or to the General Accounting Office (GAO) for claims arising from audit exceptions taken by the GAO to payments made by the FCA in accordance with 4 CFR part 105.

§ 608.806 Demand for payment.

(a) A total of three progressively stronger written demands at not more than 30-day intervals should normally be made upon a debtor, unless a response or other information indicates that additional written demands would either be unnecessary or futile. When necessary to protect the Government's interest, written demands may be preceded by other appropriate actions under Federal law, including immediate referral for litigation and/or administrative offset.

(b) The initial demand for payment shall be in writing and shall inform the debtor of the following:

(1) The amount of the debt, the date it was incurred, and the facts upon which the determination of indebtedness was made;

(2) The payment due date, which shall be 30 calendar days from the date of mailing or hand delivery of the initial demand for payment;

(3) The right of the debtor to inspect and copy the records of the agency related to the claim or to receive copies if personal inspection is impractical. The debtor shall be informed that the debtor may be assessed for the cost of copying the documents in accordance with § 608.807;

(4) The right of the debtor to obtain a review of the FCA's determination of indebtedness;

(5) The right of the debtor to offer to enter into a written agreement with the agency to repay the amount of the claim. The debtor shall be informed that the acceptance of such an agreement is discretionary with the agency;

(6) That charges for interest, penalties, and administrative costs will be assessed against the debtor, in accordance with 31 U.S.C. 3717, if payment is not received by the payment due date;

(7) That if the debtor has not entered into an agreement with the FCA to pay the debt, has not requested the FCA to review the debt, or has not paid the debt by the payment due date, the FCA intends to collect the debt by all legally available means, which may include initiating legal action against the debtor, referring the debt to a collection agency for collection, collecting the debt by offset, or asking other Federal agencies for assistance in collecting the debt by offset;

(8) The name and address of the FCA official to whom the debtor shall send all correspondence relating to the debt; and

(9) Other information, as may be appropriate.

(c) If, prior to, during, or after completion of the demand cycle, the FCA determines to collect the debt by either administrative or salary offset, the FCA shall follow, as applicable, the requirements for a Notice of Intent to Collect by Administrative Offset or a Notice of Intent to Collect by Salary Offset set forth in § 608.822.

(d) If no response to the initial demand for payment is received by the payment due date, the FCA shall take further action under this part, under the Federal Claims Collection Act of 1966, as amended, under the joint regulations (4 CFR parts 101–105), or under any other applicable State or Federal law. These actions may include reports to credit bureaus, referrals to collection agencies, termination of contracts, debarment, and salary or administrative offset.

§ 608.807 Right to inspect and copy records.

The debtor may inspect and copy the FCA records related to the claim. The debtor shall give the FCA reasonable advance notice that it intends to inspect and copy the records involved. The debtor shall pay copying costs unless they are waived by the FCA. Copying costs shall be assessed pursuant to §§ 602.11 and 602.12 of this chapter.

[59 FR 13187, Mar. 21, 1994, as amended at 71 FR 54900, Sept. 20, 2006]

§ 608.808 Right to offer to repay claim.

(a) The debtor may offer to enter into a written agreement with the FCA to repay the amount of the claim. The acceptance of such an offer and the decision to enter into such a written agreement is at the discretion of the FCA.

(b) If the debtor requests a repayment arrangement because payment of the amount due would create a financial hardship, the FCA shall analyze the debtor's financial condition. The FCA may enter into a written agreement with the debtor permitting the

Farm Credit Administration

§ 608.810

debtor to repay the debt in installments if the FCA determines, in its sole discretion, that payment of the amount due would create an undue financial hardship for the debtor. The written agreement shall set forth the amount and frequency of installment payments and shall, in accordance with § 608.812, provide for the imposition of charges for interest, penalties, and administrative costs unless waived by the FCA.

(c) The written agreement may require the debtor to execute a confess-judgment note when the total amount of the deferred installments will exceed $750. The FCA shall provide the debtor with a written explanation of the consequences of signing a confess-judgment note. The debtor shall sign a statement acknowledging receipt of the written explanation. The statement shall recite that the written explanation was read and understood before execution of the note and that the debtor signed the note knowingly and voluntarily. Documentation of these procedures will be maintained in the FCA's file on the debtor.

§ 608.809 Right to agency review.

(a) If the debtor disputes the claim, the debtor may request a review of the FCA's determination of the existence of the debt or of the amount of the debt. If only part of the claim is disputed, the undisputed portion should be paid by the payment due date.

(b) To obtain a review, the debtor shall submit a written request for review to the FCA official named in the initial demand letter, within 15 calendar days after receipt of the letter. The debtor's request for review shall state the basis on which the claim is disputed.

(c) The FCA shall promptly notify the debtor, in writing, that the FCA has received the request for review. The FCA shall conduct its review of the claim in accordance with § 608.810.

(d) Upon completion of its review of the claim, the FCA shall notify the debtor whether the FCA's determination of the existence or amount of the debt has been sustained, amended, or canceled. The notification shall include a copy of the written decision issued by the hearing official pursuant to § 608.810(e). If the FCA's determination is sustained, this notification shall contain a provision which states that the FCA intends to collect the debt by all legally available means, which may include initiating legal action against the debtor, referring the debt to a collection agency for collection, collecting the debt by offset, or asking other Federal agencies for assistance in collecting the debt by offset.

§ 608.810 Review procedures.

(a) Unless an oral hearing is required by § 608.823(d), the FCA's review shall be a review of the written record of the claim.

(b) If an oral hearing is required under § 608.823(d), the FCA shall provide the debtor with a reasonable opportunity for such a hearing. The oral hearing, however, shall not be an adversarial adjudication and need not take the form of a formal evidentiary hearing. All significant matters discussed at the hearing, however, will be carefully documented.

(c) Any review required by this part, whether a review of the written record or an oral hearing, shall be conducted by a hearing official. In the case of a salary offset, the hearing official shall not be under the supervision or control of the Chairman of the Farm Credit Administration.

(d) The FCA may be represented by legal counsel. The debtor may represent himself or herself or may be represented by an individual of the debtor's choice and at the debtor's expense.

(e) The hearing official shall issue a final written decision based on documentary evidence and, if applicable, information developed at an oral hearing. The written decision shall be issued as soon as practicable after the review but not later than 60 days after the date on which the request for review was received by the FCA, unless the debtor requests a delay in the proceedings. A delay in the proceedings shall be granted if the hearing official determines, in his or her sole discretion, that there is good cause to grant the delay. If a delay is granted, the 60-day decision period shall be extended by the number of days by which the review was postponed.

(f) Upon issuance of the written opinion, the FCA shall promptly notify the debtor of the hearing official's decision. Said notification shall include a copy of the written decision issued by the hearing official pursuant to paragraph (e) of this section.

§ 608.811 Special review.

(a) An employee subject to salary offset, under subpart C of this part, or a voluntary repayment agreement, may, at any time, request a special review by the FCA of the amount of the salary offset or voluntary repayment, based on materially changed circumstances such as, but not limited to, catastrophic illness, divorce, death, or disability.

(b) To determine whether an offset would prevent the employee from meeting essential subsistence expenses (costs incurred for food, housing, clothing, transportation, and medical care), the employee shall submit a detailed statement and supporting documents for the employee, his or her spouse, and dependents indicating:

(1) Income from all sources;
(2) Assets;
(3) Liabilities;
(4) Number of dependents;
(5) Expenses for food, housing, clothing, and transportation;
(6) Medical expenses; and
(7) Exceptional expenses, if any.

(c) If the employee requests a special review under this section, the employee shall file an alternative proposed offset or payment schedule and a statement, with supporting documents, showing why the current salary offset or payments result in an extreme financial hardship to the employee.

(d) The FCA shall evaluate the statement and supporting documents, and determine whether the original offset or repayment schedule imposes an undue financial hardship on the employee. The FCA shall notify the employee in writing of such determination, including, if appropriate, a revised offset or payment schedule.

§ 608.812 Charges for interest, administrative costs, and penalties.

(a) Except as provided in paragraph (d) of this section, the FCA shall:
(1) Assess interest on unpaid claims;
(2) Assess administrative costs incurred in processing and handling overdue claims; and
(3) Assess penalty charges not to exceed 6 percent a year on any part of a debt more than 90 days past due. The imposition of charges for interest, administrative costs, and penalties shall be made in accordance with 31 U.S.C. 3717.

(b)(1) Interest shall accrue from the date of mailing or hand delivery of the initial demand for payment or the Notice of Intent to Collect by either Administrative or Salary Offset if the amount of the claim is not paid within 30 days from the date of mailing or hand delivery of the initial demand or notice.

(2) The 30-day period may be extended on a case-by-case basis if the FCA reasonably determines that such action is appropriate. Interest shall only accrue on the principal of the claim and the interest rate shall remain fixed for the duration of the indebtedness, except, as provided in paragraph (c) of this section, in cases where a debtor has defaulted on a repayment agreement and seeks to enter into a new agreement, or if the FCA reasonably determines that a higher rate is necessary to protect the interests of the United States.

(c) If a debtor defaults on a repayment agreement and seeks to enter into a new agreement, the FCA may assess a new interest rate on the unpaid claim. In addition, charges for interest, administrative costs, and penalties which accrued but were not collected under the original repayment agreement shall be added to the principal of the claim to be paid under the new repayment agreement. Interest shall accrue on the entire principal balance of the claim, as adjusted to reflect any increase resulting from the addition of these charges.

(d) The FCA may waive charges for interest, administrative costs, and/or penalties if it determines that:

(1) The debtor is unable to pay any significant sum toward the claim within a reasonable period of time;

(2) Collection of charges for interest, administrative costs, and/or penalties would jeopardize collection of the principal of the claim;

(3) Collection of charges for interest, administrative costs, or penalties would be against equity and good conscience; or

(4) It is otherwise in the best interest of the United States, including the situation where an installment payment agreement or offset is in effect.

§ 608.813 Contracting for collection services.

The Chairman, or designee of the Chairman, may contract for collection services in accordance with 31 U.S.C. 3718 and 4 CFR 102.6 to recover debts.

§ 608.814 Reporting of credit information.

The Chairman, or designee of the Chairman, may disclose to a consumer reporting agency information that an individual is responsible for a debt owed to the United States. Information will be disclosed to reporting agencies in accordance with the terms and conditions of agreements entered into between the FCA and the reporting agencies. The terms and conditions of such agreements shall specify that all of the rights and protection afforded to the debtor under 31 U.S.C. 3711(f) have been fulfilled. The FCA shall notify each consumer reporting agency, to which a claim was disclosed, when the debt has been satisfied.

§ 608.815 Credit report.

In order to aid the FCA in making appropriate determinations regarding the collection and compromise of claims; the collection of charges for interest, administrative costs, and penalties; the use of administrative offset; the use of other collection methods; and the likelihood of collecting the claim, the FCA may institute, consistent with the provisions of the Fair Credit Reporting Act (15 U.S.C. 1681, et seq.), a credit investigation of the debtor immediately following a determination that the claim exists.

Subpart B—Administrative Offset

§ 608.820 Applicability.

(a) The provisions of this subpart shall apply to the collection of debts by administrative [or salary] offset under 31 U.S.C. 3716, 5 U.S.C. 5514, or other statutory or common law.

(b) Offset shall not be used to collect a debt more than 10 years after the Government's right to collect the debt first accrued, unless facts material to the Government's right to collect the debt were not known and could not reasonably have been known by the official or officials of the Government who were charged with the responsibility of discovering and collecting such debt.

(c) Offset shall not be used with respect to:

(1) Debts owed by other agencies of the United States or by any State or local government;

(2) Debts arising under or payments made under the Social Security Act, the Internal Revenue Code of 1986, as amended, or tariff laws of the United States; or

(3) Any case in which collection by offset of the type of debt involved is explicitly provided for or prohibited by another statute.

(d) Unless otherwise provided by contract or law, debts or payments which are not subject to offset under 31 U.S.C. 3716 or 5 U.S.C. 5514 may be collected by offset if such collection is authorized under common law or other applicable statutory authority.

§ 608.821 Collection by offset.

(a) Collection of a debt by administrative [or salary] offset shall be accomplished in accordance with the provisions of these regulations, of 4 CFR 102.3, and 5 CFR part 550, subpart K. It is not necessary for the debt to be reduced to judgment or to be undisputed for offset to be used.

(b) The Chairman, or designee of the Chairman, may determine that it is feasible to collect a debt to the United States by offset against funds payable to the debtor.

(c) The feasibility of collecting a debt by offset will be determined on a case-by-case basis. This determination shall be made by considering all relevant factors, including the following:

(1) The degree to which the offset can be accomplished in accordance with law. This determination should take into consideration relevant statutory, regulatory, and contractual requirements;

§ 608.822

(2) The degree to which the FCA is certain that its determination of the existence and amount of the debt is correct;

(3) The practicality of collecting the debt by offset. The cost, in time and money, of collecting the debt by offset and the amount of money which can reasonably be expected to be recovered through offset will be relevant to this determination; and

(4) Whether the use of offset will substantially interfere with or defeat the purpose of a program authorizing payments against which the offset is contemplated. For example, under a grant program in which payments are made in advance of the grantee's performance, the imposition of offset against such a payment may be inappropriate.

(d) The collection of a debt by offset may not be feasible when there are circumstances which would indicate that the likelihood of collection by offset is less than probable.

(e) The offset will be effected 31 days after the debtor receives a Notice of Intent to Collect by Administrative Offset (or Notice of Intent to Collect by Salary Offset if the offset is a salary offset), or upon the expiration of a stay of offset, unless the FCA determines under § 608.824 that immediate action is necessary.

(f) If the debtor owes more than one debt, amounts recovered through offset may be applied to them in any order. Applicable statutes of limitation would be considered before applying the amounts recovered to any debts owed.

§ 608.822 Notice requirements before offset.

(a) Except as provided in § 608.824, the FCA will provide the debtor with 30 calendar days' written notice that unpaid debt amounts shall be collected by administrative [or salary] offset (Notice of Intent to Collect by Administrative [or Salary] Offset) before the FCA imposes offset against any money that is to be paid to the debtor.

(b) The Notice of Intent to Collect by Administrative [or Salary] Offset shall be delivered to the debtor by hand or by mail and shall provide the following information:

(1) The amount of the debt, the date it was incurred, and the facts upon which the determination of indebtedness was made;

(2) In the case of an administrative offset, the payment due date, which shall be 30 calendar days from the date of mailing or hand delivery of the Notice;

(3) In the case of a salary offset: (i) The FCA's intention to collect the debt by means of deduction from the employee's current disposable pay account until the debt and all accumulated interest is paid in full; and

(ii) The amount, frequency, proposed beginning date, and duration of the intended deductions;

(4) The right of the debtor to inspect and copy the records of the FCA related to the claim or to receive copies if personal inspection is impractical. The debtor shall be informed that the debtor shall be assessed for the cost of copying the documents in accordance with § 608.807;

(5) The right of the debtor to obtain a review of, and to request a hearing, on the FCA's determination of indebtedness, the propriety of collecting the debt by offset, and, in the case of salary offset, the propriety of the proposed repayment schedule (i.e., the percentage of disposable pay to be deducted each pay period). The debtor shall be informed that to obtain a review, the debtor shall deliver a written request for a review to the FCA official named in the Notice, within 15 calendar days after the debtor's receipt of the Notice. In the case of a salary offset, the debtor shall also be informed that the review shall be conducted by an official arranged for by the FCA who shall be a hearing official not under the control of the Chairman of the Farm Credit Administration, or an administrative law judge;

(6) That the filing of a petition for hearing within 15 calendar days after receipt of the Notice will stay the commencement of collection proceedings;

(7) That a final decision on the hearing (if one is requested) will be issued at the earliest practical date, but not later than 60 days after the filing of the written request for review unless the employee requests, and the hearing official grants, a delay in the proceedings;

(8) The right of the debtor to offer to enter into a written agreement with the FCA to repay the amount of the claim. The debtor shall be informed that the acceptance of such an agreement is discretionary with the FCA;

(9) That charges for interest, penalties, and administrative costs shall be assessed against the debtor, in accordance with 31 U.S.C. 3717, if payment is not received by the payment due date. The debtor shall be informed that such assessments must be made unless excused in accordance with the Federal Claims Collection Standards (4 CFR parts 103 and 104);

(10) The amount of accrued interest and the amount of any other penalties or administrative costs which may have been added to the principal debt;

(11) That if the debtor has not entered into an agreement with the FCA to pay the debt, has not requested the FCA to review the debt, or has not paid the debt prior to the date on which the offset is to be imposed, the FCA intends to collect the debt by administrative [or salary] offset or by requesting other Federal agencies for assistance in collecting the debt by offset. The debtor shall be informed that the offset shall be imposed against any funds that might become available to the debtor, until the principal debt and all accumulated interest and other charges are paid in full;

(12) The date on which the offset will be imposed, which shall be 31 calendar days from the date of mailing or hand delivery of the Notice. The debtor shall be informed that the FCA reserves the right to impose an offset prior to this date if the FCA determines that immediate action is necessary;

(13) That any knowingly false or frivolous statements, representations, or evidence may subject the debtor to:

(i) Penalties under the False Claims Act, sections 3729 through 3731 of title 31, United States Code, or any other applicable statutory authority;

(ii) Criminal penalties under sections 286, 287, 1001, and 1002 of title 18, United States Code, or any other applicable statutory authority; and, with regard to employees,

(iii) Disciplinary procedures appropriate under chapter 75 of title 5, United States Code; part 752 of title 5, Code of Federal Regulations, or any other applicable statute or regulation;

(14) The name and address of the FCA official to whom the debtor shall send all correspondence relating to the debt or the offset;

(15) Any other rights and remedies available to the debtor under statutes or regulations governing the program for which the collection is being made;

(16) That unless there are applicable contractual or statutory provisions to the contrary, amounts paid on or deducted for the debt, which are later waived or found not owed to the United States, will be promptly refunded to the employee; and

(17) Other information, as may be appropriate.

(c) When the procedural requirements of this section have been provided to the debtor in connection with the same debt or under some other statutory or regulatory authority, the FCA is not required to duplicate those requirements before effecting offset.

§ 608.823 Right to review of claim.

(a) If the debtor disputes the claim, the debtor may request a review of the FCA's determination of the existence of the debt, the amount of the debt, the propriety of collecting the debt by offset, and in the case of salary offset, the propriety of the proposed repayment schedule. If only part of the claim is disputed, the undisputed portion should be paid by the payment due date.

(b) To obtain a review, the debtor shall submit a written request for review to the FCA official named in the Notice of Intent to Collect by Administrative [or Salary] Offset within 15 calendar days after receipt of the notice. The debtor's written request for review shall state the basis on which the claim is disputed and shall specify whether the debtor requests an oral hearing or a review of the written record of the claim. If an oral hearing is requested, the debtor shall explain in the request why the matter cannot be resolved by a review of the documentary evidence alone.

(c) The FCA shall promptly notify the debtor, in writing, that the FCA has received the request for review.

§ 608.824

The FCA shall conduct its review of the claim in accordance with § 608.810.

(d) The FCA's review of the claim, under this section, shall include providing the debtor with a reasonable opportunity for an oral hearing if:

(1) An applicable statute authorizes or requires the FCA to consider waiver of the indebtedness, the debtor requests waiver of the indebtedness, and the waiver determination turns on an issue of credibility or veracity; or

(2) The debtor requests reconsideration of the debt and the FCA determines that the question of the indebtedness cannot be resolved by reviewing the documentary evidence; for example, when the validity of the debt turns on an issue of credibility or veracity.

(e) A debtor waives the right to a hearing and will have his or her debt offset in accordance with the proposed offset schedule if the debtor:

(1) Fails to file a written request for review within the timeframe set forth in paragraph (b) of this section, unless the FCA determines that the delay was the result of circumstances beyond his or her control; or

(2) Fails to appear at an oral hearing of which he or she was notified unless the hearing official determines that the failure to appear was due to circumstances beyond the employee's control.

(f) Upon completion of its review of the claim, the FCA shall notify the debtor whether the FCA's determination of the existence or amount of the debt has been sustained, amended, or canceled. The notification shall include a copy of the written decision issued by the hearing official, pursuant to § 608.810(e). If the FCA's determination is sustained, this notification shall contain a provision which states that the FCA intends to collect the debt by offset or by requesting other Federal agencies for assistance in collecting the debt.

(g) When the procedural requirements of this section have been provided to the debtor in connection with the same debt or under some other statutory or regulatory authority, the FCA is not required to duplicate those requirements before effecting offset.

§ 608.824 Waiver of procedural requirements.

(a) The FCA may impose offset against a payment to be made to a debtor prior to the completion of the procedures required by this part, if:

(1) Failure to impose the offset would substantially prejudice the Government's ability to collect the debt; and

(2) The timing of the payment against which the offset will be imposed does not reasonably permit the completion of those procedures.

(b) The procedures required by this part shall be complied with promptly after the offset is imposed. Amounts recovered by offset, which are later found not to be owed to the Government, shall be promptly refunded to the debtor.

§ 608.825 Coordinating offset with other Federal agencies.

(a)(1) Any creditor agency which requests the FCA to impose an offset against amounts owed to the debtor shall submit to the FCA a claim certification which meets the requirements of this paragraph. The FCA shall submit the same certification to any agency that the FCA requests to effect an offset.

(2) The claim certification shall be in writing. It shall certify the debtor owes the debt and that all of the applicable requirements of 31 U.S.C. 3716 and 4 CFR part 102 have been met. If the intended offset is to be a salary offset, a claim certification shall instead certify that the debtor owes the debt and that the applicable requirements of 5 U.S.C. 5514 and 5 CFR part 550, subpart K, have been met.

(3) A certification that the debtor owes the debt shall state the amount of the debt, the factual basis supporting the determination of indebtedness, and the date on which payment of the debt was due. A certification that the requirements of 31 U.S.C. 3716 and 4 CFR part 102 have been met shall include a statement that the debtor has been sent a notice of Intent to Collect by Administrative Offset at least 31 calendar days prior to the date of the intended offset or a statement that pursuant to 4 CFR 102.3(b)(5) said Notice was not required to be sent. A certification that the requirements of 5

Farm Credit Administration § 608.836

U.S.C. 5514 and 5 CFR part 550, subpart K, have been met shall include a statement that the debtor has been sent a Notice of Intent to Collect by Salary Offset at least 31 calendar days prior to the date of the intended offset or a statement that pursuant to 4 CFR 102.3(b)(5) said Notice was not required to be sent.

(b)(1) The FCA shall not effect an offset requested by another Federal agency without first obtaining the claim certification required by paragraph (a) of this section. If the FCA receives an incomplete claim certification, the FCA shall return the claim certification with notice that a claim certification which complies with the requirements of paragraph (a) of this section must be submitted to the FCA before the FCA will consider effecting an offset.

(2) The FCA may rely on the information contained in the claim certification provided by a requesting creditor agency. The FCA is not authorized to review a creditor agency's determination of indebtedness.

(c) Only the creditor agency may agree to enter into an agreement with the debtor for the repayment of the claim. Only the creditor agency may agree to compromise, suspend, or terminate collection of the claim.

(d) The FCA may decline, for good cause, a request by another agency to effect an offset. Good cause includes that the offset might disrupt, directly or indirectly, essential FCA operations. The refusal and the reasons shall be sent in writing to the creditor agency.

§ 608.826 Stay of offset.

(a)(1) When a creditor agency receives a debtor's request for inspection of agency records, the offset is stayed for 10 calendar days beyond the date set for the record inspection.

(2) When a creditor agency receives a debtor's offer to enter into a repayment agreement, the offset is stayed until the debtor is notified as to whether the proposed agreement is acceptable.

(3) When a review is conducted, the offset is stayed until the creditor agency issues a final written decision.

(b) When offset is stayed, the amount of the debt and the amount of any accrued interest or other charges will be withheld from payments to the debtor. The withheld amounts shall not be applied against the debt until the stay expires. If withheld funds are later determined not to be subject to offset, they will be promptly refunded to the debtor.

(c) If the FCA is the creditor agency and the offset is stayed, the FCA will immediately notify an offsetting agency to withhold the payment pending termination of the stay.

§ 608.827 Offset against amounts payable from Civil Service Retirement and Disability Fund.

The FCA may request that monies payable to a debtor from the Civil Service Retirement and Disability Fund be administratively offset to collect debts owed to the FCA by the debtor. The FCA must certify that the debtor owes the debt, the amount of the debt, and that the FCA has complied with the requirements set forth in this part, 4 CFR 102.3, and the Office of Personnel Management regulations. The request shall be submitted to the official designated in the Office of Personnel Management regulations to receive the request.

Subpart C—Offset Against Salary

§ 608.835 Purpose.

The purpose of this subpart is to implement section 5 of the Debt Collection Act of 1982 (Pub. L. 97-365)(5 U.S.C. 5514), which authorizes the collection of debts owed by Federal employees to the Federal Government by means of salary offsets. These regulations provide procedures for the collection of a debt owed to the Government by the imposition of a salary offset against amounts payable to a Federal employee as salary. These regulations are consistent with the regulations on salary offset published by the Office of Personnel Management, codified in 5 CFR part 550, subpart K. Since salary offset is a type of administrative offset, this subpart supplements subpart B.

§ 608.836 Applicability of regulations.

(a) These regulations apply to the following cases:

43

§ 608.837

(1) Where the FCA is owed a debt by an individual currently employed by another agency;

(2) Where the FCA is owed a debt by an individual who is currently employed by the FCA; or

(3) Where the FCA currently employs an individual who owes a debt to another Federal agency. Upon receipt of proper certification from the creditor agency, the FCA will offset the debtor-employee's salary in accordance with these regulations.

(b) These regulations do not apply to the following:

(1) Debts or claims rising under the Internal Revenue Code of 1986, as amended (26 U.S.C. 1 et seq.); the Social Security Act (42 U.S.C. 301 et seq.); the tariff laws of the United States; or to any case where collection of a debt by salary offset is explicitly provided for or prohibited by another statute (e.g., travel advances in 5 U.S.C. 5705 and employee training expenses in 5 U.S.C. 4108).

(2) Any adjustment to pay arising from an employee's election of coverage or a change in coverage under a Federal benefits program requiring periodic deductions from pay if the amount to be recovered was accumulated over four pay periods or less.

(3) A claim which has been outstanding for more than 10 years after the creditor agency's right to collect the debt first accrued, unless facts material to the Government's right to collect were not known and could not reasonably have been known by the official or officials charged with the responsibility for discovery and collection of such debts.

§ 608.837 Definitions.

In this subpart, the following definitions shall apply:

(a) *Agency* means:

(1) An executive agency as defined by 5 U.S.C. 105, including the United States Postal Service and the United States Postal Rate Commission;

(2) A military department as defined in 5 U.S.C. 102;

(3) An agency or court of the judicial branch, including a court as defined in 28 U.S.C. 610, the District Court for the Northern Mariana Islands, and the Judicial Panel on Multi-district Litigation;

(4) An agency of the legislative branch, including the United States Senate and the United States House of Representatives; or

(5) Other independent establishments that are entities of the Federal Government.

(b) *Disposable pay* means, for an officially established pay interval, that part of current basic pay, special pay, incentive pay, retired pay, retainer pay, or, in the case of an employee not entitled to basic pay, other authorized pay, remaining after the deduction of any amount required by law to be withheld. The FCA shall allow the deductions described in 5 CFR 581.105 (b) through (f).

(c) *Employee* means a current employee of the FCA or other agency, including a current member of the Armed Forces or Reserve of the Armed Forces of the United States.

(d) *Waiver* means the cancellation, remission, forgiveness, or nonrecovery of a debt allegedly owed by an employee to the FCA or another agency as permitted or required by 5 U.S.C. 5584 or 8346(b), 10 U.S.C. 2774, 32 U.S.C. 716, or any other law.

§ 608.838 Waiver requests and claims to the General Accounting Office.

(a) The regulations contained in this subpart do not preclude an employee from requesting a waiver of an overpayment under 5 U.S.C. 5584 or 8346(b), 10 U.S.C. 2774, 32 U.S.C. 716, or in any way questioning the amount or validity of a debt by submitting a subsequent claim to the General Accounting Office in accordance with the procedures prescribed by the General Accounting Office.

(b) These regulations also do not preclude an employee from requesting a waiver pursuant to other statutory provisions pertaining to the particular debts being collected.

§ 608.839 Procedures for salary offset.

(a) The Chairman, or designee of the Chairman, shall determine the amount of an employee's disposable pay and the amount to be deducted from the employee's disposable pay at regular pay intervals.

Farm Credit Administration § 608.841

(b) Deductions shall begin within three official pay periods following the date of mailing or delivery of the Notice of Intent to Collect by Salary Offset.

(c)(1) If the amount of the debt is equal to or is less than 15 percent of the employee's disposable pay, such debt should be collected in one lump-sum deduction.

(2) If the amount of the debt is not collected in one lump-sum deduction, the debt shall be collected in installment deductions over a period of time not greater than the anticipated period of employment. The size and frequency of installment deductions will bear a reasonable relation to the size of the debt and the employee's ability to pay. However, the amount deducted from any pay period will not exceed 15 percent of the employee's disposable pay for that period, unless the employee has agreed in writing to the deduction of a greater amount.

(3) A deduction exceeding the 15-percent disposable pay limitation may be made from any final salary payment pursuant to 31 U.S.C. 3716 in order to liquidate the debt, whether the employee is being separated voluntarily or involuntarily.

(4) Whenever an employee subject to salary offset is separated from the FCA and the balance of the debt cannot be liquidated by offset of the final salary check pursuant to 31 U.S.C. 3716, the FCA may offset any later payments of any kind against the balance of the debt.

(d) In instances where two or more creditor agencies are seeking salary offsets against current employees of the FCA or where two or more debts are owed to a single creditor agency, the FCA, at its discretion, may determine whether one or more debts should be offset simultaneously within the 15-percent limitation. Debts owed to the FCA should generally take precedence over debts owed to other agencies.

§ 608.840 Refunds.

(a) In instances where the FCA is the creditor agency, it shall promptly refund any amounts deducted under the authority of 5 U.S.C. 5514 when:

(1) The debt is waived or otherwise found not to be owed to the United States (unless expressly prohibited by statute or regulations); or

(2) An administrative or judicial order directs the FCA to make a refund.

(b) Unless required or permitted by law or contract, refunds under this section shall not bear interest.

§ 608.841 Requesting current paying agency to offset salary.

(a) To request a paying agency to impose a salary offset against amounts owed to the debtor, the FCA shall provide the paying agency with a claim certification which meets the requirements set forth in § 608.825(a). The FCA shall also provide the paying agency with a repayment schedule determined under the provisions of § 608.839 or in accordance with a repayment agreement entered into with the debtor.

(b) If the employee separates from the paying agency before the debt is paid in full, the paying agency shall certify the total amount collected on the debt. A copy of this certification shall be sent to the employee and a copy shall be sent to the FCA. If the paying agency is aware that the employee is entitled to payments from the Civil Service Retirement and Disability Fund, or other similar payments, it must provide written notification to the agency responsible for making such payments that the debtor owes a debt (including the amount) and that the provisions of this section have been fully complied with. However, the FCA must submit a properly certified claim to the agency responsible for making such payments before the collection can be made.

(c) When an employee transfers to another paying agency, the FCA is not required to repeat the due process procedures set forth in 5 U.S.C. 5514 and this part to resume the collection. The FCA shall, however, review the debt upon receiving the former paying agency's notice of the employee's transfer to make sure the collection is resumed by the new paying agency.

(d) If a special review is conducted pursuant to § 608.811 and results in a revised offset or repayment schedule, the FCA shall provide a new claim certification to the paying agency.

45

§ 608.842 Responsibility of the FCA as the paying agency.

(a) When the FCA receives a claim certification from a creditor agency, deductions should be scheduled to begin at the next officially established pay interval. The FCA shall send the debtor written notice which provides:

(1) That the FCA has received a valid claim certification from the creditor agency;

(2) The date on which salary offset will begin;

(3) The amount of the debt; and

(4) The amount of such deductions.

(b) If, after the creditor agency has submitted the claim certification to the FCA, the employee transfers to a different agency before the debt is collected in full, the FCA must certify the total amount collected on the debt. The FCA shall send a copy of this certification to the creditor agency and a copy to the employee. If the FCA is aware that the employee is entitled to payments from the Civil Service Retirement Fund and Disability Fund, or other similar payments, it shall provide written notification to the agency responsible for making such payments that the debtor owes a debt (including the amount).

§ 608.843 Nonwaiver of rights by payments.

An employee's involuntary payment of all or any portion of a debt being collected under this subpart shall not be construed as a waiver of any rights the employee may have under 5 U.S.C. 5514 or any other provisions of a written contract or law unless there are statutory or contractual provisions to the contrary.

SUBCHAPTER B—FARM CREDIT SYSTEM

PART 609—ELECTRONIC COMMERCE

Subpart A—General Rules

Sec.
609.905 Background.
609.910 Compliance with the Electronic Signatures in Global and National Commerce Act (Public Law 106–229) (E-SIGN).
609.915 Compliance with Federal Reserve Board Regulations B, M, and Z.

Subpart B—Interpretations and Definitions

609.920 Interpretations.
609.925 Definitions.

Subpart C—Standards for Boards and Management

609.930 Policies and procedures.
609.935 Business planning.
609.940 Internal systems and controls.
609.945 Records retention.

Subpart D—General Requirements for Electronic Communications

609.950 Electronic communications.

AUTHORITY: Sec. 5.9 of the Farm Credit Act (12 U.S.C. 2243); 5 U.S.C. 301; Pub. L. 106–229 (114 Stat. 464).

SOURCE: 67 FR 16631, Apr. 8, 2002, unless otherwise noted.

Subpart A—General Rules

§ 609.905 Background.

The Farm Credit Administration (FCA) wants to create a flexible regulatory environment that facilitates electronic commerce (E-commerce) and allows Farm Credit System (System) institutions and their customers to use new technologies. System institutions may use E-commerce but must establish good business practices that ensure safety and soundness while doing so.

§ 609.910 Compliance with the Electronic Signatures in Global and National Commerce Act (Public Law 106–229) (E-SIGN).

(a) *General.* E-SIGN makes it easier to conduct E-commerce. With some exceptions, E-SIGN permits the use and establishes the legal validity of electronic contracts, electronic signatures, and records maintained in electronic rather than paper form. It governs transactions relating to the conduct of business, consumer, or commercial affairs between two or more persons. E-commerce is optional; all parties to a transaction must agree before it can be used.

(b) *Consumer transactions.* E-SIGN contains extensive consumer disclosure provisions that apply whenever another consumer protection law, such as the Equal Credit Opportunity Act, requires the disclosure of information to a consumer in writing. Consumer means an individual who obtains, through a transaction, products or services, including credit, used primarily for personal, family, or household purposes. You must follow E-SIGN's specific procedures to make the required consumer disclosures electronically. E-SIGN's special disclosure rules for consumer transactions do not apply to business transactions. Under E-SIGN, some System loans qualify as consumer transactions, while others are business transactions. You will need to distinguish between the two types of transactions to comply with E-SIGN.

(c) *Specific exceptions.* E-SIGN does not permit electronic notification for notices of default, acceleration, repossession, foreclosure, eviction, or the right to cure, under a credit agreement secured by, or a rental agreement for, a person's primary residence. These notices require paper notification. The law also requires paper notification to cancel or terminate life insurance. Thus, System institutions cannot use electronic notification to deliver some notices that must be provided under part 617, subparts A, D, E, and G of this chapter. In addition, E-SIGN does not apply to the writing or signature requirements imposed under the Uniform Commercial Code, other than sections 1–107 and 1–206 and Articles 2 and 2A.

(d) *Promissory notes.* E-SIGN establishes special technological and business process standards for electronic promissory notes secured by real estate. To treat an electronic version of

§ 609.915

such a promissory note as the equivalent of a paper promissory note, you must conform to E-SIGN's detailed requirements for transferable records. A transferable record is an electronic record that:

(1) Would be a note under Article 3 of the Uniform Commercial Code if the electronic record were in writing;

(2) The issuer of the electronic record has expressly agreed is a transferable record; and

(3) Relates to a loan secured by real property.

(e) *Effect on State and Federal law.* E-SIGN preempts most State and Federal statutes or regulations, including the Farm Credit Act of 1971, as amended (Act), and its implementing regulations, that require contracts or other business, consumer, or commercial records to be written, signed, or in non-electronic form. Under E-SIGN, an electronic record or signature generally satisfies any provision of the Act, or its implementing regulations that requires such records and signatures to be written, signed, or in paper form. Therefore, unless an exception applies or a necessary condition under E-SIGN has not been met, an electronic record or signature satisfies any applicable provision of the Act or its implementing regulations.

(f) *Document integrity and signature authentication.* Each System institution must verify the legitimacy of an E-commerce communication, transaction, or access request. Document integrity ensures that the same document is provided to all parties. Signature authentication proves the identities of all parties. The parties to the transaction may determine how to ensure document integrity and signature authentication.

(g) *Records retention.* Each System institution may maintain all records electronically even if originally they were paper records. The stored electronic record must accurately reflect the information in the original record. The electronic record must be accessible and capable of being reproduced by all persons entitled by law or regulations to review the original record.

[67 FR 16631, Apr. 8, 2002, as amended at 69 FR 10906, Mar. 9, 2004]

§ 609.915 Compliance with Federal Reserve Board Regulations B, M, and Z.

The regulations in this part require fair practices and meaningful disclosures for certain lending and leasing activities. System institutions must comply with Federal Reserve Board Regulations B (Equal Credit Opportunity), M (Consumer Leasing), and Z (Truth in Lending) (12 CFR parts 202, 213, and 226).

Subpart B—Interpretations and Definitions

§ 609.920 Interpretations.

(a) E-SIGN preempts most statutes and regulations, including the Act and its implementing regulations that require paper copies and handwritten signatures in business, consumer, or commercial transactions. E-SIGN requires that statutes and regulations be interpreted to allow E-commerce as long as the safeguards of E-SIGN are met and its exceptions recognized. Generally, an electronic record or signature satisfies any provision of the Act or its implementing regulations that require such records and signatures to be written, signed, or in paper form.

(b) System institutions may interpret the Act and its implementing regulations broadly to allow electronic transmissions, communications, records, and submissions, as provided by E-SIGN. This means that the terms address, copy, distribute, document, file, mail, notice, notify, record, provide, send, signature, sent, written, writing, and similar words generally should be interpreted to permit electronic transmissions, communications, records, and submissions in business, consumer, or commercial transactions.

§ 609.925 Definitions.

We provide the following definitions that apply to the Act and its implementing regulations:

(a) *Electronic* means relating to technology having electrical, digital, magnetic, wireless, optical, electromagnetic, or similar capabilities.

(b) *Electronic communication* means a message that can be transmitted electronically and displayed on equipment

Farm Credit Administration § 609.950

as visual text. An example is a message displayed on a personal computer monitor screen. This does not include audio- and voice-response telephone systems.

(c) *Electronic business (E-business) or electronic commerce (E-commerce)* means buying, selling, producing, or working in an electronic medium.

(d) *Electronic mail (E-mail)* means:

(1) To send or submit information electronically; or

(2) A communication received electronically.

(e) *Electronic signature* means an electronic sound, symbol, or process, attached to or logically associated with a contract or other record and executed or adopted by a person with the intent to sign the record. Electronic signature describes a category of electronic processes that can be substituted for a handwritten signature.

Subpart C—Standards for Boards and Management

§ 609.930 Policies and procedures.

The FCA supports E-commerce and wants to facilitate it and other new technologies and innovations to enhance the efficient conduct of business and the delivery of safe and sound credit and closely related services. Through E-commerce, System institutions can enhance customer service, access information, and provide alternate communication systems. At the same time, E-commerce presents challenges and risks that your board must carefully consider in advance. Before engaging in E-commerce, you must weigh its business risks against its benefits. You must also adopt E-commerce policies and procedures to ensure your institution's safety and soundness and compliance with law and regulations. Among other concerns, the policies and procedures must address, when applicable:

(a) Security and integrity of System institution and borrower data;

(b) The privacy of your customers as well as visitors to your Web site;

(c) Notices to customers or visitors to your Web site when they link to an affiliate or third party Web site;

(d) Capability of vendor or application providers;

(e) Business resumption after disruption;

(f) Fraud and money laundering;

(g) Intrusion detection and management;

(h) Liability insurance; and

(i) Prompt reporting of known or suspected criminal violations associated with E-commerce to law enforcement authorities and FCA under part 612, subpart B of this chapter.

[67 FR 16631, Apr. 8, 2002; 69 FR 42853, July 19, 2004]

§ 609.935 Business planning.

When engaging in E-commerce, the business plan required under part 618 of this chapter, subpart J, must describe the E-commerce initiative, including intended objectives, business risks, security issues, relevant markets, and legal compliance.

§ 609.940 Internal systems and controls.

When applicable, internal systems and controls must provide reasonable assurances that System institutions will:

(a) Follow and achieve business plan objectives and policies and procedures requirements regarding E-commerce; and

(b) Prevent and detect material deficiencies on a timely basis.

§ 609.945 Records retention.

Records stored electronically must be accurate, accessible, and reproducible for later reference.

Subpart D—General Requirements for Electronic Communications

§ 609.950 Electronic communications.

(a) *Agreement.* In accordance with E-SIGN, System institutions may communicate electronically in business, consumer, or commercial transactions. E-commerce transactions require the agreement of all parties when you do business.

(b) *Communications with consumers.* E-SIGN and Federal Reserve Board Regulations B, M, and Z (12 CFR parts 202, 213, and 226) outline specific disclosure requirements for communications with consumers.

(c) *Communications with parties other than consumers.* The consumer disclosure requirements of E-SIGN and of Federal Reserve Board Regulation B (12 CFR part 202) do not apply to your communications with parties other than consumers. (Federal Reserve Board Regulations M and Z (12 CFR parts 213 and 226) apply to consumers only.) Nonetheless, you must ensure that your communications, including those disclosures required under the Act and the regulations in this part, demonstrate good business practices in the delivery of credit and closely related services and in your obtaining goods and services.

PART 610—REGISTRATION OF MORTGAGE LOAN ORIGINATORS

Sec.
610.101 Authority, purpose, and scope.
610.102 Definitions.
610.103 Registration of mortgage loan originators.
610.104 Policies and procedures.
610.105 Use of unique identifier.
APPENDIX A TO PART 610—EXAMPLES OF MORTGAGE LOAN ORIGINATOR ACTIVITIES

AUTHORITY: Secs. 1.5, 1.7, 1.9, 1.10, 1.11, 1.13, 2.2, 2.4, 2.12, 5.9, 5.17, 7.2, 7.6, 7.8 of the Farm Credit Act (12 U.S.C. 2013, 2015, 2017, 2018, 2019, 2021, 2073, 2075, 2093, 2243, 2252, 2279a–2, 2279b, 2279c–10); and secs. 1501 *et seq.* of Pub. L. 110–289, 122 Stat. 2654.

SOURCE: 75 FR 44700, July 28, 2010, unless otherwise noted.

§ 610.101 Authority, purpose, and scope.

(a) *Authority.* This part is issued pursuant to the Secure and Fair Enforcement for Mortgage Licensing Act of 2008, title V of the Housing and Economic Recovery Act of 2008 (S.A.F.E. Act) (Pub. L. 110–289, 122 Stat. 2654, 12 U.S.C. 5101 *et seq.*).

(b) *Purpose.* This part implements the S.A.F.E. Act's Federal registration requirement for mortgage loan originators. The S.A.F.E. Act provides that the objectives of this registration include aggregating and improving the flow of information to and between regulators; providing increased accountability and tracking of mortgage loan originators; enhancing consumer protections; supporting anti-fraud measures; and providing consumers with easily accessible information at no charge regarding the employment history of, and publicly adjudicated disciplinary and enforcement actions against, mortgage loan originators.

(c) *Scope*—(1) *In general.* This part applies to any Farm Credit System lending institution that actually originates residential mortgage loans pursuant to its authority under sections 1.9(3), 1.11, or 2.4(a) and (b) of the Farm Credit Act of 1971, as amended, and their employees who act as mortgage loan originators.

(2) *De minimis exception.*

(i) This part and the requirements of 12 U.S.C. 5103(a)(1)(A) and (2) of the S.A.F.E. Act do not apply to any employee of a Farm Credit System institution who has never been registered or licensed through the Registry as a mortgage loan originator if during the past 12 months the employee acted as a mortgage loan originator for 5 or fewer residential mortgage loans.

(ii) Prior to engaging in mortgage loan origination activity that exceeds the exception limit in paragraph (c)(2)(i) of this section, a Farm Credit System institution employee must register with the Registry pursuant to this part.

(iii) *Evasion.* Farm Credit System institutions are prohibited from engaging in any act or practice to evade the limits of the *de minimis* exception set forth in paragraph (c)(2)(i) of this section.

§ 610.102 Definitions.

For purposes of this part, the following definitions apply:

(a) *Annual renewal period* means November 1 through December 31 of each year.

(b)(1) *Mortgage loan originator*[1] means an individual who:

(i) Takes a residential mortgage loan application; and

(ii) Offers or negotiates terms of a residential mortgage loan for compensation or gain.

(2) The term *mortgage loan originator* does not include:

---

[1] Appendix A of this part provides examples of activities that would, and would not, cause an employee to fall within this definition of mortgage loan originator.

Farm Credit Administration § 610.103

(i) An individual who performs purely administrative or clerical tasks on behalf of an individual who is described in paragraph (b)(1) of this section;

(ii) An individual who only performs real estate brokerage activities (as defined in 12 U.S.C. 5102(3)(D)) and is licensed or registered as a real estate broker in accordance with applicable State law, unless the individual is compensated by a lender, a mortgage broker, or other mortgage loan originator or by any agent of such lender, mortgage broker, or other mortgage loan originator, and meets the definition of mortgage loan originator in paragraph (b)(1) of this section; or

(iii) An individual or entity solely involved in extensions of credit related to timeshare plans, as that term is defined in 11 U.S.C. 101(53D).

(3) *Administrative or clerical tasks* means the receipt, collection, and distribution of information common for the processing or underwriting of a loan in the residential mortgage industry and communication with a consumer to obtain information necessary for the processing or underwriting of a residential mortgage loan.

(c) *Nationwide Mortgage Licensing System and Registry* or *Registry* means the system developed and maintained by the Conference of State Bank Supervisors and the American Association of Residential Mortgage Regulators for the State licensing and registration of State-licensed mortgage loan originators and the registration of mortgage loan originators pursuant to 12 U.S.C. 5107.

(d) *Registered mortgage loan originator* or *registrant* means any individual who:

(1) Meets the definition of mortgage loan originator and is an employee of a Farm Credit System institution; and

(2) Is registered pursuant to this part with, and maintains a unique identifier through, the Registry.

(e) *Residential mortgage loan* means any loan primarily for personal, family, or household use that is secured by a mortgage, deed of trust, or other equivalent consensual security interest on a dwelling (as defined in section 103(v) of the Truth in Lending Act, 15 U.S.C. 1602(v)) or residential real estate upon which is constructed or intended to be constructed a dwelling, and includes refinancings, reverse mortgages, home equity lines of credit and other first and additional lien loans that meet the qualifications listed in this definition. This definition does not amend or supersede § 613.3030(c) of this chapter.

(f) *Unique identifier* means a number or other identifier that:

(1) Permanently identifies a registered mortgage loan originator;

(2) Is assigned by protocols established by the Nationwide Mortgage Licensing System and Registry, the Federal banking agencies, and the Farm Credit Administration to facilitate:

(i) Electronic tracking of mortgage loan originators; and

(ii) Uniform identification of, and public access to, the employment history of and the publicly adjudicated disciplinary and enforcement actions against mortgage loan originators; and

(3) Must not be used for purposes other than those set forth under the S.A.F.E. Act.

§ 610.103 **Registration of mortgage loan originators.**

(a) *Registration requirement*—(1) *Employee registration.* Each employee of a Farm Credit System institution who acts as a mortgage loan originator must register with the Registry, obtain a unique identifier, and maintain this registration in accordance with the requirements of this part. Any such employee who is not in compliance with the registration and unique identifier requirements set forth in this part is in violation of the S.A.F.E. Act and this part.

(2) *Farm Credit System institution requirement*—(i) *In general.* A Farm Credit System institution that employs one or more individuals who act as a residential mortgage loan originator must require each such employee to register with the Registry, maintain this registration, and obtain a unique identifier in accordance with the requirements of this part.

(ii) *Prohibition.* A Farm Credit System institution must not permit an employee who is subject to the registration requirements of this part to act as a mortgage loan originator for the Farm Credit System institution

§ 610.103

unless such employee is registered with the Registry pursuant to this part.

(3) *Implementation period for initial registration.* An employee of a Farm Credit System institution who is a mortgage loan originator must complete an initial registration with the Registry pursuant to this part within 180 days from the date that the Farm Credit Administration provides in a public notice that the Registry is accepting registrations.

(4) *Employees previously registered or licensed through the Registry*—(i) *In general.* If an employee of a Farm Credit System institution was registered or licensed through, and obtained a unique identifier from, the Registry and has maintained this registration or license before the employee becomes subject to this part at this Farm Credit System institution, then the registration requirements of the S.A.F.E. Act and this part are deemed to be met, provided that:

(A) The employment information in paragraphs (d)(1)(i)(C) and (d)(1)(ii) of this section is updated and the requirements of paragraph (d)(2) of this section are met;

(B) New fingerprints of the employee are submitted to the Registry for a background check, as required by paragraph (d)(1)(ix) of this section, unless the employee has fingerprints on file with the Registry that are less than 3 years old;

(C) The Farm Credit System institution information required in paragraphs (e)(1)(i) (to the extent the Farm Credit System institution has not previously met these requirements) and (e)(2)(i) of this section is submitted to the Registry; and

(D) The registration is maintained pursuant to paragraphs (b) and (e)(1)(ii) of this section, as of the date that the employee becomes subject to this part.

(ii) *Rule for certain acquisitions, mergers, or reorganizations.* When registered or licensed mortgage loan originators become employees of another Farm Credit System institution as a result of a consolidation, merger, or reorganization, only the requirements of paragraphs (a)(4)(i)(A), (C), and (D) of this section must be met, and these requirements must be met within 60 days from the effective date of the consolidation, merger, or reorganization.

(b) *Maintaining registration.*

(1) A mortgage loan originator who is registered with the Registry pursuant to paragraph (a) of this section must:

(i) Except as provided in paragraph (b)(3) of this section, renew the registration during the annual renewal period, confirming the responses set forth in paragraphs (d)(1)(i) through (viii) of this section remain accurate and complete, and updating this information, as appropriate; and

(ii) Update the registration within 30 days of any of the following events:

(A) A change in the name of the registrant;

(B) The registrant ceases to be an employee of the Farm Credit System institution; or

(C) The information required under paragraphs (d)(1)(iii) through (viii) of this section becomes inaccurate, incomplete, or out-of-date.

(2) A registered mortgage loan originator must maintain his or her registration, unless the individual is no longer engaged in the activity of a mortgage loan originator.

(3) The annual registration renewal requirement set forth in paragraph (b)(1) of this section does not apply to a registered mortgage loan originator who has completed his or her registration with the Registry pursuant to paragraph (a)(1) of this section less than 6 months prior to the end of the annual renewal period.

(c) *Effective dates*—(1) *Registration.* A registration pursuant to paragraph (a)(1) of this section is effective on the date the Registry transmits notification to the registrant that the registrant is registered.

(2) *Renewals or updates.* A renewal or update pursuant to paragraph (b) of this section is effective on the date the Registry transmits notification to the registrant that the registration has been renewed or updated.

(d) *Required employee information*—(1) *In general.* For purposes of the registration required by this section, a Farm Credit System institution must require each employee who is a mortgage loan originator to submit to the Registry,

Farm Credit Administration § 610.103

or must submit on behalf of the employee, the following categories of information, to the extent this information is collected by the Registry:

(i) Identifying information, including the employee's:

(A) Name and any other names used;
(B) Home address and contact information;
(C) Principal business location address and business contact information;
(D) Social security number;
(E) Gender; and
(F) Date and place of birth;

(ii) Financial services-related employment history for the 10 years prior to the date of registration or renewal, including the date the employee became an employee of the Farm Credit System institution;

(iii) Convictions of any criminal offense involving dishonesty, breach of trust, or money laundering against the employee or organizations controlled by the employee, or agreements to enter into a pretrial diversion or similar program in connection with the prosecution for such offense(s);

(iv) Civil judicial actions against the employee in connection with financial services-related activities, dismissals with settlements, or judicial findings that the employee violated financial services-related statutes or regulations, except for actions dismissed without a settlement agreement;

(v) Actions or orders by a State or Federal regulatory agency or foreign financial regulatory authority that:

(A) Found the employee to have made a false statement or omission or been dishonest, unfair or unethical; to have been involved in a violation of a financial services-related regulation or statute; or to have been a cause of a financial services-related business having its authorization to do business denied, suspended, revoked, or restricted;

(B) Are entered against the employee in connection with a financial services-related activity;

(C) Denied, suspended, or revoked the employee's registration or license to engage in a financial services-related activity; disciplined the employee or otherwise by order prevented the employee from associating with a financial services-related business or restricted the employee's activities; or

(D) Barred the employee from association with an entity or its officers regulated by the agency or authority or from engaging in a financial services-related business;

(vi) Final orders issued by a State or Federal regulatory agency or foreign financial regulatory authority based on violations of any law or regulation that prohibits fraudulent, manipulative, or deceptive conduct;

(vii) Revocation or suspension of the employee's authorization to act as an attorney, accountant, or State or Federal contractor;

(viii) Customer-initiated financial services-related arbitration or civil action against the employee that required action, including settlements, or which resulted in a judgment; and

(ix) Fingerprints of the employee, in digital form if practicable, and any appropriate identifying information for submission to the Federal Bureau of Investigation and any governmental agency or entity authorized to receive such information in connection with a State and national criminal history background check; however, fingerprints provided to the Registry that are less than 3 years old may be used to satisfy this requirement.

(2) *Employee authorizations and attestation.* An employee registering as a mortgage loan originator or renewing or updating his or her registration under this part, and not the employing Farm Credit System institution or other employees of the Farm Credit System institution, must:

(i) Authorize the Registry and the employing institution to obtain information related to sanctions or findings in any administrative, civil, or criminal action, to which the employee is a party, made by any governmental jurisdiction;

(ii) Attest to the correctness of all information required by paragraph (d) of this section, whether submitted by the employee or on behalf of the employee by the employing Farm Credit System institution; and

(iii) Authorize the Registry to make available to the public information required by paragraphs (d)(1)(i)(A) and

§ 610.104

(C), and (d)(1)(ii) through (viii) of this section.

(3) *Submission of information.* A Farm Credit System institution may identify one or more employees of the Farm Credit System institution who may submit the information required by paragraph (d)(1) of this section to the Registry on behalf of the Farm Credit System institution's employees provided that this individual, and any employee delegated such authority, does not act as a mortgage loan originator, consistent with paragraph (e)(1)(i)(F) of this section. In addition, a Farm Credit System institution may submit to the Registry some or all of the information required by paragraphs (d)(1) and (e)(2) of this section for multiple employees in bulk through batch processing in a format to be specified by the Registry, to the extent such batch processing is made available by the Registry.

(e) *Required Farm Credit System institution information.* A Farm Credit System institution must submit the following categories of information to the Registry:

(1) *Farm Credit System institution record.*

(i) In connection with the registration of one or more mortgage loan originators:

(A) Name, main office address, and business contact information;

(B) Internal Revenue Service Employer Tax Identification Number (EIN);

(C) Research Statistics Supervision and Discount (RSSD) number, as issued by the Board of Governors of the Federal Reserve System;

(D) Identification of its primary Federal regulator;

(E) Name(s) and contact information of the individual(s) with authority to act as the Farm Credit System institution's primary point of contact for the Registry;

(F) Name(s) and contact information of the individual(s) with authority to enter the information required by paragraphs (d)(1) and (e) of this section to the Registry and who may delegate this authority to other individuals. For the purpose of providing information required by paragraph (e) of this section, this individual and their delegates must not act as mortgage loan originators unless the Farm Credit System institution has 10 or fewer full time or equivalent employees and is not a subsidiary; and

(G) If an operating subsidiary of an agricultural credit association, indication that it is a subsidiary and the RSSD number of the parent agricultural credit association.

(ii) *Attestation.* The individual(s) identified in paragraphs (e)(1)(i)(E) and (F) of this section must comply with Registry protocols to verify their identity and must attest that they have the authority to enter data on behalf of the Farm Credit System institution, that the information provided to the Registry pursuant to this paragraph (e) is correct, and that the Farm Credit System institution will keep the information required by this paragraph (e) current and will file accurate supplementary information on a timely basis.

(iii) A Farm Credit System institution must update the information required by this paragraph (e) of this section within 30 days of the date that this information becomes inaccurate.

(iv) A Farm Credit System institution must renew the information required by paragraph (e) of this section on an annual basis.

(2) *Employee information.* In connection with the registration of each employee who acts as a mortgage loan originator:

(i) After the information required by paragraph (d) of this section has been submitted to the Registry, confirmation that it employs the registrant; and

(ii) Within 30 days of the date the registrant ceases to be an employee of the Farm Credit System institution, notification that it no longer employs the registrant and the date the registrant ceased being an employee.

§ 610.104 Policies and procedures.

A Farm Credit System institution that employs one or more mortgage loan originators must adopt and follow written policies and procedures designed to assure compliance with this part. These policies and procedures must be appropriate to the nature, size, complexity, and scope of the mortgage lending activities of the Farm Credit System institution, and apply only to those employees acting within the scope of their employment at the Farm Credit System institution. At a minimum, these policies and procedures must:

(a) Establish a process for identifying which employees of the Farm Credit System institution are required to be registered mortgage loan originators;

(b) Require that all employees of the Farm Credit System institution who are mortgage loan originators be informed of the registration requirements of the S.A.F.E. Act and this part and be instructed on how to comply with such requirements and procedures;

(c) Establish procedures to comply with the unique identifier requirements in § 610.105;

(d) Establish reasonable procedures for confirming the adequacy and accuracy of employee registrations, including updates and renewals, by comparisons with its own records;

(e) Establish reasonable procedures and tracking systems for monitoring compliance with registration and renewal requirements and procedures;

(f) Provide for independent testing for compliance with this part to be conducted at least annually by Farm Credit System institution personnel or by an outside party;

(g) Provide for appropriate action in the case of any employee who fails to comply with the registration requirements of the S.A.F.E. Act, this part, or the Farm Credit System institution's related policies and procedures, including prohibiting such employees from acting as mortgage loan originators or other appropriate disciplinary actions;

(h) Establish a process for reviewing employee criminal history background reports received pursuant to this part, taking appropriate action consistent with applicable Federal law, including section 5.65(d) of the Farm Credit Act of 1971, as amended, 12 U.S.C. 2277a–14(d) and implementing regulations with respect to these reports, and maintaining records of these reports and actions taken with respect to applicable employees; and

(i) Establish procedures designed to ensure that any third party with which the Farm Credit System institution has arrangements related to mortgage loan origination has policies and procedures to comply with the S.A.F.E. Act, including appropriate licensing and/or registration of individuals acting as mortgage loan originators.

§ 610.105 Use of unique identifier.

(a) The Farm Credit System institution shall make the unique identifier(s) of its registered mortgage loan originator(s) available to consumers in a manner and method practicable to the institution.

(b) A registered mortgage loan originator shall provide his or her unique identifier to a consumer:

(1) Upon request;

(2) Before acting as a mortgage loan originator; and

(3) Through the originator's initial written communication with a consumer, if any, whether on paper or electronically.

APPENDIX A TO PART 610—EXAMPLES OF MORTGAGE LOAN ORIGINATOR ACTIVITIES

This Appendix provides examples to aid in the understanding of activities that would cause an employee of a Farm Credit System institution to fall within or outside the definition of mortgage loan originator. The examples in this Appendix are not all inclusive. They illustrate only the issue described and do not illustrate any other issues that may arise under this part. For purposes of the examples below, the term "loan" refers to a residential mortgage loan.

(a) *Taking a loan application.* The following examples illustrate when an employee takes, or does not take, a loan application.

(1) Taking an application includes: receiving information provided in connection with a request for a loan to be used to determine whether the consumer qualifies for a loan, even if the employee:

(i) Has received the consumer's information indirectly in order to make an offer or negotiate a loan;

(ii) Is not responsible for verifying information;

(iii) Is inputting information into an on-line application or other automated system on behalf of the consumer; or

(iv) Is not engaged in approval of the loan, including determining whether the consumer qualifies for the loan.

(2) Taking an application does not include any of the following activities performed solely or in combination:

(i) Contacting a consumer to verify the information in the loan application by obtaining documentation, such as tax returns or payroll receipts;

(ii) Receiving a loan application through the mail and forwarding it, without review, to loan approval personnel;

(iii) Assisting a consumer who is filling out an application by clarifying what type of information is necessary for the application or otherwise explaining the qualifications or criteria necessary to obtain a loan product;

(iv) Describing the steps that a consumer would need to take to provide information to be used to determine whether the consumer qualifies for a loan or otherwise explaining the loan application process;

(v) In response to an inquiry regarding a prequalified offer that a consumer has received from a Farm Credit System institution, collecting only basic identifying information about the consumer and forwarding the consumer to a mortgage loan originator; or

(vi) Receiving information in connection with a modification to the terms of an existing loan to a borrower as part of the Farm Credit System institution's loss mitigation efforts when the borrower is reasonably likely to default.

(b) *Offering or negotiating terms of a loan.* The following examples are designed to illustrate when an employee offers or negotiates terms of a loan, and conversely, what does not constitute offering or negotiating terms of a loan.

(1) Offering or negotiating the terms of a loan includes:

(i) Presenting a loan offer to a consumer for acceptance, either verbally or in writing, including, but not limited to, providing a disclosure of the loan terms after application under the Truth in Lending Act, even if:

(A) Further verification of information is necessary;

(B) The offer is conditional;

(C) Other individuals must complete the loan process; or

(D) Only the rate approved by the Farm Credit System institution's loan approval mechanism function for a specific loan product is communicated without authority to negotiate the rate.

(ii) Responding to a consumer's request for a lower rate or lower points on a pending loan application by presenting to the consumer a revised loan offer, either verbally or in writing, that includes a lower interest rate or lower points than the original offer.

(2) Offering or negotiating terms of a loan does not include solely or in combination:

(i) Providing general explanations or descriptions in response to consumer queries regarding qualification for a specific loan product, such as explaining loan terminology (*i.e.*, debt-to-income ratio); lending policies (*i.e.*, the loan-to-value ratio policy of the Farm Credit System institution); or product-related services;

(ii) In response to a consumer's request, informing a consumer of the loan rates that are publicly available, such as on the Farm Credit System institution's Web site, for specific types of loan products without communicating to the consumer whether qualifications are met for that loan product;

(iii) Collecting information about a consumer in order to provide the consumer with information on loan products for which the consumer generally may qualify, without presenting a specific loan offer to the consumer for acceptance, either verbally or in writing;

(iv) Arranging the loan closing or other aspects of the loan process, including communicating with a consumer about those arrangements, provided that communication with the consumer only verifies loan terms already offered or negotiated;

(v) Providing a consumer with information unrelated to loan terms, such as the best days of the month for scheduling loan closings at the Farm Credit System institution;

(vi) Making an underwriting decision about whether the consumer qualifies for a loan;

(vii) Explaining or describing the steps or process that a consumer would need to take in order to obtain a loan offer, including qualifications or criteria that would need to be met without providing guidance specific to that consumer's circumstances; or

(viii) Communicating on behalf of a mortgage loan originator that a written offer, including disclosures provided pursuant to the Truth in Lending Act, has been sent to a consumer without providing any details of that offer.

(c) *Offering or negotiating a loan for compensation or gain.* The following examples illustrate when an employee does or does not offer or negotiate terms of a loan "for compensation or gain."

(1) Offering or negotiating terms of a loan for compensation or gain includes engaging in any of the activities in paragraph (b)(1) of this Appendix in the course of carrying out employment duties, even if the employee does not receive a referral fee or commission or other special compensation for the loan.

(2) Offering or negotiating terms of a loan for compensation or gain does not include engaging in a seller-financed transaction for the employee's personal property that does not involve the Farm Credit System institution.

PART 611—ORGANIZATION

Subpart A—General

611.100 Definitions.
611.110 Meetings of stockholders.

Subpart B—Bank and Association Board of Directors

611.210 Director qualifications and training.

Farm Credit Administration

611.220 Outside directors.

Subpart C—Election of Directors and Other Voting Procedures

Sec.
611.310 Eligibility for membership on bank and association boards and subsequent employment.
611.320 Impartiality in the election of directors.
611.325 Bank and association nominating committees.
611.326 Floor nominations for open Farm Credit bank and association director positions.
611.330 Disclosures of Farm Credit bank and association director-nominees.
611.340 Confidentiality and security in voting.
611.350 Application of cooperative principles to the election of directors.

Subpart D—Rules for Compensation of Board Members

611.400 Compensation of bank board members.

Subpart E—Transfer of Authorities

611.500 General.
611.501 Procedures.
611.505 Farm Credit Administration review.
611.510 Approval procedures.
611.515 Information statement.
611.520 Plan of transfer.
611.525 Stockholder reconsideration.

Subpart F—Bank Mergers, Consolidations and Charter Amendments

611.1000 General authority.
611.1010 Bank charter amendment procedures.
611.1020 Requirements for mergers or consolidations of banks.
611.1030 [Reserved]
611.1040 Creation of new associations.

Subpart G—Mergers, Consolidations, and Charter Amendments of Associations

611.1120 General authority.
611.1121 Charter amendment procedures.
611.1122 Requirements for mergers or consolidations.
611.1123 Merger or consolidation agreements.
611.1124 Territorial adjustments.
611.1125 Treatment of associations not approving districtwide mergers.

Subpart H—Rules for Inter-System Fund Transfers

611.1130 Inter-System transfer of funds and equities.

Subpart I—Service Organizations

611.1135 Incorporation of service corporations.
611.1136 Regulation and examination of service organizations.
611.1137 Title VIII service corporations.

Subparts J–O [Reserved]

Subpart P—Termination of System Institution Status

611.1200 Applicability of this subpart.
611.1205 Definitions that apply in this subpart.
611.1210 Advance notices—commencement resolution and notice to equity holders.
611.1211 Special requirements.
611.1215 Communications with the public and equity holders.
611.1216 Public availability of documents related to the termination.
611.1217 Plain language requirements.
611.1218 Role of directors.
611.1219 Prohibited acts.
611.1220 Termination resolution.
611.1221 Submission to FCA of plan of termination and disclosure information; other required submissions.
611.1223 Plan of termination—contents.
611.1230 FCA review and approval—plan of termination.
611.1235 Plan of termination—distribution.
611.1240 Voting record date and stockholder approval.
611.1245 Stockholder reconsideration.
611.1246 Filing of termination application and its contents.
611.1247 FCA review and approval—termination.
611.1250 Preliminary exit fee estimate.
611.1255 Exit fee calculation.
611.1260 Payment of debts and assessments—terminating association.
611.1265 Retirement of a terminating association's investment in its affiliated bank.
611.1270 Repayment of obligations—terminating bank.
611.1275 Retirement of equities held by other System institutions.
611.1280 Dissenting stockholders' rights.
611.1285 Loan refinancing by borrowers.
611.1290 Continuation of borrower rights.

AUTHORITY: Secs. 1.3, 1.4, 1.13, 2.0, 2.1, 2.10, 2.11, 3.0, 3.2, 3.3, 3.7, 3.8, 3.9, 3.21, 4.3A, 4.12, 4.12A, 4.15, 4.20, 4.21, 5.9, 5.10, 5.17, 7.0–7.13, 8.5(e) of the Farm Credit Act (12 U.S.C. 2011, 2012, 2021, 2071, 2072, 2091, 2092, 2121, 2123, 2124, 2128, 2129, 2130, 2142, 2154a, 2183, 2203, 2208, 2209, 2243, 2244, 2252, 2279a–2279f–1, 2279aa–5(e)); secs. 411 and 412 of Pub. L. 100–233, 101 Stat. 1568, 1638; secs. 409 and 414 of Pub. L. 100–399, 102 Stat. 989, 1003, and 1004.

§ 611.100

SOURCE: 37 FR 11415, June 7, 1972, unless otherwise noted.

Subpart A—General

SOURCE: 75 FR 18740, Apr. 12, 2010, unless otherwise noted.

§ 611.100 Definitions.

The following definitions apply for the purpose of this part:

(a) *Mail ballot* means a ballot cast by regular or electronic mail.

(b) *Online meeting* means a meeting that is conducted over the Internet through the use of mediating technologies, such as online services, computer hardware and software, etc., where technology is used to generate objects and environments that are presented to users through a number of senses (e.g., vision and hearing). The mediating technologies allow people or objects at remote locations to appear locally present or at least allow them to be treated that way during the course of the meeting.

(c) *Online meeting space* means an online environment where Farm Credit institutions can hold stockholder meetings that allow stockholders to communicate, collaborate, and share information. Any stockholder with the necessary technology requirements and access (e.g., password-protected meetings) must be allowed to connect to his or her institution's online meeting space.

(d) *Regional election* means the apportionment of a Farm Credit institution's territory into regions in which a director or directors from a region are elected only by those voting stockholders who reside or conduct agricultural or aquatic operations in that same region.

(e) *Stockholder-association* means an association within a Farm Credit bank district holding voting stock in that bank.

(f) *Stockholder-elected director* means a director who is elected by the majority vote of the voting stockholders voting to serve as a member of a Farm Credit institution's board of directors.

§ 611.110 Meetings of stockholders.

(a) *Requirement.* Associations must have annual meetings of stockholders for the purpose of conducting annual director elections. Farm Credit banks are encouraged to hold annual or periodic meetings of stockholders. The by-laws of each Farm Credit bank and association must specify the quorum requirements for stockholder meetings. Associations must elect at least one director at each annual meeting, but the vote on the election of a director or directors by mail ballot may only occur in the period following an annual meeting. An online meeting space may be used in addition to a physical meeting space to conduct a stockholders' meeting or director election. A physical meeting space must always exist for association meetings involving director elections and other stockholders' votes.

(b) *Notice.* Each association, and those Farm Credit banks holding annual meetings, must issue an Annual Meeting Information Statement in accordance with the requirements of §§ 620.20 and 620.21 of this chapter.

(c) *Online meeting.* Each Farm Credit bank and association using an online meeting space as part of a meeting or election must have policies and procedures in place addressing how the online meeting space will be accessed and used by participants. The policies and procedures must specifically identify any technological adaptations necessary to address the confidentiality and security in voting requirements of § 611.340.

Subpart B—Bank and Association Board of Directors

SOURCE: 71 FR 5761, Feb. 2, 2006, unless otherwise noted.

§ 611.210 Director qualifications and training.

(a) *Qualifications.* (1) Each bank and association board of directors must establish and maintain a policy identifying desirable director qualifications. The policy must explain the type and level of knowledge and experience desired for board members, explaining how the desired qualifications were identified. The policy must be periodically updated and provided to the institution's nominating committee.

Farm Credit Administration §611.310

(2) Each Farm Credit institution board must have a director who is a financial expert. Boards of directors for associations with $500 million or less in total assets as of January 1 of each year may satisfy this requirement by retaining an advisor who is a financial expert. The financial advisor must report to the board of directors and be free of any affiliation with the external auditor or institution management. A financial expert is one recognized as having education or experience in: Accounting, internal accounting controls, or preparing or reviewing financial statements for financial institutions or large corporations consistent with the breadth and complexity of accounting and financial reporting issues that can reasonably be expected to be raised by the institution's financial statements.

(b) *Training.* Each bank and association board of directors must establish and maintain a policy for director training that includes appropriate implementing procedures. The policy must identify training areas supporting desired director qualifications. Each Farm Credit bank and association must require newly elected or appointed directors to complete director orientation training within 1 year of assuming their position and require incumbent directors to attend training periodically to advance their skills.

§ 611.220 Outside directors.

(a) *Eligibility, number and term.* (1) *Eligibility.* No candidate for an outside director position may be a director, officer, employee, agent, or stockholder of an institution in the Farm Credit System. Farm Credit banks and associations must make a reasonable effort to select outside directors possessing some or all of the desired director qualifications identified pursuant to § 611.210(a) of this part.

(2) *Number.* Stockholder-elected directors must constitute at least 60 percent of the members of each institution's board.

(i) Each Farm Credit bank must have at least two outside directors.

(ii) Associations with total assets exceeding $500 million as of January 1 of each year must have no fewer than two outside directors on the board. However, this requirement does not apply if it causes the percent of stockholder-elected directors to be less than 75 percent of the board.

(iii) Associations with $500 million or less in total assets as of January 1 of each year must have at least one outside director.

(3) *Terms of office.* Banks and associations may not establish a different term of office for outside directors than that established for stockholder-elected directors.

(b) *Removal.* Each institution must establish and maintain procedures for removal of outside directors. When the removal of an outside director is sought before the expiration of the outside director's term, the reason for removal must be documented. An institution's director removal procedures must allow for removal of an outside director by a majority vote of all voting stockholders voting, in person or by proxy, or by a two-thirds majority vote of the full board of directors. The outside director subject to the removal action is prohibited from voting in his or her own removal action.

Subpart C—Election of Directors and Other Voting Procedures

SOURCE: 53 FR 50392, Dec. 15, 1988, unless otherwise noted.

§ 611.310 Eligibility for membership on bank and association boards and subsequent employment.

(a) No person shall be eligible for membership on a bank or association board who is or has been, within 1 year preceding the date the term of office begins, a salaried officer or employee of any bank or association in the System.

(b) No bank or association director shall be eligible to continue to serve in that capacity and his or her office shall become vacant if after election as a member of the board, he or she becomes legally incompetent or is convicted of any criminal offense involving dishonesty or breach of trust or held liable in damages for fraud.

(c) No bank director shall, within 1 year after the date when he or she ceases to be a member of the board, serve as a salaried officer or employee of such bank, or any association with

§ 611.320

which the bank has a discount or agent relationship.

(d) No director of an association shall, within 1 year after he or she ceases to be a member of the board, serve as a salaried officer or employee of such association.

(e) No person shall be eligible for membership on a Farm Credit bank or association board of directors in the same election cycle for which the Farm Credit institution's nominating committee is identifying candidates if that person was elected to serve on that institution's nominating committee and attended any meeting called by the nominating committee.

(f) Out-of-territory borrowers who hold voting stock in the association may serve as association directors unless prohibited by the association's bylaws. If an association's bylaws prohibit it, that association must inform, in writing and at the time of loanmaking, each out-of-territory borrower that out-of-territory borrowers may not serve as directors.

[53 FR 50392, Dec. 15, 1988, as amended at 54 FR 37095, Sept. 7, 1989; 75 FR 18740, Apr. 12, 2010]

§ 611.320 Impartiality in the election of directors.

(a) Each Farm Credit institution shall adopt policies and procedures that are designed to assure that the elections of board members are conducted in an impartial manner.

(b) No employee or agent of a Farm Credit institution shall take any part, directly or indirectly, in the nomination or election of members to the board of directors of a Farm Credit institution, or make any statement, either orally or in writing, which may be construed as intended to influence any vote in such nominations, or elections. This paragraph shall not prohibit employees or agents from providing biographical and other similar information or engaging in other activities pursuant to policies and procedures for nominations and elections. This paragraph does not affect the right of an employee or agent to nominate or vote for stockholder-elected directors of an institution in which the employee or agent is a voting member.

(c) No property, facilities, or resources, including information technology and human or financial resources, of any Farm Credit institution shall be used by any candidate for nomination or election or by any other person for the benefit of any candidate for nomination or election, unless the same property, facilities, or resources are simultaneously available and made known to be available for use by all declared candidates, including floor nominees. For the limited purpose of Farm Credit bank board elections, each Farm Credit bank may allow its stockholder-associations to use stockholder-association property, facilities, or resources in support of bank director candidates. Any Farm Credit bank permitting this activity by its stockholder-associations must have a policy in place approved by its board of directors establishing reasonable standards that stockholder-associations must follow, and those standards must give appropriate consideration to the various sizes of stockholder-associations within a bank's district and include a maximum amount that a stockholder-association may expend in support of a bank director candidate.

(d) No director, employee, or agent of a Farm Credit institution shall, for the purpose of furthering the interests of any candidates for nomination or election, furnish or make use of records that are not made available for use by all declared candidates.

(e) No Farm Credit institution may in any way distribute or mail, whether at the expense of the institution or another, any campaign materials for director candidates. Institutions may request biographical information, as well as the disclosure information required under § 611.330, from all declared candidates who certify that they are eligible, restate such information in a standard format, and distribute or mail it with ballots or proxy ballots.

(f) No director of a Farm Credit institution shall, in his or her capacity as a director, make any statement, either orally or in writing, which may be construed as intending to influence any vote in that institution's director nominations or elections. This paragraph shall not prohibit director candidates from engaging in campaign activities on their own behalf.

[53 FR 50392, Dec. 15, 1988, as amended at 71 FR 5761, Feb. 2, 2006; 75 FR 18740, Apr. 12, 2010]

§ 611.325 Bank and association nominating committees.

Each Farm Credit bank and association may have only one nominating committee in any one election cycle. Each Farm Credit bank and association's board of directors must establish and maintain policies and procedures on its nominating committee, describing the formation, composition, operation, resources, and duties of the committee, consistent with current laws and regulations. Each nominating committee must conduct itself in the impartial manner prescribed by the policies and procedures adopted by its institution under § 611.320 and this section.

(a) *Composition.* The voting stockholders of each bank and association must elect a nominating committee of no fewer than three members. Unless prohibited by association bylaws, out-of-territory borrowers who hold voting stock may serve as members of an association's nominating committee. If an association's bylaws prohibit it, that association must inform, in writing and at the time of loanmaking, each out-of-territory borrower that out-of-territory borrowers may not serve on the association's nominating committee.

(b) *Election.* Farm Credit banks and associations may use in-person (including use of an online medium and proxy ballots) or mail balloting procedures to elect a nominating committee.

(1) Farm Credit banks and associations must provide voting stockholders the opportunity to vote on the candidates for each nominating committee position.

(2) Association nominating committee members may only be elected to a 1-year term. Farm Credit Banks must use weighted voting, with no cumulative voting permitted, when electing members to serve on a nominating committee. Farm Credit banks and associations may permit nominating committee members to be re-nominated and stand for re-election to serve successive terms.

(c) *Conflicts of interest.* No individual may serve on a nominating committee who, at the time of election to, or during service on, a nominating committee, is an employee, director, or agent of that bank or association. A nominating committee member may not be a candidate for election to the board in the same election for which the committee is identifying nominees. A nominating committee member may resign from the committee to run for election to the board only if the individual did not attend any nominating committee meeting.

(d) *Responsibilities.* It is the responsibility of each nominating committee to identify, evaluate, and nominate candidates for stockholder election to a Farm Credit bank or association board of directors. A nominating committee's responsibilities are limited to the following:

(1) Nominate individuals who the committee determines meet the eligibility requirements to run for open director positions. The committee must endeavor to ensure representation from all areas of the Farm Credit bank's or association's territory and, as nearly as possible, all types of agriculture practiced within the territory.

(2) Evaluate the qualifications of the director candidates. The evaluation process must consider whether there are any known obstacles preventing a candidate from performing the duties of the position.

(3) Nominate at least two candidates for each director position being voted on by stockholders. If two nominees cannot be identified, the nominating committee must provide written explanation to the existing board of the efforts to locate candidates or the reasons for disqualifying any other candidate that resulted in fewer than two nominees.

(4) Maintain records of its meetings, including a record of attendance at meetings.

(5) Identify, evaluate, and nominate eligible individuals for service on the next nominating committee, if permitted by the institution.

§ 611.326

(e) *Resources.* Each Farm Credit bank and association must provide its nominating committee reasonable access to administrative resources in order for the committee to perform its duties. Each Farm Credit bank and association must, at a minimum, provide its nominating committee with FCA regulations and guidance on nominating committees, a current list of stockholders, the most recent bylaws, the current director qualifications policy, and a copy of the policies and procedures that the bank or the association has adopted pursuant to § 611.320(a) ensuring impartial elections. On the request of the nominating committee, the institution must also provide a summary of the current board self-evaluation. The bank or association may require a pledge of confidentiality by committee members prior to releasing evaluation documents.

[75 FR 18741, Apr. 12, 2010]

§ 611.326 Floor nominations for open Farm Credit bank and association director positions.

(a) Each floor nominee must be eligible for the director position for which the person has been nominated.

(b)(1) Voting stockholders of associations must be allowed to make floor nominations for every open stockholder-elected director position. Associations using only mail ballots must allow nominations from the floor at every session of an annual meeting. Associations permitting stockholders to cast votes during annual meetings may only allow nominations from the floor at the first session of the annual meeting.

(2) If floor nominations are permitted by a Farm Credit bank's election policies and procedures, voting stockholders must be allowed to make floor nominations for every open stockholder-elected director position and a physical meeting space must exist. Before every director election by a Farm Credit bank, the bank must inform voting stockholders whether floor nominations will be accepted.

(c) Each association's board of directors must adopt policies and procedures for making and accepting floor nominations of candidates to stand for election to its board of directors. Each Farm Credit bank's board of directors allowing nominations from the floor must also adopt policies and procedures for making and accepting floor nominations. Policies and procedures for floor nominations must, at a minimum, provide that:

(1) Floor nominations may only be made after the nominating committee has provided its list of director-nominees.

(2) No more than a second by a voting stockholder to a nomination from the floor is required. After receiving a floor nomination, the floor nominee must state if he or she accepts the nomination.

(3) Floor nominees must make the disclosures required by § 611.330 of this part.

[75 FR 18741, Apr. 12, 2010]

§ 611.330 Disclosures of Farm Credit bank and association director-nominees.

(a) Each Farm Credit bank and association's board of directors must adopt policies and procedures that ensure a disclosure statement is prepared by each director-nominee. At a minimum, each disclosure statement for each nominee must:

(1) State the nominee's name, city and state of residence, business address if any, age, and business experience during the last 5 years, including each nominee's principal occupation and employment during the last 5 years.

(2) List all business interests on whose board of directors the nominee serves or is otherwise employed in a position of authority and state the principal business in which the business interest is engaged.

(3) Identify any family relationship of the nominee that would be reportable under part 612 of this chapter if elected to the institution's board.

(b)(1) Floor nominees who are not incumbent directors must provide to the Farm Credit bank or association the information referred to in this section and in § 620.5(j) and (k) of this chapter. The information must be provided in either paper or electronic form within the time period prescribed by the institution's bylaws or policies and procedures. If the institution does not have a prescribed time period, each floor

Farm Credit Administration § 611.340

nominee must provide this information to the institution within 5 business days of the nomination. If stockholders will not vote solely by mail ballot upon conclusion of the meeting, each floor nominee must provide the information at the first session at which voting is held.

(2) For each nominee who is not an incumbent director or a nominee from the floor, the nominee must provide the information referred to in this section and in § 620.5(j) and (k) of this chapter.

(c) Each Farm Credit bank and association must distribute director-nominee disclosure information to all stockholders eligible to vote in the election. Institutions may either restate such information in a standard format or provide complete copies of each nominee's disclosure statement.

(1) Disclosure information for each director-nominee must be provided as part of the Annual Meeting Information Statement (AMIS) issued for director elections.

(2) Disclosure information for each director-nominee must be distributed or mailed with ballots or proxy ballots. Farm Credit banks and associations must ensure that the disclosure information on floor nominees is provided to voting stockholders by delivering ballots for the election of directors in the same format as the comparable information contained in the AMIS.

(d) No person may be a nominee for director who does not make the disclosures required by this section.

[75 FR 18742, Apr. 12, 2010]

§ 611.340 Confidentiality and security in voting.

(a) Each Farm Credit bank and association's board of directors must adopt policies and procedures that:

(1) Ensure the security of all records and materials related to a stockholder vote including, but not limited to, ballots, proxy ballots, and other related materials.

(2) Ensure that ballots and proxy ballots are provided only to stockholders who are eligible to vote as of the record date set for the stockholder vote.

(3) Ensure that all information and materials regarding how or whether an individual stockholder has voted remain confidential, including protecting the information from disclosure to the institution's directors, stockholders, or employees, or any other person except:

(i) An independent third party tabulating the vote; or

(ii) The Farm Credit Administration.

(4) Provide for the establishment of a tellers committee or an independent third party who will be responsible for validating ballots and proxies and tabulating voting results. A tellers committee may only consist of voting stockholders who are not directors, director-nominees, or members of that election cycle's nominating committee.

(b) No Farm Credit bank or association may use signed ballots in stockholder votes. A bank or association may use balloting procedures, such as an identity code on the ballot, that can be used to identify how or whether an individual stockholder has voted only if the votes are tabulated by an independent third party. In weighted voting, the votes must be tabulated by an independent third party. An independent third party that tabulates the votes must certify in writing that such party will not disclose to any person (including the institution, its directors, stockholders, or employees) any information about how or whether an individual stockholder has voted, except that the information must be disclosed to the Farm Credit Administration if requested.

(c) Once a Farm Credit bank or association receives a ballot, the vote of that stockholder is final, except that a stockholder may withdraw a proxy ballot before balloting begins at a stockholders' meeting. A Farm Credit bank or association may give a stockholder voting by proxy an opportunity to give voting discretion to the proxy of the stockholder's choice, provided that the proxy is also a stockholder eligible to vote.

(d) Ballots and proxy ballots must be safeguarded before the time of distribution or mailing to voting stockholders and after the time of receipt by the bank or association until disposal. When stockholder meetings are held for the purpose of conducting elections or other votes, only proxy ballots may be accepted prior to any or all sessions

§ 611.350

of the stockholders' meeting and mail ballots may only be distributed after the conclusion of the meeting. In an election of directors, ballots, proxy ballots, and election records must be retained at least until the end of the term of office of the director. In other stockholder votes, ballots, proxy ballots, and records must be retained for at least 3 years after the vote.

(e) An institution and its officers, directors, and employees may not make any public announcement of the results of a stockholder vote before the tellers committee or independent third party has validated the results of the vote.

[75 FR 18742, Apr. 12, 2010]

§ 611.350 Application of cooperative principles to the election of directors.

In the election of directors, each Farm Credit institution shall comply with the following cooperative principles as well as those set forth in § 615.5230 of this chapter, unless otherwise required by statute or regulation.

(a) Each voting stockholder of an association or bank for cooperatives has only one vote, regardless of the number of shares owned or the number of loans outstanding. Each voting stockholder-association of a Farm Credit Bank has only one vote that is assigned a weight proportional to the number of that association's voting stockholders. Each voting stockholder of an agricultural credit bank has only one vote, unless another voting scheme has been approved by the Farm Credit Administration.

(b) If an association apportions its territory into geographic regions for director nomination or election purposes, out-of-territory voting stockholders must be assigned to a geographic region.

(c) All voting stockholders of a Farm Credit institution have the right to vote in any stockholder vote to remove any director.

[75 FR 18742, Apr. 12, 2010]

Subpart D—Rules for Compensation of Board Members

§ 611.400 Compensation of bank board members.

(a) Farm Credit System banks are authorized to pay fair and reasonable compensation to directors for services performed in an official capacity at a rate not to exceed the level established in section 4.21 of the Farm Credit Act of 1971, as amended, unless the FCA determines that such a level adversely affects the safety and soundness of the institution.

(b) The bank director compensation level established in section 4.21 of the Act shall be adjusted to reflect changes in the Consumer Price Index (CPI) for all urban consumers, as published by the Bureau of Labor Statistics, in the following manner: Current year's maximum compensation = Prior year's maximum compensation adjusted by the prior year's annual average percent change in the CPI for all urban consumers. Adjustments will be made to the bank director statutory compensation limit beginning from October 28, 1992 (the date of enactment of the Farm Credit Banks and Associations Safety and Soundness Act of 1992). Additionally, each year the FCA will distribute a bookletter to all FCS banks that communicates the CPI adjusted bank director statutory compensation limit.

(c)(1) A Farm Credit bank is authorized to pay a director up to 30 percent more than the statutory compensation limit in exceptional circumstances where the director contributes extraordinary time and effort in the service of the bank and its shareholders.

(2) Banks must document the exceptional circumstances justifying additional director compensation. The documentation must describe:

(i) The exceptional circumstances justifying the additional director compensation, including the extraordinary time and effort the director devoted to bank business; and

(ii) The amount and the terms and conditions of the additional director compensation.

(d) Each bank board shall adopt a written policy regarding compensation

Farm Credit Administration

§ 611.505

of bank directors. The policy shall address, at a minimum, the following areas:

(1) The activities or functions for which attendance is necessary and appropriate and may be compensated, except that a Farm Credit System bank shall not compensate any director for rendering services on behalf of any other Farm Credit System institution or a cooperative of which the director is a member, or for performing other assignments of a non-official nature;

(2) The methodology for determining each director's rate of compensation; and

(3) The exceptional circumstances under which the board would pay additional compensation for any of its directors as authorized by paragraph (c) of this section.

(e) Directors may also be reimbursed for reasonable travel, subsistence, and other related expenses in accordance with the bank's policy.

[59 FR 37411, July 22, 1994, as amended at 64 FR 16618, Apr. 6, 1999; 65 FR 8023, Feb. 17, 2000]

Subpart E—Transfer of Authorities

SOURCE: 53 FR 50393, Dec. 15, 1988, unless otherwise noted.

§ 611.500 General.

Each Farm Credit Bank or Agricultural Credit Bank is authorized, in accordance with section 7.6 of the Act, to transfer certain authorities to Federal land bank associations. The regulations in this subpart set forth the procedures and voting and approval requirements applicable to such transfers.

§ 611.501 Procedures.

(a) The boards of directors of a bank and an association which seek to transfer authorities may adopt appropriate resolutions approving such transfer and providing for the submission of such a proposal to their respective stockholders for a vote.

(b) The resolutions accompanied by the following information shall be submitted to the Farm Credit Administration for review and approval:

(1) Any proposed amendments to the charters of the institutions;

(2) A copy of the transfer plan as required under § 611.520 of this part;

(3) An information statement that complies with the requirements of § 611.515;

(4) The proposed bylaws of the bank and the association, as applicable; and

(5) Any additional information the boards of directors wish to submit in support of the request or that the Farm Credit Administration requests.

§ 611.505 Farm Credit Administration review.

(a) Upon receipt of the board of directors resolution and the accompanying documents, the Farm Credit Administration shall review the request and either deny or give its preliminary approval to the request.

(b) If the request is denied, written notice stating the reasons for the denial shall be transmitted to the chief executive officer of the bank and the association who shall promptly notify their respective boards of directors.

(c) Upon approval of the proposed transfer of authorities by the stockholders as provided in § 611.510, the secretary of the bank and the secretary of the association shall forward to the Farm Credit Administration a certified record of the results of the stockholder votes.

(d) Each institution shall notify its stockholders not later than 30 days after the stockholder vote of the final results of the vote. If no petition for reconsideration is filed with the Farm Credit Administration in accordance with § 611.525, the transfer shall be effective on the date specified in the transfer plan, or at such later date as may be required by the Farm Credit Administration to grant final approval. Notice of final approval shall be transmitted to the institutions involved.

(e) The effective date of a transfer may not be less than 35 days after mailing of the notification to stockholders of the results of the stockholder vote, or 15 days after the date of submission to the Farm Credit Administration of all required documents for

§ 611.510

the Agency's consideration of final approval, whichever occurs later. If a petition for reconsideration is filed within 35 days after the date of mailing of the notification of stockholder vote, the constituent institutions must agree on a second effective date to be used in the event the transfer is approved on reconsideration. The second effective date may not be less than 60 days after stockholder notification of the results of the first vote, or 15 days after the date of the reconsideration vote, whichever occurs later.

[53 FR 50393, Dec. 15, 1988, as amended at 63 FR 64844, Nov. 24, 1998]

§ 611.510 Approval procedures.

(a) Upon receipt of approval of a resolution by the Farm Credit Administration, the bank and the association shall call a meeting of their voting stockholders. Each institution shall notify each stockholder that the resolution has been filed and that a meeting will be held in accordance with the institution's bylaws. The stockholders meeting of the bank and the association shall be held within 60 days of receipt of the approval from the Farm Credit Administration.

(b) The notice of meeting to consider and act upon the directors' resolution shall be accompanied by an information statement that complies with the requirements of § 611.515.

(c) The proposal shall be approved if agreed to by:

(1) A majority of the stockholders of the bank voting in person or by proxy, with each association entitled to cast a number of votes equal to the number of its voting stockholders;

(2) A majority of the stockholders of the association voting, in person or by proxy;

(3) The Farm Credit Administration.

§ 611.515 Information statement.

(a) The bank and association shall prepare an information statement which will inform stockholders about the provisions of the proposed transfer of authorities and the effect of the proposal on the bank and the association.

(b) The information statement for each institution involved shall contain the following materials as applicable to the institution:

(1) A statement either on the first page of the materials or on the notice of the stockholders meeting, in capital letters and boldface type, that:

THE FARM CREDIT ADMINISTRATION HAS NEITHER APPROVED NOR PASSED UPON THE ACCURACY OR ADEQUACY OF THE INFORMATION ACCOMPANYING THE NOTICE OF MEETING OR PRESENTED AT THE MEETING AND NO REPRESENTATION TO THE CONTRARY SHALL BE MADE OR RELIED UPON.

(2) A description of the material provisions of the plan under § 611.520 and the effect of the transaction on the institution, its stockholders, and the territory to be served.

(3) A statement enumerating the potential advantages and disadvantages of the proposed transfer including, but not limited to, changes in operating efficiencies, one-stop service, branch offices, local control, and financial condition.

(4) A summary of the provisions of the charter and bylaws following the transfer that differ materially from the charter or bylaws currently existing.

(5) A brief statement by the board of directors of the institution setting forth the board's opinion on the advisability of the transfer.

(6) A presentation of the following financial data:

(i) An audited balance sheet and income statement and notes thereto of the bank or the association, as applicable, for the preceding 2 fiscal years.

(ii) If the transfer of authority includes any material transfer of assets, a balance sheet and income statement of the bank and the association showing its financial condition before the transfer of authority and a pro forma balance sheet and income statement for the bank or association, as applicable, showing its financial condition after the transfer. The statements shall meet the following conditions:

(A) Such financial statements shall be presented in columnar form, showing the financial condition as of the end of the most recent quarter of the institution, and operating results since the end of the last fiscal year through

Farm Credit Administration §611.520

the end of the most recent quarter of the institution.

(B) If the request is made within 90 days after the end of the fiscal year, the institution's financial statements shall be as of the most recent fiscal yearend.

(C) If the request is made within 45 days after the end of the most recent quarter, the institution's financial statements shall be as of the end of the quarter preceding the quarter just ended.

(D) If the request is made more than 45 days after the end of the most recent quarter, the institution's financial statements shall be as of the end of that quarter.

(E) The financial statements must be accompanied by appropriate notes, describing any assets being transferred and including data relating to high-risk assets and other property owned, allowance for loan losses, and current year-to-date chargeoffs.

(F) The amount and nature of start-up costs estimated to be associated with the transfer.

(7) A description of the type and dollar amount of any financial assistance that has been provided to the bank or the association, as applicable, during the past year; the conditions on which the financial assistance was extended, the terms of repayment or retirement, if any; and, the liability for repayment of this assistance by the bank or the association if the transfer were approved.

(8) A statement as to whether the bank or the association, as applicable, would require financial assistance during the first 3 years of operation, the estimated type and dollar amount of the assistance, and terms of repayment or retirement, if known.

(9) A statement indicating the possible tax consequences to stockholders and whether any legal opinion, ruling or external auditor's opinion has been obtained on the matter.

(10) A presentation of the association's interest rate and fee programs, interest collection policy, capitalization plan and other factors that would affect a borrower's cost of doing business with the association.

(11) A description of any event subsequent to the date of the last quarterly report, but prior to the stockholder vote, that would have a material impact on the financial condition of the bank or the association.

(12) A statement of any other material fact or circumstances that a stockholder would need in order to make an informed and responsible decision, or that would be necessary in order to provide a disclosure that is not misleading.

(13) A form of written proxy, together with instructions on its purpose, use and authorization by the stockholder. The proxy instructions must ensure the secrecy of the stockholder's ballot if the stockholder votes by proxy.

(14) A copy of the plan of transfer provided for in §611.520 of this part.

(c) No bank or association director, officer, or employee shall make any untrue or misleading statement of a material fact, or fail to disclose any material fact necessary under the circumstances to make statements made not misleading, to a stockholder of the association in connection with a transfer under this subpart.

[53 FR 50393, Dec. 15, 1988, as amended at 58 FR 48790, Sept. 20, 1993]

§611.520 Plan of transfer.

The transfer of authorities and assets, as appropriate, shall occur pursuant to a written plan which shall be agreed to by the bank and the association involved. The written plan shall include the following:

(a) An explanation of the value of the equity ownership as of the last monthend held by stockholders of the bank and the association and the impact, if any, of the transfer on the value of that equity.

(b) If the plan provides for a transfer of assets, a description of the terms and conditions upon which such transfer will occur, including, but not limited to, any warranties or representations regarding the value of such assets.

(c) A description of how the association would obtain loan funds after the transfer.

(d) A statement on how the expenses connected with the transfer are to be borne by the affected parties.

§ 611.525

(e) A statement of any conditions which must be satisfied prior to the effective date of the transfer, including but not limited to approval by stockholders and approval by the Farm Credit Administration.

(f) A statement that prior to the effective date of the transfer the board of directors of the bank or the association may rescind its resolution and void the transfer, with the concurrence of the Farm Credit Administration, on the basis that:

(1) The information disclosed to stockholders contained material errors or omissions;

(2) Material misrepresentations were made to stockholders regarding the impact of the transfer;

(3) Fraudulent activities were used to obtain the stockholders' approval; or,

(4) An event occurred between the time of the vote and the transfer that would have a significant adverse impact on the future viability of the association.

(g) A designation of those persons who have authority to carry out the plan of transfer, including the authority to execute any documents necessary to perfect title, on behalf of the bank and the association.

§ 611.525 Stockholder reconsideration.

(a) Stockholders have the right to reconsider the approval of the transfer provided that a petition signed by 15 percent of the stockholders of either institution involved in the transfer is filed with the Farm Credit Administration within 35 days after the date of mailing of the notification of the final results of the stockholder vote required under § 611.505(d) and such petition is approved by the Farm Credit Administration.

(b) A special stockholders meeting shall be called by the institution to vote on the reconsideration following the Farm Credit Administration's approval of a stockholder petition to reconsider the transfer. If a majority of stockholders of any institution involved in the transfer votes against the transfer, the transfer is not approved.

Subpart F—Bank Mergers, Consolidations and Charter Amendments

SOURCE: 53 FR 50393, Dec. 15, 1988, unless otherwise noted.

§ 611.1000 General authority.

(a) An amendment to a bank charter may relate to any provision that is properly the subject of a charter, including, but not limited to, the name of the bank, the location of its offices, or the territory served.

(b) The Farm Credit Administration may make changes in the charter of a bank as may be requested by that bank and approved by the Farm Credit Administration pursuant to § 611.1010 of this part.

(c) The Farm Credit Administration may, in accordance with the provisions of the Act, make changes in the charter of a bank as may be necessary or expedient to implement the provisions of the Act.

§ 611.1010 Bank charter amendment procedures.

(a) A bank may recommend a charter amendment to accomplish any of the following actions:

(1) A merger or consolidation with any other bank or banks operating under title I or III of the Act;

(2) A transfer of territory with any other bank operating under the same title of the Act;

(3) A change to its name or location;

(4) Any other change that is properly the subject of a bank charter;

(b) Upon approval of an appropriate resolution by the bank board, the certified resolution, together with supporting documentation, shall be submitted to the Farm Credit Administration for preliminary or final approval, as the case may be.

(c) The Farm Credit Administration shall review the material submitted and either approve or disapprove the request. The Farm Credit Administration may require submission of any supplemental materials it deems appropriate. If the request is for merger, consolidation, or transfer of territory, the approval of Farm Credit Administration will be preliminary only, with

Farm Credit Administration

§611.1121

final approval subject to a vote of the bank's stockholders.

(d) Following receipt of the Farm Credit Administration's written preliminary approval, the proposal shall be submitted for approval to the voting stockholders of the bank. A proposal shall be approved if agreed to by a majority of the stockholders of each bank voting, in person or by proxy, at a duly authorized stockholder meeting with each association entitled to cast a number of votes equal to the number of the association's voting shareholders.

(e) Upon approval by the stockholders of the bank, the request for final approval and issuance of the appropriate charter or amendments to charter for the banks involved shall be submitted to the Farm Credit Administration.

§611.1020 Requirements for mergers or consolidations of banks.

(a) As authorized under sections 7.0 and 7.12 of the Act, a bank may merge or consolidate with one or more banks operating under the same or different titles of the Act.

(b) Where two or more banks plan to merge or consolidate, the banks shall jointly submit to the Farm Credit Administration the documents itemized in §§611.1122(a)(1) through (4), (6), (7), 611.1122(e), and 611.1123. In interpreting those sections, the word "bank" shall be read for the word "association."

(c) No bank director, officer, or employee shall make any untrue or misleading statement of a material fact, or fail to disclose any material fact necessary under the circumstances to make statements made not misleading, to any stockholder of the bank in connection with a bank merger or consolidation.

(d) Upon approval of a proposed bank merger or consolidation by the stockholders of each constituent bank, the following documents shall be submitted from the constituent banks to the Farm Credit Administration for final approval and issuance of the appropriate charters or amendments to charter:

(1) A certified copy of the stockholders' resolution, on which the stockholders cast their votes, from each constituent bank;

(2) A certification of the stockholder vote from the corporate secretary of each bank or from an independent third party;

(3) An Agreement of Merger or Consolidation duly executed by those authorized to sign on behalf of each constituent bank.

§611.1030 [Reserved]

§611.1040 Creation of new associations.

Any application for the issuance of a charter to a new production credit association or Federal land bank association shall meet the requirements of sections 2.0 or 2.10, respectively, of the Act. Any application for the issuance of a charter for an agricultural credit association shall meet the requirements of section 2.0 of the Act.

Subpart G—Mergers, Consolidations, and Charter Amendments of Associations

§611.1120 General authority.

(a) An amendment to an association charter may relate to any provision that is properly the subject of a charter, including, but not limited to, the name of the association, the location of its offices, or the territory served.

(b) The Farm Credit Administration may make changes in the charter of an association as may be requested by that association and approved by the Farm Credit Administration pursuant to §611.1121 of this part.

(c) The Farm Credit Administration may, by order of the Chairman and on its own initiative, make changes in the charter of a Federal land bank association or a production credit association where the Chairman determines that the change is necessary for the accomplishment of the purposes of the Act.

[50 FR 20400, May 16, 1985, as amended at 51 FR 41945, Nov. 20, 1986]

§611.1121 Charter amendment procedures.

This section shall apply to any request by an association to amend its charter.

§ 611.1122

(a) An association which proposes to amend its charter shall submit a request to its supervising bank containing the following information:

(1) A statement of the provision(s) of the charter that the association proposes to amend and the proposed amendment(s);

(2) A statement of the reasons for the proposed amendment(s), the impact of the amendment(s) on the association and its stockholders, and the requested effective date of the amendment(s);

(3) A certified copy of the resolution of the board of directors of the association approving the amendment(s);

(4) Any additional information or documents that the association wishes to submit in support of the request or that may be requested by the supervising bank.

(b) Upon receipt of a proposed amendment from an association, the district bank shall review the materials submitted and provide the association with its analysis of the proposal within a reasonable period of time. Concurrently, the bank shall communicate its recommendation on the proposal to the Farm Credit Administration, including the reasons for the recommendation, and any analysis the bank believes appropriate. Following review by the bank, the association shall transmit the proposed amendment with attachments to the Farm Credit Administration.

(c) Upon receipt of an association's request for a charter amendment, the Farm Credit Administration shall review the materials submitted and either approve or disapprove the request. The Farm Credit Administration may require submission of any supplemental materials it deems appropriate.

(d) The Farm Credit Administration shall notify the association of its approval or disapproval of the amendment request, and provide a copy of such communication to the bank. A notification of approval shall be accompanied by a copy of the charter, as amended.

[50 FR 20400, May 16, 1985, as amended at 51 FR 32441, Sept. 12, 1986]

§ 611.1122 Requirements for mergers or consolidations.

This section shall apply to any request for approval of a proposed merger or consolidation of associations. A merger involves the combination of one or more associations into a continuing constituent association, which retains its charter and bylaws (except as amended to effect the merger proposal). A consolidation involves the combination of two or more associations into a newly organized association having a new charter and bylaws.

(a) Where two or more associations plan to merge or consolidate, or where the district board has adopted a reorganization plan for the associations in the district, the associations involved shall jointly submit a request to the district bank containing the following:

(1) In the case of a merger, a copy of the charter of the continuing association reflecting any proposed amendments. In the case of consolidation, a copy of the proposed charter of the new association;

(2) A statement of the reasons for the proposed merger or consolidation, the impact of the proposed transaction on the associations and their stockholders, and the planned effective date of the merger or consolidation;

(3)(i) A certified copy of the resolution of the board of directors of each association recommending approval of the merger or consolidation; or

(ii) In the case of a district reorganization plan, a certified copy of the resolution of the board of directors of each association recommending either approval or disapproval of the proposal.

(4) A copy of the agreement of merger or consolidation;

(5) Two signed copies of the continuing or proposed Articles of Association;

(6) All of the information specified in paragraph (e) of this section; and

(7) Any additional information or documents each association wishes to submit in support of the request or that the supervising bank or the Farm Credit Administration requests.

Farm Credit Administration §611.1122

(b) Upon receipt of a request for approval of an association merger or consolidation, the district bank shall review the materials submitted to determine whether they comply with the requirements of these regulations and shall communicate with the associations concerning any deficiency. When the bank approves the request to merge or consolidate it shall notify the associations and the Farm Credit Administration of its approval together with the reasons for its approval and any supporting analysis the bank deems appropriate. The associations shall jointly submit the proposal together with required documentation to the Farm Credit Administration for preliminary approval.

(c) Upon receipt of an association merger or consolidation request, the Farm Credit Administration shall review the request and either deny or give its preliminary approval to the request. When a request is denied, written notice stating the reasons for the denial shall be transmitted to the associations and a copy provided to the bank. When a request is preliminarily approved, written notice of the preliminary approval shall be given to the associations and a copy provided to the bank. Preliminary approval by the Farm Credit Administration shall not constitute approval of the merger or consolidation. Approval of a merger or consolidation shall be only pursuant to paragraph (g) of this section.

(d) Upon receipt of preliminary approval by the Farm Credit Administration of a merger or consolidation request, each constituent association shall call a meeting of its voting stockholders. The meeting shall be called on written notice to each stockholder entitled to vote on the transaction, and held in accordance with the terms of each association's bylaws. The affirmative vote of a majority of the voting stockholders of each association present and voting or voting by written proxy at a meeting at which a quorum is present shall be required for stockholder approval of a merger or consolidation proposal.

(e) Notice of the meeting to consider and act upon a proposed merger or consolidation of associations shall be accompanied by the following information covering each constituent association.

(1) A statement either on the first page of the materials or on the notice of the stockholders' meeting, in capital letters and bold face type, that:

THE FARM CREDIT ADMINISTRATION HAS NEITHER APPROVED NOR PASSED UPON THE ACCURACY OR ADEQUACY OF THE INFORMATION ACCOMPANYING THE NOTICE OF MEETING OR PRESENTED AT THE MEETING AND NO REPRESENTATION TO THE CONTRARY SHALL BE MADE OR RELIED UPON.

(2) A description of the material provisions of the agreement of merger or consolidation and the effect of the proposed merger or consolidation on the associations, their stockholders, the new or continuing board of directors, and the territory to be served. In addition, a copy of the agreement must be furnished with the notice to stockholders.

(3) A summary of the provisions of the charter and bylaws of the continuing or new association that differ materially from the existing charter or bylaw provisions of the constituent associations.

(4) A brief statement by the boards of directors of the constituent associations setting forth the basis for the boards' recommendation on the merger or consolidation.

(5) A description of any agreement or arrangement between a constituent association and any of its officers relating to employment or termination of employment and arising from the merger or consolidation.

(6) A presentation of the following financial data:

(i) A balance sheet and income statement for each constituent association for each of the 2 preceding fiscal years.

(ii) A balance sheet for each constituent association as of a date within 90 days of the date the request for preliminary approval is forwarded to the Farm Credit Administration presented on a comparative basis with the corresponding period of the prior fiscal year.

(iii) An income statement for the interim period between the end of the

§611.1122

last fiscal year and the date of the required balance sheet presented on a comparative basis with the corresponding period of the preceding fiscal year. The balance sheet and income statement format shall be that contained in the association's annual report to stockholders; shall contain any significant changes in accounting policies that differ from those in the latest association annual report to stockholders; and shall contain appropriate footnote disclosures, including data relating to high-risk assets and other property owned, and allowance for loan losses, including net chargeoffs as required in paragraph (e)(10) of this section.

(7) The financial statements (balance sheet and income statement) shall be in sufficient detail to show separately all significant categories of interest-earning assets and interest-bearing liabilities and the income or expense accrued thereon.

(8) Attached to the financial statements for each constituent association, either:

(i) A statement signed by the chief executive officer and each member of the board of directors of the association that the various financial statements are unaudited, but have been prepared in all material respects in accordance with generally accepted accounting principles (except as otherwise disclosed therein) and are, to the best of the knowledge of the board, a fair and accurate presentation of the financial condition of the association; or

(ii) A signed opinion by an independent certified public accountant that the various financial statements have been examined in accordance with generally accepted auditing standards and, accordingly, included such tests of the accounting records and such other auditing procedures as were considered necessary in the circumstances, and, as of the date of the statements, present fairly the financial position of the association in conformity with generally accepted accounting principles applied on a consistent basis, except as otherwise noted thereon.

(9) A presentation for each constituent association regarding its policy on accounting for loan performance, together with the number and dollar amount of loans in all performance categories, including those categorized as high-risk assets.

(10) Information of each constituent association concerning the amount of loans charged off in each of the 2 fiscal years preceding the date of the balance sheet, the current year-to-date net chargeoff amount, and the balance in the allowance for loan losses account and a statement regarding whether, in the opinion of management, the allowance for loan losses is adequate to absorb the risk currently existing in the loan portfolio. This information may be appropriately included in the footnotes to the financial statements.

(11) A management discussion and analysis of the financial condition and results of operation for the past 2 fiscal years for each constituent institution. This requirement can be satisfied by including the materials contained in the management discussion and analysis of each institution's most recent annual report.

(12) A discussion of any material changes in financial condition of each constituent institution from the end of the last fiscal year to the date of the interim balance sheet provided.

(13) A discussion of any material changes in the results of operations of each constituent institution with respect to the most recent fiscal-year-to-date period for which an income statement is provided.

(14) A discussion of any change in the tax status of the new institution from those of the constituent institutions as a result of merger or consolidation. A statement on any adverse tax consequences to the stockholders of the institution as a result of the change in tax status.

(15) A statement on the proposed institution's relationship with an independent public accountant, including any change that may occur as a result of the merger or consolidation.

(16) A pro forma balance sheet of the continuing or consolidated association presented as if the merger or consolidation had occurred as of the date on the balance sheets required in paragraph (e)(6) of this section, as recommended to the stockholders. A pro forma summary of earnings for the continuing or consolidated association presented as if

the merger or consolidation had been effective at the beginning of the interim period between the end of the last fiscal year and the date of the balance sheets.

(17) A description of the type and dollar amount of any financial assistance that has been provided during the past year or will be provided by the supervising bank or other party to assist the constituent or the continuing or new association(s), the conditions on which financial assistance has been or will be extended, the terms of repayment or retirement, if any, and the impact of the assistance on the subject association(s) or the stockholders.

(18) A presentation for each constituent association of interest rate comparisons for the last 2 fiscal years preceding the date of the balance sheet, together with a statement of the continuing or new association's proposed interest rate and fee programs, interest collection policies, capitalization rates, dividends or patronage refunds, and other factors that would affect a borrower's cost of doing business with the continuing or new association. Where agreement has not been reached on such matters, current related information shall be presented for each constituent association.

(19) A description for each constituent association of any event subsequent to the date of the financial statements, but prior to the merger or consolidation vote, that would have a material impact on the financial condition of the constituent or continuing or new association(s).

(20) A statement of any other material fact or circumstance that a stockholder would need in order to make an informed decision on the merger or consolidation proposal, or that is necessary to make the required disclosures not misleading.

(21) Where proxies are to be solicited, a form of written proxy, together with instructions on the purpose and authority for its use, and the proper method for signature by the stockholder.

(f) No bank or association, or director, officer, or employee thereof, shall make any untrue or misleading statement of a material fact, or fail to disclose any material fact necessary under the circumstances to make statements made not misleading, to a stockholder of any association in connection with an association merger or consolidation.

(g) Upon approval of a proposed merger or consolidation by the stockholders of the constituent associations, a certified copy of the stockholders' resolution shall be forwarded to the Farm Credit Administration. Each constituent association shall notify its stockholders not later than 30 days after the stockholder vote of the final results of the vote. If no petition is filed with the Farm Credit Administration to reconsider the vote, upon final approval by the FCA, the merger or consolidation shall be effective on the date specified in the merger agreement or at such later date as may be required by the Farm Credit Administration to grant final approval. Notice of final approval shall be transmitted to the associations and a copy provided to the affiliated bank.

(h) No director, officer, or employee of a bank or an association shall make an oral or written representation to any person that a preliminary or final approval by the Farm Credit Administration of an association merger or consolidation constitutes, directly or indirectly, either a recommendation on the merits of the transaction or an assurance concerning the adequacy or accuracy of any information provided to any association's stockholders in connection therewith.

(i) The notice and accompanying information required under paragraph (e) of this section shall not be sent to stockholders until preliminary approval of the merger or consolidation has been given by the Farm Credit Administration.

(j) Where a proposed merger or consolidation will involve more than three associations, the Farm Credit Administration may require the supplementation, or allow the condensation or omission of any information required under paragraph (e) of this section in furtherance of meaningful disclosure to stockholders. Any waiver sought under this paragraph shall be obtained before preparation of the financial statements and accompanying schedules required under paragraph (e) of this section.

§ 611.1123

(k) The effective date of a merger or consolidation may not be less than 35 days after the date of mailing of the notification to stockholders of the results of the stockholder vote, or 15 days after the date of submission to the Farm Credit Administration of all required documents for the Agency's consideration of final approval, whichever occurs later. If a petition for reconsideration is filed within 35 days after mailing of the notification to stockholders of the results of the stockholder vote, the constituent institutions must agree on a second effective date to be used in the event the merger or consolidation is approved on reconsideration. The second effective date may not be less than 60 days after stockholder notification of the results of the first vote, or 15 days after the date of the reconsideration vote, whichever occurs later.

[50 FR 20400, May 16, 1985; 50 FR 32165, Aug. 9, 1985, as amended at 51 FR 32441, Sept. 12, 1986; 53 FR 50396, Dec. 15, 1988; 56 FR 2674, Jan. 24, 1991; 58 FR 48790, Sept. 20, 1993; 63 FR 64844, Nov. 24, 1998]

§ 611.1123 Merger or consolidation agreements.

(a) Associations operating under the same title of the Act may merge or consolidate voluntarily only pursuant to a written agreement. The agreement shall set forth all of the terms of the transaction, including, but not limited to, the following:

(1) The proposed effective date of the merger or consolidation.

(2) The proposed name and headquarters location of the continuing or consolidated association.

(3) The names of the persons nominated to serve as directors until the first regular annual meeting of the continuing or consolidated association to be held after the effective date of the merger or consolidation. Any director of a constituent association may be designated in the agreement to serve as a director of the continuing or consolidated association for a period not to exceed his or her current term, after which he or she must stand for reelection. However, the terms of the agreement must provide for the election of at least one director at each annual meeting subsequent to the effective date of the merger or consolidation. The bylaws of the continuing or consolidated association shall reflect the provisions of the merger or consolidation agreement regarding director terms.

(4) A statement of the formula to be used to exchange the stock of the constituent associations for the stock of the continuing or consolidated association. No fractional shares of stock shall be issued.

(5) A statement of any conditions which must be satisfied prior to the effective date of the proposed transaction, including but not limited to approval by stockholders, the supervising bank, and the Farm Credit Administration.

(6) A statement of the representations or warranties, if any, made or to be made by any association, or its officers, directors, or employees that is a party to the proposed transactions.

(7) A statement that the board of directors of each constituent association can terminate the agreement before the effective date upon a determination by an association, with the concurrence of the Farm Credit Administration, that:

(i) The information disclosed to stockholders contained material errors or omissions;

(ii) Material misrepresentations were made to stockholders regarding the impact of the merger or consolidation;

(iii) Fraudulent activities were used to obtain stockholders' approval; or

(iv) An event occurred between the time of the vote and the merger that would have a significant adverse impact on the future viability of the continuing institution.

(8) A description of the legal opinions or rulings (including those related to tax matters), if any, that have been obtained or furnished by any party in connection with the proposed transaction. Also, refer to paragraph (a)(5) of this section.

(9) The capitalization plan and capital structure for the new institution and a statement that the capitalization plan shall comply with applicable FCA regulations.

(10) Provision for the employee benefits plan, its subsequent continuation or adaptation by the board of directors

of the proposed institution following the merger or consolidation.

(11) A statement of the authority of those persons designated to carry out the terms of the agreement, including the authority to waive provisions of the agreement and to execute any documents necessary to perfect title, on behalf of the constituent associations.

(b) As an attachment to the agreement, set forth those provisions of the charter and bylaws of the continuing or consolidated association which differ from the existing charter or bylaw provisions of the constituent associations.

(c) Stockholders have the right to reconsider the approval of the merger provided that a petition signed by 15 percent of the stockholders eligible to vote of one or more of the constituent institutions is filed with the Farm Credit Administration within 35 days after the date of mailing the notification of the final results of the stockholder vote required under §611.1122(g). The Farm Credit Administration will review the petition to determine whether it complies with the requirements of section 7.9 of the Act. Following a determination that the petition complies with the applicable requirements, a special stockholders meeting shall be called by the institution to reconsider the vote. If a majority of the stockholders voting, in person or by proxy, of any one of the constituent institutions that is a party to the merger vote against the merger, the merger shall not take place.

[50 FR 20400, May 16, 1985, as amended at 51 FR 32442, Sept. 12, 1986; 53 FR 50396, Dec. 15, 1988]

§ 611.1124 Territorial adjustments.

This section shall apply to any request submitted to the Farm Credit Administration to modify association charters for the purpose of transferring territory from one association to another.

(a) Territorial adjustments, except as specified in paragraph (m) of this section, require approval of a majority of the voting stockholders of each association present and voting or voting by written proxy at a duly authorized meeting at which a quorum is present.

(b) When two or more associations agree to transfer territory, each association shall submit a proposal to the district bank containing the following:

(1) A statement of the reasons for the proposed transfer and the impact the transfer will have on its stockholders and holders of participation certificates;

(2) A certified copy of the resolution of the board of directors of each association approving the proposed territory transfer;

(3) A copy of the agreement to transfer territory that contains the following information:

(i) A description of the territory to be transferred.

(ii) Transferor association's plan to transfer loans and the types of loans to be transferred.

(iii) Transferor association's plan to retire and transferee association's plan to issue equities held by holders of stock, participation certificates, and allocated equities, if any, and a statement by each association that the book value of its equities is at least equal to par.

(iv) An inventory of the assets to be sold by the transferor association and purchased by the transferee association.

(v) An inventory of the liabilities to be assumed from the transferor association by the transferee association.

(vi) A statement that the holders of stock and participation certificates whose loans are subject to transfer have 60 days from the effective date of the territory transfer to inform the transferor association of their decision to remain with the transferor association for normal servicing until the current loan is paid.

(vii) A statement that the transfer is conditioned upon the approval of the stockholders of each constituent association.

(viii) The effective date of the proposed territory transfer.

(4) A copy of the stockholder disclosure statement provided for in paragraph (f) of this section; and

(5) Any additional relevant information or documents that the association wishes to submit in support of its request or that may be required by the Farm Credit Administration.

§ 611.1124

(c) Upon receipt of documents supporting a proposed territory transfer, the district bank shall review the materials submitted and provide the associations with its analysis of the proposal within a reasonable period of time. The bank shall concurrently advise the Farm Credit Administration of its recommendation regarding the proposed territory transfer. Following review by the bank, the associations shall transmit the proposal to the Farm Credit Administration together with all required documents.

(d) Upon receipt of an association's request to transfer territory, the Farm Credit Administration shall review the request and either deny or give preliminary approval to the request. When a request is denied, written notice stating the reasons for the denial shall be transmitted to the associations, and a copy provided to the bank. When a request is preliminarily approved, written notice of the preliminary approval shall be transmitted to the associations, and a copy provided to the bank. Preliminary approval by the Farm Credit Administration shall not constitute approval of the territory transfer. Final approval shall be granted only in accordance with paragraph (h) of this section.

(e) Upon receipt of preliminary approval by the Farm Credit Administration, each constituent association shall, by written notice, and in accordance with its bylaws, call a meeting of its voting stockholders. The affirmative vote of a majority of the voting stockholders of each association present and voting or voting by written proxy at a meeting at which a quorum is present shall be required for stockholder approval of a territory transfer.

(f) Notice of the meeting to consider and act upon a proposed territory transfer shall be accompanied by the following information covering each constituent association:

(1) A statement either on the first page of the materials or on the notice of the stockholders' meeting, in capital letters and bold face type, that:

THE FARM CREDIT ADMINISTRATION HAS NEITHER APPROVED NOR PASSED UPON THE ACCURACY OR ADEQUACY OF THE INFORMATION ACCOMPANYING THE NOTICE OF MEETING OR PRESENTED AT THE MEETING AND NO REPRESENTATION TO THE CONTRARY SHALL BE MADE OR RELIED UPON.

(2) A copy of the Agreement to Transfer Territory and a summary of the major provisions of the Agreement.

(3) The reason the territory transfer is proposed.

(4) A map of the association's territory as it would look after the transfer.

(5) A summary of the differences, if any, between the transferor and transferee associations' interest rates, interest rate policies, collection policies, service fees, bylaws, and any other items of interest that would impact a borrower's lending relationship with the institution.

(6) A statement that all loans of the transferor association that finance operations located in the transferred territory shall be transferred to the transferee association except as otherwise provided for in this section or in accordance with agreements between the associations as provided for in § 614.4070 of this chapter.

(7) Where proxies are to be solicited, a form of written proxy, together with instructions on the purpose and authority for its use, and the proper method for signature by the stockholders.

(8) A statement that the associations' bylaws, financial statements for the previous 3 years, and any financial information prepared by the associations concerning the proposed transfer of territory are available on request to the stockholders of any association involved in the transaction.

(g) No bank or association, or director, officer, or employee thereof, shall make any untrue or misleading statement of a material fact, or fail to disclose any material fact necessary under the circumstances to make statements made not misleading, to a stockholder of any association in connection with a territory transfer.

(h) Upon approval of a proposed territory transfer by the stockholders of the constituent associations, a certified copy of the stockholders' resolution for each constituent association

Farm Credit Administration §611.1125

and one executed Agreement to Transfer Territory shall be forwarded to the Farm Credit Administration. The territory transfer shall be effective when thereafter finally approved and on the date as specified by the Farm Credit Administration. Notice of final approval shall be transmitted to the associations and a copy provided to the bank.

(i) No director, officer, or employee of a bank or an association shall make an oral or written representation to any person that a Preliminary or final approval by the Farm Credit Administration of a territory transfer constitutes, directly or indirectly, a recommendation on the merits of the transaction or an assurance concerning the adequacy or accuracy of any information provided to any association's stockholders in connection therewith.

(j) The notice and accompanying information required under paragraph (f) of this section shall not be sent to stockholders until preliminary approval of the territory transfer has been granted by the Farm Credit Administration.

(k) Where a territory transfer is proposed simultaneously with a merger or consolidation, both transactions may be voted on by stockholders at the same meeting. Only stockholders of a transferee or transferor association shall vote on a territory transfer.

(l) Each borrower whose real estate or operations is located in a territory that will be transferred shall be provided with a written Notice of Territory Transfer immediately after the Farm Credit Administration has given final approval of the territory transfer. The Notice shall inform the borrower of the transfer of the borrower's loan to the transferee association and the exchange of related equities for equities of like kinds and amounts in the transferee association. If a like kind of equity is not available in the transferee association, similar equities shall be offered that will not adversely affect the interest of the owner. The Notice shall give the borrower 60 days from the effective date of the territory transfer to notify the transferor association in writing if the borrower decides to stay with the transferor association for normal servicing until the current loan is paid. Any application by the borrower for renewal or for additional credit shall be made to the transferee association, except as otherwise provided for by an agreement between associations in accordance with §614.4070 of this chapter.

(m) This section shall not apply to territory transfers initiated by order of the Chairman of the Farm Credit Administration or to territory transfers due to the liquidation of the transferor association.

(n) Where a proposed action involves the transfer of a portion of an association's territory to an association operating in a different district, such proposal must comply with the provisions of this section and section 5.17(a) of the Act.

[51 FR 32442, Sept. 12, 1986, as amended at 71 FR 54901, Sept. 20, 2006]

§611.1125 Treatment of associations not approving districtwide mergers.

(a) *Issuance of charters.* When issuing charters or certificates of territory for districtwide mergers or consolidations of associations, the Farm Credit Administration will not issue any charters or certificates of territory that include the territory of one or more associations whose stockholders voted to disapprove the merger or consolidation.

(b) A district bank shall not take any of the following actions with respect to an association that has determined to not participate in a districtwide merger or consolidation:

(1) Discriminate in the provision of any financial service and assistance, including, but not limited to, access to loan funds and rates of interest on loans and discounts offered by the district bank to associations and their member/borrowers;

(2) Discriminate in the provision of any related services that are offered by the district bank to associations and their member/borrowers;

(3) Discriminate in the provision of any professional assistance that may be normally provided by the district bank to associations; or

(4) Discriminate in the provision of any technical assistance that may be normally provided by the district bank to associations.

§ 611.1130

(c) This regulation does not prohibit a district bank from taking any action with respect to an association, including, but not limited to, charging different rates of interest or different prices for services, or declining to provide financial assistance; provided that any such action is fully documented and based on an objective analysis of applicable criteria that are uniformly and consistently applied by the district bank to all associations in the district.

[51 FR 32443, Sept. 12, 1986, as amended at 60 FR 34099, June 30, 1995]

Subpart H—Rules for Inter-System Fund Transfers

§ 611.1130 Inter-System transfer of funds and equities.

(a) Section 5.17(a)(6) of the Act authorizes the FCA to regulate the borrowing, repayment, and transfer of funds and equities between institutions of the System, including banks, associations, and service organizations organized under the Act. This section sets forth the circumstances and procedures under which the FCA may direct such a transfer of funds and equities based on its determination with respect to the financial condition of one or more institutions of the System. For purposes of this section, the term "bond" refers to long-term notes, bonds, debentures, or other similar obligations, or short-term discount notes issued by one or more banks pursuant to section 4.2 of the Act.

(b) The FCA may direct a transfer of funds or equities by one or more banks of the System to another bank of the System where it determines that:

(1) The receiving institution will not be able to make payments of principal or interest on bonds for which it is primarily liable within the meaning of section 4.4(a) of the Act; or

(2) The common or preferred stock, participation certificates, or allocated equities of the receiving institution have a book value less than their par or stated values; or

(3) The total bonds outstanding for which the receiving institution is primarily liable exceed 20 times the combined capital and surplus accounts of the bank; or

(4) Based on application to it of one or more of the following ratios, the receiving institution is not financially viable in that it will not be able to continue to extend new or additional credit or financial assistance to its eligible borrowers:

(i) The ratio of stock to earned net worth (including legal reserve, unallocated and reserved surplus, undistributed earnings, and allowance for losses) exceeds 2 to 1;

(ii) The ratio of the outstanding bonds to capital and surplus exceeds 15 to 1;

(iii) Nonearning assets (any non-interest-bearing assets, including but not limited to cash, noninterest-earning loans, net fixed assets, other property owned, accrued interest receivable, and accounts receivable) exceed 15 percent of total assets;

(iv) Lendable net worth (interest-earning assets less interest-bearing liabilities) is zero or less.

(c) The FCA may direct a transfer of funds or equities between two or more Federal land bank associations or two or more production credit associations in district where it determines that such transfer:

(1) Is necessary to provide financial support to the district bank in which those associations are stockholders based on application of the criteria to the bank as set forth in paragraph (b) of this section; or

(2) Is necessary to provide financial support to one or more other like associations in the district based on application of the criteria set forth in paragraph (b)(2) or (b)(4) of this section to the associations, provided that in applying paragraph (b)(4)(ii) of this section the ratio of outstanding indebtedness to capital and surplus of the receiving association(s) shall not exceed 9 to 1; or

(3) Is an integral part of a plan that has been adopted by other institutions of the System, and approved by the FCA, under which those institutions will extend financial assistance to the district bank in which those associations are stockholders.

(d) A direction by the FCA for a transfer of funds or equities pursuant to this section shall be signed by the Chairman and shall establish the amount, timing, duration, repayment, and other terms of assessments necessary to accomplish such transfer, taking into consideration the financial condition of each institution to be assessed. Where the FCA directs a transfer of funds or equities between associations under paragraph (c) (1) or (2) of this section, it may authorize the district bank in which such associations are stockholders to accomplish the necessary assessments through debits and credits to the accounts of the bank.

[50 FR 36986, Sept. 11, 1985. Redesignated at 51 FR 8666, Mar. 13, 1986, as amended at 51 FR 41945, Nov. 20, 1986; 58 FR 48790, Sept. 20, 1993; 59 FR 21643, Apr. 26, 1994]

Subpart I—Service Organizations

SOURCE: 66 FR 16843, Mar. 28, 2001, unless otherwise noted.

§ 611.1135 Incorporation of service corporations.

(a) *What is the process for chartering a service corporation?* A Farm Credit bank or association (you or your) may organize a corporation acting alone or with other Farm Credit banks or associations to perform, for you or on your behalf, any function or service that you are authorized to perform under the Act and Farm Credit Administration (we, us, or our) regulations, with two exceptions. Those exceptions are that your corporation may not extend credit or provide insurance services. To organize a service corporation, you must submit an application to us following the applicable requirements of paragraph (c) of this section. If what you propose in your application meets the requirements of the Act, our regulations, and any other conditions we may impose, we may issue a charter for your service corporation making it a federally chartered instrumentality of the United States. Your service corporation will be subject to examination, supervision, and regulation by us.

(b) *Who may own equities in your service corporation?* (1) Your service corporation may only issue voting and non-voting stock to:

(i) One or more Farm Credit banks and associations; and

(ii) Persons that are not Farm Credit banks or associations, provided that at least 80 percent of the voting stock is at all times held by Farm Credit banks or associations.

(2) For the purposes of this subpart, we define persons as individuals or legal entities organized under the laws of the United States or any state or territory thereof.

(c) *What must be included in your application to form a service corporation?* Your application for a corporate charter must include:

(1) The certified resolution of the board of each organizing bank or association authorizing the incorporation;

(2) A request signed by the president(s) of the organizing bank(s) or association(s) to us to issue a charter, supported by a detailed statement demonstrating the need and the justification for the proposed entity; and

(3) The proposed articles of incorporation addressing, at a minimum, the following:

(i) The name of your corporation;

(ii) The city and state where the principal offices of your corporation are to be located;

(iii) The general purposes for the formation of your corporation;

(iv) The general powers of your corporation;

(v) The procedures for a Farm Credit bank or association or persons that are not Farm Credit institutions to become a stockholder;

(vi) The procedures to adopt and amend your corporation's bylaws;

(vii) The title, par value, voting and other rights, and authorized amount of each class of stock that your corporation will issue and the procedures to retire each class;

(viii) The notice and quorum requirement for a meeting of shareholders, and the vote required for shareholder action on various matters;

(ix) The procedures and shareholder voting requirements for the merger, voluntary liquidation, or dissolution of your corporation or the distribution of corporate assets;

(x) The standards and procedures for the application and distribution of your corporation's earnings; and

(xi) The length of time your corporation will exist.

§ 611.1136

(4) The proposed bylaws, which must include the provisions required by § 615.5220(b) of this chapter;

(5) A statement of the proposed amounts and sources of capitalization and operating funds;

(6) Any agreements between the organizing banks and associations relating to the organization or the operation of the corporation; and

(7) Any other supporting documentation that we may request.

(d) *What will we do with your application?* If we approve your completed application, we will issue a charter for your service corporation as a corporate body and a federally chartered instrumentality. We may condition the issuance of a charter, including imposing minimum capital requirements, as we deem appropriate. For good cause, we may deny your application.

(e) *Once your service corporation is formed, how are its articles of incorporation amended?* Your service corporation's articles of incorporation may be amended in either of two ways:

(1) The board of directors of the corporation may request that we amend the articles of incorporation by sending us a certified resolution of the board of directors of the service corporation that states the:

(i) Section(s) to be amended;

(ii) Reason(s) for the amendment;

(iii) Language of the articles of incorporation provision, as amended; and

(iv) Requisite shareholder approval has been obtained. The request will be subject to our approval as stated in paragraphs (a) and (c) of this section.

(2) We may at any time make any changes in the articles of incorporation of your service corporation that are necessary and appropriate for the accomplishment of the purposes of the Act.

(f) *When your service corporation issues equities, what are the disclosure requirements?* Your service corporation must provide the disclosures described in § 615.5255 of this chapter.

[66 FR 16843, Mar. 28, 2001, as amended at 70 FR 53907, Sept. 13, 2005; 71 FR 65386, Nov. 8, 2006]

§ 611.1136 Regulation and examination of service organizations.

(a) *What regulations apply to a service organization?* Because a service organization is formed by banks and associations, it is subject to applicable Farm Credit Administration (we, our) regulations.

(b) *Who examines a service organization?* We examine service organizations.

(c) *What types of service organizations are subject to our regulations and examination?* All incorporated service corporations and unincorporated service organizations formed by banks and associations are subject to our regulations and examination.

§ 611.1137 Title VIII service corporations.

(a) *What is a title VIII service corporation?* A title VIII service corporation is a service corporation organized for the purpose of exercising the authorities granted under title VIII of the Act to act as an agricultural mortgage marketing facility.

(b) *How do I form a title VIII service corporation?* A title VIII service corporation is formed and subject to the same requirements as a service corporation formed under § 611.1135, with one exception. The Federal Agricultural Mortgage Corporation or its affiliates may not form or own stock in a title VIII service corporation.

Subparts J–O [Reserved]

Subpart P—Termination of System Institution Status

SOURCE: 71 FR 44420, Aug. 4, 2006, unless otherwise noted.

§ 611.1200 Applicability of this subpart.

The regulations in this subpart apply to each bank and association that desires to terminate its System institution status and become chartered as a bank, savings association, or other financial institution.

Farm Credit Administration

§ 611.1205 Definitions that apply in this subpart.

Assets means all assets determined in conformity with GAAP, except as otherwise required in this subpart.

Business days means days the FCA is open for business.

Days means calendar days.

Equity holders means holders of stock, participation certificates, or other equities such as allocated equities.

GAAP means "generally accepted accounting principles" as that term is defined in § 621.2(c) of this chapter.

OFI means an "other financing institution" that has a funding and discount agreement with a Farm Credit bank under section 1.7(b)(1) of the Act.

Successor institution means the bank, savings association, or other financial institution that the terminating bank or association will become when we revoke its Farm Credit charter.

§ 611.1210 Advance notices—commencement resolution and notice to equity holders.

(a) *Adoption of commencement resolution.* Your board of directors must begin the termination process by adopting a commencement resolution stating your intention to terminate Farm Credit status under section 7.10 of the Act. Immediately after you adopt the commencement resolution, send a certified copy by overnight mail to us and to the Farm Credit System Insurance Corporation (FCSIC). If your institution is an association, also send a copy to your affiliated bank. If your institution is a bank, also send a copy to your affiliated associations, the other Farm Credit banks, and the Federal Farm Credit Banks Funding Corporation (Funding Corporation).

(b) *Advance notice.* Within 5 business days after adopting the commencement resolution, you must:

(1) Send us copies of all contracts and agreements related to the termination.

(2) Subject to paragraph (b)(2)(ii) of this section:

(i) Send an advance notice to all equity holders stating you are taking steps to terminate System status. Immediately upon mailing the notice to equity holders, you must also place it in a prominent location on your Web site. The advance notice must describe the following:

(A) The process of termination;

(B) The expected effect of termination on borrowers and other equity holders, including the effect on borrower rights and the consequences of any stock retirements before termination;

(C) The type of charter the successor institution will have; and

(D) Any bylaw creating a special class of borrower stock and participation certificates under paragraph (f) of this section.

(ii) Send us a draft of the advance notice by facsimile or electronic mail before mailing it to your equity holders. If we have not contacted you within 2 business days of our receipt of the draft notice regarding modifications, you may mail the notice to your equity holders.

(c) *Bank negotiations on joint and several liability.* If your institution is a terminating bank, within 10 days of adopting the commencement resolution, your bank and the other Farm Credit banks must begin negotiations to provide for your satisfaction of liabilities (other than your primary liability) under section 4.4 of the Act. The Funding Corporation may, at its option, be a party to the negotiations to the extent necessary to fulfill its duties with respect to financing and disclosure. The agreement must comply with the requirements in § 611.1270(c).

(d) *Disclosure to loan applicants and equity holders after commencement resolution.* Between the date your board of directors adopts the commencement resolution and the termination date, you must give the following information to your loan applicants and equity holders:

(1) For each loan applicant who is not a current stockholder, describe at the time of loan application:

(i) The effect of the proposed termination on the prospective loan; and

(ii) Whether, after the proposed termination, the borrower will continue to have any of the borrower rights provided under the Act and regulations.

(2) For any equity holders who ask to have their equities retired, explain that the retirement would extinguish

§611.1211

the holder's right to exchange those equities for an interest in the successor institution. In addition, inform holders of equities entitled to your residual assets in liquidation that retirement before termination would extinguish their right to dissent from the termination and have their equities retired.

(e) *Terminating bank's right to continue issuing debt.* Through the termination date, a terminating bank may continue to participate in the issuance of consolidated and System-wide obligations to the same extent it would be able to participate if it were not terminating.

(f) *Special class of stock.* Notwithstanding any requirements to the contrary in §615.5230(c) of this chapter, you may adopt bylaws providing for the issuance of a special class of stock and participation certificates between the date of adoption of a commencement resolution and the termination date. Your voting stockholders must approve the special class before you adopt the commencement resolution. The equities must comply with section 4.3A of the Act and be identical in all respects to existing classes of equities that are entitled to the residual assets of the institution in a liquidation, except for the value a holder will receive in a termination. In a termination, the holder of the special class of stock receives value equal to the lower of either par (or face) value, or the value calculated under §611.1280(c) and (d). A holder must have the same right to vote (if the equity is held on the voting record date) and to dissent as holders of similar equities issued before the commencement resolution. If the termination does not occur, the special classes of stock and participation certificates must automatically convert into shares of the otherwise identical equities.

[71 FR 44420, Aug. 4, 2006, as amended at 75 FR 18743, Apr. 12, 2010]

§611.1211 Special requirements.

(a) *Special assessments, analyses, studies, and rulings.* At any time after we receive your commencement resolution, and as we deem necessary or useful to evaluate your proposal, we may require you to engage independent experts, acceptable to us, to conduct assessments, analyses, or studies, or to request rulings, including, but not limited to:

(1) Assessments of fair value;

(2) Analyses and rulings on tax implications; and

(3) Studies of the effect of your proposal on equity holders (including the effect on holders in their capacity as borrowers), the System, and other parties.

(b) *Informational meetings.* After the advance notice, but before the stockholder vote, we may require you to hold regional or local informational meetings in convenient locations, at convenient times, and in a manner conducive to accommodating all equity holders that wish to attend, to discuss equity holder issues and answer questions. These meetings are subject to the plain language requirements of §611.1217(b) regarding balanced statements.

§611.1215 Communications with the public and equity holders.

(a) *Communications after commencement resolution and before termination.* The terminating institution may communicate with equity holders and the public regarding the proposed termination, as long as written communications (other than non-public communications among participants, *i.e.*, persons or entities that are parties to a proposed corporate restructuring involving the successor institution, or their agents) made in connection with or relating to the proposed termination and any related transactions are filed in accordance with paragraph (c) of this section and the conditions in this section are satisfied.

(b) To rely on this section, you must include the following legend in each communication in a prominent location:

> Equity holders should read the plan of termination that they have received or will receive (as appropriate) because it contains important information, including an enumerated statement of the anticipated benefits and potential disadvantages of the proposal.

(c) All your written communications and all written communications by your directors, employees, and agents in connection with or relating to the proposed termination or any related transactions must be filed with us

Farm Credit Administration § 611.1218

under this section on or before the date of first use.

(d) We will require you to correct communications that we deem are misleading or inaccurate.

(e) In addition to the filings we require under paragraph (c) of this section, we may require you to file timely any written communications you have knowledge of that are made by any other participants or their agents in connection with or related to the proposed termination or to any transaction related to the proposed termination.

(f) An immaterial or unintentional failure to file or a delay in filing a written communication described in this section will not result in a violation of this section, as long as:

(1) A good faith and reasonable effort was made to comply with the filing requirement; and

(2) The written communication is filed as soon as practicable after discovery of the failure to file.

(g) Communications that exist in electronic form must be filed electronically with the FCA as we direct. For communications that do not exist in electronic form, you must timely notify us by electronic mail and send us a copy by regular mail.

(h) You do not need to file a written communication that does not contain new or different information from that which you have previously publicly disclosed and filed under this section.

§ 611.1216 Public availability of documents related to the termination.

(a) We may post on our Web site, or require you to post on your Web site:

(1) Results of any special assessments, analyses, studies, and rulings required under § 611.1211;

(2) Documents you submit to us or file with us under § 611.1215; and

(3) Documents you submit to us under section 7.11 of the Act that are related directly or indirectly to the proposed termination, including but not limited to contracts entered into in connection with or relating to the proposed termination and any related transactions.

(b) We will not post confidential information on our Web site and will not require you to post it on your Web site.

(c) You may request that we treat specific information as confidential under the Freedom of Information Act, 5 U.S.C. 552 (see 12 CFR part, 602 subpart B). You should draft your request for confidential treatment narrowly to extend only to those portions of a document you consider to be confidential. If you request confidential treatment for information that we do not consider to be confidential, we may post that information on our Web site after providing notice to you. On our own initiative, we may determine that certain information should be treated as confidential and, if so, we will not make that information public.

§ 611.1217 Plain language requirements.

(a) *Plain language presentation.* All communications to equity holders required under §§ 611.1210, 611.1223, 611.1240, and 611.1280 must be clear, concise, and understandable. You must:

(1) Use short, explanatory sentences, bullet lists or charts where helpful, and descriptive headings and subheadings;

(2) Minimize the use of glossaries or defined terms;

(3) Write in the active voice when possible; and

(4) Avoid legal and highly technical business terminology.

(b) *Balanced statements.* Communications to equity holders that describe or enumerate anticipated benefits of the proposed termination should also describe or enumerate the potential disadvantages to the same degree of detail.

§ 611.1218 Role of directors.

(a) *Statements by directors.* Directors may not be prohibited by confidentiality agreements or otherwise from publicly or privately commenting orally or in writing on the termination proposal and related matters.

(b) *Directors' right to obtain independent advice.* One or more directors of a terminating institution or an institution that is considering terminating have the right to obtain independent legal and financial advice regarding the proposed termination and related transactions. The institution must pay for such advice and related expenses as

§ 611.1219

are reasonable in light of the circumstances. A request by a director or directors for the institution to pay such expenses cannot be denied unless the board of directors, by at least a two-thirds vote of the full board (the total number of current directors), denies the request. The institution must act on any request in a timely manner. For any denial of payment, the board must provide notice to the FCA within 1 business day of the denial, fully document the reasons for such a denial, and ensure that the institution discloses the nature of the request and the reasons for any denial to the terminating institution's equity holders in the plan of termination.

§ 611.1219 Prohibited acts.

(a) *Statements about termination.* Neither the institution nor any director, officer, employee, or agent may make any untrue or misleading statement of a material fact, or fail to disclose any material fact, to the FCA or a current or prospective equity holder about the proposed termination and any related transactions.

(b) *Representations regarding FCA approval.* Neither the institution nor any director, officer, employee, or agent may make an oral or written representation to anyone that our approval of the plan of termination or the termination is, directly or indirectly, either a recommendation on the merits of the proposal or an assurance that the information you give to your equity holders is adequate or accurate.

§ 611.1220 Termination resolution.

No more than 1 week before you submit your plan of termination to us, your board of directors must adopt a termination resolution stating its support for terminating your status as a System institution and authorizing:

(a) Submission to us of a plan of termination and other required submissions that comply with § 611.1223; and

(b) Submission of the plan of termination to the voting stockholders if we approve the plan of termination under § 611.1230 or, if we take no action, after the end of our approval period.

§ 611.1221 Submission to FCA of plan of termination and disclosure information; other required submissions.

(a) *Filing.* Send us an original and five copies of the plan of termination, including the disclosure information, and other required submissions. You may not file the plan of termination until at least 30 days after you mail the equity holder notice under § 611.1210(b). If you send us the plan of termination in electronic form, you must send us at least one hard copy with original signatures.

(b) *Plan contents.* The plan of termination must include your equity holder disclosure information that complies with § 611.1223.

(c) *Other submissions.* You must also submit the following:

(1) A statement of how you will transfer assets to, and have your liabilities assumed by, the successor institution;

(2) A copy of the charter application for the successor institution, with any exhibits or other supporting information; and

(3) A statement, if applicable, whether the successor institution will continue to borrow from a Farm Credit bank and how such a relationship will affect your provision for payment of debts. You must also provide evidence of any agreement and plan for satisfaction of outstanding debts.

§ 611.1223 Plan of termination—contents.

(a) *Disclaimer.* Place the following statement in boldface type in the material to be sent to equity holders, either on the notice of meeting or the first page of the plan of termination:

The Farm Credit Administration has not determined if this information is accurate or complete. You should not rely on any statement to the contrary.

(b) *Summary.* The first part of the plan of termination must be a summary that concisely explains:

(1) Which stockholders have a right to vote on the termination and related transactions;

(2) The material changes the termination will cause to the rights of borrowers and other equity holders;

(3) The effect of those changes;

Farm Credit Administration §611.1223

(4) The anticipated benefits and potential disadvantages of the termination;

(5) The right of certain equity holders to dissent and receive payment for their existing equities; and

(6) The estimated termination date.

(7) If applicable, an explanation of any corporate restructuring that the successor institution expects to engage in within 18 months after the date of termination.

(c) *Remaining requirements.* You must also disclose the following information to equity holders:

(1) *Termination resolution.* Provide a certified copy of the termination resolution required under §611.1220.

(2) *Plan of termination.* Summarize the plan of termination.

(3) *Benefits and disadvantages.* Provide an enumerated statement of the anticipated benefits and potential disadvantages of the termination.

(4) *Recommendation.* Explain the board's basis for recommending the termination.

(5) *Exit fee.* Explain the preliminary exit fee estimate, with any adjustments we require, and estimated expenses of termination and organization of the successor institution.

(6) *Initial board of directors.* List the initial board of directors and senior officers for the successor institution, with a brief description of the business experience of each person, including principal occupation and employment during the past 5 years.

(7) *Relevant contracts and agreements.* Include copies of all contracts and agreements related to the termination, including any proposed contracts in connection with the termination and subsequent operations of the successor institution. The FCA may, in its discretion, permit or require you to provide a summary or summaries of the documents in the disclosure information to be submitted to equity holders instead of copies of the documents.

(8) *Bylaws and charter.* Summarize the provisions of the bylaws and charter of the successor institution that differ materially from your bylaws and charter. The summary must state:

(i) Whether the successor institution will require a borrower to hold an equity interest as a condition for having a loan; and

(ii) Whether the successor institution will require equity holders to do business with the institution.

(9) *Changes to equity.* Explain any changes in the nature of equity investments in the successor institution, such as changes in dividends, patronage, voting rights, preferences, retirement of equities, and liquidation priority. If equities protected under section 4.9A of the Act are outstanding, the plan of termination must state that the Act's protections will be extinguished on termination.

(10) *Effect of termination on statutory and regulatory rights.* Explain the effect of termination on rights granted to equity holders by the Act and FCA regulations. You must explain the effect termination will have on borrower rights granted in the Act and part 617 of this chapter.

(11) *Loan refinancing by borrowers.*

(i) State, as applicable, that borrowers may seek to refinance their loans with the System institutions that already serve, or will be permitted to serve, your territory. State that no System institution is obligated to refinance your loans.

(ii) If we have assigned the chartered territory you serve to another System institution before the plan of termination is mailed to equity holders, or if another System institution is already chartered to make the same type of loans you make in the chartered territory, identify such institution(s) and provide the following information:

(A) The name, address, and telephone number of the institution; and

(B) An explanation of the institution's procedures for borrowers to apply for refinancing.

(iii) If we have not assigned the territory before you mail the plan of termination, give the name, address, and telephone number of the System institution specified by us and state that borrowers may contact the institution for information about loan refinancing.

(12) *Equity exchanges.* Explain the formula and procedure to exchange equity in your institution for equity in the successor institution.

§ 611.1223

(13) *Employment, retirement, and severance agreements.* Describe any employment agreement or arrangement between the successor institution and any of your senior officers or directors. Describe any severance and retirement plans that cover your employees or directors and state the costs you expect to incur under the plans in connection with the termination.

(14) *Final exit fee and its calculation.* Explain how the final exit fee will be calculated under § 611.1255 and how it will be paid.

(15) *New charter.* Describe the nature and type of financial institution the successor institution will be and any conditions of approval of the new chartering authority or regulator.

(16) *Differences in successor institution's programs and policies.* Summarize any differences between you and the successor institution on:

(i) Interest rates and fees;
(ii) Collection policies;
(iii) Services provided; and
(iv) Any other item that would affect a borrower's lending relationship with the successor institution, including whether a stockholder's ability to borrow from the institution will be restricted.

(17) *Capitalization.* Discuss expected capital requirements of the successor institution, and the amount and method of capitalization.

(18) *Sources of funding.* Explain the sources and manner of funding for the successor institution's operations.

(19) *Contingent liabilities.* Describe how the successor institution will address any contingent liability it will assume from you.

(20) *Tax status.* Summarize the differences in tax status between your institution and the successor institution, and explain how the differences may affect equity holders.

(21) *Regulatory environment.* Describe briefly how the regulatory environment for the successor institution will differ from your current regulatory environment, and any effect on the cost of doing business or the value of stockholders' equity.

(22) *Dissenters' rights.* Explain which equity holders are entitled to dissenters' rights and what those rights are. The explanation must include the estimated liquidation value of the stock, procedures for exercising dissenters' rights, and a statement of when the rights may be exercised.

(23) *Financial information.*

(i) Present the following financial data:

(A) A balance sheet and income statement for each of the 3 preceding fiscal years;

(B) A balance sheet as of a date within 90 days of the date you send the plan of termination to us, presented on a comparative basis with the corresponding period of the previous 2 fiscal years;

(C) An income statement for the interim period between the end of the last fiscal year and the date of the balance sheet required by paragraph (d)(23)(i)(B) of this section, presented on a comparative basis with the corresponding period of the previous 2 fiscal years;

(D) A pro forma balance sheet of the successor institution presented as if termination had occurred as of the date of the most recent balance sheet presented in the plan of termination; and

(E) A pro forma summary of earnings for the successor institution presented as if the termination had been effective at the beginning of the interim period between the end of the last fiscal year and the date of the balance sheet presented under paragraph (d)(23)(i)(D) of this section.

(ii) The format for the balance sheet and income statement must be the same as the format in your annual report and must contain appropriate footnote disclosures, including data on high-risk assets, other property owned, and allowance for losses.

(iii) The financial statements must include either:

(A) A statement signed by the chief executive officer and each board member that the various financial statements are unaudited but have been prepared in all material respects in conformity with GAAP (except as otherwise disclosed) and are, to the best of each signer's knowledge, a fair and accurate presentation of the financial condition of the institution; or

(B) A signed opinion by an independent certified public accountant

Farm Credit Administration § 611.1235

that the various financial statements have been examined in conformity with generally accepted auditing standards and included such tests of the accounting records and other such auditing procedures as were considered necessary in the circumstances, and, as of the date of the statements, present fairly the financial position of the institution in conformity with GAAP applied on a consistent basis, except as otherwise disclosed.

(24) *Subsequent financial events.* Describe any event after the date of the financial statements, but before the date you send the plan of termination to us, that would have a material impact on your financial condition or the condition of the successor institution.

(25) *Other subsequent events.* Describe any event after you send the plan of termination to us that could have a material impact on any information in the plan of termination.

(26) *Other material disclosures.* Describe any other material fact or circumstance that a stockholder would need to know to make an informed decision on the termination, or that is necessary to make the disclosures not misleading. We may require you to disclose any assessments, analyses, studies, or rulings we require under § 611.1211.

(27) *Ballot and proxy.* Include a ballot and proxy, with instructions on the purpose and authority for their use, and the proper method for the stockholder to sign the proxy.

(28) *Board of directors certification.* Include a certification signed by the entire board of directors as to the truth, accuracy, and completeness of the information contained in the plan of termination. If any director refuses to sign the certification, the director must inform us of the reasons for refusing.

(29) *Directors' statements.* You must include statements, if any, by directors regarding the proposed termination.

(d) *Requirement to provide updated information.* After you send us the plan of termination, you must immediately send us:

(1) Any material change to information in the plan of termination, including financial information, that occurs between the date you file the plan of termination and the termination date;

(2) Copies of any additional written information on the termination that you have given or give to current or prospective equity holders before termination; and

(3) A description of any subsequent event(s) that could have a material impact on any information in the plan of termination or on the termination.

§ 611.1230 FCA review and approval—plan of termination.

(a) *FCA review period.* No later than 60 days after we receive the plan of termination, we will review it and either approve or disapprove the plan for submission to your equity holders. If we take no action on the plan of termination within the 60 days, you may submit the plan to your equity holders. The 60-day review period under section 7.11 of the Act will begin on the date we receive a complete plan of termination. We will advise you in writing when the 60-day period begins.

(b) *FCA approval of the plan of termination.* Our approval of the plan of termination for submission to your equity holders:

(1) Is not our approval of the termination; and

(2) May be subject to any condition we impose.

§ 611.1235 Plan of termination—distribution.

(a) *Reaffirmation resolution.* Not more than 14 days before mailing the plan of termination to your equity holders, your board of directors must adopt a resolution reaffirming support of the termination. A certified copy of the resolution must be sent to us and must accompany the plan of termination when it is distributed to stockholders.

(b) *Notice of meeting and distribution of plan.* You must provide all equity holders with a notice of meeting and the plan of termination at least 45 days before the stockholder vote. You must also provide a copy of the plan to us when you provide it to your equity holders.

§ 611.1240 Voting record date and stockholder approval.

(a) *Stockholder meeting.* You must call the meeting by written notice in compliance with your bylaws. The stockholder meeting to vote on the termination must occur at least 60 days after our approval of the plan of termination (or, if we take no action, at least 60 days after the end of our approval period).

(b) *Voting record date.* The voting record date may not be more than 70 days before the stockholders' meeting.

(c) *Quorum requirement for termination vote.* At least 30 percent, unless your bylaws provide for a higher quorum, of the voting stockholders of the institution must be present at the meeting either in person or by proxy in order to hold the vote on the termination.

(d) *Approval requirement.* The affirmative vote of a majority of the voting stockholders of the institution present and voting or voting by proxy at the duly authorized meeting at which a quorum is present as prescribed in paragraph (c) of this section is required for approval of the termination.

(e) *Voting procedures.* The voting procedures must comply with § 611.340. You must have an independent third party count the ballots. If a voting stockholder notifies you of the stockholder's intent to exercise dissenters' rights, the tabulator must be able to verify to you that the stockholder voted against the termination. Otherwise, the votes of stockholders must remain confidential.

(f) *Notice to FCA and equity holders of voting results.* Within 10 days of the termination vote, you must send us a certified record of the results of the vote. You must notify all equity holders of the results within 30 days after the stockholder meeting. If the stockholders approve the termination, you must give the following information to equity holders:

(1) Stockholders who voted against termination and equity holders who were not entitled to vote have a right to dissent as provided in § 611.1280; and

(2) Voting stockholders have a right, under § 611.1245, to file a petition with the FCA for reconsideration within 35 days after the date you mail to them the notice of the results of the termination vote.

(g) *Requirement to notify new equity holders.* You must provide the information described in paragraph (f)(1) of this section to each person that becomes an equity holder after the termination vote and before termination.

[71 FR 44420, Aug. 4, 2006, as amended at 75 FR 18743, Apr. 12, 2010]

§ 611.1245 Stockholder reconsideration.

(a) *Right to reconsider termination.* Voting stockholders have the right to reconsider their approval of the termination if a petition signed by at least 15 percent of the voting stockholders is filed with us within 35 days after you mail notices to stockholders that the termination was approved. If we determine that the petition complies with the requirements of section 7.9 of the Act, you must call a special stockholders' meeting to reconsider the vote. The meeting must occur within 60 days after the date on which you mailed to stockholders the results of the termination vote.

(b) *Quorum requirement for termination reconsideration vote.* At least 30 percent, unless your bylaws provide for a higher quorum, of the voting stockholders of the institution must be present at the stockholders' meeting either in person or by proxy in order to hold the reconsideration vote. If a majority of the voting stockholders voting in person or by proxy vote against the termination, the termination may not take place.

(c) *Stockholder list and expenses.* You must, at your expense, timely give stockholders who request it a list of the names and addresses of stockholders eligible to vote in the reconsideration vote. The petitioners must pay all other expenses for the petition. You must pay expenses that you incur for the reconsideration vote.

§ 611.1246 Filing of termination application and its contents.

(a) *Filing of termination application.* Send us your termination application no later than 90 days after you send us notice of the stockholder vote approving the termination. Please send us an

Farm Credit Administration §611.1250

original and five copies of the termination application for review and approval. If you send us the termination application in electronic form, you must send us at least one hard copy with original signatures.

(b) *Contents of termination application.* The application must contain:

(1) A certified copy of the termination and reaffirmation resolutions;

(2) A certification signed by the board of directors that the board continues to support the termination, there has been no material change to any of the information contained in the plan of termination or information statement after the FCA approved the plan of termination, and there have not been any subsequent events that could have a material impact on any of the information in the plan of termination or the termination; and

(3) Any additional information that is required under this subpart, that we request or that your board of directors wishes to submit in support of the application.

§611.1247 FCA review and approval—termination.

(a) *FCA action on application.* After we receive the termination application, we will review it and either approve or disapprove the termination.

(b) *Basis for disapproval.* We will disapprove the termination if we determine that there are one or more appropriate reasons for disapproval consistent with our authorities under the Act and our regulations. We will inform you of our reason(s) for disapproval in writing.

(c) *Conditions of FCA approval.* We will approve your termination application only if:

(1) Your stockholders have voted in favor of termination in the termination vote and in any reconsideration vote;

(2) You have given us executed copies of all contracts, agreements, and other documents submitted under §§ 611.1221 and 611.1223;

(3) You have paid or made adequate provision for payment of debts, including responsibility for any contingent liabilities, and for retirement of equities;

(4) A Federal or State chartering authority has granted a new charter to the successor institution;

(5) You deposit into escrow an amount equal to 110 percent of the estimated exit fee plus 110 percent of the estimated amount you must pay to retire equities of dissenting stockholders and Farm Credit institutions, as described in § 611.1255(c); and

(6) You have fulfilled any condition of termination we impose.

(d) *Effective date of termination.* If we approve the termination, we will revoke your charter, and the termination will be effective on the date that we provide, but no earlier than the last to occur of:

(1) Fulfillment of all conditions listed in or imposed under paragraph (c) of this section;

(2) Your proposed termination date;

(3) Ninety (90) days after we receive your termination application described in § 611.1246; or

(4) Fifteen (15) days after any reconsideration vote.

§ 611.1250 Preliminary exit fee estimate.

(a) *Preliminary exit fee estimate—terminating association.* You must provide a preliminary exit fee estimate to us when you submit the plan of termination under § 611.1221. Calculate the preliminary exit fee estimate in the following order:

(1) Base your exit fee calculation on the average daily balances of assets and liabilities for the 12-month period as of the quarter end immediately before the date you send us your plan of termination.

(2) Any amounts we refer to in this section are average daily balances unless we specify that they are not. Amounts that are not average daily balances will be referred to as "dollar amount."

(3) Compute the average daily balances based on financial statements that comply with GAAP. The financial statements, as of the quarter end immediately before the date you send us your plan of termination, must be independently audited by a qualified public accountant. We may, in our discretion, waive the audit requirement if an independent audit was performed as of a

§ 611.1250

date less than 6 months before you submit the plan of termination.

(4) Make adjustments to assets as follows:

(i) Add back expenses you have incurred related to termination. Related expenses include, but are not limited to, legal services, accounting services, tax services, studies, auditing, business planning, equity holder meetings, and application fees for the termination and reorganization. Do not add back to assets expenses related to a requirement by the FCA to engage independent experts to conduct assessments, analyses, or studies, or to request rulings that solely address the impact of the termination on the System or parties other than the terminating institution and its stockholders.

(ii) Subtract the dollar amount of estimated current and deferred tax expenses, if any, due to the termination.

(iii) Add the dollar amount of estimated current and deferred tax benefits, if any, due to the termination.

(iv) Adjust for the dollar amount of significant transactions you reasonably expect to occur between the quarter end before you file your plan of termination and date of termination. Examples of these transactions include, but are not limited to, gains or losses on the sale of assets, retirements of equity, loan repayments, and patronage distributions. Do not make adjustments for future expenses related to termination, such as severance or special retirement payments, or stock retirements to dissenting stockholders and Farm Credit institutions.

(5) Subtract from liabilities any liability that we treat as regulatory capital under the capital or collateral requirements in subparts H and K of part 615 of this chapter.

(6) Make any adjustments we require under paragraph (c) of this section.

(7) After making these adjustments to assets and liabilities, subtract liabilities from assets. This is your preliminary total capital for purposes of termination.

(8) Multiply assets as adjusted above by 6 percent, and subtract this amount from preliminary total capital. This is your preliminary exit fee estimate.

(b) *Preliminary exit fee estimate—terminating bank.*

(1) Affiliated associations that are terminating with you must calculate their individual preliminary exit fee estimates as described in paragraph (a) of this section.

(2) Base your exit fee calculation on the average daily balances of assets and liabilities for the 12-month period as of the quarter end immediately before the date you send us your plan of termination.

(3) Any amounts we refer to in this section are average daily balances unless we specify that they are not. Amounts that are not average daily balances will be referred to as "dollar amount."

(4) Compute the average daily balances based on bank-only financial statements that comply with GAAP. The financial statements, as of the quarter end immediately before the date you send us your plan of termination, must be independently audited by a qualified public accountant. We may, in our discretion, waive this requirement if an independent audit was performed as of a date less than 6 months before you submit the plan of termination.

(5) Make adjustments to assets and liabilities as follows:

(i) Add back to assets the following:

(A) Expenses you have incurred related to termination. Related expenses include, but are not limited to, legal services, accounting services, tax services, studies, auditing, business planning, equity holder meetings, and application fees for the termination and reorganization. Do not add back to assets expenses related to a requirement by the FCA to engage independent experts to conduct assessments, analyses, or studies, or to request rulings that solely address the impact of the termination on the System or parties other than the terminating institution and its stockholders.

(B) Any specific allowance for losses, and a pro rata portion of any general allowance for loan losses, on direct loans to associations that you do not expect to incur before or at termination.

(ii) Subtract from your assets and liabilities an amount equal to your direct loans to your affiliated associations that are not terminating.

Farm Credit Administration §611.1250

(iii) Subtract the following from assets:

(A) Equity investments in your institution that are held by nonterminating associations and that you expect to transfer to another System bank before or at termination. A nonterminating association's investment consists of purchased equities, allocated equities, and a share of the bank's unallocated surplus calculated in accordance with the bank's bylaw provisions on liquidation. We may require a different calculation method for the unallocated surplus if we determine that using the liquidation provision would be inequitable to stockholders; and

(B) The dollar amount of estimated current and deferred tax expenses, if any, due to the termination.

(iv) Add the dollar amount of current and deferred estimated tax benefits, if any, due to the termination.

(v) Subtract from liabilities any liability that we treat as regulatory capital under the capital or collateral requirements in subparts H and K of part 615 of this chapter.

(vi) Adjust for the dollar amount of significant transactions you reasonably expect to occur between the quarter end before you file your plan of termination and date of termination. Examples of these transactions include, but are not limited to, retirements of equity, loan repayments, and patronage distributions. Do not make adjustments for future expenses related to termination, such as severance or special retirement payments, or stock retirements to dissenting stockholders and Farm Credit institutions.

(6) Make any adjustments we require under paragraph (c) of this section.

(7) After the above adjustments, combine your balance sheet with the balance sheets of your terminating associations after they have made the adjustments required in paragraph (a) of this section. Subtract liabilities from assets. This is your preliminary total capital estimate for purposes of termination.

(8) Multiply the assets of the combined balance sheet after the above adjustments by 6 percent. Subtract this amount from the preliminary total capital estimate of the combined balance sheet. The remainder is the preliminary exit fee estimate of the bank and terminating affiliated associations.

(9) Your preliminary exit fee estimate is the amount by which the preliminary exit fee estimate for the combined entity exceeds the total of the individual preliminary exit fee estimates of your affiliated terminating associations.

(c) *Adjustments.* (1) We will review your account balances, transactions over the 3 years before the date of the termination resolution under §611.1220, and any subsequent transactions. Our review will include, but not be limited to, the following:

(i) Additions to or subtractions from any allowance for losses;

(ii) Additions to assets or liabilities, or subtractions from assets or liabilities, due to transactions that are outside your ordinary course of business;

(iii) Dividends or patronage refunds exceeding your usual practices;

(iv) Changes in the institution's capital plan, or in implementing the plan, that increased or decreased the level of borrower investment;

(v) Contingent liabilities, such as loss-sharing obligations, that can be reasonably quantified; and

(vi) Assets, including real property and servicing rights, that may be overvalued, undervalued, or not recorded on your books.

(2) If we determine the account balances do not accurately show the value of your assets and liabilities (whether the assets and liabilities were booked before or during the 3-year look-back adjustment period), we will make any adjustments we deem necessary.

(3) We may require you to reverse the effect of a transaction if we determine that:

(i) You have retired capital outside the ordinary course of business;

(ii) You have taken any other actions unrelated to your core business that have the effect of changing the exit fee; or

(iii) You incurred expenses related to termination prior to the 12-month average daily balance period on which the exit fee calculation is based.

(4) We may require you to make these adjustments to the preliminary exit fee estimate that is disclosed in

§ 611.1255

the information statement, the final exit fee calculation, and the calculations of the value of equities held by dissenting stockholders, Farm Credit institutions that choose to have their equities retired at termination, and reaffiliating associations.

[67 FR 17909, Apr. 12, 2002, as amended at 71 FR 76118, Dec. 20, 2006]

§ 611.1255 Exit fee calculation.

(a) *Final exit fee calculation—terminating association.* Calculate the final exit fee in the following order:

(1) Base your exit fee calculation on the average daily balances of assets and liabilities for the 12-month period preceding the termination date. Assume for this calculation that you have not paid or accrued the items described in paragraph (a)(4)(ii) and (iii) of this section.

(2) Any amounts we refer to in this section are average daily balances unless we specify that they are not. Amounts that are not average daily balances will be referred to as "dollar amount."

(3) Compute the average daily balances based on financial statements that comply with GAAP. The financial statements, as of the termination date, must be independently audited by a qualified public accountant.

(4) Make adjustments to assets and liabilities as follows:

(i) Add back expenses related to the termination. Related expenses include, but are not limited to, legal services, accounting services, tax services, studies, auditing, business planning, payments of severance and special retirements, equity holder meetings, and application fees for the termination and reorganization. Do not add back to assets expenses related to a requirement by the FCA to engage independent experts to conduct assessments, analyses, or studies, or to request rulings that solely address the impact of the termination on the System or parties other than the terminating institution and its stockholders.

(ii) Subtract from assets the dollar amount of current and deferred tax expenses, if any, due to the termination.

(iii) Add to assets the dollar amount of current and deferred tax benefits, if any, due to the termination.

(iv) Subtract from liabilities any liability that we treat as regulatory capital under the capital or collateral requirements in subparts H and K of part 615 of this chapter.

(v) Make the adjustments that we require under § 611.1250(c). For the final exit fee, we will review and may require additional adjustments for transactions between the date you adopted the termination resolution and the termination date.

(5) After making these adjustments to assets and liabilities, subtract liabilities from assets. This is your total capital for purposes of termination.

(6) Multiply assets by 6 percent, and subtract this amount from total capital. This is your final exit fee.

(b) *Final exit fee calculation—terminating bank.*

(1) The individual exit fees of affiliated associations that are terminating with you must be calculated as described in paragraph (a) of this section.

(2) Base your exit fee calculation on the average daily balances of assets and liabilities for the 12-month period preceding the termination date. Assume for this calculation that you have not paid or accrued the items described in paragraph (b)(5)(iii)(B) and (b)(5)(iv) of this section.

(3) Any amounts we refer to in this section are average daily balances unless we specify that they are not. Amounts that are not average daily balances will be referred to as "dollar amount."

(4) Compute the average daily balances based on bank-only financial statements that comply with GAAP. The financial statements, as of the termination date, must be independently audited by a qualified public accountant.

(5) Make adjustments to assets and liabilities as follows:

(i) Add back the following to your assets:

(A) Expenses you have incurred related to termination. Related expenses include, but are not limited to, legal services, accounting services, tax services, studies, auditing, business planning, payments of severance and special retirements, equity holder meetings, and application fees for the termination and reorganization. Do not add

Farm Credit Administration §611.1260

back to assets expenses related to a requirement by the FCA to engage independent experts to conduct assessments, analyses, or studies, or to request rulings that solely address the impact of the termination on the System or parties other than the terminating institution and its stockholders.

(B) Any specific allowance for losses, and a pro rata share of any general allowance for losses, on direct loans to associations that are paid off or transferred before or at termination.

(ii) Subtract from your assets and liabilities your direct loans to affiliated associations that were paid off or transferred in the 12-month period before termination or at termination.

(iii) Subtract from your assets the following:

(A) Equity investments held in your institution by affiliated associations that you transferred at termination or during the 12 months before termination; and

(B) The dollar amount of current and deferred tax expenses, if any, due to the termination;

(iv) Add to assets, the dollar amount of estimated current and deferred tax benefits, if any, due to the termination.

(v) Subtract from liabilities any liability that we treat as regulatory capital (or that we do not treat as a liability) under the capital or collateral requirements in subparts H and K of part 615 of this chapter.

(vi) Make the adjustments that we require under §611.1250(c). For the final exit fee, we will review and may require additional adjustments for transactions between the date you adopted the termination resolution and the termination date.

(6) After the above adjustments, combine your balance sheet with the balance sheets of terminating associations after making the adjustments required in paragraph (a) of this section.

(7) Subtract combined liabilities from combined assets. This is the total capital of the combined balance sheet.

(8) Multiply the assets of the combined balance sheet after the above adjustments by 6 percent. Subtract this amount from the total capital of the combined balance sheet. This amount is the combined final exit fee for your institution and the terminating affiliated associations.

(9) Your final exit fee is the amount by which the combined final exit fee exceeds the total of the individual final exit fees of your affiliated terminating associations.

(c) *Payment of exit fee.* On the termination date, you must:

(1) Deposit into an escrow account acceptable to us and the FCSIC an amount equal to 110 percent of the preliminary exit fee estimate, adjusted to account for stock retirements to dissenting stockholders and Farm Credit institutions, and any other adjustments we require.

(2) Deposit into an escrow account acceptable to us an amount equal to 110 percent of the equity you must retire for dissenting stockholders and System institutions holding stock that would be entitled to a share of the remaining assets in a liquidation.

(d) *Pay-out of escrow.* Following the independent audit of the institution's account balances as of the termination date, we will determine the amount of the final exit fee and the amounts owed to stockholders to retire their equities. We will then direct the escrow agent to:

(1) Pay the exit fee to the Farm Credit Insurance Fund;

(2) Pay the amounts owed to dissenting stockholders and Farm Credit institutions; and

(3) Return any remaining amounts to the successor institution.

(e) *Additional payment.* If the amount held in escrow is not enough to pay the amounts under paragraph (d)(1) and (d)(2) of this section, the successor institution must pay any remaining liability to the escrow agent for distribution to the appropriate parties. The termination application must include evidence that, after termination, the successor institution will pay any remaining amounts owed.

[67 FR 17909, Apr. 12, 2002, as amended at 71 FR 76118, Dec. 20, 2006]

§611.1260 Payment of debts and assessments—terminating association.

(a) *General rule.* If your institution is a terminating association, you must pay or make adequate provision for the

§ 611.1265

payment of all outstanding debt obligations and assessments.

(b) *No OFI relationship.* If the successor institution will not become an OFI, you must either:

(1) Pay debts and assessments owed to your affiliated Farm Credit bank at termination; or

(2) With your affiliated Farm Credit bank's concurrence, arrange to pay any obligations or assessments to the bank after termination.

(c) *Obligations to other Farm Credit institutions.* You must pay or make adequate provision for payment of obligations to any Farm Credit institution (other than your affiliated bank) under any loss-sharing or other agreement.

§ 611.1265 Retirement of a terminating association's investment in its affiliated bank.

(a) *Safety and soundness restrictions.* Notwithstanding anything in this subpart to the contrary, we may prohibit a bank from retiring the equities you hold in the bank if the retirement would cause the bank to fall below its regulatory capital requirements after retirement, or if we determine that the bank would be in an unsafe or unsound condition after retirement.

(b) *Retirement agreement.* Your affiliated bank may retire the purchased and allocated equities held by your institution in the bank according to the terms of the bank's capital revolvement plan or an agreement between you and the bank.

(c) *Retirement in absence of agreement.* Your affiliated bank must retire any equities not subject to an agreement or revolvement plan no later than when you or the successor institution pays off your loan from the bank.

(d) *No retirement of unallocated surplus.* When your bank retires equities you own in the bank, the bank must pay par or face value for purchased and allocated equities, less any impairment. The bank may not pay you any portion of its unallocated surplus.

(e) *Exclusion of equities from capital ratios.* If another Farm Credit institution makes an agreement to retire equities you hold in that institution after termination, we may require that institution to exclude part or all of those equities from assets and capital when the institution calculates its capital and net collateral ratios under subparts H and K of part 615 of this chapter.

§ 611.1270 Repayment of obligations—terminating bank.

(a) *General rule.* If your institution is a terminating bank, you must pay or make adequate provision for the payment of all outstanding debt obligations, and provide for your responsibility for any probable contingent liabilities identified.

(b) *Satisfaction of primary liability on consolidated or System-wide obligations.* After consulting with the other Farm Credit banks, the Funding Corporation, and the FCSIC, you must pay or make adequate provision for payment of your primary liability on consolidated or System-wide obligations in a method that we deem acceptable. Before we make a final decision on your proposal and as we deem necessary, we may consult with the other Farm Credit banks, the Funding Corporation, and the FCSIC.

(c) *Satisfaction of joint and several liability and liability for interest on individual obligations.* (1) You and the other Farm Credit banks must enter into an agreement, which is subject to our approval, covering obligations issued under section 4.2 of the Act and outstanding on the termination date. The agreement must specify how you and your successor institution will make adequate provision for the payment of your joint and several liability to holders of obligations other than those obligations on which you are primarily liable, in the event we make calls for payment under section 4.4 of the Act. You and your successor institution must also provide for your liability under section 4.4(a)(1) of the Act to pay interest on the individual obligations issued by other System banks. As a part of the agreement, you must also agree that your successor institution will provide ongoing information to the Funding Corporation to enable it to fulfill its funding and disclosure duties. The Funding Corporation may, at its option, be a party to the agreement to the extent necessary to fulfill its duties with respect to financing and disclosure.

Farm Credit Administration

§ 611.1280

(2) If you and the other Farm Credit banks are unable to reach agreement within 90 days before the proposed termination date, we will specify the manner in which you will make adequate provision for the payment of the liabilities in question and how we will make joint and several calls for those obligations outstanding on the termination date.

(3) Notwithstanding any other provision in these regulations, the successor institution will be jointly and severally liable for consolidated and System-wide debt outstanding on the termination date (other than the obligations on which you are primarily liable). The successor institution will also be liable for interest on other banks' individual obligations as described in section 4.4(a)(1) of the Act and outstanding on the termination date. The termination application must include evidence that the successor institution will continue to be liable for consolidated and System-wide debt and for interest on other banks' individual obligations.

§ 611.1275 Retirement of equities held by other System institutions.

(a) *Retirement at option of equity holder.* If your institution is a terminating institution, System institutions that own your equities have the right to require you to retire the equities on the termination date.

(b) *Value of equity holders' interests.* You must retire the equities in accordance with the liquidation provisions in your bylaws unless we determine that the liquidation provisions would result in an inequitable distribution to stockholders. If we make such a determination, we will require you to distribute the equity in accordance with another method that we deem equitable to stockholders. Before you retire any equity, you must make the following adjustments to the amount of stockholder equity as stated in the financial statements on the termination date:

(1) Make deductions for any taxes due to the termination that have not yet been recorded;

(2) Deduct the amount of the exit fee; and

(3) Make any adjustments described under § 611.1250(c) that we may require as we deem appropriate.

(c) *Transfer of affiliated association's investment.* As an alternative to equity retirement, an affiliated association that reaffiliates with another Farm Credit bank instead of terminating with its bank has the right to require the terminating bank to transfer its investment to its new affiliated bank when it reaffiliates. If your institution is a terminating bank, at the time of reaffiliation you must transfer the purchased and allocated equities held by the association, as well as its share of unallocated surplus, to the new affiliated bank. Calculate the association's share before deduction of the exit fee as of the month end preceding the reaffiliation date (or the termination date if it is the same as the reaffiliation date) in accordance with the liquidation provisions of your bylaws, unless we determine that the liquidation provisions would result in an inequitable distribution. If we make such a determination, we will require you to distribute the association's share of your unallocated surplus in accordance with another method that we deem equitable to stockholders. Before you distribute any unallocated surplus, you must make the following adjustments to stockholder equity as stated in the financial statements as of the month end preceding the reaffiliation date (or the termination date if it is the same as the reaffiliation date):

(1) Add back any taxes due to the termination, and the exit fee; and

(2) Make any adjustments described under § 611.1250(c) that we may require as we deem appropriate.

(d) *Prohibition on certain affiliations.* No Farm Credit institution may retain an equity interest otherwise prohibited by law in a successor institution

§ 611.1280 Dissenting stockholders' rights.

(a) *Definition.* A dissenting stockholder is an equity holder (other than a System institution) in a terminating institution on the termination date who either:

(1) Was eligible to vote on the termination resolution and voted against termination;

(2) Was an equity holder on the voting record date but was not eligible to vote; or

§ 611.1285

(3) Became an equity holder after the voting record date.

(b) *Retirement at option of a dissenting stockholder.* A dissenting stockholder may require a terminating institution to retire the stockholder's equity interest in the terminating institution.

(c) *Value of a dissenting stockholder's interest.* You must pay a dissenting stockholder according to the liquidation provision in your bylaws, except that you must pay at least par or face value for eligible borrower stock (as defined in section 4.9A(d)(2) of the Act). If we determine that the liquidation provision is inequitable to stockholders, we will require you to calculate their share in accordance with another formula that we deem equitable.

(d) *Calculation of interest of a dissenting stockholder.* Before you retire any equity, you must make the following adjustments to the amount of stockholder equity as stated in the financial statements on the termination date:

(1) Deduct any taxes due to the termination that you have not yet recorded;

(2) Deduct the amount of the exit fee; and

(3) Make any adjustments described under § 611.1250(c) that we may require as we deem appropriate.

(e) *Form of payment to a dissenting stockholder.* You must pay dissenting stockholders for their equities as follows:

(1) Pay cash for the par or face value of purchased stock, less any impairment;

(2) For equities other than purchased equities, you may:

(i) Pay cash;

(ii) Cause or otherwise provide for the successor institution to issue, on the date of termination, subordinated debt to the stockholder with a face value equal to the value of the remaining equities. This subordinated debt must have a maturity date of 7 years or less, must have priority in liquidation ahead of all equity, and must carry a rate of interest not less than the rate (at the time of termination) for debt of comparable maturity issued by the U.S. Treasury plus 1 percent; or

(iii) Provide for a combination of cash and subordinated debt as described above.

(f) *Payment to holders of special class of stock.* If you have adopted bylaws under § 611.1210(f), you must pay a dissenting stockholder who owns shares of the special class of stock an amount equal to the lower of the par (or face) value or the value of such stock as determined under § 611.1280(c) and (d).

(g) *Notice to equity holders.* The notice to equity holders required in § 611.1240(f) must include a form for stockholders to send back to you, stating their intention to exercise dissenters' rights. The notice must contain the following information:

(1) A description of the rights of dissenting stockholders set forth in this section and the approximate value per share that a dissenting stockholder can expect to receive. State whether the successor institution will require borrowers to be stockholders or whether it will require stockholders to be borrowers.

(2) A description of the current book and par value per share of each class of equities, and the expected book and market value of the stockholder's interest in the successor institution.

(3) A statement that a stockholder must return the enclosed form to you within 30 days if the stockholder chooses to exercise dissenters' rights.

(h) *Notice to subsequent equity holders.* Equity holders that acquire their equities after the termination vote must also receive the notice described in paragraph (g) of this section. You must give them at least 5 business days to decide whether to request retirement of their stock.

(i) *Reconsideration.* If a reconsideration vote is held and the termination is disapproved, the right of stockholders to exercise dissenters' rights is rescinded. If a reconsideration vote is held and the termination is approved, you must retire the equities of dissenting stockholders as if there had been no reconsideration vote.

§ 611.1285 Loan refinancing by borrowers.

(a) *Disclosure of credit and loan information.* At the request of a borrower

Farm Credit Administration

§ 612.2130

seeking refinancing with another System institution before you terminate, you must give credit and loan information about the borrower to such institution.

(b) *No reassignment of territory.* If, at the termination date, we have not assigned your territory to another System institution, any System institution may lend in your territory, to the extent otherwise permitted by the Act and the regulations in this chapter.

§ 611.1290 Continuation of borrower rights.

You may not require a waiver of contractual borrower rights provisions as a condition of borrowing from and owning equity in the successor institution. Institutions that become other financing institutions on termination must comply with the applicable borrower rights provisions in the Act and part 617 of this chapter.

PART 612—STANDARDS OF CONDUCT AND REFERRAL OF KNOWN OR SUSPECTED CRIMINAL VIOLATIONS

Subpart A—Standards of Conduct

Sec.
612.2130 Definitions.
612.2135 Director and employee responsibilities and conduct—generally.
612.2140 Directors—prohibited conduct.
612.2145 Director reporting.
612.2150 Employees—prohibited conduct.
612.2155 Employee reporting.
612.2157 Joint employees.
612.2160 Institution responsibilities.
612.2165 Policies and procedures.
612.2170 Standards of Conduct Official.
612.2260 Standards of conduct for agents.
612.2270 Purchase of System obligations.

Subpart B—Referral of Known or Suspected Criminal Violations

612.2300 Purpose and scope.
612.2301 Referrals.
612.2302 Notification of board of directors and bonding company.
612.2303 Institution responsibilities.

AUTHORITY: Secs. 5.9, 5.17, 5.19 of the Farm Credit Act (12 U.S.C. 2243, 2252, 2254).

SOURCE: 59 FR 24894, May 13, 1994, unless otherwise noted.

Subpart A—Standards of Conduct

§ 612.2130 Definitions.

For purposes of this part, the following terms are defined:

(a) *Agent* means any person, other than a director or employee, who currently represents a System institution in contacts with third parties or who currently provides professional services to a System institution, such as legal, accounting, appraisal, and other similar services.

(b) A *conflict of interest* or the appearance thereof exists when a person has a financial interest in a transaction, relationship, or activity that actually affects or has the appearance of affecting the person's ability to perform official duties and responsibilities in a totally impartial manner and in the best interest of the employing institution when viewed from the perspective of a reasonable person with knowledge of the relevant facts.

(c) *Controlled entity* and *entity controlled by* mean an entity in which the individual, directly or indirectly, or acting through or in concert with one or more persons:

(1) Owns 5 percent or more of the equity;

(2) Owns, controls, or has the power to vote 5 percent or more of any class of voting securities; or

(3) Has the power to exercise a controlling influence over the management of policies of such entity.

(d) *Employee* means any salaried officer or part-time, full-time, or temporary salaried employee.

(e) *Entity* means a corporation, company, association, firm, joint venture, partnership (general or limited), society, joint stock company, trust (business or otherwise), fund, or other organization or institution.

(f) *Family* means an individual and spouse and anyone having the following relationship to either: parents, spouse, son, daughter, sibling, stepparent, stepson, stepdaughter, stepbrother, stepsister, half brother, half sister, uncle, aunt, nephew, niece, grandparent, grandson, granddaughter, and the spouses of the foregoing.

(g) *Financial interest* means an interest in an activity, transaction, property, or relationship with a person or

§ 612.2135

an entity that involves receiving or providing something of monetary value or other present or deferred compensation.

(h) *Financially obligated with* means having a joint legally enforceable obligation with, being financially obligated on behalf of (contingently or otherwise), having an enforceable legal obligation secured by property owned by another, or owning property that secures an enforceable legal obligation of another.

(i) *Material,* when applied to a financial interest or transaction or series of transactions, means that the interest or transaction or series of transactions is of such magnitude that a reasonable person with knowledge of the relevant facts would question the ability of the person who has the interest or is party to such transaction(s) to perform his or her official duties objectively and impartially and in the best interest of the institution and its statutory purpose.

(j) *Mineral interest* means any interest in minerals, oil, or gas, including, but not limited to, any right derived directly or indirectly from a mineral, oil, or gas lease, deed, or royalty conveyance.

(k) *OFI* means other financing institutions that have established an access relationship with a Farm Credit Bank or an agricultural credit bank under section 1.7(b)(1)(B) of the Act.

(l) *Officer* means the chief executive officer, president, chief operating officer, vice president, secretary, treasurer, general counsel, chief financial officer, and chief credit officer of each System institution, and any person not so designated who holds a similar position of authority.

(m) *Ordinary course of business,* when applied to a transaction, means: (1) A transaction that is usual and customary between two persons who are in business together; or

(2) A transaction with a person who is in the business of offering the goods or services that are the subject of the transaction on terms that are not preferential. Preferential means that the transaction is not on the same terms as those prevailing at the same time for comparable transactions for other persons who are not directors or employees of a System institution.

(n) *Person* means individual or entity.

(o) *Relative* means any member of the family as defined in paragraph (g) of this section.

(p) *Service organization* means each service organization authorized by section 4.25 of the Act, and each unincorporated service organization formed by one or more System institutions.

(q) *Standards of Conduct Official* means the official designated under § 612.2170 of these regulations.

(r) *Supervised institution* is a term which only applies within the context of a System bank or an employee of a System bank and refers to each association supervised by that bank.

(s) *Supervising institution* is a term that only applies within the context of an association or an employee of an association and refers to the bank that supervises that association.

(t) *System institution* and *institution* mean any bank, association, or service organization in the Farm Credit System, including the Farm Credit Banks, banks for cooperatives, agricultural credit banks, Federal land bank associations, agricultural credit associations, Federal land credit associations, production credit associations, the Federal Farm Credit Banks Funding Corporation, and service organizations.

[59 FR 24894, May 13, 1994, as amended at 71 FR 5762, Feb. 2, 2006]

§ 612.2135 Director and employee responsibilities and conduct—generally.

(a) Directors and employees of all System institutions shall maintain high standards of industry, honesty, integrity, impartiality, and conduct in order to ensure the proper performance of System business and continued public confidence in the System and each of its institutions. The avoidance of misconduct and conflicts of interest is indispensable to the maintenance of these standards.

(b) To achieve these high standards of conduct, directors and employees shall observe, to the best of their abilities, the letter and intent of all applicable local, state, and Federal laws and regulations and policy statements, instructions, and procedures of the Farm Credit Administration and System institutions and shall exercise diligence

Farm Credit Administration §612.2145

and good judgment in carrying out their duties, obligations, and responsibilities.

§612.2140 Directors—prohibited conduct.

A director of a System institution shall not:

(a) Participate, directly or indirectly, in deliberations on, or the determination of, any matter affecting, directly or indirectly, the financial interest of the director, any relative of the director, any person residing in the director's household, any business partner of the director, or any entity controlled by the director or such persons (alone or in concert), except those matters of general applicability that affect all shareholders/borrowers in a nondiscriminatory way, e.g., a determination of interest rates.

(b) Divulge or make use of, except in the performance of official duties, any fact, information, or document not generally available to the public that is acquired by virtue of serving on the board of a System institution.

(c) Use the director's position to obtain or attempt to obtain special advantage or favoritism for the director, any relative of the director, any person residing in the director's household, any business partner of the director, any entity controlled by the director or such persons (alone or in concert), any other System institution, or any person transacting business with the institution, including borrowers and loan applicants.

(d) Use the director's position or information acquired in connection with the director's position to solicit or obtain, directly or indirectly, any gift, fee, or other present or deferred compensation or for any other personal benefit on behalf of the director, any relative of the director, any person residing in the director's household, any business partner of the director, any entity controlled by the director or such persons (alone or in concert), any other System institution, or any person transacting business with the institution, including borrowers and loan applicants.

(e) Accept, directly or indirectly, any gift, fee, or other present or deferred compensation that is offered or could reasonably be viewed as being offered to influence official action or to obtain information that the director has access to by reason of serving on the board of a System institution.

(f) Knowingly acquire, directly or indirectly, except by inheritance or through public auction or open competitive bidding available to the general public, any interest in any real or personal property, including mineral interests, that was owned by the employing, supervising, or any supervised institution within the preceding 12 months and that had been acquired by any such institution as a result of foreclosure or similar action; provided, however, a director shall not acquire any such interest in real or personal property if he or she participated in the deliberations or decision to foreclose or to dispose of the property or in establishing the terms of the sale.

(g) Directly or indirectly borrow from, lend to, or become financially obligated with or on behalf of a director, employee, or agent of the employing, supervising, or a supervised institution or a borrower or loan applicant of the employing institution, unless:

(1) The transaction is with a relative or any person residing in the director's household;

(2) The transaction is undertaken in an official capacity in connection with the institution's discounting, lending, or participation relationships with OFIs and other lenders; or

(3) The Standards of Conduct Official determines, pursuant to policies and procedures adopted by the board, that the potential for conflict is insignificant because the transaction is in the ordinary course of business or is not material in amount and the director does not participate in the determination of any matter affecting the financial interests of the other party to the transaction except those matters affecting all shareholders/borrowers in a nondiscriminatory way.

(h) Violate an institution's policies and procedures governing standards of conduct.

§612.2145 Director reporting.

(a) Annually, as of the institution's fiscal year end, and at such other times as may be required to comply with

§ 612.2150

paragraph (c) of this section, each director shall file a written and signed statement with the Standards of Conduct Official that fully discloses:

(1) The names of any immediate family members as defined in § 620.1(e) of this chapter, or affiliated organizations, as defined in § 620.1(a) of this chapter, who had transactions with the institution at any time during the year;

(2) Any matter required to be disclosed by § 620.5(k) of this chapter; and

(3) Any additional information the institution may require to make the disclosures required by part 620 of this chapter.

(b) Each director shall, at such intervals as the institution's board shall determine is necessary to effectively enforce this regulation and the institution's standards-of-conduct policy adopted pursuant to § 612.2165, file a written and signed statement with the Standards of Conduct Official that contains those disclosures required by the regulations and such policy. At a minimum, these requirements shall include:

(1) The name of any relative or any person residing in the director's household, business partner, or any entity controlled by the director or such persons (alone or in concert) if the director knows or has reason to know that such individual or entity transacts business with the institution or any institution supervised by the director's institution; and

(2) The name and the nature of the business of any entity in which the director has a material financial interest or on whose board the director sits if the director knows or has reason to know that such entity transacts business with:

(i) The director's institution or any institution supervised by the director's institution; or

(ii) A borrower of the director's institution or any institution supervised by the director's institution.

(c) Any director who becomes or plans to become involved in any relationship, transaction, or activity that is required to be reported under this section or could constitute a conflict of interest shall promptly report such involvement in writing to the Standards of Conduct Official for a determination of whether the relationship, transaction, or activity is, in fact, a conflict of interest.

(d) Unless a disclosure as a director candidate under part 620 of this chapter has been made within the preceding 180 days, a newly elected or appointed director shall report matters required to be reported in paragraphs (a), (b), and (c) of this section to the Standards of Conduct Official within 30 days after the election or appointment and thereafter shall comply with the requirements of this section.

§ 612.2150 Employees—prohibited conduct.

An employee of a System institution shall not:

(a) Participate, directly or indirectly, in deliberations on, or the determination of, any matter affecting, directly or indirectly, the financial interest of the employee, any relative of the employee, any person residing in the employee's household, any business partner of the employee, or any entity controlled by the employee or such persons (alone or in concert), except those matters of general applicability that affect all shareholders/borrowers in a nondiscriminating way, e.g. a determination of interest rates.

(b) Divulge or make use of, except in the performance of official duties, any fact, information, or document not generally available to the public that is acquired by virtue of employment with a System institution.

(c) Use the employee's position to obtain or attempt to obtain special advantage or favoritism for the employee, any relative of the employee, any person residing in the employee's household, any business partner of the employee, any entity controlled by the employee or such persons (alone or in concert), any other System institution, or any person transacting business with the institution, including borrowers and loan applicants.

(d) Serve as an officer or director of an entity other than a System institution that transacts business with a System institution in the district or of any commercial bank, savings and loan, or other non-System financial institution, except employee credit unions. For the purposes of this paragraph, "transacts business" does not include loans by a System institution to a family-owned entity, service on the board of directors of the Federal Agricultural Mortgage Corporation, or transactions with nonprofit entities or entities in which the System institution has an ownership interest. With the prior approval of the board of the employing institution, an employee of a Farm Credit Bank or association may serve as a director of a cooperative that borrows from a bank for cooperatives. Prior to approving an employee request, the board shall determine whether the employee's proposed service as a director is likely to cause the employee to violate any regulations in this part or the institution's policies, e.g., the requirements relating to devotion of time to official duties.

(e) Use the employee's position or information acquired in connection with the employee's position to solicit or obtain any gift, fee, or other present or deferred compensation or for any other personal benefit for the employee, any relative of the employee, any person residing in the employee's household, any business partner of the employee, any entity controlled by the employee or such persons (alone or in concert), any other System institution, or any person transacting business with the institution, including borrowers and loan applicants.

(f) Accept, directly or indirectly, any gift, fee, or other present or deferred compensation that is offered or could reasonably be viewed as being offered to influence official action or to obtain information the employee has access to by reason of employment with a System institution.

(g) Knowingly acquire, directly or indirectly, except by inheritance, any interest in any real or personal property, including mineral interests, that was owned by the employing, supervising, or any supervised institution within the preceding 12 months and that had been acquired by any such institution as a result of foreclosure or similar action.

(h) Directly or indirectly borrow from, lend to, or become financially obligated with or on behalf of a director, employee, or agent of the employing, supervising, or a supervised institution or a borrower or loan applicant of the employing institution, unless:

(1) The transaction is with a relative or any person residing in the employee's household;

(2) The transaction is undertaken in an official capacity in connection with the institution's discounting, lending, or participation relationships with OFIs and other lenders; or

(3) The Standards of Conduct Official determines, pursuant to policies and procedures adopted by the board, that the potential for conflict is insignificant because the transaction is in the ordinary course of business or is not material in amount and the employee does not participate in the determination of any matter affecting the financial interests of the other party to the transaction except those matters affecting all shareholders/borrowers in a nondiscriminatory way.

(i) Violate an institution's policies and procedures governing standards of conduct.

(j) Act as a real estate agent or broker; provided that this paragraph shall not apply to transactions involving the purchase or sale of real estate intended for the use of the employee, a member of the employee's family, or a person residing in the employee's household.

(k) Act as an agent or broker in connection with the sale and placement of insurance; provided that this paragraph shall not apply to the sale or placement of insurance authorized by section 4.29 of the Act.

[59 FR 24894, May 13, 1994, as amended at 71 FR 5762, Feb. 2, 2006]

§ 612.2155 Employee reporting.

(a) Annually, as of the institution's fiscal yearend, and at such other times as may be required to comply with paragraph (c) of this section, each senior officer must file a written and signed statement with the Standards of Conduct Official that fully discloses:

(1) The names of any immediate family members, as defined in § 620.1(e) of this chapter, or affiliated organizations, as defined in § 620.1(a) of this chapter, who had transactions with the institution at any time during the year;

§ 612.2157

(2) Any matter required to be disclosed by § 620.5(k) of this chapter; and

(3) Any additional information the institution may require to make the disclosures required by part 620 of this chapter.

(b) Each employee shall, at such intervals as the Board shall determine necessary to effectively enforce this regulation and the institution's standards-of-conduct policy adopted pursuant to § 612.2165, file a written and signed statement with the Standards of Conduct Official that contains those disclosures required by the regulation and such policy. At a minimum, these requirements shall include:

(1) The name of any relative or any person residing in the employee's household, any business partner, or any entity controlled by the employee or such persons (alone or in concert) if the employee knows or has reason to know that such individual or entity transacts business with the employing institution or any institution supervised by the employing institution; and

(2) The name and the nature of the business of any entity in which the employee has a material financial interest or on whose board the employee sits if the employee knows or has reason to know that such entity transacts business with:

(i) The employing institution or any institution supervised by the employing institution; or

(ii) A borrower of the employing institution or any institution supervised by the employing institution.

(c) Any employee who becomes or plans to become involved in any relationship, transaction, or activity that is required to be reported under this section or could constitute a conflict of interest shall promptly report such involvement in writing to the Standards of Conduct Official for a determination of whether the relationship, transaction, or activity is, in fact, a conflict of interest.

(d) A newly hired employee shall report matters required to be reported in paragraphs (a), (b), and (c) of this section to the Standards of Conduct Official 5 business days after starting employment and thereafter shall comply with the requirements of this section.

[59 FR 24894, May 13, 1994, as amended at 71 FR 5763, Feb. 2, 2006; 71 FR 65386, Nov. 8, 2006]

§ 612.2157 Joint employees.

No officer of a Farm Credit Bank or an agricultural credit bank may serve as an employee of an association in its district and no employee of a Farm Credit Bank or an agricultural credit bank may serve as an officer of an association in its district. Farm Credit Bank or agricultural credit bank employees other than officers may serve as employees other than officers of an association in its district provided each institution appropriately reflects the expense of such employees in its financial statements.

§ 612.2160 Institution responsibilities.

Each institution shall: (a) Ensure compliance with this part by its directors and employees and act promptly to preserve the integrity of and public confidence in the institution in any matter involving a conflict of interest, whether or not specifically addressed by this part or the policies and procedures adopted pursuant to § 612.2165;

(b) Take appropriate measures to ensure that all directors and employees are informed of the requirements of this regulation and policies and procedures adopted pursuant to § 612.2165;

(c) Adopt and implement policies and procedures that will preserve the integrity of and public confidence in the institution and the System pursuant to § 612.2165;

(d) Designate a Standards of Conduct Official pursuant to § 612.2170; and

(e) Maintain all standards-of-conduct policies and procedures, reports, investigations, determinations, and evidence of compliance with this part for a minimum of 6 years.

§ 612.2165 Policies and procedures.

(a) Each institution's board of directors shall issue, consistent with this part, policies and procedures governing standards of conduct for directors and employees.

(b) Board policies and procedures issued pursuant to paragraph (a) of this section shall reflect due consideration of the potential adverse impact of any activities permitted under the policies and shall at a minimum:

(1) Establish such requirements and prohibitions as are necessary to promote public confidence in the institution and the System, preserve the integrity and independence of the supervisory process, and prevent the improper use of official property, position, or information. In developing such requirements and prohibitions, the institution shall address such issues as the hiring of relatives, political activity, devotion of time to duty, the exchange of gifts and favors among directors and employees of the employing, supervising, and supervised institution, and the circumstances under which gifts may be accepted by directors and employees from outside sources, in light of the foregoing objectives;

(2) Outline authorities and responsibilities of the Standards of Conduct Official;

(3) Establish criteria for business relationships and transactions not specifically prohibited by this part between employees or directors and borrowers, loan applicants, directors, or employees of the employing, supervised, or supervising institutions, or persons transacting business with such institutions, including OFIs or other lenders having an access or participation relationship;

(4) Establish criteria under which employees may accept outside employment or compensation;

(5) Establish conditions under which employees may receive loans from System institutions;

(6) Establish conditions under which employees may acquire an interest in real or personal property that was mortgaged to a System institution at any time within the preceding 12 months;

(7) Establish conditions under which employees may purchase any real or personal property of a System institution acquired by such institution for its operations. Farm Credit institutions must use open competitive bidding whenever they sell surplus property above a stated value (as established by the board) to their employees.

(8) Provide for a reasonable period of time for directors and employees to terminate transactions, relationships, or activities that are subject to prohibitions that arise at the time of adoption or amendment of the policies.

(9) Require new directors and new employees involved at the time of election or hiring in transactions, relationships, and activities prohibited by these regulations or internal policies to terminate such transactions within the same time period established for existing directors or employees pursuant to paragraph (b)(8) of this section, beginning with the commencement of official duties, or such shorter time period as the institution may establish.

(10) Establish procedures providing for a director's or employee's recusal from official action on any matter in which he or she is prohibited from participating under these regulations or the institution's policies.

(11) Establish documentation requirements demonstrating compliance with standards-of-conduct decisions and board policy;

(12) Establish reporting requirements, consistent with this part, to enable the institution to comply with §620.5 of this chapter, monitor conflicts of interest, and monitor recusal compliance;

(13) Establish appeal procedures available to any employee to whom any required approval has been denied;

(14) Prohibit directors and employees from purchasing or retiring any stock in advance of the release of material non-public information concerning the institution to other stockholders; and

(15) Establish when directors and employees may purchase and retire their preferred stock in the institution.

[59 FR 24894, May 13, 1994, as amended at 64 FR 43048, Aug. 9, 1999; 70 FR 53907, Sept. 13, 2005]

§ 612.2170 Standards of Conduct Official.

(a) Each institution's board shall designate a Standards of Conduct Official who shall:

(1) Advise directors, director candidates, and employees concerning the provisions of this part;

(2) Receive reports required by this part;

§ 612.2260

(3) Make such determinations as are required by this part;

(4) Maintain records of actions taken to resolve and/or make determinations upon each case reported relative to provisions of this part;

(5) Make appropriate investigations, as directed by the institution's board; and

(6) Report promptly, pursuant to part 617 of this chapter, to the institution's board and the Office of General Counsel, Farm Credit Administration, all cases where:

(i) A preliminary investigation indicates that a Federal criminal statute may have been violated;

(ii) An investigation results in the removal of a director or discharge of an employee; or

(iii) A violation may have an adverse impact on continued public confidence in the System or any of its institutions.

(b) The Standards of Conduct Official shall investigate or cause to be investigated all cases involving:

(1) Possible violations of criminal statutes;

(2) Possible violations of §§ 612.2140 and 612.2150, and applicable policies and procedures approved under § 612.2165;

(3) Complaints received against the directors and employees of such institution; and

(4) Possible violations of other provisions of this part or when the activities or suspected activities are of a sensitive nature and could affect continued public confidence in the Farm Credit System.

(c) An association board may comply with this section by contracting with the Farm Credit Bank or agricultural credit bank in its district to provide a Standards of Conduct Official.

§ 612.2260 Standards of conduct for agents.

(a) Agents of System institutions shall maintain high standards of honesty, integrity, and impartiality in order to ensure the proper performance of System business and continued public confidence in the System and all its institutions. The avoidance of misconduct and conflicts of interest is indispensable to the maintenance of these standards.

(b) System institutions shall utilize safe and sound business practices in the engagement, utilization, and retention of agents. These practices shall provide for the selection of qualified and reputable agents. Employing System institutions shall be responsible for the administration of relationships with their agents, and shall take appropriate investigative and corrective action in the case of a breach of fiduciary duties by the agent or failure of the agent to carry out other agent duties as required by contract, FCA regulations, or law.

(c) System institutions shall be responsible for exercising corresponding special diligence and control, through good business practices, to avoid or control situations that have inherent potential for sensitivity, either real or perceived. These areas include the employment of agents who are related to directors or employees of the institutions; the solicitation and acceptance of gifts, contributions, or special considerations by agents; and the use of System and borrower information obtained in the course of the agent's association with System institutions.

§ 612.2270 Purchase of System obligations.

(a) Employees and directors of System institutions, other than the Federal Farm Credit Banks Funding Corporation, may only purchase joint, consolidated, or Systemwide obligations that are:

(1) Part of an offering available to the general public; and

(2) Purchased through a dealer or dealer bank affiliated with a member of the selling group designated by the Federal Farm Credit Banks Funding Corporation or purchased in the secondary market.

(b) No director or employee of the Federal Farm Credit Banks Funding Corporation may purchase or otherwise acquire, directly or indirectly, except by inheritance, any joint, consolidated, or Systemwide obligation.

Subpart B—Referral of Known or Suspected Criminal Violations

SOURCE: 62 FR 24566, May 6, 1997, unless otherwise noted. Redesignated at 69 FR 10907, Mar. 9, 2004.

§ 612.2300 Purpose and scope.

(a) This part applies to all institutions of the Farm Credit System as defined in section 1.2(a) of the Farm Credit Act of 1971, as amended, (Act) (12 U.S.C. 2002(a)) including, but not limited to, associations, banks, service corporations chartered under section 4.25 of the Act, the Federal Farm Credit Banks Funding Corporation, the Farm Credit Leasing Services Corporation, and the Federal Agricultural Mortgage Corporation (hereinafter, institutions). The purposes of this part are to ensure public confidence in the Farm Credit System, to ensure the reporting of known or suspected criminal activity, to reduce potential losses to institutions, and to ensure the safety and soundness of institutions. This part requires that institutions use the Farm Credit Administration Criminal Referral Form (hereinafter FCA Referral Form) to notify the appropriate Federal authorities when any known or suspected Federal criminal violations of the type described in § 612.2301 are discovered by institutions.

(b) The specific referral requirements of this part apply to known or suspected criminal violations of the United States Code involving the assets, operations, or affairs of an institution. This part prescribes procedures for referring those violations to the proper Federal authorities and the Farm Credit Administration. No specific procedural requirements apply to the referral of violations of State or local laws.

(c) Nothing in this part should be construed as reducing in any way an institution's ability to report known or suspected criminal activities to the appropriate investigatory or prosecuting authorities, whether Federal, State, or local, even when the circumstances in which a report is required under § 612.2301 are not present.

(d) It shall be the responsibility of each System institution to determine whether there appears to be a reasonable basis to conclude that a criminal violation has been committed and, if so, to report the matter to the proper law enforcement authorities for consideration of prosecution.

(e) Each referral required by § 612.2301(a) shall be made on the FCA Referral Form in accordance with the FCA Referral Form instructions relating to its filing and distribution.

[62 FR 24566, May 6, 1997. Redesignated and amended at 69 FR 10907, Mar. 9, 2004; 75 FR 35968, June 24, 2010.]

§ 612.2301 Referrals.

(a) Each institution and its board of directors shall exercise due diligence to ensure the discovery, appropriate investigation, and reporting of criminal activity. Within 30 calendar days of determining that there is a known or suspected criminal violation of the United States Code involving or affecting its assets, operations, or affairs, the institution shall refer such criminal violation to the appropriate regional offices of the United States Attorney, and the Federal Bureau of Investigation or the United States Secret Service or both, using the FCA Referral Form. A copy of the completed FCA Referral Form, accompanied by any relevant documentation, shall be provided at the same time to the Farm Credit Administration's Office of General Counsel. In the event that a Farm Credit bank makes a loan through a Federal land bank association which services the loan, the Federal land bank association must inform the Farm Credit bank of any known or suspected violation involving that loan and the Farm Credit bank shall refer the violation to Federal law enforcement authorities under this section. A report is required in circumstances where there is:

(1) Any known or suspected criminal activity (e.g., theft, embezzlement), mysterious disappearance, unexplained shortage, misapplication, or other defalcation of property and/or funds, regardless of amount, where an institution employee, officer, director, agent, or other person participating in the conduct of the affairs of such an institution is suspected;

(2) Any known or suspected criminal activity involving an actual or potential loss of $5,000 or more, through false

§ 612.2302

statements or other fraudulent means, where the institution has a substantial basis for identifying a possible suspect or group of suspects and the suspect(s) is not an institution employee, officer, director, agent, or other person participating in the conduct of the affairs of such an institution;

(3) Any known or suspected criminal activity involving an actual or potential loss of $25,000 or more, through false statements or other fraudulent means, where the institution has no substantial basis for identifying a possible suspect or group of suspects; or

(4) Any known or suspected criminal activity involving a financial transaction in which the institution was used as a conduit for such criminal activity (such as money laundering/structuring schemes).

(b) In circumstances where there is a known or suspected violation of State or local criminal law, the institution shall notify the appropriate State or local law enforcement authorities.

(c) In addition to the requirements of paragraph (a) of this section, the institution shall immediately notify by telephone the appropriate Federal law enforcement authorities and FCA offices specified on the FCA Referral Form upon determining that a known or suspected criminal violation of Federal law requiring urgent attention has occurred or is ongoing. Such cases include, but are not limited to, those where:

(1) There is a likelihood that the suspect(s) will flee;

(2) The magnitude or the continuation of the known or suspected criminal violation may imperil the institution's continued operation; or

(3) Key institution personnel are involved.

§ 612.2302 Notification of board of directors and bonding company.

(a) The institution's board of directors shall be promptly notified of any criminal referral by the institution, except that if the criminal referral involves a member of the board of directors, discretion may be exercised in notifying such member of the referral.

(b) The institution involved shall promptly make all required notifications under any applicable surety bond or other contract for protection.

§ 612.2303 Institution responsibilities.

Each institution shall establish effective policies and procedures designed to ensure compliance with this part, including, but not limited to, adequate internal controls.

PART 613—ELIGIBILITY AND SCOPE OF FINANCING

Subpart A—Financing Under Titles I and II of the Farm Credit Act

Sec.
613.3000 Financing for farmers, ranchers, and aquatic producers or harvesters.
613.3005 Lending objective.
613.3010 Financing for processing or marketing operations.
613.3020 Financing for farm-related service businesses.
613.3030 Rural home financing.

Subpart B—Financing for Banks Operating Under Title III of the Farm Credit Act

613.3100 Domestic lending.
613.3200 International lending.

Subpart C—Similar Entity Authority Under Sections 3.1(11)(B) and 4.18A of the Act

613.3300 Participations and other interests in loans to similar entities.

AUTHORITY: Secs. 1.5, 1.7, 1.9, 1.10, 1.11, 2.2, 2.4, 2.12, 3.1, 3.7, 3.8, 3.22, 4.18A, 4.25, 4.26, 4.27, 5.9, 5.17 of the Farm Credit Act (12 U.S.C. 2013, 2015, 2017, 2018, 2019, 2073, 2075, 2093, 2122, 2128, 2129, 2143, 2206a, 2211, 2212, 2213, 2243, 2252).

Subpart A—Financing Under Titles I and II of the Farm Credit Act

SOURCE: 62 FR 4441, Jan. 30, 1997, unless otherwise noted.

§ 613.3000 Financing for farmers, ranchers, and aquatic producers or harvesters.

(a) *Definitions.* For purposes of this subpart, the following definitions apply:

(1) *Bona fide farmer or rancher* means a person owning agricultural land or engaged in the production of agricultural products, including aquatic products under controlled conditions.

Farm Credit Administration § 613.3010

(2) *Legal entity* means any partnership, corporation, estate, trust, or other legal entity that is established pursuant to the laws of the United States, any State thereof, the Commonwealth of Puerto Rico, the District of Columbia, or any tribal authority and is legally authorized to conduct a business.

(3) *Person* means a legal entity or an individual who is a citizen of the United States or a foreign national who has been lawfully admitted into the United States either for permanent residency pursuant to 8 U.S.C. 1101(a)(20) or on a visa pursuant to a provision in 8 U.S.C. 1101(a)(15) that authorizes such individual to own property or operate or manage a business or a legal entity.

(4) *Producer or harvester of aquatic products* means a person engaged in producing or harvesting aquatic products for economic gain in open waters under uncontrolled conditions.

(b) *Eligible borrower.* Farm Credit institutions that operate under titles I or II of the Act may provide financing to a bona fide farmer or rancher, or producer or harvester of aquatic products for any agricultural or aquatic purpose and for other credit needs.

[62 FR 4441, Jan. 30, 1997, as amended at 73 FR 30475, May 28, 2008]

§ 613.3005 Lending objective.

It is the objective of each bank and association, except for banks for cooperatives, to provide full credit, to the extent of creditworthiness, to the full-time bona fide farmer (one whose primary business and vocation is farming, ranching, or producing or harvesting aquatic products); and conservative credit to less than full-time farmers for agricultural enterprises, and more restricted credit for other credit requirements as needed to ensure a sound credit package or to accommodate a borrower's needs as long as the total credit results in being primarily an agricultural loan. However, the part-time farmer who needs to seek off-farm employment to supplement farm income or who desires to supplement off-farm income by living in a rural area and is carrying on a valid agricultural operation, shall have availability of credit for mortgages, other agricultural purposes, and family needs in the preferred position along with full-time farmers. Loans to farmers shall be on an increasingly conservative basis as the emphasis moves away from the full-time bona fide farmer to the point where agricultural needs only will be financed for the applicant whose business is essentially other than farming. Credit shall not be extended where investment in agricultural assets for speculative appreciation is a primary factor.

§ 613.3010 Financing for processing or marketing operations.

(a) *Eligible borrowers.* A borrower is eligible for financing for a processing or marketing operation under titles I and II of the Act only if the borrower:

(1) Is a bona fide farmer, rancher, or producer or harvester of aquatic products who regularly produces some portion of the throughput used in the processing or marketing operation; or

(2) Is a legal entity not eligible under paragraph (a)(1) of this section in which eligible borrowers under § 613.3000(b) own more than 50 percent of the voting stock or equity and regularly produce some portion of the throughput used in the processing or marketing operation; or

(3) Is a legal entity not eligible under paragraph (a)(1) of this section in which eligible borrowers under § 613.3000(b) own 50 percent or less of the voting stock or equity, regularly produce some portion of the throughput used in the processing or marketing operation and:

(i) Exercise majority voting control over the legal entity; or

(ii) Constitute a majority of the directors of a corporation, general partners of a limited partnership, or managing members of a limited liability company who exercise control over the legal entity by determining and overseeing the policies, business practices, management, and decision-making process of the legal entity; or

(4) Is a legal entity not eligible under paragraph (a)(1) of this section in which eligible borrowers under § 613.3000(b) meet all of the following criteria:

(i) Own at least 25 percent of the voting stock or equity in the processing or marketing operation;

(ii) Regularly produce 20 percent or more of the throughput used in the processing or marketing operation;

(iii) Maintain representation on the board of directors or in the applicable management structure of the entity.

(5) Is a legal entity not eligible under paragraph (a)(1) of this section that is a direct extension or outgrowth of an eligible borrower's operation and meets all of the following criteria:

(i) The legal entity was created for the primary purpose of processing or marketing the eligible borrower's throughput and would not exist but for the eligible borrower's involvement,

(ii) The legal entity fulfills a business need and supports the operation of the eligible borrower through product branding or other value-added business activity directly related to the operations of the eligible borrower,

(iii) The legal entity and the eligible borrower coordinate to operate in a functionally integrated manner, and

(iv) The legal entity regularly receives throughput produced by the eligible borrower representing either:

(A) At least 20 percent of the throughput used by the legal entity in the processing or marketing operation; or

(B) At least 50 percent of the eligible borrower's total output of the commodity processed or marketed.

(b) *Portfolio restrictions for certain processing and marketing loans.* Processing or marketing loans to eligible borrowers who regularly supply less than 20 percent of the throughput are subject to the following restrictions:

(1) *Bank limitation.* The aggregate of such processing and marketing loans made by a Farm Credit bank shall not exceed 15 percent of all its outstanding retail loans at the end of the preceding fiscal year.

(2) *Association limitation.* The aggregate of such processing and marketing loans made by all direct lender associations affiliated with the same Farm Credit bank shall not exceed 15 percent of the aggregate of their outstanding retail loans at the end of the preceding fiscal year. Each Farm Credit bank, in conjunction with all its affiliated direct lender associations, shall ensure that such processing or marketing loans are equitably allocated among its affiliated direct lender associations.

(3) *Calculation of outstanding retail loans.* For the purposes of this paragraph, "outstanding retail loans" includes loans, loan participations, and other interests in loans that are either bought without recourse or sold with recourse.

(c) *Reporting requirements.* Each System institution shall include information on loans made under authority of this section in the Reports of Condition and Performance required under § 621.12 of this chapter, in the format prescribed by FCA reporting instructions.

(d) *Institution policies.* The board of directors of each System institution making processing and marketing loans to legal entities under authority of this section must adopt a policy that addresses eligibility requirements for such entities and ensures that the institution, at a minimum, develops and implements:

(1) Procedures on how, at or before the time a loan is made, the institution will document:

(i) Eligible borrower ownership, control, throughput, integration of operations and other factors, as applicable, sufficient to establish eligibility of legal entities at the time a loan is made under this section; and

(ii) Each legal entity's plan and intent for maintaining eligible borrower ownership, control, throughput, and integration of operations, as applicable, during the duration of the loan;

(2) Procedures that encourage financing under paragraph (a)(4) of this section of credit-worthy entities whose operations directly benefit producers, have local community investment support and provide accessible ownership opportunities for local farmers and ranchers.

(3) Procedures for determining functional integration for loans made under paragraph (a)(5) of this section that require consideration of all relevant facts and circumstances, which include the extent to which:

(i) The operations share resources such as management, employees, facilities, and equipment;

Farm Credit Administration

§ 613.3030

(ii) The operations are conducted in coordination with or reliance upon each other; and

(iii) The eligible borrower and legal entity are dependent upon each other for economic success.

(4) Portfolio restrictions necessary to comply with paragraph (b) of this section and any board-defined limits on financing provided under this section; and

(5) Reporting requirements necessary to comply with paragraph (c) of this section and any board-defined reporting on financing provided under this section.

[62 FR 4441, Jan. 30, 1997, as amended at 73 FR 30475, May 28, 2008]

§ 613.3020 Financing for farm-related service businesses.

(a) *Eligibility.* An individual or legal entity that furnishes farm-related services to farmers and ranchers that are directly related to their agricultural production is eligible to borrow from a Farm Credit bank or association that operates under titles I or II of the Act.

(b) *Purposes of financing.* A Farm Credit Bank, agricultural credit bank, or direct lender association may finance:

(1) All of the farm-related business activities of an eligible borrower who derives more than 50 percent of its annual income (as consistently measured on either a gross sales or net sales basis) from furnishing farm-related services that are directly related to the agricultural production of farmers and ranchers; or

(2) Only the farm-related services activities of an eligible borrower who derives 50 percent or less of its annual income (as consistently measured on either a gross sales or net sales basis) from furnishing farm-related services that are directly related to the agricultural production of farmers and ranchers.

(c) *Limitation.* The authority of Farm Credit banks and associations operating under section 1.7(a) of the Act to finance eligible farm-related service businesses under paragraphs (b)(1) and (b)(2) of this section is limited to necessary capital structures, equipment, and initial working capital.

[62 FR 4441, Jan. 30, 1997, as amended at 66 FR 28643, May 24, 2001]

§ 613.3030 Rural home financing.

(a) *Definitions.* (1) *Rural homeowner* means an individual who resides in a rural area and is not a bona fide farmer, rancher, or producer or harvester of aquatic products.

(2) *Rural home* means a single-family moderately priced dwelling located in a rural area that will be owned and occupied as the rural homeowner's principal residence.

(3) *Rural area* means open country within a State or the Commonwealth of Puerto Rico, which may include a town or village that has a population of not more than 2,500 persons.

(4) *Moderately priced* means the price of any rural home that either:

(i) Satisfies the criteria in section 8.0 of the Act pertaining to rural home loans that collateralize securities that are guaranteed by the Federal Agricultural Mortgage Corporation; or

(ii) Is otherwise determined to be moderately priced for housing values for the rural area where it is located, as documented by data from a credible, independent, and recognized national or regional source, such as a Federal, State, or local government agency, or an industry source. Housing values at or below the 75th percentile of values reflected in such data will be deemed moderately priced.

(b) *Eligibility.* Any rural homeowner is eligible to obtain financing on a rural home. No borrower shall have a loan from the Farm Credit System on more than one rural home at any one time.

(c) *Purposes of financing.* Loans may be made to rural homeowners for the purpose of buying, building, remodeling, improving, repairing rural homes, and refinancing existing indebtedness thereon.

(d) *Portfolio limitations.* (1) The aggregate of retail rural home loans by any Farm Credit Bank or agricultural credit bank shall not exceed 15 percent of the total of all of its outstanding loans at any one time.

(2) The aggregate of rural home loans made by each direct lender association

§ 613.3100

shall not exceed 15 percent of the total of its outstanding loans at the end of its preceding fiscal year, except with the prior approval of its funding bank.

(3) The aggregate of rural home loans made by all direct lender associations that are funded by the same Farm Credit bank shall not exceed 15 percent of the total outstanding loans of all such associations at the end of the funding bank's preceding fiscal year.

[62 FR 4441, Jan. 30, 1997, as amended at 66 FR 28643, May 24, 2001]

Subpart B—Financing for Banks Operating Under Title III of the Farm Credit Act

SOURCE: 62 FR 4442, Jan. 30, 1997, unless otherwise noted.

§ 613.3100 Domestic lending.

(a) *Definitions.* For purposes of this subpart, the following definitions apply:

(1) *Cooperative* means any association of farmers, ranchers, producers or harvesters of aquatic products, or any federation of such associations, or a combination of such associations and farmers, ranchers, or producers or harvesters of aquatic products that conducts business for the mutual benefit of its members and has the power to:

(i) Process, prepare for market, handle, or market farm or aquatic products;

(ii) Purchase, test, grade, process, distribute, or furnish farm or aquatic supplies; or

(iii) Furnish business and financially related services to its members.

(2) *Farm or aquatic supplies and farm or aquatic business services* are any goods or services normally used by farmers, ranchers, or producers and harvesters of aquatic products in their business operations, or to improve the welfare or livelihood of such persons.

(3) *Public utility* means a cooperative or other entity that is licensed under Federal, State, or local law to provide electric, telecommunication, cable television, water, or waste treatment services.

(4) *Rural area* means all territory of a State that is not within the outer boundary of any city or town having a population of more than 20,000 inhabitants based on the latest decennial census of the United States.

(5) *Service cooperative* means a cooperative that is involved in providing business and financially related services (other than public utility services) to farmers, ranchers, aquatic producers or harvesters, or their cooperatives.

(b) *Cooperatives and other entities that serve agricultural or aquatic producers*— (1) *Eligibility of cooperatives.* A bank for cooperatives or an agricultural credit bank may lend to a cooperative that satisfies the following requirements:

(i) Unless the bank's board of directors establishes by resolution a higher voting control threshold for any type of cooperative, the percentage of voting control of the cooperative held by farmers, ranchers, producers or harvesters of aquatic products, or cooperatives shall be 80 percent except:

(A) Sixty (60) percent for a service cooperative;

(B) Sixty (60) percent for local farm supply cooperatives that have historically served the needs of a community that would not be adequately served by other suppliers and have experienced a reduction in the percentage of membership by agricultural or aquatic producers due to changed circumstances beyond their control; and

(C) Sixty (60) percent for local farm supply cooperatives that provide or will provide needed services to a community, and are or will be in competition with a cooperative specified in § 613.3100(b)(1)(i)(B);

(ii) The cooperative deals in farm or aquatic products, or products processed therefrom, farm or aquatic supplies, farm or aquatic business services, or financially related services with or for members in an amount at least equal in value to the total amount of such business it transacts with or for non-members, excluding from the total of member and non-member business, transactions with the United States, or any agencies or instrumentalities thereof, or services or supplies furnished by a public utility; and

(iii) The cooperative complies with one of the following two conditions:

(A) No member of the cooperative shall have more than one vote because

Farm Credit Administration §613.3100

of the amount of stock or membership capital owned therein; or

(B) The cooperative restricts dividends on stock or membership capital to the maximum percentage per year permitted by applicable state law.

(iv) Any cooperative that has received a loan from a bank for cooperatives or an agricultural credit bank shall, without regard to the requirements in paragraph (b)(1) of this section, continue to be eligible for as long as more than 50 percent (or such higher percentage as is established by the bank board) of the voting control of the cooperative is held by farmers, ranchers, producers or harvesters of aquatic products, or other eligible cooperatives.

(2) *Other eligible entities.* The following entities are eligible to borrow from banks for cooperatives and agricultural credit banks:

(i) Any legal entity that holds more than 50 percent of the voting control of a cooperative that is an eligible borrower under paragraph (b)(1) of this section and uses the proceeds of the loan to fund the activities of its cooperative subsidiary on the terms and conditions specified by the bank;

(ii) Any legal entity in which an eligible cooperative (or a subsidiary or other entity in which an eligible cooperative has an ownership interest) has an ownership interest, *provided that* if the percentage of ownership attributable to the eligible cooperative is less than 50 percent, financing may not exceed the percentage of ownership attributable to the eligible cooperative multiplied by the value of the total assets of such entity; or

(iii) Any creditworthy private entity operated on a non-profit basis that satisfies the requirements for a service cooperative and complies with the requirements of either paragraphs (b)(1)(i)(A) and (b)(1)(iii) of this section, or paragraph (b)(1)(iv) of this section, and any subsidiary of such entity. An entity that is eligible to borrow under this paragraph shall be organized to benefit agriculture in furtherance of the welfare of the farmers, ranchers, and aquatic producers or harvesters who are its members.

(c) *Electric and telecommunication utilities*—(1) *Eligibility.* A bank for cooperatives or an agricultural credit bank may lend to:

(i) Electric and telephone cooperatives as defined by section 3.8(a)(4)(A) of the Act that satisfy the eligibility criteria in paragraph (b)(1) of this section;

(ii) Cooperatives and other entities that:

(A) Have received a loan, loan commitment, insured loan, or loan guarantee from the Rural Utilities Service of the United States Department of Agriculture to finance rural electric and telecommunication services;

(B) Have received a loan or a loan commitment from the Rural Telephone Bank of the United States Department of Agriculture; or

(C) Are eligible under the Rural Electrification Act of 1936, as amended, for a loan, loan commitment, or loan guarantee from the Rural Utilities Service or the Rural Telephone Bank.

(iii) The subsidiaries of cooperatives or other entities that are eligible under paragraph (c)(1)(ii) of this section.

(iv) Any legal entity that holds more than 50 percent of the voting control of any public utility that is an eligible borrower under paragraph (c)(1)(ii) of this section, and uses the proceeds of the loan to fund the activities of the eligible subsidiary on the terms and conditions specified by the bank.

(v) Any legal entity in which an eligible utility under paragraph (c)(1)(ii) of this section (or a subsidiary or other entity in which an eligible utility under paragraph (c)(1)(ii) has an ownership interest) has an ownership interest, *provided that* if the percentage of ownership attributable to the eligible utility is less than 50 percent, financing may not exceed the percentage of ownership attributable to the eligible utility multiplied by the value of the total assets of such entity.

(2) *Purposes for financing.* A bank for cooperatives or agricultural credit bank may extend credit to entities that are eligible to borrow under paragraph (c)(1) of this section in order to provide electric or telecommunication services in a rural area. A subsidiary that is eligible to borrow under paragraph (c)(1)(iii) of this section may also obtain financing from a bank for cooperatives or agricultural credit bank

§ 613.3200

for energy-related or public utility-related purposes that cannot be financed by the lenders referred to in paragraph (c)(1)(ii), including, without limitation, financing to operate a licensed cable television utility.

(d) *Water and waste disposal facilities—* (1) *Eligibility.* A cooperative or a public agency, quasi-public agency, body, or other public or private entity that, under the authority of state or local law, establishes and operates water and waste disposal facilities in a rural area, as that term is defined by paragraph (a)(4) of this section, is eligible to borrow from a bank for cooperatives or an agricultural credit bank.

(2) *Purposes for financing.* A bank for cooperatives or agricultural credit bank may extend credit to entities that are eligible under paragraph (d)(1) of this section solely for installing, maintaining, expanding, improving, or operating water and waste disposal facilities in rural areas.

(e) *Domestic lessors.* A bank for cooperatives or agricultural credit bank may lend to domestic parties to finance the acquisition of facilities or equipment that will be leased to shareholders of the bank for use in their operations located inside of the United States.

[62 FR 4442, Jan. 30, 1997; 62 FR 33746, June 23, 1997, as amended at 69 FR 43514, July 21, 2004; 71 FR 65386, Nov. 8, 2006]

§ 613.3200 International lending.

(a) *Definitions.* For the purpose of this section only, the following definitions apply:

(1) *Agricultural supply* includes:

(i) A farm supply; and

(ii) Agriculture-related processing equipment, agriculture-related machinery, and other capital goods related to the storage or handling of agricultural commodities or products.

(2) *Farm supply* refers to an input that is used in a farming or ranching operation.

(b) *Import transactions.* The following parties are eligible to borrow from a bank for cooperatives or an agricultural credit bank pursuant to section 3.7(b) of the Act for the purpose of financing the import of agricultural commodities or products therefrom, aquatic products, and agricultural supplies into the United States:

(1) An eligible cooperative as defined by § 613.3100(b);

(2) A counterparty with respect to a specific import transaction with a voting stockholder of the bank for the substantial benefit of the shareholder; and

(3) Any foreign or domestic legal entity in which eligible cooperatives hold an ownership interest.

(c) *Export transactions.* Pursuant to section 3.7(b)(2) of the Act, a bank for cooperatives or an agricultural credit bank is authorized to finance the export (including the cost of freight) of agricultural commodities or products therefrom, aquatic products, or agricultural supplies from the United States to any foreign country. The board of directors of each bank for cooperatives and agricultural credit bank shall adopt policies that ensure that exports of agricultural products and commodities, aquatic products, and agricultural supplies which originate from eligible cooperatives are financed on a priority basis. The total amount of balances outstanding on loans made under this paragraph shall not, at any time, exceed 50 percent of the capital of any bank for cooperatives or agricultural credit bank for loans that:

(1) Finance the export of agricultural commodities and products therefrom, aquatic products, or agricultural supplies that are not originally sourced from an eligible cooperative; and

(2) At least 95 percent of the loan amount is not guaranteed by a department, agency, bureau, board, or commission of the United States or a corporation that is wholly owned directly or indirectly by the United States.

(d) *International business operations.* A bank for cooperatives or an agricultural credit bank may finance a domestic or foreign entity which is at least partially owned by eligible cooperatives described in § 613.3100(b), and facilitates the international business operations of such cooperatives.

(e) *Restrictions.* (1) When eligible cooperatives own less than 50 percent of a foreign or domestic legal entity, the amount of financing that a bank for cooperatives or agricultural credit bank may provide to the entity for imports,

Farm Credit Administration

exports, or international business operations shall not exceed the percentage of ownership that eligible cooperatives hold in such entity multiplied by the value of the total assets of such entity; and

(2) A bank for cooperatives or agricultural credit bank shall not finance the relocation of any plant or facility from the United States to a foreign country.

[62 FR 4442, Jan. 30, 1997, as amended at 69 FR 43514, July 21, 2004]

Subpart C—Similar Entity Authority Under Sections 3.1(11)(B) and 4.18A of the Act

§ 613.3300 Participations and other interests in loans to similar entities.

(a) *Definitions.* (1) *Participate* and *participation,* for the purpose of this section, refer to multi-lender transactions, including syndications, assignments, loan participations, subparticipations, other forms of the purchase, sale, or transfer of interests in loans, or other extensions of credit, or other technical and financial assistance.

(2) *Similar entity* means a party that is ineligible for a loan from a Farm Credit bank or association, but has operations that are functionally similar to the activities of eligible borrowers in that a majority of its income is derived from, or a majority of its assets are invested in, the conduct of activities that are performed by eligible borrowers.

(b) *Similar entity transactions.* A Farm Credit bank or a direct lender association may participate with a lender that is not a Farm Credit System institution in loans to a similar entity that is not eligible to borrow directly under § 613.3000, 613.3010, 613.3020, 613.3100, or 613.3200, for purposes similar to those for which an eligible borrower could obtain financing from the participating FCS institution.

(c) *Restrictions.* Participations by a Farm Credit bank or association in loans to a similar entity under this section are subject to the following limitations:

(1) *Lending limits.* (i) *Farm Credit banks operating under title I of the Act and direct lender associations.* The total amount of all loan participations that any Farm Credit bank, agricultural credit bank, or direct lender association has outstanding under paragraph (b) of this section to a single credit risk shall not exceed:

(A) Ten (10) percent of its total capital; or

(B) Twenty-five (25) percent of its total capital if a majority of voting stockholders voting of the respective Farm Credit bank or direct lender association so approve.

(ii) *Farm Credit banks operating under title III of the Act.* The total amount of all loan participations that any bank for cooperatives or agricultural credit bank has outstanding under paragraph (b) of this section to a single credit risk shall not exceed 10 percent of its total capital;

(2) *Percentage held in the principal amount of the loan.* The participation interest in the same loan held by one or more Farm Credit bank(s) or association(s) shall not, at any time, equal or exceed 50 percent of the principal amount of the loan; and

(3) *Portfolio limitations.* The total amount of participations that any Farm Credit bank or direct lender association has outstanding under paragraph (b) of this section shall not exceed 15 percent of its total outstanding assets at the end of its preceding fiscal year.

(d) *Approval by other Farm Credit System institutions.* A bank for cooperatives or agricultural credit bank may not participate in a loan to a similar entity under title III of the Act if the similar entity has a loan or loan commitment outstanding with a Farm Credit Bank or an association chartered under the Act, unless agreed to by the Farm Credit Bank or association.

[62 FR 4444, Jan. 30, 1997, as amended at 69 FR 43514, July 21, 2004; 75 FR 18743, Apr. 12, 2010]

PART 614—LOAN POLICIES AND OPERATIONS

Subpart A—Lending Authorities

Sec.
614.4000 Farm Credit Banks.
614.4010 Agricultural credit banks.
614.4020 Banks for cooperatives.
614.4030 Federal land credit associations.

Pt. 614

614.4040 Production credit associations.
614.4050 Agricultural credit associations.
614.4055 Federal Agricultural Mortgage Corporation loan participations.
614.4060 Affiliates established pursuant to section 8.5(e)(1) of the Farm Credit Act of 1971.

Subpart B—Chartered Territories

614.4070 Loans and chartered territory—Farm Credit Banks, agricultural credit banks, Federal land bank associations, Federal land credit associations, production credit associations, and agricultural credit associations.
614.4080 Loans and chartered territory—banks for cooperatives.

Subpart C—Bank/Association Lending Relationship

614.4100 Policies governing lending through Federal land bank associations.
614.4110 Transfer of direct lending authority to Federal land bank associations and agricultural credit associations.
614.4120 Policies governing extensions of credit to direct lender associations and OFIs.
614.4125 Funding and discount relationships between Farm Credit Banks or agricultural credit banks and direct lender associations.
614.4130 Funding and discount relationships between Farm Credit Banks or agricultural credit banks and OFIs.

Subpart D—General Loan Policies for Banks and Associations

614.4150 Lending policies and loan underwriting standards.
614.4155 Interest rates.
614.4160 Differential interest rate programs.
614.4165 Young, beginning, and small farmers and ranchers.
614.4170 General.
614.4175 Uninsured voluntary and involuntary accounts.

Subpart E—Loan Terms and Conditions

614.4200 General requirements.
614.4231 Certain seasonal commodity loans to cooperatives.
614.4232 Loans to domestic lessors.
614.4233 International loans.

Subpart F—Collateral Evaluation Requirements

614.4240 Collateral definitions.
614.4245 Collateral evaluation policies.
614.4250 Collateral evaluation standards.
614.4255 Independence requirements.
614.4260 Evaluation requirements.
614.4265 Real property evaluations.
614.4266 Personal and intangible property evaluations.
614.4267 Professional association membership; competency.

Subpart G [Reserved]

Subpart H—Loan Purchases and Sales

614.4325 Purchase and sale of interests in loans.
614.4330 Loan participations.
614.4335 Borrower stock requirements.
614.4337 Disclosure to borrowers.

Subpart I—Loss-Sharing Agreements

614.4340 General.
614.4345 Guaranty agreements.

Subpart J—Lending and Leasing Limits

614.4350 Definitions.
614.4351 Computation of lending and leasing limit base.
614.4352 Farm Credit Banks and agricultural credit banks.
614.4353 Direct lender associations.
614.4354 Federal land bank associations.
614.4355 Banks for cooperatives.
614.4356 Farm Credit Leasing Services Corporation.
614.4357 Banks for cooperatives look-through notes.
614.4358 Computation of obligations.
614.4359 Attribution rules.
614.4360 Lending and leasing limit violations.
614.4361 Transition.
614.4362 Loan and lease concentration risk mitigation policy.

Subparts K–L [Reserved]

Subpart M—Loan Approval Requirements

614.4450 General requirements.
614.4460 Loan approval responsibility.
614.4470 Loans subject to bank approval.

Subpart N [Reserved]

Subpart O—Special Lending Programs

614.4525 General.
614.4530 Special loans, production credit associations and agricultural credit associations.

Subpart P—Farm Credit Bank and Agricultural Credit Bank Financing of Other Financing Institutions

614.4540 Other financing institution access to Farm Credit Banks and agricultural credit banks for funding, discount, and other similar financial assistance.
614.4550 Place of discount.

Farm Credit Administration

§ 614.4000

614.4560 Requirements for OFI funding relationships.
614.4570 Recourse and security.
614.4580 Limitation on the extension of funding, discount and other similar financial assistance to an OFI.
614.4590 Equitable treatment of OFIs and Farm Credit System associations.
614.4595 Public disclosure about OFIs.
614.4600 Insolvency of an OFI.

Subpart Q—Banks for Cooperatives and Agricultural Credit Banks Financing International Trade

614.4700 Financing foreign trade receivables.
614.4710 [Reserved]
614.4720 Letters of credit.
614.4800 Guarantees and contracts of suretyship.
614.4810 Standby letters of credit.
614.4900 Foreign exchange.

Subpart R—Secondary Market Authorities

614.4910 Basic authorities.

Subpart S—Flood Insurance Requirements

614.4920 Purpose and scope.
614.4925 Definitions.
614.4930 Requirement to purchase flood insurance where available.
614.4935 Escrow requirement.
614.4940 Required use of standard flood hazard determination form.
614.4945 Forced placement of flood insurance.
614.4950 Determination fees.
614.4955 Notice of special flood hazards and availability of Federal disaster relief assistance.
614.4960 Notice of servicer's identity.
APPENDIX A TO SUBPART S OF PART 614—SAMPLE FORM OF NOTICE OF SPECIAL FLOOD HAZARDS AND AVAILABILITY OF FEDERAL DISASTER RELIEF ASSISTANCE

AUTHORITY: 42 U.S.C. 4012a, 4104a, 4104b, 4106, and 4128; secs. 1.3, 1.5, 1.6, 1.7, 1.9, 1.10, 1.11, 2.0, 2.2, 2.3, 2.4, 2.10, 2.12, 2.13, 2.15, 3.0, 3.1, 3.3, 3.7, 3.8, 3.10, 3.20, 3.28, 4.12, 4.12A, 4.13B, 4.14, 4.14A, 4.14C, 4.14D, 4.14E, 4.18, 4.18A, 4.19, 4.25, 4.26, 4.27, 4.28, 4.36, 4.37, 5.9, 5.10, 5.17, 7.0, 7.2, 7.6, 7.8, 7.12, 7.13, 8.0, 8.5 of the Farm Credit Act (12 U.S.C. 2011, 2013, 2014, 2015, 2017, 2018, 2019, 2071, 2073, 2074, 2075, 2091, 2093, 2094, 2097, 2121, 2122, 2124, 2128, 2129, 2131, 2141, 2149, 2183, 2184, 2201, 2202, 2202a, 2202c, 2202d, 2202e, 2206, 2206a, 2207, 2211, 2212, 2213, 2214, 2219a, 2219b, 2243, 2244, 2252, 2279a, 2279a-2, 2279b, 2279c-1, 2279f, 2279f-1, 2279aa, 2279aa-5); sec. 413 of Pub. L. 100-233, 101 Stat. 1568, 1639.

Subpart A—Lending Authorities

SOURCE: 55 FR 24880, June 19, 1990, unless otherwise noted.

§ 614.4000 Farm Credit Banks.

(a) *Long-term real estate lending.* Except to the extent such authorities are transferred pursuant to section 7.6 of the Act, Farm Credit Banks are authorized, subject to the requirements in § 614.4200 of this part, to make real estate mortgage loans with maturities of not less than 5 years nor more than 40 years and continuing commitments to make such loans.

(b) *Extensions of credit to Farm Credit direct lender associations.* Farm Credit Banks are authorized to make loans and extend other similar financial assistance to associations with direct lending authority and discount for or purchase from such associations, with the association's endorsement or guaranty, any note, draft, and other obligations for loans that have been made in accordance with the provisions of subparts D and E of part 614 of these regulations. Such extensions of credit shall be made pursuant to a written financing agreement meeting the requirements of § 614.4125.

(c) *Extensions of credit to other financing institutions.* Farm Credit Banks are authorized to make loans and extend other similar financial assistance to any national bank, State bank, trust company, agricultural credit corporation, incorporated livestock loan company, savings institution, credit union, or any association of agricultural producers or any corporation engaged in the making of loans to farmers and ranchers or producers or harvesters of aquatic products (collectively, "other financing institutions"), for purposes eligible for financing by a production credit association in accordance with § 614.4130 and subpart P of this part. Farm Credit Banks are authorized to discount for or purchase from such institutions, with the institution's endorsement or guaranty, notes, drafts, and other obligations or loans made to persons and for purposes eligible for financing by a production credit association, in accordance with § 614.4130 and subpart P of this part.

§ 614.4010

(d) *Loan participations.* Subject to the requirements of subpart H of part 614, a Farm Credit Bank may enter into loan participation agreements with:

(1) Farm Credit banks and associations that are direct lenders and lenders that are not Farm Credit institutions on loans of the type it is authorized to make under title I of the Act;

(2) Farm Credit banks and associations that are direct lenders on loans it is not authorized to make, provided the borrower eligibility, membership, term, amount, loan security, and stock or participation certificate requirements of the originating institution are met; and

(3) The Federal Agricultural Mortgage Corporation to the extent provided in § 614.4055.

(e) *Other interests in loans.* (1) Subject to the requirements of subpart H of this part, Farm Credit Banks may sell interests in loans only to:

(i) Farm Credit System institutions authorized to purchase such interests;

(ii) Other lenders that are not Farm Credit System institutions; and

(iii) Any certified agricultural mortgage marketing facility, as defined by section 8.0(3) of the Act, for the purpose of pooling and securitizing such loans under title VIII of the Act.

(2) Subject to the requirements of subpart H of this part, Farm Credit Banks may purchase interests other than participation interests in loans and nonvoting stock from other Farm Credit System institutions.

(3) Farm Credit Banks, in their capacity as certified agricultural mortgage marketing facilities under title VIII of the Act, may purchase interests in loans (other than participation interests authorized in paragraph (d) of this section) from institutions other than Farm Credit System institutions only for the purpose of pooling and securitizing such loans under title VIII of the Act.

(f) *Residual powers after the transfer of lending authority to an association.* After transferring its authority to make and participate in long-term real estate loans to an agricultural credit association or a Federal land credit association pursuant to section 7.6(a) of the Act and subpart E of part 611 of these regulations, a Farm Credit Bank retains residual authority to:

(1) Enter into loan participation agreements pursuant to paragraph (d) of this section;

(2) Purchase or sell other interests in loans in accordance with paragraph (e) of this section; and

(3) Make long-term real estate loans in accordance with paragraph (a) of this section in areas of its chartered territory where no active association operates.

[55 FR 24880, June 19, 1990, as amended at 57 FR 38246, Aug. 24, 1992; 57 FR 43290, Sept. 18, 1992; 62 FR 51013, Sept. 30, 1997; 63 FR 5723, Feb. 4, 1998; 64 FR 43049, Aug. 9, 1999; 65 FR 24102, Apr. 25, 2000; 67 FR 1285, Jan. 10, 2002]

§ 614.4010 Agricultural credit banks.

(a) *Long-term real estate lending.* Except to the extent such authorities are transferred pursuant to section 7.6 of the Act, agricultural credit banks are authorized, subject to the requirements of § 614.4200, to make real estate mortgage loans with maturities of not less than 5 years nor more than 40 years and continuing commitments to make such loans.

(b) *Extensions of credit to Farm Credit direct lender associations.* Agricultural credit banks are authorized to make loans and extend other similar financial assistance to associations with direct lending authority and discount for or purchase from such associations, with the association's endorsement or guaranty, any note, draft, and other obligations for loans made by the association in accordance with the provisions of this part. Such extensions of credit shall be made pursuant to a written financing agreement meeting the requirements of § 614.4125.

(c) *Extensions of credit to other financing institutions.* Agricultural credit banks are authorized to make loans and extend other similar financial assistance to any national bank, State bank, trust company, agricultural credit corporation, incorporated livestock loan company, savings institution, credit union, or any association of agricultural producers or corporation engaged in the making of loans to farmers, ranchers, or producers or harvesters of aquatic products (collectively, "other financing institutions"),

Farm Credit Administration §614.4010

for purposes eligible for financing by a production credit association, in accordance with §614.4130 and subpart P of this part. Agricultural credit banks are authorized to discount for or purchase from such other financing institutions, with the institution's endorsement or guaranty, notes, drafts, and other obligations or loans made to persons and for purposes eligible for financing by a production credit association, in accordance with the requirements of §614.4130 and subpart P of this part.

(d) *Extensions of credit to or on behalf of eligible cooperatives.* Agricultural credit banks are authorized to make loans and commitments and extend other technical and financial assistance, including but not limited to, collateral custody, discounting notes and other obligations, guarantees, and currency exchanges necessary to service transactions financed under paragraphs (d)(4) and (d)(5) of this section, to:

(1) Eligible cooperatives, as defined in §613.3100(b)(1), in accordance with §§614.4200, 614.4231, 614.4232, 614.4233, and subpart Q of part 614;

(2) Other eligible entities, as defined in §613.3100(b)(2), in accordance with §§614.4200, 614.4231, and 614.4232;

(3) Domestic lessors, for the purpose of providing leased assets to stockholders of the bank eligible to borrow under section 3.7(a) of the Act for use in such stockholders' operations in the United States, in accordance with §614.4232;

(4) Domestic or foreign parties with respect to a transaction with a voting stockholder of the bank, for the import of agricultural commodities, farm supplies, or aquatic products through purchases, sales or exchanges, provided such stockholder substantially benefits as a result of such extension of credit or assistance, in accordance with policies of the bank's board, §614.4233, and subpart Q of part 614; and

(5) Domestic or foreign parties in which a voting stockholder of the bank has a minimum ownership interest, for the purpose of facilitating such stockholder's import operations of the type described in paragraph (d)(4) of this section, provided the stockholder substantially benefits as a result of such extension of credit or assistance, in accordance with policies of the bank's board, §614.4233, and subpart Q of part 614.

(6) Any party, subject to the requirements in §613.3200(c) of this chapter, for the export (including the cost of freight) of agricultural commodities or products therefrom, aquatic products, or farm supplies from the United States to any foreign country, in accordance with §614.4233 and subpart Q of this part 614; and

(7) Domestic or foreign parties in which eligible cooperatives, as defined in §613.3100 of this chapter, hold an ownership interest, for the purpose of facilitating the international business operations of such cooperatives pursuant to the requirements of §613.3200 (d) and (e) of this chapter.

(e) *Loan participations.* Subject to the requirements of subpart H of this part, an agricultural credit bank may enter into loan participation agreements with:

(1) Farm Credit banks and associations that are direct lenders and lenders that are not Farm Credit institutions on loans of the type it is authorized to make under the Act;

(2) Farm Credit banks and associations that are direct lenders on loans it is not authorized to make, provided the borrower eligibility, membership, term, amount, loan security, and stock or participation certificate requirements of the originating institution are met; and

(3) The Federal Agricultural Mortgage Corporation to the extent provided in §614.4055.

(f) *Other interest in loans.* (1) Subject to subpart H of this part, agricultural credit banks may sell interests in real estate mortgage loans identified in paragraph (a) of this section to Farm Credit System institutions authorized to purchase such interests, other lenders, and certified agricultural mortgage marketing facilities for the Federal Agricultural Mortgage Corporation. Agricultural credit banks may also sell interests in the types of loans listed in paragraph (d) of this section to other Farm Credit System institutions that are authorized to purchase such interests.

(2) Subject to the requirements of subpart H of this part, agricultural

§ 614.4020

credit banks may purchase interests other than participation interests in loans and nonvoting stock from other Farm Credit System institutions.

(3) Agricultural credit banks, in their capacity as certified agricultural mortgage marketing facilities under title VIII of the Act, may purchase interests in loans (other than participation interests authorized in paragraph (e) of this section) from institutions other than Farm Credit System institutions only for the purpose of pooling and securitizing such loans under title VIII of the Act.

(g) *Residual powers after the transfer of lending authority to an association.* After transferring its authority to make and participate in long-term real estate loans to an agricultural credit association or a Federal land credit association pursuant to section 7.6(a) of the Act and subpart E of part 611 of these regulations, an agricultural credit bank retains residual authority to:

(1) Enter into loan participation agreements pursuant to paragraph (e) of this section;

(2) Purchase or sell other interests in loans in accordance with paragraph (f) of this section; and

(3) Make long-term real estate loans in accordance with paragraph (a) of this section in areas of its chartered territory where no active association operates.

[55 FR 24880, June 19, 1990, as amended at 57 FR 38246, Aug. 24, 1992; 57 FR 43290, Sept. 18, 1992; 62 FR 4445, Jan. 30, 1997; 62 FR 51013, Sept. 30, 1997; 63 FR 5723, Feb. 4, 1998; 64 FR 43049, Aug. 9, 1999; 65 FR 24102, Apr. 25, 2000; 67 FR 1285, Jan. 10, 2002; 71 FR 65387, Nov. 8, 2006]

§ 614.4020 Banks for cooperatives.

(a) Banks for cooperatives are authorized to make loans and commitments and extend other technical and financial assistance, including but not limited to, collateral custody, discounting notes and other obligations, guarantees, and currency exchanges necessary to service transactions financed under paragraphs (a)(4) and (a)(5) of this section, to:

(1) Eligible cooperatives, as defined in § 613.3100(b)(1), in accordance with §§ 614.4200, 614.4231, 614.4232, 614.4233, and subpart Q of this part;

(2) Other eligible entities as defined in § 613.3100(b)(2), in accordance with §§ 614.4200, 614.4231, and 614.4232;

(3) Domestic lessors, for the purpose of providing leased assets to stockholders of the bank eligible to borrow under section 3.7(a) of the Act for use in such stockholder's operations in the United States, in accordance with § 614.4232;

(4) Domestic or foreign parties with respect to a transaction with a voting stockholder of the bank, for the import of agricultural commodities, farm supplies, or aquatic products through purchases, sales or exchanges, provided such stockholder substantially benefits as a result of such extension of credit or assistance, in accordance with policies of the bank's board, § 614.4233, and subpart Q of this part; and

(5) Domestic or foreign parties in which a voting stockholder of the bank has an ownership interest, for the purpose of facilitating the import operations of the type described in paragraph (a)(4) of this section, in accordance with policies of the bank's board, § 614.4233, and subpart Q of this part.

(6) Any party, subject to the requirements in § 613.3200(c) of this chapter, for the export (including the cost of freight) of agricultural commodities or products therefrom, aquatic products, or farm supplies from the United States to any foreign country, in accordance with § 614.4233 and subpart Q of this part; and

(7) Domestic or foreign parties in which eligible cooperatives, as defined in § 613.3100 of this chapter, hold an ownership interest, for the purpose of facilitating the international business operations of such cooperatives pursuant to the requirements in § 613.3200 (d) and (e) of this chapter.

(b) *Loan participations.* Subject to the requirements of subpart H of this part, a bank for cooperatives may enter into loan participation agreements with:

(1) Farm Credit banks and associations that are direct lenders and lenders that are not Farm Credit institutions on loans of the type it is authorized to make under title III of the Act;

(2) Farm Credit banks and associations that are direct lenders on loans of the type it is not authorized to make,

Farm Credit Administration §614.4040

provided the borrower eligibility, membership, term, amount, loan security, and stock or participation certificate requirements of the originating institution are met; and

(3) The Federal Agricultural Mortgage Corporation to the extent provided in §614.4055.

[55 FR 24880, June 19, 1990, as amended at 62 FR 4445, Jan. 30, 1997; 62 FR 51013, Sept. 30, 1997; 67 FR 1285, Jan. 10, 2002; 71 FR 65387, Nov. 8, 2006]

§614.4030 Federal land credit associations.

(a) *Long-term real estate lending.* Federal land credit associations are authorized, subject to the requirments of §614.4200, to make real estate mortgage loans with maturities of not less than 5 years nor more than 40 years and continuing commitments to make such loans.

(b) *Loan participations.* Subject to the requirements of subpart H of this part, Federal land credit associations may enter into participation agreements with:

(1) Farm Credit banks and associations that are direct lenders and lenders that are not Farm Credit institutions on loans of the type it is authorized to make under title I of the Act;

(2) Farm Credit banks and associations that are direct lenders on loans it is not authorized to make, provided the borrower eligibility, membership, term, amount, loan security, and stock or participation certificate requirements of the originating institution are met; and

(3) The Federal Agricultural Mortgage Corporation to the extent provided in §614.4055.

(c) *Other interests in loans.* (1) Subject to the requirements of subpart H of this part and the supervision of their respective funding banks, Federal land credit associations may sell interests in loans made under paragraph (a) of this section only to:

(i) Farm Credit System institutions, as authorized by their respective funding banks;

(ii) Other lenders that are not Farm Credit System institutions, as authorized by their respective funding banks; and

(iii) Any certified agricultural mortgage marketing facility, as defined by section 8.0(3) of the Act, for the purpose of pooling and securitizing such loans under title VIII of the Act.

(2) Subject to the requirements of subpart H of this part, Federal land credit associations may purchase interests in loans that comply with the requirements of paragraph (a) of this section and nonvoting stock from Farm Credit System institutions.

(3) Federal land credit associations, in their capacity as certified agricultural mortgage marketing facilities under title VIII of the Act, may purchase interests in loans (other than participation interests under paragraph (b) of this section) from institutions other than Farm Credit System institutions for the purpose of pooling and securitizing such loans under title VIII of the Act.

[55 FR 24880, June 19, 1990, as amended at 57 FR 38247, Aug. 24, 1992; 62 FR 51013, Sept. 30, 1997; 64 FR 43049, Aug. 9, 1999; 65 FR 24102, Apr. 25, 2000; 67 FR 1285, Jan. 10, 2002]

§614.4040 Production credit associations.

(a) *Loan terms.* (1) Production credit associations are authorized to make or guarantee loans and other similar financial assistance for the following terms:

(i) Not more than 7 years

(ii) More than 7 years, but not more than 10 years, subject to authorization in policies approved by the funding bank

(iii) Not more than 15 years to producers or harvesters of aquatic products for major capital expenditures, including but not limited to the purchase of vessels, construction or purchase of shore facilities, and similar purposes directly related to the producing or harvesting operation

(2) Subject to policies approved by the funding bank, production credit associations may amortize loans over a period greater than the loan terms authorized under paragraph (a)(1) of this section, provided that:

(i) The loan is amortized over a period not to exceed 15 years

(ii) The loan may be refinanced only if the lender determines, at the time of

§ 614.4050

refinancing, that the loan meets its loan policy and underwriting criteria;

(iii) Any refinancing may not extend repayment beyond 15 years from the date of the original loan; and

(iv) The loan is not being made solely for the purpose of acquiring unimproved real estate; and

(3) Short- and intermediate-term loans shall be made with maturities that are appropriate for the purpose and underlying collateral of the loan and that comply with an institution's loan underwriting standards adopted pursuant to § 614.4150 and the general requirements of § 614.4200 of this part.

(b) *Loan participations.* Subject to the requirements of subpart H of this part, a production credit association may enter into participation agreements with:

(1) Farm Credit banks and associations that are direct lenders and lenders that are not Farm Credit institutions on loans of the type it is authorized to make under title II of the Act;

(2) Farm Credit banks and associations that are direct lenders on loans it is not authorized to make, provided the borrower eligibility, membership, term, amount, loan security, and stock or participation certificate requirements of the originating institution are met; and

(3) The Federal Agricultural Mortgage Corporation to the extent provided in § 614.4055.

(c) *Other interests in loans.* (1) Subject to the requirements of subpart H of this part and the supervision of their respective funding banks, production credit associations may sell interests in loans that are made under paragraph (a) of this section to:

(i) Banks of the Farm Credit System, as authorized by their respective funding banks; and

(ii) Any certified agricultural mortgage marketing facility, as defined by section 8.0(3) of the Act, for the purpose of pooling and securitizing such loans under title VIII of the Act.

(2) Subject to the requirements of subpart H of this part, production credit associations, as authorized by their respective funding banks, may purchase interests in loans that comply with the requirements of paragraph (a) of this section and nonvoting stock from banks of the Farm Credit System.

(3) Production credit associations, in their capacity as certified mortgage marketing facilities under title VIII of the Act, may purchase from Farm Credit System institutions and institutions that are not Farm Credit System institutions interests in loans (other than participation interests authorized by paragraph (c) of this section) for the purpose of pooling and securitizing such loans under title VIII of the Act.

[55 FR 24880, June 19, 1990; 55 FR 28511, July 11, 1990, as amended at 57 FR 38247, Aug. 24, 1992; 62 FR 51013, Sept. 30, 1997; 64 FR 43049, Aug. 9, 1999; 65 FR 24102, Apr. 25, 2000; 67 FR 1285, Jan. 10, 2002]

§ 614.4050 Agricultural credit associations.

Agricultural credit associations are authorized to make or guarantee, subject to the requirements of § 614.4200 of this part:

(a) *Long-term real estate mortgage loans* with maturities of not less than 5 nor more than 40 years, and continue commitments to make such loans; and

(b) *Short- and intermediate-term loans* and provide other similar financial assistance for a term of not more than 10 years (15 years for aquatic producers and harvesters.

(c) *Loan participations.* Subject to the requirements of subpart H of this part, agricultural credit associations may enter into participation agreements with:

(1) Farm Credit banks and associations that are direct lenders and lenders that are not Farm Credit institutions on loans of the type it is authorized to make under titles I and II of the Act;

(2) Farm Credit banks and associations that are direct lenders on loans of the type it is not authorized to make, provided the borrower eligibility, membership, term, amount, loan security, and stock or participation certificate requirements of the originating institution are met; and

(3) The Federal Agricultural Mortgage Corporation to the extent provided in § 614.4055.

(d) *Other interests in loans.* (1) Subject to the requirements of subpart H of this part and the supervision of their respective funding banks, agricultural credit associations may sell:

(i) Interests in loans made under paragraph (a) of this section only to:

(A) Farm Credit System institutions, as authorized by their respective funding banks;

(B) Lenders that are not Farm Credit System institutions, as authorized by their respective funding banks; and

(C) Any certified agricultural mortgage marketing facility, as defined by section 8.0(3) of the Act, for the purpose of pooling and securitizing such loans under title VIII of the Act.

(ii) Interests in loans made under paragraph (b) of this part only to:

(A) Banks of the Farm Credit System, as authorized by their respective funding banks; and

(B) Any certified agricultural mortgage marketing facility, as defined by section 8.0(3) of the Act, for the purpose of pooling and securitizing such loans under title VIII of the Act.

(2) Subject to the requirements of subpart H of this part, agricultural credit associations may purchase:

(i) Interests in loans that comply with the requirements in paragraph (a) of this section from institutions of the Farm Credit System;

(ii) Interests in loans that comply with the requirements of paragraph (b) of this section from banks of the Farm Credit System; and

(iii) Nonvoting stock from institutions of the Farm Credit System.

(3) Agricultural credit associations, in their capacity as certified agricultural mortgage marketing facilities under title VIII of the Act, may purchase interests in loans, other than participation interests authorized by paragraph (c) of this section, from institutions other than Farm Credit System institutions for the purpose of pooling and securitizing such loans under title VIII of the Act.

[55 FR 24880, June 19, 1990; 55 FR 28511, July 11, 1990, as amended at 57 FR 38247, Aug. 24, 1992; 62 FR 51013, Sept. 30, 1997; 64 FR 43049, Aug. 9, 1999; 65 FR 24102, Apr. 25, 2000; 67 FR 1285, Jan. 10, 2002]

§ 614.4055 Federal Agricultural Mortgage Corporation loan participations.

Subject to the requirements of subpart H of this part 614:

(a) Any Farm Credit System bank or direct lender association may buy from, and sell to, the Federal Agricultural Mortgage Corporation, participation interests in "qualified loans."

(b) The Federal Agricultural Mortgage Corporation may buy from, and sell to, any Farm Credit System bank or direct lender association, or lender that is not a Farm Credit System institution, participation interests in "qualified loans."

(c) For purposes of this section, "qualified loans" means qualified loans as defined in section 8.0(9) of the Act.

[67 FR 1285, Jan. 10, 2002]

§ 614.4060 Affiliates established pursuant to section 8.5(e)(1) of the Farm Credit Act of 1971.

An affiliate established by one or more Farm Credit System institutions pursuant to section 8.5(e)(1) of the Act and § 611.1137 of this chapter, as a certified agricultural mortgage marketing facility, may purchase loans from Farm Credit System institutions and institutions other than Farm Credit System institutions in accordance with title VIII of the Act and any applicable regulation promulgated thereunder.

[57 FR 38247, Aug. 24, 1992]

Subpart B—Chartered Territories

§ 614.4070 Loans and chartered territory—Farm Credit Banks, agricultural credit banks, Federal land bank associations, Federal land credit associations, production credit associations, and agricultural credit associations.

(a) A bank or association chartered under title I or II of the Act may finance eligible borrower operations conducted wholly within its chartered territory regardless of the residence of the applicant.

(b) A bank or association operating under title I or II of the Act may finance the operations of a borrower headquartered and operating in its territory even though the operation financed is conducted partially outside its territory, provided notice is given to all Farm Credit institutions providing similar credit in the territory(ies) in which the operations being financed are conducted. A bank or association operating under title I or II of the Act may lend to a borrower headquartered outside its territory to finance eligible borrower operations that are conducted partially within its territory and partially outside its territory only if the concurrence of Farm Credit institutions providing similar credit for the territories in which the operations are conducted is obtained.

(c) A bank or association chartered under title I or II of the Act may finance eligible borrower operations conducted wholly outside its chartered territory, provided such loans are authorized by the policies of the bank and/or association involved, do not constitute a significant shift in loan volume away from the bank or association's assigned territory, and are made and administered in accordance with paragraphs (c)(1) and (c)(2) of this section.

(1) If a loan is made to an eligible borrower whose operations are conducted wholly outside the chartered territory of the lending bank or association, the lending institution shall obtain concurrence of all Farm Credit institutions providing similar credit in the territory(ies) in which the operation being financed is conducted.

(2) Loans to finance eligible borrower operations conducted wholly outside a bank's or association's territory shall be appropriately designated by the bank or association to provide adequate identification of the number and volume of such loans, which shall be monitored by the bank or association.

(d) A bank or association chartered under title I or II of the Act may finance eligible borrower operations conducted wholly or partially outside its chartered territory through the purchase of loans from the Federal Deposit Insurance Corporation in compliance with § 614.4325(b)(3), provided:

(1) Notice is given to the Farm Credit System institution(s) chartered to serve the territory where the headquarters of the borrower's operation being financed is located; and

(2) After loan purchase, additional financing of eligible borrower operations complies with paragraphs (a), (b), and (c) of this section.

[55 FR 24882, June 19, 1990, as amended at 76 FR 30250, May 25, 2011]

§ 614.4080 Loans and chartered territory—banks for cooperatives.

Loans made under title III by banks for cooperatives and agricultural credit banks may be made to eligible domestic parties domiciled within any territory that may be served by Farm Credit institutions under section 1.2 of the Act and to eligible foreign parties without regard to domicile.

[55 FR 24882, June 19, 1990]

Subpart C—Bank/Association Lending Relationship

§ 614.4100 Policies governing lending through Federal land bank associations.

(a) Farm Credit Banks and agricultural credit banks may delegate authority to make credit decisions to Federal land bank associations that demonstrate the ability to extend and administer credit soundly, provided the association develops, implements and maintains adequate credit administration guidelines, standards, and practices.

(b) The board of directors of each Farm Credit Bank and each agricultural credit bank lending through Federal land bank associations shall adopt policies and procedures governing the exercise of statutory and delegated authorities by such associations. Policies governing the delegated authorities shall:

(1) Define authorities to be delegated;

(2) Require the documented evaluation of the capability and responsibility of individuals exercising delegated authorities;

(3) Provide for reporting of actions taken under delegated authority to the delegating bank;

(4) Provide procedures for periodic review and enforcement;

(5) Provide for withdrawal of authority where appropriate; and

Farm Credit Administration

§ 614.4125

(6) Where redelegation from the association's board to association employees is authorized, require similar control measures to be used.

[55 FR 24883, June 19, 1990]

§ 614.4110 Transfer of direct lending authority to Federal land bank associations and agricultural credit associations.

(a) Upon the transfer of authority to make and participate in long-term agricultural real estate mortgage loans by a Farm Credit Bank or agricultural credit bank to a Federal land bank association pursuant to section 7.6(a) of the Act and subpart E of part 611 of these regulations, the association shall be designated a Federal land credit association and shall have the powers set forth in § 614.4030.

(b) Upon the transfer of the authority to make and participate in long-term real estate loans by a Farm Credit Bank or agricultural credit bank to an agricultural credit association pursuant to section 7.6(d) of the Act, the association shall have all of the powers set forth in § 614.4050.

(c) An association to which such long-term lending authority is to be transferred shall have in place, prior to the transfer, policies and procedures guiding the extension and administration of credit within its territory.

[55 FR 24883, June 19, 1990]

§ 614.4120 Policies governing extensions of credit to direct lender associations and OFIs.

The board of directors of each Farm Credit Bank and agricultural credit bank shall adopt policies and procedures governing the making of direct loans to and the discounting of loans for direct lender associations and OFIs. The policies and procedures shall prescribe lending policies and loan underwriting standards that are consistent with sound financial and credit practices. The policies shall require a periodic review of the lending relationship with each direct lender association and OFI at intervals consistent with the term of the general financing agreement but in no case longer than 5 years. The policies shall require an evaluation of the creditworthiness of a direct lender association on the basis of credit factors and lending policies and loan underwriting standards set forth in part 614, subpart D, and may permit lending to such an institution on an unsecured basis only if the overall condition of the institution warrants. The stated term of a general financing agreement shall not exceed 5 years but may be automatically renewable for additional terms not to exceed 5 years if neither party objects at the time of renewal. The term of any general financing agreement that provides for unsecured lending to a direct lender association shall not exceed 1 year and may not be automatically renewed.

[63 FR 5724, Feb. 4, 1998]

§ 614.4125 Funding and discount relationships between Farm Credit Banks or agricultural credit banks and direct lender associations.

(a) A Farm Credit Bank or agricultural credit bank shall not advance funds to, or discount loans for, any direct lender association except pursuant to a general financing agreement. Each general financing agreement must require that the amount of financing available to a direct lender association not be based on loans that are ineligible under the Act and the regulations in this chapter. If financing under a general financing agreement is based on a loan that FCA determines is ineligible under the Act and the regulations in this chapter, then the amount of financing available must be recalculated without that ineligible loan.

(b) The Farm Credit Bank or agricultural credit bank shall deliver a copy of the executed general financing agreement and all related documents, such as a promissory note or security agreement, and all amendments of any of these documents, within 10 business days after any such document or amendment is executed, to the Chief Examiner, Farm Credit Administration, or to the Farm Credit Administration office that the Chief Examiner designates.

(c) The general financing agreement shall address only those matters that are reasonably related to the debtor/creditor relationship between the Farm Credit Bank or agricultural credit bank and the direct lender association.

(d) The total credit extended to a direct lender association, through direct loan or discounts, shall be consistent with the Farm Credit Bank's or agricultural credit bank's lending policies and loan underwriting standards and the creditworthiness of the direct lender association. The general financing agreement or promissory note shall establish a maximum credit limit determined by objective standards as established by the Farm Credit Bank or agricultural credit bank.

(e) A Farm Credit Bank or agricultural credit bank that provides notice to a direct lender association that it is in material default of any covenant, term, or condition of the general financing agreement, promissory note, security agreement, or other related documents simultaneously shall provide written notification to the Chief Examiner, Farm Credit Administration, or to the Farm Credit Administration office that the Chief Examiner designates and the Director, Risk Management, Farm Credit System Insurance Corporation.

(f) A direct lender association shall provide written notification to the Chief Examiner, Farm Credit Administration, or to the Farm Credit Administration office that the Chief Examiner designates, and the Director, Risk Management, Farm Credit System Insurance Corporation immediately upon receipt of a notice that it is in material default under any general financing agreement, loan agreement, promissory note, security agreement, or other related documents with a Farm Credit Bank, agricultural credit bank or non-Farm Credit institution.

(g) A Farm Credit Bank or agricultural credit bank shall obtain prior written consent of the Farm Credit Administration before it takes any action that leads to or could lead to the liquidation of a direct lender association.

(h) No direct lender association shall obtain financing from any party unless the parties agree to the requirements of this paragraph. No Farm Credit Bank, agricultural credit bank, or other party shall petition any Federal or State court to appoint a conservator, receiver, liquidation agent, or other administrator to manage the affairs of or liquidate a direct lender association.

[63 FR 5724, Feb. 4, 1998, as amended at 69 FR 43514, July 21, 2004]

§ 614.4130 Funding and discount relationships between Farm Credit Banks or agricultural credit banks and OFIs.

(a) A Farm Credit Bank or agricultural credit bank shall not advance funds to, or discount loans for, an OFI, as defined in § 611.1205 of this chapter, except pursuant to a general financing agreement.

(b) The Farm Credit Bank or agricultural credit bank shall deliver a copy of the executed general financing agreement and all related documents, such as a promissory note or security agreement, and all amendments of any of these documents, within 10 business days after any such document or amendment is executed, to the Chief Examiner, Farm Credit Administration, or to the Farm Credit Administration office that the Chief Examiner designates.

(c) The total credit extended to the OFI, through direct loan or discounts, shall be consistent with the Farm Credit Bank's or agricultural credit bank's lending policies and loan underwriting standards and the creditworthiness of the OFI. The general financing agreement or promissory note shall establish a maximum credit limit determined by objective standards as established by the Farm Credit Bank or agricultural credit bank.

[63 FR 5724, Feb. 4, 1998, as amended at 67 FR 17917, Apr. 12, 2002]

Subpart D—General Loan Policies for Banks and Associations

§ 614.4150 Lending policies and loan underwriting standards.

Under the policies of its board, each institution shall adopt written standards for prudent lending and shall issue written policies, operating procedures, and control mechanisms that reflect prudent credit practices and comply with all applicable laws and regulations. Written policies and procedures shall, at a minimum, prescribe:

Farm Credit Administration

§ 614.4165

(a) The minimum supporting credit and financial information, frequency for collection of information, and verification of information required in relation to loan size, complexity and risk exposure

(b) The procedures to be followed in credit analysis

(c) The minimum standards for loan disbursement, servicing and collections

(d) Requirements for collateral and methods for its administration

(e) Loan approval delegations and requirements for reporting to the board

(f) Loan pricing practices

(g) Loan underwriting standards that include measurable standards:

(1) For determining that an applicant has the operational, financial, and management resources necessary to repay the debt from cashflow

(2) That are appropriate for each loan program and the institution's risk-bearing ability; and

(3) That consider the nature and type of credit risk, amount of the loan, and enterprises being financed

(h) Requirements that loan terms and conditions are appropriate for the loan; and

(i) Such other requirements as are necessary for the professional conduct of a lending organization, including documentation for each loan transaction of compliance with the loan underwriting standards or the compensating factors or extenuating circumstances that establish repayment of the loan notwithstanding the failure to meet any one or more loan underwriting standard.

[62 FR 51014, Sept. 30, 1997]

§ 614.4155 Interest rates.

Loans made by each bank and direct lender association shall bear interest at a rate or rates as may be determined by the institution board. The board shall set interest rates or approve individual interest rate changes either on a case-by-case basis or pursuant to an interest rate plan within which management may establish rates. Any interest rate plan shall set loan-pricing policies and objectives, provide guidance regarding the circumstances under which management may adjust rates, and provide the upper and lower limits on management authority. Any interest rate plan adopted shall be reviewed on a continuing basis by the board, as well as in conjunction with its review and approval of the institution's operational and strategic business plan.

[62 FR 66818, Dec. 22, 1997]

§ 614.4160 Differential interest rate programs.

Pursuant to policies approved by the board of directors, differential interest rates may be established for loans based on a variety of factors that may include type, purpose, amount, quality, funding or operating costs, or similar factors or combinations of factors. Differential interest rate programs should achieve equitable rate treatment within categories of borrowers. In the adoption of differential interest rate programs, institutions may consider, among other things, the effect that such interest rate structures will have on the achievement of objectives relating to the special credit needs of young, beginning or small farmers.

[61 FR 67186, Dec. 20, 1996. Redesignated at 62 FR 66818, Dec. 22, 1997]

§ 614.4165 Young, beginning, and small farmers and ranchers.

(a) *Definitions.* (1) For purposes of this subpart, the term "credit" includes:

(i) Loans made to farmers and ranchers and producers or harvesters of aquatic products under title I or II of the Act; and

(ii) Interests in participations made to farmers and ranchers and producers or harvesters of aquatic products under title I or II of the Act.

(2) For purposes of this subpart, the term "services" includes:

(i) Leases made to farmers and ranchers and producers or harvesters of aquatic products under title I or II of the Act; and

(ii) Related services to farmers and ranchers and producers or harvesters of aquatic products under title I or II of the Act.

(b) *Farm Credit bank policies.* Each Farm Credit Bank and Agricultural Credit Bank must adopt written policies that direct:

§ 614.4165

(1) The board of each affiliated direct lender association to establish a program to provide sound and constructive credit and services to young, beginning, and small farmers and ranchers and producers or harvesters of aquatic products (YBS farmers and ranchers or YBS). The terms "bona fide farmer or rancher," and "producer or harvester of aquatic products" are defined in § 613.3000 of this chapter;

(2) Each affiliated direct lender association to include in its YBS farmers and ranchers program provisions ensuring coordination with other System institutions in the territory and other governmental and private sources of credit;

(3) Each affiliated direct lender association to provide, annually, a complete and accurate YBS farmers and ranchers operations and achievements report to its funding bank; and

(4) The bank to provide the agency a complete and accurate annual report summarizing the YBS program operations and achievements of its affiliated direct lender associations.

(c) *Direct lender association YBS programs.* The board of directors of each direct lender association must establish a program to provide sound and constructive credit and services to YBS farmers and ranchers in its territory. Such a program must include the following minimum components:

(1) A mission statement describing program objectives and specific means for achieving such objectives.

(2) Annual quantitative targets for credit to YBS farmers and ranchers that are based on an understanding of reasonably reliable demographic data for the lending territory. Such targets may include:

(i) Loan volume and loan number goals for "young," "beginning," and "small" farmers and ranchers in the territory;

(ii) Percentage goals representative of the demographics for "young," "beginning," and "small" farmers and ranchers in the territory;

(iii) Percentage goals for loans made to new borrowers qualifying as "young," "beginning," and "small" farmers and ranchers in the territory; or

(iv) Goals for capital committed to loans made to "young," "beginning," and "small" farmers and ranchers in the territory.

(3) Annual qualitative YBS goals that must include efforts to:

(i) Offer related services either directly or in coordination with others that are responsive to the needs of the "young," "beginning," and "small" farmers and ranchers in the territory;

(ii) Take full advantage of opportunities for coordinating credit and services offered with other System institutions in the territory and other governmental and private sources of credit who offer credit and services to those who qualify as "young," "beginning," and "small" farmers and ranchers; and

(iii) Implement effective outreach programs to attract YBS farmers and ranchers, which may include the use of advertising campaigns and educational credit and services programs beneficial to "young," "beginning," and "small" farmers and ranchers in the territory, as well as an advisory committee comprised of "young," "beginning," and "small" farmers and ranchers to provide views on how the credit and services of the direct lender association could best serve the credit and services needs of YBS farmers and ranchers.

(4) Methods to ensure that credit and services offered to YBS farmers and ranchers are provided in a safe and sound manner and within a direct lender association's risk-bearing capacity. Such methods could include customized loan underwriting standards, loan guarantee programs, fee waiver programs, or other credit enhancement programs.

(d) *Review and approval of YBS programs.* The YBS program of each direct lender association is subject to the review and approval of its funding bank. However, the funding bank's review and approval is limited to a determination that the YBS program contains all required components as set forth in paragraph (c) of this section. Any conclusion by the bank that a YBS program is incomplete must be communicated to the direct lender association in writing.

(e) *YBS program and the operational and strategic business plan.* Targets and goals outlined in paragraphs (c)(2) and

Farm Credit Administration

§ 614.4175

(c)(3) of this section must be included in each direct lender association's operational and strategic business plan for at least the succeeding 3 years (as set forth in § 618.8440 of this chapter).

(f) *YBS program internal controls.* Each direct lender association must have internal controls that establish clear lines of responsibility for YBS program implementation, YBS performance results, and YBS quarterly reporting to the association's board of directors.

[69 FR 16470, Mar. 30, 2004]

§ 614.4170 General.

Direct lenders shall be responsible for the servicing of the loans that they make. However, loan participation agreements may designate specific loan servicing efforts to be accomplished by a participating institution. Each direct lender shall adopt loan servicing policies and procedures to assure that loans will be serviced fairly and equitably for the borrower while minimizing the risk for the lender. Procedures shall include specific plans that help preserve the quality of sound loans and that help correct credit deficiencies as they develop.

(a) The Farm Credit Bank shall provide guidelines for the servicing of loans by the Federal land bank associations. The servicing may be accomplished either under the direct supervision of the bank or under delegated authority.

(b) The servicing of loans which are participated in by Farm Credit System institutions shall be in accordance with § 614.4325.

(c) In the development of loan servicing policies and procedures, the following criteria shall be included:

(1) *Term loans.* The objective shall be to provide borrowers with prompt and efficient service with respect to actions in such areas as personal liability, partial release of security, insurance requirements or adjustments, loan divisions or transfers, or conditional payments. Procedures shall provide for adequate inspections, reanalyses, reappraisals, controls on payment of insurance and taxes (and for payment when necessary), and prompt exercise of legal options to preserve the lender's collateral position or guard against loss. Loan servicing policies for rural home loans shall recognize the inherent differences between agricultural and rural home lending.

(2) *Operating loans.* The objective shall be to service such loans to assure disbursement in accordance with the basis of approval, repayment from the sources obligated or pledged, and to minimize risk exposure to the lender. Procedures shall require:

(i) The procurement of periodic operating data essential for maintaining control, for the proper analysis of such data, and prompt action as needed;

(ii) Inspections, reappraisals, and borrower visits appropriate to the nature and quality of the loan; and

(iii) Controls on insurance, margin requirements, warehousing, and the prompt exercise of legal options to preserve the lender's collateral position and guard against loss.

(3) *Legal entity loans.* In addition to the foregoing servicing objectives for term and operating loans, procedures for servicing these loans shall require procurement of data on changes in ownership, control, and management; review of business objectives, financing programs, organizational structure, and operating methods, and appropriate analysis of such changes with provision for action as needed.

[37 FR 11424, June 7, 1972, as amended at 40 FR 17745, Apr. 22, 1975. Redesignated at 46 FR 51878, Oct. 22, 1981 and amended at 48 FR 54475, Dec. 5, 1983; 51 FR 39502, Oct. 28, 1986; 57 FR 38250, Aug. 24, 1992; 61 FR 67187, Dec. 20, 1996. Redesignated at 75 FR 35968, June 24, 2010]

§ 614.4175 Uninsured voluntary and involuntary accounts.

(a) Borrowers may make voluntary advance payments on their loans or, under agreement with a System institution, may make voluntary advance conditional payments intended to be applied to future maturities. The monies in the advance conditional payment accounts may be available for return to the borrower in lieu of increasing his loan. System institutions may pay interest on advance conditional payments for the time the funds are held unapplied at a rate not to exceed the rate charged on the related loan(s). System institutions shall hold any advance conditional payments received in

§ 614.4200

accordance with this section in voluntary advance payment accounts.

(b) System institutions may establish involuntary payment accounts including, but not limited to, funds held for the borrower, such as loan proceeds to be disbursed for which the borrower is obligated; the unapplied insurance proceeds arising from any insured loss; and total insurance premiums and applicable taxes collected in advance in connection with any loan.

[53 FR 35454, Sept. 14, 1988. Redesignated at 75 FR 35968, June 24, 2010]

Subpart E—Loan Terms and Conditions

SOURCE: 55 FR 24884, June 19, 1990, unless otherwise noted.

§ 614.4200 General requirements.

(a) *Terms and conditions.* (1) The terms and conditions of each loan made by a Farm Credit bank or association shall be set forth in a written document or documents, such as a loan agreement, promissory note, or other instrument(s) appropriate to the type and amount of the credit extension, in order to establish loan conditions and performance requirements. Copies of all documents executed by the borrower in connection with the closing of a loan made under titles I or II of the Act shall be provided to the borrower at the time of execution and at any time thereafter that the borrower requests additional copies.

(2) The terms and conditions of all loans shall be adequately disclosed in writing to the borrower not later than loan closing. For loans made under titles I and II of the Act, the institution shall provide prompt written notice of the approval of the loan.

(3) Applicants shall be provided notification of the action taken on each credit application in compliance with the requirements of 12 CFR 202.9.

(b) *Security.* (1) Long-term real estate mortgage loans must be secured by a first lien interest in real estate, except that the loans may be secured by a second lien interest if the institution also holds the first lien on the property. No funds shall be advanced, under a legally binding commitment or otherwise, if the outstanding loan balance after the advance would exceed 85 percent (or 97 percent as provided in section 1.10(a) of the Act) of the appraised value of the real estate, except that a loan on which private mortgage insurance is obtained may exceed 85 percent of the appraised value of the real estate to the extent that the loan amount in excess of 85 percent is covered by such insurance. The real estate that is used to satisfy the loan-to-value limitation must be comprised primarily of agricultural or rural property, including agricultural land and improvements thereto, a farm-related business, a marketing or processing operation, a rural residence, or real estate used as an integral part of an aquatic operation.

(2) Notwithstanding the requirements of paragraph (b)(1) of this section, the lending institution may advance funds for the payment of taxes or insurance premiums with respect to the real estate, reschedule loan payments, grant partial releases of security interests in the real estate, and take other actions necessary to protect the lender's collateral position. Any action taken that results in exceeding the loan-to-value limitation shall be in accordance with a policy of the institution's board of directors and adequately documented in the loan file.

(3) Short- and intermediate-term loans may be secured or unsecured as the documented creditworthiness of the borrower warrants.

(4) In addition to the requirements in paragraph (b)(1) of this section, a long-term, non-farm rural home loan, including a revolving line of credit, shall be secured by a first lien on the property, except that it may be secured by a second lien if the institution also holds the first lien on the property. A short- or intermediate-term loan on a rural home, including a revolving line of credit, must be secured by a lien on the property unless the financing is provided exclusively for repairs, remodeling, or other improvements to the rural home, in which case the loan may be secured by other property or unsecured if warranted by the documented creditworthiness of the borrower.

Farm Credit Administration

(5) Except as provided in § 614.4231, loans made under title III of the Act may be secured or unsecured, as appropriate for the purpose of the loan and the documented creditworthiness of the borrower.

[62 FR 51014, Sept. 30, 1997]

§ 614.4231 Certain seasonal commodity loans to cooperatives.

Loans on certain commodities that are part of government programs shall comply with the criteria established for those programs. Security taken on program commodities shall be consistent with prudent lending practices and ensure compliance with the government program. The bank shall provide for periodic review by bank officials of any custodial activities and shall provide notice to the custodians that their activities are subject to review and examination by the Farm Credit Administration.

[62 FR 51015, Sept. 30, 1997]

§ 614.4232 Loans to domestic lessors.

Loans and financial assistance extended by banks for cooperatives and agricultural credit banks to domestic lessors to finance equipment or facilities leased by a stockholder of the bank shall be subject to the following terms and conditions:

(a) The term of the loan shall not be longer than the total period of the lease;

(b) The contract between the lessor and lessee shall establish that the leased assets are effectively under the control of the lessee and that such control shall continue in effect for essentially all of the term of the lease;

(c) The lessee must hold at least one share of stock or one participation certificate; and

(d) The leased equipment and facilities must be primarily for use in the lessee's operations in the United States.

[55 FR 24884, June 19, 1990, as amended at 64 FR 34517, June 28, 1999]

§ 614.4233 International loans.

Term loans made by banks for cooperatives and agricultural credit banks under the authority of section 3.7(b) of the Act and § 613.3200 of this chapter to foreign or domestic parties who are not shareholders of the bank shall be subject to the following conditions:

(a) The loan shall be denominated in a currency to eliminate foreign exchange risk on repayment.

(b) The borrower's obligations shall be guaranteed or insured against default under such policies as are available in the United States and other countries. Exceptions may be made where a prospective borrower has had a longstanding successful business relationship with an eligible cooperative borrower or an eligible cooperative which is not a borrower if the prospective borrower has a high credit rating as determined by the bank.

(c) For a borrower in which a voting stockholder of the bank has a majority ownership interest, financing may be extended for the full value of the transaction; otherwise, financing may be extended only to approximate the percent of ownership.

[55 FR 24884, June 19, 1990, as amended at 55 FR 28886, July 16, 1990; 55 FR 50544, Dec. 7, 1990; 56 FR 5927, Feb. 14, 1991; 62 FR 4445, Jan. 30, 1997]

Subpart F—Collateral Evaluation Requirements

SOURCE: 59 FR 46730, Sept. 12, 1994, unless otherwise noted.

§ 614.4240 Collateral definitions.

For the purposes of this part, the following definitions shall apply:

(a) *Abundance of caution*, when used to describe decisions to require collateral, means that the collateral is taken in circumstances in which:

(1) It is not required by statute, regulation, or the institution's policies; and

(2) A prudent lender would extend credit based on a borrower's income and/or other collateral, absent the real estate, and the decision to extend credit was, in fact, based on other sources of revenue or collateral.

(b) *Appraisal* means a written statement independently and impartially prepared by a qualified appraiser setting forth an opinion as to the market value of an adequately described property as of a specific date(s), supported

§614.4240

by the presentation and analysis of relevant market information.

(c) *Appraisal Foundation* means the Appraisal Foundation established on November 30, 1987, by professional appraisal organizations, as a not-for-profit corporation under the laws of Illinois, in order to enhance the quality of professional appraisals.

(d) *Appraisal Subcommittee* means the Appraisal Subcommittee of the Federal Financial Institutions Examination Council.

(e) *Business loan* means a loan or other extension of credit to any corporation, general or limited partnership, business trust, joint venture, sole proprietorship, or other business entity (including entities and individuals engaged in farming enterprises).

(f) *Cost approach* means the process by which an evaluator establishes an indicated value by measuring the current market cost to construct a reproduction of or replacement for the improvements, minus the amount of depreciation (physical deterioration, or functional and/or external obsolescence) evident in the structure from all causes, plus the market value of the land.

(g) *Evaluation* means a study of the nature, quality, or utility of, interest in, or aspects of, an asset. An evaluation may take the form of a valuation or an appraisal.

(h) *Fee appraiser* means a qualified evaluator who is not an employee of the party contracting for the completion of the evaluation and who performs an evaluation on a fee basis. For purposes of this subpart, a fee appraiser may include a staff evaluator from another Farm Credit System institution only if the employing institution is not operating under joint management with the contracting institution. In addition, for purposes of personal and intangible collateral evaluations, the term "fee appraiser" includes, but is not limited to, certified public accountants, equipment dealers, grain buyers, livestock buyers, and auctioneers.

(i) *FIRREA* means the Financial Institutions Recovery, Reform, and Enforcement Act of 1989.

(j) *Highest and best use* means the reasonable and most probable use of the property that would result in the highest market value of vacant land or improved property, as of the date of valuation; or that use, from among reasonably probable and legally alternative uses, found to be physically possible, appropriately supported, financially feasible, and which results in the highest land value.

(k) *Income capitalization approach* means the procedure that values property by measuring the present value of the expected future benefits of property ownership. This value is derived from either:

(1) Capitalizing a single year's income expectancy or an annual average of several years' income expectancies at a market-derived capitalization rate that reflects a specific income pattern, return on investment, and change in the value of the investment; or

(2) Discounting the annual cashflows for the holding period and the reversion at a specified yield rate or specified yield rates which reflect market behavior.

(l) *Market value* means the most probable price that a property should bring in a competitive and open market under all conditions requisite to a fair sale, the buyer and seller each acting prudently, knowledgeably, and assuming neither is under duress. Implicit in this definition is the consummation of a sale as of a specified date and the passing of title from seller to buyer under conditions whereby:

(1) Buyer and seller are typically motivated;

(2) Both parties are well informed or well advised, and acting in what they consider their best interests;

(3) A reasonable time is allowed for exposure in the open market;

(4) Payment is made in terms of cash in United States dollars or in terms of financial arrangements comparable thereto; and

(5) The price represents the normal consideration for the property sold unaffected by special or creative financing or sales concessions granted by anyone associated with the sale.

(m) *Personal property*, for purposes of this subpart, means all tangible and movable property not considered real property or fixtures.

Farm Credit Administration　　　　　　　　　　　　　　　　　　　§ 614.4245

(n) *Qualified evaluator* means an individual who is competent, reputable, impartial, and has demonstrated sufficient training and experience to properly evaluate property of the type that is the subject of the evaluation. For the purposes of this definition, the term "qualified evaluator" includes an appraiser or valuator.

(o) *Real estate* means an identified parcel or tract of land, including improvements, if any.

(p) *Real estate-related financial transactions* means any transaction involving:

(1) The sale, lease, purchase, investment in, or exchange of real property, including interests in property or the financing thereof; or

(2) The refinancing of real property or interests in real property; or

(3) The use of real property or interests in real property as security for a loan or investment, including mortgage-backed securities.

(q) *Real property* means all interests, benefits, and rights inherent in the ownership of real estate.

(r) *Sales comparison approach* means the procedure that values property by comparing the subject property to similar properties located in relatively close proximity, having similar size and utility, and having been recently sold in arm's-length transactions (comparable sales). The sales comparison approach requires the evaluator to estimate the degree of similarity and difference between the subject property and comparable sales. Such comparison shall be made on the basis of conditions of sale, financing terms, market conditions, location, physical characteristics, and income characteristics. Appropriate adjustments shall be made to the sales price of the comparable property based on the identified deficiencies or superiorities of the subject property to arrive at a probable price for which the subject property could be sold on the date of the collateral evaluation.

(s) *State certified appraiser* means any individual who has satisfied the requirements for and has been certified as a real estate appraiser by a State or territory whose requirements for certification currently meet or exceed the minimum criteria for certification issued by the Appraiser Qualification Board of the Appraisal Foundation. No individual shall be a State certified appraiser unless such individual has achieved a passing grade on a suitable examination administered by a State or territory that is consistent with and equivalent to the Uniform State Certification Examination issued or endorsed by the Appraiser Qualification Board of the Appraisal Foundation. In addition, the Appraisal Subcommittee must not have issued a finding that the policies, practices, or procedures of the State or territory are inconsistent with title XI of FIRREA.

(t) *State licensed appraiser* means any individual who has satisfied the requirements for licensing and has been licensed as a real estate appraiser by a State or territory in which the licensing procedures comply with title XI of FIRREA and in which the Appraisal Subcommittee has not issued a finding that the policies, practices, or procedures of the State or territory are inconsistent with title XI of FIRREA.

(u) *Transaction value* means:

(1) For loans or other extensions of credit, the amount of the loan, loan commitment, or other extensions of credit;

(2) For sales, leases, purchases, investments in, or exchanges of real property, the market value of the property interest involved; and

(3) For the pools of loans or interests in real property, the transaction value of the individual loans or the market value of the real property interests comprising the pool.

(v) *USPAP* means the Uniform Standards of Professional Appraisal Practice adopted by the Appraisal Foundation.

(w) *Valuation* means the process of estimating a defined value of an identified interest or interests in a specific asset or assets as of a given date. A valuation results from the completion of a collateral evaluation that does not require an appraisal.

§ 614.4245 **Collateral evaluation policies.**

(a) The board of directors of each Farm Credit System institution that engages in lending or leasing secured by collateral shall adopt well-defined

§ 614.4250

and effective collateral evaluation policies and standards, that comply with the regulations in this subpart, to ensure that collateral evaluations are:

(1) Sufficiently descriptive and detailed to provide ample support to the institution's related credit decisions;

(2) Performed based on criteria established for the purpose of determining the circumstances under which collateral evaluations will be required and when they will be required. Such criteria must, at a minimum:

(i) Establish when an institution will require a collateral appraisal completed under the USPAP rather than a collateral valuation; and

(ii) Take into account such factors as market trends, market volatility, and various types of credit, loan servicing, collection, and liquidation actions; and

(3) Completed by a qualified evaluator in an unbiased manner.

(b) The policies and standards required by this section shall, at a minimum, address the criteria outlined in §§ 614.4250 through 614.4267 of this subpart.

(c) A Federal land bank association shall, with the approval of its respective Farm Credit bank, adopt collateral evaluation policies that are consistent with the bank's policies and standards.

(d) An institution's board of directors may adopt specific collateral evaluation requirements, consistent with the regulations in this subpart, for loans designated as part of a minimum information program.

[59 FR 46730, Sept. 12, 1994, as amended at 62 FR 51015, Sept. 30, 1997]

§ 614.4250 Collateral evaluation standards.

(a) When real, personal, or intangible property is taken as security for a loan or is the subject of a lease, an evaluation of such property shall be performed in accordance with § 614.4260 and the institutions' policies and procedures. Such a collateral evaluation shall be identified as either a collateral valuation or a collateral appraisal. Specifically, all collateral evaluations must:

(1) Value the subject property based upon market value as defined in § 614.4240(1);

(2) Be presented in a written format;

(3) Consider the purpose for which the property will be used and the property's highest and best use, if different from the intended use;

(4) Be sufficiently descriptive to enable the reader to ascertain the reasonableness of the estimated market value and the rationale for the estimate;

(5) Provide sufficient detail (including an identification and description of the property) and depth of analysis to reflect the relevant characteristics and complexity of the subject property;

(6) Analyze and report, as appropriate, for real, intangible, and/or personal property, on:

(i) The current income producing capacity of the property;

(ii) A reasonable marketing period for the property;

(iii) The current market conditions and trends that will affect projected income, to the extent such conditions will affect the value of the property;

(iv) The appropriate deductions and discounts as they would apply to the property, including but not limited to, those based on the condition of the property, as well as the specialization of the operation and property; and

(v) Potential liabilities, including those associated with any hazardous waste or other environmental concerns; and

(7) Include in the evaluation report a certification that the evaluation was not based on a requested minimum valuation or specific valuation or approval of a loan.

(b) For purposes of determining appraisal value as required in section 1.10(a) of the Act, the definition of market value and the requirements of this subpart shall apply.

§ 614.4255 Independence requirements.

(a) *Prohibitions.* For all personal and intangible property, and for all real property exempted under § 614.4260(c) of this subpart, no person may:

(1) Perform evaluations in connection with transactions in which such person has a direct or indirect interest, financial or otherwise, in the loan or subject property;

(2) As a director, vote on or approve a loan decision on which such person performed a collateral evaluation; or

Farm Credit Administration § 614.4260

(3) As a director, perform a collateral evaluation in connection with any transaction on which such person made or will be required to make a credit decision.

(b) *Officers and employees.* If the institution's internal control procedures required by § 618.8430 of this chapter include requirements for either a prior approval or post-review of credit decisions, officers and employees may:

(1) Participate in a vote or approval involving assets on which they performed a collateral evaluation; or

(2) Perform a collateral evaluation in connection with a transaction on which they have made or will be required to make a credit decision.

(c) *Real estate appraiser.* Except as provided in § 614.4260(c) of this subpart, all evaluations of real property that serve as the primary security for a loan shall be performed by a qualified real estate appraiser who has no direct or indirect interest, financial or otherwise, in the loan or subject property and is not engaged in the marketing, lending, collection, or credit decision processes of any of the following:

(1) A Farm Credit System institution making or originating the loan;

(2) A Farm Credit System institution operating under common management with the institution making or originating the loan; or

(3) A Farm Credit System institution purchasing an interest in the loan.

(d) *Fee appraisers.* Fee appraisers shall be engaged directly by the Farm Credit System institution or its agent, and shall have no direct or indirect interest, financial or otherwise, in the property or transaction. A Farm Credit System institution may accept a real estate appraisal that was prepared by an appraiser engaged directly by another Farm Credit System institution, by a United States Government agency, a Government-Sponsored Enterprise or by a financial institution subject to title XI of FIRREA.

(e) *Loan purchases.* No employee who, acting as a State licensed or State certified appraiser, performed a real estate appraisal on any collateral supporting a loan shall subsequently participate in any decision related to the loan purchase.

§ 614.4260 Evaluation requirements.

(a) *Valuation.* Valuations of personal and intangible property, as well as real property exempted under paragraph (c) of this section, shall be performed by qualified individuals who meet the established standards of this subpart and the Farm Credit System institution obtaining the collateral valuation.

(b) *Appraisal.* (1) Appraisals for real estate-related financial transactions with transaction values of more than $250,000 shall be performed by a qualified appraiser who is a State licensed or a State certified real estate appraiser.

(2) Appraisals for real estate-related financial transactions with transaction values of more than $1,000,000 shall be performed by a qualified appraiser who is a State certified real estate appraiser.

(c) *Appraisals not required.* An appraisal performed by a State certified or State licensed appraiser is not required for any real estate-related financial transaction in which any of the following conditions are met:

(1) The transaction value is $250,000 or less;

(2) The transaction is a "business loan" as defined in § 614.4240(e) that:

(i) Has a transaction value of $1,000,000 or less; and

(ii) Is not dependent on income derived from the sale or cash rental of real estate as the primary source of repayment;

(3) A lien on real property has been taken as collateral in an abundance of caution, and the application, when evaluated on the five basic credit factors, without considering the subject real estate, would support the credit decision that was based on other sources of repayment or collateral;

(4) A lien on real estate is not statutorily required and has been taken for purposes other than the real estate's value;

(5) Subsequent loan transactions (which include but are not limited to loan servicing actions, reamortizations, modifications of loan terms, and partial releases), provided that either:

(i) The transaction does not involve the advancement of new loan funds other than funds necessary to cover reasonable closing costs; or

133

§ 614.4265

(ii) There has been no obvious and material change in market conditions or physical aspects of the property that threatens the adequacy of the Farm Credit System institution's real estate collateral protection, even with the advancement of new loan funds;

(6) A Farm Credit System institution purchases a loan or an interest in a loan, pool of loans, or interests in real property, including mortgage-backed securities, provided that:

(i) The appraisal prepared for each loan, pooled loan, or real property interest, when originated, met the standards of this subpart, other Federal regulations adopted pursuant to FIRREA, or the requirements of the government-sponsored secondary market intermediaries under whose auspices the interest is sold; and

(ii) There has been no obvious and material change in market conditions or physical aspects of the property that would threaten the Farm Credit System institution's collateral position, or

(7) A Farm Credit System institution makes or purchases a loan secured by real estate, which loan is guaranteed by an agency of the United States Government and is supported by an appraisal that conforms to the requirements of the guaranteeing agency.

To qualify for exceptions in paragraphs (c)(1) through (c)(7) of this section from the requirements of this subpart, the institution must have documentation justifying the use of such exceptions in the applicable loan file(s). In addition, the institution must document that the repayment of a "business loan" is not dependent on income derived from the sale or cash rental of real estate.

(d) *FCA-required appraisals.* The FCA reserves the right to require an appraisal under this subpart whenever it believes it is necessary to address safety and soundness issues.

(e) *Reciprocity.* The requirements of this subpart are satisfied by the use of State certified or State licensed appraisers from any State provided that:

(1) The appraiser is qualified to perform such appraisals;

(2) The applicable Farm Credit System institution has established policies providing for such interstate appraisals; and

(3) The applicable State appraiser licensing and certification agency recognizes the certification or license of the appraiser's State of permanent certification or licensure.

[59 FR 46730, Sept. 12, 1994, as amended at 60 FR 2687, Jan. 11, 1995]

§ 614.4265 Real property evaluations.

(a) Real estate shall be valued on the basis of market value.

(b) Market value shall be determined by a reasonable valuation method that:

(1) Considers the income capitalization approach, the sales comparison approach, and/or the cost approach, as appropriate, to determine market value;

(2) Explains and documents the elimination of any approach not used.

(3) Reconciles the market values of the applicable approaches; and

(c) At a minimum, the institution shall develop and document the evaluation of the income and debt servicing capacity for the property and operation where the transaction value exceeds $250,000 and the real estate taken as collateral:

(1) Is an integral part of and supports the principal source of loan repayment; or

(2) Is not an integral part of and does not support the principal source of loan repayment, but has demonstrable rental market appeal, is statutorily required, and fully or partially constitutes an integral part of an agricultural or aquatic operation.

(d) The income-earning and debt-servicing capacity established under paragraph (c) of this section on such properties shall be documented as part of the credit analysis for any related loan action, whether or not the income capitalization approach value is used as the basis for the market value conclusion stated in the evaluation report.

(e) Collateral closely aligned with, an integral part of, and normally sold with real estate (fixtures) may be included in the value of the real estate. All other collateral associated with the real estate, but designated as personal property, shall be evaluated as personal property in accordance with §§ 614.4250 and 614.4266.

(f) The evaluation shall properly identify all nonagricultural influences,

Farm Credit Administration § 614.4325

including, but not limited to, urban development, mineral deposits, and commercial building development value, and the reasoning supporting the evaluator's highest and best-use conclusion.

(g) Where an evaluation of real property is completed by a fee appraiser, as defined in § 614.4240(g), the institution's standards shall include provisions for periodic collateral inspections performed by the institution's account officer or appropriate designee.

[59 FR 46730, Sept. 12, 1994, as amended at 71 FR 65387, Nov. 8, 2006; 75 FR 35968, June 24, 2010]

§ 614.4266 Personal and intangible property evaluations.

(a) Personal property and intangibles shall be valued on the basis of market value in accordance with the institution's evaluation standards and policies.

(b) Personal property evaluations shall include a source of comparisons of value (i.e., equipment dealer listings, Blue Book, market sales reports, etc.) and a description of the property being evaluated, including location of the property and, where applicable, quantity, species/variety, measure/weight, value per unit and in total, type of identification (such as brand, bill of lading, or warehouse receipt), quality, condition, and date.

(c) Evaluations of intangibles shall include a review and description of the documents supporting the property interests and the marketability of the intangible property, including applicable terms, conditions, and restrictions contained in the document that would affect the value of the property.

(d) Where an evaluation of personal or intangible property is completed by a fee appraiser, as defined in § 614.4240(g), the institution's standards shall include provisions for periodic collateral inspections and verification by the institution's account officer or appropriate designee.

(e) When a Farm Credit System institution deems an appraisal necessary, personal or intangible property shall be appraised in accordance with procedures and standards established by the institution by individuals deemed qualified by the institution to complete the work under the USPAP Competency and Ethics Provisions.

[59 FR 46730, Sept. 12, 1994, as amended at 59 FR 50964, Oct. 6, 1994]

§ 614.4267 Professional association membership; competency.

(a) *Membership in appraisal organizations.* A State certified appraiser or a State licensed appraiser may not be excluded from consideration for an assignment for a real estate-related transaction solely by virtue of membership or lack of membership in any particular appraisal organization.

(b) *Competency.* All staff and fee evaluators, including appraisers, performing evaluations in connection with real, personal, or intangible property taken as collateral in connection with extensions of credit must meet the qualification requirements of this subpart. However, an evaluator (as defined in § 614.4240(n)) may not be considered competent solely by virtue of being certified, licensed, or accredited. Any determination of competency shall be based on the individual's experience and educational background as they relate to the particular evaluation assignment for which such individual is being considered.

Subpart G [Reserved]

Subpart H—Loan Purchases and Sales

SOURCE: 57 FR 38247, Aug. 24, 1992, unless otherwise noted.

§ 614.4325 Purchase and sale of interests in loans.

(a) *Definitions.* For the purposes of this subpart, the following definitions shall apply:

(1) *Interests in loans* means ownership interests in the principal amount, interest payments, or any aspect of a loan transaction and transactions involving a pool of loans, including servicing rights.

(2) *Lead lender* means a lending institution having a direct contractual relationship with a borrower to advance funds, which institution sells or assigns an interest or interests in such loan to one or more other lenders.

§ 614.4325

(3) *Loan* means any extension of credit or similar financial assistance of the type authorized under the Act, such as guarantees, letters of credit, and other similar transactions.

(4) *Participating institution* means an institution that purchases a participation interest in a loan originated by another lender.

(5) *Sale with recourse* means a sale of a loan or an interest in a loan in which the seller:

(i) Retains some risk of loss from the transferred asset for any cause except the seller's breach of usual and customary warranties or representations designed to protect the purchaser against fraud or misrepresentation; or

(ii) Has an obligation to make payments of principal or interest to any party resulting from:

(A) Default on the payment of principal or interest on the loan by the borrower or guarantor or any other deficiencies in the obligor's performance;

(B) Changes in the market value of the assets after transfer;

(C) Any contractual relationship between the seller and purchaser incident to the transfer that, by its terms, could continue even after final payment, default, or other termination of the assets transferred; or

(D) Any other cause, except the retention at servicing rights alone shall not constitute recourse.

(6) *Subordinated participation interest* means an interest in a loan that bears the first risk of loss, including the retention of such an interest when a loan is sold to a pooler certified by the Federal Agricultural Mortgage Corporation pursuant to title VIII of the Act, or an interest in a pool of subordinated participation interests purchased to satisfy the requirements of title VIII of the Act with respect to a loan sold to such a certified pooler.

(b) *Authority to purchase and sell interests in loans.* Loans and interests in loans may only be sold in accordance with each institution's lending authorities, as set forth in subpart A of this part. No Farm Credit System institution may purchase any interest in a loan from an institution that is not a Farm Credit System institution, except:

(1) For the purpose of pooling and securitizing such loans under title VIII of the Act;

(2) Purchases of a participation interest that qualifies under the institution's lending authority, as set forth in subpart A of this part, and meets the requirements of § 614.4330 of this subpart;

(3) Loans purchased from the Federal Deposit Insurance Corporation, provided that the Farm Credit System institution with direct lending authority under title I, II or III of the Act:

(i) Conducts a thorough due diligence prior to purchase to ensure that the loan, or pool of loans, qualifies under the institution's lending authority as set forth in subpart A of this part, and meets scope of financing and eligibility requirements in subpart A or subpart B of part 613;

(ii) Obtains funding bank approval if a Farm Credit System association purchases loans or pools of loans that exceed 10 percent of total its capital;

(iii) Establishes a program whereby each eligible borrower of the loan purchased is offered an opportunity to acquire the institution's required minimum amount of voting stock;

(iv) Determines whether each loan purchased, except for loans purchased that could be financed only by a bank for cooperatives under title III of the Act, is a distressed loan as defined in § 617.7000, and provides borrowers of purchased loans who acquire voting stock the rights afforded in § 617.7000, subparts A, and D through G if the loan is distressed; and

(v) Divests eligible purchased loans when the borrowers elect not to acquire stock under the program offered in paragraph (b)(3)(iii) of this section in the same manner it would divest loans under its current business practices.

(vi) Includes information on loans purchased under authority of this section in the Reports of Condition and Performance required under § 621.12 of this chapter, in the format prescribed by FCA reporting instructions.

(c) *Policies.* Each Farm Credit System institution that is authorized to sell or purchase interests in loans under subpart A of this part shall exercise that authority in accordance with a policy adopted by its board of directors that addresses the following matters:

(1) The types of purchasers to which the institution is authorized to sell interests in loans;

(2) The types of loans in which the institution may purchase or sell an interest and the types of interests which may be purchased or sold;

(3) The underwriting standards to be applied in the purchase of interests in loans:

(4) Such limitations on the aggregate principal amount of interests in loans that the institution may purchase from a single institution as are necessary to diversify risk, and such limitations on the aggregate amount the institution may purchase from all institutions as are necessary to assure that service to the territory is not impeded;

(5) Provision for the identification and reporting of loans in which interests are sold or purchased;

(6) Requirements for providing and securing in a timely manner adequate credit and other information needed to make an independent credit judgment; and

(7) Any limitations or conditions to which sales or purchases are subject that the board deems appropriate, including arbitration.

(d) *Purchase and sale agreements.* Agreements to purchase or sell an interest in a loan shall, at a minimum:

(1) Identify the particular loan(s) to be covered by the agreement;

(2) Provide for the transfer of credit and other borrower information on a timely and continuing basis;

(3) Provide for sharing, dividing, or assigning collateral;

(4) Identify the nature of the interest(s) sold or purchased;

(5) Set forth the rights and obligations of the parties and the terms and conditions of the sale; and

(6) Contain any terms necessary for the appropriate administration of the loan and the protection of the interests of the Farm Credit System institution.

(e) *Independent credit judgment.* Each institution that purchases an interest in a loan shall make a judgment on the creditworthiness of the borrower that is independent of the originating or lead lender and any intermediary seller or broker prior to the purchase of the interest and prior to any servicing action that alters the terms of the original agreement, which judgment shall not be delegated to any person(s) not employed by the institution. A Farm Credit System institution that purchases a loan or any interest therein may use information, such as appraisals or collateral inspections, furnished by the originating or lead lender, or any intermediary seller or broker; however, the purchasing Farm Credit System institution shall independently evaluate such information when exercising its independent credit judgment. No employee who performed a real estate appraisal on any collateral supporting a loan shall participate in the decision to purchase that loan. The independent credit judgment shall be documented by a credit analysis that considers factors set forth in the loan underwriting standards adopted pursuant to §614.4150 of this part and is independent of the originating institution and any intermediary seller or broker. The credit analysis shall consider such credit and other borrower information as would be required by a prudent lender and shall include an evaluation of the capacity and reliability of the servicer. Boards of directors of jointly managed institutions shall adopt procedures to ensure that the interests of their respective shareholders are protected in participation between such institutions.

(f) *Limitations.* The aggregate principal amount of interests in loans purchased from a single lead lender and the aggregate principal amount of interests in loans purchased from other institutions shall not exceed the limits set in the institution's policy.

(g) *Sales with recourse.* When a loan or interest in a loan is sold with recourse, it shall be accorded the following treatment:

(1) The loan shall be considered, to the extent of the recourse, an extension of credit by the purchaser to the seller, as well as an extension of credit from the seller to the borrower(s), for the purpose of determining whether credit extensions to a borrower are within the lending limits established in subpart J of this part.

§ 614.4330

(2) The amount of the loan subject to the recourse agreement shall be considered a loan sold with recourse for the purpose of computing permanent capital ratios.

(h) *Transactions through agents.* Transactions pertaining to purchases of loans, including the judgement on creditworthiness, may be performed through an agent, provided that:

(1) The institution establishes the necessary criteria in a written agency agreement that outlines, at a minimum, the scope of the agency relationship and obligates the agent to comply with the institution's underwriting standards;

(2) The institution periodically reviews the agency relationship to determine if the agent's actions are in the best interest of the institution;

(3) The agent must be independent of the seller or intermediate broker in the transaction; and

(4) If an association's funding bank serves as its agent, the agency agreement must provide that:

(i) The association can terminate the agreement upon no more than 60 days notice to the bank;

(ii) The association may, in its discretion, require the bank to purchase from the association any interest in a loan that the association determines does not comply with the terms of the agency agreement or the association's loan underwriting standards.

[57 FR 38247, Aug. 24, 1992, as amended at 58 FR 40321, July 28, 1993; 62 FR 51015, Sept. 30, 1997; 64 FR 34517, June 28, 1999; 67 FR 1285, Jan. 10, 2002; 76 FR 30250, May 25, 2011]

§ 614.4330 Loan participations.

Agreements to purchase or sell a participation interest shall be subject to the provisions of § 614.4325 of this subpart, and, in addition, shall satisfy the requirements of this section.

(a) *Participation agreements.* Agreements to purchase or sell a participation interest in a loan shall, in addition to meeting the requirements of § 614.4325(d) of this subpart, at a minimum:

(1) Define the duties and responsibilities of the participating institution and the lead lender, and/or the servicing institution, if different from the lead lender.

(2) Provide for loan servicing and monitoring of the servicer;

(3) Set forth authorization and conditions for action in the event of borrower distress or default;

(4) Provide for sharing of risk;

(5) Set forth conditions for the offering and acceptance of the loan participation and termination of the agreement;

(6) Provide for sharing of fees, interest charges, and costs between participating institutions;

(7) Provide for a method of resolution of disagreements arising under the agreement between two or more institutions;

(8) Specify whether the contract is assignable by either party; and

(9) Provide for the issuance of certificates evidencing a participation interest in a loan.

(b) *Intrasystem participations.* Loans participated between or among Farm Credit System institutions shall meet the borrower eligibility, membership, loan term, loan amount, loan security, and stock purchase requirements of the originating lender.

[57 FR 38247, Aug. 24, 1992, as amended at 67 FR 1285, Jan. 10, 2002]

§ 614.4335 Borrower stock requirements.

(a) *In general.* Except as provided in paragraph (b) of this section, a borrower shall meet the minimum borrower stock purchase requirements as a condition of obtaining a loan.

(b) *Loans designated for sale into a secondary market.* (1) An institution's bylaws may provide that the institution's minimum borrower stock purchase requirements do not apply if a loan is designated, at the time it is made, for sale into a secondary market.

(2) If a loan designated for sale under paragraph (b)(1) of this section is not sold into a secondary market during the 180-day period that begins on the date of designation, the institution's minimum borrower stock purchase requirements shall apply.

(c) *Retirement of borrower stock*—(1) *In general.* Borrower stock may be retired only if the institution meets the minimum permanent capital requirements imposed by the FCA pursuant to the

Farm Credit Administration

§ 614.4340

Act or regulations and, except as provided in paragraph (c)(2) of this section, in accordance with the following:

(i) Borrower stock may be retired if the entire loan is sold without recourse, provided that when the loan is sold without recourse to another Farm Credit System institution, the borrower may elect to hold stock in either the selling or purchasing institution.

(ii) Borrower stock may not be retired when the entire loan is sold with recourse.

(iii) When an interest in a loan is sold without recourse, a proportionate amount of borrower stock may be retired, but in no event may stock be retired below the institution's minimum stock purchase requirements for the interest retained.

(iv) If an institution repurchases a loan on which the stock has been retired, the borrower shall be required to repurchase stock in the amount of the minimum stock purchase requirement.

(2) *Loans sold into a secondary market.* An institution's bylaws may provide that all outstanding voting stock held by a borrower with respect to a loan shall be retired when the loan is sold into a secondary market.

(d) *Applicability.* In the case of a loan sold into a secondary market under title VIII of the Act, paragraphs (b)(1) and (c)(2) of this section apply regardless of whether the institution retains a subordinated participation interest in a loan or pool of loans or contributes to a cash reserve.

[62 FR 63646, Dec. 2, 1997]

§ 614.4337 Disclosure to borrowers.

When a loan or an interest in a loan other than a participation interest is sold with servicing rights, the disclosure shall be made to the borrower in accordance with this section:

(a) The selling institution shall disclose to the borrower at least 10 days prior to the borrower's next payment date;

(1) The name, address, and telephone number of the purchasing institution;

(2) The name and address of the party to whom payment is to be made;

(3) A description of the impact of the sale on statutory borrower rights after the sale;

(4) Any terms in the agreement that would permit a purchaser to change the terms or conditions of the loan.

(b) A Farm Credit System institution that purchases a loan or a non-participation interest therein shall not take any servicing action that adversely affects the borrower until it ensures that disclosure has been made to the borrower of:

(1) The name, address, and telephone number of the purchasing institution; and

(2) The address where the payment should be sent.

Subpart I—Loss-Sharing Agreements

§ 614.4340 General.

(a) Upon the approval of the board of directors of the respective Farm Credit System institutions, any System bank, association, or service corporation or service association may enter into an agreement to share loan and other losses with any other institution(s) of the System. As appropriate, a loss-sharing agreement may contain provisions relating to definitions of terms, terms and conditions for activation, determinations of assessment formulas, limitations on assessments, reimbursements, administration, arbitration, and provisions for amendment and termination.

(b) System institutions may agree among themselves to share losses for the purpose of protecting against the impairment of capital stock or participation certificates, or for any other purpose. Agreements may provide for sharing losses that arise in the future or that were recognized by one or more of the signatory institutions before the date of the agreement. Agreements may contain provisions that are not entirely reciprocal among the signatories to the agreement. Loss-sharing agreements can provide for the sharing of loan losses, operating losses, casualty losses, losses on high risk assets, or any other losses.

[49 FR 48910, Dec. 17, 1984, as amended at 54 FR 1151, Jan. 12, 1989; 54 FR 50736, Dec. 11, 1989]

§ 614.4345 Guaranty agreements.

Guaranty agreements under which a percentage of the risk associated with specific loans is assumed may be entered into by or among System banks and associations.

[49 FR 48910, Dec. 17, 1984, as amended at 54 FR 1151, Jan. 12, 1989; 54 FR 50736, Dec. 11, 1989]

Subpart J—Lending and Leasing Limits

SOURCE: 58 FR 40321, July 28, 1993, unless otherwise noted.

§ 614.4350 Definitions.

For purposes of this subpart, the following definitions shall apply:

(a) *Borrower* means an individual, partnership, joint venture, trust, corporation, or other business entity to which an institution has made a loan or a commitment to make a loan either directly or indirectly. Excluded are a Farm Credit System association or other financing institution that comply with the criteria in section 1.7(b) of the Act and the regulations in subpart P of this part. For the purposes of this subpart, the term "borrower" includes any customer to whom an institution has made a lease or a commitment to make a lease.

(b) *Commitment* means a legally binding obligation to extend credit, enter into lease financing, purchase or participate in loans or leases, or pay the obligation of another, which becomes effective at the time such commitment is made.

(c) *Loan* means any extension of, or commitment to extend, credit authorized under the Act whether it results from direct negotiations between a lender and a borrower or is purchased from or discounted for another lender. This includes participation interests. The term "loan" includes loans and leases outstanding, obligated but undisbursed commitments to lend or lease, contracts of sale, notes receivable, other similar obligations, guarantees, and all types of leases. An institution "makes a loan or lease" when it enters into a commitment to lend or lease, advances new funds, substitutes a different borrower or lessee for a borrower or lessee who is released, or where any other person's liability is added to the outstanding loan, lease or commitment.

(d) *Primary liability* means an obligation to repay that is not conditioned upon an unsuccessful prior demand on another party.

(e) *Secondary liability* means an obligation to repay that only arises after an unsuccessful demand on another party.

[58 FR 40321, July 28, 1993, as amended at 64 FR 34517, June 28, 1999]

§ 614.4351 Computation of lending and leasing limit base.

(a) *Lending and leasing limit base.* An institution's lending and leasing limit base is composed of the permanent capital of the institution, as defined in § 615.5201 of this chapter, with adjustments applicable to the institution provided for in § 615.5207 of this chapter, and with the following further adjustments:

(1) Where one institution invests in another institution in connection with the sale of a loan participation interest, the amount of investment in the institution purchasing this participation interest that is owned by the institution originating the loan shall be counted in the lending and leasing limit base of the originating institution and shall not be counted in the lending and leasing limit base of the purchasing institution.

(2) Stock protected under section 4.9A of the Act may be included in the lending and leasing limit base until January 1, 1998.

(3) Any amounts of preferred stock not eligible to be included in total surplus as defined in § 615.5301(i) of this chapter must be deducted from the lending limit base.

(b) *Timing of calculation.* The lending limit base will be calculated on a monthly basis as of the preceding month end.

[58 FR 40321, July 28, 1993, as amended at 59 FR 37403, July 22, 1994; 64 FR 34517, June 28, 1999; 70 FR 35348, June 17, 2005; 70 FR 53907, Sept. 13, 2005]

§ 614.4352 Farm Credit Banks and agricultural credit banks.

(a) *Farm Credit Banks.* No Farm Credit Bank may make or discount a loan to a borrower, if the consolidated amount of all loans outstanding and undisbursed commitments to that borrower exceed 25 percent of the bank's lending and leasing limit base.

(b) *Agricultural credit banks.* (1) No agricultural credit bank may make or discount a loan to a borrower under the authority of title I of the Act, if the consolidated amount of all loans outstanding and undisbursed commitments to that borrower exceeds 25 percent of the bank's lending and leasing limit base.

(2) No agricultural credit bank may make or discount a loan to a borrower under the authority of title III of the Act, if the consolidated amount of all loans outstanding and undisbursed commitments to that borrower exceeds the lending and leasing limits prescribed in § 614.4355 of this subpart.

[58 FR 40321, July 28, 1993, as amended at 64 FR 34517, June 28, 1999]

EFFECTIVE DATE NOTE: At 76 FR 29997, May 24, 2011, § 614.4352 was amended by removing the comma after the word "borrower" and removing the number "25" and adding in its place, the number "15" in paragraph (a); removing the comma after the word "Act" and removing "exceeds 25" and adding in its place "exceed 15" in paragraph (b)(1); and removing the comma after the word "Act" and removing "exceeds" and adding in its place "exceed" in paragraph (b)(2), effective July 1, 2012.

§ 614.4353 Direct lender associations.

No association may make a loan to a borrower, if the consolidated amount of all loans outstanding and undisbursed commitments to that borrower exceeds 25 percent of the association's lending and leasing limit base.

[58 FR 40321, July 28, 1999, as amended at 64 FR 34517, June 28, 1999]

EFFECTIVE DATE NOTE: At 76 FR 29997, May 24, 2011, § 614.4353 was amended by adding the words "direct lender" after the word "No"; removing the comma after the word "borrower"; and removing "exceeds 25" and adding in its place "exceed 15", effective July 1, 2012.

§ 614.4354 Federal land bank associations.

No Federal land bank association may assume endorsement liability on any loan if the total amount of the association's endorsement liability on loans outstanding and undisbursed commitments to that borrower would exceed 25 percent of the association's lending and leasing limit base.

[58 FR 40321, July 28, 1999, as amended at 64 FR 34517, June 28, 1999]

EFFECTIVE DATE NOTE: At 76 FR 29997, May 24, 2011, § 614.4354 was removed, effective July 1, 2012.

§ 614.4355 Banks for cooperatives.

No bank for cooperatives may make a loan if the consolidated amount of all loans outstanding and undisbursed commitments to that borrower exceeds the following percentages of the lending and leasing limit base of the bank:

(a) *Basic limit.* (1) Term loans to eligible cooperatives: 25 percent.

(2) Term loans to foreign and domestic parties: 10 percent.

(3) Lease loans qualifying under § 614.4020(a)(3) and applying to the lessee: 25 percent.

(4) Standby letters of credit qualifying under § 614.4810: 35 percent.

(5) Guarantees qualifying under § 614.4800: 35 percent.

(6) Seasonal loans exclusive of commodity loans qualifying under § 614.4231: 35 percent.

(7) Foreign trade receivables qualifying under § 614.4700: 50 percent.

(8) Commodity loans qualifying under § 614.4231: 50 percent.

(9) Export and import letters of credit qualifying under § 614.4720: 50 percent.

(b) *Total limit.* (1) The sum of term and seasonal loans exclusive of commodity loans qualifying under § 614.4231: 35 percent.

(2) The sum of paragraphs (a)(1) through (a)(9) of this section: 50 percent.

[58 FR 40321, July 28, 1993, as amended at 62 FR 51015, Sept. 30, 1997; 64 FR 34517, June 28, 1999; 71 FR 65387, Nov. 8, 2006]

§ 614.4356 Farm Credit Leasing Services Corporation.

The Farm Credit Leasing Services Corporation may enter into a lease agreement with a lessee if the consolidated amount of all leases and undisbursed commitments to that lessee or any related entities does not exceed 25 percent of its lending and leasing limit base.

[64 FR 34517, June 28, 1999]

EFFECTIVE DATE NOTE: At 76 FR 29997, May 24, 2011, § 614.4356 was amended by removing the number "25" and adding in its place, the number "15", effective July 1, 2012.

§ 614.4357 Banks for cooperatives look-through notes.

Where a bank for cooperatives makes a loan to an eligible borrower that is secured by notes of individuals or business entities, the basic lending limits provided in § 614.4355 may be applied to each original notemaker rather than to the loan to the eligible borrower, if:

(a) Each note is current and carries a full recourse endorsement or unconditional guarantee by the borrower;

(b) The bank determines the financial condition, repayment capacity, and other credit factors of the loan to the original maker reasonably justify the credit granted by the endorser; and

(c) The loans are fully supported by documented loan files, which include, at a minimum:

(1) A credit report supporting the bank's finding that the financial condition, repayment capacity, and other factors of the maker of the notes being pledged justify the credit extended by the bank and/or endorser;

(2) A certification by a bank officer designated for that purpose by the loan or executive committee that the financial responsibility of the original notemaker has been evaluated by the loan committee and the bank is relying primarily on each such maker for the payment of the obligation; and

(3) Other credit information normally required of a borrower when making and administering a loan.

[58 FR 40321, July 28, 1993. Redesignated at 64 FR 34517, June 28, 1999]

§ 614.4358 Computation of obligations.

(a) *Inclusions.* The computation of total loans to each borrower for the purpose of computing their lending and leasing limit shall include:

(1) The total unpaid principal of all loans and lease balances outstanding and the total amount of undisbursed commitments except as excluded by paragraph (b) of this section. This amount shall include loans that have been charged off on the books of the institution in whole or in part but have not been collected, except to the extent that such amounts are not legally collectible;

(2) Purchased interests in loans, including participation interests, to the extent of the amount of the purchased interest, including any undisbursed commitment;

(3) Loans attributed to a borrower in accordance with § 614.4359.

(b) *Exclusions.* The following loans when adequately documented in the loan file, may be excluded from loans to a borrower subject to the lending and leasing limit:

(1) Any loan or portion of a loan that carries a full faith and credit performance guaranty or surety of any department, agency, bureau, board, commission, or establishment of the United States government, provided there is no evidence to suggest that the guaranty has become unenforceable and the institution can demonstrate that it is in compliance with the terms and conditions of the guaranty.

(2) Any loan or portion of a loan guaranteed by a Farm Credit System institution, pursuant to the provisions of § 614.4345 on guaranty agreements. This exclusion does not apply to the institution providing the guaranty.

(3) Any loan or portion of a loan that is secured by bonds, notes, certificates of indebtedness, or Treasury bills of the United States or by other obligations guaranteed as to principal and interest by the United States government, provided the loans are fully secured by the current market value of such obligations. If the market value of the collateral declines to below the balance of the loan, and the entire loan, individually, or when combined

Farm Credit Administration § 614.4359

with other loans and undisbursed commitments to or attributed to the borrower, causes the borrower's total indebtedness to exceed the institution's lending limit, the institution shall have 5 business days to bring the loan into conformance before it shall be deemed to be in violation of the lending limit.

(4) Interests in loans sold, including participation interests, when the sale agreement meets the following requirements:

(i) The interest must be sold without recourse; and

(ii) The agreement under which the interest is sold must provide for the sharing of all payments of principal, collection expenses, collateral proceeds, and risk of loss on a pro rata basis according to the percentage interest in the principal amount of the loan. Agreements that provide for the pro rata sharing to commence at the time of default or similar event, as defined in the agreement under which the interest is sold, shall be considered to be pro rata agreements, notwithstanding the fact that advances are made and payments are distributed on a basis other than pro rata prior to that time.

(5) Interests in leases sold when the sale agreement provides that:

(i) The interest sold must be:

(A) An undivided interest in all the lease payments or the residual value of all the leased property; or

(B) A fractional undivided interest in the total lease transaction;

(ii) The interest must be sold without recourse; and

(iii) Sharing of all lease payments must be on a pro rata basis according to the percentage interest in the lease payments.

(6) Loans sold in their entirety to a pooler certified by the Federal Agricultural Mortgage Corporation, if an interest in a pool of subordinated participation interests is purchased to satisfy the requirements of title VIII of the Act.

[58 FR 40321, July 28, 1993. Redesignated and amended at 64 FR 34517, June 28, 1999; 67 FR 1285, Jan. 10, 2002]

§ 614.4359 Attribution rules.

(a) For the purpose of applying the lending and leasing limit to the indebtedness of a borrower, loans to a related borrower shall be combined with loans outstanding to the borrower and attributed to the borrower when any one of the following three conditions exist:

(1) *Liability.* (i) The borrower has primary or secondary liability on a loan made to the related borrower. The amount of such loan attributable to the borrower is limited to the amount of the borrower's liability.

(ii) This section does not require attribution of a guarantee taken out of an abundance of caution. To qualify for the abundance of caution exception to the requirements of this subpart, the institution must document in the loan file that the loan, when evaluated under the loan underwriting standards adopted pursuant to § 614.4150 of this part without considering the guarantee, would support the credit decision under the same basic terms and conditions.

(iii) For the banks for cooperatives and agricultural credit banks operating under title III authorities of the Act, look-through notes are exempt from the lending limit provisions provided they meet the criteria of § 614.4357.

(2) *Financial interdependence.* The operations of a borrower and related borrower are financially interdependent. Financial interdependence exists if the borrower is the primary source of repayment for a related borrower's loan, or if the operations of the borrower and the related borrower are commingled.

(i) The borrower shall be considered the primary source of repayment on the loan to the related borrower if the borrower is obligated to supply 50 percent or more of the related borrower's annual gross receipts, *and* reliance on the income from one another is such that, regardless of the solvency and liquidity of the borrower's operations, the debt service obligation of the related borrower could not be met if income flow from the borrower is interrupted or terminated. For the purpose of this paragraph, gross receipts include, but are not limited to, revenues, intercompany loans, dividends and capital contributions.

§ 614.4359

(ii) The assets or operations of the borrower and related borrower are considered to be commingled if they cannot be separated without materially impacting the economic survival of the individual operations and their ability to repay their loans.

(3) *Control.* The borrower directly or indirectly controls the related borrower. A borrower is deemed to control a related borrower if either paragraph (a)(3)(i) or (a)(3)(ii) of this section exist:

(i) The borrower, directly or acting through one or more other persons, owns 50 percent or more of the stock of the related borrower; or

(ii) The borrower, directly or acting through one or more other persons, owns or has the power to vote 25 percent or more of the voting stock of a related borrower, and meets at least one of the following three conditions:

(A) The borrower shares a common directorate or management with a related borrower. A common directorate is deemed to exist when a majority of the directors, trustees, or other persons performing similar functions of one borrower also serves the other borrower in a like capacity. A common management is deemed to exist if any employee of the borrower holds the position of chief executive officer, chief operating officer, chief financial officer, or an equivalent position in the related borrower's organization.

(B) The borrower controls in any manner the election of a majority of directors of a related borrower.

(C) The borrower exercises or has the power to exercise a controlling influence over management of a related borrower's operations through the provisions of management placement or marketing agreements, or providing services such as insurance carrier or bookkeeping.

(b) Each institution shall make provisions for appropriately designating loans to a related borrower that are combined with the borrower's loan and attributed to the borrower to ensure that loans to the borrower are within the lending and leasing limits.

(c) *Attribution rules table.* For the purposes of applying the lending and leasing limit to the indebtedness of a borrower, loans to a related borrower shall be combined with loans outstanding to the borrower and attributed to the borrower when any one of three attribution rules are met as outlined in Table 1.

TABLE 1

Attribution rule	Criteria per § 614.4359	Attribute
(A) Liability .... *to the extent of the borrower's liability.	Borrower has primary or secondary liability .... Borrower's liability is taken out of an abundance of caution .... Look-through notes (BC only)	Yes.* No.* No.
(B) Financial Interdependence .... (Economic survival of the borrower's operation will materially impact economic survival of the related borrowers operation).	Source of Repayment: Borrower is obligated to supply 50 percent or more of related borrower's annual gross receipts, *and* reliance on the income from one another is such that the debt service of the related borrower could not be met if income flow from the borrower is interrupted or terminated. Commingled Operations: Assets or operations of the borrowers are commingled and cannot be separated without materially impacting the borrowers' repayment capacity	Yes. Yes.
(C) Control .... (The borrower, directly or indirectly, controls the related borrower).	The borrower owns 50 percent or more of the stock of the related borrower. The borrower owns or has the power to vote 25 percent or more of the voting stock of a related borrower, and (1) Shares a common directorate or management with a related borrower, or (2) Controls the election of a majority of directors of a related borrower, or (3) Exercises a controlling influence over management of a related borrower's operations through the provisions of management placement or marketing agreements, or providing services such as insurance carrier or bookkeeping.	Yes. Yes.

[58 FR 40321, July 28, 1993, as amended at 62 FR 51015, Sept. 30, 1997. Redesignated and amended at 64 FR 34517, June 28, 1999]

§ 614.4360 Lending and leasing limit violations.

(a) Each loan, except loans that are grandfathered under the provisions of § 614.4361, shall be in compliance with the lending and leasing limit on the date the loan is made, and at all times thereafter. Except as provided for in paragraph (b) of this section, loans which are in violation of the lending and leasing limit shall comply with the provisions of § 615.5090 of this chapter.

(b) Under the following conditions a loan that violates the lending and leasing limit shall be exempt from the provisions of § 615.5090 of this chapter:

(1) A loan in which the total amount of principal outstanding and undisbursed commitments exceed the lending and leasing limit because of a decline in permanent capital after the loan was made.

(2) Loans on which funds are advanced pursuant to a commitment that was within the lending and leasing limit at the time the commitment was made, even if the lending and leasing limit subsequently declines.

(3) A loan that exceeds the lending and leasing limit as a result of the consolidation of the debt of two or more borrowers as a consequence of a merger or the acquisition of one borrower's operations by another borrower. Such a loan may be extended or renewed, for a period not to exceed 1 year from the date of such merger or acquisition, during which period the institution may advance and/or readvance funds not to exceed the greater of:

(i) 110 percent of the advances to the borrower in the prior calendar year; or

(ii) 110 percent of the average of the advances to the borrower in the past 3 calendar years.

(c) For all lending and leasing limit violations except those exempted under § 614.4360(b)(3), within 90 days of the identification of the violation, the institution must develop a written plan prescribing the specific actions that will be taken by the institution to bring the total amount of loans and commitments outstanding or attributed to that borrower within the new lending and leasing limit, and must document the plan in the loan file.

(d) All leases, except those permitted under § 614.4361, reading "effective date of this subpart" in § 614.4361(a) and "effective date of these regulations" in § 614.4361(b) as "effective date of this amendment," must comply with the lending and leasing limit on the date the lease is made, and at all times after that.

(e) Nothing in this section limits the authority of the FCA to take administrative action, including, but not limited to, monetary penalties, as a result of lending and leasing limit violations.

[58 FR 40321, July 28, 1993. Redesignated and amended at 64 FR 34517, June 28, 1999]

§ 614.4361 Transition.

(a) A loan (not including a commitment) made or attributed to a borrower prior to the effective date of this subpart, which does not comply with the limits contained in this subpart, will not be considered a violation of the lending and leasing limits during the existing contract terms of such loans. A new loan must conform with the rules set forth in this subpart. A new loan includes but is not limited to:

(1) Funds advanced in excess of existing commitment;

(2) A different borrower is substituted for a borrower who is subsequently released; or

(3) An additional person becomes an obligor on the loan.

(b) A commitment made prior to the effective date of these regulations which exceeds the lending and leasing limit may be funded to the full extent of the legal commitment. Any advances that exceed the lending and leasing limit are subject to the provisions prescribed in § 614.4360.

[58 FR 40321, July 28, 1993. Redesignated and amended at 64 FR 34517, 34518, June 28, 1999]

§ 614.4362 Loan and lease concentration risk mitigation policy.

The board of directors of each title I, II, and III System institution must adopt and ensure implementation of a written policy to effectively measure, limit and monitor exposures to concentration risks resulting from the institution's lending and leasing activities.

(a) *Policy elements.* The policy must include:

(1) A purpose and objective;

§ 614.4450

(2) Clearly defined and consistently used terms;

(3) Quantitative methods to measure and limit identified exposures to significant and reasonably foreseeable loan and lease concentration risks (as set forth in paragraph (b) of this section); and

(4) Internal controls that delineate authorities delegated to management, authorities retained by the board, and a process for addressing exceptions and reporting requirements.

(b) *Quantitative methods.* (1) At a minimum, the quantitative methods included in the policy must measure and limit identified exposures to significant and reasonably foreseeable concentration risks emanating from:

(i) A single borrower;

(ii) A single-industry sector;

(iii) A single counterparty; or

(iv) Other lending activities unique to the institution because of its territory, the nature and scope of its activities and its risk-bearing capacity.

(2) In determining concentration limits, the policy must consider other risk factors that could identify significant and reasonably foreseeable loan and lease losses. Such risk factors could include borrower risk ratings, the institution's relationship with the borrower, the borrower's knowledge and experience, loan structure and purpose, type or location of collateral (including loss given default ratings), loans to emerging industries or industries outside of an institution's area of expertise, out-of-territory loans, counterparties, or weaknesses in due diligence practices.

[76 FR 29997, May 24, 2011]

EFFECTIVE DATE NOTE: At 76 FR 29997, May 24, 2011, § 614.4362 was added, effective July 1, 2012.

Subparts K–L [Reserved]

Subpart M—Loan Approval Requirements

§ 614.4450 General requirements.

Authority for loan approval is vested in the Farm Credit banks and associations.

[51 FR 41947, Nov. 20, 1986]

§ 614.4460 Loan approval responsibility.

Approval of the following loans is the responsibility of each district board of directors. The responsibility may be discharged by prior approval of such loans by the appropriate bank board, or establishment of a policy under which the authority to approve such loans is delegated to bank management (except paragraphs (d) and (e) of this section which cannot be delegated to management). If the approval of such loans is to be delegated to bank management, the loans are to be submitted promptly for post review by the bank board and a report disclosing all material facts relating to the credit relationship involved shall be submitted annually by bank management to the district board.

(a) Loans to a member of the Farm Credit Administration Board.

(b) Loans to a member of the district board.

(c) Loans to a cooperative of which a member of a bank board of directors is a member of the board of directors, an officer, or employee.

(d) Loans to the president of a Farm Credit bank.

(e) Loans to employees of the Farm Credit Administration.

(f) Loans where directors, officers or employees designated above:

(1) Are to receive proceeds of the loan in excess of an amount prescribed by an appropriate bank board, or

(2) Are stockholders or owners of equity in a legal entity to which the loan is to be made wherein they have a significant personal or beneficial interest in the loan proceeds thereof or the security, or

(3) Are endorsers, guarantors or co-makers in excess of an amount prescribed by an appropriate bank board.

[38 FR 27837, Oct. 9, 1973, as amended at 39 FR 29585, Aug. 16, 1974. Redesignated at 46 FR 51878, Oct. 22, 1981, and amended at 51 FR 41947, Nov. 20, 1986; 54 FR 1151, Jan. 12, 1989; 54 FR 50736, Dec. 11, 1989; 56 FR 2674, Jan. 24, 1991]

§ 614.4470 Loans subject to bank approval.

(a) The following loans (unless such loans are of a type prohibited under part 612) shall be subject to prior approval of the bank supervising the association in which the loan application originates:

(1) Loans to a director of the association.

(2) Loans to a director of an association which is under joint management when the application originates in one of the associations.

(3) Loans to an employee of the association.

(4) Loans to an employee of an association which is under joint management when the application originates in one of the associations.

(5) Loans to bank employees when the application originates in one of the associations supervised by the employing bank.

(b) Loans to any borrower shall be subject to the prior approval of the bank supervising the association in which the loan application originates whenever a director or an employee of the association or an employee of the bank supervising the association:

(1) Will receive proceeds of the loan in excess of the amount prescribed by the supervising bank board, or

(2) Has a significant personal or beneficial interest in the loan, the proceeds, or the security, or controls the borrower, or

(3) Is an endorser, guarantor, or comaker with respect to the loan in excess of an amount prescribed by the supervising bank board.

(c) Any loan which will result in any one borrower being obligated (as defined in subpart J of this part) in excess of an amount established by the supervising bank under its policies for delegation of authority to associations shall be subject to prior approval of the supervising bank.

[47 FR 49832, Nov. 3, 1982, as amended at 58 FR 40324, July 28, 1993; 60 FR 20010, Apr. 24, 1995]

Subpart N [Reserved]

Subpart O—Special Lending Programs

§ 614.4525 General.

(a) To provide the best possible credit service to farmers, ranchers, and producers or harvesters of aquatic products, bank and association boards may adopt policies permitting the bank or association to enter into agreements with agents, dealers, cooperatives, other lenders, and individuals to facilitate its making of loans to eligible farmers, ranchers, and producers or harvesters of aquatic products.

(b) A bank or association, pursuant to its board policies, may enter into an agreement with third parties that will accrue to the benefit of the borrower and the lender to perform functions in the making or servicing of loans other than the evaluation and approval of loans. When such an agreement is developed, and the territory covered by the agreement extends outside the territorial limits of the originating association or bank, the written consent of all affected banks or associations is required. Reasonable compensation may be paid for services rendered.

(c) Production credit associations and agricultural credit associations may enter into agreements with private dealers or cooperatives permitting them to take applications for loans from the association to purchase farm or aquatic equipment, supplies, and machinery. Such agreements shall normally be limited to persons or businesses selling to farmers, ranchers, or producers or harvesters of aquatic products and shall contain credit limits consistent with sound credit standards. When the sales territory of a dealer or cooperative extends outside the territory of the originating association or the Farm Credit district, written consent of each bank and association affected shall be obtained before making such loans. Reasonable compensation may be paid or charged to a dealer or cooperative for services rendered in connection with such programs.

(d) Farm Credit System institutions that are direct lenders may enter into memoranda of understanding among themselves or with other lenders for the simultaneous processing and closing of loans to a mutual borrower. The

§ 614.4530

basic policies and principles of each System lender shall apply.

[47 FR 12146, Mar. 22, 1982. Redesignated at 53 FR 35454, Sept. 14, 1988, and amended at 55 FR 24886, June 19, 1990; 61 FR 67187, Dec. 20, 1996]

§ 614.4530 Special loans, production credit associations and agricultural credit associations.

Under policies approved by the bank board and procedures developed by the bank, production credit associations and agricultural credit associations may make the following special types of loans on commodities covered by price support programs. Notwithstanding the regulations covering other loans made by an association, loans may be made to members on any commodity for which a Commodity Credit Corporation price support program is in effect, at such rate of interest and upon such terms as the bank board may prescribe subject to the following conditions:

(a) The commodity offered as security for the loan shall be eligible for price support under a Commodity Credit Corporation price support program and shall be stored in a bonded public warehouse, holding storage agreement for such commodity approved by Commodity Credit Corporation.

(b) The member shall have complied with all Commodity Credit Corporation eligibility requirements.

(c) The loan shall mature not later than 30 days prior to the expiration of the period during which the Commodity Credit Corporation loan or other price support may be obtained on the commodity and shall be secured by pledge of negotiable warehouse receipts covering the commodity.

(d) The borrower shall appoint the association as his attorney-in-fact to obtain a Commodity Credit Corporation loan (or other such price support as is available) in the event that the borrower fails to do so prior to maturity or repayment of the loan.

[37 FR 11424, June 7, 1972. Redesignated at 46 FR 51878, Oct. 22, 1981, and amended at 55 FR 24886, June 19, 1990]

Subpart P—Farm Credit Bank and Agricultural Credit Bank Financing of Other Financing Institutions

SOURCE: 63 FR 36547, July 7, 1998, unless otherwise noted.

§ 614.4540 Other financing institution access to Farm Credit Banks and agricultural credit banks for funding, discount, and other similar financial assistance.

(a) *Basic criteria for access.* Any national bank, State bank, trust company, agriculture credit corporation, incorporated livestock loan company, savings association, credit union, or any association of agricultural producers engaged in the making of loans to farmers and ranchers, and any corporation engaged in the making of loans to producers or harvesters of aquatic products may become an other financing institution (OFI) that funds, discounts, and obtains other similar financial assistance from a Farm Credit Bank or agricultural credit bank in order to extend short- and intermediate-term credit to eligible borrowers for authorized purposes pursuant to sections 1.10(b) and 2.4(a) and (b) of the Act. Each OFI shall be duly organized and qualified to make loans and leases under the laws of each jurisdiction in which it operates.

(b) *Assured access.* Each Farm Credit Bank or agricultural credit bank must fund, discount, or provide other similar financial assistance to any creditworthy OFI that:

(1) Maintains at least 15 percent of its loan volume at a seasonal peak in loans and leases to farmers, ranchers, aquatic producers and harvesters. The Farm Credit Bank or agricultural credit bank shall not include the loan assets of the OFI's parent, affiliates, or subsidiaries when determining compliance with the requirement of this paragraph; and

(2) Executes a general financing agreement with the Farm Credit Bank or agricultural credit bank that establishes a financing or discount relationship for at least 2 years.

(c) *Underwriting standards.* Each Farm Credit Bank and agricultural credit bank shall establish objective

Farm Credit Administration § 614.4560

policies, procedures, pricing guidelines, and loan underwriting standards for determining the creditworthiness of each OFI applicant. A copy of such policies, procedures, guidelines, and standards shall be made available, upon request to each OFI and OFI applicant.

(d) *Denial of OFI access.* A Farm Credit Bank or an agricultural credit bank may deny the funding request of any creditworthy OFI that meets the conditions in paragraph (b) of this section only when such request would:

(1) Adversely affect a Farm Credit Bank or agricultural credit bank's ability to:

(i) Achieve and maintain established or projected capital levels; or

(ii) Raise funds in the money markets; or

(2) Otherwise expose the Farm Credit Bank or agricultural credit bank to safety and soundness risks.

(e) *Notice to applicants.* Each Farm Credit Bank or agricultural credit bank shall render its decision on an OFI application in as expeditious a manner as is practicable. Upon reaching a decision on an application, the Farm Credit Bank or agricultural credit bank shall provide prompt written notice of its decision to the applicant. When the Farm Credit Bank or agricultural credit bank makes an adverse credit decision on an application, the written notice shall include the specific reason(s) for the decision.

(f) *Reports to the board of directors.* Each Farm Credit Bank and agricultural credit bank shall provide its board of directors with a written annual report regarding the scope of OFI program activities during the preceding fiscal year.

[63 FR 36547, July 7, 1998, as amended at 69 FR 29862, May 26, 2004]

§ 614.4550 Place of discount.

A Farm Credit Bank or agricultural credit bank may provide funding, discounting, or other similar financial assistance to any OFI applicant. However, a Farm Credit Bank or agricultural credit bank cannot fund, discount, or extend other similar financial assistance to an OFI that maintains its headquarters, or has more than 50 percent of its outstanding loan volume to eligible borrowers who conduct agricultural or aquatic operations in the chartered territory of another Farm Credit bank unless it notifies such bank in writing within five (5) business days of receiving the OFI's application for financing. Two or more Farm Credit banks cannot simultaneously fund the same OFI.

[69 FR 29863, May 26, 2004]

§ 614.4560 Requirements for OFI funding relationships.

(a) As a condition for extending funding, discount and other similar financial assistance to an OFI, each Farm Credit Bank or agricultural credit bank shall require every OFI to:

(1) Execute a general financing agreement pursuant to the regulations in subpart C of part 614; and

(2) Purchase non-voting stock in its Farm Credit Bank or agricultural credit bank pursuant to the bank's bylaws.

(b) A Farm Credit Bank or agricultural credit bank shall extend funding, discount and other similar financial assistance to an OFI only for purposes and terms authorized under sections 1.10(b) and 2.4(a) and (b) of the Act.

(c) Rural home loans to borrowers who are not *bona fide* farmers, ranchers, and aquatic producers and harvesters are subject to the restrictions in § 613.3030 of this chapter. Loans that an OFI makes to processing and marketing operators who supply less than 20 percent of the throughput shall be included in the calculation that § 613.3010(b)(1) of this chapter establishes for Farm Credit Banks and agricultural credit banks.

(d) The borrower rights requirements in part C of title IV of the Act, and the regulations in part 617 of this chapter shall apply to all loans that an OFI funds or discounts through a Farm Credit Bank or agricultural credit bank, unless such loans are subject to the Truth-in-Lending Act, 15 U.S.C. 1601 *et seq.*

(e) As a condition for obtaining funding, discount and other similar financial assistance from a Farm Credit Bank or agricultural credit bank, all State banks, trust companies, or State-chartered savings associations shall execute a written consent that authorizes their State regulators to furnish

§ 614.4570

examination reports to the Farm Credit Administration upon its request. Any OFI that is not a depository institution shall consent in writing to examination by the Farm Credit Administration as a condition precedent for obtaining funding, discount and other similar financial assistance from a Farm Credit Bank or agricultural credit bank, and file such consent with its Farm Credit funding bank.

[63 FR 36547, July 7, 1998, as amended at 69 FR 10906, Mar. 9, 2004; 69 FR 29863, May 26, 2004]

§ 614.4570 Recourse and security.

(a) *Full recourse and guarantee.* All obligations that are funded or discounted through a Farm Credit Bank or agricultural credit bank shall be endorsed with the full recourse or unconditional guarantee of the OFI.

(b) *General collateral.* (1) Each Farm Credit Bank and agricultural credit bank shall take as collateral all notes, drafts, and other obligations that it funds or discounts for each OFI; and

(2) Each Farm Credit Bank and agricultural credit bank shall perfect, in accordance with State law, a senior security interest in any and all obligations and the proceeds thereunder that the OFI pledges as collateral.

(c) *Supplemental collateral.* (1) Each Farm Credit Bank and agricultural credit bank shall develop policies and loan underwriting standards that establish uniform and objective requirements to determine the need and amount of supplemental collateral or other credit enhancements that each OFI shall provide as a condition for obtaining funding, discount and other similar financial assistance from such Farm Credit bank.

(2) The amount, type, and quality of supplemental collateral or other credit enhancements required for each OFI shall be established in the general financing agreement and shall be proportional to the level of risk that the OFI poses to the Farm Credit Bank or agricultural credit bank.

§ 614.4580 Limitation on the extension of funding, discount and other similar financial assistance to an OFI.

(a) No obligation shall be purchased from or discounted for and no loan shall be made or other similar financial assistance extended by a Farm Credit Bank or agricultural credit bank to an OFI if the amount of such obligation added to the aggregate liabilities of such OFI, whether direct or contingent (other than *bona fide* deposit liabilities), exceeds ten times the paid-in and unimpaired capital and surplus of such OFI or the amount of such liabilities permitted under the laws of the jurisdiction creating such OFI, whichever is less.

(b) It shall be unlawful for any national bank that is indebted to any Farm Credit Bank or agricultural credit bank, on paper discounted or purchased, to incur any additional indebtedness, if by virtue of such additional indebtedness its aggregate liabilities, direct or contingent, will exceed the limitation described in paragraph (a) of this section.

§ 614.4590 Equitable treatment of OFIs and Farm Credit System associations.

(a) Each Farm Credit Bank and agricultural credit bank shall apply comparable and objective loan underwriting standards and pricing requirements to both OFIs and Farm Credit System direct lender associations.

(b) The total charges that a Farm Credit Bank or agricultural credit bank assesses an OFI through capitalization requirements, interest rates, and fees shall be comparable to the charges that the same Farm Credit Bank or agricultural credit bank imposes on its direct lender associations. Any variation between the overall funding costs that OFIs and direct lender associations are charged by the same funding bank shall result from differences in credit risk and administrative costs to the Farm Credit Bank or agricultural credit bank.

(c) Upon request, each Farm Credit Bank or agricultural credit bank must provide each OFI and OFI applicant, that has or is seeking to establish a funding relationship with the Farm Credit Bank or agricultural credit bank, a copy of its policies, procedures, loan underwriting standards, and pricing guidelines for OFIs. The pricing guidelines must identify the specific components that make up the cost of

Farm Credit Administration § 614.4700

funds for OFIs, and the amount of these components expressed in basis points.

(d) Upon request of any OFI or OFI applicant, that has or is seeking to establish a funding relationship with the Farm Credit Bank or agricultural credit bank, the bank must explain in writing the reasons for any variation in the overall funding costs it charges to OFIs and affiliated direct lender associations. The written explanation must compare the cost of funds that the Farm Credit Bank or agricultural credit bank charges the OFIs and affiliated direct lender associations. When possible, the written explanation shall compare the costs of funding that the bank charges several OFIs and Farm Credit associations that are similar in size. However, the Farm Credit Bank or agricultural credit bank must not disclose financial or confidential information about any individual Farm Credit association.

[63 FR 36547, July 7, 1998, as amended at 69 FR 29863, May 26, 2004]

§ 614.4595 Public disclosure about OFIs.

A Farm Credit Bank or agricultural credit bank may disclose to members of the public the name, address, telephone number, and Internet Web site address of any affiliated OFI only if such OFI, through a duly authorized officer, consents in writing. Each Farm Credit Bank and agricultural credit bank must adopt policies and procedures for requesting, obtaining, and maintaining the consent of its OFIs and for disclosing this information to the public.

[69 FR 29863, May 26, 2004]

§ 614.4600 Insolvency of an OFI.

If an OFI that is indebted to a Farm Credit Bank or agricultural credit bank becomes insolvent, is in process of liquidation, or fails to service its loans properly, the Farm Credit Bank or agricultural credit bank may take over such loans and other assets that the OFI pledged as collateral. Once the Farm Credit Bank or agricultural credit bank exercises its remedies, it shall have the authority to make additional advances, to grant renewals and extensions, and to take such other actions as may be necessary to collect and service loans to the OFI's borrower. The funding Farm Credit Bank or agricultural credit bank may also liquidate the OFI's loans and other assets in order to achieve repayment of the debt.

Subpart Q—Banks for Cooperatives and Agricultural Credit Banks Financing International Trade

§ 614.4700 Financing foreign trade receivables.

(a) Banks for cooperatives and agricultural credit banks, under policies adopted by their boards of directors, are authorized to finance foreign trade receivables on behalf of eligible cooperatives to include the following:

(1) Advances against collections;
(2) Trade acceptances;
(3) Factoring; and
(4) Open accounts.

(b) To reduce credit, political, and other risks associated with foreign trade receivable financing, the banks for cooperatives and agricultural credit banks shall avail themselves of such guarantee and insurance plans as are available in the United States and other countries, such as the Foreign Credit Insurance Association and the Export-Import Bank of the United States. Exceptions may be made where a prospective borrower has had a long-standing successful business relationship with the eligible cooperative borrower or an eligible cooperative which is not a borrower if the prospective borrower has a high credit rating as determined by the bank.

(c) When financing a draft drawn on a foreign importer, the banks should retain recourse to the exporter unless their credit evaluation of and experience with the importer indicate recourse is not necessary or unless appropriate guarantees or insurance plans are used.

(d) The financing of foreign trade receivables shall be limited by the policies of each bank's board of directors. The policies shall provide a method of determining the maximum amount in dollars, by country, to be financed and establishing a maximum percentage of

§ 614.4710

the amount of a draft drawn on a foreign party against which the bank may advance funds. The banks shall take into consideration the following factors:

(1) The reputation and financial strength of the foreign importer.

(2) The reputation and payment record of the class of importers in the same country as the subject importer in regard to prompt payment of drafts drawn upon them.

(3) The quality of the supporting documents offered with the draft.

(4) The degree of ease with which necessary foreign exchange conversion can be made, or the extent to which foreign currency exposure may be hedged by forward or future contracts.

(5) The reputation and financial strength of the exporter.

(e) The banks may establish foreign trade receivable financing programs by which eligible parties pledge collections to the bank, and then may borrow from the bank up to a stated maximum percentage of the total amount of receivables pledged at any one time.

(f) When financing foreign trade receivables, the banks shall take such precautions and obtain such credit information as necessary to ascertain that all parties to the transaction(s) being financed are reputable and capable of performing their responsibilities under the contract of sale.

(g) When financing foreign trade receivables, the banks shall determine that all shipments are covered by maritime insurance while on the high seas.

(h) Countries where credit is to be extended will be analyzed periodically and systematically on a centralized basis. The resulting country studies will be disseminated to all banks for cooperatives and agricultural credit banks to be used as inputs in credit grading decisions.

[46 FR 51879, Oct. 22, 1981, as amended at 55 FR 24886, June 19, 1990; 62 FR 4445, Jan. 30, 1997]

§ 614.4710 [Reserved]

§ 614.4720 Letters of credit.

Banks for cooperatives and agricultural credit banks, under policies adopted by their boards of directors, may issue, advise, or confirm import or export letters of credit in accordance with the Uniform Commercial Code, or the Uniform Customs and Practice for Documentary Credits, to or on behalf of its customers. In addition, as a matter of sound banking practice, letters of credit shall be issued in conformity with the list which follows.

(a) Each letter of credit shall be in writing and shall conspicuously state that it is a letter of credit, or be conspicuously entitled as such.

(b) The letter of credit shall contain a specified expiration date or be for a definite term.

(c) The letter of credit shall contain a sum certain.

(d) The bank's obligation to pay should arise only upon fulfilling the terms and conditions as specified in the letter of credit. The bank must not be called upon to determine questions of fact or law at issue between the account party and the beneficiary.

(e) The bank's customer should have an unqualified obligation to reimburse the bank for payments made under the letter of credit.

(f) All letters of credit shall be irrevocable.

[46 FR 51879, Oct. 22, 1981, as amended at 55 FR 24887, June 19, 1990; 62 FR 4445, Jan. 30, 1997; 64 FR 43049, Aug. 9, 1999]

§ 614.4800 Guarantees and contracts of suretyship.

A bank for cooperatives or an agricultural credit bank, under a policy approved by the bank's board of directors, may lend its credit, be itself a surety to indemnify another, or otherwise become a guarantor if an eligible cooperative substantially benefits from the performance of the transaction involved. A bank may guarantee the debt of eligible cooperatives and foreign parties or otherwise agree to make payments on the occurrence of readily ascertainable events if the guarantee or agreement specifies a maximum monetary liability. Guarantees may be secured or unsecured, and can include, but are not limited to, such events as nonpayment of taxes, rentals, customs duties, costs of transport, and loss of or nonconformance of shipping documents. The bank's customer shall have an unqualified obligation to reimburse the bank for payments made under a guarantee or surety.

[55 FR 24887, June 19, 1990, as amended at 62 FR 4445, Jan. 30, 1997]

§ 614.4810 Standby letters of credit.

(a) The banks for cooperatives and agricultural credit banks are authorized to issue on behalf of parties eligible for financing under regulations § 614.4010(d) or § 614.4020 standby letters of credit that represent an obligation to the beneficiary on the part of the issuer:

(1) To repay money borrowed by, advanced to, or for the account of the account party, or

(2) To make payment on account of any indebtedness undertaken by the account party, or

(3) To make payment on account of any default by the account party in the performance of an obligation.

(b) As a matter of sound banking practice, banks for cooperatives and agricultural credit banks shall evaluate applications for standby letters of credit on the basis of the loan underwriting standards adopted pursuant to § 614.4150 of the regulations.

[46 FR 51879, Oct. 22, 1981, as amended at 55 FR 24887, June 19, 1990; 62 FR 4445, Jan. 30, 1997; 62 FR 51015, Sept. 30, 1997]

§ 614.4900 Foreign exchange.

(a) Before a bank for cooperatives or an agricultural credit bank may engage in any financial transaction which transports monetary instruments from any place within the United States to or through any place outside the United States or to any place within the United States, the bank must have policies adopted by the bank's board of directors governing such transactions and must have established bank procedures to safeguard the interests of the stockholders of the bank in regard to such transactions.

(b) Under policies adopted by the bank's board of directors, a bank for cooperatives or an agricultural credit bank may engage in currency exchange activities necessary to service individual transactions that may be financed under the regulations authorizing export, import, and other internationally related credit and financial services. These currency exchange activities shall not include any loans or commitments intended to finance speculative futures transactions by eligible borrowers in foreign currencies. The bank may engage, on behalf of the eligible borrowers or on its own behalf, in bona fide hedging transactions and positions, where such transactions or positions normally reduce risks in the conduct and management of international financial activities. The bank's policies should include established guidelines for:

(1) Net overnight positions, by currency.

(2) Maturity distribution, by currency, of foreign currency assets, liabilities, and foreign exchange contracts.

(3) Outstanding contracts with individual customers and banks.

(4) Credit approval procedures safeguarding against delivery or settlement risk.

(5) Total value of outstanding contracts—spot and forward.

(c) A bank for cooperatives or an agricultural credit bank is responsible for its compliance with the laws of the United States in regard to reporting requirements of the Department of the Treasury pertaining to currency exchange activities and international transfers of monetary instruments.

(d) A bank for cooperatives or an agricultural credit bank engaged in foreign exchange trading shall have written policies describing the scope of trading activity authorized, delegation of authority, types of services offered, trading limits, reporting requirements, and internal accounting controls.

(e) The bank's trading guideline policies should provide for reporting procedures adequate to inform management properly of trading activities and to facilitate detection of lack of compliance with policy directives.

(f) The bank's policies shall establish foreign exchange delivery limits for eligible customers with relationship to the customer's financial capability to bear the financial risks assumed. The bank will be expected to maintain documentary evidence that a customer's delivery exposure is reasonable, and

§ 614.4910

that responsible bank officers routinely review outstanding delivery exposure of individual customers.

(g) The bank's personnel policies shall include written standards of conduct for those involved with foreign exchange activities, including the following which should be prohibited:

(1) Trading with entities affiliated with the bank or with members of the board of directors.

(2) Foreign exchange and deposit transactions with other bank employees.

(3) Personal business relationships with foreign exchange and money brokers with whom the bank deals.

(h) The bank's policies should provide detailed instructions regarding the need for bank officers to disclose the limits of responsibility and liability of the bank when it holds positions or executes contracts for the account of eligible parties. The bank's policies regarding the respective procedures should provide reasonable assurance that reports on trading activities are current and complete, and that the opportunity for concealment of unauthorized transactions is kept at the absolute minimum.

(i) The banks for cooperatives and agricultural credit banks shall use the Funding Corporation for purposes of trading foreign exchange. All foreign exchange transactions shall be made by the Funding Corporation on behalf of the banks consistent with instructions received from the respective banks.

(j) Guidelines (b) through (i) of this section will not apply if a bank purchases or sells foreign exchange through a commercial bank and has no foreign exchange risk exposure.

[46 FR 51879, Oct. 22, 1981, as amended at 55 FR 24887, June 19, 1990; 62 FR 4445, Jan. 30, 1997]

Subpart R—Secondary Market Authorities

§ 614.4910 Basic authorities.

(a) Any bank or association of the Farm Credit System, except a bank for cooperatives, with direct lending authority may originate agricultural real estate loans for sale to one or more certified agricultural mortgage marketing facilities under title VIII of the Act.

(b) Any bank or association of the Farm Credit System, except a bank for cooperatives, may operate as an agricultural mortgage marketing facility under title VIII of the Act, either acting alone or jointly with other banks and/or associations, if so certified by the Federal Agricultural Mortgage Corporation.

[54 FR 1155, Jan. 12, 1989]

Subpart S—Flood Insurance Requirements

SOURCE: 61 FR 45711, Aug. 29, 1996, unless otherwise noted.

§ 614.4920 Purpose and scope.

(a) *Purpose.* This subpart implements the requirements of the National Flood Insurance Act of 1968 (1968 Act), as amended, and the Flood Disaster Protection Act of 1973 (1973 Act), as amended (42 U.S.C. 4001–4129).

(b) *Scope.* This subpart, except for §§ 614.4940 and 614.4950, applies to loans of Farm Credit System (System) institutions that are secured by buildings or mobile homes located or to be located in areas determined by the Director of the Federal Emergency Management Agency to have special flood hazards. Sections 614.4940 and 614.4950 apply to loans secured by buildings or mobile homes, regardless of location.

§ 614.4925 Definitions.

(a) *Building* means a walled and roofed structure, other than a gas or liquid storage tank, that is principally above ground and affixed to a permanent site, and a walled and roofed structure while in the course of construction, alteration, or repair.

(b) *Community* means a State or a political subdivision of a State that has zoning and building code jurisdiction over a particular area having special flood hazards.

(c) *Designated loan* means a loan secured by a building or a mobile home that is located or to be located in a special flood hazard area in which flood insurance is available under the 1968 Act.

Farm Credit Administration

§ 614.4935

(d) *Director of FEMA* means the Director of the Federal Emergency Management Agency.

(e) *Mobile home* means a structure, transportable in one or more sections, that is built on a permanent chassis and designed for use with or without a permanent foundation when attached to the required utilities. The term *mobile home* does not include a recreational vehicle. For purposes of this subpart, the term *mobile home* means a mobile home on a permanent foundation. The term *mobile home* includes a manufactured home as that term is used in the NFIP.

(f) *NFIP* means the National Flood Insurance Program authorized under the 1968 Act.

(g) *Residential improved real estate* means real estate upon which a home or other residential building is located or to be located.

(h) *Servicer* means the person responsible for:

(1) Receiving any scheduled, periodic payments from a borrower under the terms of a loan, including amounts for taxes, insurance premiums, and other charges with respect to the property securing the loan; and

(2) Making payments of principal and interest and any other payments from the amounts received from the borrower as may be required under the terms of the loan.

(i) *Special flood hazard area* means the land in the flood plain within a community having at least a one percent chance of flooding in any given year, as designated by the Director of FEMA.

(j) *Table funding* means a settlement at which a loan is funded by a contemporaneous advance of loan funds and an assignment of the loan to the person advancing the funds.

§ 614.4930 Requirement to purchase flood insurance where available.

(a) *In general.* A System institution shall not make, increase, extend or renew any designated loan unless the building or mobile home and any personal property securing the loan are covered by flood insurance for the term of the loan. The amount of insurance must be at least equal to the outstanding principal balance of the designated loan or the maximum limit of coverage available for the particular type of property under the 1968 Act. Flood insurance coverage under the Act is limited to the overall value of the property securing the designated loan minus the value of the land on which the property is located.

(b) *Table funded loans.* A System institution that acquires a loan from a mortgage broker or other entity through table funding shall be considered to be making a loan for purposes of this part.

(c) *Exemptions.* The flood insurance requirement of paragraph (a) of this section does not apply with respect to:

(1) Any State-owned property covered under a policy of self-insurance satisfactory to the Director of FEMA, who publishes and periodically revises the list of States falling within this exemption; or

(2) Property securing any loan with an original principal balance of $5,000 or less and a repayment term of one year or less.

§ 614.4935 Escrow requirement.

If a System institution requires the escrow of taxes, insurance premiums, fees, or any other charges for a loan secured by *residential* improved real estate or a mobile home that is made, increased, extended or renewed on or after October 4, 1996, the institution shall also require the escrow of all premiums and fees for any flood insurance required under § 614.4930. The institution, or a servicer acting on behalf of the institution, shall deposit the flood insurance premiums on behalf of the borrower in an escrow account. This escrow account will be subject to escrow requirements adopted pursuant to section 10 of the Real Estate Settlement Procedures Act of 1974 (12 U.S.C. 2609) (RESPA), which generally limits the amount that may be maintained in escrow accounts for certain types of loans and requires escrow account statements for those accounts, only if the loan is otherwise subject to RESPA. Following receipt of a notice from the Director of FEMA or other provider of flood insurance that premiums are due, the institution, or a servicer acting on behalf of the institution, shall pay the amount owed to the

§ 614.4940

insurance provider from the escrow account by the date when such premiums are due.

§ 614.4940 Required use of standard flood hazard determination form.

(a) *Use of form.* System institutions must use the standard flood hazard determination form developed by the Director of FEMA when determining whether the building or mobile home offered as collateral security for a loan is or will be located in a special flood hazard area in which flood insurance is available under the 1968 Act. The standard flood hazard determination form may be used in a printed, computerized, or electronic manner. A System institution may obtain the standard flood hazard determination form by written request to FEMA, P.O. Box 2012, Jessup, MD 20794-2012.

(b) *Retention of form.* System institutions shall retain a copy of the completed standard flood hazard determination form, in either hard copy or electronic form, for the period of time the institution owns the loan.

[61 FR 45711, Aug. 29, 1996, as amended at 64 FR 71274, Dec. 21, 1999]

§ 614.4945 Forced placement of flood insurance.

If a System institution, or a servicer acting on behalf of the institution, determines at any time during the term of a designated loan, that the building or mobile home and any personal property securing the designated loan are not covered by flood insurance or are covered by flood insurance in an amount less than the amount required under § 614.4930(a), then the institution or its servicer shall notify the borrower that the borrower should obtain flood insurance, at the borrower's expense, in an amount at least equal to the amount required under § 614.4930(a), for the remaining term of the loan. If the borrower fails to obtain flood insurance within 45 days after notification, then the institution or its servicer shall purchase insurance on the borrower's behalf. The institution or its servicer may charge the borrower for the cost of premiums and fees incurred in purchasing the insurance.

§ 614.4950 Determination fees.

(a) *General.* Notwithstanding any Federal or State law other than the 1973 Act, any System institution, or a servicer acting on behalf of the institution, may charge a reasonable fee for determining whether the building or mobile home securing the loan is located or will be located in a special flood hazard area. A determination fee may also include, but is not limited to, a fee for life-of-loan monitoring.

(b) *Borrower fee.* The determination fee authorized by paragraph (a) of this section may be charged to the borrower if the determination:

(1) Is made in connection with a making, increasing, extending, or renewing of the loan that is initiated by the borrower;

(2) Reflects the Director of FEMA's revision or updating of floodplain areas or flood-risk zones;

(3) Reflects the Director of FEMA's publication of a notice or compendium that:

(i) Affects the area in which the building or mobile home securing the loan is located; or

(ii) By determination of the Director of FEMA, may reasonably require a determination whether the building or mobile home securing the loan is located in a special flood hazard area; or

(4) Results in the purchase of flood insurance coverage under § 614.4945.

(c) *Purchaser or transferee fee.* The determination fee authorized by paragraph (a) of this section may be charged to the purchaser or transferee of a loan in the case of the sale or transfer of the loan.

§ 614.4955 Notice of special flood hazards and availability of Federal disaster relief assistance.

(a) *Notice requirement.* When a System institution makes, increases, extends, or renews a loan secured by a building or a mobile home located or to be located in a special flood hazard area, the institution shall mail or deliver a written notice containing the information specified in paragraph (b) of this section to the borrower and to the servicer of the loan. Notice is required whether or not flood insurance is available under the 1968 Act for the collateral securing the loan.

Farm Credit Administration **Pt. 614, Subpt. S, App. A**

(b) *Contents of notice.* The written notice must include the following information:

(1) A warning, in a form approved by the Director of FEMA, that the building or the mobile home is or will be located in a special flood hazard area;

(2) A description of the flood insurance purchase requirements set forth in section 102(b) of the 1973 Act (42 U.S.C. 4012a(b));

(3) A statement, where applicable, that flood insurance coverage is available under the NFIP and also may be available from private insurers; and

(4) A statement whether Federal disaster relief assistance may be available in the event of damage to the building or the mobile home caused by flooding in a Federally declared disaster.

(c) *Timing of notice.* The institution shall provide the notice required by paragraph (a) of this section to the borrower within a reasonable time before the completion of the transaction, and to the servicer as promptly as practicable after the institution provides notice to the borrower and in any event no later than the time the institution provides other similar notices to the servicer concerning hazard insurance and taxes. Notice to the servicer may be made electronically or may take the form of a copy of the notice to the borrower.

(d) *Record of receipt.* Each institution shall retain a record of the receipt of the notices by the borrower and the servicer for the period of time the institution owns the loan.

(e) *Alternate method of notice.* Instead of providing the notice to the borrower required by paragraph (a) of this section, an institution may obtain satisfactory written assurance from a seller or lessor that, within a reasonable time before the completion of the sale or lease transaction, the seller or lessor has provided such notice to the purchaser or lessee. The institution shall retain a record of the written assurance from the seller or lessor for the period of time the institution owns the loan.

(f) *Use of prescribed form of notice.* An institution will be considered to be in compliance with the requirements of this section for notice to the borrower by providing written notice to the borrower containing the language presented in appendix A to this subpart within a reasonable time before the completion of the transaction. The notice presented in appendix A to this subpart satisfies the borrower notice requirements of the 1968 Act.

§ 614.4960 **Notice of servicer's identity.**

(a) *Notice requirement.* When a System institution makes, increases, extends, renews, sells, or transfers a loan secured by a building or mobile home located or to be located in a special flood hazard area, the institution shall notify the Director of FEMA (or the Director's designee) in writing of the identity of the servicer of the loan. The Director of FEMA has designated the insurance provider to receive the institution's notice of the servicer's identity. This notice may be provided electronically if electronic transmission is satisfactory to the Director of FEMA's designee.

(b) *Transfer of servicing rights.* The institution shall notify the Director of FEMA (or the Director's designee) of any change in the servicer of a loan described in paragraph (a) of this section within 60 days after the effective date of the change. This notice may be provided electronically if electronic transmission is satisfactory to the Director of FEMA's designee. Upon any change in the servicing of a loan described in paragraph (a) of this section, the duty to provide notice under this paragraph (b) shall transfer to the transferee servicer.

APPENDIX A TO SUBPART S OF PART 614—SAMPLE FORM OF NOTICE OF SPECIAL FLOOD HAZARDS AND AVAILABILITY OF FEDERAL DISASTER RELIEF ASSISTANCE

We are giving you this notice to inform you that:

The building or mobile home securing the loan for which you have applied is or will be located in an area with special flood hazards. The area has been identified by the Director of the Federal Emergency Management Agency (FEMA) as a special flood hazard area using FEMA's *Flood Insurance Rate Map* or the *Flood Hazard Boundary Map* for the following community: _____. This area has at least a one percent (1%) chance of a flood equal to or exceeding the base flood elevation (a 100-year flood) in any given year. During the life of a 30-year mortgage loan, the risk of a 100-year flood in a special flood hazard area is 26 percent (26%).

Federal law allows a lender and borrower jointly to request the Director of FEMA to review the determination of whether the property securing the loan is located in a special flood hazard area. If you would like to make such a request, please contact us for further information.

_____ The community in which the property securing the loan is located participates in the National Flood Insurance Program (NFIP). Federal law will not allow us to make you the loan that you have applied for if you do not purchase flood insurance. The flood insurance must be maintained for the life of the loan. If you fail to purchase or renew flood insurance on the property, Federal law authorizes and requires us to purchase the flood insurance for you at your expense.

• Flood insurance coverage under the NFIP may be purchased through an insurance agent who will obtain the policy either directly through the NFIP or through an insurance company that participates in the NFIP. Flood insurance also may be available from private insurers that do not participate in the NFIP.

• At a minimum, flood insurance purchased must cover *the lesser of:*

(1) The outstanding principal balance of the loan; *or*

(2) The maximum amount of coverage allowed for the type of property under the NFIP.

Flood insurance coverage under the NFIP is limited to the overall value of the property securing the loan minus the value of the land on which the property is located.

• Federal disaster relief assistance (usually in the form of a low-interest loan) may be available for damages incurred in excess of your flood insurance if your community's participation in the NFIP is in accordance with NFIP requirements.

_____ Flood insurance coverage under the NFIP is not available for the property securing the loan because the community in which the property is located does not participate in the NFIP. In addition, if the nonparticipating community has been identified for at least one year as containing a special flood hazard area, properties located in the community will not be eligible for Federal disaster relief assistance in the event of a Federally-declared flood disaster.

PART 615—FUNDING AND FISCAL AFFAIRS, LOAN POLICIES AND OPERATIONS, AND FUNDING OPERATIONS

Subpart A—Funding

Sec.
615.5000 General responsibilities.
615.5010 Funding Corporation.
615.5030 Borrowings from commercial banks.
615.5040 Borrowings from financial institutions other than commercial banks.

Subpart B—Collateral

615.5045 Definitions.
615.5050 Collateral requirements.
615.5060 Special collateral requirement.
615.5090 Reduction in carrying value of collateral.

Subpart C—Issuance of Bonds, Notes, Debentures and Similar Obligations

615.5100 Authority to issue.
615.5101 Requirements for issuance.
615.5102 Issuance of debt obligations through the Funding Corporation.
615.5103–615.5104 [Reserved]
615.5105 Consolidated Systemwide notes.

Subpart D—Other Funding

615.5110 Authority to issue (other funding).
615.5120 Purchase eligibility requirement.
615.5130 Procedures.

Subpart E—Investment Management

615.5131 Definitions.
615.5132 Investment purposes.
615.5133 Investment management.
615.5134 Liquidity reserve requirement.
615.5135 Management of interest rate risk.
615.5136 Emergencies impeding normal access of Farm Credit banks to capital markets.
615.5140 Eligible investments.
615.5141 Stress tests for mortgage securities.
615.5142 Association investments.
615.5143 Disposal of ineligible investments.
615.5144 Banks for cooperatives and agricultural credit banks.

Subpart F—Property, Transfers of Capital, and Other Investments

615.5170 Real and personal property.
615.5171 Transfer of capital from banks to associations.
615.5172 Production credit association and agricultural credit association investment in farmers' notes given to cooperatives and dealers.

Farm Credit Administration

615.5173 Stock of the Federal Agricultural Mortgage Corporation.
615.5174 Farmer Mac securities.
615.5175 Investments in Farm Credit System institution preferred stock.

Subpart G—Risk Assessment and Management

615.5180 Interest rate risk management by banks—general.
615.5181 Bank interest rate risk management program.
615.5182 Interest rate risk management by associations and other Farm Credit System institutions other than banks.

Subpart H—Capital Adequacy

615.5200 Capital planning.
615.5201 Definitions.
615.5205 Minimum permanent capital standards.
615.5206 Permanent capital ratio computation.
615.5207 Capital adjustments and associated reductions to assets.
615.5208 Allotment of allocated investments.
615.5209 Deferred-tax assets.
615.5210 Risk-adjusted assets.
615.5211 Risk categories—balance sheet assets.
615.5212 Credit conversion factors—off-balance sheet items.
615.5215 Distribution of earnings.
615.5216 [Reserved]

Subpart I—Issuance of Equities

615.5220 Capitalization bylaws.
615.5230 Implementation of cooperative principles.
615.5240 Permanent capital requirements.
615.5245 Limitations on association preferred stock.
615.5250 Disclosure requirements for borrower stock.
615.5255 Disclosure and review requirements for other equities.

Subpart J—Retirement of Equities and Payment of Dividends

615.5260 Retirement of eligible borrower stock.
615.5270 Retirement of other equities.
615.5280 Retirement in event of default.
615.5290 Retirement of capital stock and participation certificates in event of restructuring.
615.5295 Payment of dividends.

Subpart K—Surplus and Collateral Requirements

615.5301 Definitions.
615.5330 Minimum surplus ratios.
615.5335 Bank net collateral ratio.

615.5336 Compliance and reporting.

Subpart L—Establishment of Minimum Capital Ratios for an Individual Institution

615.5350 General—Applicability.
615.5351 Standards for determination of appropriate individual institution minimum capital ratios.
615.5352 Procedures.
615.5353 Relation to other actions.
615.5354 Enforcement.

Subpart M—Issuance of a Capital Directive

615.5355 Purpose and scope.
615.5356 Notice of intent to issue a capital directive.
615.5357 Response to notice.
615.5358 Decision.
615.5359 Issuance of a capital directive.
615.5360 Reconsideration based on change in circumstances.
615.5361 Relation to other administrative actions.

Subpart N [Reserved]

Subpart O—Book-Entry Procedures for Farm Credit Securities

615.5450 Definitions.
615.5451 Book-entry and definitive securities.
615.5452 Law governing rights and obligations of Federal Reserve Banks, Farm Credit banks, and Funding Corporation; rights of any person against Federal Reserve Banks, Farm Credit banks, and Funding Corporation.
615.5453 Law governing other interests.
615.5454 Creation of participant's security entitlement; security interests.
615.5455 Obligations of the Farm Credit banks and the Funding Corporation; no adverse claims.
615.5456 Authority of Federal Reserve Banks.
615.5457 Withdrawal of eligible book-entry securities for conversion to definitive form.
615.5458 Waiver of regulations.
615.5459 Liability of Farm Credit banks, Funding Corporation and Federal Reserve Banks.
615.5460 Additional provisions.
615.5461 Lost, stolen, destroyed, mutilated or defaced Farm Credit securities, including coupons.
615.5462 Restrictive endorsement of bearer securities.

Subpart P—Global Debt Securities

615.5500 Definitions.
615.5502 Issuance of global debt securities.

§ 615.5000

Subpart Q—Bankers Acceptances

615.5550 Bankers' acceptances.

Subpart R [Reserved]

Subpart S—Federal Agricultural Mortgage Corporation Securities

615.5570 Book-entry procedures for Federal Agricultural Mortgage Corporation securities.

AUTHORITY: Secs. 1.5, 1.7, 1.10, 1.11, 1.12, 2.2, 2.3, 2.4, 2.5, 2.12, 3.1, 3.7, 3.11, 3.25, 4.3, 4.3A, 4.9, 4.14B, 4.25, 5.9, 5.17, 6.20, 6.26, 8.0, 8.3, 8.4, 8.6, 8.8, 8.10, 8.12 of the Farm Credit Act (12 U.S.C. 2013, 2015, 2018, 2019, 2020, 2073, 2074, 2075, 2076, 2093, 2122, 2128, 2132, 2146, 2154, 2154a, 2160, 2202b, 2211, 2243, 2252, 2278b, 2278b–6, 2279aa, 2279aa–3, 2279aa–4, 2279aa–6, 2279aa–8, 2279aa–10, 2279aa–12); sec. 301(a) of Pub. L. 100–233, 101 Stat. 1568, 1608.

Subpart A—Funding

§ 615.5000 General responsibilities.

(a) The System banks, acting through the Federal Farm Credit Banks Funding Corporation (Funding Corporation), have the primary responsibility for obtaining funds for the lending operations of the System institutions.

(b) The System's funding operations have a significant impact upon the investment community, the general public, and the national economy in both the volume and the manner by which funds are raised. The Farm Credit Administration supervises compliance with the statutory collateral requirements for the debt obligations issued. The Chairman of the Farm Credit Administration, under policies adopted by the Board, consults with the Secretary of the Treasury concerning the System's funding activities, pursuant to section 5.10 of the Act.

[54 FR 1158, Jan. 12, 1989]

§ 615.5010 Funding Corporation.

(a) The Funding Corporation shall issue, market, and handle the obligations of the banks issued under section 4.2(b) through (d) of the Act and interbank or intersystem flow of funds as may from time to time be required, and, upon request of the banks, shall handle investment portfolios. The Funding Corporation shall maintain accurate and timely records. The System banks shall provide for the sale of such obligations through the Funding Corporation by negotiation, offer, bid, or syndicate sale, and for the delivery of such obligations by book entry, wire transfer, or such other means as may be appropriate.

(b) The interaction of the System with the financial community shall be conducted principally through the Funding Corporation. The Funding Corporation shall be subject to regulation and examination by the Farm Credit Administration.

[54 FR 1158, Jan. 12, 1989]

§ 615.5030 Borrowings from commercial banks.

Each System bank board, by resolution, shall authorize all commercial bank borrowings by that System bank.

[54 FR 1159, Jan. 12, 1989, as amended at 75 FR 35968, June 24, 2010]

§ 615.5040 Borrowings from financial institutions other than commercial banks.

The Farm Credit banks may borrow from other financial institutions, such as insurance companies, Federal agencies, or Federal reserve banks.

[37 FR 11434, June 7, 1972, as amended at 54 FR 1151, Jan. 12, 1989; 54 FR 50736, Dec. 11, 1989]

Subpart B—Collateral

SOURCE: 54 FR 1159, Jan. 12, 1989, unless otherwise noted.

§ 615.5045 Definitions.

(a) *Cost* means the actual amount paid for any asset.

(b) *Market value* means the price at which a willing seller would sell to a willing buyer, neither under any compulsion to buy or sell.

(c) *Unpaid balance* means total principal and accrued interest owed.

(d) *Secured interbank loan* means a loan from one Farm Credit System bank to another Farm Credit System bank, secured by assets of the borrowing Farm Credit System bank.

§ 615.5050 Collateral requirements.

(a) Each bank shall have on hand at the time of issuance of any notes,

Farm Credit Administration § 615.5060

bonds, debentures, or other similar obligations, and at all times thereafter maintain, free from any lien or other pledge, assets consisting of notes and other obligations representing loans made under the authority of the Act, real or personal property acquired in connection with loans made under the Act, obligations of the United States or any agency thereof direct or fully guaranteed, other bank assets (including marketable securities) approved by the Farm Credit Administration, cash, or cash equivalents approved by the Farm Credit Administration, in an aggregate value equal to the total amount of notes, bonds, debentures, or other similar obligations outstanding for which the bank is primarily liable.

(b) The collateral value of eligible investments (as defined in § 615.5140) shall be the lower of cost or market value.

(c)(1) Except as otherwise provided in this paragraph, the collateral value of notes and other obligations representing loans made under the authority of any Farm Credit Act shall be the unpaid balance of such loans adjusted for any allowance for loan losses (except as provided for in § 615.5090).

(2) The collateral value of loans in process of liquidation or foreclosure, judgments, and sales contracts shall be the unpaid balance of such loans, judgments, and contracts adjusted for any allowance for losses.

(3) The collateral value of loans which have been restructured by any action, such as an extension, deferment, or partial release, shall be the new unpaid balance of the loans adjusted for any allowance for losses.

(4) The collateral value of property acquired in the liquidation of loans shall be the book value of such property adjusted for any allowance for losses.

(5) Collateral shall not include the amount of any loan that exceeds the maximum amount authorized under the Act or part 614 of these regulations.

(6) Collateral may include the collateral value of secured interbank loans, computed as provided in § 615.5050(c)(1), provided that the assets securing the loan could serve as collateral supporting the issuance of obligations under § 615.5050(a). In computing its eligible collateral, the borrowing bank shall not count the assets securing such loan.

(d) Each bank shall have procedures which will ensure that the bank is in compliance with the statutory requirements for maintenance of collateral. Such procedures shall include provisions for:

(1) Adequate safekeeping facilities;

(2) Methods to determine that debt instruments meet all requirements of law and regulations;

(3) A report signed by an authorized bank officer at each regular meeting of the board of directors certifying the eligibility and the adequacy of collateral. Items to be reported will include but not be limited to the total amount of eligible collateral, amount of ineligible loans, amount of deductions, and the amount of excess collateral; and

(4) Written procedures and practices to ensure that there will be a high degree of accuracy in protecting and accounting for the collateral.

§ 615.5060 Special collateral requirement.

(a) An attorney lien certification need not be obtained at the time a note is accepted as collateral if the counsel for the bank or association has determined, in writing, that the bank or association procedures provide sufficient safeguards to ensure that a real estate mortgage loan, within the meaning of section 1.7(a) of the Act, made by the bank or association will be secured by a first lien or its equivalent on the borrower's interest in the primary real estate security. However, the note shall be withdrawn from collateral upon the expiration of 1 year from the date of the loan closing, unless, before the end of such period:

(1) An attorney has certified that the bank or association has a first lien or its equivalent from a security standpoint in the primary real estate security for the loan; or

(2) The bank or association has obtained a title insurance policy insuring that it has a first lien or its equivalent from a security standpoint in the primary real estate security for the loan, and all of the following requirements are satisfied:

(i) The final policy was issued by a title insurance company that has been

§ 615.5090

licensed to issue such policies by the appropriate state insurance regulatory body or bodies, has not been barred or suspended, and has been approved by the lending institution;

(ii) The standard form on which the final policy was issued has been approved by the counsel for the lending institution;

(iii) The final policy was issued for an amount at least equal to the balance outstanding on the real estate mortgage loan or, if separate policies are issued to insure separate tracts, the minimum amount insured by each policy shall bear the same ratio to the outstanding balance of the loan that the appraised value of the tract insured by that policy bears to the appraised value of all the real estate security for the loan; and

(iv) Personnel meeting written standards of training and experience in real estate title matters prescribed by the counsel for the lending institution certified in writing that:

(A) They reviewed the final policy and that the policy complies with standards prescribed by such counsel; and

(B) The final policy insures that a first lien or its equivalent from a security standpoint has been obtained on the primary real estate security for the loan.

(b) A loan participation agreement to which a System bank or association is a participant and involving a loan originated by another lender shall constitute an obligation meeting the collateral requirements of § 615.5050(a).

[54 FR 1159, Jan. 12, 1989, as amended at 59 FR 3787, Jan. 27, 1994]

§ 615.5090 Reduction in carrying value of collateral.

When the bank or Farm Credit Administration determines that a loan did not conform to the requirements of the law or regulations at the time the loan was closed, such loan shall be withdrawn from collateral until the cause of ineligibility is remedied. When a loan has been classified as a loss loan, the bank shall adjust the collateral value of the loan accordingly.

Subpart C—Issuance of Bonds, Notes, Debentures and Similar Obligations

§ 615.5100 Authority to issue.

The Act authorizes each bank of the System, subject to the collateral requirements of section 4.3(c) of the Act, to issue:

(a) Notes, bonds, debentures, or other similar obligations;

(b) Consolidated obligations, together with any or all banks organized and operating under the same title of the Act;

(c) Systemwide obligations, together with other banks of the System; and

(d) Investment bonds to the authorized purchasers subject to the limitations contained in the regulations set forth in subpart D.

[54 FR 1160, Jan. 12, 1989]

§ 615.5101 Requirements for issuance.

Except as provided in section 4.2(e) of the Act, each debt obligation shall meet the following requirements:

(a) Each debt obligation shall be issued through the Federal Farm Credit Banks Funding Corporation acting for System banks.

(b) Each debt obligation shall be authorized by resolution of the board(s) of directors of the issuer(s). Each participating bank shall provide, in its authorizing resolution, for its primary liability on the portion of any consolidated or Systemwide obligation issued on its behalf and be jointly and severally liable for the payment of any additional sums as called upon by the Farm Credit Administration, in accordance with section 4.4 of the Act, in the event any bank primarily liable therefor is unable to pay.

(c) Each issuance of debt obligations shall meet the collateral requirements set forth in subpart B.

(d) Each issuance of debt obligations shall be approved by the Farm Credit Administration.

(e)(1) Consultation with the Secretary of the Treasury required by 31 U.S.C. 9108 shall be conducted by System representatives and shall have occurred prior to each debt issuance.

Farm Credit Administration

(2) Under policies adopted by the Board of the Farm Credit Administration, the Chairman will consult with the Secretary of the Treasury on a regular basis concerning the exercise by the System of the powers conferred under section 4.2 of the Act.

[54 FR 1160, Jan. 12, 1989]

§ 615.5102 Issuance of debt obligations through the Funding Corporation.

(a) The amount, maturities, rates or interest, terms and conditions of participation by the System banks in each issue of joint, consolidated or Systemwide obligations shall be determined by the Funding Corporation established pursuant to section 4.9 of the Act, acting for the banks of the System, subject to the approval of the Farm Credit Administration in accordance with § 615.5102.

(b) The Funding Corporation shall plan and develop funding guidelines, priorities, and objectives based upon the asset/liability management policies of the System institutions and the requirements of the market. The guidelines, priorities, and objectives shall be designed to ensure that the debt marketing responsibilities of the Funding Corporation will continue to provide flexibility for the banks and are fiscally sound.

(c) For all debt issuances conducted by the Funding Corporation, the specific prior approval of the Farm Credit Administration must be obtained prior to the distribution and sale of the obligation pursuant to section 4.9 of the Act.

[54 FR 1160, Jan. 12, 1989]

§§ 615.5103–615.5104 [Reserved]

§ 615.5105 Consolidated Systemwide notes.

Consolidated Systemwide notes authorized under § 615.5100(b) shall be subject to the following provisions unless otherwise approved by the Farm Credit Administration:

(a) Maturities shall be not less than five days nor more than 365 days.

(b) Prices shall be on a discount yield basis or as determined by the Funding Corporation.

[42 FR 32227, June 24, 1977, as amended at 47 FR 28609, July 1, 1982; 54 FR 1160, Jan. 12, 1989; 60 FR 20011, Apr. 24, 1995]

Subpart D—Other Funding

§ 615.5110 Authority to issue (other funding).

Any Farm Credit bank may issue Farm Credit Investment Bonds directly to those eligible as set forth in § 615.5120(a). The bonds are subject to the limitations contained in the Federal Reserve Board's Regulation Q.

[43 FR 47489, Oct. 16, 1978; 43 FR 55239, Nov. 27, 1978]

§ 615.5120 Purchase eligibility requirement.

(a) *Limitations.* Eligibility to purchase Farm Credit Investment Bonds shall be limited to members and employees of the Farm Credit banks and associations, except any bank officers, directors, and employees who are involved in setting the term or rate, to retired employees who are beneficiaries of a pension or retirement program of the Farm Credit banks or associations, and to retired employees of the Farm Credit Administration. A member of a Farm Credit association or a bank for cooperatives need not be an active borrower to be eligible. A member of any Farm Credit institution may purchase investment bonds from any of the institutions in the district which offer the purchase program. Patrons, members, employees, or stockholder of other financing institutions discounting loans with a Farm Credit Bank or agricultural credit bank or of any legal entity which is a borrower from any Farm Credit institution as such are ineligible as they are not members of a Farm Credit institution. Stock or participation certificates shall not be sold merely to qualify a party for the purchase of Farm Credit Investment Bonds. For purposes of this section "member" means a stockholder or participation certificate holder who acquired stock or participation certificates to obtain a loan, to purchase stock for investment or to qualify for

§ 615.5130

other services of the association or bank. A person who assumes a loan is not a member unless he becomes a stockholder or participation certificate holder in connection with that loan. Employee means a regular full-time employee of a Farm Credit bank or association. Retired employee means a retiree who is a direct beneficiary of a pension or retirement program of a Farm Credit bank or association or the Farm Credit Administration under civil service retirement.

(b) *Form and ownership.* Farm Credit Investment Bonds are registered bonds issued in definitive or book-entry form depending on investor preference. The registration used must express the actual ownership of an interest in the bond and will be considered by the issuing institution as conclusive of such ownership and interest. No designation of an attorney, agent, or other representative to request or receive payment on behalf of the owner or coowner, nor any restriction on the right of the owner or coowner to receive payment of the bond or interest, except as provided in this section may be made in the registration or otherwise. Registrations requested in applications for the purchase shall be clear, accurate, complete, and conform with one of the registration provisions set forth in this section, and include the appropriate taxpayer identifying number. Registrations requested will be inscribed on the face of the bond if in definitive form or on the confirmation of investment if in book-entry form. The following provisions shall apply for registration of Farm Credit Investment Bonds:

(1) In all cases the member's name (whether a natural person, fiduciary, or legal entity) or employee's name must appear as owner of the bond.

(2) A bond may be registered in the name of a fiduciary only if the fiduciary is in fact the member.

(3) A member or employee may not use a form of registration (such as a gift to a minor, irrevocable trust, etc.) which would divest himself of ownership. However, a minor may be named as coowner or beneficiary.

(4) If a member is a natural person, a second natural person, member or nonmember, may be named as coowner or beneficiary. Coownership may not involve a fiduciary or private organization.

(5) In the coownership form the connective "or" shall serve the same purpose as "joint tenants with right of survivorship."

[43 FR 47489, Oct. 16, 1978; 43 FR 55239, Nov. 27, 1978, as amended at 56 FR 2675, Jan. 24, 1991; 61 FR 67187, Dec. 20, 1996]

§ 615.5130 Procedures.

Procedures relating to issuance, pricing, payment of interest, redemption, replacement of lost or stolen bonds and other matters shall be promulgated under the authority of this regulation as operating instructions to banks and associations.

[37 FR 11434, June 7, 1972]

Subpart E—Investment Management

§ 615.5131 Definitions.

For purposes of this subpart, the following definitions apply:

(a) *Asset-backed securities (ABS)* mean investment securities that provide for ownership of a fractional undivided interest or collateral interests in specific assets of a trust that are sold and traded in the capital markets. For the purposes of this subpart, ABS exclude mortgage securities that are defined in § 615.5131(h).

(b) *Eurodollar time deposit* means a non-negotiable deposit denominated in United States dollars and issued by an overseas branch of a United States bank or by a foreign bank outside the United States.

(c) *Final maturity* means the last date on which the remaining principal amount of a security is due and payable (matures) to the registered owner. It does not mean the call date, the expected average life, the duration, or the weighted average maturity.

(d) *General obligations* of a State or political subdivision means:

(1) The full faith and credit obligations of a State, the District of Columbia, the Commonwealth of Puerto Rico, a territory or possession of the United States, or a political subdivision thereof that possesses general powers of taxation, including property taxation; or

Farm Credit Administration

§ 615.5133

(2) An obligation that is unconditionally guaranteed by an obligor possessing general powers of taxation, including property taxation.

(e) *Liquid investments* are assets that can be promptly converted into cash without significant loss to the investor. In the money market, a security is liquid if the spread between its bid and ask price is narrow and a reasonable amount can be sold at those prices.

(f) *Loans* are defined by § 621.2(f) of this chapter and they are calculated quarterly (as of the last day of March, June, September, and December) by using the average daily balance of loans during the quarter.

(g) *Market risk* means the risk to the financial condition of your institution because the value of your holdings may decline if interest rates or market prices change. Exposure to market risk is measured by assessing the effect of changing rates and prices on either the earnings or economic value of an individual instrument, a portfolio, or the entire institution.

(h) *Mortgage securities* means securities that are either:

(1) Pass-through securities or participation certificates that represent ownership of a fractional undivided interest in a specified pool of residential (excluding home equity loans), multifamily or commercial mortgages, or

(2) A multiclass security (including collateralized mortgage obligations and real estate mortgage investment conduits) that is backed by a pool of residential, multifamily or commercial real estate mortgages, pass-through mortgage securities, or other multiclass mortgage securities.

(i) *Nationally Recognized Statistical Rating Organization (NRSRO)* means a rating organization that the Securities and Exchange Commission recognizes as an NRSRO.

(j) *Revenue bond* means an obligation of a municipal government that finances a specific project or enterprise but it is not a full faith and credit obligation. The obligor pays a portion of the revenue generated by the project or enterprise to the bondholders.

(k) *Weighted average life (WAL)* means the average time until the investor receives the principal on a security, weighted by the size of each principal payment and calculated under specified prepayment assumptions.

(l) *You* means a Farm Credit bank, association, or service corporation.

[64 FR 28895, May 28, 1999, as amended at 70 FR 51589, Aug. 31, 2005]

§ 615.5132 Investment purposes.

Each Farm Credit bank is allowed to hold eligible investments, listed under § 615.5140, in an amount not to exceed 35 percent of its total outstanding loans, to comply with the liquidity reserve requirement of § 615.5134, manage surplus short-term funds, and manage interest rate risk under § 615.5135.

[70 FR 51589, Aug. 31, 2005]

§ 615.5133 Investment management.

(a) *Responsibilities of Board of Directors.* Your board must adopt written policies for managing your investment activities. Your board of directors must also ensure that management complies with these policies and that appropriate internal controls are in place to prevent loss. Annually, the board of directors must review these investment policies and make any changes that are needed.

(b) *Investment policies.* Your board's written investment policies must address the purposes and objectives of investments, risk tolerance, delegations of authority, and reporting requirements. Investment policies must be appropriate for the size, types, and risk characteristics of your investments.

(c) *Risk tolerance.* Your investment policies must establish risk limits and diversification requirements for the various classes of eligible investments and for the entire investment portfolio. These policies must ensure that you maintain appropriate diversification of your investment portfolio. Risk limits must be based on your institutional objectives, capital position, and risk tolerance. Your policies must identify the types and quantity of investments that you will hold to achieve your objectives and control credit, market, liquidity, and operational risks. The policy of any association or service corporation that holds significant investments and each bank must establish risk limits for the following four types of risk.

§ 615.5134

(1) *Credit risk.* Investment policies must establish:

(i) Credit quality standards, limits on counterparty risk, and risk diversification standards that limit concentrations based on a single or related counterparty(ies), a geographical area, industries or obligations with similar characteristics.

(ii) Criteria for selecting brokers, dealers, and investment bankers (collectively, securities firms). You must buy and sell eligible investments with more than one securities firm. As part of your annual review of your investment policies, your board of directors must review the criteria for selecting securities firms and determine whether to continue your existing relationships with them.

(iii) Collateral margin requirements on repurchase agreements.

(2) *Market risk.* Investment policies must set market risk limits for specific types of investments, the investment portfolio, or your institution. Your board of directors must establish market risk limits in accordance with these regulations and our other policies.

(3) *Liquidity risk.* Investment policies must describe the liquidity characteristics of eligible investments that you will hold to meet your liquidity needs and institutional objectives.

(4) *Operational risk.* Investment policies must address operational risks, including delegations of authority and internal controls in accordance with paragraphs (d) and (e) of this section.

(d) *Delegation of authority.* All delegations of authority to specified personnel or committees must state the extent of management's authority and responsibilities for investments.

(e) *Internal controls.* You must:

(1) Establish appropriate internal controls to detect and prevent loss, fraud, embezzlement, conflicts of interest, and unauthorized investments.

(2) Establish and maintain a separation of duties and supervision between personnel who execute investment transactions and personnel who approve, revaluate, and oversee investments.

(3) Maintain management information systems that are appropriate for the level and complexity of your investment activities.

(f) *Securities valuation.* (1) Before you purchase a security, you must evaluate its credit quality and its price sensitivity to changes in market interest rates. You must also verify the value of a security that you plan to purchase, other than a new issue, with a source that is independent of the broker, dealer, counterparty or other intermediary to the transaction.

(2) You must determine the fair market value of each security in your portfolio and the fair market value of your whole investment portfolio at least monthly. You must also evaluate the credit quality and price sensitivity to change in market interest rates of all investments that you hold on an ongoing basis.

(3) Before you sell a security, you must verify its value with a source that is independent of the broker, dealer, counterparty, or other intermediary to the transaction.

(g) *Reports to the board.* Each quarter, management must report to the board of directors or a board committee on the performance and risk of each class of investments and the entire investment portfolio. These reports must identify all gains and losses that you incur during the quarter on individual securities that you sold before maturity. Reports must also identify potential risk exposure to changes in market interest rates and other factors that may affect the value of your bank's investment holdings. Management's report must discuss how investments affect your bank's overall financial condition and must evaluate whether the performance of the investment portfolio effectively achieves the board's objectives. Any deviations from the board's policies must be specifically identified in the report.

[64 FR 28895, May 28, 1999]

§ 615.5134 Liquidity reserve requirement.

(a) Each Farm Credit bank must maintain a liquidity reserve, discounted in accordance with paragraph (c) of this section, sufficient to fund 90 days of the principal portion of maturing obligations and other borrowings of the bank at all times. The liquidity reserve may only be funded from cash, including cash due from traded but not yet settled debt, and the eligible investments under § 615.5140. Money market instruments, floating, and fixed rate debt securities used to fund the liquidity reserve must be backed by the full faith and credit of the United States or rated in one of the two highest NRSRO credit categories. If not rated, the issuer's NRSRO credit rating, if one of the two highest, may be used.

(b) All investments that the bank holds for the purpose of meeting the liquidity reserve requirement of this section must be free of lien.

(c) The liquid assets of the liquidity reserve are discounted as follows:

(1) Multiply cash and overnight investments by 100 percent.

(2) Multiply money market instruments and floating rate debt securities that are below the contractual cap rate by 95 percent of the market value.

(3) Multiply fixed rate debt securities and floating rate debt securities that meet or exceed the contractual cap rate by 90 percent of the market value.

(4) Multiply individual securities in diversified investment funds by the discounts that would apply to the securities if held separately.

(d) Each Farm Credit bank must have a contingency plan to address liquidity shortfalls during market disruptions. The board of directors must review the plan each year, making all needed changes. Farm Credit banks may incorporate these requirements into their § 615.5133 investment management policies.

[58 FR 63056, Nov. 30, 1993, as amended at 64 FR 28896, May 28, 1999; 70 FR 51590, Aug. 31, 2005]

§ 615.5135 Management of interest rate risk.

The board of directors of each Farm Credit Bank, bank for cooperatives, and agricultural credit bank shall develop and implement an interest rate risk management program as set forth in subpart G of this part. The board of directors shall adopt an interest rate risk management section of an asset/liability management policy which establishes interest rate risk exposure limits as well as the criteria to determine compliance with these limits. At a minimum, the interest rate risk management section shall establish policies and procedures for the bank to:

(a) Identify and analyze the causes of risks within its existing balance sheet structure;

(b) Measure the potential impact of these risks on projected earnings and market values by conducting interest rate shock tests and simulations of multiple economic scenarios at least on a quarterly basis;

(c) Explore and implement actions needed to obtain its desired risk management objectives;

(d) Document the objectives that the bank is attempting to achieve by purchasing eligible investments that are authorized by § 615.5140 of this subpart;

(e) Evaluate and document, at least quarterly, whether these investments have actually met the objectives stated under paragraph (d) of this section.

[58 FR 63056, Nov. 30, 1993, as amended at 63 FR 39225, July 22, 1998]

§ 615.5136 Emergencies impeding normal access of Farm Credit banks to capital markets.

An emergency shall be deemed to exist whenever a financial, economic, agricultural or national defense crisis could impede the normal access of Farm Credit banks to the capital markets. Whenever the Farm Credit Administration determines after consultations with the Federal Farm Credit Banks Funding Corporation that such an emergency exists, the Farm Credit Administration Board shall, in its sole discretion, adopt a resolution that:

(a) Increases the amount of eligible investments that Farm Credit Banks, banks for cooperatives and agricultural credit banks are authorized to hold pursuant to § 615.5132 of this subpart; and/or

(b) Modifies or waives the liquidity reserve requirement in § 615.5134 of this subpart.

[58 FR 63057, Nov. 30, 1993]

§ 615.5140 Eligible investments.

(a) You may hold only the following types of investments listed in the Investment Eligibility Criteria Table. These investments must be denominated in United States dollars.

Investment Eligibility Criteria Table

ASSET CLASS	FINAL MATURITY LIMIT	NRSRO CREDIT RATING	OTHER REQUIREMENTS	INVESTMENT PORTFOLIO LIMIT
(1) Obligations of the United States	None	NA	None	None
• Treasuries				
• Agency securities (except mortgage securities)				
• Other obligations fully insured or guaranteed by the United States, its agencies, instrumentalities and corporations				
(2) Municipal Securities				
• General obligations	10 years	One of the highest two	None	None
• Revenue bonds	5 years	Highest	At the time of purchase, you must document that the issue is actively traded in an established secondary market	15%
(3) International and Multilateral Development Bank Obligations	None	None	The United States must be a voting shareholder	None
(4) Money Market Instruments				
• Federal funds	1 day or continuously callable up to 100 days	One of the two highest short-term	None	None
• Negotiable certificates of deposit	1 year		None	None
• Bankers acceptances	None		Issued by a depository institution	None
• Commercial paper	270 days			None
• Non-callable Term Federal funds and Eurodollar time deposits	100 days	Highest short-term	None	20%
• Master notes	270 days			20%
• Repurchase agreements collateralized by eligible investments or marketable securities rated in the highest credit rating category by an NRSRO	100 days	NA	If counterparty defaults, you must divest non-eligible securities under § 615.5143	None

Farm Credit Administration

§ 615.5140

ASSET CLASS	FINAL MATURITY LIMIT	NRSRO CREDIT RATING	OTHER REQUIREMENTS	INVESTMENT PORTFOLIO LIMIT
(5) Mortgage Securities				
• Issued or guaranteed by the United States	None	NA	Stress testing under § 615.5141	None
• Fannie Mae or Freddie Mac mortgage securities	None	NA	Stress testing under § 615.5141	50%
• Non-Agency securities that comply 15 U.S.C. 77d(5) or 15 U.S.C. 78c(a)(41)	None	Highest	Stress testing under § 615.5141	15%
• Commercial mortgage-backed securities	None	Highest	• Security must be backed by a minimum of 100 loans. • Loans from a single mortgagor cannot exceed 5% of the pool • Pool must be geographically diversified pursuant to the board's policy • Stress testing under § 615.5141	
(6) Asset-Backed Securities secured by: • Credit card receivables • Automobile loans • Home equity loans • Wholesale automobile dealer loans • Student loans • Equipment loans • Manufactured housing loans	None	Highest	5-year WAL for fixed rate or floating rate ABS at their contractual interest rate caps 7-year WAL for floating rate ABS that remain below their contractual interest rate cap	20%
(7) Corporate Debt Securities	5 years	One of the two highest	Cannot be convertible to equity securities	20%
(8) Diversified Investment Funds Shares of an investment company registered under section 8 of the Investment Company Act of 1940	NA	NA	The portfolio of the investment company must consist solely of eligible investments authorized by §§ 615.5140 and 615.5174. The investment company's risk and return objectives and use of derivatives must be consistent with FCA guidance and your investment policies.	None, if your shares in each investment company comprise 10% or less of your portfolio. Otherwise counts toward limit for each type of investment.

(b) *Rating of foreign countries.* Whenever the obligor or issuer of an eligible investment is located outside the United States, the host country must maintain the highest sovereign rating for political and economic stability by an NRSRO.

(c) *Marketable securities.* All eligible investments, except money market instruments, must be marketable. An eligible investment is marketable if you can sell it quickly at a price that closely reflects its fair value in an active and universally recognized secondary market.

(d) *Obligor limits.* (1) You may not invest more than 20 percent of your total capital in eligible investments issued by any single institution, issuer, or obligor. This obligor limit does not apply to obligations, including mortgage securities, that are issued or guaranteed as to interest and principal by the United States, its agencies, instrumentalities, or corporations.

(2) *Obligor limits for your holdings in an investment company.* You must count securities that you hold through an investment company towards the obligor limit of this section unless the investment company's holdings of the security of any one issuer do not exceed five (5) percent of the investment company's total portfolio.

(e) *Other investments approved by the FCA.* You may purchase and hold other investments that we approve. Your request for our approval must explain the risk characteristics of the investment and your purpose and objectives for making the investment.

[64 FR 28896, May 28, 1999]

§ 615.5141 Stress tests for mortgage securities.

Mortgage securities are not eligible investments unless they pass a stress test. You must perform stress tests to determine how interest rate changes will affect the cashflow and price of each mortgage security that you purchase and hold, except for adjustable rate securities that reprice at intervals of 12 months or less and are tied to an index. You must also use stress tests to gauge how interest rate fluctuations on mortgage securities affect your institution's capital and earnings. You may conduct the stress tests as described in either paragraph (a) or (b) of this section.

(a) Mortgage securities must comply with the following three tests at the time of purchase and each following quarter:

(1) *Average Life Test.* The expected WAL of the instrument does not exceed 5 years.

(2) *Average Life Sensitivity Test.* The expected WAL does not extend for more than 2 years, assuming an immediate and sustained parallel shift in the yield curve of plus 300 basis points, nor shorten for more than 3 years, assuming an immediate and sustained parallel shift in the yield curve of minus 300 basis points.

(3) *Price Sensitivity Test.* The estimated change in price is not more than thirteen (13) percent due to an immediate and sustained parallel shift in the yield curve of plus or minus 300 basis points.

(4) *Exemption.* A floating rate mortgage security is subject only to the price sensitivity test in paragraph (a)(3) of this section if at the time of purchase and each quarter thereafter it bears a rate of interest that is below its contractual cap.

(b) You may use an alternative stress test to evaluate the price sensitivity of your mortgage securities. An alternative stress test must be able to measure the price sensitivity of mortgage instruments over different interest rate/yield curve scenarios. The methodology that you use to analyze mortgage securities must be appropriate for the complexity of the instrument's structure and cashflows. Prior to purchase and each quarter thereafter, you must use the stress test to determine that the risk in the mortgage security is within the risk limits of your board's investment policies. The stress test must enable you to determine at the time of purchase and each subsequent quarter that the mortgage security does not expose your capital or earnings to excessive risks.

(c) You must rely on verifiable information to support all your assumptions, including prepayment and interest rate volatility assumptions, when you apply the stress tests in either paragraph (a) or (b) of this section. You must document the basis for all assumptions that you use to evaluate the security and its underlying mortgages. You must also document all subsequent changes in your assumptions. If at any time after purchase, a mortgage security no longer complies with requirements in this section, you must divest it in accordance with § 615.5143.

[64 FR 28899, May 28, 1999]

§ 615.5142 Association investments.

An association may hold eligible investments listed in § 615.5140, with the approval of its funding bank, for the purposes of reducing interest rate risk and managing surplus short-term funds. Each bank must review annually the investment portfolio of every association that it funds.

[64 FR 28899, May 28, 1999]

§ 615.5143 Disposal of ineligible investments.

You must dispose of an ineligible investment within 6 months unless we approve, in writing, a plan that authorizes you to divest the instrument over a longer period of time. An acceptable divestiture plan must require you to dispose of the ineligible investment as quickly as possible without substantial financial loss. Until you actually dispose of the ineligible investment, the managers of your investment portfolio must report at least quarterly to your board of directors about the status and performance of the ineligible instrument, the reasons why it remains ineligible, and the managers' progress in disposing of the investment.

[64 FR 28899, May 28, 1999]

§ 615.5144 Banks for cooperatives and agricultural credit banks.

As may be authorized by the banks for cooperatives' or agricultural credit banks boards of directors ownership investment may be made in foreign business entities solely for the purpose of obtaining credit information and other services needed to facilitate transactions which may be financed under section 3.7(b) of the Farm Credit Act Amendments of 1980. Such an investment shall not exceed the level required to access credit and other services of the entity and shall not be made for earnings purposes. The business entity shall be deemed to be principally engaged in providing credit information to and performing such servicing functions for its members where such activities constitute a materially important line of business to its members. Also, investments must be made by a bank for cooperatives or agricultural credit bank for its own account and not on behalf of its members. The bank for cooperatives or agricultural credit bank shall use only those services provided by the business entity as necessary to facilitate transactions authorized by section 3.7(b) of the Farm Credit Act Amendments of 1980.

[46 FR 55088, Nov. 6, 1981, as amended at 54 FR 1151, Jan. 12, 1989; 54 FR 50736, Dec. 11, 1989; 61 FR 67187, Dec. 20, 1996. Redesignated at 64 FR 28899, May 28, 1999]

Subpart F—Property, Transfers of Capital, and Other Investments

§ 615.5170 Real and personal property.

Real estate and personal property may be acquired, held, or disposed of by any Farm Credit institution for the necessary and normal operations of its business. The purchase, lease, or construction of office quarters shall be limited to facilities reasonably necessary to meet the foreseeable requirements of the institution. Property shall not be acquired if it involves, or appears to involve, a bank or association in the real estate or other unrelated business.

[50 FR 48554, Nov. 26, 1985. Redesignated at 58 FR 63056, Nov. 30, 1993, and amended at 60 FR 20011, Apr. 24, 1995]

§ 615.5171 Transfer of capital from banks to associations.

(a) *Definitions for this section*—(1) *Transfer of capital* means any payment or forbearance by a Farm Credit Bank or agricultural credit bank (collectively, bank) to an affiliated association, including but not limited to:

(i) The purchase of nonvoting stock or participation certificates;

(ii) The payment of cash;

(iii) Debt forgiveness or reduction;

(iv) Interest rate concessions or interest-free loans;

(v) The transfer of loans at other than fair market value;

(vi) The reduction or elimination of standard loan servicing or other fees; and

§ 615.5172

(vii) The assumption of operating or other expenses, such as legal fees or insurance premiums.

(2) *Preferential transfer of capital* means a transfer of capital that is not available to all similarly situated affiliated associations.

(3) *Nonroutine transfer of capital* means a transfer of capital that is not available in the ordinary course of business.

(b) *Considerations for preferential or nonroutine transfers of capital.* Before authorizing a preferential or nonroutine transfer of capital, a bank board of directors must take into account and document whether:

(1) The transfer of capital is in the best interests of all of the shareholders;

(2) The bank will be able to achieve its capital adequacy and business plan goals after making the transfer of capital; and

(3) The transfer of capital is the "least cost" alternative available and will enable the association to maintain sound, adequate, and constructive service to borrowers.

(c) *Notification requirements.* At least 30 days before making a preferential or nonroutine transfer of capital to an affiliated association, banks must provide shareholders and the Chief Examiner of the Farm Credit Administration with a description of the transfer and the documentation required by paragraph (b) of this section.

[64 FR 49961, Sept. 15, 1999]

§ 615.5172 Production credit association and agricultural credit association investment in farmers' notes given to cooperatives and dealers.

(a) In accordance with policies prescribed by the board of directors of the Farm Credit Bank or agricultural credit bank and each production credit association and agricultural credit association (hereinafter association(s)), such association(s) may invest in notes, conditional sales contracts, and other similar obligations given to cooperatives and private dealers by farmers and ranchers eligible to borrow from such associations.

(b) Such notes and other obligations evidencing purchases of farm machinery, supplies, equipment, home appliances, and other items of a capital nature handled by cooperatives and private dealers will be eligible for purchase as investments.

(c) The total amount which an association may invest in such obligations at any one time shall not exceed 15 percent of the balance of its loans outstanding at the close of the association's preceding fiscal year. In addition, the total amount which an association may invest in such obligations that are originated by any one cooperative or private dealer, at any one time, shall not exceed 50 percent of association capital and surplus.

(d) All notes in which an association invests shall be endorsed with full recourse against the cooperative or dealer. The association shall contact each notemaker who meets the association's credit standards to encourage him to become a borrower.

[54 FR 1158, Jan. 12, 1989, as amended at 55 FR 24888, June 19, 1990; 55 FR 38313, Sept. 18, 1990. Redesignated at 58 FR 63056, Nov. 30, 1993]

§ 615.5173 Stock of the Federal Agricultural Mortgage Corporation.

Banks and associations of the Farm Credit System are authorized to purchase and hold Class B common stock of the Federal Agricultural Mortgage Corporation pursuant to section 8.4 of the Farm Credit Act.

[58 FR 63058, Nov. 30, 1993]

§ 615.5174 Farmer Mac securities.

(a) *General authority.* You may purchase and hold mortgage securities that are issued or guaranteed as to both principal and interest by the Federal Agricultural Mortgage Corporation (Farmer Mac securities). You may purchase and hold Farmer Mac securities for the purposes of managing credit and interest rate risks, and furthering your mission to finance agriculture. The total value of your Farmer Mac securities cannot exceed your total outstanding loans, as defined by § 615.5131(f).

(b) *Board and management responsibilities.* Your board of directors must adopt written policies that will govern your investments in Farmer Mac securities. All delegations of authority to specified personnel or committees

Farm Credit Administration §615.5182

must state the extent of management's authority and responsibilities for managing your investments in Farmer Mac securities. The board of directors must also ensure that appropriate internal controls are in place to prevent loss, in accordance with §615.5133(e). Management must submit quarterly reports to the board of directors on the performance of all investments in Farmer Mac securities. Annually, your board of directors must review these policies and the performance of your Farmer Mac securities and make any changes that are needed.

(c) *Policies.* Your board of directors must establish investment policies for Farmer Mac securities that include your:

(1) *Objectives* for holding Farmer Mac securities.

(2) *Credit risk* parameters including:

(i) The quantities and types of Farmer Mac mortgage securities that are collateralized by qualified agricultural mortgages, rural home loans, and loans guaranteed by the Farm Service Agency.

(ii) Product and geographic diversification for the loans that underlie the security; and

(iii) Minimum pool size, minimum number of loans in each pool, and maximum allowable premiums or discounts on these securities.

(3) *Liquidity risk* tolerance and the liquidity characteristics of Farmer Mac securities that are suitable to meet your institutional objectives. A bank may not include Farmer Mac mortgage securities in the liquidity reserve maintained to comply with §615.5134.

(4) *Market risk* limits based on the effects that the Farmer Mac securities have on your capital and earnings.

(d) *Stress Test.* You must perform stress tests on mortgage securities that are issued or guaranteed by Farmer Mac in accordance with the requirements of §615.5141(b) and (c). If a Farmer Mac security fails a stress test, you must divest it as required by §615.5143.

[64 FR 28899, May 28, 1999, as amended at 70 FR 51590, Aug. 31, 2005]

§ 615.5175 **Investments in Farm Credit System institution preferred stock.**

Except as provided for in §615.5171, Farm Credit banks, associations and service corporations may only purchase preferred stock issued by another Farm Credit System institution, including the Federal Agricultural Mortgage Corporation, with the written prior approval of the Farm Credit Administration. The request for approval should explain the terms and risk characteristics of the investment and the purpose and objectives for making the investment.

[70 FR 53908, Sept. 13, 2005]

Subpart G—Risk Assessment and Management

SOURCE: 63 FR 39225, July 22, 1998, unless otherwise noted.

§ 615.5180 **Interest rate risk management by banks—general.**

The board of directors of each Farm Credit Bank, bank for cooperatives, and agricultural credit bank shall develop and implement an interest rate risk management program tailored to the needs of the institution and consistent with the requirements set forth in §615.5135 of this part. The program shall establish a risk management process that effectively identifies, measures, monitors, and controls interest rate risk.

§ 615.5181 **Bank interest rate risk management program.**

(a) The board of directors of each Farm Credit Bank, bank for cooperatives, and agricultural credit bank is responsible for providing effective oversight to the interest rate risk management program and must be knowledgeable of the nature and level of interest rate risk taken by the institution.

(b) Senior management is responsible for ensuring that interest rate risk is properly managed on both a long-range and a day-to-day basis.

§ 615.5182 **Interest rate risk management by associations and other Farm Credit System institutions other than banks.**

Any association or other Farm Credit System institution other than banks, excluding the Federal Agricultural Mortgage Corporation, with interest rate risk that could lead to significant

173

§ 615.5200

declines in net income or in the market value of capital shall comply with the requirements of §§ 615.5180 and 615.5181. The interest rate risk management program required under § 615.5181 shall be commensurate with the level of interest rate risk of the institution.

Subpart H—Capital Adequacy

SOURCE: 53 FR 39247, Oct. 6, 1988, unless otherwise noted.

§ 615.5200 Capital planning.

(a) The Board of Directors of each Farm Credit System institution shall determine the amount of total capital, core surplus, total surplus, and unallocated surplus needed to assure the institution's continued financial viability and to provide for growth necessary to meet the needs of its borrowers. The minimum capital standards specified in this part are not meant to be adopted as the optimal capital level in the institution's capital adequacy plan. Rather, the standards are intended to serve as minimum levels of capital that each institution must maintain to protect against the credit and other general risks inherent in its operations.

(b) Each Board of Directors shall establish, adopt, and maintain a formal written capital adequacy plan as a part of the financial plan required by § 618.8440 of this chapter. The plan shall include the capital targets that are necessary to achieve the institution's capital adequacy goals as well as the minimum permanent capital and surplus standards. The plan shall address any projected dividends, patronage distribution, equity requirements, or other action that may decrease the institution's capital or the components thereof for which minimum amounts are required by this part. The plan shall set forth the circumstances in which retirements or revolvements of stock or equities may occur. If the plan provides for retirement or revolvement of equities included in core surplus, in connection with a loan default or the death of a former borrower, the plan must require the institution to make a prior determination that such retirement or revolvement is in the best interest of the institution, and also require the institution to charge off an amount of the indebtedness on the loan equal to the amount of the equities that are retired or canceled. In addition to factors that must be considered in meeting the minimum standards, the board of directors shall also consider at least the following factors in developing the capital adequacy plan:

(1) Capability of management and the board of directors;

(2) Quality of operating policies, procedures, and internal controls;

(3) Quality and quantity of earnings;

(4) Asset quality and the adequacy of the allowance for losses to absorb potential loss within the loan and lease portfolios;

(5) Sufficiency of liquid funds;

(6) Needs of an institution's customer base; and

(7) Any other risk-oriented activities, such as funding and interest rate risks, potential obligations under joint and several liability, contingent and off-balance-sheet liabilities or other conditions warranting additional capital.

[53 FR 39247, Oct. 6, 1988, as amended at 62 FR 4446, Jan. 30, 1997; 71 FR 5763, Feb. 2, 2006]

§ 615.5201 Definitions.

For the purpose of this subpart, the following definitions apply:

Allocated investment means earnings allocated but not paid in cash by a System bank to an association or other recipient.

Bank means an institution that:

(1) Engages in the business of banking;

(2) Is recognized as a bank by the bank supervisory or monetary authority of the country of its organization or principal banking operations;

(3) Receives deposits to a substantial extent in the regular course of business; and

(4) Has the power to accept demand deposits.

Commitment means any arrangement that legally obligates an institution to:

(1) Purchase loans or securities;

(2) Participate in loans or leases;

(3) Extend credit in the form of loans or leases;

(4) Pay the obligation of another;

(5) Provide overdraft, revolving credit, or underwriting facilities; or

Farm Credit Administration §615.5201

(6) Participate in similar transactions.

Credit conversion factor means that number by which an off-balance sheet item is multiplied to obtain a credit equivalent before placing the item in a risk-weight category.

Credit derivative means a contract that allows one party (the protection purchaser) to transfer the credit risk of an asset or off-balance sheet credit exposure to another party (the protection provider). The value of a credit derivative is dependent, at least in part, on the credit performance of a "reference asset."

Credit-enhancing interest-only strip—

(1) The term credit-enhancing interest-only strip means an on-balance sheet asset that, in form or in substance:

(i) Represents the contractual right to receive some or all of the interest due on transferred assets; and

(ii) Exposes the institution to credit risk directly or indirectly associated with the transferred assets that exceeds its pro rata claim on the assets, whether through subordination provisions or other credit enhancement techniques.

(2) FCA reserves the right to identify other cash flows or related interests as credit-enhancing interest-only strips. In determining whether a particular interest cash flow functions as a credit-enhancing interest-only strip, FCA will consider the economic substance of the transaction.

Credit-enhancing representations and warranties—

(1) The term credit-enhancing representations and warranties means representations and warranties that:

(i) Are made or assumed in connection with a transfer of assets (including loan-servicing assets), and

(ii) Obligate an institution to protect investors from losses arising from credit risk in the assets transferred or loans serviced.

(2) Credit-enhancing representations and warranties include promises to protect a party from losses resulting from the default or nonperformance of another party or from an insufficiency in the value of the collateral.

(3) Credit-enhancing representations and warranties do not include:

(i) Early-default clauses and similar warranties that permit the return of, or premium refund clauses covering, loans for a period not to exceed 120 days from the date of transfer. These warranties may cover only those loans that were originated within 1 year of the date of the transfer;

(ii) Premium refund clauses covering assets guaranteed, in whole or in part, by the United States Government, a United States Government agency, or a United States Government-sponsored agency, provided the premium refund clause is for a period not to exceed 120 days from the date of transfer;

(iii) Warranties that permit the return of assets in instances of fraud, misrepresentation, or incomplete documentation; or

(iv) Clean-up calls if the agreements to repurchase are limited to 10 percent or less of the original pool balance (except where loans 30 days or more past due are repurchased).

Deferred-tax assets that are dependent on future income or future events means:

(1) Deferred-tax assets arising from deductible temporary differences dependent upon future income that exceed the amount of taxes previously paid that could be recovered through loss carrybacks if existing temporary differences (both deductible and taxable and regardless of where the related tax-deferred effects are recorded on the institution's balance sheet) fully reverse;

(2) Deferred-tax assets dependent upon future income arising from operating loss and tax carryforwards;

(3) Deferred-tax assets arising from temporary differences that could be recovered if existing temporary differences that are dependent upon other future events (both deductible and taxable and regardless of where the related tax-deferred effects are recorded on the institution's balance sheet) fully reverse.

Direct credit substitute means an arrangement in which an institution assumes, in form or in substance, credit risk directly or indirectly associated with an on-or off-balance sheet asset or exposure that was not previously owned by the institution (third-party asset) and the risk assumed by the institution exceeds the pro rata share of

§ 615.5201

the institution's interest in the third-party asset. If the institution has no claim on the third-party asset, then the institution's assumption of any credit risk is a direct credit substitute. Direct credit substitutes include, but are not limited to:

(1) Financial standby letters of credit that support financial claims on a third party that exceed an institution's pro rata share in the financial claim;

(2) Guarantees, surety arrangements, credit derivatives, and similar instruments backing financial claims that exceed an institution's pro rata share in the financial claim;

(3) Purchased subordinated interests that absorb more than their pro rata share of losses from the underlying assets;

(4) Credit derivative contracts under which the institution assumes more than its pro rata share of credit risk on a third-party asset or exposure;

(5) Loans or lines of credit that provide credit enhancement for the financial obligations of a third party;

(6) Purchased loan-servicing assets if the servicer is responsible for credit losses or if the servicer makes or assumes credit-enhancing representations and warranties with respect to the loans serviced. Servicer cash advances as defined in this section are not direct credit substitutes; and,

(7) Clean-up calls on third-party assets. However, clean-up calls that are 10 percent or less of the original pool balance and that are exercisable at the option of the institution are not direct credit substitutes.

Direct lender institution means an institution that extends credit in the form of loans or leases to eligible borrowers in its own right and carries such loan or lease assets on its books.

Externally rated means that an instrument or obligation has received a credit rating from at least one NRSRO.

Face amount means:

(1) The notional principal, or face value, amount of an off-balance sheet item;

(2) The amortized cost of an asset not held for trading purposes; and

(3) The fair value of a trading asset.

Financial asset means cash or other monetary instrument, evidence of debt, evidence of an ownership interest in an entity, or a contract that conveys a right to receive from or exchange cash or another financial instrument with another party.

Financial standby letter of credit means a letter of credit or similar arrangement that represents an irrevocable obligation to a third-party beneficiary:

(1) To repay money borrowed by, or advanced to, or for the account of, a second party (the account party); or

(2) To make payment on behalf of the account party, in the event that the account party fails to fulfill its obligation to the beneficiary.

Government agency means an agency or instrumentality of the United States Government whose obligations are fully and explicitly guaranteed as to the timely repayment of principal and interest by the full faith and credit of the United States Government.

Government-sponsored agency means an agency, instrumentality, or corporation chartered or established to serve public purposes specified by the United States Congress but whose obligations are not explicitly guaranteed by the full faith and credit of the United States Government, including but not limited to any Government-sponsored enterprise.

Institution means a Farm Credit Bank, Federal land bank association, Federal land credit association, production credit association, agricultural credit association, Farm Credit Leasing Services Corporation, bank for cooperatives, agricultural credit bank, and their successors.

Nationally recognized statistical rating organization (NRSRO) means a rating organization that the Securities and Exchange Commission recognizes as an NRSRO.

Non-OECD bank means a bank and its branches (foreign and domestic) organized under the laws of a country that does not belong to the OECD group of countries.

Nonagreeing association means an association that does not have an allotment agreement in effect with a Farm Credit Bank or agricultural credit bank pursuant to § 615.5207(b)(2).

Farm Credit Administration §615.5201

OECD means the group of countries that are full members of the Organization for Economic Cooperation and Development, regardless of entry date, as well as countries that have concluded special lending arrangements with the International Monetary Fund's General Arrangement to Borrow, excluding any country that has rescheduled its external sovereign debt within the previous 5 years.

OECD bank means a bank and its branches (foreign and domestic) organized under the laws of a country that belongs to the OECD group of countries. For purposes of this subpart, this term includes U.S. depository institutions.

Preferred stock means stock that is permanent capital and has dividend and/or liquidation preference over common stock.

Performance-based standby letter of credit means any letter of credit, or similar arrangement, however named or described, that represents an irrevocable obligation to the beneficiary on the part of the issuer to make payment as a result of any default by a third party in the performance of a nonfinancial or commercial obligation.

Permanent capital, subject to adjustments as described in §615.5207, includes:

(1) Current year retained earnings;

(2) Allocated and unallocated earnings (which, in the case of earnings allocated in any form by a System bank to any association or other recipient and retained by the bank, must be considered, in whole or in part, permanent capital of the bank or of any such association or other recipient as provided under an agreement between the bank and each such association or other recipient);

(3) All surplus;

(4) Stock issued by a System institution, except:

(i) Stock that may be retired by the holder of the stock on repayment of the holder's loan, or otherwise at the option or request of the holder;

(ii) Stock that is protected under section 4.9A of the Act or is otherwise not at risk;

(iii) Farm Credit Bank equities required to be purchased by Federal land bank associations in connection with stock issued to borrowers that is protected under section 4.9A of the Act;

(iv) Capital subject to revolvement, unless:

(A) The bylaws of the institution clearly provide that there is no express or implied right for such capital to be retired at the end of the revolvement cycle or at any other time; and

(B) The institution clearly states in the notice of allocation that such capital may only be retired at the sole discretion of the board of directors in accordance with statutory and regulatory requirements and that no express or implied right to have such capital retired at the end of the revolvement cycle or at any other time is thereby granted;

(5) [Reserved]

(6) Financial assistance provided by the Farm Credit System Insurance Corporation that the FCA determines appropriate to be considered permanent capital; and

(7) Any other debt or equity instruments or other accounts the FCA has determined are appropriate to be considered permanent capital. The FCA may permit one or more institutions to include all or a portion of such instrument, entry, or account as permanent capital, permanently or on a temporary basis, for purposes of this part.

Qualified residential loan—

(1) The term qualified residential loan means:

(i) A rural home loan, as authorized by §613.3030, and

(ii) A single-family residential loan to a bona fide farmer, rancher, or producer or harvester of aquatic products.

(2) A qualified residential loan must be secured by a separate first lien mortgage or deed of trust on the residential property alone (not on any adjoining agricultural property or any other nonresidential property), must have been approved in accordance with prudent underwriting standards suitable for residential property, must not be past due 90 days or more or carried in nonaccrual status, and must have a monthly amortization schedule. In addition, the mortgage or deed of trust securing the residential property must be written and recorded in accordance with all state and local requirements governing its enforceability as a first

lien and the secured residential property must have a permanent right-of-way access.

Qualifying bilateral netting contract means a bilateral netting contract that meets at least the following conditions:

(1) The contract is in writing;

(2) The contract is not subject to a walkaway clause, defined as a provision that permits a non-defaulting counterparty to make lower payments than it would make otherwise under the contract, or no payment at all, to a defaulter or to the estate of a defaulter, even if the defaulter or the estate of the defaulter is a net creditor under the contract;

(3) The contract creates a single obligation either to pay or receive the net amount of the sum of positive and negative mark-to-market values for all derivative contracts subject to the qualifying bilateral netting contract;

(4) The institution receives a legal opinion that represents, to a high degree of certainty, that in the event of legal challenge the relevant court and administrative authorities would find the institution's exposure to be the net amount;

(5) The institution establishes a procedure to monitor relevant law and to ensure that the contracts continue to satisfy the requirements of this section; and

(6) The institution maintains in its files adequate documentation to support the netting of a derivatives contract.

Qualifying securities firm means:

(1) A securities firm incorporated in the United States that is a broker-dealer that is registered with the Securities and Exchange Commission (SEC) and that complies with the SEC's net capital regulations (17 CFR 240.15c3–1); and

(2) A securities firm incorporated in any other OECD-based country, if the institution is able to demonstrate that the securities firm is subject to supervision and regulation (covering its direct and indirect subsidiaries, but not necessarily its parent organizations) comparable to that imposed on depository institutions in OECD countries. Such regulation must include risk-based capital requirements comparable to those imposed on depository institutions under the Accord on International Convergence of Capital Measurement and Capital Standards (1988, as amended in 1998) (Basel Accord).

Recourse means an institution's retention, in form or in substance, of any credit risk directly or indirectly associated with an asset it has sold (in accordance with GAAP) that exceeds a pro rata share of the institution's claim on the asset. If an institution has no claim on an asset it has sold, then the retention of any credit risk is recourse. A recourse obligation typically arises when an institution transfers assets in a sale and retains an explicit obligation to repurchase assets or to absorb losses due to a default on the payment of principal or interest or any other deficiency in the performance of the underlying obligor or some other party. Recourse may also exist implicitly if an institution provides credit enhancement beyond any contractual obligation to support assets it has sold. Recourse obligations include, but are not limited to:

(1) Credit-enhancing representations and warranties made on transferred assets;

(2) Loan-servicing assets retained pursuant to an agreement under which the institution will be responsible for losses associated with the loans serviced. Servicer cash advances as defined in this section are not recourse obligations;

(3) Retained subordinated interests that absorb more than their pro rata share of losses from the underlying assets;

(4) Assets sold under an agreement to repurchase, if the assets are not already included on the balance sheet;

(5) Loan strips sold without contractual recourse where the maturity of the transferred portion of the loan is shorter than the maturity of the commitment under which the loan is drawn;

(6) Credit derivatives issued that absorb more than the institution's pro rata share of losses from the transferred assets; and

(7) Clean-up call on assets the institution has sold. However, clean-up calls that are 10 percent or less of the

Farm Credit Administration

§ 615.5201

original pool balance and that are exercisable at the option of the institution are not recourse arrangements.

Residual interest—

(1) The term residual interest means any on-balance sheet asset that:

(i) Represents an interest (including a beneficial interest) created by a transfer that qualifies as a sale (in accordance with generally accepted accounting principles) of financial assets, whether through a securitization or otherwise; and

(ii) Exposes an institution to credit risk directly or indirectly associated with the transferred asset that exceeds a pro rata share of the institution's claim on the asset, whether through subordination provisions or other credit enhancement techniques.

(2) Residual interests generally include credit-enhancing interest-only strips, spread accounts, cash collateral accounts, retained subordinated interests (and other forms of overcollateralization), and similar assets that function as a credit enhancement.

(3) Residual interests further include those exposures that, in substance, cause the institution to retain the credit risk of an asset or exposure that had qualified as a residual interest before it was sold.

(4) Residual interests generally do not include interests purchased from a third party. However, purchased credit-enhancing interest-only strips are residual interests.

Risk-adjusted asset base means the total dollar amount of the institution's assets adjusted in accordance with § 615.5207 and weighted on the basis of risk in accordance with §§ 615.5211 and 615.5212.

Risk participation means a participation in which the originating party remains liable to the beneficiary for the full amount of an obligation (*e.g.*, a direct credit substitute) notwithstanding that another party has acquired a participation in that obligation.

Rural Business Investment Company has the definition given in 7 U.S.C. 2009cc(14).

Securitization means the pooling and repackaging by a special purpose entity or trust of assets or other credit exposures that can be sold to investors. Securitization includes transactions that create stratified credit risk positions whose performance is dependent upon an underlying pool of credit exposures, including loans and commitments.

Servicer cash advance means funds that a mortgage servicer advances to ensure an uninterrupted flow of payments, including advances made to cover foreclosure costs or other expenses to facilitate the timely collection of the loan. A servicer cash advance is not a recourse obligation or a direct credit substitute if:

(1) The servicer is entitled to full reimbursement and this right is not subordinated to other claims on the cash flows from the underlying asset pool; or

(2) For any one loan, the servicer's obligation to make nonreimbursable advances is contractually limited to an insignificant amount of the outstanding principal amount on that loan.

Stock means stock and participation certificates.

Term preferred stock means preferred stock with an original maturity of at least 5 years and on which, if cumulative, the board of directors has the option to defer dividends, provided that, at the beginning of each of the last 5 years of the term of the stock, the amount that is eligible to be counted as permanent capital is reduced by 20 percent of the original amount of the stock (net of redemptions).

Total capital means assets minus liabilities, valued in accordance with generally accepted accounting principles, except that liabilities do not include obligations to retire stock protected under section 4.9A of the Act.

Traded position means a position retained, assumed, or issued that is externally rated, where there is a reasonable expectation that, in the near future, the rating will be relied upon by:

(1) Unaffiliated investors to purchase the position; or

(2) An unaffiliated third party to enter into a transaction involving the position, such as a purchase, loan, or repurchase agreement.

§ 615.5205

U.S. depository institution means branches (foreign and domestic) of federally insured banks and depository institutions chartered and headquartered in the 50 states of the United States, the District of Columbia, Puerto Rico, and United States territories and possessions. The definition encompasses banks, mutual or stock savings banks, savings or building and loan associations, cooperative banks, credit unions, international banking facilities of domestic depository institutions, and U.S.-chartered depository institutions owned by foreigners. The definition excludes branches and agencies of foreign banks located in the U.S. and bank holding companies.

[70 FR 35348, June 17, 2005, as amended at 70 FR 53908, Sept. 13, 2005]

§ 615.5205 Minimum permanent capital standards.

Each institution shall at all times maintain permanent capital at a level of at least 7 percent of its risk-adjusted asset base.

[62 FR 4446, Jan. 30, 1997]

§ 615.5206 Permanent capital ratio computation.

(a) The institution's permanent capital ratio is determined on the basis of the financial statements of the institution prepared in accordance with generally accepted accounting principles except that the obligations of the Farm Credit System Financial Assistance Corporation issued to repay banks in connection with the capital preservation and loss-sharing agreements described in section 6.9(e)(1) of the Act shall not be considered obligations of any institution subject to this regulation prior to their maturity.

(b) The institution's asset base and permanent capital are computed using average daily balances for the most recent 3 months.

(c) The institution's permanent capital ratio is calculated by dividing the institution's permanent capital, adjusted in accordance with § 615.5207 (the numerator), by the risk-adjusted asset base (the denominator) as determined in § 615.5210, to derive a ratio expressed as a percentage.

(d) Until September 27, 2002, payments of assessments to the Farm Credit System Financial Assistance Corporation, and any part of the obligation to pay future assessments to the Farm Credit System Financial Assistance Corporation that is recognized as an expense on the books of a bank or association, shall be included in the capital of such bank or association for the purpose of determining its compliance with regulatory capital requirements, to the extent allowed by section 6.26(c)(5)(G) of the Act. If the bank directly or indirectly passes on all or part of the payments to its affiliated associations pursuant to section 6.26(c)(5)(D) of the Act, such amounts shall be included in the capital of the associations and shall not be included in the capital of the bank. After September 27, 2002, no payments of assessments or obligations to pay future assessments may be included in the capital of the bank or association.

[70 FR 35351, June 17, 2005]

§ 615.5207 Capital adjustments and associated reductions to assets.

For the purpose of computing the institution's permanent capital ratio, the following adjustments must be made prior to assigning assets to risk-weight categories and computing the ratio:

(a) Where two Farm Credit System institutions have stock investments in each other, such reciprocal holdings must be eliminated to the extent of the offset. If the investments are equal in amount, each institution must deduct from its assets and its total capital an amount equal to the investment. If the investments are not equal in amount, each institution must deduct from its total capital and its assets an amount equal to the smaller investment. The elimination of reciprocal holdings required by this paragraph must be made prior to making the other adjustments required by this section.

(b) Where a Farm Credit Bank or an agricultural credit bank is owned by one or more Farm Credit System institutions, the double counting of capital is eliminated in the following manner:

(1) All equities of a Farm Credit Bank or agricultural credit bank that have been purchased by other Farm Credit institutions are considered to be

Farm Credit Administration § 615.5208

permanent capital of the Farm Credit Bank or agricultural credit bank.

(2) Each Farm Credit Bank or agricultural credit bank and each of its affiliated associations may enter into an agreement that specifies, for the purpose of computing permanent capital only, a dollar amount and/or percentage allotment of the association's allocated investment between the bank and the association. Section 615.5208 provides conditions for allotment agreements or defines allotments in the absence of such agreements.

(c) A Farm Credit Bank or agricultural credit bank and a recipient, other than an association, of allocated earnings from such bank may enter into an agreement specifying a dollar amount and/or percentage allotment of the recipient's allocated earnings in the bank between the bank and the recipient. Such agreement must comply with the provisions of paragraph (b) of this section, except that, in the absence of an agreement, the allocated investment must be allotted 100 percent to the allocating bank and 0 percent to the recipient. All equities of the bank that are purchased by a recipient are considered as permanent capital of the issuing bank.

(d) A bank for cooperatives and a recipient of allocated earnings from such bank may enter into an agreement specifying a dollar amount and/or percentage allotment of the recipient's allocated earnings in the bank between the bank and the recipient. Such agreement must comply with the provisions of paragraph (b) of this section, except that, in the absence of an agreement, the allocated investment must be allotted 100 percent to the allocating bank and 0 percent to the recipient. All equities of a bank that are purchased by a recipient shall be considered as permanent capital of the issuing bank.

(e) Where a bank or association invests in an association to capitalize a loan participation interest, the investing institution must deduct from its total capital an amount equal to its investment in the participating institution.

(f) The double counting of capital by a service corporation chartered under section 4.25 of the Act and its stockholder institutions must be eliminated by deducting an amount equal to the institution's investment in the service corporation from its total capital.

(g) Each institution must deduct from its total capital an amount equal to all goodwill, whenever acquired.

(h) To the extent an institution has deducted its investment in another Farm Credit institution from its total capital, the investment may be eliminated from its asset base.

(i) Where a Farm Credit Bank and an association have an enforceable written agreement to share losses on specifically identified assets on a predetermined quantifiable basis, such assets must be counted in each institution's risk-adjusted asset base in the same proportion as the institutions have agreed to share the loss.

(j) The permanent capital of an institution must exclude the net effect of all transactions covered by the definition of "accumulated other comprehensive income" contained in the Statement of Financial Accounting Standards No. 130, as promulgated by the Financial Accounting Standards Board.

(k) For purposes of calculating capital ratios under this part, deferred-tax assets are subject to the conditions, limitations, and restrictions described in § 615.5209.

(l) Capital may also need to be reduced for potential loss exposure on any recourse obligations, direct credit substitutes, residual interests, and credit-enhancing interest-only-strips in accordance with § 615.5210.

[70 FR 35351, June 17, 2005]

§ 615.5208 Allotment of allocated investments.

(a) The following conditions apply to agreements that a Farm Credit Bank or agricultural credit bank enters into with an affiliated association pursuant to § 615.5207(b)(2):

(1) The agreement must be for a term of 1 year or longer.

(2) The agreement must be entered into on or before its effective date.

(3) The agreement may be amended according to its terms, but no more frequently than annually except in the event that a party to the agreement is merged or reorganized.

(4) On or before the effective date of the agreement, a certified copy of the

§ 615.5208

agreement, and any amendments thereto, must be sent to the field office of the Farm Credit Administration responsible for examining the institution. A copy must also be sent within 30 calendar days of adoption to the bank's other affiliated associations.

(5) Unless the parties otherwise agree, if the bank and the association have not entered into a new agreement on or before the expiration of an existing agreement, the existing agreement will automatically be extended for another 12 months, unless either party notifies the Farm Credit Administration in writing of its objection to the extension prior to the expiration of the existing agreement.

(b) In the absence of an agreement between a Farm Credit Bank or an agricultural credit bank and one or more associations, or in the event that an agreement expires and at least one party has timely objected to the continuation of the terms of its agreement, the following formula applies with respect to the allocated investments held by those associations with which there is no agreement (nonagreeing associations), and does not apply to the allocated investments held by those associations with which the bank has an agreement (agreeing associations):

(1) The allotment formula must be calculated annually.

(2) The permanent capital ratio of the Farm Credit Bank or agricultural credit bank must be computed as of the date that the existing agreement terminates, using a 3-month average daily balance, excluding the allocated investment from nonagreeing associations but including any allocated investments of agreeing associations that are allotted to the bank under applicable allocation agreements. The permanent capital ratio of each nonagreeing association must be computed as of the same date using a 3-month average daily balance, and must be computed excluding its allocated investment in the bank.

(3) If the permanent capital ratio for the Farm Credit Bank or agricultural credit bank calculated in accordance with § 615.5208(b)(2) is 7 percent or above, the allocated investment of each nonagreeing association whose permanent capital ratio calculated in accordance with § 615.5208(b)(2) is 7 percent or above must be allotted 50 percent to the bank and 50 percent to the association.

(4) If the permanent capital ratio of the Farm Credit Bank or agricultural credit bank calculated in accordance with § 615.5208(b)(2) is 7 percent or above, the allocated investment of each nonagreeing association whose capital ratio is below 7 percent must be allotted to the association until the association's capital ratio reaches 7 percent or until all of the investment is allotted to the association, whichever occurs first. Any remaining unallotted allocated investment must be allotted 50 percent to the bank and 50 percent to the association.

(5) If the permanent capital ratio of the Farm Credit Bank or agricultural credit bank calculated in accordance with § 615.5208(b)(2) is less than 7 percent, the amount of additional capital needed by the bank to reach a permanent capital ratio of 7 percent must be determined, and an amount of the allocated investment of each nonagreeing association must be allotted to the Farm Credit Bank or agricultural credit bank, as follows:

(i) If the total of the allocated investments of all nonagreeing associations is greater than the additional capital needed by the bank, the allocated investment of each nonagreeing association must be multiplied by a fraction whose numerator is the amount of capital needed by the bank and whose denominator is the total amount of allocated investments of the nonagreeing associations, and such amount must be allotted to the bank. Next, if the permanent capital ratio of any nonagreeing association is less than 7 percent, a sufficient amount of unallotted allocated investment must then be allotted to each nonagreeing association, as necessary, to increase its permanent capital ratio to 7 percent, or until all such remaining investment is allotted to the association, whichever occurs first. Any unallotted allocated investment still remaining must be allotted 50 percent to the bank and 50 percent to the nonagreeing association.

(ii) If the additional capital needed by the bank is greater than the total of

Farm Credit Administration §615.5210

the allocated investments of the nonagreeing associations, all of the remaining allocated investments of the nonagreeing associations must be allotted to the bank.

(c) If a payment or part of a payment to the Farm Credit System Financial Assistance Corporation pursuant to section 6.9(e)(3)(D)(ii) of the Act would cause a bank to fall below its minimum permanent capital requirement, the bank and one or more associations shall amend their allocation agreements to increase the allotment of the allocated investment to the bank sufficiently to enable the bank to make the payment to the Farm Credit System Financial Assistance Corporation, provided that the associations would continue to meet their minimum permanent capital requirement. In the case of a nonagreeing association, the Farm Credit Administration may require a revision of the allotment sufficient to enable the bank to make the payment to the Farm Credit System Financial Assistance Corporation, provided that the association would continue to meet its minimum permanent capital requirement. The Farm Credit Administration may, at the request of one or more of the institutions affected, waive the requirements of this paragraph if the FCA deems it is in the overall best interest of the institutions affected.

[70 FR 35351, June 17, 2005]

§ 615.5209 Deferred-tax assets.

For purposes of calculating capital ratios under this part, deferred-tax assets are subject to the conditions, limitations, and restrictions described in this section.

(a) Each institution must deduct an amount of deferred-tax assets, net of any valuation allowance, from its assets and its total capital that is equal to the greater of:

(1) The amount of deferred-tax assets that is dependent on future income or future events in excess of the amount that is reasonably expected to be realized within 1 year of the most recent calendar quarter-end date, based on financial projections for that year, or

(2) The amount of deferred-tax assets that is dependent on future income or future events in excess of 10 percent of the amount of core surplus that exists before the deduction of any deferred-tax assets.

(b) For purposes of this calculation:

(1) The amount of deferred-tax assets that can be realized from taxes paid in prior carryback years and from the reversal of existing taxable temporary differences may not be deducted from assets and from equity capital.

(2) All existing temporary differences should be assumed to fully reverse at the calculation date.

(3) Projected future taxable income should not include net operating loss carryforwards to be used within 1 year or the amount of existing temporary differences expected to reverse within that year.

(4) Financial projections must include the estimated effect of tax-planning strategies that are expected to be implemented to minimize tax liabilities and realize tax benefits. Financial projections for the current fiscal year (adjusted for any significant changes that have occurred or are expected to occur) may be used when applying the capital limit at an interim date within the fiscal year.

(5) The deferred tax effects of any unrealized holding gains and losses on available-for-sale debt securities may be excluded from the determination of the amount of deferred-tax assets that are dependent upon future taxable income and the calculation of the maximum allowable amount of such assets. If these deferred-tax effects are excluded, this treatment must be followed consistently over time.

[70 FR 35351, June 17, 2005]

§ 615.5210 Risk-adjusted assets.

(a) *Computation.* Each asset on the institution's balance sheet and each off-balance-sheet item, adjusted by the appropriate credit conversion factor in § 615.5212, is assigned to one of the risk categories specified in § 615.5211. The aggregate dollar value of the assets in each category is multiplied by the percentage weight assigned to that category. The sum of the weighted dollar values from each of the risk categories comprises "risk-adjusted assets," the denominator for computation of the permanent capital ratio.

§ 615.5210

(b) *Ratings-based approach.* (1) Under the ratings-based approach, a rated position in a securitization (provided it satisfies the criteria specified in paragraph (b)(3) of this section) is assigned to the appropriate risk-weight category based on its external rating.

(2) Provided they satisfy the criteria specified in paragraph (b)(3) of this section, the following positions qualify for the ratings-based approach:

(i) Recourse obligations;
(ii) Direct credit substitutes;
(iii) Residual interests (other than credit-enhancing interest-only strips); and
(iv) Asset-or mortgage-backed securities.

(3) A position specified in paragraph (b)(2) of this section qualifies for a ratings-based approach provided it satisfies the following criteria:

(i) If the position is traded and externally rated, its long-term external rating must be one grade below investment grade or better (*e.g.*, BB or better) or its short-term external rating must be investment grade or better (*e.g.*, A–3, P–3). If the position receives more than one external rating, the lowest rating applies.

(ii) If the position is not traded and is externally rated,

(A) It must be externally rated by more than one NRSRO;

(B) Its long-term external rating must be one grade below investment grade or better (*e.g.*, BB or better) or its short-term external rating must be investment grade or better (*e.g.*, A–3, P–3 or better). If the ratings are different, the lowest rating applies;

(C) The ratings must be publicly available; and

(D) The ratings must be based on the same criteria used to rate traded positions.

(c) *Positions in securitizations that do not qualify for a ratings-based approach.* The following positions in securitizations do not qualify for a ratings-based approach. They are treated as indicated.

(1) For any residual interest that is not externally rated, the institution must deduct from capital and assets the face amount of the position (dollar-for-dollar reduction).

(2) For any credit-enhancing interest-only strip, the institution must deduct from capital and assets the face amount of the position (dollar-for-dollar reduction).

(3) For any position that has a long-term external rating that is two grades below investment grade or lower (*e.g.*, B or lower) or a short-term external rating that is one grade below investment grade or lower (*e.g.*, B or lower, Not Prime), the institution must deduct from capital and assets the face amount of the position (dollar-for-dollar reduction).

(4) Any recourse obligation or direct credit substitute (*e.g.*, a purchased subordinated security) that is not externally rated is risk weighted using the amount of the recourse obligation or direct credit substitute and the full amount of the assets it supports, *i.e.*, all the more senior positions in the structure. This treatment is subject to the low-level exposure rule set forth in paragraph (e) of this section. This amount is then placed into a risk-weight category according to the obligor or, if relevant, the guarantor or the nature of the collateral.

(5) Any stripped mortgage-backed security or similar instrument, such as an interest-only strip that is not credit-enhancing or a principal-only strip (including such instruments guaranteed by Government-sponsored agencies), is assigned to the 100-percent risk-weight category described in § 615.5211(d)(7).

(d) *Senior positions not externally rated.* For a position in a securitization that is not externally rated but is senior in all features to a traded position (including collateralization and maturity), an institution may apply a risk weight to the face amount of the senior position based on the traded position's external rating. This section will apply only if the traded position provides substantial credit support for the entire life of the unrated position.

(e) *Low-level exposure rule.* If the maximum contractual exposure to loss retained or assumed by an institution in connection with a recourse obligation or a direct credit substitute is less than the effective risk-based capital requirement for the credit-enhanced assets, the risk-based capital required

Farm Credit Administration § 615.5211

under paragraph (c)(4) of this section is limited to the institution's maximum contractual exposure, less any recourse liability account established in accordance with generally accepted accounting principles. This limitation does not apply when an institution provides credit enhancement beyond any contractual obligation to support assets it has sold.

(f) *Reservation of authority.* The FCA may, on a case-by-case basis, determine the appropriate risk weight for any asset or credit equivalent amount that does not fit wholly within one of the risk categories set forth in § 615.5211 or that imposes risks that are not commensurate with the risk weight otherwise specified in § 615.5211 for the asset or credit equivalent. In addition, the FCA may, on a case-by-case basis, determine the appropriate credit conversion factor for any off-balance sheet item that does not fit wholly within one of the credit conversion factors set forth in § 615.5212 or that imposes risks that are not commensurate with the credit conversion factor otherwise specified in § 615.5212 for the item. In making this determination, the FCA will consider the similarity of the asset or off-balance sheet item to assets or off-balance sheet items explicitly treated in §§ 615.5211 or 615.5212, as well as other relevant factors.

[70 FR 35351, June 17, 2005]

§ 615.5211 Risk categories—balance sheet assets.

Section 615.5210(c) specifies certain balance sheet assets that are not assigned to the risk categories set forth below. All other balance sheet assets are assigned to the percentage risk categories as follows:

(a) *Category 1: 0 Percent.*

(1) Cash (domestic and foreign).

(2) Balances due from Federal Reserve Banks and central banks in other OECD countries.

(3) Direct claims on, and portions of claims unconditionally guaranteed by, the U.S. Treasury, government agencies, or central governments in other OECD countries.

(4) Portions of local currency claims on, or unconditionally guaranteed by, non-OECD central governments (including non-OECD central banks), to the extent the institution has liabilities booked in that currency.

(5) Claims on, or guaranteed by, qualifying securities firms that are collateralized by cash held by the institution or by securities issued or guaranteed by the United States (including U.S. Government agencies) or OECD central governments, provided that a positive margin of collateral is required to be maintained on such a claim on a daily basis, taking into account any change in the institution's exposure to the obligor or counterparty under the claim in relation to the market value of the collateral held in support of the claim.

(b) *Category 2: 20 Percent.* (1) Cash items in the process of collection.

(2) Loans and other obligations of and investments in Farm Credit institutions.

(3) All claims (long- and short-term) on, and portions of claims (long- and short-term) guaranteed by, OECD banks.

(4) Short-term (remaining maturity of 1 year or less) claims on, and portions of short-term claims guaranteed by, non-OECD banks.

(5) Portions of loans and other claims conditionally guaranteed by the U.S. Treasury, government agencies, or central governments in other OECD countries and portions of local currency claims conditionally guaranteed by non-OECD central governments to the extent that the institution has liabilities booked in that currency.

(6) All securities and other claims on, and portions of claims guaranteed by, Government-sponsored agencies.

(7) Portions of loans and other claims (including repurchase agreements) collateralized by securities issued or guaranteed by the U.S. Treasury, government agencies, Government-sponsored agencies or central governments in other OECD countries.

(8) Portions of loans and other claims collateralized by cash held by the institution or its funding bank.

(9) General obligation claims on, and portions of claims guaranteed by, the full faith and credit of states or other political subdivisions or OECD countries, including U.S. state and local governments.

§ 615.5211

(10) Claims on, and portions of claims guaranteed by, official multinational lending institutions or regional development institutions in which the U.S. Government is a shareholder or a contributing member.

(11) Portions of claims collateralized by securities issued by official multilateral lending institutions or regional development institutions in which the U.S. Government is a shareholder or contributing member.

(12) Investments in shares of mutual funds whose portfolios are permitted to hold only assets that qualify for the zero or 20-percent risk categories.

(13) Recourse obligations, direct credit substitutes, residual interests (other than credit-enhancing interest-only strips) and asset-or mortgage-backed securities that are externally rated in the highest or second highest investment grade category, *e.g.*, AAA, AA, in the case of long-term ratings, or the highest rating category, *e.g.*, A–1, P–1, in the case of short-term ratings.

(14) Claims on, and claims guaranteed by, qualifying securities firms provided that:

(i) The qualifying securities firm, or at least one issue of its long-term debt, has a rating in one of the highest two investment grade rating categories from an NRSRO (if the securities firm or debt has more than one NRSRO rating the lowest rating applies); or

(ii) The claim is guaranteed by a qualifying securities firm's parent company with such a rating.

(15) Certain collateralized claims on qualifying securities firms without regard to satisfaction of the rating standard, provided that the claim arises under a contract that:

(i) Is a reverse repurchase/repurchase agreement or securities lending/borrowing transaction executed under standard industry documentation;

(ii) Is collateralized by liquid and readily marketable debt or equity securities;

(iii) Is marked-to-market daily;

(iv) Is subject to a daily margin maintenance requirement under the standard documentation; and

(v) Can be liquidated, terminated, or accelerated immediately in bankruptcy or similar proceedings, and the security or collateral agreement will not be stayed or avoided, under applicable law of the relevant country.

(16) Claims on other financing institutions provided that:

(i) The other financing institution qualifies as an OECD bank or it is owned and controlled by an OECD bank that guarantees the claim, or

(ii) The other financing institution has a rating in one of the highest three investment-grade rating categories from a NRSRO or the claim is guaranteed by a parent company with such a rating, and

(iii) The other financing institution has endorsed all obligations it pledges to its funding Farm Credit bank with full recourse.

(c) *Category 3: 50 Percent.* (1) All other investment securities with remaining maturities under 1 year, if the securities are not eligible for the ratings-based approach or subject to the dollar-for-dollar capital treatment.

(2) Qualified residential loans.

(3) Recourse obligations, direct credit substitutes, residual interests (other than credit-enhancing interest-only strips) and asset-or mortgage-backed securities that are rated in the third highest investment grade category, *e.g.*, A, in the case of long-term ratings, or the second highest rating category, *e.g.*, A–2, P–2, in the case of short-term ratings.

(4) Revenue bonds or similar obligations, including loans and leases, that are obligations of state or political subdivisions of the United States or other OECD countries but for which the government entity is committed to repay the debt only out of revenue from the specific projects financed.

(5) Claims on other financing institutions that:

(i) Are not covered by the provisions of paragraph (b)(17) of this section, but otherwise meet similar capital, risk identification and control, and operational standards, or

(ii) Carry an investment-grade or higher NRSRO rating or the claim is guaranteed by a parent company with such a rating, and

(iii) The other financing institution has endorsed all obligations it pledges to its funding Farm Credit bank with full recourse.

Farm Credit Administration § 615.5212

(d) *Category 4: 100 Percent.* This category includes all assets not specified in the categories above or below nor deducted dollar-for-dollar from capital and assets as discussed in § 615.5210(c). This category comprises standard risk assets such as those typically found in a loan or lease portfolio and includes:

(1) All other claims on private obligors.

(2) Claims on, or portions of claims guaranteed by, non-OECD banks with a remaining maturity exceeding 1 year.

(3) Claims on, or portions of claims guaranteed by, non-OECD central governments that are not included in paragraphs (a)(4) or (b)(4) of this section, and all claims on non-OECD state and local governments.

(4) Industrial-development bonds and similar obligations issued under the auspices of states or political subdivisions of the OECD-based group of countries for the benefit of a private party or enterprise where that party or enterprise, not the government entity, is obligated to pay the principal and interest.

(5) Premises, plant, and equipment; other fixed assets; and other real estate owned.

(6) Recourse obligations, direct credit substitutes, residual interests (other than credit-enhancing interest-only strips) and asset-or mortgage-backed securities that are rated in the lowest investment grade category, *e.g.*, BBB, in the case of long-term ratings, or the third highest rating category, *e.g.*, A–3, P–3, in the case of short-term ratings.

(7) Stripped mortgage-backed securities and similar instruments, such as interest-only strips that are not credit-enhancing and principal-only strips (including such instruments guaranteed by Government-sponsored agencies).

(8) Investments in Rural Business Investment Companies.

(9) If they have not already been deducted from capital:

(i) Investments in unconsolidated companies, joint ventures, or associated companies.

(ii) Deferred-tax assets.

(iii) Servicing assets.

(10) All non-local currency claims on foreign central governments, as well as local currency claims on foreign central governments that are not included in any other category.

(11) Claims on other financing institutions that do not otherwise qualify for a lower risk-weight category under this section; and

(12) All other assets not specified above, including but not limited to leases and receivables.

(e) *Category 5: 200 Percent.* Recourse obligations, direct credit substitutes, residual interests (other than credit-enhancing interest-only strips) and asset-or mortgage-backed securities that are rated one category below the lowest investment grade category, *e.g.*, BB.

[70 FR 35351, June 17, 2005]

§ 615.5212 Credit conversion factors—off-balance sheet items.

(a) The face amount of an off-balance sheet item is generally incorporated into risk-weighted assets in two steps. For most off-balance sheet items, the face amount is first multiplied by a credit conversion factor. (In the case of direct credit substitutes and recourse obligations the full amount of the assets enhanced are multiplied by a credit conversion factor). The resultant credit equivalent amount is assigned to the appropriate risk-weight category described in § 615.5211 according to the obligor or, if relevant, the guarantor or the collateral.

(b) Conversion factors for various types of off-balance sheet items are as follows:

(1) *0 Percent.* (i) Unused commitments with an original maturity of 14 months or less;

(ii) Unused commitments with an original maturity greater than 14 months if:

(A) They are unconditionally cancellable by the institution; and

(B) The institution has the contractual right to, and in fact does, make a separate credit decision based upon the borrower's current financial condition before each drawing under the lending arrangement.

(2) *20 Percent.* Short-term, self-liquidating, trade-related contingencies, including but not limited to commercial letters of credit.

§ 615.5215

(3) *50 Percent.* (i) Transaction-related contingencies (*e.g.*, bid bonds, performance bonds, warranties, and performance-based standby letters of credit related to a particular transaction).

(ii) Unused loan commitments with an original maturity greater than 14 months, including underwriting commitments and commercial credit lines.

(iii) Revolving underwriting facilities (RUFs), note issuance facilities (NIFs) and other similar arrangements pursuant to which the institution's customer can issue short-term debt obligations in its own name, but for which the institution has a legally binding commitment to either:

(A) Purchase the obligations its customer is unable to sell by a stated date; or

(B) Advance funds to its customer if the obligations cannot be sold.

(4) *100 Percent.* (i) The full amount of the assets supported by direct credit substitutes and recourse obligations for which an institution directly or indirectly retains or assumes credit risk. For risk participations in such arrangements acquired by the institution, the full amount of assets supported by the main obligation multiplied by the acquiring institution's percentage share of the risk participation. The capital requirement under this paragraph is limited to the institution's maximum contractual exposure, less any recourse liability account established under generally accepted accounting principles.

(ii) Acquisitions of risk participations in bankers acceptances.

(iii) Sale and repurchase agreements, if not already included on the balance sheet.

(iv) Forward agreements (*i.e.*, contractual obligations) to purchase assets, including financing facilities with certain drawdown.

(c) *Credit equivalents of interest rate contracts and foreign exchange contracts.* (1) Credit equivalents of interest rate contracts and foreign exchange contracts (except single-currency floating/floating interest rate swaps) are determined by adding the replacement cost (mark-to-market value, if positive) to the potential future credit exposure, determined by multiplying the notional principal amount by the following credit conversion factors as appropriate.

CONVERSION FACTOR MATRIX
(In percent)

Remaining maturity	Interest rate	Exchange rate	Commodity
1 year or less	0.0	1.0	10.0
Over 1 to 5 years	0.5	5.0	12.0
Over 5 years	1.5	7.5	15.0

(2) For any derivative contract that does not fall within one of the categories in the above table, the potential future credit exposure is to be calculated using the commodity conversion factors. The net current exposure for multiple derivative contracts with a single counterparty and subject to a qualifying bilateral netting contract is the net sum of all positive and negative mark-to-market values for each derivative contract. The positive sum of the net current exposure is added to the adjusted potential future credit exposure for the same multiple contracts with a single counterparty. The adjusted potential future credit exposure is computed as $A_{net} = (0.4 \times A_{gross}) + 0.6 (NGR \times A_{gross})$ where:

(i) A_{net} is the adjusted potential future credit exposure;

(ii) A_{gross} is the sum of potential future credit exposures determined by multiplying the notional principal amount by the appropriate credit conversion factor; and

(iii) NGR is the ratio of the net current credit exposure divided by the gross current credit exposure determined as the sum of only the positive mark-to-markets for each derivative contract with the single counterparty.

(3) Credit equivalents of single-currency floating/floating interest rate swaps are determined by their replacement cost (mark-to-market).

[70 FR 35351, June 17, 2005]

§ 615.5215 Distribution of earnings.

The boards of directors of System institutions may not reduce the permanent capital of the institution through the payment of patronage refunds or dividends, or the retirement of stock or allocated equities except retirements pursuant to §§ 615.5280 and 615.5290 if, after or due to the action, the permanent capital of the institution would

Farm Credit Administration

§ 615.5220

fail to meet the minimum permanent capital adequacy standard established under § 615.5205 for that period. This limitation shall not apply to the payment of noncash patronage refunds by any institution exempt from Federal income tax if the entire refund paid qualifies as permanent capital at the issuing institution. Any System institution subject to Federal income tax may pay patronage refunds partially in cash if the cash portion of the refund is the minimum amount required to qualify the refund as a deductible patronage distribution for Federal income tax purposes and the remaining portion of the refund paid qualifies as permanent capital.

[53 FR 39247, Oct. 6, 1988, as amended at 53 FR 40046, Oct. 13, 1988]

§ 615.5216 [Reserved]

Subpart I—Issuance of Equities

SOURCE: 53 FR 40046, Oct. 13, 1988, unless otherwise noted.

§ 615.5220 Capitalization bylaws.

(a) The board of directors of each System bank and association shall, pursuant to section 4.3A of the Farm Credit Act of 1971 (Act), adopt capitalization bylaws, subject to the approval of its voting shareholders that set forth:

(1) Classes of equities and the manner in which they shall be issued, transferred, converted and retired;

(2) For each class of equities, a description of the class(es) of persons to whom such stock may be issued, voting rights, dividend rights and preferences, and priority upon liquidation, including rights, if any, to share in the distribution of the residual estate;

(3) The number of shares and par value of equities authorized to be issued for each class of equities. However, the bylaws need not state a number or value limit for these equities:

(i) Equities that are required to be purchased as a condition of obtaining a loan, lease, or related service.

(ii) Non-voting stock resulting from the conversion of voting stock due to repayment of a loan.

(iii) Non-voting equities that are issued to an association's funding bank in conjunction with any agreement for a transfer of capital between the association and the bank.

(iv) Equities resulting from the distribution of earnings.

(4) For Farm Credit Banks, agricultural credit banks (with respect to loans other than to cooperatives), and associations, the percentage or dollar amount of equity investment (which may be expressed as a range within which the board of directors may from time to time determine the requirement) that will be required to be purchased as a condition for obtaining a loan, which shall be not less than, 2 percent of the loan amount or $1,000, whichever is less;

(5) For banks for cooperatives and agricultural credit banks (with respect to loans to cooperatives), the percentage or dollar amount of equity or guaranty fund investment (which may be expressed as a range within which the board may from time to time determine the requirement) that serves as a target level of investment in the bank for patronage-sourced business, which shall not be less than, 2 percent of the loan amount or $1,000, whichever is less;

(6) The manner in which equities will be retired, including a provision stating that equities other than those protected under section 4.9A of the Act are retirable at the sole discretion of the board, provided minimum permanent capital adequacy standards established in subpart H of this part are met;

(7) The manner in which earnings will be allocated and distributed, including the basis on which patronage refunds will paid, which shall be in accord with cooperative principles; and

(8) For Farm Credit banks, the manner in which the capitalization requirements of the Farm Credit Bank shall be allocated and equalized from time to time among its owners.

(b) The board of directors of each service corporation (including the Farm Credit Leasing Services Corporation) shall adopt capitalization bylaws, subject to the approval of its voting shareholders, that set forth the requirements of paragraphs (a)(1), (a)(2), and (a)(3) of this section to the extent applicable. Such bylaws shall also set forth the manner in which equities will

§ 615.5230

be retired and the manner in which earnings will be distributed.

[53 FR 40046, Oct. 13, 1988, as amended at 62 FR 4446, Jan. 30, 1997; 63 FR 39227, July 22, 1998; 66 FR 16844, Mar. 28, 2001]

§ 615.5230 Implementation of cooperative principles.

(a) Voting stockholders of Farm Credit banks and associations shall be accorded full voting rights in accordance with cooperative principles, including those set forth in § 611.350 of this chapter. Except as otherwise required by statute or regulation, and except as modified by paragraphs (b) and (c) of this section, the voting rights of each voting shareholder are as follows:

(1) Each voting stockholder of a Farm Credit Bank has only one vote that is assigned a weight proportional to the number of that association's voting stockholders and has the right to vote in the election of each stockholder-elected director and to cumulate such votes and distribute them among the candidates in the stockholder's discretion, except that cumulative voting for directors may be eliminated if 75 percent of the associations that are stockholders of the Farm Credit Bank vote in favor of elimination. In a vote to eliminate cumulative voting, each association shall be accorded one vote.

(2) Each voting stockholder of an agricultural credit bank has only one vote, unless another voting scheme has been approved by the Farm Credit Administration.

(3) Each voting stockholder of an association or bank for cooperatives has only one vote, regardless of the number of shares owned or the number of loans outstanding. Unless regional election of directors is provided for in the bylaws pursuant to § 615.5230(b), each voting stockholder of an association or bank for cooperatives has the right to vote in the election of each stockholder-elected director. Unless otherwise provided in the capitalization bylaws, each voting stockholder of an association or bank for cooperatives is allowed to cumulate such votes and distribute them among the candidates in the stockholder's discretion. Cumulative voting is not allowed in the regional election of stockholder-elected directors.

(b) The regional election of stockholder-elected directors is only permitted under the following conditions:

(1) A bylaw establishing regional elections is approved by a majority of voting stockholders, voting in person or by proxy, prior to implementation.

(2) The bylaw provides that the use of regional election of stockholder-elected directors does not prevent all voting stockholders of the institution, regardless of the region where they reside or conduct agricultural or aquatic operations, from voting in any stockholder vote to remove a director.

(3) There are an approximately equal number of voting stockholders in each of the institution's voting regions. Regions will have an approximately equal number of voting stockholders if the number of voting stockholders in any one region does not exceed the number of voting stockholders in any other region by more than 25 percent. At least once every 3 years, the institution must count the number of voting stockholders in each region and, if the regions do not have an approximately equal number of stockholders, the regional boundaries must be adjusted to achieve such result.

(4) An institution may provide for more than one director to represent a region. Institutions providing for more than one director to represent a region will determine the equitability of the regions by dividing the number of voting stockholders in that region by the number of director positions representing that region, and the resulting quotient shall be the number that is compared to the number of voting stockholders in other regions.

(5) Each voting stockholder is accorded the right to vote in the election of each stockholder-elected director for his or her region.

(c) Each equityholder of each institution shall be equitably treated in the operation of the institution.

(1) Each issuance of preferred stock (other than preferred stock outstanding on October 5, 1988, and stock into which such outstanding stock is converted that has substantially similar preferences) shall be approved by a majority of the shares voting of each

class of equities adversely affected by the preference, voting as a class, whether or not such classes are otherwise authorized to vote;

(2) Any dividends paid to the holders of common stock and participation certificates shall be on a per share basis and without preference as to rate or priority of payment between classes of common stock, between classes of participation certificates, between classes of common stock and classes of participation certificates, or between holders of the same class of stock or participation certificates, except that any class of common stock or participation certificates that result from the conversion of allocated surplus may be subordinated to other classes of common stock and participation certificates in the payment of dividends.

(3) Any patronage refunds that are paid shall be paid in accordance with cooperative principles, on an equitable and nondiscriminatory basis determined by the board of directors in accordance with the capitalization bylaws, provided that any earning pools that may be established for the payment of patronage shall be established on a rational and equitable basis that will ensure that each patron of the institution receives its fair share of the earnings of the institution and bears its fair share of the expenses of the institution.

(4) All classes of common stock and participation certificates (except those resulting from a conversion of allocated surplus) must be accorded the same priority with respect to impairment and restoration of impairment and have the same rights and priority upon liquidation.

[53 FR 40046, Oct. 13, 1988, as amended at 54 FR 6118, Feb. 8, 1989; 60 FR 57921, Nov. 24, 1995; 62 FR 4446, Jan. 30, 1997; 62 FR 49908, Sept. 24, 1997; 63 FR 39228, July 22, 1998; 70 FR 53908, Sept. 13, 2005; 71 FR 5763, Feb. 2, 2006; 75 FR 18743, Apr. 12, 2010]

§ 615.5240 Permanent capital requirements.

(a) The capitalization bylaws shall enable the institution to meet the capital adequacy standards established under subparts H and K of this part and the total capital requirements established by the board of directors of the institution.

(b) In order to qualify as permanent capital, equities issued under the bylaws must meet the following requirements:

(1) Retirement must be solely at the discretion of the board of directors and not upon a date certain (other than the original maturity date of preferred stock) or upon the happening of any event, such as repayment of the loan, and not pursuant to any automatic retirement or revolvement plan;

(2) Retirement must be at not more than book value;

(3) The institution must have made the disclosures required by this subpart;

(4) For common stock and participation certificates, dividends must be noncumulative and payable only at the discretion of the board; and

(5) For cumulative preferred stock, the board of directors must have discretion to defer payment of dividends.

[70 FR 53908, Sept. 13, 2005]

§ 615.5245 Limitations on association preferred stock.

(a) The board of directors of each association offering preferred stock must adopt a policy that addresses the association's conditions or limits on the amount of preferred stock that any one holder, or small number of holders may acquire.

(b) Each association offering preferred stock must make the stock available for purchase to each of its members on the same basis.

(c) An association may not extend credit for purchases of preferred stock in the association.

[70 FR 53908, Sept. 13, 2005]

§ 615.5250 Disclosure requirements for borrower stock.

(a) For sales of borrower stock, which for this subpart means equities purchased as a condition for obtaining a loan, an institution must provide a prospective borrower with the following documents prior to loan closing:

(1) The institution's most recent annual report filed under part 620 of this chapter;

§ 615.5255

(2) The institution's most recent quarterly report filed under part 620 of this chapter, if more recent than the annual report;

(3) A copy of the institution's capitalization bylaws; and

(4) A written description of the terms and conditions under which the equity is issued. In addition to specific terms and conditions, the description must disclose:

(i) That the equity is an at-risk investment and not a compensating balance;

(ii) That the equity is retireable only at the discretion of the board of directors and only if minimum permanent capital standards established under subpart H of this part are met;

(iii) Whether the institution presently meets its minimum permanent capital standards;

(iv) Whether the institution knows of any reason the institution may not meet its permanent capital standard on the next earnings distribution date; and

(v) The rights, if any, to share in patronage distributions.

(b) Notwithstanding the provisions of paragraph (a) of this section, no materials previously provided to a purchaser (except the disclosures required by paragraph (a)(4) of this section) need be provided again unless the purchaser requests such materials.

[70 FR 53908, Sept. 13, 2005]

§ 615.5255 Disclosure and review requirements for other equities.

(a) A bank, association, or service corporation must submit a proposed disclosure statement to the Farm Credit Administration (FCA) for review and clearance prior to the proposed sale of any other equities, which for this subpart means equities not purchased as a condition for obtaining a loan.

(b) An institution may not offer to sell other equities until a disclosure statement is reviewed and cleared by FCA.

(c) A disclosure statement must include:

(1) All of the information required by part 620 of this chapter in the annual report to shareholders as of a date within 135 days of the proposed sale. An institution may incorporate by reference its most recent annual report to shareholders and the most recent quarterly report filed with the FCA in satisfaction of this requirement;

(2) The information required by § 615.5250(a)(3) and (a)(4); and

(3) A discussion of the intended use of the sale proceeds.

(d) An institution is not required to provide the materials identified in paragraphs (c)(1) and (c)(2) of this section to a purchaser who previously received them unless the purchaser requests it.

(e) For any class of stock where each purchaser and each subsequent transferee acquires at least $250,000 of the stock and meets the definition of "accredited investor" or "qualified institutional buyer" contained in 17 CFR 230.501 and 230.144A (or successor provisions), a disclosure statement submitted pursuant to this section is deemed reviewed and cleared by FCA and an institution may treat stock that meets all requirements of part 615 as permanent capital for the purpose of meeting the minimum permanent capital standards established under subpart H unless FCA notifies the institution to the contrary within 30 days of receipt of a complete disclosure statement submission. A complete disclosure statement submission includes the proposed disclosure statement plus any additional materials requested by FCA.

(f) For all other issuances, a disclosure statement submitted pursuant to this section is deemed cleared by FCA, and an institution may treat stock that meets all requirements of part 615 as permanent capital for the purpose of meeting the minimum permanent capital standards established under subpart H unless FCA notifies the institution to the contrary within 60 days of receipt of a complete disclosure statement submission. A complete disclosure statement submission includes the proposed disclosure statement plus any additional materials requested by FCA.

(g) Upon request, FCA will inform the institution how it will treat the proposed issuance for other regulatory capital ratios or computations.

(h) No institution, officer, director, employee, or agent shall, in connection

Farm Credit Administration § 615.5270

with the sale of equities, make any disclosure, through a disclosure statement or otherwise, that is inaccurate or misleading, or omit to make any statement needed to prevent other disclosures from being misleading.

(i) Each bank and association must establish a method to disclose and make information on insider preferred stock purchases and retirements readily available to the public. At a minimum, each institution offering preferred stock must make this information available upon request.

(j) The requirements of this section do not apply to the sale of Farm Credit System institution equities to:

(1) Other Farm Credit System institutions,

(2) Other financing institutions in connection with a lending or discount relationship, or

(3) Non-Farm Credit System lenders that purchase equities in connection with a loan participation transaction.

(k) In addition to the requirements of this section, each institution is responsible for ensuring its compliance with all applicable Federal and state securities laws.

[70 FR 53908, Sept. 13, 2005]

Subpart J—Retirement of Equities and Payment of Dividends

§ 615.5260 **Retirement of eligible borrower stock.**

(a) *Definitions.* For the purposes of this subpart the following definitions shall apply:

(1) *Eligible borrowers stock* means:

(i) Stock, participation certificates or allocated equities outstanding on January 6, 1988, or purchased as a condition of obtaining a loan prior to the earlier of the date of shareholder approval of capitalization bylaws under section 4.3A of the Act or October 6, 1988; and

(ii) Any stock, participation certificates or allocated equities for which such eligible borrower stock is exchanged in connection with a merger, consolidation, or other reorganization or a transfer of territory. *Eligible borrower stock* does not include equities for which eligible borrower stock is required to be exchanged pursuant to the bylaws adopted under section 4.3A or equities for which eligible borrower stock is voluntarily exchanged except in connection with a merger, consolidation or other reorganization or a transfer of territory.

(2) *Retirement in the ordinary course of business* means:

(i) Retirement upon repayment of a loan or under a retirement or revolvement plan in effect prior to January 6, 1988, and for eligible borrower stock issued after that date, at the time the loan was made; or

(ii) Retirement pursuant to §§ 615.5280 and 615.5290.

(3) *Par value* means:

(i) In the case of stock, par value;

(ii) In the case of participation certificates and other equities, face or equivalent value; or

(iii) In the case of participation certificates and allocated surplus subject to retirement under a revolving cycle and retired out or order pursuant to §§ 615.5280 and 615.5290 or otherwise under the Act, par or face value discounted at a rate determined by the institution to reflect the present value of the equity as of the date of such retirement.

(b) When an institution retires eligible borrower stock in the ordinary course of business, such equities shall be retired at par, even if book value is less than par.

(c) When a Farm Credit Bank retires stock for the sole purpose of enabling an association to retire eligible borrower stock that was issued in connection with a long term real estate loan, such stock shall be retired at par even if its book value is less than par.

[53 FR 40048, Oct. 13, 1988; 54 FR 7029, Feb. 16, 1989, as amended at 62 FR 4447, Jan. 30, 1997; 63 FR 39228, July 22, 1998]

§ 615.5270 **Retirement of other equities.**

(a) Equities other than eligible borrower stock shall be retired at not more than their book value.

(b) No equities shall be retired, except pursuant to §§ 615.5280 and 615.5290, or term stock at its stated maturity unless after the retirement the institution would continue to meet the minimum permanent capital standards established under subpart H of this part.

§ 615.5280

(c) A bank, association, or service corporation board of directors may delegate authority to retire at-risk stock to institution management if:

(1) The board has determined that the institution's capital position is adequate;

(2) All retirements are in accordance with the institution's capital adequacy plan or capital restoration plan;

(3) The institution's permanent capital ratio will be in excess of 9 percent after any retirements;

(4) The institution will continue to satisfy all applicable minimum surplus and collateral standards after any retirements; and

(5) Management reports the aggregate amount and net effect of stock purchases and retirements to the board of directors each quarter.

(d) Each board of directors of a bank, association, or service corporation that issues preferred stock must adopt a written policy covering the retirement of preferred stock. The policy must, at a minimum:

(1) Establish any delegations of authority to retire preferred stock and the conditions of delegation, which must meet the requirements of paragraph (c) of this section and include minimum levels for total surplus and core surplus commensurate with the volatility of the preferred stock.

(2) Identify limitations on the amount of stock that may be retired during a single quarterly (or shorter) time period;

(3) Ensure that all stockholder requests for retirement are treated fairly and equitably;

(4) Prohibit any insider, including institution officers, directors, employees, or agents, from retiring any preferred stock in advance of the release of material non-public information concerning the institution to other stockholders; and

(5) Establish when insiders may retire their preferred stock.

(e) The institution's board must review its policy at least annually to ensure that it continues to be appropriate for the institution's current financial condition and consistent with its long-term goals established in its capital adequacy plan.

[53 FR 40048, Oct. 13, 1988; 54 FR 7029, Feb. 16, 1989, as amended at 62 FR 4447, Jan. 30, 1997; 70 FR 53909, Sept. 13, 2005]

§ 615.5280 Retirement in event of default.

(a) When the debt of a holder of eligible borrower stock issued by a production credit association, Federal land bank association, Federal land credit association or agricultural credit association is in default, such institution may, but shall not be required to, retire at par eligible borrower stock owned by such borrower on which the institution has a lien, in total or partial liquidation of the debt.

(b) When the debt of a holder of stock, participation certificates or other equities issued by a production credit association, Federal land bank association, Federal land credit association or agricultural credit association is in default, such institution may, but shall not be required to, retire at book value not to exceed par all or part of such equities, other than eligible borrower stock as defined in § 615.5260(a)(1), owned by such borrower on which the institution has a lien, in total or partial liquidation of the debt.

(c) When the debt of a holder of equities or guaranty fund certificates issued by a bank for cooperatives or agricultural credit bank is in default the bank may, but shall not be required to, retire all or part of such equities qualify or guaranty fund investments owned by the borrower on which the bank has a lien, in total or partial liquidation of the debt. If such investments qualify as eligible borrower stock, it shall be retired at par, as defined in § 615.5260(a)(3). All other investments shall be retired at a rate determined by the institution to reflect its present value on the date of retirement.

(d) When the debt of a holder of the equities of a Farm Credit Bank or agricultural credit bank is in default the bank may, but shall not be required to, retire all or part of such equities owned by the borrower on which the bank has a lien, in total or partial liquidation of the debt. If such equities qualify as eligible borrower stock or are retired

Farm Credit Administration § 615.5295

solely to permit a Federal land bank association to retire eligible borrower stock under § 615.5280(a), they shall be retired at par. All other equities shall be retired at book value not to exceed par.

(e) Any retirements made under this section by a Federal land bank association shall be made only upon the specific approval of, or in accordance with, approval procedures issued by the association's funding bank.

(f) Prior to making any retirement pursuant to this section, except retirements pursuant to paragraphs (c) and (d) of this section, the institution shall provide the borrower with written notice of the following matters;

(1) A statement that the institution has declared the borrower's loan to be in default;

(2) A statement that the institution will retire all or part of the equities of the borrower in total or partial liquidation of his or her loan;

(3) A description of the effect of the retirement on the relationship of the borrower to the institution;

(4) A statement of the amount of the outstanding debt that will be owed to the institution after the retirement of the borrower's equities; and

(5) The date on which the institution will retire the equities of the borrower.

(g) The notice required by this section shall be provided in person at least 10 days prior to the retirement of any equities of a holder, or by mailing a copy of the notice by first class mail to the last known address of the equity holder at least 13 days prior to the retirement of such person's equities.

(h) The requirements of this section may be satisfied by notices given pursuant to §§ 617.7405, 617.7410, 617.7420, and 617.7425 of this chapter that contain the information required by this section.

[53 FR 40048, Oct. 13, 1988; 54 FR 7029, Feb. 16, 1989, as amended at 61 FR 67187, Dec. 20, 1996; 62 FR 13213, Mar. 19, 1997; 69 FR 10907, Mar. 9, 2004]

§ 615.5290 Retirement of capital stock and participation certificates in event of restructuring.

(a) If a Farm Credit Bank or agricultural credit bank forgives and writes off, under § 617.7415, any of the principal outstanding on a loan made to any borrower, where appropriate the Federal land bank association of which the borrower is a member and stockholder shall cancel the same dollar amount of borrower stock held by the borrower in respect of the loan, up to the total amount of such stock, and to the extent provided for in the bylaws of the Bank relating to its capitalization, the Farm Credit Bank or agricultural credit bank shall retire an equal amount of stock owned by the Federal land bank association.

(b) If a production credit association or merged association forgives and writes off, under § 617.7415, any of the principal outstanding on a loan made to any borrower, the association shall cancel the same dollar amount of borrower stock held by the borrower in respect of the loan, up to the total amount of such loan.

(c) Notwithstanding paragraphs (a) and (b) of this section, the borrower shall be entitled to retain at least one share of stock to maintain the borrower's membership and voting interest.

[53 FR 35457, Sept. 14, 1988, as amended at 61 FR 67188, Dec. 20, 1996; 69 FR 10907, Mar. 9, 2004]

§ 615.5295 Payment of dividends.

(a) The board of directors of a bank, association, or service corporation must declare a dividend on a class of stock before any dividends may be paid to stockholders.

(b) No bank, association, or service corporation may declare or pay any dividend unless after declaration or payment of the dividend the institution would continue to meet its regulatory capital standards under this part.

(c) Each bank, association, and service corporation must exclude any accrued but unpaid dividends from regulatory capital computations under this part.

[70 FR 53909, Sept. 13, 2005]

Subpart K—Surplus and Collateral Requirements

SOURCE: 62 FR 4447, Jan. 30, 1997, unless otherwise noted.

§ 615.5301 Definitions.

For the purposes of this subpart, the following definitions shall apply:

(a) The terms *deferred-tax assets that are dependent on future income or future events*, *institution*, *permanent capital*, and *total capital* shall have the meanings set forth in § 615.5201.

(b) *Core surplus*. (1) Core surplus means:

(i) Undistributed earnings/unallocated surplus less, for associations only, an amount equal to the net investment in the bank;

(ii) Nonqualified allocated equities (including stock) that are not distributed according to an established plan or practice, *provided that*, in the event that a nonqualified patronage allocation is distributed, other than as required by section 4.14B of the Act, or in connection with a loan default or the death of an equityholder whose loan has been repaid (to the extent provided for in the institution's capital adequacy plan), any remaining nonqualified allocations that were allocated in the same year will be excluded from core surplus.

(iii) Perpetual common or noncumulative perpetual preferred stock (other than allocated stock) that is not retired according to an established plan or practice, *provided that*, in the event that stock held by a borrower is retired, other than as required by section 4.14B of the Act or in connection with a loan default to the extent provided for in the institution's capital plan, the remaining perpetual stock of the same class or series shall be excluded from core surplus;

(iv) A capital instrument or a particular balance sheet entry or account that the Farm Credit Administration has determined to be the functional equivalent of a component of core surplus. The Farm Credit Administration may permit an institution to include all or a portion of such instrument, entry, or account as core surplus, permanently or on a temporary basis, for purposes of this subpart.

(2) For associations only, other allocated equities may also be included in the core surplus ratio to the extent permitted by § 615.5330(b) if the following conditions are met:

(i) The allocated equities are includible in total surplus; and

(ii) The allocated equities, if subject to a plan or practice of revolvement or retirement, are not scheduled or intended to be revolved or retired during the next 3 years, provided that, in the event that such allocated equities included in core surplus are retired, other than as required by section 4.14B of the Act, or in connection with a loan default or the death of an equityholder whose loan has been repaid (to the extent provided for in the institution's capital adequacy plan), any remaining such allocated equities that were allocated in the same year will be excluded from core surplus.

(3) The deductions that must be made by an institution in the computation of its permanent capital pursuant to § 615.5207(f), (g), (i), and (k) shall also be made in the computation of its core surplus. Deductions required by § 615.5207(a) shall also be made to the extent that they do not duplicate deductions calculated pursuant to this section and required by § 615.5330(b)(2).

(4) Equities issued by System institutions and held by other System institutions shall not be included in the core surplus of the issuing institution or of the holder, unless approved pursuant to paragraph (b)(1)(iv) of this section, except that equities held in connection with a loan participation shall not be excluded by the holder. This paragraph shall not apply to investments by an association in its affiliated bank, which are governed by § 615.5301(b)(1)(i).

(5) The core surplus of an institution shall exclude the net effect of all transactions covered by the definition of "accumulated other comprehensive income" contained in the Statement of Financial Accounting Standards No. 130, as promulgated by the Financial Accounting Standards Board.

(6) The Farm Credit Administration may, if it finds that a particular component, balance sheet entry, or account has characteristics or terms that diminish its contribution to an institution's ability to absorb losses, require the deduction of all or a portion of such component, entry, or account from core surplus.

(c) *Net collateral* means the value of a bank's collateral as defined by § 615.5050

Farm Credit Administration § 615.5301

(except that eligible investments as described in § 615.5140 are to be valued at their amortized cost), less an amount equal to that portion of the allocated investments of affiliated associations that is not counted as permanent capital by the bank.

(d) *Net collateral ratio* means a bank's net collateral, divided by the bank's total liabilities.

(e) *Net investment in the bank* means the total investment by an association in its affiliated bank, less reciprocal investments and investments resulting from a loan originating/service agency relationship, including participations.

(f) *Nonqualified allocated equities* means allocations of earnings designated to the institution's members that are not deducted from the gross taxable income of the allocating institution at the time of allocation.

(g) *Perpetual stock or equity* means stock or equity not having a maturity date, not redeemable at the option of the holder, and having no other provisions that will require the future redemption of the issue.

(h) *Qualified allocated equities* means allocations of earnings that are deducted from the gross taxable income of the allocating institution and designated to the institution's members.

(i) *Total surplus* means:

(1) Undistributed earnings/unallocated surplus;

(2) Allocated equities, including allocated surplus and stock, that are not subject to a plan or practice of revolvement or retirement of 5 years or less and are eligible to be included in permanent capital pursuant to paragraph (4)(iv) of the definition of permanent capital in § 615.5201; and

(3) Common and perpetual preferred stock (other than allocated stock) that is not purchased or held as a condition of obtaining a loan, provided that the institution has no established plan or practice of retiring such stock;

(4) Term preferred stock that is not purchased or held as a condition of obtaining a loan, up to a maximum of 25 percent of the institution's permanent capital (as calculated after deductions required in the permanent capital ratio computation). The amount of includible term stock must be reduced by 20 percent (net of redemptions) at the beginning of each of the last 5 years of the term of the instrument;

(5) The total surplus of an institution shall exclude the net effect of all transactions covered by the definition of "accumulated other comprehensive income" contained in the Statement of Financial Accounting Standards No. 130, as promulgated by the Financial Accounting Standards Board.

(6) A capital instrument or a particular balance sheet entry or account that the Farm Credit Administration has determined to be the functional equivalent of a component of total surplus. The Farm Credit Administration may permit one or more institutions to include all or a portion of such instrument, entry, or account as total surplus, permanently or on a temporary basis, for purposes of this subpart.

(7) The Farm Credit Administration may, if it finds that a particular component, balance sheet entry, or account has characteristics or terms that diminish its contribution to an institution's ability to absorb losses, require the deduction of all or a portion of such component, entry, or account from total surplus.

(8) Any deductions made by an institution in the computation of its permanent capital pursuant to § 615.5207 shall also be made in the computation of its total surplus.

(j) *Total liabilities* means liabilities valued in accordance with generally accepted accounting principles (GAAP), except that total liabilities shall exclude the following:

(1) As set forth in Statement of Financial Accounting Standards No. 133, *Accounting for Derivative Instruments and Hedging Activities*, as promulgated by the Financial Accounting Standards Board—

(i) Adjustments to the carrying amount of any liability designated as being hedged; and

(ii) Any derivative recognized as a liability that is designated as a hedging instrument.

(2) Term preferred stock to the extent such stock is included as total surplus in the computation of the

§ 615.5330

bank's total surplus ratio pursuant to § 615.5301(i).

[62 FR 4447, Jan. 30, 1997; 62 FR 19219, Apr. 21, 1997; 63 FR 39228, July 22, 1998; 68 FR 18534, Apr. 16, 2003; 70 FR 35356, June 17, 2005]

§ 615.5330 Minimum surplus ratios.

(a) *Total surplus.* (1) Each institution shall achieve and at all times maintain a ratio of at least 7 percent of total surplus to the risk-adjusted asset base.

(2) The risk-adjusted asset base is the total dollar amount of the institution's assets adjusted in accordance with § 615.5301(i)(7) and weighted on the basis of risk in accordance with § 615.5210.

(b) *Core surplus.* (1) Each institution shall achieve and at all times maintain a ratio of core surplus to the risk-adjusted asset base of at least 3.5 percent, of which no more than 2 percentage points may consist of allocated equities otherwise includible pursuant to § 615.5301(b).

(2) Each association shall compute its core surplus ratio by deducting an amount equal to the net investment in the bank from its core surplus.

(3) The risk-adjusted asset base is the total dollar amount of the institution's assets adjusted in accordance with §§ 615.5301(b)(3) and 615.5330(b)(2), and weighted on the basis of risk in accordance with § 615.5210.

(c) An institution shall compute its risk-adjusted asset base, total surplus, and core surplus ratios using average daily balances for the most recent 3 months.

[63 FR 39228, July 22, 1998, as amended at 70 FR 35356, June 17, 2005; 75 FR 18744, Apr. 12, 2010]

§ 615.5335 Bank net collateral ratio.

(a) Each bank shall achieve and at all times maintain a net collateral ratio of at least 103 percent.

(b) At a minimum, a bank shall compute its net collateral ratio as of the end of each month. A bank shall have the capability to compute its net collateral ratio a day after the close of a business day using the daily balances outstanding for assets and liabilities for that date.

[63 FR 39229, July 22, 1998]

§ 615.5336 Compliance and reporting.

(a) *Noncompliance and reporting.* An institution that meets the minimum applicable surplus ratios and net collateral ratio established in §§ 615.5330 and 615.5335 at or after the end of the quarter in which these regulations become effective and subsequently falls below one or more minimum requirements shall be in violation of the applicable regulations. Such institution shall report its noncompliance to the Farm Credit Administration within 20 calendar days following the month end in which the institution initially determines that it is not in compliance with the requirements.

(b) *Initial compliance and reporting requirements.* (1) An institution that fails to satisfy one or more of its minimum applicable surplus and net collateral ratios at the end of the quarter in which these regulations become effective shall report its initial noncompliance to the Farm Credit Administration within 20 days following such quarter end and shall also submit a capital restoration plan for achieving and maintaining the standards, demonstrating appropriate annual progress toward meeting the goal, to the Farm Credit Administration within 60 days following such quarter end. If the capital restoration plan is not approved by the Farm Credit Administration, the Agency shall inform the institution of the reasons for disapproval, and the institution shall submit a revised capital restoration plan within the time specified by the Farm Credit Administration.

(2) *Approval of compliance plans.* In determining whether to approve a capital restoration plan submitted under this section, the FCA shall consider the following factors, as applicable:

(i) The conditions or circumstances leading to the institution's falling below minimum levels, the exigency of those circumstances, and whether or not they were caused by actions of the institution or were beyond the institution's control;

(ii) The overall condition, management strength, and future prospects of the institution and, if applicable, affiliated System institutions;

Farm Credit Administration

§ 615.5351

(iii) The institution's capital, adverse assets (including nonaccrual and nonperforming loans), allowance for loss, and other ratios compared to the ratios of its peers or industry norms;

(iv) How far an institution's ratios are below the minimum requirements;

(v) The estimated rate at which the institution can reasonably be expected to generate additional earnings;

(vi) The effect of the business changes required to increase capital;

(vii) The institution's previous compliance practices, as appropriate;

(viii) The views of the institution's directors and senior management regarding the plan; and

(ix) Any other facts or circumstances that the FCA deems relevant.

(3) An institution shall be deemed to be in compliance with the surplus and collateral requirements of this subpart if it is in compliance with a capital restoration plan that is approved by the Farm Credit Administration within 180 days following the end of the quarter in which these regulations become effective.

Subpart L—Establishment of Minimum Capital Ratios for an Individual Institution

SOURCE: 62 FR 4448, Jan. 30, 1997, unless otherwise noted.

§ 615.5350 General—Applicability.

(a) The rules and procedures specified in this subpart are applicable to a proceeding to establish required minimum capital ratios that would otherwise be applicable to an institution under §§ 615.5205, 615.5330, and 615.5335. The Farm Credit Administration is authorized to establish such minimum capital requirements for an institution as the Farm Credit Administration, in its discretion, deems to be necessary or appropriate in light of the particular circumstances of the institution. Proceedings under this subpart also may be initiated to require an institution having capital ratios greater than those set forth in §§ 615.5205, 615.5330, or 615.5335 to continue to maintain those higher ratios.

(b) The Farm Credit Administration may require higher minimum capital ratios for an individual institution in view of its circumstances. For example, higher capital ratios may be appropriate for:

(1) An institution receiving special supervisory attention;

(2) An institution that has, or is expected to have, losses resulting in capital inadequacy;

(3) An institution with significant exposure due to operational risk, interest rate risk, the risks from concentrations of credit, certain risks arising from other products, services, or related activities, or management's overall inability to monitor and control financial risks presented by concentrations of credit and related services activities;

(4) An institution exposed to a high volume of, or particularly severe, problem loans;

(5) An institution that is growing rapidly; or

(6) An institution that may be adversely affected by the activities or condition of System institutions with which it has significant business relationships or in which it has significant investments.

(7) An institution with significant exposures to declines in net income or in the market value of its capital due to a change in interest rates and/or the exercising of embedded or explicit options.

[62 FR 4448, Jan. 30, 1997, as amended at 63 FR 39229, July 22, 1998]

§ 615.5351 Standards for determination of appropriate individual institution minimum capital ratios.

The appropriate minimum capital ratios for an individual institution cannot be determined solely through the application of a rigid mathematical formula or wholly objective criteria. The decision is necessarily based in part on subjective judgment grounded in Agency expertise. The factors to be considered in the determination will vary in each case and may include, for example:

(a) The conditions or circumstances leading to the Farm Credit Administration's determination that higher minimum capital ratios are appropriate or necessary for the institution;

(b) The exigency of those circumstances or potential problems;

§ 615.5352

(c) The overall condition, management strength, and future prospects of the institution and, if applicable, affiliated institutions;

(d) The institution's capital, adverse assets (including nonaccrual and nonperforming loans), allowance for loss, and other ratios compared to the ratios of its peers or industry norms; and

(e) The views of the institution's directors and senior management.

§ 615.5352 Procedures.

(a) *Notice.* When the Farm Credit Administration determines that minimum capital ratios greater than those set forth in §§ 615.5205, 615.5330, or 615.5335 are necessary or appropriate for a particular institution, the Farm Credit Administration will notify the institution in writing of the proposed minimum capital ratios and the date by which they should be reached (if applicable) and will provide an explanation of why the ratios proposed are considered necessary or appropriate for the institution.

(b) *Response.* (1) The institution may respond to any or all of the items in the notice. The response should include any matters which the institution would have the Farm Credit Administration consider in deciding whether individual minimum capital ratios should be established for the institution, what those capital ratios should be, and, if applicable, when they should be achieved. The response must be in writing and delivered to the designated Farm Credit Administration official within 30 days after the date on which the institution received the notice. In its discretion, the Farm Credit Administration may extend the time period for good cause. The Farm Credit Administration may shorten the time period with the consent of the institution or when, in the opinion of the Farm Credit Administration, the condition of the institution so requires, provided that the institution is informed promptly of the new time period.

(2) Failure to respond within 30 days or such other time period as may be specified by the Farm Credit Administration shall constitute a waiver of any objections to the proposed minimum capital ratios or the deadline for their achievement.

(c) *Decision.* After the close of the institution's response period, the Farm Credit Administration will decide, based on a review of the institution's response and other information concerning the institution, whether individual minimum capital ratios should be established for the institution and, if so, the ratios and the date the requirements will become effective. The institution will be notified of the decision in writing. The notice will include an explanation of the decision, except for a decision not to establish individual minimum capital requirements for the institution.

(d) *Submission of plan.* The decision may require the institution to develop and submit to the Farm Credit Administration, within a time period specified, an acceptable plan to reach the minimum capital ratios established for the institution by the date required.

(e) *Reconsideration based on change in circumstances.* If, after the Farm Credit Administration's decision in paragraph (c) of this section, there is a change in the circumstances affecting the institution's capital adequacy or its ability to reach the required minimum capital ratios by the specified date, either the institution or the Farm Credit Administration may propose a change in the minimum capital ratios for the institution, the date when the minimums must be achieved, or the institution's plan (if applicable). The Farm Credit Administration may decline to consider proposals that are not based on a significant change in circumstances or are repetitive or frivolous. Pending a decision on reconsideration, the Farm Credit Administration's original decision and any plan required under that decision shall continue in full force and effect.

§ 615.5353 Relation to other actions.

In lieu of, or in addition to, the procedures in this subpart, the required minimum capital ratios for an institution may be established or revised through a written agreement or cease and desist proceedings under part C of title V of the Act, or as a condition for approval of an application.

Farm Credit Administration

§ 615.5354 Enforcement.

An institution that does not have or maintain the minimum capital ratios applicable to it, whether required in subparts H and K of this part, in a decision pursuant to this subpart, in a written agreement or temporary or final order under part C of title V of the Act, or in a condition for approval of an application, or an institution that has failed to submit or comply with an acceptable plan to attain those ratios, will be subject to such administrative action or sanctions as the Farm Credit Administration considers appropriate. These sanctions may include the issuance of a capital directive pursuant to subpart M of this part or other enforcement action, assessment of civil money penalties, and/or the denial or condition of applications.

Subpart M—Issuance of a Capital Directive

SOURCE: 62 FR 4449, Jan. 30, 1997, unless otherwise noted.

§ 615.5355 Purpose and scope.

(a) This subpart is applicable to proceedings by the Farm Credit Administration to issue a capital directive under sections 4.3(b) and 4.3A(e) of the Act. A capital directive is an order issued to an institution that does not have or maintain capital at or greater than the minimum ratios set forth in §§ 615.5205, 615.5330, and 615.5335; or established for the institution under subpart L, by a written agreement under part C of title V of the Act, or as a condition for approval of an application. A capital directive may order the institution to:

(1) Achieve the minimum capital ratios applicable to it by a specified date;

(2) Adhere to a previously submitted plan to achieve the applicable capital ratios;

(3) Submit and adhere to a plan acceptable to the Farm Credit Administration describing the means and time schedule by which the institution shall achieve the applicable capital ratios;

(4) Take other action, such as reduction of assets or the rate of growth of assets, restrictions on the payment of dividends or patronage, or restrictions on the retirement of stock, to achieve the applicable capital ratios, or reduce levels of interest rate and other risk exposures, or strengthen management expertise, or improve management information and measurement systems; or

(5) A combination of any of these or similar actions.

(b) A capital directive may also be issued to the board of directors of an institution, requiring such board to comply with the requirements of section 4.3A(d) of the Act prohibiting the reduction of permanent capital.

(c) A capital directive issued under this rule, including a plan submitted under a capital directive, is enforceable in the same manner and to the same extent as an effective and outstanding cease and desist order which has become final as defined in section 5.25 of the Act. Violation of a capital directive may result in assessment of civil money penalties in accordance with section 5.32 of the Act.

[62 FR 4449, Jan. 30, 1997, as amended at 63 FR 39229, July 22, 1998]

§ 615.5356 Notice of intent to issue a capital directive.

The Farm Credit Administration will notify an institution in writing of its intention to issue a capital directive. The notice will state:

(a) The reasons for issuance of the capital directive;

(b) The proposed contents of the capital directive, including the proposed date for achieving the minimum capital requirement; and

(c) Any other relevant information concerning the decision to issue a capital directive.

§ 615.5357 Response to notice.

(a) An institution may respond to the notice by stating why a capital directive should not be issued and/or by proposing alternative contents for the capital directive or seeking other appropriate relief. The response shall include any information, mitigating circumstances, documentation, or other relevant evidence that supports its position. The response may include a plan for achieving the minimum capital ratios applicable to the institution. The

§ 615.5358

response must be in writing and delivered to the Farm Credit Administration within 30 days after the date on which the institution received the notice. In its discretion, the Farm Credit Administration may extend the time period for good cause. The Farm Credit Administration may shorten the 30-day time period:

(1) When, in the opinion of the Farm Credit Administration, the condition of the institution so requires, provided that the institution shall be informed promptly of the new time period;

(2) With the consent of the institution; or

(3) When the institution already has advised the Farm Credit Administration that it cannot or will not achieve its applicable minimum capital ratios.

(b) Failure to respond within 30 days or such other time period as may be specified by the Farm Credit Administration shall constitute a waiver of any objections to the proposed capital directive.

§ 615.5358 Decision.

After the closing date of the institution's response period, or receipt of the institution's response, if earlier, the Farm Credit Administration may seek additional information or clarification of the response. Thereafter, the Farm Credit Administration will determine whether or not to issue a capital directive, and if one is to be issued, whether it should be as originally proposed or in modified form.

§ 615.5359 Issuance of a capital directive.

(a) A capital directive will be served by delivery to the institution. It will include or be accompanied by a statement of reasons for its issuance.

(b) A capital directive is effective immediately upon its receipt by the institution, or upon such later date as may be specified therein, and shall remain effective and enforceable until it is stayed, modified, or terminated by the Farm Credit Administration.

§ 615.5360 Reconsideration based on change in circumstances.

Upon a change in circumstances, an institution may request the Farm Credit Administration to reconsider the terms of its capital directive or may propose changes in the plan to achieve the institution's applicable minimum capital ratios. The Farm Credit Administration also may take such action on its own motion. The Farm Credit Administration may decline to consider requests or proposals that are not based on a significant change in circumstances or are repetitive or frivolous. Pending a decision on reconsideration, the capital directive and plan shall continue in full force and effect.

§ 615.5361 Relation to other administrative actions.

A capital directive may be issued in addition to, or in lieu of, any other action authorized by law, including cease and desist proceedings, civil money penalties, or the conditioning or denial of applications. The Farm Credit Administration also may, in its discretion, take any action authorized by law, in lieu of a capital directive, in response to an institution's failure to achieve or maintain the applicable minimum capital ratios.

Subpart N [Reserved]

Subpart O—Book-Entry Procedures for Farm Credit Securities

SOURCE: 61 FR 67192, Dec. 20, 1996, unless otherwise noted.

§ 615.5450 Definitions.

In this subpart, unless the context otherwise requires or indicates:

(a) *Adverse claim* means a claim that a claimant has a property interest in a security and that it is a violation of the rights of the claimant for another person to hold, transfer, or deal with the security.

(b) *Book-entry security* means a Farm Credit security issued or maintained in the Book-entry System.

(c) *Book-entry System* means the automated book-entry system operated by the Federal Reserve Banks, acting as the fiscal agent for the Farm Credit banks, through which book-entry securities are issued, recorded, transferred and maintained in book-entry form.

(d) *Definitive Farm Credit security* means a Farm Credit security in engraved or printed form, or that is otherwise represented by a certificate.

(e) *Eligible book-entry security* means a book-entry security issued or maintained in the Book-entry System, which by the terms of its securities documentation, is eligible to be converted from book-entry into definitive form.

(f) *Entitlement Holder* means a person to whose account an interest in a book-entry security is credited on the records of a securities intermediary.

(g) *Farm Credit banks* means one or more Farm Credit Banks, agricultural credit banks, and banks for cooperatives.

(h) *Farm Credit securities* means consolidated notes, bonds, debentures, or other similar obligations of the Farm Credit banks and Systemwide notes, bonds, debentures, or similar obligations of the Farm Credit banks issued under sections 4.2(c) and 4.2(d), respectively, of the Act, or laws repealed thereby.

(i) *Federal Reserve Bank* means a Federal Reserve Bank or Branch acting as agent for the Farm Credit banks and the Funding Corporation.

(j) *Federal Reserve Bank Operating Circular* means the publication issued by each Federal Reserve Bank that sets forth the terms and conditions under which the Federal Reserve Bank maintains book-entry securities accounts and transfers book-entry securities.

(k) *Funding Corporation* means the Federal Farm Credit Banks Funding Corporation established pursuant to section 4.9 of the Act, which issues Farm Credit securities on behalf of the Farm Credit banks.

(l) *Funds Account* means a reserve and/or clearing account at a Federal Reserve Bank to which debits or credits are posted for transfers against payment, book-entry securities transaction fees, or principal and interest payments.

(m) *Participant* means a person that maintains a participant's securities account with a Federal Reserve Bank.

(n) *Participant's Securities Account* means an account in the name of a participant at a Federal Reserve Bank to which book-entry securities held for a participant are or may be credited.

(o) *Person* means an individual, corporation, company, governmental entity, association, firm, partnership, trust, estate, representative and any other similar organization, but does not mean the United States, a Farm Credit bank, the Funding Corporation or a Federal Reserve Bank.

(p) *Revised Article 8* means Uniform Commercial Code, Revised Article 8, Investment Securities (with Conforming and Miscellaneous Amendments to Articles 1, 3, 4, 5, 9, and 10) 1994 Official Text, and has the same meaning as in 31 CFR 357.2.

(q) *Securities Documentation* means the applicable statement of terms, trust indenture, securities agreement, offering circular or other documents establishing the terms of a book-entry security.

(r) *Securities Intermediary* means:

(1) A person that is registered as a "clearing agency" under the Federal securities laws; a Federal Reserve Bank; any other person that provides clearance or settlement services with respect to a book-entry security that would require it to register as a clearing agency under the Federal securities laws but for an exclusion or exemption from the registration requirement, if its activities as a clearing corporation, including promulgation of rules, are subject to regulation by a Federal or State governmental authority; or

(2) A person (other than an individual, unless such individual is registered as a broker or dealer under the Federal securities laws) including a bank or broker, that in the ordinary course of its business maintains securities accounts for others and is acting in that capacity.

(s) *Security* means a Farm Credit security as defined in paragraph (h) of this section.

(t) *Security Entitlement* means the rights and property interest of an entitlement holder with respect to a book-entry security.

(u) *State* means any State of the United States, the District of Columbia, Puerto Rico, the Virgin Islands, or any other territory or possession of the United States.

§ 615.5451

(v) *Transfer Message* means an instruction of a participant to a Federal Reserve Bank to effect a transfer of a book-entry security maintained in the Book-entry System, as set forth in Federal Reserve Bank Operating Circulars.

[61 FR 67192, Dec. 20, 1996, as amended at 62 FR 53229, Oct. 14, 1997]

§ 615.5451 Book-entry and definitive securities.

Subject to subpart C of this part:

(a) Farm Credit banks operating under the same title of the Act may issue consolidated securities in book-entry form.

(b) Farm Credit banks may issue Systemwide securities in book-entry form.

(c) Consolidated and Systemwide securities also may be issued in either registered or bearer definitive form.

[61 FR 67192, Dec. 20, 1996, as amended at 62 FR 53229, Oct. 14, 1997]

§ 615.5452 Law governing rights and obligations of Federal Reserve Banks, Farm Credit banks, and Funding Corporation; rights of any person against Federal Reserve Banks, Farm Credit banks, and Funding Corporation.

(a) Except as provided in paragraph (b) of this section, the following are governed solely by the regulations contained in this subpart O, the securities documentation, and Federal Reserve Bank Operating Circulars:

(1) The rights and obligations of the Farm Credit banks, the Funding Corporation, and the Federal Reserve Banks with respect to:

(i) A book-entry security or security entitlement, and

(ii) The operation of the Book-entry System as it applies to Farm Credit securities; and

(2) The rights of any person, including a participant, against the Farm Credit banks, the Funding Corporation, and the Federal Reserve Banks with respect to:

(i) A book-entry security or security entitlement, and

(ii) The operation of the Book-entry System as it applies to Farm Credit securities.

(b) A security interest in a security entitlement that is in favor of a Federal Reserve Bank from a participant and that is not recorded on the books of a Federal Reserve Bank pursuant to § 615.5454(c)(1) of this subpart, is governed by the law (not including the conflict-of-law rules) of the jurisdiction where the head office of the Federal Reserve Bank maintaining the participant's securities account is located. A security interest in a security entitlement that is in favor of a Federal Reserve Bank from a person that is not a participant, and that is not recorded on the books of a Federal Reserve Bank pursuant to § 615.5454(c)(1) of this subpart, is governed by the law determined in the manner specified in § 615.5453 of this subpart.

(c) If the jurisdiction specified in the first sentence of paragraph (b) of this section is a State that has not adopted revised Article 8 (see 31 CFR 357.2) then the law specified in paragraph (b) of this section shall be the law of that State as though revised Article 8 had been adopted by that State.

[61 FR 67192, Dec. 20, 1996, as amended at 62 FR 53229, Oct. 14, 1997]

§ 615.5453 Law governing other interests.

(a) To the extent not inconsistent with these regulations, the law (not including the conflict-of-law rules) of a securities intermediary's jurisdiction governs:

(1) The acquisition of a security entitlement from the securities intermediary;

(2) The rights and duties of the securities intermediary and entitlement holder arising out of a security entitlement;

(3) Whether the securities intermediary owes any duties to an adverse claimant to a security entitlement;

(4) Whether an adverse claim can be asserted against a person who acquires a security entitlement from the securities intermediary or a person who purchases a security entitlement or interest therein from an entitlement holder; and

(5) Except as otherwise provided in paragraph (c) of this section, the perfection, effect of perfection or non-perfection and priority of a security interest in a security entitlement.

Farm Credit Administration §615.5454

(b) The following rules determine a "securities intermediary's jurisdiction" for purposes of this section:

(1) If an agreement between the securities intermediary and its entitlement holder specifies that it is governed by the law of a particular jurisdiction, that jurisdiction is the securities intermediary's jurisdiction.

(2) If an agreement between the securities intermediary and its entitlement holder does not specify the governing law as provided in paragraph (b)(1) of this section, but expressly specifies that the securities account is maintained at an office in a particular jurisdiction, that jurisdiction is the securities intermediary's jurisdiction.

(3) If an agreement between the securities intermediary and its entitlement holder does not specify a jurisdiction as provided in paragraph (b)(1) or (b)(2) of this section, the securities intermediary's jurisdiction is the jurisdiction in which is located the office identified in an account statement as the office serving the entitlement holder's account.

(4) If an agreement between the securities intermediary and its entitlement holder does not specify a jurisdiction as provided in paragraph (b)(1) or (b)(2) of this section and an account statement does not identify an office serving the entitlement holder's account as provided in paragraph (b)(3) of this section, the securities intermediary's jurisdiction is the jurisdiction in which is located the chief executive office of the securities intermediary.

(c) Notwithstanding the general rule in paragraph (a)(5) of this section, the law (but not the conflict-of-law rules) of the jurisdiction in which the person creating a security interest is located governs whether and how the security interest may be perfected automatically or by filing a financing statement.

(d) If the jurisdiction specified in paragraph (b) of this section is a State that has not adopted revised Article 8 (see 31 CFR 357.2), then the law for the matters specified in paragraph (a) of this section shall be the law of that State as though revised Article 8 had been adopted by that State. For purposes of the application of the matters specified in paragraph (a) of this section, the Federal Reserve Bank maintaining the securities account is a clearing corporation, and the participant's interest in a book-entry security is a security entitlement.

§ 615.5454 **Creation of participant's security entitlement; security interests.**

(a) A participant's security entitlement is created when a Federal Reserve Bank indicates by book entry that a book-entry security has been credited to a participant's securities account.

(b) A security interest in a security entitlement of a participant in favor of the United States to secure deposits of public money, including without limitation deposits to the Treasury tax and loan accounts, or other security interest in favor of the United States that is required by Federal statute, regulation, or agreement, and that is marked on the books of a Federal Reserve Bank is thereby effected and perfected, and has priority over any other interest in the securities. Where a security interest in favor of the United States in a security entitlement of a participant is marked on the books of a Federal Reserve Bank, such Federal Reserve Bank may rely, and is protected in relying, exclusively on the order of an authorized representative of the United States directing the transfer of the security. For purposes of this paragraph, an "authorized representative of the United States" is the official designated in the applicable regulations or agreement to which a Federal Reserve Bank is a party, governing the security interest.

(c)(1) The Farm Credit Banks, the Funding Corporation, and the Federal Reserve Banks have no obligation to agree to act on behalf of any person or to recognize the interest of any transferee of a security interest or other limited interest in favor of any person except to the extent of any specific requirement of Federal law or regulation or to the extent set forth in any specific agreement with the Federal Reserve Bank on whose books the interest of the participant is recorded. To the extent required by such law or regulation or set forth in an agreement with a Federal Reserve Bank, or the Federal

§ 615.5455

Reserve Bank Operating Circular, a security interest in a security entitlement that is in favor of a Federal Reserve Bank, a Farm Credit Bank, the Funding Corporation, or a person may be created and perfected by a Federal Reserve Bank marking its books to record the security interest. Except as provided in paragraph (b) of this section, a security interest in a security entitlement marked on the books of a Federal Reserve Bank shall have priority over any other interest in the securities.

(2) In addition to the method provided in paragraph (c)(1) of this section, a security interest, including a security interest in favor of a Federal Reserve Bank, may be perfected by any method by which a security interest may be perfected under applicable law as described in § 615.5452(b) or § 615.5453 of this subpart. The perfection, effect of perfection or non-perfection and priority of a security interest are governed by that applicable law. A security interest in favor of a Federal Reserve Bank shall be treated as a security interest in favor of a clearing corporation in all respects under that law, including with respect to the effect of perfection and priority of the security interest. A Federal Reserve Bank Operating Circular shall be treated as a rule adopted by a clearing corporation for such purposes.

[62 FR 67192, Dec. 20, 1996, as amended at 62 FR 53229, Oct. 14, 1997]

§ 615.5455 Obligations of the Farm Credit banks and the Funding Corporation; no adverse claims.

(a) Except in the case of a security interest in favor of the United States or a Federal Reserve Bank or otherwise as provided in § 615.5454(c)(1), for the purposes of this subpart O, the Farm Credit banks, the Funding Corporation and the Federal Reserve Banks shall treat the participant to whose securities account an interest in a book-entry security has been credited as the person exclusively entitled to issue a transfer message, to receive interest and other payments with respect thereof and otherwise to exercise all the rights and powers with respect to such security, notwithstanding any information or notice to the contrary. The Federal Reserve Banks, the Farm Credit banks, and the Funding Corporation are not liable to a person asserting or having an adverse claim to a security entitlement or to a book-entry security in a participant's securities account, including any such claim arising as a result of the transfer or disposition of a book-entry security by a Federal Reserve Bank pursuant to a transfer message that the Federal Reserve Bank reasonably believes to be genuine.

(b) The obligation of the Farm Credit banks and the Funding Corporation to make payments (including payments of interest and principal) with respect to book-entry securities is discharged at the time payment in the appropriate amount is made as follows:

(1) Interest or other payments on book-entry securities are either credited by a Federal Reserve Bank to a funds account maintained at the Federal Reserve Bank or otherwise paid as directed by the participant.

(2) Book-entry securities are redeemed in accordance with their terms by a Federal Reserve Bank withdrawing the securities from the participant's securities account in which they are maintained and by either crediting the amount of the redemption proceeds, including both principal and interest, where applicable, to a funds account at the Federal Reserve Bank or otherwise paying such principal and interest as directed by the participant. No action by the participant is required in connection with the redemption of a book-entry security.

[61 FR 67192, Dec. 20, 1996, as amended at 62 FR 53229, Oct. 14, 1997]

§ 615.5456 Authority of Federal Reserve Banks.

(a) Each Federal Reserve Bank is hereby authorized as fiscal agent of the Farm Credit banks and the Funding Corporation to perform functions with respect to the issuance of book-entry securities offered and sold by the Farm Credit banks and the Funding Corporation to which this subpart applies, in accordance with the terms of the securities documentation and the provisions of this subpart:

(1) To service and maintain book-entry securities in accounts established for such purposes;

(2) To make payments of principal and interest, as directed by the Farm Credit banks and the Funding Corporation;

(3) To effect transfer of book-entry securities between participants' securities accounts as directed by the participants;

(4) To effect conversions between book-entry securities and definitive Farm Credit securities with respect to those securities as to which conversion rights are available pursuant to the applicable securities documentation; and

(5) To perform such other duties as fiscal agent as may be requested by the Farm Credit banks and the Funding Corporation.

(b) Each Federal Reserve Bank may issue Operating Circulars not inconsistent with this subpart, governing the details of its handling of book-entry securities, security entitlements, and the operation of the Book-entry System under this subpart.

§ 615.5457 Withdrawal of eligible book-entry securities for conversion to definitive form.

(a) Eligible book-entry securities may be withdrawn from the Book-entry System by requesting delivery of like definitive Farm Credit securities.

(b) A Federal Reserve Bank shall, upon receipt of appropriate instructions to withdraw eligible book-entry securities from book-entry in the Book-entry System, convert such securities into definitive Farm Credit securities and deliver them in accordance with such instructions.

(c) Farm Credit securities which are to be delivered upon withdrawal may be issued in either registered or bearer form, to the extent permitted by the applicable securities documentation.

(d) All requests for withdrawal of eligible book-entry securities must be made prior to the maturity or the applicable date of call of the Farm Credit securities.

[61 FR 67192, Dec. 20, 1996, as amended at 62 FR 53230, Oct. 14, 1997]

§ 615.5458 Waiver of regulations.

The Farm Credit Administration reserves the right, in the Farm Credit Administration's discretion, to waive any provision(s) of the regulations in this subpart in any case or class of cases for the convenience of the Farm Credit banks and the Funding Corporation or in order to relieve any person(s) of unnecessary hardship, if such action is not inconsistent with law, does not adversely affect any substantial existing rights, and the Farm Credit Administration is satisfied that such action will not subject the Farm Credit banks and the Funding Corporation to any substantial expense or liability.

§ 615.5459 Liability of Farm Credit banks, Funding Corporation and Federal Reserve Banks.

The Farm Credit banks, the Funding Corporation, and the Federal Reserve Banks may rely on the information provided in a transfer message or other transaction documentation, and are not required to verify the information. The Farm Credit banks, the Funding Corporation, and the Federal Reserve Banks shall not be liable for any action taken in accordance with the information set out in the transfer message, other transaction documentation, or evidence submitted in support thereof.

§ 615.5460 Additional provisions.

(a) *Additional requirements.* In any case or any class of cases arising under the regulations in this subpart, the Farm Credit banks and the Funding Corporation may require such additional evidence and a bond of indemnity, with or without surety, as may in the judgment of the Farm Credit banks and the Funding Corporation be necessary for the protection of the interests of the Farm Credit banks and the Funding Corporation.

(b) *Notice of attachment for Farm Credit securities in the Book-entry System.* The interest of a debtor in a security entitlement may be reached by a creditor only by legal process upon the securities intermediary with whom the debtor's securities account is maintained, except where a security entitlement is maintained in the name of a secured party, in which case the debtor's interest may be reached by legal

§ 615.5461

process upon the secured party. These regulations do not purport to establish whether a Federal Reserve Bank is required to honor an order or other notice of attachment in any particular case or class of cases.

(c) *Conversion of definitive securities into book-entry securities.* Definitive Farm Credit securities may be converted to book-entry form in accordance with the terms of the applicable securities documentation and Federal Reserve Operating Circular.

[61 FR 67192, Dec. 20, 1996, as amended at 62 FR 53230, Oct. 14, 1997]

§ 615.5461 **Lost, stolen, destroyed, mutilated or defaced Farm Credit securities, including coupons.**

(a) Relief on the account of the loss, theft, destruction, mutilation, or defacement of any definitive consolidated or Systemwide securities of the Farm Credit banks and coupons of such securities may be granted on the same basis and to the same extent as relief may be granted under the statutes of the United States and the regulations of the Department of the Treasury on the account of the loss, theft, destruction, mutilation, or defacement of United States securities and coupons of such securities.

(b) Applicants for relief under paragraph (a) of this section, shall present claims and proof of loss:

(1) To the Division of Special Investments, Bureau of the Public Debt, P.O. Box 396, Parkersburg, WV 26102–0396, in the case of consolidated or Systemwide securities of the Farm Credit banks issued prior to May 1, 1978; or

(2) To the Federal Farm Credit Banks Funding Corporation, 10 Exchange Place, Suite 1401, Jersey City, NJ 07302, in the case of consolidated or Systemwide securities issued on or after May 1, 1978.

§ 615.5462 **Restrictive endorsement of bearer securities.**

When consolidated and Systemwide bearer securities of the Farm Credit banks are being presented to Federal Reserve Banks, for redemption, exchange, or conversion to book entry, such securities may be restrictively endorsed. The restrictive endorsement shall be placed thereon in substantially the same manner and with the same effects as prescribed in United States Treasury Department regulations, now or hereafter in force, governing like transactions in United States bonds; and consolidated or Systemwide securities of the Farm Credit banks so endorsed shall be prepared for shipment and shipped in the manner prescribed in such regulations for United States bearer securities. (See 31 CFR part 328.)

Subpart P—Global Debt Securities

§ 615.5500 **Definitions.**

In this subpart, unless the context otherwise requires or indicates:

(a) *Global debt securities* means consolidated Systemwide debt securities issued by the Funding Corporation on behalf of the Farm Credit banks under section 4.2(d) of the Act through a fiscal agent or agents and distributed either exclusively outside the United States or simultaneously inside and outside the United States.

(b) *Global agent* means any fiscal agent, other than the Federal Reserve Banks, used by the Funding Corporation to facilitate the sale of global debt securities.

[60 FR 57919, Nov. 24, 1995]

§ 615.5502 **Issuance of global debt securities.**

(a) The Funding Corporation may provide for the sale of global debt securities on behalf of the Farm Credit banks through a global agent or agents by negotiation, offer, bid, or syndicate sale, and deliver such obligations by book-entry, wire transfer, or such other means as may be appropriate.

(b) The Funding Corporation Board of Directors shall establish appropriate criteria for the selection of global agents and shall approve each global agent.

[60 FR 57919, Nov. 24, 1995]

Subpart Q—Bankers' Acceptances

§ 615.5550 **Bankers' acceptances.**

Banks for cooperatives may rediscount with other purchasers the acceptances they have created. The bank for cooperatives' board of directors,

Farm Credit Administration

under established policies, may delegate this authority to management.

[71 FR 65387, Nov. 8, 2006]

Subpart R [Reserved]

PART 616—LEASING

Sec.
616.6000 Definitions.
616.6100 Purchase and sale of interests in leases.
616.6200 Out-of-territory leasing.
616.6300 Leasing policies, procedures, and underwriting standards.
616.6400 Documentation.
616.6500 Investment in leased assets.
616.6600 Leasing limit.
616.6700 Stock purchase requirements.
616.6800 Disclosure requirements.

AUTHORITY: Secs. 1.3, 1.5, 1.6, 1.7, 1.9, 1.10, 1.11, 2.0, 2.2, 2.3, 2.4, 2.10, 2.12, 2.13, 2.15, 3.0, 3.1, 3.3, 3.7, 3.8, 3.9, 3.10, 3.20, 3.28, 4.3, 4.3A, 4.13, 4.13A, 4.13B, 4.14, 4.14A, 4.14C, 4.14D, 4.14E, 4.18, 4.18A, 4.25, 4.26, 4.27, 4.28, 4.36, 4.37, 5.9, 5.10, 5.17, 7.0, 7.2, 7.3, 7.6, 7.8, 7.12, 7.13 of the Farm Credit Act (12 U.S.C. 2011, 2013, 2014, 2015, 2017, 2018, 2019, 2071, 2073, 2074, 2075, 2091, 2093, 2094, 2097, 2121, 2122, 2124, 2128, 2129, 2130, 2131, 2141, 2149, 2154, 2154a, 2199, 2200, 2201, 2202, 2202a, 2202c, 2202d, 2202e, 2206, 2206a, 2211, 2212, 2213, 2214, 2219a, 2219b, 2243, 2244, 2252, 2279a, 2279a–2, 2279a–3, 2279b, 2279c–1, 2279f, 2279f–1).

SOURCE: 64 FR 34518, June 28, 1999, unless otherwise noted.

§ 616.600 Definitions.

For the purposes of this part, the following definitions apply:

(a) *Interests in leases* means ownership interests in any aspect of a lease transaction, including, but not limited to, servicing rights.

(b) *Lease* means any contractual obligation to own and lease, or lease with the option to purchase, equipment or facilities used in the operations of persons eligible to borrow under part 613 of this chapter.

(c) *Sale with recourse* means a sale of a lease or an interest in a lease in which the seller:

(1) Retains some risk of loss from the transferred asset for any cause except the seller's breach of usual and customary warranties or representations designed to protect the purchaser against fraud or misrepresentation; or

(2) Has an obligation to make payments to any party resulting from:

(i) Default on the lease by the lessee or guarantor or any other deficiencies in the lessee's performance;

(ii) Changes in the market value of the assets after transfer;

(iii) Any contractual relationship between the seller and purchaser incident to the transfer that, by its terms, could continue even after final payment, default, or other termination of the assets transferred; or

(iv) Any other cause, except that the retention of servicing rights alone shall not constitute recourse.

§ 616.6100 Purchase and sale of interests in leases.

(a) *Authority to buy interests in leases.* A Farm Credit System institution may buy leases and interests in leases.

(b) *Policies.* Each Farm Credit System institution that sells or buys interests in leases must do so only under a policy adopted by its board of directors that addresses the following:

(1) The types of leases in which the institution may buy or sell an interest and the types of interests which may be bought or sold;

(2) The underwriting standards for the purchase of interests in leases;

(3) Such limits on the aggregate lease payments and residual amount of interests in leases that the institution may buy from a single institution as are necessary to diversify risk, and such limits on the aggregate amounts the institution may buy from all institutions as are necessary to assure that service to the territory is not impeded;

(4) Identification and reporting of leases in which interests are sold or bought;

(5) Requirements for securing from the selling lessor in a timely manner adequate financial and other information about the lessee needed to make an independent judgment; and

(6) Any limits or conditions to which sales or purchases are subject that the board considers appropriate, including arbitration.

(c) *Purchase and sale agreements.* Each agreement to buy or sell an interest in a lease must, at a minimum:

(1) Identify the particular lease(s) to be covered by the agreement;

§ 616.6200

(2) Provide for the transfer of lessee information on a timely and continuing basis;

(3) Identify the nature of the interest(s) sold or bought;

(4) Specify the rights and obligations of the parties and the terms and conditions of the sale;

(5) Contain any terms necessary for the appropriate administration of the lease, including lease servicing and monitoring of the servicer and authorization and conditions for action in the event of lessee distress or default;

(6) Provide for a method of resolution of disagreements arising under the agreement;

(7) Specify whether the contract is assignable by either party; and

(8) In the case of lease transactions through agents, comply with § 614.4325(h) of this chapter, reading the term "lease" or "leases" in place of the term "loan" or "loans," as applicable.

(d) *Independent judgment.* Each institution that buys an interest in a lease must make a judgment on the payment ability of the lessee that is independent of the originating or lead lessor and any intermediary seller or broker. This must occur before the purchase of the interest and before any servicing action that alters the terms of the original agreement. The institution must not delegate such judgment to any person(s) not employed by the institution. A Farm Credit System institution that buys a lease or any interest in a lease may use information, such as appraisals or inspections, provided by the originating or lead lessor, or any intermediary seller or broker; however, the buying Farm Credit System institution must independently evaluate such information when exercising its judgment. The independent judgment must be documented by a payment analysis that considers factors set forth in § 616.6300. The payment analysis must consider such financial and other lessee information as would be required by a prudent lessor and must include an evaluation of the capacity and reliability of the servicer. Boards of directors of jointly managed institutions must adopt procedures to ensure the interests of their respective shareholders are protected in participation between such institutions.

(e) *Sales with recourse.* When a lease or interest in a lease is sold with recourse:

(1) For the purpose of determining the lending and leasing limit in subpart J of part 614 of this chapter, the lease must be considered, to the extent of the recourse or guaranty, a lease by the buyer to the seller, and in addition, the seller must aggregate the lease with other obligations of the lessee; and

(2) The lease subject to the recourse agreement must be considered an asset sold with recourse for the purpose of computing capital ratios.

(f) *Similar entity lease transactions.* The provisions of § 613.3300 of this chapter that apply to interests in loans made to similar entities apply to interests in leases made to similar entities. In applying these provisions, the term "loan" shall be read to include the term "lease" and the term "principal amount" shall be read to include the term "lease amount."

§ 616.6200 Out-of-territory leasing.

A System institution may make leases outside its chartered territory.

§ 616.6300 Leasing policies, procedures, and underwriting standards.

The board of each institution engaged in lease underwriting must adopt a written policy (or policies). Management, at the direction of the board, must develop procedures that reflect lease practices that control risk and comply with all applicable laws and regulations. Any leasing activity must comply with the lending policies and loan underwriting requirements in § 614.4150 of this chapter. An institution engaged in the making, buying, or syndicating of leases also must adopt written policies and procedures that address the additional risks associated with leasing. Written policies and procedures must address the following, if applicable:

(a) Appropriateness of the lease amount, purpose, and terms and conditions, including the residual value established at the inception of the lease;

(b) Process for estimating the leased asset's market value during the lease term;

(c) Types of equipment and facilities the institution will lease;

(d) Remarketing of leased property and associated risks;

(e) Property tax and sales tax reporting;

(f) Title and ownership of leased assets;

(g) Title and licensing for motor vehicles;

(h) Liability associated with ownership, including any environmental hazards or risks;

(i) Insurance requirements for both the lessor and lessee;

(j) Classification of leases in accordance with generally accepted accounting principles; and

(k) Tax treatment of lease transactions and associated risks.

§ 616.6400 Documentation.

Each institution must document that any asset it leases is within its statutory authority.

§ 616.6500 Investment in leased assets.

An institution may acquire property to be leased that is consistent with current or planned leasing programs.

§ 616.6600 Leasing limit.

All leases made by Farm Credit System institutions shall be subject to the lending and leasing limit in subpart J of part 614 of this chapter.

§ 616.6700 Stock purchase requirements.

(a) Each System institution, except the Farm Credit Leasing Services Corporation, making an equipment lease under titles II or III of the Act must require the lessee to buy or own at least one share of stock or one participation certificate in the institution making the lease, in accordance with its bylaws.

(b) The disclosure requirements of § 615.5250(a) and (b) of this chapter apply to stock (or participation certificates) bought as a condition for obtaining a lease.

§ 616.6800 Disclosure requirements.

(a) Each System institution must give to each lessee a copy of all lease documents signed by the lessee within a reasonable time following lease closing.

(b) Each System institution must make its decision on a lease application as soon as possible and provide prompt written notice of its decision to the applicant.

PART 617—BORROWER RIGHTS

Subpart A—General

Sec.
617.7000 Definitions
617.7005 When may electronic communications be used in the borrower rights process?
617.7010 May borrower rights be waived?
617.7015 What happens to borrower rights when a loan is sold?

Subpart B—Disclosure of Effective Interest Rates

617.7100 Who must make and who is entitled to receive an effective interest rate disclosure?
617.7105 When must a qualified lender disclose the effective interest rate to a borrower?
617.7110 How should a qualified lender disclose the cost of borrower stock or participation certificates?
617.7115 How should a qualified lender disclose loan origination charges?
617.7120 How should a qualified lender present the disclosures to a borrower?
617.7125 How should a qualified lender determine the effective interest rate?
617.7130 What initial disclosures must a qualified lender make to a borrower?
617.7135 What subsequent disclosures must a qualified lender make to a borrower?

Subpart C—Disclosure of Differential Interest Rates

617.7200 What disclosures must a qualified lender make to a borrower on loans offered with more than one rate of interest?

Subpart D—Actions on Applications; Review of Credit Decisions

617.7300 When acting on a loan application, what are the notice requirements and review rights?
617.7305 What is a CRC and who are the members?
617.7310 What is the review process of the CRC?

§ 617.7000

617.7315 What records must the qualified lender maintain on behalf of the CRC?

Subpart E—Distressed Loan Restructuring; State Agricultural Loan Mediation Programs

617.7400 What protections exist for borrowers who meet all loan obligations?
617.7405 On what policies are loan restructurings based?
617.7410 When and how does a qualified lender notify a borrower of the right to seek loan restructuring?
617.7415 How does a qualified lender decide to restructure a loan?
617.7420 How will a decision on an application for restructuring be issued?
617.7425 What type of notice should be given to a borrower before foreclosure?
617.7430 Are institutions required to participate in state agricultural loan mediation programs?

Subpart F—Distressed Loan Restructuring Directive

617.7500 What is a directive used for and what may it require?
617.7505 How will the qualified lender know when FCA is considering issuing a distressed loan restructuring directive?
617.7510 What should the qualified lender do when it receives notice of a distressed loan restructuring directive?
617.7515 How does the FCA decide whether to issue a directive?
617.7520 How does the FCA issue a directive and when will it be effective?
617.7525 May FCA use other enforcement actions?

Subpart G—Right of First Refusal

617.7600 What are the definitions used in this subpart?
617.7605 How should System institutions document whether the borrower had the financial resources to avoid foreclosure?
617.7610 What should the System institution do when it decides to sell acquired agricultural real estate?
617.7615 What should the System institution do when it decides to lease acquired agricultural real estate?
617.7620 What should the System institution do when it decides to sell acquired agricultural real estate at a public auction?
617.7625 Whom should the System institution notify?
617.7630 Does this Federal requirement affect any state property laws?

AUTHORITY: Secs. 4.13, 4.13A, 4.13B, 4.14, 4.14A, 4.14C, 4.14D, 4.14E, 4.36, 5.9, 5.17 of the Farm Credit Act (12 U.S.C. 2199, 2200, 2201, 2202, 2202a, 2202c, 2202d, 2202e, 2219a, 2243, 2252).

SOURCE: 69 FR 10907, 10908, Mar. 9, 2004, unless otherwise noted.

Subpart A—General

§ 617.7000 Definitions.

For the purposes of this part, the following terms apply:

Adjustable rate loan means a loan where the interest rate payable over the term of the loan may change. This includes adjustable rate, variable rate, or other similarly designated loans.

Adverse credit decision means a credit decision where a qualified lender:

(1) Decides not to make a loan to an applicant;

(2) Approves a loan in an amount less than the applicant requested; or

(3) Denies an application for restructuring.

Applicant means any person who completes and executes a loan application from a qualified lender.

Application for restructuring means a written request from a borrower to restructure a distressed loan. The request must be submitted on the appropriate forms prescribed by the qualified lender and accompanied by sufficient financial information and repayment projections, where appropriate, as required by the qualified lender to support a sound credit decision.

Distressed loan means a loan that the borrower does not have the financial capacity to pay according to its terms, as determined by the qualified lender, and exhibits one or more of the following characteristics:

(1) The borrower is demonstrating adverse financial and repayment trends.

(2) The loan is delinquent or past due under the terms of the loan contract.

(3) One or both of the factors listed in paragraphs (1) and (2) of this section, together with inadequate collateralization, present a high probability of loss to the qualified lender.

Effective interest rate means a measure of the cost of credit, expressed as an annual percentage rate, that shows the effect of the following costs, if any, on the interest rate on a loan charged by a qualified lender to a borrower:

(1) The amount of any stock or participation certificates that a borrower is required to buy to obtain the loan; and

Farm Credit Administration § 617.7010

(2) Any loan origination charges paid by a borrower to a qualified lender to obtain the loan.

Foreclosure proceeding means:
(1) A foreclosure or similar legal proceeding to enforce a lien on property, whether real or personal, that secures a non-interest-earning asset or distressed loan; or
(2) The seizing of and realizing on non-real property collateral, other than collateral subject to a statutory lien arising under titles I and II of the Act, to effect collection of a non-accrual or distressed loan.

Independent evaluator means an individual who is a qualified evaluator and who satisfies the standards of § 614.4260, subpart F of this chapter, and the standards set by the qualified lender for the type of property to be evaluated. The independent evaluator may not be an employee or agent of a qualified lender or have a relationship with the lender or any of its officers or directors in contravention of part 612 of this chapter.

Interest rate means the stated contract rate of interest.

Loan means an extension of credit made to a farmer, rancher, or producer or harvester of aquatic products, for any agricultural or aquatic purpose and other credit needs of the borrower, including financing for basic processing and marketing that directly relates to the borrower's operations and those of other eligible farmers, ranchers, and producers or harvesters of aquatic products.

Loan application means a complete oral or written request for an extension of credit made in accordance with a qualified lender's procedures for the type of credit requested. An application is complete when the qualified lender receives all the information normally obtained and used in evaluating applications for credit. This information may include credit reports, supporting information for the credit requested, and reports by governmental agencies or other persons necessary to guarantee, insure, or provide security for the credit or collateral.

Qualified lender means:
(1) A System institution, except a bank for cooperatives, that makes loans as defined in this section; and

(2) Each bank, institution, corporation, company, credit union, and association described in section 1.7(b)(1)(B) of the Act (commonly referred to as an other financing institution), but only with respect to loans discounted or pledged under section 1.7(b)(1).

Restructure and restructuring of a loan means a reamortization, renewal, deferral of principal or interest, monetary concessions, or the taking of any other action to modify the terms of, or forbear on, a loan.

[69 FR 10907, 10908, Mar. 9, 2004, as amended at 69 FR 16459, Mar. 30, 2004]

§ 617.7005 When may electronic communications be used in the borrower rights process?

Qualified lenders may use, with the parties' agreement, electronic commerce (E-commerce), including electronic communications for borrower rights disclosures. Part 609 of this chapter addresses when a qualified lender may use E-commerce. Consistent with these rules, a qualified lender should interpret part 617 broadly to allow electronic transmissions, communications, records, and submissions. However, electronic communications may not be used for a notice of default, acceleration, repossession, foreclosure, eviction, or the right to cure when a borrower's primary residence secures the loan. In these instances, a qualified lender must use paper disclosures.

§ 617.7010 May borrower rights be waived?

(a) A qualified lender may not obtain a waiver of borrower rights, except as indicated in paragraphs (b) and (c) of this section.

(b) A borrower may waive rights relating to distressed loan restructuring, credit reviews, and the right of first refusal when a loan is guaranteed by the Small Business Administration or in connection with a loan sale as provided in § 617.7015. Waivers obtained pursuant to this paragraph must be voluntary and in writing. The document evidencing the waiver must clearly explain the rights the borrower is being asked to waive.

(c) A borrower may waive all borrower rights provided for in part 617 of these regulations in connection with a

§ 617.7015

loan syndication transaction with non-System lenders that are otherwise not required by section 4.14A(a)(6) of the Act to provide borrower rights. For purposes of this paragraph, a "loan syndication" is a multi-lender transaction in which each member of the lending syndicate has a direct contractual relationship with the borrower, but does not include a transaction created for the primary purpose of avoiding borrower rights. Waivers obtained pursuant to this paragraph must be voluntary and in writing. The document evidencing the waiver must clearly disclose the rights the borrower is waiving. Additionally, the borrower's written waiver must contain a statement that the borrower was represented by legal counsel in connection with execution of the waiver.

[69 FR 10907, 10908, Mar. 9, 2004, as amended at 70 FR 18968, Apr. 12, 2005]

§ 617.7015 What happens to borrower rights when a loan is sold?

(a) *What happens when a qualified lender sells a loan to another qualified lender?* A loan made by a qualified lender and subsequently sold, in whole or in part, to another qualified lender is subject to the borrower rights provisions of title IV of the Act.

(b) *What happens when a qualified lender sells a loan into the secondary market?* (1) Except as provided in paragraph (b)(2) of this section, the borrower rights provisions of sections 4.14, 4.14A, 4.14B, 4.14C, 4.14D, and 4.36 of the Act do not apply to a loan made on or after February 10, 1996, and designated for sale into a secondary market at the time the loan was made.

(2) Borrower rights apply to a loan designated for sale under paragraph (b)(1) of this section but not sold into a secondary market during the 180-day period that begins on the date of designation. The provisions of paragraph (b)(1) of this section will subsequently apply on the date of sale if the loan is later sold into a secondary market.

(c) *What happens when a qualified lender sells a loan to a nonqualified lender?* (1) Except for loans sold to another qualified lender or designated for sale into a secondary market, a qualified lender must comply with one of the following requirements before selling a loan or interest in a loan subject to borrower rights:

(i) The qualified lender and borrower must agree to include provisions in the loan contract with the borrower, or a written modification thereto, that ensure that the buyer of the loan will be obligated to provide the borrower the same rights a qualified lender must provide; or

(ii) The qualified lender must obtain from the borrower a signed written consent to the sale, which clearly states the borrower waives statutory borrower rights.

(2) Before the qualified lender obtains the borrower's consent to the sale of the loan and the waiver of borrower rights under paragraph (c)(1)(ii) of this section, the qualified lender must disclose in writing to the borrower:

(i) A complete description of the statutory rights the borrower will waive;

(ii) Any changes in the loan terms or conditions that will occur if the qualified lender does not sell the loan;

(iii) That waiving borrower rights will not become effective unless the qualified lender sells the loan; and

(iv) That borrower rights will become effective again if any qualified lender repurchases the loan or any interest in the loan.

(3) The consent to the loan sale and waiver of borrower rights shall have no effect until the qualified lender sells the loan. Borrower rights become effective again if any qualified lender repurchases the loan or any interest in the loan.

(4) A qualified lender may not make a loan conditioned on the borrower consenting to the loan's sale and a waiver of borrower rights.

Subpart B—Disclosure of Effective Interest Rates

SOURCE: 69 FR 16459, Mar. 30, 2004, unless otherwise noted.

§ 617.7100 Who must make and who is entitled to receive an effective interest rate disclosure?

(a) A qualified lender must make the disclosures required by subparts B and C of this part to borrowers for all loans

Farm Credit Administration § 617.7125

not subject to the Truth in Lending Act.

(b) For a single loan involving more than one borrower, a qualified lender is required to provide only one set of disclosures to borrowers. All borrowers may designate, in writing, one person who will receive the effective interest rate disclosure. If the borrowers do not designate a particular recipient, the lender may provide the disclosure to at least one of the borrowers who is primarily liable for repayment of the loan.

§ 617.7105 When must a qualified lender disclose the effective interest rate to a borrower?

(a) *Disclosure to prospective borrowers.* A qualified lender must provide written effective interest rate disclosure for each loan no later than the time of loan closing.

(b) *Disclosure to existing borrowers.* (1) A qualified lender must provide a new effective interest rate disclosure to an existing borrower on or before the date:

(i) The borrower executes a new promissory note or other comparable evidence of indebtedness;

(ii) The borrower purchases additional stock or participation certificates as a condition of obtaining new funds from the qualified lender; or

(iii) The borrower pays an additional loan origination charge to the qualified lender as a condition of obtaining new funds.

(2) A qualified lender is not required to provide a new effective interest rate disclosure when it advances new funds to an existing borrower if none of the conditions of paragraph (b)(1) of this section apply and the advance is made pursuant to a preexisting contract that specifically provides for future advances.

§ 617.7110 How should a qualified lender disclose the cost of borrower stock or participation certificates?

The cost of borrower stock or participation certificates must be included in the effective interest rate calculation at the time the stock or participation certificate is purchased in connection with a loan transaction. For subsequent loans to existing borrowers, only the cost of new stock or participation certificates, if any, purchased in connection with a new loan or advance of new funds must be included in the effective interest rate calculation for the transaction.

§ 617.7115 How should a qualified lender disclose loan origination charges?

Any one-time charge paid by a borrower to a qualified lender in consideration for making a loan must be included in the effective interest rate as a loan origination charge. These include, but are not limited to, loan origination fees, application fees, and conversion fees. Loan origination charges also include any payments made by a borrower to a qualified lender to reduce the interest rate that would otherwise be charged, including any charges designated as "points."

§ 617.7120 How should a qualified lender present the disclosures to a borrower?

A qualified lender must:

(a) Disclose the effective interest rate and other information required by subparts B and C of this part clearly and conspicuously in writing, in a form that is easy to read and understand and that the borrower may keep; and

(b) Not combine the disclosures with any information not directly related to the information required by §§ 617.7130 and 617.7135.

§ 617.7125 How should a qualified lender determine the effective interest rate?

(a) A qualified lender must calculate the effective interest rate on a loan using the discounted cash flow method showing the effect of the time value of money.

(b) For all loans, the cash flow stream used for calculating the effective interest rate of a loan must include:

(1) Principal and interest;

(2) The cost of stock or participation certificates that a borrower is required to purchase in connection with the loan; and

(3) Loan origination charges described in § 617.7115.

(c) A qualified lender must establish policies and procedures for EIR disclosures that clearly show the effect of

§ 617.7130

the cost of borrower stock (or participation certificates) and loan origination charges on the interest rate of a loan. A qualified lender must also establish policies and procedures for determining major assumptions used in calculating the effective interest rate, *e.g.*, criteria on how the cost of borrower stock (or participation certificates) and loan origination charges are assigned or allocated among multiple loans obtained by a borrower simultaneously.

§ 617.7130 What initial disclosures must a qualified lender make to a borrower?

(a) *Required disclosures—in general.* A qualified lender must disclose in writing:

(1) The interest rate on the loan;

(2) The effective interest rate of the loan;

(3) The amount of stock or participation certificates that a borrower is required to purchase in connection with the loan and included in the calculation of the effective interest rate of the loan;

(4) All loan origination charges included in the effective interest rate;

(5) That stock or participation certificates that borrowers are required to purchase are at risk and may only be retired at the discretion of the board of the institution; and

(6) The various types of loan options available to borrowers, with an explanation of the terms and borrower rights that apply to each type of loan.

(b) *Adjustable rate loans.* A qualified lender must provide the following information for adjustable rate loans in addition to the requirements of paragraph (a) of this section:

(1) The circumstances under which the rate can be adjusted;

(2) How much the rate can be adjusted at any one time and how much the rate can be adjusted during the term of the loan;

(3) How often the rate can be adjusted;

(4) Any limitations on the amount or frequency of adjustments;

(5) The specific factors that the qualified lender may take into account in making adjustments to the interest rate on the loan; and

(6) If the borrower's interest rate is directly tied to a widely publicized external index:

(i) How and where the borrower may obtain information on changes to the index; and

(ii) When the qualified lender will provide written notice of changes to the borrower's interest rate.

[69 FR 16459, Mar. 30, 2004, , as amended at 74 FR 67972, Dec. 22, 2009]

§ 617.7135 What subsequent disclosures must a qualified lender make to a borrower?

(a) *Notice of interest rate change.* (1) A qualified lender must provide written notice to a borrower of any change in interest rate on the borrower's existing loan, containing the following information:

(i) The new interest rate on the loan;

(ii) The date on which the new rate is effective; and

(iii) The factors used to adjust the interest rate on the loan.

(2) If the borrower's interest rate is directly tied to a widely publicized external index, a qualified lender must provide written notice to the borrower of the rate change either:

(i) Within forty-five (45) days after the effective date of the change; or

(ii) As part of the borrower's first regularly scheduled billing statement affected by the rate change.

(3) If the borrower's interest rate is not directly tied to a widely publicized external index, a qualified lender must send written notice to the borrower of the rate change within ten (10) days after the effective date of the change.

(b) *Notice to adjustable rate loan borrowers with interest rates directly tied to a widely publicized external index.* A qualified lender must provide the written disclosure required by § 617.7130(b)(6) to applicable borrowers who were not previously given the disclosure no later than the qualified lender's next regularly scheduled correspondence to those borrowers occurring after April 1, 2010.

(c) *Notice of increase in stock purchase requirement.* If a qualified lender increases the amount of stock (or participation certificates) a borrower must own during the term of a loan, the lender must send a written notice to

Farm Credit Administration § 617.7310

the borrower at least ten (10) days prior to the effective date of the increase. The notice must state:

(1) The new effective interest rate on the outstanding balance for the remaining term of the borrower's loan;

(2) The date on which the new rate is effective; and

(3) The reason for the increase in the borrower stock (or participation certificates) purchase requirement.

[69 FR 16459, Mar. 30, 2004, , as amended at 74 FR 67972, Dec. 22, 2009]

Subpart C—Disclosure of Differential Interest Rates

§ 617.7200 **What disclosures must a qualified lender make to a borrower on loans offered with more than one rate of interest?**

A qualified lender that offers more than one rate of interest to borrowers must notify each borrower of the right to request a review of the interest rate charged on his or her loan no later than the time of loan closing. At the request of a borrower, the lender must:

(a) Provide a review of the loan to determine if the proper interest rate has been established;

(b) Explain to the borrower in writing the basis for the interest rate charged; and

(c) Explain to the borrower in writing how the credit status of the borrower may be improved to receive a lower interest rate on the loan.

[69 FR 16459, Mar. 30, 2004]

Subpart D—Actions on Applications; Review of Credit Decisions

§ 617.7300 **When acting on a loan application, what are the notice requirements and review rights?**

Each qualified lender must make its decision on a loan application as quickly as possible. The qualified lender must provide prompt written notice of its decision to the applicant. The qualified lender is required to notify all primary applicants. If a loan application has more than one primary applicant, the qualified lender may send the original notice to the applicant designated to receive notices and may send copies to all other applicants. If the qualified lender makes an adverse credit decision on a loan application, the notice must include:

(a) The specific reasons for the qualified lender's decision;

(b) A statement that the applicant may request a review of the decision;

(c) A statement that a written request for review must be made within 30 days after the applicant receives the qualified lender's notice; and

(d) A brief explanation of the process for seeking review of the decision, including the independent collateral evaluation review process, whom to contact for access to information, and the applicant's right to appear in person before the credit review committee (CRC).

§ 617.7305 **What is a CRC and who are the members?**

The board of directors of each qualified lender must establish one or more CRCs to review adverse credit decisions made by a qualified lender. The CRC may only review adverse credit decisions at the request of the applicant or borrower. The CRC has the ultimate decision-making authority on the loan or application under review. CRC members are selected by the board of directors of each qualified lender and must include at least one of the qualified lender's farmer-elected board members. The loan officer involved in the adverse credit decision being reviewed may not serve on the CRC when it reviews that loan.

§ 617.7310 **What is the review process of the CRC?**

(a) *How will an applicant or borrower know when the CRC will consider the review request?* The qualified lender must inform the applicant or borrower 15 days in advance of the CRC meeting where the applicant or borrower's request will be reviewed.

(b) *Who may make a personal appearance before the CRC?* Each applicant or borrower who has requested a review may appear in person before the CRC. The applicant or borrower may be accompanied by counsel or other representative when seeking a reversal of a decision on a loan or an application for restructuring.

§ 617.7315

(c) *What documents may the CRC consider?* An applicant or borrower may submit any documents or other evidence to support the information contained in the loan or application for restructuring. The documents should demonstrate that the application for a loan or restructuring satisfies the credit standards of the qualified lender and is an eligible loan or application for restructuring. Additionally, the applicant or borrower is entitled to a copy of each independent collateral evaluation used by the qualified lender.

(d) *May an applicant obtain a new collateral evaluation even if collateral was not a reason for the adverse credit decision?* As part of a CRC review, an applicant may request an independent collateral evaluation of the agricultural real estate securing the loan or being offered as security, regardless of whether collateral was an identified reason for the adverse credit decision. The independent collateral evaluation may be for any interest(s) in the property securing the loan, except stock or participation certificates issued by the qualified lender and held by the applicant or borrower.

(1) *Who may conduct an independent collateral evaluation?* The independent collateral evaluation must be conducted by an independent evaluator. The CRC must provide the applicant or borrower with a list of three independent evaluators approved by the qualified lender within 30 days of the request for an independent collateral evaluation. The applicant or borrower must select and engage the services of an evaluator from the list. The evaluation must comply with the collateral evaluation requirements of part 614, subpart F, of this chapter. The qualified lender must provide the applicant or borrower a copy of part 614, subpart F, for presentation to the selected independent evaluator. A copy of part 614, subpart F, signed by the evaluator is a required exhibit in the subsequent evaluation report.

(2) *When must an applicant or borrower obtain the independent collateral evaluation and who pays for the evaluation?* The applicant or borrower must enter into a contractual arrangement for evaluation services within 30 days of receiving the names of three approved independent evaluators. The contractual arrangement must be a written contract for services that complies with the lender's appraisal standards. The evaluation must be completed within a reasonable period of time, taking into consideration any extenuating circumstance. The applicant or borrower is responsible for the costs of the independent evaluation.

(3) *How does the CRC use an independent collateral evaluation when making a decision?* The CRC will consider the results of any independent collateral evaluation before making a final determination with respect to the loan or restructuring, except the CRC is not required to consider a collateral evaluation that does not conform to the collateral evaluation standards described in part 614, subpart F, of this chapter.

(e) *When must the CRC issue a decision?* The CRC must reach a decision, and it must be the final decision of the qualified lender, not later than 30 days after the meeting on the request under review. The CRC must make every reasonable effort to conduct reviews and render decisions in as expeditious a manner as possible. After making its decision, the committee must promptly notify the applicant or borrower in writing of the decision and the reasons for the decision.

§ 617.7315 **What records must the qualified lender maintain on behalf of the CRC?**

A qualified lender must maintain a complete file of all requests for CRC reviews, including participation in state mediation programs, the minutes of each CRC meeting, and the disposition of each review by the CRC.

Subpart E—Distressed Loan Restructuring; State Agricultural Loan Mediation Programs

§ 617.7400 **What protections exist for borrowers who meet all loan obligations?**

(a) A qualified lender may not foreclose on a loan because the borrower failed to post additional collateral when the borrower has made all accrued payments of principal, interest, and penalties on the loan.

Farm Credit Administration §617.7410

(b) A qualified lender may not require a borrower to reduce the outstanding principal balance of a loan by any amount that exceeds the regularly scheduled principal installment when due and payable, unless:

(1) The borrower sells or otherwise disposes of part, or all, of the collateral without the prior approval of the qualified lender and the proceeds from the sale or disposition are not applied to the loan; or

(2) The parties agree otherwise in writing.

(c) After a borrower has made all accrued payments of principal, interest, and penalties on a loan, the qualified lender may not enforce acceleration of the borrower's repayment schedule due to the borrower's untimely payment of those principal, interest, or penalty payments.

(d) If a qualified lender places a loan in non-interest-earning status and this results in an adverse action being taken against the borrower, such as revoking any undisbursed loan commitment, the lender must document the change of status and promptly notify the borrower in writing of the action and the reasons for taking it. If the borrower was not delinquent on any principal, interest, or penalty payment at the time of such action and the borrower's request to have the loan placed back into accrual status is denied, the borrower may obtain a review of the denial before the CRC pursuant to §617.7310 of this part. The borrower must request this review within 30 days after receiving the lender's notice.

§617.7405 On what policies are loan restructurings based?

Loan restructurings must be made in accordance with the policy adopted by the supervising bank board of directors under section 4.14A(g) of the Act.

§617.7410 When and how does a qualified lender notify a borrower of the right to seek loan restructuring?

(a) *What are the notice requirements?* When a qualified lender determines that a loan is, or has become, distressed, the lender must provide one of the following written notices to the borrower stating that the loan may be suitable for restructuring.

(1) A notice stating that the loan has been identified as distressed and that the borrower has the right to request a restructuring of the loan (nonforeclosure notice).

(2) A notice that the loan has been identified as distressed, that the borrower has the right to request a restructuring of the loan, and that the alternative to restructuring may be foreclosure (45-day notice). The qualified lender must provide this notice to the borrower no later than 45 days before the qualified lender begins foreclosure proceedings with respect to any loan outstanding to the borrower. This notice must specifically state that if the loan is restructured and the borrower does not perform under the restructure agreement (as described in §617.7410(e)), the qualified lender may initiate foreclosure proceedings without further notice.

(b) *What should each notice include?* (1) A copy of the policy the qualified lender established governing the treatment of distressed loans; and

(2) All materials necessary for the borrower to submit an application for restructuring.

(c) *What notice should a qualified lender send to a borrower who is a debtor in a bankruptcy proceeding?* The qualified lender should send a notice that identifies the loan as distressed and the statutory right to file an application for a restructuring. The notice may also restate the language from the automatic stay provision to emphasize that the notice is not intended as an attempt to collect, assess, or recover a claim.

(d) *Whom should the qualified lender notify?* The qualified lender is required to notify all primary obligors. If the obligors identify one party to receive notices, the qualified lender should send the original notice to that person and send copies to the other obligors. For borrowers in a bankruptcy proceeding, the qualified lender should send the notice to the borrower and, if retained, the borrower's counsel.

(e) *When is a qualified lender required to send another restructure notice to a borrower whose loan was previously restructured?* A qualified lender must notify a borrower of the right to file another application to restructure the loan if the qualified lender sent the

219

§ 617.7415

nonforeclosure notice to the borrower and the borrower has performed on the previous restructure agreement. Performance means that a borrower has made six consecutive monthly payments, four consecutive quarterly payments, three consecutive semiannual payments, or two consecutive annual payments. However, a qualified lender is not required to send another notice if they previously sent a 45-day notice, as described in §617.7410(a)(2), and a borrower did not perform under a restructure agreement, as described above.

(f) *Does the borrower have the opportunity to meet with the qualified lender after receiving the restructure notice?* The qualified lender must provide any borrower to whom a notice has been sent with a reasonable opportunity to meet personally with a representative of the lender. The borrower and lender may meet to review the status of the loan, the financial condition of the borrower, and the suitability of the loan for restructuring. A meeting to discuss a loan that is in a non-interest-earning status may also involve developing a plan for restructuring, if the qualified lender determines the loan is suitable for restructuring.

(g) *May the qualified lender voluntarily consider restructuring for a borrower who did not submit a restructuring application?* A qualified lender may, in the absence of an application for restructuring from a borrower, propose restructuring to an individual borrower.

§ 617.7415 How does a qualified lender decide to restructure a loan?

(a) *What criteria does a qualified lender use to evaluate an application for restructuring?* The qualified lender should consider the following:

(1) Whether the cost to the lender of restructuring the loan is equal to or less than the cost of foreclosure, considering all relevant criteria. These criteria include:

(i) The present value of interest and principal foregone by the lender in carrying out the application for restructuring;

(ii) Reasonable and necessary administrative expenses involved in working with the borrower to finalize and implement the application for restructuring;

(iii) Whether the borrower's application for restructuring included a preliminary restructuring plan and cash flow analysis, taking into account income from all sources to be applied to the debt and all assets to be pledged, that show a reasonable probability that orderly debt retirement will occur as a result of the proposed restructuring; and

(iv) Whether the borrower has furnished, or is willing to furnish, complete and current financial statements in a form acceptable to the qualified lender.

(2) Whether the borrower is applying all income over and above necessary and reasonable living and operating expenses to the payment of primary obligations;

(3) Whether the borrower has the financial capacity and the management skills to protect the collateral from diversion, dissipation, or deterioration;

(4) Whether the borrower is capable of working out existing financial difficulties, taking into consideration any prior restructuring of the loan, reestablishing a viable operation, and repaying the loan on a rescheduled basis; and

(5) In the case of a distressed loan that is not delinquent, whether restructuring consistent with sound lending practices may be taken to reasonably ensure that the loan will not have to be placed into non-interest-earning status in the future.

(b) *What should be included in determining the cost of foreclosure?* (1) The difference between the outstanding balance due, as provided by the loan documents, and the liquidation value of the loan, taking into consideration the borrower's repayment capacity and the liquidation value of the collateral used to secure the loan;

(2) The estimated cost of maintaining a loan classified as a high-risk asset;

(3) The estimated cost of administrative and legal actions necessary to foreclose a loan and dispose of property acquired as the result of the foreclosure, including attorneys' fees and court costs;

(4) The estimated cost of value changes in collateral used to secure a

Farm Credit Administration §617.7425

loan during the period beginning on the date of the initiation of an action to foreclose or liquidate the loan and ending on the date of the disposition of the collateral; and

(5) All other costs incurred as the result of the foreclosure or liquidation of a loan.

(c) *What should the qualified lender do if the borrower and the qualified lender cannot agree on the financial projections used in the application for restructuring?* If the borrower and lender are not able to agree on supportable or realistic financial projections, the lender may use benchmarks to determine the operational input costs and chattel security values. These benchmarks may include, but are not limited to, the borrower's 5-year production average; averages in the county where the farming operation is located, based on data from United States Department of Agriculture, local colleges or universities, or other recognized authority; and other such reasonable sources.

(d) *How does the qualified lender decide whether to restructure or foreclose?* If a qualified lender determines the potential cost to the lender of restructuring the loan as proposed in the application for restructuring is less than or equal to the potential cost of foreclosure, the qualified lender must restructure the loan. If two or more restructuring alternatives are available, the qualified lender must restructure the loan using the alternative that results in the least cost to the lender.

(e) *What documentation should the qualified lender retain?* In the event that an application for restructuring is denied, a qualified lender must maintain sufficient documentation to demonstrate compliance with paragraphs (a), (b), and (c) of this section, as applicable.

§ 617.7420 **How will a decision on an application for restructuring be issued?**

(a) *When must a qualified lender make a decision on an application for restructuring?* Each qualified lender must provide a written decision on an application for restructuring and provide this decision to the borrower within 15 days from the conclusion of the negotiations used to develop the application for restructuring.

(b) *How does a qualified lender notify the borrower of the decision?* On reaching a decision on an application for restructuring, the qualified lender must provide written notice in any manner that requires a primary obligor to acknowledge receipt of the lender's decision. In the case of a loan involving one or more primary obligors, the original notice may be provided to the primary obligor identified to receive such notice, with copies provided by regular mail to the other obligors.

(c) *What notice is required if the restructuring request is denied?* When an application for restructuring is denied, the notice must include:

(1) The specific reason(s) for the denial and any critical assumptions and relevant information on which the specific reasons are based, except that any confidential information shall not be disclosed;

(2) A statement that the borrower may request a review of the denial;

(3) A statement that any request for review must be made in writing within 7 days after receiving such notice.

(4) A brief explanation of the process for seeking review of the denial, including the appraisal review process and the right to appear before the CRC, pursuant to § 617.7310 of this part, accompanied by counsel or any other representative, if the borrower chooses.

§ 617.7425 **What type of notice should be given to a borrower before foreclosure?**

The qualified lender must send the 45-day notice, as described in § 617.7410(a)(2), no later than 45 days before any qualified lender begins foreclosure proceedings. The notice informs the borrower in writing that the loan may be suitable for restructuring and that the qualified lender will review any suitable loan for possible restructuring. The 45-day notice must include a copy of the policy and the materials described in § 617.7410(b). The notice must also state that if the loan is restructured, the borrower must perform under this restructure agreement. If the borrower does not perform, the qualified lender may initiate foreclosure.

221

§ 617.7430

(a) *Does the notice have to inform the borrower that foreclosure is possible?* The notice must inform the borrower that the alternative to restructuring may be foreclosure. If the notice does not inform the borrower of potential foreclosure, then the qualified lender must send a second notice at least 45 days before foreclosure is initiated.

(b) *How are borrowers who are debtors in a bankruptcy proceeding notified?* A qualified lender must restate the language from the automatic stay provision to emphasize that the notice is not intended to be an attempt to collect, assess, or recover a claim. The qualified lender should send the notice to the borrower and, if retained, the borrower's counsel.

(c) *May a qualified lender foreclose on a loan when there is a restructuring application on file?* No qualified lender may foreclose or continue any foreclosure proceeding with respect to a distressed loan before the lender has completed consideration of any pending application for restructuring and CRC consideration, if applicable. This section does not prevent a lender from taking any action necessary to avoid the dissipation of assets or the diversion, dissipation, or deterioration of collateral if the lender has reasonable grounds to believe that such diversion, dissipation, or deterioration may occur.

§ 617.7430 Are institutions required to participate in state agricultural loan mediation programs?

(a) If initiated by a borrower, System institutions must participate in state mediation programs certified under section 501 of the Agricultural Credit Act of 1987 and present and explore debt restructuring proposals advanced in the course of such mediation. If provided in the certified program, System institutions may initiate mediation at any time.

(b) System institutions must cooperate in good faith with requests for information or analysis of information made in the course of mediation under any loan mediation program.

(c) No System institution may make a loan secured by a mortgage or lien on agricultural property to a borrower on the condition that the borrower waive any right under the agricultural loan mediation program of any state.

(d) A state mediation may proceed at the same time as the loan restructuring process of § 617.7415 or at any other appropriate time.

Subpart F—Distressed Loan Restructuring Directive

§ 617.7500 What is a directive used for and what may it require?

(a) A distressed loan restructuring directive is an order issued to a qualified lender when FCA has determined that the lender has violated section 4.14A of the Act.

(b) A distressed loan restructuring directive requires the qualified lender to comply with the specific distressed loan restructuring requirements in the Act.

(c) A distressed loan restructuring directive is enforceable in the same manner and to the same extent as an effective and outstanding cease and desist order that has become final. Any violation of a distressed loan restructuring directive may result in FCA assessing civil money penalties or seeking a court order pursuant to section 5.31 or 5.32 of the Act.

§ 617.7505 How will the qualified lender know when FCA is considering issuing a distressed loan restructuring directive?

When FCA intends to issue a distressed loan restructuring directive, it will notify the qualified lender in writing. The notice will state:

(a) The reasons FCA intends to issue a distressed loan restructuring directive;

(b) The proposed contents of the distressed loan restructuring directive; and

(c) Any other relevant information.

§ 617.7510 What should the qualified lender do when it receives notice of a distressed loan restructuring directive?

(a) A qualified lender should respond to the notice by stating why FCA should not issue a distressed loan restructuring directive, by proposing changes to the directive, or by seeking other suitable relief. The response must include any information, documentation, or other relevant evidence that supports the qualified lender's position. The response may include a plan for achieving compliance with the distressed loan restructuring requirements of the Act. The response must be in writing and delivered to FCA within 30 days after the date on which the qualified lender received the notice. In its discretion, FCA may extend the time period for good cause. FCA may shorten the 30-day period with the consent of the qualified lender or when FCA determines that providing the full 30 days would result in a borrower not receiving distressed loan restructuring rights.

(b) If the qualified lender fails to respond within 30 days or such other time period specified by FCA, this failure will constitute a waiver of any objections to the proposed distressed loan restructuring directive.

§ 617.7515 How does the FCA decide whether to issue a directive?

After the closing date of the qualified lender's response period, or following receipt of the qualified lender's response, FCA must decide if there is sufficient information to support the issuance of a directive or if additional information is necessary. Once FCA has received sufficient information, it must decide whether to issue a directive as originally proposed or as modified.

§ 617.7520 How does the FCA issue a directive and when will it be effective?

A distressed loan restructuring directive is effective immediately on receipt by the qualified lender, or on such later date as may be specified by FCA, and will remain effective and enforceable until it is stayed, modified, or terminated by FCA.

§ 617.7525 May FCA use other enforcement actions?

FCA may issue a distressed loan restructuring directive in addition to, or instead of, any other action allowed by law, including cease and desist proceedings, civil money penalties, or the granting or conditioning of any application or other requests by the System institution.

Subpart G—Right of First Refusal

§ 617.7600 What are the definitions used in this subpart?

In addition to the definitions in § 617.7000, the following definitions apply to this subpart.

Acquired agricultural real estate or property means agricultural real estate acquired by a System institution as a result of a loan foreclosure or a voluntary conveyance by a borrower who, as determined by the institution, does not have the financial resources to avoid foreclosure.

Previous owner means:

(1) The prior record owner who was a borrower from a System institution and did not have the financial resources, as determined by the institution, to avoid foreclosure on acquired agricultural real estate; or

(2) The prior record owner who is not a borrower and whose acquired agricultural real estate was used as collateral for a loan to a System borrower.

System institution means a Farm Credit System institution, except a bank for cooperatives, which makes loans as defined in § 617.7000.

§ 617.7605 How should System institutions document whether the borrower had the financial resources to avoid foreclosure?

The right of first refusal applies only to borrowers who did not have the financial resources to avoid foreclosure or voluntary conveyance. A System institution must clearly document in its files whether the borrower had the resources to avoid foreclosure or voluntary conveyance.

§ 617.7610 What should the System institution do when it decides to sell acquired agricultural real estate?

(a) Notify the previous owner,

(1) Within 15 days of the System institution's decision to sell acquired agricultural real estate, it must notify the previous owner, by certified mail, of the property's appraised fair market value as established by an accredited appraiser and of the previous owner's right to:

§ 617.7615

(i) Buy the property at the appraised fair market value, or

(ii) Offer to buy the property at a price less than the appraised value.

(2) That any offer must be received within 30 days of receipt of the notice.

(b) Act on an offer to buy the acquired agricultural real estate at the appraised value. Within 15 days after the receipt of the previous owner's offer to buy the acquired agricultural real estate at the appraised value, the System institution must accept the offer and sell the property to the previous owner if the offer was received within 30 days of the notice required in paragraph (a)(2) of this section.

(c) Act on an offer to buy the acquired agricultural real estate at less than the appraised value.

(1) The System institution must consider the offer if it was received within 30 days of the notice required in paragraph (a)(2) of this section.

(2) If the System institution accepts this offer, it must notify the previous owner of the decision and sell the acquired agricultural real estate to the previous owner within 15 days of receiving the offer to buy the acquired agricultural real estate at a value less than the appraised value.

(3) If the System institution rejects this offer, it must notify the previous owner of the decision within 15 days of receiving the offer to buy the acquired agricultural real estate at a value less than the appraised value. The previous owner has 15 days from receipt of the notice to submit an offer to buy at such price or under such terms and conditions. The System institution may not sell the acquired agricultural real estate to any other person:

(i) At a price equal to, or less than, that offered by the previous owner; or

(ii) On different terms or conditions than those extended to the previous owner without first notifying the previous owner by certified mail and providing an opportunity to buy the property at such price or under such terms and conditions.

(d) For purposes of this section, financing by the System institution is not a term or condition of the sale of acquired agricultural real estate. A System institution is not required to provide financing to the previous owner for purchase of acquired agricultural real estate.

§ 617.7615 What should the System institution do when it decides to lease acquired agricultural real estate?

(a) Notify the previous owner,

(1) Within 15 days of the System institution's decision to lease acquired agricultural real estate, it must notify the previous owner, by certified mail, of the property's appraised rental value, as established by an accredited appraiser, and of the previous owner's right to:

(i) Lease the property at a rate equivalent to the appraised rental value of the property, or

(ii) Offer to lease the property at rate that is less than the appraised rental value of the property.

(2) That any offer must be received within 15 days of receipt of the notice.

(b) Act on an offer to lease the acquired agricultural real estate at a rate equivalent to the appraised rental value of the property.

(1) Within 15 days after receipt of such offer, the System institution may accept the offer to lease the property at the appraised rental value and lease the property to the previous owner, or

(2) Within 15 days after receipt of such offer, the System institution may reject the offer to lease the property at the appraised rental value when the institution determines that the previous owner:

(i) Does not have the resources available to conduct a successful farming or ranching operation; or

(ii) Cannot meet all the payments, terms, and conditions of such lease.

(c) Act on an offer to lease the acquired agricultural real estate at a rate that is less than the appraised rental value of the property.

(1) The System institution must consider the offer to lease the property at a rate that is less than the appraised rental value of the property. Notice of the decision to accept or reject such offer must be provided to the previous owner within 15 days of receipt of the offer.

(2) If the System institution accepts the offer to lease the property at less than the appraised rental value, it must notify the previous owner and

Farm Credit Administration

lease the property to the previous owner.

(3) If the institution rejects the offer, the System institution must notify the previous owner of this decision. The previous owner has 15 days after receipt of the notice in which to agree to lease the property at such rate or under such terms and conditions. The System institution may not lease the property to any other person:

(i) At a rate equal to or less than that offered by the previous owner; or

(ii) On different terms and conditions than those that were extended to the previous owner without first informing the previous owner by certified mail and providing an opportunity to lease the property at such rate or under such terms and conditions.

§ 617.7620 What should the System institution do when it decides to sell acquired agricultural real estate at a public auction?

System institutions electing to sell or lease acquired agricultural real estate or a portion of it through a public auction, competitive bidding process, or other similar public offering must:

(a) Notify the previous owner, by certified mail, of the availability of such property. The notice must contain the minimum amount, if any, required to qualify a bid as acceptable to the institution and any terms or conditions to which such sale or lease will be subject;

(b) Accept the offer by the previous owner if the System institution receives two or more qualified bids in the same amount, the bids are the highest received, and one of the qualified bids is from the previous owner; and

(c) Not discriminate against a previous owner in these proceedings.

§ 617.7625 Whom should the System institution notify?

Each certified mail notice requirement in this section is fully satisfied by mailing one certified mail notice to the last known address of the previous owner or owners.

§ 617.7630 Does this Federal requirement affect any state property laws?

The rights provided under section 4.36 of the Act and this section do not affect any right of first refusal under the law of the state in which the property is located.

PART 618—GENERAL PROVISIONS

Subpart A—Related Services

Sec.
618.8000 Definitions.
618.8005 Eligibility.
618.8010 Related services authorization process.
618.8015 Policy guidelines.
618.8020 Feasibility requirements.
618.8025 Feasibility reviews.
618.8030 Out-of-territory related services.

Subpart B—Member Insurance

618.8040 Authorized insurance services.

Subparts C–F [Reserved]

Subpart G—Releasing Information

618.8300 General regulation.
618.8310 Lists of borrowers and stockholders.
618.8320 Data regarding borrowers and loan applicants.
618.8325 Disclosure of loan documents.
618.8330 Production of documents and testimony during litigation.
618.8340 [Reserved]

Subpart H—Disposition of Obsolete Records

618.8360 [Reserved]
618.8370 [Reserved]

Subpart I [Reserved]

Subpart J—Internal Controls

618.8430 Internal controls.
618.8440 Planning.

AUTHORITY: Secs. 1.5, 1.11, 1.12, 2.2, 2.4, 2.5, 2.12, 3.1, 3.7, 4.12, 4.13A, 4.25, 4.29, 5.9, 5.10, 5.17 of the Farm Credit Act (12 U.S.C. 2013, 2019, 2020, 2073, 2075, 2076, 2093, 2122, 2128, 2183, 2200, 2211, 2218, 2243, 2244, 2252).

Subpart A—Related Services

SOURCE: 60 FR 34099, June 30, 1995, unless otherwise noted.

§ 618.8000 Definitions.

For the purposes of this subpart, the following definitions shall apply:

(a) *Program* means the method or procedures used to deliver a related service. This distinguishes the particulars

§ 618.8005

of how a related service will be provided from the type of activity or concept.

(b) *Related service* means any service or type of activity provided by a System bank or association that is appropriate to the recipient's operations, including control of related financial matters. The term "related service" includes, but is not limited to, technical assistance, financial assistance, financially related services and insurance, but does not include lending or leasing activities.

(c) *System banks and associations* means Farm Credit Banks, agricultural credit banks, banks for cooperatives, agricultural credit associations, production credit associations, Federal land bank associations, Federal land credit associations, and service corporations formed pursuant to section 4.25 of the Act.

[60 FR 34099, June 30, 1995, as amended at 69 FR 43514, July 21, 2004]

§ 618.8005 Eligibility.

(a) Farm Credit Banks and associations may offer related services appropriate to on-farm and aquatic operations to persons eligible to borrow as defined in §§ 613.3000 (a) and (b), 613.3010, and 613.3300 of this chapter.

(b) Banks for cooperatives may offer related services to entities eligible to borrow as defined in §§ 613.3100, 613.3200, and 613.3300 of this chapter.

(c) Agricultural credit banks may offer related services appropriate to on-farm and aquatic operations of persons eligible to borrow specified in paragraph (a) of this section and may offer related services to entities eligible to borrow as specified in paragraph (b) of this section.

(d) Service corporations formed pursuant to section 4.25 of the Act may offer related services to persons eligible to borrow from the owners of the service corporation, pursuant to paragraphs (a), (b), (c), and (e) of this section.

(e) System banks and associations may provide related services to recipients that do not otherwise meet the requirements of this section in connection with loan applications, loan servicing, and other transactions between these recipients and persons eligible to borrow as defined in paragraphs (a), (b), or (c) of this section, as long as the service provided is requested by an eligible borrower or necessary to the transaction between the parties. Such services include, but are not limited to, fee appraisals of agricultural assets provided to any Federal agency, commercial banks, and other lenders.

[60 FR 34099, June 30, 1995, as amended at 62 FR 4450, Jan. 30, 1997; 69 FR 43514, July 21, 2004]

§ 618.8010 Related services authorization process.

(a) *Authorities.* System banks and associations may only offer related services that meet the criteria specified in this regulation and are authorized by the FCA.

(b) *New service proposals.* (1) A System bank or association that proposes or intends to offer a related service that the FCA has not previously authorized must submit to the FCA, in writing, a proposal that includes a description of the service, a statement of how it meets the regulatory definition of "related services" in § 618.8000(b), and the risk analysis cited in § 618.8020(b)(3). The FCA will evaluate the proposed service based on the information submitted, and may also consider whether there are extenuating circumstances or other compelling reasons that justify the proposed service or support a determination that the service is not authorized. This evaluation will focus primarily on Systemwide issues rather than on institution or program-specific factors.

(2) When authorizing a proposed related service, at its discretion, the FCA may impose special conditions or limitations on any related service or program to offer a related service.

(3) At its discretion the FCA may, at any time during its evaluation of a proposed related service, publish the proposed related service in the FEDERAL REGISTER for public comment.

(4) Within 60 days of the FCA receiving a completed proposal, including any additional information the FCA may require, the FCA will act on the request to authorize a new service. The FCA shall approve the request, deny the request, or publish the service for

Farm Credit Administration § 618.8020

public comment in the FEDERAL REGISTER. For good cause and prior to the expiration of the 60 days, the FCA may extend this period for an additional 60 days.

(5) Within the time period established in paragraph (b)(4) of this section, the FCA shall notify the requesting institution of its actions. Following notification of the requesting institution, the FCA will notify all System banks and associations of its determination on the proposed service by bookletter or other means. If a service is not authorized, the reasons for denial will be included in the notifications to the System and the requesting institution.

(c) *Previously authorized services.* (1) For related services that have been authorized by the FCA, any System bank or association may develop a program and subsequently offer the related service to eligible recipients, subject to any special conditions or institutional limits placed by the FCA. These programs will be subject to review and evaluation during the examination and enforcement process.

(2) The FCA shall make available to all System banks and associations a list of such related services ("related services list" or "list") and will update the list in accordance with paragraph (b)(5) of this section. The list will contain the following:

(i) A description of each related service; and

(ii) The types of institutions authorized to offer each type of related service;

(iii) Identification of any special conditions on how the related service may be offered. The special conditions and description of the service will be fully detailed in FCA's notice to System institutions under paragraph (b)(5) of this section.

(3) At least 10 business days prior to implementing a related service program already on the list, the System bank or association must notify the FCA Office of Examination field office responsible for examining that institution in writing and provide it with a description of the proposed related service program.

§ 618.8015 **Policy guidelines.**

(a) The board of directors of each System bank or association providing related services must adopt a policy addressing related services. The policy shall include clearly stated purposes, objectives, and operating parameters for offering related services and a requirement that each service offered be consistent with the institution's business plan and long-term strategic goals. Such policy shall also be subject to review under an appropriate internal control policy.

(b) All related services must be offered to recipients on an optional basis. If the institution requires a related service as a condition to borrow, it must inform the recipient that the related service can be obtained from the institution or from any other person or entity offering the same or similar related services.

(c) All fees for related services must be separately identified from loan interest charges and disclosed to the recipient of the service prior to providing or implementing the service.

§ 618.8020 **Feasibility requirements.**

For every related service program a System bank or association provides, it must document program feasibility. The feasibility analysis shall include the following:

(a) Support for the determination that the related service is authorized; and

(b) An overall cost-benefit analysis that demonstrates program feasibility, taking into consideration the following items:

(1) An analysis of how the program relates to or promotes the institution's business plan and strategic goals, and whether offering the service is consistent with the long-term goals described in its capital plan;

(2) An analysis of the expected financial returns of the program which, at a minimum, must include an evaluation of market, pricing, competition issues, and expected profitability. This analysis should include an explanation of how the program will contribute to the overall financial health of the institution; and

(3) An analysis of the risk in the program, including:

(i) An evaluation of the operational costs and risks involved in offering the program, such as management and personnel requirements, training requirements, and capital outlays;

(ii) An evaluation of the financial liability that may be incurred as a result of offering the program and any insurance or other measures that are necessary to minimize these risks; and

(iii) An evaluation of the conflicts of interest, whether real or perceived, that may arise as a result of offering the program and any steps that are necessary to eliminate or appropriately manage these conflicts.

§ 618.8025 Feasibility reviews.

(a) Prior to an association offering a related service program for the first time or offering a service that it did not offer during the most recently completed business cycle (generally 1 year), the board of directors of the funding bank must verify that the association has performed a feasibility analysis pursuant to § 618.8020. The bank review is limited to a determination that the feasibility analysis is complete and that the analysis establishes that it is feasible for the association to provide the program. Any conclusion by the bank that the feasibility analysis is incomplete or fails to demonstrate program feasibility must be fully supported and communicated to the association in writing within 60 days of its submission to the bank.

(b) Prior to a service corporation offering a service for the first time or offering a service that it did not offer during the most recently completed business cycle (generally 1 year), the owners of the service corporation must verify that the service corporation has performed a feasibility analysis pursuant to § 618.8020. If the owners all agree, one bank with a significant ownership interest can be delegated this responsibility.

[60 FR 34099, June 30, 1995; 60 FR 42029, Aug. 15, 1995]

§ 618.8030 Out-of-territory related services.

(a) System banks and associations may offer related services outside their chartered territories subject to the following conditions:

(1) The System bank or association obtains consent from all chartered institutions currently offering the same type of service in the territory in which the service is to be provided; or

(2) If no System bank or association is currently offering the same type of service in the territory, then the out-of-territory institution must obtain the consent of at least one direct lender institution chartered in the territory in which the related service is to be provided.

(3) The consent obtained pursuant to paragraphs (a)(1) and (a)(2) of this section shall be in the form of a written agreement with specific terms and conditions including timeframes.

(b) System banks and associations providing out-of-territory services must fulfill all requirements of subparts A and B of this part 618.

(c) An institution that consents to another bank or association providing a related service in its chartered territory must meet the requirements of this section, but need not comply with the other requirements of subparts A and B of this part 618, unless the program consented to imposes a financial obligation on the consenting institution. If a financial obligation exists, then the consenting institution must comply with §§ 618.8015, 618.8020 and 618.8025.

(d) Service corporations must follow the requirements of this section in offering related services out-of-territory. A service corporation cannot consent to an out-of-territory institution providing services in its chartered territory.

Subpart B—Member Insurance

§ 618.8040 Authorized insurance services.

(a) Farm Credit System banks (excluding banks for cooperatives) (hereinafter banks) and associations may sell to their members and borrowers, on an optional basis, credit or term life and credit disability insurance appropriate to protect the loan commitment in the event of death or disability of the debtors. The sale of other insurance necessary to protect a member's or borrower's farm or aquatic unit is

Farm Credit Administration

§ 618.8040

permitted, but limited to hail and multiple-peril crop insurance, title insurance, and insurance necessary to protect the facilities and equipment of aquatic members and borrowers. A member or borrower shall have the option, without coercion from the bank or association, to accept or reject such insurance.

(b) Bank and association board policies governing the provision of member insurance programs shall be established within the following general guidelines:

(1) A System bank or association may provide credit or term-life or credit-disability insurance only to persons who have a loan or lease with any System bank or association, without regard to whether such institution is the provider. Term-life insurance coverage may continue after the loan has been repaid or the lease terminated, provided the member can reasonably be expected to borrow again within 2 years, and provided the continuation of insurance is not contrary to state law.

(2) A debtor-creditor relationship is not required for the sale of other insurance specified in paragraph (a) of this section, as long as purchasers are members of a System bank or association. For the purposes of this section, "member" means someone eligible to borrow who is a stockholder or participation certificate holder and who acquired stock or participation certificates to obtain a loan, for investment purposes, or to qualify for other services of the association or bank.

(3) In making insurance available through private insurers, each bank shall approve the programs of more than two insurers for each type of insurance offered in the bank's chartered territory, provided that more than two insurers for each type of insurance have proposed programs to the bank that will, in all likelihood, have long-term viability, and meet the requirements of § 618.8040(b)(4)(i) of this section. The banks shall make a reasonable and good faith effort to attract more than two qualified insurers for each insurance program offered to borrowers in all States of the bank's chartered territory. Where the bank is unable to approve more than two insurers, the bank shall document its efforts to attract additional qualified insurers for the affected insurance program and State. The banks may provide comparative information relating to costs and quality of approved programs and the financial condition of approved companies.

(4) Member insurance services may be offered only if:

(i) The insurance program has been approved by the bank or association from among eligible programs made available to it by insurers—

(A) Meeting reasonable financial and quality of service standards prescribed by the bank; and

(B) Licensed under State law to do business in the State(s) in which the insurance is offered:

(ii) The bank or association has the capacity to render authorized insurance services in an effective and efficient manner;

(iii) There exists the probability that the service will generate sufficient revenue to cover all costs;

(iv) Rendering the insurance service will not have an adverse effect on the credit or other operations of the bank or association; and

(v) In making insurance available through approved insurers, the board of directors of the bank or association shall make a reasonable and good faith effort to select and offer at least two approved insurers for each type of insurance made available to the members and borrowers. In the event that the bank or association has selected less than two insurers for any insurance program, such bank or association shall document the reasons why it is unable to offer members and borrowers additional insurers for the affected insurance program.

(5) All costs to members and borrowers for insurance services provided shall be disclosed separately from interest charges.

(6) Bank and association personnel shall not benefit from insurance sales by receipt of commissions or gifts from underwriting insurance companies. However, employees may participate in an incentive plan under which incentive compensation is provided based on the sale of insurance.

§ 618.8300

(i) In any single year, for all employees except full-time insurance personnel or full-time supervisors or managers of insurance departments, incentive compensation attributable to sales of all types of insurance cannot exceed an amount equivalent to 5 percent of the recipient's annual base salary.

(ii) In any single year, for full-time insurance personnel and full-time supervisors and managers of insurance departments, incentive compensation for sales of credit life and similar types of insurance (i.e. insurance that pays on a loan or mortgage upon the death or disability of the debtor) cannot exceed an amount equivalent to 5 percent of the recipient's annual base salary.

(iii) No incentive compensation limit applies to sales of other insurance (crop, title, etc.) by full-time insurance personnel or full-time supervisors or managers of insurance departments.

(7) Term insurance may be written for the amount of coverage desired by the member or borrower, but in no case may the amount of term insurance, credit life insurance, or a combination of the two with an institution of the System, be in excess of total loan commitments to the member or borrower by the institution writing the insurance.

(8) The banks may, only by agreement with an insurer, offer services traditionally furnished by insurers to the Farm Credit System. This shall include master marketers when considering the sale of Federal crop insurance. The banks shall not underwrite insurance, adjust claim payments or settlements, or train and school or service adjustors or insurance agents.

(9) No bank or association shall, directly or indirectly, condition the extension of credit or provision of other service on the purchase of insurance sold or endorsed by a bank or association. At the time insurance sold or endorsed by a bank or association is offered to a member or borrower, a bank or association shall present a written notice that the service is optional. The notice shall be in prominent type and separately signed by the member or borrower. The bank or association shall explain to the member or borrower that purchase of insurance from the association is optional and that the member or borrower will not be discriminated against for obtaining the insurance elsewhere.

(10) No bank or association shall, directly or indirectly, discriminate in any manner against any agent, broker, or insurer that is not affiliated with such bank or association, or against any party who purchases insurance through any such nonaffiliated insurance agent, broker, or insurer.

(11) Bank supervision shall ensure that insurance services offered by approved insurers consistently provide members or borrowers with a high quality and cost-effective service as prescribed by policies of the bank's board of directors, but such supervision shall be without any coercion or suasion from any bank in favor of any agent or insurer.

(12) Records must be maintained by banks and associations in sufficient detail to facilitate the review and supervision required herein.

[47 FR 38867, Sept. 3, 1982, as amended at 53 FR 35305, Sept. 13, 1988; 56 FR 65990, Dec. 20, 1991. Redesignated and amended at 60 FR 34099, 34101, June 30, 1995]

Subparts C–F [Reserved]

Subpart G—Releasing Information

§ 618.8300 General regulation.

Except as necessary in performing official duties or as authorized in the following paragraphs, no director or employee of a bank, association, or agency thereof shall disclose information of a type not ordinarily contained in published reports or press releases regarding any such banks or associations or their borrowers or members.

[37 FR 11442, June 7, 1972. Redesignated at 47 FR 12151, Mar. 22, 1982]

§ 618.8310 Lists of borrowers and stockholders.

(a) Any System institution, for the purpose of protecting the security position of the institution, may provide lists of borrowers to buyers, warehousemen, and others who deal in produce or livestock of the kind that secures such loans, except to the extent such actions are prohibited by State laws adopted in accordance with

Farm Credit Administration § 618.8320

the Food Security Act of 1985, Pub. L. 99–198, 99 Stat. 1354. Lists of borrowers or stockholders shall not otherwise be released by any bank or association except in accordance with paragraph (b) of this section.

(b)(1) Within 7 days after receipt of a written request by a stockholder, each Farm Credit bank or association must provide a current list of its stockholders' names, addresses, and classes of stock held to such requesting stockholder. As a condition to providing the list, the bank or association may only require that the stockholder agree and certify in writing that the stockholder will:

(i) Utilize the list exclusively for communicating with stockholders for permissible purposes; and

(ii) Not make the list available to any person, other than the stockholder's attorney or accountant, without first obtaining the written consent of the institution.

(2) As an alternative to receiving a list of stockholders, a stockholder may request the institution mail or otherwise furnish to each stockholder a communication for a permissible purpose on behalf of the requesting stockholder. This alternative may be used at the discretion of the requesting stockholder, provided that the requester agrees to defray the reasonable costs of the communication. In the event the requester decides to exercise this option, the institution must provide the requester with a written estimate of the costs of handling and mailing the communication as soon as practicable after receipt of the stockholder's request to furnish a communication. However, a stockholder may not exercise this option when requesting the list to distribute campaign material for election to the institution board or board committees. Farm Credit banks and associations are prohibited from distributing or mailing campaign material under § 611.320(e) of this chapter.

(3) For purposes of paragraph (b) of this section "permissible purpose" is defined to mean matters relating to the business operations of the institutions. This includes matters relating to the effectiveness of management, the use of institution assets, the distribution by stockholder candidates of campaign material for election to the institution board or board committees, and the performance of directors and officers. This does not include communications involving commercial, social, political, or charitable causes, communications relating to the enforcement of a personal claim or the redress of a personal grievance, or proposals advocating that the bank or association violate any Federal, State, or local law or regulation.

[51 FR 39503, Oct. 28, 1986, as amended at 53 FR 35457, Sept. 14, 1988; 61 FR 67188, Dec. 20, 1996; 71 FR 5763, Feb. 2, 2006]

§ 618.8320 Data regarding borrowers and loan applicants.

(a) Except as provided in paragraph (b) of this section, the directors, officers, and employees of every bank and association shall hold in strict confidence all information regarding the character, credit standing, and property of borrowers and applicants for loans. They shall not exhibit or quote the following documents: Loan applications; supplementary statements by applicants; letters and statements relative to the character, credit standing, and property of borrowers and applicants; recommendations of loan committees; and reports of inspectors, fieldmen, investigators, and appraisers.

(b) The requirements of paragraph (a) of this section are subject to the following exceptions.

(1) Examiners and other authorized representatives of the Farm Credit Administration and the bank concerned shall have free access to all information, records, and files.

(2) In connection with a legitimate law enforcement inquiry, accredited representatives of any agency or department of the United States may be given access to information upon presentation of official identification and a written request specifying:

(i) The particular information desired; and

(ii) That the information is relevant to the law enforcement inquiry and will be used only for the purpose for which it is sought.

(3) The chairman of the presidents committees and the presidents of the banks may supply statistical and other impersonal information pertaining to

groups of borrowers, applicants, and loans, in response to requests from any department or independent office of the Government of the United States, or responsible private organizations, with the understanding that the information will not be published.

(4) Information concerning borrowers may be given for the confidential use of any Farm Credit institution in contemplation of the extension of credit, administration of credit, or the collection of loans.

(5) Impersonal information based solely on transactions or experience with a borrower, such as amounts of loans, terms, and payment records, may be given by a bank or association to any reliable organization for its confidential use in contemplation of the extension of credit or to a consumer reporting agency.

(6) Credit information concerning any borrower may be given when such borrower consents thereto in writing.

(7) An unsuccessful applicant for credit which primarily is for personal, family, or household purposes, if his application was rejected either wholly or partly because of information contained in a consumer report from a consumer reporting agency shall be advised as required in section 615(a) of the Fair Credit Reporting Act (84 Stat. 1133), and if his application was rejected either wholly or partly because of information obtained from a person other than a consumer reporting agency shall be advised as required in section 615(b) thereof.

(8)(i) Any information or analysis of information requested during the course of mediation by a State agency, governor's office or mediator under any State mediation program certified under section 501 of the Agricultural Credit Act of 1987, may be provided to the State agency, governor's office or mediator, with the approval of the borrower.

(ii) Information concerning borrowers contained in an appraisal report may be given by a Farm Credit institution to any State agency certifying and licensing real estate appraisers provided that the Farm Credit institution:

(A) Certifies that the information is required in connection with an employee's application for certification and licensure and that the institution has taken appropriate steps to protect the confidentiality of any borrower information that is not essential to the State's evaluation of the application; and

(B) Determines that the State certification and licensing program makes reasonable provisions for protecting the confidentiality of the borrower information contained in the appraisal report.

(9) Collateral evaluation reports may be released to a loan applicant, when required by the Equal Credit Opportunity Act or related regulations.

(c) The exceptions in paragraph (b) of this section shall be exercised by Farm Credit institutions with full awareness of the requirements of the Fair Credit Reporting Act.

[37 FR 11442, June 7, 1972. Redesignated at 47 FR 12151, Mar. 22, 1982, and amended at 53 FR 35457, Sept. 14, 1988; 56 FR 2675, Jan. 24, 1991; 58 FR 51994, Oct. 6, 1993; 59 FR 46734, Sept. 12, 1994; 61 FR 67188, Dec. 20, 1996; 62 FR 25831, May 12, 1997; 64 FR 43049, Aug. 9, 1999; 75 FR 35968, June 24, 2010]

§ 618.8325 Disclosure of loan documents.

(a) For purposes of this section, the following definitions shall apply:

(1) *Borrower* means any signatory to a loan contract who is either primarily or secondarily liable on such contract, including guarantors, endorsers, co-signers or the like.

(2) *Execution of the loan* means the time at which the borrower and the qualified lender have entered into a legal, binding, and enforceable loan contract and any subsequent amendment or modification of such contract.

(3) *Loan* means a loan made to a farmer, rancher, or producer or harvester of aquatic products, for any agricultural or aquatic purpose and other credit needs of the borrower, including financing for basic processing and marketing directly related to the borrower's operations and those of other eligible farmers, ranchers, and producers or harvesters of aquatic products.

(4) *Loan contract* means any written agreement under which a qualified lender lends or agrees to lend funds to a borrower in consideration for, among

Farm Credit Administration § 618.8430

other things, the borrower's promise to repay the loaned funds at an agreed-upon rate of interest.

(5) *Loan document* means any form, application, agreement, contract, instrument, or other writing to which a borrower affixes his signature or seal and which the qualified lender intends to retain in its files as evidence relating to the loan contract entered into between it and the borrower, but shall not include any document related to a loan which the borrower has not signed.

(6) *Qualified lender* means:

(i) A System institution that makes loans (as defined in paragraph (a)(3) of this section) except a bank for cooperatives; and

(ii) Each bank, institution, corporation, company, union, and association described in section 1.7(b)(1)(B) of the Act, but only with respect to loans discounted or pledged under section 1.7(b)(1) of the Act.

(b) Each qualified lender shall provide a copy of all loan documents to the borrower or the borrower's legal representative at the execution of the loan. Subsequently, upon written request of a borrower or a borrower's legal representative, a qualified lender shall provide, as soon as practicable, a copy of any loan documents signed by the borrower, a copy of other documents delivered by such borrower to that qualified lender, and a copy of each collateral evaluation of the borrower's assets made or used by the qualified lender. To the extent that a collateral evaluation may contain confidential third party information, the lender may protect such confidential third party information by withholding any information that would disclose identifying characteristics of the third party or his property. One copy shall be furnished free of charge. The lender may assess reasonable copying charges for any additional copies requested by the borrower.

(c) Each System bank and association shall have available in its offices copies of the institution's articles of incorporation or charter and bylaws for inspection and shall furnish a copy of such documents to any owner of stock or participation certificates upon request.

[51 FR 39504, Oct. 28, 1986, as amended at 53 FR 35458, Sept. 14, 1988; 56 FR 2675, Jan. 24, 1991; 59 FR 46734, Sept. 12, 1994; 61 FR 67188, Dec. 20, 1996]

§ 618.8330 Production of documents and testimony during litigation.

(a) If your bank or association is a party to litigation with a borrower or a successor in interest, you or your directors, officers, or employees may disclose confidential information about that borrower or the successor in interest during the litigation.

(b) If the Government or your bank or association is not a party to litigation, you or your directors, officers, or employees may produce confidential documents or testimony only if a court of competent jurisdiction issues a lawful order signed by a judge.

[64 FR 43049, Aug. 9, 1999]

§ 618.8340 [Reserved]

Subpart H—Disposition of Obsolete Records

§ 618.8360 [Reserved]

§ 618.8370 [Reserved]

Subpart I [Reserved]

Subpart J—Internal Controls

§ 618.8430 Internal controls.

Each Farm Credit institution's board of directors must adopt an internal control policy, providing adequate direction to the institution in establishing effective control over, and accountability for, operations, programs, and resources. The policy must include, at a minimum, the following:

(a) Direction to management which assigns responsibility for the internal control function (financial, credit, credit review, collateral, and administrative) to an officer (or officers) of the institution.

(b) Adoption of internal audit and control procedures that evidence responsibility for review and maintenance of comprehensive and effective internal controls.

§ 618.8440

(c) Direction for the operation of a program to review and assess its assets. These policies shall include standards which address the administration of this program, described in the list which follows:

(1) Loan, loan-related assets, and appraisal review standards, including standards for scope of review selection and standards for workpapers and supporting documentation.

(2) Asset quality classification standards to be utilized in accordance with a standardized classification system consistent among associations within a district and their funding Farm Credit Bank or agricultural credit bank.

(3) Standards for assessing credit administration, including the appraisal of collateral.

(4) Standards for the training required to initiate the program.

(d) The role of the audit committee in providing oversight and review of the institution's internal controls.

[55 FR 24888, June 19, 1990, as amended at 71 FR 5763, Feb. 2, 2006]

§ 618.8440 Planning.

(a) No later than 30 days after the commencement of each calendar year, the board of directors of each Farm Credit System institution shall adopt an operational and strategic business plan for at least the succeeding 3 years.

(b) The plan must include, at a minimum, the following:

(1) A mission statement.

(2) An annual review of the internal and external factors likely to affect the institution during the planning period. The review must include:

(i) An assessment of management capabilities,

(ii) An assessment of the needs of the board, based on the annual self-evaluation of the board's performance, and

(iii) Strategies for correcting identified weaknesses.

(3) Quantifiable goals and objectives.

(4) Pro forma financial statements for each year of the plan.

(5) A detailed operating budget for the first year of the plan.

(6) The capital adequacy plan adopted pursuant to §§ 615.5200(b), 615.5330 (c), and 615.5335(b).

[53 FR 39250, Oct. 6, 1988, as amended at 62 FR 4450, Jan. 30, 1997; 64 FR 34519, June 28, 1999; 71 FR 5764, Feb. 2, 2006]

PART 619—DEFINITIONS

Sec.
619.9000 The Act.
619.9010 Additional security.
619.9015 Agricultural credit associations.
619.9020 Agricultural credit banks.
619.9025 Agricultural land.
619.9050 Associations.
619.9060 Bank for cooperatives.
619.9110 Consolidation.
619.9130 Differential interest rates.
619.9135 Direct lender.
619.9140 Farm Credit bank(s).
619.9145 Farm Credit Bank.
619.9146 Farm Credit institutions.
619.9155 Federal land credit association.
619.9170 Fixed interest rate.
619.9180 Fixed interest spread.
619.9185 Funding Corporation.
619.9195 [Reserved]
619.9200 Loss-sharing agreements.
619.9210 Merger.
619.9230 Open-end mortgage loan plans.
619.9235 Outside director.
619.9240 Participation agreement.
619.9250 Participation certificates.
619.9260 Primary security.
619.9270 Qualified Public Accountant or External Auditor.
619.9310 Senior officer.
619.9320 Shareholder or stockholder.
619.9330 Speculative purposes.
619.9340 Variable interest rate.

AUTHORITY: Secs. 1.4, 1.7, 2.1, 2.4, 2.11, 3.2, 3.21, 4.9, 5.9, 5.17, 5.18, 5.19, 7.0, 7.1, 7.6, 7.8, and 7.12 of the Farm Credit Act (12 U.S.C. 2012, 2015, 2072, 2075, 2092, 2123, 2142, 2160, 2243, 2252, 2253, 2254, 2279a, 2279a–1, 2279b, 2279c–1, 2279f).

SOURCE: 37 FR 11446, June 7, 1972, unless otherwise noted.

§ 619.9000 The Act.

The Farm Credit Act of 1971; Pub. L. 92–181 and amendments.

§ 619.9010 Additional security.

Supplementary collateral to the primary security taken in connection with the loan.

§ 619.9015 Agricultural credit associations.

Agricultural credit associations are associations created by the merger of

Farm Credit Administration § 619.9170

one or more Federal land bank associations or Federal land credit associations and one or more production credit associations and which have received a transfer of authority to make and participate in long-term real estate mortgage loans pursuant to section 7.6 of the Act.

[55 FR 24888, June 19, 1990]

§ 619.9020 Agricultural credit banks.

Agricultural credit banks are those banks created by the merger of a Farm Credit Bank and a bank for cooperatives pursuant to section 7.0 of the Act.

[55 FR 24888, June 19, 1990]

§ 619.9025 Agricultural land.

Land improved or unimproved which is devoted to or available for the production of crops and other products such as but not limited to fruits and timber or for the raising of livestock.

[37 FR 11446, June 7, 1972. Redesignated at 55 FR 24888, June 19, 1990]

§ 619.9050 Associations.

The term *associations* includes (individually or collectively) Federal land bank associations, Federal land credit associations, production credit associations, and agricultural credit associations.

[55 FR 24888, June 19, 1990]

§ 619.9060 Bank for cooperatives.

A bank for cooperatives is a bank that is operating under section 3.0 of the Act.

[61 FR 67188, Dec. 20, 1996]

§ 619.9110 Consolidation.

Creation of one new organizational entity from two or more existing entities or parts thereof.

§ 619.9130 Differential interest rates.

An interest rate program under which different rates of interest may be made applicable to individual or classes of loans on the basis of type, purpose, amount, quality of loan, or a combination of these factors.

§ 619.9135 Direct lender.

The term *direct lender* refers to Farm Credit banks and associations (production credit associations, agricultural credit associations, and Federal land credit associations) authorized to lend to eligible borrowers identified in § 613.3000.

[55 FR 24889, June 19, 1990]

§ 619.9140 Farm Credit bank(s).

Except as otherwise defined, the term *Farm Credit bank(s)* includes Farm Credit Banks, agricultural credit banks, and banks for cooperatives.

[55 FR 24889, June 19, 1990]

§ 619.9145 Farm Credit Bank.

The term *Farm Credit Bank* refers to a bank resulting from the mandatory merger of the Federal land bank and the Federal intermediate credit bank in each Farm Credit district pursuant to section 410 of the Agricultural Credit Act of 1987, Pub. L. 100-233, or any bank resulting from a merger of two or more Farm Credit Banks.

[55 FR 24889, June 19, 1990]

§ 619.9146 Farm Credit institutions.

Except as otherwise defined, the term *Farm Credit institutions* refers to all institutions chartered and regulated by the Farm Credit Administration as described in section 1.2 of the Act, and to the Funding Corporation.

[55 FR 24889, June 19, 1990, as amended at 56 FR 2675, Jan. 24, 1991]

§ 619.9155 Federal land credit association.

The term *Federal land credit association* refers to a Federal land bank association that has received a transfer of direct long-term real estate lending authority pursuant to section 7.6 of the Act.

[55 FR 24889, June 19, 1990]

§ 619.9170 Fixed interest rate.

The rate of interest specified in the note or loan document which will prevail as the maximum rate chargeable to the borrower during the period of the loan.

§ 619.9180 Fixed interest spread.

A percentage to be added to the cost of money to the bank or association as the means of establishing a lending rate.

§ 619.9185 Funding Corporation.

The term *Funding Corporation* refers to the Federal Farm Credit Banks Funding Corporation established pursuant to section 4.9 of the Act.

[55 FR 24889, June 19, 1990]

§ 619.9195 [Reserved]

§ 619.9200 Loss-sharing agreements.

A contractual arrangement under which the parties agree to share losses associated with loans or otherwise, as may be provided for in the agreement.

[42 FR 20457, Apr. 20, 1977]

§ 619.9210 Merger.

Combining of one or more organizational entities into another similar entity.

§ 619.9230 Open-end mortgage loan plans.

A mortgage loan which permits the borrower to obtain additional sums during the term of the loan.

§ 619.9235 Outside director.

A member of a board of directors selected or appointed by the board, who is not a director, officer, employee, agent, or stockholder of any Farm Credit System institution.

[71 FR 5764, Feb. 2, 2006]

§ 619.9240 Participation agreement.

A contract under which a lender agrees to sell a portion of a loan to one or more purchasers under specific terms set forth in the agreement.

§ 619.9250 Participation certificates.

Evidence of investment in a bank or association to which all the rights and obligations of stock attach with the exception of the right to vote in the affairs of the institution.

§ 619.9260 Primary security.

The basic collateral securing the loan.

§ 619.9270 Qualified Public Accountant or External Auditor.

A qualified public accountant or external auditor is a person who:

(a) Holds a valid and unrevoked certificate, issued to such person by a legally constituted State authority, identifying such person as a certified public accountant;

(b) Is licensed to practice as a public accountant by an appropriate regulatory authority of a State or other political subdivision of the United States;

(c) Is in good standing as a certified and licensed public accountant under the laws of the State or other political subdivision of the United States in which is located the home office or corporate office of the institution that is to be audited;

(d) Is not suspended or otherwise barred from practice as an accountant or public accountant before the Securities and Exchange Commission (SEC) or any other appropriate Federal or State regulatory authority; and

(e) Is independent of the institution that is to be audited. For the purposes of this definition, the term "independent" has the same meaning as under the rules and interpretations of the authoritative body governing overall audit performance. At a minimum, an accountant hired to audit a System institution is not independent if he or she functions in the role of management, audits his or her own work, or serves in an advocacy role for the institution.

[71 FR 76119, Dec. 20, 2006, as amended at 74 FR 28599, June 17, 2009]

§ 619.9310 Senior officer.

The Chief Executive Officer, the Chief Operations Officer, the Chief Financial Officer, the Chief Credit Officer, and the General Counsel, or persons in similar positions; and any other person responsible for a major policymaking function.

[71 FR 5764, Feb. 2, 2006]

§ 619.9320 Shareholder or stockholder.

A holder of any equity interest in a Farm Credit institution.

[75 FR 18744, Apr. 12, 2010]

Farm Credit Administration

§ 619.9330 Speculative purposes.

To buy or sell with the expectation of profiting by fluctuations in price.

[40 FR 49078, Oct. 21, 1975]

§ 619.9340 Variable interest rate.

An interest rate on the outstanding loan balances, which may be changed from time to time during the period of the loan, if provision is made in the note or loan document.

PART 620—DISCLOSURE TO SHAREHOLDERS

Subpart A—General

Sec.
620.1 Definitions.
620.2 Preparing and filing the reports.
620.3 Accuracy of reports and assessment of internal control over financial reporting.

Subpart B—Annual Report to Shareholders

620.4 Preparing and providing the annual report.
620.5 Contents of the annual report to shareholders.

Subpart C—Quarterly Report

620.10 Preparing the quarterly report.
620.11 Content of quarterly report to shareholders.

Subpart D—Notice to Shareholders

620.15 Notice.
620.17 Contents of the notice.

Subpart E—Subpart E—Annual Meeting Information Statements and Other Information To Be Furnished in Connection with Annual Meetings and Director Elections

620.20 Preparing and distributing the information statement.
620.21 Contents of the information statement and other information to be furnished in connection with the annual meeting or director elections.

Subpart F—Bank and Association Audit and Compensation Committees

620.30 Audit committees.
620.31 Compensation committees.

AUTHORITY: Secs. 4.19, 5.9, 5.17, 5.19, 8.11 of the Farm Credit Act (12 U.S.C. 2207, 2243, 2252, 2254, 2279aa–11); sec. 424 of Pub. L. 100–233, 101 Stat. 1568, 1656; sec. 514 of Pub. L. 102–552, 106 Stat. 4102.

Subpart A—General

§ 620.1 Definitions.

For the purpose of this part, the following definitions shall apply:

(a) *Affiliated organization* means any organization, other than a Farm Credit organization, of which a director, senior officer or nominee for director of the reporting institution is a partner, director, officer, or majority shareholder.

(b) *Association* means any of the associations as described in § 619.9050 of this chapter.

(c) *Bank* means any of the Farm Credit banks as described in § 619.9140 of this chapter.

(d) *Direct lender association* means any association that is a direct lender as described in § 619.9135 of this chapter.

(e) *Immediate family* means spouse, parents, siblings, children, mothers- and fathers-in-law, brothers- and sisters-in-law, and sons- and daughters-in-law.

(f) *Institution* means any bank or association chartered by the Act.

(g) *Loan* means any extension of credit or lease that is recorded as an asset of a reporting institution, whether made directly or purchased from another lender. The term "loan" includes, but is not limited to, loans originated through direct negotiations between the reporting institution and a borrower; purchased loans or interests in loans, including participation interests, retained subordinated participation interests in loans sold, interests in pools of subordinated participation interests that are held in lieu of retaining a subordinated participation interest in loans sold; contracts of sale; notes receivable; and other similar obligations and lease financings.

(h) *Material.* The term *material*, when used to qualify a requirement to furnish information as to any subject, limits the information required to those matters to which there is a substantial likelihood that a reasonable person would attach importance in making shareholder decisions or determining the financial condition of the institution.

(i) *Normal risk of collectibility* means the ordinary risk inherent in the lending operation. Loans that are deemed

§ 620.2

to have more than a normal risk of collectibility include, but are not limited to, any adversely classified loans.

(j) *Permanent capital* shall have the same meaning as set forth in § 615.5201 of this chapter.

(k) *Protected borrower capital* means eligible borrower stock as defined in § 615.5260 of this chapter.

(l) *Related association* means an association within the reporting bank's chartered territory that generates loans for the bank or whose operations the bank funds.

(m) *Related bank* means a reporting association's funding bank or the bank for which it generates loans.

(n) *Related organization* means any Farm Credit institution that is a shareholder of the reporting institution or in which the reporting institution has an ownership interest.

(o) *Report* refers to the annual report, quarterly report, notice, or information statement, regardless of form, required by this part unless otherwise specified.

(p) *Signed*, when referring to paper form, means a manual signature, and, when referring to electronic form, means marked in a manner that authenticates each signer's identity.

(q) *Significant event* means any event that is likely to have a material impact on the reporting institution's financial condition, results of operations, cost of funds, or reliability of sources of funds. The term "significant event" includes, but is not limited to, actual or probable noncompliance with the regulatory minimum permanent capital standards or capital adequacy requirements, stock impairment, the imposition of or entering into enforcement actions, execution of financial assistance agreements with other institutions, collateral deficiencies that impact a bank's ability to obtain loan funds, or defaults on debt obligations.

[51 FR 8656, Mar. 13, 1986, as amended at 51 FR 42086, Nov. 21, 1986; 53 FR 3337, Feb. 5, 1988; 56 FR 29421, June 27, 1991; 56 FR 42649, Aug. 28, 1991; 58 FR 48791, Sept. 20, 1993; 59 FR 37406, July 22, 1994; 62 FR 15092, Mar. 31, 1997; 63 FR 39229, July 22, 1998; 67 FR 16633, Apr. 8, 2002; 70 FR 35357, June 17, 2005; 71 FR 5764, Feb. 2, 2006; 75 FR 18744, Apr. 12, 2010]

§ 620.2 Preparing and filing the reports.

For the purposes of this part, the following shall apply:

(a) Copies of each report required by this part, including financial statements and related schedules, exhibits, and all other papers and documents that are a part of the report, must be sent to the Farm Credit Administration according to our instructions. Submissions must comply with the requirements of § 620.3 of this part. The Farm Credit Administration must receive the report within the period prescribed under applicable subpart sections.

(b) The reports must be available for public inspection at the issuing institution and the Farm Credit Administration office with which the reports are filed. Farm Credit bank reports must also be available for public inspection at each related association's office(s).

(c) The reports sent to shareholders must comply with the requirements of § 620.3 of this part. Shareholders must agree to electronic disclosures of reports required by this part.

(d) Information in any part of this report may be incorporated by reference in answer or partial answer to any other item of the report.

(e) All items of essentially the same character as items required to be reported in the reports of condition and performance pursuant to part 621 of this chapter shall be prepared in accordance with the rules set forth in part 621.

(f) No disclosure required by subparts B and E of this part shall be deemed to violate any regulation of the Farm Credit Administration.

(g) Each Farm Credit institution shall present its reports in accordance with generally accepted accounting principles and in a manner that provides the most meaningful disclosure to shareholders.

(1) Any Farm Credit institution that presents its annual and quarterly financial statements on a combined or consolidated basis shall also include in the report the statement of condition and statement of income of the institution on a stand-alone basis. The stand-alone statements may be in summary form and shall disclose the basis of

Farm Credit Administration § 620.3

presentation if different from accounting policies of the combined or consolidated statements.

(2) Any bank that prepares its financial statements on a stand-alone basis shall provide in the footnotes accompanying its annual report supplemental information containing a condensed statement of condition and statement of income for the bank's related associations on a combined basis. The condensed statements may be unaudited and shall disclose the basis of presentation if different from accounting policies of the bank-only statements.

(h)(1) Each institution's annual report or notice must state, in a prominent location within the report or notice:

(i) That the institution's quarterly reports are available free of charge on request;

(ii) The approximate dates the quarterly reports will be available; and

(iii) The telephone numbers and addresses (including information on any other distribution method the institution makes available) where shareholders can request or obtain copies of the quarterly reports.

(2) Each association must state, in a prominent location within each report:

(i) That the shareholders' investment in the association may be materially affected by the financial condition and results of operations of the related bank;

(ii) That (if not otherwise provided) a copy of the bank's financial reports to shareholders will be made available free of charge on request; and

(iii) The telephone numbers and addresses (including information on any other distribution method the association makes available) where shareholders can request or obtain copies of the related bank's financial reports.

(3) Each institution shall, after receiving a request for a report, provide the report to the requestor. The first copy of the requested report shall be provided to the requestor free of charge.

(i) Any events that have affected one or more related organizations of the reporting institution that are likely to have a material effect on the financial condition, results of operations, cost of funds, or reliability of sources of funds of the reporting institution shall be considered significant events for the reporting institution and shall be disclosed in the reports. Any significant event affecting the reporting institution that occurred during the preceding fiscal quarters that continues to have a material effect on the reporting institution shall be considered significant events of the current fiscal quarter and shall be disclosed in the reports.

[51 FR 8656, Mar. 13, 1986, as amended at 51 FR 21340, June 12, 1986; 56 FR 29421, June 27, 1991; 58 FR 27923, May 12, 1993; 58 FR 48791, Sept. 20, 1993; 62 FR 15092, Mar. 31, 1997; 66 FR 14301, Mar. 12, 2001; 67 FR 16633, Apr. 8, 2002; 71 FR 76119, Dec. 20, 2006]

§ 620.3 Accuracy of reports and assessment of internal control over financial reporting.

(a) *Prohibition against incomplete, inaccurate, or misleading disclosures.* No institution and no employee, officer, director, or nominee for director of the institution shall make any disclosure to shareholders or the general public concerning any matter required to be disclosed by this part that is incomplete, inaccurate, or misleading. When any such person makes disclosure that, in the judgment of the Farm Credit Administration, is incomplete, inaccurate, or misleading, whether or not such disclosure is made in disclosure statements required by this part, such institution or person shall make such additional or corrective disclosure as is necessary to provide shareholders and the general public with a full and fair disclosure.

(b) *Signatures.* The name and position title of each person signing the report must be printed beneath his or her signature. If any person required to sign the report has not signed the report, the name and position title of the individual and the reason(s) such individual is unable or refuses to sign must be disclosed in the report. All reports must be dated and signed on behalf of the institution by:

(1) The chief executive officer (CEO);

(2) The chief financial officer (CFO), or if the institution has no CFO, the officer responsible for preparing financial reports; and

(3) A board member formally designated by action of the board to certify reports on behalf of individual board members.

(c) *Certification of financial accuracy.* The report must be certified as financially accurate by the signatories to the report. If any signatory is unable to, or refuses to, certify the report, the institution must disclose the individual's name and position title and the reason(s) such individual is unable or refuses to certify the report. At a minimum, the certification must include a statement that:

(1) The signatories have reviewed the report,

(2) The report has been prepared in accordance with all applicable statutory or regulatory requirements, and

(3) The information is true, accurate, and complete to the best of signatories' knowledge and belief.

(d) *Management assessment of internal control over financial reporting.* Annual reports of those institutions with over $1 billion in total assets (as of the end of the prior fiscal year) must include a report by management assessing the effectiveness of the institution's internal control over financial reporting. The assessment must be conducted during the reporting period and be reported to the institution's board of directors. Quarterly and annual reports for those institutions with over $1 billion in total assets (as of the end of the prior fiscal year) must disclose any material change(s) in the internal control over financial reporting occurring during the reporting period.

[71 FR 76119, Dec. 20, 2006, as amended at 74 FR 28599, June 17, 2009]

Subpart B—Annual Report to Shareholders

§ 620.4 Preparing and providing the annual report.

(a) Each institution of the Farm Credit System must:

(1) Prepare and send to the Farm Credit Administration an electronic copy of its annual report within 75 calendar days of the end of its fiscal year;

(2) Publish a copy of its annual report on its Web site when it sends the report electronically to the Farm Credit Administration;

(3) Provide prior written notification to its shareholders that the institution will publish its annual report on the institution's Web site when the report is sent electronically to the Farm Credit Administration; and

(4) Within 90 calendar days of the end of its fiscal year, prepare and provide to its shareholders an annual report substantively identical to the copy of the report sent to the Farm Credit Administration under paragraph (a)(1) of this section.

(b)(1) A bank must provide its annual report to the shareholders of all related associations if the bank experiences a significant event that has a material effect on those associations.

(2) Any bank that is required by paragraph (b)(1) of this section to provide its annual report must coordinate its distribution with its related associations.

(c) The report shall contain, at a minimum, the information required by § 620.5 and, in addition, such other information as is necessary to make the required statements, in light of the circumstances under which they are made, not misleading.

[51 FR 8656, Mar. 13, 1986. Redesignated and amended at 56 FR 29421, 29422, June 27, 1991; 62 FR 15093, Mar. 31, 1997; 66 FR 14301, Mar. 12, 2001; 67 FR 16633, Apr. 8, 2002; 71 FR 76119, Dec. 20, 2006; 72 FR 68061, Dec. 4, 2007]

§ 620.5 Contents of the annual report to shareholders.

The report must contain the following items in substantially the same order:

(a) *Description of business.* The description must include a brief discussion of the following items:

(1) The territory served;

(2) The persons eligible to borrow;

(3) The types of lending activities engaged in and related services offered. Each bank shall also briefly describe the lending and related services offered by its related associations, as well as related services offered to the borrowers in the bank's chartered territory by any service organization in which it has an ownership interest. Each association shall briefly describe the lending and related services offered by its related organizations or incorporate by reference relevant portions

Farm Credit Administration

§ 620.5

of the related bank's report, if such report is provided to association shareholders;

(4) Any significant developments within the last 5 years that had or could have a material impact on earnings, interest rates to borrowers, patronage, or dividends, including, but not limited to, changes in the reporting entity, changes in patronage policies and practices, and financial assistance provided by or to the institution through loss-sharing or capital preservation agreements or from any other source;

(5) Any acquisition or disposition of material assets during the last fiscal year, other than in the ordinary course of business;

(6) Any material change during the last fiscal year in the manner of conducting the business;

(7) Any seasonal characteristics of the institution's business;

(8) Any concentrations of more than 10 percent of its assets in particular commodities or particular types of agricultural activity or business, and the institution's dependence, if any, upon a single customer, or a few customers, including other financing institutions (OFIs), the loss of any one of which would have a material effect on the institution; and

(9) A brief description of the business of any related Farm Credit institution, as described in § 619.9146 of this chapter, and the nature of the institution's relationship with such organization.

(10) For associations, in a separate section of the annual report, discuss the interdependent relationship between the association and its funding bank, including, but not limited to, the financial relationship, a service provider relationship, other material operational relationships, and other specific issues or areas that create a material interdependent relationship between the association and its funding bank. This separate section may incorporate by reference information from other sections of the annual report. At a minimum, the separate section must include the statement required by § 620.2(h)(2)(i) of this part and the following information required elsewhere in this section, if applicable:

(i) The association's obligation to borrow only from the bank unless the bank gives the association approval to borrow elsewhere;

(ii) The major terms of any capital preservation, loss sharing, or financial assistance agreements between the association and the bank;

(iii) Any statutory or bank bylaw provisions authorizing bank access to the capital of the association; and

(iv) The extent the bank assumed the association's exposure to interest rate risk.

(b) *Description of property.* State the location of and briefly describe the principal offices, i.e., headquarters, and major facilities where the institution makes and services its loans, and other materially important physical properties (other than property acquired in the course of collecting a loan) of the institution.

(c) *Legal proceedings and enforcement actions.* (1) Describe briefly any material pending legal proceedings, other than ordinary routine litigation incidental to the business, to which the institution is a party, of which any of its property is the subject, or which involved claims that the institution may be required by contract or operation of law, to satisfy.

(2) Describe the type of and reason for each enforcement action in effect, i.e., agreements, cease and desist orders, temporary cease and desist orders, prohibitions and removals of officers or directors, or civil money penalties, if any, imposed or assessed on the institution or its officers or directors and the amount of any civil money penalties assessed.

(d) *Description of capital structure.* (1) Describe each class of stock and participation certificates the institution is authorized to issue and the rights, duties, and liabilities of each class. The description shall include:

(i) The number of shares of each class outstanding;

(ii) The par or face value;

(iii) The voting and dividend rights;

(iv) The order of priority upon impairment or liquidation;

(v) The institution's retirement policies and restrictions on transfer;

§ 620.5

(vi) The statutory requirement that a borrower purchase stock as a condition to obtaining a loan;

(vii) The manner in which the stock is purchased (i.e., promissory note to the issuer, or cash not advanced by issuing institution);

(viii) The statutory authority of the institution to require additional capital contributions, if any; and

(ix) The statutory and regulatory restriction regarding retirement of stock and distribution of earnings pursuant to § 615.5215, and any requirements to add capital under a plan approved by the Farm Credit Administration pursuant to §§ 615.5330, 615.5335, 615.5351, or 615.5357.

(2) Describe regulatory minimum capital standards, and the institution's compliance with such standards. For banks, also discuss any related associations that are not currently in compliance with the standards.

(3) State whether the institution is currently prohibited from retiring stock or distributing earnings by the statutory and regulatory restrictions described in paragraph (d)(1)(ix) of this section, or knows of any reason such prohibitions may apply during the fiscal year subsequent to the fiscal year just ended.

(4) Describe the institution's capital adequacy requirements and the minimum stock purchase requirement in effect.

(e) *Description of liabilities.* (1) Describe separately the institution's insured and uninsured debt, indicating the type, amount, maturity, and interest rates of each category of obligations outstanding at the end of the fiscal year just ended. Describe the nature of the insurance provided under part E of title V of the Act. Describe any applicable statutory and regulatory restrictions on the institution's ability to incur debt.

(2) Describe fully the institution's rights and obligations under any agreement, formal or informal, between the institution and any other person or entity having to do with capital preservation, loss sharing, or any other form of financial assistance.

(3) Describe any statutory authorities or obligations to contribute to or on behalf of another institution of the Farm Credit System.

(f) *Selected financial data.* Furnish in comparative columnar form for each of the last 5 fiscal years the following financial data, if material:

(1) *For banks and direct lender associations.*

(i) *Balance sheet.*
(A) Total assets.
(B) Investments.
(C) Loans.
(D) Allowance for losses.
(E) Net loans.
(F) Other property owned.
(G) Total liabilities.
(H) Obligations with maturities less than 1 year.
(I) Obligations with maturities longer than 1 year.
(J) Protected borrower capital.
(K) *At-risk capital.*
(*1*) Stock and participation certificates.
(*2*) Allocated surplus.
(*3*) Unallocated surplus.

(ii) *Statement of income.*
(A) Net interest income.
(B) Provision for loan losses.
(C) Extraordinary items.
(D) Net income.

(iii) *Key financial ratios.*
(A) Return on average assets.
(B) Return on average protected borrower capital and at-risk capital.
(C) Net interest margin as a percentage of average earning assets.
(D) Protected and at-risk capital-to-total assets.
(E) Net chargeoffs-to-average loans.
(F) Allowance for loan losses-to-loans.

(iv) *Net income distributed.*
(A) Dividends.
(B) *Patronage refunds.*
(*1*) Cash.
(*2*) Stock.
(*3*) Allocated surplus.

(2) *For all banks* (on a bank-only basis):
(i) Permanent capital ratio.
(ii) Total surplus ratio.
(iii) Core surplus ratio.
(iv) Net collateral ratio.

(3) *For all associations:*
(i) Permanent capital ratio.
(ii) Total surplus ratio.
(iii) Core surplus ratio.

(g) *Management's discussion and analysis of financial condition and results of operations.* Fully discuss any material aspects of the institution's financial condition, changes in financial condition, and results of operations during the last 2 fiscal years, identifying favorable and unfavorable trends, and significant events or uncertainties. In addition to the items enumerated below, the discussion shall provide such other information as is necessary to an understanding of the institution's financial condition, changes in financial condition, and results of operations.

(1) *Loan portfolio.* (i) Describe the types of loans in the portfolio by major category (e.g., agricultural real estate mortgage loans, rural home loans, agricultural production loans, processing and marketing loans, farm business loans, and international loans), indicating the approximate percentage of the total dollar portfolio represented by each major category. Associations that make agricultural production loans shall provide the information required for such loans by major subcategory (e.g., cash grains, field crops, livestock, dairy, poultry, and timber). For each category and subcategory, discuss any special features of the loans that may be material to the evaluation of risk and any economic or business conditions that have had or are likely to have a material impact on their collectibility. For banks, also disclose separately the aggregate amount of loans outstanding to related associations and other financial institutions.

(ii) Describe the geographic distribution of the loan portfolio by State or other significant geographic division, if any.

(iii) *Purchases and sales of loans.* (A) Describe any material participation in the Federal Agricultural Mortgage Corporation program or origination of loans for resale.

(B) Disclose the amount of purchased loans, loans sold with recourse, retained subordinated participation interests in loans sold, and interests in pools of subordinated participation interests that are held in lieu of retaining a subordinated participation interest in the loans sold.

(iv) *Risk exposure.* For the periods covered by the financial statements provide:

(A) An analysis of high-risk assets and loan performance categories, to include, but not limited to, a discussion of the nature and extent of significant potential credit risks within the loan portfolio, or other information that could adversely impact performance of the loan portfolio in the near future;

(B) An analysis of the allowance for loan losses that includes the ratios of the allowance to loans and net chargeoffs to average loans, and a discussion of the adequacy of the allowance for losses;

(C) Financial assistance given or received under districtwide or Systemwide loss-sharing or capital preservation agreements or otherwise;

(D) For banks, a description in the aggregate of the recent loss experience of related associations that are its shareholders, including the items enumerated in paragraphs (g)(1)(iv) (A), (B), and (C) of this section.

(E) Describe any material obligations with respect to loans sold and the amount of any material contributions made in connection with loans sold into the secondary market. Further disclose the amount of risk of loss associated with such obligations and the amount included in the allowance for losses to provide for such risk.

(2) *Results of operations.* (i) Describe, on a comparative basis, changes in the major components of net interest income during the last 2 fiscal years, describing significant factors that contributed to the changes and quantifying the amount of change(s) due to an increase in volume or the introduction of new services and the amount due to changes in interest rates earned and paid, based on averages for each period.

(ii) Describe any unusual or infrequent events or transactions or any significant economic changes, including, but not limited to, financial assistance received or paid that materially affected reported income. In each case, indicate the extent to which income was so affected.

(iii) Discuss the factors underlying the material changes, if any, in the return on average assets, the return on average protected borrower capital and at-risk capital, and the permanent capital ratio as determined in accordance

§ 620.5

with part 615, subpart H of this chapter. An explanation of the basis of the calculation of ratios relating to permanent capital and at-risk capital shall be included.

(iv) Describe, on a comparative basis, the major components of operating expense, indicating the reasons for significant increases or decreases.

(v) Describe any other significant components of income or expense, including, but not limited to, income from investments, that should be described in order to understand the institution's results of operations.

(vi) Discuss any events affecting a related organization that are likely to have a material effect on the reporting institution's financial condition, results of operations, cost of funds, or reliability of sources of funds.

(vii) Describe any known trends or uncertainties that have had, or that the institution reasonably expects will have, a material impact on net interest income or net income. Disclose any events known to management that will cause a material change in the relationship between costs and revenues.

(3) *Liquidity and funding sources*—(i) *Funding sources.* (A) Describe the average and year end amounts, maturities, and interest rates on outstanding consolidated System-wide debt obligations, bond obligations, or any other obligations used to fund the institution's lending operations.

(B) Describe existing lines of credit and their terms.

(C) Describe the institution's capital accounts and other sources of lendable funds.

(ii) *Liquidity.* (A) Discuss the institution's liquidity policy and the components of asset liquidity, including, but not limited to, cash, investment securities, and maturing loan repayments. Assess the ability of the institution to generate adequate amounts of cash to fund its operations and meet its obligations.

(B) Discuss any known trends that are likely to result in a liquidity deficiency and the course of action management intends to take to resolve it. Discuss any material increase or decrease in liquidity that is likely to occur.

(C) Discuss the institution's participation in the Federal Agricultural Mortgage Corporation secondary market programs authorized by title VIII of the Act and the origination of loans for resale under other authorities, if any.

(iii) *Funds management.* (A) Discuss the institution's interest rate programs and the institution's ability to control interest rate margins.

(B) Discuss changes in net interest margin (net interest income as a percentage of average earning assets), explaining the reasons therefor.

(4) *Capital resources.* (i) Describe any material commitments to purchase capital assets and the anticipated sources of funding.

(ii) Describe any material trends or changes in the mix and cost of debt and capital resources. The discussion shall consider changes in permanent capital, core and total surplus, and net collateral requirements, debt, and any off-balance-sheet financial arrangements.

(iii) Describe any favorable or unfavorable trends in the institution's capital resources.

(iv) Discuss and explain any material changes in capital ratios, noting any material adverse variances from regulatory guidelines.

(v) Discuss the adequacy of the current capital position and any material changes in the capital plan adopted pursuant to § 615.5200 of this chapter, to the extent that such changes may have an effect on the institution's minimum stock purchase requirements and its ability to retire stock and distribute earnings.

(vi) Discuss any trends, commitments, contingencies, or events that are reasonably likely to have a materially adverse effect upon the institution's ability to meet the regulatory minimum capital standards and capital adequacy requirements.

(h) *Directors and senior officers.* (1) List the names of all directors and senior officers of the institution, indicating the position title and term of office of each director, and the position, title, and date each senior officer commenced employment in his or her current position.

(2) Briefly describe the business experience during the past 5 years of each

Farm Credit Administration § 620.5

director and senior officer, including each person's principal occupation and employment during the past 5 years.

(3) For each director and senior officer, list any other business interest where the director or senior officer serves on the board of directors or as a senior officer. Name the position held and state the principal business in which the business is engaged.

(i) *Compensation of directors and senior officers*—(1) *Director compensation.* Describe the arrangements under which directors of the institution are compensated for all services as a director (including total cash compensation and noncash compensation). Noncash compensation with an annual aggregate value of less than $5,000 does not have to be reported. State the total cash and reportable noncash compensation paid to all directors as a group during the last fiscal year. For the purposes of this paragraph, disclosure of compensation paid to and days served by directors applies to any director who served in that capacity at any time during the reporting period. If applicable, describe any exceptional circumstances justifying the additional director compensation as authorized by § 611.400(c) of this chapter. For each director, state:

(i) The number of days served at board meetings;

(ii) The total number of days served in other official activities, including any board committee(s);

(iii) Any additional compensation paid for service on a board committee, naming the committee; and

(iv) The total cash and noncash compensation paid to each director during the last fiscal year. Reportable compensation includes cash and the value of noncash items provided by a third party to a director for services rendered by the director on behalf of the reporting Farm Credit institution. Noncash compensation with an annual aggregate value of less than $5,000 does not have to be reported.

(2) *Senior officer compensation.* Disclose the information on senior officer compensation and compensation plans as required by this paragraph. Farm Credit System associations may disclose the information required by this paragraph in the Annual Meeting Information Statement (AMIS) required under subpart E of this part. Associations exercising this option must include a reference in the annual report stating that the senior officer compensation information is included in the AMIS and that the AMIS is available for public inspection at the reporting association offices pursuant to § 620.2(b).

(i) The institution must disclose the total amount of compensation paid to senior officers in substantially the same manner as the tabular form specified in the following Summary Compensation Table (table):

SUMMARY COMPENSATION TABLE

Name of individual or number in group	Year	Annual Salary	Bonus	Deferred/ perquisite	Other	Total
(a)	(b)	(c)	(d)	(e)	(f)	(g)
CEO	20XX 20XX 20XX					
Aggregate number of senior officers: (X) .... (X) .... (X)	20XX 20XX 20XX					

(A) For each of the last 3 completed fiscal years, report the total amount of compensation paid and the amount of each component of compensation paid to the institution's chief executive officer (CEO), naming the individual. If more than one person served in the capacity of CEO during any given fiscal year, individual compensation disclosures must be provided for each CEO.

(B) For each of the last 3 completed fiscal years, report the aggregate

245

amount of compensation paid, and the components of compensation paid, to all senior officers as a group, stating the number of officers in the group without naming them. If applicable, include in the aggregate the amount of compensation paid to those officers who are not senior officers but whose total annual compensation is among the five highest amounts paid by the institution for the reporting period.

(C) Amounts shown as "Salary" (column (c)) and "Bonus" (column (d)) must reflect the dollar value of salary and bonus earned by the senior officer during the fiscal year. Amounts contributed during the fiscal year by the senior officer pursuant to a plan established under section 401(k) of the Internal Revenue Code, or similar plan, must be included in the salary column or bonus column, as appropriate. If the amount of salary or bonus earned during the fiscal year is not calculable by the time the report is prepared, the reporting institution must provide its best estimate of the compensation amount(s) and disclose that fact in a footnote to the table.

(D) Amounts shown as "deferred/perquisites" (column (e)) must reflect the dollar value of other annual compensation not properly categorized as salary or bonus, including but not limited to:

(1) Deferred compensation earned during the fiscal year, whether or not paid in cash; or

(2) Perquisites and other personal benefits, including the value of noncash items, unless the annual aggregate value of such perquisites is less than $5,000. Reportable perquisites include cash and the value of noncash items provided by a third party to a senior officer for services rendered by the officer on behalf of the reporting institution.

(E) Compensation amounts reported under the category "Other" (column (f)) shall reflect the dollar value of all other compensation not properly reportable in any other column. Items reported in this column shall be specifically identified and described in a footnote to the table. Such compensation includes, but is not limited to:

(1) The amount paid to the senior officer pursuant to a plan or arrangement in connection with the resignation, retirement, or termination of such officer's employment with the institution; or

(2) The amount of contributions by the institution on behalf of the senior officer to a vested or unvested defined contribution plan unless the plan is made available to all employees on the same basis.

(F) Amounts displayed under "Total" (column (g)) shall reflect the sum total of amounts reported in columns (c), (d), (e), and (f).

(ii) Provide a description of all plans pursuant to which cash or noncash compensation was paid or distributed during the last fiscal year, or is proposed to be paid or distributed in the future for performance during the last fiscal year, to those individuals described in paragraph (i)(2)(i) of this section. The description of each plan must include, but not be limited to:

(A) A summary of how the plan operates and who is covered by the plan;

(B) The criteria used to determine amounts payable, including any performance formula or measure;

(C) The time periods over which the measurement of compensation will be determined;

(D) Payment schedules; and

(E) Any material amendments to the plan during the last fiscal year.

(iii) The annual report or AMIS must include a statement that disclosure of information on the total compensation paid during the last fiscal year to any senior officer or to any other officer included in the aggregate is available and will be disclosed to shareholders of the institution and shareholders of related associations (if applicable) upon request.

(3) *Travel, subsistence, and other related expenses.* (i) Briefly describe your policy addressing reimbursements for travel, subsistence, and other related expenses as it applies to directors and senior officers. The report shall include a statement that a copy of the policy is available to shareholders of the institution and shareholders of related associations (if applicable) upon request.

(ii) For each of the last 3 fiscal years, state the aggregate amount of reimbursement for travel, subsistence, and other related expenses for all directors as a group.

(j) *Transactions with senior officers and directors.* (1) State the institution's policies, if any, on loans to and transactions with officers and directors of the institution.

(2) *Transactions other than loans.* For each person who served as a senior officer or director on January 1 of the year following the fiscal year of which the report is filed, or at any time during the fiscal year just ended, describe briefly any transaction or series of transactions other than loans that occurred at any time since the last annual meeting between the institution and such person, any member of the immediate family of such person, or any organization with which such person is affiliated.

(i) For transactions relating to the purchase or retirement of preferred stock issued by the institution, state the name of each senior officer or director that held preferred stock issued by the institution during the reporting period, the current amount of preferred stock held by the senior officer or director, the average dividend rate on the preferred stock currently held, and the amount of purchases and retirements by the individual during the reporting period.

(ii) For all other transactions, state the name of the senior officer or director who entered into the transaction or whose immediate family member or affiliated organization entered into the transaction, the nature of the person's interest in the transaction, and the terms of the transaction. No information need be given where the purchase price, fees, or charges involved were determined by competitive bidding or where the amount involved in the transaction (including the total of all periodic payments) does not exceed $5,000, or the interest of the person arises solely as a result of his or her status as a stockholder of the institution and the benefit received is not a special or extra benefit not available to all stockholders.

(3) *Loans to senior officers and directors.* (i) To the extent applicable, state that the institution (or in the case of an association that does not carry loans to its senior officers and directors on its books, its related bank) has had loans outstanding during the last full fiscal year to date to its senior officers and directors, their immediate family members, and any organizations with which such senior officers or directors are affiliated that:

(A) Were made in the ordinary course of business; and

(B) Were made on the same terms, including interest rate, amortization schedule, and collateral, as those prevailing at the time for comparable transactions with other persons.

(ii) To the extent applicable, state that no loan to a senior officer or director, or to any organization affiliated with such person, or to any immediate family member who resides in the same household as such person or in whose loan or business operation such person has a material financial or legal interest, involved more than the normal risk of collectibility; provided that no such statement need be made with respect to any director or senior officer who has resigned before the time for filing the applicable report with the Farm Credit Administration (but in no case later than the actual filing), or whose term of office will expire or terminate no later than the date of the meeting of stockholders to which the report relates.

(iii) If the conditions stated in paragraphs (j)(3)(i) and (ii) of this section do not apply to the loans of the persons or organizations specified therein, with respect to such loans state:

(A) The name of the officer or director to whom the loan was made or to whose relative or affiliated organization the loan was made.

(B) The largest aggregate amount of each indebtedness outstanding at any time during the last fiscal year.

(C) The nature of the loan(s).

(D) The amount outstanding as of the latest practicable date.

(E) The reasons the loan does not comply with the criteria contained in paragraphs (j)(3)(i) and (j)(3)(ii) of this section.

(F) If the loan does not comply with paragraph (j)(3)(i)(B) of this section, the rate of interest payable on the loan and the repayment terms.

(G) If the loan does not comply with paragraph (j)(3)(ii) of this section, the amount past due, if any, and the reason

§ 620.5

the loan is deemed to involve more than a normal risk of collectibility.

(k) *Involvement in certain legal proceedings.* Describe any of the following events that occurred during the past 5 years and that are material to an evaluation of the ability or integrity of any person who served as director or senior officer on January 1 of the year following the fiscal year for which the report is filed or at any time during the fiscal year just ended:

(1) A petition under the Federal bankruptcy laws or any State insolvency law was filed by or against, or a receiver, fiscal agent, or similar officer was appointed by a court for the business or property of such person, or any partnership in which such person was a general partner at or within 2 years before the time of such filing, or any corporation or business association of which such person was a senior officer at or within 2 years before the time of such filing;

(2) Such person was convicted in a criminal proceeding or is a named party in a pending criminal proceeding (excluding traffic violations and other misdemeanors);

(3) Such person was the subject of any order, judgment, or decree, not subsequently reversed, suspended, or vacated, by any court of competent jurisdiction, permanently or temporarily enjoining or otherwise limiting such person from engaging in any type of business practice.

(l) *Relationship with qualified public accountant.* (1) If a change or changes in qualified public accountants have taken place since the last annual report to shareholders or if a disagreement with a qualified public accountant has occurred that the institution would be required to report to the Farm Credit Administration under part 621 of this chapter, the information required by § 621.4(c) and (d) of this chapter must be disclosed.

(2) Disclose the total fees, by the category of services provided, paid during the reporting period to the qualified public accountant engaged to conduct the institution's financial statement audit. At a minimum, identify fees paid for audit services, tax services, and non-audit related services. The types of non-audit services must be identified and indicate audit committee approval of the services.

(m) *Financial statements.* (1) Furnish financial statements and related footnotes that have been prepared in accordance with generally accepted accounting principles and instructions and other requirements of the Farm Credit Administration and that have been audited in accordance with generally accepted auditing standards by a qualified public accountant and an opinion expressed thereon. The statements shall include the following statements and related footnotes for the last 3 fiscal years: balance sheet, statement of income, statement of changes in protected borrower capital and at-risk capital, and statement of cash flows.

(2) State that the financial statements were prepared under the oversight of the audit committee, identifying the members of the audit committee.

(n) *Credit and services to young, beginning, and small farmers and ranchers and producers or harvesters of aquatic products.* (1) Each direct lender association must describe the YBS demographics in its territory and the source of the demographic data. If there are differences in the methods by which the demographic and YBS data are presented, these differences must be described.

(2) Each direct lender association must provide a description of its YBS program, including a status report on each program component as set forth in § 614.4165(c) of this chapter and the definitions of "young," "beginning," and "small" farmers and ranchers. The discussion must provide such other information necessary for a comprehensive understanding of the direct lender association's YBS program and its results.

(3) Each Farm Credit bank must include a summary report of the quantitative YBS data from its affiliated direct lender associations as described in FCA's instructions for the annual YBS yearend report. The report must include the definitions of "young," "beginning," and "small" farmers and ranchers. A narrative report may be

Farm Credit Administration § 620.11

necessary for an ample understanding of the YBS mission results.

[51 FR 8656, Mar. 13, 1986, as amended at 69 FR 16471, Mar. 30, 2004; 70 FR 53909, Sept. 13, 2005; 71 FR 5764, Feb. 2, 2006; 71 FR 76119, Dec. 20, 2006; 72 FR 4414, Jan. 31, 2007; 74 FR 28599, June 17, 2009; 75 FR 18744, Apr. 12, 2010]

Subpart C—Quarterly Report

§ 620.10 Preparing the quarterly report.

(a) Each institution of the Farm Credit System must:

(1) Prepare and send, to the Farm Credit Administration, an electronic copy of its quarterly report within 40 calendar days after the end of each fiscal quarter, except that no report need be prepared for the fiscal quarter that coincides with the end of the fiscal year of the institution; and

(2) Publish a copy of its quarterly report on its Web site when it electronically sends the report to the Farm Credit Administration.

(b) The report shall contain, at a minimum, the information specified in § 620.11 and, in addition, such other material information (including significant events) as is necessary to make the required disclosures, in light of the circumstances under which they are made, not misleading.

[62 FR 15093, Mar. 31, 1997, as amended at 71 FR 76120, Dec. 20, 2006; 74 FR 28600, June 17, 2009]

§ 620.11 Content of quarterly report to shareholders.

(a) *General.* The information required to be included in the quarterly report may be presented in any format deemed suitable by the institution, except as otherwise required by this section. The report must be organized in an easily understandable format and not presented in a manner that is misleading.

(b) *Rules for condensation.* For purposes of this section, major captions to be provided in the financial statements are the same as those provided in the financial statements contained in the institution's annual report to shareholders, except that the financial statements included in the quarterly report may be condensed into major captions in accordance with the rules prescribed under this paragraph and paragraph (f) of this section.

(1) *Interim balance sheets.* When any major balance sheet caption is less than 10 percent of total assets and the amount in the caption has not increased or decreased by more than 25 percent since the end of the preceding fiscal year, the caption may be combined with others.

(2) *Interim statements of income.* When any major income statement caption is less than 15 percent of average net income for the 3 most recent fiscal years and the amount in the caption has not increased or decreased by more than 20 percent since the corresponding interim period of the preceding fiscal year, the caption may be combined with others. In calculating average net income, loss years should be excluded. If losses were incurred in each of the 3 most recent fiscal years, the average loss shall be used for purposes of this test.

(3) The interim financial information shall include disclosure either on the face of the financial statements or in accompanying footnotes sufficient to make the interim information presented not misleading. Institutions may presume that users of the interim financial information have read or have access to the audited financial statements for the preceding fiscal year and the adequacy of additional disclosure needed for a fair presentation may be determined in that context. Accordingly, footnote disclosure that would substantially duplicate the disclosure contained in the most recent audited financial statements (such as a statement of significant accounting policies and practices), and details of accounts that have not changed significantly in amount or composition since the end of the most recent completed fiscal year may be omitted. However, disclosure shall be provided of events occurring subsequent to the end of the most recent fiscal year that have a material impact on the institution. Disclosures should encompass, for example, significant changes since the end of the most recently completed fiscal year in such items as accounting principles and practices; estimates inherent in the preparation of financial

§ 620.11

statements; status of long-term contracts; capitalization, including significant new indebtedness or modification of existing financing agreements; and the reporting entity resulting from business combinations or dispositions.

(4) The interim financial statements furnished shall reflect all adjustments that are, necessary to a fair statement of the results for the interim periods presented. A statement to that effect shall be included. Furnish any material information necessary to make the information called for not misleading, such as a statement that the results for interim periods are not necessarily indicative of results to be expected for the year.

(c) *Management's discussion and analysis of financial condition and results of operations.* Discuss material changes, if any, to the information provided to shareholders pursuant to § 620.5(g) that have occurred during the periods specified in paragraphs (d)(1) and (2) of this section. Such additional information as is needed to enable the reader to assess material changes in financial condition and results of operations between the periods specified in paragraphs (d)(1) and (2) of this section shall be provided.

(1) *Material changes in financial condition.* Discuss any material changes in financial condition from the end of the preceding fiscal year to the date of the most recent interim balance sheet provided. If the interim financial statements include an interim balance sheet as of the corresponding interim date of the preceding fiscal year, any material changes in financial conditions from that date to the date of the most recent interim balance sheet provided also shall be discussed. If discussions of changes from both the end and the corresponding interim date of the preceding fiscal year are required, the discussions may be combined at the discretion of the institution.

(2) *Material changes in results of operations.* Discuss any material changes in the institution's results of operations with respect to the most recent fiscal year-to-date period for which an income statement is provided and the corresponding year-to-date period of the preceding fiscal year. Such discussion also shall cover material changes with respect to that fiscal quarter and the corresponding fiscal quarter in the preceding fiscal year. In addition, if the institution has elected to provide an income statement for the 12-month period ended as of the date of the most recent interim balance sheet provided, the discussion also shall cover material changes with respect to that 12-month period and the 12-month period ended as of the corresponding interim balance sheet date of the preceding fiscal year.

(d) *Financial statements.* The following financial statements must be provided:

(1) An interim balance sheet as of the end of the most recent fiscal quarter and as of the end of the preceding fiscal year. A balance sheet for the comparable quarter of the preceding fiscal year is optional.

(2) Interim statements of income for the most recent fiscal quarter, for the period between the end of the preceding fiscal year and the end of the most recent fiscal quarter, and for the comparable periods for the previous fiscal year.

(3) Interim statements of changes in protected borrower capital and at-risk capital for the period between the end of the preceding fiscal year and the end of the most recent fiscal quarter, and for the comparable period for the preceding fiscal year.

(4) For banks, interim statements of cash flows for the period between the end of the preceding fiscal year and the end of the most recent fiscal quarter, and for the comparable period for the preceding fiscal year. For associations, interim statements of cash flows are optional.

(5) State that the financial statements were prepared under the oversight of the audit committee.

(e) *Review by a qualified public accountant or external auditor.* The interim financial information need not be audited or reviewed by a qualified public accountant or external auditor prior to filing. If, however, a review of the data is made in accordance with the established professional standards and procedures for such a review, the institution may state that a qualified public accountant or external auditor has performed such a review under the supervision of the institution's audit committee. If such a statement is made, the report of a qualified public accountant or external auditor on such review must accompany the interim financial information.

(f) If any amount that would otherwise be required to be shown by this subpart with respect to any item is not material, it need not be separately shown. The combination of insignificant items is permitted.

[51 FR 21341, June 12, 1986, as amended at 53 FR 3337, Feb. 5, 1988. Redesignated and amended at 56 FR 29421, 29424, June 27, 1991; 67 FR 16633, Apr. 8, 2002; 71 FR 5765, Feb. 2, 2006; 74 FR 28600, June 17, 2009]

Subpart D—Notice to Shareholders

SOURCE: 62 FR 15093, Mar. 31, 1997, unless otherwise noted.

§ 620.15 Notice.

(a) Each Farm Credit bank and direct lender association shall prepare and provide the Farm Credit Administration and shareholders a notice, within 30 days following the month end that the institution initially determines that it is not in compliance with the minimum permanent capital standard prescribed under § 615.5205 of this chapter.

(b) An institution that has given notice to shareholders pursuant to paragraph (a) of this section or subsequent notice pursuant to this paragraph shall also prepare and provide the Farm Credit Administration and shareholders a notice within 45 days following the end of any subsequent quarter at which the institution's permanent capital ratio decreases by one-half of 1 percent or more from the level reported in the most recent notice provided to shareholders.

(c) Each institution required to prepare a notice under paragraphs (a) or (b) of this section shall provide the notice to shareholders or publish it in any publication with circulation wide enough to be reasonably assured that all of the institution's shareholders have access to the information in a timely manner.

[67 FR 16634, Apr. 8, 2002]

§ 620.17 Contents of the notice.

(a) The information required to be in a notice must be conspicuous, easily understandable, and not misleading.

(b) A notice, at a minimum, shall include:

(1) A statement that:

(i) Briefly describes the regulatory minimum permanent capital standard established by the Farm Credit Administration and the notice requirement of § 620.15(a);

(ii) Indicates the institution's current level of permanent capital; and

(iii) Notifies shareholders that the institution's permanent capital is below the Farm Credit Administration regulatory minimum standard.

(2) A statement of the effect that noncompliance has had on the institution and its shareholders, including whether the institution is currently prohibited by statute or regulation from retiring stock or distributing earnings or whether the Farm Credit Administration has issued a capital directive or other enforcement action to the institution.

(3) A complete description of any event(s) that may have significantly contributed to the institution's noncompliance with the minimum permanent capital standard.

(4) A statement that the institution is required by regulation to provide another notice to shareholders within 45 days following the end of any subsequent quarter at which the institution's permanent capital ratio decreases by one half of one percent or more from the level reported in the notice.

[62 FR 15093, Mar. 31, 1997, as amended at 67 FR 16634, Apr. 8, 2002]

Subpart E—Annual Meeting Information Statements and Other Information To Be Furnished in Connection with Annual Meetings and Director Elections

§ 620.20 Preparing and distributing the information statement.

(a)(1) Each Farm Credit bank and association must prepare and provide an information statement ("statement" or "AMIS") to its shareholders at least

§ 620.21

10 business days, but not more than 30 business days, before any annual meeting or any director elections.

(2) Each Farm Credit bank and association must provide the Farm Credit Administration an electronic copy of the AMIS when issued.

(3) In addition to the mailed AMIS, each Farm Credit bank and association may post its AMIS on its Web site. Any AMIS posted on an institution's Web site must remain on the Web site for a reasonable period of time, but not less than 30 calendar days.

(b) Every AMIS must be dated and signed in accordance with the requirements of § 620.3(b) of this part.

(c) Every AMIS must be available for public inspection at all offices of the issuing institution pursuant to § 620.2(b) of this part.

[75 FR 18744, Apr. 12, 2010]

§ 620.21 Contents of the information statement.

(a) An AMIS must, at a minimum, address the following items:

(1) *Date, time, and place of the meeting(s).* Notice of the date, time, and meeting location(s) must be provided at least 10 business days, but no more than 30 business days, before the meeting. If the Farm Credit bank or association will use an online meeting space as part of its meeting, the notice must also specify the date, time, and means of accessing the online meeting space. This information does not need to be part of an AMIS issued by a Farm Credit bank if no meeting is held.

(2) *Voting shareholders.* For each class of stock entitled to vote at the meeting, state the number of shareholders entitled to vote and, when shareholders are asked to vote on preferred stock, the number of shares entitled to vote. State the record date as of which the shareholders entitled to vote will be determined and the voting requirements for each matter to be voted upon. If association directors are nominated or elected by region, describe the regions and state the number of voting shareholders entitled to vote in each region.

(3) *Financial updates.* Each AMIS must reference the most recently issued annual report required by subpart B of this part. The AMIS must also include such other information considered material and necessary to make the required contents of the AMIS, in light of the circumstances under which it is made, not misleading.

(i) If any transactions between the institution and its senior officers and directors of the type required to be disclosed in the annual report to shareholders under § 620.5(j), or any of the events required to be disclosed in the annual report to shareholders under § 620.5(k) have occurred since the end of the last fiscal year and were not disclosed in the annual report to shareholders, the disclosures required by § 620.5(j) and (k) shall be made with respect to such transactions or events in the information statement. If any material change in the matters disclosed in the annual report to shareholders pursuant to § 620.5(j) and (k) has occurred since the annual report to shareholders was prepared, disclosure shall be made of such change in the information statement.

(ii) If a Farm Credit institution has had a change or changes in its external auditor(s) since the last annual report to shareholders, or if a disagreement with an external auditor has occurred, the institution shall disclose the information required by § 621.4(c) and (d) of this chapter.

(4) *Directors.* State the names and ages of persons currently serving as directors of the institution, their terms of office, and the periods during which such persons have served. Institutions must also state the type or types of agriculture or aquaculture engaged in by each director. No information need be given with respect to any director whose term of office as a director will not continue after any meeting to which the statement relates.

(i) Identify by name any incumbent director who attended fewer than 75 percent of the board meetings or any meetings of board committees on which he or she served during the last fiscal year.

(ii) If any director resigned or declined to stand for reelection since the last annual meeting because of a policy disagreement with the board, and if the director has provided a notice requesting disclosure of the nature of the disagreement, state the date of the director's resignation and summarize the director's description of the disagreement. If the institution holds a different view of the disagreement, the institution's view may be summarized as well.

(b) An AMIS issued for director elections must also include the information required by this paragraph.

(1) Provide the nominating committee's slate of director-nominees. If fewer than two director-nominees for each position are named, describe the efforts of the nominating committee to locate two willing nominees.

(2) Provide, as part of the AMIS, the director-nominee disclosure information collected under §611.330 of this chapter. Institutions may either restate such information in a standard format or provide complete copies of each nominee's disclosure statement.

(3) State whether nominations will be accepted from the floor and explain the procedures for making floor nominations.

(c) When the nominating committee will be elected during director elections, notice to voting shareholders of this event must be included in the AMIS. The AMIS must describe the balloting procedures that will be used to elect the nominating committee, including whether floor nominations for committee members will be permitted. The AMIS must state the number of committee positions to be filled and the names of the nominees for the committee.

(d) If shareholders are asked to vote on matters not normally required to be submitted to shareholders for approval, the AMIS must describe fully the material circumstances surrounding the matter, the reason shareholders are asked to vote, and the vote required for approval of the proposition. The AMIS must describe any other matter that will be discussed at the meeting upon which shareholder vote is not required.

[75 FR 18744, Apr. 12, 2010]

Subpart F—Bank and Association Audit and Compensation Committees

SOURCE: 71 FR 5766, Feb. 2, 2006, unless otherwise noted.

§ 620.30 Audit committees.

Each Farm Credit bank and association must establish and maintain an audit committee. An audit committee is established by adopting a written charter describing the committee's composition, authorities, and responsibilities in accordance with this section. All audit committees must maintain records of meetings, including attendance, for at least 3 fiscal years.

(a) *Composition.* Each member of an audit committee must be a member of the Farm Credit institution's board of directors. An audit committee may not consist of less than three members and must include any director designated as a financial expert under §611.210(a)(2) of this chapter. All audit committee members should be knowledgeable in at least one of the following: Public and corporate finance, financial reporting and disclosure, or accounting procedures.

(b) *Independence.* Every audit committee member must be free from any relationship that, in the opinion of the board, would interfere with the exercise of independent judgment as a committee member.

(c) *Resources.* Farm Credit institutions must permit their audit committees to contract for independent legal counsel and expert advisors. If an institution hires a financial expert advisor pursuant to §611.210(a)(2), that advisor will also serve as an advisor to the audit committee. Each institution is responsible for providing monetary and nonmonetary resources to enable its audit committee to contract for external auditors, outside advisors, and ordinary administrative expenses. A two-thirds majority vote of the full board of directors is required to deny an audit committee's request for resources.

(d) *Duties.* Each audit committee must report only to the board of directors. In its capacity as a committee of the board, the audit committee is responsible for the following:

§ 620.31

(1) *Financial reports.* Each audit committee must oversee management's preparation of the report to shareholders; review the impact of any significant accounting and auditing developments; review accounting policy changes relating to preparation of financial statements; and review annual and quarterly reports prior to release. After the audit committee reviews a financial policy, procedure, or report, it must record in its minutes its agreement or disagreement with the item(s) under review.

(2) *External auditors.* The external auditor must report directly to the audit committee. Each audit committee must:

(i) Determine the appointment, compensation, and retention of external auditors issuing audit reports of the institution;

(ii) Review the external auditor's work;

(iii) Give prior approval for any non-audit services performed by the external auditor, except the audit committee may not approve those non-audit services specifically prohibited by FCA regulation; and

(iv) Comply with the auditor independence provisions of part 621 of this chapter.

(3) *Internal controls.* Each audit committee must oversee the institution's system of internal controls relating to preparation of financial reports, including controls relating to the institution's compliance with applicable laws and regulations. Any internal audit functions of the institution must also be subject to audit committee review and supervision.

[53 FR 50339, Dec. 15, 1988, as amended at 71 FR 76120, Dec. 20, 2006]

§ 620.31 Compensation committees.

Each Farm Credit bank and association must establish and maintain a compensation committee by adopting a written charter describing the committee's composition, authorities, and responsibilities in accordance with this section. All compensation committees will be required to maintain records of meetings, including attendance, for at least 3 fiscal years.

(a) *Composition.* Each compensation committee must consist of at least three members. Each committee member must be a member of the institution's board of directors. Every member must be free from any relationship that, in the opinion of the board, would interfere with the exercise of independent judgment as a committee member.

(b) *Duties.* Each compensation committee must report only to the board of directors. In its capacity as a committee of the board, the compensation committee is responsible for reviewing the compensation policies and plans for senior officers and employees. Each compensation committee must approve the overall compensation program for senior officers.

(c) *Resources.* Each institution must provide monetary and nonmonetary resources to enable its compensation committee to function.

PART 621—ACCOUNTING AND REPORTING REQUIREMENTS

Subpart A—Purpose and Definitions

Sec.
621.1 Purpose and applicability.
621.2 Definitions.

Subpart B—General Rules

621.3 Application of generally accepted accounting principles.
621.4 Audit by qualified public accountant.
621.5 Accounting for the allowance for loan losses and chargeoffs.

Subpart C—Loan Performance and Valuation Assessment

621.6 Performance categories and other property owned.
621.7 Rule of aggregation.
621.8 Application of payments and income recognition on nonaccrual loans.
621.9 Reinstatement to accrual status.
621.10 Monitoring of performance categories and other property owned.

Subpart D—Report of Condition and Performance

621.12 Applicability and general instructions.
621.13 Content and standards—general rules.
621.14 Certification of correctness.

Subpart E—Auditor Independence

621.30 General.
621.31 Non-audit services.

Farm Credit Administration § 621.2

621.32 Conflicts of interest and rotation.

AUTHORITY: Secs. 5.17, 8.11 of the Farm Credit Act (12 U.S.C. 2252, 2279aa–11); sec. 514 of Pub. L. 102–552.

SOURCE: 58 FR 48786, Sept. 20, 1993, unless otherwise noted.

Subpart A—Purpose and Definitions

§ 621.1 Purpose and applicability.

This part sets forth accounting and reporting requirements to be followed by all banks, associations, and service organizations chartered under the Act; the Federal Farm Credit Banks Funding Corporation; and, where specifically indicated, the Federal Agricultural Mortgage Corporation. The requirements set forth in this part are of both general and specific applicability. Certain requirements focus on areas of financial condition and operating performance that are of special importance for generating, presenting, and disclosing accurate and reliable information.

§ 621.2 Definitions.

For the purposes of this part, the following definitions shall apply:

(a) *Accrual basis of accounting* means the accounting method in which expenses are recorded when incurred, whether paid or unpaid, and income is reported when earned, whether received or not received.

(b) *Borrowing entity* means the individual(s), partnership, joint venture, trust, corporation, or other business entity, or any combination thereof, that is primarily obligated on the loan instrument.

(c) *Generally accepted accounting principles* means that body of conventions, rules, and procedures necessary to define accepted accounting practices at a particular time, as promulgated by the Financial Accounting Standards Board (FASB) and other authoritative sources recognized as setting standards for the accounting profession in the United States. Generally accepted accounting principles include not only broad guidelines of general application but also detailed practices and procedures that constitute standards by which financial presentations are evaluated.

(d) *Generally accepted auditing standards* means the standards and guidelines that are generally accepted in the United States of America and that are adopted by the authoritative body that governs the overall quality of audit performance.

(e) *Institution* means any bank, association, or service organization chartered under the Act; the Federal Farm Credit Banks Funding Corporation, and where specifically noted, the Federal Agricultural Mortgage Corporation.

(f) *Loan* means any extension of credit or lease that is recorded as an asset of a reporting institution, whether made directly or purchased from another lender. The term "loan" includes, but is not limited to:

(1) Loans originated through direct negotiations between the reporting institution and a borrower;

(2) Purchased loans or interests in loans, including participation interests, retained subordinated participation interests in loans sold, and interests in pools of subordinated participation interests that are held in lieu of retaining a subordinated participation interest in loans sold;

(3) Contracts of sale; notes receivable; and

(4) Other similar obligations and lease financing.

(g) *Material* means the magnitude of an omission or misstatement of accounting information that, in light of surrounding circumstances, makes it probable that the judgment of a reasonable person relying on the information would have been changed or influenced by the omission or misstatement.

(h) *Net realizable value* means the net amount the lender would expect to be realized from the acquisition and subsequent sale or disposition of a loan's underlying collateral. Generally, net realizable value is equal to the estimated selling price in the ordinary course of business, less estimated costs of acquisition, completion, and disposal.

(i) *Recorded investment* means the face amount of the loan increased or decreased by applicable accrued interest

§ 621.3

and unamortized premium, discount, finance charges, or acquisition costs, and may also reflect a previous direct write-down of the investment.

[58 FR 48786, Sept. 20, 1993, as amended at 71 FR 76120, Dec. 20, 2006; 74 FR 28600, June 17, 2009]

Subpart B—General Rules

§ 621.3 Application of generally accepted accounting principles.

Each institution shall:

(a) Prepare and maintain, on an accrual basis, accurate and complete records of its business transactions as necessary to prepare financial statements and reports, including reports to the Farm Credit Administration, in accordance with generally accepted accounting principles, except as otherwise directed by statutory and regulatory requirements;

(b) Prepare its financial statements and reports, including reports to the shareholders, investors, boards of directors, institution management and the Farm Credit Administration, in accordance with generally accepted accounting principles, except as otherwise directed by statutory and regulatory requirements; and

(c) Prepare and maintain its books and records in such a manner as to facilitate reconciliation with financial statements and reports prepared from them.

§ 621.4 Audit by qualified public accountant.

(a) Each institution shall, at least annually, have its financial statements audited by a qualified public accountant in accordance with generally accepted auditing standards.

(b) The qualified public accountant's opinion of each institution's financial statements must be included as a part of each annual report to shareholders. The accountant must comply with the auditor independence provisions of subpart E of this part.

(c) If an institution disagrees with the opinion of a qualified public accountant required by paragraph (b) of this section, the following actions shall be taken immediately:

(1) The institution shall prepare a brief but thorough written description of the scope and content of the disagreement, noting each point of disagreement and citing, in all cases, the specific provisions of generally accepted accounting principles and generally accepted auditing standards upon which the institution's position in the disagreement is based;

(2) A copy of the institution's final description of the disagreement shall be given to the accountant who provided the opinion with which the institution disagrees;

(3) The accountant shall have 10 business days to develop and provide a brief but thorough final response to the institution's description of the disagreement, including all items believed to be incorrect or incomplete, and citing, in all cases, the specific provisions of generally accepted accounting principles and generally accepted auditing standards upon which the accountant's position in the disagreement is based;

(4) Both the institution's final description of the disagreement and the accountant's final response to it shall be included in the institution's annual report to shareholders directly following the accountant's opinion of the institution's financial statements; and

(5) The institution shall immediately notify the Chief Examiner, Farm Credit Administration, of any disagreement with its accountant and shall furnish the Farm Credit Administration with the written documentation required by paragraphs (c) (1) through (4) of this section.

(d) If an institution selects a qualified public accountant to audit its financial statements and provide an opinion thereon for its annual report who is different from the accountant whose opinion appeared in the institution's most recent annual report, the following items shall be sent to the Farm Credit Administration no later than 15 days after the end of the month in which the change took place and shall be included in the institution's annual meeting information statement and annual report to shareholders for the year in which the change of accountants took place:

(1) The name and address of the accountant whose opinion appeared in the institution's most recent annual report to shareholders;

(2) A brief but thorough statement of the reasons the accountant selected for the most recent annual report was not selected for the current annual report. If the change resulted from a disagreement with the accountant, the statement shall describe the institution's disagreement with the accountant's opinion and the accountant's final response to the institution's disagreement prepared pursuant to paragraph (c) of this section; and

(3) The identification of the highest ranking officer, committee of officers, or board of directors, as appropriate, that recommended, approved, or otherwise made the decision to change qualified public accountants.

[58 FR 48786, Sept. 20, 1993, as amended at 71 FR 76120, Dec. 20, 2006]

§ 621.5 Accounting for the allowance for loan losses and chargeoffs.

Each institution shall:

(a) Maintain at all times an allowance for loan losses that is determined according to generally accepted accounting principles.

(b) Develop, adopt, and consistently apply policies and procedures governing the establishment and maintenance of the allowance for loan losses which, at a minimum, conform to the rules, definitions, and standards set forth in this part and any other applicable requirements.

(c) Charge-off loans, wholly or partially, as appropriate, at the time they are determined to be uncollectible.

(d) Ensure that when an institution or the Farm Credit Administration determines that the value of a loan or other asset recorded on its books and records exceeds the amount that can reasonably be expected to be collectible, or when the documentation supporting the recorded asset value is inadequate, the institution shall immediately charge off the asset in the amount determined to be uncollectible. If the amount determined to be uncollectible by the institution is different from the amount determined to be uncollectible by the Farm Credit Administration, the institution shall charge off such amount as the Farm Credit Administration shall direct.

[58 FR 48786, Sept. 20, 1993, as amended at 74 FR 28600, June 17, 2009]

Subpart C—Loan Performance and Valuation Assessment

§ 621.6 Performance categories and other property owned.

Each institution shall employ the following practices with respect to categorizing high-risk loans and loan-related assets. No loan shall be put into more than one performance category. At a minimum, loans meeting the criteria for both nonaccrual and another performance category shall be classified as nonaccrual.

(a) *Nonaccrual loans.* A loan shall be considered nonaccrual if it meets any of the following conditions:

(1) Collection of any amount of outstanding principal and all past and future interest accruals, considered over the full term of the asset, is not expected;

(2) Any portion of the loan has been charged off, except in cases where the prior chargeoff was taken as part of a formal restructuring of the loan; or

(3) The loan is 90 days past due and is not both adequately secured and in process of collection.

(i) A loan is considered adequately secured only if:

(A) It is secured by real or personal property having a net realizable value sufficient to discharge the debt in full; or

(B) It is guaranteed by a financially responsible party in an amount sufficient to discharge the debt in full.

(ii) A loan is considered in process of collection only if collection efforts are proceeding in due course and, based on a probable and specific event, are expected to result in the prompt repayment of the debt or its restoration to current status. There must be documented evidence that collection in full of amounts due and unpaid is expected to occur within a reasonable time period, not to exceed 180 days from the date that payment was due. The commencement of collection efforts through legal action, including bankruptcy or foreclosure, or through collection efforts not involving legal action, including ongoing workouts and reamortizations, do not, in and of themselves, provide sufficient cause to keep a loan out of nonaccrual status. If

§ 621.7

full collection of the debt or its restoration to current status is dependent upon completion of any action by the borrower, the institution must obtain the borrower's written agreement to complete all such actions by the specific dates set forth in agreement.

(b) *Formally restructured loans.* A loan is considered formally restructured if it meets the "troubled debt restructuring" definition set forth in Statement of Financial Accounting Standards No. 15, Accounting by Debtors and Creditors for Troubled Debt Restructurings, as promulgated by the FASB.

(c) *Loans 90 days past due still accruing interest.* (1) Loans 90 days past due still accruing interest means loans that are 90 days or more contractually past due, and that are both adequately secured and in process of collection, as described in this section.

(2) A loan shall be considered contractually past due when any principal repayment or interest payment required by the loan instrument is not received on or before the due date. A loan shall remain contractually past due until it is formally restructured or until the entire amount past due, including principal, accrued interest, and penalty interest incurred as the result of past due status, is collected or otherwise discharged in full.

(d) *Other property owned* means any real or personal property, other than an interest-earning asset, that has been acquired as a result of full or partial liquidation of a loan, through foreclosure, deed in lieu of foreclosure, or other means.

§ 621.7 Rule of aggregation.

(a) When one loan to a borrower is placed in nonaccrual, an institution must immediately evaluate whether its other loans to that borrower, or related borrowers, should also be placed in nonaccrual. All loans on which a borrowing entity, or a component of a borrowing entity, is primarily obligated to the reporting institution shall be considered as one loan unless a review of all pertinent facts supports a reasonable determination that a particular loan constitutes an independent credit risk and such determination is adequately documented in the loan file.

(1) A loan shall be considered an independent credit risk if a substantial portion of the loan is guaranteed as to principal and interest by a government agency.

(2) Other loans shall be considered independent credit risks if and so long as:

(i) The primary sources of repayment are independent for each loan;

(ii) The loans are not cross-collateralized; and

(iii) The principal obligors are different person(s) and/or entity(ies). Related loans will not be considered independent credit risks if the operations of a related borrower are so financially interdependent with the borrower's operations that the economic survival of one will materially affect the economic survival of the other, determined in accordance with § 614.4359(a)(2) of this chapter.

(b) If the evaluation required by paragraph (a) of this section results in a determination that the borrower's other loans with the institution do not represent an independent credit risk, and full collection of such loans is not expected, then all of the borrower's loans must be aggregated and classified as nonaccrual. If such other loans represent an independent credit risk and are fully collectible, then they may remain in their current performance category.

(c) When an institution becomes aware that a borrower has a loan that has been classified nonaccrual by any other lender, the institution must re-evaluate the credit risk in its loan to the borrower and then determine whether an independent credit risk exists.

[58 FR 48786, Sept. 20, 1993, as amended at 64 FR 34519, June 28, 1999]

§ 621.8 Application of payments and income recognition on nonaccrual loans.

Each institution shall employ the following practices with respect to application of cash payments on nonaccrual loans:

(a) If the ultimate collectibility of the recorded investment, in whole or in part, is in doubt, any payment received on such loan shall be applied to reduce

Farm Credit Administration § 621.10

the recorded investment to the extent necessary to eliminate such doubt.

(b) Once the ultimate collectibility of the recorded investment is no longer in doubt, payments received in cash on such loan may qualify for recognition as interest income if all of the following characteristics are met at the time the payment is received:

(1) The loan does not have a remaining unrecovered prior chargeoff associated with it, except in cases where the prior chargeoff was taken as part of a formal restructuring of the loan;

(2) The payment received has come from a source of repayment detailed in the plan of collection;

(3) The loan, after considering the payment, is not contractually past due more than 90 days and is not expected to become 90 days past due, or a repayment pattern has been established that reasonably demonstrates future repayment capacity.

(c) The institution shall employ the following practices with respect to earned but uncollected interest income on loans, leases, contracts, and similar assets that are determined not to be fully collectible:

(1) Earned but uncollected interest income that was accrued in the current fiscal year and is determined to be uncollectible shall be reversed from interest income; and

(2) Earned but uncollected interest income that was accrued in prior fiscal years and is determined to be uncollectible shall be charged off against the allowance for loan losses.

§ 621.9 Reinstatement to accrual status.

A loan may be reinstated to accrual status, when each of the following criteria are met:

(a) All contractual principal and interest due on the loan is paid and the loan is current;

(b) Prior chargeoffs are recovered, except for troubled debt restructures;

(c) No reasonable doubt remains regarding the willingness and ability of the borrower to perform in accordance with the contractual terms of the loan agreement; and

(d) Reinstatement is supported by a period of sustained performance in accordance with the contractual terms of the note and/or loan agreement. Sustained performance will generally be demonstrated by 6 consecutive monthly payments, 4 consecutive quarterly payments, 3 consecutive semi-annual payments, or 2 consecutive annual payments.

§ 621.10 Monitoring of performance categories and other property owned.

(a) Each institution shall:

(1) Account for, report, and disclose to shareholders, investors, boards of directors, and the Farm Credit Administration all material items with respect to performance categories and other property owned in accordance with the rules and definitions set forth in this part and any other applicable requirements;

(2) In accordance with § 620.5(g)(1)(iv)(A) of this chapter, disclose to shareholders, investors, boards of directors, and the Farm Credit Administration the nature and extent of significant potential credit risks within the loan portfolio, or other information that could adversely impact performance of the loan portfolio in the near future;

(3) Develop, adopt, and consistently apply policies and procedures governing performance categories and other property owned, which, at a minimum, conform to the definitions, rules, and standards set forth in this part and such other requirements and procedures as may be required by the Farm Credit Administration;

(4) Review the loan portfolio at least quarterly to ensure that all high-risk loans have been assigned the appropriate performance category; and

(5) Review all high-risk loans in the loan portfolio at least quarterly to determine the collectibility of accrued but uncollected income, if any.

(b) Measures taken to enhance the collectibility of a loan shall not be deemed to relieve an institution of the requirement to monitor and evaluate the loan for the purpose of determining its performance status.

Subpart D—Report of Condition and Performance

§ 621.12 Applicability and general instructions.

(a) Each institution, including the Federal Agricultural Mortgage Corporation, shall prepare and file such reports of condition and performance as may be required by the Farm Credit Administration.

(b) Reports of condition and performance shall be filed four times each year, and at such other times as the Farm Credit Administration may require. The reports shall be prepared on the accrual basis of accounting and shall fairly represent the financial condition and performance of each institution at the end of, and over the period of, each calendar quarter, provided that such additional reports as may be necessary to ensure timely, complete, and accurate monitoring and evaluation of the affairs, condition, and performance of Farm Credit institutions may be required, as determined by the Chief Examiner, Farm Credit Administration.

(c) All reports of condition and performance shall be submitted electronically in accordance with the instructions prescribed by the Farm Credit Administration and located on its Web site.

[58 FR 48786, Sept. 20, 1993, as amended at 74 FR 28600, June 17, 2009]

§ 621.13 Content and standards—general rules.

Each institution, including the Federal Agricultural Mortgage Corporation, shall prepare reports of condition and performance:

(a) In accordance with all applicable laws, regulations, standards, and such instructions and specifications and on such media as may be prescribed by the Farm Credit Administration;

(b) In accordance with generally accepted accounting principles and such other accounting requirements, standards, and procedures as may be prescribed by the Farm Credit Administration; and

(c) In such manner as to facilitate their reconciliation with the books and records of reporting institutions.

§ 621.14 Certification of correctness.

Each report of financial condition and performance filed with the Farm Credit Administration shall be certified as having been prepared in accordance with all applicable regulations and instructions and to be a true and accurate representation of the financial condition and performance of the institution to which it applies. The reports shall be certified by the officer of the reporting institution named for that purpose by action of the reporting institution's board of directors. If the board of directors of the institution has not acted to name an officer to certify the correctness of its reports of condition and performance, then the reports shall be certified by the president or chief executive officer of the reporting institution.

Subpart E—Auditor Independence

SOURCE: 71 FR 76120, Dec. 20, 2006, unless otherwise noted.

§ 621.30 General.

Each Farm Credit institution must ensure the independence of all qualified public accountants conducting the institution's audit by establishing and maintaining policies and procedures governing the engagement of external auditors. The policies and procedures must incorporate the provisions of this subpart and § 612.2260 of this chapter.

§ 621.31 Non-audit services.

Non-audit services are any professional services provided by a qualified public accountant during the period of an audit engagement which are not connected to an audit or review of an institution's financial statements.

(a) A qualified public accountant engaged to conduct a Farm Credit institution's audit may not perform the following non-audit services for that institution:

(1) Bookkeeping,

(2) Financial information systems design,

(3) Appraisal and valuation services,

(4) Actuarial services,

(5) Internal audit outsourcing services,

Farm Credit Administration

(6) Management or human resources functions,

(7) Legal and expert services unrelated to the audit, and

(8) Advocating an institution's interests in litigation, regulatory or administrative investigations and proceedings unrelated to external audit work.

(b) A qualified public accountant engaged to conduct a Farm Credit institution's audit may only perform non-audit services, not otherwise prohibited in this section, if the institution's audit committee pre-approves the services and the services are fully disclosed in the annual report.

§ 621.32 Conflicts of interest and rotation.

(a) *Conflicts of interest.* (1) A Farm Credit institution may not engage a qualified public accountant to conduct the institution's audit if the accountant uses a partner, concurring partner, or lead member in the audit engagement team who was a director, officer or employee of the Farm Credit institution within the past year.

(2) A Farm Credit institution may not make an employment offer to a partner, concurring partner, or lead member serving on the institution's audit engagement team during the audit or within 1 year of the conclusion of the audit engagement.

(b) *Rotation.* Each institution may engage the same lead and reviewing audit partners of a qualified public accountant to conduct the institution's audit for no more than 5 consecutive years. The institution must then require the lead and reviewing audit partners assigned to the institution's audit team to rotate out of the audit team for 5 years. At the end of 5 years, the institution may again engage the audit services of those lead and reviewing audit partners.

PART 622—RULES OF PRACTICE AND PROCEDURE

Subpart A—Rules Applicable to Formal Hearings

Sec.
622.1 Scope of regulations.
622.2 Definitions.
622.3 Appearance and practice.
622.4 Commencement of proceedings.
622.5 Answer.
622.6 Opportunity for informal settlement.
622.7 Conduct of hearings.
622.8 Rules of evidence.
622.9 Subpoenas.
622.10 Depositions.
622.11 Motions.
622.12 Proposed findings and conclusions; recommended decision.
622.13 Exceptions.
622.14 Briefs.
622.15 Oral argument before the Board.
622.16 Notice of submission to the Board.
622.17 Decision of the Board.
622.18 Filing.
622.19 Service.
622.20 Documents in proceedings confidential.
622.21 Computing time.
622.22 Retained authority.
622.23–622.50 [Reserved]

Subpart B—Rules and Procedures for Assessment and Collection of Civil Money Penalties

622.51 Definitions.
622.52 Purpose and scope.
622.53–622.54 [Reserved]
622.55 Notice of assessment of civil money penalty.
622.56 Request for formal hearing on assessment.
622.57 Waiver of hearing; consent.
622.58 Hearing on assessment.
622.59 Assessment order.
622.60 Payment of civil money penalty.
622.61 Adjustment of civil money penalties by the rate of inflation under the Federal Civil Penalties Inflation Adjustment Act of 1990, as amended.
622.62–622.75 [Reserved]

Subpart C—Rules and Procedures Applicable to Suspension or Removal of an Individual Where Certain Crimes are Charged or Proven

622.76 Definitions.
622.77 Purpose and scope.
622.78 Suspension, prohibition or removal.
622.79 Petition for informal hearing.
622.80 Informal hearing.
622.81 Default.
622.82 Decision of the Board.
622.83–622.100 [Reserved]

Subpart D—Rules and Procedures Applicable to Formal Investigations

622.101 Definitions.
622.102 Scope.
622.103 Formal investigations are confidential.
622.104 Order to conduct formal investigation.

§ 622.1

622.105 Conduct of investigation.
622.106 Service of subpoena and payment of witness fees.
622.107 Transcripts.

AUTHORITY: Secs. 5.9, 5.10, 5.17, 5.25–5.37 of the Farm Credit Act (12 U.S.C. 2243, 2244, 2252, 2261–2273); 28 U.S.C. 2461 note; and 42 U.S.C. 4012a(f).

SOURCE: 51 FR 21139, June 11, 1986, unless otherwise noted.

Subpart A—Rules Applicable to Formal Hearings

§ 622.1 Scope of regulations.

This subpart prescribes rules of practice and procedure in connection with any formal hearing before the Farm Credit Administration (FCA) that is required by the Farm Credit Act of 1971, as amended (Act) or is ordered for other reasons by the FCA. In connection with any particular matter, reference should also be made to any special requirements of practice and procedure that may be contained in applicable provisions of the Act or the rules adopted by the FCA in subpart B of this part, which special requirements are controlling. The rules in subpart A do not apply to the informal hearings described in subpart C of this part, to any other informal hearing that may be ordered by the FCA, or to formal investigations described in subpart D of this part.

§ 622.2 Definitions.

As used in this part:
(a) *Act* means the Farm Credit Act of 1971, as amended. 12 U.S.C. 2001, *et seq.*
(b) *FCA* means the Farm Credit Administration.
(c) *Board* means the Farm Credit Administration Board.
(d) The terms *institution in the System, System institution* and *institution* mean all institutions enumerated in section 1.2 of the Act, any institution chartered pursuant to or established by the Act, except for the Farm Credit System Assistance Board and the Farm Credit System Insurance Corporation, and any service organization chartered under part E of title IV of the Act.
(e) *Party* means the FCA or a person or institution named as a party in any notice that commences a proceeding, or any person or institution who is ad-

mitted as a party or who has filed a written request and is entitled as of right to be a party.
(f) *Presiding officer* means an administrative law judge or any FCA employee or other person designated by the Board to conduct a hearing.
(g) *Ex parte communication* means an oral or written communication not on the record with respect to which reasonable prior notice to all parties is not given. It does not include requests for status reports.

[51 FR 21139, June 11, 1986, as amended at 53 FR 27284, July 19, 1988]

§ 622.3 Appearance and practice.

(a) *Appearance before the Board or a presiding officer*—(1) *By nonattorneys.* An individual may appear in his or her own behalf; a member of a partnership may represent the partnership; a duly authorized officer or other agent of a corporation, trust association or other entity not specifically listed herein may represent the corporation, trust association, or other entity; and a duly authorized officer or employee of any government unit, agency or authority may represent that unit, agency or authority. Any person appearing in a representative capacity shall file a written notice of appearance with the Board which shall contain evidence of his or her authority to act in such capacity.

(2) *By attorneys.* A party may be represented by an attorney who is a member in good standing of the bar of the highest court of any State, possession, territory, Commonwealth or the District of Columbia, and who has not been suspended or debarred from practice before the FCA in accordance with the provisions of part 623 of this chapter. Prior to appearing, an attorney representing a person in a proceeding shall file a written notice of appearance with the Board, which shall contain a declaration that he or she is currently qualified as provided by paragraph (a)(2) of this section and is authorized to represent the party on whose behalf he or she acts.

(3) *Representation of multiple interests.* A person shall not represent more than one party without informing each party of any actual or potential conflict of interest that may be involved

Farm Credit Administration §622.6

in such representation. Such person shall file a statement with the Board indicating that such disclosure has been made. The presiding officer has authority to take protective measures at any stage of a proceeding, including the authority to prohibit multiple representation when deemed appropriate.

(b) *Summary suspension.* Dilatory, obstructionist, egregious, contemptuous, contumacious, or other unethical or improper conduct at any proceeding before the Board or a presiding officer shall be grounds for exclusion therefrom and suspension for the duration of the proceeding, or other appropriate action by the Board or presiding officer.

§622.4 Commencement of proceedings.

Proceedings under this subpart are commenced by the issuance of a notice by the Board. Such notice shall state the time, place, and nature of the hearing, the name and address of the presiding officer if one has been designated, and a statement of the matters of fact and law constituting the grounds for the hearing. The matters of fact and law alleged in a notice may be amended by the Board at any stage of the proceeding and such amended notice may require an answer from the party or parties served and may set a new hearing date. A copy of any notice served by the FCA on any System association, director, officer or other person participating in the conduct of the affairs of the association will also be sent to the supervisory bank.

§622.5 Answer.

(a) *Answer is required.* Unless a different period is specified by the Board, a party who does not wish to consent to a final order must file an answer within 20 days after being served with a notice that commences the proceeding. Any subsequent notice which contains amended allegations and by its terms requires an answer must similarly be answered within 20 days after service.

(b) *Requirements of answer; effect of failure to deny.* An answer filed under this section shall concisely state any defenses and specifically admit or deny each allegation in the notice. A party who lacks information or knowledge sufficient to form a belief as to the truth of any particular allegation shall so state and this shall have the effect of a denial. Any allegation not denied shall be deemed to be admitted. A party who intends in good faith to deny only a part of or to qualify an allegation shall specify so much of it as is true and shall deny only the remainder.

(c) *Admitted allegations.* If a party filing an answer under this section elects not to contest any of the allegations of fact set forth in the notice, the answer shall consist of a statement admitting all of the allegations to be true. Such answer constitutes a waiver of hearing as to the facts alleged in the notice, and together with the notice will provide a record basis on which the presiding officer shall file with the Board a recommended decision in accordance with 5 U.S.C. 557. The recommended decision shall be served on the party, who may file exceptions thereto within the time provided in §622.13.

(d) *Effect of failure to answer.* Failure of a party to file an answer required by this section within the time provided constitutes a waiver of the party's right to appear and contest the allegations in the notice and authorizes the presiding officer, without further notice to the party, to find the facts to be as alleged in the notice and to file with the Board a recommended decision containing such findings and appropriate conclusions. The Board or the presiding officer may, for good cause shown, permit the filing of a delayed answer after the time for filing and the answer has expired.

§622.6 Opportunity for informal settlement.

Any interested party may at any time submit to the Board for consideration written offers or proposals for settlement of a proceeding, without prejudice to the rights of the parties. No offer or proposal shall be admissible into evidence over the objection of any party in any hearing in connection with such proceeding. The foregoing provisions of this section shall not preclude settlement of any proceeding through the regular adjudicatory process by the filing of an answer as provided in §622.5(c), or by submission of the case to the presiding officer on a stipulation of facts and an agreed order.

§ 622.7 Conduct of hearings.

(a) *Authority of presiding officer.* All hearings governed by this subpart shall be conducted in accordance with the provisions of chapter 5 of title 5 of the United States Code. The presiding officer designated by the Board to preside at any such hearing shall have complete charge of the hearing, shall have the duty to conduct it in a fair and impartial manner and shall take all necessary action to avoid delay in the disposition of the proceeding. Such officer shall have all powers necessary to that end, including the following:

(1) To administer oaths and affirmations;

(2) To issue subpoenas and subpoenas duces tecum, as authorized by law, and to revoke, quash, or modify any such subpoena;

(3) To receive relevant evidence and to rule upon the admission of evidence and offers of proof;

(4) To take or cause depositions to be taken;

(5) To regulate the course of the hearing and the conduct of the parties and their counsel;

(6) To hold conferences for the settlement or simplification of issues or for any proper purpose; and

(7) To consider and rule upon, as justice may require, all procedural and other motions appropriate in a proceeding under this subpart, except that a presiding officer shall not have power to decide any motion to dismiss the proceeding or other motion which results in a final determination of the merits of the proceeding. This power rests only with the Board. Without limitation on the foregoing, the presiding officer shall, subject to the provisions of this subpart, have all the authority set forth in 5 U.S.C. 556(c).

(b) *Prehearing conference.* The presiding officer may, on his or her own initiative or at the request of any party, direct counsel for all parties to meet with him or her at a specified time and place prior to the hearing, or to submit suggestions to him or her in writing, for the purpose of considering any or all of the following:

(1) Simplification and clarification of the issues;

(2) Stipulations, admissions of fact and of the contents and authenticity of documents;

(3) Matters of which official notice will be taken; and

(4) Such other matters as may aid in the orderly disposition of the proceeding.

At the conclusion of such conference(s) the presiding officer shall enter an order which recites the results of the conference. Such order shall include the presiding officer's rulings upon matters considered at the conference, together with appropriate directions, if any, to the parties. Such order shall control the subsequent course of the proceeding, unless modified at the hearing for good cause shown.

(c) *Exchange of information.* Thirty (30) days prior to the hearing, parties shall exchange a list of the names of witnesses with a general description of their expected testimony, and a list and one copy of all documents or other physical exhibits which will be introduced in evidence in the course of the proceeding.

(d) *Attendance at hearings.* All hearings shall be private and shall be attended only by the parties, their counsel or authorized representatives, witnesses while testifying, and other persons having an official interest in the proceeding. However, if the Board, in its discretion, after fully considering the views of the party afforded the hearing, determines that a public hearing is necessary to protect the public interest, the Board may in its sole discretion order that the hearing be public.

(e) *Transcript of testimony.* Hearings shall be recorded. A copy of the transcript of the testimony taken at any hearing, duly certified by the reporter, together with all exhibits accepted into evidence shall be filed with the presiding officer. The presiding officer shall promptly serve notice upon all parties of such filing. The parties shall make their own arrangements with the person recording the testimony for copies of the testimony and exhibits. The presiding officer shall have authority to correct the record sua sponte with notice to all parties and to rule upon

Farm Credit Administration § 622.8

motions to correct the record. In the event the hearing is public, transcripts will be furnished to interested persons upon payment of the cost thereof.

(f) *Continuances and changes or extensions of time and changes of place of hearing.* Except as otherwise provided by law, the presiding officer may extend time limits prescribed by these rules or by any notice or order issued in the proceedings, may change the time for beginning any hearing, continue or adjourn a hearing from time to time, and/or change the location of the hearing. Prior to the appointment of a presiding officer and after the filing of a recommended decision pursuant to § 622.12, the Board may grant such extensions or changes. Subject to the approval of the presiding officer, the parties may by stipulation change the time limits specified by these rules or any notice or order issued hereunder.

(g) *Closing of hearing.* The record of the hearing shall be closed by an announcement to that effect by the presiding officer when the taking of evidence has been concluded. In the discretion of the presiding officer, the record may be closed as of a future date in order to permit the admission into the record, under circumstances determined by the presiding officer, of exhibits to be prepared.

(h) *Call for further evidence, oral arguments, briefs, reopening of hearing.* The presiding officer may call for the production of further evidence upon any issue, may permit oral argument and submission of briefs at the hearing and, upon appropriate notice, may reopen any hearing at any time prior to the filing of his or her recommended decision. The Board may reopen the record at anytime permitted by law.

(i) *Order of procedure.* The FCA shall open and close.

(j) *Ex parte communications.* (1) No person shall make or knowingly cause to be made an ex parte communication relevant to the merits of the proceeding to the presiding officer or anyone who is or may reasonably be expected to be involved in the decisional process.

(2) No person who is or may reasonably be expected to be involved in the decisional process shall make or knowingly cause to be made an ex parte communication relevant to the merits of the proceeding to any person.

(3) Except as authorized by law, the presiding officer shall not consult anyone on any fact in issue, unless upon notice and opportunity for all parties to participate. The presiding officer shall not be responsible to, or subject to the supervision or direction of, any officer, employee, or agent of the FCA engaged in the performance of investigative or prosecuting functions. An officer, employee or agent engaged in the performance of such functions in any case shall not, in that case or a factually related case, participate or advise in the decision of the presiding officer, except as a witness or counsel in the proceedings, or as otherwise authorized by law.

(4) If an ex parte communication is made or knowingly caused to be made, all such communications, and any responses, shall be placed in the record.

(5) Upon receipt of a communication knowingly made or caused to be made in violation of paragraph (j) of this section, the responsible party may be required to show cause why such party's claim or interest should not be dismissed, denied, or otherwise adversely affected. To the extent consistent with the interests of justice, a knowing violation of paragraph (j) of this section may be grounds for a decision adverse to a party in violation.

(6) The prohibitions against ex parte communications apply from the time a proceeding is noticed for hearing. However, when the person responsible for the communication has knowledge that the proceeding will be noticed, the prohibitions apply from the time such knowledge is acquired.

§ 622.8 **Rules of evidence.**

(a) *Evidence.* Every party shall have the right to present a case or defense by oral and documentary evidence, to submit rebuttal evidence, and to conduct such cross-examination as may be required for a full and true disclosure of the facts. Irrelevant, immaterial or unduly repetitious evidence shall be excluded.

(b) *Objections.* Objections to the admission or exclusion of evidence shall be in short form, stating the grounds of objection relied upon but no argument thereon shall be permitted, except as ordered, allowed, or requested by the presiding officer. Rulings on such objections and all other matters shall be part of the transcript. Failure to object timely to the admission or exclusion of evidence or to any ruling constitutes a waiver of such objection.

(c) *Stipulations.* Independently of the orders or rulings issued as provided by § 622.7(b), the parties may stipulate as to any relevant matters of fact or the authenticity of any relevant documents. Such stipulations may be received in evidence at the hearing, and when so received shall be binding on the parties with respect to the matters therein stipulated.

(d) *Official notice.* All matters officially noticed by the presiding officer shall appear on the record.

§ 622.9 Subpoenas.

(a) *Issuance.* The presiding officer or, in the event he or she is unavailable, the Board may issue subpoenas and subpoena duces tecum at the request of any party requiring the attendance of witnesses or the production of documents at a designated place. The person seeking the subpoena may be required, as a condition precedent to the issuance of the subpoena, to show the general relevance and reasonable scope of the testimony or other evidence sought. Where it appears to the presiding officer that a subpoena may be unreasonable, oppressive, excessive in scope, unduly burdensome, or delay the proceeding, the presiding officer has discretion to refuse to issue a subpoena or to issue it only upon such conditions as fairness requires.

(b) *Motions to quash.* Any person to whom a subpoena is directed may, prior to the time specified therein for compliance but in no event more than 10 days after the date the subpoena was served, with notice to the party requesting the subpoena, apply to the presiding officer, or in the event he or she is unavailable to the Board, to quash or modify the subpoena, accompanying such application with a brief statement of the reasons therefor. The presiding officer may deny the application or, upon notice to the party on whose behalf the subpoena was issued and after affording that party an opportunity to reply, may quash or modify the subpoena or impose reasonable conditions including, in the case of a subpoena duces tecum, a requirement that the party on whose behalf the subpoena was issued pay in advance the reasonable cost of copying and transporting the documentary evidence to the designated place.

(c) *Service of subpoena.* A subpoena may be served upon the person named therein by personal service or certified mail with a return receipt to the last known address of the person. The fees for one day's attendance and mileage as specified in paragraph (d) of this section must be tendered at the time of service unless the subpoena is issued on behalf of the FCA. If personal service is made by a U.S. marshal, a deputy U.S. marshal, or an employee of the FCA, such service shall be evidenced by the return thereon. If personal service is made by any other person, such person shall sign an affidavit describing the manner in which service is made, and return such affidavit with a copy of the subpoena. In case of failure to make service, reasons for the failure shall be stated on the original subpoena. The original or a copy of the subpoena, bearing or accompanied by the required return, affidavit, statement or return receipt, shall be returned without delay to the presiding officer.

(d) *Attendance of witnesses.* The attendance of witnesses at a designated place may be required from any place in any State or territory subject to the jurisdiction of the United States. Witnesses who are subpoenaed shall be paid the same fees and mileage that are paid witnesses in the district courts of the United States. Fees required by this paragraph shall be paid by the party upon whose application the subpoena is issued.

(e) *Production of documents.* The production of documents at a designated place may be required from any place in any State or territory subject to the jurisdiction of the United States. In lieu of an original document, a certified or authenticated copy may be produced. However, any party has the right to inspect the original document.

Farm Credit Administration

§ 622.10 Depositions.

(a) *Application to take deposition.* Any party desiring to take the deposition of any person shall make written application to the presiding officer setting forth the name and address of the witness, the subject matter concerning which the witness is expected to testify, its relevance, the time and place of the deposition, and the reasons why such deposition should be taken. The application may include a request that specified documents be produced at the deposition. A copy of the application shall be served on the other parties at the same time the application is filed with the presiding officer.

(b) *Subpoena; notice to other parties.* Upon a showing that the testimony or other evidence sought will be material, and the taking of the deposition will not result in any undue burden to the witness or any party or undue delay of the proceedings, the presiding officer may issue a subpoena or subpoena duces tecum. Notice of the issuance of such subpoena shall be served upon all parties at least 10 days in advance of the date set for deposition.

(c) *Deposition by notice.* The requirements of paragraphs (a) and (b) of this section may be waived by agreement of the parties and the witness whose testimony or documentary evidence is sought. Such agreement shall be embodied in a stipulation which becomes part of the record and may provide for the taking of depositions upon notice without leave of the presiding officer.

(d) *Procedure on deposition.* Depositions may be taken before any person having the power to administer oaths. Each witness whose testimony is taken by deposition shall be duly sworn before any question is propounded. Examination and cross-examination of deponents may proceed as permitted at the hearing. Objections to questions or documents shall be in short form, stating the grounds relief upon for the objection. Failure to object to questions or evidence is deemed a waiver if the ground of the objection is one which might have been obviated or removed if presented at that time. The questions propounded and the answers thereto, together with all objections made (but not including argument or debate) shall be recorded by or under the direction of the person before whom the deposition is taken. The deposition shall be signed by the witness, unless the parties by stipulation waive the signing or the witness is physically unable to sign, cannot be found, or refuses to sign. The deposition shall also be certified as a true and complete transcript by the person recording the testimony. If the deposition is not signed by the witness, the person recording the testimony shall state this fact and the reason therefor on the record. The person before whom the deposition is taken shall promptly file the transcript and all exhibits with the presiding officer. Interested parties shall make their own arrangements with the person recording the testimony for copies of the testimony and exhibits.

(e) *Introduction as evidence.* Subject to appropriate rulings by the presiding officer on such objections and answers as were noted at the time the deposition was taken or as would be valid were the witness personally present and testifying at the hearing, the deposition or any part thereof may be received in evidence by the presiding officer in his or her discretion. Only such part of a deposition as is received in evidence at a hearing shall constitute a part of the record upon which a decision may be based.

(f) *Payment of fees.* Deponents whose depositions are taken and the reporter taking the same shall be entitled to the same fees as are paid for like services in the district courts of the United States, which fees shall be paid by the party upon whose application the deposition is taken.

§ 622.11 Motions.

(a) *How made.* An application or request for an order or ruling not otherwise specifically provided for in this subpart, unless made during a hearing, shall be made by written motion supported by a memorandum which concisely states the grounds therefor.

(b) *Opposition.* Within 10 days after service of any written motion, or within such other period of time as may be fixed by the presiding officer, any party may file a memorandum in opposition thereto. The moving party has no right to reply except as permitted by the presiding officer. The presiding

§ 622.12

officer has discretion to waive the requirements of this section as to motions for extension of time and may rule upon such motions ex parte.

(c) *Oral argument.* No oral argument will be heard on motions except as otherwise directed by the presiding officer or the Board.

(d) *Rulings and orders.* Except as otherwise provided in this subpart, the presiding officer shall rule on all motions and may issue appropriate orders, except that motions may be referred to the Board if the presiding officer is unavailable or determines that such motion should be referred to the Board. Prior to the appointment of a presiding officer and after a recommended decision is filed pursuant to § 622.12, the Board shall rule on motions filed by the parties.

(e) *Appeal from rulings on motions.* All answers, motions, objections and rulings shall become part of the record. Rulings of a presiding officer on any motion may not be appealed to the Board prior to its consideration of the presiding officer's recommended decision, except by special permission of the Board. However, such rulings shall be considered by the Board in reviewing the record. Requests to the Board for special permission to appeal from a ruling of the presiding officer shall be filed in writing within 5 days of the ruling, and shall briefly state the grounds relied on. The moving party shall immediately serve a copy thereof on every other party to the proceeding who may then respond to such request within 5 days after service.

(f) *Continuation of hearing.* Unless otherwise ordered by the presiding officer or the Board, the hearing shall continue pending the determination of any request or motion by the Board.

§ 622.12 Proposed findings and conclusions; recommended decision.

(a) *Proposed findings and conclusions by parties.* Within 30 days after the hearing transcript has been filed, any party may file proposed findings of fact and conclusions of law. Such proposals shall be supported by citation of such statutes, decisions, and other authorities, and by specific page references to such portions of the record as may be relevant. All such proposals shall become a part of the record.

(b) *Recommended decision by presiding officer.* Within 30 days after the expiration of time allowed under paragraph (a) of this section, or within such further time as the Board for good cause allows, the presiding officer shall file the entire hearing record, including a recommended decision and findings and conclusions, the transcript, exhibits (including on request of any of the parties any exhibits excluded from evidence or tender of proof), exceptions, rulings and all briefs and memoranda filed in connection with the hearing. Promptly upon such filing, the presiding officer shall serve a copy of the recommended decision, findings and conclusions upon each party to the proceeding.

(c) *Board as presiding officer.* In proceedings in which the Board or one or more of its members has presided at the reception of evidence, the presiding officer's recommended decision, findings of fact, and conclusions of law will be omitted. In such proceedings the proposed findings and conclusions, briefs, and other submissions permitted under paragraph (a) of this section shall be filed with the Board for consideration.

§ 622.13 Exceptions.

(a) *Filing.* Within 15 days after service of the recommended decision of the presiding officer, any party may file exceptions thereto or to any portion thereof, or to the failure of the presiding officer to make any recommendation, finding, or conclusion, or to the admission or exclusion of evidence, or to any other ruling of the presiding officer.

(b) *Contents.* Each exception shall be supported by a concise argument and by citation of such statutes, decisions and other authorities, and by page references to such portions of the record as may be relevant. If the exception relates to the admission or exclusion of evidence, the substance of the evidence admitted or excluded shall be set forth in the brief with appropriate references to the transcript.

(c) *Waiver.* Failure of a party to file exceptions to those matters specified in paragraph (a) of this section within

Farm Credit Administration

§ 622.19

the time prescribed shall be a waiver of objection thereto.

§ 622.14 Briefs.

(a) *Contents.* Any brief filed in a proceeding shall be confined to the particular matters in issue, citing statutes, decisions, and other authorities, and page references to such portions of the record or the recommended decision of the presiding officer as may be relevant.

(b) *Reply briefs.* Reply briefs may be filed within 10 days after service of original briefs of opposing parties, and shall be confined to matters in such briefs. Further briefs may be filed only with permission of the presiding officer or the Board with respect to a matter before the Board.

(c) *Delayed filing.* Briefs not filed on or before the time fixed in this subpart or by the presiding officer will be received only upon special permission of the Board.

§ 622.15 Oral argument before the Board.

Upon its own initiative or upon written request by any party, the Board, in its discretion, may order the matter to be set down for oral argument before the Board or one or more members thereof. Any request for oral argument by a party filing exceptions shall be made within the time prescribed for filing such exceptions, or by any other party, within the time prescribed for the filing of a reply brief. Oral argument before the Board shall be recorded unless otherwise ordered by the Board.

§ 622.16 Notice of submission to the Board.

Upon the filing of the record with the Board, and upon the expiration of the time for the filing of exceptions and all briefs, including reply briefs or any further briefs permitted by the presiding officer or the Board, and upon the hearing of oral argument by the Board, if ordered by the Board, the Board shall notify the parties in writing that the case has been submitted for final decision.

§ 622.17 Decision of the Board.

Any person who has not engaged in the performance of investigative or prosecuting functions in the case, or in a factually related case, may advise and assist the Board in the consideration of the case. Copies of the decision and order of the Board shall be served upon the parties. A copy of the order will also be sent to the supervisory bank if the order relates to a System association, director, officer, or other person participating in the conduct of the affairs of the association.

§ 622.18 Filing.

(a) *Filing.* Papers required or permitted to be filed with the Board shall be filed with the Chairman of the Board, FCA, 1501 Farm Credit Drive, McLean, VA 22102–5090 or with the person designated to receive papers for the agency in a proceeding. Papers sent by mail must be postmarked or received within the prescribed time limit for filing. Papers sent by any other means must be received within the prescribed time limit for filing.

(b) *Formal requirements.* All filed papers shall be printed, typewritten, or otherwise reproduced, and copies shall be clear and legible. The original of all papers filed by a party shall be signed and dated as of the date of execution by the party filing the same, or a duly authorized agent or attorney. The signer's address and telephone number must appear on the original. Counsel for the FCA shall sign the original of all papers filed on behalf of the FCA. All papers filed must name in the heading or on a title page, the parties, the docket number and the subject of the papers.

(c) *Copies.* Parties shall file an original and three copies of all documents and papers required or permitted to be filed under this subpart (except the transcript of testimony and exhibits), unless otherwise specifically provided by the Board.

§ 622.19 Service.

(a) *Service.* Except as otherwise provided in these rules, each party who files papers is responsible for serving a copy thereof upon the presiding officer and upon every other party or the attorney or representative of record of

§ 622.20

that party. A copy of all papers filed by the presiding officer or the Board, except for the transcript of testimony and exhibits, shall be served upon each of the parties. Service may be by personal service, private delivery service, or by express, certified or regular first-class mail. If a party is not represented, service shall be made at the last known address of the party or an officer thereof as shown on the records of the FCA.

(b) *Proof of service.* Proof of service of papers filed by a party shall be filed before action is to be taken thereon. The proof shall show the date and manner of service, and may be by written acknowledgment of service, by declaration of the person making service, or by certificate of an attorney or other representative of record. Failure to make proof of service shall not affect the validity of service. The presiding officer may allow the proof to be amended or supplied, unless to do so would result in material prejudice to a party.

§ 622.20 Documents in proceedings confidential.

Unless otherwise ordered by the Board or required by law, the entire record in any proceeding under this subpart, including the notice of hearing, transcript, exhibits, proposed findings and conclusions, recommended decision of the presiding officer, exceptions thereto, decision and order of the Board, and any other papers which are filed in connection with the proceeding shall not be made public, and shall be for the confidential use only of the FCA and its staff, the presiding officer, the parties, and other appropriate supervisory authorities.

§ 622.21 Computing time.

(a) *General rule.* In computing any period of time prescribed or allowed by this subpart, the date of the act or event from which the designated period of time begins to run is not to be included. The last day so computed shall be included, unless it is a Saturday, Sunday or Federal holiday, in which event the period shall run until the end of the next day which is not a Saturday, Sunday, or Federal holiday. When the period of time prescribed or allowed is 10 days or less, intermediate Saturdays, Sundays, and Federal holidays shall not be included in the computation.

(b) *Service by mail.* Whenever any party has the right or is required to do some act within the period of time prescribed in this subpart after the service upon the party of any document or other paper of any kind, and such service is made by mail, three days shall be added to the prescribed period from the date when the matter served is deposited in the United States mail.

§ 622.22 Retained authority.

Nothing is this part is in derogation of powers of examination and investigation conferred on the FCA by any provision of law.

§§ 622.23–622.50 [Reserved]

Subpart B—Rules and Procedures for Assessment and Collection of Civil Money Penalties

SOURCE: 53 FR 27284, July 19, 1988, unless otherwise noted.

§ 622.51 Definitions.

Unless noted otherwise, the definitions set forth in § 622.2 of subpart A shall apply to this subpart.

§ 622.52 Purpose and scope.

The rules and procedures specified in this subpart and in subpart A are applicable to proceedings by the FCA to assess and collect civil money penalties:

(a) For violations of the terms of a final cease and desist order issued under section 5.25 or 5.26 of the Act;

(b) For violations of any provision of the Act or any regulation issued under the Act; or

(c) For violations of the National Flood Insurance Reform Act (Reform Act) as set forth in 42 U.S.C. 4012a(f) or any regulation issued under the Reform Act.

[51 FR 21139, June 11, 1986, as amended at 70 FR 12584, Mar. 15, 2005]

Farm Credit Administration

§§ 622.53–622.54 [Reserved]

§ 622.55 Notice of assessment of civil money penalty.

(a) *Notice of assessment.* The notice of assessment for a civil money penalty will state:

(1) The legal authority for the assessment;

(2) The amount of the civil money penalty being assessed;

(3) The date by which the civil money penalty must be paid;

(4) The matter of fact or law constituting the grounds for assessment of the civil money penalty;

(5) The right of the institution or person being assessed to a formal hearing to challenge the assessment;

(6) That failure to request a hearing constitutes a waiver of the opportunity for a hearing and the notice of assessment will constitute a final and unappealable order; and

(7) The time limit to request such a formal hearing.

(b) *Service.* The notice of assessment may be served upon the institution or person being assessed by personal service or by certified mail with a return receipt to the institution's or the person's last known address. Such service constitutes issuance of the notice.

[51 FR 21139, June 11, 1986, as amended at 70 FR 12585, Mar. 15, 2005]

§ 622.56 Request for formal hearing on assessment.

An institution or person being assessed may request a formal hearing to challenge the assessment of a civil money penalty. The request must be filed in writing, within 10 days of the issuance of the notice of assessment, with the Chairman of the Board, FCA, 1501 Farm Credit Drive, McLean, VA 22102–5090.

§ 622.57 Waiver of hearing; consent.

(a) *Waiver.* Failure to request a hearing pursuant to § 622.56 constitutes a waiver of the opportunity for a hearing and the notice of assessment issued pursuant to § 622.55 will constitute a final and unappealable order.

(b) *Consent.* Any party afforded a hearing who does not appear at the hearing personally or by a duly authorized representative is deemed to have consented to the issuance of an assessment order.

[51 FR 21139, June 11, 1986, as amended at 70 FR 12585, Mar. 15, 2005]

§ 622.58 Hearing on assessment.

(a) *Time and place.* An institution or person requesting a hearing will be informed by order of the Board of the time and place set for hearing.

(b) *Answer; procedures.* The hearing order may require the institution or person requesting the hearing to file an answer as prescribed in § 622.5 of subpart A. The procedures of the Administrative Procedure Act (5 U.S.C. 554–557) and subpart A of these rules will apply to the hearing.

[51 FR 21139, June 11, 1986, as amended at 70 FR 12585, Mar. 15, 2005]

§ 622.59 Assessment order.

(a) *Consent.* In the event of consent of the parties concerned to an assessment, or if, upon the record made at a hearing ordered under this subpart, the Board finds that the grounds for having assessed the penalty have been established, the Board may issue an order of assessment of civil money penalty. In its assessment order, the Board may reduce the amount of the penalty specified in the notice of assessment.

(b) *Effective date and period.* An assessment order is effective immediately upon issuance, or upon such other date as may be specified therein, and will remain effective and enforceable unless it is stayed, modified, terminated, or set aside by action of the board or a reviewing court.

(c) *Service.* An assessment order may be served by personal service or by certified mail with a return receipt to the last known address of the institution or person being assessed. Such service constitutes issuance of the order.

[51 FR 21139, June 11, 1986, as amended at 70 FR 12585, Mar. 15, 2005]

§ 622.60 Payment of civil money penalty.

(a) *Payment date.* Generally, the date designated in the notice of assessment for payment of the civil money penalty will be 60 days from the issuance of the notice. If, however, the Board finds, in a specific case, that the purposes of the

§ 622.61

relevant statutes would be better served if the 60-day period were changed, the Board may shorten or lengthen the period or make the civil money penalty payable immediately upon receipt of the notice of assessment. If a timely request for a formal hearing to challenge an assessment of a civil money penalty is filed, payment of the penalty will not be required unless and until the Board issues a final order of assessment following the hearing. If an assessment order is issued, it will specify the date by which the civil money penalty is to be paid or collected.

(b) *Method of payment.* Checks in payment of civil money penalties must be made payable to the "Farm Credit Administration." Upon collection, the FCA will forward payment for penalties described in § 622.52(a) and (b) to the United States Department of Treasury. The FCA will forward payment for penalties described in § 622.52(c) to the National Flood Mitigation Fund as required by 42 U.S.C. 4012a(f)(8).

[70 FR 12585, Mar. 15, 2005]

§ 622.61 Adjustment of civil money penalties by the rate of inflation under the Federal Civil Penalties Inflation Adjustment Act of 1990, as amended.

(a) The maximum amount of each civil money penalty within FCA's jurisdiction is adjusted in accordance with the Federal Civil Penalties Inflation Adjustment Act of 1990, as amended (28 U.S.C. 2461 note), as follows:

(1) Amount of civil money penalty imposed under section 5.32 of the Act for violation of a final order issued under section 5.25 or 5.26 of the Act: The maximum daily amount is $1,100.

(2) Amount of civil money penalty for violation of the Act or regulations: The maximum daily amount is $550 for each violation that occurs before March 16, 2005, $650 for each violation that occurs on or after March 16, 2005, but before January 16, 2009, and $750 for each violation that occurs on or after January 16, 2009.

(b) The maximum civil money penalty amount assessed under 42 U.S.C. 4012a(f) is $350 for each violation that occurs before March 16, 2005, with total

12 CFR Ch. VI (1–1–12 Edition)

penalties under such statute not to exceed $110,000 for any single institution during any calendar year. For violations that occur on or after March 16, 2005, but before January 16, 2009, the maximum civil money penalty is $385 for each violation, with total penalties under such statute not to exceed $110,000 for any single institution during any calendar year. For violations that occur on or after January 16, 2009, the maximum civil money penalty is $385 for each violation, with total penalties under such statute not to exceed $120,000 for any single institution during any calendar year.

[74 FR 2341, Jan. 15, 2009]

§§ 622.62–622.75 [Reserved]

Subpart C—Rules and Procedures Applicable to Suspension or Removal of an Individual Where Certain Crimes Are Charged or Proven

§ 622.76 Definitions.

Unless noted otherwise, the definitions set forth in § 622.2 of subpart A shall apply to this subpart.

§ 622.77 Purpose and scope.

The rules and procedures set forth in this subpart apply to informal hearings afforded to any officer, director, or other person participating in the conduct of the affairs of a System institution who has been suspended or removed from office or prohibited from further participation in any manner in the conduct of the institution's affairs by a notice or order issued by the Board upon the grounds set forth in section 5.29 of the Act.

§ 622.78 Suspension, prohibition or removal.

(a) *Content.* The Board may serve a notice of suspension or prohibition or order of removal upon a director, officer or other person participating in the conduct of the affairs of an institution. A copy of such notice or order shall also be served upon the institution, whereupon the individual concerned shall immediately cease service to the institution or participation in the affairs of the institution. Any notice or

Farm Credit Administration § 622.80

order shall indicate the basis for the suspension, prohibition, or removal and shall inform the individual of the right to request in writing, within 30 days of being served with such notice or order, an opportunity to show at an informal hearing that continued service to or participation in the conduct of the affairs of the institution does not, or is not likely to, pose a threat to the interests of the institution's shareholders or the investors in Farm Credit System obligations or threaten to impair public confidence in the institution or the Farm Credit System.

(b) *Service.* A notice or order of suspension, removal or prohibition may be served by personal service or by certified mail with a return receipt to the last known address of the person being served.

§ 622.79 Petition for informal hearing.

(a) *Filing.* To obtain a hearing, the subject individual must file an original and three copies of a petition with the Board within 30 days of being served with the notice or order.

(b) *Content.* The petition shall:

(1) State whether the petitioner is requesting termination or modification of the notice or order;

(2) State with particularity how the petitioner intends to show that his or her continued service to or participation in the conduct of the affairs of the institution would not, or is not likely to, pose a threat to the interests of the institution's shareholders or the investors in Farm Credit System obligations or threaten to impair public confidence in the institution or the Farm Credit System;

(3) Include a request to present oral testimony or witnesses at the hearing, if the petitioner desires to do so. The request should specify the names of the witnesses and a summary of their expected testimony; and

(4) Indicate whether the petitioner desires oral argument or elects to have the matter determined solely on the basis of written submissions.

§ 622.80 Informal hearing.

(a) *Time and place.* Upon receipt of a timely petition for a hearing, the Board shall notify the petitioner of the time and place fixed for the hearing and shall designate one or more Board members or FCA employees to preside ("designated FCA representative"). The hearing shall be scheduled to be held no later than 30 days from the date a petition for hearing is received unless the time is extended at the request of the petitioner. Notice of the hearing shall also be sent to the FCA's Office of General Counsel.

(b) *Appearance.* A petitioner may appear personally or through counsel to submit relevant written materials and oral argument. An attorney is subject to all the requirements and limitations imposed on attorneys in § 622.3 of subpart A. A representative(s) of the FCA's Office of General Counsel may participate in the hearing to the extent such representative deems appropriate.

(c) *Written material.* Any written material the petitioner wishes to have considered must be submitted to the designated FCA representative and the FCA's Office of General Counsel at least 10 days prior to the date of the hearing.

(d) *Oral testimony.* Oral testimony may be presented only if expressly permitted by the Board in the notice of hearing. The designated FCA representative may ask questions of any witness.

(e) *Transcripts.* Oral testimony, if any, and oral argument shall be recorded. A copy of the transcript shall be filed with the designated FCA representative, who shall have authority to correct the record sua sponte upon notice, or upon the motion of the petitioner or the representative of the FCA's Office of General Counsel. The designated FCA representative shall promptly serve notice upon the petitioner and the FCA's Office of General Counsel of such filing. Such parties shall make arrangements with the person recording the testimony or argument for copies of the transcript.

(f) *Closing of record.* Upon the request of the petitioner or representative of the FCA's Office of General Counsel, the record shall remain open for a period of 5 business days following the hearing, during which time additional submissions for the record may be made. Thereafter, the record shall be closed.

(g) *Rules of evidence and procedure.* Neither the formal rules of evidence nor the adjudicative procedures of the Administrative Procedure Act (5 U.S.C. 554–557) or subpart A of these rules shall apply to the informal hearing ordered under this subpart unless the Board orders that they apply in whole or in part.

§ 622.81 Default.

If the subject individual fails to file a petition for a hearing, or fails to appear at a hearing, either in person or by an attorney, or fails to submit a written argument where oral argument has been waived, the notice shall remain in effect until the information, indictment, or complaint is finally disposed of and the order shall remain in effect until terminated by the Board.

§ 622.82 Decision of the Board.

(a) *Recommended decision.* Within 30 days of the hearing, the designated FCA representative shall make a recommendation with findings and conclusions to the Board concerning the notice or order of suspension, removal, or prohibition.

(b) *Final decision.* Within 60 days of the hearing, the Board shall notify the subject individual and the FCA's Office of General Counsel whether the suspension or removal from office, or prohibition from participation in any manner in the affairs of the institution, will be continued, terminated, or otherwise modified. The Board's final decision, if adverse to the individual, shall contain a statement of the basis thereof. The Board may satisfy this requirement where it adopts the recommended decision of the designated FCA representative.

(c) *Guilt not an issue.* In deciding upon any suspension of prohibition by notice, the ultimate question of the guilt or innocence of the individual with respect to the criminal charge that is outstanding will not be considered. A finding of not guilty or other disposition of the charge shall not preclude the Board from thereafter instituting removal proceedings pursuant to section 5.28 of the Act.

(d) *Effective period.* A removal or prohibition by order remains in effect until terminated by the Board. A suspension or prohibition by notice remains in effect until the criminal charge is finally disposed of or until terminated by the Board.

(e) *Reconsideration.* A suspended or removed individual may petition the Board to reconsider the decision any time after the expiration of a 12-month period from the date of the decision, but no petition for reconsideration may be made within 12 months of a previous petition. A petition shall state with particularity the relief sought and the grounds therefor and may be accompanied by a supporting memorandum and any other documentation the petitioner wishes to have considered. No hearing need be granted on the petition for reconsideration.

§§ 622.83–622.100 [Reserved]

Subpart D—Rules and Procedures Applicable to Formal Investigations

§ 622.101 Definitions.

Unless noted otherwise, the definitions set forth in § 622.2 of subpart A shall apply to this subpart.

§ 622.102 Scope.

The rules in this subpart apply to formal investigations initiated by order of the Board and pertain to the exercise of powers specified in section 5.37 of the Act. These rules do not restrict or in any way affect the authority of the FCA, including but not limited to the powers enumerated in section 5.37 of the Act, to conduct examinations of System institutions.

§ 622.103 Formal investigations are confidential.

Information or documents obtained or testimony recorded in the course of a formal investigation shall be confidential and shall be disclosed only in accordance with the provisions of 12 CFR part 602.

§ 622.104 Order to conduct formal investigation.

A formal investigation begins with the issuance of an order by the Board. The order shall designate the person or persons who will conduct the investigation, issue, revoke, quash or modify subpoenas and subpoenas duces tecum, take or cause to be taken depositions, administer oaths, and receive affirmations as to any matter under investigation by the FCA. Upon application and for good cause shown, the Board may limit, modify, or withdraw the order at any stage of the proceeding.

§ 622.105   Conduct of investigation.

(a) *Review of order.* Any person who is compelled or requested to furnish testimony, documentary evidence, or other information with respect to any matter under formal investigation shall upon request be shown the order initiating such investigation.

(b) *Right to counsel.* Any person who, in a formal investigation, is compelled to appear and testify or who appears and testifies by request or permission of the Board may be accompanied, represented, and advised by counsel. The right to be accompanied, represented, and advised by counsel shall mean the right of a person testifying to have an attorney present at all times while testifying and to have this attorney:

(1) Advise such person before, during and after the conclusion of testimony;

(2) Question such person briefly at the conclusion of testimony to clarify any of the answers given; and

(3) Make summary notes during the testimony solely for the use of such person.

(c) *Appearance.* The provisions of § 622.3 are applicable to this subpart.

(d) *Exclusion.* (1) Any person who has given or will give testimony, and counsel representing such person, may be excluded from the taking of testimony of any other witness in the discretion of the designated FCA representative conducting the investigation.

(2) The designated FCA representative conducting the investigation shall report to the Board any instances where any person has been guilty of dilatory, obstructionist, egregious, contemptuous, contumacious or other unethical or improper conduct during the course of the proceeding or any other instance involving a violation of these rules. The Board may thereupon take such action as the circumstances may warrant, including exclusion of the offending individual or individual from participation in the proceeding.

§ 622.106   Service of subpoena and payment of witness fees.

(a) *Service.* A subpoena may be served upon the person named therein by personal service or certified mail with a return receipt to the last known address of the person. Witnesses who are subpoenaed shall be paid the same fees and mileage that are paid witnesses in the district courts of the United States. The fees and mileage need not be tendered at the time a subpoena is served.

(b) *Motions to quash.* Any person to whom a subpoena is directed may, prior to the time specified therein for compliance, but in no event more than 5 days after the date of service of such subpoena, apply to the FCA representative authorized in the order, or if unavailable to the Board, to quash or modify such subpoena, accompanying such application with a brief statement of the reasons therefor. The FCA representative, or the Board, may:

(1) Deny the application;

(2) Quash or revoke the subpoena;

(3) Modify the subpoena; or

(4) Condition the granting of the application on such terms as the FCA representative or the Board, determines in his, her, or its discretion, to be just, reasonable, and proper.

§ 622.107   Transcripts.

Transcripts, if any, of an investigative proceeding shall be recorded by any means authorized by the designated FCA representative conducting the investigation. A person who has given testimony in an investigative proceeding (or counsel for such person) upon proper identification shall have the right to inspect the transcript of the person's testimony but may not obtain a copy if the FCA's representative conducting the investigation has cause to believe that the contents should not be disclosed.

PART 623—PRACTICE BEFORE THE FARM CREDIT ADMINISTRATION

Sec.
623.1   Scope of part.
623.2   Definitions.

§ 623.1

623.3 Who may practice.
623.4 Suspension and debarment.
623.5 Reinstatement.
623.6 Duty to file information concerning adverse judicial or administrative action.
623.7 Proceeding under this part.

AUTHORITY: Secs. 5.9, 5.10, 5.17, 5.25–5.37; 12 U.S.C. 2243, 2244, 2252, 2261–2273.

SOURCE: 51 FR 21147, June 11, 1986, unless otherwise noted.

§ 623.1 Scope of part.

This part prescribes rules with regard to persons who may practice before the Farm Credit Administration and the circumstances under which attorneys, accountants, appraisers, or other persons may be suspended or debarred, either temporarily or permanently, from practicing before the Farm Credit Administration. In connection with any particular matter, reference also should be made to any special requirements of procedure and practice that may be contained in the particular statute involved or the rules and forms adopted by the Farm Credit Administration thereunder, which special requirements are controlling. In addition to any suspension hereunder, a person may be excluded from further participation in a particular adjudicative proceeding in accordance with § 622.3 or in a formal investigation in accordance with § 622.105.

§ 623.2 Definitions.

As used in this part:

(a) *FCA* means the Farm Credit Administration.

(b) *Board* means the Farm Credit Administration Board.

(c) *Act* means the Farm Credit Act of 1971, as amended. 12 U.S.C. 2001, et seq.

(d) The terms *institution in the System*, *System institution* and *institution* mean all institutions enumerated in section 1.2 of the Act, any institution chartered pursuant to or established by the Act, except for the Farm Credit System Assistance Board and the Farm Credit System Insurance Corporation and any service organization chartered under part E of title IV of the Act.

(e) The term *presiding officer* includes the Board, one or more members thereof, FCA employees, or an administrative law judge. As used in this part, the term shall be construed to refer to whichever of the above-identified individuals presides at a hearing or other proceeding, except as otherwise specified in the text;

(f) The term *attorney* means any person who is a member in good standing of the bar of the highest court of any State, possession, territory, Commonwealth or the District of Columbia;

(g) The term *practice* means transacting any business with the FCA, including but not limited to:

(1) The representation of another person at any adjudicatory, investigatory, removal or rulemaking proceeding conducted before the FCA or a presiding officer;

(2) The preparation or certification of any statement, opinion, report of financial condition and performance, financial statement, appraisal report, audit report, or other document or report by any attorney, accountant, appraiser or other person which is filed with or submitted to the FCA, with such person's consent or knowledge in connection with any filing with the FCA;

(3) A presentation to the FCA or a presiding officer at a conference or meeting relating to an institution's or person's rights, privileges or liabilities under the laws administered by the FCA and rules and regulations promulgated thereunder;

(4) Any business correspondence or communication with the FCA or a presiding officer; and

(5) The transaction of any other business with the FCA on behalf of another, in the capacity of an attorney, accountant, appraiser, licensed expert or any other capacity.

[51 FR 21147, June 11, 1986, as amended at 53 FR 27285, July 19, 1988]

§ 623.3 Who may practice.

(a) *By nonattorneys.* (1) An individual may appear on his or her own behalf; a member of a partnership may represent the partnership; a bona fide and duly authorized officer or other designated representative of a corporation, trust, association or other entity not specifically listed herein may represent the corporation, trust, association or other entity; and an authorized officer or other designated representative of any

Farm Credit Administration § 623.4

government unit, agency or authority may represent that unit, agency or authority.

(2) Any accountant, appraiser or licensed expert may practice before the FCA in a professional capacity.

(b) *By attorneys.* Any entity noted in paragraph (a) of this section may be represented in any proceeding or other matter before the FCA by an attorney.

(c) Any person transacting business with the FCA in a representative capacity may be required to show evidence of his or her authority to act in such capacity and certification of credentials.

§ 623.4 Suspension and debarment.

(a) *Grounds.* The Board may censure any person practicing before the FCA or may deny, temporarily or permanently, the privilege of any person to practice before the FCA if such person is found by the Board, after notice of and opportunity for hearing in the matter:

(1) Not to possess the requisite qualifications to represent others;

(2) To be lacking in character or professional integrity;

(3) To have engaged in any dilatory, obstructionist, egregious, contemptuous, contumacious or other unethical or improper conduct before FCA; or

(4) To have willfully violated, or willfully aided and abetted the violation of, any provision of the laws administered by the FCA or the rules and regulations promulgated thereunder.

(b) *Automatic suspension.* (1) Any person who, after being licensed as a professional or expert by any competent authority, has been convicted by a Federal or State court of a felony, or of a misdemeanor involving moral turpitude, personal dishonesty or breach of trust, shall be suspended automatically from practicing before the FCA without a hearing.

(2) Any accountant, appraiser or licensed expert whose license to practice has been revoked in any State, possession, territory, Commonwealth or the District of Columbia, or who has been suspended or otherwise barred from practice before any Federal or State regulatory authority, shall be suspended automatically from practicing before the FCA without a hearing.

(3) Any attorney who has been suspended or disbarred by a court of the United States or in any State, possession, territory, Commonwealth or the District of Columbia, shall be suspended automatically from practicing before the FCA without a hearing.

(4) A conviction (including a judgment or order on a plea of nolo contendere), revocation, suspension or disbarment under paragraphs (b)(1), (2) and (3) of this section shall be deemed to have occurred when the convicting, revoking, suspending or disbarring agency or tribunal enters its judgment or order, regardless of whether an appeal is pending or could be taken.

(5) For purposes of this section, it shall be irrelevant that any attorney, accountant, appraiser or licensed expert who has been suspended, disbarred or otherwise disqualified from practice before a court, regulatory authority, or in a jurisdiction continues in professional good standing before other courts, regulatory authorities, or in other jurisdictions.

(c) *Temporary suspension.* (1) The Board, with due regard to the public interest and without preliminary hearing, by order, may temporarily suspend any person from appearing or practicing before it who by name, has been:

(i) Permanently enjoined (whether by consent, default or summary judgment or after trial) by any court of competent jurisdiction or by the Board in a final administrative order, by reason of his or her misconduct in any action brought by the FCA based upon violations of, or aiding and abetting the violation of any provision of any law that is administered by the FCA or of any rule or regulation promulgated thereunder; or

(ii) Found by any court of competent jurisdiction (whether by consent, default, upon summary judgment or after hearing) or in any administrative proceeding in which the FCA is a complainant and he or she is a party, to have willfully committed, caused, aided or abetted a violation of any provision of any law that is administered by the FCA, or of any rule or regulation promulgated thereunder.

(2) An order of temporary suspension shall become effective when served by

§ 623.5

certified mail with a return receipt directed to the last known business or residential address of the person involved. No order of temporary suspension shall be entered by the Board pursuant to paragraph (c)(1) of this section more than 3 months after the final judgment or order entered in a judicial or administrative proceeding described in paragraph (c)(1) (i) or (ii) of this section has become effective and all review or appeal procedures have been completed or are no longer available.

(3) Any person temporarily suspended from appearing and practicing before the FCA in accordance with paragraph (c)(1) of this section may, within 30 days after service of the order of temporary suspension, petition the Board to lift such suspension. If no petition is received by the Board within 30 days, the suspension shall become permanent.

(4) Within 30 days after the filing of a petition in accordance with paragraph (c)(3) of this section, the Board shall either lift the temporary suspension or set the matter down for hearing at a time and place to be designated by the Board, or both. After opportunity for hearing, the Board may censure the petitioner or may suspend the petitioner from appearing or practicing before the FCA temporarily or permanently. In any case in which the temporary suspension has not been lifted, the hearing and any other action taken pursuant to this paragraph shall be expedited by the Board in order to ensure the petitioner's right to address the allegations.

(5) In any hearing held on a petition filed in accordance with paragraph (c)(3) of this section, a showing that the petitioner has been enjoined or has been found to have committed, caused, aided or abetted violations as described in paragraph (c)(1) of this section, without more, may be a basis for suspension or debarment; that showing having been made, the burden shall then be on the petitioner to show why the petitioner should not be censured or be temporarily or permanently suspended or debarred. A petitioner will not be permitted to contest any findings against the petitioner or any admissions made by the petitioner in the judicial or administrative proceedings upon which the proposed censure, suspension or debarment is based. A petitioner who has consented to the entry of a permanent injunction or order as described in paragraph (c)(1)(i) of this section, without admitting the facts set forth in the complaint, shall nevertheless be presumed for all purposes under this section to have been enjoined or ordered by reason of the misconduct alleged in the complaint.

§ 623.5 Reinstatement.

(a) Any person who is suspended from practicing before the FCA under § 623.4 (a) or (c) of this part may file an application for reinstatement at any time. Denial of the privilege of practicing before the FCA shall continue unless and until the applicant has been reinstated by order of the Board for good cause shown.

(b) Any person suspended under § 623.4(b) shall be reinstated by the Board, upon appropriate application, if all of the grounds for application of the provisions of that paragraph are removed subsequently by a reversal of the conviction or termination of the suspension, disbarment of revocation. An application for reinstatement on any other grounds by any person suspended under § 623.4(b) may be filed at any time. Such application shall state with particularity the relief requested and the grounds therefor and shall include supporting evidence, when available. The applicant shall be accorded an opportunity for an informal hearing in the matter, unless the applicant has waived a hearing in the application and, instead, has elected to have the matter determined on the basis of written submissions. Such hearing shall utilize the procedures established in part 622, subpart C. However, such suspension shall continue unless and until the applicant has been reinstated by order of the Board for good cause shown.

§ 623.6 Duty to file information concerning adverse judicial or administrative action.

Any person appearing or practicing before the FCA who has been or is the subject of a conviction, suspension, debarment, license revocation, injunction or other finding of the kind described in § 623.4 (b) or (c) of this part is an action not instituted by the FCA shall promptly file a copy of the relevant order, judgment or decree with the Board together with any related opinion or statement of the agency or tribunal involved. Any person who fails to file a copy of such an order, judgment or decree within 30 days after the later of the entry of the order, judgment or decree, or the date such person initiates practice before the FCA, for that reason alone may be disqualified from practicing before the FCA until such time as the appropriate filing shall be made, but neither the filing of these documents nor the failure of a person to file them shall in any way impair the operation of any other provision of this part.

§ 623.7 Proceeding under this part.

(a) *Rules.* All hearings required or permitted to be held under paragraphs (a) and (c) of § 623.4 of this part shall be held before a presiding officer utilizing the procedures established in the rules of practice and procedure under part 622, subpart A.

(b) *Closed hearings.* All hearings held under this part shall be closed to the public unless the Board directs otherwise on its own motion or upon the request of a party.

(c) *Collateral proceedings.* Any proceeding brought under any section of this part shall not preclude a proceeding under any other section of this part or any other part of the FCA's regulations.

PART 624 [RESERVED]

PART 625—APPLICATION FOR AWARD OF FEES AND OTHER EXPENSES UNDER THE EQUAL ACCESS TO JUSTICE ACT

Subpart A—General Provisions

Sec.
625.1 Purpose.
625.2 Proceedings covered.
625.3 Eligibility of applicants.
625.4 Standards for awards.
625.5 Allowable fees and expenses.
625.6 Rulemaking on maximum rates for attorney fees.
625.7 Awards against other agencies.

Subpart B—Applicant Information Required

625.10 Contents of application.
625.11 Net worth exhibit.
625.12 Documentation of fees and expenses.
625.13 When an application may be filed.

Subpart C—Procedures for Considering Applications

625.20 Settlement.
625.21 Filing and service of documents.
625.22 Answer to application.
625.23 Reply.
625.24 Comments by other parties.
625.25 Further proceedings.
625.26 Recommended decision.
625.27 Board decision.
625.28 Judicial review.
625.29 Payment of award.

AUTHORITY: 5 U.S.C. 504, 12 U.S.C. 2252.

SOURCE: 57 FR 60109, Dec. 18, 1992, unless otherwise noted.

Subpart A—General Provisions

§ 625.1 Purpose.

These rules implement the Equal Access to Justice Act, 5 U.S.C. 504 (EAJA). The EAJA provides for the award of attorney fees and other expenses to eligible individuals and entities who are parties to certain administrative proceedings (designated by the EAJA as "adversary adjudications") before Federal agencies. An eligible party may receive an award when it prevails over an agency, unless the agency's position was substantially justified or special circumstances make an award unjust. The rules in this part explain how the EAJA applies to Farm Credit Administration (FCA) proceedings. The rules describe the parties eligible for awards, how such parties may apply for awards, and the procedures and standards that govern FCA consideration of applications.

§ 625.2 Proceedings covered.

(a) The EAJA applies to adversary adjudications conducted by the FCA either on its own behalf or in connection with any other agency of the United States that participates in or in any way is a part of the adversary adjudication. Adversary adjudications are:

(1) Adjudications under 5 U.S.C. 554 in which the position of the FCA or other agency is presented by an attorney or other representative who enters

§ 625.3

an appearance and participates in the proceeding; and

(2) Enforcement proceedings under 12 U.S.C. 2261–2273.

(b) The failure of the FCA to identify a type of proceeding as an adversary adjudication shall not preclude the filing of an application by a party who believes that the proceeding is covered by the EAJA; whether the proceeding is covered shall then be an issue for resolution in proceedings on the application.

(c) If a proceeding includes both matters covered and excluded from coverage by the EAJA, any award made will include only fees and expenses related to covered issues.

(d) Proceedings under this part may be conducted by the FCA Board (Board) or by the presiding officer (referred to as the "adjudicative officer" in the EAJA), as defined in § 622.2(f) of this chapter. If the Board conducts proceedings, reference to the "presiding officer" in this part shall mean the Board, in applicable context. Where the Board presides, the recommended decision under § 625.26 of this part will be omitted and the Board will make a final decision on the application in accordance with § 625.27 of this part.

(e) If a court reviews the underlying decision of the adversary adjudication, an award for fees and other expenses may be made only pursuant to 28 U.S.C. 2412(d)(3).

§ 625.3 Eligibility of applicants.

(a) To be eligible for an award under the EAJA, an applicant must be a prevailing party named or admitted to the adversary adjudication for which an award is sought. The applicant must show that it meets all conditions of eligibility set out in this subpart and in subpart B of this part.

(b) The types of eligible applicants are as follows:

(1) An individual with a net worth of $2 million or less;

(2) The sole owner of an unincorporated business who has both a net worth of $7 million or less (including personal and business interests), and 500 or fewer employees;

(3) A charitable or other tax-exempt organization described in section 501(c)(3) of the Internal Revenue Code (26 U.S.C. 501(c)(3)) with 500 or fewer employees;

(4) A cooperative association as defined in section 15(a) of the Agricultural Marketing Act (12 U.S.C. 1141j(a)) with 500 or fewer employees; and

(5) Any other partnership, corporation, association, unit of local government, or organization with a net worth of $7 million or less and 500 or fewer employees.

(c) For eligibility purposes, the net worth and number of employees of an applicant shall be determined as of the date the adversary adjudication was initiated.

(d) An applicant who owns an unincorporated business will be considered as an "individual" rather than a "sole owner of an unincorporated business" if the issues on which the applicant prevails are related primarily to personal interests rather than to business interests.

(e) The employees of an applicant include all persons who regularly perform services for remuneration for that applicant, under the applicant's direction and control. Part-time employees shall be included on a proportional basis.

(f) The net worth and number of employees of the applicant and all of its affiliates shall be aggregated to determine eligibility unless the presiding officer determines that aggregation would be unjust and contrary to the purposes of the EAJA in light of the actual relationship between the affiliated entities.

(1) For purposes of this part, an affiliate is:

(i) Any individual, corporation, or other entity that directly or indirectly controls or owns a majority of the voting shares or other interests of the applicant; or

(ii) Any corporation or other entity of which the applicant directly or indirectly owns or controls a majority of the voting shares or other interests.

(2) The presiding officer may determine that financial relationships of the applicant other than those described in paragraph (f)(1) of this section constitute special circumstances that would make an award unjust.

(g) An applicant that participates in an adversary adjudication primarily on

Farm Credit Administration

§ 625.7

behalf of one or more other persons or entities that would be ineligible is not itself eligible for an award.

§ 625.4 Standards for awards.

(a) If an eligible applicant prevails over the FCA in an adversary adjudication, or in a significant and discrete substantive portion thereof, the applicant may receive an award for fees and expenses incurred in the adjudication, or portion thereof, unless the position of the FCA over which the applicant prevailed was substantially justified.

(b) The position of the FCA includes:
(1) The position taken by the FCA in the adversary adjudication; and
(2) The action or inaction of the FCA upon which the adversary adjudication is based.

(c) Except as provided in paragraph (d) of this section, the FCA must prove that its position was substantially justified before an award may be denied to an otherwise eligible applicant.

(d) An award will be reduced or denied if the applicant has unduly or unreasonably protracted the adversary adjudication or if special circumstances make the award sought unjust.

§ 625.5 Allowable fees and expenses.

(a) Awards will be based on rates customarily charged by persons engaged in the business of acting as attorneys, agents, and expert witnesses, even if the services were made available without charge or at a reduced rate to the applicant.

(b) No award for the fee of an attorney or agent under these rules may exceed $75 per hour. No award to compensate an expert witness may exceed the highest rate at which the FCA pays expert witnesses. However, an award also may include the reasonable expenses of the attorney, agent, or expert witness as a separate item, if the attorney, agent, or expert witness ordinarily charges clients separately for such expenses.

(c) In determining the reasonableness of the fee sought for an attorney, agent, or expert witness, the presiding officer shall consider the following:
(1) If the attorney, agent, or expert witness is in private practice, his or her customary fees for similar services, or, if an employee of the applicant, the fully allocated costs of the services;
(2) The prevailing rate for similar services in the community in which the attorney, agent, or expert witness ordinarily performs services;
(3) The time actually spent in the representation of the applicant;
(4) The time reasonably spent in light of the difficulty or complexity of the issues in the adversary adjudication; and
(5) Such other factors as may bear on the value of the services provided.

(d) The reasonable cost of any study, analysis, audit, engineering report, test, project, or similar matter prepared on behalf of a party may be awarded, to the extent that the charge for the service does not exceed the prevailing rate for similar services, and the study or other matter was necessary for the preparation of the applicant's case.

§ 625.6 Rulemaking on maximum rates for attorney fees.

(a) If warranted by an increase in the cost of living or by special circumstances (such as limited availability of attorneys qualified to handle certain types of proceedings), the FCA may adopt regulations providing that attorney fees may be awarded at a rate higher than $75 per hour in some or all of the types of proceedings covered by this part. The FCA will conduct any rulemaking proceedings for this purpose under the informal rulemaking procedures of the Administrative Procedure Act.

(b) Any person may file with the FCA a petition for rulemaking to increase the maximum rate for attorney fees. The petition should identify the rate the petitioner believes the FCA should establish and the types of proceedings in which the rate should be used. It should also explain fully the reasons why the higher rate is warranted. The FCA will respond to the petition within 90 days after it is filed, by initiating a rulemaking proceeding, denying the petition, or taking other appropriate action.

§ 625.7 Awards against other agencies.

If an applicant is entitled to an award because it prevails over another

§ 625.10

agency of the United States that participates in or in any way is a part of an adversary adjudication before the FCA and that agency's position is not substantially justified, the award or an appropriate portion of the award shall be made against that agency.

Subpart B—Applicant Information Required

§ 625.10 Contents of application.

(a) An application for an award of fees and other expenses under the EAJA shall identify the applicant and the adversary adjudication for which an award is sought. The application shall show that the applicant has prevailed in the adversary adjudication. If the application is made on the basis of significant and discrete substantive issues on which the applicant prevailed, the issues must be specifically identified. The application also shall identify each position of the FCA or other agencies that the applicant alleges was not substantially justified. Unless the applicant is an individual, the application shall describe briefly the type and purpose of its organization or business and state the number of persons employed.

(b) The application shall include a statement that the applicant's net worth does not exceed $2 million (if an individual) or $7 million (for all other applicants, including their affiliates). However, an applicant may omit this statement if:

(1) It states that it has 500 employees or fewer and attaches a copy of a ruling by the Internal Revenue Service that it qualifies as an organization described in section 501(c)(3) of the Internal Revenue Code (26 U.S.C. 501(c)(3)) or, in the case of a tax-exempt organization not required to obtain a ruling from the Internal Revenue Service on its exempt status, a statement that describes the basis for the applicant's belief that it qualifies under such section; or

(2) It states that it is a cooperative association as defined in section 15(a) of the Agricultural Marketing Act (12 U.S.C. 1141j(a)) with 500 or fewer employees.

(c) The application shall state the total amount of fees and other expenses for which an award is sought.

(d) The application may include any other relevant matters that the applicant wishes the FCA to consider in determining whether and in what amount an award should be made.

(e) The application shall be signed by the applicant or an authorized officer or attorney of the applicant. The application must contain a written verification under oath or under penalty of perjury that the information provided in the application and any supporting documents is accurate.

§ 625.11 Net worth exhibit.

(a) Each applicant, except a qualified tax-exempt organization or cooperative association, must provide with its application a detailed exhibit showing the net worth of the applicant and any affiliates (as defined in § 625.3(f)(1) of this part) as of the date when the adversary adjudication was initiated. The exhibit may be in any convenient form that provides full disclosure of the assets and liabilities of the applicant and its affiliates and is otherwise sufficient to demonstrate that the applicant qualifies under the standards in this part. The presiding officer may require an applicant to file additional information supporting its eligibility for an award.

(b) An applicant that objects to public disclosure of information in any portion of the net worth exhibit and believes there are legal grounds for withholding it from disclosure may submit that portion of the exhibit directly to the presiding officer in a sealed envelope labeled "Confidential Financial Information," accompanied by a motion under § 622.11 of this chapter to withhold the information from public disclosure. The motion shall describe the information sought to be withheld and explain, in detail, why it falls within one or more of the specific exemptions from mandatory disclosure under the Freedom of Information Act, 5 U.S.C. 552(b) (1)–(9), why public disclosure of the information would adversely affect the applicant, and why disclosure is not required in the public interest. The material in question shall be served on counsel representing the FCA, but need not be served on any other party to the application proceeding. If the presiding officer, or the

Farm Credit Administration

§ 625.22

FCA Board pursuant to § 622.11(e) of this chapter, finds that the information should not be withheld from disclosure, it shall be placed in the public record of the application proceeding. Otherwise, any request to inspect or copy the exhibit shall be treated in accordance with the FCA's procedures regarding release of information (12 CFR part 602).

§ 625.12 Documentation of fees and expenses.

The application shall be accompanied by full documentation of the fees and expenses, including the cost of any study, analysis, audit, engineering report, test, project, or similar matter, for which an award is sought. A separate itemized statement shall be submitted for each professional firm or individual whose services are covered by the application, showing the hours spent in connection with the proceeding by each individual, a description of the specific services performed, the rates at which each fee has been computed, any expenses for which reimbursement is sought, and the total amount paid or payable by the applicant or by any other person or entity for the services provided. Under § 625.25 of this part, the presiding officer may require the applicant to provide vouchers, receipts, logs, or other substantiation for any fees or expenses claimed.

§ 625.13 When an application may be filed.

(a) An application may be filed whenever the applicant has prevailed in the adversary adjudication, or in a significant and discrete substantive portion thereof, but in no case later than 30 days after the FCA's final disposition of the adversary adjudication.

(b) For purposes of this rule, final disposition means the date on which a decision or order disposing of the merits of the adversary adjudication is issued or any other complete resolution of the adversary adjudication, such as a settlement or voluntary dismissal, becomes final and is unreviewable by the FCA, any other administrative body, or the courts.

(c) If review, reconsideration, or appeal is sought or taken of an adversary adjudication decision as to which an applicant believes it has prevailed, application proceedings for any award of fees and other expenses shall be stayed pending final disposition of the underlying controversy.

Subpart C—Procedures for Considering Applications

§ 625.20 Settlement.

A prevailing party and the FCA through its counsel may agree on a proposed settlement of an award at any time, either in connection with a settlement of the underlying adversary adjudication or after the underlying adversary adjudication has been concluded. If a prevailing party and the FCA counsel agree on a proposed settlement of an award, the proposed settlement must be submitted to the presiding officer for a recommended decision pursuant to § 625.26 of this part. If it has not been previously filed, the application must be submitted to the presiding officer along with the proposed settlement.

§ 625.21 Filing and service of documents.

Any application for an award or other pleading or document related to an application shall be filed and served on all parties to the adversary adjudication in the same manner as other pleadings in the adversary adjudication (see §§ 622.18 and 622.19 of this chapter), except as provided in § 625.11(b) of this part for confidential financial information.

§ 625.22 Answer to application.

(a) Within 30 days after service, counsel for the FCA may file an answer to the application. Unless the FCA counsel requests an extension of time for filing or a statement of intent to negotiate under paragraph (c) of this section is filed, the presiding officer, upon a satisfactory showing of entitlement by the applicant, may make an award for the applicant's fees and other expenses under the EAJA.

(b) The answer shall set forth any objections to the requested award and identify the facts relied on in support of the FCA's position. If the answer is based on any alleged facts not already

§ 625.23

in the record of the adversary adjudication, the FCA counsel shall include with the answer either supporting affidavits or a request for further proceedings under § 625.25 of this part.

(c) If the FCA counsel and the applicant believe that the issues in the fee application can be settled, they may jointly file a statement of their intent to negotiate a settlement. The filing of this statement shall extend the time for filing an answer for an additional 30 days, and further extensions may be granted by the presiding officer upon request by the FCA counsel and the applicant.

§ 625.23 Reply.

Within 15 days after service of an answer, the applicant may file a reply. If the reply is based on any alleged facts not already in the record of the adversary adjudication, the applicant shall include with the reply either supporting affidavits or a request for further proceedings under § 625.25 of this part.

§ 625.24 Comments by other parties.

Any party to a proceeding other than the applicant and FCA counsel may file comments on an application within 30 days after it is served or on an answer within 15 days after it is served. A commenting party may not participate further in proceedings on the application unless the presiding officer determines that the public interest requires such participation in order to permit full exploration of matters raised in the comments.

§ 625.25 Further proceedings.

(a) The determination of an award shall be made on the basis of the written record unless the presiding officer finds that further proceedings are necessary for full and fair resolution of the issues arising from the application. Such further proceedings may be at the request of either the applicant or the FCA counsel, or on the presiding officer's own initiative, and shall be conducted as promptly as possible. Further proceedings may include an informal conference, oral argument, additional written submissions, or other actions required by the presiding officer, but may not include discovery or an evidentiary hearing with respect to the issue of whether the agency's position was substantially justified.

(b) Whether or not the position of the agency was substantially justified shall be determined on the basis of the administrative record, as a whole, which is made in the adversary adjudication for which fees and other expenses are sought.

(c) A request that the presiding officer order further proceedings under this section shall specifically identify the information sought or the disputed issues and shall explain why the additional proceedings are necessary to resolve the issues.

§ 625.26 Recommended decision.

The presiding officer shall file a recommended decision within 30 days after completion of proceedings on the application, and, promptly upon filing, shall serve a copy of the recommended decision upon each party to the proceedings. The decision shall include written findings and conclusions on the applicant's eligibility, status as a prevailing party, the recommended amount of the award, if any, and an explanation of the reasons for any difference between the amount requested and the amount awarded. The decision shall also include, if at issue, findings on whether the FCA's position was substantially justified, whether the applicant unduly protracted the adversary adjudication, or whether special circumstances make an award unjust. If the applicant has sought an award against more than one agency, the decision shall allocate responsibility for payment of any award made among the agencies, and shall explain the reasons for the allocation made.

§ 625.27 Board decision.

Following filing of the recommended decision with the Board, the Board shall render a final decision on the application. The Board maintains full discretion to uphold, reverse, remand, or alter the recommended decision. The Board may order further proceedings (including those set forth in §§ 622.11 and 622.13 through 622.16 of this chapter) upon request by any party to the application proceeding or on its own initiative, but such proceedings may not include discovery or an evidentiary hearing with respect to the issue of whether the agency's position was substantially justified.

§ 625.28 Judicial review.

Judicial review of final FCA decisions on awards may be sought as provided in 5 U.S.C. 504(c)(2).

§ 625.29 Payment of award.

(a) An applicant seeking payment of an award shall submit to the Secretary to the Board a copy of the final decision granting the award, accompanied by a certification that the applicant will not seek judicial review of the decision. The required submission and certification should be sent to: Secretary to the Board, Farm Credit Administration, 1501 Farm Credit Drive, McLean, Virginia 22102–5090.

(b) The FCA will pay the amount awarded to the applicant within 60 days of receipt of the applicant's submission and certification.

PART 626—NONDISCRIMINATION IN LENDING

Sec.
626.6000 Definitions.
626.6005 Nondiscrimination in lending and other services.
626.6010 Nondiscrimination in applications.
626.6015 Nondiscriminatory appraisal.
626.6020 Nondiscriminatory advertising.
626.6025 Equal housing lender poster.
626.6030 Complaints.

AUTHORITY: Secs. 1.5, 2.2, 2.12, 3.1, 5.9, 5.17 of the Farm Credit Act (12 U.S.C. 2013, 2073, 2093, 2122, 2243, 2252); 42 U.S.C. 3601 et seq.; 15 U.S.C. 1691 et seq.; 12 CFR 202, 24 CFR 100, 109, 110.

SOURCE: Subpart E of part 613 added at 37 FR 11421, June 7, 1972, and 57 FR 13637, Apr. 17, 1992. Redesignated as part 626 at 62 FR 4441, Jan. 30, 1997.

§ 626.6000 Definitions.

For the purpose of this subpart, the following definitions shall apply:

(a) *Applicant* means any person who requests or who has received an extension of credit from a creditor and includes any person who is or may become contractually liable regarding an extension of credit.

(b) *Dwelling* means any building, structure, or portion thereof which is occupied as, or designed or intended for occupancy as, a residence by one or more families, and any vacant land which is offered for sale or lease for the construction or location thereon of any such building, structure, or portion thereof.

(c) *Familial status* means one or more individuals (who have not attained the age of 18 years) being domiciled with:

(1) A parent or another person having legal custody of such individual or individuals; or

(2) The designee of such parent or other person having such custody, with the written permission of such parent or other person.

The protections afforded against discrimination on the basis of familial status shall apply to any person who is pregnant or is in the process of securing legal custody of any individual who has not attained the age of 18 years.

(d) *Handicap* means, with respect to a person:

(1) A physical or mental impairment which substantially limits one or more of such person's major life activities,

(2) A record of having such an impairment, or

(3) Being regarded as having such an impairment,

but such term does not include current, illegal use of or addiction to a controlled substance (as defined in section 102 of the Controlled Substances Act (21 U.S.C. 802)).

(e) *Residential real estate-related transaction* means any of the following:

(1) The making or purchasing of loans or providing other financial assistance:

(i) For purchasing, constructing, improving, repairing, or maintaining a dwelling; or

(ii) Secured by residential real estate.

(2) The selling, brokering, or appraising of residential real property.

[57 FR 13637, Apr. 17, 1992. Redesignated at 62 FR 4441, Jan. 30, 1997]

§ 626.6005 Nondiscrimination in lending and other services.

(a) No Farm Credit institution may discriminate in making credit or other financial assistance available in a residential real estate-related transaction, or in the terms or conditions of such a

§ 626.6010

transaction, because of race, color, religion, sex, handicap, familial status, or national origin.

(b) No Farm Credit institution may discriminate in any aspect of a credit transaction or a financial service involving a credit transaction because of:

(1) Race, color, religion, national origin, sex, marital status, or age (provided that the applicant has the capacity to enter into a binding contract); or

(2) The fact that all or part of the applicant's income derives from any public assistance program; or

(3) The fact that the applicant has in good faith exercised any right under title VII (Equal Credit Opportunity Act) of the Consumer Credit Protection Act.

(c) Prohibited practices under this section include, but are not limited to, discrimination in fixing the amount, interest rate, duration, or other terms or conditions of any loan or a financial service involving a credit transaction or in the purchase of loans and securities on the basis of race, color, religion, sex, handicap, familial status (having one or more children under the age of 18), marital status, age (provided the applicant has the capacity to enter into a binding contract), or national origin.

(d) Nothing in this subpart shall be deemed to change the eligibility requirements imposed by the Farm Credit Act of 1971, as amended, or any Farm Credit Administration regulation adopted pursuant thereto.

[57 FR 13638, Apr. 17, 1992. Redesignated at 62 FR 4441, Jan. 30, 1997]

§ 626.6010 Nondiscrimination in applications.

(a) No Farm Credit institution may discourage or refuse to allow, receive, or consider any application, request, or inquiry regarding an eligible loan or other eligible credit service or discriminate in imposing conditions upon, or in processing, any such application, request, or inquiry on the basis of:

(1) Race, color, religion, sex, marital status, age (provided that the applicant has the capacity to enter into a binding contract), or national origin, as prescribed under title VII (the Equal Credit Opportunity Act) of the Consumer Credit Protection Act, as amended by the Equal Credit Opportunity Act Amendments of 1976 (15 U.S.C. 1601 et seq.), and the Board of Governors of the Federal Reserve System's implementing regulation (12 CFR part 202); and

(2) Race, color, religion, sex, national origin, handicap, or familial status, as prescribed under title VIII (the Fair Housing Act) of the Civil Rights Act of 1968, as amended by the Fair Housing Amendments Act of 1988 (42 U.S.C. 3601 et seq.), and the Department of Housing and Urban Development's implementing regulations (24 CFR part 100).

(b) The provisions of paragraph (a) of this section shall apply whenever:

(1) An application is made for any such loan or other credit service; or

(2) A request is made for forms or papers to be used to make application for any such loan or other credit service; or

(3) An inquiry is made about the availability of such loan or other credit service.

[57 FR 13638, Apr. 17, 1992. Redesignated at 62 FR 4441, Jan. 30, 1997]

§ 626.6015 Nondiscriminatory appraisal.

No Farm Credit institution shall discriminate against any person on the basis of race, color, religion, sex, handicap, familial status, or national origin when conducting, using, or relying upon an appraisal of residential real property that is subject to sale, rental, or other financing transaction.

[57 FR 13638, Apr. 17, 1992. Redesignated at 62 FR 4441, Jan. 30, 1997]

§ 626.6020 Nondiscriminatory advertising.

(a) A Farm Credit institution that directly or through third parties engages in any form of advertising shall not use words, phrases, symbols, directions, forms, or models in such advertising which express, imply or suggest a policy of discrimination or exclusion in violation of the provisions of title VIII (the Fair Housing Act) of the Civil Rights Act of 1968, as amended by the Fair Housing Amendments Act of 1988 (42 U.S.C. 3601–3631); the Department of Housing and Urban Development's implementing regulations (24 CFR parts 100 and 109), and title VII (the Equal

Farm Credit Administration § 626.6025

Credit Opportunity Act) of the Consumer Credit Protection Act, as amended by the Equal Credit Opportunity Act Amendments of 1976 (15 U.S.C. 1691–1691f); and the Board of Governors of the Federal Reserve System's implementing regulation (12 CFR part 202), or this subpart.

(b) Written advertisements relating to dwellings shall include a facsimile of the following logotype and legend:

[37 FR 16932, Aug. 23, 1972, as amended at 57 FR 13638, Apr. 17, 1992. Redesignated at 62 FR 4441, Jan. 30, 1997]

§ 626.6025 Equal housing lender poster.

(a) Each Farm Credit institution that makes loans for the purpose of purchasing, constructing, improving, repairing, or maintaining a dwelling or any loan secured by a dwelling shall post and maintain an Equal Housing Lender Poster in the lobby of each of its offices. The poster shall be in a prominent place readily apparent to all persons seeking such loans.

(b) The Equal Housing Lender Poster shall be at least 11 inches by 14 inches in size, and shall bear the logotype and legend set forth in § 626.6020(b) of this subpart and the following text:

WE DO BUSINESS IN ACCORDANCE WITH FEDERAL FAIR LENDING LAWS

(The Civil Rights Act of 1968, as amended by the Fair Housing Amendments Act of 1988)

UNDER THE FEDERAL FAIR HOUSING ACT, IT IS ILLEGAL, ON THE BASIS OF RACE, COLOR, NATIONAL ORIGIN, RELIGION, SEX, HANDICAP, OR FAMILIAL STATUS (HAVING CHILDREN UNDER THE AGE OF 18), TO:

• Deny a loan for the purpose of purchasing, constructing, improving, repairing, or maintaining a dwelling, or deny any loan secured by a dwelling; or

• Discriminate in fixing the amount, interest rate, duration, application procedures, or other terms or conditions of such a loan, or in appraising property.

IF YOU BELIEVE YOU HAVE BEEN DISCRIMINATED AGAINST, YOU SHOULD SEND A COMPLAINT TO:

Assistant Secretary for Fair Housing and Equal Opportunity, Department of Housing and Urban Development, Washington, DC 20410, 1–800–669–9777 (Toll Free), 1–800–927–9275 (TDD), for processing under the Federal Fair Housing Act

AND TO:

Farm Credit Administration, Office of Congressional and Public Affairs, 1501 Farm Credit Drive, McLean, VA 22102–5090, 703–883–4056, 703–883–4444 (TDD), for processing under Farm Credit Administration Regulations

UNDER THE EQUAL CREDIT OPPORTUNITY ACT

(The Consumer Credit Protection Act, as amended by the Equal Credit Opportunity Act Amendments of 1976)

IT IS ILLEGAL TO DISCRIMINATE IN ANY CREDIT TRANSACTION:

• On the basis of race, color, national origin, religion, sex, marital status, or age,

• Because income is from public assistance, or

• Because a right was exercised under the Consumer Credit Protection Act.

IF YOU BELIEVE YOU HAVE BEEN DISCRIMINATED AGAINST, YOU SHOULD SEND A COMPLAINT TO:

Farm Credit Administration, Office of Congressional and Public Affairs, 1501 Farm Credit Drive, McLean, VA 22102–5090, 703–883–4056, 703–883–4444 (TDD).

[57 FR 13638, Apr. 17, 1992. Redesignated at 62 FR 4441, Jan. 30, 1997, as amended at 62 FR 4451, Jan. 30, 1997]

§ 626.6030 Complaints.

(a) Complaints regarding discrimination in lending by a Farm Credit institution under the Fair Housing Act shall be referred to the Assistant Secretary for Fair Housing and Equal Opportunity, United States Department of Housing and Urban Development, Washington, DC 20410, and to the Office of Congressional and Public Affairs, Farm Credit Administration, McLean, Virginia 22102–5090.

(b) Complaints regarding discrimination in lending by a Farm Credit institution under the Equal Credit Opportunity Act shall be referred to the Office of Congressional and Public Affairs, Farm Credit Administration, McLean, Virginia 22102–5090.

[57 FR 13639, Apr. 17, 1992. Redesignated at 62 FR 4441, Jan. 30, 1997]

PART 627—TITLE IV CONSERVATORS, RECEIVERS, AND VOLUNTARY LIQUIDATIONS

Subpart A—General

Sec.
627.2700 General—applicability.
627.2705 Definitions.
627.2710 Grounds for appointment of conservators and receivers.
627.2715 Action for removal of conservator or receiver.

Subpart B—Receivers and Receiverships

627.2720 Appointment of receiver.
627.2725 Powers and duties of the receiver.
627.2726 Treatment by the conservator or receiver of financial assets transferred in connection with a securitization or participation.
627.2730 Preservation of equity.
627.2735 Notice to holders of uninsured accounts and stockholders.
627.2740 Creditors' claims.
627.2745 Priority of claims—associations.
627.2750 Priority of claims—banks.
627.2752 Priority of claims—other Farm Credit institutions.
627.2755 Payment of claims.
627.2760 Inventory, audit, and reports.
627.2765 Final discharge and release of the receiver.

Subpart C—Conservators and Conservatorships

627.2770 Conservators.
627.2775 Appointment of a conservator.
627.2780 Powers and duties of conservators.
627.2785 Inventory, examination, audit, and reports to stockholders.
627.2790 Final discharge and release of the conservator.

Subpart D—Voluntary Liquidation

627.2795 Voluntary liquidation.
627.2797 Preservation of equity.

AUTHORITY: Secs. 4.2, 5.9, 5.10, 5.17, 5.51, 5.58, 5.61 of the Farm Credit Act (12 U.S.C. 2183, 2243, 2244, 2252, 2277a, 2277a–7, 2277a–10).

SOURCE: 57 FR 46482, Oct. 9, 1992, unless otherwise noted.

Subpart A—General

§ 627.2700 General—applicability.

The provisions of this part shall apply to conservatorships, receiverships, and voluntary liquidations.

[63 FR 5724, Feb. 4, 1998]

§ 627.2705 Definitions.

For purposes of this part the following definitions apply:

(a) *Act* means the Farm Credit Act of 1971, as amended.

(b) *Farm Credit institution(s)* or *institution(s)* means all associations, banks, service corporations chartered under title IV of the Act, the Federal Farm Credit Banks Funding Corporation, and the Farm Credit System Financial Assistance Corporation.

(c) *Conservator* means the Farm Credit System Insurance Corporation acting in its capacity as conservator.

(d) *Insurance Corporation* means the Farm Credit System Insurance Corporation.

(e) *Receiver* means the Insurance Corporation acting in its capacity as receiver.

[57 FR 46482, Oct. 9, 1992, as amended at 75 FR 35968, June 24, 2010]

§ 627.2710 Grounds for appointment of conservators and receivers.

(a) Upon a determination by the Farm Credit Administration Board of the existence of one or more of the factors set forth in paragraph (b) of this section, with respect to any bank, association, or other institution of the System, the Farm Credit Administration Board may, in its discretion, appoint a conservator or receiver for such institution. After January 5, 1993, the Insurance Corporation shall be the sole entity to be appointed as conservator or receiver.

(b) The grounds for the appointment of a conservator or receiver for a System institution are:

(1) The institution is insolvent, in that the assets of the institution are less than its obligations to creditors and others, including its members. For purposes of determining insolvency, "obligations to members" shall not include stock or allocated equities held by current or former borrowers.

(2) There has been a substantial dissipation of the assets or earnings of the institution due to the violation of any law, rule, or regulation, or the conduct of an unsafe or unsound practice;

(3) The institution is in an unsafe or unsound condition to transact business, including having insufficient capital or otherwise. For purposes of this regulation, "unsafe or unsound condition" shall include, but shall not be limited to, the following conditions:

(i) For banks, a net collateral ratio below 102 percent.

(ii) For associations, a default by the association of one or more terms of its general financing agreement with its affiliated bank that the Farm Credit Administration determines to be a material default.

(iii) For all institutions, permanent capital of less than one-half the minimum required level for the institution.

(iv) For all institutions, a total surplus ratio of less than 2 percent.

(v) For associations, stock impairment.

(4) The institution has committed a willful violation of a final cease-and-desist order issued by the Farm Credit Administration Board; or

(5) The institution is concealing its books, papers, records, or assets, or is refusing to submit its books, papers, records, assets, or other material relating to the affairs of the institution for inspection to any examiner or to any lawful agent of the Farm Credit Administration Board.

(6) The institution is unable to make a timely payment of principal or interest on any insured obligation (as defined in section 5.51(3) of the Act) issued by the institution individually, or on which it is primarily liable.

[51 FR 32443, Sept. 12, 1986, as amended at 54 FR 1148, Jan. 12, 1989. Redesignated and amended at 46487, Oct. 9, 1992; 63 FR 39229, July 22, 1998]

§ 627.2715 Action for removal of conservator or receiver.

Upon the appointment of a conservator or receiver for a Farm Credit institution by the Farm Credit Administration Board pursuant to § 627.2710 of this part, the institution may, within 30 days of such appointment, bring an action in the United States District Court for the judicial district in which the home office of the institution is located, or in the United States District Court for the District of Columbia, for an order requiring the Farm Credit Administration Board to remove such conservator or receiver and, if the charter has been canceled, to rescind the cancellation of the charter. Notwithstanding any other provision of subpart B or C of this part, the institution's board of directors is empowered to meet subsequent to such appointment and authorize the filing of an action for removal. An action for removal may be authorized only by such institution's board of directors.

Subpart B—Receivers and Receiverships

§ 627.2720 Appointment of receiver.

(a) The Farm Credit Administration Board may, in its discretion, appoint ex parte and without notice a receiver for any Farm Credit institution in accordance with the grounds for appointment set forth in § 627.2710 of this part.

(b) The receiver appointed for a Farm Credit institution shall be the Insurance Corporation.

(c) Upon the appointment of the Insurance Corporation as receiver, the Chairman of the Farm Credit Administration Board shall immediately notify the institution, and its district bank in the case of an association, and shall publish a notice of the appointment in the FEDERAL REGISTER.

(d) In the case of the voluntary or involuntary liquidation of an association, the district bank shall institute appropriate measures to minimize the adverse effect of the liquidation on those borrowers whose loans are purchased by or otherwise transferred to another System institution.

(e) Upon the issuance of the order placing a Farm Credit institution into liquidation and appointing the Insurance Corporation as receiver, all rights, privileges, and powers of the board of directors, officers, and employees of the institution shall be vested exclusively in the receiver. The Farm Credit Administration Board may simultaneously, or any time thereafter, cancel the charter of the institution.

[57 FR 46482, Oct. 9, 1992, as amended at 63 FR 5724, Feb. 4, 1998]

§ 627.2725 Powers and duties of the receiver.

(a) *General.* (1) Upon appointment as receiver, the receiver shall take possession of a Farm Credit institution pursuant to 12 U.S.C. 2183 and § 627.2710 of this part in order to wind up the business operations of such institution, collect the debts owed to the institution, liquidate its property and assets, pay its creditors, and distribute the remaining proceeds to stockholders. The receiver is authorized to exercise all powers necessary to the efficient termination of an institution's operation as provided for in this subpart.

(2) Upon its appointment as receiver, the receiver automatically succeeds to—

(i) All rights, titles, powers and privileges of the institution and of any stockholder, officer, or director of such institution with respect to the institution and the assets of the institution; and

(ii) Title to the books, records, and assets of any previous conservator or other legal custodian of such institution.

(3) The receiver of a Farm Credit institution serves as the trustee of the receivership estate and conducts its operations for the benefit of the creditors and stockholders of the institution.

(b) *Specific powers.* The receiver may:

(1) Exercise all powers as are conferred upon the officers and directors of the institution under law and the charter, articles, and bylaws of the institution.

(2) Take any action the receiver considers appropriate or expedient to carry on the business of the institution during the process of liquidating its assets and winding up its affairs.

(3) Extend credit to existing borrowers as necessary to honor existing commitments and to effectuate the purposes of the receivership.

(4) Borrow such sums as necessary to effectuate the purposes of the receivership.

(5) Pay any sum the receiver deems necessary or advisable to preserve, conserve, or protect the institution's assets or property or rehabilitate or improve such property and assets.

(6) Pay any sum the receiver deems necessary or advisable to preserve, conserve, or protect any asset or property on which the institution has a lien or in which the institution has a financial or property interest, and pay off and discharge any liens, claims, or charges of any nature against such property.

(7) Investigate any matter related to the conduct of the business of the institution, including, but not limited to, any claim of the institution against any individual or entity, and institute appropriate legal or other proceedings to prosecute such claims.

(8) Institute, prosecute, maintain, defend, intervene, and otherwise participate in any legal proceeding by or against the institution or in which the institution or its creditors or members have any interest, and represent in every way the institution, its members, and creditors.

(9) Employ attorneys, accountants, appraisers, and other professionals to give advice and assistance to the receivership generally or on particular matters, and pay their retainers, compensation, and expenses, including litigation costs.

(10) Hire any agents or employees necessary for proper administration of the receivership.

(11) Execute, acknowledge, and deliver, in person or through a general or specific delegation, any instrument necessary for any authorized purpose, and any instrument executed under this paragraph shall be valid and effective as if it had been executed by the

institution's officers by authority of its board of directors.

(12) Sell for cash or otherwise any mortgage, deed of trust, chose in action, note contract, judgment or decree, stock, or debt owed to the institution, or any property (real or personal, tangible or intangible).

(13) Purchase or lease office space, automobiles, furniture, equipment, and supplies, and purchase insurance, professional, and technical services necessary for the conduct of the receivership.

(14) Release any assets or property of any nature, regardless of whether the subject of pending litigation, and repudiate, with cause, any lease or executory contract the receiver considers burdensome.

(15) Settle, release, or obtain release of, for cash or other consideration, claims and demands against or in favor of the institution or receiver.

(16) Pay, out of the assets of the institution, all expenses of the receivership and all costs of carrying out or exercising the rights, powers, privileges, and duties as receiver.

(17) Pay out of the assets of the institution all approved claims of indebtedness in accordance with priorities established in this subpart.

(18) Take all actions and have such rights, powers, and privileges as are necessary and incident to the exercise of any specific power.

(19) Take such actions, and have such additional rights, powers, privileges, immunities, and duties as the Farm Credit Administration Board authorizes by order or by amendment of any order or by regulation.

(c) *Authority to pay claims.* The receiver of a bank is also empowered to pay claims of holders of notes, bonds, debentures, or other obligations issued by the bank under 12 U.S.C. 2153(c) or (d) in accordance with procedures specified by the Insurance Corporation pursuant to § 627.2740(d) of this part.

§ 627.2726 Treatment by the conservator or receiver of financial assets transferred in connection with a securitization or participation.

(a) *Definitions.* For the purposes of this section, the following definitions apply:

Beneficial interest means debt or equity (or mixed) interests or obligations of any type issued by a special purpose entity that entitle their holders to receive payments that depend primarily on the cash flow from financial assets owned by the special purpose entity.

Financial asset means cash or a contract or instrument that conveys to one entity a contractual right to receive cash or another financial instrument from another entity.

Participation means the transfer or assignment of an undivided interest in all or part of a loan or a lease from a seller, known as the "lead", to a buyer, known as the "participant", without recourse to the lead, pursuant to an agreement between the lead and the participant. *Without recourse* means that the participation is not subject to any agreement that requires the lead to repurchase the participant's interest or to otherwise compensate the participant due to a default on the underlying obligation.

Securitization means the issuance by a special purpose entity of beneficial interests:

(1) The most senior class of which at the time of issuance is rated in one of the four highest categories assigned to long-term debt or in an equivalent short-term category (within either of which there may be sub-categories or gradations indicating relative standing) by one or more nationally recognized statistical rating organizations, or

(2) Which are sold in transactions by an issuer not involving any public offering for purposes of section 4 of the Securities Act of 1933 (15 U.S.C. 77d), as amended, or in transactions exempt from registration under such Act pursuant to Regulation S thereunder (or any successor regulation).

Special purpose entity means a trust, corporation, or other entity demonstrably distinct from the Farm Credit institution that is primarily engaged in acquiring and holding (or transferring to another special purpose entity) financial assets, and in activities related or incidental thereto, in connection with the issuance by such special purpose entity (or by another special purpose entity that acquires financial assets directly or indirectly from such

§ 627.2730

special purpose entity) of beneficial interests.

(b) The receiver shall not, by exercise of its authority to repudiate contracts under § 627.2725(b)(2) and (b)(14), reclaim, recover, or recharacterize as property of the institution or the receivership any financial assets transferred by a Farm Credit institution in connection with a securitization or participation, provided that such transfer meets all conditions for sale accounting treatment under generally accepted accounting principles, other than the "legal isolation" condition as it applies to institutions for which the FCSIC may be appointed as receiver which is addressed by this section.

(c) Paragraph (b) of this section shall not apply unless the Farm Credit institution received adequate consideration for the transfer of financial assets at the time of the transfer, and the documentation effecting the transfer of financial assets reflects the intent of the parties to treat the transaction as a sale, and not as a secured borrowing, for accounting purposes.

(d) Paragraph (b) of this section shall not be construed as waiving, limiting, or otherwise affecting the power of the receiver to disaffirm or repudiate any agreement imposing continuing obligations or duties upon the institution in receivership.

(e) Paragraph (b) of this section shall not be construed as waiving, limiting or otherwise affecting the rights or powers of the receiver to take any action or to exercise any power not specifically limited by this section, including, but not limited to, any rights, powers or remedies of the receiver regarding transfers taken in contemplation of the institution's insolvency or with the intent to hinder, delay, or defraud the institution or the creditors of such institution, or that is a fraudulent transfer under applicable law.

(f) The receiver shall not seek to avoid an otherwise legally enforceable securitization agreement or participation agreement executed by a Farm Credit institution solely because such agreement does not meet the "contemporaneous" requirement of section 5.61(d) of the Act.

(g) This section may be repealed or amended by the Farm Credit Administration, but any such repeal or amendment shall not apply to any transfers of financial assets made in connection with a securitization or participation that was in effect before such repeal or modification.

[70 FR 55515, Sept. 22, 2005]

§ 627.2730 Preservation of equity.

(a) Except as provided for upon final distribution of the assets of the institution, no capital stock, participation certificates, equity reserves, or other allocated equities of an institution in receivership shall be issued, allocated, retired, sold, distributed, transferred, assigned, or applied against any indebtedness of the owners of such equities.

(b) Notwithstanding paragraph (a) of this section, eligible borrower stock shall be retired in accordance with section 4.9A of the Act.

[57 FR 46482, Oct. 9, 1992, as amended at 63 FR 5724, Feb. 4, 1998]

§ 627.2735 Notice to holders of uninsured accounts and stockholders.

(a) Upon the placing of an institution in liquidation, the receiver shall immediately notify every borrower who has an uninsured account (voluntary or involuntary) as described in § 614.4175 of this chapter that the funds ceased earning interest when the receivership was instituted and will be applied against the outstanding indebtedness of any loans of such borrower unless, within 15 days of such notice, the borrower directs the receiver to otherwise apply such funds in the manner provided for in existing loan documents.

(b) As soon as practicable after the receiver takes possession of the institution, the receiver shall notify, by first class mail, each holder of stock and participation certificates of the following matters:

(1) The number of shares such holder owns;

(2) That the stock and other equities of the institution may not be retired or transferred until the liquidation is completed, whereupon the receiver will distribute a liquidating dividend, if any, to the owners of such equities; and

(3) Such other matters as the receiver or the Farm Credit Administration deems necessary.

[57 FR 46482, Oct. 9, 1992, as amended at 75 FR 35968, June 24, 2010]

§ 627.2740 Creditors' claims.

(a) The receiver shall publish promptly a notice to creditors to present their claims against the institution, with proof thereof, to the receiver by a date specified in the notice, which shall be not less than 90 calendar days after the first publication. The notice shall be republished approximately 30 days and 60 days after the first publication. The receiver shall promptly send, by first class mail, a similar notice to any creditor shown on the institution's books at the creditor's last address appearing thereon. Claims filed after the specified date shall be disallowed, except as the receiver may approve them for full or partial payment from the institution's assets remaining undistributed at the time of approval.

(b) The receiver shall allow any claim that is timely received and proved to the receiver's satisfaction. The receiver may disallow in whole or in part any creditor's claim or claim of security, preference, or priority which is not proved to the receiver's satisfaction or is not timely received and shall notify the claimant of the disallowance and reason therefor. Sending the notice of disallowance by first class mail to the claimant's address appearing on the proof of claim shall be sufficient notice. The disallowance shall be final, unless, within 30 days after the notice of disallowance is mailed, the claimant files a written request for payment regardless of the disallowance. The receiver shall reconsider any claim upon the timely request of the claimant and may approve or disapprove such claim in whole or in part.

(c) Creditors' claims that are allowed shall be paid by the receiver from time to time, to the extent funds are available therefor and in accordance with the priorities established in this subpart and in such manner and amounts as the receiver deems appropriate. In the event the institution has a claim against a creditor of the institution, the receiver shall offset the amount of such claim against the claim asserted by such creditor.

(d) The claims of holders of notes, bonds, debentures, or other obligations issued by a bank under 12 U.S.C. 2153 (c) or (d) shall be made, if deemed necessary or appropriate, in accordance with procedures formulated by the Insurance Corporation. In the formulation of such procedures, the Insurance Corporation shall consult with the Farm Credit Administration.

§ 627.2745 Priority of claims—associations.

The following priority of claims shall apply to the distribution of the assets of an association in liquidation:

(a) All costs, expenses, and debts incurred by the receiver in connection with the administration of the receivership.

(b) Administrative expenses of the association, provided that such expenses were incurred within 60 days prior to the receiver's taking possession, and that such expenses shall be limited to reasonable expenses incurred for services actually provided by accountants, attorneys, appraisers, examiners, or management companies, or reasonable expenses incurred by employees which were authorized and reimbursable under a pre-existing expense reimbursement policy, that, in the opinion of the receiver, are of benefit to the receivership, and shall not include wages or salaries of employees of the association.

(c) If authorized by the receiver, claims for wages and salaries, including vacation pay, earned prior to the appointment of the receiver by an employee of the association whom the receiver determines it is in the best interest of the receivership to engage or retain for a reasonable period of time.

(d) If authorized by the receiver, claims for wages and salaries, including vacation pay, earned prior to the appointment of the receiver, up to a maximum of three thousand dollars ($3,000) per person as adjusted for inflation, by an employee of the association not engaged or retained by the receiver. The adjustment for inflation shall be the percentage by which the Consumer Price Index (as prepared by the Department of Labor) for the calendar year preceding the appointment of the receiver exceeds the Consumer Price Index for the calendar year 1992.

(e) All claims for taxes.

(f) All claims of creditors, including the district bank, which are secured by assets or equities of the association in accordance with applicable Federal or State law.

(g) All claims of the district bank other than those provided for in paragraph (f) of this section, based on the financing agreement between the association and the bank, including interest accrued before and after the appointment of the receiver, minus any setoff for stock or other equity of the district bank owned by the association made in accordance with this paragraph or paragraph (f) of this section. Prior to making such setoff, the district bank must obtain the approval of the Farm Credit Administration Board for the retirement of such equities.

(h) All claims of general creditors.

(i) All claims that, by their terms, are subordinated in whole or in part to the claims of general creditors, other than distributions covered under § 627.2755(b). Such claims shall receive the priority specified in the written instruments that evidence the claims and, to the extent that the written documents provide different priorities for different categories of such claims, each category shall be considered a class of claims for purposes of § 627.2755(a).

[57 FR 46482, Oct. 9, 1992, as amended at 72 FR 54527, Sept. 26, 2007]

§ 627.2750 Priority of claims—banks.

The following priority of claims shall apply to the distribution of the assets of a bank in liquidation:

(a) All costs, expenses, and debts incurred by the receiver in connection with the administration of the receivership.

(b) Administrative expenses of the bank, provided that such expenses were incurred within 60 days prior to the receiver's taking possession, and that such expenses shall be limited to reasonable expenses incurred for services actually provided by accountants, attorneys, appraisers, examiners, or management companies, or reasonable expenses incurred by employees which were authorized and reimbursable under a pre-existing expense reimbursement policy, that, in the opinion of the receiver, are of benefit to the receivership, and shall not include wages or salaries of employees of the bank.

(c) If authorized by the receiver, claims for wages and salaries, including vacation pay, earned prior to the appointment of the receiver by an employee of the bank whom the receiver determines it is in the best interest of the receivership to engage or retain for a reasonable period of time.

(d) If authorized by the receiver, claims for wages and salaries, including vacation pay, earned prior to the appointment of the receiver, up to a maximum of three thousand dollars ($3,000) per person as adjusted for inflation, by an employee of the bank not engaged or retained by the receiver. The adjustment for inflation shall be the percentage by which the Consumer Price Index (as prepared by the Department of Labor) for the calendar year preceding the appointment of the receiver exceeds the Consumer Price Index for the calendar year 1992.

(e) All claims for taxes.

(f) All claims of creditors which are secured by specific assets or equities of the bank, with priority of conflicting claims of creditors within this same class to be determined in accordance with priorities of applicable Federal or State law.

(g) All claims of holders of bonds issued by the bank individually to the extent such are collateralized in accordance with 12 U.S.C. 2154.

(h) All claims of holders of consolidated and System-wide bonds and all claims of the other Farm Credit banks arising from their payments on consolidated and System-wide bonds pursuant to 12 U.S.C. 2155 or pursuant to an agreement among the banks to reallocate the payments, provided the agreement is in writing and approved by the Farm Credit Administration.

(i) All claims of general creditors.

(j) All claims that, by their terms, are subordinated in whole or in part to the claims of general creditors, other than distributions covered under § 627.2755(b). Such claims shall receive

Farm Credit Administration § 627.2760

the priority specified in the written instruments that evidence the claims and, to the extent that the written documents provide different priorities for different categories of such claims, each category shall be considered a class of claims for purposes of § 627.2755(a).

[57 FR 46482, Oct. 9, 1992, as amended at 72 FR 54527, 54529 Sept. 26, 2007]

§ 627.2752 Priority of claims—other Farm Credit institutions.

The following priority of claims shall apply to the distribution of the assets of an institution, other than a bank or association, in liquidation:

(a) All costs, expenses, and debts incurred by the receiver in connection with the administration of the receivership.

(b) Administrative expenses of the institution, provided that such expenses were incurred within 60 days prior to the receiver's taking possession, and that such expenses shall be limited to reasonable expenses incurred for services actually provided by accountants, attorneys, appraisers, examiners, or management companies, or reasonable expenses incurred by employees which were authorized and reimbursable under a pre-existing expense reimbursement policy, that, in the opinion of the receiver, are of benefit to the receivership, and shall not include wages or salaries of employees of the institution.

(c) If authorized by the receiver, claims for wages and salaries, including vacation pay, earned prior to the appointment of the receiver by an employee of the institution whom the receiver determines it is in the best interest of the receivership to engage or retain for a reasonable period of time.

(d) If authorized by the receiver, claims for wages and salaries, including vacation pay, earned prior to the appointment of the receiver, up to a maximum of three thousand dollars ($3,000) per person as adjusted for inflation, by an employee of the institution not engaged or retained by the receiver. The adjustment for inflation shall be the percentage by which the Consumer Price Index (as prepared by the Department of Labor) for the calendar year preceding the appointment of the receiver exceeds the Consumer Price Index for the calendar year 1992.

(e) All claims for taxes.

(f) All claims of creditors which are secured by specific assets or equities of the institution, with priority of conflicting claims of creditors within this same class to be determined in accordance with priorities of applicable Federal or State law.

(g) All claims of general creditors.

(h) All claims that, by their terms, are subordinated in whole or in part to the claims of general creditors, other than distributions covered under § 627.2755(b). Such claims shall receive the priority specified in the written instruments that evidence the claims and, to the extent that the written documents provide different priorities for different categories of such claims, each category shall be considered a class of claims for purposes of § 627.2755(a).

[57 FR 46482, Oct. 9, 1992, as amended at 72 FR 54527, Sept. 26, 2007]

§ 627.2755 Payment of claims.

(a) All claims of each class described in § 627.2745, § 627.2750, or § 627.2752 of this part, respectively, shall be paid in full, or provisions shall be made for such payment, prior to the payment of any claim of a lesser priority. If there are insufficient funds to pay in full any class of claims described, distribution on such class shall be on a pro rata basis.

(b) Following the payment of all claims, the receiver shall distribute the remainder of the assets of the institution to the owners of stock, participation certificates, and other equities in accordance with the priorities for impairment set forth in the bylaws of the institution.

(c) Notwithstanding this section, eligible borrower stock shall be retired in accordance with section 4.9A of the Act.

[57 FR 46482, Oct. 9, 1992, as amended at 72 FR 54529, Sept. 26, 2007]

§ 627.2760 Inventory, audit, and reports.

(a) As soon as practicable after taking possession of an institution, the receiver shall make an inventory of the assets and liabilities as of the date possession was taken.

(b) The institution in receivership shall be audited on an annual basis by a certified public accountant selected by the receiver.

(c) With respect to each receivership, the receiver shall make an annual accounting or report, as appropriate, available upon request to any stockholder of the institution in receivership or any member of the public, with a copy provided to the Farm Credit Administration.

(d) Upon the final liquidation of the institution, the receiver shall send to each stockholder of record a report summarizing the disposition of the assets of the receivership and claims against the receivership.

§ 627.2765 **Final discharge and release of the receiver.**

After the receiver has made a final distribution of the assets of the receivership, the receivership shall be terminated, the charter shall be canceled by the Farm Credit Administration Board if such cancellation has not previously occurred, and the receiver shall be finally discharged and released.

Subpart C—Conservators and Conservatorships

§ 627.2770 **Conservators.**

(a) The Insurance Corporation shall be appointed as conservator by the Farm Credit Administration Board pursuant to section 4.12 of the Act and § 627.2710 of this part to take possession of an institution in accordance with the terms of the appointment. Upon appointment, the conservator shall direct the institution's further operation until the Farm Credit Administration Board decides whether to place the institution into receivership. Upon correction or resolution of the problem or condition that provided the basis for the appointment and upon a determination by the Farm Credit Administration Board that the institution can be returned to normal operations, the Farm Credit Administration Board may turn the institution over to such management as the Farm Credit Administration Board may direct.

(b) The conservator shall exercise all powers necessary to continue the ongoing operations of the institution, to conserve and preserve the institution's assets and property, and otherwise protect the interests of the institution, its stockholders, and creditors as provided in this subpart.

§ 627.2775 **Appointment of a conservator.**

(a) The Farm Credit Administration Board may appoint ex parte and without notice a conservator for any Farm Credit institution provided that one or more of the grounds for appointment as set forth in § 627.2710 exist.

(b) Upon the appointment of a conservator, the Chairman of the Farm Credit Administration shall immediately notify the institution and, in the case of an association, the district bank, and notice of the appointment shall be published in the FEDERAL REGISTER. As soon as practicable after the conservator takes possession of the institution, the conservator shall notify, by first class mail, each holder of stock and participation certificates in the institution of the establishment of the conservatorship and shall describe the effect of the conservatorship on the institution's operations and on the borrower's loan and equity holdings.

(c) Upon the issuance of the order placing a Farm Credit institution in conservatorship, all rights, privileges, and powers of the members, board of directors, officers, and employees of the institution are vested exclusively in the conservator.

(d) The conservator is responsible for conserving and preserving the assets of the institution and continuing the ongoing operations of the institution until the conservatorship is terminated by order of the Farm Credit Administration Board.

(e) The Board may, at any time, terminate the conservator and direct the conservator to turn over the institution's operations to such management as the Board may designate, in which event the provisions of this subpart shall no longer apply.

§ 627.2780 Powers and duties of conservators.

(a) The conservator of an institution serves as the trustee of the institution and conducts its operations for the benefit of the creditors and stockholders of the institution.

(b) The conservator may, with respect to Farm Credit institutions, exercise the powers that a receiver of an institution may exercise under any of the provisions of § 627.2725(b) of this part, except paragraphs § 627.2725 (b)(2) and (b)(17). The provisions of § 627.2726 shall also apply to the conservator of a Farm Credit institution. In interpreting the applicable paragraphs for purposes of this section, the terms "conservator" and "conservatorship" shall be read for "receiver" and "receivership."

(c) The conservator may extend credit to new and existing borrowers as is necessary to the continuing operation of the institution and to effectuate the purposes of the conservatorship.

(d) The conservator may also take any other action the conservator considers appropriate or expedient to the continuing operation of the institution.

[57 FR 46482, Oct. 9, 1992, as amended at 70 FR 55515, Sept. 22, 2005]

§ 627.2785 Inventory, examination, audit, and reports to stockholders.

(a) As soon as practicable after taking possession of a Farm Credit institution the conservator shall make an inventory of the assets and liabilities of the institution as of the date possession was taken. One copy of the inventory shall be filed with the Farm Credit Administration.

(b) The institution in conservatorship shall be examined by the Farm Credit Administration in accordance with section 5.19 of the Act. The institution must also be audited by a qualified public accountant in accordance with part 621 of this chapter.

(c) Each institution in conservatorship shall prepare and file with the Farm Credit Administration financial reports in accordance with the requirements of part 621 of this chapter. The conservator of the institution shall provide the certification required in § 621.14 of this chapter.

(d) Each institution in conservatorship must prepare and issue published financial reports in accordance with the provisions of part 620 of this chapter, and the certifications and signatures of the board of directors or management provided for in § 620.3 of this chapter must be provided by the conservator of the institution.

[57 FR 46482, Oct. 9, 1992, as amended at 58 FR 48791, Sept. 20, 1993; 71 FR 76121, Dec. 20, 2006]

§ 627.2790 Final discharge and release of the conservator.

At such time as the conservator shall be relieved of its conservatorship duties, the conservator shall file a report on the conservator's activities with the Farm Credit Administration. The conservator shall thereupon be completely and finally released.

Subpart D—Voluntary Liquidation

SOURCE: 63 FR 5725, Feb. 4, 1998, unless otherwise noted.

§ 627.2795 Voluntary liquidation.

(a) A Farm Credit institution may voluntarily liquidate by a resolution of its board of directors, but only with the consent of, and in accordance with a plan of liquidation approved by, the Farm Credit Administration Board. Upon adoption of such resolution to liquidate, the Farm Credit institution shall submit the proposed voluntary liquidation plan to the Farm Credit Administration for preliminary approval. The Farm Credit Administration Board, in its discretion, may appoint a receiver as part of an approved liquidation plan. If a receiver is appointed for the Farm Credit institution as part of a voluntary liquidation, the receivership shall be conducted pursuant to subpart B of this part, except to the extent that an approved plan of liquidation provides otherwise.

(b) If the Farm Credit Administration Board gives preliminary approval to the liquidation plan, the board of directors of the Farm Credit institution shall submit the resolution to liquidate and the liquidation plan to the stockholders for approval.

(c) The resolution to liquidate and the liquidation plan shall be approved by the stockholders if agreed to by at least a majority of the voting stockholders of the institution voting, in person or by written proxy, at a duly authorized stockholders' meeting.

(d) The Farm Credit Administration Board will consider final approval of the liquidation plan after an affirmative stockholder vote on the resolution to liquidate.

(e) Any subsequent amendments, modifications, revisions, or adjustments to the liquidation plan shall require Farm Credit Administration Board approval.

(f) The Farm Credit Administration Board, in its discretion, reserves the right to terminate or modify the liquidation plan at any time.

§ 627.2797 Preservation of equity.

(a) Immediately upon the adoption of a resolution by its board of directors to voluntarily liquidate a Farm Credit institution, the capital stock, participation certificates, equity reserves, and allocated equities of the Farm Credit institution shall not be issued, allocated, retired, sold, distributed, transferred, assigned, or applied against any indebtedness of the owners of such equities. Such activities could resume if the stockholders of the Farm Credit institution disapprove the resolution to liquidate or the Farm Credit Administration Board disapproves the liquidation plan. In the event the resolution to liquidate is approved by the stockholders of the Farm Credit institution and the liquidation plan is approved by the Farm Credit Administration Board, the liquidation plan shall govern disposition of the equities of the Farm Credit institution, except that if the Farm Credit institution is placed in receivership, the provisions of § 627.2730(a) shall govern further disposition of the equities of the Farm Credit institution.

(b) Notwithstanding paragraph (a) of this section, eligible borrower stock shall be retired in accordance with section 4.9A of the Act.

PART 630—DISCLOSURE TO INVESTORS IN SYSTEMWIDE AND CONSOLIDATED BANK DEBT OBLIGATIONS OF THE FARM CREDIT SYSTEM

Subpart A—General

Sec.
630.1 Purpose.
630.2 Definitions.
630.3 Publishing and filing the report to investors.
630.4 Responsibilities for preparing the report to investors.
630.5 Prohibition against incomplete, inaccurate, or misleading disclosure.
630.6 Funding Corporation committees.

Subpart B—Annual Report to Investors

630.20 Contents of the annual report to investors.

Subpart C—Quarterly Reports to Investors

630.40 Contents of the quarterly report to investors.
APPENDIX A TO PART 630—SUPPLEMENTAL INFORMATION DISCLOSURE GUIDELINES

AUTHORITY: Secs. 5.17, 5.19 of the Farm Credit Act (12 U.S.C. 2252, 2254).

SOURCE: 59 FR 46742, Sept. 12, 1994, unless otherwise noted.

Subpart A—General

§ 630.1 Purpose.

This part sets forth the requirements for preparation and publication by the Farm Credit System (FCS or System) of annual and quarterly reports to investors and potential investors in Systemwide and consolidated bank debt obligations of the System and to other users of the reports in the general public.

§ 630.2 Definitions.

For purposes of this part, the following definitions shall apply:

(a) *Bank* means any bank chartered under the Farm Credit Act of 1971, as amended (Act).

(b) *Combined financial statements* means financial statements prepared on a combined basis by a group of affiliated entities that share the same financial interest, regardless of whether any of the entities has the ability to exercise control over another. For purposes of this part, unless otherwise specified, combined financial data of a bank and its related associations includes financial data of the bank's consolidated subsidiaries.

(c) *Disclosure entity* means any Farm Credit bank and the Federal Farm Credit Banks Funding Corporation (Funding Corporation).

(d) *Engagement letter* means the proposal, contract, letter, and other documents reflecting the understandings between the audit committee or board of directors of a bank or an association and its independent public accountant regarding the scope, terms, and nature of the audit services to be performed.

(e) *Farm Credit System* means, collectively, the banks, associations, and such other institutions that are or may be made a part of the System under the Act, all of which are chartered by and subject to regulation by the Farm Credit Administration (FCA). For purposes of this part, the System does not include the Federal Agricultural Mortgage Corporation (Farmer Mac).

(f) *FCS debt obligation* means, collectively, notes, bonds, debentures, and other debt securities issued by banks pursuant to section 4.2(c) (consolidated bank debt securities) and section 4.2(d) (Systemwide debt securities) of the Act.

(g) *Report to investors* or *report* means a report that presents the Systemwide combined financial statements, supplemental financial statement information, and related financial and nonfinancial information pertaining to the System required by this part.

(h) *Systemwide combined financial statements* means the combined financial statements required by this part.

[59 FR 46742, Sept. 12, 1994, as amended at 71 FR 76121, Dec. 20, 2006]

§ 630.3 Publishing and filing the report to investors.

(a) The disclosure entities shall jointly publish the following reports in order to provide meaningful information pertaining to the financial condition and results of operations of the System to investors and potential investors in FCS debt obligations and other users of the report:

(1) An annual report to investors within 75 calendar days after the end of each fiscal year;

(2) A quarterly report to investors within 45 calendar days after the end of each quarter, except for the quarter that coincides with the end of the fiscal year.

(3) Interim reports, as required by the Funding Corporation's written policies and procedures, disclosing significant events or material changes in information occurring since the most recently published report to investors.

(b) Each report to investors shall present Systemwide combined financial statements and related footnotes deemed appropriate for the purpose of the report to provide investors with the most meaningful presentation pertaining to the financial condition and results of operations of the System.

(c) All items of essentially the same character as items required to be reported in the reports of condition and performance pursuant to part 621 of this chapter shall be prepared in accordance with the rules set forth in part 621 of this chapter.

(d) Each report to investors shall contain the information required by subparts B and C of this part, as applicable, and such other information as is necessary to make the required statements, in light of the circumstances under which they are made, not misleading.

(e) Information in any part of the report may be referenced or incorporated in answer or partial answer to any other item of the report. Information required by this part may be presented in any order deemed suitable by the Funding Corporation.

(f) Information in documents prepared for investors in connection with the offering of debt securities issued through the Funding Corporation may be incorporated by reference in the annual and quarterly reports in answer or partial answer to any item required in the reports under this part. A complete description of any offering documents incorporated by reference must be clearly identified in the report (e.g., Federal Farm Credit Banks Consolidated System-wide Bonds and Discount

§ 630.4

Notes—Offering Circular issued on [insert date]). Offering documents incorporated by reference in either an annual or quarterly report prepared under this part must be filed with the Farm Credit Administration according to our instructions either prior to or at the time of submission of the report under paragraph (h) of this section. Any offering document incorporated by reference is subject to the delivery and availability requirements set forth in § 630.4(a)(5) and (a)(6).

(g) The report shall include a statement in a prominent location that Systemwide debt securities and consolidated bank debt obligations are joint and several liabilities of individual banks and that copies of each bank's recent periodic reports to shareholders are available upon request. The report shall also include addresses and telephone numbers where copies of the report to investors and the periodic reports of individual banks can be obtained. Copies of the report to investors shall be available for public inspection at the Funding Corporation.

(h) Complete copies of the report must be filed with the Farm Credit Administration according to our instructions. All copies must comply with the requirements of § 630.5 of this part.

[59 FR 46724, Sept. 12, 1994, as amended at 62 FR 15094, Mar. 31, 1997; 71 FR 76121, Dec. 20, 2006]

§ 630.4 Responsibilities for preparing the report to investors.

(a) *Responsibilities of the Funding Corporation.* The Funding Corporation shall:

(1) Prepare the reports to investors required by § 630.3(a), including the Systemwide combined financial statements and notes thereto, and such other disclosures, supplemental information, and related analysis as are required by this part to make the reports meaningful and not misleading.

(2) Establish a system of internal controls sufficient to reasonably ensure that any information it releases to investors and the general public concerning any matter required to be disclosed by this part is true and that there are no omissions of material information. The system of internal controls, at a minimum, shall require that the Funding Corporation:

(i) Maintain written policies and procedures, approved by the System Audit Committee, to be carried out by the disclosure entities for preparation of the report to investors;

(ii) Provide instructions to the disclosure entities regarding the information needed for preparation of the Systemwide combined financial statements and disclosures required to be presented in the report to investors;

(iii) Review the information submitted to it for preparation of the report to investors, and make reasonable inquiries to ascertain whether the information is reliable, accurate, and complete; and

(iv) Specify procedures for monitoring interim disclosures of System institutions and disclose, in a timely manner, any material changes in information contained in the most recently published report to investors.

(3) Collect from each disclosure entity financial data and related analyses and other information needed for preparation of the report to investors, including any information that is material to the disclosure entity.

(4) File the reports with the FCA in accordance with § 630.3(f) and (h) and § 630.5.

(5) Ensure prompt delivery of sufficient copies of each report to selling group dealers for distribution to investors and potential investors in FCS debt obligations.

(6) Make the report available to the general public upon request.

(7) Notify the FCA if it is unable to prepare and publish the report to investors in compliance with the requirements of this part because one or more banks have failed to comply with the requirements of paragraph (c) of this section. A notification, signed by the officer(s) designated by the board of directors of the Funding Corporation to certify the report to investors and by the chief executive officer, shall be made to the FCA as soon as the Funding Corporation becomes aware of its inability to comply. The Funding Corporation shall explain the reasons for the notification and may request that the FCA extend the due date for the report to investors.

(8) Include in the report a statement that briefly explains the respective responsibilities of the disclosure entities and states that the Funding Corporation has policies and procedures in place to ensure, to the best of the knowledge and belief of management and the board of the Funding Corporation, that the information contained in the report is true, accurate, and complete. The statement shall be signed by the chief executive officer and the chairperson of the board of the Funding Corporation.

(9) Request the FCA to provide information regarding the content of the latest Reports of Examination of any banks and related associations, if such information is necessary for preparation of a report that is meaningful and not misleading and is not forthcoming from a bank in accordance with paragraph (c) of this section. The request shall be made to the Chief Examiner, Farm Credit Administration, McLean, Virginia 22102–5090.

(b) *Responsibilities of banks.* Each bank shall:

(1) Provide to the Funding Corporation annual, quarterly, and interim financial and other information in accordance with instructions of the Funding Corporation for preparation of the report to investors, including:

(i) Financial data of the bank or, if the bank is required under generally accepted accounting principles (GAAP) to prepare its financial statements on a consolidated basis with its subsidiaries, consolidated financial data of the bank and its consolidated subsidiaries; and

(ii) Combined financial data of the bank (including any consolidated subsidiaries of the bank) and related associations of the bank.

(2) Respond to Funding Corporation inquiries and provide any followup information requested by the Funding Corporation in connection with the preparation of the report to investors in accordance with instructions of the Funding Corporation.

(3) Notify the Funding Corporation promptly of any events occurring subsequent to publication of the report that may be material either to the financial condition and results of operations of the bank or to the combined financial condition and results of operations of the bank and its related associations. Furnish the Funding Corporation with any information necessary to provide interim Systemwide disclosure to investors to make the most recently published report to investors not misleading.

(4) Respond to inquiries from the Funding Corporation relating to preparation of the report.

(5) Certify to the Funding Corporation that all information needed for preparation of the report to investors has been submitted in accordance with the instructions of the Funding Corporation and the information submitted complies with the signature and certification provisions of §620.3(b) and (c), respectively.

(c) *Responsibilities of associations.* Each association must:

(1) Provide its related bank with the information necessary to allow the bank to provide accurate and complete information regarding the bank and its related associations to the Funding Corporation for preparation of the report. The financial information provided by the association to its related bank must be signed and certified in the same manner as provided in §620.3(b) and (c), respectively.

(2) Respond to inquiries of the related bank pertaining to preparation of the combined financial data of the association and its related bank.

[59 FR 46724, Sept. 12, 1994, as amended at 71 FR 76121, Dec. 20, 2006]

§ 630.5 **Accuracy of reports and assessment of internal control over financial reporting.**

(a) *Prohibition against incomplete, inaccurate, or misleading disclosure.* Neither the Funding Corporation, nor any institution supplying information to the Funding Corporation under this part, nor any employee, officer, director, or nominee for director of the Funding Corporation or of such institutions, shall make or cause to be made any disclosure to investors and the general public required by this part that is incomplete, inaccurate, or misleading. When any such institution or person makes or causes to be made disclosure under this part that, in the judgment of the FCA, is incomplete, inaccurate, or misleading, whether or not

§ 630.6

such disclosure is made in published statements required by this part, such institution or person shall promptly furnish to the Funding Corporation, and the Funding Corporation shall promptly publish, such additional or corrective disclosure as is necessary to provide full and fair disclosure to investors and the general public. Nothing in this section shall prevent the FCA from taking additional actions to enforce this section pursuant to its authority under title V, part C of the Act.

(b) *Signatures.* The name and position title of each person signing the report must be printed beneath his or her signature. If any person required to sign the report has not signed the report, the name and position title of the individual and the reasons such individual is unable to, or refuses to, sign must be disclosed in the report. All reports must be dated and signed on behalf of the Funding Corporation by:

(1) The chief executive officer (CEO);

(2) The officer in charge of preparing financial statements; and

(3) A board member formally designated by action of the board to certify reports of condition and performance on behalf of individual board members.

(c) *Certification of financial accuracy.* The report must be certified as financially accurate by the signatories to the report. If any signatory is unable to, or refuses to, certify the report, the institution must disclose the individual's name and position title and the reason(s) such individual is unable or refuses to certify the report. At a minimum, the certification must include a statement that:

(1) The signatories have reviewed the report,

(2) The report has been prepared in accordance with all applicable statutory or regulatory requirements, and

(3) The information is true, accurate, and complete to the best of signatories' knowledge and belief.

(d) *Management assessment of internal control over financial reporting.* (1) Annual reports must include a report by the Funding Corporation's management assessing the effectiveness of the internal control over financial reporting for the System-wide report to investors. The assessment must be conducted during the reporting period and be reported to the Funding Corporation's board of directors. Quarterly and annual reports must disclose any material change(s) in the internal control over financial reporting occurring during the reporting period.

(2) The Funding Corporation must require its external auditor to issue an attestation report, which must express an opinion on the effectiveness of internal control over financial reporting. The resulting attestation report must accompany management's assessment and be included in the annual report.

[71 FR 76121, Dec. 20, 2006, as amended at 72 FR 64130, Nov. 15, 2007]

§ 630.6 Funding Corporation committees.

(a) *System Audit Committee.* The Funding Corporation must establish and maintain a System Audit Committee (SAC) by adopting a written charter describing the committee's composition, authorities, and responsibilities in accordance with this section. The SAC must maintain records of meetings, including attendance, for at least 3 fiscal years.

(1) *Composition.* All SAC members should be knowledgeable in at least one of the following: Public and corporate finance, financial reporting and disclosure, or accounting procedures.

(i) At least one-third of the SAC members must be representatives from the Farm Credit System.

(ii) The SAC may not consist of less than three members and at least one member must be a financial expert. A financial expert is one who either has experience with internal controls and procedures for financial reporting or experience in preparing or auditing financial statements.

(iii) The chair of the SAC must be a financial expert.

(2) *Independence.* Every audit committee member must be free from any relationship that, in the opinion of the Funding Corporation board, would interfere with the exercise of independent judgment as a committee member.

(3) *Resources.* The Funding Corporation must permit the SAC to contract for independent legal counsel and expert advisors. The Funding Corporation

Farm Credit Administration § 630.20

is responsible for providing monetary and nonmonetary resources to enable the SAC to contract for external auditors, outside advisors, and ordinary administrative expenses. A two-thirds majority vote of the full Funding Corporation board of directors is required to deny any SAC request for resources.

(4) *Duties.* The SAC reports only to the Funding Corporation board of directors. In its capacity as a committee of the board, the SAC is responsible for the following:

(i) *Financial reports.* The SAC must oversee the Funding Corporation's preparation of the report to stockholders and investors; review the impact of any significant accounting and auditing developments; review accounting policy changes relating to preparation of the System-wide combined financial statements; and review annual and quarterly reports prior to release. After the SAC reviews a financial policy, procedure, or report, it must record in its minutes its agreement or disagreement with the item(s) under review.

(ii) *External auditors.* The external auditor must report directly to the SAC. The SAC must:

(A) Determine the appointment, compensation, and retention of external auditors issuing System-wide audit reports;

(B) Review the external auditor's work;

(C) Give prior approval for any nonaudit services performed by the external auditor, except the audit committee may not approve those nonaudit services specifically prohibited by FCA regulation; and

(D) Comply with the auditor independence provisions of part 621 of this chapter.

(iii) *Internal controls.* The SAC must oversee the Funding Corporation's system of internal controls relating to preparation of financial reports, including controls relating to the Farm Credit System's compliance with applicable laws and regulations.

(b) *Compensation committee.* The Funding Corporation must establish and maintain a compensation committee by adopting a written charter describing the committee's composition, authorities, and responsibilities in accordance with this section. The compensation committee will be required to maintain records of meetings, including attendance, for at least 3 fiscal years.

(1) *Composition.* The committee must consist of at least three members. Each committee member must be a member of the Funding Corporation's board of directors. Every member must be free from any relationship that, in the opinion of the board, would interfere with the exercise of independent judgment as a committee member.

(2) *Duties.* The compensation committee must report only to the board of directors. In its capacity as a committee of the board, the compensation committee is responsible for reviewing the compensation policies and plans for senior officers and employees. The compensation committee must approve the overall compensation program for senior officers.

(3) *Resources.* The Funding Corporation must provide monetary and nonmonetary resources to enable its compensation committee to function.

[71 FR 5767, Feb. 2, 2006, as amended at 71 FR 76122, Dec. 20, 2006]

Subpart B—Annual Report to Investors

§ 630.20 Contents of the annual report to investors.

The annual report must contain the following:

(a) *Description of business.* (1) The description shall include a brief discussion of the following:

(i) The System's overall organizational structure, its lending institutions by type and their respective authorities, the relationships between different types of institutions, and the overall geographic area and eligible borrowers served by those institutions;

(ii) The types of lending activities engaged in and financial services offered by System institutions;

(iii) Any significant developments within the last 5 years that have had or could have a material impact on the System's organizational structure and the manner in which System institutions conduct business, including, but not limited to, statutory or regulatory changes, mergers or liquidations of

§ 630.20

System institutions, terminations of System institution status, and financial assistance provided by or to System institutions through loss-sharing or capital preservation agreements or from any other source;

(iv) Any acquisition or disposition of material assets during the last fiscal year that took place outside the ordinary course of business;

(v) Any concentrations of more than 10 percent of total assets in particular types of agricultural activities or businesses, and any dependence of an institution or a group of institutions of the System upon a specific activity or business, a single customer, or a few customers, including other financing institutions (OFIs), the loss of any one of which would have a material effect on the System; and

(vi) The authority of System institutions to purchase and sell interests in loans in secondary markets and the risk involved in such activities.

(2) List the address of the headquarters of each disclosure entity and service organization of the System.

(b) *Federal regulation and insurance—* (1) *Farm Credit Administration.* Describe the regulatory and enforcement authority of the FCA over System institutions under the Act.

(2) *Farm Credit System Insurance Corporation.* (i) Describe the role and authorities of the Farm Credit System Insurance Corporation (FCSIC) under part E of title V of the Act. Describe specifically the role of the FCSIC in insuring the timely payment of principal and interest on FCS debt obligations and in providing assistance to System institutions.

(ii) Describe the FCSIC's status as a Government corporation and state that System institutions have no control over the management of the FCSIC or the discretionary expenditures from the Farm Credit Insurance Fund (Insurance Fund), which are the sole prerogative of the FCSIC.

(c) *Description of legal proceedings and enforcement actions.* (1) Describe any material pending legal proceedings in which one or more System institutions are a party, or that involve claims that a System institution(s) may be required by contract or operation of law to satisfy, and the potential impact of

12 CFR Ch. VI (1–1–12 Edition)

such proceedings, to the extent known, on the System.

(2) Provide a summary of the types of enforcement actions in effect during the year, and any material impact of such proceedings on the System.

(d) *Description of liabilities.* (1) Describe how the System funds its lending operations, including:

(i) System banks' authority to borrow, and issue notes, bonds, debentures, and other obligations, and limitations thereof under section 4.2 of the Act;

(ii) A description of the types of debt obligations authorized to be issued under the Act, the types of debt obligations currently issued, the manner and form in which they are issued, rights of securities holders, risk factors, use of proceeds, tax effects of holding securities, market information, and other pertinent information;

(iii) For each of the types of obligations that may be issued, whether it is insured, and the extent of any joint and several liability for the obligations; and

(iv) Any applicable statutory and regulatory requirements affecting a bank's ability to incur debt.

(2) Describe agreements among System banks and the Funding Corporation affecting a bank's ability to incur debt.

(3) Describe agreements among System institutions regarding capital preservation, loss sharing, or any other forms of financial assistance.

(e) *Description of capital.* (1) Describe the capitalization of the System, including capital structure, types of stock and participation certificates, and voting rights of holders of stock and participation certificates.

(2) Describe the statutory requirement that a borrower purchase stock as a condition of obtaining a loan; how such stock is purchased, transferred, and retired; and how earnings are distributed.

(3) Describe any statutory or other authority of a System institution to require additional capital contributions from stockholders.

(4) Describe regulatory minimum permanent capital standards and capital adequacy requirements for banks and associations. State the number of

Farm Credit Administration §630.20

institutions, if any, categorized by banks and associations, that are not currently in compliance with such standards and include a brief discussion of the reasons for the noncompliance.

(5) Describe any statutory and regulatory restrictions on retirement of stock and distribution of earnings by System institutions. State the number of System institutions, if any, categorized by banks and associations, that are currently affected by such restrictions and provide a summary of the causes of such prohibitions.

(f) *Selected financial data.* At a minimum, furnish the following combined financial data of the System in comparative columnar form for each of the last 5 fiscal years, if material.

(1) *Balance sheet.*
(i) Loans.
(ii) Allowance for losses.
(iii) Net loans.
(iv) Cash and investments.
(v) Other property owned.
(vi) Total assets.
(vii) FCS debt obligations and other bonds, notes, debentures, and obligations, presented by type, with a descriptive title.
(viii) Total liabilities.
(ix) Capital stock and surplus.

(2) *Statement of income.*
(i) Net interest income.
(ii) Net other expenses.
(iii) Provision for loan losses.
(iv) Extraordinary items.
(v) Provision for income taxes.
(vi) Net income (loss).

(3) *Key financial ratios.* (i) Return on average assets.
(ii) Return on average capital stock and surplus.
(iii) Net interest income as a percentage of average earning assets.
(iv) Net loan chargeoffs as a percentage of average loans.
(v) Allowance for loan losses as a percentage of gross loans outstanding at yearend.
(vi) Capital stock and surplus as a percentage of total assets at yearend.
(vii) Debt to capital stock and surplus at yearend.

(g) *Discussion and analysis.* Fully discuss any material aspects of financial condition, changes in financial condition, and results of operations of System institutions, on a combined basis, for the comparative years required by paragraph (g)(6)(ii) of this section or such other time periods specified in the following paragraphs of this section. Identify favorable and unfavorable trends, and significant events or uncertainties necessary to understand the financial condition and results of operations of the System. At a minimum, the discussion shall include the following:

(1) *Loan portfolio*—(i) *Categorization.* Describe the loan portfolio of the System by major loan purpose category, indicating the amount and approximate percentage of the total dollar portfolio represented by each major category.

(ii) *Risk exposure.* (A) Describe and analyze all high-risk assets, including an analysis of the nature and extent of significant current and potential credit risks within the loan portfolio and of other information that could adversely affect the loan portfolio and other property owned.

(B) Provide an analysis of the allowance for loan losses that includes the ratios of the allowance for loan losses to loans (outstanding at yearend) and net chargeoffs to average loans, and a discussion of the adequacy of the allowance for loan losses to absorb the risk inherent in the loan portfolio and the basis for such determination.

(iii) *Secondary market activities.* (A) If material, quantify System institutions' secondary market activities and the risk involved in such activities.

(B) If material, provide an analysis of historical loss experience and the amount provided for risk of loss associated with secondary market activities.

(2) *Results of operations.* (i) Describe, on a comparative basis, changes in the major components of net interest income. Include a discussion of significant factors that contributed to the changes and quantify the amount of change(s) due to an increase or decrease in volume and the amount due to changes in interest rates earned and paid, based on averages for each period.

(ii) Describe any unusual or infrequent events or transactions, or any significant economic changes that materially affected reported income and,

§ 630.20

in each case, indicate the extent to which income was so affected.

(iii) Discuss the factors underlying any material changes in the return on average assets and return on average capital stock and surplus.

(iv) Describe, on a comparative basis, the major components of operating expense and any other significant components of income or expense, indicating the reasons for any significant increases or decreases.

(v) Describe any known trends or uncertainties that have had, or that are reasonably expected to have, a material impact on net interest income or net income. Disclose any known events that will cause a material change in the relationship between costs and revenues.

(vi) Explain the changes that have taken place, by major components on a comparative basis, in Insurance Fund assets and related restricted capital and how such changes affected reported income.

(3) *Funding sources and liquidity*—(i) *Funding sources.* (A) Provide, in tabular form, the component amounts and the total amount of FCS debt obligations, debt obligations issued by banks individually, and Financial Assistance Corporation debt obligations outstanding at yearend for each of the past 2 fiscal years. List debt obligations issued by System institutions separately by type, also separating insured obligations from uninsured obligations. For each type of debt obligation listed, provide the following, at a minimum, for each fiscal year listed:

(*1*) The beginning balance, the total amount of debt issued, the total amount of debt retired, and the yearend balance; and

(*2*) The average maturities and average interest rates on debt outstanding at yearend, and the average maturities and average interest rates of new debt issued during the year.

(B) Summarize any other sources of funds, including lines of credit with commercial lenders, and their terms.

(ii) *Liquidity.* (A) Include a brief overview of any FCA regulations or System policies with regard to liquidity and liquidity reserves.

(B) Identify any known trends, demands, commitments, events, or uncertainties that will result in, or that are reasonably likely to result in, System liquidity increasing or decreasing in any material way. If a material liquidity deficiency is identified, indicate the course of action that has been taken or is proposed to be taken by management of affected System institutions to remedy the deficiency.

(iii) *Investment.* Provide a brief overview of the System's investment policies and objectives, any regulatory limitations thereon, and the contents of the System's existing investment portfolio.

(iv) *Interest rate sensitivity.* (A) Provide a brief overview of the System's asset and liability management practices, including interest rate risk measurement systems, and methods used to control interest rate risk, such as the use of investments, derivatives, and other off-balance-sheet transactions.

(B) Provide an analysis of the System's exposure to interest rate risk and its ability to control such risk.

(4) *Capital resources.* (i) Describe any material commitments to purchase capital assets and the anticipated sources of funding.

(ii) Describe any material trends, favorable or unfavorable, in the System's capital resources, including any material changes in the mix of capital and debt, the relative cost of capital resources, and any off-balance- sheet financing arrangements.

(iii) Provide a general discussion of any trends, commitments, contingencies, or events that are reasonably likely to have a material adverse effect on System institutions' ability to comply with regulatory capital standards.

(5) *Insurance Fund.* (i) Describe the purposes for which expenditures from the Insurance Fund may be made and the statutory requirements for making such expenditures.

(ii) Provide a schedule itemizing the amount of Insurance Fund assets that have been specifically identified by the FCSIC for payment of estimated obligations of the FCSIC and the amount of Insurance Fund assets for which no specific use has been identified or designated by the FCSIC. Information provided shall be as of the end of the most recent fiscal year.

Farm Credit Administration §630.20

(iii) Explain how FCSIC expenditures or designations of Insurance Fund assets for payment of future obligations affect the combined assets and capital of the System, and quantify the effect, if any.

(6) *Instructions for discussion and analysis.* (i) The purpose of the discussion and analysis (D&A) shall be to provide to investors and other users information relevant to an assessment of the combined financial condition and results of operations of System institutions as determined by evaluating the amounts and certainty of cashflows from operations and from outside sources. The information provided pursuant to this section need only include that which is available to System institutions and which does not clearly appear in the combined financial statements.

(ii) The D&A of the financial statements and other statistical data shall be presented in a manner designed to enhance a reader's understanding of the combined financial condition, results of operations, cashflows, and changes in capital of System institutions. Unless otherwise specified in §630.20(g), the discussion shall cover the period covered by the financial statements and shall use year-to-year comparisons or any other understandable format. Where trend information is relevant, reference to the 5-year selected financial data required by paragraph (f) of this section may be necessary.

(iii) The D&A shall focus specifically on material events and uncertainties known at the time of reporting that would cause reported financial information not to be necessarily indicative of future operating results or of future financial condition. This should include descriptions and amounts of:

(A) Matters that would have an impact on future operations but that have not had an impact in the past; and

(B) Matters that have had an impact on reported operations but are not expected to have an impact on future operations.

(h) *Directors and management*—(1) *Board of directors.* Briefly describe the composition of boards of directors of the disclosure entities. List the name of each director of such entities, including the director's term of office and principal occupation during the past 5 years, or state that such information is available upon request.

(2) *Senior officers.* List the names of all senior officers employed by the disclosure entities, including position title and length of service at current position.

(i) *Compensation of directors and senior officers.* State that information on the compensation of directors and senior officers of Farm Credit banks is contained in each bank's annual report to shareholders and that the annual report of each bank is available to investors upon request pursuant to §630.3(g).

(j) *Related party transactions.* (1) Briefly describe how System institutions, in the ordinary course of business and subject to regulation by the FCA, may enter into loan transactions with related parties, including their directors, officers, and employees, the immediate family members (as defined in §620.1(e) of this chapter) of such persons, and any organizations with which such persons and their immediate family members are affiliated.

(2) On a comparative basis for each of the fiscal years covered by the balance sheet, state the aggregate amount of the following:

(i) Loans made to related parties;

(ii) Loans outstanding at yearend to related parties;

(iii) Loans outstanding at yearend to related parties that are made on more favorable terms than those prevailing at the time for comparable transactions with unrelated borrowers; and

(iv) Loans outstanding at yearend to related parties that involve more than a normal risk of collectibility (as defined in §620.1(i) of this chapter).

(k) *Relationship with qualified public accountant.* (1) If a change in the qualified public accountant who has previously examined and expressed an opinion on the System-wide combined financial statements has taken place since the last annual report to investors or if a disagreement with a qualified public accountant has occurred that the Funding Corporation would be required to report to the FCA under part 621 of this chapter, disclose the information required by §621.4(c) and (d).

§ 630.20

(2) Disclose the total fees paid during the reporting period to the qualified public accountant by the category of services provided. At a minimum, identify fees paid for audit services, tax services, and non-audit services. The types of non-audit services must be identified and indicate audit committee approval of the services.

(l) *Financial statements.* Furnish System-wide combined financial statements and related footnotes prepared in accordance with GAAP, and accompanied by supplemental information prepared in accordance with the requirements of § 630.20(m). The Systemwide combined financial statements shall provide investors and potential investors in FCS debt obligations with the most meaningful presentation pertaining to the financial condition and results of operations of the System. The System-wide combined financial statement and accompanying supplemental information shall be audited in accordance with generally accepted auditing standards by a qualified public accountant. The System-wide combined financial statements shall include the following:

(1) A balance sheet as of the end of each of the 2 most recent fiscal years; and

(2) Statements of income, statements of changes in capital stock and surplus (or, if applicable, statements of changes in protected borrower capital and capital stock and surplus), and statements of cash flows for each of the 3 most recent fiscal years.

(m) *Supplemental information.* Furnish supplemental information regarding the components of the Systemwide combined financial statements that has been prepared in accordance with the requirements of this paragraph and any additional guidance or instructions provided by the FCA.

(1) At a minimum, the supplemental information shall include the following:

(i) Supplemental balance sheet information as of the end of the most recent fiscal year; and

(ii) Supplemental income statement information for the most recently completed fiscal year.

(2) At a minimum, the report shall present supplemental information showing combined financial data for the following components on a stand-alone basis:

(i) Banks;

(ii) Associations;

(iii) Combined financial data of the System without the Insurance Fund;

(iv) The Insurance Fund and related combination entries; and

(v) Combined financial data of the System with the Insurance Fund.

(3) The supplemental information shall be presented in a columnar format and include, at a minimum, the selected financial data listed in the schedules in appendix A of this part. The prescribed components shall be designated as column headings and they may be abbreviated in the schedules. The financial data required by § 630.20(m)(2)(i) shall include the financial data required to be submitted by each bank pursuant to the requirement of § 630.4(c)(1)(i).

(4) The supplemental information may be presented separately or in accompanying notes to the Systemwide combined financial statements and shall contain additional disclosures sufficient to explain the basis of the presentation of the supplemental information, the components, and any adjustments contained therein to enable readers to understand the effect of each component on the Systemwide combined financial statements.

(n) List the names of the System Audit Committee members in the report to investors.

(o) Include a detailed index setting forth the major disclosure captions of this subpart and the page or pages on which the required information appears in the report.

(p) *Credit and services to young, beginning, and small farmers and ranchers and producers or harvesters of aquatic products.* The Farm Credit banks must include a report on consolidated YBS lending data of their affiliated associations. The report must include the definitions of "young," "beginning," and "small" farmers and ranchers. A narrative report may be necessary for an ample understanding of the YBS mission results.

[59 FR 46742, Sept. 12, 1994, as amended at 63 FR 36549, July 7, 1998; 69 FR 16471, Mar. 30, 2004; 71 FR 5767, Feb. 2, 2006; 71 FR 76122, Dec. 20, 2006]

Subpart C—Quarterly Reports to Investors

§ 630.40 Contents of the quarterly report to investors.

(a) *General.* The quarterly report to investors shall contain the information specified in this section along with any other material information necessary to make the required disclosures, in light of the circumstances under which they are made, not misleading. The quarterly report must be presented in a format that is easily understandable and not misleading.

(b) *Rules for condensation.* For purposes of this subpart, major captions to be provided in interim financial statements are the same as those provided in the financial statements contained in the annual report to investors, except that the financial statements included in the quarterly report may be condensed into major captions in accordance with the rules prescribed under this paragraph.

(1) *Interim balance sheets.* When any major balance sheet caption is less than 10 percent of total assets and the amount in the caption has not increased or decreased by more than 25 percent since the end of the preceding fiscal year, the caption may be combined with others.

(2) *Interim statements of income.* When any major income statement caption is less than 15 percent of average net income for the 3 most recent fiscal years and the amount in the caption has not increased or decreased by more than 20 percent since the corresponding interim period of the preceding fiscal year, the caption may be combined with others. In calculating average net income, loss years should be excluded. If losses were incurred in each of the 3 most recent fiscal years, the average loss shall be used for purposes of this test.

(3) The interim financial information shall include disclosure either on the face of the financial statements or in accompanying footnotes sufficient to make the interim information presented not misleading. It may be presumed that users of the interim financial information have read or have access to the audited financial statements for the preceding fiscal year, and the adequacy of additional disclosure needed for a fair presentation may be determined in that context. Accordingly, footnote disclosure that would substantially duplicate the disclosure contained in the most recent audited financial statements (such as a statement of significant accounting policies and practices) and details of accounts that have not changed significantly in amount or composition since the end of the most recently completed fiscal year may be omitted.

(4) Interim reports shall disclose events that have occurred subsequent to the end of the most recently completed fiscal year that have a material impact on the System. Disclosures should encompass, for example, significant changes since the end of the most recently completed fiscal year in such items as accounting principles and practices, estimates used in the preparation of financial statements, status of long-term contracts, capitalization, significant new indebtedness or modification of existing financing agreements, financial assistance received, significant business combinations and liquidations of System institutions, and terminations of System institution status. Notwithstanding the provisions of this paragraph, where material contingencies exist, disclosure of such matters shall be provided even though a significant change since yearend may not have occurred.

(5) In addition to meeting the reporting requirements specified by existing accounting pronouncements for accounting changes, state the date of any material accounting change and the reasons for making it.

(6) Any material prior period adjustment made during any period covered by the interim financial statements shall be disclosed, together with its effect upon net income and upon the balance of surplus for any prior period included. If results of operations for any period presented have been adjusted

§ 630.40

retroactively by such an item subsequent to the initial reporting of such period, similar disclosure of the effect of the change shall be made.

(7) Interim financial statements furnished shall reflect all adjustments that are necessary to a fair statement of the results for the interim periods presented. A statement to that effect shall be included. Furnish any material information necessary to make the information called for not misleading, such as a statement that the results for interim periods are not necessarily indicative of results to be expected for the year.

(8) If any amount that would otherwise be required to be shown by this section with respect to any item is not material, it need not be separately shown. The combination of insignificant items is permitted.

(c) *Discussion and analysis of interim financial condition and results of operations.* Discuss any material changes to the information disclosed to investors pursuant to § 630.20(g) that have occurred during the periods specified in paragraphs (d)(1) and (d)(2) of this section. Provide any additional information needed to enable the reader to assess material changes in financial condition and results of operations between the periods specified in paragraphs (d)(1) and (d)(2) of this section.

(1) *Material changes in financial condition.* Discuss any material changes in financial condition from the end of the preceding fiscal year to the date of the most recent interim balance sheet provided.

(2) *Material changes in results of operations.* Discuss any material changes in the combined results of operations of the System with respect to the most recent fiscal year-to-date period for which an income statement is provided and the corresponding year-to-date period of the preceding fiscal year. Such discussion shall also cover material changes with respect to the most recent fiscal quarter and the corresponding fiscal quarter in the preceding fiscal year.

(d) *Financial statements.* Interim combined financial statements must be provided in the quarterly report to investors as set forth in paragraphs (d)(1) through (4). Indicate that the financial statements were prepared under the oversight of the System Audit Committee.

(1) An interim balance sheet as of the end of the most recent fiscal quarter and a balance sheet as of the end of the preceding fiscal year.

(2) Interim statements of income for the most recent fiscal quarter, for the period between the end of the preceding fiscal year and the end of the most recent fiscal quarter, and for the comparable periods for the previous fiscal year.

(3) Interim statements of changes in capital stock and surplus (or, if applicable, interim statements of changes in protected borrower capital and capital stock and surplus) for the period between the end of the preceding fiscal year and the end of the most recent fiscal quarter, and for the comparable period for the preceding fiscal year.

(4) Interim statements of cash flows for the period between the end of the preceding fiscal year and the end of the most recent fiscal quarter, and for the comparable period for the preceding fiscal year.

(e) *Supplemental information.* The interim report shall present supplemental information in accordance with the requirements of § 630.20 (m)(2), (m)(3), and (m)(4), as well as other requirements and instructions of the FCA, and shall include, at a minimum, the following:

(1) Supplemental balance sheet information as of the end of the most recent quarter; and

(2) Supplemental income statement information for the period between the end of the preceding fiscal year and the end of the most recent fiscal quarter.

(f) *Review by independent public accountant.* Unless otherwise ordered by the FCA as a result of a supervisory action, the interim financial statements and supplemental information need not be audited or reviewed by an independent public accountant prior to filing. If, however, a review of the report is made in accordance with the established professional standards and procedures for such a review, a statement that the independent accountant has performed such a review may be included. If such a statement is made,

Farm Credit Administration   **Pt. 630, App. A**

the report of the independent accountant on such review shall accompany the interim financial information.

[59 FR 46742, Sept. 12, 1994, as amended at 71 FR 5768, Feb. 2, 2006]

APPENDIX A TO PART 630—SUPPLEMENTAL INFORMATION DISCLOSURE GUIDELINES

Supplemental information required by §§ 630.20(m) and 630.40(e) shall contain, at a minimum, the current year financial data for the components listed in the following tables and be presented in the columnar format illustrated in the following tables:

TABLE A—SUPPLEMENTAL BALANCE SHEET INFORMATION

	Banks[1]	Associations[2]	Financial assistance corporation	Eliminations	Combined without Insurance fund[3]	Insurance fund and related combination entries	Combined with insurance fund
Cash and investments							
Net loans							
Restricted assets							
Other Assets							
Total assets							
Total liabilities							
Protected borrower capital[4]							
Restricted capital							
Capital stock and surplus							
Total liabilities, protected borrower capital, and capital stock and surplus							

[1] Provide combined financial data of all FCS banks, including any consolidated subsidiaries of the banks.
[2] Provide association-only combined financial data of all FCS associations.
[3] Provide the combined financial data of all columns on the left.
[4] Any item that is no longer applicable, e.g., protected borrower stock, may be omitted.

TABLE B—SUPPLEMENTAL INCOME STATEMENT INFORMATION

	Banks[1]	Associations[2]	Financial assistance corporation	Eliminations	Combined without Insurance fund[3]	Insurance fund and related combination entries	Combined with insurance fund
Net interest income							
Provision for loan losses							
Other income							
Other expenses							
Net income							

[1] Provide combined financial data of all FCS banks, including any consolidated subsidiaries of the banks.
[2] Provide association-only combined financial data of all FCS associations.
[3] Provide the combined financial data of all columns on the left.

PART 650—FEDERAL AGRICULTURAL MORTGAGE CORPORATION GENERAL PROVISIONS

Sec.
650.1 Grounds for appointment of a receiver or conservator.
650.5 Action for removal of receiver or conservator.
650.10 Voluntary liquidation.
650.15 Appointment of a receiver.
650.20 Powers and duties of the receiver.
650.25 Report to Congress.
650.30 Preservation of equity.
650.35 Notice to stockholders.
650.40 Creditor claims.
650.45 Priority of claims.
650.50 Payment of claims.
650.55 Inventory, audit, and reports.
650.60 Final discharge and release of the receiver.
650.65 Appointment of a conservator.
650.70 Powers and duties of the conservator.
650.75 Inventory, examination, and reports to stockholders.
650.80 Final discharge and release of the conservator.

AUTHORITY: Secs. 4.12, 5.9, 5.17, 8.11, 8.31, 8.32, 8.33, 8.34, 8.35, 8.36, 8.37, 8.41 of the Farm Credit Act (12 U.S.C. 2183, 2243, 2252, 2279aa–11, 2279bb, 2279bb–1, 2279bb–2, 2279bb–3, 2279bb–4, 2279bb–5, 2279bb–6, 2279cc); sec. 514 of Pub. L. 102–552, 106 Stat. 4102; sec. 118 of Pub. L. 104–105, 110 Stat. 168.

SOURCE: 62 FR 43636, Aug. 15, 1997. Redesignated at 70 FR 40650, July 14, 2005, unless otherwise noted.

§ 650.1 Grounds for appointment of a receiver or conservator.

(a) The grounds for the appointment of a receiver or conservator for the Corporation are:

(1) The Corporation is insolvent. For purposes of this paragraph, insolvent means:

(i) The assets of the Corporation are less than its obligations to its creditors and others; or

(ii) The Corporation is unable to pay its debts as they fall due in the ordinary course of business;

(2) There has been a substantial dissipation of the assets or earnings of the Corporation due to the violation of any law, rule, or regulation, or the conduct of an unsafe or unsound practice;

(3) The Corporation is in an unsafe or unsound condition to transact business;

(4) The Corporation has committed a willful violation of a final cease-and-desist order issued by the Farm Credit Administration Board;

(5) The Corporation is concealing its books, papers, records, or assets, or is refusing to submit its books, papers, records, assets, or other material relating to the affairs of the Corporation for inspection to any examiner or any lawful agent of the Farm Credit Administration Board.

(b) In addition to the grounds set forth in paragraph (a) of this section, a receiver can be appointed for the Corporation if the Farm Credit Administration Board determines that the appointment of a conservator would not be appropriate when one of the following conditions exists:

(1) The authority of the Corporation to purchase qualified loans or issue or guarantee loan-backed securities is suspended; or

(2) The Corporation is classified under section 8.35 of the Act as within enforcement level III or IV and the alternative actions available under subtitle B of title VIII of the Act are not satisfactory.

(c) In addition to the grounds set forth in paragraph (a) of this section, a conservator can be appointed for the Corporation if:

(1) The Corporation is classified under section 8.35 of the Act as within enforcement level III or IV; or

(2) The authority of the Corporation to purchase qualified loans or issue or guarantee loan-backed securities is suspended.

§ 650.5 Action for removal of receiver or conservator.

Upon the appointment of a receiver or conservator for the Corporation by the Farm Credit Administration Board pursuant to § 650.50 of this subpart, the Corporation may, within 30 days of such appointment, bring an action in the United States District Court for the District of Columbia, for an order requiring the Farm Credit Administration Board to remove the receiver or conservator and, if the charter has been canceled, to rescind the cancellation of the charter. Notwithstanding any other provision of this part, the Corporation's board of directors is empowered to meet subsequent to such appointment and authorize the filing of

§ 650.10

an action for removal. An action for removal may be authorized only by the Corporation's board of directors.

§ 650.10 Voluntary liquidation.

(a) The Corporation may voluntarily liquidate by a resolution of its board of directors, but only with the consent of, and in accordance with a plan of liquidation approved by, the Farm Credit Administration Board. Upon adoption of such resolution, the Corporation shall submit the resolution and proposed voluntary liquidation plan to the Farm Credit Administration Board for preliminary approval. The Farm Credit Administration Board, in its discretion, may appoint a receiver as part of an approved liquidation plan. If a receiver is appointed for the Corporation as part of a voluntary liquidation, the receivership shall be conducted pursuant to the regulations of this part, except to the extent that an approved plan of liquidation provides otherwise.

(b) If the Farm Credit Administration Board gives preliminary approval to the liquidation plan, the board of directors of the Corporation shall submit the resolution to liquidate to the stockholders for a vote in accordance with the bylaws of the Corporation.

(c) The Farm Credit Administration Board will consider final approval of the resolution to voluntarily liquidate and the liquidation plan after an affirmative stockholder vote on the resolution.

§ 650.15 Appointment of a receiver.

(a) The Farm Credit Administration Board may in its discretion appoint, ex parte and without prior notice, a receiver for the Corporation provided that one or more of the grounds for appointment as set forth in § 650.50 of this subpart exist.

(b) Upon the appointment of the receiver, the Chairman of the Farm Credit Administration Board shall immediately notify the Corporation and shall publish a notice of the appointment in the FEDERAL REGISTER.

(c) Upon the issuance of the order placing the Corporation into liquidation and appointing the receiver, all rights, privileges, and powers of the board of directors, officers, and employees of the Corporation shall be vested exclusively in the receiver. The Farm Credit Administration Board may cancel the charter of the Corporation on such date as the Farm Credit Administration Board determines is appropriate, but not later than the conclusion of the receivership and discharge of the receiver.

§ 650.20 Powers and duties of the receiver.

(a) *General.* (1) Upon appointment as receiver, the receiver shall take possession of the Corporation in order to wind up the business operations of the Corporation, collect the debts owed to the Corporation, liquidate its property and assets, pay its creditors, and distribute the remaining proceeds to stockholders. The receiver is authorized to exercise all powers necessary to the efficient termination of the Corporation's operation as provided for in this part.

(2) Upon its appointment as receiver, the receiver automatically succeeds to:

(i) All rights, titles, powers, and privileges of the Corporation and of any stockholder, officer, or director of the Corporation with respect to the Corporation and the assets of the Corporation; and

(ii) Title to the books, records, and assets of the Corporation in the possession of any other legal custodian of the Corporation.

(3) The receiver of the Corporation serves as the trustee of the receivership estate and conducts its operations for the benefit of the creditors and stockholders of the Corporation.

(b) *Specific powers.* The receiver may:

(1) Exercise all powers as are conferred upon the officers and directors of the Corporation under law and the charter, articles, and bylaws of the Corporation.

(2) Take any action the receiver considers appropriate or expedient to carry on the business of the Corporation during the process of liquidating its assets and winding up its affairs.

(3) Borrow funds in accordance with section 8.41(f) of the Act to meet the ongoing administrative expenses or other liquidity needs of the receivership.

Farm Credit Administration § 650.30

(4) Pay any sum the receiver deems necessary or advisable to preserve, conserve, or protect the Corporation's assets or property or rehabilitate or improve such property and assets.

(5) Pay any sum the receiver deems necessary or advisable to preserve, conserve, or protect any asset or property on which the Corporation has a lien or in which the Corporation has a financial or property interest, and pay off and discharge any liens, claims, or charges of any nature against such property.

(6) Investigate any matter related to the conduct of the business of the Corporation, including, but not limited to, any claim of the Corporation against any individual or entity, and institute appropriate legal or other proceedings to prosecute such claims.

(7) Institute, prosecute, maintain, defend, intervene, and otherwise participate in any legal proceeding by or against the Corporation or in which the Corporation or its creditors or stockholders have any interest, and represent in every way the Corporation, its stockholders and creditors.

(8) Employ attorneys, accountants, appraisers, and other professionals to give advice and assistance to the receivership generally or on particular matters, and pay their retainers, compensation, and expenses, including litigation costs.

(9) Hire any agents or employees necessary for proper administration of the receivership.

(10) Execute, acknowledge, and deliver, in person or through a general or specific delegation, any instrument necessary for any authorized purpose, and any instrument executed under this paragraph shall be valid and effective as if it had been executed by the Corporation's officers by authority of its board of directors.

(11) Sell for cash or otherwise any mortgage, deed of trust, chose in action, note, contract, judgment or decree, stock, or debt owed to the Corporation, or any property (real or personal, tangible or intangible).

(12) Purchase or lease office space, automobiles, furniture, equipment, and supplies, and purchase insurance, professional, and technical services necessary for the conduct of the receivership.

(13) Release any assets or property of any nature, regardless of whether the subject of pending litigation, and repudiate, with cause, any lease or executory contract the receiver considers burdensome.

(14) Settle, release, or obtain release of, for cash or other consideration, claims and demands against or in favor of the Corporation or receiver.

(15) Pay, out of the assets of the Corporation, all expenses of the receivership (including compensation to personnel employed to represent or assist the receiver) and all costs of carrying out or exercising the rights, powers, privileges, and duties as receiver.

(16) Pay, out of the assets of the Corporation, all approved claims of indebtedness in accordance with the priorities established in this part.

(17) Take all actions and have such rights, powers, and privileges as are necessary and incident to the exercise of any specific power.

(18) Take such actions, and have such additional rights, powers, privileges, immunities, and duties as the Farm Credit Administration Board authorizes by order or by amendment of any order or by regulation.

§ 650.25 Report to Congress.

On a determination by the receiver that there are insufficient assets of the receivership to pay all valid claims against the receivership, the receiver shall submit to the Secretary of the Treasury and Congress a report on the financial condition of the receivership.

§ 650.30 Preservation of equity.

(a) Except as provided for upon final distribution of the assets of the Corporation pursuant to § 650.62 of this subpart, no capital stock, equity reserves, or other allocated equities of the Corporation in receivership shall be issued, allocated, retired, sold, distributed, transferred, or assigned.

(b) Immediately upon the adoption of a resolution by its board of directors to voluntarily liquidate the Corporation, the capital stock, equity reserves, and allocated equities of the Corporation shall not be issued, allocated, retired,

§ 650.35

sold, distributed, transferred, or assigned. Such activities could resume if the stockholders of the Corporation or the Farm Credit Administration Board disapprove the resolution. In the event the resolution is approved by the stockholders of the Corporation and the Farm Credit Administration Board, the liquidation plan shall govern disposition of the equities of the Corporation as provided in § 650.52 of this subpart.

§ 650.35 Notice to stockholders.

As soon as practicable after a receiver takes possession of the Corporation, the receiver shall notify, by first class mail, each holder of stock of the following matters:

(a) The number of shares such holder owns;

(b) That the stock and other equities of the Corporation may not be retired or transferred until the liquidation is completed, whereupon the receiver will distribute a liquidating dividend, if any, to the stockholders; and

(c) Such other matters as the receiver or the Farm Credit Administration Board deems necessary.

§ 650.40 Creditor claims.

(a) Upon appointment, the receiver shall promptly publish a notice to creditors to present their claims against the Corporation, with proof thereof, to the receiver by a date specified in the notice, which shall be not less than 90 calendar days after the first publication. The notice shall be republished approximately 30 days and 60 days after the first publication. The receiver shall promptly send, by first class mail, a similar notice to any creditor shown on the Corporation's books at the creditor's last address appearing thereon. Claims filed after the specified date shall be disallowed except as the receiver may approve them for full or partial payment from the Corporation's assets remaining undistributed at the time of approval.

(b) The receiver shall allow any claim that is timely received and proved to the receiver's satisfaction. The receiver may disallow in whole or in part any creditor's claim or claim of security, preference, or priority that is not proved to the receiver's satisfac-

12 CFR Ch. VI (1–1–12 Edition)

tion or is not timely received and shall notify the claimant of the disallowance and reason therefor. Sending the notice of disallowance by first class mail to the claimant's address appearing on the proof of claim shall be sufficient notice. The disallowance shall be final unless, within 30 days after the notice of disallowance is mailed, the claimant files a written request for payment regardless of the disallowance. The receiver shall reconsider any claim upon the timely request of the claimant and may approve or disapprove such claim in whole or in part.

(c) Creditors' claims that are allowed shall be paid by the receiver from time to time, to the extent funds are available therefor and in accordance with the priorities established in this part and in such manner and amounts as the receiver deems appropriate. In the event the Corporation has a claim against a creditor of the Corporation, the receiver shall offset the amount of such claim against the claim asserted by such creditor.

§ 650.45 Priority of claims.

The following priority of claims shall apply to the distribution of the assets of the Corporation in liquidation:

(a) All costs, expenses, and debts incurred by the receiver in connection with the administration of the receivership, all Farm Credit Administration assessments for the costs of supervising and examining the Corporation, and any amounts borrowed pursuant to § 650.56(b)(3).

(b) Administrative expenses of the Corporation, provided that such expenses were incurred within 60 days prior to the receiver's taking possession, and that such expenses shall be limited to reasonable expenses incurred for services actually provided by accountants, attorneys, appraisers, examiners, or management companies, or reasonable expenses incurred by employees that were authorized and reimbursable under a preexisting expense reimbursement policy and that, in the opinion of the receiver, are of benefit to the receivership, and shall not include wages or salaries of employees of the Corporation.

Farm Credit Administration § 650.65

(c) If authorized by the receiver, claims for wages and salaries, including vacation pay, earned prior to the appointment of the receiver by an employee of the Corporation whom the receiver determines it is in the best interest of the receivership to engage or retain for a reasonable period of time.

(d) If authorized by the receiver, claims for wages and salaries, including vacation pay, earned prior to the appointment of the receiver, up to a maximum of three thousand dollars ($3,000) per person as adjusted for inflation, by an employee of the Corporation not engaged or retained by the receiver. The adjustment for inflation shall be the percentage by which the Consumer Price Index (as prepared by the Department of Labor) for the calendar year preceding the appointment of the receiver exceeds the Consumer Price Index for the calendar year 1992.

(e) All claims for taxes.

(f) All claims of creditors which are secured by specific assets of the Corporation, with priority of conflicting claims of creditors within this same class to be determined in accordance with priorities of applicable Federal or State law.

(g) All claims of general creditors.

§ 650.50 Payment of claims.

(a) All claims of each class described in § 650.61 of this subpart shall be paid in full or provisions shall be made for such payment prior to the payment of any claim of a lesser priority. If there are insufficient funds to pay all claims in a class in full, distribution to that class will be on a pro rata basis.

(b) Following the payment of all claims, the receiver shall distribute the remainder of the assets of the Corporation, if any, to the owners of stock and other equities in accordance with the priorities for impairment set forth in section 8.4(e)(3) of the Act and the bylaws of the Corporation.

§ 650.55 Inventory, audit, and reports.

(a) As soon as practicable after taking possession of the Corporation, the receiver shall take an inventory of the assets and liabilities as of the date possession was taken.

(b) The receivership shall be audited on an annual basis by a certified public accountant selected by the receiver.

(c) The receiver shall make an annual accounting or report, as appropriate, available for review upon request to any stockholder of the Corporation or any member of the public, with a copy provided to the Farm Credit Administration.

(d) As soon as practicable after final distribution, the receiver shall send to each stockholder of record a report summarizing the disposition of the assets of the receivership and claims against the receivership.

§ 650.60 Final discharge and release of the receiver.

After the receiver has made a final distribution of the assets of the receivership, the receivership shall be terminated, the charter shall be canceled by the Farm Credit Administration Board if such cancellation has not previously occurred, and the receiver shall be finally discharged and released.

§ 650.65 Appointment of a conservator.

(a) The Farm Credit Administration Board may in its discretion appoint, ex parte and without prior notice, a conservator for the Corporation provided that one or more of the grounds for appointment as set forth in § 650.50 of this subpart exist;

(b) Upon the appointment of a conservator, the Chairman of the Farm Credit Administration shall immediately notify the Corporation and shall publish a notice of the appointment in the FEDERAL REGISTER.

(c) As soon as practicable after the conservator takes possession of the Corporation, the conservator shall notify, by first class mail, each holder of stock in the Corporation of the establishment of the conservatorship and shall describe the effect of the conservatorship on the Corporation's operations and equity holdings.

(d) Upon the issuance of the order placing the Corporation in conservatorship, all rights, privileges, and powers of the board of directors, officers, and employees of the Corporation are vested exclusively in the conservator.

(e) The Farm Credit Administration Board may, at any time, terminate the

§ 650.70

conservatorship and direct the conservator to turn over the Corporation's operations to such management as the Farm Credit Administration Board may designate, in which event the provisions of this subpart shall no longer apply.

§ 650.70 Powers and duties of the conservator.

(a) The conservator shall direct the Corporation's further operation until the Farm Credit Administration Board decides that the Corporation can operate without the conservatorship or places the Corporation into receivership. Upon correction or resolution of the problem or condition that provided the basis for the appointment, the Farm Credit Administration Board may turn the Corporation over to such management as the Farm Credit Administration Board may direct.

(b) The conservator shall exercise all powers necessary to continue the ongoing operations of the Corporation, to conserve and preserve the Corporation's assets and property, and otherwise protect the interests of the Corporation, its stockholders, and creditors as provided in this subpart.

(c) The conservator serves as the trustee of the Corporation and conducts its operations for the benefit of the creditors and stockholders of the Corporation.

(d) The conservator may exercise the powers that a receiver of the Corporation may exercise under any of the provisions of § 650.56(b) of this subpart, except paragraphs (b)(2) and (b)(16). In interpreting the applicable paragraphs for purposes of this section, the terms "conservator" and "conservatorship" shall be read for "receiver" and "receivership".

(e) The conservator may also take any other action the conservator considers appropriate or expedient to the continuing operation of the Corporation.

§ 650.75 Inventory, examination, and reports to stockholders.

(a) As soon as practicable after taking possession of the Corporation, the conservator shall take an inventory of the assets and liabilities of the Corporation as of the date possession was taken. One copy of the inventory shall be filed with the Farm Credit Administration.

(b) The conservatorship shall be examined by the Farm Credit Administration in accordance with section 8.11 of the Act.

(c) The conservatorship shall prepare and file financial reports and other documents in accordance with the requirements of § 655.1 and part 621 of this chapter. The conservator of the Corporation shall provide the certification required in § 621.14 of this chapter.

[62 FR 43636, Aug. 15, 1997. Redesignated and amended at 70 FR 40650, 40651, July 14, 2005]

§ 650.80 Final discharge and release of the conservator.

At such time as the conservator shall be relieved of its conservatorship duties, the conservator shall file a report on the conservator's activities with the Farm Credit Administration. The conservator shall thereupon be completely and finally released.

PART 651—FEDERAL AGRICULTURAL MORTGAGE CORPORATION GOVERNANCE

Sec.
651.1 Definitions.
651.2 Conflict-of-interest policy.
651.3 Implementation of policy.
651.4 Director, officer, employee, and agent responsibilities.

AUTHORITY: Secs. 4.12, 5.9, 5.17, 8.11, 8.31, 8.32, 8.33, 8.34, 8.35, 8.36, 8.37, 8.41 of the Farm Credit Act (12 U.S.C. 2183, 2243, 2252, 2279aa–11, 2279bb, 2279bb–1, 2279bb–2, 2279bb–3, 2279bb–4, 2279bb–5, 2279bb–6, 2279cc); sec. 514 of Pub. L. 102–552, 106 Stat. 4102; sec. 118 of Pub. L. 104–105, 110 Stat. 168.

SOURCE: 59 FR 9626, Mar. 1, 1994. Redesignated at 70 FR 40644, 40650, July 14, 2005, unless otherwise noted.

§ 651.1 Definitions.

(a) *Agent* means any person (other than a director, officer, or employee of the Corporation) who represents the Corporation in contacts with third parties or who provides professional services such as legal, accounting, or appraisal services to the Corporation.

(b) *Affiliate* means any entity established under authority granted to the Corporation under section 8.3(c)(14) of the Farm Credit Act of 1971, as amended.

(c) *Corporation* means the Federal Agricultural Mortgage Corporation and its affiliates.

(d) *Employee* means any salaried individual working part-time, full-time, or temporarily for the Corporation.

(e) *Entity* means a corporation, company, association, firm, joint venture, partnership (general or limited), society, joint stock company, trust (business or otherwise), fund, or other organization or institution.

(f) *Material*, when applied to a potential conflict of interest, means the conflicting interest is of sufficient magnitude or significance that a reasonable observer with knowledge of the relevant facts would question the ability of the person having such interest to discharge official duties in an objective and impartial manner in furtherance of the interests and statutory purposes of the Corporation.

(g) *Officer* means the salaried president, vice presidents, secretary, treasurer, and general counsel, or other person, however designated, who holds a position of similar authority in the Corporation.

(h) *Person* means individual or entity.

(i) *Potential conflict of interest* means a director, officer, or employee of the Corporation has an interest in a transaction, relationship, or activity that might adversely affect, or appear to adversely affect, the ability of the director, officer, or employee to perform his official duties on behalf of the Corporation in an objective and impartial manner in furtherance of the interest of the Corporation and its statutory purposes. For the purpose of determining whether a potential conflict of interest exists, the following interests shall be imputed to a person subject to this regulation as if they were that person's own interests:

(1) Interests of that person's spouse;

(2) Interests of that person's minor child;

(3) Interests of that person's general partner;

(4) Interests of an organization or entity that the person serves as officer, director, trustee, general partner or employee; and

(5) Interests of a person, organization, or entity with which that person is negotiating for or has an arrangement concerning prospective employment.

(j) *Resolved*, when applied to a potential conflict of interest that the Corporation has determined is material, means that circumstances have been altered so that a reasonable observer with knowledge of the relevant facts would conclude that the conflicting interest would not adversely affect the person's performance of official duties in an objective and impartial manner in furtherance of the interests and statutory purposes of the Corporation.

[59 FR 9626, Mar. 1, 1994, as amended at 76 FR 23467, April 27, 2011]

§ 651.2 Conflict-of-interest policy.

The Corporation shall establish and administer a conflict-of-interest policy that will provide reasonable assurance that the directors, officers, employees, and agents of the Corporation discharge their official responsibilities in an objective and impartial manner in furtherance of the interests and statutory purposes of the Corporation. The policy shall, at a minimum:

(a) Define the types of transactions, relationships, or activities that could reasonably be expected to give rise to potential conflicts of interest.

(b) Require each director, officer, and employee to report in writing, annually, and at such other times as conflicts may arise, sufficient information about financial interests, transactions, relationships, and activities to inform the Corporation of potential conflicts of interest;

(c) Require each director, officer, and employee who had no transaction, relationship, or activity required to be reported under paragraph (b) of this section at any time during the year to file a signed statement to that effect;

(d) Establish guidelines for determining when a potential conflict is material in accordance with this subpart;

(e) Establish procedures for resolving or disclosing material conflicts of interest.

(f) Provide internal controls to ensure that reports are filed as required and that conflicts are resolved or disclosed in accordance with this subpart.

§ 651.3

(g) Notify directors, officers, and employees of the conflict-of-interest policy and any subsequent changes thereto and allow them a reasonable period of time to conform to the policy.

§ 651.3 Implementation of policy.

(a) The Corporation shall disclose any unresolved material conflicts of interest involving its directors, officers, and employees to:

(1) Shareholders through annual reports and proxy statements; and

(2) Investors and potential investors through disclosure documents supplied to them.

(b) The Corporation shall make available to any shareholder, investor, or potential investor, upon request, a copy of its policy on conflicts of interest. The Corporation may charge a nominal fee to cover the costs of reproduction and handling.

(c) The Corporation shall maintain all reports of all potential conflicts of interest and documentation of materiality determinations and resolutions of conflicts of interest for a period of 6 years.

§ 651.4 Director, officer, employee, and agent responsibilities.

(a) Each director, officer, employee, and agent of the Corporation shall:

(1) Conduct the business of the Corporation following high standards of honesty, integrity, impartiality, loyalty, and care, consistent with applicable law and regulation in furtherance of the Corporation's public purpose;

(2) Adhere to the requirements of the conflict-of-interest policy established by the Corporation and provide any information the Corporation deems necessary to discharge its responsibilities under this subpart.

(b) Directors, officers, employees, and agents of the Corporation shall be subject to the penalties of part C of title V of the Farm Credit Act of 1971, as amended, for violations of this regulation, including failure to adhere to the conflict-of-interest policy established by the Corporation.

PART 652—FEDERAL AGRICULTURAL MORTGAGE CORPORATION FUNDING AND FISCAL AFFAIRS

Subpart A—Investment Management

Sec.
652.1 Purpose.
652.5 Definitions.
652.10 Investment management and requirements.
652.15 Interest rate risk management and requirements.
652.20 Liquidity reserve management and requirements.
652.25 Non-program investment purposes and limitation.
652.30 Temporary regulatory waivers or modifications for extraordinary situations.
652.35 Eligible non-program investments.
652.40 Stress tests for mortgage securities.
652.45 Divestiture of ineligible non-program investments.

Subpart B—Risk-Based Capital Requirements

652.50 Definitions.
652.55 General.
652.60 Corporation board guidelines.
652.65 Risk-based capital stress test.
652.70 Risk-based capital level.
652.75 Your responsibility for determining the risk-based capital level.
652.80 When you must determine the risk-based capital level.
652.85 When to report the risk-based capital level.
652.90 How to report your risk-based capital determination.
652.95 Failure to meet capital requirements.
652.100 Audit of the risk-based capital stress test.

APPENDIX A TO SUBPART B—RISK-BASED CAPITAL STRESS TEST

AUTHORITY: Secs. 4.12, 5.9, 5.17, 8.11, 8.31, 8.32, 8.33, 8.34, 8.35, 8.36, 8.37, 8.41 of the Farm Credit Act (12 U.S.C. 2183, 2243, 2252, 2279aa–11, 2279bb, 2279bb–1, 2279bb–2, 2279bb–3, 2279bb–4, 2279bb–5, 2279bb–6, 2279cc); sec. 514 of Pub. L. 102–552, 106 Stat. 4102; sec. 118 of Pub. L. 104–105, 110 Stat. 168.

SOURCE: 70 FR 40644, July 14, 2005, unless otherwise noted.

Subpart A—Investment Management

§ 652.1 Purpose.

This subpart contains the Farm Credit Administration's (FCA) rules for governing liquidity and non-program investments held by the Federal Agricultural Mortgage Corporation (Farmer Mac). The purpose of this subpart is to ensure safety and soundness, continuity of funding, and appropriate use of non-program investments considering Farmer Mac's special status as a Government-sponsored enterprise (GSE). The subpart contains requirements for Farmer Mac's board of directors to adopt policies covering such areas as investment management, interest rate risk, and liquidity reserves. The subpart also requires Farmer Mac to comply with various reporting requirements.

§ 652.5 Definitions.

For purposes of this subpart, the following definitions will apply:

Affiliate means any entity established under authority granted to the Corporation under section 8.3(c)(14) of the Farm Credit Act of 1971, as amended.

Asset-backed securities (ABS) means investment securities that provide for ownership of a fractional undivided interest or collateral interests in specific assets of a trust that are sold and traded in the capital markets. For the purposes of this subpart, ABS exclude mortgage securities that are defined below.

Eurodollar time deposit means a non-negotiable deposit denominated in United States dollars and issued by an overseas branch of a United States bank or by a foreign bank outside the United States.

Farmer Mac, Corporation, you, and your means the Federal Agricultural Mortgage Corporation and its affiliates.

FCA, our, or we means the Farm Credit Administration.

Final maturity means the last date on which the remaining principal amount of a security is due and payable (matures) to the registered owner. It does not mean the call date, the expected average life, the duration, or the weighted average maturity.

General obligations of a state or political subdivision means:

(1) The full faith and credit obligations of a state, the District of Columbia, the Commonwealth of Puerto Rico, a territory or possession of the United States, or a political subdivision thereof that possesses general powers of taxation, including property taxation; or

(2) An obligation that is unconditionally guaranteed by an obligor possessing general powers of taxation, including property taxation.

Government agency means an agency or instrumentality of the United States Government whose obligations *are* fully and explicitly guaranteed as to the timely repayment of principal and interest by the full faith and credit of the United States Government.

Government-sponsored agency means an agency, instrumentality, or corporation chartered or established to serve public purposes specified by the United States Congress but whose obligations *are not* explicitly guaranteed by the full faith and credit of the United States Government, including but not limited to any Government-sponsored enterprise.

Liquid investments are assets that can be promptly converted into cash without significant loss to the investor. A security is liquid if the spread between its bid price and ask price is narrow and a reasonable amount can be sold at those prices promptly.

Long-Term Standby Purchase Commitment (LTSPC) is a commitment by Farmer Mac to purchase specified eligible loans on one or more undetermined future dates. In consideration for Farmer Mac's assumption of the credit risk on the specified loans underlying an LTSPC, Farmer Mac receives an annual commitment fee on the outstanding balance of those loans in monthly installments based on the outstanding balance of those loans.

Market risk means the risk to your financial condition because the value of your holdings may decline if interest rates or market prices change. Exposure to market risk is measured by assessing the effect of changing rates and prices on either the earnings or economic value of an individual instrument, a portfolio, or the entire Corporation.

Maturing obligations means maturing debt and other obligations that may be expected, such as buyouts of long-term standby purchase commitments or repurchases of agricultural mortgage securities.

§ 652.10

Mortgage securities means securities that are either:

(1) Pass-through securities or participation certificates that represent ownership of a fractional undivided interest in a specified pool of residential (excluding home equity loans), multifamily or commercial mortgages, or

(2) A multiclass security (including collateralized mortgage obligations and real estate mortgage investment conduits) that is backed by a pool of residential, multifamily or commercial real estate mortgages, pass-through mortgage securities, or other multiclass mortgage securities.

(3) This definition does not include agricultural mortgage-backed securities guaranteed by Farmer Mac itself.

Nationally recognized statistical rating organization (NRSRO) means a rating organization that the Securities and Exchange Commission recognizes as an NRSRO.

Non-program investments means investments other than those in:

(1) "Qualified loans" as defined in section 8.0(9) of the Farm Credit Act of 1971, as amended; or

(2) Securities collateralized by "qualified loans."

Program assets means on-balance sheet "qualified loans" as defined in section 8.0(9) of the Farm Credit Act of 1971, as amended.

Program obligations means off-balance sheet "qualified loans" as defined in section 8.0(9) of the Farm Credit Act of 1971, as amended.

Regulatory capital means your core capital plus an allowance for losses and guarantee claims, as determined in accordance with generally accepted accounting principles.

Revenue bond means an obligation of a municipal government that finances a specific project or enterprise, but it is not a full faith and credit obligation. The obligor pays a portion of the revenue generated by the project or enterprise to the bondholders.

Weighted average life (WAL) means the average time until the investor receives the principal on a security, weighted by the size of each principal payment and calculated under specified prepayment assumptions.

[70 FR 40644, July 14, 2005, as amended at 76 FR 23467, April 27, 2011]

§ 652.10 Investment management and requirements.

(a) *Investment policies—board responsibilities.* Your board of directors must adopt written policies for managing your non-program investment activities. Your board must also ensure that management complies with these policies and that appropriate internal controls are in place to prevent loss. At least annually, your board, or a designated subcommittee of the board, must review these investment policies. Any changes to the policies must be adopted by the board. You must report any changes to these policies to FCA's Office of Secondary Market Oversight within 10 business days of adoption.

(b) *Investment policies—general requirements.* Your investment policies must address the purposes and objectives of investments, risk tolerance, delegations of authority, exception parameters, securities valuation, internal controls, and reporting requirements. Furthermore, the policies must address the means for reporting, and approvals needed for, exceptions to established policies. Investment policies must be sufficiently detailed, consistent with, and appropriate for the amounts, types, and risk characteristics of your investments.

(c) *Investment policies—risk tolerance.* Your investment policies must establish risk limits and diversification requirements for the various classes of eligible investments and for the entire investment portfolio. These policies must ensure that you maintain prudent diversification of your investment portfolio. Risk limits must be based on the Corporation's objectives, capital position, and risk tolerance. Your policies must identify the types and quantity of investments that you will hold to achieve your objectives and control credit, market, liquidity, and operational risks. Your policies must establish risk limits for the following four types of risk:

(1) *Credit risk.* Your investment policies must establish:

(i) Credit quality standards, limits on counterparty risk, and risk diversification standards that limit concentrations based on a single or related counterparty(ies), a geographical area,

Farm Credit Administration § 652.10

industries or obligations with similar characteristics.

(ii) *Criteria for selecting brokers, dealers, and investment bankers (collectively, securities firms).* You must buy and sell eligible investments with more than one securities firm. As part of your annual review of your investment policies, your board of directors, or a designated subcommittee of the board, must review the criteria for selecting securities firms. Any changes to the criteria must be approved by the board. Also, as part of your annual review, the board, or a designated subcommittee of the board, must review existing relationships with securities firms. In addition, the board, or a designated subcommittee of the board, must be notified before any changes to securities firms are made.

(iii) *Collateral margin requirements on repurchase agreements.* You must regularly mark the collateral to market and ensure appropriate controls are maintained over collateral held.

(2) *Market risk.* Your investment policies must set market risk limits for specific types of investments, and for the investment portfolio or for Farmer Mac generally. Your board of directors must establish market risk limits in accordance with these regulations (including, but not limited to, §§ 652.15 and 652.40) and our other policies and guidance. You must document in the Corporation's records or minutes any analyses used in formulating your policies or amendments to the policies.

(3) *Liquidity risk.* Your investment policies must describe the liquidity characteristics of eligible investments that you will hold to meet your liquidity needs and the Corporation's objectives.

(4) *Operational risk.* Investment policies must address operational risks, including delegations of authority and internal controls in accordance with paragraphs (d) and (e) of this section.

(d) *Delegation of authority.* All delegations of authority to specified personnel or committees must state the extent of management's authority and responsibilities for investments.

(e) *Internal controls.* You must:

(1) Establish appropriate internal controls to detect and prevent loss, fraud, embezzlement, conflicts of interest, and unauthorized investments.

(2) Establish and maintain a separation of duties and supervision between personnel who execute investment transactions and personnel who approve, revaluate, and oversee investments.

(3) Maintain records and management information systems that are appropriate for the level and complexity of your investment activities.

(f) *Securities valuations.* (1) Before you purchase a security, you must evaluate its credit quality and price sensitivity to changes in market interest rates. You must also verify the value of a security that you plan to purchase, other than a new issue, with a source that is independent of the broker, dealer, counterparty, or other intermediary to the transaction. Your investment policies must fully address the extent of the prepurchase analysis that management needs to perform for various classes of instruments. For example, you should specifically describe the stress tests in § 652.40 that must be performed on various types of mortgage securities.

(2) At least monthly, you must determine the fair market value of each security in your portfolio and the fair market value of your whole investment portfolio. In doing so you must also evaluate the credit quality and price sensitivity to the change in market interest rates of each security in your portfolio and your whole investment portfolio.

(3) Before you sell a security, you must verify its value with a source that is independent of the broker, dealer, counterparty, or other intermediary to the transaction.

(g) *Reports to the board of directors.* At least quarterly, Farmer Mac's management must report to the Corporation's board of directors, or a designated subcommittee of the board:

(1) On the performance and risk of each class of investments and the entire investment portfolio;

(2) All gains and losses that you incur during the quarter on individual securities that you sold before maturity and why they were liquidated;

(3) Potential risk exposure to changes in market interest rates and

§ 652.15

any other factors that may affect the value of your investment holdings;

(4) How investments affect your overall financial condition;

(5) Whether the performance of the investment portfolio effectively achieves the board's objectives; and

(6) Any deviations from the board's policies. These deviations must be formally approved by the board of directors.

§ 652.15 Interest rate risk management and requirements.

(a) The board of directors of Farmer Mac must provide effective oversight (direction, controls, and supervision) to the interest rate risk management program and must be knowledgeable of the nature and level of interest rate risk taken by Farmer Mac.

(b) The management of Farmer Mac must ensure that interest rate risk is properly managed on both a long-range and a day-to-day basis.

(c) The board of directors of Farmer Mac must adopt an interest rate risk management policy that establishes appropriate interest rate risk exposure limits based on the Corporation's risk-bearing capacity and reporting requirements in accordance with paragraphs (d) and (e) of this section. At least annually, the board of directors, or a designated subcommittee of the board, must review the policy. Any changes to the policy must be approved by the board of directors. You must report any changes to the policy to FCA's Office of Secondary Market Oversight within 10 business days of adoption.

(d) The interest rate risk management policy must, at a minimum:

(1) Address the purpose and objectives of interest rate risk management;

(2) Identify and analyze the causes of interest rate risks within Farmer Mac's existing balance sheet structure;

(3) Require Farmer Mac to measure the potential impact of these risks on projected earnings and market values by conducting interest rate shock tests and simulations of multiple economic scenarios at least quarterly;

(4) Describe and implement actions needed to obtain Farmer Mac's desired risk management objectives;

(5) Document the objectives that Farmer Mac is attempting to achieve by purchasing eligible investments that are authorized by § 652.35 of this subpart;

(6) Require Farmer Mac to evaluate and document, at least quarterly, whether these investments have actually met the objectives stated under paragraph (d)(4) of this section;

(7) Identify exception parameters and post approvals needed for any exceptions to the policy's requirements;

(8) Describe delegations of authority; and

(9) Describe reporting requirements, including exceptions to policy limits.

(e) At least quarterly, Farmer Mac's management must report to the Corporation's board of directors, or a designated subcommittee of the board, describing the nature and level of interest rate risk exposure. Any deviations from the board's policy on interest rate risk must be specifically identified in the report and approved by the board, or a designated subcommittee of the board.

§ 652.20 Liquidity reserve management and requirements.

(a) *Minimum liquidity reserve requirement.* Within 24 months of this rule becoming effective, and thereafter, Farmer Mac must hold cash, eligible non-program investments under § 652.35 of this subpart, and/or on-balance sheet securities backed by portions of Farmer Mac program assets (loans) that are guaranteed by the United States Department of Agriculture as described in section 8.0(9)(B) of the Act (in accordance with the requirements of paragraphs (b) and (c) of this section), to maintain sufficient liquidity to fund a minimum of 60 days of maturing obligations, interest expense, and operating expenses at all times. You must document your compliance with this minimum reserve requirement at least once each month as of the last day of the month using month end data. Liquid asset values must be marked to market. In addition, you must have the capability and information systems in place to be able to calculate the minimum reserve requirement on a daily basis.

(b) *Free of lien.* All investments held for the purpose of meeting the liquidity reserve requirement of this section

Farm Credit Administration § 652.20

must be free of liens or other encumbrances.

(c) *Discounts.* The amount that may be counted to meet the minimum liquidity reserve requirement is as follows:

(1) For cash and overnight investments, multiply the cash and investments by 100 percent;

(2) For money market instruments with maturities of 5 business days or less, multiply the instruments by 97 percent of market value;

(3) For money market instruments with maturities greater than 5 business days and floating rate debt and preferred stock securities, multiply the instruments and securities by 95 percent of market value;

(4) For diversified investment funds, multiply the individual securities in the funds by the discounts that would apply to the securities if held separately;

(5) For fixed rate debt and preferred stock securities, multiply the securities by 90 percent of market value;

(6) For securities backed by Farmer Mac program assets (loans) guaranteed by the United States Department of Agriculture as described in section 8.0(9)(B) of the Act, multiply the securities by 75 percent; and

(7) We reserve the authority to modify or determine the appropriate discount for any investment used to meet the minimum liquidity reserve requirement if the otherwise applicable discount does not accurately reflect the liquidity of that investment or if the investment does not fit wholly within one of the specified investment categories. In making any modification or determination, we will consider the liquidity of the investment as well as any other relevant factors. We will provide notice of at least 20 business days before any modified discounts will take effect.

(d) *Liquidity reserve policy—board responsibilities.* Farmer Mac's board of directors must adopt a liquidity reserve policy. The board must also ensure that management uses adequate internal controls to ensure compliance with the liquidity reserve policy standards, limitations, and reporting requirements established pursuant to this paragraph and to paragraphs (e), (f), and (g) of this section. At least annually, the board of directors or a designated subcommittee of the board must review and validate the liquidity policy's adequacy. The board of directors must approve any changes to the policy. You must provide a copy of the revised policy to FCA's Office of Secondary Market Oversight within 10 business days of adoption.

(e) *Liquidity reserve policy—content.* Your liquidity reserve policy must contain at a minimum the following:

(1) The purpose and objectives of liquidity reserves;

(2) A listing of specific assets, debt, and arrangements that can be used to meet liquidity objectives;

(3) Diversification requirements of your liquidity reserve portfolio;

(4) Maturity limits and credit quality standards for non-program investments used to meet the minimum liquidity reserve requirement of paragraph (a) of this section;

(5) The minimum and target (or optimum) amounts of liquidity that the board believes are appropriate for Farmer Mac;

(6) The maximum amount of non-program investments that can be held for meeting Farmer Mac's liquidity needs, as expressed as a percentage of program assets and program obligations;

(7) Exception parameters and post approvals needed;

(8) Delegations of authority; and

(9) Reporting requirements.

(f) *Liquidity reserve reporting—periodic reporting requirements.* At least quarterly, Farmer Mac's management must report to the Corporation's board of directors or a designated subcommittee of the board describing, at a minimum, liquidity reserve compliance with the Corporation's policy and this section. Any deviations from the board's liquidity reserve policy (other than requirements specified in § 652.20(e)(5)) must be specifically identified in the report and approved by the board of directors.

(g) *Liquidity reserve reporting—special reporting requirements.* Farmer Mac's management must immediately report to its board of directors any noncompliance with board policy requirements that are specified in § 652.20(e)(5). Farmer Mac must report, in writing, to FCA's Office of Secondary Market

§ 652.25

Oversight no later than the next business day following the discovery of any breach of the minimum liquidity reserve requirement at § 652.20(a).

§ 652.25 Non-program investment purposes and limitation.

(a) Farmer Mac is authorized to hold eligible non-program investments listed under § 652.35 for the purposes of complying with the interest rate risk requirements of § 652.15, complying with the liquidity reserve requirements of § 652.20, and managing surplus short-term funds.

(b) Non-program investments cannot exceed the greater of $1.5 billion or thirty-five (35) percent of program assets and program obligations, excluding 75 percent of the program assets that are guaranteed by the United States Department of Agriculture as described in section 8.0(9)(B) of the Farm Credit Act of 1971, as amended.

§ 652.30 Temporary regulatory waivers or modifications for extraordinary situations.

Whenever the FCA determines that an extraordinary situation exists that necessitates a temporary regulatory waiver or modification, the FCA may, in its sole discretion:

(a) Modify or waive the minimum liquidity reserve requirement in § 652.20 of this subpart; and/or

(b) Modify the amount, qualities, and types of eligible investments that you are authorized to hold pursuant to § 652.25 of this subpart.

§ 652.35 Eligible non-program investments.

(a) You may hold only the types, quantities, and qualities of non-program investments listed in the following Non-Program Investment Eligibility Criteria Table. These investments must be denominated in United States dollars.

Farm Credit Administration § 652.35

Non-Program Investment Eligibility Criteria Table

ASSET CLASS	FINAL MATURITY LIMIT	NRSRO ISSUE OR ISSUER CREDIT RATING REQUIREMENT	OTHER REQUIREMENTS	MAXIMUM PERCENTAGE OF TOTAL NON-PROGRAM INVESTMENT PORTFOLIO
(1) Obligations of the United States • Treasuries • Other obligations (except mortgage securities) fully insured or guaranteed by the United States Government or a Government agency.	None	NA	None	None
(2) Obligations of Government-sponsored agencies • Government-sponsored agency securities (except mortgage securities). • Other obligations (except mortgage securities) fully insured or guaranteed by Government-sponsored agencies.	None	NA	None	None
(3) Municipal Securities				
• General obligations	10 years	One of the two highest.	None	None
• Revenue bonds	5 years for fixed rate bonds and 10 years for index/floating rate bonds	Highest	None	15%
(4) International and Multilateral Development Bank Obligations	None	None	The United States must be a voting shareholder.	None
(5) Money Market Instruments				
• Federal funds	1 day or continuously callable up to 100 days	One of the two highest short-term.	None	None
• Negotiable certificates of deposit	1 year	One of the two highest short-term.	None	None
• Bankers acceptances	None	One of the two highest short-term.	Issued by a depository institution.	None
• Prime commercial paper	270 days	Highest short-term.	None	None
• Non-callable term Federal funds and Eurodollar time deposits.	100 days	Highest short-term.	None	20%
• Master notes	270 days	Highest short-term.	None	20%
• Repurchase agreements collateralized by eligible investments or marketable securities rated in the highest credit rating category by an NRSRO.	100 days	NA	If counterparty defaults, you must divest non-eligible securities as required under § 652.45.	None

Note: You must also comply with requirements of paragraphs (b), (c), and (d) of this section, and § 651.40 when applicable. "NA" means not applicable.

§ 652.35

ASSET CLASS	FINAL MATURITY LIMIT	NRSRO ISSUE OR ISSUER CREDIT RATING REQUIREMENT	OTHER REQUIREMENTS	MAXIMUM PERCENTAGE OF TOTAL NON-PROGRAM INVESTMENT PORTFOLIO
(6) Mortgage Securities				
• Issued or guaranteed by the United States or a Government agency.	None	NA	Stress testing under § 652.40.	None
• Government-sponsored agency mortgage securities.	None	One of the two highest.	Stress testing under § 652.40.	50%
• Non-Government agency or Government-sponsored agency securities that comply with 15 U.S.C. 77d(5) or 15 U.S.C. 78c(a)(41).	None	Highest	Stress testing under § 652.40.	15% combined
• Commercial mortgage-backed securities.	None	Highest	• Security must be backed by a minimum of 100 loans. • Loans from a single mortgagor cannot exceed 5% of the pool. • Pool must be geographically diversified pursuant to the board's policy. • Stress testing under § 652.40.	
(7) Asset-Backed Securities secured by: • Credit card receivables • Automobile loans • Home equity loans • Wholesale automobile dealer loans • Student loans • Equipment loans • Manufactured housing loans	None	Highest	Maximum of 5-year WAL for fixed rate or floating rate ABS at their contractual interest rate caps.	25% combined
(8) Corporate Debt Securities	5 years	One of the highest two for maturities greater than 3 years, and one of the highest three for maturities of three years or less.	Cannot be convertible to equity securities.	25%
(9) Diversified Investment Funds Shares of an investment company registered under section 8 of the Investment Company Act of 1940.	NA	NA	The portfolio of the investment company must consist solely of eligible investments authorized by this section. The investment company's risk and return objectives and use of derivatives must be consistent with FCA guidance and your investment policies.	None, if your shares in each investment company comprise less than 10% of your portfolio. Otherwise counts toward limit for each type of investment.

Note: You must also comply with requirements of paragraphs (b), (c), and (d) of this section, and § 651.40 when applicable. "NA" means not applicable.

(b) *Rating of foreign countries.* Whenever the obligor or issuer of an eligible investment is located outside the United States, the host country must maintain the highest sovereign rating for political and economic stability by an NRSRO.

(c) *Marketable investments.* All eligible investments, except money market instruments, must be readily marketable. An eligible investment is marketable if you can sell it promptly at a price that closely reflects its fair value in an active and universally recognized secondary market. You must evaluate and document the size and liquidity of the secondary market for the investment at time of purchase.

(d) *Obligor limits.* (1) You may not invest more than 25 percent of your regulatory capital in eligible investments issued by any single entity, issuer or obligor. This obligor limit does not apply to Government-sponsored agencies or Government agencies. You may not invest more than 100 percent of your regulatory capital in any one Government-sponsored agency. There are no obligor limits for Government agencies.

(2) *Obligor limits for your holdings in an investment company.* You must count securities that you hold through an investment company towards the obligor limits of this section unless the investment company's holdings of the security of any one issuer do not exceed 5 percent of the investment company's total portfolio.

(e) *Preferred stock and other investments approved by the FCA.* (1) You may purchase non-program investments in preferred stock issued by other Farm Credit System institutions only with our written prior approval. You may also purchase non-program investments other than those listed in the Non-Program Investment Eligibility Criteria Table at paragraph (a) of this section only with our written prior approval.

(2) Your request for our approval must explain the risk characteristics of the investment and your purpose and objectives for making the investment.

§ 652.40 Stress tests for mortgage securities.

(a) You must perform stress tests to determine how interest rate changes will affect the cashflow and price of each mortgage security that you purchase and hold, except for adjustable rate mortgage securities that reprice at intervals of 12 months or less and are tied to an index. You must also use stress tests to gauge how interest rate fluctuations on mortgage securities affect your capital and earnings. The stress tests must be able to measure the price sensitivity of mortgage instruments over different interest rate/yield curve scenarios and be consistent with any asset liability management and interest rate risk policies. The methodology that you use to analyze mortgage securities must be appropriate for the complexity of the instrument's structure and cashflows. Prior to purchase and each quarter thereafter, you must use the stress tests to determine that the risk in the mortgage securities is within the risk limits of your board's investment policies. The stress tests must enable you to determine at the time of purchase and each subsequent quarter that the mortgage security does not expose your capital or earnings to excessive risks.

(b) You must rely on verifiable information to support all your assumptions, including prepayment and interest rate volatility assumptions. You must document the basis for all assumptions that you use to evaluate the security and its underlying mortgages. You must also document all subsequent changes in your assumptions. If at any time after purchase, a mortgage security no longer complies with requirements in this section, Farmer Mac's management must report to the Corporation's board of directors in accordance with § 652.10(g).

§ 652.45 Divestiture of ineligible non-program investments.

(a) *Divestiture requirements*—(1) *Initial divestiture requirements.* Within 6 months of this rule's effective date, you must divest of all ineligible non-program investments or securities unless we approve, in writing, a plan that authorizes you to divest the instruments over a longer period of time. An acceptable plan generally would require you to divest of the ineligible investments or securities as quickly as possible without substantial financial loss.

(2) *Subsequent divestiture requirements.* Subsequent to the initial divestiture

§ 652.50

period set forth in paragraph (a)(1) of this section, you must divest of an ineligible non-program investment or security within 6 months unless we approve, in writing, a plan that authorizes you to divest the instrument over a longer period of time. An acceptable plan generally would require you to divest of the ineligible investment or security as quickly as possible without substantial financial loss.

(b) *Reporting requirements.* Until you divest of the ineligible non-program investment or security, you must report at least quarterly to your board of directors and to FCA's Office of Secondary Market Oversight about the status and performance of the ineligible instrument, the reasons why it remains ineligible, and the manager's progress in divesting of the investment.

Subpart B—Risk-Based Capital Requirements

SOURCE: 71 FR 77253, Dec. 26, 2006, unless otherwise noted.

§ 652.50 Definitions.

For purposes of this subpart, the following definitions will apply:

AgVantage Plus means both the product by that name used by Farmer Mac and other similarly structured program volume that Farmer Mac might finance in the future under other names. Those AgVantage securities with initial principal amounts under $25 million and whose issuers were part of the original AgVantage program are excluded from this definition.

Farmer Mac, Corporation, you, and your means the Federal Agricultural Mortgage Corporation and its affiliates as defined in subpart A of this part.

Our, us, or we means the Farm Credit Administration.

Regulatory capital means the sum of the following as determined in accordance with generally accepted accounting principles:

(1) The par value of outstanding common stock;

(2) The par value of outstanding preferred stock;

(3) Paid-in capital, which is the amount of owner investment in Farmer Mac in excess of the par value of stock;

(4) Retained earnings; and,

(5) Any allowances for losses on loans and guaranteed securities.

Risk-based capital means the amount of regulatory capital sufficient for Farmer Mac to maintain positive capital during a 10-year period of stressful conditions as determined by the risk-based capital stress test described in § 652.65.

Rural utility guarantee fee means the actual guarantee fee charged for off-balance sheet volume and the earnings spread over Farmer Mac's funding costs for on-balance sheet volume on rural utility loans.

[71 FR 77253, Dec. 26, 2006, as amended at 76 FR 23467, April 27, 2011]

§ 652.55 General.

You must hold risk-based capital in an amount determined in accordance with this subpart.

§ 652.60 Corporation board guidelines.

(a) Your board of directors is responsible for ensuring that you maintain total capital at a level that is sufficient to ensure continued financial viability and—provide for growth. In addition, your capital must be sufficient to meet statutory and regulatory requirements.

(b) No later than 65 days after the beginning of Farmer Mac's planning year, your board of directors must adopt an operational and strategic business plan for at least the next 3 years. The plan must include:

(1) A mission statement;

(2) A review of the internal and external factors that are likely to affect you during the planning period;

(3) Measurable goals and objectives;

(4) Forecasted income, expense, and balance sheet statements for each year of the plan; and,

(5) A capital adequacy plan.

(c) The capital adequacy plan must include capital targets necessary to achieve the minimum, critical and risk-based capital standards specified by the Act and this subpart as well as your capital adequacy goals. The plan must address any projected dividends, equity retirements, or other action that may decrease your capital or its components for which minimum amounts are required by this subpart.

Farm Credit Administration

§ 652.65

You must specify in your plan the circumstances in which stock or equities may be retired. In addition to factors that must be considered in meeting the statutory and regulatory capital standards, your board of directors must also consider at least the following factors in developing the capital adequacy plan:

(1) Capability of management;

(2) Strategies and objectives in your business plan;

(3) Quality of operating policies, procedures, and internal controls;

(4) Quality and quantity of earnings;

(5) Asset quality and the adequacy of the allowance for losses to absorb potential losses in your retained mortgage portfolio, securities guaranteed as to principal and interest, commitments to purchase mortgages or securities, and other program assets or obligations;

(6) Sufficiency of liquidity and the quality of investments; and,

(7) Any other risk-oriented activities, such as funding and interest rate risks, contingent and off-balance sheet liabilities, or other conditions warranting additional capital.

§ 652.65 Risk-based capital stress test.

You will perform the risk-based capital stress test as described in summary form below and as described in detail in appendix A to this subpart. The risk-based capital stress test spreadsheet is also available electronically at *http://www.fca.gov*. The risk-based capital stress test has five components:

(a) *Data requirements.* You will use the following data to implement the risk-based capital stress test.

(1) You will use Corporation loan-level data to implement the credit risk component of the risk-based capital stress test.

(2) You will use Call Report data as the basis for Corporation data over the 10-year stress period supplemented with your interest rate risk measurements and tax data.

(3) You will use other data, including the 10-year Constant Maturity Treasury (CMT) rate and the applicable Internal Revenue Service corporate income tax schedule, as further described in appendix A to this subpart.

(b) *Credit risk.* The credit risk part estimates loan losses during a period of sustained economic stress.

(1) For each loan in the Farmer Mac I portfolio, you will determine a default probability by using the logit functions specified in appendix A to this subpart with each of the following variables:

(i) Borrower's debt-to-asset ratio at loan origination;

(ii) Loan-to-value ratio at origination, which is the loan amount divided by the value of the property;

(iii) Debt-service-coverage ratio at origination, which is the borrower's net income (on- and off-farm) plus depreciation, capital lease payments, and interest, less living expenses and income taxes, divided by the total term debt payments;

(iv) The origination loan balance stated in 1997 dollars based on the consumer price index; and,

(v) The worst-case percentage change in farmland values (23.52 percent).

(2) You will then calculate the loss rate by multiplying the default probability for each loan by the estimated loss-severity rate, which is the average loss of the defaulted loans in the data set (20.9 percent).

(3) You will calculate losses by multiplying the loss rate by the origination loan balances stated in 1997 dollars.

(4) You will adjust the losses for loan seasoning, based on the number of years since loan origination, according to the functions in appendix A to this subpart.

(5) You will calculate loss rates on rural utility loans as further described in Appendix A.

(6) You will further adjust losses for loans that collateralize the general obligation of AgVantage Plus volume, and for loans where the program loan counterparty retains a subordinated interest in accordance with Appendix A to this subpart.

(7) The losses must be applied in the risk-based capital stress test as specified in appendix A to this subpart.

(c) *Interest rate risk.* (1) During the first year of the stress period, you will adjust interest rates for two scenarios, an increase in rates and a decrease in rates. You must determine your risk-

331

§ 652.70

based capital level based on whichever scenario would require more capital.

(2) You will calculate the interest rate stress based on changes to the quarterly average of the 10-year CMT. The starting rate is the 3-month average of the most recent CMT monthly rate series. To calculate the change in the starting rate, determine the average yield of the preceding 12 monthly 10-year CMT rates. Then increase and decrease the starting rate by:

(i) 50 percent of the 12-month average if the average rate is less than 12 percent; or

(ii) 600 basis points if the 12-month average rate is equal to or higher than 12 percent.

(3) Following the first year of the stress period, interest rates remain at the new level for the remainder of the stress period.

(4) You will apply the interest rate changes scenario as indicated in appendix A to this subpart.

(5) You may use other interest rate indices in addition to the 10-year CMT subject to our concurrence, but in no event can your risk-based capital level be less than that determined by using only the 10-year CMT.

(d) *Cashflow generator.* (1) You must adjust your financial statements based on the credit risk inputs and interest rate risk inputs described above to generate pro forma financial statements for each year of the 10-year stress test. The cashflow generator produces these financial statements. You may use the cashflow generator spreadsheet that is described in appendix A to this subpart and available electronically at *http://www.fca.gov.* You may also use any reliable cashflow program that can develop or produce pro forma financial statements using generally accepted accounting principles and widely recognized financial modeling methods, subject to our concurrence. You may disaggregate financial data to any greater degree than that specified in appendix A to this subpart, subject to our concurrence.

(2) You must use model assumptions to generate financial statements over the 10-year stress period. The major assumption is that cashflows generated by the risk-based capital stress test are based on a steady-state scenario. To implement a steady-state scenario, when on- and off-balance sheet assets and liabilities amortize or are paid down, you must replace them with similar assets and liabilities (AgVantage Plus volume is not replaced when it matures). Replace amortized assets from discontinued loan programs with current loan programs. In general, keep assets with small balances in constant proportions to key program assets.

(3) You must simulate annual pro forma balance sheets and income statements in the risk-based capital stress test using Farmer Mac's starting position, the credit risk and interest rate risk components, resulting cashflow outputs, current operating strategies and policies, and other inputs as shown in appendix A to this subpart and the electronic spreadsheet available at *http://www.fca.gov.*

(e) *Calculation of capital requirement.* The calculations that you must use to solve for the starting regulatory capital amount are shown in appendix A to this subpart and in the electronic spreadsheet available at *http://www.fca.gov.*

[71 FR 77253, Dec. 26, 2006, as amended at 73 FR 31940, June 5, 2008; 76 FR 23467, April 27, 2011]

§ 652.70 Risk-based capital level.

The risk-based capital level is the sum of the following amounts:

(a) *Credit and interest rate risk.* The amount of risk-based capital determined by the risk-based capital test under § 652.65.

(b) *Management and operations risk.* Thirty (30) percent of the amount of risk-based capital determined by the risk-based capital test in § 652.65.

§ 652.75 Your responsibility for determining the risk-based capital level.

(a) You must determine your risk-based capital level using the procedures in this subpart, appendix A to this subpart, and any other supplemental instructions provided by us. You will report your determination to us as prescribed in § 652.90. At any time, however, we may determine your risk-based capital level using the procedures in § 652.65 and appendix A to this subpart, and you must hold risk-based capital in the amount we determine is appropriate.

(b) You must at all times comply with the risk-based capital levels established by the risk-based capital stress test and must be able to determine your risk-based capital level at any time.

(c) If at any time the risk-based capital level you determine is less than the minimum capital requirements set forth in section 8.33 of the Act, you must maintain the statutory minimum capital level.

§ 652.80 When you must determine the risk-based capital level.

(a) You must determine your risk-based capital level at least quarterly, or whenever changing circumstances occur that have a significant effect on capital, such as exposure to a high volume of, or particularly severe, problem loans or a period of rapid growth.

(b) In addition to the requirements of paragraph (a) of this section, we may require you to determine your risk-based capital level at any time.

(c) If you anticipate entering into any new business activity that could have a significant effect on capital, you must determine a pro forma risk-based capital level, which must include the new business activity, and report this pro forma determination to the Director, Office of Secondary Market Oversight, at least 10-business days prior to implementation of the new business program.

§ 652.85 When to report the risk-based capital level.

(a) You must file a risk-based capital report with us each time you determine your risk-based capital level as required by § 652.80.

(b) You must also report to us at once if you identify in the interim between quarterly or more frequent reports to us that you are not in compliance with the risk-based capital level required by § 652.70.

(c) If you make any changes to the data used to calculate your risk-based capital requirement that cause a material adjustment to the risk-based capital level you reported to us, you must file an amended risk-based capital report with us within 5-business days after the date of such changes;

(d) You must submit your quarterly risk-based capital report for the last day of the preceding quarter by the earlier of the reporting deadlines for Securities and Exchange Commission Forms 10–K and 10–Q, or the 40th day after each of the quarters ending March 31st, June 30th, and September 30th, and the 75th day after the quarter ending on December 31st.

[71 FR 77253, Dec. 26, 2006, as amended at 73 FR 31940, June 5, 2008]

§ 652.90 How to report your risk-based capital determination.

(a) Your risk-based capital report must contain at least the following information:

(1) All data integral for determining the risk-based capital level, including any business policy decisions or other assumptions made in implementing the risk-based capital test;

(2) Other information necessary to determine compliance with the procedures for determining risk-based capital as specified in appendix A to this subpart; and

(3) Any other information we may require in written instructions to you.

(b) You must submit each risk-based capital report in such format or medium, as we require.

§ 652.95 Failure to meet capital requirements.

(a) *Determination and notice.* At any time, we may determine that you are not meeting your risk-based capital level calculated according to § 652.65, your minimum capital requirements specified in section 8.33 of the Act, or your critical capital requirements specified in section 8.34 of the Act. We will notify you in writing of this fact and the date by which you should be in compliance (if applicable).

(b) *Submission of capital restoration plan.* Our determination that you are not meeting your required capital levels may require you to develop and submit to us, within a specified time period, an acceptable plan to reach the appropriate capital level(s) by the date required.

§ 652.100 Audit of the risk-based capital stress test.

You must have a qualified, independent external auditor review your implementation of the risk-based capital stress test every 3 years and submit a copy of the auditor's opinion to us.

APPENDIX A TO SUBPART B OF PART 652— RISK-BASED CAPITAL STRESS TEST

2.0 Credit Risk.
2.1 Loss-Frequency and Loss-Severity Models for All Types of Loans, Except Rural Utility Loans.
2.2 Loan-Seasoning Adjustment for All Types of Loans, Except Rural Utility Loans.
2.3 Example Calculation of Dollar Loss on One Loan for All Types of Loans, Except Rural Utility Loans.
2.4 Treatment of Loans Backed by an Obligation of the Counterparty and Loans for Which Pledged Loan Collateral Volume Exceeds Farmer Mac-Guaranteed Volume.
2.5 Calculation of Loss Rates for Use in the Stress Test for All Types of Loans, Except Rural Utility Loans.
2.6 Calculation of Loss Rates on Rural Utility Volume for Use in the Stress Test.
3.0 Interest Rate Risk.
3.1 Process for Calculating the Interest Rate Movement.
4.0 Elements Used in Generating Cashflows.
4.1 Data Inputs.
4.2 Assumptions and Relationships.
4.3 Risk Measures.
4.4 Loan and Cashflow Accounts.
4.5 Income Statements.
4.6 Balance Sheets.
4.7 Capital.
5.0 Capital Calculations.
5.1 Method of Calculation.

1.0 INTRODUCTION

a. Appendix A provides details about the risk-based capital stress test (stress test) for Farmer Mac. The stress test calculates the risk-based capital level required by statute under stipulated conditions of credit risk and interest rate risk. The stress test uses loan-level data from Farmer Mac's agricultural mortgage portfolio or proxy data as described in section 4.1 d.(3) below, as well as quarterly Call Report and related information to generate pro forma financial statements and calculate a risk-based capital requirement. The stress test also uses historic agricultural real estate mortgage performance data, rural utility guarantee fees, relevant economic variables, and other inputs in its calculations of Farmer Mac's capital needs over a 10-year period.

b. Appendix A establishes the requirements for all components of the stress test. The key components of the stress test are: Specifications of credit risk, interest rate risk, the cashflow generator, and the capital calculation. Linkages among the components ensure that the measures of credit and interest rate risk pass into the cashflow generator. The linkages also transfer cashflows through the financial statements to represent values of assets, liabilities, and equity capital. The 10-year projection is designed to reflect a steady state in the scope and composition of Farmer Mac's assets.

2.0 CREDIT RISK

Loan loss rates are determined by applying the loss-frequency equation and the loss-severity factor to Farmer Mac loan-level data. Using this equation and severity factor, you must calculate loan losses under stressful economic conditions assuming Farmer Mac's portfolio remains at a "steady state." Steady state assumes the underlying characteristics and risks of Farmer Mac's portfolio remain constant over the 10 years of the stress test. Loss rates discussed in this section apply to all loans, unless otherwise indicated. Loss rates are computed from estimated dollar losses for use in the stress test. The loan volume subject to loss throughout the stress test is then multiplied by the loss rate. Lastly, the stress test allocates losses to each of the 10 years assuming a time pattern for loss occurrence as discussed in section 4.3, "Risk Measures."

2.1 Loss-Frequency and Loss-Severity Models for All Types of Loans, Except Rural Utility Loans

a. Credit risks are modeled in the stress test using historical time series loan-level data to measure the frequency and severity of losses on agricultural mortgage loans. The model relates loss frequency and severity to loan-level characteristics and economic conditions through appropriately specified regression equations to account explicitly for the effects of these characteristics on loan losses. Loan losses for Farmer Mac are estimated from the resulting loss-frequency equation combined with the loss-severity factor by substituting the respective values of Farmer Mac's loan-level data or proxy data as described in section 4.1 d.(3) below, and applying stressful economic inputs.

b. The loss-frequency equation and loss-severity factor were estimated from historical agricultural real estate mortgage loan data from the Farm Credit Bank of Texas (FCBT). Due to Farmer Mac's relatively short history, its own loan-level data are insufficiently developed for use in estimating the default frequency equation and loss-severity factor. In the future, however, expansions in both the scope and historic length of Farmer

Farm Credit Administration
Pt. 652, Subpt. B, App. A

Mac's lending operations may support the use of its data in estimating the relationships.

c. To estimate the equations, the data used included FCBT loans, which satisfied three of the four underwriting standards Farmer Mac currently uses (estimation data). The four standards specify: (1) The debt-to-assets ratio (D/A) must be less than 0.50, (2) the loan-to-value ratio (LTV) must be less than 0.70, (3) the debt-service-coverage ratio (DSCR) must exceed 1.25, (4) and the current ratio (current assets divided by current liabilities) must exceed 1.0. Furthermore, the D/A and LTV ratios were restricted to be less than or equal to 0.85.

d. Several limitations in the FCBT loan-level data affect construction of the loss-frequency equation. The data contained loans that were originated between 1979 and 1992, but there were virtually no losses during the early years of the sample period. As a result, losses attributable to specific loans are only available from 1986 through 1992. In addition, no prepayment information was available in the data.

e. The FCBT data used for estimation also included as performing loans, those loans that were re-amortized, paid in full, or merged with a new loan. Including these loans may lead to an understatement of loss-frequency probabilities if some of the re-amortized, paid, or merged loans experience default or incur losses. In contrast, when the loans that are re-amortized, paid in full, or merged are excluded from the analysis, the loss-frequency rates are overstated if a higher proportion of loans that are re-amortized, paid in full, or combined (merged) into a new loan are non-default loans compared to live loans.[1]

f. The structure of the historical FCBT data supports estimation of loss frequency based on origination information and economic conditions. Under an origination year approach, each observation is used only once in estimating loan default. The underwriting variables at origination and economic factors occurring over the life of the loan are then used to estimate loan-loss frequency.

g. The final loss-frequency equation is based on origination year data and represents a lifetime loss-frequency model. The final equation for loss frequency is:

$p = 1/(1+\exp(-(BX))$

Where:

$BX = (-12.62738) + 1.91259 \cdot X_1 + (-0.33830) \cdot X_2 / (1 + 0.0413299)^{Periods} + (-0.19596) \cdot X_3 + 4.55390 \cdot (1-\exp((-0.00538178) \cdot X_4) + 2.49482 \cdot X_5$

Where:

- p is the probability that a loan defaults and has positive losses (Pr (Y=1 | x));
- X_1 is the LTV ratio at loan origination raised to the power 5.3914596;[2]
- X_2 is the largest annual percentage decline in FCBT farmland values during the life of the loan dampened with a factor of 0.0413299 per year;[3]
- X_3 is the DSCR at loan origination;
- X_4 is 1 minus the exponential of the product of negative 0.00538178 and the original loan balance in 1997 dollars expressed in thousands; and
- X_5 is the D/A ratio at loan origination.

h. The estimated logit coefficients and p-values are:[4]

---

[1] Excluding loans with defaults, 11,527 loans were active and 7,515 loans were paid in full, re-amortized or merged as of 1992. A t-test[2] of the differences in the means for the group of defaulted loans and active loans indicated that active loans had significantly higher D/A and LTV ratios, and lower current ratios than defaulted loans where loss occurred. These results indicate that, on average, active loans have potentially higher risk than loans that were re-amortized, paid in full, or merged.

[2] Loss probability is likely to be more sensitive to changes in LTV at higher values of LTV. The power function provides a continuous relationship between LTV and defaults.

[3] The dampening function reflects the declining effect that the maximum land value decline has on the probability of default when it occurs later in a loan's life.

[4] The nonlinear parameters for the variable transformations were simultaneously estimated using SAS version 8e NLIN procedure. The NLIN procedure produces estimates of the parameters of a nonlinear transformation for LTV, dampening factor, and loan-size variables. To implement the NLIN procedure, the loss-frequency equation and its variables are declared and initial parameter values supplied. The NLIN procedure is an iterative process that uses the initial parameter values as the starting values for the first iteration and continues to iterate until acceptable parameters are solved. The initial values for the power function and dampening function are based on the proposed rule. The procedure for the initial values for the size variable parameter is provided in an Excel spreadsheet posted at *http://www.fca.gov*. The Gauss-Newton method is the selected iterative solving process. As described in the preamble, the loss-frequency function for the nonlinear model is the negative of the log-likelihood function, thus producing maximum likelihood estimates. In order to obtain statistical properties for the loss-frequency equation and verify the logistic coefficients, the estimates for the nonlinear transformations are applied to the FCBT

Continued

	Coefficients	p-value
Intercept	−12.62738	<0.0001
X_1: LTV variable	1.91259	0.0001
X_2: Max land value decline variable	0.33830	<0.0001
X_3: DSCR	−0.19596	0.0002
X_4: Loan size variable	4.55390	<0.0001
X_5: D/A ratio	2.49482	<0.0000

i. The low p-values on each coefficient indicate a highly significant relationship between the probability ratio of loan-loss frequency and the respective independent variables. Other goodness-of-fit indicators are:

Hosmer and Lemeshow goodness-of-fit p-value	0.1718
Max-rescaled R^2	0.2015
Concordant	85.2%
Disconcordant	12.0%
Tied	2.8%

j. These variables have logical relationships to the incidence of loan default and loss, as evidenced by the findings of numerous credit-scoring studies in agricultural finance.[5] Each of the variable coefficients has directional relationships that appropriately capture credit risk from underwriting variables and, therefore, the incidence of loan-loss frequency. The frequency of loan loss was found to differ significantly across all of the loan characteristics and lending conditions. Farmland values represent an appropriate variable for capturing the effects of exogenous economic factors. It is commonly accepted that farmland values at any point in time reflect the discounted present value of expected returns to the land.[6] Thus, changes in land values, as expressed in the loss-frequency equation, represent the combined effects of the level and growth rates of farm income, interest rates, and inflationary expectations—each of which is accounted for in the discounted, present value process.

k. When applying the equation to Farmer Mac's portfolio, you must get the input values for X_1, X_3, X_4, and X_5 for each loan in Farmer Mac's portfolio on the date at which the stress test is conducted, using either submitted data or proxy data as described in section 4.1 d.(3) below. For the variable X_2, the stressful input value from the benchmark loss experience is −23.52 percent. You must apply this input to all Farmer Mac loans subject to loss to calculate loss frequency under stressful economic conditions.[7] The maximum land value decline from the benchmark loss experience is the simple average of annual land value changes for Iowa, Illinois, and Minnesota for the years 1984 and 1985.[8]

l. Forecasting with data outside the range of the estimation data requires special treatment for implementation. While the estimation data embody Farmer Mac values for various loan characteristics, the maximum farmland price decline experienced in Texas was −16.69 percent, a value below the benchmark experience of −23.52 percent. To control for this effect, you must apply a procedure that restricts the slope of all the independent variables to that observed at the maximum land value decline observed in the estimation data. Essentially, you must approximate the slope of the loss-frequency equation at the point −16.69 percent in order to adjust the probability of loan default and loss occurrence for data beyond the range in the estimating data. The adjustment procedure is shown in step 4 of section 2.3 entitled, "Example Calculation of Dollar Loss on One Loan."

m. Loss severity was not found to vary systematically and was considered constant across the tested loan characteristics and lending conditions. Thus, the simple weighted average by loss volume of 20.9 percent is used in the stress test.[9] You must multiply loss severity with the probability estimate computed from the loss-frequency equation to determine the loss rate for a loan.

n. Using original loan balance results in estimated probabilities of loss frequency over

---

data and the loss-frequency model is re-estimated using the SAS Logistic procedure. The SAS procedures, output reports and Excel spreadsheet used to estimate the parameters of the loss-frequency equation are located on the Web site *http://www.fca.gov*.

[5] Splett, N.S., P. J. Barry, B. Dixon, and P. Ellinger. "A Joint Experience and Statistical Approach to Credit Scoring," *Agricultural Finance Review*, 54(1994):39–54.

[6] Barry, P. J., P. N. Ellinger, J. A. Hopkin, and C. B. Baker. *Financial Management in Agriculture*, 5th ed., Interstate Publishers, 1995.

[7] On- and off-balance sheet Farmer Mac I agricultural mortgage program assets booked after the 1996 Act amendments are subject to the loss calculation.

[8] While the worst-case losses, based on origination year, occurred during 1983 and 1984, this benchmark was determined using annual land value changes that occurred 2 years later.

[9] We calculated the weighted-average loss severity from the estimation data.

Farm Credit Administration

the entire life of a loan. To account for loan seasoning, you must reduce the loan-loss exposure by the cumulative probability of loss already experienced by each loan as discussed in section 2.2 entitled, "Loan-Seasoning Adjustment." This subtraction is based on loan age and reduces the loss estimated by the loss-frequency and loss-severity equations. The result is an age-adjusted lifetime dollar loss that can be used in subsequent calculations of loss rates as discussed in section 2.4, "Calculation of Loss Rates for Use in the Stress Test."

2.2 Loan-Seasoning Adjustment for All Types of Loans, Except Rural Utility Loans

a. You must use the seasoning function supplied by FCA to adjust the calculated probability of loss for each Farmer Mac loan for the cumulative loss exposure already experienced based on the age of each loan. The seasoning function is based on the same data used to determine the loss-frequency equation and an assumed average life of 14 years for agricultural mortgages. If we determine that the relationship between the loss experience in Farmer Mac's portfolio over time and the seasoning function can be improved, we may augment or replace the seasoning function.

b. The seasoning function is parameterized as a beta distribution with parameters of p = 4.288 and q = 5.3185.[10] How the loan-seasoning distribution is used is shown in Step 7 of section 2.3, "Example Calculation of Dollar Loss on One Loan."

2.3 Example Calculation of Dollar Loss on One Loan for All Types of Loans, Except Rural Utility Loans

Here is an example of the calculation of the dollar losses for an individual loan with the following characteristics and input values:[11]

Loan Origination Year	1996
Loan Origination Balance ..	$1,250,000
LTV at Origination	0.5
D/A at Origination	0.5
DSCR at Origination	1.3984

---

[10] We estimated the loan-seasoning distribution from portfolio aggregate charge-off rates from the estimation data. To do so, we arrayed all defaulting loans where loss occurred according to the time from origination to default. Then, a beta distribution, β(p, q), was fit to the estimation data scaled to the maximum time a loan survived (14 years).

[11] In the examples presented we rounded the numbers, but the example calculation is based on a larger number of significant digits. The stress test uses additional digits carried at the default precision of the software.

Pt. 652, Subpt. B, App. A

Maximum Percentage Land Price Decline (MAX)	−23.52

Step 1: Convert 1996 Origination Value to 1997 dollar value (LOAN) based on the consumer price index and transform as follows:
$1,278,500 = $1,250,000 · 1.0228
0.998972 = 1 − exp((−.00538178) · $1,278,500 / 1000)

Step 2: Calculate the default probabilities using −16.64 percent and −16.74 percent land value declines as follows:[12]
Where:

Z_1 = (−12.62738) + 1.91259 · $LTV^{5.3914596}$ − 0.33830 · (−16.6439443) − 0.19596 · DSCR + 4.55390 · 0.998972 + 2.49482 · DA = (−1.428509)
Default Loss Frequency at (−16.64%) =
$1/1 + exp^{-(-1.428509)}$ = 0.19333111
And
Z_1 = (−12.62738) + 1.91259 · $LTV^{5.3914596}$ − 0.33830 · (−16.7439443) − 0.19596 · DSCR + 4.55390 · 0.998972 + 2.49482 · DA = (−1.394679)
Loss Frequency Probability at (−16.74%) =
$1/1 + exp^{-(-1.394679)}$ = 0.19866189

Step 3: Calculate the slope adjustment. You must calculate slope by subtracting the difference between "Loss-Frequency Probability at −16.64 percent" and "Loss-Frequency Probability at −16.74 percent" and dividing by −0.1 (the difference between −16.64 percent and −16.74 percent) as follows:

0.05330776 = (0.19333111 − 0.19866189) / −0.1

Step 4: Make the linear adjustment. You make the adjustment by increasing the loss-frequency probability where the dampened stressed farmland value input is less than −16.69 percent to reflect the stressed farmland value input, appropriately discounted. As discussed previously, the stressed land value input is discounted to reflect the declining effect that the maximum land value decline has on the probability of default when it occurs later in a loan's life.[13] The linear adjustment is the difference between −16.69 percent land value decline and the adjusted stressed maximum land value decline input of −23.52 multiplied by the slope estimated in Step 3 as follows:

Loss Frequency at −16.69 percent =
Z_1 = (−12.62738) + (1.91259)($LTV^{5.3914596}$) − (0.33830)(−16.6939443) − (0.19596)(DSCR) + (4.55390)(0.998972) + (2.49482)(DA) = −1.411594
And
$1/1 + exp^{-(-1.411594)}$ = 0.19598279

---

[12] This process facilitates the approximation of slope needed to adjust the loss probabilities for land value declines greater than observed in the estimation data.

[13] The dampened period is the number of years from the beginning of the origination year to the current year (i.e., January 1, 1996 to January 1, 2000 is 4 years).

Dampened Maximum Land Price Decline = (−20.00248544) = (−23.52)(1.0413299)⁻⁴
Slope Adjustment = 0.17637092 = 0.053312247 · (−16.6939443 − (−20.00248544))
Loan Default Probability = 0.37235371 = 0.19598279 + 0.17637092

Step 5: Multiply loan default probability times the average severity of 0.209 as follows: 0.077821926 = 0.37235371 · 0.209

Step 6: Multiply the loss rate times the origination loan balance as follows:
$97,277 = $1,250,000 · 0.077821926

Step 7: Adjust the origination based dollar losses for 4 years of loan seasoning as follows:
$81,987 = $97,277 − $97,277 · (0.157178762)[14]

2.4 Treatment of Loans Backed by an Obligation of the Counterparty and Loans for Which Pledged Loan Collateral Volume Exceeds Farmer Mac-Guaranteed Volume

You must calculate the age-adjusted loss rates for these loans that include adjustments to scale losses according to the proportion of total submitted collateral to the guaranteed amount as provided for in the "Dollar Losses" column of the transformed worksheets in the Credit Loss Module based on new data inputs required in the "Coefficients" worksheet of the Credit Loss Module. Then, you must adjust the calculated loss rates as follows.

a. For loans in which the seller retains a subordinated interest, subtract from the total estimated age-adjusted dollar losses on the pool the amount equal to current unpaid principal times the subordinated interest percentage.

b. Some pools of loans underlying specific transactions could include loan collateral volume pledged to Farmer Mac in excess of Farmer Mac's guarantee amount ("overcollateral"). Overcollateral can be either: (i) Contractually required according to the terms of the transaction, or (ii) not contractually required, but pledged in addition to the contractually required amount at the discretion of the counterparty, often for purposes of administrative convenience regarding the collateral substitution process, or (iii) both (i) and (ii).

1. If a pool of loans includes collateral pledged in excess of the guaranteed amount, you must adjust the age-adjusted, loan-level dollar losses by a factor equal to the ratio of the guarantee amount to total submitted collateral. For example, consider a pool of two loans serving as security for a Farmer Mac guarantee on a note with a total issuance face value of $2 million and on which the counterparty has submitted 10-percent overcollateral. The two loans in the example have the following characteristics and adjustments.

Loan	Origination balance	Age-adjusted loss rate (percent)	Estimated age-adjusted losses	Guarantee amount scaling adjustment (2/2.2) (Percent)	Losses adjusted for overcollateral
1	$1,080,000	7.0	$75,600	90.91	$68,727
2	1,120,000	5.0	56,000	90.91	50,909

2. If a pool of loans includes collateral pledged in excess of the guaranteed amount that is required under the terms of the transaction, you must further adjust the dollar losses as follows. Calculate the total losses on the subject portfolio of loans after age adjustments and any adjustments related to total submitted overcollateral as described in "1." above. Calculate the total dollar amount of contractually required overcollateral in the subject pool. Subtract the total dollars of contractually required overcollateral from the adjusted total losses on the subject pool. If the result is less than or equal to zero, input a loss rate of zero for this transaction pool in the Data Inputs worksheet of the RBCST. A new category must be created for each such transaction in the RBCST. If the loss rate after subtracting contractually required overcollateral is greater than zero, proceed to additional adjustment for the risk-reducing effects of the counterparty's general obligation described in "3." below.

3. Loans with a positive loss estimate remaining after adjustments in "1." and "2." above are further adjusted for the security provided by the general obligation of the counterparty. To make this adjustment in our example, multiply the estimated dollar losses remaining after adjustments in "1." and "2." above by the appropriate general obligation adjustment (GOA) factor based on the counterparty's whole-letter issuer credit rating by a nationally recognized statistical rating organization (NRSRO) and the ratio of the counterparty's concentration of risk in the same industry sector as the loans

---

[14] The age of adjustment of 0.157178762 is determined from the beta distribution for a 4-year-old loan.

Farm Credit Administration

Pt. 652, Subpt. B, App. A

backing the AgVantage Plus volume, as determined by the Director.

A. The Director will make final determinations of concentration ratios on a case-by-case basis by using publicly reported data on counterparty portfolios, non-public data submitted and certified by Farmer Mac as part of its RBCST submissions, and will generally recognize rural electric cooperatives and rural telephone cooperatives as separate rural utility sectors. The following table sets forth the GOA factors and their components by whole-letter credit rating (Adjustment Factor = Default Rate × Severity Rate × 3), which may be further adjusted for industry sector concentration by the Director.[15]

A	B	C	D	E	F	G
Whole-letter rating	Default rate (percent)	Severity rate (percent)	V3.0 GOA factor (percent)	V4.0 GOA factors (D × 3) (percent)	Concentration ratio (e.g., 25%) (percent)	Factor with concentration adjustment 1 − ((1 − E) × (1 − F)) (percent)
AAA	0.897	54	0.48	1.41	25.00	26.06
AA	2.294	54	1.24	3.70	25.00	27.78
A	2.901	54	1.57	5.13	25.00	28.84
BBB	7.061	54	3.82	11.48	25.00	33.61
Below BBB and Unrated	26.827	54	14.50	44.52	25.00	58.39

B. The adjustment factors will be updated annually as Moody's annual report on Default and Recovery Rates of Corporate Bond Issuers becomes available, normally in January or February of each year. In the event that there is an interruption of Moody's publication of this annual report, or FCA determines that the format of the report has changed enough to prevent or call into question the identification of updated factors, the prior year's factors will remain in effect until FCA revises the process through rulemaking.

4. Continuing the previous example, the pool contains two loans on which Farmer Mac is guaranteeing a total of $2 million and with total submitted collateral of 110 percent of the guaranteed amount. Of the 10-percent total overcollateral, 5 percent is contractually required under the terms of the transaction. The pool consists of two loans of slightly over $1 million. Total overcollateral is $200,000 of which $100,000 is contractually required. The counterparty has a single "A" credit rating, a 25-percent concentration ratio, and after adjusting for contractually required overcollateral, estimated losses are greater than zero. The net loss rate is calculated as described in the steps in the table below.

		Loan A	Loan B
1	Guaranteed Volume.	$2,000,000	
2	Origination Balance of 2-Loan Portfolio.	$1,080,000	$1,120,000.
3	Age-Adjusted Loss Rate.	7%	5%.
4	Estimated Age-Adjusted Losses.	$75,600	$56,000.

---

[15] Emery, K., Ou S., Tennant, J., Kim F., Cantor R., "Corporate Default and Recovery Rates, 1920—2007," published by Moody's Investors Service, February 2008—the most recent edition as of March 2008; Default Rates, page 24, Recovery Rates (Severity Rate = 1 minus Senior Unsecured Average Recovery Rate) page 20.

Pt. 652, Subpt. B, App. A

	Loan A	Loan B
5 Guarantee Volume Scaling Factor.	90.91%	90.91%.
6 Losses Adjusted for Total Overcollateral.	$68,727	$50,909.
7 Contractually Required Overcollateral on Pool (5%).	$100,000	
8 Net Losses on Pool Adjusted for Contractually Required Overcollateral.	$19,636	
9 GOA Factor for "A" Issuer with 25% Concentration Ratio.	28.84%	
10 Losses Adjusted for "A" General Obligation.	$5,664	
11 Loss Rate Input in the RBCST for this Pool.	0.28%	

A. The net, fully adjusted losses are distributed over time on a straight-line basis. When a transaction reaches maturity within the 10-year modeling horizon, the losses are distributed on a straightline over a timepath that ends in the year of the transaction's maturity.

B. [Reserved]

2.5 Calculation of Loss Rates for Use in the Stress Test for All Types of Loans, Except Rural Utility Loans

a. You must compute the loss rates by state as the dollar weighted average seasoned loss rates from the Cash Window and Standby loan portfolios by state. The spreadsheet entitled, "Credit Loss Module.XLS" can be used for these calculations. This spreadsheet is available for download on our Web site, *www.fca.gov*, or will be provided upon request. The blended loss rates for each state are copied from the "Credit Loss Module" to the stress test spreadsheet for determining Farmer Mac's regulatory capital requirement.

b. The stress test use of the blended loss rates is further discussed in section 4.3, "Risk Measures."

2.6 Calculation of Loss Rates on Rural Utility Volume for-Use in the Stress Test

You must submit the outstanding principal, maturity date of the loan, maturity date of the AgVantage Plus contract (if applicable), and the rural utility guarantee fee percentage for each loan in Farmer Mac's

Farm Credit Administration

Pt. 652, Subpt. B, App. A

rural utility loan portfolio on the date at which the stress test is conducted. You must multiply the rural utility guarantee fee by two to calculate the loss rate on rural utility loans under stressful economic conditions and then multiply the loss rate by the total outstanding principal. To arrive at the net rural utility loan losses, you must next apply the steps "5" through "11" of section 2.4.b.4 of this Appendix. For loans under an AgVantage Plus-type structure, the calculated losses are distributed over time on a straight-line basis. For loans that are not part of an AgVantage Plus-type structure, losses are distributed over the 10-year modeling horizon, consistent with other non-AgVantage Plus loan volume.

3.0 INTEREST RATE RISK

The stress test explicitly accounts for Farmer Mac's vulnerability to interest rate risk from the movement in interest rates specified in the statute. The stress test considers Farmer Mac's interest rate risk position through the current structure of its balance sheet, reported interest rate risk shock-test results,[16] and other financial activities. The stress test calculates the effect of interest rate risk exposure through market value changes of interest-bearing assets, liabilities, and off-balance sheet transactions, and thereby the effects to equity capital. The stress test also captures this exposure through the cashflows on rate-sensitive assets and liabilities. We discuss how to calculate the dollar impact of interest rate risk in section 4.6, "Balance Sheets."

3.1 Process for Calculating the Interest Rate Movement

a. The stress test uses the 10-year Constant Maturity Treasury (10-year CMT) released by the Federal Reserve in HR. 15, "Selected Interest Rates." The stress test uses the 10-year CMT to generate earnings yields on assets, expense rates on liabilities, and changes in the market value of assets and liabilities. For stress test purposes, the starting rate for the 10-year CMT is the 3-month average of the most recent monthly rate series published by the Federal Reserve. The 3-month average is calculated by summing the latest monthly series of the 10-year CMT and dividing by three. For instance, you would calculate the initial rate on June 30, 1999, as:

Month end	10-year CMT monthly series
04/1999	5.18
05/1999	5.54

---

[16] See paragraph c. of section 4.1 entitled, "Data Inputs," for a description of the interest rate risk shock-reporting requirement.

Month end	10-year CMT monthly series
06/1999	5.90
Average	5.54

b. The amount by which the stress test shocks the initial rate up and down is determined by calculating the 12-month average of the 10-year CMT monthly series. If the resulting average is less than 12 percent, the stress test shocks the initial rate by an amount determined by multiplying the 12-month average rate by 50 percent. However, if the average is greater than or equal to 12 percent, the stress test shocks the initial rate by 600 basis points. For example, determine the amount by which to increase and decrease the initial rate for June 30, 1999, as follows:

Month end	10-year CMT monthly series
07/1998	5.46
08/1998	5.34
09/1998	4.81
10/1998	4.53
11/1998	4.83
12/1998	4.65
01/1999	4.72
02/1999	5.00
03/1999	5.23
04/1999	5.18
05/1999	5.54
06/1999	5.90
12-Month Average	5.10

Calculation of shock amount	
12-Month Average Less than 12%	Yes.
12-Month Average	5.10.
Multiply the 12-Month Average by	50%.
Shock in basis points equals	255.

c. You must run the stress test for two separate changes in interest rates: (i) An immediate increase in the initial rate by the shock amount; and (ii) immediate decrease in the initial rate by the shock amount. The stress test then holds the changed interest rate constant for the remainder of the 10-year stress period. For example, at June 30, 1999, the stress test would be run for an immediate and sustained (for 10 years) upward movement in interest rates to 8.09 percent (5.54 percent plus 255 basis points) and also for an immediate and sustained (for 10 years) downward movement in interest rates to 2.99 percent (5.54 percent minus 255 basis points). The movement in interest rates that results in the greatest need for capital is then used to determine Farmer Mac's risk-based capital requirement.

4.0 ELEMENTS USED IN GENERATING CASHFLOWS

a. This section describes the elements that are required for implementation of the stress test and assessment of Farmer Mac capital performance through time. An Excel spreadsheet named FAMC RBCST, available at *http://www.fca.gov*, contains the stress test, including the cashflow generator. The spreadsheet contains the following seven worksheets:

(1) Data Input;
(2) Assumptions and Relationships;
(3) Risk Measures (credit risk and interest rate risk);
(4) Loan and Cash Flow Accounts;
(5) Income Statements;
(6) Balance Sheets; and
(7) Capital.

b. Each of the components is described in further detail below with references where appropriate to the specific worksheets within the Excel spreadsheet. The stress test may be generally described as a set of linked financial statements that evolve over a period of 10 years using generally accepted accounting conventions and specified sets of stressed inputs. The stress test uses the initial financial condition of Farmer Mac, including earnings and funding relationships, and the credit and interest rate stressed inputs to calculate Farmer Mac's capital performance through time. The stress test then subjects the initial financial conditions to the first period set of credit and interest rate risk stresses, generates cashflows by asset and liability category, performs necessary accounting postings into relevant accounts, and generates an income statement associated with the first interval of time. The stress test then uses the income statement to update the balance sheet for the end of period 1 (beginning of period 2). All necessary capital calculations for that point in time are then performed.

c. The beginning of the period 2 balance sheet then serves as the departure point for the second income cycle. The second period's cashflows and resulting income statement are generated in similar fashion as the first period's except all inputs (*i.e.*, the periodic loan losses, portfolio balance by category, and liability balances) are updated appropriately to reflect conditions at that point in time. The process evolves forward for a period of 10 years with each pair of balance sheets linked by an intervening set of cashflow and income statements. In this and the following sections, additional details are provided about the specification of the income-generating model to be used by Farmer Mac in calculating the risk-based capital requirement.

4.1 Data Inputs

The stress test requires the initial financial statement conditions and income generating relationships for Farmer Mac. The worksheet named "Data Inputs" contains the complete data inputs and the data form used in the stress test. The stress test uses these data and various assumptions to calculate pro forma financial statements. For stress test purposes, Farmer Mac is required to supply:

a. *Call Report Schedules RC: Balance Sheet and RI: Income Statement.* These schedules form the starting financial position for the stress test. In addition, the stress test calculates basic financial relationships and assumptions used in generating pro forma annual financial statements over the 10-year stress period. Financial relationships and assumptions are in section 4.2, "Assumptions and Relationships."

b. *Cashflow Data for Asset and Liability Account Categories.* The necessary cashflow data for the spreadsheet-based stress test are book value, weighted average yield, weighted average maturity, conditional prepayment rate, weighted average amortization, and weighted average guarantee fees and rural utility guarantee fees. The spreadsheet uses this cashflow information to generate starting and ending account balances, interest earnings, guarantee fees, rural utility guarantee fees, and interest expense. Each asset and liability account category identified in this data requirement is discussed in section 4.2 "Assumptions and Relationships."

c. *Interest Rate Risk Measurement Results.* The stress test uses the results from Farmer Mac's interest rate risk model to represent changes in the market value of assets, liabilities, and off-balance sheet positions during upward and downward instantaneous shocks in interest rates of 300, 250, 200, 150, and 100 basis points. The stress test uses these data to calculate a schedule of estimated effective durations representing the market value effects from a change in interest rates. The stress test uses a linear interpolation of the duration schedule to relate a change in interest rates to a change in the market value of equity. This calculation is described in section 4.4 entitled, "Loan and Cashflow Accounts," and is illustrated in the referenced worksheet of the stress test.

d. *Loan-Level Data for all Farmer Mac I Program Assets.*

(1) The stress test requires loan-level data for all Farmer Mac I program assets to determine lifetime age-adjusted loss rates. The specific loan data fields required for running the credit risk component are:

Farmer Mac I Program Loan Data Fields

Loan Number
Ending Scheduled Balance
Group

Farm Credit Administration

Pt. 652, Subpt. B, App. A

Pre/Post Act
Property State
Product Type
Origination Date
Loan Cutoff Date
Original Loan Balance
Original Scheduled P&I
Original Appraised Value
Loan-to-Value Ratio
Debt-to-Assets Ratio
Current Assets
Current Liabilities
Total Assets
Total Liabilities
Gross Farm Revenue
Net Farm Income
Depreciation
Interest on Capital Debt
Capital Lease Payments
Living Expenses
Income & FICA Taxes
Net Off-Farm Income
Total Debt Service
Guarantee/Commitment Fee
Seasoned Loan Flag

(2) From the loan-level data, you must identify the geographic distribution by state of Farmer Mac's loan portfolio and enter the current loan balance for each state in the "Data Inputs" worksheet. The lifetime age-adjustment of origination year loss rates was discussed in section 2.0, "Credit Risk." The lifetime age-adjusted loss rates are entered in the "Risk Measures" worksheet of the stress test. The stress test application of the loss rates is discussed in section 4.3, "Risk Measures."

(3) Under certain circumstances, described below, you must substitute the following data proxies for the variables LTV, DSCR, and D/A: LTV = 0.70, DSCR = 1.25, and D/A = 0.50. The substitution must be done whenever any of these data are missing, i.e., cells are blank, or one or more of the conditions in the following table is true.

Condition	Apply
1. Total Assets = 0	Proxy D/A.
2. Total Liabilities = 0	Proxy D/A.
3. Total assets less total liabilities <0	Proxy D/A.
4. Total debt service = 0 or not calculable	Proxy DSCR.
5. Net farm income = 0	Proxy DSCR.
6. LTV ratio = 0	Proxy LTV.
7. Total assets less than original appraised value	Proxy LTV, D/A.
8. Total liabilities less than the original loan amount	Proxy D/A.
9. Total debt service is less than original scheduled principal and interest payment	Proxy DSCR.
10. Depreciation, interest on capital debt, capital lease payments, or living expenses are reported as less than zero.	Proxy DSCR.
11. Original Scheduled Principal and Interest is greater than Total Debt Service	Proxy DSCR.
12. Calculated LTV (original loan amount divided by original appraised value) does not equal the submitted LTV ratio.	The greater of the two LTV ratios.
13. Any of the fields referenced in "1." through "12." above are blank or contain spaces, periods, zeros, negative amounts, or fonts formatted to any setting other than numbers.	Proxy all related ratios.

In addition, the following loan data adjustments must be made in response to the situations listed below:

Situation	Data adjustment
Original loan balance is less than scheduled loan balance	Substitute scheduled balance for origination.
Purchase (commitment) date (a.k.a. "cutoff" date) field and Origination date field are both blank.	Insert the quarter end "as of" date of the RBCST submission.
Origination date field is blank	Model based on Cutoff date.
Seasoned Standby loans that include loan data	Proxy data applied.*

*Application of proxy data recognizes that underwriting data on seasoned Standby loans are not reviewed by Farmer Mac in favor of other criteria and frequently not origination data.

Further, because it would not be possible to compile an exhaustive list of loan data anomalies, FCA reserves the authority to require an explanation on other data anomalies it identifies and to apply the loan data proxies on such cases until the anomaly is adequately addressed by the Corporation.

e. *Loan-Level Data for All Rural Utility Program Volume.* The stress test requires loan-level data for all rural utility program volume. The specific loan data fields required for calculating the credit risk are outstanding principal, maturity date of the loan, maturity date of the AgVantage Plus contract (if applicable), and the rural utility guarantee fee percentage for each loan in Farmer Mac's rural utility loan portfolio on the date at which the stress test is conducted.

Pt. 652, Subpt. B, App. A

f. *Weighted Haircuts for Non-Program Investments.* For non-program investments, the stress test adjusts the weighted average yield data referenced in section 4.1.b. to reflect counterparty risk. Non-program investments are defined in § 652.5. The Corporation must calculate the haircut to be applied to each investment based on the lowest whole-letter credit rating the investment received from an NRSRO using the haircut levels in effect at the time. Haircut levels shall be the same amounts calculated for the GOA factor in section 2.4.b.3 above. The first table provides the mappings of NRSRO ratings to whole-letter ratings for purposes of applying haircuts. Any "+" or "−" signs appended to NRSRO ratings that are not shown in the table should be ignored for purposes of mapping NRSRO ratings to FCA whole-letter ratings. The second table provides the haircut levels by whole-letter rating category.

FCA WHOLE-LETTER CREDIT RATINGS MAPPED TO RATING AGENCY CREDIT RATINGS

FCA Ratings Category.	AAA	AA	A	BBB	Below BBB and Unrated.
Standard & Poor's Long-Term.	AAA	AA	A	BBB	Below BBB and Unrated.
Fitch Long-Term	AAA	AA	A	BBB	Below BBB and Unrated.
Standard & Poor's Short-Term.	A–1+ / SP–1+	A–1 / SP–1	A–2 / SP–2	A–3	SP–3, B, or Below and Unrated.
Fitch Short-Term	F–1+	F–1	F–2	F–3	Below F–3 and Unrated.
Moody's		Prime-MIG12. VMIg1	Prime-2 MIG2 VMIG2.	Prime-3 MIG3 VMIG3.	Not Prime, SG and Unrated.
Fitch Bank Ratings	A	B / A/B	C / B/C	D / C/D	E. / D/E.
Moody's Bank Financial Strength Rating.	A	B	C	D	E.

FARMER MAC RBCST MAXIMUM HAIRCUT BY RATINGS CLASSIFICATION

Ratings classification	Non-program investment counterparties (excluding derivatives) (percent)
Cash	0.00
AAA	1.41
AA	3.70
A	5.13
BBB	11.48
Below BBB or Unrated	44.52

1. Certain special cases will receive the following treatment. For an investment structured as a collateralized obligation backed by the issuer's general obligation and, in turn, a pool of collateral, reference the Issuer Rating or Financial Strength Rating of that issuer as the credit rating applicable to the security. Unrated securities that are fully guaranteed by Government-sponsored enterprises (GSE) such as the Federal National Mortgage Corporation (Fannie Mae) will receive the same treatment as AAA securities. Unrated securities backed by the full faith and credit of the U.S. Government will not receive a haircut. Unrated securities that are not fully guaranteed by a GSE will receive the haircut level in place at that time for "Below BBB and Unrated" investments unless the Director, at the Director's discretion, determines to apply a lesser haircut. In making this determination, the Director will consider the risk characteristics associated with the structure of individual instruments.

2. If portions of investments are later sold by Farmer Mac according to their specific risk characteristics, the Director will take reasonable measures to adjust the haircut level applied to the investment to recognize the change in the risk characteristics of the retained portion. The Director will consider relevant similar methods for dealing with capital requirements adopted by other Federal financial institution regulators in similar situations.

3. Individual investment haircuts must then be aggregated into weighted-average haircuts by investment category and submitted in the "Data Inputs" worksheet. The spreadsheet uses these inputs to reduce the weighted-average yield on the investment category to account for counterparty insolvency according to a 10-year linear phase-in of the haircuts. Each asset account category

Farm Credit Administration

identified in this data requirement is discussed in section 4.2, "Assumptions and Relationships."

4.2 Assumptions and Relationships

a. The stress test assumptions are summarized on the worksheet called "Assumptions and Relationships." Some of the entries on this page are direct user entries. Other entries are relationships generated from data supplied by Farmer Mac or other sources as discussed in section 4.1, "Data Inputs." After current financial data are entered, the user selects the date for running the stress test. This action causes the stress test to identify and select the appropriate data from the "Data Inputs" worksheet. The next section highlights the degree of disaggregation needed to maintain reasonably representative financial characterizations of Farmer Mac in the stress test. Several specific assumptions are established about the future relationships of account balances and how they evolve.

b. From the data and assumptions, the stress test computes pro forma financial statements for 10 years. The stress test must be run as a "steady state" with regard to program balances (with the exception of AgVantage Plus volume, in which case maturities are recognized by the model), and where possible, will use information gleaned from recent financial statements and other data supplied by Farmer Mac to establish earnings and cost relationships on major program assets that are applied forward in time. As documented in the stress test, entries of "1" imply no growth and/or no change in account balances or proportions relative to initial conditions with the exception of pre-1996 loan volume being transferred to post-1996 loan volume. The interest rate risk and credit loss components are applied to the stress test through time. The individual sections of that worksheet are:

(1) *Elements related to cashflows, earnings rates, and disposition of discontinued program assets.*

(A) The stress test accounts for earnings rates by asset class and cost rates on funding. The stress test aggregates investments into the categories of: Cash and money market securities; commercial paper; certificates of deposit; agency mortgage-backed securities and collateralized mortgage obligations; and other investments. With FCA's concurrence, Farmer Mac is permitted to further disaggregate these categories. Similarly, we may require new categories for future activities to be added to the stress test. Loan items requiring separate accounts include the following:

(i) Farmer Mac I program assets post-1996 Act;

(ii) Farmer Mac I program assets post-1996 Act Swap balances;

(iii) Farmer Mac I program assets pre-1996 Act;

(iv) Farmer Mac I AgVantage securities;

(v) Loans held for securitization;

(vi) Farmer Mac II program assets; and

(vii) Rural Utility program volume on balance sheet.

(B) The stress test also uses data elements related to amortization and prepayment experience to calculate and process the implied rates at which asset and liability balances terminate or "roll off" through time. Further, for each category, the stress test has the capacity to track account balances that are expected to change through time for each of the above categories. For purposes of the stress test, all assets are assumed to maintain a "steady state" with the implication that any principal balances retired or prepaid are replaced with new balances. The exceptions are that expiring pre-1996 Act program assets are replaced with post-1996 Act program assets and AgVantage Plus volume maturities are recognized by the model.

(2) *Elements related to other balance sheet assumptions through time.* As well as interest earning assets, the other categories of the balance sheet that are modeled through time include interest receivable, guarantee fees receivable, rural utility guarantee fees receivable, prepaid expenses, accrued interest payable, accounts payable, accrued expenses, reserves for losses (loans held and guaranteed securities), and other off-balance sheet obligations. The stress test is consistent with Farmer Mac's existing reporting categories and practices. If reporting practices change substantially, the above list will be adjusted accordingly. The stress test has the capacity to have the balances in each of these accounts determined based upon existing relationships to other earning accounts, to keep their balances either in constant proportions of loan or security accounts, or to evolve according to a user-selected rule. For purposes of the stress test, these accounts are to remain constant relative to the proportions of their associated balance sheet accounts that generated the accrued balances.

(3) *Elements related to income and expense assumptions.* Several other parameters that are required to generate pro forma financial statements may not be easily captured from historic data or may have characteristics that suggest that they be individually supplied. These parameters are the gain on agricultural mortgage-backed securities (AMBS) sales, miscellaneous income, operating expenses, reserve requirement, guarantee fees, rural utility guarantee fees, and loan loss resolution timing.

(A) The stress test applies the actual weighted average gain rate on sales of AMBS over the most recent 3 years to the dollar

Pt. 652, Subpt. B, App. A

amount of AMBS sold during the most recent four quarters in order to estimate gain on sale of AMBS over the stress period.

(B) The stress test assumes miscellaneous income at a level equal to the average of the most recent 3-year's actual miscellaneous income as a percent of the sum of; cash, investments, guaranteed securities, and loans held for investment.

(C) The stress test assumes that short-term cost of funds is incurred in relation to the amount of defaulting loans purchased from off-balance sheet pools. The remaining unpaid principal balance on this loan volume is the origination amount reduced by the proportion of the total portfolio that has amortized as of the end of the most recent quarter. This volume is assumed to be funded at the short-term cost of funds and this expense continues for a period equal to the loan loss resolution timing period (LLRT) period minus 1. We will calculate the LLRT period from Farmer Mac data. In addition, during the LLRT period, all guarantee income associated with the loan volume ceases.

(D) The stress test generates no interest income on the estimated volume of defaulted on-balance sheet loan volume required to be carried during the LLRT period, but continues to accrue funding costs during the remainder of the LLRT period.

(E) You must update the LLRT period in response to changes in the Corporation's actual experience with each quarterly submission.

(F) Operating costs are determined in the model using weighted moving average of operating expenses as a percentage of the sum of on-balance sheet assets and off-balance sheet program activities over the previous four quarters inclusive of the current submission date. The share will then be applied forward to the balances of the same categories throughout the 10-year period of the RBCST model. As additional data accumulate, the specification will be re-examined and modified if we deem changing the specification results in a more appropriate representation of operating expenses.

(G) The reserve requirement as a fraction of loan assets can also be specified. However, the stress test is run with the reserve requirement set to zero. Setting the parameter to zero causes the stress test to calculate a risk-based capital level that is comparable to regulatory capital, which includes reserves. Thus, the risk-based capital requirement contains the regulatory capital required, including reserves. The amount of total capital that is allocated to the reserve account is determined by GAAP. The stress test applies quarterly updates of the weighted average guarantee rates for post-1996 Farmer Mac I assets, pre-1996 Farmer Mac I assets, and Farmer Mac II assets.

12 CFR Ch. VI (1–1–12 Edition)

(4) *Elements related to earnings rates and funding costs.*

(A) The stress test can accommodate numerous specifications of earnings and funding costs. In general, both relationships are tied to the 10-year CMT interest rate. Specifically, each investment account, each loan item, and each liability account can be specified as fixed rate, or fixed spread to the 10-year CMT with initial rates determined by actual data. The stress test calculates specific spreads (weighted average yield less initial 10-year CMT) by category from the weighted average yield data supplied by Farmer Mac as described earlier. For example, the fixed spread for Farmer Mac I program post-1996 Act mortgages is calculated as follows:

Fixed Spread = Weighted Average Yield less 10-year CMT 0.014 = 0.0694—0.0554

(B) The resulting fixed spread of 1.40 percent is then added to the 10-year CMT when it is shocked to determine the new yield. For instance, if the 10-year CMT is shocked upward by 300 basis points, the yield on Farmer Mac I program post-1996 Act loans would change as follows:

Yield = Fixed Spread + 10-year CMT .0994 = .014 + .0854

(C) The adjusted yield is then used for income calculations when generating pro forma financial statements. All fixed-spread asset and liability classes are computed in an identical manner using starting yields provided as data inputs from Farmer Mac. The fixed-yield option holds the starting yield data constant for the entire 10-year stress test period. You must run the stress test using the fixed-spread option for all accounts except for discontinued program activities, such as Farmer Mac I program loans made before the 1996 Act. For discontinued loans, the fixed-rate specification must be used if the loans are primarily fixed-rate mortgages.

(5) *Elements related to interest rate shock test.* As described earlier, the interest rate shock test is implemented as a single set of forward interest rates. The stress test applies the up-rate scenario and down-rate scenario separately. The stress test also uses the results of Farmer Mac's shock test, as described in paragraph c. of section 4.1, "Data Inputs," to calculate the impact on equity from a stressful change in interest rates as discussed in section 3.0 titled, "Interest Rate Risk." The stress test uses a schedule relating a change in interest rates to a change in the market value of equity. For instance, if interest rates are shocked upward so that the percentage change is 262 basis points, the linearly interpolated effective estimated duration of equity is −6.7405 years given Farmer Mac's interest rate measurement results at 250 and 300 basis points of −6.7316 and 76.7688

Farm Credit Administration

Pt. 652, Subpt. B, App. A

years, respectively found on the effective duration schedule. The stress test uses the linearly interpolated estimated effective duration for equity to calculate the market value change by multiplying duration by the base value of equity before any rate change from Farmer Mac's interest rate risk measurement results with the percentage change in interest rates.

4.3 Risk Measures

a. This section describes the elements of the stress test in the worksheet named "Risk Measures" that reflect the interest rate shock and credit loss requirements of the stress test.

b. As described in section 3.1, the stress test applies the statutory interest rate shock to the initial 10-year CMT rate. It then generates a series of fixed annual interest rates for the 10-year stress period that serve as indices for earnings yields and cost of funds rates used in the stress test. (See the "Risk Measures" worksheet for the resulting interest rate series used in the stress test.)

c. The Credit Loss Module's state-level loss rates, as described in section 2.4 entitled, "Calculation of Loss Rates for Use in the Stress Test," are entered into the "Risk Measures" worksheet and applied to the loan balances that exist in each state. The distribution of loan balances by state is used to allocate new loans that replace loan products that roll off the balance sheet through time. The loss rates are applied both to the initial volume and to new loan volume that replaces expiring loans. The total life of loan losses that are expected at origination are then allocated through time based on a set of user entries describing the time-path of losses.

d. The loss rates estimated in the credit risk component of the stress test are based on an origination year concept, adjusted for loan seasoning. All losses arising from loans originated in a particular year are expressed as lifetime age-adjusted losses irrespective of when the losses actually occur. The fraction of the origination year loss rates that must be used to allocate losses through time are 43 percent to year 1, 17 percent to year 2, 11.66 percent to year 3, and 4.03 percent for the remaining years. The total allocated losses in any year are expressed as a percent of loan volume in that year to reflect the conversion to exposure year.

e. The credit loss exposure on rural utility volume, described in section 2.6, "Calculation of Loss Rates on Rural Utility Volume for Use in the Stress Test," is entered into the "Risk Measures" worksheet applied to the volume balance. All losses arising from rural utility loans are expressed as annual loss rates and distributed over the weighted average maturity of the rural utility AgVantage Plus Volume, or as annual loss across the full 10-year modeling horizon in the case of rural utility Cash Window loans.

4.4 Loan and Cashflow Accounts

The worksheet labeled "Loan and Cashflow Data" contains the categorized loan data and cashflow accounting relationships that are used in the stress test to generate projections of Farmer Mac's performance and condition. The steady-state formulation results in account balances that remain constant except for the effects of discontinued programs, maturing AgVantage Plus positions, and the LLRT adjustment. For assets with maturities under 1 year, the results are reported for convenience as though they matured only one time per year with the additional convention that the earnings/cost rates are annualized. For the pre-1996 Act assets, maturing balances are added back to post-1996 Act account balances. The liability accounts are used to satisfy the accounting identity, which requires assets to equal liabilities plus owner equity. In addition to the replacement of maturities under a steady state, liabilities are increased to reflect net losses or decreased to reflect resulting net gains. Adjustments must be made to the long- and short-term debt accounts to maintain the same relative proportions as existed at the beginning period from which the stress test is run with the exception of changes associated with the funding of defaulted loans during the LLRT period. The primary receivable and payable accounts are also maintained on this worksheet, as is a summary balance of the volume of loans subject to credit losses.

4.5 Income Statements

a. Information related to income performance through time is contained on the worksheet named "Income Statements." Information from the first period balance sheet is used in conjunction with the earnings and cost-spread relationships from Farmer Mac supplied data to generate the first period's income statement. The same set of accounts is maintained in this worksheet as "Loan and Cashflow Accounts" for consistency in reporting each annual period of the 10-year stress period of the test with the exception of the line item labeled "Interest reversals to carry loan losses" which incorporates the LLRT adjustment to earnings from the "Risk Measures" worksheet. Loans that defaulted do not earn interest or guarantee and commitment fees during LLRT period. The income from each interest-bearing account is calculated, as are costs of interest-bearing liabilities. In each case, these entries are the associated interest rate for that period multiplied by the account balances.

b. The credit losses described in section 2.0, "Credit Risk," are transmitted through the provision account, as is any change needed

347

to re-establish the target reserve balance. For determining risk-based capital, the reserve target is set to zero as previously indicated in section 4.2. Under the income tax section, it must first be determined whether it is appropriate to carry forward tax losses or recapture tax credits. The tax section then establishes the appropriate income tax liability that permits the calculation of final net income (loss), which is credited (debited) to the retained earnings account.

4.6 Balance Sheets

a. The worksheet named "Balance Sheets" is used to construct pro forma balance sheets from which the capital calculations can be performed. As can be seen in the Excel spreadsheet, the worksheet is organized to correspond to Farmer Mac's normal reporting practices. Asset accounts are built from the initial financial statement conditions, and loan and cashflow accounts. Liability accounts including the reserve account are likewise built from the previous period's results to balance the asset and equity positions. The equity section uses initial conditions and standard accounts to monitor equity through time. The equity section maintains separate categories for increments to paid-in-capital and retained earnings and for mark-to-market effects of changes in account values. The process described below in the "Capital" worksheet uses the initial retained earnings and paid-in-capital account to test for the change in initial capital that permits conformance to the statutory requirements. Therefore, these accounts must be maintained separately for test solution purposes.

b. The market valuation changes due to interest rate movements must be computed utilizing the linearly interpolated schedule of estimated equity effects due to changes in interest rates, contained in the "Assumptions & Relationships" worksheet. The stress test calculates the dollar change in the market value of equity by multiplying the base value of equity before any rate change from Farmer Mac's interest rate risk measurement results, the linearly interpolated estimated effective duration of equity, and the percentage change in interest rates. In addition, the earnings effect of the measured dollar change in the market value of equity is estimated by multiplying the dollar change by the blended cost of funds rate found on the "Assumptions & Relationships" worksheet. Next, divide by 2 the computed earnings effect to approximate the impact as a theoretical shock in the interest rates that occurs at the mid-point of the income cycle from period t_0 to period t_1. The measured dollar change in the market value of equity and related earnings effect are then adjusted to reflect any tax-related benefits. Tax adjustments are determined by including the measured dollar change in the market value of equity and the earnings effect in the tax calculations found in the "Income Statements" worksheet. This approach ensures that the value of equity reflects the economic loss or gain in value of Farmer Mac's capital position from a change in interest rates and reflects any immediate tax benefits that Farmer Mac could realize. Any tax benefits in the module are posted through the income statement by adjusting the net taxes due before calculating final net income. Final net income is posted to accumulated unretained earnings in the shareholders' equity portion of the balance sheet. The tax section is also described in section 4.5 entitled, "Income Statements."

c. After one cycle of income has been calculated, the balance sheet as of the end of the income period is then generated. The "Balance Sheet" worksheet shows the periodic pro forma balance sheets in a format convenient to track capital shifts through time.

d. The stress test considers Farmer Mac's balance sheet as subject to interest rate risk and, therefore, the capital position reflects mark-to-market changes in the value of equity. This approach ensures that the stress test captures interest rate risk in a meaningful way by addressing explicitly the loss or gain in value resulting from the change in interest rates required by the statute.

4.7 Capital

The "Capital" worksheet contains the results of the required capital calculations as described below, and provides a method to calculate the level of initial capital that would permit Farmer Mac to maintain positive capital throughout the 10-year stress test period.

5.0 CAPITAL CALCULATION

a. The stress test computes regulatory capital as the sum of the following:
(1) The par value of outstanding common stock;
(2) The par value of outstanding preferred stock;
(3) Paid-in capital;
(4) Retained earnings; and
(5) Reserve for loan and guarantee losses.

b. Inclusion of the reserve account in regulatory capital is an important difference compared to minimum capital as defined by the statute. Therefore, the calculation of reserves in the stress test is also important because reserves are reduced by loan and guarantee losses. The reserve account is linked to the income statement through the provision for loan-loss expense (provision). Provision expense reflects the amount of current income necessary to rebuild the reserve account to acceptable levels after loan losses reduce the account or as a result of increases

Farm Credit Administration

in the level of risky mortgage positions, both on- and off-balance sheet. Provision reversals represent reductions in the reserve levels due to reduced risk of loan losses or loan volume of risky mortgage positions. The liabilities section of the "Balance Sheets" worksheet also includes separate line items to disaggregate the Guarantee and commitment obligation related to the Financial Accounting Standards Board Interpretation No. 45 (FIN 45) Guarantor's Accounting and Disclosure Requirements for Guarantees, Including Indirect Guarantees of Indebtedness of Others. This item is disaggregated to permit accurate calculation of regulatory capital post-adoption of FIN 45. When calculating the stress test, the reserve is maintained at zero to result in a risk-based capital requirement that includes reserves, thereby making the requirement comparable to the statutory definition of regulatory capital. By setting the reserve requirement to zero, the capital position includes all financial resources Farmer Mac has at its disposal to withstand risk.

5.1 Method of Calculation

a. Risk-based capital is calculated in the stress test as the minimum initial capital that would permit Farmer Mac to remain solvent for the ensuing 10 years. To this amount, an additional 30 percent is added to account for managerial and operational risks not reflected in the specific components of the stress test.

b. The relationship between the solvency constraint (i.e., future capital position not less than zero) and the risk-based capital requirement reflects the appropriate earnings and funding cost rates that may vary through time based on initial conditions. Therefore, the minimum capital at a future point in time cannot be directly used to determine the risk-based capital requirement. To calculate the risk-based capital requirement, the stress test includes a section to solve for the minimum initial capital value that results in a minimum capital level over the 10 years of zero at the point in time that it would actually occur. In solving for initial capital, it is assumed that reductions or additions to the initial capital accounts are made in the retained earnings accounts, and balanced in the debt accounts at terms proportionate to initial balances (same relative proportion of long- and short-term debt at existing initial rates). Because the initial capital position affects the earnings, and hence capital positions and appropriate discount rates through time, the initial and future capital are simultaneously determined and must be solved iteratively. The resulting minimum initial capital from the stress test is then reported on the "Capital" worksheet of the stress test. The "Capital" worksheet includes an element that uses Excel's "solver" or "goal seek" capability to calculate the minimum initial capital that, when added (subtracted) from initial capital and replaced with debt, results in a minimum capital balance over the following 10 years of zero.

[71 FR 77253, Dec. 26, 2006, as amended at 73 FR 31940, June 5, 2008; 76 FR 23467, April 27, 2011]

PARTS 653–654 [RESERVED]

PART 655—FEDERAL AGRICULTURAL MORTGAGE CORPORATION DISCLOSURE AND REPORTING REQUIREMENTS

Subpart A—Annual Report of Condition of the Federal Agricultural Mortgage Corporation

Sec.
655.1 Content, timing, and providing of the Federal Agricultural Mortgage Corporation's annual report of condition.

Subpart B—Reports Relating to Securities Activities of the Federal Agricultural Mortgage Corporation

655.50 Form and content.

AUTHORITY: Sec. 8.11 of the Farm Credit Act (12 U.S.C. 2279aa–11).

Subpart A—Annual Report of Condition of the Federal Agricultural Mortgage Corporation

§ 655.1 Content, timing, and providing of the Federal Agricultural Mortgage Corporation's annual report of condition.

(a) The Federal Agricultural Mortgage Corporation shall prepare and publish an annual report of its condition that is equivalent in content to the annual report to shareholders required by section 14 of the Securities and Exchange Act of 1934.

(b) The Corporation shall provide the annual report of condition to its shareholders within 120 days of its fiscal year-end.

(c) Upon receiving a request for an annual report of condition, the Corporation shall promptly provide the requester the most recent annual report described in this section.

(d) The Corporation shall provide copies of the annual report of condition

§ 655.50

to the Farm Credit Administration's Office of Secondary Market Oversight within 120 days of its fiscal year-end. If providing paper copies, send three copies to Office of Secondary Market Oversight, Farm Credit Administration, 1501 Farm Credit Drive, McLean, VA 22102–5090. If providing electronic copies, send according to our instructions to you.

[58 FR 48791, Sept. 20, 1993. Redesignated at 62 FR 15093, Mar. 31, 1997, as amended at 67 FR 16634, Apr. 8, 2002. Redesignated at 70 FR 40643, July 14, 2005]

Subpart B—Reports Relating to Securities Activities of the Federal Agricultural Mortgage Corporation

§ 655.50 Form and content.

(a) The Federal Agricultural Mortgage Corporation (Corporation) shall provide the Office of Secondary Market Oversight with three copies of any filings made with the SEC pursuant to the Securities Act of 1933 or the Securities and Exchange Act of 1934. Such copies shall be filed with the FCA no later than 1 business day after any SEC filing.

(b) The Corporation shall make the following filings with the Office of Secondary Market Oversight for securities either issued or guaranteed by the Corporation that are not registered under the Securities Act of 1933.

(1) Three copies of any offering circular, private placement memorandum, or information statement prepared in connection with the securities offering shall be filed with the Office of Secondary Market Oversight at or before the time of the securities offering.

(2) For securities backed by qualified loans as defined in section 8.0(9)(A) of the Act, the Corporation shall file one copy of the following within 1 business day of the finalization of the transaction:

(i) The private placement memoranda for securities sold to investors; and

(ii) The pooling and servicing agreement when the security is purchased by the Corporation as authorized by section 8.6(g) of the Act.

(3) For securities backed by qualified loans as defined in section 8.0(9)(B) of the Act, the Corporation shall provide summary information on such securities issued during each calendar quarter in the form prescribed by the Office of Secondary Market Oversight. Such summary information shall be provided with each report of condition and performance filed pursuant to § 621.12, and at such other times as the Office of Secondary Market Oversight may require.

(c) The Corporation shall file with the Office of Secondary Market Oversight copies of all substantive correspondence between the Corporation and the Securities and Exchange Commission and the Department of the Treasury relating to securities activities or regulatory compliance. Such correspondence must be filed no later than the date of filing of the report of condition and performance for the calendar quarter in which the correspondence was received or sent.

(d) The Corporation shall promptly notify the Office of Secondary Market Oversight if it becomes exempt or claims exemption from the filing requirements of the Securities and Exchange Act of 1934.

[58 FR 48786, Sept. 20, 1993. Redesignated at 70 FR 40643, July 14, 2005.Amended at 71 FR 77262, Dec. 26, 2006]

CHAPTER VII—NATIONAL CREDIT UNION ADMINISTRATION

EDITORIAL NOTE: For FEDERAL REGISTER citations to interpretations and policy statements to Chapter VII, see the List of CFR Sections Affected, which appears in the Finding Aids section of the printed volume and at *www.fdsys.gov*.

SUBCHAPTER A—REGULATIONS AFFECTING CREDIT UNIONS

Part		Page
700	Definitions	353
701	Organization and operation of Federal credit unions	353
702	Prompt corrective action	514
703	Investment and deposit activities	542
704	Corporate credit unions	554
705	Community Development Revolving Loan Fund access for credit unions	615
706	Unfair or deceptive acts or practices	622
707	Truth in savings	624
708a	Bank conversions and mergers	680
708b	Mergers of federally-insured credit unions; voluntary termination or conversion of insured status	701
709	Involuntary liquidation of Federal credit unions and adjudication of creditor claims involving federally insured credit unions in liquidation	716
710	Voluntary liquidation	726
711	Management official interlocks	728
712	Credit union service organizations (CUSOs)	732
713	Fidelity bond and insurance coverage for Federal credit unions	737
714	Leasing	739
715	Supervisory Committee audits and verifications	741
716	Privacy of consumer financial information	748
717	Fair credit reporting	775
721	Incidental powers	808
722	Appraisals	812
723	Member business loans	816
724	Trustees and custodians of certain tax-advantaged savings plans	823

Part		Page
725	National Credit Union Administration Central Liquidity Facility	824
740	Accuracy of advertising and notice of insured status	831
741	Requirements for insurance	834
742	Regulatory flexibility program	851
745	Share insurance and appendix	853
747	Administrative actions, adjudicative hearings, rules of practice and procedure, and investigations	872
748	Security program, report of suspected crimes, suspicious transactions, catastrophic acts and Bank Secrecy Act compliance	920
749	Records Preservation Program and Appendices—record retention guidelines; Catastrophic Act preparedness guidelines	929
750	Golden parachute and indemnification payments	932
760	Loans in areas having special flood hazards	939
761	Registration of residential mortgage loan originators	943

SUBCHAPTER B—REGULATIONS AFFECTING THE OPERATIONS OF THE NATIONAL CREDIT UNION ADMINISTRATION

790	Description of NCUA; requests for agency action	951
791	Rules of NCUA Board procedure; promulgation of NCUA rules and regulations; public observation of NCUA Board meetings	955
792	Requests for information under the Freedom of Information Act and Privacy Act, and by subpoena; security procedures for classified information	962
793	Tort claims against the Government	987
794	Enforcement of nondiscrimination on the basis of handicap in programs or activities conducted by the National Credit Union Administration	991
796	Post-employment restrictions for certain NCUA examiners	997
797	Procedures for debt collection	998

SUBCHAPTER A—REGULATIONS AFFECTING CREDIT UNIONS

PART 700—DEFINITIONS

Sec.
700.1 Scope.
700.2 Definitions.

AUTHORITY: 12 U.S.C. 1752, 1757(6), 1766.

§ 700.1 Scope.

The definitions in § 700.2 apply to terms used in this chapter. Many additional definitions appear in the parts where the terms are used.

[66 FR 65624, Dec. 20, 2001]

§ 700.2 Definitions.

As used in this chapter:

Act means the Federal Credit Union Act (73 Stat. 628, 84 Stat. 944, 12 U.S.C. 1751 through 1790).

Administration means the National Credit Union Administration.

Board means the Board of the National Credit Union Administration.

Credit Union means a credit union chartered under the Federal Credit Union Act or, as the context permits, under the laws of any State.

Insolvency. (1) A credit union will be determined to be insolvent when the total amount of its shares exceeds the present cash value of its assets after providing for liabilities unless:

(i) It is determined by the Board that the facts that caused the deficient share-asset ratio no longer exist; and

(ii) The likelihood of further depreciation of the share-asset ratio is not probable; and

(iii) The return of the share-asset ratio to its normal limits within a reasonable time for the credit union concerned is probable; and

(iv) The probability of a further potential loss to the insurance fund is negligible.

(2) For purposes of this section, the following definitions are used:

(i) *Cash value of assets.* Recorded value will be considered the cash value of any asset account providing accepted accounting principles and practices are followed and the provisions of law, regulation, and bylaws are met.

(ii) *Liabilities.* Recorded liabilities which are due and payable, excluding shares of members and non-members, are considered liabilities.

Net worth. Unless otherwise noted, the term "net worth," as applied to credit unions, has the same meaning as set forth in § 702.2(f) of this chapter.

Paid-in and unimpaired capital and surplus means shares plus post-closing, undivided earnings. This does not include regular reserves or special reserves required by law, regulation or special agreement between the credit union and its regulator or share insurer. "Paid-in and unimpaired capital and surplus" for purposes of the Central Liquidity Facility is defined in § 725.2(o) of this chapter.

Regional Director means the representative of the Administration in the designated geographical area in which the office of the Federal credit union is located.

Regional Office means the office of the Administration located in the designated geographical areas in which the office of the Federal credit union is located.

State means a State of the United States, the District of Columbia, any of the several territories and possessions of the United States, the Panama Canal Zone, and the Commonwealth of Puerto Rico.

Unimpaired capital and surplus means the same as "paid-in and unimpaired capital and surplus," as defined in paragraph (f) of this section.

[36 FR 23794, Dec. 15, 1971; 37 FR 329, Jan. 11, 1972, as amended at 37 FR 10342, May 20, 1972; 45 FR 47121, July 14, 1980; 54 FR 48234, Nov. 22, 1989; 54 FR 52015, Dec. 20, 1989; 55 FR 1794, Jan. 19, 1990; 57 FR 47985, Oct. 21, 1992; 58 FR 40042, July 27, 1993; 65 FR 44966, July 20, 2000. Redesignated and amended at 66 FR 65624, Dec. 20, 2001; 73 FR 30477, May 28, 2008; 76 FR 60366, Sept. 29, 2011]

PART 701—ORGANIZATION AND OPERATION OF FEDERAL CREDIT UNIONS

Sec.
701.1 Federal credit union chartering, field of membership modifications, and conversions.
701.2 Federal credit union bylaws.

701.3 Member inspection of credit union books, records, and minutes.
701.4 General authorities and duties of Federal credit union directors.
701.5 [Reserved]
701.6 Fees paid by Federal credit unions.
701.7–701.13 [Reserved]
701.14 Change in official or senior executive officer in credit unions that are newly chartered or are in troubled condition.
701.15–701.18 [Reserved]
701.19 Benefits for employees of Federal credit unions.
701.20 Suretyship and guaranty.
701.21 Loans to members and lines of credit to members.
701.22 Loan participation.
701.23 Purchase, sale, and pledge of eligible obligations.
701.24 Refund of interest.
701.25 Charitable contributions and donations.
701.26 Credit union service contracts.
701.27–701.29 [Reserved]
701.30 Services for nonmembers within the field of membership.
701.31 Nondiscrimination requirements.
701.32 Payment on shares by public units and nonmembers.
701.33 Reimbursement, insurance, and indemnification of officials and employees.
701.34 Designation of low income status; Acceptance of secondary capital accounts by low-income designated credit unions.
701.35 Share, share draft, and share certificate accounts.
701.36 FCU ownership of fixed assets.
701.37 Treasury tax and loan depositaries; depositaries and financial agents of the Government.
701.38 Borrowed funds from natural persons.
701.39 Statutory lien.
APPENDIX A TO PART 701—FEDERAL CREDIT UNION BYLAWS
APPENDIX B TO PART 701—CHARTERING AND FIELD OF MEMBERSHIP MANUAL

AUTHORITY: 12 U.S.C. 1752(5), 1755, 1756, 1757, 1758, 1759, 1761a, 1761b, 1766, 1767, 1782, 1784, 1786, 1787, 1789. Section 701.6 is also authorized by 15 U.S.C. 3717. Section 701.31 is also authorized by 15 U.S.C. 1601 *et seq.*; 42 U.S.C. 1981 and 3601–3610. Section 701.35 is also authorized by 42 U.S.C. 4311–4312.

§ 701.1 Federal credit union chartering, field of membership modifications, and conversions.

National Credit Union Administration policies concerning chartering, field of membership modifications, and conversions, also known as the Chartering and Field of Membership Manual, are set forth in appendix B to this part and are available on-line at *http://www.ncua.gov*.

[75 FR 36263, June 25, 2010]

§ 701.2 Federal credit union bylaws.

(a) Federal credit unions must operate in accordance with their approved bylaws. The Federal Credit Union Bylaws are hereby published as appendix A to part 701 pursuant to 5 U.S.C. 552(a)(1) and accompanying regulations. Federal credit unions may adopt amendments to their bylaws as provided in the Bylaws, with the approval of the Board.

(b) Copies of the Federal Credit Union Bylaws may be obtained at *http://www.ncua.gov* or by request addressed to *ogc-mail@ncua.gov* or National Credit Union Administration, 1775 Duke Street, Alexandria, VA 22314.

(c) The National Credit Union Administration may issue revisions or amendments of the Federal Credit Union Bylaws from time to time. An historic file of amendments or revisions is maintained and made available for inspection at the National Credit Union Administration, 1775 Duke Street, Alexandria, VA 22314.

[72 FR 61500, Oct. 31, 2007]

§ 701.3 Member inspection of credit union books, records, and minutes.

(a) *Member inspection rights.* A group of members of a Federal credit union has the right, upon submission of a petition to the credit union as described in paragraph (b) of this section, to inspect and copy nonconfidential portions of the credit union's:

(1) Accounting books and records; and

(2) Minutes of the proceedings of the credit union's members, board of directors, and committees of directors.

(b) *Petition for inspection.* The petition must describe the particular records to be inspected and state a proper purpose for the inspection, that is, a purpose related to the protection of the members' financial interests in the credit union. The petition must state that the petitioners as a whole, or certain named petitioners, agree to pay the direct and reasonable costs associated with search and duplication of requested material. The petition must also state that the inspection is not desired for any purpose other than the stated purpose; that the members signing the petition will not sell or offer for sale any information obtained from the credit union; and that the members signing the petition have not within five years preceding the signature date sold or offered for sale any information acquired from the credit union or aided or abetted any person in procuring any information from the credit union for purposes of sale. The petition must name one member, and one alternate member, who will represent the petitioners on issues such as inspection procedures, costs, and potential disputes. At least one percent of the credit union's members, with a minimum of 20 members and a maximum of 500 members, must sign the petition. Each member who signs the petition must have been a member of the credit union for at least 180 days at the time the petitioners submit the petition to the credit union.

(c) *Inspection procedures.* (1) A Federal credit union must respond to petitioners within 14 days of receiving a petition. In its response, a credit union must inform petitioners either that it will provide inspection of the requested material and, if so, when, or, if a credit union is going to withhold all or part of the requested material, it must inform petitioners what part of the requested material it intends to withhold and the reasons for withholding the requested material. As soon as possible after receiving a petition, a credit union must schedule inspection and copying of nonconfidential requested material it determines petitioners may inspect and copy.

(2) Inspection may be made in person or by agent or attorney and at any reasonable time or times. The credit union may, at its option, skip inspection and deliver copies of requested documents directly to the petitioners. Member inspection rights under this section are in addition to any other member inspection rights afforded by the credit union's charter or bylaws or other Federal law or Federal regulation.

(3) If the credit union denies inspection because the petitioners have failed to obtain the minimum number of valid signatures, the credit union must inform the petitioners which signatures were not valid and why.

(d) *Confidential books, records, and minutes.* Members do not have the right to inspect any portion of the books, records, or minutes of a Federal credit union if:

(1) Federal law or regulation prohibits disclosure of that portion;

(2) The publication of that portion could cause the credit union predictable and substantial financial harm;

(3) That portion contains nonpublic personal information as defined in §716.3 of this part; or

(4) That portion contains information about credit union employees or officials the disclosure of which would constitute a clearly unwarranted invasion of personal privacy.

(e) *Costs.* A Federal credit union may charge petitioners the direct and reasonable costs associated with search and duplication. The credit union may not charge for other costs, including indirect costs or attorney's fees.

(f) *Dispute resolution.* (1) In the event of a dispute between a federal credit union and its members concerning a petition for inspection or the associated costs, either party may submit the dispute to the regional director. The regional director, after obtaining the views of both parties, will direct the credit union either to withhold the disputed materials or to make them available for member inspection and copying. The regional director may place conditions upon release. The decision of the regional director is a final agency decision and is not appealable to the Board.

(2) The regional director has the discretion to refer any dispute to the credit union's supervisory committee for review and resolution. If petitioners are not satisfied with the supervisory committee's response, they may resubmit the dispute to the regional director.

[72 FR 56253, Oct. 3, 2007]

§701.4 General authorities and duties of Federal credit union directors.

(a) *General direction and control of a Federal credit union.* The board of directors is responsible for the general direction and control of the affairs of

§ 701.5

each Federal credit union. While a Federal credit union board of directors may delegate the execution of operational functions to Federal credit union personnel, the ultimate responsibility of each Federal credit union's board of directors for that Federal credit union's direction and control is non-delegable.

(b) *Duties of Federal credit union directors.* Each Federal credit union director has the duty to:

(1) Carry out his or her duties as a director in good faith, in a manner such director reasonably believes to be in the best interests of the membership of the Federal credit union as a whole, and with the care, including reasonable inquiry, as an ordinarily prudent person in a like position would use under similar circumstances;

(2) Administer the affairs of the Federal credit union fairly and impartially and without discrimination in favor of or against any particular member;

(3) At the time of election or appointment, or within a reasonable time thereafter, not to exceed six months, have at least a working familiarity with basic finance and accounting practices, including the ability to read and understand the Federal credit union's balance sheet and income statement and to ask, as appropriate, substantive questions of management and the internal and external auditors; and

(4) Direct management's operations of the Federal credit union in conformity with the requirements set forth in the Federal Credit Union Act, this chapter, other applicable law, and sound business practices.

(c) *Authority regarding staff and outside consultants.* (1) In carrying out its duties and responsibilities, each Federal credit union's board of directors and all its committees have authority to retain staff and outside counsel, independent accountants, financial advisors, and other outside consultants at the expense of the Federal credit union.

(2) Federal credit union staff providing services to the board of directors or any committee of the board under paragraph (c)(1) of this section may be required by the board of directors or such committee to report directly to the board or such committee, as appropriate.

(3) In discharging board or committee duties a director who does not have knowledge that makes reliance unwarranted is entitled to rely on information, opinions, reports or statements, including financial statements and other financial data, prepared or presented by any of the persons specified in paragraph (d).

(d) *Reliance.* A director may rely on:

(1) One or more officers or employees of the Federal credit union who the director reasonably believes to be reliable and competent in the functions performed or the information, opinions, reports or statements provided;

(2) Legal counsel, independent public accountants, or other persons retained by the Federal credit union as to matters involving skills or expertise the director reasonably believes are matters:

(i) Within the particular person's professional or expert competence, and

(ii) As to which the particular person merits confidence; and

(3) A committee of the board of directors of which the director is not a member if the director reasonably believes the committee merits confidence.

[75 FR 81385, Dec. 28, 2010]

§ 701.5 [Reserved]

§ 701.6 Fees paid by Federal credit unions.

(a) *Basis for assessment.* Each calendar year or as otherwise directed by the Board, each Federal credit union shall pay to the Administration for the current National Credit Union Administration fiscal year (January 1 to December 31) an operating fee in accordance with a schedule as fixed from time to time by the National Credit Union Administration Board based on the total assets of each Federal credit union as of December 31 of the preceding year or as otherwise determined pursuant to paragraph (b) of this section. The operating fee is determined based on total assets less the assets created on the books of a natural person Federal credit union by investments made in a corporate credit union under the Credit Union System Investment Program or the Credit Union Homeowners Affordability Relief Program.

(b) *Coverage.* The operating fee shall be paid by each Federal credit union engaged in operations as of January 1 of each calendar year, except as otherwise provided by this paragraph.

(1) *New charters.* A newly chartered Federal credit union will not pay an operating fee until the year following the first full calendar year after the date chartered.

(2) *Conversions.* A state chartered credit union that converts to Federal charter will pay an operating fee in the year following the conversion. Federal credit unions converting to state charter will not receive a refund of the operating fee paid to the Administration in the year in which the conversion takes place.

(3) *Mergers.* A continuing Federal credit union that has merged with another credit union will pay an operating fee in the following year based on the combined total assets of the merged credit union and the continuing Federal credit union as of December 31 of the year in which the merger took place. For purposes of this requirement, a purchase and assumption transaction wherein the continuing Federal credit union purchases all or essentially all of the assets of another credit union shall be deemed a merger. Federal credit unions merging with other Federal or state credit unions will not receive a refund of the operating fee paid to the Administration in the year in which the merger took place.

(4) *Liquidations.* A Federal credit union placed in liquidation will not pay any operating fee after the date of liquidation.

(c) *Notification.* Each Federal credit union shall be notified at least 30 days in advance of the schedule of fees to be paid. A Federal credit union may submit written comments to the Board for consideration regarding the existing fee schedule. Any subsequent revision to the schedule shall be provided to each Federal credit union at least 15 days before payment is due.

(d) *Assessment of Administrative Fee and Interest for Delinquent Payment.* Each Federal credit union shall pay to the Administration an administrative fee, the costs of collection, and interest on any delinquent payment of its operating fee. A payment will be considered delinquent if it is postmarked later than the date stated in the notice to the credit union provided under §701.6(c). The National Credit Union Administration may waive or abate charges or collection of interest if circumstances warrant.

(1) The administrative fee for a delinquent payment shall be an amount fixed from time to time by the National Credit Union Administration Board and based upon the administrative costs of such delinquent payments to the Administration in the preceding year.

(2) The costs of collection shall be the actual hours expended by Administration personnel multiplied by the average hourly salary and benefits costs of such personnel as determined by the National Credit Union Administration Board.

(3) The interest rate charged on any delinquent payment shall be the U.S. Department of the Treasury Tax and Loan Rate in effect on the date when the payment is due as provided in 31 U.S.C. 3717.

(4) If a credit union makes a combined payment of its operating fee and its share insurance deposit as provided in §741.4 of this chapter and such payment is delinquent, only one administrative fee will be charged and interest will be charged on the total combined payment.

[44 FR 27380, May 10, 1979, as amended at 50 FR 20745, May 20, 1985; 55 FR 1799, Jan. 19, 1990; 59 FR 33421, June 29, 1994; 60 FR 58503, Nov. 28, 1995; 74 FR 29936, June 24, 2009]

§§ 701.7–701.13 [Reserved]

§ 701.14 Change in official or senior executive officer in credit unions that are newly chartered or are in troubled condition.

(a) *Statement of scope and purpose.* Section 212 of the Federal Credit Union Act (12 U.S.C. 1790a) sets forth conditions under which a credit union must notify NCUA in writing of any proposed changes in its board of directors, committee members or senior executive staff. The regulation only applies

§ 701.14

in cases of newly chartered credit unions and credit unions in troubled condition.

(b) *Definitions.* For the purposes of this section:

(1) *Committee member* means any individual who serves as an official of the credit union in the capacity of a credit committee member or supervisory committee member.

(2) *Senior executive officer* means a credit union's chief executive officer (typically this individual holds the title of president or treasurer/manager), any assistant chief executive officer (e.g., any assistant president, any vice president or any assistant treasurer/manager) and the chief financial officer (controller). The term "senior executive officer" also includes employees of an entity, such as a consulting firm, hired to perform the functions of positions covered by the regulation.

(3) Except as provided in paragraph (b)(4) of this section for corporate credit unions, "troubled condition" means any insured credit union that has one or a combination of the following conditions:

(i) Has been assigned

(A) A 4 or 5 CAMEL composite rating by the NCUA in the case of a federal credit union, or

(B) An equivalent 4 or 5 CAMEL composite rating by the state supervisor in the case of a federally insured, state-chartered credit union, or

(C) A 4 or 5 CAMEL composite rating by NCUA based on core workpapers received from the state supervisor in the case of a federally insured, state-chartered credit union in a state that does ot use the CAMEL system. In this case, the state supervisor will be notified in writing by the Regional Director in the Region in which the credit union is located that the credit union has been designated by NCUA as a troubled institution;

(ii) Has been granted assistance as outlined under sections 208 or 216 of the Federal Credit Union Act.

(4) In the case of a corporate credit union, "troubled condition" means any insured corporate credit union that has one or a combination of the following conditions:

(i) Has been assigned

(A) A 4 or 5 Corporate Risk Information System (CRIS) rating by NCUA in either the Financial Risk or Risk Management composites, in the case of a federal corporate credit union, or

(B) An equivalent 4 or 5 CRIS rating in either the Financial Risk or Risk Management composites by the state supervisor in the case of a federally insured, state-chartered corporate credit union in a state that has adopted the CRIS system, or an equivalent 4 or 5 CAMEL composite rating by the state supervisor in the case of a federally insured, state-chartered corporate credit union in a state that uses the CAMEL system, or

(C) A 4 or 5 CRIS rating in either the Financial Risk or Risk Management composites by NCUA based on core workpapers received from the state supervisor in the case of a federally insured, state-chartered credit union in a state that does not use either the CRIS or CAMEL system. In this case, the state supervisor will be notified in writing by the Director of the Office of Corporate Credit Unions that the corporate credit union has been designated by NCUA as a troubled institution;

(ii) Has been granted assistance as outlined under sections 208 or 216 of the Federal Credit Union Act.

(c) *Procedures for Notice of Proposed Change in Official or Senior Executive Officer*—(1) *Prior Notice Requirement.* An insured credit union must give NCUA written notice at least 30 days before the effective date of any addition or replacement of a member of the board of directors or committee member or the employment or change in responsibilities of any individual to a position of senior executive officer if:

(i) The credit union has been chartered for less than two years; or

(ii) The credit union meets the definition of troubled condition in paragraph (b)(3) or (4) of this section.

(2) *Waiver of Prior Notice*—(i) *Waiver requests.* Parties may petition the appropriate Regional Director for a waiver of the prior notice required under this section. Waiver may be granted if it is found that delay could harm the credit union or the public interest.

(ii) *Automatic waiver.* In the case of the election of a new member of the

National Credit Union Administration

§ 701.14

board of directors or credit committee member at a meeting of the members of a federally insured credit union, the prior 30-day notice is automatically waived and the individual may immediately begin serving, provided that a complete notice is filed with the appropriate Regional Director within 48 hours of the election. If NCUA disapproves a director or credit committee member, the board of directors of the credit union may appoint its own alternate, to serve until the next annual meeting, contingent on NCUA approval.

(iii) *Effect on disapproval authority.* A waiver does not affect the authority of NCUA to issue a Notice of Disapproval within 30 days of the waiver or within 30 days of any subsequent required notice.

(3) *Filing procedures*—(i) *Where to file.* Notices will be filed with the appropriate Regional Director or, in the case of a corporate credit union, with the Director of the Office of Corporate Credit Unions. All references to Regional Director will, for corporate credit unions, mean the Director of Office of Corporate Credit Unions. State-chartered federally insured credit unions will also file a copy of the notice with their state supervisor.

(ii) *Contents.* The notice must contain information about the competence, experience, character, or integrity of the individual on whose behalf the notice is submitted. The Regional Director or his or her designee may require additional information. The information submitted must include the identity, personal history, business background, and experience of the individual, including material business activities and affiliations during the past five years, and a description of any material pending legal or administrative proceedings in which the individual is a party and any criminal indictment or conviction of the individual by a state or federal court. Each individual on whose behalf the notice is filed must attest to the validity of the information filed. At the option of the individual, the information may be forwarded to the Regional Director by the individual; however, in such cases, the credit union must file a notice to that effect.

(iii) *Processing.* Within ten calendar days after receiving the notice, the Regional Director will inform the credit union either that the notice is complete or that additional, specified information is needed and must be submitted within 30 calendar days. If the initial notice is complete, the Regional Director will issue a written decision of approval or disapproval to the individual and the credit union within 30 calendar days of receipt of the notice. If the initial notice is not complete, the Regional Director will issue a written decision within 30 calendar days of receipt of the original notice plus the amount of time the credit union takes to provide the requested additional information. If the additional information is not submitted within 30 calendar days of the Regional Director's request, the Regional Director may either disapprove the proposed individual or review the notice based on the information provided. If the credit union and the individual have submitted all requested information and the Regional Director has not issued a written decision within the applicable time period, the individual is approved.

(d) *Commencement of Service.* A proposed director, committee member, or senior executive officer may begin service after the end of the 30-day period or any other additional period as provided under paragraph (c)(3)(iii) of this section, unless the NCUA disapproves the notice before the end of the period.

(e) *Notice of disapproval.* NCUA may disapprove the individual's serving as a director, committee member or senior executive officer if it finds that the competence, experience, character, or integrity of the individual with respect to whom a notice under this section is submitted indicates that it would not be in the best interests of the members of the credit union or of the public to permit the individual to be employed by, or associated with, the credit union. The Notice of Disapproval will advise the parties of their rights of appeal pursuant to 12 CFR part 747 subpart J, of NCUA's Regulations.

[55 FR 43086, Oct. 26, 1990, as amended at 59 FR 36042, July 15, 1994; 60 FR 31911, June 19, 1995; 64 FR 28717, May 27, 1999; 66 FR 65624, Dec. 20, 2001; 69 FR 62562, Oct. 27, 2004; 75 FR 34620, June 18, 2010]

§§ 701.15–701.18 [Reserved]

§ 701.19 Benefits for employees of Federal credit unions.

(a) *General authority.* A federal credit union may provide employee benefits, including retirement benefits, to its employees and officers who are compensated in conformance with the Act and the bylaws, individually or collectively with other credit unions. The kind and amount of these benefits must be reasonable given the federal credit union's size, financial condition, and the duties of the employees.

(b) *Plan trustees and custodians.* Where a federal credit union is the benefit plan trustee or custodian, the plan must be authorized and maintained in accordance with the provisions of part 724 of this chapter. Where the benefit plan trustee or custodian is a party other than a federal credit union, the benefit plan must be maintained in accordance with applicable laws governing employee benefit plans, including any applicable rules and regulations issued by the Secretary of Labor, the Secretary of the Treasury, or any other federal or state authority exercising jurisdiction over the plan.

(c) *Investment authority.* A federal credit union investing to fund an employee benefit plan obligation is not subject to the investment limitations of the Act and part 703 or, as applicable, part 704, of this chapter and may purchase an investment that would otherwise be impermissible if the investment is directly related to the federal credit union's obligation or potential obligation under the employee benefit plan and the federal credit union holds the investment only for as long as it has an actual or potential obligation under the employee benefit plan.

(d) *Defined benefit plans.* Under paragraph (c) of this section, a federal credit union may invest to fund a defined benefit plan if the investment meets the conditions provided in that paragraph. If a federal credit union invests to fund a defined benefit plan that is not subject to the fiduciary responsibility provisions of part 4 of the Employee Retirement Income Security Act of 1974, it should diversify its investment portfolio to minimize the risk of large losses unless it is clearly prudent not to do so under the circumstances.

(e) *Liability insurance.* No federal credit union may occupy the position of a fiduciary, as defined in the Employee Retirement Income Security Act of 1974 and the rules and regulations issued by the Secretary of Labor, unless it has obtained appropriate liability insurance as described and permitted by Section 410(b) of the Employee Retirement Income Security Act of 1974.

(f) *Definitions.* For this section, defined benefit plan has the same meaning as in 29 U.S.C. 1002(35) and employee benefit plan has the same meaning as in 29 U.S.C. 1002(3).

[68 FR 23027, Apr. 30, 2003]

§ 701.20 Suretyship and guaranty.

(a) *Scope.* This section authorizes a federal credit union to enter into a suretyship or guaranty agreement as an incidental powers activity. This section does not apply to the guaranty of public deposits or the assumption of liability for member accounts.

(b) *Definitions.* A *suretyship* binds a federal credit union with its principal to pay or perform an obligation to a third person. Under a *guaranty* agreement, a federal credit union agrees to satisfy the obligation of the principal only if the principal fails to pay or perform. The *principal* is the person primarily liable, for whose performance of his obligation the surety or guarantor has become bound.

(c) *Requirements.* The suretyship or guaranty agreement must be for the benefit of a principal that is a member and is subject to the following conditions:

(1) The federal credit union limits its obligations under the agreement to a fixed dollar amount and a specified duration;

(2) The federal credit union's performance under the agreement creates

an authorized loan that complies with the applicable lending regulations, including the limitations on loans to one member or associated members or officials for purposes of §§ 701.21(c)(5), (d); 723.2 and 723.8; and

(3) The federal credit union obtains a segregated deposit from the member that is sufficient in amount to cover the federal credit union's total potential liability.

(d) *Collateral.* A segregated deposit under this section includes collateral:

(1) In which the federal credit union has perfected its security interest (for example, if the collateral is a printed security, the federal credit union must have obtained physical control of the security, and, if the collateral is a book entry security, the federal credit union must have properly recorded its security interest); and

(2) That has a market value, at the close of each business day, equal to 100 percent of the federal credit union's total potential liability and is composed of:

(i) Cash;

(ii) Obligations of the United States or its agencies;

(iii) Obligations fully guaranteed by the United States or its agencies as to principal and interest; or

(iv) Notes, drafts, or bills of exchange or banker's acceptances that are eligible for rediscount or purchase by a Federal Reserve Bank; or

(3) That has a market value equal to 110 percent of the federal credit union's total potential liability and is composed of:

(i) Real estate, the value of which is established by a signed appraisal or evaluation in accordance with part 722 of this chapter. In determining the value of the collateral, the federal credit union must factor in the value of any existing senior mortgages, liens or other encumbrances on the property except those held by the principal to the suretyship or guaranty agreement; or

(ii) Marketable securities that the federal credit union is authorized to invest in. The federal credit union must ensure that the value of the security is 110 percent of the obligation at all times during the term of the agreement.

[69 FR 8547, Feb. 25, 2004]

§ 701.21 Loans to members and lines of credit to members.

(a) *Statement of scope and purpose.* Section 701.21 complements the provisions of section 107(5) of the Federal Credit Union Act (12 U.S.C. 1757(5)) authorizing Federal credit unions to make loans to members and issue lines of credit (including credit cards) to members. Section 107(5) of the Act contains limitations on matters such as loan maturity, rate of interest, security, and prepayment penalties. Section 701.21 interprets and implements those provisions. In addition, § 701.21 states the NCUA Board's intent concerning preemption of state laws, and expands the authority of Federal credit unions to enforce due-on-sale clauses in real property loans. Also, while § 701.21 generally applies to Federal credit unions only, its provisions may be used by state-chartered credit unions with respect to alternative mortgage transactions in accordance with 12 U.S.C. 3801 *et seq.*, and certain provisions apply to loans made by federally insured state-chartered credit unions as specified in § 741.203 of this chapter. Part 722 of this chapter sets forth requirements for appraisals for certain real estate secured loans made under § 701.21 and any other applicable lending authority. Finally, it is noted that § 701.21 does not apply to loans by Federal credit unions to other credit unions (although certain statutory limitations in section 107 of the Act apply), nor to loans to credit union organizations which are governed by section 107(5)(D) of the Act and part 712 of this chapter.

(b) *Relation to other laws*—(1) *Preemption of state laws.* Section 701.21 is promulgated pursuant to the NCUA Board's exclusive authority as set forth in section 107(5) of the Federal Credit Union Act (12 U.S.C 1757(5)) to regulate the rates, terms of repayment and other conditions of Federal credit union loans and lines of credit (including credit cards) to members. This exercise of the Board's authority preempts any state law purporting to limit or affect:

§ 701.21

(i)(A) Rates of interest and amounts of finance charges, including:
(1) The frequency or the increments by which a variable interest rate may be changed;
(2) The index to which a variable interest rate may be tied;
(3) The manner or timing of notifying the borrower of a change in interest rate;
(4) The authority to increase the interest rate on an existing balance;
(B) Late charges; and
(C) Closing costs, application, origination, or other fees;
(ii) Terms of repayment, including:
(A) The maturity of loans and lines of credit;
(B) The amount, uniformity, and frequency of payments, including the accrual of unpaid interest if payments are insufficient to pay all interest due;
(C) Balloon payments; and
(D) Prepayment limits;
(iii) Conditions related to:
(A) The amount of the loan or line of credit;
(B) The purpose of the loan or line of credit;
(C) The type or amount of security and the relation of the value of the security to the amount of the loan or line of credit;
(D) Eligible borrowers; and
(E) The imposition and enforcement of liens on the shares of borrowers and accommodation parties.
(2) *Matters not preempted.* Except as provided by paragraph (b)(1) of this section, it is not the Board's intent to preempt state laws that do not affect rates, terms of repayment and other conditions described above concerning loans and lines of credit, for example:
(i) Insurance laws;
(ii) Laws related to transfer of and security interests in real and personal property (see, however, paragraph (g)(6) of this section concerning the use and exercise of due-on-sale clauses);
(iii) Conditions related to:
(A) Collection costs and attorneys' fees;
(B) Requirements that consumer lending documents be in "plain language;" and
(C) The circumstances in which a borrower may be declared in default and may cure default.

12 CFR Ch. VII (1-1-12 Edition)

(3) *Other Federal law.* Except as provided by paragraph (b)(1) of this section, it is not the Board's intent to preempt state laws affecting aspects of credit transactions that are primarily regulated by Federal law other than the Federal Credit Union Act, for example, state laws concerning credit cost disclosure requirements, credit discrimination, credit reporting practices, unfair credit practices, and debt collection practices. Applicability of state law in these instances should be determined pursuant to the preemption standards of the relevant Federal law and regulations.
(4) *Examination and enforcement.* Except as otherwise agreed by the NCUA Board, the Board retains exclusive examination and administrative enforcement jurisdiction over Federal credit unions. Violations of Federal or applicable state laws related to the lending activities of a Federal credit union should be referred to the appropriate NCUA regional office.
(5) *Definition of State law.* For purposes of paragraph (b) of this section "state law" means the constitution, laws, regulations and judicial decisions of any state, the District of Columbia, the several territories and possessions of the United States, and the Commonwealth of Puerto Rico.
(c) *General rules*—(1) *Scope.* The following general rules apply to all loans to members and, where indicated, all lines of credit (including credit cards) to members, except as otherwise provided in the remaining provisions of § 701.21.
(2) *Written policies.* The board of directors of each Federal credit union shall establish written policies for loans and lines of credit consistent with the relevant provisions of the Act, NCUA's regulations, and other applicable laws and regulations.
(3) *Credit applications and overdrafts.* Consistent with policies established by the board of directors, the credit committee or loan officer shall ensure that a credit application is kept on file for each borrower supporting the decision to make a loan or establish a line of credit. A credit union may advance money to a member to cover an account deficit without having a credit application from the borrower on file if

National Credit Union Administration § 701.21

the credit union has a written overdraft policy. The policy must: set a cap on the total dollar amount of all overdrafts the credit union will honor consistent with the credit union's ability to absorb losses; establish a time limit not to exceed forty-five calendar days for a member either to deposit funds or obtain an approved loan from the credit union to cover each overdraft; limit the dollar amount of overdrafts the credit union will honor per member; and establish the fee and interest rate, if any, the credit union will charge members for honoring overdrafts.

(4) *Maturity.* The maturity of a loan to a member may not exceed 15 years. Lines of credit are not subject to a statutory or regulatory maturity limit. Amortization of line of credit balances and the type and amount of security on any line of credit shall be as determined by contract between the Federal credit union and the member/borrower.

(5) *Ten percent limit.* No loan or line of credit advance may be made to any member if such loan or advance would cause that member to be indebted to the Federal credit union upon loans and advances made to the member in an aggregate amount exceeding 10% of the credit union's total unimpaired capital and surplus. In the case of member business loans as defined in §723.1 of this chapter, additional limitations apply as set forth in §§723.8 and 723.9 of this chapter.

(6) *Early payment.* A member may repay a loan, or outstanding balance on a line of credit, prior to maturity in whole or in part on any business day without penalty.

(7) *Loan interest rates*—(i) *General.* Except when the Board establishes a higher maximum rate, federal credit unions may not extend credit to members at rates exceeding 15 percent per year on the unpaid balance inclusive of all finance charges. Federal credit unions may use variable rates of interest but only if the effective rate over the term of a loan or line of credit does not exceed the maximum permissible rate.

(ii) *Temporary rates.* (A) At least every 18 months, the Board will determine if federal credit unions may extend credit to members at an interest rate exceeding 15 percent. After consultation with appropriate congressional committees, the Department of Treasury, and other federal financial institution regulatory agencies, the Board may establish a rate exceeding the 15 percent per year rate, if it determines money market interest rates have risen over the preceding six-month period and prevailing interest rate levels threaten the safety and soundness of individual federal credit unions as evidenced by adverse trends in liquidity, capital, earnings, and growth.

(B) When the Board establishes a higher maximum rate, the Board will provide notice to federal credit unions of the adjusted rate by issuing a *Letter to Federal Credit Unions*, as well as providing information in other NCUA publications and in a statement for the press.

(C) Federal credit unions may continue to charge rates exceeding the established maximum rate only on existing loans or lines of credit made before the effective date of any lowering of the maximum rate.

(iii) *Short-term, small amount Loans (STS loans).* (A) Notwithstanding the provisions in §701.21(c)(7)(ii), a Federal credit union may charge an interest rate of 1000 basis points above the maximum interest rate as established by the Board, provided the Federal credit union is making a closed-end loan in accordance with the following conditions:

(*1*) The principal of the loan is not less than $200 or more than $1000;

(*2*) The loan has a minimum maturity term of one month and a maximum maturity term of six months;

(*3*) The Federal credit union does not make more than three STS loans in any rolling six-month period to any one borrower and makes no more than one short-term, small amount loan at a time to a borrower;

(*4*) The Federal credit union must not roll-over any STS loan;

(A) The prohibition against roll-overs does not apply to an extension of the loan term within the maximum loan terms in paragraph (c)(7)(iii)(*3*) provided the Federal credit union does not charge any additional fees or extend any new credit.

(B) [Reserved]

§ 701.21

(5) The Federal credit union fully amortizes the loan;

(6) The Federal credit union sets a minimum length of membership requirement of at least one month;

(7) The Federal credit union charges an application fee to all members applying for a new loan that reflects the actual costs associated with processing the application, but in no case may the application fee exceed $20; and

(8) The Federal credit union includes, in its written lending policies, a limit on the aggregate dollar amount of loans made under this section of a maximum of 20% of net worth and implements appropriate underwriting guidelines to minimize risk; for example, requiring a borrower to verify employment by producing at least two recent pay stubs.

(B) *STS Loan Program Guidance and Best Practices.* In developing a successful STS loan program, a Federal credit union should consider how the program will help benefit a member's financial well-being while considering the higher degree of risk associated with this type of lending. The guidance and best practices are intended to help Federal credit unions minimize risk and develop a successful program, but are not an exhaustive checklist and do not guarantee a successful program with a low degree of risk.

(1) *Program Features.* Several features that may increase the success of an STS loan program and enhance member benefit include adding a savings component, financial education, reporting of members' payment of STS loans to credit bureaus, or electronic loan transactions as part of an STS program. In addition, although a Federal credit union cannot require members to authorize a payroll deduction, a Federal credit union should encourage or incentivize members to utilize payroll deduction.

(2) *Underwriting.* Federal credit unions need to develop minimum underwriting standards that account for a member's need for quickly available funds, while adhering to principles of responsible lending. Underwriting standards should address required documentation for proof of employment or income, including at least two recent paycheck stubs. FCUs should be able to use a borrower's proof of recurring income as the key criterion in developing standards for maturity lengths and loan amounts so a borrower can manage repayment of the loan. For members with established accounts, FCUs should only need to review a member's account records and proof of recurring income or employment.

(3) *Risk Avoidance.* Federal credit unions need to consider risk avoidance strategies, including: requiring members to participate in direct deposit and conducting a thorough evaluation of the Federal credit union's resources and ability to engage in an STS loan program.

(8)(i) Except as otherwise provided herein, no official or employee of a Federal credit union, or immediate family member of an official or employee of a Federal credit union, may receive, directly or indirectly, any commission, fee, or other compensation in connection with any loan made by the credit union.

(ii) For the purposes of this section:

Compensation includes non-monetary items, except those of nominal value.

Immediate family member means a spouse or other family member living in the same household.

Loan includes line of credit.

Official means any member of the board of directors or a volunteer committee.

Person means an individual or an organization.

Senior management employee means the credit union's chief executive officer (typically, this individual holds the title of President or Treasurer/Manager), any assistant chief executive officers (e.g., Assistant President, Vice President, or Assistant Treasurer/Manager), and the chief financial officer (Comptroller).

Volunteer official means an official of a credit union who does not receive compensation from the credit union solely for his or her service as an official.

(iii) This section does not prohibit:

(A) Payment, by a Federal credit union, of salary to employees;

(B) Payment, by a Federal credit union, of an incentive or bonus to an employee based on the credit union's overall financial performance;

National Credit Union Administration § 701.21

(C) Payment, by a Federal credit union, of an incentive or bonus to an employee, other than a senior management employee, in connection with a loan or loans made by the credit union, provided that the board of directors of the credit union establishes written policies and internal controls in connection with such incentive or bonus and monitors compliance with such policies and controls at least annually.

(D) Receipt of compensation from a person outside a Federal credit union by a volunteer official or non-senior-management employee of the credit union, or an immediate family member of a volunteer official or employee of the credit union, for a service or activity performed outside the credit union, provided that no referral has been made by the credit union or the official, employee, or family member.

(d) *Loans and lines of credit to officials*—(1) *Purpose.* Sections 107(5)(A) (iv) and (v) of the Act require the approval of the board of directors of the Federal credit union in any case where the aggregate of loans to an official and loans on which the official serves as endorser or guarantor exceeds $20,000 plus pledged shares. This paragraph implements the requirement by establishing procedures for determining whether board of directors's approval is required. The section also prohibits preferential treatment of officials.

(2) *Official.* An "official" is any member of the board of directors, credit committee or supervisory committee.

(3) *Initial approval.* All applications for loans or lines of credit on which an official will be either a direct obligor or an endorser, cosigner or guarantor shall be initially acted upon by either the board of directors, the credit committee or a loan officer, as specified in the Federal credit union's bylaws.

(4) *Board of Directors' review.* The board of directors shall, in any case, review and approve or deny an application on which an official is a direct obligor, endorser, cosigner or guarantor if the following computation produces a total in excess of $20,000:

(i) Add:

(A) The amount of the current application.

(B) The outstanding balances of loans, including the used portion of an approved line of credit, extended to or endorsed, cosigned or guaranteed by the official.

(C) The total unused portion of approved lines of credit extended to or endorsed, cosigned or guaranteed by the official.

(ii) From the above total subtract:

(A) The amount of shares pledged by the official on loans or lines of credit extended to or endorsed, cosigned or guaranteed by the official.

(B) The amount of shares to be pledged by the official on the loan or line of credit applied for.

(5) *Nonpreferential treatment.* The rates, terms and conditions on any loan or line of credit either made to, or endorsed or guaranteed by—

(i) An official,

(ii) An immediate family member of an official, or

(iii) Any individual having a common ownership, investment or other pecuniary interest in a business enterprise with an official or with an immediate family member of an official

shall not be more favorable than the rates, terms and conditions for comparable loans or lines of credit to other credit union members. "Immediate family member" means a spouse or other family member living in the same household.

(e) *Insured, Guaranteed and Advance Commitment Loans.* A loan secured, in full or in part, by the insurance or guarantee of, or with an advance commitment to purchase the loan, in full or in part, by the Federal Government, a State government or any agency of either, may be made for the maturity and under the terms and conditions, including rate of interest, specified in the law, regulations or program under which the insurance, guarantee or commitment is provided.

(f) *20-Year Loans.* (1) Notwithstanding the general 15-year maturity limit on loans to members, a federal credit union may make loans with maturities of up to 20 years in the case of:

(i) A loan to finance the purchase of a mobile home if the mobile home will be used as the member-borrower's residence and the loan is secured by a first lien on the mobile home, and the mobile home meets the requirements for

§ 701.21

the home mortgage interest deduction under the Internal Revenue Code,

(ii) A second mortgage loan (or a nonpurchase money first mortgage loan in the case of a residence on which there is no existing first mortgage) if the loan is secured by a residential dwelling which is the residence of the member-borrower, and

(iii) A loan to finance the repair, alteration, or improvement of a residential dwelling which is the residence of the member-borrower.

(2) For purposes of this paragraph (f), mobile home may include a recreational vehicle, house trailer or boat.

(3) Notwithstanding the general 20-year maturity limit on second mortgage loans, a federal credit union participating in the Department of the Treasury's Making Home Affordable Program may extend the term of a modified second mortgage to match the term of a modified first mortgage, in accordance with applicable program guidelines.

(g) *Long-Term Mortgage Loans*—(1) *Authority.* A federal credit union may make residential real estate loans to members, including loans secured by manufactured homes permanently affixed to the land, with maturities of up to 40 years, or such longer period as may be permitted by the NCUA Board on a case-by-case basis, subject to the conditions of this paragraph (g).

(2) *Statutory limits.* The loan shall be made on a one to four family dwelling that is or will be the principal residence of the member-borrower and the loan shall be secured by a perfected first lien in favor of the credit union on such dwelling (or a perfected first security interest in the case of either a residential cooperative or a leasehold or ground rent estate).

(3) *Loan application.* The loan application shall be a completed standard Federal Housing Administration, Veterans Administration, Federal Home Loan Mortgage Corporation, Federal National Mortgage Association or Federal Home Loan Mortgage Corporation/Federal National Mortgage Association application form. In lieu of use of a standard application the Federal credit union may have a current attorney's opinion on file stating that the forms in use meet the requirements of applicable Federal, state and local laws.

(4) *Security instrument and note.* The security instrument and note shall be executed on the most current version of the FHA, VA, FHLMC, FNMA, or FHLMC/FNMA Uniform Instruments for the jurisdiction in which the property is located. No prepayment penalty shall be allowed, although a Federal credit union may require that any partial prepayments be made on the date monthly installments are due and be in the amount of that part of one or more monthly installments that would be applicable to principal. In lieu of use of a standard security instrument and note, the Federal credit union may have a current attorney's opinion on file stating that the security instrument and note in use meet the requirements of applicable Federal, state and local laws.

(5) *First lien, territorial limits.* The loan shall be secured by a perfected first lien or first security interest in favor of the credit union supported by a properly executed and recorded security instrument. No loan shall be secured by a residence located outside the United States of America, its territories and possessions, or the Commonwealth of Puerto Rico.

(6) *Due-on-sale clauses.* (i) Except as otherwise provided herein, the exercise of a due-on-sale clause by a Federal credit union is governed exclusively by section 341 of Pub. L. 97–320 and by any regulations issued by the Federal Home Loan Bank Board implementing section 341.

(ii) In the case of a contract involving a long-term (greater than fifteen years), fixed rate first mortgage loan which was made or assumed, including a transfer of the liened property subject to the loan, during the period beginning on the date a State adopted a constitutional provision or statute prohibiting the exercise of due-on-sale clauses, or the date on which the highest court of such state has rendered a decision (or if the highest court has not so decided, the date on which the next highest court has rendered a decision resulting in a final judgment if such decision applies statewide) prohibiting such exercise, and ending on October

National Credit Union Administration § 701.21

15, 1982, a Federal credit union may exercise a due-on-sale clause in the case of a transfer which occurs on or after November 18, 1982, unless exercise of the due-on-sale clause would be based on any of the following:

(A) The creation of a lien or other encumbrance subordinate to the lender's security instrument which does not relate to a transfer of rights of occupancy in the property;

(B) The creation of a purchase money security interest for household appliances;

(C) A transfer by devise, descent, or operation of law on the death of a joint tenant or tenant by the entirety;

(D) The granting of a leasehold interest of 3 years or less not containing an option to purchase;

(E) A transfer to a relative resulting from the death of a borrower;

(F) A transfer where the spouse or children of the borrower become an owner of the property;

(G) A transfer resulting from a decree of a dissolution of marriage, a legal separation agreement, or from an incidental property settlement agreement, by which the spouse of the borrower becomes an owner of the property;

(H) A transfer into an inter vivos trust in which the borrower is and remains a beneficiary and which does not relate to a transfer of rights of occupancy in the property; or

(I) Any other transfer or disposition described in regulations promulgated by the Federal Home Loan Bank Board.

(7) *Assumption of real estate loans by nonmembers.* A Federal credit union may permit a nonmember to assume a member's mortgage loan in conjunction with the nonmember's purchase of the member's principal residence, provided that the nonmember assumes only the remaining unpaid balance of the loan, the terms of the loan remain unchanged, and there is no extension of the original maturity date specified in the loan agreement with the member. An assumption is impermissible if the original loan was made with the intent of having a nonmember assume the loan.

(h) *Third-party servicing of indirect vehicle loans.* (1) A federally-insured credit union must not acquire any vehicle loan, or any interest in a vehicle loan, serviced by a third-party servicer if the aggregate amount of vehicle loans and interests in vehicle loans serviced by that third-party servicer and its affiliates would exceed:

(i) 50 percent of the credit union's net worth during the initial thirty months of that third-party servicing relationship; or

(ii) 100 percent of the credit union's net worth after the initial thirty months of that third-party servicing relationship.

(2) Regional directors may grant a waiver of the limits in paragraph (h)(1) of this section to permit greater limits upon written application by a credit union. In determining whether to grant or deny a waiver, a regional director will consider:

(i) The credit union's understanding of the third-party servicer's organization, business model, financial health, and the related program risks;

(ii) The credit union's due diligence in monitoring and protecting against program risks;

(iii) If contracts between the credit union and the third-party servicer grant the credit union sufficient control over the servicer's actions and provide for replacing an inadequate servicer; and

(iv) Other factors relevant to safety and soundness.

(3) A regional director will provide a written determination on a waiver request within 45 calendar days after receipt of the request; however, the 45-day period will not begin until the requesting credit union has submitted all necessary information to the regional director. If the regional director does not provide a written determination within the 45-day period the request is deemed denied. A credit union may appeal any part of the determination to the NCUA Board. Appeals must be submitted through the regional director within 30 days of the date of the determination.

(4) For purposes of paragraph (h) of this section:

(i) The term "third-party servicer" means any entity, other than a federally-insured depository institution or a wholly-owned subsidiary of a federally-

§ 701.21

insured depository institution, that receives any scheduled, periodic payments from a borrower pursuant to the terms of a loan and distributes payments of principal and interest and any other payments with respect to the amounts received from the borrower as may be required pursuant to the terms of the loan. The term also excludes any servicing entity that meets the following three requirements:

(A) Has a majority of its voting interests owned by federally-insured credit unions;

(B) Includes in its servicing agreements with credit unions a provision that the servicer will provide NCUA with complete access to its books and records and the ability to review its internal controls as deemed necessary by NCUA in carrying out NCUA's responsibilities under the Act; and

(C) Has its credit union clients provide a copy of the servicing agreement to their regional directors.

(ii) The term "its affiliates," as it relates to the third-party servicer, means any entities that:

(A) Control, are controlled by, or are under common control with, that third-party servicer; or

(B) Are under contract with that third-party servicer or other entity described in paragraph (h)(4)(ii)(A) of this section.

(iii) The term "vehicle loan" means any installment vehicle sales contract or its equivalent that is reported as an asset under generally accepted accounting principles. The term does not include:

(A) Loans made directly by a credit union to a member, or

(B) Loans in which neither the third-party servicer nor any of its affiliates are involved in the origination, underwriting, or insuring of the loan or the process by which the credit union acquires its interest in the loan.

(iv) The term "net worth" means the retained earnings balance of the credit union at quarter end as determined under generally accepted accounting principles and as further defined in § 702.2(f) of this chapter.

(i) *Put option purchases in managing increased interest-rate risk for real estate loans produced for sale on the secondary market—*

(1) *Definitions.* For purposes of § 701.21(i):

(i) *Financial options contract* means an agreement to make or take delivery of a standardized financial instrument upon demand by the holder of the contract at any time prior to the expiration date specified in the agreement, under terms and conditions established either by:

(A) A contract market designated for trading such contracts by the Commodity Futures Trading Commission, or

(B) By a Federal credit union and a primary dealer in Government securities that are counterparties in an over-the-counter transaction.

(ii) *FHLMC security* means obligations or other securities which are or ever have been sold by the Federal Home Loan Mortgage Corporation pursuant to section 305 or 306 of the Federal Home Loan Mortgage Corporation Act (12 U.S.C. 1454 and 1455).

(iii) *FNMA security* means an obligation, participation, or any instrument of or issued by, or fully guaranteed as to principal and interest by, the Federal National Mortgage Association.

(iv) *GNMA security* means an obligation, participation, or any instrument of or issued by, or fully guaranteed as to principal and interest by, the Government National Mortgage Association.

(v) *Long position* means the holding of a financial options contract with the option to make or take delivery of a financial instrument.

(vi) *Primary dealer in Government securities* means:

(A) A member of the Association of Primary Dealers in United States Government Securities; or

(B) Any parent, subsidiary, or affiliated entity of such primary dealer where the member guarantees (to the satisfaction of the FCU's board of directors) over-the-counter sales of financial options contracts by the parent, subsidiary, or affiliated entity to a Federal credit union.

(vii) *Put* means a financial options contract which entitles the holder to sell, entirely at the holder's option, a specified quantity of a security at a specified price at any time until the stated expiration date of the contract.

(2) *Permitted options transactions.* A Federal credit union may, to manage risk of loss through a decrease in value of its commitments to originate real estate loans at specified interest rates, enter into long put positions on GNMA, FNMA, and FHLMC securities:

(i) If the real estate loans are to be sold on the secondary market within ninety (90) days of closing;

(ii) If the positions are entered into:

(A) Through a contract market designated by the Commodity Futures Trading Commission for trading such contracts, or

(B) With a primary dealer in Government securities;

(iii) If the positions are entered into pursuant to written policies and procedures which are approved by the Federal credit union's board of directors, and include, at a minimum:

(A) The Federal credit union's strategy in using financial options contracts and its analysis of how the strategy will reduce sensitivity to changes in price or interest rates in its commitments to originate real estate loans at specified interest rates;

(B) A list of brokers or other intermediaries through which positions may be entered into;

(C) Quantitative limits (e.g., position and stop loss limits) on the use of financial options contracts;

(D) Identification of the persons involved in financial options contract transactions, including a description of these persons' qualifications, duties, and limits of authority, and description of the procedures for segregating these persons' duties,

(E) A requirement for written reports for review by the Federal credit union's board of directors at its monthly meetings, or by a committee appointed by the board on a monthly basis, of:

(*1*) The type, amount, expiration date, correlation, cost of, and current or projected income or loss from each position closed since the last board review, each position currently open and current gains or losses from such positions, and each position planned to be entered into prior to the next board review;

(*2*) Compliance with limits established on the policies and procedures; and

(*3*) The extent to which the positions described contributed to reduction of sensitivity to changes in prices or interest rates in the Federal credit union's commitments to originate real estate loans at a specified interest rate; and

(iv) If the Federal credit union has received written permission from the appropriate NCUA Regional Director to engage in financial options contracts transactions in accordance with this §701.21(i) and its policies and procedures as written.

(3) *Recordkeeping and reporting.* (i) The reports described in §701.21(i)(2)(iii)(E) for each month must be submitted to the appropriate NCUA Regional Office by the end of the following month. This monthly reporting requirement may be waived by the appropriate NCUA Regional Director on a case-by-case basis for those Federal credit unions with a proven record of responsible use of permitted financial options contracts.

(ii) The records described in §701.21(i)(2)(iii)(E) must be retained for two years from the date the financial options contracts are closed.

(4) *Accounting.* A federal credit union must account for financial options contracts transactions in accordance with generally accepted accounting principles.

[49 FR 30685, Aug. 1, 1984]

EDITORIAL NOTE: For FEDERAL REGISTER citations affecting §701.21, see the List of CFR Sections Affected, which appears in the Finding Aids section of the printed volume and at *www.fdsys.gov.*

§701.22 Loan participation.

(a) For purposes of this section:

(1) *Participation loan* means a loan where one or more eligible organizations participates pursuant to a written agreement with the originating lender.

(2) *Eligible organizations* means a credit union, credit union organization, or financial organization.

(3) *Credit union* means any Federal or State chartered credit union.

(4) *Credit union organization* means any credit union service organization meeting the requirements of part 712 of this chapter. This term does not include trade associations or membership

organizations principally composed of credit unions.

(5) *Financial organization* means any federally chartered or federally insured financial institution; and any state or federal government agency and their subdivisions.

(6) *Originating lender* means the participant with which the member contracts.

(b) Subject to the provisions of this section any Federal credit union may participate in making loans with eligible organizations within the limitations of the board of director's written participation loan policies, *Provided:*

(1) No Federal credit union shall obtain an interest in a participation loan if the sum of that interest and any (other) indebtedness owing to the Federal credit union by the borrower exceeds 10 per centum of the Federal credit union's unimpaired capital and surplus;

(2) A written master participation agreement shall be properly executed, acted upon by the Federal credit union's board of directors, or if the board has so delegated in its policy, the investment committee or senior management official(s) and retained in the Federal credit union's office. The master agreement shall include provisions for identifying, either through a document which is incorporated by reference into the master agreement or directly in the master agreement, the participation loan or loans prior to their sale; and

(3) A Federal credit union may sell to or purchase from any participant the servicing of any loan in which it owns a participation interest.

(c) An originating lender which is a Federal credit union shall:

(1) Originate loans only to its members;

(2) Retain an interest of at least 10 per centum of the face amount of each loan;

(3) Retain the original or copies of the loan documents; and

(4) Require the credit committee or loan officer to use the same underwriting standards for participation loans used for loans that are not being sold in a participation agreement unless there is a participation agreement in place prior to the disbursement of the loan. Where a participation agreement is in place prior to disbursement, either the credit union's loan policies or the participation agreement shall address any variance from non-participation loan underwriting standards.

(d) A participant Federal credit union that is not an originating lender shall:

(1) Participate only in loans it is empowered to grant, having a participation policy in place which sets forth the loan underwriting standards prior to entering into a participation agreement;

(2) Participate in participation loans only if made to its own members or members of another participating credit union;

(3) Retain the original or a copy of the written participation loan agreement and a schedule of the loans covered by the agreement; and

(4) Obtain the approval of the board of directors or investment committee of the disbursement of proceeds to the originating lender.

[43 FR 51610, Nov. 6, 1978, as amended at 46 FR 38680, July 29, 1981; 46 FR 43830, Sept. 1, 1981; 47 FR 1371, Jan. 13, 1982; 47 FR 54428, Dec. 3, 1982. Redesignated and amended at 49 FR 30688, Aug. 1, 1984; 60 FR 58204, Nov. 27, 1995; 68 FR 75111, Dec. 30, 2003]

§ 701.23 Purchase, sale, and pledge of eligible obligations.

(a) For purposes of this section:

(1) *Eligible obligation* means a loan or group of loans.

(2) *Student loan* means a loan granted to finance the borrower's attendance at an institution of higher education or at a vocational school, which is secured by and on which payment of the outstanding principal and interest has been deferred in accordance with the insurance or guarantee of the Federal Government, of a State government, or any agency of either.

(b) *Purchase.* (1) A Federal credit union may purchase, in whole or in part, within the limitations of the board of directors' written purchase policies:

(i) Eligible obligations of its members, from any source, if either: (A) They are loans it is empowered to grant or (B) they are refinanced with the consent of the borrowers, within 60

National Credit Union Administration

§ 701.23

days after they are purchased, so that they are loans it is empowered to grant;

(ii) Eligible obligations of a liquidating credit union's individual members, from the liquidating credit union;

(iii) Student loans, from any source, if the purchaser is granting student loans on an ongoing basis and if the purchase will facilitate the purchasing credit union's packaging of a pool of such loans to be sold or pledged on the secondary market; and

(iv) Real estate-secured loans, from any source, if the purchaser is granting real estate-secured loans pursuant to § 701.21 on an ongoing basis and if the purchase will facilitate the purchasing credit union's packaging of a pool of such loans to be sold or pledged on the secondary mortage market. A pool must include a substantial portion of the credit union's members' loans and must be sold promptly.

(2) A Federal credit union may make purchases in accordance with this paragraph (b), provided:

(i) The board of directors or investment committee approves the purchase;

(ii) A written agreement and a schedule of the eligible obligations covered by the agreement are retained in the purchasers office; and

(iii) For purchases under paragraph (b)(1)(ii) of this section, any advance written approval required by § 741.8 of this chapter is obtained before consummation of such purchase.

(3) The aggregate of the unpaid balance of eligible obligations purchased under paragraph (b) of this section shall not exceed 5 percent of the unimpaired capital and surplus of the purchaser. The following can be exculded in calculating this 5 percent limitation:

(i) Student loans purchased in accordance with paragraph (b)(1)(iii) of this section;

(ii) Real estate loans purchased in accordance with paragraph (b)(1)(iv) of this section;

(iii) Eligible obligations purchased in accordance with paragraph (b)(1)(i) of this section that are refinanced by the purchaser so that it is a loan it is empowered to grant;

(iv) An indirect lending or indirect leasing arrangement that is classified as a loan and not the purchase of an eligible obligation because the Federal credit union makes the final underwriting decision and the sales or lease contract is assigned to the Federal credit union very soon after it is signed by the member and the dealer or leasing company.

(c) *Sale.* A Federal credit union may sell, in whole or in part, to any source, eligible obligations of its members, eligible obligations purchased in accordance with paragraph (b)(1)(ii) of this section, student loans purchased in accordance with paragraph (b)(1)(iii) of this section, and real estate loans purchased in accordance with paragraph (b)(1)(iv) of this section, within the limitations of the board of directors' written sale policies, *Provided:*

(1) The board of directors or investment committee approves the sale; and

(2) A written agreement and a schedule of the eligible obligations covered by the agreement are retained in the seller's office.

(d) *Pledge.* (1) A Federal credit union may pledge, in whole or in part, to any source, eligible obligations of its members, eligible obligations purchased in accordance with paragraph (b)(1)(ii) of this section, student loans purchased in accordance with paragraph (b)(1)(iii) of this section, and real estate loans purchased in accordance with paragraph (b)(1)(iv) of this section, within the limitations of the board of directors' written pledge policies, *Provided:*

(i) The board of directors or investment committee approves the pledge;

(ii) Copies of the original loan documents are retained; and

(iii) A written agreement covering the pledging arrangement is retained in the office of the credit union that pledges the eligible obligations.

(2) The pledge agreement shall identify the eligible obligations covered by the agreement.

(e) *Servicing.* A Federal credit union may agree to service any eligible obligation it purchases or sells in whole or in part.

(f) *10 Percent limitation.* The total indebtedness owing to any Federal credit union by any person, inclusive of retained and reacquired interests, shall

§ 701.24

not exceed 10 percent of its unimpaired capital and surplus.

(g)(1) *Conflicts of interest.* No federal credit union official, employee, or their immediate family member may receive, directly or indirectly, any compensation in connection with that credit union's purchase, sale, or pledge of an eligible obligation under the provisions of § 701.23.

(2) *Permissible payments.* This section does not prohibit:

(i) A federal credit union's payment of salary to employees;

(ii) A federal credit union's payment of an incentive or bonus to an employee based on the credit union's overall financial performance;

(iii) A federal credit union's payment of an incentive or bonus to an employee, other than a senior management employee, in connection with that credit union's purchase, sale or pledge of an eligible obligation. This payment is permissible if the board of directors establishes a written policy and internal controls for the incentive or bonus program and monitors compliance with the policy and controls at least annually; and

(iv) Payment by a person other than the federal credit union of compensation to a volunteer official, non-senior management employee, or their immediate family member, for a service or activity performed outside the credit union provided that the federal credit union, the official, employee, or their immediate family member has not made a referral.

(3) *Business associates and family members.* All transactions under this section with business associates or family members not specifically prohibited by paragraph (g)(1) of this section must be conducted at arm's length and in the interest of the federal credit union.

(4) *Definitions.* The definitions in § 701.21(c)(8)(ii) of this part apply to this section.

[44 FR 27071, May 9, 1979, as amended at 46 FR 38680, July 29, 1981. Redesignated at 49 FR 30688, Aug. 1, 1984, and amended at 53 FR 4844, Feb. 18, 1988; 56 FR 15286, Apr. 15, 1991; 56 FR 35811, July 29, 1991; 60 FR 58504, Nov. 28, 1995; 63 FR 70998, Dec. 23, 1998; 72 FR 65442, Nov. 21, 2007]

§ 701.24 Refund of interest.

(a) The board of directors of a Federal credit union may authorize an interest refund to members who paid interest to the credit union during any dividend period and who are members of record at the close of business on the last day of such dividend period. Interest refunds may be made for a dividend period only if dividends on share accounts have been declared and paid for that period.

(b) The amount of interest refund to each member shall be determined as a percentage of the interest paid by the member. Such percentage may vary according to the type of extension of credit and the interest rate charged.

(c) The board of directors may exclude from an interest refund:

(1) A particular type of extension of credit;

(2) Any extension of credit made at a particular interest rate; and

(3) Any extension of credit that is presently delinquent or has been delinquent within the period for which the refund is being made.

[53 FR 19747, May 31, 1988]

§ 701.25 Charitable contributions and donations.

(a) A federal credit union may make charitable contributions and/or donate funds to recipients not organized for profit that are located in or conduct activities in a community in which the federal credit union has a place of business or to organizations that are tax exempt organizations under Section 501(c)(3) of the Internal Revenue Code and operate primarily to promote and develop credit unions.

(b) The board of directors must approve charitable contributions and/or donations, and the approval must be based on a determination by the board of directors that the contributions and/or donations are in the best interests of the federal credit union and are reasonable given the size and financial condition of the federal credit union. The board of directors, if it chooses, may establish a budget for charitable contributions and/or donations and authorize appropriate officials of the federal credit union to select recipients

National Credit Union Administration

§ 701.31

and disburse budgeted funds among those recipients.

[64 FR 19443, Apr. 21, 1999]

§ 701.26 Credit union service contracts.

A Federal credit union may act as a representative of and enter into a contractual agreement with one or more credit unions or other organizations for the purpose of sharing, utilizing, renting, leasing, purchasing, selling, and/or joint ownership of fixed assets or engaging in activities and/or services which relate to the daily operations of credit unions. Agreements must be in writing, and shall advise all parties subject to the agreement that the goods and services provided shall be subject to examination by the NCUA Board to the extent permitted by law.

[47 FR 30462, July 14, 1982, as amended at 63 FR 10756, Mar. 5, 1998]

§§ 701.27–701.29 [Reserved]

§ 701.30 Services for nonmembers within the field of membership.

Federal credit unions may provide the following services to persons within their fields of membership, regardless of membership status:

(a) Selling negotiable checks including travelers checks, money orders, and other similar money transfer instruments (including international and domestic electronic fund transfers and remittance transfers, as defined in section 919 of the Electronic Fund Transfer Act); and

(b) Cashing checks and money orders for a fee.

[71 FR 62876, Oct. 27, 2006, as amended at 76 FR 44762, July 27, 2011]

§ 701.31 Nondiscrimination requirements.

(a) *Definitions.* As used in this part, the term:

(1) *Application* carries the meaning of that term as defined in 12 CFR 202.2(f) (Regulation B), which is as follows:

An oral or written request for an extension of credit that is made in accordance with procedures established by a creditor for the type of credit requested;

(2) *Dwelling* carries the meaning of that term as defined in 42 U.S.C. 3602(b) (Fair Housing Act), which is as follows: "Any building, structure, or portion thereof which is occupied as, or designed or intended for occupancy as, a residence by one or more families, and any vacant land which is offered for sale or lease for the construction or location thereon of any building, structure, or portion thereof"; and

(3) *Real estate-related loan* means any loan for which application is made to finance or refinance the purchase, construction, improvement, repair, or maintenance of a dwelling.

(b) *Nondiscrimination in Lending.* (1) A Federal credit union may not deny a real estate-related loan, nor may it discriminate in setting or exercising its rights pursuant to the terms or conditions of such a loan, nor may it discourage an application for such a loan, on the basis of the race, color, national origin, religion, sex, handicap, or familial status (having children under the age of 18) of:

(i) Any applicant or joint applicant;

(ii) Any person associated, in connection with a real estate-related loan application, with an applicant or joint applicant;

(iii) The present or prospective owners, lessees, tenants, or occupants of the dwelling for which a real estate-related loan is requested;

(iv) The present or prospective owners, lessees, tenants, or occupants of other dwellings in the vicinity of the dwelling for which a real estate-related loan is requested.

(2) With regard to a real estate-related loan, a Federal credit union may not consider a lending criterion or exercise a lending policy which has the effect of discriminating on the basis of race, color, national origin, religion, sex, handicap, or familial status (having children under the age of 18). Guidelines concerning possible exceptions to this provision appear in paragraph (e)(1) of this section.

(3) Consideration of any of the following factors in connection with a real estate-related loan is not necessary to a Federal credit union's business, generally has a discriminatory effect, and is therefore prohibited:

(i) The age or location of the dwelling;

§ 701.31

(ii) Zip code of the applicant's current residence;
(iii) Previous home ownership;
(iv) The age or location of dwellings in the neighborhood of the dwelling;
(v) The income level of residents in the neighborhood of the dwelling.

Guidelines concerning possible exceptions to this provision appear in paragraph (e)(2) of this section.

(c) *Nondiscrimination in appraisals.* (1) A Federal credit union may not rely upon an appraisal of a dwelling if it knows or should know that the appraisal is based upon consideration of the race, color, national origin, religion, sex, handicap, or familial status (having children under the age of 18) of:

(i) Any applicant or joint applicant;
(ii) Any person associated, in connection with a real estate-related loan application, with an applicant or joint applicant;
(iii) The present or prospective owners, lessees, tenants, or occupants of the dwelling for which a real estate-related loan is requested;
(iv) The present or prospective owners, lessees, tenants, or occupants of other dwellings in the vicinity of the dwelling for which a real estate-related loan is requested.

(2) With respect to a real-estate related loan, a Federal credit union may not rely upon an appraisal of a dwelling if it knows or should know that the appraisal is based upon consideration of a criterion which has the effect of discriminating on the basis of race, color, national origin, religion, sex, handicap, or familial status (having children under the age of 18). Guidelines concerning possible exceptions to this provision appear in paragraph (e)(1) of this section.

(3) A Federal credit union may not rely upon an appraisal that it knows or should know is based upon consideration of any of the following criteria, for such criteria generally have a discriminatory effect, and are not necessary to a Federal credit union's business:

(i) The age or location of the dwelling;
(ii) The age or location of dwellings in the neighborhood of the dwelling;
(iii) The income level of the residents in the neighborhood of the dwelling.

(4) Notwithstanding paragraph (c)(3) of this section, it is recognized that there may be factors concerning location of the dwelling which can be properly considered in an appraisal. If any such factor(s) is relied upon, it must be specifically documented in the appraisal, accompanied by a brief statement demonstrating the necessity of using such factor(s). Guidelines concerning the consideration of location factors appear in paragraph (e)(3) of this section.

(5) Each Federal credit union shall make available, to any requesting member/applicant, a copy of the appraisal used in connection with that member's real estate-related loan application. The appraisal shall be available for a period of 25 months after the applicant has received notice from the Federal credit union of the action taken by the Federal credit union on the real estate-related loan application.

(d) *Nondiscrimination in advertising.* No federal credit union may engage in any form of advertising of real estate-related loans that indicates the credit union discriminates on the basis of race, color, religion, national origin, sex, handicap, or familial status in violation of the Fair Housing Act. Advertisements must not contain any words, symbols, models or other forms of communication that suggest a discriminatory preference or policy of exclusion in violation of the Fair Housing Act or the Equal Credit Opportunity Act.

(1) *Advertising notice of nondiscrimination compliance.* Any federal credit union that advertises real estate-related loans must prominently indicate in such advertisement, in a manner appropriate to the advertising medium and format used, that the credit union makes such loans without regard to race, color, religion, national origin, sex, handicap, or familial status.

(i) With respect to written and visual advertisements, a credit union may satisfy the notice requirement by including in the advertisement a copy of the logotype, with the legend "Equal Housing Lender," from the poster described in paragraph (d)(3) of this section or a copy of the logotype, with the legend "Equal Housing Opportunity," from the poster described in § 110.25(a)

National Credit Union Administration §701.31

of the United States Department of Housing and Urban Development's (HUD) regulations (24 CFR 110.25(a)).

(ii) With respect to oral advertisements, a credit union may satisfy the notice requirement by a spoken statement that the credit union is an "Equal Housing Lender" or an "Equal Opportunity Lender."

(iii) When an oral advertisement is used in conjunction with a written or visual advertisement, the use of either of the methods specified in paragraphs (d)(1)(i) or (ii) of this section will satisfy the notice requirement.

(iv) A credit union may use any other method reasonably calculated to satisfy the notice requirement.

(2) *Lobby notice of nondiscrimination.* Every federal credit union that engages in real estate-related lending must display a notice of nondiscrimination. The notice must be placed in the public lobby of the credit union and in the public area of each office where such loans are made and must be clearly visible to the general public. The notice must incorporate either a facsimile of the logotype and language appearing in paragraph (d)(3) of this section or the logotype and language appearing at 24 CFR 110.25(a). Posters containing the logotype and language appearing in paragraph (d)(3) of this section may be obtained from the regional offices of the National Credit Union Administration.

(3) *Logotype and notice of nondiscrimination compliance.* The logotype and text of the notice required in paragraph (d)(2) of this section shall be as follows:

§ 701.31   12 CFR Ch. VII (1–1–12 Edition)

EQUAL HOUSING LENDER
We Do Business In Accordance With
Federal Fair Lending Laws

UNDER THE FEDERAL FAIR HOUSING ACT, IT IS ILLEGAL, ON THE BASIS OF RACE, COLOR, NATIONAL ORIGIN, RELIGION, SEX, HANDICAP, OR FAMILIAL STATUS (HAVING CHILDREN UNDER THE AGE OF 18), TO:

- Deny a loan for the purpose of purchasing, constructing, improving, repairing or maintaining a dwelling, or deny any loan secured by a dwelling; or
- Discriminate in fixing the amount, interest rate, duration, application procedures or other terms or conditions of such a loan, or in appraising property.

IF YOU BELIEVE YOU HAVE BEEN DISCRIMINATED
AGAINST, YOU SHOULD SEND A COMPLAINT TO:

Assistant Secretary for Fair Housing and Equal Opportunity
Department of Housing & Urban Development
Washington, D.C. 20410
For processing under the Federal Fair Housing Act
and to:
National Credit Union Administration
Office of Examination and Insurance
Washington, D.C. 20456
For processing under NCUA Regulations

UNDER THE EQUAL CREDIT OPPORTUNITY ACT, IT IS ILLEGAL
TO DISCRIMINATE IN ANY CREDIT TRANSACTION:

- On the basis of race, color, national origin, religion, sex, marital status, or age,
- Because income is from public assistance, or
- Because a right was exercised under the Consumer Credit Protection Act.

IF YOU BELIEVE YOU HAVE BEEN DISCRIMINATED
AGAINST, YOU SHOULD SEND A COMPLAINT TO:

National Credit Union Administration
Office of Examination and Insurance
Washington, D.C. 20456

NCUA 1503 (Rev. 3/90)

(e) *Guidelines*. (1) Compliance with the Fair Housing Act is achieved when each loan applicant's creditworthiness is evaluated on an individual basis, without presuming that the applicant has certain characteristics of a group.

National Credit Union Administration § 701.31

If certain lending policies or procedures do presume group characteristics, they may violate the Fair Housing Act, even though the characteristics are not based upon race, color, sex, national origin, religion, handicap, or familial status. Such a violation occurs when otherwise facially nondiscriminatory lending procedures (either general lending policies or specific criteria used in reviewing loan applications) have the effect of making real estate-related loans unavailable or less available on the basis of race, color, sex, national origin, religion, handicap, or familial status. Note, however, that a policy or criterion which has a discriminatory effect is not a violation of the Fair Housing Act if its use achieves a legitimate business necessity which cannot be achieved by using less discriminatory standards. It is also important to note that the Equal Credit Opportunity Act and Regulation B prohibit discrimination, either per se or in effect, on the basis of the applicant's age, marital status, receipt of public assistance, or the exercise of any rights under the Consumer Credit Protection Act.

(2) Paragraph (b)(3) of this section prohibits consideration of certain factors because of their likely discriminatory effect and because they are not necessary to make sound real estate-related loans. For purposes of clarification, the prohibited use of location factors in this section is intended to prevent abandonment of areas in which a Federal credit union's members live or want to live. It is not intended to require loans in those areas that are geographically remote from the FCU's main or branch offices or that contravene the parameters of a Federal credit union's charter. Further, this prohibition does not preclude requiring a borrower to obtain flood insurance protection pursuant to the National Flood Insurance Act and part 760 of NCUA's Rules and Regulations, nor does it preclude involvement with Federal or state housing insurance programs which provide for lower interest rates for the purchase of homes in certain urban or rural areas. Also, the legitimate use of location factors in an appraisal does not constitute a violation of the provision of paragraph (b)(3) of this section, which prohibits consideration of location of the dwelling. Finally, the prohibited use of prior home ownership does not preclude a Federal credit union from considering an applicant's payment history on a loan which was made to obtain a home. Such action entails consideration of the payment record on a previous loan in determining creditworthiness; it does not entail consideration of prior home ownership.

(3)(i) Paragraph (c)(3) of this section prohibits consideration of the age or location of a dwelling in a real estate-related loan appraisal. These restrictions are intended to prohibit the use of unfounded or unsubstantiated assumptions regarding the effect upon loan risk of the age of a dwelling or the physical or economic characteristics of an area. Appraisals should be based on the present market value of the property offered as security (including consideration of specific improvements to be made by the borrower) and the likelihood that the property will retain an adequate value over the term of the loan.

(ii) The term "age of the dwelling" does not encompass structural soundness. In addition, the age of the dwelling may be used by an appraiser as a basis for conducting further inspections of certain structural aspects of the dwelling. Paragraph (c)(3) of this section does, however, prohibit an unsubstantiated determination that a house over X years in age is not structurally sound.

(iii) With respect to location factors, paragraph (c)(4) of this section recognizes that there may be location factors which may be considered in an appraisal, and requires that the use of any such factors be specifically documented in the appraisal. These factors will most often be those location factors which may negatively affect the short range future value (up to 3-5 years) of a property. Factors which in some cases may cause the market value of a property to decline are recent zoning changes or a significant number of abandoned homes in the immediate vicinity of the property. However, not all zoning changes will cause a decline in property values, and proximity to abandoned buildings may not

§ 701.32

affect the market value of a property because the cause of abandonment is unrelated to high risk. Proper considerations include the condition and utility of the improvement and various physical factors such as street conditions, amenities such as parks and recreation areas, availability of public utilities and municipal services, and exposure to flooding and land faults.

[54 FR 46223, Nov. 2, 1989, as amended at 59 FR 36041, July 15, 1994; 66 FR 48206, Sept. 19, 2001]

§ 701.32 Payment on shares by public units and nonmembers.

(a) *Authority.* A Federal credit union may, to the extent permitted under Section 107(6) of the Act and this section, receive payments on shares, (regular shares, share certificates, and share draft accounts) from public units and political subdivisions thereof (as those terms are defined in § 745.1) and nonmember credit unions, and to the extent permitted under the Act, this section and § 701.34, receive payments on shares (regular shares, share certificates, and share draft accounts) from other nonmembers.

(b) *Limitations.* (1) Unless a greater amount has been approved by the Regional Director, the maximum amount of all public unit and nonmember shares shall not, at any given time, exceed 20% of the total shares of the federal credit union or $1.5 million, whichever is greater.

(2) Before accepting any public unit or nonmember shares in excess of 20% of total shares, the board of directors must adopt a specific written plan concerning the intended use of these shares and forward a copy of the plan to the Regional Director. The plan must include:

(i) A statement of the credit union's needs, sources and intended uses of public unit and nonmember shares;

(ii) Provision for matching maturities of public unit and nonmember shares with corresponding assets, or justification for any mismatch; and

(iii) Provision for adequate income spread between public unit and nonmember shares and corresponding assets.

(3) A federal credit union seeking an exemption from the limits of paragraph (b)(1) of this section must submit to the Regional Director a written request including:

(i) The new maximum level of public unit and nonmember shares requested, either as a dollar amount or a percentage of total shares;

(ii) The current plan adopted by the credit union's board of directors concerning the use of new public unit and nonmember shares;

(iii) A copy of the credit union's latest financial statement; and

(iv) A copy of the credit union's loan and investment policies.

(4) Where the financial condition and management of the credit union are sound and the credit union's plan for the funds is reasonable, there will be a presumption in favor of granting the request. When granted, exemptions will normally be for a two-year period. The Regional Director will provide a written explanation for an exemption that is granted for a lesser time period.

(5) The Regional Director will provide a written determination on an exemption request within 30 calendar days after receipt of the request. The 30 day period will not begin to run until all necessary information has been submitted to the Regional Director. All denials may be appealed to the NCUA Board in a timely manner. Appeals should be submitted through the Regional Director.

(6) Upon expiration of an exemption, nonmember shares currently in the credit union in excess of the limits established pursuant to (b)(1) of this section will continue to be insured by the National Credit Union Insurance Fund within applicable limits. No new shares in excess of the limits established pursuant to (b)(1) of this section shall be accepted. Existing share certificates in excess of the limits established pursuant to (b)(1) of this section may remain in the credit union only until maturity.

(c) The limitations herein do not apply to accounts maintained in accordance with § 701.37 (Treasury Tax and Loan Depositaries; Depositaries and Financial Agents of the Government) and matching funds required by § 705.5(g) (Community Development Revolving Loan Program for Credit Unions). Once a loan granted pursuant

National Credit Union Administration § 701.33

to part 705 is repaid, nonmember share deposits accepted to meet the matching requirement are subject to this section.

[54 FR 31184, July 27, 1989, as amended at 54 FR 51384, Dec. 15, 1989; 55 FR 1794, Jan. 19, 1990; 58 FR 21645, Apr. 23, 1993; 59 FR 26102, May 19, 1994; 61 FR 3790, Feb. 2, 1996; 76 FR 67587, Nov. 2, 2011]

§ 701.33 Reimbursement, insurance, and indemnification of officials and employees.

(a) *Official.* An *official* is a person who is or was a member of the board of directors, credit committee or supervisory committee, or other volunteer committee established by the board of directors.

(b) *Compensation.* (1) Only one board officer, if any, may be compensated as an officer of the board. The bylaws must specify the officer to be compensated, if any, as well as the specific duties of each of the board officers. No other official may receive compensation for performing the duties or responsibilities of the board or committee position to which the person has been elected or appointed.

(2) For purposes of this section, the term *compensation* specifically excludes:

(i) Payment (by reimbursement to an official or direct credit union payment to a third party) for reasonable and proper costs incurred by an official in carrying out the responsibilities of the position to which that person has been elected or appointed, if the payment is determined by the board of directors to be necessary or appropriate in order to carry out the official business of the credit union, and is in accordance with written policies and procedures, including documentation requirements, established by the board of directors. Such payments may include the payment of travel costs for officials and one guest per official;

(ii) Provision of reasonable health, accident and related types of personal insurance protection, supplied for officials at the expense of the credit union: *Provided,* that such insurance protection must exclude life insurance; must be limited to areas of risk, including accidental death and dismemberment, to which the official is exposed by reason of carrying out the duties or responsibilities of the official's credit union position; must cease immediately upon the insured person's leaving office, without providing residual benefits other than from pending claims, if any; except that a credit union must comply with federal and state laws providing departing officials the right to maintain health insurance coverage at their own expense and

(iii) Indemnification and related insurance consistent with paragraph (c) of this section.

(c) *Indemnification.* (1) A Federal credit union may indemnify its officials and current and former employees for expenses reasonably incurred in connection with judicial or administrative proceedings to which they are or may become parties by reason of the performance of their official duties.

(2) Indemnification shall be consistent either with the standards applicable to credit unions generally in the state in which the principal or home office of the credit union is located, or with the relevant provisions of the Model Business Corporation Act. A Federal credit union that elects to provide indemnification shall specify whether it will follow the relevant state law or the Model Business Corporation Act. Indemnification and the method of indemnification may be provided for by charter or bylaw amendment, contract or board resolution, consistent with the procedural requirements of the applicable state law or the Model Business Corporation Act, as specified. A charter or bylaw amendment must be approved by the National Credit Union Administration.

(3) A Federal credit union may purchase and maintain insurance on behalf of its officials and employees against any liability asserted against them and expenses incurred by them in their official capacities and arising out of the performance of their official duties to the extent such insurance is permitted by the applicable state law or the Model Business Corporation Act.

(4) Notwithstanding paragraphs (c)(1) through (3) of this section, a federal credit union may not indemnify a dual employee for duties performed for any employer other than the federal credit union. For purposes of this subsection,

§ 701.34

a dual employee is a federal credit union employee who also performs work functions for another entity as part of a sharing arrangement between the federal credit union and the other entity.

(5) Notwithstanding paragraphs (c)(1) through (3) of this section, a Federal credit union may not indemnify an official or employee for personal liability related to any decision made by that individual on a matter significantly affecting the fundamental rights and interests of the Federal credit union's members where the decision giving rise to the claim for indemnification is determined by a court to have constituted gross negligence, recklessness, or willful misconduct. Matters affecting the fundamental rights and interests of Federal credit union members include charter and share insurance conversions and terminations.

(6) A Federal credit union may, before final disposition of a proceeding referred to in paragraph (c)(5) of this section, advance funds to pay for or reimburse the expenses, including legal fees, reasonably incurred in connection with the proceeding by an official or employee who is a party to the proceeding because that individual is or was an official or employee of the credit union if:

(i) The disinterested members of the credit union's board of directors (or in the event there are fewer than two disinterested directors, the supervisory committee), in good faith, determine in writing after due investigation and consideration that the official or employee acted in good faith and in a manner he or she reasonably believed to be in the best interests of the credit union's members;

(ii) The disinterested members of the credit union's board of directors (or the supervisory committee, as the case may be), in good faith, determine in writing after due investigation and consideration that the payment or reimbursement of the expenses will not materially adversely affect the credit union's safety and soundness; and

(iii) The official or employee provides:

(A) A written affirmation of the individual's reasonable good faith belief that the relevant standard of conduct described in § 701.4(b) of this chapter has been met by the individual; and

(B) A written undertaking to repay the credit union for any funds advanced or reimbursed, to the extent not covered by payments from insurance, if the official or employee is not entitled to indemnification under paragraph (c)(5) of this section.

(7) To the extent a Federal credit union has elected to follow State law or the Model Business Corporation Act in accordance with paragraph (c)(2) of this section, the credit union must substitute the phrase "in the best interests of the members" for any language indicating that fiduciary duties are owed to persons or entities other than the members of the credit union, including, but not limited to, language such as "in the best interests of the credit union" or "in the best interests of the corporation."

[53 FR 29642, Aug. 8, 1988, as amended at 57 FR 54503, Nov. 19, 1992; 66 FR 65629, Dec. 20, 2001; 72 FR 30246, May 31, 2007; 75 FR 81386, Dec. 28, 2010]

§ 701.34 Designation of low income status; Acceptance of secondary capital accounts by low-income designated credit unions.

(a) *Designation of low-income status.* (1) Based on data obtained through examinations, NCUA will notify a federal credit union that it qualifies for designation as a low-income credit union if a majority of its membership qualifies as low-income members. A federal credit union that wishes to receive the designation will notify NCUA in writing within 30 days of receipt of NCUA's notification.

(2) Low-income members are those members whose family income is 80% or less than the median family income for the metropolitan area where they live or national metropolitan area, whichever is greater, or those members who earn 80% or less than the total median earnings for individuals for the metropolitan area where they live or national metropolitan area, whichever is greater. NCUA will use the statewide or national, non-metropolitan area median family income instead of the metropolitan area or national metropolitan area median family income for members living outside a metropolitan

National Credit Union Administration

§ 701.34

area. Member earnings will be estimated based on data reported by the U.S. Census Bureau for the geographic area where the member lives. The term "low-income members" also includes those members enrolled as students in a college, university, high school, or vocational school.

(3) Federal credit unions that do not receive notification that they qualify for a low-income credit union designation but believe they qualify may submit information to NCUA to demonstrate they qualify for a low-income credit union designation. For example, federal credit unions may provide actual member income from loan applications or surveys to demonstrate a majority of their membership is low-income members. Actual member income data must be compared to a like category of statistical data, for example, actual individual member income may only be compared to total median earnings for individuals for the metropolitan area where they live or national metropolitan area, whichever is greater. A Federal credit union may rely on a sample of membership income data drawn from loan files or a member survey provided the Federal credit union can demonstrate the sample is a statistically valid, random sample by submitting with its data a narrative describing its sampling technique and evidence supporting the validity of the analysis, including the actual data set used in the analysis. The random sample must be representative of the membership, must be sufficient in both number and scope on which to base conclusions, and must have a minimum confidence level of 95% and a confidence interval of 5%. A Federal credit union must draw the sample either entirely from loan files or entirely from the survey, and must not combine a loan file review with a survey. NCUA will provide a response to the Federal credit union within 60 days of its submission.

(4) If NCUA determines a low-income designated federal credit union no longer meets the criteria for the designation, NCUA will notify the federal credit union in writing, and the federal credit union must, within five years, meet the criteria for the designation or come into compliance with the regulatory requirements applicable to federal credit unions that do not have a low-income designation. The designation will remain in effect during the five-year period. If a federal credit union does not requalify and has secondary capital or nonmember deposit accounts with a maturity beyond the five-year period, NCUA may extend the time for a federal credit union to come into compliance with regulatory requirements to allow the federal credit union to satisfy the terms of any account agreements. A federal credit union may appeal NCUA's determination that the credit union no longer meets the criteria for a low-income designation to the Board within 60 days of the date of the notice from NCUA. An appeal must be submitted through NCUA.

(5) Any credit union with a low-income credit union designation on January 1, 2009 will have five years from that date to meet the criteria for low-income designation under paragraph (a)(1) of this section, unless NCUA determines a longer time is required to allow the low-income credit union to satisfy the terms of a secondary capital or nonmember deposit account agreement.

(6) *Definitions.* The following definitions apply to this section:

Median family income and *total median earnings for individuals* are income statistics reported by the U.S. Census Bureau. The applicable income data can be obtained via the American FactFinder on the Census Bureau's webpage at *http://factfinder.census.gov/home/saff/main.html?_lang=en.*

Metropolitan area means an area designated by the Office of Management and Budget pursuant to 31 U.S.C. 1104(d), 44 U.S.C. 3504(c), and Executive Order 10253, 16 FR 5605 (June 13, 1951) (as amended).

(b) *Acceptance of secondary capital accounts by low-income designated credit unions.* A federal credit union having a designation of low-income status pursuant to paragraph (a) of this section may accept secondary capital accounts from nonnatural person members and nonnatural person nonmembers subject to the following conditions:

(1) *Secondary capital plan.* Before accepting secondary capital, a low-income credit union ("LICU") shall adopt, and forward to NCUA for approval, a written "Secondary Capital Plan" that, at a minimum:

(i) States the maximum aggregate amount of uninsured secondary capital the LICU plans to accept;

(ii) Identifies the purpose for which the aggregate secondary capital will be used, and how it will be repaid;

(iii) Explains how the LICU will provide for liquidity to repay secondary capital upon maturity of the accounts;

(iv) Demonstrates that the planned uses of secondary capital conform to the LICU's strategic plan, business plan and budget; and

(v) Includes supporting pro forma financial statements, including any off-balance sheet items, covering a minimum of the next two years.

(2) *Decision on plan.* If a LICU is not notified within 45 days of receipt of a Secondary Capital Plan that the plan is approved or disapproved, the LICU may proceed to accept secondary capital accounts pursuant to the plan.

(3) *Nonshare account.* The secondary capital account must be established as an uninsured secondary capital account or other form of non-share account.

(4) *Minimum maturity.* The maturity of the secondary capital account must be a minimum of five years.

(5) *Uninsured account.* The secondary capital account will not be insured by the National Credit Union Share Insurance Fund or any governmental or private entity.

(6) *Subordination of claim.* The secondary capital account investor's claim against the LICU must be subordinate to all other claims including those of shareholders, creditors and the National Credit Union Share Insurance Fund.

(7) *Availability to cover losses.* Funds deposited into a secondary capital account, including interest accrued and paid into the secondary capital account, must be available to cover operating losses realized by the LICU that exceed its net available reserves (exclusive of secondary capital and allowance accounts for loan and lease losses), and to the extent funds are so used, the LICU must not restore or replenish the account under any circumstances. The LICU may, in lieu of paying interest into the secondary capital account, pay accrued interest directly to the investor or into a separate account from which the secondary capital investor may make withdrawals. Losses must be distributed pro-rata among all secondary capital accounts held by the LICU at the time the losses are realized. In instances where a LICU accepted secondary capital from the United States Government or any of its subdivisions under the Community Development Capital Initiative of 2010 ("CDCI secondary capital") and matching funds were required under the Initiative and are on deposit in the form of secondary capital at the time a loss is realized, a LICU must apply either of the following pro-rata loss distribution procedures to its secondary capital accounts with respect to the loss:

(i) If not inconsistent with any agreements governing other secondary capital on deposit at the time a loss is realized, the CDCI secondary capital may be excluded from the calculation of the pro-rata loss distribution until all of its matching secondary capital has been depleted, thereby causing the CDCI secondary capital to be held as senior to all other secondary capital until its matching secondary capital is exhausted. The CDCI secondary capital should be included in the calculation of the pro-rata loss distribution and is available to cover the loss only after all of its matching secondary capital has been depleted.

(ii) Regardless of any agreements applicable to other secondary capital, the CDCI secondary capital and its matching secondary capital may be considered a single account for purposes of determining a pro-rata share of the loss and the amount determined as the pro-rata share for the combined account must first be applied to the matching secondary capital account, thereby causing the CDCI secondary capital to be held as senior to its matching secondary capital. The CDCI secondary capital is available to cover the loss only after all of its matching secondary capital has been depleted.

(8) *Security.* The secondary capital account may not be pledged or provided

by the account investor as security on a loan or other obligation with the LICU or any other party.

(9) *Merger or dissolution.* In the event of merger or other voluntary dissolution of the LICU, other than merger into another LICU, the secondary capital accounts will be closed and paid out to the account investor to the extent they are not needed to cover losses at the time of merger or dissolution.

(10) *Contract agreement.* A secondary capital account contract agreement must be executed by an authorized representative of the account investor and of the LICU reflecting the terms and conditions mandated by this section and any other terms and conditions not inconsistent with this section.

(11) *Disclosure and acknowledgement.* An authorized representative of the LICU and of the secondary capital account investor each must execute a "Disclosure and Acknowledgment" as set forth in the appendix to this section at the time of entering into the account agreement. The LICU must retain an original of the account agreement and the "Disclosure and Acknowledgment" for the term of the agreement, and a copy must be provided to the account investor.

(12) *Prompt corrective action.* As provided in §§ 702.204(b)(11), 702.304(b) and 702.305(b) of this chapter, the NCUA Board may prohibit a LICU classified "critically undercapitalized" or, if "new," as "moderately capitalized", "marginally capitalized", "minimally capitalized" or "uncapitalized", as the case may be, from paying principal, dividends or interest on its uninsured secondary capital accounts established after August 7, 2000, except that unpaid dividends or interest will continue to accrue under the terms of the account to the extent permitted by law.

(c) *Accounting treatment; Recognition of net worth value of accounts*—(1) *Equity account.* A LICU that issues secondary capital accounts pursuant to paragraph (b) of this section must record the funds on its balance sheet in an equity account entitled "uninsured secondary capital account."

(2) Schedule for recognizing net worth value. The LICU's reflection of the net worth value of the accounts in its financial statement may never exceed the full balance of the secondary capital on deposit after any early redemptions and losses. For accounts with remaining maturities of less than five years, the LICU must reflect the net worth value of the accounts in its financial statement in accordance with the lesser of:

(i) The remaining balance of the accounts after any redemptions and losses; or

(ii) The amounts calculated based on the following schedule:

Remaining maturity	Net worth value of original balance (percent)
Four to less than five years	80
Three to less than four years	60
Two to less than three years	40
One to less than two years	20
Less than one year	0

(3) *Financial statement.* The LICU must reflect the full amount of the secondary capital on deposit in a footnote to its financial statement.

(d) *Redemption of secondary capital.* With the written approval of NCUA, secondary capital that is not recognized as net worth under paragraph (c)(2) of this section ("discounted secondary capital" recategorized as subordinated debt) may be redeemed according to the remaining maturity schedule in paragraph (d)(3) of this section.

(1) *Request to redeem secondary capital.* A request for approval to redeem discounted secondary capital may be submitted in writing at any time, must specify the increment(s) to be redeemed and the schedule for redeeming all any part of each eligible increment, and must demonstrate to the satisfaction of NCUA that:

(i) The LICU will have a post-redemption net worth classification of "adequately capitalized" under part 702 of this chapter;

(ii) The discounted secondary capital has been on deposit at least two years;

(iii) The discounted secondary capital will not be needed to cover losses prior to final maturity of the account;

(iv) The LICU's books and records are current and reconciled;

(v) The proposed redemption will not jeopardize other current sources of funding, if any, to the LICU; and

§ 701.34

(vi) The request to redeem is authorized by resolution of the LICU's board of directors.

(2) *Decision on request.* A request to redeem discounted secondary capital may be granted in whole or in part. If a LICU is not notified within 45 days of receipt of a request for approval to redeem secondary capital that its request is either granted or denied, the LICU may proceed to redeem secondary capital accounts as proposed.

(3) *Schedule for redeeming secondary capital.*

Remaining maturity	Redemption limit as percent of original balance
Four to less than five years	20
Three to less than four years	40
Two to less than three years	60
One to less than two years	80

(4) *Early redemption exception.* Subject to the written approval of NCUA obtained pursuant to the requirements of paragraphs (d)(1) and (2) of this section, a LICU can redeem all or part of secondary capital accepted from the United States Government or any of its subdivisions at any time after the secondary capital has been on deposit for two years. If the secondary capital was accepted under conditions that required matching secondary capital from a source other than the Federal Government, the matching secondary capital may also be redeemed in the manner set forth in the preceding sentence. For purposes of obtaining NCUA's approval, all secondary capital a LICU accepts from the United States Government or any of its subdivisions, as well as its matching secondary capital, if any, is eligible for early redemption regardless of whether any part of the secondary capital has been discounted pursuant to paragraph (c)(2) of this section.

APPENDIX TO § 701.34

A LICU that is authorized to accept uninsured secondary capital accounts and each investor in such an account shall execute and date the following "Disclosure and Acknowledgment" form, a signed original of which must be retained by the credit union:

DISCLOSURE AND ACKNOWLEDGMENT

[Name of CU] and [Name of investor] hereby acknowledge and agree that [Name of investor] has committed [amount of funds] to a secondary capital account with [name of credit union] under the following terms and conditions:

1. *Term.* The funds committed to the secondary capital account are committed for a period of ____ years.

2. *Redemption prior to maturity.* Subject to the conditions set forth in 12 CFR 701.34, the funds committed to the secondary capital account are redeemable prior to maturity only at the option of the LICU and only with the prior approval of NCUA.

3. *Uninsured, non-share account.* The secondary capital account is not a share account and the funds committed to the secondary capital account are not insured by the National Credit Union Share Insurance Fund or any other governmental or private entity.

4. *Prepayment risk.* Redemption of U.S.C. prior to the account's original maturity date may expose the account investor to the risk of being unable to reinvest the repaid funds at the same rate of interest for the balance of the period remaining until the original maturity date. The investor acknowledges that it understands and assumes responsibility for prepayment risk associated with the [name of credit union]'s redemption of the investor's U.S.C. account prior to the original maturity date.

5. *Availability to cover losses.* The funds committed to the secondary capital account and any interest paid into the account may be used by [name of credit union] to cover any and all operating losses that exceed the credit union's net worth exclusive of allowance accounts for loan losses, and in the event the funds are so used, (name of credit union) will under no circumstances restore or replenish those funds to [name of institutional investor]. Dividends are not considered operating losses and are not eligible to be paid out of secondary capital.

6. *Accrued interest.* By initialing below, [name of credit union] and [name of institutional investor] agree that accrued interest will be:

____Paid into and become part of the secondary capital account;

____Paid directly to the investor;

____Paid into a separate account from which the investor may make withdrawals; or

____Any combination of the above provided the details are specified and agreed to in writing.

7. *Subordination of claims.* In the event of liquidation of [name of credit union], the funds committed to the secondary capital account will be subordinate to all other claims on the assets of the credit union, including claims of member shareholders, creditors and the National Credit Union Share Insurance Fund.

National Credit Union Administration

§ 701.36

8. *Prompt Corrective Action.* Under certain net worth classifications (*see* 12 CFR 702.204(b)(11), 702.304(b) and 702.305(b), as the case may be), the NCUA Board may prohibit [name of credit union] from paying principal, dividends or interest on its uninsured secondary capital accounts established after August 7, 2000, except that unpaid dividends or interest will continue to accrue under the terms of the account to the extent permitted by law.

ACKNOWLEDGED AND AGREED TO this ___ day of [month and year] by:

_____
[name of investor's official]
[title of official]
[name of investor]
[address and phone number of investor]
[investor's tax identification number]

_____
[name of credit union official]
[title of official]

[61 FR 3790, Feb. 2, 1996, as amended at 61 FR 50695, 50697, Sept. 27, 1996; 64 FR 72270, Dec. 27, 1999; 65 FR 21131, Apr. 20, 2000; 71 FR 4238, Jan. 26, 2006; 73 FR 71912, Nov. 26, 2008; 75 FR 7342, Feb. 19, 2010; 75 FR 47172, Aug. 5, 2010; 75 FR 57843, Sept. 23, 2010; 76 FR 36979, June 24, 2011; 76 FR 80227, Dec. 23, 2011]

§ 701.35 Share, share draft, and share certificate accounts.

(a) Federal credit unions may offer share, share draft, and share certificate accounts in accordance with section 107(6) of the Act (12 U.S.C. 1757(6)) and the board of directors may declare dividends on such accounts as provided in section 117 of the Act (12 U.S.C. 1763).

(b) A Federal credit union shall accurately represent the terms and conditions of its share, share draft, and share certificate accounts in all advertising, disclosures, or agreements, whether written or oral

(c) A Federal credit union may, consistent with this section, parts 707 and 740 of this subchapter, other federal law, and its contractual obligations, determine the types of fees or charges and other matters affecting the opening, maintaining and closing of a share, share draft or share certificate account. State laws regulating such activities are not applicable to federal credit unions.

(d) For purposes of this section, "state law" means the constitution, statutes, regulations, and judicial decisions of any state, the District of Columbia, the several territories and possessions of the United States, and the Commonwealth of Puerto Rico.

[47 FR 17979, Apr. 27, 1982, as amended at 50 FR 4637, Feb. 1, 1985; 59 FR 50445, Sept. 27, 1993]

§ 701.36 FCU ownership of fixed assets.

(a) *Investment in Fixed Assets.* (1) No Federal credit union with $1,000,000 or more in assets may invest in any fixed assets if the investment would cause the aggregate of all such investments to exceed five percent of the credit union's shares and retained earnings.

(2) The NCUA may waive the prohibition in paragraph (a)(1) of this section.

(i) A Federal credit union desiring a waiver must submit a written request to the NCUA regional office having jurisdiction over the geographical area in which the credit union's main office is located. The request must describe in detail the contemplated investment and the need for the investment. The request must also indicate the approximate aggregate amount of fixed assets, as a percentage of shares and retained earnings, that the credit union would hold after the investment.

(ii) The regional director will inform the requesting credit union, in writing, of the date the request was received and of any additional documentation that the regional director might require in support of the waiver request.

(iii) The regional director will approve or disapprove the waiver request in writing within 45 days after receipt of the request and all necessary supporting documentation. If the regional director approves the waiver, the regional director will establish an alternative limit on aggregate investments in fixed assets, either as a dollar limit or as a percentage of the credit union's shares and retained earnings. Unless otherwise specified by the regional director, the credit union may make future acquisition of fixed assets only if the aggregate all of such future investments in fixed assets does not exceed an additional one percent of the shares and retained earnings of the credit union over the amount approved by the regional director.

(iv) If the regional director does not notify the credit union of the action taken on its request within 45 calendar

§ 701.36

days of the receipt of the waiver request or the receipt of additional requested supporting information, whichever occurs later, the credit union may proceed with its proposed investment in fixed assets. The investment, and any future investments in fixed assets, must not cause the credit union to exceed the aggregate investment limit described in its waiver request.

(b) *Premises Not Currently Used To Transact Credit Union Business.* (1) When a Federal credit union acquires premises for future expansion and does not fully occupy the space within one year, the credit union must have a board resolution in place by the end of that year with definitive plans for full occupation. Premises are fully occupied when the credit union, or a combination of the credit union, CUSOs, or vendors, use the entire space on a full-time basis. CUSOs and vendors must be using the space primarily to support the credit union or to serve the credit union's members. The credit union must make any plans for full occupation available to an NCUA examiner upon request.

(2) When a Federal credit union acquires premises for future expansion, the credit union must partially occupy the premises within a reasonable period, not to exceed three years. Premises are partially occupied when the credit union is using some part of the space on a full-time basis. The NCUA may waive this partial occupation requirement in writing upon written request. The request must be made within 30 months after the property is acquired.

(3) A Federal credit union must make diligent efforts to dispose of abandoned premises and any other real property not intended for use in the conduct of credit union business. The credit union must seek fair market value for the property, and record its efforts to dispose of abandoned premises. After premises have been abandoned for four years, the credit union must publicly advertise the property for sale. Unless otherwise approved in writing by the NCUA, the credit union must complete the sale within five years of abandonment.

(c) *Prohibited Transactions.* (1) Without the prior written approval of the NCUA, no federal credit union may invest in premises through an acquisition or a lease of one year or longer from any of the following:

(i) A director, member of the credit committee or supervisory committee, or senior management employee of the federal credit union, or immediate family member of any such individual.

(ii) A corporation in which any director, member of the credit committee or supervisory committee, official, or senior management employee, or immediate family members of any such individual, is an officer or director, or has a stock interest of 10 percent or more.

(iii) A partnership, limited liability company, or other entity in which any director, member of the credit committee or supervisory committee, or senior management employee, or immediate family members of any such individual, is a general partner, or a limited partner or entity member with an interest of 10 percent or more.

(2) The prohibition contained in paragraph (c)(1) of this section also applies to a lease from any other employee if the employee is directly involved in investments in fixed assets unless the board of directors determines that the employee's involvement does not present a conflict of interest.

(3) All transactions with business associates or family members not specifically prohibited by this paragraph (c) must be conducted at arm's length and in the interest of the credit union.

(d) *Regulatory Flexibility Program.* Federal credit unions that meet Regulatory Flexibility Program standards, as determined pursuant to Part 742 of this chapter, are exempt from the three-year partial occupancy requirement described in paragraph (b) of this section when acquiring unimproved land for future expansion pursuant to the terms of section 742.4(a)(3) of this chapter. For a Federal credit union eligible for the Regulatory Flexibility Program that subsequently loses eligibility:

(1) Section 742.3 of this chapter provides that NCUA may require the credit union to divest any existing fixed assets for substantive safety and soundness reasons; and

(2) The credit union may not make any new investments in fixed assets if,

National Credit Union Administration

§ 701.37

after the investment, the credit union's total investments in fixed assets would exceed the five percent limitation described in paragraph (a) of this section. The regional director may waive this prohibition to allow for new investments.

(e) *Definitions*—As used in this section:

(1) *Abandoned premises* means real property previously used to transact credit union business but no longer used for that purpose and real property originally acquired for future expansion for which the credit union no longer contemplates such use.

(2) *Fixed assets* means premises, furniture, fixtures and equipment.

(3) *Furniture, fixtures, and equipment* means all office furnishings, office machines, computer hardware and software, automated terminals, and heating and cooling equipment.

(4) *Investments in fixed assets* means:

(i) Any investment in improved or unimproved real property which is being used or is intended to be used as premises;

(ii) Any leasehold improvement on premises;

(iii) The aggregate of all capital and operating lease payments on fixed assets, without discounting commitments for future payments to present value; and

(iv) Any investment in furniture, fixtures and equipment.

(5) *Immediate family* member means a spouse or other family members living in the same household.

(6) *Premises* means any office, branch office, suboffice, service center, parking lot, other facility, or real estate where the credit union transacts or will transact business.

(7) *Senior management employee* means the credit union's chief executive officer (typically this individual holds the title of President or Treasurer/Manager), any assistant chief executive officers (*e.g.*, Assistant President, Vice President or Assistant Treasurer/Manager) and the chief financial officer (Comptroller).

(8) *Shares* means regular shares, share drafts, share certificates, other savings.

(9) *Retained earnings* means undivided earnings, regular reserve, reserve for contingencies, supplemental reserves, reserve for losses, and other appropriations from undivided earnings as designated by management or the Administration.

[69 FR 58042, Sept. 29, 2004, as amended at 74 FR 13083, Mar. 26, 2009; 75 FR 66297, Oct. 28, 2010]

§ 701.37 Treasury tax and loan depositaries; depositaries and financial agents of the Government.

(a) *Definitions.* (1) *Treasury Tax and Loan (TT&L) Remittance Account* means a nondividend-paying account, the balance of which is subject to the right of immediate withdrawal, established for receipt of payments of Federal taxes and certain United States obligations under United States Treasury Department regulations.

(2) *TT&L Note Account* means an account subject to the right of immediate call, evidencing funds held by depositaries electing the note option under United States Treasury Department regulations.

(3) *Treasury General Account* means an account, established under United States Treasury Department regulations, in which a zero balance may be maintained and from which the entire balance may be withdrawn by the depositor immediately under all circumstances except closure of the credit union.

(4) *U.S. Treasury Time Deposit—Open Account* means a nondividend-bearing account, established under United States Treasury Department regulations, which generally may not be withdrawn until the expiration of 14 days after the date of the United States Treasury Department's written notice of intent to withdraw.

(b) Subject to regulation of the United States Treasury Department, a Federal credit union may serve as a Treasury tax and loan depositary, a depositary of Federal taxes, a depositary of public money, and a financial agent of the United States Government. In serving in these capacities, a Federal credit union may maintain the accounts defined in subsection (a), pledge collateral, and perform the services described under United States Treasury Department regulations for institutions acting in these capacities.

§ 701.38

(c) Funds held in a TT&L Remittance Account, a TT&L Note Account, a Treasury General Account, and a U.S. Treasury Time Deposit—Open Account shall be considered deposits of public funds. Funds held in a TT&L Remittance Account and a TT&L Note Account shall be added together and insured up to a maximum of $100,000 in the aggregate. Funds held in a Treasury General Account and a U.S. Treasury Time Deposit—Open Account shall be added together and insured up to a maximum of $100,000 in the aggregate.

(d) Funds held in a TT&L Remittance Account, a TT&L Note Account, a Treasury General Account, and U.S. Treasury Time Deposit—Open Account are not subject to the 60-day notice requirement of Article III, section 5(a) of the Federal Credit Union Bylaws.

[54 FR 18471, May 1, 1989]

§ 701.38 Borrowed funds from natural persons.

(a) Federal credit unions may borrow from a natural person, provided:

(1) The borrowing is evidenced by a signed promissory note which sets forth the terms and conditions regarding maturity, prepayment, interest rate, method of computation, and method of payment;

(2) The promissory note and any advertisement for such funds contains conspicuous langauge indicating that:

(i) The note represents money borrowed by the credit union;

(ii) The note does not represent shares and, therefore, is *not* insured by the National Credit Union Share Insurance Fund.

(b) Federal credit unions must comply with the maximum borrowing authority of § 741.2 of this chapter.

[45 FR 29271, May 2, 1980, as amended at 47 FR 17979, Apr. 27, 1982; 72 FR 30246, May 31, 2007]

§ 701.39 Statutory lien.

(a) *Definitions.* Within this section, each of the following terms has the meaning prescribed below:

(1) *Except as otherwise provided by law* or *except as otherwise provided by federal law* is a qualifying phrase referring to a federal and/or state law, as the case may be, which supersedes a requirement of this section. It is the responsibility of the credit union to ascertain whether such statutory or case law exists and is applicable;

(2) *Impress* means to attach to a member's account and is the act which makes the lien enforceable against that account;

(3) *Member* means any member who is primarily, secondarily or otherwise responsible for an outstanding financial obligation to the credit union, including without limitation an obligor, maker, co-maker, guarantor, co-signer, endorser, surety or accommodation party;

(4) *Notice* means written notice to a member disclosing, in plain language, that the credit union has the right to impress and enforce a statutory lien against the member's shares and dividends in the event of failure to satisfy a financial obligation, and may enforce the right without further notice to the member. Such notice must be given at the time, or at any time before, the member incurs the financial obligation;

(5) *Statutory lien* means the right granted by section 107(11) of the Federal Credit Union Act, 12 U.S.C. 1757(11), to a federal credit union to establish a right in or claim to a member's shares and dividends equal to the amount of that member's outstanding financial obligation to the credit union, as that amount varies from time to time.

(b) *Superior claim.* Except as otherwise provided by law, a statutory lien gives the federal credit union priority over other creditors when claims are asserted against a member's account(s).

(c) *Impressing a statutory lien.* Except as otherwise provided by federal law, a credit union can impress a statutory lien on a member's account(s)—

(1) *Account records.* By giving notice thereof in the member's account agreement(s) or other account opening documentation; or

(2) *Loan documents.* In the case of a loan, by giving notice thereof in a loan document signed or otherwise acknowledged by the member(s); or

(3) *By-Law or policy.* Through a duly adopted credit union by-law or policy

of the board of directors, of which the member is given notice.

(d) *Enforcing a statutory lien*—(1) *Application of funds.* Except as otherwise provided by federal law, a federal credit union may enforce its statutory lien against a member's account(s) by debiting funds in the account and applying them to the extent of any of the member's outstanding financial obligations to the credit union.

(2) *Default required.* A federal credit union may enforce its statutory lien against a member's account(s) only when the member fails to satisfy an outstanding financial obligation due and payable to the credit union.

(3) *Neither judgment nor set-off required.* A federal credit union need not obtain a court judgment on the member's debt, nor exercise the equitable right of set-off, prior to enforcing its statutory lien against the member's account.

[64 FR 56956, Oct. 22, 1999]

APPENDIX A TO PART 701—FEDERAL CREDIT UNION BYLAWS

INTRODUCTION

A. Effective date. After consideration of public comment, the National Credit Union Administration (NCUA) Board adopted these Bylaws and incorporated them as appendix A to Part 701 of NCUA's regulations on November 30, 2007. Unless a federal credit union has adopted bylaws before November 30, 2007, it must adopt these revised bylaws.

B. Adoption of all or part of these bylaws. Although federal credit unions may retain any previously approved version of the bylaws, the NCUA Board encourages federal credit unions to adopt the revised bylaws because it believes they provide greater clarity and flexibility for credit unions and their officials and members. Federal credit unions may also adopt portions of the revised bylaws and retain the remainder of previously approved bylaws, but the NCUA Board cautions federal credit unions to be extremely careful. Federal credit unions must be careful because they run the risk of having inconsistent or conflicting provisions because of the various options the revised bylaws provide as well as other revisions in the text.

C. Bylaw amendments. 1. The FCU Bylaws contain several provisions allowing FCU boards to select from an option or range of options and fill in a blank. Changes to "fill-in-the-blank" provisions are, in fact, changes to the FCU's bylaws and require a two-thirds vote of the board. As long as the FCU selects from the permissible options for completing the blank, the FCU need not submit the change for NCUA approval using the process outlined below.

2. Federal credit unions continue to have the flexibility to request other bylaw amendments if the need arises. NCUA must approve any bylaw amendments; federal credit unions may no longer adopt amendments from the "Standard Bylaw Amendments" booklet because the 1999 revisions to the bylaws included sufficient flexibility to make the separate list of standard bylaw amendments superfluous. Thus, NCUA no longer differentiates between "standard" and "non-standard" bylaw amendments.

3. The procedure for approval of bylaw amendments is as follows:

a. The federal credit union wishing to adopt a bylaw amendment must file a request with its regional director.

b. The request must include the section of the bylaws to be amended; the reason for or purpose of the amendment, including an explanation of why the amendment is desirable and what it will accomplish for the credit union; and the specific, proposed wording of the amendment.

c. After review by the regional director and consultation within the agency, the regional director will advise the credit union if a proposed amendment is approved.

4. Federal credit unions considering an amendment may find it useful to review the bylaws section of the agency Web site, which includes Office of General Counsel opinions about proposed bylaw amendments. Opinions issued after April 2006 will include the language of approved amendments. Even if an amendment has been previously approved, the credit union must submit a proposed amendment to NCUA for review under the procedure listed above to ensure the amendment is identical. Credit unions requesting previously approved amendments will receive notice of the regional office's decision within 15 business days of the receipt of the request.

D. The nature of the bylaws. 1. The Federal Credit Union Act requires the NCUA Board to prepare bylaws for federal credit unions. 12 U.S.C. 1758. The bylaws address a broad range of matters concerning a credit union's organization and governance, the relationship of the credit union to its members, and the procedures and rules a credit union follows. The bylaws supplement the broad provisions of: A federal credit union's charter, which establishes the existence of a federal credit union; the Federal Credit Union Act, which establishes the powers of federal credit unions; and NCUA regulations, which implement the Federal Credit Union Act. As a legal matter, a federal credit union's bylaws must conform to and cannot be inconsistent with any provision of its charter, the Federal Credit Union Act, NCUA regulations or other

Pt. 701, App. A

laws or regulations applicable to its operations.

2. NCUA expects federal credit unions and their members will make every effort to resolve bylaw disputes using the credit union's internal member complaint resolution process. If a bylaw dispute cannot be resolved internally, however, credit union officials or members should contact the regional office with jurisdiction for the credit union for assistance in resolving the dispute.

3. NCUA has discretion to take administrative actions when a credit union is not in compliance with its bylaws. If a potential violation is identified, NCUA will carefully consider all of the facts and circumstances in deciding whether to take enforcement action. NCUA will not take action against minor or technical violations, but emphasizes that it retains discretion to enforce the bylaws in appropriate cases, such as safety and soundness concerns or threats to fundamental, material credit union member rights.

TABLE OF CONTENTS

Page

Article I. Name—Purposes
Article II. Qualifications for Membership
Article III. Shares of Members
Article IV. Meetings of Members
Article V. Elections
Article VI. Board of Directors
Article VII. Board Officers, Management Officials and Executive Committee
Article VIII. Credit Committee or Loan Officers
Article IX. Supervisory Committee
Article X. Organization Meeting
Article XI. Loans and Lines of Credit to Members
Article XII. Dividends
Article XIII. Reserved
Article XIV. Expulsion and Withdrawal
Article XV. Minors
Article XVI. General
Article XVII. Amendments of Bylaws and Charter
Article XVIII. Definitions

BYLAWS

FEDERAL CREDIT UNION, CHARTER NO._____

(A corporation chartered under the laws of the United States)

ARTICLE I. NAME—PURPOSES

Section 1. Name. The name of this credit union is as stated in Section 1 of the charter (approved organization certificate) of this credit union.

Section 2. Purposes. This credit union is a member-owned, democratically operated, not-for-profit organization managed by a volunteer board of directors, with the specified mission of meeting the credit and savings needs of consumers, especially persons of modest means. The purpose of this credit union is to promote thrift among its members by affording them an opportunity to accumulate their savings and to create for them a source of credit for provident or productive purposes. *The credit union may add business as one of its purposes by placing a comma after "provident" and inserting "business."*

ARTICLE II. QUALIFICATIONS FOR MEMBERSHIP

Section 1. *Field of membership.* The field of membership of this credit union is limited to that stated in Section 5 of its charter.

Section 2. *Membership application procedures.* Applications for membership from persons eligible for membership under Section 5 of the charter must be signed by the applicant on forms approved by the board. The applicant is admitted to membership after approval of an application by a majority of the directors, a majority of the members of a duly authorized executive committee, or by a membership officer, and after subscription to at least one share of this credit union and the payment of the initial installment, and the payment of a uniform entrance fee if required by the board. If a person whose membership application is denied makes a written request, the credit union must explain the reasons for the denial in writing.

Section 3. *Maintenance of membership share required.* A member who withdraws all shareholdings or fails to comply with the time requirements for restoring his or her account balance to par value in Article III, Section 3, ceases to be a member. By resolution, the board may require persons readmitted to membership to pay another entrance fee.

Section 4. *Continuation of membership.* Once a member becomes a member that person may remain a member until the person or organization chooses to withdraw or is expelled in accordance with the Act and Article XIV of these bylaws. A member who is disruptive to credit union operations may be subject to limitations on services and access to credit union facilities. *A credit union that wishes to restrict services to members no longer within the field of membership should specify the restrictions in this section.*

Staff commentary on qualifications for membership:

Entrance fee—FCUs may not vary the entrance fee among different classes of members because the Act requires a uniform fee. FCUs may, however, eliminate the entrance fee for all applicants.

ARTICLE III. SHARES OF MEMBERS

Section 1. *Par value.* The par value of each share will be $_____. Subscriptions to shares

National Credit Union Administration

are payable at the time of subscription, or in installments of at least $____ per month.

Section 2. *Cap on shares held by one person.* The board may establish, by resolution, the maximum amount of shares that any one member may hold.

Section 3. *Time periods for payment and maintenance of membership share.* A member who fails to complete payment of one share within ____ of admission to membership, or within ____ from the increase in the par value of shares, or a member who reduces the share balance below the par value of one share and does not increase the balance to at least the par value of one share within ____ of the reduction will be terminated from membership.

Section 4. *Transferability.* Shares may only be transferred from one member to another by an instrument in a form as the board may prescribe. Shares that accrue credits for unpaid dividends retain those credits when transferred.

Section 5. *Withdrawals.* Money paid in on shares or installments of shares may be withdrawn as provided in these bylaws or regulation on any day when payment on shares may be made, provided, however, that;

(a) The board has the right, at any time, to require members to give up to 60 days written notice of intention to withdraw the whole or any part of the amounts paid in by them.

(b) Reserved.

(c) No member may withdraw any shareholdings below the amount of the member's primary or contingent liability to the credit union if the member is delinquent as a borrower, or if borrowers for whom the member is comaker, endorser, or guarantor are delinquent, without the written approval of the credit committee or loan officer. Coverage of overdrafts under an overdraft protection policy does not constitute delinquency for purposes of this paragraph. Shares issued in an irrevocable trust as provided in Section 6 of this article are not subject to withdrawal restrictions except as stated in the trust agreement.

(d) The share account of a deceased member (other than one held in joint tenancy with another member) may be continued until the close of the dividend period in which the administration of the deceased's estate is completed.

(e) The board will have the right, at any time, to impose a fee for excessive share withdrawals from regular share accounts. The number of withdrawals not subject to a fee and the amount of the fee will be established by board resolution and will be subject to regulations applicable to the advertising and disclosure of terms and conditions on member accounts.

Section 6. *Trusts.* Shares may be issued in a revocable or irrevocable trust, subject to the following:

When shares are issued in a revocable trust, the settlor must be a member of this credit union in his or her own right. When shares are issued in an irrevocable trust, either the settlor or the beneficiary must be a member of this credit union. The name of the beneficiary must be stated in both a revocable and irrevocable trust. For purposes of this section, shares issued pursuant to a pension plan authorized by the rules and regulations will be treated as an irrevocable trust unless otherwise indicated in the rules and regulations.

Section 7. *Joint accounts and membership requirements. Select one option and check the box corresponding to that option.*

__ *Option A—Separate account not required to establish membership*

Owners of a joint account may both be members of the credit union without opening separate accounts. For joint membership, both owners are required to fulfill all of the membership requirements including each member purchasing and maintaining at least one share in the account.

__ *Option B—Separate account required to establish membership*

Each member must purchase and maintain at least one share in a share account that names the member as the sole or primary owner. Being named as a joint owner of a joint account is insufficient to establish membership.

Staff commentary on shares:

i. Installments—FCUs may insert zero for the number of installments. The FCU Act allows membership upon the payment of the initial installment of a membership share, but NCUA no longer views this provision as requiring FCUs to offer the option of paying for the membership share in installments.

ii. Par value—FCUs may establish differing par values for different classes of members or types of accounts, provided this action does not violate any federal, state or local antidiscrimination laws. For example, an FCU may want to establish a higher par value for recent credit union members, without requiring long-time members to bring their accounts up to the new par value. A differing par value may also be permissible for different types of accounts, such as requiring a higher par value for a member with only a share draft account. If a credit union adopts differing par values, all of the possible par values should be stated in Section 1.

iii. Reduction in share balance below par value—When a member's account balance falls below the par value, Section 3 requires FCUs to allow members a minimum time period to restore their account balance to the par value before membership is terminated.

FCUs may not delete this requirement or delete references to this requirement in Article II, Section 3.

ARTICLE IV. MEETINGS OF MEMBERS

Section 1. *Annual meeting.* The annual meeting of the members must be held [insert time for annual meeting, for example, "during the month of March/on the third Saturday of April/ no later than March 31"], in the county in which any office of the credit union is located or within a radius of 100 miles of an office, at the time and place as the board determines and announces in the notice of the annual meeting.

Section 2. *Notice of meetings required.* a. At least 30 but no more than 75 days before the date of any annual meeting or at least 7 days before the date of any special meeting of the members, the secretary must give written notice to each member. Notice may be by written notice delivered in person or by mail to the member's address, or, for members who have opted to receive statements and notices electronically, by electronic mail. Notice of the annual meeting may be given by posting the notice in a conspicuous place in the office of this credit union where it may be read by the members, at least 30 days before the meeting, if the annual meeting is to be held during the same month as that of the previous annual meeting and if this credit union maintains an office that is readily accessible to members where regular business hours are maintained. Any meeting of the members, whether annual or special, may be held without prior notice, at any place or time, if all the members entitled to vote, who are not present at the meeting, waive notice in writing, before, during, or after the meeting.

b. Notice of any special meeting must state the purpose for which it is to be held, and no business other than that related to this purpose may be transacted at the meeting.

Section 3. *Special meetings.* a. Special meetings of the members may be called by the chair or the board of directors upon a majority vote, or by the supervisory committee as provided in these bylaws. The chair must call a special meeting, meaning the meeting must be held, within 30 days of the receipt of a written request of 25 members or 5% of the members as of the date of the request, whichever number is larger. However, a request of no more than 750 members may be required to call a special meeting.

b. The notice of a special meeting must be given as provided in Section 2 of this article. Special meetings may be held at any location permitted for the annual meeting.

Section 4. *Items of business for annual meeting and rules of order for annual and special meetings.* The suggested order of business at annual meetings of members is—

(a) Ascertainment that a quorum is present.

(b) Reading and approval or correction of the minutes of the last meeting.

(c) Report of directors, if there is one. For credit unions participating in the Community Development Revolving Loan Program, the directors must report on the credit union's progress on providing needed community services, if required by NCUA Regulations.

(d) Report of the financial officer or the chief management official.

(e) Report of the credit committee, if there is one.

(f) Report of the supervisory committee, as required by Section 115 of the Act.

(g) Unfinished business.

(h) New business other than elections.

(i) Elections, as required by Section 111 of the Act.

(j) Adjournment.

(k) To the extent consistent with these bylaws, all meetings of the members will be conducted according to _____. The order of business for the annual meeting may vary from the suggested order, provided it includes all required items and complies with the rules of procedure adopted by the credit union.

The credit union must fill in the blank with one of the following authorities, noting the edition to be used: Democratic Rules of Order, The Modern Rules of Order, Robert's Rules of Order, or Sturgis' Standard Code of Parliamentary Procedure.

Section 5. *Quorum.* Except as otherwise provided, 15 members constitute a quorum at annual or special meetings. If no quorum is present, an adjournment may be taken to a date at least 7 but not more than 14 days thereafter. The members present at any adjourned meeting will constitute a quorum, regardless of the number of members present. The same notice must be given for the adjourned meeting as is prescribed in Section 2 of this article for the original meeting, except that the notice must be given at least 5 days before the date of the meeting as fixed in the adjournment.

ARTICLE V. ELECTIONS

The Credit Union must select one of the four voting options. This may be done by printing the credit union's bylaws with the option selected or retaining this copy and checking the box of the option selected. All options continue with Section 3 of this article.

Option A1—In-Person Elections; Nominating Committee and Nominations From Floor

Section 1. *Nomination procedures.* At least 30 days before each annual meeting, the chair will appoint a nominating committee of three or more members. It is the duty of the nominating committee to nominate at least one member for each vacancy, including any unexpired term vacancy, for which elections are being held, and to determine that the members nominated are agreeable to the placing of their names in nomination and will accept office if elected.

Section 2. *Election procedures.* After the nominations of the nominating committee have been placed before the members, the chair calls for nominations from the floor. When nominations are closed, the chair appoints the tellers, ballots are distributed, the vote is taken and tallied by the tellers, and the results announced. All elections are determined by plurality vote and will be by ballot except where there is only one nominee for the office.

Option A2—In-Person Elections; Nominating Committee and Nominations by Petition

Section 1. *Nomination procedures.* a. At least 120 days before each annual meeting the chair will appoint a nominating committee of three or more members. It is the duty of the nominating committee to nominate at least one member for each vacancy, including any unexpired term vacancy, for which elections are being held, and to determine that the members nominated are agreeable to the placing of their names in nomination and will accept office if elected.

b. The nominating committee files its nominations with the secretary of the credit union at least 90 days before the annual meeting, and the secretary notifies in writing all members eligible to vote at least 75 days before the annual meeting that nominations for vacancies may also be made by petition signed by 1% of the members with a minimum of 20 and a maximum of 500. The secretary may use electronic mail to notify members who have opted to receive notices or statements electronically.

c. The written notice must indicate that the election will not be conducted by ballot and there will be no nominations from the floor when the number of nominees equals the number of positions to be filled. A brief statement of qualifications and biographical data in a form approved by the board of directors will be included for each nominee submitted by the nominating committee with the written notice to all eligible members. Each nominee by petition must submit a similar statement of qualifications and biographical data with the petition. The written notice must state the closing date for receiving nominations by petition. In all cases, the period for receiving nominations by petition must extend at least 30 days from the date that the petition requirement and the list of nominating committee's nominees are mailed to all members. To be effective, nominations by petition must be accompanied by a signed certificate from the nominee or nominees stating that they are agreeable to nomination and will serve if elected to office. Nominations by petition must be filed with the secretary of the credit union at least 40 days before the annual meeting and the secretary will ensure that nominations by petition, along with those of the nominating committee, are posted in a conspicuous place in each credit union office at least 35 days before the annual meeting.

Section 2. *Election procedures.* a. All persons nominated by either the nominating committee or by petition must be placed before the members. When nominations are closed, the chair appoints the tellers, ballots are distributed, the vote is taken and tallied by the tellers, and the results announced. All elections are determined by plurality vote and will be by ballot except where there is only one nominee for each position to be filled.

b. If sufficient nominations are made by the nominating committee or by petition to provide at least as many nominees as positions to be filled, nominations cannot be made from the floor. In the event nominations from the floor are permitted and result in more nominees than positions to be filled, when nominations have been closed, the chair appoints the tellers, ballots are distributed, the vote is taken and tallied by the tellers, and the results announced. When the number of nominees equals the number of positions to be filled, the chair may take a voice vote or declare each nominee elected by general consent or acclamation at the annual meeting.

Option A3—Election by Ballot Boxes or Voting Machine; Nominating Committee and Nomination by Petition

Section 1. *Nomination procedures.* a. At least 120 days before each annual meeting, the chair will appoint a nominating committee of three or more members. It is the duty of the nominating committee to nominate at least one member for each vacancy, including any unexpired term vacancy, for which elections are being held, and to determine that the members nominated are agreeable to the placing of their names in nomination and will accept office if elected.

b. The nominating committee files its nominations with the secretary of the credit union at least 90 days before the annual meeting, and the secretary notifies in writing all members eligible to vote at least 75 days before the annual meeting that nominations for vacancies may also be made by petition signed by 1% of the members with a minimum of 20 and a maximum of 500. The secretary may use electronic mail to notify members who have opted to receive notices or statements electronically.

c. The written notice must indicate that the election will not be conducted by ballot and there will be no nominations from the floor when the number of nominees equals the number of positions to be filled. A brief statement of qualifications and biographical data in a form approved by the board of directors will be included for each nominee submitted by the nominating committee with the written notice to all eligible members. Each nominee by petition must submit a similar statement of qualifications and biographical data with the petition. The written notice must state the closing date for receiving nominations by petition. In all cases, the period for receiving nominations by petition must extend at least 30 days from the date of the petition requirement and the list of nominating committee's nominees are mailed to all members. To be effective, nominations by petition must be accompanied by a signed certificate from the nominee or nominees stating that they are agreeable to nomination and will serve if elected to office. Nominations by petition must be filed with the secretary of the credit union at least 40 days before the annual meeting and the secretary will ensure that nominations by petition along with those of the nominating committee are posted in a conspicuous place in each credit union office at least 35 days before the annual meeting.

Section 2. *Election procedures.* All elections are determined by plurality vote. The election will be conducted by ballot boxes or voting machines, subject to the following conditions:

(a) The board of directors will appoint the election tellers;

(b) If sufficient nominations are made by the nominating committee or by petition to provide more nominees than positions to be filled, the secretary, at least 10 days before the annual meeting, will cause ballot boxes and printed ballots, or voting machines, to be placed in conspicuous locations, as determined by the board of directors with the names of the candidates posted near the boxes or voting machines. The name of each candidate will be followed by a brief statement of qualifications and biographical data in a form approved by the board of directors;

(c) After the members have been given 24 hours to vote at conspicuous locations as determined by the board of directors, the ballot boxes or voting machines will be opened, the vote tallied by the tellers, the tallies placed in the ballot boxes, and the ballot boxes resealed. The tellers are responsible at all times for the ballot boxes or voting machines and the integrity of the vote. A record must be kept of all persons voting and the tellers must assure themselves that each person voting is entitled to vote; and

(d) The tellers will take the ballot boxes to the annual meeting. At the annual meeting, printed ballots will be distributed to those in attendance who have not voted and their votes will be deposited in the ballot boxes placed by the tellers, before the beginning of the meeting, in conspicuous locations with the names of the candidates posted near them. After those members have been given an opportunity to vote at the annual meeting, balloting will be closed, the ballot boxes opened, the vote tallied by the tellers and added to the previous count, and the chair will announce the result of the vote.

Option A4—Election by Electronic Device (Including But Not Limited To Telephone and Electronic Mail) or Mail Ballot; Nominating Committee and Nominations by Petition

Section 1. *Nomination procedures.* a. At least 120 days before each annual meeting, the chair will appoint a nominating committee of three or more members. It is the duty of the nominating committee to nominate at least one member for each vacancy, including any unexpired term vacancy, for which elections are being held, and to determine that the members nominated are agreeable to the placing of their names in nomination and will accept office if elected.

b. The nominating committee files its nominations with the secretary of the credit union at least 90 days before the annual meeting, and the secretary notifies in writing all members eligible to vote at least 75 days before the annual meeting that nominations for vacancies may also be made by petition signed by 1% of the members with a minimum of 20 and a maximum of 500. The secretary may use electronic mail to notify members who have opted to receive notices or statements electronically.

c. The notice must indicate that the election will not be conducted by ballot and there will be no nominations from the floor when the number of nominees equals the number of positions to be filled. A brief statement of qualifications and biographical data in a form approved by the board of directors will be included for each nominee submitted by the nominating committee with the notice to all eligible members. Each nominee by petition must submit a similar statement of qualifications and biographical data with the petition. The notice must state the closing date for receiving nominations by petition. In all cases, the period for receiving nominations by petition must extend at least 30 days from the date of the petition requirement and the list of nominating committee's nominees are mailed to all members. To be effective, nominations by petition must be accompanied by a signed certificate from the nominee or nominees stating that they are agreeable to nomination and will serve if elected to office. Nominations by petition must be filed with the secretary of the credit union at least 40 days before the annual meeting and the secretary will ensure that nominations by petition, along with those of the nominating committee, are posted in a conspicuous place in each credit union office at least 35 days before the annual meeting.

National Credit Union Administration

Section 2. *Election procedures.* All elections are determined by plurality vote. All elections will be by electronic device or mail ballot, subject to the following conditions:

(a) The board of directors will appoint the election tellers;

(b) If sufficient nominations are made by the nominating committee or by petition to provide more nominees than positions to be filled, the secretary, at least 30 days before the annual meeting, will cause either a printed ballot or notice of ballot to be mailed to all members eligible to vote. Electronic mail may be used to provide the notice of ballot to members who have opted to receive notices or statements electronically;

(c) If the credit union is conducting its elections electronically, the secretary will cause the following materials to be transmitted to each eligible voter and the following procedures will be followed:

(1) One notice of balloting stating the names of the candidates for the board of directors and the candidates for other separately identified offices or committees. The name of each candidate must be followed by a brief statement of qualifications and biographical data in a form approved by the board of directors. Electronic mail may be used to provide the notice of ballot to members who have opted to receive notices or statements electronically.

(2) One mail ballot that conforms to Section 2(d) of this article and one instruction sheet stating specific instructions for the electronic election procedure, including how to access and use the system, and the period of time in which votes will be taken. The instruction will state that members without the requisite electronic device necessary to vote on the system may vote by submitting the enclosed mail ballot and specify the date the mail ballot must be received by the credit union. For members who have opted to receive notices or statements electronically, the mail ballot is not required and electronic mail may be used to provide the instructions for the electronic election procedure.

(3) It is the duty of the tellers of election to verify, or cause to be verified the name of the voter and the credit union account number as they are registered in the electronic balloting system. It is the duty of the teller to test the integrity of the balloting system at regular intervals during the election period.

(4) Ballots must be received no later than midnight, 5 calendar days before the annual meeting.

(5) The vote will be tallied by the tellers. The result must be verified at the annual meeting and the chair will make the result of the vote public at the annual meeting.

(6) In the event of malfunction of the electronic balloting system, the board of directors may in its discretion order elections be held by mail ballot only. The mail ballots must conform to Section 2(d) of this article and must be mailed once more to all eligible members 30 days before the annual meeting. The board may make reasonable adjustments to the voting time frames above, or postpone the annual meeting when necessary, to complete the elections before the annual meeting.

(d) If the credit union is conducting its election by mail ballot, the secretary will cause the following materials to be mailed to each member and the following procedures will be followed:

(1) One ballot, clearly identified as the ballot on which the names of the candidates for the board of directors and the candidates for other separately identified offices or committees are printed in random order. The name of each candidate will be followed by a brief statement of qualifications and biographical data in a form approved by the board of directors;

(2) One ballot envelope clearly marked with instructions that the completed ballot must be placed in that envelope and sealed;

(3) One identification form to be completed so as to include the name, address, signature and credit union account number of the voter;

(4) One mailing envelope in which the voter, following instructions provided with the mailing envelope, must insert the sealed ballot envelope and the identification form, and which must have postage prepaid and be preaddressed for return to the tellers;

(5) When properly designed with features that preserve the secrecy of the ballot, one form can be printed that represents a combined ballot and identification form, and postage prepaid and preaddressed return envelope;

(6) It is the duty of the tellers to verify, or cause to be verified, the name and credit union account number of the voter as appearing on the identification form; to place the verified identification form and the sealed ballot envelope in a place of safekeeping pending the count of the vote; in the case of a questionable or challenged identification form, to retain the identification form and sealed ballot envelope together until the verification or challenge has been resolved;

(7) Ballots mailed to the tellers must be received by the tellers no later than midnight 5 days before the date of the annual meeting;

(8) The vote will be tallied by the tellers. The result will be verified at the annual meeting and the chair will make the result of the vote public at the annual meeting.

All Options Continue Here

Section 3. *Order of nominations.* Nominations may be in the following order:

(a) Nominations for directors.

(b) Nominations for credit committee members, if applicable. Elections may be by separate ballots following the same order as the above nominations or, if preferred, may be by one ballot for all offices.

Section 4. *Proxy and agent voting.* Members cannot vote by proxy. A member other than a natural person may vote through an agent designated in writing for the purpose.

Section 5. *One vote per member.* Irrespective of the number of shares, no member has more than one vote.

Section 6. *Submission of information regarding credit union officials to NCUA.* The names and addresses of members of the board, board officers, executive committee, and members of the credit committee, if applicable, and supervisory committees must be forwarded to the Administration in accordance with the Act and regulations in the manner as may be required by the Administration.

Section 7. *Minimum age requirement.* Members must be at least __ years of age by the date of the meeting (or for appointed offices, the date of appointment) in order to vote at meetings of the members, hold elective or appointive office, sign nominating petitions, or sign petitions requesting special meetings.

The Credit Union's board should adopt a resolution inserting an age no greater than 18, or the age of majority under the state law applicable to the credit union, in the blank space.

The Credit Union may select the absentee ballot provision in conjunction with the voting procedure it has selected. This may be done by printing the credit union's bylaws with this provision or by retaining this copy and checking the box.

__ Section 8. *Absentee ballots.* The board of directors may authorize the use of absentee ballots in conjunction with the other procedures authorized in this article, subject to the following conditions:

(a) The board of directors will appoint the election tellers;

(b) If sufficient nominations are made by the nominating committee or by petition to provide more than one nominee for any position to be filled, the secretary, at least 30 days before the annual meeting, will cause printed ballots to be mailed to all members of the credit union who are eligible to vote and who have submitted a written or electronic request for an absentee ballot;

(c) The secretary will cause the following materials to be mailed to each eligible voter who has submitted a written or electronic request for an absentee ballot:

(1) One ballot, clearly identified as the ballot on which the names of the candidates for the board of directors and the candidates for other separately identified offices or committees are printed in random order. The name of each candidate will be followed by a brief statement of qualifications and biographical data in a form approved by the board of directors;

(2) One ballot envelope clearly marked with instructions that the completed ballot must be placed in that envelope and sealed;

(3) One identification form to be completed so as to include the name, address, signature and credit union account number of the voter;

(4) One mailing envelope in which the voter, pursuant to instructions provided with the envelope, must insert the sealed ballot envelope and the identification form, and which must have postage prepaid and be preaddressed for return to the tellers;

(5) When properly designed with features that preserve the secrecy of the ballot, one form can be printed that represents a combined ballot and identification form, and postage prepaid and preaddressed return envelope;

(d) It is the duty of the election tellers to verify, or cause to be verified, the name and credit union account number of the voter as appearing on the identification form; to place the verified identification and the sealed ballot envelope in a place of safekeeping pending the count of the vote; in the case of a questionable or challenged identification form, to retain the identification form and the sealed ballot envelope together until the verification or challenge has been resolved; and in the event that more than one voting procedure is used, to verify that no eligible voter has voted more than one time;

(e) Ballots mailed to the tellers must be received by the tellers no later than midnight 5 days before the date of the annual meeting;

(f) Absentee ballots will be deposited in the ballot boxes to be taken to the annual meeting or included in a precount in accordance with procedures specified in Article V, Section 2; and

(g) If a member has chosen to receive statements and notices electronically, the credit union may provide notices required in this section by email and provide instructions for voting via electronic means instead of mail ballots.

Staff commentary on the election process:

i. *Eligibility Requirements:* The Act and the FCU Bylaws contain the only eligibility requirements for membership on an FCU's board of directors, which are as follows:

(a) The individual must be a member of the FCU before distribution of ballots;

(b) the individual cannot have been convicted of a crime involving dishonesty or breach of trust unless the NCUA Board has waived the prohibition for the conviction; and

(c) the individual meets the minimum age requirement established under Article V, Section 7 of the FCU Bylaws.

Anyone meeting the three eligibility requirements may run for a seat on the board of directors if properly nominated. It is the nominating committee's duty to ascertain that all nominated candidates, including those nominated by petition, meet the eligibility requirements.

ii. Nomination Criteria for Nominating Committee: The FCU Act and the FCU Bylaws do not prohibit a board of directors from establishing reasonable criteria, in addition to the eligibility requirements, for a nominating committee to follow in making its nominations, such as financial experience, years of membership, or conflict of interest provisions. The board's nomination criteria, however, applies only to individuals nominated by the nominating committee; they cannot be imposed on individuals who meet the eligibility requirements and are properly nominated from the floor or by petition.

iii. Candidates' Names on Ballots: When producing an election ballot, the FCU's secretary may order the names of the candidates on the ballot using any method for selection provided it is random and used consistently from year to year so as to avoid manipulation or favoritism.

iv. Secret Ballots: An FCU must establish an election process that assures members their votes remain confidential and secret from all interested parties. If the election process does not separate the member's identity from the ballot, FCUs should use a third-party teller that has sole control over completed ballots. If the ballots are designed so that members' identities remain secret and are not disclosed on the ballot, FCUs may use election tellers from the FCU. In any case, FCU employees, officials, and members must not have access to ballots identifying members or to information that links members' votes to their identities.

v. Plurality Voting: At least one nominee must be nominated for each vacant seat. When there are more nominees than seats open for election, the nominees who receive the greatest number of votes are elected to the vacant seats.

vi. Minimum Age Requirement: The age the board selects may not be greater than the age of majority under the state law applicable to the credit union.

ARTICLE VI. BOARD OF DIRECTORS

Section 1. *Number of members.* The board consists of _____ members, all of whom must be members of this credit union. The number of directors may be changed to an odd number not fewer than 5 nor more than 15 by resolution of the board. No reduction in the number of directors may be made unless corresponding vacancies exist as a result of deaths, resignations, expiration of terms of office, or other actions provided by these bylaws. A copy of the resolution of the board covering any increase or decrease in the number of directors must be filed with the official copy of the bylaws of this credit union.

Section 2. *Composition of board.* _____ (Fill in the number, which may be zero) directors or committee members may be a paid employee of the credit union. _____ (Fill in the number, which may be zero) immediate family members of a director or committee member may be a paid employee of the credit union. In no case may employees, family members, or employees and family members constitute a majority of the board. The board may appoint a management official who _____ (may or may not) be a member of the board and one or more assistant management officials who _____ (may or may not) be a member of the board. If the management official or assistant management official is permitted to serve on the board, he or she may not serve as the chair.

Section 3. *Terms of office.* Regular terms of office for directors must be for periods of either 2 or 3 years as the board determines. All regular terms must be for the same number of years and until the election and qualification of successors. Regular terms must be fixed at the first meeting, or upon any increase or decrease in the number of directors, so that approximately an equal number of regular terms must expire at each annual meeting.

Section 4. *Vacancies.* Any vacancy on the board, credit committee, if applicable, or supervisory committee will be filled as soon as possible by vote of a majority of the directors then holding office. If all director positions become vacant simultaneously, the supervisory committee immediately becomes the temporary board of directors and must follow the procedures in Article IX, Section 3. Directors and credit committee members appointed to fill a vacancy will hold office only until the next annual meeting, at which any unexpired terms will be filled by vote of the members, and until the qualification of their successors. Members of the supervisory committee appointed to fill a vacancy will hold office until the first regular meeting of the board following the next annual meeting of members, at which the regular term expires, and until the appointment and qualification of their successors.

Section 5. *Regular and special meetings.* A regular meeting of the board must be held each month at the time and place fixed by resolution of the board. One regular meeting each calendar year must be conducted in person. If a quorum is present in person for the annual in person meeting, the remaining board members may participate using audio or video teleconference methods. The other regular meetings may be conducted using audio or video teleconference methods. The chair, or in the chair's absence the ranking vice chair, may call a special meeting of the board at any time and must do so upon written request of a majority of the directors then holding office. Unless the board prescribes otherwise, the chair, or in the chair's absence the ranking vice chair, will fix the time and place of special meetings. Notice of all meetings will be given in the manner the board may from time to time by resolution prescribe. Special meetings may be conducted using audio or video teleconference methods.

Section 6. *Board responsibilities.* The board has the general direction and control of the affairs of this credit union and is responsible for performing all the duties customarily performed by boards of directors. This includes but is not limited to the following:

(a) Directing the affairs of the credit union in accordance with the Act, these bylaws, the rules and regulations and sound business practices.

(b) Establishing programs to achieve the purposes of this credit union as stated in Article I, Section 2, of these bylaws.

(c) Establishing a loan collection program and authorizing the chargeoff of uncollectible loans.

(d) Establishing a policy to address training for newly elected and incumbent directors and volunteer officials, in areas such as ethics and fiduciary responsibility, regulatory compliance, and accounting and determining that all persons appointed or elected by this credit union to any position requiring the receipt, payment or custody of money or other property of this credit union, or in its custody or control as collateral or otherwise, are properly bonded in accordance with the Act and regulations.

(e) Performing additional acts and exercising additional powers as may be required or authorized by applicable law.

If the credit union has an elected credit committee, you do not need to check a box. If the credit union has no credit committee check Option 1 and if it has an appointed credit committee check Option 2.

__ *Option 1 No Credit Committee.*

(f) Reviewing denied loan applications of members who file written requests for review.

(g) Appointing one or more loan officers and delegating to those officers the power to approve or disapprove loans, lines of credit or advances from lines of credit.

(h) In its discretion, appointing a loan review committee to review loan denials and delegating to the committee the power to overturn denials of loan applications. The committee will function as a mid-level appeal committee for the board. Any denial of a loan by the committee must be reviewed by the board upon written request of the member. The committee must consist of three members and the regular term of office of the committee member will be for two years. Not more than one member of the committee may be appointed as a loan officer.

__ *Option 2. Appointed Credit Committee.*

(f) Appointing an odd number of credit committee members as provided in Article VIII of these bylaws.

Section 7. *Quorum.* A majority of the number of directors, including any vacant positions, constitutes a quorum for the transaction of business at any meeting, except that vacancies may be filled by a quorum consisting of a majority of the directors holding office as provided in Section 4 of this article. Fewer than a quorum may adjourn from time to time until a quorum is in attendance.

Section 8. *Attendance and removal.* a. If a director or a credit committee member, if applicable, fails to attend regular meetings of the board or credit committee, respectively, for 3 consecutive months, or 4 meetings within a calendar year, or otherwise fails to perform any of the duties as a director or a credit committee member, the office may be declared vacant by the board and the vacancy filled as provided in the bylaws.

b. The board may remove any board officer from office for failure to perform the duties thereof, after giving the officer reasonable notice and opportunity to be heard.

When any board officer, membership officer, executive committee member or investment committee member is absent, disqualified, or otherwise unable to perform the duties of the office, the board may by resolution designate another member of this credit union to fill the position temporarily. The board may also, by resolution, designate another member or members of this credit union to act on the credit committee when necessary in order to obtain a quorum.

Section 9. *Suspension of supervisory committee members.* Any member of the supervisory committee may be suspended by a majority vote of the board of directors. The members of this credit union will decide, at a special meeting held not fewer than 7 nor more than 14 days after any suspension, whether the suspended committee member will be removed from or restored to the supervisory committee.

ARTICLE VII. BOARD OFFICERS, MANAGEMENT OFFICIALS AND EXECUTIVE COMMITTEE

Section 1. *Board officers.* The board officers of this credit union are comprised of a chair, one or more vice chairs, a financial officer, and a secretary, all of whom are elected by the board and from their number. The board determines the title and rank of each board officer and records them in the addendum to this article. One board officer, the _____, may be compensated for services as determined by the board. If more than one vice chair is elected, the board determines their rank as first vice chair, second vice chair, and so on. The offices of the financial officer and secretary may be held by the same person. If a management official or assistant management official is permitted to serve on the board, he or she may not serve as the chair. Unless removed as provided in these bylaws, the board officers elected at the first meeting of the board hold office until the first meeting of the board following the first annual meeting of the members and until the election and qualification of their respective successors.

Section 2. *Election and term of office.* Board officers elected at the meeting of the board next following the annual meeting of the members, which must be held not later than 7 days after the annual meeting, hold office for a term of 1 year and until the election and qualification of their respective successors: provided, however, that any person elected to fill a vacancy caused by the death, resignation, or removal of an officer is elected by the board to serve only for the unexpired term of that officer and until a successor is duly elected and qualified.

Section 3. *Duties of Chair.* The chair presides at all meetings of the members and at all meetings of the board, unless disqualified through suspension by the supervisory committee. The chair also performs other duties customarily assigned to the office of the chair or duties he or she is directed to perform by resolution of the board not inconsistent with the Act and regulations and these bylaws.

Section 4. *Approval required.* The board must approve all individuals who are authorized to sign all notes of this credit union and all checks, drafts and other orders for disbursement of credit union funds.

Section 5. *Vice chair.* The ranking vice chair has and may exercise all the powers, authority, and duties of the chair during the chair's absence or inability to act.

Section 6. *Duties of financial officer.* i. The financial officer manages this credit union under the control and direction of the board unless the board has appointed a management official to act as general manager. Subject to limitations, controls and delegations the board may impose, the financial officer will:

(a) Have custody of all funds, securities, valuable papers and other assets of this credit union.

(b) Provide and maintain full and complete records of all the assets and liabilities of this credit union in accordance with forms and procedures prescribed in regulations and other guidance approved by the Administration, including, for small credit unions, the Accounting Manual for Federal Credit Unions.

(c) Within 20 days after the close of each month, ensure that a financial statement showing the condition of this credit union as of the end of the month, including a summary of delinquent loans is prepared and submitted to the board and post a copy of the statement in a conspicuous place in the office of the credit union where it will remain until replaced by the financial statement for the next succeeding month.

(d) Ensure that financial and other reports the Administration may require are prepared and sent.

(e) Within standards and limitations prescribed by the board, employ tellers, clerks, bookkeepers, and other office employees, and have the power to remove these employees.

(f) Perform other duties customarily assigned to the office of the financial officer or duties he or she is directed to perform by resolution of the board not inconsistent with the Act, regulations and these bylaws.

ii. The board may employ one or more assistant financial officers, none of whom may also hold office as chair or vice chair, and may authorize them, under the direction of the financial officer, to perform any of the duties devolving on the financial officer, including the signing of checks. When designated by the board, any assistant financial officer may also act as financial officer during the financial officer's temporary absence or temporary inability to act.

Section 7. *Duties of management official and assistant management official.* The board may appoint a management official who is under the direction and control of the board or of the financial officer as determined by the board. The management official may be assigned any or all of the responsibilities of the financial officer described in Section 6 of this article. The board will determine the title and rank of each management official and record them in the addendum to this article. The board may employ one or more assistant management officials. The board may authorize assistant management officials under the direction of the management official, to perform any of the duties devolving on the management official, including the signing of checks. When designated by the board, any assistant management official may also act as management official during the management official's temporary absence or temporary inability to act.

Section 8. *Board powers regarding employees.* The board employs, fixes the compensation, and prescribes the duties of employees as necessary, and has the power to remove employees, unless it has delegated these powers to the financial officer or management official. Neither the board, the financial officer, nor the management official has the power or duty to employ, prescribe the duties of, or remove necessary clerical and auditing assistance employed or used by the supervisory committee and, if there is a credit committee, the power or duty to employ, prescribe the duties of, or remove any loan officer appointed by the credit committee.

Section 9. *Duties of secretary.* The secretary prepares and maintains full and correct records of all meetings of the members and of the board, which records will be prepared within 7 days after the respective meetings.

The secretary must promptly inform the Administration in writing of any change in the address of the office of this credit union or the location of its principal records. The secretary will give or cause to be given, in the manner prescribed in these bylaws, proper notice of all meetings of the members, and perform other duties he or she may be directed to perform by resolution of the board not inconsistent with the Act, regulations and these bylaws. The board may employ one or more assistant secretaries, none of whom may also hold office as chair, vice chair, or financial officer, and may authorize them under direction of the secretary to perform any of the duties assigned to the secretary.

Section 10. *Executive committee.* As authorized by the Act, the board may appoint an executive committee of not fewer than three directors to serve at its pleasure, to act for it with respect to the board's specifically delegated functions. When making delegations to the executive committee, the board must be specific with regard to the committee's authority and limitations related to the particular delegation. The board may also authorize any of the following to approve membership applications under conditions the board and these bylaws may prescribe: an executive committee; a membership officer(s) appointed by the board from the membership, other than a board member paid as an officer; the financial officer; any assistant to the paid officer of the board or to the financial officer; or any loan officer. No executive committee member or membership officer may be compensated as such.

Section 11. *Investment committee.* The board may appoint an investment committee composed of not less than two, to serve at its pleasure to have charge of making investments under rules and procedures established by the board. No member of the investment committee may be compensated as such. Addendum: The board must list the positions of the board officers and management officials of this credit union. They are as follows:

Select Option 1 if the credit union has a credit committee and Option 2 if it does not have a credit committee.

ARTICLE VIII. OPTION 1 CREDIT COMMITTEE

Section 1. *Credit committee members.* The credit committee consists of ___ members. All the members of the credit committee must be members of this credit union. The number of members of the credit committee must be an odd number and may be changed to not fewer than 3 nor more than 7 by resolution of the board. No reduction in the number of members may be made unless corresponding vacancies exist as a result of deaths, resignations, expiration of terms of office, or other actions provided by these bylaws. A copy of the resolution of the board covering any increase or decrease in the number of committee members must be filed with the official copy of the bylaws of this credit union.

Section 2. *Terms of office.* Regular terms of office for elected credit committee members are for periods of either 2 or 3 years as the board determines: provided, however, that all regular terms are for the same number of years and until the election and qualification of successors. The regular terms are fixed at the beginning, or upon any increase or decrease in the number of committee members, that approximately an equal number of regular terms expire at each annual meeting. Regular terms of office for appointed credit committee members are for periods as determined by the board and as noted in the board's minutes.

Section 3. *Officers of credit committee.* The credit committee chooses from their number a chair and a secretary. The secretary of the committee prepares and maintains full and correct records of all actions taken by it, and those records must be prepared within 3 days after the action. The offices of the chair and secretary may be held by the same person.

Section 4. *Credit committee powers.* The credit committee may, by majority vote of its members, appoint one or more loan officers to serve at its pleasure, and delegate to them the power to approve application for loans or lines of credit, share withdrawals, releases and substitutions of security, within limits specified by the committee and within limits of applicable law and regulations. Not more than one member of the committee may be appointed as a loan officer. Each loan officer must furnish to the committee a record of each approved or not approved transaction within 7 days of the date of the filing of the application or request, and this record becomes a part of the records of the committee. All applications or requests not approved by a loan officer must be acted upon by the committee. No individual may disburse funds of this credit union for any application or share withdrawal which the individual has approved as a loan officer.

Section 5. *Credit committee meetings.* The credit committee holds meetings as the business of this credit union may require, and not less frequently than once a month. Notice of meetings will be given to members of the committee in a manner as the committee may from time to time, by resolution, prescribe.

Section 6. *Credit committee duties.* For each loan or line of credit, the credit committee or loan officer must inquire into the character and financial condition of the applicant and the applicant's sureties, if any, to ascertain their ability to repay fully and promptly the obligations incurred by them and to determine whether the loan or line of credit will be of probable benefit to the borrower. The credit committee and its appointed loan officers should endeavor diligently to assist applicants in solving their financial problems.

Section 7. *Unapproved loans prohibited.* No loan or line of credit may be made unless approved by the committee or a loan officer in accordance with applicable law and regulations.

Section 8. *Lending procedures.* Subject to the limits imposed by applicable law and regulations, these bylaws, and the general policies of the board, the credit committee, or a loan officer, determines the security, if any, required for each application and the terms of repayment. The security furnished must be adequate in quality and character and consistent with sound lending practices. When funds are not available to make all the loans and lines of credit for which there are applications, preference should be given, in all cases, to the smaller applications if the need and credit factors are nearly equal.

ARTICLE VIII. OPTION 2 LOAN OFFICERS (NO CREDIT COMMITTEE)

Section 1. *Records of loan officer; prohibition on loan officer disbursing funds.* Each loan officer must maintain a record of each approved or not approved transaction within 7 days of the filing of the application or request, and that record becomes a part of the records of the credit union. No individual may disburse funds of this credit union for any application or share withdrawal which the individual has approved as a loan officer.

Section 2. *Duties of loan officer.* For each loan or line of credit, the loan officer must inquire into the character and financial condition of the applicant and the applicant's sureties, if any, to ascertain their ability to repay fully and promptly the obligations incurred by them and to determine whether the loan or line of credit will be of probable benefit to the borrower. The loan officers should endeavor diligently to assist applicants in solving their financial problems.

Section 3. *Unapproved loans prohibited.* No loan or line of credit may be made unless approved by a loan officer in accordance with applicable law and regulations.

Section 4. *Lending procedures.* Subject to the limits imposed by law and regulations, these bylaws, and the general policies of the board, a loan officer determines the security if any required for each application and the terms of repayment. The security furnished must be adequate in quality and character and consistent with sound lending practices. When funds are not available to make all the loans and lines of credit for which there are applications, preference should be given, in all cases, to the applications for lesser amounts if the need and credit factors are nearly equal.

ARTICLE IX. SUPERVISORY COMMITTEE

Section 1. *Appointment and membership.* The supervisory committee is appointed by the board from among the members of this credit union, one of whom may be a director other than the financial officer or the compensated officer of the board. The board determines the number of members on the committee, which may not be fewer than 3 nor more than 5. No member of the credit committee, if applicable, or any employee of this credit union may be appointed to the committee. Regular terms of committee members are for periods of 1, 2, or 3 years as the board determines: Provided, however, that all regular terms are for the same number of years and until the appointment and qualification of successors. The regular terms are fixed at the beginning, or upon any increase or decrease in the number of committee members, so that approximately an equal number of regular terms expires at each annual meeting.

Section 2. *Officers of supervisory committee.* The supervisory committee members choose from among their number a chair and a secretary. The secretary of the supervisory committee prepares, maintains, and has custody of full and correct records of all actions taken by it. The offices of chair and secretary may be held by the same person.

Section 3. *Duties of supervisory committee.* a. The supervisory committee makes, or causes to be made, the audits, and prepares and submits the written reports required by the Act and regulations. The committee may employ and use clerical and auditing assistance required to carry out its responsibilities prescribed by this article, and may request the board to provide compensation for this assistance. It will prepare and forward to the Administration required reports.

b. If all director positions become vacant simultaneously, the supervisory committee immediately assumes the role of the board of directors. The supervisory committee acting as the board must generally call and hold a special meeting to elect a board that will serve until the next annual meeting. The special meeting must occur at least 7 but no more than 14 days after all director positions became vacant, and candidates for the board at the special meeting may be nominated by petition or from the floor. However, if the next annual meeting has been scheduled and will occur within 45 days after all the director positions become vacant, the supervisory committee may decide to forego the special meeting and continue serving as the board until the election of new directors at the annual meeting.

c. If the next annual meeting has not been scheduled, but the month and day of the previous year's meeting plus 7 days falls within

45 days after all the director positions become vacant, the supervisory committee acting as the board may decide to forego the special meeting to elect new directors. In this case, the supervisory committee must schedule the annual meeting within 7 days before or after the month and day of the previous annual meeting and continue to serve as the board until directors are elected at the annual meeting.

d. The supervisory committee acting as the board may not act on policy matters. However, directors elected at a special meeting have the same powers as directors elected at the annual meeting.

Section 4. *Verification of accounts.* The supervisory committee will cause the verification of the accounts of members with the records of the financial officer from time to time and not less frequently than as required by the Act and regulations. The committee must maintain a record of this verification.

Section 5. *Powers of supervisory committee—removal of directors and credit committee members.* By unanimous vote, the supervisory committee may suspend until the next meeting of the members any director, board officer, or member of the credit committee. In the event of any suspension, the supervisory committee must call a special meeting of the members to act on the suspension, which meeting must be held not fewer than 7 nor more than 14 days after the suspension. The chair of the committee acts as chair of the meeting unless the members select another person to act as chair.

Section 6. *Powers of supervisory committee—special meetings.* By the affirmative vote of a majority of its members, the supervisory committee may call a special meeting of the members to consider any violation of the provisions of the Act, the regulations, or of the charter or the bylaws of this credit union, or to consider any practice of this credit union which the committee deems to be unsafe or unauthorized.

ARTICLE X. ORGANIZATION MEETING

Section 1. *Initial meeting.* When application is made for a federal credit union charter, the subscribers to the organization certificate must meet for the purpose of electing a board of directors and a credit committee, if applicable. Failure to commence operations within 60 days following receipt of the approved organization certificate is cause for revocation of the charter unless a request for an extension of time has been submitted to and approved by the Regional Director.

Section 2. *Election of directors and credit committee.* The subscribers elect a chair and a secretary for the meeting. The subscribers then elect from their number, or from those eligible to become members of this credit union, a board of directors and a credit committee, if applicable, all to hold office until the first annual meeting of the members and until the election and qualification of their respective successors. If not already a member, every person elected under this section or appointed under Section 3 of this article, must qualify within 30 days by becoming a member. If any person elected as a director or committee member or appointed as a supervisory committee member does not qualify as a member within 30 days of election or appointment, the office will automatically become vacant and be filled by the board.

Section 3. *Election of board officers.* Promptly following the elections held under the provisions of Section 2 of this article, the board must meet and elect the board officers who will hold office until the first meeting of the board of directors following the first annual meeting of the members and until the election and qualification of their respective successors. The board also appoints a supervisory committee at this meeting as provided in Article IX, Section 1, of these bylaws and a credit committee, if applicable. The members so appointed hold office until the first regular meeting of the board following the first annual meeting of the members and until the appointment and qualification of their respective successors.

ARTICLE XI. LOANS AND LINES OF CREDIT TO MEMBERS

Section 1. *Loan purposes.* Loans may only be made to members and for provident or productive purposes in accordance with applicable law and regulations.

The credit union may add business as one of its purposes by placing a comma after "provident" and inserting "business."

Section 2. *Delinquency.* Any member whose loan is delinquent may be required to pay a late charge as determined by the board of directors.

ARTICLE XII. DIVIDENDS

Section 1. *Power of board to declare dividends.* The board establishes dividend periods and declares dividends as permitted by the Act and applicable regulations.

ARTICLE XIII. RESERVED

ARTICLE XIV. EXPULSION AND WITHDRAWAL

Section 1. *Expulsion procedure; expulsion or withdrawal does not affect members' liability or shares.* A member may be expelled by a two-thirds vote of the members present at special meeting called for that purpose, but only after the member has been given the opportunity to be heard. A member also may be expelled under a nonparticipation policy adopted by the board of directors and provided to each member in accordance with the Act. Expulsion or withdrawal will not operate to relieve a member of any liability to this credit union. All amounts paid in on shares by expelled or withdrawing members, before their expulsion or withdrawal, will be paid to them in the order of their withdrawal or expulsion, but only as funds become available and only after deducting any amounts due to this credit union.

ARTICLE XV. MINORS

Section 1. *Minors permitted to own shares.* Shares may be issued in the name of a minor. State law governs the rights of minors to transact business with this credit union.

ARTICLE XVI. GENERAL

Section 1. *Compliance with law and regulation.* All power, authority, duties, and functions of the members, directors, officers, and employees of this credit union, pursuant to the provisions of these bylaws, must be exercised in strict conformity with the provisions of applicable law and regulations, and of the charter and the bylaws of this credit union.

Section 2. *Confidentiality.* The officers, directors, members of committees and employees of this credit union must hold in confidence all transactions of this credit union with its members and all information respecting their personal affairs, except when permitted by state or federal law.

Section 3. *Removal of directors and committee members.* Notwithstanding any other provisions in these bylaws, any director or committee member of this credit union may be removed from office by the affirmative vote of a majority of the members present at a special meeting called for the purpose, but only after an opportunity has been given to be heard. If member votes at a special meeting result in the removal of all directors, the supervisory committee immediately becomes the temporary board of directors and must follow the procedures in Article IX, Section 3.

Section 4. *Conflicts of interest prohibited.* No director, committee member, officer, agent, or employee of this credit union may participate in any manner, directly or indirectly, in the deliberation upon or the determination of any question affecting his or her pecuniary or personal interest or the pecuniary interest of any corporation, partnership, or association (other than this credit union) in which he or she is directly or indirectly interested. In the event of the disqualification of any director respecting any matter presented to the board for deliberation or determination, that director must withdraw from the meeting plus the disqualified director or directors constitute a quorum, the remaining qualified directors may exercise with respect to this matter, by majority vote, all the powers of the board. In the event of the disqualification of any member of the credit committee, if applicable, or the supervisory committee, that committee member must withdraw from the deliberation or determination.

Section 5. *Records.* Copies of the organization certificate of this credit union, its bylaws and any amendments to the bylaws, and any special authorizations by the Administration must be preserved in a place of safekeeping. Copies of the organization certificate and field of membership amendments should be attached as an appendix to these bylaws. Returns of nominations and elections and proceedings of all regular and special meetings of the members and directors must be recorded in the minute books of this credit union. The minutes of the meetings of the members, the board, and the committees must be signed by their respective chairmen or presiding officers and by the persons who serve as secretaries of those meetings.

Section 6. *Availability of credit union records.* All books of account and other records of this credit union must be available at all times to the directors and committee members of this credit union provided they have a proper purpose for obtaining the records. The charter and bylaws of this credit union must be made available for inspection by any member and, if the member requests a copy, it will be provided for a reasonable fee.

Section 7. *Member contact information.* Members must keep the credit union informed of their current address.

Section 8. *Indemnification.* (a) Subject to the limitations in §701.33(c)(5) through (c)(7) of the regulations, the credit union may elect to indemnify to the extent authorized by (check one)

[ ] Law of the State of _____:
[ ] Model Business Corporation Act:

the following individuals from any liability asserted against them and expenses reasonably incurred by them in connection with judicial or administrative proceedings to which they are or may become parties by reason of the performance of their official duties (check as appropriate).

[ ] Current officials
[ ] Former officials
[ ] Current employees
[ ] Former employees

(b) The credit union may purchase and maintain insurance on behalf of the individuals indicated in (a) above against any liability asserted against them and expenses reasonably incurred by them in their official capacities and arising out of the performance of their official duties to the extent such insurance is permitted by the applicable State law or the Model Business Corporation Act.

(c) The term "official" in this bylaw means a person who is a member of the board of directors, credit committee, supervisory committee, other volunteer committee (including elected or appointed loan officers or membership officers), established by the board of directors.

ARTICLE XVII. AMENDMENTS OF BYLAWS AND CHARTER

Section 1. *Amendment procedures.* Amendments of these bylaws may be adopted and amendments of the charter requested by the affirmative vote of two-thirds of the authorized number of members of the board at any duly held meeting of the board if the members of the board have been given prior written notice of the meeting and the notice has contained a copy of the proposed amendment or amendments. No amendment of these bylaws or of the charter may become effective, however, until approved in writing by the NCUA Board.

ARTICLE XVIII. DEFINITIONS

Section 1. *General definitions.* When used in these bylaws the terms:

"Act" means the Federal Credit Union Act, as amended.

"Administration" means the National Credit Union Administration.

"Applicable law and regulations" means the Federal Credit Union Act and rules and regulations issued thereunder or other applicable federal and state statutes and rules and regulations issued thereunder as the context indicates (such as The Higher Education Act of 1965).

"Board" means board of directors of the federal credit union.

"Immediate family member" means spouse, child, sibling, parent, grandparent, grandchild, stepparents, stepchildren, stepsiblings, and adoptive relationships.

"NCUA Board" means the Board of the National Credit Union Administration.

"Regulation" or "regulations" means rules and regulations issued by the NCUA Board.

"Share" or "shares" means all classes of shares and share certificates that may be held in accordance with applicable law and regulations.

[72 FR 61500, Oct. 31, 2007, as amended at 75 FR 34620, June 18, 2010; 75 FR 81386, Dec. 28, 2010]

APPENDIX B TO PART 701—CHARTERING AND FIELD OF MEMBERSHIP MANUAL

CHAPTER 1

FEDERAL CREDIT UNION CHARTERING

I—GOALS OF NCUA CHARTERING POLICY

The National Credit Union Administration's (NCUA) chartering and field of membership policies are directed toward achieving the following goals:
• To encourage the formation of credit unions;
• To uphold the provisions of the Federal Credit Union Act;
• To promote thrift and credit extension;
• To promote credit union safety and soundness; and
• To make quality credit union service available to all eligible persons.

NCUA may grant a charter to single occupational/associational groups, multiple groups, or communities if:
• The occupational, associational, or multiple groups possess an appropriate common bond or the community represents a well-defined local community, neighborhood, or rural district;
• The subscribers are of good character and are fit to represent the proposed credit union; and
• The establishment of the credit union is economically advisable.

Generally, these are the primary criteria that NCUA will consider. In unusual circumstances, however, NCUA may examine other factors, such as other federal law or public policy, in deciding if a charter should be approved.

Unless otherwise noted, the policies outlined in this manual apply only to federal credit unions.

II—TYPES OF CHARTERS

The Federal Credit Union Act recognizes three types of federal credit union charters—single common bond (occupational and associational), multiple common bond (more than one group each having a common bond of occupation or association), and community.

The requirements that must be met to charter a federal credit union are described in Chapter 2. Special rules for credit unions serving low-income groups are described in Chapter 3.

If a federal credit union charter is granted, Section 5 of the charter will describe the credit union's field of membership, which defines those persons and entities eligible for membership. Generally, federal credit unions are only able to grant loans and provide services to persons within the field of membership who have become members of the credit union.

III—SUBSCRIBERS

Federal credit unions are generally organized by persons who volunteer their time and resources and are responsible for determining the interest, commitment, and economic advisability of forming a federal credit union. The organization of a successful federal credit union takes considerable planning and dedication.

National Credit Union Administration

Persons interested in organizing a federal credit union should contact one of the credit union trade associations or the NCUA regional office serving the state in which the credit union will be organized. Lists of NCUA offices and credit union trade associations are shown in the appendices. NCUA will provide information to groups interested in pursuing a federal charter and will assist them in contacting an organizer.

While anyone may organize a credit union, a person with training and experience in chartering new federal credit unions is generally the most effective organizer. However, extensive involvement by the group desiring credit union service is essential.

The functions of the organizer are to provide direction, guidance, and advice on the chartering process. The organizer also provides the group with information about a credit union's functions and purpose as well as technical assistance in preparing and submitting the charter application. Close communication and cooperation between the organizer and the proposed members are critical to the chartering process.

The Federal Credit Union Act requires that seven or more natural persons—the "subscribers"—present to NCUA for approval a sworn organization certificate stating at a minimum:

- The name of the proposed federal credit union;
- The location of the proposed federal credit union and the territory in which it will operate;
- The names and addresses of the subscribers to the certificate and the number of shares subscribed by each;
- The initial par value of the shares;
- The detailed proposed field of membership; and
- The fact that the certificate is made to enable such persons to avail themselves of the advantages of the Federal Credit Union Act.

False statements on any of the required documentation filed in obtaining a federal credit union charter may be grounds for federal criminal prosecution.

IV—ECONOMIC ADVISABILITY

IV.A—General

Before chartering a federal credit union, NCUA must be satisfied that the institution will be viable and that it will provide needed services to its members. Economic advisability, which is a determination that a potential charter will have a reasonable opportunity to succeed, is essential in order to qualify for a credit union charter.

NCUA will conduct an independent on-site investigation of each charter application to ensure that the proposed credit union can be successful. In general, the success of any credit union depends on: (a) The character and fitness of management; (b) the depth of the members' support; and (c) present and projected market conditions.

IV.B—Proposed Management's Character and Fitness

The Federal Credit Union Act requires NCUA to ensure that the subscribers are of good "general character and fitness." Prospective officials and employees will be the subject of credit and background investigations. The investigation report must demonstrate each applicant's ability to effectively handle financial matters. Employees and officials should also be competent, experienced, honest and of good character. Factors that may lead to disapproval of a prospective official or employee include criminal convictions, indictments, and acts of fraud and dishonesty. Further, factors such as serious or unresolved past due credit obligations and bankruptcies disclosed during credit checks may disqualify an individual.

NCUA also needs reasonable assurance that the management team will have the requisite skills—particularly in leadership and accounting—and the commitment to dedicate the time and effort needed to make the proposed federal credit union a success.

Section 701.14 of NCUA's Rules and Regulations sets forth the procedures for NCUA approval of officials of newly chartered credit unions. If the application of a prospective official or employee to serve is not acceptable to the regional director, the group can propose an alternate to act in that individual's place. If the charter applicant feels it is essential that the disqualified individual be retained, the individual may appeal the regional director's decision to the NCUA Board. If an appeal is pursued, action on the application may be delayed. If the appeal is denied by the NCUA Board, an acceptable new applicant must be provided before the charter can be approved.

IV.C—Member Support

Economic advisability is a major factor in determining whether the credit union will be chartered. An important consideration is the degree of support from the field of membership. The charter applicant must be able to demonstrate that membership support is sufficient to ensure viability.

NCUA has not set a minimum field of membership size for chartering a federal credit union. Consequently, groups of any size may apply for a credit union charter and be approved if they demonstrate economic advisability. However, it is important to note that often the size of the group is indicative of the potential for success. For that reason, a charter application with fewer than 3,000 primary potential members (e.g., employees of a corporation or members of an association) may not be economically advisable. Therefore, a charter applicant with a proposed field of membership of fewer than 3,000 primary potential members may have to provide more support than an applicant with a larger field of membership. For example, a small occupational or associational group may be required to demonstrate a commitment for long-term support from the sponsor.

IV.D—Present and Future Market Conditions— Business Plan

The ability to provide effective service to members, compete in the marketplace, and to adapt to changing market conditions are key to the survival of any enterprise. Before NCUA will charter a credit union, a business plan based on realistic and supportable projections and assumptions must be submitted.

The business plan should contain, at a minimum, the following elements:
- Mission statement;
- Analysis of market conditions, including if applicable, geographic, demographic, employment, income, housing, and other economic data;
- Evidence of member support;
- Goals for shares, loans, and for number of members;
- Financial services needed/desired;
- Financial services to be provided to members of all segments within the field of membership;
- How/when services are to be implemented;
- Organizational/management plan addressing qualification and planned training of officials/employees;
- Continuity plan for directors, committee members and management staff;
- Operating facilities, to include office space/equipment and supplies, safeguarding of assets, insurance coverage, etc.;
- Type of record keeping and data processing system;
- Detailed semiannual pro forma financial statements (balance sheet, income and expense projections) for 1st and 2nd year, including assumptions—e.g., loan and dividend rates;
- Plans for operating independently;
- Written policies (shares, lending, investments, funds management, capital accumulation, dividends, collections, etc.);
- Source of funds to pay expenses during initial months of operation, including any subsidies, assistance, etc., and terms or conditions of such resources; and
- Evidence of sponsor commitment (or other source of support) if subsidies are critical to success of the federal credit union. Evidence may be in the form of letters, contracts, financial statements from the sponsor, and any other such document on which the proposed federal credit union can substantiate its projections.

While the business plan may be prepared with outside assistance, the subscribers and proposed officials must understand and support the submitted business plan.

V—Steps in Organizing a Federal Credit Union

V.A—Getting Started

Following the guidance contained throughout this policy, the organizers should submit wording for the proposed field of membership (the persons, organizations and other legal entities the credit union will serve) to NCUA early in the application process for written preliminary approval. The proposed field of membership must meet all common bond or community requirements.

Once the field of membership has been given preliminary approval, and the organizer is satisfied the application has merit, the organizer should conduct an organizational meeting to elect seven to ten persons to serve as subscribers. The subscribers should locate willing individuals capable of serving on the board of directors, credit committee, supervisory committee, and as chief operating officer/manager of the proposed credit union.

Subsequent organizational meetings may be held to discuss the progress of the charter investigation, to announce the proposed slate of officials, and to respond to any questions posed at these meetings.

If NCUA approves the charter application, the subscribers, as their final duty, will elect the board of directors of the proposed federal credit union. The new board of directors will then appoint the supervisory committee.

V.B—Charter Application Documentation

V.B.1—General

As discussed previously in this Chapter, the organizer of a federal credit union charter must, at a minimum, provide evidence that:
- The group(s) possess an appropriate common bond or the geographical area to be served is a well-defined local community, neighborhood, or rural district;
- The subscribers, prospective officials, and employees are of good character and fitness; and
- The establishment of the credit union is economically advisable.

As part of the application process, the organizer must submit the following forms, which are available in appendix 4 of this Manual:
- Federal Credit Union Investigation Report, NCUA 4001;
- Organization Certificate, NCUA 4008;
- Report of Official and Agreement To Serve, NCUA 4012;
- Application and Agreements for Insurance of Accounts, NCUA 9500; and

National Credit Union Administration

• Certification of Resolutions, NCUA 9501. Each of these forms is described in more detail in the following sections.

V.B.2—Federal Credit Union Investigation Report, NCUA 4001

The application for a new federal credit union will be submitted on NCUA 4001. State-chartered credit unions applying for conversion to a federal charter will use NCUA 4000. (See Chapter 4 for a full discussion.) The organizer is required to certify the information and recommend approval or disapproval, based on the investigation of the request.

V.B.3—Organization Certificate, NCUA 4008

This document, which must be completed by the subscribers, includes the seven criteria established by the Federal Credit Union Act. NCUA staff assigned to the case will assist in the proper completion of this document.

V.B.4—Report of Official and Agreement To Serve, NCUA 4012

This form documents general background information of each official and employee of the proposed federal credit union. Each official and employee must complete and sign this form. The organizer must review each of the NCUA 4012s for elements that would prevent the prospective official or employee from serving. Further, such factors as serious, unresolved past due credit obligations and bankruptcies disclosed during credit checks may disqualify an individual.

V.B.5—Application and Agreements for Insurance of Accounts, NCUA 9500

This document contains the agreements with which federal credit unions must comply in order to obtain National Credit Union Share Insurance Fund (NCUSIF) coverage of member accounts. The document must be completed and signed by both the chief executive officer and chief financial officer. A federal credit union must qualify for federal share insurance.

V.B.6—Certification of Resolutions, NCUA 9501

This document certifies that the board of directors of the proposed federal credit union has resolved to apply for NCUSIF insurance of member accounts and has authorized the chief executive officer and recording officer to execute the Application and Agreements for Insurance of Accounts. Both the chief executive officer and recording officer of the proposed federal credit union must sign this form.

VI—NAME SELECTION

It is the responsibility of the federal credit union organizers or officials of an existing credit union to ensure that the proposed federal credit union name or federal credit union name change does not constitute an infringement on the name of any corporation in its trade area. This responsibility also includes researching any service marks or trademarks used by any other corporation (including credit unions) in its trade area. NCUA will ensure, to the extent possible, that the credit union's name:

• Is not already being officially used by another federal credit union;
• Will not be confused with NCUA or another federal or state agency, or with another credit union; and
• Does not include misleading or inappropriate language.

The last three words in the name of every credit union chartered by NCUA must be "Federal Credit Union."

The word "community," while not required, can only be included in the name of federal credit unions that have been granted a community charter.

VII—NCUA REVIEW

VII.A—General

Once NCUA receives a complete charter application package, an acknowledgment of receipt will be sent to the organizer. At some point during the review process, a staff member will be assigned to perform an on-site contact with the proposed officials and others having an interest in the proposed federal credit union.

NCUA staff will review the application package and verify its accuracy and reasonableness. A staff member will inquire into the financial management experience and the suitability and commitment of the proposed officials and employees, and will make an assessment of economic advisability. The staff member will also provide guidance to the subscribers in the proper completion of the Organization Certificate, NCUA 4008.

Credit and background investigations may be conducted concurrently by NCUA with other work being performed by the organizer and subscribers to reduce the likelihood of delays in the chartering process.

The staff member will analyze the prospective credit union's business plan for realistic projections, attainable goals, adequate service to all segments of the field of membership, sufficient start-up capital, and time commitment by the proposed officials and employees. Any concerns will be reviewed with the organizer and discussed with the prospective credit union's officials. Additional on-site contacts by NCUA staff may be necessary. The organizer and subscribers will be expected to take the steps necessary to resolve any issues or concerns. Such resolution efforts may delay processing the application.

NCUA staff will then make a recommendation to the regional director regarding the charter application. The recommendation may include specific provisions to be included in a Letter of Understanding and Agreement. In most cases, NCUA will require the prospective officials to adhere to certain operational guidelines. Generally, the agreement is for a limited term of two to four years. A sample Letter of Understanding and Agreement is found in appendix 2.

VII.B—Regional Director Approval

Once approved, the board of directors of the newly formed federal credit union will receive a signed charter and standard bylaws from the regional director. Additionally, the officials will be advised of the name of the examiner assigned responsibility for supervising and examining the credit union.

VII.C—Regional Director Disapproval

When a regional director disapproves any charter application, in whole or in part, the organizer will be informed in writing of the specific reasons for the disapproval. Where applicable, the regional director will provide information concerning options or suggestions that the applicant could consider for gaining approval or otherwise acquiring credit union service. The letter of denial will include the procedures for appealing the decision.

VII.D—Appeal of Regional Director Decision

If the regional director denies a charter application, in whole or in part, that decision may be appealed to the NCUA Board. An appeal must be sent to the appropriate regional office within 60 days of the date of denial and must address the specific reasons for denial. The regional director will then forward the appeal to the NCUA Board. NCUA central office staff will make an independent review of the facts and present the appeal with a recommendation to the NCUA Board.

Before appealing, the prospective group may, within 30 days of the denial, provide supplemental information to the regional director for reconsideration. A reconsideration will contain new and material evidence addressing the reasons for the initial denial. The regional director will have 30 days from the date of the receipt of the request for reconsideration to make a final decision. If the request is again denied, the applicant may proceed with the appeal process within 60 days of the date of the last denial. A second request for reconsideration will be treated as an appeal to the NCUA Board.

VII.E—Commencement of Operations

Assistance in commencing operations is generally available through the various credit union trade organizations listed in appendix 5.

All new federal credit unions are also encouraged to establish a mentor relationship with a knowledgeable, experienced credit union individual or an existing, well-operated credit union. The mentor should provide guidance and assistance to the new credit union through attendance at meetings and general oversight. Upon request, NCUA will provide assistance in finding a qualified mentor.

VIII—FUTURE SUPERVISION

Each federal credit union will be examined regularly by NCUA to determine that it remains in compliance with applicable laws and regulations and to determine that it does not pose undue risk to the NCUSIF. The examiner will contact the credit union officials shortly after approval of the charter in order to arrange for the initial examination (usually within the first six months of operation).

The examiner will be responsible for monitoring the progress of the credit union and providing the necessary advice and guidance to ensure it is in compliance with applicable laws and regulations. The examiner will also monitor compliance with the terms of any required Letter of Understanding and Agreement. Typically, the examiner will require the credit union to submit copies of monthly board minutes and financial statements.

The Federal Credit Union Act requires all newly chartered credit unions, up to two years after the charter anniversary date, to obtain NCUA approval prior to appointment of any new board member, credit or supervisory committee member, or senior executive officer. Section 701.14 of the NCUA Rules and Regulations sets forth the notice and application requirements. If NCUA issues a Notice of Disapproval, the newly chartered credit union is prohibited from making the change.

NCUA may disapprove an individual serving as a director, committee member or senior executive officer if it finds that the competence, experience, character, or integrity of the individual indicates it would not be in the best interests of the members of the credit union or of the public to permit the individual to be employed by or associated with the credit union. If a Notice of Disapproval is issued, the credit union may appeal the decision to the NCUA Board.

IX—CORPORATE FEDERAL CREDIT UNIONS

A corporate federal credit union is one that is operated primarily for the purpose of serving other credit unions. Corporate federal credit unions operate under and are administered by the NCUA Office of Corporate Credit Unions.

X—GROUPS SEEKING CREDIT UNION SERVICE

NCUA will attempt to assist any group in chartering a credit union or joining an existing credit union. If the group is not eligible for federal credit union service, NCUA will refer the group to the appropriate state supervisory authority where different requirements may apply.

XI—FIELD OF MEMBERSHIP DESIGNATIONS

NCUA will designate a credit union based on the following criteria:

Single Occupational: If a credit union serves a single occupational sponsor, such as ABC Corporation, it will be designated as an occupational credit union. A single occupational common bond credit union may also serve a trade, industry, or profession (TIP), such as all teachers.

Single Associational: If a credit union serves a single associational sponsor, such as the Knights of Columbus, it will be designated as an associational credit union.

Multiple Common Bond: If a credit union serves more than one group, each of which has a common bond of occupation and/or association, it will be designated as a multiple common bond credit union.

Community: All community credit unions will be designated as such, followed by a description of their geographic boundaries (e.g., city or county).

Credit unions desiring to confirm or submit an application to change their designations should contact the appropriate NCUA regional office.

XII—FOREIGN BRANCHING

Federal credit unions are permitted to serve foreign nationals within their fields of membership wherever they reside provided they have the ability, resources, and management expertise to serve such persons. Before a credit union opens a branch outside the United States, it must submit an application to do so and have prior written approval of the regional director. A federal credit union may establish a service facility on a United States military installation or United States embassy without prior NCUA approval.

CHAPTER 2

FIELD OF MEMBERSHIP REQUIREMENTS FOR FEDERAL CREDIT UNIONS

I—INTRODUCTION

I.A.1—General

As set forth in Chapter 1, the Federal Credit Union Act provides for three types of federal credit union charters—single common bond (occupational or associational), multiple common bond (multiple groups), and community. Section 109 (12 U.S.C. 1759) of the Federal Credit Union Act sets forth the membership criteria for each of these three types of credit unions.

The field of membership, which is specified in Section 5 of the charter, defines those persons and entities eligible for membership. A single common bond federal credit union consists of one group having a common bond of occupation or association. A multiple common bond federal credit union consists of more than one group, each of which has a common bond of occupation or association. A community federal credit union consists of persons or organizations within a well-defined local community, neighborhood, or rural district.

Once chartered, a federal credit union can amend its field of membership; however, the same common bond or community requirements for chartering the credit union must be satisfied. Since there are differences in the three types of charters, special rules, which are fully discussed in the following sections of this Chapter, may apply to each.

I.A.2—Special Low-Income Rules

Generally, federal credit unions can only grant loans and provide services to persons who have joined the credit union. The Federal Credit Union Act states that one of the purposes of federal credit unions is "to serve the productive and provident credit needs of individuals of modest means." Although field of membership requirements are applicable, special rules set forth in Chapter 3 may apply to low-income designated credit unions and those credit unions assisting low-income groups or to a federal credit union that adds an underserved community to its field of membership.

II—OCCUPATIONAL COMMON BOND

II.A.1—General

A single occupational common bond federal credit union may include in its field of membership all persons and entities who share that common bond. NCUA permits a person's membership eligibility in a single occupational common bond group to be established in five ways:

• Employment (or a long-term contractual relationship equivalent to employment) in a single corporation or other legal entity makes that person part of a single occupational common bond;

• Employment in a corporation or other legal entity with a controlling ownership interest (which shall not be less than 10 percent) in or by another legal entity makes that person part of a single occupational common bond;

• Employment in a corporation or other legal entity which is related to another legal entity (such as a company under contract and possessing a strong dependency relationship with another company) makes that person part of a single occupational common bond;

• Employment or attendance at a school makes that person part of a single occupational common bond (see Chapter 2, Section III.A.1); or

• Employment in the same Trade, Industry, or Profession (TIP) (see Chapter 2, Section II.A.2).

A geographic limitation is not a requirement for a single occupational common bond. However, for purposes of describing the field of membership, the geographic areas being served may be included in the charter. For example:

• Employees, officials, and persons who work regularly under contract in Miami, Florida for ABC Corporation and subsidiaries;

• Employees of ABC Corporation who are paid from * * *;

• Employees of ABC Corporation who are supervised from * * *;

• Employees of ABC Corporation who are headquartered in * * *; and/or

• Employees of ABC Corporation who work in the United States.

The corporation or other legal entity (i.e., the employer) may also be included in the common bond—e.g., "ABC Corporation." The corporation or legal entity will be defined in the last clause in Section 5 of the credit union's charter.

A charter applicant must provide documentation to establish that the single occupational common bond requirement has been met.

Some examples of single occupational common bonds are:

• Employees of the Hunt Manufacturing Company who work in West Chester, Pennsylvania. (common bond—same employer with geographic definition);

• Employees of the Buffalo Manufacturing Company who work in the United States. (common bond—same employer with geographic definition);

• Employees, elected and appointed officials of municipal government in Parma, Ohio. (common bond—same employer with geographic definition);

• Employees of Johnson Soap Company and its majority owned subsidiary, Johnson Toothpaste Company, who work in, are paid from, are supervised from, or are headquartered in Augusta and Portland, Maine. (common bond—parent and subsidiary company with geographic definition);

• Employees of MMLLJS contractor who work regularly at the U.S. Naval Shipyard in Bremerton, Washington. (common bond—employees of contractors with geographic definition);

• Employees, doctors, medical staff, technicians, medical and nursing students who work in or are paid from the Newport Beach Medical Center, Newport Beach, California. (single corporation with geographic definition);

• Employees of JLS, Incorporated and MJM, Incorporated working for the LKM Joint Venture Company in Catalina Island, California. (common bond—same employer—ongoing dependent relationship);

• Employees of and students attending Georgetown University. (common bond—same occupation);

• Employees of all the schools supervised by the Timbrook Board of Education in Timbrook, Georgia. (common bond—same employer); or

• All licensed nurses in Fairfax County, Virginia. (occupational common bond TIP).

Some examples of insufficiently defined single occupational common bonds are:

• Employees of manufacturing firms in Seattle, Washington. (no defined occupational sponsor; overly broad TIP);

• Persons employed or working in Chicago, Illinois. (no occupational common bond).

II.A.2—Trade, Industry, or Profession

A common bond based on employment in a trade, industry, or profession can include employment at any number of corporations or other legal entities that—while not under common ownership—have a common bond by virtue of producing similar products, providing similar services, or participating in the same type of business.

While proposed or existing single common bond credit unions have some latitude in defining a trade, industry, or profession occupational common bond, it cannot be defined so broadly as to include groups in fields which are not closely related. For example, the manufacturing industry, energy industry, communications industry, retail industry, or entertainment industry would not qualify as a TIP because each industry lacks the necessary commonality. However, textile workers, realtors, nurses, teachers, police officers, or U.S. military personnel are closely related and each would qualify as a TIP.

The common bond relationship must be one that demonstrates a narrow commonality of interests within a specific trade, industry, or profession. If a credit union wants to serve a physician TIP, it can serve all physicians, but that does not mean it can also serve all clerical staff in the physicians' offices. However, if the TIP is based on the health care industry, then clerical staff would be able to be served by the credit union because they work in the same industry and have the same commonality of interests.

National Credit Union Administration

If a credit union wants to include the airline services industry, it can serve airline and airport personnel but not passengers. Clients or customers of the TIP are not eligible for credit union membership (e.g., patients in hospitals). Any company that is involved in more than one industry cannot be included in an industry TIP (e.g., a company that makes tobacco products, food products, and electronics). However, employees of these companies may be eligible for membership in a variety of trade/profession occupational common bond TIPs.

Since a TIP must be narrowly defined, it cannot include third party vendors and other suppliers. For example, the steel suppliers to the automobile industry would not be part of the automobile industry TIP. However, the automobile industry includes manufacturers and their automobile dealerships.

In general, except for credit unions currently serving a national field of membership or operating in multiple states, a geographic limitation is required for a TIP credit union. The geographic limitation will be part of the credit union's charter and generally correspond to its current or planned operational area. More than one federal credit union may serve the same trade, industry, or profession, even if both credit unions are in the same geographic location.

This type of occupational common bond is only available to single common bond credit unions. A TIP cannot be added to a multiple common bond or community field of membership.

To obtain a TIP designation, the proposed or existing credit union must submit a request to the regional director. New charter applicants must follow the documentation requirements in Chapter 1. New charter applicants and existing credit unions must submit a business plan on how the credit union will serve the group with the request to serve the TIP. The business plan also must address how the credit union will verify the TIP. Examples of such verification include state licenses, professional licenses, organizational memberships, pay statements, union membership, or employer certification. The regional director must approve this type of field of membership before a credit union can serve a TIP. Credit unions converting to a TIP can retain members of record but cannot add new members from its previous group or groups, unless it is part of the TIP.

Section II.B on Occupational Common Bond Amendments does not apply to a TIP common bond. Removing or changing a geographical limitation will be processed as a housekeeping amendment. If safety and soundness concerns are present, the regional director may require additional information before the request can be processed.

Section II.H, on Other Persons Eligible for Credit Union Membership, applies to TIP based credit unions except for the corporate account provision which only applies to industry based TIPs. Credit unions with industry based TIPs may include corporations as members because they have the same commonality of interests as all employees in the industry. For example, an airline service TIP (industry) can serve an airline carrier (corporate account); however, a nurses TIP (profession) could not serve a hospital (corporate account) because not everyone working in the hospital shares the same profession.

If a TIP designated credit union wishes to convert to a different TIP or employer-based occupational common bond, or different charter type, it only retains members of record after the conversion. The regional director, for safety and soundness reasons, may approve a TIP designated credit union to convert to its original field of membership.

II.B—Occupational Common Bond Amendments

II.B.1—General

Section 5 of every single occupational federal credit union's charter defines the field of membership the credit union can legally serve. Only those persons or legal entities specified in the field of membership can be served. There are a number of instances in which Section 5 must be amended by NCUA.

First, a group sharing the credit union's common bond is added to the field of membership. This may occur through various ways including agreement between the group and the credit union directly, or through a merger, corporate acquisition, purchase and assumption (P&A), or spin-off.

Second, if the entire field of membership is acquired by another corporation, the credit union can serve the employees of the new corporation and any subsidiaries after receiving NCUA approval.

Third, a federal credit union qualifies to change its common bond from:

• A single occupational common bond to a single associational common bond;
• A single occupational common bond to a community charter; or
• A single occupational common bond to a multiple common bond.

Fourth, a federal credit union removes a portion of the group from its field of membership through agreement with the group, a spin-off, or because a portion of the group is no longer in existence.

An existing single occupational common bond federal credit union that submits a request to amend its charter must provide documentation to establish that the occupational common bond requirement has been met. The regional director must approve all amendments to an occupational common bond credit union's field of membership.

II.B.2—Corporate Restructuring

If the single common bond group that comprises a federal credit union's field of membership undergoes a substantial restructuring, the result is often that portions of the group are sold or spun off. This requires a change to the credit union's field of membership. NCUA will not permit a single common bond credit union to maintain in its field of membership a sold or spun-off group to which it has been providing service unless the group otherwise qualifies for membership in the credit union or the credit union converts to a multiple common bond credit union.

If the group comprising the single common bond of the credit union merges with, or is acquired by, another group, the credit union can serve the new group resulting from the merger or acquisition after receiving a housekeeping amendment.

II.B.3—Economic Advisability

Prior to granting a common bond expansion, NCUA will examine the amendment's likely effect on the credit union's operations and financial condition. In most cases, the information needed for analyzing the effect of adding a particular group will be available to NCUA through the examination and financial and statistical reports; however, in particular cases, a regional director may require additional information prior to making a decision.

II.B.4—Documentation Requirements

A federal credit union requesting a common bond expansion must submit an Application for Field of Membership Amendment (NCUA 4015-EZ) to the appropriate NCUA regional director. An authorized credit union representative must sign the request.

II.C—NCUA'S PROCEDURES FOR AMENDING THE FIELD OF MEMBERSHIP

II.C.1—General

All requests for approval to amend a federal credit union's charter must be submitted to the appropriate regional director.

II.C.2—Regional Director's Decision

NCUA staff will review all amendment requests in order to ensure compliance with NCUA policy.

Before acting on a proposed amendment, the regional director may require an on-site review. In addition, the regional director may, after taking into account the significance of the proposed field of membership amendment, require the applicant to submit a business plan addressing specific issues.

The financial and operational condition of the requesting credit union will be considered in every instance. NCUA will carefully consider the economic advisability of expanding the field of membership of a credit union with financial or operational problems.

In most cases, field of membership amendments will only be approved for credit unions that are operating satisfactorily. Generally, if a federal credit union is having difficulty providing service to its current membership, or is experiencing financial or other operational problems, it may have more difficulty serving an expanded field of membership.

Occasionally, however, an expanded field of membership may provide the basis for reversing current financial problems. In such cases, an amendment to expand the field of membership may be granted notwithstanding the credit union's financial or operational problems. The applicant credit union must clearly establish that the expanded field of membership is in the best interest of the members and will not increase the risk to the NCUSIF.

II.C.3—Regional Director Approval

If the regional director approves the requested amendment, the credit union will be issued an amendment to Section 5 of its charter.

II.C.4—Regional Director Disapproval

When a regional director disapproves any application, in whole or in part, to amend the field of membership under this chapter, the applicant will be informed in writing of the:

• Specific reasons for the action;
• Options to consider, if appropriate, for gaining approval; and
• Appeal procedure.

II.C.5—Appeal of Regional Director Decision

If a field of membership expansion request, merger, or spin-off is denied by the regional director, the federal credit union may appeal the decision to the NCUA Board. An appeal must be sent to the appropriate regional office within 60 days of the date of denial, and must address the specific reason(s) for the denial. The regional director will then forward the appeal to the NCUA Board. NCUA central office staff will make an independent review of the facts and present the appeal to the Board with a recommendation.

Before appealing, the credit union may, within 30 days of the denial, provide supplemental information to the regional director for reconsideration. A reconsideration will contain new and material evidence addressing the reasons for the initial denial. The regional director will have 30 days from the date of the receipt of the request for reconsideration to make a final decision. If the request is again denied, the applicant may proceed with the appeal process within 60 days

National Credit Union Administration

of the date of the last denial. A second request for reconsideration will be treated as an appeal to the NCUA Board.

II.D—MERGERS, PURCHASE AND ASSUMPTIONS, AND SPIN-OFFS

In general, other than the addition of common bond groups, there are three additional ways a federal credit union with a single occupational common bond can expand its field of membership:
- By taking in the field of membership of another credit union through a common bond or emergency merger;
- By taking in the field of membership of another credit union through a common bond or emergency purchase and assumption (P&A); or
- By taking a portion of another credit union's field of membership through a common bond spin-off.

II.D.1—Mergers

Generally, the requirements applicable to field of membership expansions found in this chapter apply to mergers where the continuing credit union has a federal charter. That is, the two credit unions must share a common bond.

Where the merging credit union is state-chartered, the common bond rules applicable to a federal credit union apply.

Mergers must be approved by the NCUA regional director where the continuing credit union is headquartered, with the concurrence of the regional director of the merging credit union, and, as applicable, the state regulators.

If a single occupational credit union wants to merge into a multiple common bond or community credit union, Section IV.D or Section V.D of this Chapter, respectively, should be reviewed.

II.D.2—Emergency Mergers

An emergency merger may be approved by NCUA without regard to common bond or other legal constraints. An emergency merger involves NCUA's direct intervention and approval. The credit union to be merged must either be insolvent or in danger of insolvency, as defined in the Glossary, and NCUA must determine that:
- An emergency requiring expeditious action exists;
- Other alternatives are not reasonably available; and
- The public interest would best be served by approving the merger.

If not corrected, conditions that could lead to insolvency include, but are not limited to:
- Abandonment by management;
- Loss of sponsor;
- Serious and persistent recordkeeping problems; or
- Serious and persistent operational concerns.

In an emergency merger situation, NCUA will take an active role in finding a suitable merger partner (continuing credit union). NCUA is primarily concerned that the continuing credit union has the financial strength and management expertise to absorb the troubled credit union without adversely affecting its own financial condition and stability.

As a stipulated condition to an emergency merger, the field of membership of the merging credit union may be transferred intact to the continuing federal credit union without regard to any common bond restrictions. Under this authority, therefore, a single occupational common bond federal credit union may take into its field of membership any dissimilar charter type.

The common bond characteristic of the continuing credit union in an emergency merger does not change. That is, even though the merging credit union is a multiple common bond or community, the continuing credit union will remain a single common bond credit union. Similarly, if the merging credit union is also an unlike single common bond, the continuing credit union will remain a single common bond credit union. Future common bond expansions will be based on the continuing credit union's original single common bond.

Emergency mergers involving federally insured credit unions in different NCUA regions must be approved by the regional director where the continuing credit union is headquartered, with the concurrence of the regional director of the merging credit union and, as applicable, the state regulators.

II.D.3—Purchase and Assumption (P&A)

Another alternative for acquiring the field of membership of a failing credit union is through a consolidation known as a P&A. A P&A has limited application because, in most cases, the failing credit union must be placed into involuntary liquidation. In the few instances where a P&A may be appropriate, the assuming federal credit union, as with emergency mergers, may acquire the entire field of membership if the emergency merger criteria are satisfied. However, if the P&A does not meet the emergency merger criteria, it must be processed under the common bond requirements.

In a P&A processed under the emergency criteria, specified loans, shares, and certain other designated assets and liabilities, without regard to common bond restrictions, may also be acquired without changing the character of the continuing federal credit union for purposes of future field of membership amendments.

If the purchased and/or assumed credit union's field of membership does not share a common bond with the purchasing and/or assuming credit union, then the continuing credit union's original common bond will be controlling for future common bond expansions.

P&As involving federally insured credit unions in different NCUA regions must be approved by the regional director where the continuing credit union is headquartered, with the concurrence of the regional director of the purchased and/or assumed credit union and, as applicable, the state regulators.

II.D.4—Spin-Offs

A spin-off occurs when, by agreement of the parties, a portion of the field of membership, assets, liabilities, shares, and capital of a credit union are transferred to a new or existing credit union. A spin-off is unique in that usually one credit union has a field of membership expansion and the other loses a portion of its field of membership.

All common bond requirements apply regardless of whether the spun-off group becomes a new credit union or goes to an existing federal charter.

The request for approval of a spin-off must be supported with a plan that addresses, at a minimum:
- Why the spin-off is being requested;
- What part of the field of membership is to be spun off;
- Whether the affected credit unions have a common bond (applies only to single occupational credit unions);
- Which assets, liabilities, shares, and capital are to be transferred;
- The financial impact the spin-off will have on the affected credit unions;
- The ability of the acquiring credit union to effectively serve the new members;
- The proposed spin-off date; and
- Disclosure to the members of the requirements set forth above.

The spin-off request must also include current financial statements from the affected credit unions and the proposed voting ballot.

For federal credit unions spinning off a group, membership notice and voting requirements and procedures are the same as for mergers (see Part 708 of the NCUA Rules and Regulations), except that only the members directly affected by the spin-off—those whose shares are to be transferred—are permitted to vote. Members whose shares are not being transferred will not be afforded the opportunity to vote. All members of the group to be spun off (whether they voted in favor, against, or not at all) will be transferred if the spin-off is approved by the voting membership. Voting requirements for federally insured state credit unions are governed by state law.

Spin-offs involving federally insured credit unions in different NCUA regions must be approved by all regional directors where the credit unions are headquartered and the state regulators, as applicable. Spin-offs in the same region also require approval by the state regulator, as applicable.

II.E—Overlaps

II.E.1—General

An overlap exists when a group of persons is eligible for membership in two or more credit unions. NCUA will permit single occupational federal credit unions to overlap any other charter without performing an overlap analysis.

II.E.2—Organizational Restructuring

A federal credit union's field of membership will always be governed by the common bond descriptions contained in Section 5 of its charter. Where a sponsor organization expands its operations internally, by acquisition or otherwise, the credit union may serve these new entrants to its field of membership if they are part of the common bond described in Section 5. NCUA will permit a complete overlap of the credit unions' fields of membership.

If a sponsor organization sells off a group, new members can no longer be served unless they otherwise qualify for membership in the credit union or it converts to a multiple common bond charter.

Credit unions must submit documentation explaining the restructuring and providing information regarding the new organizational structure.

II.E.3—Exclusionary Clauses

An exclusionary clause is a limitation precluding the credit union from serving the primary members of a portion of a group otherwise included in its field of membership. NCUA no longer grants exclusionary clauses. Those granted prior to the adoption of this new chartering manual will remain in effect unless the credit unions agree to remove them or one of the affected credit unions submits a housekeeping amendment to have it removed.

II.F—Charter Conversion

A single occupational common bond federal credit union may apply to convert to a community charter provided the field of membership requirements of the community charter are met. Groups within the existing charter which cannot qualify in the new charter cannot be served except for members of record, or groups or communities obtained in an emergency merger or P&A. A credit union must notify all groups that will be removed from the field of membership as a result of conversion. Members of record can continue to be served. Also, in order to support a case for a conversion, the applicant federal credit union may be required to develop a detailed business plan as specified in Chapter 2, Section V.A.3.

A single occupational common bond federal credit union may apply to convert to a multiple common bond charter by adding a non-common bond group that is within a reasonable proximity of a service facility. Groups within the existing charter may be retained and continue to be served. However, future amendments, including any expansions of the original single common bond group, must be done in accordance with multiple common bond policy.

II.G—REMOVAL OF GROUPS FROM THE FIELD OF MEMBERSHIP

A credit union may request removal of a portion of the common bond group from its field of membership for various reasons. The most common reasons for this type of amendment are:
- The group is within the field of membership of two credit unions and one wishes to discontinue service;
- The federal credit union cannot continue to provide adequate service to the group;
- The group has ceased to exist;
- The group does not respond to repeated requests to contact the credit union or refuses to provide needed support; or
- The group initiates action to be removed from the field of membership.

When a federal credit union requests an amendment to remove a group from its field of membership, the regional director will determine why the credit union desires to remove the group. If the regional director concurs with the request, membership will continue for those who are already members under the "once a member, always a member" provision of the Federal Credit Union Act.

II.H—OTHER PERSONS ELIGIBLE FOR CREDIT UNION MEMBERSHIP

A number of persons, by virtue of their close relationship to a common bond group, may be included, at the charter applicant's option, in the field of membership. These include the following:
- Spouses of persons who died while within the field of membership of this credit union;
- Employees of this credit union;
- Persons retired as pensioners or annuitants from the above employment;
- Volunteers;
- Members of the immediate family or household;
- Organizations of such persons; and
- Corporate or other legal entities in this charter.

Immediate family is defined as spouse, child, sibling, parent, grandparent, or grandchild. This includes stepparents, stepchildren, stepsiblings, and adoptive relationships.

Household is defined as persons living in the same residence maintaining a single economic unit.

Membership eligibility is extended only to individuals who are members of an "immediate family or household" of a credit union member. It is not necessary for the primary member to join the credit union in order for the immediate family or household member of the primary member to join, provided the immediate family or household clause is included in the field of membership. However, it is necessary for the immediate family member or household member to first join in order for that person's immediate family member or household member to join the credit union. A credit union can adopt a more restrictive definition of immediate family or household.

Volunteers, by virtue of their close relationship with a sponsor group, may be included. Examples include volunteers working at a hospital or school.

Under the Federal Credit Union Act, once a person becomes a member of the credit union, such person may remain a member of the credit union until the person chooses to withdraw or is expelled from the membership of the credit union. This is commonly referred to as "once a member, always a member." The "once a member, always a member" provision does not prevent a credit union from restricting services to members who are no longer within the field of membership.

III—ASSOCIATIONAL COMMON BOND

III.A.1—General

A single associational federal credit union may include in its field of membership, regardless of location, all members and employees of a recognized association. A single associational common bond consists of individuals (natural persons) and/or groups (non-natural persons) whose members participate in activities developing common loyalties, mutual benefits, and mutual interests. Separately chartered associational groups can establish a single common bond relationship if they are integrally related and share common goals and purposes. For example, two or more churches of the same denomination, Knights of Columbus Councils, or locals of the same union can qualify as a single associational common bond.

Individuals and groups eligible for membership in a single associational credit union can include the following:
- Natural person members of the association (for example, members of a union or church members);
- Non-natural person members of the association;

- Employees of the association (for example, employees of the labor union or employees of the church); and
- The association.

Generally, a single associational common bond does not include a geographic definition and can operate nationally. However, a proposed or existing federal credit union may limit its field of membership to a single association or geographic area. NCUA may impose a geographic limitation if it is determined that the applicant credit union does not have the ability to serve a larger group or there are other operational concerns. All single associational common bonds should include a definition of the group that may be served based on the association's charter, bylaws, and any other equivalent documentation.

The common bond for an associational group cannot be established simply on the basis that the association exists. In determining whether a group satisfies associational common bond requirements for a federal credit union charter, NCUA will consider the totality of the circumstances, which includes:
- Whether members pay dues;
- Whether members participate in the furtherance of the goals of the association;
- Whether the members have voting rights. To meet this requirement, members need not vote directly for an officer, but may vote for a delegate who in turn represents the members' interests;
- Whether the association maintains a membership list;
- Whether the association sponsors other activities;
- The association's membership eligibility requirements; and
- The frequency of meetings.

A support group whose members are continually changing or whose duration is temporary may not meet the single associational common bond criteria. Each class of member will be evaluated based on the totality of the circumstances. Individuals or honorary members who only make donations to the association are not eligible to join the credit union.

Educational groups—for example, parent-teacher organizations, alumni associations, and student organizations in any school—and church groups may constitute associational common bonds.

Student groups (e.g., students enrolled at a public, private, or parochial school) may constitute either an associational or occupational common bond. For example, students enrolled at a church sponsored school could share a single associational common bond with the members of that church and may qualify for a federal credit union charter. Similarly, students enrolled at a university, as a group by itself, or in conjunction with the faculty and employees of the school, could share a single occupational common bond and may qualify for a federal credit union charter.

The terminology "Alumni of Jacksonville State University" is insufficient to demonstrate an associational common bond. To qualify as an association, the alumni association must meet the requirements for an associational common bond. The alumni of a school must first join the alumni association, and not merely be alumni of the school to be eligible for membership.

Homeowner associations, tenant groups, consumer groups, and other groups of persons having an "interest in" a particular cause and certain consumer cooperatives may also qualify as an association.

Associations based primarily on a client-customer relationship do not meet associational common bond requirements. However, having an incidental client-customer relationship does not preclude an associational charter as long as the associational common bond requirements are met. For example, a fraternal association that offers insurance, which is not a condition of membership, may qualify as a valid associational common bond.

Applicants for a single associational common bond federal credit union charter or a field of membership amendment to include an association must provide, at the request of the regional director, a copy of the association's charter, bylaws, or other equivalent documentation, including any legal documents required by the state or other governing authority.

The associational sponsor itself may also be included in the field of membership—e.g., "Sprocket Association"—and will be shown in the last clause of the field of membership.

III.A.2—Subsequent Changes to Association's Bylaws

If the association's membership or geographical definitions in its charter and bylaws are changed subsequent to the effective date stated in the field of membership, the credit union must submit the revised charter or bylaws for NCUA's consideration and approval prior to serving members of the association added as a result of the change.

III.A.3—Sample Single Associational Common Bonds

Some examples of associational common bonds are:
- Regular members of Locals 10 and 13, IBEW, in Florida, who qualify for membership in accordance with their charter and bylaws in effect on May 20, 2001;
- Members of the Hoosier Farm Bureau in Grant, Logan, or Lee Counties of Indiana, who qualify for membership in accordance with its charter and bylaws in effect on March 7, 1997;

- Members of the Shalom Congregation in Chevy Chase, Maryland;
- Regular members of the Corporate Executives Association, located in Westchester, New York, who qualify for membership in accordance with its charter and bylaws in effect on December 1, 1997;
- Members of the University of Wisconsin Alumni Association, located in Green Bay, Wisconsin;
- Members of the Marine Corps Reserve Officers Association; or
- Members of St. John's Methodist Church and St. Luke's Methodist Church, located in Toledo, Ohio.

Some examples of insufficiently defined single associational common bonds are:
- All Lutherans in the United States (too broadly defined); or
- Veterans of U.S. military service (group is too broadly defined; no formal association of all members of the group).

Some examples of unacceptable single associational common bonds are:
- Alumni of Amos University (no formal association);
- Customers of Fleetwood Insurance Company (policyholders or primarily customer/client relationships do not meet associational standards);
- Employees of members of the Reston, Virginia, Chamber of Commerce (not a sufficiently close tie to the associational common bond); or
- Members of St. John's Lutheran Church and St. Mary's Catholic Church located in Anniston, Alabama (churches are not of the same denomination).

III.B—ASSOCIATIONAL COMMON BOND AMENDMENTS

III.B.1—General

Section 5 of every associational federal credit union's charter defines the field of membership the credit union can legally serve. Only those persons who, or legal entities that, join the credit union and are specified in the field of membership can be served. There are three instances in which Section 5 must be amended by NCUA.

First, a group that shares the credit union's common bond is added to the field of membership. This may occur through various ways including agreement between the group and the credit union directly, or through a merger, purchase and assumption (P&A), or spin-off.

Second, a federal credit union qualifies to change its common bond from:
- A single associational common bond to a single occupational common bond;
- A single associational common bond to a community charter; or
- A single associational common bond to a multiple common bond.

Third, a federal credit union removes a portion of the group from its field of membership through agreement with the group, a spin-off, or a portion of the group that is no longer in existence.

An existing single associational federal credit union that submits a request to amend its charter must provide documentation to establish that the associational common bond requirement has been met. The regional director must approve all amendments to an associational common bond credit union's field of membership.

III.B.2—Organizational Restructuring

If the single common bond group that comprises a federal credit union's field of membership undergoes a substantial restructuring, the result is often that portions of the group are sold or spun off. This is an event requiring a change to the credit union's field of membership. NCUA may not permit a single associational credit union to maintain in its field of membership a sold or spun-off group to which it has been providing service unless the group otherwise qualifies for membership in the credit union or the credit union converts to a multiple common bond credit union.

If the group comprising the single common bond of the credit union merges with, or is acquired by, another group, the credit union can serve the new group resulting from the merger or acquisition after receiving a housekeeping amendment.

III.B.3—Economic Advisability

Prior to granting a common bond expansion, NCUA will examine the amendment's likely impact on the credit union's operations and financial condition. In most cases, the information needed for analyzing the effect of adding a particular group will be available to NCUA through the examination and financial and statistical reports; however, in particular cases, a regional director may require additional information prior to making a decision.

III.B.4—Documentation Requirements

A federal credit union requesting a common bond expansion must submit an Application for Field of Membership Amendment (NCUA 4015-EZ) to the appropriate NCUA regional director. An authorized credit union representative must sign the request.

III.C—NCUA PROCEDURES FOR AMENDING THE FIELD OF MEMBERSHIP

III.C.1—General

All requests for approval to amend a federal credit union's charter must be submitted to the appropriate regional director.

III.C.2—Regional Director's Decision

NCUA staff will review all amendment requests in order to ensure conformance to NCUA policy.

Before acting on a proposed amendment, the regional director may require an on-site review. In addition, the regional director may, after taking into account the significance of the proposed field of membership amendment, require the applicant to submit a business plan addressing specific issues.

The financial and operational condition of the requesting credit union will be considered in every instance. The economic advisability of expanding the field of membership of a credit union with financial or operational problems must be carefully considered.

In most cases, field of membership amendments will only be approved for credit unions that are operating satisfactorily. Generally, if a federal credit union is having difficulty providing service to its current membership, or is experiencing financial or other operational problems, it may have more difficulty serving an expanded field of membership.

Occasionally, however, an expanded field of membership may provide the basis for reversing current financial problems. In such cases, an amendment to expand the field of membership may be granted notwithstanding the credit union's financial or operational problems. The applicant credit union must clearly establish that the expanded field of membership is in the best interest of the members and will not increase the risk to the NCUSIF.

III.C.3—Regional Director Approval

If the regional director approves the requested amendment, the credit union will be issued an amendment to Section 5 of its charter.

III.C.4—Regional Director Disapproval

When a regional director disapproves any application, in whole or in part, to amend the field of membership under this chapter, the applicant will be informed in writing of the:
- Specific reasons for the action;
- Options to consider, if appropriate, for gaining approval; and
- Appeal procedures.

III.C.5—Appeal of Regional Director Decision

If a field of membership expansion request, merger, or spin-off is denied by the regional director, the federal credit union may appeal the decision to the NCUA Board. An appeal must be sent to the appropriate regional office within 60 days of the date of denial and must address the specific reason(s) for the denial. The regional director will then forward the appeal to the NCUA Board. NCUA central office staff will make an independent review of the facts and present the appeal to the NCUA Board with a recommendation.

Before appealing, the credit union may, within 30 days of the denial, provide supplemental information to the regional director for reconsideration. A reconsideration will contain new and material evidence addressing the reasons for the initial denial. The regional director will have 30 days from the date of the receipt of the request for reconsideration to make a final decision. If the request is again denied, the applicant may proceed with the appeal process within 60 days of the date of the last denial. A second request for reconsideration will be treated as an appeal to the NCUA Board.

III.D—MERGERS, PURCHASE AND ASSUMPTIONS, AND SPIN-OFFS

In general, other than the addition of common bond groups, there are three additional ways a federal credit union with a single associational common bond can expand its field of membership:
- By taking in the field of membership of another credit union through a common bond or emergency merger;
- By taking in the field of membership of another credit union through a common bond or emergency purchase and assumption (P&A); or
- By taking a portion of another credit union's field of membership through a common bond spin-off.

III.D.1—Mergers

Generally, the requirements applicable to field of membership expansions found in this section apply to mergers where the continuing credit union is a federal charter. That is, the two credit unions must share a common bond.

Where the merging credit union is state-chartered, the common bond rules applicable to a federal credit union apply.

Mergers must be approved by the NCUA regional director where the continuing credit union is headquartered, with the concurrence of the regional director of the merging credit union, and, as applicable, the state regulators.

If a single associational credit union wants to merge into a multiple common bond or community credit union, Section IV.D or Section V.D of this Chapter, respectively, should be reviewed.

III.D.2—Emergency Mergers

An emergency merger may be approved by NCUA without regard to common bond or other legal constraints. An emergency merger involves NCUA's direct intervention and approval. The credit union to be merged

must either be insolvent or in danger of insolvency, as defined in the Glossary, and NCUA must determine that:
• An emergency requiring expeditious action exists;
• Other alternatives are not reasonably available; and
• The public interest would best be served by approving the merger.

If not corrected, conditions that could lead to insolvency include, but are not limited to:
• Abandonment by management;
• Loss of sponsor;
• Serious and persistent record keeping problems; or
• Serious and persistent operational concerns.

In an emergency merger situation, NCUA will take an active role in finding a suitable merger partner (continuing credit union). NCUA is primarily concerned that the continuing credit union has the financial strength and management expertise to absorb the troubled credit union without adversely affecting its own financial condition and stability.

As a stipulated condition to an emergency merger, the field of membership of the merging credit union may be transferred intact to the continuing federal credit union without regard to any common bond restrictions. Under this authority, therefore, a single associational common bond federal credit union may take into its field of membership any dissimilar charter type.

The common bond characteristic of the continuing credit union in an emergency merger does not change. That is, even though the merging credit union is a multiple common bond or community, the continuing credit union will remain a single common bond credit union. Similarly, if the merging credit union is an unlike single common bond, the continuing credit union will remain a single common bond credit union. Future common bond expansions will be based on the continuing credit union's single common bond.

Emergency mergers involving federally insured credit unions in different NCUA regions must be approved by the regional director where the continuing credit union is headquartered, with the concurrence of the regional director of the merging credit union and, as applicable, the state regulators.

III.D.3—Purchase and Assumption (P&A)

Another alternative for acquiring the field of membership of a failing credit union is through a consolidation known as a P&A. A P&A has limited application because, in most cases, the failing credit union must be placed into involuntary liquidation. In the few instances where a P&A may be appropriate, the assuming federal credit union, as with emergency mergers, may acquire the entire field of membership if the emergency merger criteria are satisfied. However, if the P&A does not meet the emergency merger criteria, it must be processed under the common bond requirements.

In a P&A processed under the emergency criteria, specified loans, shares, and certain other designated assets and liabilities, without regard to common bond restrictions, may also be acquired without changing the character of the continuing federal credit union for purposes of future field of membership amendments.

If the purchased and/or assumed credit union's field of membership does not share a common bond with the purchasing and/or assuming credit union, then the continuing credit union's original common bond will be controlling for future common bond expansions.

P&As involving federally insured credit unions in different NCUA regions must be approved by the regional director where the continuing credit union is headquartered, with the concurrence of the regional director of the purchased and/or assumed credit union and, as applicable, the state regulators.

III.D.4—Spin-Offs

A spin-off occurs when, by agreement of the parties, a portion of the field of membership, assets, liabilities, shares, and capital of a credit union are transferred to a new or existing credit union. A spin-off is unique in that usually one credit union has a field of membership expansion and the other loses a portion of its field of membership.

All common bond requirements apply regardless of whether the spun-off group becomes a new credit union or goes to an existing federal charter.

The request for approval of a spin-off must be supported with a plan that addresses, at a minimum:
• Why the spin-off is being requested;
• What part of the field of membership is to be spun off;
• Whether the affected credit unions have the same common bond (applies only to single associational credit unions);
• Which assets, liabilities, shares, and capital are to be transferred;
• The financial impact the spin-off will have on the affected credit unions;
• The ability of the acquiring credit union to effectively serve the new members;
• The proposed spin-off date; and
• Disclosure to the members of the requirements set forth above.

The spin-off request must also include current financial statements from the affected credit unions and the proposed voting ballot.

For federal credit unions spinning off a group, membership notice and voting requirements and procedures are the same as for mergers (see Part 708 of the NCUA Rules and Regulations), except that only the members directly affected by the spin-off—those whose shares are to be transferred—are permitted to vote. Members whose shares are not being transferred will not be afforded the opportunity to vote. All members of the group to be spun off (whether they voted in favor, against, or not at all) will be transferred if the spin-off is approved by the voting membership. Voting requirements for federally insured state credit unions are governed by state law.

Spin-offs involving federally insured credit unions in different NCUA regions must be approved by all regional directors where the credit unions are headquartered and the state regulators, as applicable. Spin-offs in the same region also require approval by the state regulator, as applicable.

III.E—Overlaps

III.E.1—General

An overlap exists when a group of persons is eligible for membership in two or more credit unions. NCUA will permit single associational federal credit unions to overlap any other charters without performing an overlap analysis.

III.E.2—Organizational Restructuring

A federal credit union's field of membership will always be governed by the common bond descriptions contained in Section 5 of its charter. Where a sponsor organization expands its operations internally, by acquisition or otherwise, the credit union may serve these new entrants to its field of membership if they are part of the common bond described in Section 5. NCUA will permit a complete overlap of the credit unions' fields of membership. If a sponsor organization sells off a group, new members can no longer be served unless they otherwise qualify for membership in the common union or it converts to a multiple common bond.

Credit unions must submit documentation explaining the restructuring and providing information regarding the new organizational structure.

III.E.3—Exclusionary Clauses

An exclusionary clause is a limitation precluding the credit union from serving the primary members of a portion of a group otherwise included in its field of membership. NCUA no longer grants exclusionary clauses. Those granted prior to the adoption of this new chartering manual will remain in effect unless the credit unions agree to remove them or one of the affected credit unions submits a housekeeping amendment to have it removed.

III.F—Charter Conversions

A single associational common bond federal credit union may apply to convert to a community charter provided the field of membership requirements of the community charter are met. Groups within the existing charter which cannot qualify in the new charter cannot be served except for members of record, or groups or communities obtained in an emergency merger or P&A. A credit union must notify all groups that will be removed from the field of membership as a result of conversion. Members of record can continue to be served. Also, in order to support a case for a conversion, the applicant federal credit union may be required to develop a detailed business plan as specified in Chapter 2, Section V.A.3.

A single associational common bond federal credit union may apply to convert to a multiple common bond charter by adding a non-common bond group that is within a reasonable proximity of a service facility. Groups within the existing charter may be retained and continue to be served. However, future amendments, including any expansions of the original single common bond group, must be done in accordance with multiple common bond policy.

III.G—Removal of Groups From the Field of Membership

A credit union may request removal of a portion of the common bond group from its field of membership for various reasons. The most common reasons for this type of amendment are:

• The group is within the field of membership of two credit unions and one wishes to discontinue service;
• The federal credit union cannot continue to provide adequate service to the group;
• The group has ceased to exist;
• The group does not respond to repeated requests to contact the credit union or refuses to provide needed support; or
• The group initiates action to be removed from the field of membership.

When a federal credit union requests an amendment to remove a group from its field of membership, the regional director will determine why the credit union desires to remove the group. If the regional director concurs with the request, membership will continue for those who are already members under the "once a member, always a member" provision of the Federal Credit Union Act.

III.H—Other Persons Eligible for Credit Union Membership

A number of persons by virtue of their close relationship to a common bond group may be included, at the charter applicant's option, in the field of membership. These include the following:

• Spouses of persons who died while within the field of membership of this credit union;
• Employees of this credit union;
• Volunteers;

National Credit Union Administration

- Members of the immediate family or household;
- Organizations of such persons; and
- Corporate or other legal entities in this charter.

Immediate family is defined as spouse, child, sibling, parent, grandparent, or grandchild. This includes stepparents, stepchildren, stepsiblings, and adoptive relationships.

Household is defined as persons living in the same residence maintaining a single economic unit.

Membership eligibility is extended only to individuals who are members of an "immediate family or household" of a credit union member. It is not necessary for the primary member to join the credit union in order for the immediate family or household member of the primary member to join, provided the immediate family or household clause is included in the field of membership. However, it is necessary for the immediate family member or household member to first join in order for that person's immediate family member or household member to join the credit union. A credit union can adopt a more restrictive definition of immediate family or household.

Volunteers, by virtue of their close relationship with a sponsor group, may be included. One example is volunteers working at a church.

Under the Federal Credit Union Act, once a person becomes a member of the credit union, such person may remain a member of the credit union until the person chooses to withdraw or is expelled from the membership of the credit union. This is commonly referred to as "once a member, always a member." The "once a member, always a member" provision does not prevent a credit union from restricting services to members who are no longer within the field of membership.

IV—MULTIPLE OCCUPATIONAL/ ASSOCIATIONAL COMMON BONDS

IV.A.1—General

A federal credit union may be chartered to serve a combination of distinct, definable single occupational and/or associational common bonds. This type of credit union is called a multiple common bond credit union. Each group in the field of membership must have its own occupational or associational common bond. For example, a multiple common bond credit union may include two unrelated employers, or two unrelated associations, or a combination of two or more employers or associations. Additionally, these groups must be within reasonable geographic proximity of the credit union. That is, the groups must be within the service area of one of the credit union's service facilities. These groups are referred to as select groups.

A multiple common bond credit union cannot include a TIP or expand using single common bond criteria.

A federal credit union's service area is the area that can reasonably be served by the service facilities accessible to the groups within the field of membership. The service area will most often coincide with that geographic area primarily served by the service facility. Additionally, the groups served by the credit union must have access to the service facility. The non-availability of other credit union service is a factor to be considered in determining whether the group is within reasonable proximity of a credit union wishing to add the group to its field of membership.

A service facility for multiple common bond credit unions is defined as a place where shares are accepted for members' accounts, loan applications are accepted or loans are disbursed. This definition includes a credit union owned branch, a mobile branch, an office operated on a regularly scheduled weekly basis, a credit union owned ATM, or a credit union owned electronic facility that meets, at a minimum, these requirements. A service facility also includes a shared branch or a shared branch network if either: (1) the credit union has an ownership interest in the service facility either directly or through a CUSO or similar organization; or (2) the service facility is local to the credit union and the credit union is an authorized participant in the service center. This definition does not include the credit union's Internet Web site.

The select group as a whole will be considered to be within a credit union's service area when:

- A majority of the persons in a select group live, work, or gather regularly within the service area;
- The group's headquarters is located within the service area; or
- The group's "paid from" or "supervised from" location is within the service area.

IV.A.2—Sample Multiple Common Bond Field of Membership

An example of a multiple common bond field of membership is:

"The field of membership of this federal credit union shall be limited to the following:

1. Employees of Teltex Corporation who work in Wilmington, Delaware;

2. Partners and employees of Smith & Jones, Attorneys at Law, who work in Wilmington, Delaware;

3. Members of the M&L Association in Wilmington, Delaware, who qualify for membership in accordance with its charter and by-laws in effect on December 31, 1997."

IV.B—MULTIPLE COMMON BOND AMENDMENTS

IV.B.1—General

Section 5 of every multiple common bond federal credit union's charter defines the field of membership and select groups the credit union can legally serve. Only those persons or legal entities specified in the field of membership can be served. There are a number of instances in which Section 5 must be amended by NCUA.

First, a new select group is added to the field of membership. This may occur through agreement between the group and the credit union directly, or through a merger, corporate acquisition, purchase and assumption (P&A), or spin-off.

Second, a federal credit union qualifies to change its charter from:
- A single occupational or associational charter to a multiple common bond charter;
- A multiple common bond to a single occupational or associational charter;
- A multiple common bond to a community charter; or
- A community to a multiple common bond charter.

Third, a federal credit union removes a group from its field of membership through agreement with the group, a spin-off, or because the group no longer exists.

IV.B.2—Numerical Limitation of Select Groups

An existing multiple common bond federal credit union that submits a request to amend its charter must provide documentation to establish that the multiple common bond requirements have been met. The regional director must approve all amendments to a multiple common bond credit union's field of membership.

NCUA will approve groups to a credit union's field of membership if the agency determines in writing that the following criteria are met:
- The credit union has not engaged in any unsafe or unsound practice, as determined by the regional director, which is material during the one year period preceding the filing to add the group;
- The credit union is "adequately capitalized." NCUA defines adequately capitalized to mean the credit union has a net worth ratio of not less than 6 percent. For low-income credit unions or credit unions chartered less than ten years, the regional director may determine that a net worth ratio of less than 6 percent is adequate if the credit union is making reasonable progress toward meeting the 6 percent net worth requirement. For any other credit union, the regional director may determine that a net worth ratio of less than 6 percent is adequate if the credit union is making reasonable progress toward meeting the 6 percent net worth requirement, and the addition of the group would not adversely affect the credit union's capitalization level;
- The credit union has the administrative capability to serve the proposed group and the financial resources to meet the need for additional staff and assets to serve the new group;
- Any potential harm the expansion may have on any other credit union and its members is clearly outweighed by the probable beneficial effect of the expansion. With respect to a proposed expansion's effect on other credit unions, the requirements on overlapping fields of membership set forth in Section IV.E of this Chapter are also applicable; and
- If the formation of a separate credit union by such group is not practical and consistent with reasonable standards for the safe and sound operation of a credit union.

A detailed analysis is required for groups of 3,000 or more primary potential members requesting to be added to a multiple common bond credit union. It is incumbent upon the credit union to demonstrate that the formation of a separate credit union by such a group is not practical. The group must provide evidence that it lacks sufficient volunteer and other resources to support the efficient and effective operations of a credit union or does not meet the economic advisability criteria outlined in Chapter 1. If this can be demonstrated, the group may be added to a multiple common bond credit union's field of membership.

IV.B.3—Documentation Requirements

A multiple common bond credit union requesting a select group expansion must submit a formal written request, using the Application for Field of Membership Amendment (NCUA 4015 or NCUA 4015–EZ) to the appropriate NCUA regional director. An authorized credit union representative must sign the request.

The NCUA 4015–EZ (for groups less than 3,000 potential members) must be accompanied by the following:
- A letter, or equivalent documentation, from the group requesting credit union service. This letter must indicate:
  ○ That the group wants to be added to the applicant federal credit union's field of membership;
  ○ The number of persons currently included within the group to be added and their locations; and
  ○ The group's proximity to credit union's nearest service facility.
- The most recent copy of the group's charter and bylaws or equivalent documentation (for associational groups).

The NCUA 4015 (for groups of 3,000 or more primary potential members) must be accompanied by the following:

National Credit Union Administration

- A letter, or equivalent documentation, from the group requesting credit union service. This letter must indicate:
  - That the group wants to be added to the federal credit union's field of membership;
  - Whether the group presently has other credit union service available;
  - The number of persons currently included within the group to be added and their locations;
  - The group's proximity to credit union's nearest service facility, and
  - Why the formation of a separate credit union for the group is not practical or consistent with safety and soundness standards. A credit union need not address every item on the list, simply those issues that are relevant to its particular request:

Member location—whether the membership is widely dispersed or concentrated in a central location.

Demographics—the employee turnover rate, economic status of the group's members, and whether the group is more apt to consist of savers and/or borrowers.

Market competition—the availability of other financial services.

Desired services and products—the type of services the group desires in comparison to the type of services a new credit union could offer.

Sponsor subsidies—the availability of operating subsidies.

The desire of the sponsor—the extent of the sponsor's interest in supporting a credit union charter.

Employee interest—the extent of the employees' interest in obtaining a credit union charter.

Evidence of past failure—whether the group previously had its own credit union or previously filed for a credit union charter.

Administrative capacity to provide services—will the group have the management expertise to provide the services requested.

- If the group is eligible for membership in any other credit union, documentation must be provided to support inclusion of the group under the overlap standards set forth in Section IV.E of this Chapter; and
- The most recent copy of the group's charter and bylaws or equivalent documentation (for associational groups).

IV.B.4—Corporate Restructuring

If a select group within a federal credit union's field of membership undergoes a substantial restructuring, a change to the credit union's field of membership may be required if the credit union is to continue to provide service to the select group. NCUA permits a multiple common bond credit union to maintain in its field of membership a sold, spun-off, or merged select group to which it has been providing service. This type of amendment to the credit union's charter is not considered an expansion; therefore, the criteria relating to adding new groups are not applicable.

When two groups merge and each is in the field of membership of a credit union, then both (or all affected) credit unions can serve the resulting merged group, subject to any existing geographic limitation and without regard to any overlap provisions. However, the credit unions cannot serve the other multiple groups that may be in the field of membership of the other credit union.

IV.C—NCUA'S PROCEDURES FOR AMENDING THE FIELD OF MEMBERSHIP

IV.C.1—General

All requests for approval to amend a federal credit union's charter must be submitted to the appropriate regional director.

IV.C.2—Regional Director's Decision

NCUA staff will review all amendment requests in order to ensure conformance to NCUA policy.

Before acting on a proposed amendment, the regional director may require an on-site review. In addition, the regional director may, after taking into account the significance of the proposed field of membership amendment, require the applicant to submit a business plan addressing specific issues.

The financial and operational condition of the requesting credit union will be considered in every instance. An expanded field of membership may provide the basis for reversing adverse trends. In such cases, an amendment to expand the field of membership may be granted notwithstanding the credit union's adverse trends. The applicant credit union must clearly establish that the approval of the expanded field of membership meets the requirements of Section IV.B.2 of this Chapter and will not increase the risk to the NCUSIF.

IV.C.3—Regional Director Approval

If the regional director approves the requested amendment, the credit union will be issued an amendment to Section 5 of its charter.

IV.C.4—Regional Director Disapproval

When a regional director disapproves any application, in whole or in part, to amend the field of membership under this chapter, the applicant will be informed in writing of the:

- Specific reasons for the action;
- Options to consider, if appropriate, for gaining approval; and
- Appeal procedure.

IV.C.5—Appeal of Regional Director Decision

If a field of membership expansion request, merger, or spin-off is denied by the regional director, the federal credit union may appeal the decision to the NCUA Board. An appeal must be sent to the appropriate regional office within 60 days of the date of denial, and must address the specific reason(s) for the denial. The regional director will then forward the appeal to the NCUA Board. NCUA central office staff will make an independent review of the facts and present the appeal to the Board with a recommendation.

Before appealing, the credit union may, within 30 days of the denial, provide supplemental information to the regional director for reconsideration. A reconsideration will contain new and material evidence addressing the reasons for the initial denial. The regional director will have 30 days from the date of the receipt of the request for reconsideration to make a final decision. If the request is again denied, the applicant may proceed with the appeal process within 60 days of the date of the last denial. A second request for reconsideration will be treated as an appeal to the NCUA Board.

IV.D—Mergers, Purchase and Assumptions, and Spin-Offs

In general, other than the addition of select groups, there are three additional ways a multiple common bond federal credit union can expand its field of membership:
- By taking in the field of membership of another credit union through a merger;
- By taking in the field of membership of another credit union through a purchase and assumption (P&A); or
- By taking a portion of another credit union's field of membership through a spin-off.

IV.D.1—Voluntary Mergers

a. All Select Groups in the Merging Credit Union's Field of Membership Have Less Than 3,000 Primary Potential Members

A voluntary merger of two or more federal credit unions is permissible as long as each select group in the merging credit union's field of membership has less than 3,000 primary potential members. While the merger requirements outlined in Section 205 of the Federal Credit Union Act must still be met, the requirements of Chapter 2, Section IV.B.2 of this manual are not applicable.

b. One or More Select Groups in the Merging Credit Union's Field of Membership Has 3,000 or More Primary Potential Members

If the merging credit unions serve the same group, and the group consists of 3,000 or more primary potential members, then the ability to form a separate credit union analysis is not required for that group. If the merging credit union has any other groups consisting of 3,000 or more primary potential members, special requirements apply. NCUA will analyze each group of 3,000 or more primary potential members, except as noted above, to determine whether the formation of a separate credit union by such a group is practical. If the formation of a separate credit union by such a group is not practical because the group lacks sufficient volunteer and other resources to support the efficient and effective operations of a credit union or does not meet the economic advisable criteria outlined in Chapter 1, the group may be merged into a multiple common bond credit union. If the formation of a separate credit union is practical, the group must be spun-off before the merger can be approved.

c. Merger of a Single Common Bond Credit Union Into a Multiple Common Bond Credit Union

A financially healthy single common bond credit union with a primary potential membership of 3,000 or more cannot merge into a multiple common bond credit union, absent supervisory reasons, unless the continuing credit union already serves the same group.

d. Merger Approval

If the merger is approved, the qualifying groups within the merging credit union's field of membership will be transferred intact to the continuing credit union and can continue to be served.

Where the merging credit union is state-chartered, the field of membership rules applicable to a federal credit union apply.

Mergers must be approved by the NCUA regional director where the continuing credit union is headquartered, with the concurrence of the regional director of the merging credit union, and, as applicable, the state regulators.

IV.D.2—Supervisory Mergers

The NCUA may approve the merger of any federally insured credit union when safety and soundness concerns are present without regard to the 3,000 numerical limitation. The credit union need not be insolvent or in danger of insolvency for NCUA to use this statutory authority. Examples constituting appropriate reasons for using this authority are: abandonment of the management and/or officials and an inability to find replacements, loss of sponsor support, serious and persistent record keeping problems, sustained material decline in financial condition, or other serious or persistent circumstances.

IV.D.3—Emergency Mergers

An emergency merger may be approved by NCUA without regard to common bond or other legal constraints. An emergency merger involves NCUA's direct intervention and approval. The credit union to be merged

must either be insolvent or in danger of insolvency, as defined in the Glossary, and NCUA must determine that:
- An emergency requiring expeditious action exists;
- Other alternatives are not reasonably available; and
- The public interest would best be served by approving the merger.

If not corrected, conditions that could lead to insolvency include, but are not limited to:
- Abandonment by management;
- Loss of sponsor;
- Serious and persistent record keeping problems; or
- Serious and persistent operational concerns.

In an emergency merger situation, NCUA will take an active role in finding a suitable merger partner (continuing credit union). NCUA is primarily concerned that the continuing credit union has the financial strength and management expertise to absorb the troubled credit union without adversely affecting its own financial condition and stability.

As a stipulated condition to an emergency merger, the field of membership of the merging credit union may be transferred intact to the continuing federal credit union without regard to any field of membership restrictions including numerical limitation requirements. Under this authority, any single occupational or associational common bond, multiple common bond, or community charter may merger into a multiple common bond credit union and that credit union can continue to serve the merging credit union's field of membership. Subsequent field of membership expansions of the continuing multiple common bond credit union must be consistent with multiple common bond policies.

Emergency mergers involving federally insured credit unions in different NCUA regions must be approved by the regional director where the continuing credit union is headquartered, with the concurrence of the regional director of the merging credit union and, as applicable, the state regulators.

IV.D.4—Purchase and Assumption (P&A)

Another alternative for acquiring the field of membership of a failing credit union is through a consolidation known as a P&A. Generally, the requirements applicable to field of membership expansions found in this chapter apply to purchase and assumptions where the purchasing credit union is a federal charter.

A P&A has limited application because, in most cases, the failing credit union must be placed into involuntary liquidation. However, in the few instances where a P&A may occur, the assuming federal credit union, as with emergency mergers, may acquire the entire field of membership if the emergency criteria are satisfied. Specified loans, shares, and certain other designated assets and liabilities, without regard to field of membership restrictions, may also be acquired without changing the character of the continuing federal credit union for purposes of future field of membership amendments. Subsequent field of membership expansions must be consistent with multiple common bond policies.

P&As involving federally insured credit unions in different NCUA regions must be approved by the regional director where the continuing credit union is headquartered, with the concurrence of the regional director of the purchased and/or assumed credit union and, as applicable, the state regulators.

IV.D.5—Spin-Offs

A spin-off occurs when, by agreement of the parties, a portion of the field of membership, assets, liabilities, shares, and capital of a credit union are transferred to a new or existing credit union. A spin-off is unique in that usually one credit union has a field of membership expansion and the other loses a portion of its field of membership.

All common bond requirements apply regardless of whether the spun-off group becomes a new charter or goes to an existing federal charter.

The request for approval of a spun-off group must be supported with a plan that addresses, at a minimum:
- Why the spin-off is being requested;
- What part of the field of membership is to be spun off;
- Which assets, liabilities, shares, and capital are to be transferred;
- The financial impact the spin-off will have on the affected credit unions;
- The ability of the acquiring credit union to effectively serve the new members;
- The proposed spin-off date; and
- Disclosure to the members of the requirements set forth above.

The spin-off request must also include current financial statements from the affected credit unions and the proposed voting ballot.

For federal credit unions spinning off a group, membership notice and voting requirements and procedures are the same as for mergers (see Part 708 of the NCUA Rules and Regulations), except that only the members directly affected by the spin-off—those whose shares are to be transferred—are permitted to vote. Members whose shares are not being transferred will not be afforded the opportunity to vote. All members of the group to be spun off (whether they voted in favor, against, or not at all) will be transferred if the spin-off is approved by the voting membership. Voting requirements for federally insured state credit unions are governed by state law.

Spin-offs involving federally insured credit unions in different NCUA regions must be approved by all regional directors where the credit unions are headquartered and the state regulators, as applicable. Spin-offs in the same region also require approval by the state regulator, as applicable.

IV.E—OVERLAPS

IV.E.1—General

An overlap exists when a group of persons is eligible for membership in two or more credit unions, including state charters. An overlap is permitted when the expansion's beneficial effect in meeting the convenience and needs of the members of the group proposed to be included in the field of membership clearly outweighs any adverse effect on the overlapped credit union.

Credit unions must investigate the possibility of an overlap with federally insured credit unions prior to submitting an expansion request if the group has 3,000 or more primary potential members. If cases arise where the assurance given to a regional director concerning the unavailability of credit union service is inaccurate, the misinformation may be grounds for removal of the group from the federal credit union's charter.

When an overlap situation requiring analysis does arise, officials of the expanding credit union must ascertain the views of the overlapped credit union. If the overlapped credit union does not object, the applicant must submit a letter or other documentation to that effect. If the overlapped credit union does not respond, the expanding credit union must notify NCUA in writing of its attempt to obtain the overlapped credit union's comments.

NCUA will approve an overlap if the expansion's beneficial effect in meeting the convenience and needs of the members of the group clearly outweighs any adverse effect on the overlapped credit union.

In reviewing the overlap, the regional director will consider:
• The view of the overlapped credit union(s);
• Whether the overlap is incidental in nature—the group of persons in question is so small as to have no material effect on the original credit union;
• Whether there is limited participation by members or employees of the group in the original credit union after the expiration of a reasonable period of time;
• Whether the original credit union fails to provide requested service;
• Financial effect on the overlapped credit union;
• The desires of the group(s);
• The desire of the sponsor organization; and
• The best interests of the affected group and the credit union members involved.

Generally, if the overlapped credit union does not object, and NCUA determines that there is no safety and soundness problem, the overlap will be permitted.

Potential overlaps of a federally insured state credit union's field of membership by a federal credit union will generally be analyzed in the same way as if two federal credit unions were involved. Where a federally insured state credit union's field of membership is broadly stated, NCUA will exclude its field of membership from any overlap protection.

NCUA will permit multiple common bond federal credit unions to overlap community charters without performing an overlap analysis.

IV.E.2—Overlap Issues as a Result of Organizational Restructuring

A federal credit union's field of membership will always be governed by the field of membership descriptions contained in Section 5 of its charter. Where a sponsor organization expands its operations internally, by acquisition or otherwise, the credit union may serve these new entrants to its field of membership if they are part of any select group listed in Section 5. Where acquisitions are made which add a new subsidiary, the group cannot be served until the subsidiary is included in the field of membership through a housekeeping amendment.

Overlaps may occur as a result of restructuring or merger of the parent organization. When such overlaps occur, each credit union must request a field of membership amendment to reflect the new groups each wishes to serve. The credit union can continue to serve any current group in its field of membership that is acquiring a new group or has been acquired by a new group. The new group cannot be served by the credit union until the field of membership amendment is approved by NCUA.

Credit unions affected by organizational restructuring or merger should attempt to resolve overlap issues among themselves. Unless an agreement is reached limiting the overlap resulting from the corporate restructuring, NCUA will permit a complete overlap of the credit unions' fields of membership. When two groups merge, or one group is acquired by the other, and each is in the field of membership of a credit union, both (or all affected) credit unions can serve the resulting merged or acquired group, subject to any existing geographic limitation and without regard to any overlap provisions. This is accomplished through a housekeeping amendment.

Credit unions must submit to NCUA documentation explaining the restructuring and provide information regarding the new organizational structure.

National Credit Union Administration

IV.E.3—*Exclusionary Clauses*

An exclusionary clause is a limitation precluding the credit union from serving the primary members of a portion of a group otherwise included in its field of membership. NCUA no longer grants exclusionary clauses. Those granted prior to the adoption of this new chartering manual will remain in effect unless the credit unions agree to remove them or one of the affected credit unions submits a housekeeping amendment to have it removed.

IV.F—CHARTER CONVERSION

A multiple common bond federal credit union may apply to convert to a community charter provided the field of membership requirements of the community charter are met. Groups within the existing charter which cannot qualify in the new charter cannot be served except for members of record, or groups or communities obtained in an emergency merger or P&A. A credit union must notify all groups that will be removed from the field of membership as a result of conversion. Members of record can continue to be served. Also, in order to support a case for a conversion, the applicant federal credit union may be required to develop a detailed business plan as specified in Chapter 2, Section V.A.3.

A multiple common bond federal credit union may apply to convert to a single occupational or associational common bond charter provided the field of membership requirements of the new charter are met. Groups within the existing charter, which do not qualify in the new charter, cannot be served except for members of record, or groups or communities obtained in an emergency merger or P&A. A credit union must notify all groups that will be removed from the field of membership as a result of conversion.

IV.G—REMOVAL OF GROUPS FROM THE FIELD OF MEMBERSHIP

A credit union may request removal of a group from its field of membership for various reasons. The most common reasons for this type of amendment are:

• The group is within the field of membership of two credit unions and one wishes to discontinue service;
• The federal credit union cannot continue to provide adequate service to the group;
• The group has ceased to exist;
• The group does not respond to repeated requests to contact the credit union or refuses to provide needed support;
• The group initiates action to be removed from the field of membership; or
• The federal credit union wishes to convert to a single common bond.

When a federal credit union requests an amendment to remove a group from its field of membership, the regional director will determine why the credit union desires to remove the group. If the regional director concurs with the request, membership will continue for those who are already members under the "once a member, always a member" provision of the Federal Credit Union Act.

IV.H—OTHER PERSONS ELIGIBLE FOR CREDIT UNION MEMBERSHIP

A number of persons, by virtue of their close relationship to a common bond group, may be included, at the charter applicant's option, in the field of membership. These include the following:

• Spouses of persons who died while within the field of membership of this credit union;
• Employees of this credit union;
• Persons retired as pensioners or annuitants from the above employment;
• Volunteers;
• Members of the immediate family or household;
• Organizations of such persons; and
• Corporate or other legal entities in this charter.

Immediate family is defined as spouse, child, sibling, parent, grandparent, or grandchild. This includes stepparents, stepchildren, stepsiblings, and adoptive relationships.

Household is defined as persons living in the same residence maintaining a single economic unit.

Membership eligibility is extended only to individuals who are members of an "immediate family or household" of a credit union member. It is not necessary for the primary member to join the credit union in order for the immediate family or household member of the primary member to join, provided the immediate family or household clause is included in the field of membership. However, it is necessary for the immediate family member or household member to first join in order for that person's immediate family member or household member to join the credit union. A credit union can adopt a more restrictive definition of immediate family or household.

Volunteers, by virtue of their close relationship with a sponsor group, may be included. Examples include volunteers working at a hospital or church.

Under the Federal Credit Union Act, once a person becomes a member of the credit union, such person may remain a member of the credit union until the person chooses to withdraw or is expelled from the membership of the credit union. This is commonly referred to as "once a member, always a member." The "once a member, always a member" provision does not prevent a credit union from restricting services to members who are no longer within the field of membership.

V—COMMUNITY CHARTER REQUIREMENTS

V.A.1—General

There are two types of community charters. One is based on a single, geographically well-defined local community or neighborhood; the other is a rural district. More than one credit union may serve the same community.

NCUA recognizes four types of affinity on which both a community charter and a rural district can be based—persons who live in, worship in, attend school in, or work in the community or rural district. Businesses and other legal entities within the community boundaries or rural district may also qualify for membership.

NCUA has established the following requirements for community charters:
- The geographic area's boundaries must be clearly defined; and
- The area is a well-defined local community or a rural district.

V.A.2—DEFINITION OF WELL-DEFINED LOCAL COMMUNITY AND RURAL DISTRICT

In addition to the documentation requirements in Chapter 1 to charter a credit union, a community credit union applicant must provide additional documentation addressing the proposed area to be served and community service policies.

An applicant has the burden of demonstrating to NCUA that the proposed community area meets the statutory requirements of being: (1) well-defined, and (2) a local community or rural district.

"Well-defined" means the proposed area has specific geographic boundaries. Geographic boundaries may include a city, township, county (single, multiple, or portions of a county) or their political equivalent, school districts, or a clearly identifiable neighborhood. Although congressional districts and state boundaries are well-defined areas, they do not meet the requirement that the proposed area be a local community or rural district.

The well-defined local community requirement is met if:
- Single Political Jurisdiction—The area to be served is in a recognized single political jurisdiction, *i.e.*, a city, county, or their political equivalent, or any contiguous portion thereof.
- Statistical Area—
- The area is a designated Core Based Statistical Area (CBSA) or allowing part thereof, or in the case of a CBSA with Metropolitan Divisions, the area is a Metropolitan Division or part thereof; and
- The CBSA or Metropolitan Division must have a population of 2.5 million or less people.

The rural district requirement is met if:
- Rural District—
- The district has well-defined, contiguous geographic boundaries;
- More than 50% of the district's population resides in census blocks or other geographic areas that are designated as rural by the United States Census Bureau; and
- The total population of the district does not exceed 200,000 people; *or*
- The district has well-defined, contiguous geographic boundaries;
- The district does not have a population density in excess of 100 people per square mile; and
- The total population of the district does not exceed 200,000 people.

The affinities that apply to rural districts are the same as those that apply to well defined local communities. The OMB definitions of CBSA and Metropolitan Division may be found at 65 FR82238 (Dec. 27, 2000). They are incorporated herein by reference. Access to these definitions is available through the main page of the FEDERAL REGISTER Web site at *http://www.gpoaccess.gov/fr/index.html* and on NCUA's Web site at *http://www.ncua.gov*.

The requirements in Chapter 2, Sections V.A.4 through V.G. also apply to a credit union that serves a rural district.

V.A.3—PREVIOUSLY APPROVED COMMUNITIES

If prior to July 26, 2010 NCUA has determined that a specific geographic area is a well defined local community, then a new applicant need not reestablish that fact as part of its application to serve the exact area. The new applicant must, however, note NCUA's previous determination as part of its overall application. An applicant applying for an area after that date that is not exactly the same as the previously approved well defined local community must comply with the current criteria in place for determining a well defined local community.

V.A.4—BUSINESS PLAN REQUIREMENTS FOR A COMMUNITY CREDIT UNION

A community credit union is frequently more susceptible to competition from other local financial institutions and generally does not have substantial support from any single sponsoring company or association. As a result, a community credit union will often encounter financial and operational factors that differ from an occupational or associational charter. Its diverse membership may require special marketing programs targeted to different segments of the community. For example, the lack of payroll deduction creates special challenges in the development and promotion of savings programs and in the collection of loans. Accordingly, to support an application for a community charter, an applicant Federal credit union must develop a business plan incorporating the following data:

National Credit Union Administration

• Pro forma financial statements for a minimum of 24 months after the proposed conversion, including the underlying assumptions and rationale for projected member, share, loan, and asset growth;
• Anticipated financial impact on the credit union, including the need for additional employees and fixed assets, and the associated costs;
• A description of the current and proposed office/branch structure, including a general description of the location(s); parking availability, public transportation availability, drive-through service, lobby capacity, or any other service feature illustrating community access;
• A marketing plan addressing how the community will be served for the 24-month period after the proposed conversion to a community charter, including detailing: how the credit union will implement its business plan; the unique needs of the various demographic groups in the proposed community; how the credit union will market to each group, particularly underserved groups; which community-based organizations the credit union will target in its outreach efforts; the credit union's marketing budget projections dedicating greater resources to reaching new members; and the credit union's timetable for implementation, not just a calendar of events;
• Details, terms and conditions of the credit union's financial products, programs, and services to be provided to the entire community; and
• Maps showing the current and proposed service facilities, ATMs, political boundaries, major roads, and other pertinent information.

An existing Federal credit union may apply to convert to a community charter. Groups currently in the credit union's field of membership, but outside the new community credit union's boundaries, may not be included in the new community charter. Therefore, the credit union must notify groups that will be removed from the field of membership as a result of the conversion. Members of record can continue to be served.

Before approval of an application to convert to a community credit union, NCUA must be satisfied that the credit union will be viable and capable of providing services to its members.

Community credit unions will be expected to regularly review and to follow, to the fullest extent economically possible, the marketing and business plans submitted with their applications. Additionally, NCUA will follow-up with an FCU every year for three years after the FCU has been granted a new or expanded community charter, and at any other intervals NCUA believes appropriate, to determine if the FCU is satisfying the terms of its marketing and business plans. An FCU failing to satisfy those terms will be subject to supervisory action. As part of this review process, the regional office will report to the NCUA Board instances where an FCU is failing to satisfy the terms of its marketing and business plan and indicate what supervisory actions the region intends to take.

V.A.5—COMMUNITY BOUNDARIES

The geographic boundaries of a community Federal credit union are the areas defined in its charter. The boundaries can usually be defined using political borders, streets, rivers, railroad tracks, or other static geographical feature.

A community that is a recognized legal entity may be stated in the field of membership—for example, "Gus Township, Texas," "Isabella City, Georgia," or "Fairfax County, Virginia."

A community that is a recognized CBSA must state in the field of membership the political jurisdiction(s) that comprise the CBSA.

V.A.6—SPECIAL COMMUNITY CHARTERS

A community field of membership may include persons who work or attend school in a particular industrial park, shopping mall, office complex, or similar development. The proposed field of membership must have clearly defined geographic boundaries.

V.A.7—SAMPLE COMMUNITY FIELDS OF MEMBERSHIP

A community charter does not have to include all four affinities (*i.e.*, live, work, worship, or attend school in a community). Some examples of community fields of membership are:

• Persons who live, work, worship, or attend school in, and businesses located in the area of Johnson City, Tennessee, bounded by Fern Street on the north, Long Street on the east, Fourth Street on the south, and Elm Avenue on the west;
• Persons who live or work in Green County, Maine;
• Persons who live, worship, work (or regularly conduct business in), or attend school on the University of Dayton campus, in Dayton, Ohio;
• Persons who work for businesses located in Clifton Country Mall, in Clifton Park, New York;
• Persons who live, work, or worship in the Binghamton, New York, CBSA, consisting of Broome and Tioga Counties, New York (a qualifying CBSA in its entirety);
• Persons who live, work, worship, or attend school in the portion of the Oklahoma City, OK MSA that includes Canadian and Oklahoma counties, Oklahoma (two contiguous counties in a portion of a qualifying CBSA that has seven counties in total); or

- Persons who live, work, worship, or attend school in Uinta County or Lincoln County, Wyoming, a rural district.

Some examples of insufficiently defined local communities, neighborhoods, or rural districts are:

- Persons who live or work within and businesses located within a ten-mile radius of Washington, DC (using a radius does not establish a well-defined area);
- Persons who live or work in the industrial section of New York, New York. (not a well-defined neighborhood, community, or rural district); or
- Persons who live or work in the greater Boston area. (not a well-defined neighborhood, community, or rural district).

Some examples of unacceptable local communities, neighborhoods, or rural districts are:

- Persons who live or work in the State of California. (does not meet the definition of local community, neighborhood, or rural district);
- Persons who live in the first congressional district of Florida. (does not meet the definition of local community, neighborhood, or rural district).

V.B—Field of Membership Amendments

A community credit union may amend its field of membership by adding additional affinities or removing exclusionary clauses. This can be accomplished with a housekeeping amendment.

A community credit union also may expand its geographic boundaries. Persons who live, work, worship, or attend school within the proposed well-defined local community, neighborhood or rural district must have common interests and/or interact. The credit union must follow the requirements of Section V.A.3 of this chapter.

V.C—NCUA Procedures for Amending the Field of Membership

V.C.1—General

All requests for approval to amend a community credit union's charter must be submitted to the appropriate regional director. If a decision cannot be made within a reasonable period of time, the regional director will notify the credit union.

V.C.2—NCUA's Decision

The financial and operational condition of the requesting credit union will be considered in every instance. The economic advisability of expanding the field of membership of a credit union with financial or operational problems must be carefully considered.

In most cases, field of membership amendments will only be approved for credit unions that are operating satisfactorily. Generally, if a federal credit union is having difficulty providing service to its current membership, or is experiencing financial or other operational problems, it may have more difficulty serving an expanded field of membership.

Occasionally, however, an expanded field of membership may provide the basis for reversing current financial problems. In such cases, an amendment to expand the field of membership may be granted notwithstanding the credit union's financial or operational problems. The applicant credit union must clearly establish that the expanded field of membership is in the best interest of the members and will not increase the risk to the NCUSIF.

V.C.3—NCUA Approval

If the requested amendment is approved by NCUA, the credit union will be issued an amendment to Section 5 of its charter.

V.C.4—NCUA Disapproval

When NCUA disapproves any application to amend the field of membership, in whole or in part, under this chapter, the applicant will be informed in writing of the:

- Specific reasons for the action;
- If appropriate, options or suggestions that could be considered for gaining approval; and
- Appeal procedures.

V.C.5—Appeal of Regional Director Decision

If a field of membership expansion request, merger, or spin-off is denied by the regional director, the federal credit union may appeal the decision to the NCUA Board. An appeal must be sent to the appropriate regional office within 60 days of the date of denial and must address the specific reason(s) for the denial. The regional director will then forward the appeal to the NCUA Board. NCUA central office staff will make an independent review of the facts and present the appeal to the NCUA Board with a recommendation.

Before appealing, the credit union may, within 30 days of the denial, provide supplemental information to the regional director for reconsideration. A reconsideration will contain new and material evidence addressing the reasons for the initial denial. The regional director will have 30 days from the date of the receipt of the request for reconsideration to make a final decision. If the request is again denied, the applicant may proceed with the appeal process within 60 days of the date of the last denial. A second request for reconsideration will be treated as an appeal to the NCUA Board.

V.D—Mergers, Purchase and Assumptions, and Spin-offs

There are three additional ways a community federal credit union can expand its field of membership:
- By taking in the field of membership of another credit union through a merger;
- By taking in the field of membership through a purchase and assumption (P&A); or
- By taking a portion of another credit union's field of membership through a spin-off.

V.D.1—Standard Mergers

Generally, the requirements applicable to field of membership expansions apply to mergers where the continuing credit union is a community federal charter.

Where both credit unions are community charters, the continuing credit union must meet the criteria for expanding the community boundaries. A community credit union cannot merge into a single occupational/associational, or multiple common bond credit union, except in an emergency merger. However, a single occupational or associational, or multiple common bond credit union can merge into a community charter as long as the merging credit union has a service facility within the community boundaries or a majority of the merging credit union's field of membership would qualify for membership in the community charter. While a community charter may take in an occupational, associational, or multiple common bond credit union in a merger, it will remain a community charter.

Groups within the merging credit union's field of membership located outside of the community boundaries may not continue to be served. The merging credit union must notify groups that will be removed from the field of membership as a result of the merger. However, the credit union may continue to serve members of record.

Where a state-chartered credit union is merging into a community federal credit union, the continuing federal credit union's field of membership will be worded in accordance with NCUA policy. Any subsequent field of membership expansions must comply with applicable amendment procedures.

Mergers must be approved by the NCUA regional director where the continuing credit union is headquartered, with the concurrence of the regional director of the merging credit union, and, as applicable, the state regulators.

V.D.2—Emergency Mergers

An emergency merger may be approved by NCUA without regard to common bond or other legal constraints. An emergency merger involves NCUA's direct intervention and approval. The credit union to be merged must either be insolvent or in danger of insolvency, as defined in the Glossary, and NCUA must determine that:
- An emergency requiring expeditious action exists;
- Other alternatives are not reasonably available; and
- The public interest would best be served by approving the merger.

If not corrected, conditions that could lead to insolvency include, but are not limited to:
- Abandonment by management;
- Loss of sponsor;
- Serious and persistent record keeping; or
- Serious and persistent operational concerns.

In an emergency merger situation, NCUA will take an active role in finding a suitable merger partner (continuing credit union). NCUA is primarily concerned that the continuing credit union has the financial strength and management expertise to absorb the troubled credit union without adversely affecting its own financial condition and stability.

As a stipulated condition to an emergency merger, the field of membership of the merging credit union may be transferred intact to the continuing federal credit union without regard to any field of membership restrictions, including the service facility requirement. Under this authority, a federal credit union may take in any dissimilar field of membership.

Even though the merging credit union is a single common bond credit union or multiple common bond credit union or community credit union, the continuing credit union will remain a community charter. Future community expansions will be based on the continuing credit union's original community area.

Emergency mergers involving federally insured credit unions in different NCUA regions must be approved by the regional director where the continuing credit union is headquartered, with the concurrence of the regional director of the merging credit union and, as applicable, the state regulators.

V.D.3—Purchase and Assumption (P&A)

Another alternative for acquiring the field of membership of a failing credit union is through a consolidation known as a P&A. Generally, the requirements applicable to community expansions found in this chapter apply to purchase and assumptions where the purchasing credit union is a federal charter.

A P&A has limited application because, in most instances, the failing credit union must be placed into involuntary liquidation. However, in the few instances where a P&A may occur, the assuming federal credit union, as with emergency mergers, may acquire the entire field of membership if the emergency criteria are satisfied.

In a P&A processed under the emergency criteria, specified loans, shares, and certain other designated assets and liabilities may also be acquired without regard to field of membership restrictions and without changing the character of the continuing federal credit union for purposes of future field of membership amendments.

If the P&A does not meet the emergency criteria, then only members of record can be obtained unless they otherwise qualify for membership in the community charter.

P&As involving federally insured credit unions in different NCUA regions must be approved by the regional director where the continuing credit union is headquartered, with the concurrence of the regional director of the purchased and/or assumed credit union and, as applicable, the state regulators.

V.D.4—Spin-Offs

A spin-off occurs when, by agreement of the parties, a portion of the field of membership, assets, liabilities, shares, and capital of a credit union are transferred to a new or existing credit union. A spin-off is unique in that usually one credit union has a field of membership expansion and the other loses a portion of its field of membership.

All field of membership requirements apply regardless of whether the spun-off group goes to a new or existing federal charter.

The request for approval of a spin-off must be supported with a plan that addresses, at a minimum:

- Why the spin-off is being requested;
- What part of the field of membership is to be spun off;
- Whether the field of membership requirements are met;
- Which assets, liabilities, shares, and capital are to be transferred;
- The financial impact the spin-off will have on the affected credit unions;
- The ability of the acquiring credit union to effectively serve the new members;
- The proposed spin-off date; and
- Disclosure to the members of the requirements set forth above.

The spin-off request must also include current financial statements from the affected credit unions and the proposed voting ballot.

For federal credit unions spinning off a portion of the community, membership notice and voting requirements and procedures are the same as for mergers (see Part 708 of the NCUA Rules and Regulations), except that only the members directly affected by the spin-off—those whose shares are to be transferred—are permitted to vote. Members whose shares are not being transferred will not be afforded the opportunity to vote. All members of the group to be spun off (whether they voted in favor, against, or not at all) will be transferred if the spin-off is approved by the voting membership. Voting requirements for federally insured state credit unions are governed by state law.

V.E—OVERLAPS

V.E.1—General

Generally, an overlap exists when a group of persons is eligible for membership in two or more credit unions. NCUA will permit community credit unions to overlap any other charters without performing an overlap analysis.

V.E.2—Exclusionary Clauses

An exclusionary clause is a limitation precluding the credit union from serving the primary members of a portion of a group or community otherwise included in its field of membership. NCUA no longer grants exclusionary clauses. Those granted prior to the adoption of this new chartering manual will remain in effect unless the credit unions agree to remove them or one of the affected credit unions submits a housekeeping amendment to have it removed.

V.F—CHARTER CONVERSIONS

A community federal credit union may convert to a single occupational or associational, or multiple common bond credit union. The converting credit union must meet all occupational, associational, and multiple common bond requirements, as applicable. The converting credit union may continue to serve members of record of the prior field of membership as of the date of the conversion, and any groups or communities obtained in an emergency merger or P&A. A change to the credit union's field of membership and designated common bond will be necessary.

A community credit union may convert to serve a new geographical area provided the field of membership requirements of V.A.3 of this chapter are met. Members of record of the original community can continue to be served.

V.G—OTHER PERSONS WITH A RELATIONSHIP TO THE COMMUNITY

A number of persons who have a close relationship to the community may be included, at the charter applicant's option, in the field of membership. These include the following:

- Spouses of persons who died while within the field of membership of this credit union;
- Employees of this credit union;
- Volunteers in the community;
- Members of the immediate family or household; and
- Organizations of such persons

Immediate family is defined as spouse, child, sibling, parent, grandparent, or grandchild. This includes stepparents, stepchildren, stepsiblings, and adoptive relationships.

National Credit Union Administration

Household is defined as persons living in the same residence maintaining a single economic unit.

Membership eligibility is extended only to individuals who are members of an "immediate family or household" of a credit union member. It is not necessary for the primary member to join the credit union in order for the immediate family or household member of the primary member to join, provided the immediate family or household clause is included in the field of membership. However, it is necessary for the immediate family member or household member to first join in order for that person's immediate family member or household member to join the credit union. A credit union can adopt a more restrictive definition of immediate family or household.

Under the Federal Credit Union Act, once a person becomes a member of the credit union, such person may remain a member of the credit union until the person chooses to withdraw or is expelled from the membership of the credit union. This is commonly referred to as "once a member, always a member." The "once a member, always a member" provision does not prevent a credit union from restricting services to members who are no longer within the field of membership.

CHAPTER 3

LOW-INCOME CREDIT UNIONS AND CREDIT UNIONS SERVING UNDERSERVED AREAS

I—INTRODUCTION

One of the primary reasons for the creation of federal credit unions was to make credit available to people of modest means for provident and productive purposes. To help NCUA fulfill this mission, the agency has established special operational policies for federal credit unions that serve low-income groups and underserved areas. The policies provide a greater degree of flexibility that will enhance and invigorate capital infusion into low-income groups, low-income communities, and underserved areas. These unique policies are necessary to provide credit unions serving low-income groups with financial stability and potential for controlled growth and to encourage the formation of new charters as well as the delivery of credit union services in low-income communities.

II—LOW-INCOME CREDIT UNION

II.A—Defined

A credit union serving predominantly low-income members may be designated as a low-income credit union. Section 701.34 of NCUA's Rules and Regulations defines the term "low-income members" as those members:

- Who make less than 80 percent of the average for all wage earners as established by the Bureau of Labor Statistics; or
- Whose annual household income falls at or below 80 percent of the median household income for the nation as established by the Census Bureau.

The term "low-income members" also includes members who are full-time or part-time students in a college, university, high school, or vocational school.

To obtain a low-income designation from NCUA, an existing credit union must establish that a majority of its members meet the low-income definition. An existing community credit union that serves a geographic area where a majority of residents meet the annual income standard is presumed to be serving predominantly low-income members. A low-income designation for a new credit union charter may be based on a majority of the potential membership.

II.B—SPECIAL PROGRAMS

A credit union with a low-income designation has greater flexibility in accepting nonmember deposits insured by the NCUSIF, are exempt from the aggregate loan limit on business loans, and may offer secondary capital accounts to strengthen its capital base. It also may participate in special funding programs such as the Community Development Revolving Loan Program for Credit Unions (CDRLP) if it is involved in the stimulation of economic development and community revitalization efforts.

The CDRLP provides both loans and grants for technical assistance to low-income credit unions. The requirements for participation in the revolving loan program are in Part 705 of the NCUA Rules and Regulations. Only operating credit unions are eligible for participation in this program.

II.C—LOW-INCOME DOCUMENTATION

A federal credit union charter applicant or existing credit union wishing to receive a low-income designation should forward a separate request for the designation to the regional director, along with appropriate documentation supporting the request.

For community charter applicants, the supporting material should include the median household income or annual wage figures for the community to be served. If this information is unavailable, the applicant should identify the individual zip codes or census tracts that comprise the community and NCUA will assist in obtaining the necessary demographic data.

Similarly, if single occupational or associational or multiple common bond charter applicants cannot supply income data on its potential members, they should provide the regional director with a list which includes the number of potential members, sorted by their residential zip codes, and NCUA will assist in obtaining the necessary demographic data.

An existing credit union can perform a loan or membership survey to determine if the credit union is primarily serving low-income members.

II.D—THIRD PARTY ASSISTANCE

A low-income federal credit union charter applicant may contract with a third party to assist in the chartering and low-income designation process. If the charter is granted, a low-income credit union may contract with a third party to provide necessary management services. Such contracts should not exceed the duration of one year subject to renewal.

II.E—SPECIAL RULES FOR LOW-INCOME FEDERAL CREDIT UNIONS

In recognition of the unique efforts needed to help make credit union service available to low-income groups, NCUA has adopted special rules that pertain to low-income credit union charters, as well as field of membership additions for low-income credit unions. These special rules provide additional latitude to enable underserved, low-income individuals to gain access to credit union service.

NCUA permits credit union chartering and field of membership amendments based on associational groups formed for the sole purpose of making credit union service available to low-income persons. The association must be defined so that all of its members will meet the low-income definition of Section 701.34 of the NCUA Rules and Regulations. Any multiple common bond credit union can add low-income associations to their fields of membership.

A low-income designated community federal credit union has additional latitude in serving persons who are affiliated with the community. In addition to serving members who live, work, worship, or attend school in the community, a low-income community federal credit union may also serve persons who participate in programs to alleviate poverty or distress, or who participate in associations headquartered in the community.

Examples of a low-income designated community and an associational-based low-income federal credit union are as follows:

• Persons who live in [the target area]; persons who work, worship, attend school, or participate in associations headquartered in [the target area]; persons participating in programs to alleviate poverty or distress which are located in [the target area]; incorporated and unincorporated organizations located in [the target area] or maintaining a facility in [the target area]; and organizations of such persons.

• Members of the Canarsie Economic Assistance League, in Brooklyn, NY, an association whose members all meet the low-income definition of Section 701.34 of the NCUA Rules and Regulations.

III—SERVICE TO UNDERSERVED COMMUNITIES

III.A—General

A multiple common bond federal credit union may include in its field of membership, without regard to location, an "underserved area" as defined by the Federal Credit Union Act. 12 U.S.C. 1759(c)(2). The addition of an "underserved area" will not change the charter type of the multiple common bond federal credit union. More than one multiple common-bond federal credit union can serve the same "underserved area," provided each credit union is approved as provided below.

By adding an "underserved area," a multiple common bond federal credit union does not become eligible to receive the benefits afforded to low-income designated credit unions, such as expanded use of nonmember deposits and access to the Community Development Revolving Loan Program for Credit Unions.

III.B—"Underserved Area" Defined

The Federal Credit Union Act defines an "underserved area" as (1) a "local community, neighborhood, or rural district" that (2) meets the definition of an "investment area" under section 103(16) of the Community Development Banking and Financial Institutions Act of 1994 ("CDFI"), 12 U.S.C. 4702(16), and (3) is "underserved by other depository institutions" based on data of the NCUA Board and the federal banking agencies.

III.B.1—Local Community

To be eligible for approval as "underserved," a proposed area must be a well-defined local community, neighborhood, or rural district as defined in Chapter 2, sections V.A.1. and V.A.2. of this Manual.

III.B.2—Investment Area

To be approved as an "underserved area," the proposed area must meet the CDFI definition of an "investment area." Id. §4702(16). A proposed area that, at the time the credit union applies, is designated in its entirety as an Empowerment Zone or Enterprise Community (id. §1391) automatically qualifies as an "investment area"; no further criteria of an "investment area" must be met. Id. §4702(16)(B). A proposed area that is not designated as such must qualify as an "investment area" under "the objective criteria of economic distress" developed by the CDFI Fund ("distress criteria") based on current decennial U.S. Census data, and also must have "significant unmet needs" for loans and

National Credit Union Administration

financial services that credit unions are authorized to offer to their members. *Id.* § 4702(16)(A).

III.B.2.a—*Economic Distress Criteria*

Geographic Unit(s) By Proposed Area's Location. The location of a proposed "underserved area" either within or outside of an MSA corresponding to the most recent completed decennial census published by the U.S. Bureau of the Census ("decennial Census") determines the geographic unit(s) that apply to determine whether the area meets the distress criteria.

Within MSA. For a proposed area located, in whole or in part, within an MSA, the permissible geographic units ("Metro units") for implementing the economic distress criteria are: (i) a census tract; (ii) a block group; and (iii) an American Indian or Alaskan Native area. 12 CFR 1805.201(b)(3)(ii)(B) (2008). For ease of implementation, it is advisable to use a census tract as the proposed area's Metro unit.

Outside MSA. For a proposed area that is located entirely outside an MSA, the permissible units ("Non-Metro units") for implementing the economic distress criteria are: (i) a county or equivalent area; (ii) a minor civil division that is a unit of local government; (iii) an incorporated place; (iv) a census tract; (v) a block numbering area; (vi) a block group; and (vii) an American Indian or Alaskan Native area. *Id.* For ease of implementation, it is advisable to use either a census tract or county, as the case may be, as the proposed area's Non-Metro unit.

Proposed Area Consisting of a Single Metro Unit. A proposed area consisting of a single whole Metro unit (*e.g.*, a single census tract located within an MSA) must meet one of the following distress criteria, as reported by the most recent decennial Census:

- *Unemployment.* The proposed area's unemployment rate is at least 1.5 times the national average; or
- *Poverty.* At least 20 percent (20%) of the proposed area's population lives in poverty; or
- *Median Family Income.* The proposed area's Median Family Income ("MFI") is at or below 80 percent (80%) of either the MFI of the corresponding MSA, or the national MFI for Metro Areas, whichever is greater; or
- *Other Criterion.* Any other economic distress criterion the CDFI Fund may adopt in the future.

Id. § 1805.201(b)(3)(ii)(D)(1), (2)(i) and (3) (2008).

Proposed Area Consisting of a Single Non-Metro Unit. A proposed area consisting of a single whole Non-Metro unit (*e.g.*, a single county located outside an MSA) must meet one of the following distress criteria, as reported by the most recent decennial Census:

- *Unemployment.* The proposed area's unemployment rate is at least 1.5 times the national average; or
- *Poverty.* At least 20 percent (20%) of the proposed area's population lives in poverty; or
- *Median Family Income.* The proposed area's MFI is at or below 80 percent (80%) of either the corresponding state's Non-Metro MFI or the national MFI for Non-Metro Areas, whichever is greater; or
- *Other Criterion.* Any other economic distress criterion the CDFI Fund may adopt in the future.

Id. § 1805.201(b)(3)(ii)(D)(1), (2)(ii) and (3) (2008). Alternatively, a proposed area consisting of a single Non-Metro county (located outside an MSA) may instead meet either of the following two criteria, as reported by the decennial Census:

- *County Population Loss.* County's population loss of at least 10 percent (10%) between the most recent and the preceding decennial Census; or
- *County Migration Loss.* County's net migration loss of at least 5 percent (5%) in the 5-year period preceding the most recent decennial Census.

Id. § 1805.201(b)(3)(ii)(D)(4)–(5) (2008).

Proposed Area Consisting of Multiple Contiguous Units. When a proposed area consists of either multiple contiguous Metro units (*e.g.*, a group of adjoining census tracts) or multiple contiguous Non-Metro units (*e.g.*, a group of adjoining counties), a population threshold applies when implementing the economic distress criteria. At least 85 percent (85%) of the area's total population must reside within the units that are "distressed," *i.e*, that meet one of the applicable economic distress criteria above, as reported by the decennial Census (Unemployment, Poverty and MFI for census tracts plus, for counties only, Population Loss and Migration Loss); the balance of the area's population may reside in the non-"distressed" tract(s). The population threshold is met, and the whole proposed area qualifies as "distressed," when the "distressed" units represent at least 85 percent of the area's total population.

III.B.2.b—*Proposed Area's "Significant Unmet Needs"*

A proposed area that is "distressed" also must display "significant unmet needs" for loans or for one or more of the financial services credit unions are authorized to offer. To meet this criterion, the credit union must include within its Business Plan a section, one page in length, entitled "Significant Unmet Needs for Credit Union Services" ("SUN section") that establishes the existence of such unmet needs by identifying the credit and depository needs of the community and detailing how the credit union plans to serve those needs. The credit union may choose which among the following "credit and depository needs" to address in the SUN section: loans, share draft accounts, savings accounts, check cashing, money orders, certified checks, automated teller machines, deposit taking, safe deposit box services, and similar services. The existence of each "credit and depository need" the credit union identifies and plans to serve must be supported by objective reasons and/or accompanying documentation derived from an identified, authoritative source of the credit union's choice. Third party documentation generally is the most compelling.

III.B.3—Underserved by Other Depository Institutions

A proposed area that meets the CDFI definition of an "investment area" (i.e, is "distressed" and has "significant unmet needs") must also be underserved by other insured depository institutions, including credit unions. 12 U.S.C. 1759(c)(2)(A)(ii). This statutory criterion is met when the concentration of depository institution facilities among the population of the proposed area's non-"distressed" tracts—which sets a benchmark level of adequate service—is greater than the concentration of facilities among the population of all of the proposed area's census tracts combined. If there are no non-"distressed" tracts within a proposed area, a non-"distressed" census tract or larger geographic unit (e.g., city or county) of the credit union's choice that adjoins the proposed area may be used to set the benchmark concentration ratio.

Without regard to a proposed area's location within or outside an MSA, this criterion compares two ratios: the ratio of facilities to the population of the non-"distressed" tracts (the benchmark) versus the same facilities-to-population ratio among all the tracts of the proposed area as a whole. If the benchmark ratio is greater than the ratio for the whole area, then the area is "underserved by other depository institutions," and vice versa.

III.C—NCUA Approval

If NCUA approves the request to add an "underserved area," the credit union will be issued an amendment to Section 5 of its charter.

III.D—Approval to Serve an Already Approved "Underserved Area"

Once a credit union is initially approved to serve an "underserved area," other credit unions that subsequently apply may be approved to serve the same area. To be approved, the area must qualify as "underserved" at the time the new applicant applies. An applicant must demonstrate the area continues to be "distressed", as provided above, only if a new decennial Census has been published since the date the area was last approved. In any case, the applicant must demonstrate that the area still has "significant unmet needs" for loans or credit union services (to qualify as an "investment area"), and remains "underserved by other depository institutions" (to qualify as "underserved").

III.E—Business Plan

A federal credit union that desires to include an underserved community in its field of membership must first develop, and submit for approval, a business plan specifying how it will serve the community. In addition, the business plan must include a SUN section as provided in section III.B.2.b. above. The credit union will be expected to regularly review the business plan to determine if the community is being adequately served. The regional director may require periodic service status reports from a credit union about the "underserved area" to ensure that the needs of the community are being met, and must require such reports before NCUA allows a multiple common bond federal credit union to add an additional "underserved area."

III.F—Service Facility

Once an "underserved area" has been added to a federal credit union's field of membership, the credit union must establish within two years, and maintain, an office or service facility in the community. A service facility is defined as a place where shares are accepted for members' accounts, loan applications are accepted and loans are disbursed. By definition, a service facility includes a credit union-owned branch, a shared branch, a mobile branch, or an office operated on a regularly scheduled weekly basis or a credit union owned electronic facility that meets, at a minimum, the above requirements. This definition does not include an ATM or the credit union's Internet Web site.

IV—APPEAL PROCEDURES FOR DENIAL OF UNDERSERVED AREA

IV.A—NCUA Disapproval

When NCUA disapproves any application to add an "underserved area" in whole or in part, under this chapter, the applicant will be informed in writing of the:
• Specific reasons for the action;
• Options to consider, if appropriate, for gaining approval; and
• Appeal procedures.

IV.B—Appeal of Regional Director Decision

If the regional director denies an "underserved area" request, the federal credit union may appeal the decision to the NCUA Board. An appeal must be sent to the appropriate regional office within 60 days of the

National Credit Union Administration

date of denial and must address the specific reason(s) for the denial. The regional director will then forward the appeal to the NCUA Board. NCUA central office staff will make an independent review of the facts and present the appeal to the NCUA Board with a recommendation.

Before appealing, the credit union may, within 30 days of the denial, provide supplemental information to the regional director for reconsideration. A reconsideration will contain new and material evidence addressing the reasons for the initial denial. The regional director will have 30 days from the date of the receipt of the request for reconsideration to make a final decision. If the request is again denied, the applicant may proceed with the appeal process within 60 days of the date of the last denial. A second request for reconsideration will be treated as an appeal to the NCUA Board.

CHAPTER 4

CHARTER CONVERSIONS

I—INTRODUCTION

A charter conversion is a change in the jurisdictional authority under which a credit union operates.

Federal credit unions receive their charters from NCUA and are subject to its supervision, examination, and regulation.

State-chartered credit unions are incorporated in a particular state, receiving their charter from the state agency responsible for credit unions and subject to the state's regulator. If the state-chartered credit union's deposits are federally insured, it will also fall under NCUA's jurisdiction.

A federal credit union's power and authority are derived from the Federal Credit Union Act and NCUA Rules and Regulations. State-chartered credit unions are governed by state law and regulation. Certain federal laws and regulations also apply to federally insured state chartered credit unions.

There are two types of charter conversions: federal charter to state charter and state charter to federal charter. Common bond and community requirements are not an issue from NCUA's standpoint in the case of a federal to state charter conversion. The procedures and forms relevant to both types of charter conversion are included in appendix 4.

II—CONVERSION OF A STATE CREDIT UNION TO A FEDERAL CREDIT UNION

II.A—General Requirements

Any state-chartered credit union may apply to convert to a federal credit union. In order to do so it must:

• Comply with state law regarding conversion and file proof of compliance with NCUA;
• File the required conversion application, proposed federal credit union organization certificate, and other documents with NCUA;
• Comply with the requirements of the Federal Credit Union Act, e.g., chartering and reserve requirements; and
• Be granted federal share insurance by NCUA.

Conversions are treated the same as any initial application for a federal charter, including an on-site examination by NCUA where appropriate. NCUA will also consult with the appropriate state authority regarding the credit union's current financial condition, management expertise, and past performance. Since the applicant in a conversion is an ongoing credit union, the economic advisability of granting a charter is more readily determinable than in the case of an initial charter applicant.

A converting state credit union's field of membership must conform to NCUA's chartering policy. The field of membership will be phrased in accordance with NCUA chartering policy. However, if the converting credit union is a multiple group charter and the new federal charter is a multiple group, then the new federal charter may retain in its field of membership any group that the state credit union was serving at the time of conversion. Subsequent changes must conform to NCUA chartering policy in effect at that time.

If the converting credit union is a community charter and the new federal charter is community-based, it must meet the community field of membership requirements set forth in Chapter 2, Section V of this manual. If the state-chartered credit union's community boundary is more expansive than the approved federal boundary, only members of record outside of the new community boundary may continue to be served.

The converting credit union, regardless of charter type, may continue to serve members of record. The converting credit union may retain in its field of membership any group or community added pursuant to state emergency provisions.

II.B—SUBMISSION OF CONVERSION PROPOSAL TO NCUA

The following documents must be submitted with the conversion proposal:

• Conversion of State Charter to Federal Charter (NCUA 4000);
• Organization Certificate (NCUA 4008). Only Part (3) and the signature/notary section should be completed and, where applicable, signed by the credit union officials.
• Report of Officials and Agreement to Serve (NCUA 4012);
• The Application to Convert From State Credit Union to Federal Credit Union (NCUA 4401);
• The Application and Agreements for Insurance of Accounts (NCUA 9500);

- Certification of Resolution (NCUA 9501);
- Written evidence regarding whether the state regulator is in agreement with the conversion proposal; and
- Business plan, as appropriate, including the most current financial report and delinquent loan schedule.

If the state charter is applying to become a federal community charter, it must also comply with the documentation requirements included in Chapter 2, Section V.A.2 of this manual.

II.C—NCUA Consideration of Application To Convert

II.C.1—Review by the Regional Director

The application will be reviewed to determine that it is complete and that the proposal is in compliance with Section 125 of the Federal Credit Union Act. This review will include a determination that the state credit union's field of membership is in compliance with NCUA's chartering policies. The regional director may make further investigation into the proposal and may require the submission of additional information to support the request to convert.

II.C.2—On-Site Review

NCUA may conduct an on-site examination of the books and records of the credit union. Non-federally insured credit unions will be assessed an insurance application fee.

II.C.3—Approval by the Regional Director and Conditions to the Approval

The conversion will be approved by the regional director if it is in compliance with Section 125 of the Federal Credit Union Act and meets the criteria for federal insurance. Where applicable, the regional director will specify any special conditions that the credit union must meet in order to convert to a federal charter, including changes to the credit union's field of membership in order to conform to NCUA's chartering policies. Some of these conditions may be set forth in a Letter of Understanding and Agreement (LUA), which requires the signature of the officials and the regional director.

II.C.4—Notification

The regional director will notify both the credit union and the state regulator of the decision on the conversion.

II.C.5—NCUA Disapproval

When NCUA disapproves any application to convert to a federal charter, the applicant will be informed in writing of the:
- Specific reasons for the action;
- Options to consider, if appropriate, for gaining approval; and
- Appeal procedures.

II.C.6—Appeal of Regional Director Decision

If a conversion to a federal charter is denied by the regional director, the applicant credit union may appeal the decision to the NCUA Board. An appeal must be sent to the appropriate regional office within 60 days of the date of denial and must address the specific reason(s) for the denial. The regional director will then forward the appeal to the NCUA Board. NCUA central office staff will make an independent review of the facts and present the appeal to the NCUA Board with a recommendation.

Before appealing, the credit union may, within 30 days of the denial, provide supplemental information to the regional director for reconsideration. The request will not be considered as an appeal, but a request for reconsideration by the regional director. The regional director will have 30 business days from the date of the receipt of the request for reconsideration to make a final decision. If the application is again denied, the credit union may proceed with the appeal process to the NCUA Board within 60 days of the date of the last denial by the regional director.

II.D—Action by Board of Directors

II.D.1—General

Upon being informed of the regional director's preliminary approval, the board must:
- Comply with all requirements of the state regulator that will enable the credit union to convert to a federal charter and cease being a state credit union;
- Obtain a letter or official statement from the state regulator certifying that the credit union has met all of the state requirements and will cease to be a state credit union upon its receiving a federal charter. A copy of this document must be submitted to the regional director;
- Obtain a letter from the private share insurer (includes excess share insurers), if applicable, certifying that the credit union has met all withdrawal requirements. A copy of this document must be submitted to the regional director; and
- Submit a statement of the action taken to comply with any conditions imposed by the regional director in the preliminary approval of the conversion proposal and, if applicable, submit the signed LUA.

II.D.2—Application for a Federal Charter

When the regional director has received evidence that the board of directors has satisfactorily completed the actions described above, the federal charter and new Certificate of Insurance will be issued.

The credit union may then complete the conversion as discussed in the following section. A denial of a conversion application

National Credit Union Administration

can be appealed. Refer to Section II.C.6 of this chapter.

II.E—COMPLETION OF THE CONVERSION

II.E.1—Effective Date of Conversion

The date on which the regional director approves the Organization Certificate and the Application and Agreements for Insurance of Accounts is the date on which the credit union becomes a federal credit union. The regional director will notify the credit union and the state regulator of the date of the conversion.

II.E.2—Assumption of Assets and Liabilities

As of the effective date of the conversion, the federal credit union will be the owner of all of the assets and will be responsible for all of the liabilities and share accounts of the state credit union.

II.E.3—Board of Directors' Meeting

Upon receipt of its federal charter, the board will hold its first meeting as a federal credit union. At this meeting, the board will transact such business as is necessary to complete the conversion as approved and to operate the credit union in accordance with the requirements of the Federal Credit Union Act and NCUA Rules and Regulations.

As of the commencement of operations, the accounting system, records, and forms must conform to the standards established by NCUA.

II.E.4—Credit Union's Name

Changing of the credit union's name on all signage, records, accounts, investments, and other documents should be accomplished as soon as possible after conversion. The credit union has 180 days from the effective date of the conversion to change its signage and promotional material. This requires the credit union to discontinue using any remaining stock of "state credit union" stationery immediately, and discontinue using credit cards, ATM cards, etc., within 180 days after the effective date of the conversion, or the reissue date, whichever is later. The regional director has the discretion to extend the timeframe for an additional 180 days. Member share drafts with the state-chartered name can be used by the members until depleted.

II.E.5—Reports to NCUA

Within 10 business days after commencement of operations, the recently converted federal credit union must submit to the regional director the following:
• Report of Officials (NCUA 4501); and
• Financial and Statistical Reports, as of the commencement of business of the federal credit union.

III—CONVERSION OF A FEDERAL CREDIT UNION TO A STATE CREDIT UNION

III.A—GENERAL REQUIREMENTS

Any federal credit union may apply to convert to a state credit union. In order to do so, it must:
• Notify NCUA prior to commencing the process to convert to a state charter and state the reason(s) for the conversion;
• Comply with the requirements of Section 125 of the Federal Credit Union Act that enable it to convert to a state credit union and to cease being a federal credit union; and
• Comply with applicable state law and the requirements of the state regulator.

It is important that the credit union provide an accurate disclosure of the reasons for the conversion. These reasons should be stated in specific terms, not as generalities. The federal credit union converting to a state charter remains responsible for the entire operating fee for the year in which it converts.

III.B—SPECIAL PROVISIONS REGARDING FEDERAL SHARE INSURANCE

If the federal credit union intends to continue federal share insurance after the conversion to a state credit union, it must submit an Application for Insurance of Accounts (NCUA 9600) to the regional director at the time it requests approval of the conversion proposal. The regional director has the authority to approve or disapprove the application.

If the converting federal credit union does not intend to continue federal share insurance or if its application for continued insurance is denied, insurance will cease in accordance with the provisions of Section 206 of the Federal Credit Union Act.

If, upon its conversion to a state credit union, the federal credit union will be terminating its federal share insurance or converting from federal to non-federal share insurance, it must comply with the membership notice and voting procedures set forth in Section 206 of the Federal Credit Union Act and Part 708 of NCUA's Rules and Regulations, and address the criteria set forth in Section 205(c) of the Federal Credit Union Act.

Where the state credit union will be non-federally insured, federal insurance ceases on the effective date of the charter conversion. If it will be otherwise uninsured, then federal insurance will cease one year after the date of conversion subject to the restrictions in Section 206(d)(1) of the Federal Credit Union Act. In either case, the state credit union will be entitled to a refund of the federal credit union's NCUSIF capitalization deposit after the final date on which any of its shares are federally insured.

The NCUA Board reserves the right to delay the refund of the capitalization deposit for up to one year if it determines that payment would jeopardize the NCUSIF.

III.C—Submission of Conversion Proposal to NCUA

Upon approval of a proposition for conversion by a majority vote of the board of directors at a meeting held in accordance with the federal credit union's bylaws, the conversion proposal will be submitted to the regional director and will include:
- A current financial report;
- A current delinquent loan schedule;
- An explanation and appropriate documents relative to any changes in insurance of member accounts;
- A resolution of the board of directors;
- A proposed Notice of Special Meeting of the Members (NCUA 4221);
- A copy of the ballot to be sent to all members (NCUA 4506);
- If the credit union intends to continue with federal share insurance, an application for insurance of accounts (NCUA 9600);
- Evidence that the state regulator is in agreement with the conversion proposal; and
- A statement of reasons supporting the request to convert.

III.D—Approval of Proposal to Convert

III.D.1—Review by the Regional Director

The proposal will be reviewed to determine that it is complete and is in compliance with Section 125 of the Federal Credit Union Act. The regional director may make further investigation into the proposal and require the submission of additional information to support the request.

III.D.2—Conditions to the Approval

The regional director will specify any special conditions that the credit union must meet in order to proceed with the conversion.

III.D.3—Approval by the Regional Director

The proposal will be approved by the regional director if it is in compliance with Section 125 and, in the case where the state credit union will no longer be federally insured, the notice and voting requirements of Section 206 of the Federal Credit Union Act.

III.D.4—Notification

The regional director will notify both the credit union and the state regulator of the decision on the proposal.

III.D.5—NCUA Disapproval

When NCUA disapproves any application to convert to a state charter, the applicant will be informed in writing of the:
- Specific reasons for the action;
- If appropriate, options or suggestions that could be considered for gaining approval; and
- Appeal procedures.

III.D.6—Appeal of Regional Director Decision

If the regional director denies a conversion to a state charter, the applicant credit union may appeal the decision to the NCUA Board. An appeal must be sent to the appropriate regional office within 60 days of the date of denial and must address the specific reason(s) for the denial. The regional director will then forward the appeal to the NCUA Board. NCUA central office staff will make an independent review of the facts and present the appeal to the NCUA Board with a recommendation.

Before appealing, the credit union may, within 30 days of the denial, provide supplemental information to the regional director for reconsideration. The request will not be considered as an appeal, but a request for reconsideration by the regional director. The regional director will have 30 business days from the date of the receipt of the request for reconsideration to make a final decision. If the application is again denied, the credit union may proceed with the appeal process to the NCUA Board within 60 days of the date of the last denial by the regional director.

III.E—Approval of Proposal by Members

The members may not vote on the proposal until it is approved by the regional director. Once approval of the proposal is received, the following actions will be taken by the board of directors:
- The proposal must be submitted to the members for approval and a date set for a meeting to vote on the proposal. The proposal may be acted on at the annual meeting or at a special meeting for that purpose. The members must also be given the opportunity to vote by written ballot to be filed by the date set for the meeting.
- Members must be given advance notice (NCUA 4221) of the meeting at which the proposal is to be submitted. The notice must:
  ○ Specify the purpose, time and place of the meeting;
  ○ Include a brief, complete, and accurate statement of the reasons for and against the proposed conversion, including any effects it could have upon share holdings, insurance of member accounts, and the policies and practices of the credit union;
  ○ Specify the costs of the conversion, i.e., changing the credit union's name, examination and operating fees, attorney and consulting fees, tax liability, etc.;
  ○ Inform the members that they have the right to vote on the proposal at the meeting, or by written ballot to be filed not later than the date and time announced for the annual

meeting, or at the special meeting called for that purpose;
  ○ Be accompanied by a Federal to State Conversion—Ballot for Conversion Proposal (NCUA 4506); and
  ○ State in **bold** face type that the issue will be decided by a majority of members who vote.
• The proposed conversion must be approved by a majority of all of the members who vote on the proposal, a quorum being present, in order for the credit union to proceed further with the proposition, provided federal insurance is maintained. If the proposed state-chartered credit union will not be federally insured, 20 percent of the total membership must participate in the voting, and of those, a majority must vote in favor of the proposal. Ballots cast by members who did not attend the meeting but who submitted their ballots in accordance with instructions above will be counted with votes cast at the meeting. In order to have a suitable record of the vote, the voting at the meeting should be by written ballot as well.
• The board of directors shall, within 10 days, certify the results of the membership vote to the regional director. The statement shall be verified by affidavits of the Chief Executive Officer and the Recording Officer on NCUA 4505.

III.F—COMPLIANCE WITH STATE LAWS

If the proposal for conversion is approved by a majority of all members who voted, the board of directors will:
• Ensure that all requirements of state law and the state regulator have been accommodated;
• Ensure that the state charter or the license has been received within 90 days from the date the members approved the proposal to convert; and
• Ensure that the regional director is kept informed as to progress toward conversion and of any material delay or of substantial difficulties which may be encountered.

If the conversion cannot be completed within the 90-day period, the regional director should be informed of the reasons for the delay. The regional director may set a new date for the conversion to be completed.

III.G—COMPLETION OF CONVERSION

In order for the conversion to be completed, the following steps are necessary:
• The board of directors will submit a copy of the state charter to the regional director within 10 days of its receipt. This will be accompanied by the federal charter and the federal insurance certificate. A copy of the financial reports as of the preceding month-end should be submitted at this time.
• The regional director will notify the credit union and the state regulator in writing of the receipt of evidence that the credit union has been authorized to operate as a state credit union.
• The credit union shall cease to be a federal credit union as of the effective date of the state charter.
• If the regional director finds a material deviation from the provisions that would invalidate any steps taken in the conversion, the credit union and the state regulator shall be promptly notified in writing. This notice may be either before or after the copy of the state charter is filed with the regional director. The notice will inform the credit union as to the nature of the adverse findings. The conversion will not be effective and completed until the improper actions and steps have been corrected.
• Upon ceasing to be a federal credit union, the credit union shall no longer be subject to any of the provisions of the Federal Credit Union Act, except as may apply if federal share insurance coverage is continued. The successor state credit union shall be immediately vested with all of the assets and shall continue to be responsible for all of the obligations of the federal credit union to the same extent as though the conversion had not taken place. Operation of the credit union from this point will be in accordance with the requirements of state law and the state regulator.
• If the regional director is satisfied that the conversion has been accomplished in accordance with the approved proposal, the federal charter will be canceled.
• There is no federal requirement for closing the records of the federal credit union at the time of conversion or for the manner in which the records shall be maintained thereafter. The converting credit union is advised to contact the state regulator for applicable state requirements.
• The credit union shall neither use the words "Federal Credit Union" in its name nor represent itself in any manner as being a federal credit union.
• Changing of the credit union's name on all signage, records, accounts, investments, and other documents should be accomplished as soon as possible after conversion. Unless it violates state law, the credit union has 180 days from the effective date of the conversion to change its signage and promotional material. This requires the credit union to discontinue using any remaining stock of "federal credit union" stationery immediately, and discontinue using credit cards, ATM cards, etc., within 180 days after the effective date of the conversion, or the reissue date, whichever is later. The regional director has the discretion to extend the timeframe for an additional 180 days. Member share drafts with the federal chartered name can be used by the members until depleted. If

the state credit union is not federally insured, it must change its name and must immediately cease using any credit union documents referencing federal insurance.

• If the state credit union is to be federally insured, the regional director will issue a new insurance certificate.

(Approved by the Office of Management and Budget under control numbers 3133–0015 and 3133–0116)

APPENDIX 1

GLOSSARY

These definitions apply only for use with this Manual. Definitions are not intended to be all inclusive or comprehensive. This Manual, the Federal Credit Union Act, and NCUA Rules and Regulations, as well as state laws, may be used for further reference.

Adequately capitalized - A credit union is considered adequately capitalized when it has a net worth ratio of at least 6 percent. A multiple common bond credit union must be adequately capitalized in order to add new groups to its charter. The regional director may determine that a net worth ratio of less than 6 percent is adequate if the credit union is making reasonable progress toward meeting the 6 percent net worth requirement, and the addition of the group would not adversely affect the credit union's capitalization level.

Affinity - A relationship upon which a community charter is based. Acceptable affinities include living, working, worshiping, or attending school in a community.

Appeal - The right of a credit union or charter applicant to request a formal review of a regional director's adverse decision by the National Credit Union Administration Board.

Associational common bond - A common bond comprised of members and employees of a recognized association. It includes individuals (natural persons) and/or groups (non-natural persons) whose members participate in activities developing common loyalties, mutual benefits, and mutual interests.

Business plan - Plan submitted by a charter applicant or existing federal credit union addressing the economic advisability of a proposed charter or field of membership addition.

Charter - The document which authorizes a group to operate as a credit union and defines the fundamental limits of its operating authority, generally including the persons the credit union is permitted to accept for membership. Charters are issued by the National Credit Union Administration for federal credit unions and by the designated state chartering authority for credit unions organized under the laws of that state.

Common bond - The characteristic or combination of characteristics which distinguishes a particular group of persons from the general public. There are two common bonds which can serve as a basis for a group forming a federal credit union or being included in an existing federal credit union's field of membership: occupational - employment by the same company, related companies or in a trade, industry, or profession (TIP); and associational - membership in the same association.

National Credit Union Administration   **Pt. 701, App. B**

Community credit union - A credit union whose field of membership consists of persons who live, work, worship, or attend school in the same well-defined local community, neighborhood, or rural district.

Credit union - A member-owned, not-for-profit cooperative financial institution formed to permit those in the field of membership specified in the charter to save, borrow, and obtain related financial services.

Economic advisability - An overall evaluation of the credit union's or charter applicant's ability to operate successfully.

Emergency merger - Pursuant to Section 205(h) of the Federal Credit Union Act, authority of NCUA to merge two credit unions without regard to common bond policy.

Exclusionary clause - A limitation, written in a credit union's charter, which precludes the credit union from serving a portion of a group which otherwise could be included in its field of membership.

Federal share insurance - Insurance coverage provided by the National Credit Union Share Insurance Fund and administered by the National Credit Union Administration. Coverage is provided for qualified accounts in all federal credit unions and participating state credit unions.

Field of membership - The persons (including organizations and other legal entities) a credit union is permitted to accept for membership.

Household - Persons living in the same residence maintaining a single economic unit.

Housekeeping Amendment - A field of membership amendment to delete groups, change group names, change group locations, remove exclusionary clauses, and to add other persons eligible for credit union membership by virtue of their close relationship to a common bond group or the community for community charters.

Immediate family member - A spouse, child, sibling, parent, grandparent, or grandchild. This includes stepparents, stepchildren, stepsiblings, and adoptive relationships.

In danger of insolvency - In making the determination that a particular credit union is in danger of insolvency, NCUA will establish that the credit union falls into one or more of the following categories:

1. The credit union's net worth is declining at a rate that will render it insolvent within 24 months. In projecting future net worth, NCUA may relay on data in addition to Call Report data. The trend must be supported by at least 12 months of historic data.

2. The credit union's net worth is declining at a rate that will take it under two percent (2%) net worth within 12 months. In projecting future net worth, NCUA may rely on data in addition to Call Report data. The trend must be supported by at least 12 months of historic data.

3. The credit union's net worth, as self-reported on its Call Report, is significantly undercapitalized, and NCUA determines that there is no reasonable prospect of the credit union becoming adequately capitalized in the succeeding 36 months. In making its determination on the prospect of achieving adequate capitalization, NCUA will assume that, if adverse economic conditions are affecting the value of the credit union's assets and liabilities, including property values and loan delinquencies related to unemployment, these adverse conditions will not further deteriorate.

Letter of Understanding and Agreement - Agreement between NCUA and federal credit union officials not to engage in certain activities and/or to establish reasonable operational goals. These are normally entered into with new charter applicants for a limited time.

Mentor - An individual who provides guidance and assistance to newly chartered, small, or low-income credit unions. All new federal credit unions are encouraged to establish a mentor relationship with a trained, experienced credit union individual or an existing credit union.

Metropolitan Statistical Area (MSA) - The Office of Management and Budget defines a metropolitan statistical area as an urbanized area that has at least one urbanized area in excess of 50,000 and "comprises the central county or counties containing the core, plus adjacent outlying counties having a high degree of social and economic integration with the central county as measured through commuting."

Merger - Absorption by one credit union of all of the assets, liabilities and equity of another credit union. Mergers must be approved by the National Credit Union Administration and by the appropriate state regulator whenever a state credit union is involved.

Multiple common bond credit union - A credit union whose field of membership consists of more than one group, each of which has a common bond of occupation or association.

Occupational common bond - Employment by the same entity or related entities or a Trade, Industry, or Profession.

Once a member, always a member - A provision of the Federal Credit Union Act which permits an individual to remain a member of the credit union until he or she chooses to withdraw or is expelled from the membership of the credit union. Under this

National Credit Union Administration   Pt. 701, App. B

provision, leaving a group that is named in the credit union's charter does not terminate an individual's membership in the credit union.

Organizations of such persons - An organization or organizations composed exclusively of persons who are within the field of membership of the credit union.

Overlap - The situation which results when a group is eligible for membership in more than one credit union.

Primary potential members - Members or employees who belong to an associational or occupational group.

Purchase and assumption - Purchase of all or part of the assets of and assumption of all or part of the liabilities of one credit union by another credit union. The purchased and assumed credit union must first be placed into involuntary liquidation.

Service area - The area that can reasonably be served by the service facilities accessible to the groups within the field of membership.

Service facility - A place where shares are accepted for members' accounts, loan applications are accepted or loans are disbursed. This definition includes a credit union owned branch, a mobile branch, an office operated on a regularly scheduled weekly basis, a credit union owned ATM, or a credit union owned electronic facility that meets, at a minimum, these requirements. A service facility also includes a shared branch or a shared branch network if either: (1) the credit union has an ownership interest in the service facility either directly or through a CUSO or similar organization; or (2) the service facility is local to the credit union and the credit union is an authorized participant in the service center. This definition does not include the credit union's Internet website. A service facility does not include an ATM or interest in a shared branch network for purposes of serving an underserved area.

Single associational common bond credit union - A credit union whose field of membership includes members and employees of a recognized association.

Single common bond credit union - A credit union whose field of membership consists of one group which has a common bond of occupation or association.

Single occupational common bond credit union - A credit union whose field of membership consists of employees of the same entity or related entities or part of a Trade, Industry, or Profession (TIP).

Spin-off - The transfer of a portion of the field of membership, assets, liabilities, shares, and capital of one credit union to a new or existing credit union.

Subscribers - For a federal credit union, at least seven individuals who sign the charter application and pledge at least one share.

Trade, Industry, or Profession (TIP) - A single occupational common bond credit union based on employment in a trade, industry, or profession including employment at any number of corporations or other legal entities that while not under common ownership – have a common bond by virtue of producing similar products, providing similar services, or participating in the same type of business.

Underserved community - A local community, neighborhood, or rural district that is an "investment area" as defined in Section 103(16) of the Community Development Banking and Financial Institutions Act of 1994. The area must also be underserved based on other NCUA and federal banking agency data.

Unsafe or unsound practice - Any action, or lack of action, which would result in an abnormal risk or loss to the credit union, its members, or the National Credit Union Share Insurance Fund.

National Credit Union Administration   Pt. 701, App. B

APPENDIX 2

LETTER OF UNDERSTANDING AND AGREEMENT

To the Board of Directors and Other Officials
_____ Federal Credit Union

Since the purposes of credit unions are to promote thrift and to make funds available for loans to credit union members for provident and productive purposes, and since newly chartered credit unions do not generally have sufficient reserves to cover large losses on loans or meet unduly large liquidity requirements, Federal insurance coverage of member accounts under the National Credit Union Share Insurance Fund will be granted to the above named credit union subject to the conditions listed in this Letter of Understanding and Agreement and in the Organization Certificate and Application and Agreements for Insurance of Accounts. These terms are listed below and are subject to acceptance by authorized credit union officials.

1. The credit union will refrain from soliciting or accepting brokered fund deposits from any source without the prior written approval of the Regional Director.

2. The credit union will refrain from the making of large loans, that is, loans in excess of 5 percent of unimpaired capital and surplus, to any one member or group of members without the prior written approval of the Regional Director.

3. The credit union will not establish or invest in a Credit Union Service Organization (CUSO) without the prior written approval of the Regional Director.

4. The credit union will not enter into any insurance programs whereby the credit union member finances the payment of insurance premiums through loans from the credit union.

5. Any special insurance plan/program, that is, insurance other than usual and normal surety bonding or casualty or liability or loan protection and life savings insurance coverage, which the credit union officials intend to undertake, will be submitted to the Regional Director of the National Credit Union Administration for written approval prior to the officials committing the credit union thereto.

6. The credit union will prepare and mail to the district examiner financial and statistical reports as required by the Federal Credit Union Act and Bylaws by the 20th of each month following that for which the report is prepared.

7. As the credit union's officials gain experience and the credit union achieves target levels of growth and profitability, the above terms and conditions may be renegotiated by the two parties.

We, the undersigned officials of the _____ Federal Credit Union, as authorized by the board of directors, acknowledge receipt of and agree to the attached Letter of Understanding and Agreement dated _____.

This Letter of Understanding and Agreement has been voluntarily entered into with the National Credit Union Administration. We agree to comply with all terms and conditions expressed in this Letter of Understanding and Agreement.

Should the NCUA Board determine that these terms and conditions have not been complied with or that the board of directors or other officials have not conducted the affairs of the credit union in a sound and prudent manner, the NCUA Board may terminate insurance coverage of the credit union. If actions by the officials, in violation of this Letter of Understanding and Agreement, cause the credit union to become insolvent, the officials assume such personal liability as may result from their actions.

The term of this Letter of Understanding and Agreement shall be for the period of at least 24 months from the date the credit union is insured. This Letter of Understanding and Agreement may, at the option of the Regional Director, be extended for an additional 24 months at the end of the initial term of this agreement.

Dated this _____ of _____ _____.
　　　　　　　　(day)　　　　(month)　　(year)

NATIONAL CREDIT UNION ADMINISTRATION BOARD
ON BEHALF OF THE NATIONAL CREDIT UNION SHARE INSURANCE FUND

_____
Regional Director

_____Federal Credit Union

By:

_____
Chief Executive Officer　　　　　　Date

_____
Chief Financial Officer　　　　　　　Date

_____
Secretary　　　　　　　　　　　　　Date

National Credit Union Administration	Pt. 701, App. B

APPENDIX 3- NCUA OFFICES

CENTRAL OFFICE,
1775 Duke Street, Alexandria, VA 22314-3428, Phone: 703-518-6300.

REGION I – Albany,
9 Washington Square, Washington Avenue Extension, Albany, NY 12205-5512, Phone: 518-862-7400, FAX: 518-862-7420.

Connecticut, Maine, Massachusetts, Michigan, New Hampshire, New York, Rhode Island, Vermont.

REGION II - Capital

1775 Duke Street, Suite 4206, Alexandria, VA 22314-3437, Phone: 703-519-4600, FAX: 703-519-4620.

Delaware, District of Columbia, Maryland, New Jersey, Pennsylvania, Virginia, West Virginia.

REGION III - Atlanta

7000 Central Parkway, Suite 1600Atlanta, GA 30328-4598, Phone: 678-443-3000, FAX: 678-443-3020.

Alabama, Florida, Georgia, Indiana, Kentucky, Mississippi, North Carolina, Ohio, Puerto Rico, South Carolina, Tennessee, Virgin Islands.

REGION IV - Austin

4807 Spicewood Springs Road, Suite 5200, Austin, TX 78759-8490, Phone: 512-342-5600, FAX: 512-342-5620.

Arkansas, Illinois, Iowa, Kansas, Louisiana, Minnesota, Missouri, Nebraska, North Dakota, Oklahoma, South Dakota, Texas, Wisconsin.

REGION V - Tempe

1230 W. Washington Street, Suite 301, Tempe, AZ 85281, Phone: 602-302-6000, FAX: 602-302-6024.

Alaska, Arizona, American Samoa, California, Colorado, Guam, Hawaii, Idaho, Montana, Nevada, New Mexico, Oregon, Utah, Washington, Wyoming.

APPENDIX 2
NCUA FORMS

Form Number	Form Title
NCUA 4000	Conversion of State Charter to a Federal Charter – Federal Credit Union Investigation Report
NCUA 4001	Federal Credit Union Investigation Report
NCUA 4008	Organization Certificate
NCUA 4009	Approval of Organization Certificate and Certification of Insurance
NCUA 4012	Report of Official and Agreement to Serve
NCUA 4015	Application for Field of Membership Amendment
NCUA 4015-EZ	Application for Field of Membership Amendment (use for all single common bond expansions and multiple common bond expansions of less than 3,000)
NCUA 4221	Notice of Meeting of Members to Convert from a Federal to State Chartered Credit Union
NCUA 4401	Application to Convert from a State to a Federal Credit Union
NCUA 4505	Affidavit - Proof of Results of Membership Vote - Proposed Conversion From Federal Credit Union to State Credit Union
NCUA 4506	Federal to State Conversion - Ballot for Conversion Proposal
NCUA 9500	Application and Agreements for Insurance of Accounts
NCUA 9501	Certification of Resolutions
NCUA 9600	Information to be Provided in Support of the Application of a State Chartered Credit Union for Insurance of Accounts

National Credit Union Administration   Pt. 701, App. B

CONVERSION OF STATE CHARTER TO FEDERAL CHARTER

FEDERAL CREDIT UNION INVESTIGATION REPORT

This report must be filled in completely and submitted with the other completed forms listed in Chapter 4 and in the instructions for this form.

A. INFORMATION FOR CHARTER AND BYLAWS

1. Proposed Name: _____ Federal Credit Union
Second Choice of Name: _____ Federal Credit Union

2. Contact Person_____
Bus. Tel. No./Area Code: _____ Res. Tel. No./Area Code_____

3. The credit union will maintain its office at:

    _____ _____ _____ _____
        (City)   (County)   (State)   (Zip)

4. Permanent mailing address of credit union:
    _____
    _____
    _____

5. Define proposed field of membership (Attach a copy of current state charter field of membership):
_____
_____
_____
_____
_____
_____
_____
_____
_____
_____

6. The board will have (an odd number 5 to 15) _____ members; the credit committee (an odd number, 3 to 7) _____ members; the supervisory committee (3 to 5) _____ members. Each official must complete a Report of Official and Agreement to Serve (NCUA 4012) which is to be submitted with this investigation report.

NCUA 4000   PAGE 1

Pt. 701, App. B   12 CFR Ch. VII (1-1-12 Edition)

B. CHARACTER AND FITNESS OF SUBSCRIBERS

7. Type or print the list of the subscribers who have signed the organization certificate (7 not more than 10 persons). Names should be IDENTICAL to signatures on the Organization Certificate (NCUA 4008). Each subscriber listed below has subscribed to at least one share in accordance with Section 103 of the Federal Credit Union Act:

Name:	*Address:*
Occupation:	*Years of Membership:*
Name:	*Address:*
Occupation:	*Years of Membership:*
Name:	*Address:*
Occupation:	*Years of Membership:*
Name:	*Address:*
Occupation:	*Years of Membership:*
Name:	*Address:*
Occupation:	*Years of Membership:*
Name:	*Address:*
Occupation:	*Years of Membership:*
Name:	*Address:*
Occupation:	*Years of Membership:*
Name:	*Address:*
Occupation:	*Years of Membership:*
Name:	*Address:*
Occupation:	*Years of Membership:*

NCUA 4000   **PAGE 2**

National Credit Union Administration   Pt. 701, App. B

ANY ADDITIONAL COMMENTS OR INFORMATION THAT IS DEEMED PERTINENT OR HELPFUL IN GIVING CONSIDERATION TO THIS APPLICATION SHOULD BE INCLUDED AS AN ATTACHMENT.

The undersigned certifies that to the best of his/her knowledge and belief the above information is true and correct.

I do (do not) recommend that a charter be granted to this group.

Signature _____, Organizer

Organizer's Address: _____
_____
_____

Pt. 701, App. B 12 CFR Ch. VII (1-1-12 Edition)

FORM 4000 INSTRUCTIONS

A. INFORMATION FOR CHARTERS AND BYLAWS

The subscriber should select a name for the proposed credit union. It is the responsibility of the federal credit union organizers to ensure that the proposed federal credit union name does not constitute an infringement on the name of any corporation in its trade area. The last three words in the name must be "Federal Credit Union." Since the name selected should not duplicate exactly the name of an existing credit union, item 1 provides space for a second choice.

The territory of operations of a Federal credit union is described in the field of membership, item 5. The principal office of the credit union will usually be maintained at a location described in the field of membership.

The proposed field of membership should be defined so clearly that it leaves no room for any doubt as to whom the credit union is to serve or the area which it is to operate. Corporations and other organizations referred to in the definition of the field of membership should be designated by the exact names rather than by some local or popular contraction of these names. Any segment of a larger organization should be identified with the parent. The field of membership for each type of common bond and samples are discussed in detail in Chapter 2 of the *Chartering and Field of Membership Manual.*"

With the guidance of the organizer, the subscribers to the Organization Certificate decide on the number of directors and credit committee members. The board and credit committee must be composed of an odd number of members. The supervisory committee is appointed by the board of directors.

B. CHARACTER AND FITNESS OF SUBSCRIBERS

The names and address of the subscribers should be recorded legibly and completely in item 7 of this report. It is from this information that the National Credit Union Administration prepares Section 3 of the charter. The names of the subscribers must be IDENTICAL to their signatures on the Organization Certificate.

National Credit Union Administration
Pt. 701, App. B

C. SUBMITTAL OF CHARTER APPLICATION

In addition to this Investigation Report, the following should be submitted to the appropriate regional director of NCUA:

1. Application to Convert, NCUA 4401 – one original;

2. Written evidence regarding whether the state regulator is in agreement with the conversion proposal;

3. Application and Agreements for Insurance of Accounts, NCUA 9500 - one original;

4. Certificate of Resolution, NCUA 9501 - one original;

5. Organization Certificate, NCUA 4008 - one notarized original. At least seven, *but no more than ten persons*, must sign the organization certificate. The person administering the oath must not be one of the subscribers. The oath on the organization certificate must be executed and show the notary's seal and date the commission expires as required by State law;

6. Report of Official and Agreement to Serve, NCUA 4012 – one original for each board member, credit committee member, and supervisory committee member;

7. Most current financial report and delinquent loan schedule; and

8. Business Plan - refer to Chapter 1 of the *Chartering and Field of Membership Manual* for a discussion of the components of an acceptable business plan.

Pt. 701, App. B   12 CFR Ch. VII (1-1-12 Edition)

FEDERAL CREDIT UNION INVESTIGATION REPORT

This form must be filled in completely and submitted with the other completed forms listed in the instructions to this form.

A. INFORMATION FOR CHARTER AND BYLAWS

1. Proposed name: _____ Federal Credit Union

   Second choice: _____ Federal Credit Union

2. Contact Person: _____
   Business Tel.: _____
   Residence Tel.: _____
   Address: _____
   _____
   _____

3. The credit union will maintain its offices at:
   _____
   (City, State, County, Zip Code)

3a. Proposed permanent mailing address of credit union:
   _____
   _____
   _____

4. Define proposed field of membership: _____
   _____
   _____
   _____
   _____
   _____
   _____
   _____
   _____

5. The board will have (an odd number, 5 to 15) _____members; the credit committee will have (an odd number, 3 to 7) _____members; the supervisory committee will have (3 to 5) _____members. Each official must complete a Report of Official and Agreement to Serve (NCUA 4012) which is to be submitted with this investigation report.

NCUA 4001   PAGE 1

National Credit Union Administration

Pt. 701, App. B

B. ECONOMIC ADVISABILITY OF ORGANIZING PROPOSED CREDIT UNION

(Attach a separate sheet if space available is not adequate.)

GENERAL INFORMATION

1. Potential membership: _____

   NOTE: Number of employees for occupational, active members for associational (or families for religious groups), or population per most recent census for community-type fields of membership.

2. Potential interest (survey results).

   NOTE: Sample must consist of a minimum of 250 potential members. Copy of survey form(s) utilized should be attached.

   Number of people surveyed: _____
   Number of people responding to survey: _____
   Number of people pledging an initial deposit: _____
   Total dollars pledged: $_____
   Number pledging systematic savings: _____
   Total dollars pledged (per month): $_____

3. Number of persons attending the charter-organization meeting: _____

4. Attach a business plan containing, at a minimum, the following elements:

   - mission statement;

   - analysis of market conditions, including if applicable, geographic, demographic, employment, income, housing, and other economic data;

   - evidence of member support;

   - goals for shares, loans, and for number of members;

   - financial services needed/desired;

   - financial services to be provided to members of all segments within the field of membership;

   - how/when services are to be implemented;

   - organizational/management plan addressing qualification and planned training of officials/employees;

NCUA 4001   PAGE 2

Pt. 701, App. B   12 CFR Ch. VII (1-1-12 Edition)

- continuity plan for directors, committee members, and management staff;
- operating facilities, to include office space/equipment and supplies, safeguarding of assets, insurance coverage, etc.;
- type of record keeping and data processing system;
- detailed semiannual pro forma financial statements (balance sheet, income and expense projections) for 1st and 2nd year, including assumptions - e.g., loan and dividend rates;
- plans for operating independently;
- written policies (shares, lending, investments, funds management, capital accumulation, dividends, collections, etc.);
- source of funds to pay expenses during initial months of operation, including any subsidies, assistance, etc., and terms or conditions of such resources; and
- evidence of sponsor commitment (or other source of support) if subsidies are critical to success of the federal credit union. Evidence may be in the form of letters, contracts, financial statements from the sponsor, and any other such document on which the proposed federal credit union can substantiate its projections.

5. What potential difficulties do you detect in the elected officials carrying out their management responsibilities or in the FCU achieving its stated objectives?

_____
_____
_____
_____

6. What provisions have been made to overcome potential difficulties?

_____
_____
_____
_____

Dates of planned contacts by organizer to determine progress and to assist the group:

First Contact Date: _____
Second Contact Date: _____
Third Contact Date: _____

NCUA 4001   PAGE 3

National Credit Union Administration	Pt. 701, App. B

SPECIFIC INFORMATION - OCCUPATIONAL (same company) CHARTER APPLICANTS

1. How long has the sponsor company been in existence? _____

2. What was the highest number of employees during the past three years? _____ Lowest number during the past three years? _____ If a large variance, please explain. _____
_____
_____
_____
_____

3. Are there any contemplated changes in the corporate structure of the company? _____ If yes, explain. _____
_____
_____
_____

4. Have there been any significant changes in the corporate structure in the past three years? _____ If yes, please explain. _____
_____
_____
_____

5. Are there any negotiations now in progress between management and labor that could lead to work stoppages? _____ If yes, please explain. _____
_____
_____
_____

6. If the credit union cannot operate on the employer's property, explain how the credit union will be able to transact business effectively with the members.
_____
_____
_____

NCUA 4001	PAGE 4

Pt. 701, App. B   12 CFR Ch. VII (1–1–12 Edition)

7. If the employees to be served by the credit union work in more than one location or city, identify each location with the corresponding number of employees working at each.

_____
_____
_____
_____
_____

8. Are there other employees of the company who are not being included in the proposed field of membership? _____ If so, give the number and location of the other employees and explain why they are not included in the proposed credit union's field of membership.

_____
_____
_____
_____
_____

National Credit Union Administration   Pt. 701, App. B

SPECIFIC INFORMATION - OCCUPATIONAL (trade, industry or profession) CHARTER APPLICANTS

1. Explain how the credit union will be able to transact business effectively with the members. _____
_____
_____
_____
_____
_____
_____
_____

Pt. 701, App. B   **12 CFR Ch. VII (1–1–12 Edition)**

SPECIFIC INFORMATION - ASSOCIATIONAL CHARTER APPLICANTS

1. State the purpose and goals of the organization sponsoring this charter.
_____
_____
_____
_____
_____
_____
_____

2. List the types of activities and their frequency, which the organization sponsors that provide contact among the members and from which common loyalties, mutual benefits, and mutual interests are developed. _____
_____
_____
_____
_____
_____
_____
_____
_____

3. In what year was the organization established? _____ Is it incorporated? _____ Where is the headquarters located? _____

4. Give statistics as to trends in membership during the last five years. _____
_____
_____
_____

5. What is the frequency of membership meetings? _____
Average attendance: _____ Dues required: $_____

6. State the geographic territory where members reside. _____
_____
_____
_____

NCUA 4001   PAGE 7

National Credit Union Administration Pt. 701, App. B

7. Submit a copy of the current bylaws of the association, the constitution, articles of incorporation, or equivalent documentation and recent financial statements, i.e. balance sheet, and income and expense statement, with this application.

8. If the bylaws, constitution, articles of incorporation, or equivalent documentation provide for more than one type of membership and if all classes of membership are to be included in the credit union's field of membership, provide justification for the inclusion of other than "regular" members.

Pt. 701, App. B

SPECIFIC INFORMATION – MULTIPLE COMMON BOND CHARTER APPLICANTS

1. Explain how the credit union will be able to transact business effectively with the members. _____
_____
_____
_____
_____
_____
_____

National Credit Union Administration

Pt. 701, App. B

SPECIFIC INFORMATION - COMMUNITY CHARTER APPLICANTS

1. Community charters must be based on a well-defined local community, neighborhood, or rural district where individuals have common interests and/or interact. Please refer to Chapter 2, Section V of the *"Chartering and Field of Membership Manual"* when answering this question.

2. Provide a map which clearly outlines the credit union's proposed community boundaries and identify proposed service facilities.

NCUA 4001 PAGE 10

Pt. 701, App. B

C. CHARACTER AND FITNESS OF SUBSCRIBERS

1. List of subscribers who have signed the Organization Certificate (7 not more than 10 persons). Names should be IDENTICAL to signature on the Organization Certificate (NCUA 4008). Each subscriber listed below has subscribed to at least one share in accordance with Section 103 of the Federal Credit Union Act:

Name: _____
Address: _____
_____
Occupation: _____
Years of Residence: _____

Name: _____
Address: _____
_____
Occupation: _____
Years of Residence: _____

Name: _____
Address: _____
_____
Occupation: _____
Years of Residence: _____

Name: _____
Address: _____
_____
Occupation: _____
Years of Residence: _____

Name: _____
Address: _____
_____
Occupation: _____
Years of Residence: _____

Name: _____
Address: _____
_____
Occupation: _____
Years of Residence: _____

National Credit Union Administration Pt. 701, App. B

Name: _____
Address: _____
_____
Occupation: _____
Years of Residence: _____

Name: _____
Address: _____
_____
Occupation: _____
Years of Residence: _____

Name: _____
Address: _____
_____
Occupation: _____
Years of Residence: _____

Name: _____
Address: _____
_____
Occupation: _____
Years of Residence: _____

2. Are all of the subscribers within the field of membership? _____ Do they appear to be representative of the group described in the definition of the field of membership? _____ If not, explain. _____
_____
_____
_____

3. Does your investigation indicate that the subscribers are persons of good character? _____ If not, explain. _____
_____
_____
_____

NCUA 4001   PAGE 12

Pt. 701, App. B

12 CFR Ch. VII (1-1-12 Edition)

4. From your investigation, is it your judgment that the directors and committee members are persons of good character, and that they have the ability and determination to operate a credit union satisfactorily? _____ If not, explain. _____

_____
_____
_____
_____

5. Does it appear that there are any factions within the group which may render smooth and efficient credit union operations difficult? _____ If so, explain. _____

_____
_____
_____
_____

6. Is there any indication that the proposed credit union would be used for selfish gain by any person or group of persons within the group to be served?_____

_____
_____
_____
_____

7. Is an application for a State Charter now pending? _____

8. Has the group ever had a credit union? _____ If so, when did it liquidate or merge? _____

ANY ADDITIONAL COMMENTS OR INFORMATION THAT IS DEEMED PERTINENT OR HELPFUL IN GIVING CONSIDERATION TO THIS APPLICATION SHOULD BE INCLUDED AS AN ATTACHMENT.

The undersigned certifies that to the best of their knowledge and belief the above information is true and correct.

I do (do not) recommend that a charter be granted to this group.

Signature: _____, Organizer
Organizer's Address: _____
_____
_____

Telephone No.: _____ Date: _____

NCUA 4001

National Credit Union Administration   **Pt. 701, App. B**

FORM 4001 INSTRUCTIONS

A. INFORMATION FOR CHARTER AND BYLAWS

The subscriber should select a name for the proposed credit union. It is the responsibility of the federal credit union organizers to ensure that the proposed federal credit union name does not constitute an infringement on the name of any corporation in its trade area. The last three words in the name must be "Federal Credit Union." Since the name selected should not duplicate exactly the name of an existing credit union, Item 1 provides space for a second choice.

The territory of operations of a Federal Credit Union is described in the field of membership, item 4. The principal office of the credit union will usually be maintained at a location described in the field of membership.

The proposed field of membership should be defined so clearly that it leaves no room for any doubt as to whom the credit union is to serve or the area which it is to operate. Corporations and other organizations referred to in the definition of the field of membership should be designated by the exact names rather than by some local or popular contraction of these names. The field of membership for each type of common bond and samples are discussed in detail in Chapter 2 of the *"Chartering and Field of Membership Manual."*

With the guidance of the organizer, the subscribers to the Organization Certificate decide on the number of directors and credit committee members. The board and credit committee must be composed of an odd number of members. The supervisory committee is appointed by the board of directors.

B. ECONOMIC ADVISABILITY OF ORGANIZING PROPOSED CREDIT UNION

This section of the report contains information on the required business plan elements and other information needed to make a decision on the economic advisability of chartering the proposed credit union.

C. CHARACTER AND FITNESS OF SUBSCRIBERS

The names and addresses of the subscribers should be recorded legibly and completely in item C. 1. of this report. It is from this information that the National Credit Union Administration prepares Section 3 of the charter. The names of the subscribers must be IDENTICAL to their signatures on the Organization Certificate.

Pt. 701, App. B   12 CFR Ch. VII (1-1-12 Edition)

D. SUBMITTAL OF CHARTER APPLICATION

In addition to this Investigation Report, the following should be submitted to the appropriate regional director of NCUA:

1. Organization Certificate, NCUA 4008 - one notarized original. At least seven, *but no more than ten persons*, must sign the organization certificate. The person administering the oath must not be one of the subscribers. The oath on the organization certificate must be executed and show the notary's seal and date the commission expires as required by State law;

2. Report of Official and Agreement to Serve, NCUA 4012 – one original for each board member, credit committee member, and supervisory committee member;

3. Business Plan - refer to Part B, question 4 of this form and Chapter 1 of the *Chartering and Field of Membership Manual* for a discussion of the components of an acceptable business plan;

4. Application and Agreements for Insurance of Accounts, NCUA 9500 - one original; and

5. Certification of Resolutions, NCUA 9501 - one original.

NATIONAL CREDIT UNION ADMINISTRATION

FEDERAL CREDIT UNION

(A corporation chartered under the laws of the United States)

CHARTER NO. _____

NCUA 4008
PAGE 1

Pt. 701, App. B   12 CFR Ch. VII (1-1-12 Edition)

ORGANIZATION CERTIFICATE

_____ FEDERAL CREDIT UNION

Charter No. _____

TO NATIONAL CREDIT UNION ADMINISTRATION:

We, the undersigned, do hereby associate ourselves as a Federal Credit Union for the purposes indicated in and in accordance with the provisions of the Federal Credit Union Act, (12 U.S.C. 1751 et seq.). We hereby request approval of this organization certificate; we hereby apply for insurance of member accounts; we agree to comply with the requirements of said Act, with the terms of this organization certificate and with all laws, rules, and regulations now or hereafter applicable to Federal Credit Unions.

(1) **The name of this credit union shall be** _____ **Federal Credit Union.**

(2) This credit union will maintain its office and will operate in the territory de-scribed in the field of membership.

NCUA 4008
PAGE 2

National Credit Union Administration Pt. 701, App. B

(3) The names and addresses of the subscribers to this certificate and the number of shares subscribed by each are as follows:

NAME	ADDRESS	SHARES

(4) The par value of the shares of this credit union will be stated in the bylaws.

(5) The field of membership shall be limited to those having the following common bond:_____
_____
_____
_____
_____
_____

NCUA 4008
PAGE 3

Pt. 701, App. B   12 CFR Ch. VII (1-1-12 Edition)

(6) The term of this credit union's existence shall be perpetual: Provided, however, that upon the finding that this credit union is bankrupt or insolvent or has violated any provision of this organization certificate, of the bylaws, of the Federal Credit Union Act including any amendments thereto or thereof, or of any regulations issued thereunder, this organization certificate may be suspended or revoked under the provisions of Section 120(b) of the Federal Credit Union Act.

(7) This certificate is made to enable the undersigned to avail themselves of the advantages of said Act.

(8) The management of this credit union, the conduct of its affairs, and the powers, duties, and privileges of its directors, officers, committees and membership shall be set forth in the approved bylaws and any approved amendments thereto or thereof.

IN WITNESS THEREOF we[1] have here unto subscribed our names this

_____   _____   _____
(day)   (month)   (year)

_____   _____
_____   _____
_____   _____
_____   _____

Subscribed before me, an officer competent to administer oaths, at _____
                                    CITY/STATE

this _____   _____   _____
     (day)   (month)   (year)

Signed _____

Title _____
         (Notary public or other competent officer)

1 At least seven signers none of whom should administer the oath.

NCUA 4008
PAGE 4

474

National Credit Union Administration — Pt. 701, App. B

APPROVAL OF ORGANIZATION CERTIFICATE

AND

CERTIFICATION OF INSURANCE

Pursuant to the provisions of the Federal Credit Union Act (12 U.S.C. 1751 et. Seq.), the foregoing organization certificate and insurance of member accounts of _____ Federal Credit Union are approved this _____

_____   _____   _____
(day)   (month)   (year)

_____
CHAIRPERSON
NATIONAL CREDIT UNION ADMINISTRATION

NCUA 4009   PAGE 1

Pt. 701, App. B   12 CFR Ch. VII (1-1-12 Edition)

REPORT OF OFFICIAL AND AGREEMENT TO SERVE

TO: NATIONAL CREDIT UNION ADMINISTRATION

Proposed _____ Federal Credit Union

Title of Prospective Position: _____

Name: _____
      Mr./Ms./Mrs. Last, First, Middle

Maiden Name (If Different From Above): _____

Address (Res.): _____
      Street,   City,   State, Zip Code

Telephone Number: (___) _____

Place of Birth: _____ Date of Birth: _____
      City/State/Country

Employer: _____

Social Security Number (Optional): _____

Type of Business: _____

Number of years with present employer: _____ Your position title: _____

Education background (enter highest grade completed)
    High School: _____ College: _____ Major Field of Study: _____

Other training or experience:
_____
_____
_____

Are you willing to accept the position of trust for which you have been selected and to remain in office until a qualified successor is found? ___ YES ___ NO

Have you been informed as to the general duties and responsibilities of an official of the proposed Federal Credit Union and are you willing to devote the time necessary to familiarize yourself with and to perform your duties?
___ YES ___ NO

National Credit Union Administration   Pt. 701, App. B

Estimated number of hours per month you will be able to volunteer:_____

IF THE ANSWER IS <u>YES</u> TO THE FOLLOWING QUESTION, PLEASE PROVIDE INFORMATION AS INSTRUCTED ON THE FOLLOWING PAGE:

Have you ever been convicted of any CRIMINAL OFFENSE involving dishonesty or a breach of trust? ___ YES ___ NO

To facilitate the process of obtaining a credit and background check, please provide the following:

    1. Any other names which you have used: _____and,
    2. Previous address, (if your address changed over the past 2 years):

        _____
        _____
        _____

    3. Name of Spouse: _____

READ THE FOLLOWING CAREFULLY BEFORE SIGNING

CERTIFICATION AND AGREEMENT TO SERVE

I certify that the information provided on this form is true and correct. Further, I, the undersigned, having been duly designated to occupy the position(s) indicated above, do hereby agree to serve in the above-stated office(s) of this proposed credit union until the first annual meeting held in accordance with the Federal Credit Union Act and the bylaws of this credit union and until the election of my successor(s). I further pledge to carry out the duties and responsibilities commensurate with said office(s) as promulgated by the Federal Credit Union Act and the bylaws of this credit union. I have read the Privacy Act Notice that follows.

Date	Signature	Witness

NCUA 4012   PAGE 2

Pt. 701, App. B   12 CFR Ch. VII (1-1-12 Edition)

PRIVACY ACT NOTICE

The Privacy Act of 1974 (Public Law 93-579) requires that you be advised as to the legal authority, purpose and uses of the information solicited by this form. Pursuant to Sections 104 and 205(d) of the Federal Credit Union Act, the information in this form is requested for the purpose of completing the investigation required for a new Federal credit union. The information in this form will be primarily used in considering the soundness of the management for the proposed Federal credit union. However, this form may be disclosed to any of the following sources: a congressional office in response to your inquiry to that office; an appropriate Federal, state or local authority in the investigation or enforcement of a statute or regulation; or employees of a Federal agency for audit purposes. Failure to complete this form or omission of any item of information, except for disclosure of your social security number, may result in a delay in the process for chartering the proposed Federal credit union. In accordance with Section 792.68 of NCUA's regulations, you are not required to furnish your social security number on this form. Your social security number, if voluntarily provided, will be used to more easily verify the information required by this form. No penalty will result to you as a management official or to the chartering of the proposed Federal credit union if you do not provide your social security number.

Further information needed if answer to CRIMINAL OFFENSE question on the previous page was YES:

CRIMINAL OFFENSE:

    Nature of offense: _____
    Date of occurrence: _____ Date of conviction: _____
    Sentence conferred: _____
    (Attach a separate sheet if space provided is not adequate)

NCUA 4012   PAGE 3

CRIMINAL OFFENSE GUIDELINES

The Federal Credit Union Act, Subchapter II, Section 205(d), requires that, except with the written consent of the NCUA Board, no person shall serve as director, officer, committee member, or employee of an insured credit union who has been convicted or who is hereafter convicted, of any criminal offense involving dishonesty or breach of trust. To assist the NCUA Board in making a determination of the fitness of a person who is selected to serve and who the organizer believes is qualified to serve as an official, the specific information above will need to be furnished.

If the NCUA Board believes that, in view of the facts presented and the date of the offense, they can give their consent to the appointment they will so advise that person in writing. If on the other hand, the NCUA Board believes after careful consideration that they cannot in good conscience give their written consent to the appointment they will contact the organizer and ask that another person be selected for the position. The person selected will have to complete a Report of Official and Agreement to Serve.

An indication of whether the bonding company would agree to provide coverage should be included if the person is to serve as treasurer. Bonding company agrees to provide coverage: ___ YES ___ NO

AUTHORIZATION TO OBTAIN A CREDIT REPORT

The National Credit Union Administration (NCUA) may evaluate the competence, experience, character, and integrity of any individual who is to serve as an official, employee, or committee member of a federally insured credit union, in accordance with §1790a of the Federal Credit Union Act and Chapter 1, §V.B.4 of the NCUA Chartering and Field of Membership Manual.

NCUA may disapprove any individual whose employment it believes will not be in the best interest of the credit union or of the public. To assist in the evaluation process, NCUA may obtain and review an individual's credit report.

Your signature on this document authorizes NCUA to obtain a copy of your credit report.

_____v
Last   First   Middle

Social Security Number: _____

Date of Birth: _____

_____
Signature   Date

NCUA 4012

National Credit Union Administration   Pt. 701, App. B

APPLICATION FOR FIELD OF MEMBERSHIP AMENDMENT
NCUA FORM 4015

USE FOR MULTIPLE COMMON BOND EXPANSION FOR GROUPS OF 3,000 OR MORE PERSONS

Attach a separate application for each group included in your request for expansion. The application must be complete or it will be returned unprocessed.

1. Name and address of credit union: Telephone Number: _____
   _____   Charter Number: _____
   _____
   _____

2. Name and address of group: Telephone Number: _____
   _____
   _____
   _____

   If the group is an association, include a copy of the association's Charter/Bylaws or other equivalent organizational documentation.

3. Provide the proposed field of membership wording. Use the example wording found in NCUA's *Chartering and Field of Membership Manual,* Chapter 2, Section IV.A.2.
   _____
   _____
   _____

4. How many primary potential members (excluding immediate family and household members) are in the group:
   _____

5. (a) What is the distance between the group's location and your credit union's nearest service facility[1] to which the group has access (Reference Chapter 2, Section IV.A.1):
   _____
   _____

   (b) What is the address of this service facility:
   _____
   _____
   _____

---

[1] A service facility is defined as a place where shares are accepted for members' accounts, loan applications are accepted or loans are disbursed.

NCUA 4015   PAGE 1

481

Pt. 701, App. B　　　　　　　　　　　　　　**12 CFR Ch. VII (1–1–12 Edition)**

(c) Describe the service area[2] primarily served by the above service facility:

_____
_____
_____
_____

6. Is the group in the field of membership of <u>any</u> other credit union? Yes___ No___

   If yes, and the overlapped credit union is not a community credit union or a non-federally insured credit union, please address the following:

   ☐ Provide the name and location of the other servicing credit union:

   _____
   _____
   _____

   ☐ Include a letter from the overlapped credit union indicating whether it concurs or objects to the overlap. If the overlapped credit union objects or fails to respond, document attempts to resolve the issue:

   _____
   _____
   _____
   _____

   ☐ Explain how the expansion's beneficial effect in meeting the convenience and needs of the members of the group clearly outweighs any adverse effect on the overlapped credit union:

   _____
   _____
   _____
   _____

---

[2] A federal credit union's service area is the area that can reasonably be served by the service facility accessible to the groups within the field of membership. It will most often coincide with that geographic area primarily served by the service facility.

NCUA 4015　　　　　　　　　　　　　　**PAGE 2**

National Credit Union Administration
Pt. 701, App. B

7. Attach a letter, or equivalent documentation, from the group requesting credit union service indicating:

   ☐ that the group wants to be added to the federal credit union's field of membership;
   ☐ whether the group presently has other credit union service available;
   ☐ the number of persons currently included within the group to be added and the group's location(s);
   ☐ the group's proximity to the credit union's nearest service facility; and
   ☐ why the formation of a separate credit union for the group is not practical or consistent with safety and soundness standards. *The formation of a separate credit union may not be practical if the group lacks sufficient volunteers or resources to support the operation of a credit union or does not meet the economic advisability criteria outlined in Chapter 1 of NCUA's Chartering and Field of Membership Manual.*

8. Other comments:
_____
_____
_____
_____
_____
_____

Name and title of credit union board-authorized representative (e.g., President/CEO):

_____ _____ _____
(Typed/Printed Name)   (Signature)   (Date)

NCUA 4015   PAGE 3

Pt. 701, App. B 12 CFR Ch. VII (1–1–12 Edition)

APPLICATION FOR FIELD OF MEMBERSHIP AMENDMENT
NCUA FORM 4015-EZ

USE FOR MULTIPLE COMMON BOND EXPANSIONS OF LESS THAN 3,000 PERSONS AND ALL SINGLE COMMON BOND EXPANSIONS

Attach a separate application for each group included in your request for expansion. The application must be complete or it will be returned unprocessed.

1. Name and address of credit union: _____ Telephone Number: _____
   _____ Charter Number: _____
   _____

2. Name and address of group: _____ Telephone Number: _____
   _____
   _____

   If the group is an association, include a copy of the association's Charter/Bylaws or other equivalent organizational documentation.

3. Provide the proposed field of membership wording: _____
   _____
   _____

4. **Multiple Common Bond Expansions Only:** Attach a letter, or equivalent documentation, from the group requesting credit union service indicating:

   ☐ that the group wants to be added to the federal credit union's field of membership;
   ☐ the number of persons to be added and the group's location(s); and
   ☐ the group's distance to the credit union's nearest service facility.

5. **Single Common Bond Expansions Only:** How the group shares the occupational or associational common bond_____
   How many primary potential members (excluding immediate family and household members) are in the group: _____

Name and title of credit union board-authorized representative (e.g., President/CEO):

_____ _____ _____
(Typed/Printed Name and Title) (Signature) (Date)

NCUA 4401 PAGE 1

National Credit Union Administration Pt. 701, App. B

NOTICE OF MEETING OF MEMBERS TO CONVERT FROM A FEDERAL TO A STATE CHARTERED CREDIT UNION

_____ FEDERAL CREDIT UNION

_____   _____
(City)   (State)

THIS PROPOSITION WILL BE DECIDED BY A MAJORITY OF THE MEMBERS WHO VOTE.

Notice is hereby given that a meeting of the members of _____ Federal Credit Union has been called and will be held at_____ _____ on _____, at _____ o'clock, __.M. for the purpose of considering and voting upon the following resolution:

"RESOLVED, That the _____ Federal Credit Union be converted to a credit union chartered under the laws of the State of _____ and that its operation under Federal charter be discontinued.

RESOLVED FURTHER, That the board of directors and the officers of this credit union and are hereby authorized and directed to do all things necessary to effect and to complete the conversion of this credit union from a Federal to State-chartered credit union."

The board of directors of this credit union has given careful consideration to the advantages and the disadvantages of the proposed conversion and believes it to be in the best interest of the members for the following reasons:

NCUA 4401   PAGE 2

Pt. 701, App. B   **12 CFR Ch. VII (1–1–12 Edition)**

The proposed conversion would result in the following disadvantages or adverse changes in services and benefits to the members of the credit union:

The proposed conversion would result in the following costs of conversion (i.e. changing the credit unions name, examination and operating fees, attorney and consulting fees, tax liability, etc):

The board of directors recommends that the members approve the proposal to convert to a State charter.

The members' accounts will ☐ will not ☐ continue to be insured by the National Credit Union Share Insurance Fund.

NCUA 4401   PAGE 3

National Credit Union Administration — Pt. 701, App. B

Attached is your ballot. You are urged to bring your ballot to the meeting and to cast your vote after hearing the discussion of the proposal. If you cannot attend the meeting, you are urged to mark your vote, date and sign your ballot, and return it to the following address by no later than the date and the time announced for the meeting of the members:

BY ORDER OF THE BOARD OF DIRECTORS

TITLE: _____
(CHAIRPERSON)

TITLE: _____
(BOARD SECRETARY)

Pt. 701, App. B   12 CFR Ch. VII (1-1-12 Edition)

APPLICATION TO CONVERT FROM A STATE TO A FEDERAL CREDIT UNION

The _____ Credit Union of _____ (city), _____ (State), incorporated under the laws of the State of _____ on _____ by decision of its board of directors, hereby makes application to the National Credit Union Administration to convert to a Federal credit union.

1. Field of membership. Provide a copy of the credit union's charter, articles of incorporation or bylaws, as amended to date.
   _____
   _____
   _____

2. Is proposed Federal charter to cover same field of membership? Yes ☐ No ☐ If answer is "No," explain fully: _____
   _____
   _____
   _____

3. Standard financial and statistical reports as of _____ or comparable forms of reports, certified correct by the treasurer and verified by the affidavit of the president or vice-president, are attached.

4. A schedule of delinquent loans classified 2 to 6 months, 6 to 12 months, and 12 months and over delinquent is attached.

5. The following policies on loans to members are currently in effect in this credit union:

   a. Interest rates on loans: _____

   b. Charges incident to making loans which are passed on to borrowers: _____

   c. Maturity limits: _____

   d. Unsecured loan limit: _____

   e. Secured loan limit: _____

   f. Types of security accepted: _____

   g. Requirements of amortization (Repayment requirements): _____

6. Attached is a list of unsecured loans in excess of the amounts stipulated in the Act. (For each loan show account number, original amount, terms, and unpaid balance.)

NCUA 4401   PAGE 5

National Credit Union Administration

Pt. 701, App. B

7. Attached is a list of loans with maturities in excess of periods stipulated in the Act and the NCUA Rules and Regulations. (For each loan show account number, original amount, terms, unpaid balance, and security.)

8. Types of accounts which members are required or are permitted to maintain: Share ☐ Deposit ☐ Other ☐ (describe): _____

_____

9. Describe any real estate owned by credit union, including a list of its current market value: _____

_____

10. Describe and list any investments which are outside of the investment powers of Federal credit unions (Refer to Section 107(7), Federal Credit Union Act):_____

_____

11. Names and locations of any depository institutions in which the credit union deposits its funds but which are beyond the purview of deposit powers authorized by Section 107(8) of the Federal Credit Union Act: _____

_____

12. Describe any services rendered to or on behalf of members or of the public, other than accepting and maintaining accounts of members and making loans to members:

_____

_____

13. Describe what you propose to do about any policies, procedures, assets or liabilities which do not comply with the Federal Credit Union Act: _____

_____

14. Give specific reasons as to why you desire to convert to a Federal credit union:

_____

We hereby authorize the National Credit Union Administration to examine our books and our records.

NCUA 4401 PAGE 6

Pt. 701, App. B   12 CFR Ch. VII (1-1-12 Edition)

We, the undersigned _____ Chief Executive Officer and _____ Chief Financial Officer of the _____ Credit Union of _____ State of _____ certify: That we are the duly elected Chairperson and the Chief Financial Officer, respectfully, of said credit union; that the statements made in this Application to Convert from a State to a Federal Credit Union and the schedules attached hereto are true, complete, and correct to the best of our knowledge and belief and are made in good faith.

TITLE: _____
(CHAIRPERSON)

TITLE: _____
(CHIEF FINANCIAL OFFICER)

National Credit Union Administration   Pt. 701, App. B

AFFIDAVIT
PROOF OF RESULTS OF MEMBERSHIP VOTE - PROPOSED CONVERSION FROM FEDERAL CREDIT UNION TO STATE CREDIT UNION

We, the undersigned _____ chairperson and _____ secretary of the _____ Federal Credit Union, hereby swear or affirm as follows:

1. That the conversion proposal as set forth in the attached Notice of Meeting of the Members was fully explained to the members present at said meeting of members.

2. That on the date of the said meeting of members there were _____ members of this credit union qualified to vote; _____ members were present at said meeting; of those members present, _____ members voted in favor of the conversion and _____ members voted against the conversion; of those members not present at the meeting but who filed ballots, _____ members voted in favor of the conversion and _____ members voted against the conversion; and that, without duplication of the votes of any member, a total of _____ members voted in favor of the conversion and _____ members voted against the conversion.

NCUA 4505   PAGE 1

Pt. 701, App. B   **12 CFR Ch. VII (1–1–12 Edition)**

3. That the action of the members of this credit union at said meeting is fully and completely recorded in the minutes of said meeting and all ballots cast by the members on the question of conversion, either at the meeting or by delivery to the credit union, are on file with the secretary of this credit union.

TITLE: _____
(CHAIRPERSON)

TITLE: _____
(BOARD SECRETARY)

_____

FEDERAL CREDIT UNION

Subscribed before me, an officer competent to administer oaths, at _____
_____, **this** _____
                                                 (day)   (month)   (year)

Signed _____

(SEAL)

Title _____
(Notary Public or other competent officer)

My Commission Expires _____, _____
                                (year)

NCUA 4505   PAGE 2

National Credit Union Administration   Pt. 701, App. B

FEDERAL TO STATE CONVERSION

BALLOT FOR CONVERSION PROPOSAL

I have read the notice concerning the meeting of the members of the _____ Federal Credit Union called for _____ to consider and to vote upon the following proposition:

"RESOLVED, That the _____ Federal Credit Union be converted to a credit union chartered under the laws of the State of _____ and operation under Federal Charter Number _____ be discontinued.

RESOLVED FURTHER, That the board of directors and the officers of this credit union are hereby authorized and directed to do all things necessary to effect and to complete the conversion of this credit union from a Federal to State-chartered credit union."

I hereby cast my vote on the proposition: (Place an X in the square opposite the appropriate statement.)

I vote for the conversion ☐

I vote against the conversion ☐

_____   _____
(Account Number)   (Signature of Member)

Date: _____

NCUA 4506

Pt. 701, App. B 12 CFR Ch. VII (1-1-12 Edition)

APPLICATION AND AGREEMENTS FOR INSURANCE OF ACCOUNTS

Date: _____

TO: The National Credit Union Administration Board (Board)

The proposed _____ Federal Credit Union

_____
(Street Address)

_____
(City)   (State)   (Zip Code)

applies for insurance of its accounts as provided in Title II of the Federal Credit Union Act, and in consideration of the granting of insurance, hereby agrees:

1. To pay the reasonable cost of such examinations as the Board may deem necessary in connection with determining the eligibility of the application for insurance.

2. To permit and pay the reasonable cost of such examinations as in the judgment of the Board may from time to time be necessary for the protection of the fund and other insured credit unions.

3. To permit the Board to have access to any information or report with respect to any examination made by or for any public regulatory authority and furnish such additional information with respect thereto as the Board may require.

4. To provide protection and indemnity against burglary, defalcation, and other similar insurable losses, of the type, in the form, and in an amount at least equal to that required by the laws under which the credit union is organized and operates.

5. To maintain such special reserves as the Board, by regulation or in special cases, may require for protecting the interest of members.

6. Not to issue or have outstanding any account or security the form of which, by regulation or in special cases, has not been approved by the Board.

7. To pay and maintain the capitalization deposit required by Title II of the Federal Credit Union Act.

8. To pay the premium charges for insurance imposed by Title II of the Federal Credit Union Act.

NCUA 9500   PAGE 1

National Credit Union Administration   Pt. 701, App. B

9. To comply with the requirements of Title II of the Federal Credit Union Act and of regulations prescribed by the Board pursuant thereto.

10. To permit the Board to have access to all records and information concerning the affairs of the credit union and to furnish such information pertinent thereto that the Board may require.

11. To comply with Title 18 of the United States Code and other pertinent Federal statutes as they may exist or may be hereafter promulgated or amended.

We, the undersigned, certify to the correctness of the information submitted. We, the undersigned, further certify that to the best of our knowledge and belief no proposed officer, committee member, or employee of this credit union has been convicted of any criminal offense involving dishonesty or a breach of trust, except as noted in attachments to this application. We further agree to notify the Board if any proposed or future officer commits a criminal offense.

_____   _____
Chairperson   Chief Financial Officer

Note: A willfully false certification is a criminal offense. U.S. Code, Title 18, Sec. 1001.

NCUA 9500   PAGE 2

Pt. 701, App. B   12 CFR Ch. VII (1–1–12 Edition)

CERTIFICATION OF RESOLUTIONS

_____ FEDERAL CREDIT UNION (PROPOSED)

We certify that we are the duly elected and qualified chief executive officer and recording officer of the above-named proposed Federal credit union and that at the charter-organization meeting, the board of directors passed the following resolution and recorded it in its minutes:

"Be it resolved that this credit union apply to the National Credit Union Administration Board for insurance of its accounts as provided in Title II of the Federal Credit Union Act.

Be it further resolved that the president and treasurer be authorized and directed to execute the Application and Agreements for Insurance of Accounts as prescribed by the Board and any other papers and documents required in connection therewith; to pay all expenses and do all other things necessary or proper to secure and continue in force such insurance."

_____
Chief Executive Officer

_____
Recording Officer, Board of Directors

NCUA 9501

National Credit Union Administration Pt. 701, App. B

INFORMATION TO BE PROVIDED IN SUPPORT OF THE APPLICATION OF A STATE CHARTERED CREDIT UNION FOR INSURANCE OF ACCOUNTS

Existing credit unions must complete the entire application. All other applicants do not have to complete questions 8, 11, 12, 13, 15, and 16.

_____Credit Union

1. Show below the location of the credit union's books and records.

   _____
   (Street Address)

   _____
   (City)   (State)   (Zip)   (Telephone)

2. Show the date (month, day, year) in which the credit union was chartered. _____

3. Attach a copy of the credit union's field of membership as shown in the charter, articles of incorporation and/or bylaws, as amended to date. Please identify it as the first schedule in the consecutive number sequence as discussed in the instructions. Schedule No. _____

4. Potential membership (total number of persons who could be served including present members). _____

5. Identify charter type (e.g., single common bond, multiple common bond, community).
   _____

6. Does the credit union operate under standard bylaws provided by the state supervisory authority? Yes ☐   No ☐   (Complete a.)

   a. Attach a copy of the current official bylaws under which the credit union operated. Schedule No. _____

7. Is the credit union under any administrative restraints by the State Supervisory Authority? Yes ☐   No ☐   (Complete a.)

   a. Explain fully on an attached schedule. Schedule No. _____

NCUA 9600   Page 1

Pt. 701, App. B

8. Attach a copy of the latest State supervisory authority examination. Copies of any correspondence from the accountant's report if made in lieu of a State supervisory authority examination. Copies of any correspondence from the State supervisory authority which accompanied the examination report should also be included.

9. Attach copies of the Balance Sheet and Statement of Income and Expense (or Financial and Statistical Report) for the month preceding the date of this application and for the same month of the preceding year.
Schedule Nos. _____

10. Reserves

    Show below the requirements of the State law and/or your bylaws for transfer of earnings to reserves (either monthly or at the end of each accounting period).
    _____

11. Delinquent Loans and Charged-off Loans

    a. Attach a copy of the delinquent loan list as of the month-end preceding the date of this application. See instructions pertaining to Item No. 11a. Schedule No. _____

    b. List below the requested information on delinquent loans for the latest four calendar quarters preceding the date of the application (March 31, June 30, September 30 and December 31). Also show total share and loan balances for all members for the same period.

(a) *Other Delinquent Categories	(b) Delinquent Categories	Date	Date	Date	Date
	2 to less than 6 mos.	$	$	$	$
	6 to less than 12 mos.	$	$	$	$
	12 mos. and over	$	$	$	$
	Totals	$	$	$	$
	Share Balances	$	$	$	$
	Loan Balances	$	$	$	$

*See instructions pertaining to Item No. 11 b.

NCUA 9600

National Credit Union Administration Pt. 701, App. B

c. List below the requested information on loans charged off during the last three years and the current year. List total of all reserves both revocable and irrevocable for the same period as (balance at year-end and or current period).

	Year	Year	Year	Current Yr. To Date	*Totals Since Organization
Total Charged Off					
Total Recovered					
Net Charged Off					

*If this information is available.

12. Does the credit union have any unrecorded or contingent liabilities, (including pending law suits or civil actions)? Yes ☐ No ☐ Complete a.

    a. List on an attached schedule the complete description of such liabilities, including amounts, status of the items, and a description of the circumstances creating the liabilities or contingent liabilities. Schedule No. _____

13. Do any asset accounts other than loans to members, investments, and real estate have actual values less than the book values shown on the Balance Sheet?

    List on a separate schedule a description of such assets, showing at least the following information; account number, description of item, book value and actual value. Schedule No. _____

14. List below or on an attached schedule, any investments or real estate as discussed in the instructions pertaining to Item No. 14. Schedule No. _____ . Attach a copy of the credit union's current investment policies. Investments/Loans to Credit Union Service Organization (CUSO) should be listed separately.

Description of Item	Current Market Value	Current Book Value
	$	$
	$	$
	$	$

NCUA 9600

Pt. 701, App. B

15. Individual Share and Loan Ledgers:

   a. Were the totals of the trial balance of the individual share and loan ledgers in agreement with the balances of the respective general ledger control accounts as of the month-end preceding the date of this application? _____

   b. What are the differences as of the month and preceding the date of this application?

	Shares	Loans
Balances in General Ledger	$	$
Totals of the trial balance of the individual ledgers	$	$
Differences	$	$

16. Supervisory Committee:

   a. What is the effective date of the last complete comprehensive annual audit performed by the supervisory committee?
   Effective Date _____

   (1) If the effective date of the annual audit is not within the last 18 months what is the supervisory committee's target date for completion of a comprehensive audit?
   Date _____

   b. Show the effective date of the supervisory committee's last controlled verification of all members' accounts:
   Effective Date _____

   (1) If all members' accounts have not been verified under controlled conditions during the last two years, what is the supervisory committee's target date for completion of the verification program?
   Date _____

   c. If it is necessary to complete either 16a(1) or 16 b(1); please describe the directors' plans for seeing that the target dates are met. (Discuss below or on an attached schedule.) Schedule No. _____

NCUA 9600

National Credit Union Administration **Pt. 701, App. B**

17. List below the credit union's surety bond coverage.

    a. Name of carrier _____

    b. Standard form number of the bond (i.e., 23, 576, 577, 578, 581, 562 CU-1, other) _____

    c. Basic amount of coverage $_____

    d. Bond premium paid to (date) _____

    e. What is the amount of coverage required by State law or your bylaws? _____

    f. Riders to the bond (list below) (i.e., faithful performance, forgery, misplacement, etc.) _____
    _____

18. Does the credit union render any services to or perform any functions on behalf of the members, non-members, organizations, or the public other than the usual savings and loan services for members? _____

    Attach a schedule describing each activity in full. Schedule No. _____

19. Does the board of directors or management know of any adverse economic condition that is affecting or will affect the credit union's present or future operation or that of the sponsor organization? _____

    Attach a schedule describing the condition and its possible effect on the credit union's future. Schedule No. _____

20. To the best of the credit union's knowledge and belief, has any director, officer, committee member, or employee been convicted of any criminal offense involving dishonesty or breach of trust? _____

    a. Attach a statement describing the circumstances. Schedule No. _____

21. Lending policies and practices:

    a. Complete the following schedule showing the present policies and practices on loans to members.

    b. Complete the following schedule of largest loans with the attached instructions pertaining to Item No. 21.

NCUA 9600 Page 5

Pt. 701, App. B   12 CFR Ch. VII (1-1-12 Edition)

LENDING POLICIES AND PRACTICES

	Maximum Loan Amount	Maximum Period of Repayment	Required Amount of Down Payment (Equity)
1. Credit Union Policies and Practices			
a. Unsecured Loan Limits			
b. Secured Loan Limits			
(1) New Auto Collateral			
(2) Used Auto Collateral			
(3) Real Estate			
(a) First Mortgage			
(b) Second Mortgage			
(4) Comakers			
(5) Others (describe)			
c. Loans to Organizations			
d. Loans to Directors, Officers, or Committee Members			
2. State Credit Union Law; Bylaws			
a. Unsecured Loan Limits			
b. Secured Loan Limits			
c. Loans to Directors, Officers, or Committee Members			

NCUA 9600   Page 6

502

National Credit Union Administration Pt. 701, App. B

List on an attached page, any additional policies, including the interest rates applied to members' loans and the method of assessing and accounting for interest income, i.e.: add-on, discount or unpaid balance.

SCHEDULE OF LARGEST LOANS
Complete this form as discussed in the instructions pertaining to Item 21b.

Account No.	Unpaid Bal.	Repayment Period (Mths)	Repayment Status Current	Repayment Status Mths Delq.	Appraised Collateral Value*	Collateral Description

NCUA 9600

*If there is more than one type of collateral assign value to each type.

National Credit Union Administration   Pt. 701, App. B

CREDIT UNION SERVICE ORGANIZATION
(CUSO)

1. Name of CUSO _____

2. Date of CUSO'S Organization _____
   (Date of obtaining charter from State)

3. Type of organization (check one):

   a. General Partnership ☐   c. Joint Ownership ☐

   b. Limited Partnership ☐   d. Corporation ☐

4. Owners of CUSO (list name, charter number if FCU, and percentage of ownership, if possible).

   a. _____ _____ _____
        Name   *Charter Number (If FCU)*   *%*

   b. _____ _____ _____
        Name   *Charter Number (If FCU)*   *%*

   (Continue on reverse side if additional space is required)

5. Capitalization (list investors and amount of investment in CUSO).

   a. _____ _____ _____
        Name   *Charter Number (If FCU)*   *Amount*

   b. _____ _____ _____
        Name   *Charter Number (If FCU)*   *Amount*

   (Continue on reverse side if additional space is required)

NCUA 9600

Pt. 701, App. B 12 CFR Ch. VII (1-1-12 Edition)

6. List all known services which are being offered by CUSO (be as specific as possible)._____
_____
_____

7. Comments (include all other pertinent information, if applicable, not previously discussed). _____
_____
_____

8. Attach the latest Financial and Statistical Report of CUSO, if available.

NCUA 9600   Page 10

National Credit Union Administration **Pt. 701, App. B**

FORM 9600 INSTRUCTION

APPLICATION OF A STATE CHARTERED CREDIT UNION
FOR INSURANCE OF ACCOUNTS

The application and all supporting documents should be prepared, photocopied, and submitted in accordance with these instructions. Additional schedules may be included if deemed appropriate.

Existing credit unions must complete the entire application. All other applicants do not have to complete questions 8, 11, 12, 13, 15, and 16.

Existing credit unions must submit current policies and financial statements as noted in the application. All other applicants must submit proposed policies and pro forma financial statements for the first and second year of operation.

When an item specifies that a schedule should be prepared and attached, please assign a schedule number in consecutive order, starting with number one. Please show the schedule number at the top right-hand corner of the schedule.

Some of the items are self-explanatory and require no special instructions. Other items, however, need special explanations, definitions, and instructions for completion. These are listed below, identified by the same item numbers as appear in Exhibit A.

Item No. 10: Reserves: The term "reserves" means that account, or accounts, which represents segregated portions of earnings as provided by the law, bylaws, and/or the credit union's management for the absorption of losses relating to loans to members.

Item No. 11a: The delinquent loan list requested should include, for each delinquent loan, the account number of the borrower, date of loan, original amount of loan, unpaid balance, date of last payment of principle, excluding transfers from pledged shares, collateral, and comments regarding the collectability of each loan in the categories 6 months to less than 12 months and 12 months and over. Payments of interest only should be so identified.

Item No. 11b: The schedule provided for the delinquent loan information is set up in delinquency categories of 2 months to less than 6 months, 6 to less than 12 months, and 12 months and over. Credit unions that compute delinquency using categories other than shown in column (b) may use these other categories and show them in column (a). Credit unions using column (a) need not show the delinquencies in the column (b) categories. It is not necessary to report on loans which are delinquent less than 2 months.

Adverse Trends: If items 8, 9, or 11 indicate adverse trends such as significant decreases in shares, loans or reserves, increases in loan delinquency or loan charge-offs, or unresolved

Pt. 701, App. B

serious exceptions shown in the State examination report, the credit union may attach an explanation and identify it as "Explanation of Adverse Trends or

Unresolved Examination Exceptions" and assign it a schedule number.

Item No. 14: This item need be completed only if the credit union owns any of the following:

A. Investments in U.S. Government securities guaranteed as to principle and interest or Federal Agency securities, the market value of which is now less than the book value.

B. Real estate other than that used entirely for the credit union's own office(s).

C. Other investments of any type except:

   1. Loans to other credit unions.
   2. Certificates of, or accounts in, federally insured financial institutions.
   3. Deposits or accounts in corporate credit unions.

If corporate bonds are listed, please show maturity date, rate of interest on bonds and current yield rate.

If stocks are listed, please show number of shares and bid price.

Please identify the source of the market valuation information and the date of such information.

Item No. 21b: In selecting the largest loans for this Exhibit, list the largest outstanding unpaid loan balance and proceed in descending order by dollar amount until the number specified below has been shown. The number of such loans to be listed will be determined as follows:

If your credit union has the following no. of outstanding loans	You should list the following no. of the largest unpaid balances

NCUA 9600   Page 12

508

National Credit Union Administration — Pt. 701, App. B

Under 100	5
100 to 199	10
200 to 299	15
300 to 399	20
400 or more	25

If any of the above loans are delinquent, please show the number of months delinquent in the appropriate "Status of Re-payment" column.

Complete the Credit Union Service Organization (CUSO) schedule for each investment/loan to a CUSO.

TERMINATION OF INSURANCE

Should the credit union, after obtaining insurance of member accounts, desire to terminate its insured status, this could be accomplished by complying with the provisions of Section 206(a), (c) and (d) of Title II of the Federal Credit Union Act. This action would require approval by a vote of the majority of the members, and ninety days written notice of the proposed termination date to NCUA. Member accounts would continue to be insured for one year following termination of insurance and the insurance premium would be paid during that period. After termination of insurance, the credit union shall give prompt and reasonable notice to all members whose accounts are insured that it has ceased to be an insured credit union.

Sections 206(a)(2) and 206(d)(2) and (3) of the Act provide that an insured credit union may also terminate its insurance by converting from its status as an insured credit union under the Act to insurance from a corporation authorized and duly licensed to insure member accounts. In this event, approval is required by a majority of all the directors and by affirmative vote of a majority of the members voting, provided that at least 20 percent of the members have voted on the proposition. Under this provision for termination, insurance of member accounts would cease as of the date of termination.

Pt. 701, App. B   12 CFR Ch. VII (1-1-12 Edition)

APPLICATION AND AGREEMENTS FOR INSURANCE OF ACCOUNTS
STATE CHARTERED CREDIT UNION

TO: The National Credit Union Administration Board   Date _____

The _____ Credit Union,

Insurance Certificate Number _____ (if applicable)

_____
(mailing address)   (city)   (state)   (zip code)

applies for insurance of its accounts as provided in Title II of the Federal Credit Union Act, and in consideration of the granting of insurance, hereby agrees:

1. To permit and pay the cost of such examinations as the NCUA Board deems necessary for the protection of the interests of the National Credit Union Share Insurance Fund.

2. To permit the Board to have access to all records and information concerning the affairs of the credit union, including any information or report related to an examination made by or for any other regulating authority, and to furnish such records, information, and reports upon request of the NCUA Board.

3. To possess such fidelity coverage and such coverage against burglary, robbery, and other losses as is required by Parts 713 and 741 of NCUA's regulations.

4. To meet, at a minimum, the statutory reserve and full and fair disclosure requirements imposed on Federal Credit Unions by Part 702 of NCUA's regulations, and to maintain such special reserves as the NCUA Board may be regulation or on a case-by-case basis determine are necessary to protect the interests of members. Any waivers of the statutory reserve or full and fair disclosure requirements or any direct charges to the statutory reserve other than loss loans must have the prior written approval of the NCUA Board. In addition, corporate credit unions shall be subject to the reserve requirements specified in Part 704 of NCUA's regulations.

5. Not to issue or have outstanding any account or security the form of which has not been approved by the NCUA Board, except accounts authorized by state law for state credit unions.

6. To maintain the deposit and pay the insurance premium charges imposed as a condition of insurance pursuant to Title II (Share Insurance) of the Federal Credit Union Act.

NCUA 9600   Page 14

National Credit Union Administration   **Pt. 701, App. B**

7. To comply with the requirement of Title II (Share Insurance) of the Federal Credit Union Act and of regulations prescribed by the NCUA Board pursuant thereto.

8. For any investments other than loans to members and obligations or securities expressly authorized in Title I of the Federal Credit Union Act, as amended to establish now and maintain at the end of each accounting period and prior to payment of any dividend, an Investment Valuation Reserve Account in an amount at least equal to the net excess of book value over current market value of the investments. If the market value cannot be determined, an amount equal to the full book value will be established. When, as of the end of any dividend period, the amount in the Investment Valuation Reserve exceeds the difference between book value and market value, the board of directors may authorize the transfer of the excess to Undivided Earnings.

9. When a state-chartered credit union is permitted by state law to accept nonmember shares or deposits from sources other than other credit unions and public units, such nonmember accounts shall be identified as nonmember shares or deposits on any statement or report required by the NCUA Board for insurance purposes. Immediately after a state-chartered credit union receives notice from NCUA that its member accounts are federally insured, the credit union will advise any present nonmember share and deposit holders by letter that their accounts are not insured by the National Credit Union Share Insurance Fund. Also, future nonmember share and deposit fund holders will be so advised by letter as they open accounts.

10. In the event a state-chartered credit union chooses to terminate its status as a federally-insured credit union, then it shall meet the requirements imposed by Sections 206(a)(1) and 206(c) of the Federal Credit Union Act and Part 741.208 of NCUA's regulations.

11. In the event a state-chartered credit union chooses to convert from federal insurance to some other insurance from a corporation authorized and duly licensed to insure member accounts, then it shall meet the requirements imposed by Sections 206(a)(2), 206(c), 206(d)(2), and 206(d)(3) of the Federal Credit Union Act and any other applicable federal law.

Pt. 701, App. B **12 CFR Ch. VII (1-1-12 Edition)**

In support of this application we submit the following schedules:

Schedule No.	Title

National Credit Union Administration   Pt. 701, App. B

CERTIFICATIONS AND RESOLUTIONS

We, the undersigned, certify that we are the duly elected and qualified presiding officer and recording officer of the credit union and that at a properly called and regular or special meeting of its board of directors, at which a quorum was present, the following resolutions were passed and recorded in its minutes:

We, the undersigned, certify to the correctness of the information submitted.

Be it resolved that this credit union apply to the National Credit Union Administration Board for insurance of its accounts as provided in Title II of the Federal Credit Union Act.

Be it resolved that the presiding officer and recording officer be authorized and directed to execute the Application and Agreement for Insurance of Accounts as prescribed by the NCUA Board and any other papers and documents required in connection therewith and to pay all expenses and do all such other things necessary or proper to secure and continue in force such insurance.

We further certify that to the best of our knowledge and belief no existing or proposed officer, committee member, or employee of this credit union has been convicted of any criminal offense involving dishonesty or breach of trust, except as noted in attachments to this application. We further agree to notify the Board if any existing, proposed or future officer, committee member or employee is indicted for such an offense.

_____
(Signature) Chairperson, Board of Directors

_____
(Print or type Chairperson's Name)

_____
(Signature) Secretary, Board of Directors

_____
(Print or type Secretary's Name)

NCUA 9600

APPENDIX 5

TRADE ASSOCIATIONS

Credit Union National Association (CUNA)
P.O. Box 431
Madison, WI 53701
608-231-4000

National Association of Federal Credit Unions (NAFCU)
3138 N. 10th Street, Suite 300
Arlington, VA 22201
703-522-4770

National Association of State Credit Union Supervisors (NASCUS)
1655 North Fort Myer Drive, Suite 300
Arlington, VA 22209
703-528-8351

National Federation of Community Development Credit Unions (NFCDCU)
120 Wall Street, 10th Floor
New York, NY 10005-3902
212-809-1850

[73 FR 73398, Dec. 2, 2008, as amended at 75 FR 36263, 36263, June 25, 2010]

PART 702—PROMPT CORRECTIVE ACTION

Sec.
702.1 Authority, purpose, scope and other supervisory authority.
702.2 Definitions.

Subpart A—Net Worth Classification

702.101 Measure and effective date of net worth classification.
702.102 Statutory net worth categories.
702.103 Applicability of risk-based net worth requirement.
702.104 Risk portfolios defined.

National Credit Union Administration

§ 702.2

702.105 Weighted-average life of investments.
702.106 Standard calculation of risk-based net worth requirement.
702.107 Alternative components for standard calculation.
702.108 Risk mitigation credit.
APPENDIXES A–H TO SUBPART A

Subpart B—Mandatory and Discretionary Supervisory Actions

702.201 Prompt corrective action for "adequately capitalized" credit unions.
702.202 Prompt corrective action for "undercapitalized" credit unions.
702.203 Prompt corrective action for "significantly undercapitalized" credit unions.
702.204 Prompt corrective action for "critically undercapitalized" credit unions.
702.205 Consultation with State officials on proposed prompt corrective action.
702.206 Net worth restoration plans.

Subpart C—Alternative Prompt Corrective Action for New Credit Unions

702.301 Scope and definition.
702.302 Net worth categories for new credit unions.
702.303 Prompt corrective action for "adequately capitalized" new credit unions.
702.304 Prompt corrective action for "moderately capitalized," "marginally capitalized" and "minimally capitalized" new credit unions.
702.305 Prompt corrective action for "uncapitalized" new credit unions.
702.306 Revised business plans for new credit unions.
702.307 Incentives for new credit unions.

Subpart D—Reserves

702.401 Reserves.
702.402 Full and fair disclosure of financial condition.
702.403 Payment of dividends.

AUTHORITY: 12 U.S.C. 1766(a), 1790d.

SOURCE: 65 FR 8584, Feb. 18, 2000, unless otherwise noted.

§ 702.1 Authority, purpose, scope and other supervisory authority.

(a) *Authority.* Subparts A, B and C of this part and subpart L of part 747 of this chapter are issued by the National Credit Union Administration pursuant to section 216 of the Federal Credit Union Act (FCUA), 12 U.S.C. 1790d (section 1790d), as added by section 301 of the Credit Union Membership Access Act, Pub. L. No. 105–219, 112 Stat. 913 (1998). Subpart D of this part is issued pursuant to FCUA section 120, 12 U.S.C. 1766.

(b) *Purpose.* The express purpose of prompt corrective action under section 1790d is to resolve the problems of federally-insured credit unions at the least possible long-term loss to the National Credit Union Share Insurance Fund. This part carries out the purpose of prompt corrective action by establishing a framework of mandatory and discretionary supervisory actions, applicable according to a credit union's net worth ratio, designed primarily to restore and improve the net worth of federally-insured credit unions.

(c) *Scope.* This part implements the provisions of section 1790d as they apply to federally-insured credit unions, whether federally- or state-chartered; to such credit unions defined as "new" pursuant to section 1790d(b)(2); and to such credit unions defined as "complex" pursuant to section 1790d(d). Certain of these provisions also apply to officers and directors of federally-insured credit unions. This part does not apply to corporate credit unions. Procedures for issuing, reviewing and enforcing orders and directives issued under this part are set forth in subpart L of part 747 of this chapter, 12 CFR 747.2001 et seq.

(d) *Other supervisory authority.* Neither § 1790d nor this part in any way limits the authority of the NCUA Board or appropriate State official under any other provision of law to take additional supervisory actions to address unsafe or unsound practices or conditions, or violations of applicable law or regulations. Action taken under this part may be taken independently of, in conjunction with, or in addition to any other enforcement action available to the NCUA Board or appropriate State official, including issuance of cease and desist orders, orders of prohibition, suspension and removal, or assessment of civil money penalties, or any other actions authorized by law.

§ 702.2 Definitions.

Except as provided below, the terms used in this part have the same meanings as set forth in FCUA sections 101 and 216, 12 U.S.C. 1752, 1790d.

§ 702.2

(a) *Appropriate regional director* means the director of the NCUA regional office having jurisdiction over federally-insured credit unions in the state where the affected credit union is principally located.

(b) *Appropriate State official* means the commission, board or other supervisory authority having jurisdiction over credit unions chartered by the State which chartered the affected credit union.

(c) *Credit union* means a federally-insured, natural person credit union, whether federally- or State-chartered, as defined by 12 U.S.C. 1752(6).

(d) *CUSO* means a credit union service organization as described in 12 CFR 712 et seq. for federally-chartered credit unions, and as defined under State law for State-chartered credit unions.

(e) *NCUSIF* means the National Credit Union Share Insurance Fund as defined by 12 U.S.C. 1783.

(f) *Net Worth* means (1) The retained earnings balance of the credit union at quarter-end as determined under generally accepted accounting principles, subject to paragraph (f)(3) of this section. Retained earnings consists of undivided earnings, regular reserves, and any other appropriations designated by management or regulatory authorities;

(2) For a low income-designated credit union, net worth also includes secondary capital accounts that are uninsured and subordinate to all other claims, including claims of creditors, shareholders and the NCUSIF; and

(3) For a credit union that acquires another credit union in a mutual combination, net worth includes the retained earnings of the acquired credit union, or of an integrated set of activities and assets, less any bargain purchase gain recognized in either case to the extent the difference between the two is greater than zero. The acquired retained earnings must be determined at the point of acquisition under generally accepted accounting principles. A mutual combination is a transaction in which a credit union acquires another credit union or acquires an integrated set of activities and assets that is capable of being conducted and managed as a credit union.

(4) The term "net worth" also includes loans to and accounts in an insured credit union established pursuant to section 208 of the Act [12 U.S.C. 1788], provided such loans and accounts:

(i) Have a remaining maturity of more than 5 years;

(ii) Are subordinate to all other claims including those of shareholders, creditors and the National Credit Union Share Insurance Fund;

(iii) Are not pledged as security on a loan to, or other obligation of, any party;

(iv) Are not insured by the National Credit Union Share Insurance Fund;

(v) Have non-cumulative dividends;

(vi) Are transferable; and

(vii) Are available to cover operating losses realized by the insured credit union that exceed its available retained earnings.

(g) *Net worth ratio* means the ratio of the net worth of the credit union (as defined in paragraph (f) of this section) to the total assets of the credit union (as defined by a measure chosen under paragraph (j) of this section).

(h) *New credit union* means a federally-insured credit union which both has been in operation for less than ten (10) years and has $10,000,000 or less in total assets.

(i) *Senior executive officer* means a senior executive officer as defined by 12 CFR 701.14(b)(2).

(j) *Shares* means deposits, shares, share certificates, share drafts, or any other depository account authorized by federal or state law.

(k) *Total assets.* (1) Total assets means a credit union's total assets as measured by either—

(i) *Average quarterly balance.* The average of quarter-end balances of the current and three preceding calendar quarters; or

(ii) *Average monthly balance.* The average of month-end balances over the three calendar months of the calendar quarter; or

(iii) *Average daily balance.* The average daily balance over the calendar quarter; or

(iv) *Quarter-end balance.* The quarter-end balance of the calendar quarter as reported on the credit union's Call Report.

(2) For each quarter, a credit union must elect a measure of total assets

from paragraph (k)(1) of this section to apply for all purposes under this part except §§ 702.103 through 702.108 [risk-based net worth requirement].

(l) *Weighted-average life* means the weighted-average time to the return of a dollar of principal, calculated by multiplying each portion of principal received by the time at which it is expected to be received (based on a reasonable and supportable estimate of that time), and then summing and dividing by the total amount of principal.

[65 FR 8584, Feb. 18, 2000, as amended at 65 FR 44966, July 20, 2000; 67 FR 71087, Nov. 29, 2002; 73 FR 72691, Dec. 1, 2008; 75 FR 34620, June 18, 2010; 76 FR 60367, Sept. 29, 2011]

Subpart A—Net Worth Classification

§ 702.101 Measures and effective date of net worth classification.

(a) *Net worth measures.* For purposes of this part, a credit union must determine its net worth category classification at the end of each calendar quarter using two measures:

(1) The net worth ratio as defined in § 702.2(g); and

(2) If determined to be applicable under § 702.103, a risk-based net worth requirement.

(b) *Effective date of net worth classification.* For purposes of this part, the effective date of a federally-insured credit union's net worth category classification shall be the most recent to occur of:

(1) *Quarter-end effective date.* The last day of the calendar month following the end of the calendar quarter; or

(2) *Corrected net worth category.* The date the credit union received subsequent written notice from NCUA or, if State-chartered, from the appropriate State official, of a decline in net worth category due to correction of an error or misstatement in the credit union's most recent Call Report; or

(3) *Reclassification to lower category.* The date the credit union received written notice from NCUA or, if State-chartered, the appropriate State official, of reclassification on safety and soundness grounds as provided under §§ 702.102(b) or 702.302(d).

(c) *Notice to NCUA by filing Call Report.* (1) Other than by filing a Call Report, a federally-insured credit union need not notify the NCUA Board of a change in its net worth ratio that places the credit union in a lower net worth category;

(2) Failure to timely file a Call Report as required under this section in no way alters the effective date of a change in net worth classification under this paragraph (b) of this section, or the affected credit union's corresponding legal obligations under this part.

[65 FR 8584, Feb. 18, 2000; 65 FR 55439, Sept. 14, 2000, as amended at 67 FR 12464, Mar. 19, 2002; 67 FR 71087, Nov. 29, 2002]

§ 702.102 Statutory net worth categories.

(a) *Net worth categories.* Except for credit unions defined as "new" under subpart B of this part, a federally-insured credit union shall be classified (Table 1)—

(1) *Well capitalized* if it has a net worth ratio of seven percent (7%) or greater and also meets any applicable risk-based net worth requirement under §§ 702.103 through 702.108; or

(2) *Adequately capitalized* if it has a net worth ratio of six percent (6%) or more but less than seven percent (7%), and also meets any applicable risk-based net worth requirement under §§ 702.103 through 702.108 below; or

(3) *Undercapitalized* if it has a net worth ratio of four percent (4%) or more but less than six percent (6%), or fails to meet any applicable risk-based net worth requirement under §§ 702.103 through 702.108; or

(4) *Significantly undercapitalized* if it

(i) Has a net worth ratio of two percent (2%) or more but less than four percent (4%); or

(ii) Has a net worth ratio of four percent (4%) or more but less than five percent (5%), and either—

(A) Fails to submit an acceptable net worth restoration plan within the time prescribed in § 702.206; or

(B) Materially fails to implement a net worth restoration plan approved by the NCUA Board; or

(5) *Critically undercapitalized* if it has a net worth ratio of less than two percent (2%).

§ 702.103   12 CFR Ch. VII (1–1–12 Edition)

TABLE 1 – STATUTORY NET WORTH CATEGORY CLASSIFICATION

A credit union's net worth category is...	if its net worth ratio is...	and subject to the following condition(s)...
"Well Capitalized"	7% or above	Meets applicable risk-based net worth (RBNW) requirement
"Adequately Capitalized"	6% to 6.99%	Meets applicable RBNW requirement
"Undercapitalized"	4% to 5.99%	Or fails applicable RBNW requirement
"Significantly Undercapitalized"	2% to 3.99%	Or if "undercapitalized" at <5% net worth ratio and fails to timely submit or materially implement Net Worth Restoration Plan
"Critically Undercapitalized"	Less than 2%	None

(b) *Reclassification based on supervisory criteria other than net worth.* The NCUA Board may reclassify a "well capitalized" credit union as "adequately capitalized" and may require an "adequately capitalized" or "undercapitalized" credit union to comply with certain mandatory or discretionary supervisory actions as if it were in the next lower net worth category (each of such actions hereinafter referred to generally as "reclassification") in the following circumstances:

(1) *Unsafe or unsound condition.* The NCUA Board has determined, after notice and opportunity for hearing pursuant to § 747.2003 of this chapter, that the credit union is in an unsafe or unsound condition; or

(2) *Unsafe or unsound practice.* The NCUA Board has determined, after notice and opportunity for hearing pursuant to § 747.2003 of this chapter, that the credit union has not corrected a material unsafe or unsound practice of which it was, or should have been, aware.

(c) *Non-delegation.* The NCUA Board may not delegate its authority to reclassify a credit union under paragraph (b) of this section.

(d) *Consultation with State officials.* The NCUA Board shall consult and seek to work cooperatively with the appropriate State official before reclassifying a federally-insured State-chartered credit union under paragraph (b) of this section, and shall promptly notify the appropriate State official of its decision to reclassify.

[65 FR 8584, Feb. 18, 2000, as amended at 65 FR 44966, July 20, 2000; 67 FR 71087, Nov. 29, 2002]

§ 702.103 Applicability of risk-based net worth requirement.

For purposes of § 702.102, a credit union is defined as "complex" and a risk-based net worth requirement is applicable only if the credit union meets both of the following criteria as reflected in its most recent Call Report:

(a) *Minimum asset size.* Its quarter-end total assets exceed ten million dollars ($10,000,000); and

(b) *Minimum RBNW calculation.* Its risk-based net worth requirement as calculated under § 702.106 exceeds six percent (6%).

[65 FR 44966, July 20, 2000, as amended by 67 FR 13464, Mar. 19, 2002; 67 FR 71088, Nov. 29, 2002; 75 FR 34620, June 18, 2010]

§ 702.104 Risk portfolios defined.

A risk portfolio is a portfolio of assets, liabilities, or contingent liabilities as specified below, each expressed as a percentage of the credit union's quarter-end total assets reflected in its most recent Call Report, rounded to two decimal places (Table 2):

(a) *Long-term real estate loans.* Total real estate loans and real estate lines of credit outstanding, exclusive of those outstanding that will contractually refinance, reprice or mature within the next five (5) years, and exclusive of all member business loans (as defined in 12 CFR 723.1 or as approved under 12 CFR 723.20);

(b) *Member business loans outstanding.* All member business loans as defined in 12 CFR 723.1 or as approved under 12 CFR 723.20;

(c) *Investments.* Investments as defined by 12 CFR 703.150 or applicable State law, including investments in CUSOs (as defined by § 702.2(d));

(d) *Low-risk assets.* Cash on hand (*e.g.,* coin and currency, including vault, ATM and teller cash), the NCUSIF deposit, and debt instruments unconditionally guaranteed by the National Credit Union Administration;

(e) *Average-risk assets.* One hundred percent (100%) of total assets minus the sum of the risk portfolios in paragraphs (a) through (d) of this section;

(f) *Loans sold with recourse.* Outstanding balance of loans sold or swapped with recourse, excluding loans sold to the secondary mortgage market that have representations and warranties consistent with those customarily required by the U.S. Government and government sponsored enterprises;

(g) *Unused member business loan commitments.* Unused commitments for member business loans as defined in 12 CFR 723.1 or as approved under 12 CFR 723.20; and

(h) *Allowance.* The Allowance for Loan and Lease Losses not to exceed the equivalent of one and one-half percent (1.5%) of total loans outstanding.

TABLE 2 -- §702.104 RISK PORTFOLIOS DEFINED

Risk portfolio	Assets, liabilities or contingent liabilities
(a) Long-term real estate loans	Total real estate loans and real estate lines of credit (excluding MBLs) with a maturity (and next rate adjustment period if variable rate) greater than 5 years
(b) MBLs outstanding	Member business loans outstanding
(c) Investments	As defined by federal regulation or applicable State law.
(d) Low-risk assets	Cash on hand and NCUSIF deposit.
(e) Average-risk assets	100% of total assets minus sum of risk portfolios above
(f) Loans sold with recourse	Outstanding balance of loans sold or swapped with recourse, except for loans sold to the secondary mortgage market with a recourse period of 1 year or less.
(g) Unused MBL commitments	Unused commitments for MBLs
(h) Allowance	Allowance for Loan and Lease Losses limited to equivalent of 1.50 percent of total loans

[65 FR 44966, July 20, 2000, as amended at 67 FR 71088, Nov. 29, 2002; 75 FR 66300, Oct. 28, 2010]

§ 702.105 Weighted-average life of investments.

Except as provided below (Table 3), the weighted-average life of an investment for purposes of §§ 702.106(c) and 702.107(c) is defined pursuant to § 702.2(m):

(a) *Registered investment companies and collective investment funds.* (1) For investments in registered investment companies (*e.g.,* mutual funds) and collective investment funds, the weighted-average life is defined as the maximum weighted-average life disclosed, directly or indirectly, in the prospectus or trust instrument;

(2) For investments in money market funds, as defined in 17 CFR 270.2a–7, and collective investment funds operated in

§ 702.106

accordance with short-term investment fund rules set forth in 12 CFR 9.18(b)(4)(ii)(B)(1)–(3), the weighted-average life is defined as one (1) year or less; and

(3) For other investments in registered investment companies or collective investment funds, the weighted-average life is defined as greater than five (5) years, but less than or equal to seven (7) years;

(b) *Callable fixed-rate debt obligations and deposits.* For fixed-rate debt obligations and deposits that are callable in whole, the weighted-average life is defined as the period remaining to the maturity date;

(c) *Variable-rate debt obligations and deposits.* For variable-rate debt obligations and deposits, the weighted-average life is defined as the period remaining to the next rate adjustment date;

(d) *Capital in mixed-ownership Government corporations and corporate credit unions.* For capital stock in mixed-ownership Government corporations, as defined in 31 U.S.C. 9101(2), and perpetual and nonperpetual capital in corporate credit unions, as defined in 12 CFR 704.2, the weighted-average life is defined as greater than one (1) year, but less than or equal to three years;

(e) *Investments in CUSOs.* For investments in CUSOs (as defined in § 702.2(d)), the weighted-average life is defined as greater than one (1) year, but less than or equal to three (3) years; and

(f) *Other equity securities.* For other equity securities, the weighted average life is defined as greater than ten (10) years.

TABLE 3 -- § 702.105 WEIGHTED-AVERAGE LIFE OF INVESTMENTS

Investment	Weighted-average life
(a) Registered investment companies and collective investment funds	i. *Registered investment companies and collective investment funds*: As disclosed in prospectus or trust instrument, but if not disclosed, greater than five (5) years, but less than or equal to seven (7) years. ii. *Money market funds and STIFs*: One (1) year or less.
(b) Callable fixed-rate debt obligations and deposits	Period remaining to maturity date.
(c) Variable-rate debt obligations and deposits	Period remaining to next rate adjustment date.
(d) Capital in mixed-ownership Government corporations and corporate credit unions	Greater than one (1) year, but less than or equal to three (3) years.
(e) Investments in CUSOs	Greater than one (1) year, but less than or equal to three (3) years.
(f) Other equity securities	Greater than ten (10) years.

[65 FR 44966, July 20, 2000, as amended at 67 FR 71088, Nov. 29, 2002; 75 FR 64826, Oct. 20, 2010]

§ 702.106 Standard calculation of risk-based net worth requirement.

A credit union's risk-based net worth requirement is the aggregate of the following standard component amounts, each expressed as a percentage of the credit union's quarter-end total assets as reflected in its most recent Call Report, rounded to two decimal places (Table 4):

(a) *Long-term real estate loans.* The sum of:

(1) Six percent (6%) of the amount of long-term real estate loans less than or equal to twenty-five percent (25%) of total assets; and

(2) Fourteen percent (14%) of the amount in excess of twenty-five percent (25%) of total assets;

(b) *Member business loans outstanding.* The sum of:

(1) Six percent (6%) of the amount of member business loans outstanding less than or equal to fifteen percent (15%) of total assets;

(2) Eight percent (8%) of the amount of member business loans outstanding greater than fifteen percent (15%), but less than or equal to twenty-five percent (25%), of total assets; and

(3) Fourteen percent (14%) of the amount in excess of twenty-five percent (25%) of total assets;

(c) *Investments.* The sum of:

(1) Three percent (3%) of the amount of investments with a weighted-average life (as specified in § 702.105 above) of one (1) year or less;

(2) Six percent (6%) of the amount of investments with a weighted-average life greater than one (1) year, but less than or equal to three (3) years;

(3) Twelve percent (12%) of the amount of investments with a weighted-average life greater than three (3) years, but less than or equal to ten (10) years; and

(4) Twenty percent (20%) of the amount of investments with a weighted-average life greater than ten (10) years;

(d) *Low-risk assets.* Zero percent (0%) of the entire portfolio of low-risk assets;

(e) *Average-risk assets.* Six percent (6%) of the entire portfolio of average-risk assets;

(f) *Loans sold with recourse.* Six percent (6%) of the entire portfolio of loans sold with recourse;

(g) *Unused member business loan commitments.* Six percent (6%) of the entire portfolio of unused member business loan commitments; and

(h) *Allowance.* Negative one hundred percent (−100%) of the balance of the Allowance for Loan and Lease Losses account, not to exceed the equivalent of one and one-half percent (1.5%) of total loans outstanding.

§ 702.107   12 CFR Ch. VII (1–1–12 Edition)

TABLE 4 — § 702.106 STANDARD CALCULATION OF RBNW REQUIREMENT

Risk portfolio	Amount of risk portfolio (as percent of quarter-end total assets) to be multiplied by risk weighting	Risk weighting
(a) Long-term real estate loans	0 to 25.00% over 25.00%	.06 .14
(b) MBLs outstanding	0 to 15.00% >15.00% to 25.00% over 25.00%	.06 .08 .14
(c) Investments	*By weighted-average life*: 0 to 1 year >1 year to 3 years >3 years to 10 years >10 years	.03 .06 .12 .20
(d) Low-risk assets	All %	.00
(e) Average-risk assets	All %	.06
(f) Loans sold with recourse	All %	.06
(g) Unused MBL commitments	All %	.06
(h) Allowance	Limited to equivalent of 1.50% of total loans (expressed as a percent of total assets)	(1.00)

A credit union's RBNW requirement is the sum of eight standard components. A standard component is calculated for each of the eight risk portfolios, equal to the sum of each amount of a risk portfolio times its risk weighting. A credit union is classified "undercapitalized" if its net worth ratio is less than its applicable RBNW requirement.

[65 FR 44966, July 20, 2000, as amended at 67 FR 71088, Nov. 29, 2002; 68 FR 56547, Oct. 1, 2003]

§ 702.107 Alternative components for standard calculation.

A credit union may substitute one or more alternative components below, in place of the corresponding standard components in § 702.106 above, when any alternative component amount, expressed as a percentage of the credit union's quarter-end total assets as reflected in its most recent Call Report, rounded to two decimal places, is smaller (Table 5):

(a) *Long-term real estate loans.* The sum of:

(1) *Non-callable.* Non-callable long-term real estate loans as follows:

(i) Eight percent (8%) of the amount of such loans with a remaining maturity of greater than 5 years, but less than or equal to 12 years;

(ii) Twelve percent (12%) of the amount of such loans with a remaining maturity of greater than 12 years, but less than or equal to 20 years; and

(iii) Fourteen percent (14%) of the amount of such loans with a remaining maturity greater than 20 years;

(2) *Callable.* Long-term real estate loans callable in 5 years or less as follows:

(i) Six percent (6%) of the amount of such loans with a documented call provision of 5 years or less and with a remaining maturity of greater than 5 years, but less than or equal to 12 years;

(ii) Ten percent (10%) of the amount of such loans with a documented call provision of 5 years or less and with a remaining maturity of greater than 12 years, but less than or equal to 20 years; and

(iii) Twelve percent (12%) of the amount of such loans with a documented call provision of 5 years or less and with a remaining maturity of greater than 20 years;

(b) *Member business loans outstanding.* The sum of:

(1) *Fixed rate.* Fixed-rate member business loans outstanding as follows:

(i) Six percent (6%) of the amount of such loans with a remaining maturity of 3 or fewer years;

National Credit Union Administration § 702.107

(ii) Nine percent (9%) of the amount of such loans with a remaining maturity greater than 3 years, but less than or equal to 5 years;

(iii) Twelve percent (12%) of the amount of such loans with a remaining maturity greater than 5 years, but less than or equal to 7 years;

(iv) Fourteen percent (14%) of the amount of such loans with a remaining maturity greater than 7 years, but less than or equal to 12 years; and

(v) Sixteen percent (16%) of the amount of such loans with a remaining maturity greater than 12 years; and

(2) *Variable-rate.* Variable-rate member business loans outstanding as follows:

(i) Six percent (6%) of the amount of such loans with a remaining maturity of 3 or fewer years;

(ii) Eight percent (8%) of the amount of such loans with a remaining maturity greater than 3 years, but less than or equal to 5 years;

(iii) Ten percent (10%) of the amount of such loans with a remaining maturity greater than 5 years, but less than or equal to 7 years;

(iv) Twelve percent (12%) of the amount of such loans with a remaining maturity greater than 7 years, but less than or equal to 12 years; and

(v) Fourteen percent (14%) of the amount of such loans with a remaining maturity greater than 12 years.

(c) *Investments.* The sum of:

(1) Three percent (3%) of the amount of investments with a weighted-average life (as specified in § 702.105 above) of one (1) year or less;

(2) Six percent (6%) of the amount of investments with a weighted-average life greater than one (1) year, but less than or equal to three (3) years;

(3) Eight percent (8%) of the amount of investments with a weighted-average life greater than three (3) years, but less than or equal to five (5) years;

(4) Twelve percent (12%) of the amount of investments with a weighted-average life greater than five (5) years, but less than or equal to seven (7) years;

(5) Sixteen percent (16%) of the amount of investments with a weighted-average life greater than seven (7) years, but less than or equal to ten (10) years; and

(6) Twenty percent (20%) of the amount of investments with a weighted-average life greater than ten (10) years.

(d) *Loans sold with recourse.* The alternative component is the sum of:

(1) Six percent (6%) of the amount of loans sold with contractual recourse obligations of six percent (6%) or greater; and

(2) The weighted average recourse percent of the amount of loans sold with contractual recourse obligations of less than six percent (6%), as computed by the credit union.

§ 702.107

TABLE 5—§ 702.107 ALTERNATIVE COMPONENTS FOR STANDARD CALCULATION

(a) LONG-TERM REAL ESTATE LOANS

Amount of long-term real estate loans by remaining maturity	Alternative risk weighting
Non-callable long-term real estate loans	
Remaining maturity:	
> 5 years to 12 years	.08
> 12 years to 20 years	.12
> 20 years	.14
Long-term real estate loans callable in 5 years or less	
Remaining maturity:	
> 5 years to 12 years	.06
> 12 years to 20 years	.10
> 20 years	.12

The "alternative component" is the sum of each amount of the "long-term real estate loans" risk portfolio by non-"callable" and "callable" characteristic and by remaining maturity (as a percent of quarter-end total assets) times its alternative factor. Substitute for corresponding standard component if smaller.

(b) MEMBER BUSINESS LOANS

Amount of member business loans by remaining maturity	Alternative risk weighting
Fixed-rate MBLs	
0 to 3 years	.06
> 3 years to 5 years	.09
> 5 years to 7 years	.12
> 7 years to 12 years	.14
> 12 years	.16
Variable-rate MBLs	
0 to 3 years	.06
> 3 years to 5 years	.08
> 5 years to 7 years	.10
> 7 years to 12 years	.12
> 12 years	.14

The "alternative component" is the sum of each amount of the member business loans risk portfolio by fixed and variable rate and by remaining maturity (as a percent of quarter-end total assets) times its alternative factor. Substitute for corresponding standard component if smaller.

(c) INVESTMENTS

Amount of investments by weighted-average life	Alternative risk weighting
0 to 1 year	.03
>1 year to 3 years	.06
>3 years to 5 years	.08
>5 years to 7 years	.12
>7 years to 10 years	.16
> 10 years	.20

The "alternative component" is the sum of each amount of the Investments risk portfolio by weighted-average life (as a percent of quarter-end total assets) times its alternative factor. Substitute for corresponding standard component if smaller.

(d) LOANS SOLD WITH RECOURSE

Amount of loans by recourse	Alternative risk weighting
Recourse 6% or greater	.06
Recourse <6%	Weighted average recourse percent

The "alternative component" is the sum of each amount of the "loans sold with recourse" risk portfolio by level of recourse (as a percent of quarter-end total assets) times its alternative factor. The alternative factor for loans sold with recourse of less than 6% is equal to the weighted average recourse percent on such loans. A credit union must compute the weighted average recourse percent for its loans sold with recourse of less than six percent (6%). Substitute for corresponding standard component if smaller.

[65 FR 44966, July 20, 2000, as amended at 67 FR 71088, Nov. 29, 2002]

§ 702.108 Risk mitigation credit.

(a) *Who may apply.* A credit union may apply for a risk mitigation credit if on any of the current or three preceding effective dates of classification it either failed an applicable RBNW requirement or met it by less than 100 basis points.

(b) *Application for credit.* Upon application pursuant to guidelines duly adopted by the NCUA Board, the NCUA Board may in its discretion grant a credit to reduce a risk-based net worth requirement under §§ 702.106 and 702.107 upon proof of mitigation of:

(1) Credit risk; or

(2) Interest rate risk as demonstrated by economic value exposure measures.

(c) *Application by FISCU.* In the case of a FISCU seeking a risk mitigation credit—

(1) Before an application under paragraph (a) above may be submitted to the NCUA Board, it must be submitted in duplicate to the appropriate State official and the appropriate Regional Director; and

(2) The NCUA Board, when evaluating the application of a FISCU, shall consult and seek to work cooperatively with the appropriate State official, and shall provide prompt notice of its decision to the appropriate State official.

[65 FR 44971, July 20, 2000, as amended at 67 FR 71089, Nov. 29, 2002]

APPENDIXES A–H TO SUBPART A OF PART 702

APPENDIX A – EXAMPLE STANDARD COMPONENTS FOR RBNW REQUIREMENT, §702.106
(EXAMPLE CALCULATION IN BOLD)

Risk portfolio	Dollar balance	Amount as percent of quarter-end total assets	Risk weighting	Amount times risk weighting	Standard component
Quarter-end total assets	200,000,000	100.0000 %			
(a) Long-term real estate loans	60,000,000	30.0000 % =			2.20 %
Threshold amount: 0 to 25%		25.0000 %	.06	1.5000 %	
Excess amount: over 25%		5.0000 %	.14	0.7000 %	
(b) MBLs outstanding	35,000,000	17.5000 % =			1.10 %
Threshold amount: 0 to 15%		15.0000 %	.06	0.9000 %	
Intermediate tier: >15% to 25%		2.5000 %	.08	0.2000 %	
Excess amount: over 25%		0.0 %	.14	0.0 %	
(c) Investments	50,000,000 =	25.0000 % =			1.51 %
Weighted-average life:					
0 to 1 year	24,000,000	12.0000 %	.03	0.3600 %	
>1 year to 3 years	15,000,000	7.5000 %	.06	0.4500 %	
>3 years to 10 years	10,000,000	5.0000 %	.12	0.6000 %	
>10 years	1,000,000	0.5000 %	.20	0.1000 %	
(d) Low-risk assets	4,000,000	2.0000 %	.00		0 %
Sum of risk portfolios (a) through (d) above	149,000,000	74.5.000%			
(e) Average-risk assets	51,000,000	25.5000 %[a]	.06		1.53 %
(f) Loans sold with recourse	40,000,000	20.0000 %	.06		1.20 %
(g) Unused MBL commitments	5,000,000	2.5000 %	.06		0.15 %
(h) Allowance	2,040,000.00 [b]	1.0200 %	(1.00)		(1.02) %
Sum of standard components: RBNW requirement [c]					6.67 %

[a] The Average-risk assets risk portfolio percent of quarter-end total assets equals 100 percent minus the sum of the percentages in the four risk portfolios above (i.e., Long-term real estate loans, MBLs outstanding, Investments, and Low-risk assets).

[b] The Allowance risk portfolio is limited to the equivalent of 1.50 percent of total loans. For an example computation of the permitted dollar balance of Allowance, see worksheet in Appendix B below.

[c] A credit union is classified "undercapitalized" if its net worth ratio is less than its applicable RBNW requirement. The dollar equivalent of RBNW requirement may be computed for informational purposes as the RBNW requirement percent of total assets.

APPENDIX B – ALLOWANCE RISK PORTFOLIO DOLLAR BALANCE WORKSHEET
(EXAMPLE CALCULATION IN BOLD)

Balance sheet account	Dollar balance	Percent of total loans	Range of ALL permitted	Permitted ALL percent of total loans	Permitted dollar balance of Allowance
Allowance for Loan and Lease Losses (ALL)	2,400,000	1.7647%	0 to 1.50%	1.50%	2,040,000
Total loans	136,000,000				

APPENDIX C – EXAMPLE LONG-TERM REAL ESTATE LOANS ALTERNATIVE COMPONENT, §702.107(a)
(EXAMPLE CALCUATION IN BOLD)

Remaining maturity	Dollar balance of Long-term real estate loans by remaining maturity	Percent of total assets by remaining maturity	Alternative risk weighting	Alternative component
Non-callable long-term real estate loans				
> 5 years to 12 years	15,000,000	7.5000 %	.08	0.6000 %
> 12 years to 20 years	2,500,000	1.2500 %	.12	0.1500 %
> 20 years	2,500,000	1.2500 %	.14	0.1750 %
Long-term real estate loans callable in 5 years or less				
> 5 years to 12 years	35,000,000	17.5000 %	.06	1.0500 %
> 12 years to 20 years	5,000,000	2.5000 %	.10	0.2500 %
> 20 years	0	0.000 %	.12	0.000 %
Sum of above equals Alternative Component*				2.23 %

*Substitute for standard component if lower.

APPENDIX D – EXAMPLE OF MEMBER BUSINESS LOANS ALTERNATIVE COMPONENT, §702.107(b)
(EXAMPLE CALCULATION IN BOLD)

Remaining maturity	Dollar balance of MBLs by remaining maturity	Percent of total assets by remaining maturity	Alternative risk weighting	Alternative component
Fixed-rate MBLs				
0 to 3 years	6,000,000	3.0000 %	.06	0.1800 %
> 3 years to 5 years	4,000,000	2.0000 %	.09	0.1800 %
> 5 years to 7 years	2,000,000	1.0000 %	.12	0.1200 %
> 7 years to 12 years	0	0.0000 %	.14	0.0000 %
> 12 years	0	0.0000 %	.16	0.0000 %
Variable-rate MBLs				
0 to 3 years	17,000,000	8.5000 %	.06	0.5100 %
> 3 years to 5 years	4,000,000	2.0000 %	.08	0.1600 %
> 5 years to 7 years	2,000,000	1.0000 %	.10	0.1000 %
> 7 years to 12 years	0	0.0000 %	.12	0.0000 %
>12 years	0	0.0000 %	.14	0.0000 %
Sum of above equals Alternative component*				1.25 %

* Substitute for standard component if lower.

Pt. 702, Apps.

APPENDIX E -- EXAMPLE OF INVESTMENTS ALTERNATIVE COMPONENT, §702.107(c)
(EXAMPLE CALCULATION IN BOLD)

Weighted-average life	Dollar balance of investments by weighted-average life	Percent of total assets by weighted-average life	Alternative risk weighting	Alternative component
0 to 1 year	24,000,000	12.0000 %	.03	0.3600 %
> 1 year to 3 years	15,000,000	7.5000 %	.06	0.4500 %
> 3 years to 5 years	8,000,000	4.0000 %	.08	0.3200 %
> 5 years to 7 years	1,000,000	0.5000 %	.12	0.0600 %
> 7 years to 10 years	1,000,000	0.5000 %	.16	0.0800 %
> 10 years	1,000,000	0.5000 %	.20	0.1000 %
Sum of above equals Alternative component*				1.37 %

* Substitute for standard component if lower.

APPENDIX F -- EXAMPLE LOANS SOLD WITH RECOURSE ALTERNATIVE COMPONENT, §702.107(d)
(EXAMPLE CALCULATION IN BOLD)

Percent of contractual recourse obligation	Dollar balance of Loans sold with recourse	Percent of total assets	Alternative risk weighting	Alternative component
Recourse 6 % or greater	5,000,000	2.5000 %	.06	0.1500 %
Recourse < 6 %	35,000,000	17.5000 %	.0500 ʷ	0.8750 %
Sum of above equals Alternative component*				1.03 %

* Substitute for corresponding standard component if lower.
ʷ The credit union must calculate this alternative risk weighting for loans sold with recourse of less than 6 %. For an example computation, see worksheet in Appendix G below.

APPENDIX G -- WORKSHEET FOR ALTERNATIVE RISK WEIGHTING OF LOANS SOLD WITH CONTRACTUAL RECOURSE OBLIGATIONS OF LESS THAN 6 %
(EXAMPLE CALCULATION IN BOLD)

Percent of contractual recourse obligation less than 6%	Dollar balance of loans sold with recourse	Dollars of recourse	Alternative risk weighting
5.50 %	5,000,000	275,000	
5.00 %	25,000,000	1,250,000	
4.50 %	5,000,000	225,000	
Sum of above equals	35,000,000	1,750,000	
Dollar of recourse divided by dollar balance equals (expressed as %)			5.00 %

Appendix H -- Example RBNW requirement using Alternative Components
(Example Calculation in Bold)

Risk portfolio	Standard component	Alternative component	Lower of standard or alternative component
(a) Long-term real estate loans	2.20 %	2.85 %	2.20 %
(b) MBLs outstanding	1.10 %	1.25 %	1.10 %
(c) Investments	1.51 %	1.37 %	1.37 %
(f) Loans sold with recourse	1.20%	1.03%	1.03% Standard component
(d) Low-risk assets			0 %
(e) Average-risk assets			1.53 %
(g) Unused MBL commitments			0.15 %
(h) Allowance			(1.02) %
RBNW requirement* Compare to Net Worth Ratio			6.53 %

* A credit union is "undercapitalized" if its net worth ratio is less than its applicable RBNW requirement

[65 FR 44971, July 20, 2000, as amended at 67 FR 71089, 71090, 71091, Nov. 29, 2002; 68 FR 56548, 56549, 56550, Oct. 1, 2003]

Subpart B—Mandatory and Discretionary Supervisory Actions

§ 702.201 Prompt corrective action for "adequately capitalized" credit unions.

(a) *Earnings retention.* Beginning the effective date of classification as "adequately capitalized" or lower, a federally-insured credit union must increase the dollar amount of its net worth quarterly either in the current quarter, or on average over the current and three preceding quarters, by an amount equivalent to at least 1/10th percent (0.1%) of its total assets, and must quarterly transfer that amount (or more by choice) from undivided earnings to its regular reserve account until it is "well capitalized."

(b) *Decrease in retention.* Upon written application received no later than 14 days before the quarter end, the NCUA Board, on a case-by-case basis, may permit a credit union to increase the dollar amount of its net worth and quarterly transfer an amount that is less than the amount required under paragraph (a) of this section, to the extent the NCUA Board determines that such lesser amount—

(1) Is necessary to avoid a significant redemption of shares; and

(2) Would further the purpose of this part.

(c) *Decrease by FISCU.* The NCUA Board shall consult and seek to work cooperatively with the appropriate State official before permitting a federally-insured State-chartered credit union to decrease its earnings retention under paragraph (b) of this section.

(d) *Periodic review.* A decision under paragraph (b) of this section to permit a credit union to decrease its earnings retention is subject to quarterly review and revocation except when the credit union is operating under an approved net worth restoration plan that provides for decreasing its earnings retention as provided under paragraph (b).

[67 FR 71091, Nov. 29, 2002]

§ 702.202 Prompt corrective action for "undercapitalized" credit unions.

(a) *Mandatory supervisory actions by credit union.* A federally-insured credit union which is "undercapitalized" must—

§ 702.202

(1) *Earnings retention.* Increase net worth and transfer earnings to its regular reserve account in accordance with § 702.201;

(2) *Submit net worth restoration plan.* Submit a net worth restoration plan pursuant to § 702.206, *provided however,* that a credit union in this category having a net worth ratio of less than five percent (5%) which fails to timely submit such a plan, or which materially fails to implement an approved plan, is classified "significantly undercapitalized" pursuant to § 702.102(a)(4)(ii) above;

(3) *Restrict increase in assets.* Beginning the effective date of classification as "undercapitalized" or lower, not permit the credit union's assets to increase beyond its total assets (per § 702.2(j)) for the preceding quarter unless—

(i) *Plan approved.* The NCUA Board has approved a net worth restoration plan which provides for an increase in total assets and—

(A) The assets of the credit union are increasing consistent with the approved plan; and

(B) The credit union is implementing steps to increase the net worth ratio consistent with the approved plan;

(ii) *Plan not approved.* The NCUA Board has not approved a net worth restoration plan and total assets of the credit union are increasing because of increases since quarter-end in balances of:

(A) Total accounts receivable and accrued income on loans and investments; or

(B) Total cash and cash equivalents; or

(C) Total loans outstanding, not to exceed the sum of total assets (per § 702.2(j)) plus the quarter-end balance of unused commitments to lend and unused lines of credit provided however that a credit union which increases a balance as permitted under paragraphs (A), (B) or (C) cannot offer rates on shares in excess of prevailing rates on shares in its relevant market area, and cannot open new branches;

(4) *Restrict member business loans.* Beginning the effective date of classification as "undercapitalized" or lower, not increase the total dollar amount of member business loans (defined as loans outstanding and unused commitments to lend) as of the preceding quarter-end unless it is granted an exception under 12 U.S.C. 1757a(b).

(b) *"Second tier" discretionary supervisory actions by NCUA.* Subject to the applicable procedures for issuing, reviewing and enforcing directives set forth in subpart L of part 747 of this chapter, the NCUA Board may, by directive, take one or more of the following actions with respect to an "undercapitalized" credit union having a net worth ratio of less than five percent (5%), or a director, officer or employee of such a credit union, if it determines that those actions are necessary to carry out the purpose of this part:

(1) *Requiring prior approval for acquisitions, branching, new lines of business.* Prohibit a credit union from, directly or indirectly, acquiring any interest in any business entity or financial institution, establishing or acquiring any additional branch office, or engaging in any new line of business, unless the NCUA Board has approved the credit union's net worth restoration plan, the credit union is implementing its plan, and the NCUA Board determines that the proposed action is consistent with and will further the objectives of that plan;

(2) *Restricting transactions with and ownership of CUSO.* Restrict the credit union's transactions with a CUSO, or require the credit union to reduce or divest its ownership interest in a CUSO;

(3) *Restricting dividends paid.* Restrict the dividend rates the credit union pays on shares to the prevailing rates paid on comparable accounts and maturities in the relevant market area, as determined by the NCUA Board, except that dividend rates already declared on shares acquired before imposing a restriction under this paragraph may not be retroactively restricted;

(4) *Prohibiting or reducing asset growth.* Prohibit any growth in the credit union's assets or in a category of assets, or require the credit union to reduce its assets or a category of assets;

(5) *Alter, reduce or terminate activity.* Require the credit union or its CUSO

to alter, reduce, or terminate any activity which poses excessive risk to the credit union;

(6) *Prohibiting nonmember deposits.* Prohibit the credit union from accepting all or certain nonmember deposits;

(7) *Dismissing director or senior executive officer.* Require the credit union to dismiss from office any director or senior executive officer, *provided however,* that a dismissal under this clause shall not be construed to be a formal administrative action for removal under 12 U.S.C. 1786(g);

(8) *Employing qualified senior executive officer.* Require the credit union to employ qualified senior executive officers (who, if the NCUA Board so specifies, shall be subject to its approval); and

(9) *Other action to carry out prompt corrective action.* Restrict or require such other action by the credit union as the NCUA Board determines will carry out the purpose of this part better than any of the actions prescribed in paragraphs (b)(1) through (8) of this section.

(c) *"First tier" application of discretionary supervisory actions.* An "undercapitalized" credit union having a net worth ratio of five percent (5%) or more, or which is classified "undercapitalized" by reason of failing to satisfy a risk-based net worth requirement under § 702.105 or 702.106, is subject to the discretionary supervisory actions in paragraph (b) of this section if it fails to comply with any mandatory supervisory action in paragraph (a) of this section or fails to timely implement an approved net worth restoration plan under § 702.206, including meeting its prescribed steps to increase its net worth ratio.

[65 FR 8584, Feb. 18, 2000, as amended at 67 FR 71092, Nov. 29, 2002]

§ 702.203 Prompt corrective action for "significantly undercapitalized" credit unions.

(a) *Mandatory supervisory actions by credit union.* A federally-insured credit union which is "significantly undercapitalized" must—

(1) *Earnings retention.* Increase net worth and transfer earnings to its regular reserve account in accordance with § 702.201;

(2) *Submit net worth restoration plan.* Submit a net worth restoration plan pursuant to § 702.206;

(3) *Restrict increase in assets.* Not permit the credit union's total assets to increase except as provided in § 702.202(a)(3) and

(4) *Restrict member business loans.* Not increase the total dollar amount of member business loans (defined as loans outstanding and unused commitments to lend) as provided in § 702.202(a)(4).

(b) *Discretionary supervisory actions by NCUA.* Subject to the applicable procedures for issuing, reviewing and enforcing directives set forth in subpart L of part 747 of this chapter, the NCUA Board may, by directive, take one or more of the following actions with respect to any "significantly undercapitalized" credit union, or a director, officer or employee of such credit union, if it determines that those actions are necessary to carry out the purpose of this part:

(1) *Requiring prior approval for acquisitions, branching, new lines of business.* Prohibit a credit union from, directly or indirectly, acquiring any interest in any business entity or financial institution, establishing or acquiring any additional branch office, or engaging in any new line of business, except as provided in § 702.202(b)(1);

(2) *Restricting transactions with and ownership of CUSO.* Restrict the credit union's transactions with a CUSO, or require the credit union to divest or reduce its ownership interest in a CUSO;

(3) *Restricting dividends paid.* Restrict the dividend rates that the credit union pays on shares as provided in § 702.202(b)(3);

(4) *Prohibiting or reducing asset growth.* Prohibit any growth in the credit union's assets or in a category of assets, or require the credit union to reduce assets or a category of assets;

(5) *Alter, reduce or terminate activity.* Require the credit union or its CUSO(s) to alter, reduce, or terminate any activity which poses excessive risk to the credit union;

(6) *Prohibiting nonmember deposits.* Prohibit the credit union from accepting all or certain nonmember deposits;

§ 702.204

(7) *New election of directors.* Order a new election of the credit union's board of directors;

(8) *Dismissing director or senior executive officer.* Require the credit union to dismiss from office any director or senior executive officer, *provided however,* that a dismissal under this clause shall not be construed to be a formal administrative action for removal under 12 U.S.C. 1786(g);

(9) *Employing qualified senior executive officer.* Require the credit union to employ qualified senior executive officers (who, if the NCUA Board so specifies, shall be subject to its approval);

(10) *Restricting senior executive officers' compensation.* Except with the prior written approval of the NCUA Board, limit compensation to any senior executive officer to that officer's average rate of compensation (excluding bonuses and profit sharing) during the four (4) calendar quarters preceding the effective date of classification of the credit union as "significantly undercapitalized," and prohibit payment of a bonus or profit share to such officer;

(11) *Other actions to carry out prompt corrective action.* Restrict or require such other action by the credit union as the NCUA Board determines will carry out the purpose of this part better than any of the actions prescribed in paragraphs (b)(1) through (10) of this section; and

(12) *Requiring merger.* Require the credit union to merge with another financial institution if one or more grounds exist for placing the credit union into conservatorship pursuant to 12 U.S.C. 1786(h)(1)(F), or into liquidation pursuant to 12 U.S.C. 1787(a)(3)(A)(i).

(c) *Discretionary conservatorship or liquidation if no prospect of becoming "adequately capitalized."* Notwithstanding any other actions required or permitted to be taken under this section, when a credit union becomes "significantly undercapitalized" (including by reclassification under section 702.102(b) above), the NCUA Board may place the credit union into conservatorship pursuant to 12 U.S.C. 1786(h)(1)(F), or into liquidation pursuant to 12 U.S.C. 1787(a)(3)(A)(i), provided that the credit union has no reasonable prospect of becoming "adequately capitalized."

[65 FR 8584, Feb. 18, 2000, as amended at 67 FR 71092, Nov. 29, 2002]

§ 702.204 Prompt corrective action for "critically undercapitalized" credit unions

(a) *Mandatory supervisory actions by credit union.* A federally-insured credit union which is "critically undercapitalized" must—

(1) *Earnings retention.* Increase net worth and transfer earnings to its regular reserve account in accordance with § 702.201;

(2) *Submit net worth restoration plan.* Submit a net worth restoration plan pursuant to § 702.206;

(3) *Restrict increase in assets.* Not permit the credit union's total assets to increase except as provided in § 702.202(a)(3); and

(4) *Restrict member business loans.* Not increase the total dollar amount of member business loans (defined as loans outstanding and unused commitments to lend) as provided in § 702.202(a)(4).

(b) *Discretionary supervisory actions by NCUA.* Subject to the applicable procedures for issuing, reviewing and enforcing directives set forth in subpart L of part 747 of this chapter, the NCUA Board may, by directive, take one or more of the following actions with respect to any "critically undercapitalized" credit union, or a director, officer or employee of such credit union, if it determines that those actions are necessary to carry out the purpose of this part:

(1) *Requiring prior approval for acquisitions, branching, new lines of business.* Prohibit a credit union from, directly or indirectly, acquiring any interest in any business entity or financial institution, establishing or acquiring any additional branch office, or engaging in any new line of business, except as provided by § 702.202(b)(1);

(2) *Restricting transactions with and ownership of CUSO.* Restrict the credit union's transactions with a CUSO, or require the credit union to divest or reduce its ownership interest in a CUSO;

(3) *Restricting dividends paid.* Restrict the dividend rates that the credit

National Credit Union Administration § 702.204

union pays on shares as provided in § 702.202(b)(3);

(4) *Prohibiting or reducing asset growth.* Prohibit any growth in the credit union's assets or in a category of assets, or require the credit union to reduce assets or a category of assets;

(5) *Alter, reduce or terminate activity.* Require the credit union or its CUSO(s) to alter, reduce, or terminate any activity which poses excessive risk to the credit union;

(6) *Prohibiting nonmember deposits.* Prohibit the credit union from accepting all or certain nonmember deposits;

(7) *New election of directors.* Order a new election of the credit union's board of directors;

(8) *Dismissing director or senior executive officer.* Require the credit union to dismiss from office any director or senior executive officer, *provided however,* that a dismissal under this clause shall not be construed to be a formal administrative action for removal under 12 U.S.C. 1786(g);

(9) *Employing qualified senior executive officer.* Require the credit union to employ qualified senior executive officers (who, if the NCUA Board so specifies, shall be subject to its approval);

(10) *Restricting senior executive officers' compensation.* Reduce or, with the prior written approval of the NCUA Board, limit compensation to any senior executive officer to that officer's average rate of compensation (excluding bonuses and profit sharing) during the four (4) calendar quarters preceding the effective date of classification of the credit union as "critically undercapitalized," and prohibit payment of a bonus or profit share to such officer;

(11) *Restrictions on payments on uninsured secondary capital.* Beginning 60 days after the effective date of classification of a credit union as "critically undercapitalized," prohibit payments of principal, dividends or interest on the credit union's uninsured secondary capital accounts established after August 7, 2000, except that unpaid dividends or interest shall continue to accrue under the terms of the account to the extent permitted by law;

(12) *Requiring prior approval.* Require a "critically undercapitalized" credit union to obtain the NCUA Board's prior written approval before doing any of the following:

(i) Entering into any material transaction not within the scope of an approved net worth restoration plan (or approved revised business plan under subpart C of this part);

(ii) Extending credit for transactions deemed highly leveraged by the NCUA Board or, if State-chartered, by the appropriate State official;

(iii) Amending the credit union's charter or bylaws, except to the extent necessary to comply with any law, regulation, or order;

(iv) Making any material change in accounting methods; and

(v) Paying dividends or interest on new share accounts at a rate exceeding the prevailing rates of interest on insured deposits in its relevant market area;

(13) *Other action to carry out prompt corrective action.* Restrict or require such other action by the credit union as the NCUA Board determines will carry out the purpose of this part better than any of the actions prescribed in paragraphs (b)(1) through (12) of this section; and

(14) *Requiring merger.* Require the credit union to merge with another financial institution if one or more grounds exist for placing the credit union into conservatorship pursuant to 12 U.S.C. 1786(h)(1)(F), or into liquidation pursuant to 12 U.S.C. 1787(a)(3)(A)(i).

(c) *Mandatory conservatorship, liquidation or action in lieu thereof*—(1) *Action within 90 days.* Notwithstanding any other actions required or permitted to be taken under this section (and regardless of a credit union's prospect of becoming "adequately capitalized"), the NCUA Board must, within 90 calendar days after the effective date of classification of a credit union as "critically undercapitalized"—

(i) *Conservatorship.* Place the credit union into conservatorship pursuant to 12 U.S.C. 1786(h)(1)(G); or

(ii) *Liquidation.* Liquidate the credit union pursuant to 12 U.S.C. 1787(a)(3)(A)(ii); or

(iii) *Other corrective action.* Take other corrective action, in lieu of conservatorship or liquidation, to better achieve the purpose of this part, provided that the NCUA Board documents why such action in lieu of conservatorship or liquidation would do so, *provided however*, that other corrective action may consist, in whole or in part, of complying with the quarterly timetable of steps and meeting the quarterly net worth targets prescribed in an approved net worth restoration plan.

(2) *Renewal of other corrective action.* A determination by the NCUA Board to take other corrective action in lieu of conservatorship or liquidation under paragraph (c)(1)(iii) of this section shall expire after an effective period ending no later than 180 calendar days after the determination is made, and the credit union shall be immediately placed into conservatorship or liquidation under paragraphs (c)(1)(i) and (ii), unless the NCUA Board makes a new determination under paragraph (c)(1)(iii) of this section before the end of the effective period of the prior determination;

(3) *Mandatory liquidation after 18 months*—(i) *Generally.* Notwithstanding paragraphs (c)(1) and (2) of this section, the NCUA Board must place a credit union into liquidation if it remains "critically undercapitalized" for a full calendar quarter, on a monthly average basis, following a period of 18 months from the effective date the credit union was first classified "critically undercapitalized."

(ii) *Exception.* Notwithstanding paragraph (c)(3)(i) of this section, the NCUA Board may continue to take other corrective action in lieu of liquidation if it certifies that the credit union—

(A) Has been in substantial compliance with an approved net worth restoration plan requiring consistent improvement in net worth since the date the net worth restoration plan was approved;

(B) Has positive net income or has an upward trend in earnings that the NCUA Board projects as sustainable; and

(C) Is viable and not expected to fail.

(iii) *Review of exception.* The NCUA Board shall, at least quarterly, review the certification of an exception to liquidation under paragraph (c)(3)(ii) of this section and shall either—

(A) Recertify the credit union if it continues to satisfy the criteria of paragraph (c)(3)(ii) of this section; or

(B) Promptly place the credit union into liquidation, pursuant to 12 U.S.C. 1787(a)(3)(A)(ii), if it fails to satisfy the criteria of paragraph (c)(3)(ii) of this section.

(4) *Nondelegation.* The NCUA Board may not delegate its authority under paragraph (c) of this section, unless the credit union has less than $5,000,000 in total assets. A credit union shall have a right of direct appeal to the NCUA Board of any decision made by delegated authority under this section within ten (10) calendar days of the date of that decision.

(d) *Mandatory liquidation of insolvent federal credit union.* In lieu of paragraph (c) of this section, a "critically undercapitalized" federal credit union that has a net worth ratio of less than zero percent (0%) may be placed into liquidation on grounds of insolvency pursuant to 12 U.S.C. 1787(a)(1)(A).

[65 FR 8584, Feb. 18, 2000, as amended at 67 FR 71092, Nov. 29, 2002; 75 FR 34620, June 18, 2010]

§ 702.205 Consultation with State officials on proposed prompt corrective action.

(a) *Consultation on proposed conservatorship or liquidation.* Before placing a federally-insured State-chartered credit union into conservatorship (pursuant to 12 U.S.C. 1786(h)(1)(F) or (G)) or liquidation (pursuant to 12 U.S.C. 1787(a)(3)) as permitted or required under subparts B or C of this part to facilitate prompt corrective action—

(1) The NCUA Board shall seek the views of the appropriate State official (as defined in § 702.2(b)), and give him or her an opportunity to take the proposed action;

(2) The NCUA Board shall, upon timely request of the appropriate State official, promptly provide him or her with a written statement of the reasons for the proposed conservatorship or liquidation, and reasonable time to respond to that statement; and

(3) If the appropriate State official makes a timely written response that disagrees with the proposed conservatorship or liquidation and gives reasons for that disagreement, the

NCUA Board shall not place the credit union into conservatorship or liquidation unless it first considers the views of the appropriate State official and determines that—

(i) The NCUSIF faces a significant risk of loss if the credit union is not placed into conservatorship or liquidation; and

(ii) Conservatorship or liquidation is necessary either to reduce the risk of loss, or to reduce the expected loss, to the NCUSIF with respect to the credit union.

(b) *Nondelegation.* The NCUA Board may not delegate any determination under paragraph (a)(3) of this section.

(c) *Consultation on proposed discretionary action.* The NCUA Board shall consult and seek to work cooperatively with the appropriate State official before taking any discretionary supervisory action under §§ 702.202(b), 702.203(b), 702.204(b), 702.304(b) and 702.305(b) with respect to a federally-insured State-chartered credit union; shall provide prompt notice of its decision to the appropriate State official; and shall allow the appropriate State official to take the proposed action independently or jointly with NCUA.

[65 FR 8584, Feb. 18, 2000, as amended at 67 FR 71092, Nov. 29, 2002; 75 FR 34620, June 18, 2010]

§ 702.206 Net worth restoration plans.

(a) *Schedule for filing*—(1) *Generally.* A federally-insured credit union shall file a written net worth restoration plan (NWRP) with the appropriate Regional Director and, if State-chartered, the appropriate State official, within 45 calendar days of the effective date of classification as either "undercapitalized," "significantly undercapitalized" or "critically undercapitalized," unless the NCUA Board notifies the credit union in writing that its NWRP is to be filed within a different period.

(2) *Exception.* An otherwise "adequately capitalized" credit union that is reclassified "undercapitalized" on safety and soundness grounds under § 702.102(b) is not required to submit a NWRP solely due to the reclassification, unless the NCUA Board notifies the credit union that it must submit an NWRP.

(3) *Filing of additional plan.* Notwithstanding paragraph (a)(1) of this section, a credit union that has already submitted and is operating under a NWRP approved under this section is not required to submit an additional NWRP due to a change in net worth category (including by reclassification under § 702.102(b)), unless the NCUA Board notifies the credit union that it must submit a new NWRP. A credit union that is notified to submit a new or revised NWRP shall file the NWRP in writing with the appropriate Regional Director within 30 calendar days of receiving such notice, unless the NCUA Board notifies the credit union in writing that the NWRP is to be filed within a different period.

(4) *Failure to timely file plan.* When a credit union fails to timely file an NWRP pursuant to this paragraph, the NCUA Board shall promptly notify the credit union that it has failed to file an NWRP and that it has 15 calendar days from receipt of that notice within which to file an NWRP.

(b) *Assistance to small credit unions.* Upon timely request by a credit union having total assets of less than $10 million (regardless how long it has been in operation), the NCUA Board shall provide assistance in preparing an NWRP required to be filed under paragraph (a) of this section.

(c) *Contents of NWRP.* An NWRP must—

(1) Specify—

(i) A quarterly timetable of steps the credit union will take to increase its net worth ratio so that it becomes "adequately capitalized" by the end of the term of the NWRP, and to remain so for four (4) consecutive calendar quarters. If "complex," the credit union is subject to a risk-based net worth requirement that may require a net worth ratio higher than six percent (6%) to become "adequately capitalized";

(ii) The projected amount of earnings to be transferred to the regular reserve account in each quarter of the term of the NWRP as required under § 702.201(a), or as permitted under § 702.201(b);

(iii) How the credit union will comply with the mandatory and any discretionary supervisory actions imposed on

§ 702.301

it by the NCUA Board under this subpart;

(iv) The types and levels of activities in which the credit union will engage; and

(v) If reclassified to a lower category under § 702.102(b), the steps the credit union will take to correct the unsafe or unsound practice(s) or condition(s);

(2) Include pro forma financial statements, including any off-balance sheet items, covering a minimum of the next two years; and

(3) Contain such other information as the NCUA Board has required.

(d) *Criteria for approval of NWRP.* The NCUA Board shall not accept a NWRP plan unless it—

(1) Complies with paragraph (c) of this section;

(2) Is based on realistic assumptions, and is likely to succeed in restoring the credit union's net worth; and (3) Would not unreasonably increase the credit union's exposure to risk (including credit risk, interest-rate risk, and other types of risk).

(e) *Consideration of regulatory capital.* To minimize possible long-term losses to the NCUSIF while the credit union takes steps to become "adequately capitalized," the NCUA Board shall, in evaluating an NWRP under this section, consider the type and amount of any form of regulatory capital which may become established by NCUA regulation, or authorized by State law and recognized by NCUA, which the credit union holds, but which is not included in its net worth.

(f) *Review of NWRP*—(1) *Notice of decision.* Within 45 calendar days after receiving an NWRP under this part, the NCUA Board shall notify the credit union in writing whether the NWRP has been approved, and shall provide reasons for its decision in the event of disapproval.

(2) *Delayed decision.* If no decision is made within the time prescribed in paragraph (f)(1) of this section, the NWRP is deemed approved.

(3) *Consultation with State officials.* In the case of an NWRP submitted by a federally-insured State-chartered credit union (whether an original, new, additional, revised or amended NWRP), the NCUA Board shall, when evaluating the NWRP, seek and consider the views of the appropriate State official, and provide prompt notice of its decision to the appropriate State official.

(g) *NWRP not approved* (1) *Submission of revised NWRP.* If an NWRP is rejected by the NCUA Board, the credit union shall submit a revised NWRP within 30 calendar days of receiving notice of disapproval, unless it is notified in writing by the NCUA Board that the revised NWRP is to be filed within a different period.

(2) *Notice of decision on revised NWRP.* Within 30 calendar days after receiving a revised NWRP under paragraph (g)(1) of this section, the NCUA Board shall notify the credit union in writing whether the revised NWRP is approved. The Board may extend the time within which notice of its decision shall be provided.

(3) *Disapproval of reclassified credit union's NWRP.* A credit union which has been classified "significantly undercapitalized" under § 702.102(a)(4)(ii) shall remain so classified pending NCUA Board approval of a new or revised NWRP.

(h) *Amendment of NWRP.* A credit union that is operating under an approved NWRP may, after prior written notice to, and approval by the NCUA Board, amend its NWRP to reflect a change in circumstance. Pending approval of an amended NWRP, the credit union shall implement the NWRP as originally approved.

(i) *Publication.* An NWRP need not be published to be enforceable because publication would be contrary to the public interest.

[65 FR 8584, Feb. 18, 2000, as amended at 67 FR 71092, Nov. 29, 2002]

Subpart C—Alternative Prompt Corrective Action for New Credit Unions

§ 702.301 Scope and definition.

(a) *Scope.* This subpart C applies in lieu of subpart B of this part exclusively to credit unions defined in paragraph (b) of this section as "new" pursuant to 12 U.S.C. 1790d(b)(2).

(b) *New credit union defined.* A "new" credit union for purposes of this subpart is a federally-insured credit union that both has been in operation for less than ten (10) years and has total assets of not more than $10 million. A credit union which exceeds $10 million in total assets may become "new" if its total assets subsequently decline below $10 million while it is still in operation for less than 10 years.

(c) *Effect of spin-offs.* A credit union formed as the result of a "spin-off" of a group from the field of membership of an existing credit union is deemed to be in operation since the effective date of the "spin-off." A credit union whose total assets decline below $10 million because a group within its field of membership has been "spun-off" is deemed "new" if it has been in operation less than 10 years.

(d) *Actions to evade prompt corrective action.* If the NCUA Board determines that a credit union was formed, or was reduced in asset size as a result of a "spin-off," or was merged, primarily to qualify as "new" under this subpart, the credit union shall be deemed subject to prompt corrective action under subpart A of this part.

§ 702.302 Net worth categories for new credit unions.

(a) *Net worth measures.* For purposes of this part, a new credit union must determine its net worth category classification quarterly according to its net worth ratio as defined in § 702.2(g).

(b) *Effective date of net worth classification of new credit union.* For purposes of subpart C, the effective date of a new federally-insured credit union's classification within a net worth category in paragraph (c) of this section shall be determined as provided in § 702.101(b); and written notice to the NCUA Board of a decline in net worth category in paragraph (c) of this section shall be given as required by section 702.101(c).

(c) *Net worth categories.* A federally-insured credit union defined as "new" under this section shall be classified (Table 6)—

(1) *Well capitalized* if it has a net worth ratio of seven percent (7%) or greater;

(2) *Adequately capitalized* if it has a net worth ratio of six percent (6%) or more but less than seven percent (7%);

(3) *Moderately capitalized* if it has a net worth ratio of three and one-half percent (3.5%) or more but less than six percent (6%);

(4) *Marginally capitalized* if it has a net worth ratio of two percent (2%) or more but less than three and one-half percent (3.5%);

(5) *Minimally capitalized* if it has a net worth ratio of zero percent (0%) or greater but less than two percent (2%); and

(6) *Uncapitalized* if it has a net worth ratio of less than zero percent (0%) (*e.g.*, a deficit in retained earnings).

TABLE 6 -- NET WORTH CATEGORY CLASSIFICATION FOR "NEW" CREDIT UNIONS

A "new" credit union's net worth category is . . .	if its net worth ratio is . . .
"Well Capitalized"	7% or above
"Adequately Capitalized"	6% to 6.99%
"Moderately Capitalized"	3.5% to 5.99%
"Marginally Capitalized"	2% to 3.49%
"Minimally Capitalized"	0% to 1.99%
"Uncapitalized"	Less than 0%

(d) *Reclassification based on supervisory criteria other than net worth.* Subject to § 702.102(b) and (c), the NCUA Board may reclassify a "well capitalized," "adequately capitalized" or "moderately capitalized" new credit union to the next lower net worth category (each of such actions is hereinafter referred to generally as "reclassification") in either of the circumstances prescribed in § 702.102(b).

§ 702.303

(e) *Consultation with State officials.* The NCUA Board shall consult and seek to work cooperatively with the appropriate State official before reclassifying a federally-insured State-chartered credit union under paragraph (d) of this section, and shall promptly notify the appropriate State official of its decision to reclassify.

[65 FR 8584, Feb. 18, 2000, as amended at 65 FR 44974, July 20, 2000; 65 FR 55439, Sept. 14, 2000; 67 FR 71092, Nov. 29, 2002]

§ 702.303 Prompt corrective action for "adequately capitalized" new credit unions.

Beginning on the effective date of classification, an "adequately capitalized" new credit union must increase the dollar amount of its net worth by the amount reflected in its approved initial or revised business plan in accordance with § 702.304(a)(2), or in the absence of such a plan, in accordance with § 702.201, and quarterly transfer that amount from undivided earnings to its regular reserve account, until it is "well capitalized."

[67 FR 71092, Nov. 29, 2002]

§ 702.304 Prompt corrective action for "moderately capitalized," "marginally capitalized" or "minimally capitalized" new credit unions.

(a) *Mandatory supervisory actions by new credit union.* Beginning on the date of classification as "moderately capitalized," "marginally capitalized" or "minimally capitalized" (including by reclassification under § 702.302(d)), a new credit union must—

(1) *Earnings retention.* Increase the dollar amount of its net worth by the amount reflected in its approved initial or revised business plan and quarterly transfer that amount from undivided earnings to its regular reserve account;

(2) *Submit revised business plan.* Submit a revised business plan within the time provided by § 702.306 if the credit union either:

(i) Has not increased its net worth ratio consistent with its then-present approved business plan;

(ii) Has no then-present approved business plan; or

(iii) Has failed to comply with paragraph (a)(3) of this section; and

(3) *Restrict member business loans.* Not increase the total dollar amount of member business loans (defined as loans outstanding and unused commitments to lend) as of the preceding quarter-end unless it is granted an exception under 12 U.S.C. 1757a(b).

(b) *Discretionary supervisory actions by NCUA.* Subject to the applicable procedures set forth in subpart L of part 747 of this chapter for issuing, reviewing and enforcing directives, the NCUA Board may, by directive, take one or more of the actions prescribed in § 702.204(b) if the credit union's net worth ratio has not increased consistent with its then-present business plan, or the credit union has failed to undertake any mandatory supervisory action prescribed in paragraph (a) of this section.

(c) *Discretionary conservatorship or liquidation.* Notwithstanding any other actions required or permitted to be taken under this section, the NCUA Board may place a new credit union which is "moderately capitalized," "marginally capitalized" or "minimally capitalized" (including by reclassification under § 702.302(d)) into conservatorship pursuant to 12 U.S.C. 1786(h)(1)(F), or into liquidation pursuant to 12 U.S.C. 1787(a)(3)(A)(i), provided that the credit union has no reasonable prospect of becoming "adequately capitalized."

[65 FR 8584, Feb. 18, 2000, as amended at 67 FR 71093, Nov. 29, 2002]

§ 702.305 Prompt corrective action for "uncapitalized" new credit unions.

(a) *Mandatory supervisory actions by new credit union.* Beginning on the effective date of classification as "uncapitalized," a new credit union must—

(1) *Earnings retention.* Increase the dollar amount of its net worth by the amount reflected in the credit union's approved initial or revised business plan;

(2) *Submit revised business plan.* Submit a revised business plan within the time provided by § 702.306, providing for alternative means of funding the credit union's earnings deficit, if the credit union either:

National Credit Union Administration

§ 702.306

(i) Has not increased its net worth ratio consistent with its then-present approved business plan;

(ii) Has no then-present approved business plan; or

(iii) Has failed to comply with paragraph (a)(3) of this section; and

(3) *Restrict member business loans.* Not increase the total dollar amount of member business loans as provided in § 702.304(a)(3).

(b) *Discretionary supervisory actions by NCUA.* Subject to the procedures set forth in subpart L of part 747 of this chapter for issuing, reviewing and enforcing directives, the NCUA Board may, by directive, take one or more of the actions prescribed in § 702.204(b) if the credit union's net worth ratio has not increased consistent with its then-present business plan, or the credit union has failed to undertake any mandatory supervisory action prescribed in paragraph (a) of this section.

(c) *Mandatory liquidation or conservatorship.* Notwithstanding any other actions required or permitted to be taken under this section, the NCUA Board—

(1) *Plan not submitted.* May place into liquidation pursuant to 12 U.S.C. 1787(a)(3)(A)(ii), or conservatorship pursuant to 12 U.S.C. 1786(h)(1)(F), an "uncapitalized" new credit union which fails to submit a revised business plan within the time provided under paragraph (a)(2) of this section; or

(2) *Plan rejected, approved, implemented.* Except as provided in paragraph (c)(3) of this section, must place into liquidation pursuant to 12 U.S.C. 1787(a)(3)(A)(ii), or conservatorship pursuant to 12 U.S.C. 1786(h)(1)(F), an "uncapitalized" new credit union that remains "uncapitalized" one hundred twenty (120) calendar days after the later of:

(i) The effective date of classification as "uncapitalized"; or

(ii) The last day of the calendar month following expiration of the time period provided in the credit union's initial business plan (approved at the time its charter was granted) to remain "uncapitalized," regardless whether a revised business plan was rejected, approved or implemented.

(3) *Exception.* The NCUA Board may decline to place a new credit union into liquidation or conservatorship as provided in paragraph (c)(2) of this section if the credit union documents to the NCUA Board why it is viable and has a reasonable prospect of becoming "adequately capitalized."

(d) *Mandatory liquidation of "uncapitalized" federal credit union.* In lieu of paragraph (c) of this section, an "uncapitalized" federal credit union may be placed into liquidation on grounds of insolvency pursuant to 12 U.S.C. 1787(a)(1)(A).

[65 FR 8584, Feb. 18, 2000, as amended at 67 FR 71093, Nov. 29, 2002]

§ 702.306 Revised business plans for new credit unions.

(a) *Schedule for filing*—(1) *Generally.* Except as provided in paragraph (a)(2) of this section, a new credit union classified "moderately capitalized" or lower must file a written revised business plan (RBP) with the appropriate Regional Director and, if State-chartered, with the appropriate State official, within 30 calendar days of either:

(i) The last of the calendar month following the end of the calendar quarter that the credit union's net worth ratio has not increased consistent with its the-present approved business plan;

(ii) The effective date of classification as less than "adequately capitalized" if the credit union has no then-present approved business plan; or

(iii) The effective date of classification as less than "adequately capitalized" if the credit union has increased the total amount of member business loans in violation of § 702.304(a)(3).

(2) *Exception.* The NCUA Board may notify the credit union in writing that its RBP is to be filed within a different period or that it is not necessary to file an RBP.

(3) *Failure to timely file plan.* When a new credit union fails to file an RBP as provided under paragraphs (a)(1) or (a)(2) of this section, the NCUA Board shall promptly notify the credit union that it has failed to file an RBP and that it has 15 calendar days from receipt of that notice within which to do so.

(b) *Contents of revised business plan.* A new credit union's RBP must, at a minimum—

539

§ 702.306

(1) Address changes, since the new credit union's current business plan was approved, in any of the business plan elements required for charter approval under Chapter 1, section IV.D. of NCUA's *Chartering and Field of Membership Manual* (IRPS 99–1), 63 FR 71998, 72019 (Dec. 30, 1998), or its successor(s), or for State-chartered credit unions under applicable State law;

(2) Establish a timetable of quarterly targets for net worth during each year in which the RBP is in effect so that the credit union becomes "adequately capitalized" by the time it no longer qualifies as "new" per § 702.301(b);

(3) Specify the projected amount of earnings to be transferred quarterly to its regular reserve as provided under § 702.304(a)(1) or 702.305(a)(1);

(4) Explain how the new credit union will comply with the mandatory and discretionary supervisory actions imposed on it by the NCUA Board under this subpart;

(5) Specify the types and levels of activities in which the new credit union will engage;

(6) In the case of a new credit union reclassified to a lower category under § 702.302(d), specify the steps the credit union will take to correct the unsafe or unsound condition or practice; and

(7) Include such other information as the NCUA Board may require.

(c) *Criteria for approval.* The NCUA Board shall not approve a new credit union's RBP unless it—

(1) Addresses the items enumerated in paragraph (b) of this section;

(2) Is based on realistic assumptions, and is likely to succeed in building the credit union's net worth; and

(3) Would not unreasonably increase the credit union's exposure to risk (including credit risk, interest-rate risk, and other types of risk).

(d) *Consideration of regulatory capital.* To minimize possible long-term losses to the NCUSIF while the credit union takes steps to become "adequately capitalized," the NCUA Board shall, in evaluating an RBP under this section, consider the type and amount of any form of regulatory capital which may become established by NCUA regulation, or authorized by State law and recognized by NCUA, which the credit union holds, but which is not included in its net worth.

(e) *Review of revised business plan*—(1) *Notice of decision.* Within 30 calendar days after receiving an RBP under this section, the NCUA Board shall notify the credit union in writing whether its RBP is approved, and shall provide reasons for its decision in the event of disapproval. The NCUA Board may extend the time within which notice of its decision shall be provided.

(2) *Delayed decision.* If no decision is made within the time prescribed in paragraph (e)(1) of this section, the RBP is deemed approved.

(3) *Consultation with State officials.* When evaluating an RBP submitted by a federally-insured State-chartered new credit union (whether an original, new or additional RBP), the NCUA Board shall seek and consider the views of the appropriate State official, and provide prompt notice of its decision to the appropriate State official.

(f) *Plan not approved*—(1) *Submission of new revised plan.* If an RBP is rejected by the NCUA Board, the new credit union shall submit a new RBP within 30 calendar days of receiving notice of disapproval of its initial RBP, unless it is notified in writing by the NCUA Board that the new RBP is to be filed within a different period.

(2) *Notice of decision on revised plan.* Within 30 calendar days after receiving an RBP under paragraph (f)(1) of this section, the NCUA Board shall notify the credit union in writing whether the new RBP is approved. The Board may extend the time within which notice of its decision shall be provided.

(g) *Amendment of plan.* A credit union that has filed an approved RBP may, after prior written notice to and approval by the NCUA Board, amend it to reflect a change in circumstance. Pending approval of an amended RBP, the new credit union shall implement its existing RBP as originally approved.

(h) *Publication.* An RBP need not be published to be enforceable because publication would be contrary to the public interest.

[65 FR 8584, Feb. 18, 2000, as amended at 67 FR 71093, Nov. 29, 2002]

§ 702.307 Incentives for new credit unions.

(a) *Assistance in revising business plans.* Upon timely request by a credit union having total assets of less than $10 million (regardless how long it has been in operation), the NCUA Board shall provide assistance in preparing a revised business plan required to be filed under § 702.306.

(b) *Assistance.* Management training and other assistance to new credit unions will be provided in accordance with policies approved by the NCUA Board.

(c) *Small credit union program.* A new credit union is eligible to join and receive comprehensive benefits and assistance under NCUA's Small Credit Union Program.

Subpart D—Reserves

§ 702.401 Reserves.

(a) *Special reserve.* Each federally-insured credit union shall establish and maintain such reserves as may be required by the FCUA, by state law, by regulation, or in special cases by the NCUA Board or appropriate State official.

(b) *Regular reserve.* Each federally-insured credit union shall establish and maintain a regular reserve account for the purpose of absorbing losses that exceed undivided earnings and other appropriations of undivided earnings, subject to paragraph (c) of this section. Earnings required to be transferred annually to a credit union's regular reserve under subparts B or C of this part shall be held in this account.

(c) *Charges to regular reserve after depleting undivided earnings.* The board of directors of a federally-insured credit union may authorize losses to be charged to the regular reserve after first depleting the balance of the undivided earnings account and other reserves, provided that the authorization states the amount and provides an explanation of the need for the charge, and either—

(1) The charge will not cause the credit union's net worth classification to fall below "adequately capitalized" under subparts B or C of this part; or

(2) If the charge will cause the net worth classification to fall below "adequately capitalized," the appropriate Regional Director and, if State-chartered, the appropriate State official, have given written approval (in an NWRP or otherwise) for the charge.

(d) *Transfers to regular reserve.* The transfer of earnings to a federally-insured credit union's regular reserve account when required under subparts B or C of this part must occur after charges for loan or other losses are addressed as provided in paragraph (c) of this section and § 702.402(d), but before payment of any dividends to members.

[65 FR 8584, Feb. 18, 2000, as amended at 67 FR 71093, Nov. 29, 2002]

§ 702.402 Full and fair disclosure of financial condition.

(a) *Full and fair disclosure defined.* "Full and fair disclosure" is the level of disclosure which a prudent person would provide to a member of a federally-insured credit union, to NCUA, or, at the discretion of the board of directors, to creditors to fairly inform them of the financial condition and the results of operations of the credit union.

(b) *Full and fair disclosure implemented.* The financial statements of a federally-insured credit union shall provide for full and fair disclosure of all assets, liabilities, and members' equity, including such valuation (allowance) accounts as may be necessary to present fairly the financial condition; and all income and expenses necessary to present fairly the statement of income for the reporting period.

(c) *Declaration of officials.* The Statement of Financial Condition, when presented to members, to creditors or to the NCUA, shall contain a dual declaration by the treasurer and the chief executive officer, or in the latter's absence, by any other officer designated by the board of directors of the reporting credit union to make such declaration, that the report and related financial statements are true and correct to the best of their knowledge and belief and present fairly the financial condition and the statement of income for the period covered.

(d) *Charges for loan losses.* Full and fair disclosure demands that a credit union properly address charges for loan losses as follows:

§ 702.403

(1) Charges for loan losses shall be made in accordance with generally accepted accounting principles (GAAP);

(2) The allowance for loan and lease losses (ALL) established for loans must fairly present the probable losses for all categories of loans and the proper valuation of loans. The valuation allowance must encompass specifically identified loans, as well as estimated losses inherent in the loan portfolio, such as loans and pools of loans for which losses have been incurred but are not identifiable on a specific loan-by-loan basis;

(3) Adjustments to the valuation ALL will be recorded in the expense account "Provision for Loan and Lease Losses";

(4) The maintenance of an ALL shall not affect the requirement to transfer earnings to a credit union's regular reserve when required under subparts B or C of this part; and

(5) At a minimum, adjustments to the ALL shall be made prior to the distribution or posting of any dividend to the accounts of members.

§ 702.403 Payment of dividends.

(a) *Restriction on dividends.* Dividends shall be available only from undivided earnings, if any.

(b) *Payment of dividends if undivided earnings depleted.* The board of directors of a "well capitalized" federally-insured credit union that has depleted the balance of its undivided earnings account may authorize a transfer of funds from the credit union's regular reserve account to undivided earnings to pay dividends, provided that either—

(1) The payment of dividends will not cause the credit union's net worth classification to fall below "adequately capitalized" under subpart B or C of this part; or

(2) If the payment of dividends will cause the net worth classification to fall below "adequately capitalized," the appropriate Regional Director and, if State-chartered, the appropriate State official, have given prior written approval (in an NWRP or otherwise) to pay a dividend.

[65 FR 8584, Feb. 18, 2000, as amended at 67 FR 71093, Nov. 29, 2002]

PART 703—INVESTMENT AND DEPOSIT ACTIVITIES

Sec.
703.1 Purpose and scope.
703.2 Definitions.
703.3 Investment policies.
703.4 Recordkeeping and documentation requirements.
703.5 Discretionary control over investments and investment advisers.
703.6 Credit analysis.
703.7 Notice of non-compliant investments.
703.8 Broker-dealers.
703.9 Safekeeping of investments.
703.10 Monitoring non-security investments.
703.11 Valuing securities.
703.12 Monitoring securities.
703.13 Permissible investment activities.
703.14 Permissible investments.
703.15 Prohibited investment activities.
703.16 Prohibited investments.
703.17 Conflicts of interest.
703.18 Grandfathered investments.
703.19 Investment pilot program.

AUTHORITY: 12 U.S.C. 1757(7), 1757(8), 1757(15).

SOURCE: 68 FR 32960, June 3, 2003, unless otherwise noted.

§ 703.1 Purpose and scope.

(a) This part interprets several of the provisions of Sections 107(7), 107(8), and 107(15) of the Federal Credit Union Act (Act), 12 U.S.C. 1757(7), 1757(8), 1757(15), which list those securities, deposits, and other obligations in which a Federal credit union may invest. Part 703 identifies certain investments and deposit activities permissible under the Act and prescribes regulations governing those investments and deposit activities on the basis of safety and soundness concerns. Additionally, part 703 identifies and prohibits certain investments and deposit activities. Investments and deposit activities that are permissible under the Act and not prohibited or otherwise regulated by part 703 remain permissible for Federal credit unions.

(b) This part does not apply to:

(1) Investment in loans to members and related activities, which is governed by §§ 701.21, 701.22, 701.23, and part 723 of this chapter;

(2) The purchase of real estate-secured loans pursuant to Section 107(15)(A) of the Act, which is governed by § 701.23 of this chapter, except those real estate-secured loans purchased as

a part of an investment repurchase transaction, which is governed by §§ 703.13 and 703.14 of this chapter;

(3) Investment in credit union service organizations, which is governed by part 712 of this chapter;

(4) Investment in fixed assets, which is governed by § 701.36 of this chapter;

(5) Investment by corporate credit unions, which is governed by part 704 of this chapter; or

(6) Investment activity by State-chartered credit unions, except as provided in § 741.3(a)(2) and § 741.219 of this chapter.

[68 FR 32960, June 3, 2003, as amended at 69 FR 27828, May 17, 2004; 71 FR 76124, Dec 20, 2006]

§ 703.2 Definitions.

The following definitions apply to this part:

Adjusted trading means selling an investment to a counterparty at a price above its current fair value and simultaneously purchasing or committing to purchase from the counterparty another investment at a price above its current fair value.

Associated personnel means a person engaged in the investment banking or securities business who is directly or indirectly controlled by a National Association of Securities Dealers (NASD) member, whether or not this person is registered or exempt from registration with NASD. Associated personnel includes every sole proprietor, partner, officer, director, or branch manager of any NASD member.

Banker's acceptance means a time draft that is drawn on and accepted by a bank and that represents an irrevocable obligation of the bank.

Bank note means a direct, unconditional, and unsecured general obligation of a bank that ranks equally with all other senior unsecured indebtedness of the bank, except deposit liabilities and other obligations that are subject to any priorities or preferences.

Borrowing repurchase transaction means a transaction in which the Federal credit union agrees to sell a security to a counterparty and to repurchase the same or an identical security from that counterparty at a specified future date and at a specified price.

Call means an option that gives the holder the right to buy a specified quantity of a security at a specified price during a fixed time period.

Collateralized Mortgage Obligation (CMO) means a multi-class mortgage related security.

Collective investment fund means a fund maintained by a national bank under 12 CFR part 9 (Comptroller of the Currency's regulations).

Commercial mortgage related security means a mortgage related security, as defined below, except that it is collateralized entirely by commercial real estate, such as a warehouse or office building, or a multi-family dwelling consisting of more than four units.

Counterparty means the party on the other side of the transaction.

Custodial Agreement means a contract in which one party agrees to hold securities in safekeeping for others.

Delivery versus payment means payment for an investment must occur simultaneously with its delivery.

Deposit note means an obligation of a bank that is similar to a certificate of deposit but is rated.

Derivatives means any derivative instrument as defined under generally accepted accounting principles (GAAP).

Embedded option means a characteristic of an investment that gives the issuer or holder the right to alter the level and timing of the cash flows of the investment. Embedded options include call and put provisions and interest rate caps and floors. Since a prepayment option in a mortgage is a type of call provision, a mortgage-backed security composed of mortgages that may be prepaid is an example of an investment with an embedded option.

Eurodollar deposit means a U.S. dollar-denominated deposit in a foreign branch of a United States depository institution.

European financial options contract means an option that can be exercised only on its expiration date.

Exchangeable Collateralized Mortgage Obligation means a class of a collateralized mortgage obligation (CMO) that, at the time of purchase, represents beneficial ownership interests in a combination of two or more underlying classes of the same CMO

§ 703.2

structure. The holder of an exchangeable CMO may pay a fee and take delivery of the underlying classes of the CMO.

Fair value means the amount at which an instrument could be exchanged in a current, arms-length transaction between willing parties, as opposed to a forced or liquidation sale.

Financial options contract means an agreement to make or take delivery of a standardized financial instrument upon demand by the holder of the contract as specified in the agreement.

Immediate family member means a spouse or other family member living in the same household.

Independent qualified agent means an agent independent of an investment repurchase counterparty that does not receive a transaction fee from the counterparty and has at least two years experience assessing the value of mortgage loans.

Industry-recognized information provider means an organization that obtains compensation by providing information to investors and receives no compensation for the purchase or sale of investments.

Investment means any security, obligation, account, deposit, or other item authorized for purchase by a Federal credit union under Sections 107(7), 107(8), or 107(15) of the Act, or this part, other than loans to members.

Investment repurchase transaction means a transaction in which an investor agrees to purchase a security from a counterparty and to resell the same or an identical security to that counterparty at a specified future date and at a specified price.

Maturity means the date the last principal amount of a security is scheduled to come due and does not mean the call date or the weighted average life of a security.

Mortgage related security means a security as defined in Section 3(a)(41) of the Securities Exchange Act of 1934 (15 U.S.C. 78c(a)(41)), *e.g.*, a privately-issued security backed by first lien mortgages secured by real estate upon which is located a dwelling, mixed residential and commercial structure, residential manufactured home, or commercial structure, that is rated in one of the two highest rating categories by at least one nationally-recognized statistical rating organization.

Mortgage servicing rights means a contractual obligation to perform mortgage servicing and the right to receive compensation for performing those services. Mortgage servicing is the administration of a mortgage loan, including collecting monthly payments and fees, providing recordkeeping and escrow functions, and, if necessary curing defaults and foreclosing.

Negotiable instrument means an instrument that may be freely transferred from the purchaser to another person or entity by delivery, or endorsement and delivery, with full legal title becoming vested in the transferee.

Net worth means the retained earnings balance of the credit union at quarter end as determined under generally accepted accounting principles and as further defined in § 702.2(f) of this chapter.

Official means any member of a Federal credit union's board of directors, credit committee, supervisory committee, or investment-related committee.

Ordinary care means the degree of care, which an ordinarily prudent and competent person engaged in the same line of business or endeavor should exercise under similar circumstances.

Pair-off transaction means an investment purchase transaction that is closed or sold on, or before the settlement date. In a pair-off, an investor commits to purchase an investment, but then pairs-off the purchase with a sale of the same investment before or on the settlement date.

Put means an option that gives the holder the right to sell a specified quantity of a security at a specified price during a fixed time period.

Registered investment company means an investment company that is registered with the Securities and Exchange Commission under the Investment Company Act of 1940 (15 U.S.C. 80a). Examples of registered investment companies are mutual funds and unit investment trusts.

Regular way settlement means delivery of a security from a seller to a buyer within the time frame that the securities industry has established for immediate delivery of that type of security.

National Credit Union Administration § 703.3

For example, regular way settlement of a Treasury security includes settlement on the trade date (cash), the business day following the trade date (regular way), and the second business day following the trade date (skip day).

Residual interest means the remainder cash flows from collateralized mortgage obligations/real estate mortgage investment conduits (CMOs/REMICs), or other mortgage-backed security transaction, after payments due bondholders and trust administrative expenses have been satisfied.

Securities lending means lending a security to a counterparty, either directly or through an agent, and accepting collateral in return.

Security means a share, participation, or other interest in property or in an enterprise of the issuer or an obligation of the issuer that:

(1) Either is represented by an instrument issued in bearer or registered form or, if not represented by an instrument, is registered in books maintained to record transfers by or on behalf of the issuer;

(2) Is of a type commonly dealt in on securities exchanges or markets or, when represented by an instrument, is commonly recognized in any area in which it is issued or dealt in as a medium for investment; and

(3) Either is one of a class or series or by its terms is divisible into a class or series of shares, participations, interests, or obligations.

Senior management employee means a Federal credit union's chief executive officer (typically this individual holds the title of President or Treasurer/Manager), an assistant chief executive officer, and the chief financial officer.

Small business related security means a security as defined in Section 3(a)(53) of the Securities Exchange Act of 1934 (15 U.S.C. 78c(a)(53), *e.g.*, a security that is rated in 1 of the 4 highest rating categories by at least one nationally recognized statistical rating organization, and represents an interest in one or more promissory notes or leases of personal property evidencing the obligation of a small business concern and originated by an insured depository institution, insured credit union, insurance company, or similar institution which is supervised and examined by a Federal or State authority, or a finance company or leasing company. This definition does not include Small Business Administration securities permissible under § 107(7) of the Act.

Weighted average life means the weighted-average time to the return of a dollar of principal, calculated by multiplying each portion of principal received by the time at which it is expected to be received (based on a reasonable and supportable estimate of that time) and then summing and dividing by the total amount of principal.

When-issued trading of securities means the buying and selling of securities in the period between the announcement of an offering and the issuance and payment date of the securities.

Yankee dollar deposit means a deposit in a United States branch of a foreign bank licensed to do business in the State in which it is located, or a deposit in a State-chartered, foreign controlled bank.

Zero coupon investment means an investment that makes no periodic interest payments but instead is sold at a discount from its face value. The holder of a zero coupon investment realizes the rate of return through the gradual appreciation of the investment, which is redeemed at face value on a specified maturity date.

[68 FR 32960, June 3, 2003, as amended at 69 FR 39831, July 1, 2004; 71 FR 76124, Dec. 20, 2006]

§ 703.3 Investment policies.

A Federal credit union's board of directors must establish written investment policies consistent with the Act, this part, and other applicable laws and regulations and must review the policy at least annually. These policies may be part of a broader, asset-liability management policy. Written investment policies must address the following:

(a) The purposes and objectives of the Federal credit union's investment activities;

(b) The characteristics of the investments the Federal credit union may make including the issuer, maturity, index, cap, floor, coupon rate, coupon

§ 703.4

formula, call provision, average life, and interest rate risk;

(c) How the Federal credit union will manage interest rate risk;

(d) How the Federal credit union will manage liquidity risk;

(e) How the Federal credit union will manage credit risk including specifically listing institutions, issuers, and counterparties that may be used, or criteria for their selection, and limits on the amounts that may be invested with each;

(f) How the Federal credit union will manage concentration risk, which can result from dealing with a single or related issuers, lack of geographic distribution, holding obligations with similar characteristics like maturities and indexes, holding bonds having the same trustee, and holding securitized loans having the same originator, packager, or guarantor;

(g) Who has investment authority and the extent of that authority. Those with authority must be qualified by education or experience to assess the risk characteristics of investments and investment transactions. Only officials or employees of the Federal credit union may be voting members of an investment-related committee;

(h) The broker-dealers the Federal credit union may use;

(i) The safekeepers the Federal credit union may use;

(j) How the Federal credit union will handle an investment that, after purchase, is outside of board policy or fails a requirement of this part; and

(k) How the Federal credit union will conduct investment trading activities, if applicable, including addressing:

(1) Who has purchase and sale authority;

(2) Limits on trading account size;

(3) Allocation of cash flow to trading accounts;

(4) Stop loss or sale provisions;

(5) Dollar size limitations of specific types, quantity and maturity to be purchased;

(6) Limits on the length of time an investment may be inventoried in a trading account; and

(7) Internal controls, including segregation of duties.

§ 703.4 Recordkeeping and documentation requirements.

(a) Federal credit unions with assets of $10,000,000 or greater must comply with all generally accepted accounting principles applicable to reports or statements required to be filed with NCUA. Federal credit unions with assets less than $10,000,000 are encouraged to do the same, but are not required to do so.

(b) A Federal credit union must maintain documentation for each investment transaction for as long as it holds the investment and until the documentation has been audited in accordance with § 715.4 of this chapter and examined by NCUA. The documentation should include, where applicable, bids and prices at purchase and sale and for periodic updates, relevant disclosure documents or a description of the security from an industry-recognized information provider, financial data, and tests and reports required by the Federal credit union's investment policy and this part.

(c) A Federal credit union must maintain documentation its board of directors used to approve a broker-dealer or a safekeeper for as long as the broker-dealer or safekeeper is approved and until the documentation has been audited in accordance with § 715.4 of this chapter and examined by NCUA.

(d) A Federal credit union must obtain an individual confirmation statement from each broker-dealer for each investment purchased or sold.

[68 FR 32960, June 3, 2003, as amended at 69 FR 27828, May 17, 2004; 72 FR 30246, May 31, 2007]

§ 703.5 Discretionary control over investments and investment advisers.

(a) Except as provided in paragraph (b) of this section, a Federal credit union must retain discretionary control over its purchase and sale of investments. A Federal credit union has not delegated discretionary control to an investment adviser when the Federal credit union reviews all recommendations from investment advisers and is required to authorize a recommended purchase or sale transaction before its execution.

(b)(1) A Federal credit union may delegate discretionary control over the purchase and sale of investments to a person other than a Federal credit union official or employee:

(i) Provided the person is an investment adviser registered with the Securities and Exchange Commission under the Investment Advisers Act of 1940 (15 U.S.C. 80b); and

(ii) In an amount up to 100 percent of its net worth in the aggregate at the time of delegation.

(2) At least annually, the Federal credit union must adjust the amount of funds held under discretionary control to comply with the 100 percent of net worth cap. The Federal credit union's board of directors must receive notice as soon as possible, but no later than the next regularly scheduled board meeting, of the amount exceeding the net worth cap and notify in writing the appropriate regional director within 5 days after the board meeting. The credit union must develop a plan to comply with the cap within a reasonable period of time.

(3) Before transacting business with an investment adviser, a Federal credit union must analyze his or her background and information available from State or Federal securities regulators, including any enforcement actions against the adviser, associated personnel, and the firm for which the adviser works.

(c) A Federal credit union may not compensate an investment adviser with discretionary control over the purchase and sale of investments on a per transaction basis or based on capital gains, capital appreciation, net income, performance relative to an index, or any other incentive basis.

(d) A Federal credit union must obtain a report from its investment adviser at least monthly that details the investments under the adviser's control and their performance.

§ 703.6 Credit analysis.

A Federal credit union must conduct and document a credit analysis on an investment and the issuing entity before purchasing it, except for investments issued or fully guaranteed as to principal and interest by the U.S. government or its agencies, enterprises, or corporations or fully insured (including accumulated interest) by the National Credit Union Administration or the Federal Deposit Insurance Corporation. A Federal credit union must update this analysis at least annually for as long as it holds the investment.

§ 703.7 Notice of non-compliant investments.

A Federal credit union's board of directors must receive notice as soon as possible, but no later than the next regularly scheduled board meeting, of any investment that either is outside of board policy after purchase or has failed a requirement of this part. The board of directors must document its action regarding the investment in the minutes of the board meeting, including a detailed explanation of any decision not to sell it. The Federal credit union must notify in writing the appropriate regional director of an investment that has failed a requirement of this part within 5 days after the board meeting.

§ 703.8 Broker-dealers.

(a) A Federal credit union may purchase and sell investments through a broker-dealer as long as the broker-dealer is registered as a broker-dealer with the Securities and Exchange Commission under the Securities Exchange Act of 1934 (15 U.S.C. 78a *et seq.*) or is a depository institution whose broker-dealer activities are regulated by a Federal or State regulatory agency.

(b) Before purchasing an investment through a broker-dealer, a Federal credit union must analyze and annually update the following:

(1) The background of any sales representative with whom the Federal credit union is doing business;

(2) Information available from State or Federal securities regulators and securities industry self-regulatory organizations, such as the National Association of Securities Dealers and the North American Securities Administrators Association, about any enforcement actions against the broker-dealer, its affiliates, or associated personnel; and

(3) If the broker-dealer is acting as the Federal credit union's counterparty, the ability of the broker-dealer and its subsidiaries or affiliates to fulfill commitments, as evidenced

by capital strength, liquidity, and operating results. The Federal credit union should consider current financial data, annual reports, reports of nationally-recognized statistical rating organizations, relevant disclosure documents, and other sources of financial information.

(c) The requirements of paragraph (a) of this section do not apply when the Federal credit union purchases a certificate of deposit or share certificate directly from a bank, credit union, or other depository institution.

[68 FR 32960, June 3, 2003, as amended at 69 FR 39831, July 1, 2004]

§ 703.9 Safekeeping of investments.

(a) A Federal credit union's purchased investments and repurchase collateral must be in the Federal credit union's possession, recorded as owned by the Federal credit union through the Federal Reserve Book-Entry System, or held by a board-approved safekeeper under a written custodial agreement that requires the safekeeper to exercise, at least, ordinary care.

(b) Any safekeeper used by a Federal credit union must be regulated and supervised by either the Securities and Exchange Commission, a Federal or State depository institution regulatory agency, or a State trust company regulatory agency.

(c) A Federal credit union must obtain and reconcile monthly a statement of purchased investments and repurchase collateral held in safekeeping.

(d) Annually, the Federal credit union must analyze the ability of the safekeeper to fulfill its custodial responsibilities, as evidenced by capital strength, liquidity, and operating results. The Federal credit union should consider current financial data, annual reports, reports of nationally-recognized statistical rating organizations, relevant disclosure documents, and other sources of financial information.

[68 FR 32960, June 3, 2003, as amended at 69 FR 39831, July 1, 2004]

§ 703.10 Monitoring non-security investments.

(a) At least quarterly, a Federal credit union must prepare a written report listing all of its shares and deposits in banks, credit unions, and other depository institutions, that have one or more of the following features:

(1) Embedded options;

(2) Remaining maturities greater than 3 years; or

(3) Coupon formulas that are related to more than one index or are inversely related to, or multiples of, an index.

(b) The requirement of paragraph (a) of this section does not apply to shares and deposits that are securities.

(c) If a Federal credit union does not have an investment-related committee, then each member of its board of directors must receive a copy of the report described in paragraph (a) of this section. If a Federal credit union has an investment-related committee, then each member of the committee must receive a copy of the report, and each member of the board must receive a summary of the information in the report.

§ 703.11 Valuing securities.

(a) Before purchasing or selling a security, a Federal credit union must obtain either price quotations on the security from at least two broker-dealers or a price quotation on the security from an industry-recognized information provider. This requirement to obtain price quotations does not apply to new issues purchased at par or at original issue discount.

(b) At least monthly, a Federal credit union must determine the fair value of each security it holds. It may determine fair value by obtaining a price quotation on the security from an industry-recognized information provider, a broker-dealer, or a safekeeper.

(c) At least annually, the Federal credit union's supervisory committee or its external auditor must independently assess the reliability of monthly price quotations received from a broker-dealer or safekeeper. The Federal credit union's supervisory committee or external auditor must follow generally accepted auditing standards, which require either re-computation or reference to market quotations.

(d) If a Federal credit union is unable to obtain a price quotation required by this section for a particular security, then it may obtain a quotation for a security with substantially similar characteristics.

§ 703.12 Monitoring securities.

(a) At least monthly, a Federal credit union must prepare a written report setting forth, for each security held, the fair value and dollar change since the prior month-end, with summary information for the entire portfolio.

(b) At least quarterly, a Federal credit union must prepare a written report setting forth the sum of the fair values of all fixed and variable rate securities held that have one or more of the following features:

(1) Embedded options;

(2) Remaining maturities greater than 3 years; or

(3) Coupon formulas that are related to more than one index or are inversely related to, or multiples of, an index.

(c) Where the amount calculated in paragraph (b) of this section is greater than a Federal credit union's net worth, the report described in that paragraph must provide a reasonable and supportable estimate of the potential impact, in percentage and dollar terms, of an immediate and sustained parallel shift in market interest rates of plus and minus 300 basis points on:

(1) The fair value of each security in the Federal credit union's portfolio;

(2) The fair value of the Federal credit union's portfolio as a whole; and

(3) The Federal credit union's net worth.

(d) If the Federal credit union does not have an investment-related committee, then each member of its board of directors must receive a copy of the reports described in paragraphs (a) through (c) of this section. If the Federal credit union has an investment-related committee, then each member of the committee must receive copies of the reports, and each member of the board of directors must receive a summary of the information in the reports.

§ 703.13 Permissible investment activities.

(a) *Regular way settlement and delivery versus payment basis.* A Federal credit union may only contract for the purchase or sale of a security as long as the delivery of the security is by regular way settlement and the transaction is accomplished on a delivery versus payment basis.

(b) *Federal funds.* A Federal credit union may sell Federal funds to an institution described in Section 107(8) of the Act and credit unions, as long as the interest or other consideration received from the financial institution is at the market rate for Federal funds transactions.

(c) *Investment repurchase transaction.* A Federal credit union may enter into an investment repurchase transaction so long as:

(1) Any securities the Federal credit union receives are permissible investments for Federal credit unions, the Federal credit union, or its agent, either takes physical possession or control of the repurchase securities or is recorded as owner of them through the Federal Reserve Book Entry Securities Transfer System, the Federal credit union, or its agent, receives a daily assessment of their market value, including accrued interest, and the Federal credit union maintains adequate margins that reflect a risk assessment of the securities and the term of the transaction; and

(2) The Federal credit union has entered into signed contracts with all approved counterparties.

(d) *Borrowing repurchase transaction.* A Federal credit union may enter into a borrowing repurchase transaction so long as:

(1) The transaction meets the requirements of paragraph (c) of this section;

(2) Any cash the Federal credit union receives is subject to the borrowing limit specified in Section 107(9) of the Act, and any investments the Federal credit union purchases with that cash are permissible for Federal credit unions; and

(3) The investments referenced in paragraph (d)(2) of this section mature no later than the maturity of the borrowing repurchase transaction.

(e) *Securities lending transaction.* A Federal credit union may enter into a securities lending transaction so long as:

(1) The Federal credit union receives written confirmation of the loan;

(2) Any collateral the Federal credit union receives is a legal investment for

§ 703.14

Federal credit unions, the Federal credit union, or its agent, obtains a first priority security interest in the collateral by taking physical possession or control of the collateral, or is recorded as owner of the collateral through the Federal Reserve Book Entry Securities Transfer System; and the Federal credit union, or its agent, receives a daily assessment of the market value of the collateral, including accrued interest, and maintains adequate margin that reflects a risk assessment of the collateral and the term of the loan;

(3) Any cash the Federal credit union receives is subject to the borrowing limit specified in Section 107(9) of the Act, and any investments the Federal credit union purchases with that cash are permissible for Federal credit unions and mature no later than the maturity of the transaction; and

(4) The Federal credit union has executed a written loan and security agreement with the borrower.

(f)(1) *Trading securities.* A Federal credit union may trade securities, including engaging in when-issued trading and pair-off transactions, so long as the Federal credit union can show that it has sufficient resources, knowledge, systems, and procedures to handle the risks.

(2) A Federal credit union must record any security it purchases or sells for trading purposes at fair value on the trade date. The trade date is the date the Federal credit union commits, orally or in writing, to purchase or sell a security.

(3) At least monthly, the Federal credit union must give its board of directors or investment-related committee a written report listing all purchase and sale transactions of trading securities and the resulting gain or loss on an individual basis.

§ 703.14 Permissible investments.

(a) *Variable rate investment.* A Federal credit union may invest in a variable rate investment, as long as the index is tied to domestic interest rates and not, for example, to foreign currencies, foreign interest rates, or domestic or foreign commodity prices, equity prices, or inflation rates. For purposes of this part, the U.S. dollar-denominated London Interbank Offered Rate (LIBOR) is a domestic interest rate.

(b) *Corporate credit union shares or deposits.* A Federal credit union may purchase shares or deposits in a corporate credit union, except where the NCUA Board has notified it that the corporate credit union is not operating in compliance with part 704 of this chapter. A Federal credit union's aggregate amount of perpetual and nonperpetual capital, as defined in part 704 of this chapter, in one corporate credit union is limited to two percent of the federal credit union's assets measured at the time of investment or adjustment. A Federal credit union's aggregate amount of contributed capital in all corporate credit unions is limited to four percent of assets measured at the time of investment or adjustment.

(c) *Registered investment company.* A Federal credit union may invest in a registered investment company or collective investment fund, as long as the prospectus of the company or fund restricts the investment portfolio to investments and investment transactions that are permissible for Federal credit unions.

(d) *Collateralized mortgage obligation/real estate mortgage investment conduit.* A Federal credit union may invest in a fixed or variable rate collateralized mortgage obligation/real estate mortgage investment conduit.

(e) *Municipal security.* A Federal credit union may purchase and hold a municipal security, as defined in Section 107(7)(K) of the Act, only if a nationally-recognized statistical rating organization has rated it in one of the four highest rating categories.

(f) *Instruments issued by institutions described in Section 107(8) of the Act.* A Federal credit union may invest in the following instruments issued by an institution described in Section 107(8) of the Act:

(1) Yankee dollar deposits;
(2) Eurodollar deposits;
(3) Banker's acceptances;
(4) Deposit notes; and
(5) Bank notes with original weighted average maturities of less than 5 years.

(g) *European financial options contract.* A Federal credit union may purchase a European financial options contract or a series of European financial options

National Credit Union Administration § 703.14

contracts only to fund the payment of dividends on member share certificates where the dividend rate is tied to an equity index provided:

(1) The option and dividend rate are based on a domestic equity index;

(2) Proceeds from the options are used only to fund dividends on the equity-linked share certificates;

(3) Dividends on the share certificates are derived solely from the change in the domestic equity index over a specified period;

(4) The options' expiration dates are no later than the maturity date of the share certificate.

(5) The certificate may be redeemed prior to the maturity date only upon the member's death or termination of the corresponding option;

(6) The total costs associated with the purchase of the option is known by the Federal credit union prior to effecting the transaction;

(7) The options are purchased at the same time the certificate is issued to the member.

(8) The counterparty to the transaction is a domestic counterparty and has been approved by the Federal credit union's board of directors;

(9) The counterparty to the transaction:

(i) Has a long-term, senior, unsecured debt rating from a nationally-recognized statistical rating organization of AA− (or equivalent) or better at the time of the transaction, and the contract between the counterparty and the Federal credit union specifies that if the long-term, senior, unsecured debt rating declines below AA− (or equivalent) then the counterparty agrees to post collateral with an independent party in an amount fully securing the value of the option; or

(ii) Posts collateral with an independent party in an amount fully securing the value of the option if the counterparty does not have a long-term, senior unsecured debt rating from a nationally-recognized statistical rating organization.

(10) Any collateral posted by the counterparty is a permissible investment for Federal credit unions and is valued daily by an independent third party along with the value of the option;

(11) The aggregate amount of equity-linked member share certificates does not exceed the credit union's net worth;

(12) The terms of the share certificate include a guarantee that there can be no loss of principal to the member regardless of changes in the value of the option unless the certificate is redeemed prior to maturity; and

(13) The Federal credit union provides its board of directors with a monthly report detailing at a minimum:

(i) The dollar amount of outstanding equity-linked share certificates;

(ii) Their maturities; and

(iii) The fair value of the options as determined by an independent third party.

(h) *Mortgage note repurchase transactions.* A federal credit union may invest in securities that are offered and sold pursuant to section 4(5) of the Securities Act of 1933, 15 U.S.C. 77d(5), only as a part of an investment repurchase agreement under §703.13(c), subject to the following conditions:

(1) The aggregate of the investments with any one counterparty is limited to 25 percent of the credit union's net worth and 100 percent of its net worth with all counterparties;

(2) At the time a federal credit union purchases the securities, the counterparty, or a party fully guaranteeing the transaction, must have outstanding debt with a long-term rating no lower than A− or its equivalent and outstanding debt with a short-term rating, if any, no lower than A-1 or its equivalent;

(3) The federal credit union must obtain a daily assessment of the market value of the securities under §703.13(c)(1) using an independent qualified agent;

(4) The mortgage note repurchase transaction is limited to a maximum term of 90 days;

(5) All mortgage note repurchase transactions will be conducted under tri-party custodial agreements; and

(6) A federal credit union must obtain an undivided interest in the securities.

[68 FR 32960, June 3, 2003, as amended at 69 FR 39831, July 1, 2004; 71 FR 76124, Dec. 20, 2006; 75 FR 64826, Oct. 20, 2010]

§ 703.15 Prohibited investment activities.

Adjusted trading or short sales. A Federal credit union may not engage in adjusted trading or short sales.

§ 703.16 Prohibited investments.

(a) *Derivatives.* A Federal credit union may not purchase or sell financial derivatives, such as futures, options, interest rate swaps, or forward rate swaps. This prohibition does not apply to:

(1) Any derivatives permitted under §§ 701.21(i) and 703.14(g) of this chapter;

(2) Embedded options not required under GAAP to be accounted for separately from the host contract; and

(3) Interest rate lock commitments or forward sales commitments made in connection with a loan originated by the Federal credit union.

(b) *Zero coupon investments.* A Federal credit union may not purchase a zero coupon investment with a maturity date that is more than 10 years from the settlement date;

(c) *Mortgage servicing rights.* A Federal credit union may not purchase mortgage servicing rights as an investment but may perform mortgage servicing functions as a financial service for a member as long as the mortgage loan is owned by a member;

(d) A Federal credit union may not purchase a commercial mortgage related security that is not otherwise permitted by Section 107(7)(E) of the Act; and

(e) *Stripped mortgage backed securities (SMBS).* A Federal credit union may not invest in SMBS or securities that represent interests in SMBS except as described in paragraphs (1) and (3) below.

(1) A Federal credit union may invest in and hold exchangeable collateralized mortgage obligations (exchangeable CMOs) representing beneficial ownership interests in one or more interest-only classes of a CMO (IO CMOs) or principal-only classes of a CMO (PO CMOs), but only if:

(i) At the time of purchase, the ratio of the market price to the remaining principal balance is between .8 and 1.2, meaning that the discount or premium of the market price to par must be less than 20 points;

(ii) The offering circular or other official information available at the time of purchase indicates that the notional principal on each underlying IO CMO should decline at the same rate as the principal on one or more of the underlying non-IO CMOs, and that the principal on each underlying PO CMO should decline at the same rate as the principal, or notional principal, on one or more of the underlying non-PO CMOs; and

(iii) The credit union staff has the expertise dealing with exchangeable CMOs to apply the conditions in paragraphs (e)(1)(i) and (e)(1)(ii) of this section.

(2) A Federal credit union that invests in an exchangeable CMO may exercise the exchange option only if all of the underlying CMOs are permissible investments for that credit union.

(3) A Federal credit union may accept an exchangeable CMO representing beneficial ownership interests in one or more IO CMOs or PO CMOs as an asset associated with an investment repurchase transaction or as collateral in a securities lending transaction. When the exchangeable CMO is associated with one of these two transactions, it need not conform to the conditions in paragraphs (e)(1)(i) and (ii) of this section.

(f) *Other prohibited investments.* A Federal credit union may not purchase residual interests in collateralized mortgage obligations, real estate mortgage investment conduits, or small business related securities.

[68 FR 32960, June 3, 2003, as amended at 69 FR 39832, July 1, 2004]

§ 703.17 Conflicts of interest.

(a) A Federal credit union's officials and senior management employees, and their immediate family members, may not receive anything of value in connection with its investment transactions. This prohibition also applies to any other employee, such as an investment officer, if the employee is directly involved in investments, unless the Federal credit union's board of directors determines that the employee's involvement does not present a conflict of interest. This prohibition does not include compensation for employees.

National Credit Union Administration § 703.19

(b) A Federal credit union's officials and employees must conduct all transactions with business associates or family members that are not specifically prohibited by paragraph (a) of this section at arm's length and in the Federal credit union's best interest.

§ 703.18 Grandfathered investments.

(a) Subject to safety and soundness considerations, a Federal credit union may hold a CMO/REMIC residual, stripped mortgage-backed securities, or zero coupon security with a maturity greater than 10 years, if it purchased the investment:

(1) Before December 2, 1991; or

(2) On or after December 2, 1991, but before January 1, 1998, if for the purpose of reducing interest rate risk and if the Federal credit union meets the following:

(i) The Federal credit union has a monitoring and reporting system in place that provides the documentation necessary to evaluate the expected and actual performance of the investment under different interest rate scenarios;

(ii) The Federal credit union uses the monitoring and reporting system to conduct and document an analysis that shows, before purchase, that the proposed investment will reduce its interest rate risk;

(iii) After purchase, the Federal credit union evaluates the investment at least quarterly to determine whether or not it actually has reduced the interest rate risk; and

(iv) The Federal credit union accounts for the investment consistent with generally accepted accounting principles.

(b) All grandfathered investments are subject to the valuation and monitoring requirements of §§ 703.10, 703.11, and 703.12 of this part.

§ 703.19 Investment pilot program.

(a) Under the investment pilot program, NCUA will permit a limited number of Federal credit unions to engage in investment activities prohibited by this part but permitted by the Act.

(b) Except as provided in paragraph (c) of this section, before a Federal credit union may engage in additional activities it must obtain written approval from NCUA. To obtain approval, a Federal credit union must submit a request to its regional director that addresses the following items:

(1) Certification that the Federal credit union is "well-capitalized" under part 702 of this chapter;

(2) Board policies approving the activities and establishing limits on them;

(3) A complete description of the activities, with specific examples of how they will benefit the Federal credit union and how they will be conducted;

(4) A demonstration of how the activities will affect the Federal credit union's financial performance, risk profile, and asset-liability management strategies;

(5) Examples of reports the Federal credit union will generate to monitor the activities;

(6) Projections of the associated costs of the activities, including personnel, computer, audit, and so forth;

(7) Descriptions of the internal systems that will measure, monitor, and report the activities;

(8) Qualifications of the staff and officials responsible for implementing and overseeing the activities; and

(9) Internal control procedures that will be implemented, including audit requirements.

(c) A third-party seeking approval of an investment pilot program must submit a request to the Director of the Office of Capital Markets and Planning that addresses the following items:

(1) A complete description of the activities with specific examples of how a credit union will conduct and account for them, and how they will benefit a Federal credit union;

(2) A description of any risks to a Federal credit union from participating in the program; and

(3) Contracts that must be executed by the Federal credit union.

(d) A Federal credit union need not obtain individual written approval to engage in investment activities prohibited by this part but permitted by statute where the activities are part of a third-party investment program that NCUA has approved under this section.

[68 FR 32960, June 3, 2003, as amended at 69 FR 39832, July 1, 2004; 70 FR 55517, Sept. 22, 2005]

PART 704—CORPORATE CREDIT UNIONS

Sec.
704.1　Scope.
704.2　Definitions.
704.3　Corporate credit union capital.
704.4　Prompt corrective action
704.5　Investments.
704.6　Credit risk management.
704.7　Lending.
704.8　Asset and liability management.
704.9　Liquidity management.
704.10　Investment action plan.
704.11　Corporate Credit Union Service Organizations (Corporate CUSOs).
704.12　Permissible services.
704.13　Board responsibilities.
704.14　Representation.
704.15　Audit and reporting requirements.
704.16　Contracts/written agreements.
704.17　State-chartered corporate credit unions.
704.18　Fidelity bond coverage.
704.19　Disclosure of executive and director compensation.
704.21　Enterprise risk management.
704.22　Membership fees.
APPENDIX A TO PART 704—CAPITAL PRIORITIZATION AND MODEL FORMS
APPENDIX B TO PART 704—EXPANDED AUTHORITIES AND REQUIREMENTS
APPENDIX C TO PART 704—RISK-BASED CAPITAL CREDIT RISK-WEIGHT CATEGORIES

AUTHORITY: 12 U.S.C. 1766(a), 1781, 1789.

SOURCE: 62 FR 12938, Mar. 19, 1997, unless otherwise noted.

§ 704.1 Scope.

(a) This part establishes special rules for all federally insured corporate credit unions. Non federally insured corporate credit unions must agree, by written contract, to both adhere to the requirements of this part and submit to examinations, as determined by NCUA, as a condition of receiving shares or deposits from federally insured credit unions. This part grants certain additional authorities to federal corporate credit unions. Except to the extent that they are inconsistent with this part, other provisions of NCUA's Rules and Regulations (12 CFR chapter VII) and the Federal Credit Union Act apply to federally chartered corporate credit unions and federally insured state-chartered corporate credit unions to the same extent that they apply to other federally chartered and federally insured state-chartered credit unions, respectively.

(b) The Board has the authority to issue orders which vary from this part. This authority is provided under Section 120(a) of the Federal Credit Union Act, 12 U.S.C. 1766(a). Requests by state-chartered corporate credit unions for waivers to this part and for expansions of authority under appendix B of this part must be approved by the state regulator before being submitted to NCUA.

§ 704.2 Definitions.

As used in this part:

Adjusted core capital means core capital modified as follows:

(1) Deduct an amount equal to the amount of the corporate credit union's intangible assets that exceed one half percent of the corporate credit union's moving daily average net assets, but the NCUA, on its own initiative, upon petition by the applicable state regulator, or upon application from a corporate credit union, may direct that a particular corporate credit union add some or all of these excess intangibles back to the credit union's adjusted core capital;

(2) Deduct investments, both equity and debt, in unconsolidated credit union service organizations (CUSOs);

(3) If the corporate credit union, on or after October 20, 2011, contributes any perpetual contributed capital (PCC), or maintains any NCAs, at another corporate credit union, deduct an amount equal to this PCC or NCA;

(4) Beginning on October 20, 2016, and ending on October 20, 2020, deduct any amount of perpetual contributed capital (PCC) that causes PCC minus retained earnings, all divided by moving daily net average assets, to exceed two percent; and

(5) Beginning after October 20, 2020, deduct any amount of PCC that causes PCC to exceed retained earnings.

Adjusted trading means any method or transaction whereby a corporate credit union sells a security to a vendor at a price above its current market price and simultaneously purchases or commits to purchase from the vendor another security at a price above its current market price.

Applicable state regulator means the prudential state regulator of a state chartered corporate credit union.

National Credit Union Administration §704.2

Asset-backed commercial paper program (ABCP program) means a program that primarily issues commercial paper that has received a credit rating from an NRSRO and that is backed by assets or other exposures held in a bankruptcy-remote special purpose entity. The term *sponsor of an ABCP program* means a corporate credit union that:

(1) Establishes an ABCP program;

(2) Approves the sellers permitted to participate in an ABCP program;

(3) Approves the asset pools to be purchased by an ABCP program; or

(4) Administers the ABCP program by monitoring the assets, arranging for debt placement, compiling monthly reports, or ensuring compliance with the program documents and with the program's credit and investment policy.

Asset-backed security (ABS) means a security that is primarily serviced by the cashflows of a discrete pool of receivables or other financial assets, either fixed or revolving, that by their terms convert into cash within a finite time period plus any rights or other assets designed to assure the servicing or timely distribution of proceeds to the security holders. Mortgage-backed securities are a type of asset-backed security.

Available to cover losses that exceed retained earnings means that the funds are available to cover operating losses realized, in accordance with generally accepted accounting principles (GAAP), by the corporate credit union that exceed retained earnings net of equity acquired in a combination. Likewise, *available to cover losses that exceed retained earnings and perpetual contributed capital (PCC)* means that the funds are available to cover operating losses realized, in accordance with GAAP, by the corporate credit union that exceed retained earnings net of equity acquired in a combination and PCC. Any such losses must be distributed *pro rata* at the time the loss is realized first among the holders of PCC, and when all PCC is exhausted, then *pro rata* among all nonperpetual capital accounts (NCAs) and unconverted membership capital accounts, all subject to the optional prioritization described in Appendix A of this Part. To the extent that any contributed capital funds are used to cover losses, the corporate credit union must not restore or replenish the affected capital accounts under any circumstances. In addition, contributed capital that is used to cover losses in a calendar year previous to the year of liquidation has no claim against the liquidation estate.

Capital means the same as *total capital*, defined below.

Capital ratio means the corporate credit union's capital divided by its moving daily average net assets.

Collateralized debt obligation (CDO) means a debt security collateralized by mortgage-backed securities, asset-backed securities, or corporate obligations in the form of loans or debt. Senior tranches of Re-REMIC's consisting of senior mortgage- and asset-backed securities are excluded from this definition.

Collateralized mortgage obligation (CMO) means a multi-class mortgage-backed security.

Commercial mortgage-backed security (CMBS) means a mortgage-backed security collateralized primarily by multi-family and commercial property loans.

Compensation means all salaries, fees, wages, bonuses, severance payments, current year contributions to employee benefit plans (for example, medical, dental, life insurance, and disability), current year contributions to deferred compensation plans and future severance payments, including payments in connection with a merger or similar combination (whether or not funded; whether or not vested; and whether or not the deferred compensation plan is a qualified plan under Section 401(a) of the IRS Code). Compensation also includes expense accounts and other allowances (for example, the value of the personal use of housing, automobiles or other assets owned by the corporate credit union; expense allowances or reimbursements that recipients must report as income on their separate income tax return; payments made under indemnification arrangements; and payments made for the benefit of friends or relatives). In calculating required compensation disclosures, reasonable estimates may be used if precise cost figures are not readily available.

§ 704.2

Consolidated Credit Union Service Organization (Consolidated CUSO) means any corporation, partnership, business trust, joint venture, association or similar organization in which a corporate credit union directly or indirectly holds an ownership interest (as permitted by § 704.11 of this Part) and the assets of which are consolidated with those of the corporate credit union for purposes of reporting under Generally Accepted Accounting Principles (GAAP). Generally, consolidated CUSOs are majority-owned CUSOs.

Contributed capital means either perpetual or nonperpetual capital.

Core capital means the sum of:

(1) Retained earnings;

(2) Perpetual contributed capital;

(3) The retained earnings of any acquired credit union, or of an integrated set of activities and assets, calculated at the point of acquisition, if the acquisition was a mutual combination; and

(4) Minority interests in the equity accounts of CUSOs that are fully consolidated. However, minority interests in consolidated ABCP programs sponsored by a corporate credit union are excluded from the credit unions' core capital or total capital base if the corporate credit union excludes the consolidated assets of such programs from risk-weighted assets pursuant to appendix C of this part.

Core capital ratio means the corporate credit union's core capital divided by its moving daily average net assets.

Corporate credit union means an organization that:

(1) Is chartered under Federal or state law as a credit union;

(2) Receives shares from and provides loan services to credit unions;

(3) Is operated primarily for the purpose of serving other credit unions;

(4) Is designated by NCUA as a corporate credit union;

(5) Limits natural person members to the minimum required by state or federal law to charter and operate the credit union; and

(6) Does not condition the eligibility of any credit union to become a member on that credit union's membership in any other organization.

Credit-enhancing interest-only strip. (1) Credit-enhancing interest-only strip means an on-balance sheet asset that, in form or in substance:

(i) Represents the contractual right to receive some or all of the interest due on transferred assets; and

(ii) Exposes the corporate credit union to credit risk directly or indirectly associated with the transferred assets that exceeds its *pro rata* share of the corporate credit union's claim on the assets whether through subordination provisions or other credit enhancement techniques.

(2) NCUA reserves the right to identify other cash flows or related interests as a credit-enhancing interest-only strip. In determining whether a particular interest cash flow functions as a credit-enhancing interest-only strip, NCUA will consider the economic substance of the transaction.

Critical accounting policies means those policies that are most important to the portrayal of a corporate credit union's financial condition and results and that require management's most difficult, subjective, or complex judgments, often as a result of the need to make estimates about the effect of matters that are inherently uncertain.

Daily average net assets means the average of net assets calculated for each day during the period.

Daily average net risk-weighted assets means the average of net risk-weighted assets calculated for each day during the period.

Derivatives means a financial contract whose value is derived from the values of one or more underlying assets, reference rates, or indices of asset values or reference rates. Derivative contracts include interest rate derivative contracts, exchange rate derivative contracts, equity derivative contracts, commodity derivative contracts, credit derivative contracts, and any other instrument that poses similar counterparty credit risks.

Dollar roll means the purchase or sale of a mortgage-backed security to a counterparty with an agreement to resell or repurchase a substantially identical security at a future date and at a specified price.

Eligible ABCP liquidity facility means a legally binding commitment to provide liquidity support to asset-backed commercial paper by lending to, or purchasing assets from any structure, program or conduit in the event that funds are required to repay maturing asset-backed commercial paper and that meets the following criteria:

(1)(i) At the time of the draw, the liquidity facility must be subject to an asset quality test that precludes funding against assets that are 90 days or more past due or in default; and

(ii) If the assets that the liquidity facility is required to fund against are assets or exposures that have received a credit rating by an NRSRO at the time the inception of the facility, the facility can be used to fund only those assets or exposures that are rated investment grade by an NRSRO at the time of funding; or

(2) If the assets that are funded under the liquidity facility do not meet the criteria described in paragraph (1) of this definition, the assets must be guaranteed, conditionally or unconditionally, by the United States Government, its agencies, or the central government of an Organization for Economic Cooperation and Development (OECD) country.

Embedded option means a characteristic of certain assets and liabilities which gives the issuer of the instrument the ability to change the features such as final maturity, rate, principal amount and average life. Options include, but are not limited to, calls, caps, and prepayment options.

Enterprise risk management means the process of addressing risk on an entity-wide basis. The purpose of this process is not to eliminate risk but, rather, to provide the knowledge the board of directors and management need to effectively measure, monitor, and control risk and to then plan appropriate strategies to achieve the entity's business objectives with a reasonable amount of risk taking.

Equity investment means investments in real property, equity securities, and any other ownership interests, including, for example, investments in partnerships and limited liability companies.

Equity security means any security representing an ownership interest in an enterprise (for example, common, preferred, or other capital stock) or the right to acquire (for example, warrants and call options) or dispose of (for example, put options) an ownership interest in an enterprise at fixed or determinable prices. However, the term does not include convertible debt or preferred stock that by its terms either must be redeemed by the issuing enterprise or is redeemable at the option of the investor.

Examination of internal control means an engagement of an independent public accountant to report directly on internal control or on management's assertions about internal control. An examination of internal control over financial reporting includes controls over the preparation of financial statements in accordance with accounting principles generally accepted in the United States of America (GAAP) and NCUA regulatory reporting requirements.

Exchangeable collateralized mortgage obligation means a class of a collateralized mortgage obligation (CMO) that, at the time of purchase, represents beneficial ownership interests in a combination of two or more underlying classes of the same CMO structure. The holder of an exchangeable CMO may pay a fee and take delivery of the underlying classes of the CMO.

Fair value means the price that would be received to sell an asset or paid to transfer a liability in an orderly transaction between market participants at the measurement date. If there is a principal market for the asset or liability, the fair value measurement is the price in that market (whether that price is directly observable or otherwise determined using a valuation technique), even if the price in a different market is potentially more advantageous at the measurement date. In the absence of a principal market, the fair value measurement occurs in the most advantageous market for the asset or liability. The fair value of the asset or liability shall be determined based on the assumptions that market participants would use in pricing the asset or liability. In developing those assumptions, the corporate need not identify specific market participants. Rather, the corporate should identify characteristics that distinguish market participants generally, considering

§ 704.2

factors specific to all of the following: the asset or liability; the principal (or most advantageous) market for the asset or liability; and market participants with whom the corporate would transact in that market. To increase consistency and comparability in fair value measurements and related disclosures, the fair value hierarchy prioritizes the inputs to valuation techniques used to measure fair value into three broad levels. The fair value hierarchy gives the highest priority to quoted prices (unadjusted) in active markets for identical assets or liabilities (Level 1) and the lowest priority to unobservable inputs (Level 3). Examples of valuation techniques include the present value of estimated future cash flows, option-pricing models, and option-adjusted spread models.

Federal funds transaction means a short-term or open-ended unsecured transfer of immediately available funds by one depository institution to another depository institution or entity.

Financial statements means the presentation of a corporate credit union's financial data, including accompanying notes, derived from accounting records of the credit union, and intended to disclose the credit union's economic resources or obligations at a point in time, or the changes therein for a period of time, in conformity with GAAP. Each of the following is considered to be a financial statement: a balance sheet or statement of financial condition; statement of income or statement of operations; statement of undivided earnings; statement of cash flows; statement of changes in members' equity; statement of revenue and expenses; and statement of cash receipts and disbursements.

Financial statement audit means an audit of the financial statements of a corporate credit union performed in accordance with generally accepted auditing standards by an independent person who is licensed by the appropriate State or jurisdiction. The objective of a financial statement audit is to express an opinion as to whether those financial statements of the credit union present fairly, in all material respects, the financial position and the results of its operations and its cash flows in conformity with GAAP.

Foreign bank means an institution which is organized under the laws of a country other than the United States, is engaged in the business of banking, and is recognized as a bank by the banking supervisory authority of the country in which it is organized.

Generally accepted auditing standards (GAAS) means the standards approved and adopted by the American Institute of Certified Public Accountants which apply when an independent, licensed certified public accountant audits private company financial statements in the United States of America. Auditing standards differ from auditing procedures in that procedures address acts to be performed, whereas standards measure the quality of the performance of those acts and the objectives to be achieved by use of the procedures undertaken. In addition, auditing standards address the auditor's professional qualifications as well as the judgment exercised in performing the audit and in preparing the report of the audit.

Immediate family member means a spouse or other family member living in the same household.

Independent public accountant (IPA) means a person who is licensed by, or otherwise authorized by, the appropriate State or jurisdiction to practice public accounting. An IPA must be able to exercise fairness toward credit union officials, members, creditors and others who may rely upon the report of a supervisory committee audit and to demonstrate the impartiality necessary to produce dependable findings. As used in this part, IPA is synonymous with the terms "auditor" and "accountant." The term IPA does not include a licensed person working in his or her capacity as an employee of an unlicensed entity and issuing an audit opinion in the unlicensed entity's name, *e.g.*, a licensed league auditor or licensed retired examiner working for a non-licensed entity.

Intangible assets means assets considered to be intangible assets under GAAP. These assets include, but are not limited to, core deposit premiums, purchased credit card relationships, favorable leaseholds, and servicing assets (mortgage and non-mortgage). Interest-only strips receivable are not intangible assets under this definition.

National Credit Union Administration § 704.2

Internal control means the process, established by the corporate credit union's board of directors, officers and employees, designed to provide reasonable assurance of reliable financial reporting and safeguarding of assets against unauthorized acquisition, use, or disposition. A credit union's internal control structure generally consists of five components: Control environment; risk assessment; control activities; information and communication; and monitoring. Reliable financial reporting refers to preparation of Call Reports that meet management's financial reporting objectives. Internal control over safeguarding of assets against unauthorized acquisition, use, or disposition refers to prevention or timely detection of transactions involving such unauthorized access, use, or disposition of assets which could result in a loss that is material to the financial statements.

Internal control framework means criteria such as that established in *Internal Control—Integrated Framework,* issued by the Committee of Sponsoring Organizations of the Treadway Commission (COSO), or comparable, reasonable, and U.S.-recognized criteria.

Internal control over financial reporting means a process effected by those charged with governance, management, and other personnel, designed to provide reasonable assurance regarding the preparation of reliable financial statements in accordance with accounting principles generally accepted in the United States of America. A corporate credit union's internal control over financial reporting includes those policies and procedures that:

(1) Pertain to the maintenance of records that, in reasonable detail, accurately and fairly reflect the transactions and dispositions of the assets of the entity;

(2) Provide reasonable assurance that transactions are recorded as necessary to permit preparation of financial statements in accordance with accounting principles generally accepted in the United States of America, and that receipts and expenditures of the entity are being made only in accordance with authorizations of management and those charged with governance; and

(3) Provide reasonable assurance regarding prevention, or timely detection and correction, of unauthorized acquisition, use, or disposition of the entity's assets that could have a material effect on the financial statements.

Leverage ratio means, before October 21, 2013, the ratio of total capital to moving daily average net assets. This is the interim leverage ratio.

Leverage ratio means, on or after October 21, 2013, the ratio of adjusted core capital to moving daily average net assets. This is the permanent leverage ratio.

Limited liquidity investment means a private placement or funding agreement.

Member reverse repurchase transaction means an integrated transaction in which a corporate credit union purchases a security from one of its member credit unions under agreement by that member credit union to repurchase the same security at a specified time in the future. The corporate credit union then sells that same security, on the same day, to a third party, under agreement to repurchase it on the same date on which the corporate credit union is obligated to return the security to its member credit union.

Mortgage-backed security (MBS) means a security backed by first or second mortgages secured by real estate upon which is located a dwelling, mixed residential and commercial structure, residential manufactured home, or commercial structure.

Moving daily average net assets means the average of daily average net assets for the month being measured and the previous eleven (11) months.

Moving monthly average net risk-weighted assets means the average of the net risk-weighted assets for the month being measured and the previous eleven (11) months. Measurements must be taken on the last day of each month.

Mutual combination means a transaction or event in which a corporate credit union acquires another credit union, or acquires an integrated set of activities and assets that is capable of being conducted and managed as a credit union.

Nationally Recognized Statistical Rating Organization (NRSRO) means any

§ 704.2

entity that has applied for, and been granted permission, to be considered an NRSRO by the United States Securities and Exchange Commission.

NCUA means NCUA Board (Board), unless the particular action has been delegated by the Board.

Net assets means total assets less loans guaranteed by the NCUSIF and member reverse repurchase transactions. For its own account, a corporate credit union's payables under reverse repurchase agreements and receivables under repurchase agreements may be netted out if the GAAP conditions for offsetting are met. Also, any amounts deducted from core capital in calculating adjusted core capital are also deducted from net assets.

Net economic value (NEV) means the fair value of assets minus the fair value of liabilities. All fair value calculations must include the value of forward settlements and embedded options. Perpetual contributed capital, and the unamortized portion of nonperpetual capital that is, the portion that qualifies as capital for purposes of any of the minimum capital ratios, is excluded from liabilities for purposes of this calculation. The NEV ratio is calculated by dividing NEV by the fair value of assets.

Net interest margin security means a security collateralized by residual interests in collateralized mortgage obligations, residual interests in real estate mortgage investment conduits, or residual interests in other asset-backed securities.

Net risk-weighted assets means risk-weighted assets less Central Liquidity Facility (CLF) stock subscriptions, CLF loans guaranteed by the NCUSIF, and member reverse repurchase transactions. For its own account, a corporate credit union's payables under reverse repurchase agreements and receivables under repurchase agreements may be netted out if the GAAP conditions for offsetting are met. Also, any amounts deducted from core capital in calculating adjusted core capital are also deducted from net risk-weighted assets.

Nonperpetual capital means funds contributed by members or nonmembers that: are term certificates with an original minimum term of five years or that have an indefinite term (*i.e.*, no maturity) with a minimum withdrawal notice of five years; are available to cover losses that exceed retained earnings and perpetual contributed capital; are not insured by the NCUSIF or other share or deposit insurers; and cannot be pledged against borrowings. In the event the corporate is liquidated, the holders of nonperpetual capital accounts (NCAs) will claim equally. These claims will be subordinate to all other claims (including NCUSIF claims), except that any claims by the holders of perpetual contributed capital (PCC) will be subordinate to the claims of holders of NCAs.

Obligor means the primary party obligated to repay an investment, *e.g.*, the issuer of a security, such as a Qualified Special Purpose Entity (QSPE) trust; the taker of a deposit; or the borrower of funds in a federal funds transaction. Obligor does not include an originator of receivables underlying an asset-backed security, the servicer of such receivables, or an insurer of an investment.

Official means any director or committee member.

Pair-off transaction means a security purchase transaction that is closed out or sold at, or prior to, the settlement or expiration date.

Perpetual contributed capital (PCC) means accounts or other interests of a corporate credit union that: are perpetual, non-cumulative dividend accounts; are available to cover losses that exceed retained earnings; are not insured by the NCUSIF or other share or deposit insurers; and cannot be pledged against borrowings. In the event the corporate is liquidated, any claims made by the holders of perpetual contributed capital will be subordinate to all other claims (including NCUSIF claims).

Private label security means a security that is not issued or guaranteed by the U.S. government, its agencies, or its government-sponsored enterprises (GSEs).

Quoted market price means a recent sales price or a price based on current bid and asked quotations.

Repurchase transaction means a transaction in which a corporate credit union agrees to purchase a security

National Credit Union Administration § 704.2

from a counterparty and to resell the same or any identical security to that counterparty at a specified future date and at a specified price.

Residential mortgage-backed security (RMBS) means a mortgage-backed security collateralized primarily by mortgage loans on residential properties.

Residential properties means houses, condominiums, cooperative units, and manufactured homes. This definition does not include boats or motor homes, even if used as a primary residence, or timeshare properties.

Residual interest means the ownership interest in remainder cash flows from a CMO or ABS transaction after payments due bondholders and trust administrative expenses have been satisfied.

Retained earnings means retained earnings as defined under Generally Accepted Accounting Principles (GAAP).

Risk-weighted assets means a corporate credit union's risk-weighted assets as calculated in accordance with Appendix C of this part.

Section 107(8) institution means an institution described in Section 107(8) of the Federal Credit Union Act (12 U.S.C. 1757(8)).

Securities lending means lending a security to a counterparty, either directly or through an agent, and accepting collateral in return.

Securitization means the pooling and repackaging by a special purpose entity of assets or other credit exposures that can be sold to investors. Securitization includes transactions that create stratified credit risk positions whose performance is dependent upon an underlying pool of credit exposures, including loans and commitments.

Senior executive officer means a chief executive officer, any assistant chief executive officer (*e.g.*, any assistant president, any vice president or any assistant treasurer/manager), and the chief financial officer (controller). This term also includes employees of any entity hired to perform the functions described above.

Settlement date means the date originally agreed to by a corporate credit union and a counterparty for settlement of the purchase or sale of a security.

Short sale means the sale of a security not owned by the seller.

Small business related security means a security that is rated in 1 of the 4 highest rating categories by at least one nationally recognized statistical rating organization, and represents an interest in one or more promissory notes or leases of personal property evidencing the obligation of a small business concern and originated by an insured depository institution, insured credit union, insurance company, or similar institution which is supervised and examined by a Federal or State authority, or a finance company or leasing company. This definition does not include Small Business Administration securities permissible under § 107(7) of the Act.

State means any one of the several states of the United States of America, the District of Columbia, Puerto Rico, and the territories and possessions of the United States.

Stripped mortgage-backed security means a security that represents either the principal-only or interest-only portion of the cash flows of an underlying pool of mortgages.

Subordinated security means a security that, at the time of purchase, has a junior claim on the underlying collateral or assets to other securities in the same issuance. If a security is junior only to money market fund eligible securities in the same issuance, the former security is not subordinated for purposes of this definition.

Supervisory committee means, for federally chartered corporate credit unions, the supervisory committee as defined in Section 111(b) of the Federal Credit Union Act, 12 U.S.C. 1761(b). For state chartered corporate credit unions, the term supervisory committee refers to the audit committee, or similar committee, designated by state statute or regulation.

Supplementary Capital means the sum of the following items:

(1) Nonperpetual capital accounts, as amortized under § 704.3(b)(3);

(2) Allowance for loan and lease losses calculated under GAAP to a maximum of 1.25 percent of risk-weighted assets; and

561

§ 704.3

(3) Forty-five percent of unrealized gains on available-for-sale equity securities with readily determinable fair values. Unrealized gains are unrealized holding gains, net of unrealized holding losses, calculated as the amount, if any, by which fair value exceeds historical cost. The NCUA may disallow such inclusion in the calculation of supplementary capital if the NCUA determines that the securities are not prudently valued.

Tier 1 capital means adjusted core capital. *Tier 1 risk-based capital ratio* means the ratio of Tier 1 capital to the moving monthly average net risk-weighted assets.

Tier 2 capital means supplementary capital plus any perpetual contributed capital deducted from adjusted core capital.

Total assets means the sum of all a corporate credit union's assets as calculated under GAAP.

Total capital means the sum of a corporate credit union's adjusted core capital and its supplementary capital, less the corporate credit union's equity investments not otherwise deducted when calculating adjusted core capital.

Total risk-based capital ratio means the ratio of total capital to moving monthly average net risk-weighted assets.

Trade date means the date a corporate credit union originally agrees, whether orally or in writing, to enter into the purchase or sale of a security.

Trigger means an event in a securitization that will redirect cashflows if predefined thresholds are breached. Examples of triggers are delinquency and cumulative loss triggers.

Weighted average life means the weighted-average time to the return of a dollar of principal, calculated by multiplying each portion of principal received by the time at which it is expected to be received (based on a reasonable and supportable estimate of that time) and then summing and dividing by the total amount of principal. The calculation of weighted average life for interest only securities means the weighted-average time to the return of a dollar of interest, calculated by multiplying each portion of interest received by the time at which it is expected to be received (based on a reasonable and supportable estimate of that time) and then summing and dividing by the total amount of interest to be received.

When-issued trading means the buying and selling of securities in the period between the announcement of an offering and the issuance and payment date of the securities.

[75 FR 64829, Oct. 20, 2010, as amended at 76 FR 23867, Apr. 29, 2011]

EFFECTIVE DATE NOTE: At 76 FR 79533, Dec. 22, 2011, § 704.2 was amended by removing the definition of "daily average net risk-weighted assets" and revising the definition of "net assets", effective Jan. 23, 2012. For the convenience of the user, the revised text is set forth as follows:

§ 704.2 Definitions.

* * * * *

Net assets means total assets less Central Liquidity Facility (CLF) stock subscriptions, loans guaranteed by the NCUSIF, and member reverse repurchase transactions. For its own account, a corporate credit union's payables under reverse repurchase agreements and receivables under repurchase agreements may be netted out if the GAAP conditions for offsetting are met. Also, any amounts deducted from core capital in calculating adjusted core capital are also deducted from net assets.

* * * * *

§ 704.3 Corporate credit union capital.

(a) *Capital requirements.* (1) A corporate credit union must maintain at all times:

(i) A leverage ratio of 4.0 percent or greater;

(ii) A Tier 1 risk-based capital ratio of 4.0 percent or greater; and

(iii) A total risk-based capital ratio of 8.0 percent or greater.

(2) To ensure it meets its capital requirements, a corporate credit union must develop and ensure implementation of written short- and long-term capital goals, objectives, and strategies which provide for the building of capital consistent with regulatory requirements, the maintenance of sufficient capital to support the risk exposures that may arise from current and projected activities, and the periodic review and reassessment of the capital position of the corporate credit union.

National Credit Union Administration § 704.3

(3) Beginning with the first call report submitted on or after October 21, 2013, a corporate credit union must calculate and report to NCUA the ratio of its retained earnings to its moving daily average net assets. If this ratio is less than 0.45 percent, the corporate credit union must, within 30 days, submit a retained earnings accumulation plan to the NCUA for NCUA's approval. The plan must contain a detailed explanation of how the corporate credit union will accumulate earnings sufficient to meet all its future minimum leverage ratio requirements, including specific semiannual milestones for accumulating retained earnings. In the case of a state-chartered corporate credit union, the NCUA will consult with the appropriate state supervisory authority (SSA) before making a determination to approve or disapprove the plan, and will provide the SSA a copy of the completed plan. If the corporate credit union fails to submit a plan acceptable to NCUA, or fails to comply with any element of a plan approved by NCUA, the corporate will immediately be classified as significantly undercapitalized or, if already significantly undercapitalized, as critically undercapitalized for purposes of prompt corrective actions. The corporate credit union will be subject to all the associated actions under § 704.4.

(b) *Requirements for nonperpetual capital accounts (NCAs)*—(1) Form. NCA funds may be in the form of a term certificate or a no-maturity notice account.

(2) Disclosure. The terms and conditions of a nonperpetual capital account must be disclosed to the recorded owner of the account at the time the account is opened and at least annually thereafter.

(i) The initial NCA disclosure must be signed by either all of the directors of the member credit union or, if authorized by board resolution, the chair and secretary of the board; and

(ii) The annual disclosure notice must be signed by the chair of the corporate credit union. The chair must sign a statement that certifies that the notice has been sent to all entities with NCAs. The certification must be maintained in the corporate credit union's files and be available for examiner review.

(3) Five-year remaining maturity. When a no-maturity NCA has been placed on notice, or a term account has a remaining maturity of less than five years, the corporate will reduce the amount of the account that can be considered as nonperpetual capital by a constant monthly amortization that ensures the capital is fully amortized one year before the date of maturity or one year before the end of the notice period. The full balance of an NCA being amortized, not just the remaining non-amortized portion, is available to absorb losses in excess of the sum of retained earnings and perpetual contributed capital until the funds are released by the corporate credit union at the time of maturity or the conclusion of the notice period.

(4) Release. Nonperpetual capital may not be released due solely to the merger, charter conversion, or liquidation of the account holder. In the event of a merger, the capital account transfers to the continuing entity. In the event of a charter conversion, the capital account transfers to the new institution. In the event of liquidation, the corporate may release a member capital account to facilitate the payout of shares, but only with the prior written approval of the NCUA.

(5) Redemption. A corporate credit union may redeem NCAs prior to maturity or prior to the end of the notice period only with the prior approval of the NCUA and, for state chartered corporate credit unions, the approval of the appropriate state regulator.

(6) Sale. A member may transfer its interest in a nonperpetual capital account to another member or to a nonmember (other than a natural person). At least 14 days before consummating such a transfer, the member must notify the corporate credit union of the pending transfer. The corporate credit union must, within 10 days of such notice, provide the member and the potential transferee all financial information about the corporate credit union that is available to the public or that the corporate credit union has provided to its members, including any

§ 704.3

call report data submitted by the corporate credit union to NCUA but not yet posted on NCUA's Web site.

(7) *Merger.* In the event of a merger of a corporate credit union, nonperpetual capital will transfer to the continuing corporate credit union. The minimum five-year notice period for withdrawal of no-maturity capital remains in effect.

(c) *Requirements for perpetual contributed capital (PCC)*—(1) *Disclosure.* The terms and conditions of any perpetual contributed capital instrument must be disclosed to the recorded owner of the instrument at the time the instrument is created and must be signed by either all of the directors of the member credit union or, if authorized by board resolution, the chair and secretary of the board.

(2) *Release.* Perpetual contributed capital may not be released due solely to the merger, charter conversion or liquidation of a member credit union. In the event of a merger, the perpetual contributed capital transfers to the continuing credit union. In the event of a charter conversion, the perpetual contributed capital transfers to the new institution. In the event of liquidation, the perpetual contributed capital may be released to facilitate the payout of shares with NCUA's prior written approval.

(3) *Callability.* A corporate credit union may call perpetual contributed capital instruments only with the prior approval of the NCUA and, for state chartered corporate credit unions, the applicable state regulator. Perpetual contributed capital accounts are callable on a pro-rata basis across an issuance class.

(4) *Perpetual contributed capital.* A corporate credit union may issue perpetual contributed capital to both members and nonmembers.

(5) The holder of a PCC instrument may transfer its interests in the instrument to another member or to a nonmember (other than a natural person). At least 14 days before consummating such a transfer, the member must notify the corporate credit union of the pending transfer. The corporate credit union must, within 10 days of such notice, provide the member and the potential transferee all financial information about the corporate credit union that is available to the public or that the corporate credit union has provided to its members, including any call report data submitted by the corporate credit union to NCUA but not yet posted on NCUA's Web site.

(6) A corporate credit union is permitted to condition membership, services, or prices for services on a member's ownership of PCC, provided the corporate credit union gives existing members at least six months written notice of:

(i) The requirement to purchase PCC, including specific amounts; and

(ii) The effects of a failure to purchase the requisite PCC on the pricing of services or on the member's access to membership or services.

(d) *Individual minimum capital requirements.*

(1) *General.* The rules and procedures specified in this paragraph apply to the establishment of an individual minimum capital requirement for a corporate credit union that varies from any of the risk-based capital requirement(s) or leverage ratio requirements that would otherwise apply to the corporate credit union under this part.

(2) *Appropriate considerations for establishing individual minimum capital requirements.* Minimum capital levels higher than the risk-based capital requirements or the leverage ratio requirement under this part may be appropriate for individual corporate credit unions. The NCUA may establish increased individual minimum capital requirements, including modification of the minimum capital requirements related to being either significantly and critically undercapitalized for purposes of § 704.4 of this part, upon a determination that the corporate credit union's capital is or may become inadequate in view of the credit union's circumstances. For example, higher capital levels may be appropriate when NCUA determines that:

(i) A corporate credit union is receiving special supervisory attention;

(ii) A corporate credit union has or is expected to have losses resulting in capital inadequacy;

(iii) A corporate credit union has a high degree of exposure to interest rate

National Credit Union Administration § 704.3

risk, prepayment risk, credit risk, concentration risk, certain risks arising from nontraditional activities or similar risks, or a high proportion of off-balance sheet risk including standby letters of credit;

(iv) A corporate credit union has poor liquidity or cash flow;

(v) A corporate credit union is growing, either internally or through acquisitions, at such a rate that supervisory problems are presented that are not dealt with adequately by other NCUA regulations or other guidance;

(vi) A corporate credit union may be adversely affected by the activities or condition of its CUSOs or other persons or entities with which it has significant business relationships, including concentrations of credit;

(vii) A corporate credit union with a portfolio reflecting weak credit quality or a significant likelihood of financial loss, or has loans or securities in nonperforming status or on which borrowers fail to comply with repayment terms;

(viii) A corporate credit union has inadequate underwriting policies, standards, or procedures for its loans and investments;

(ix) A corporate credit union has failed to properly plan for, or execute, necessary retained earnings growth, or

(ix) A corporate credit union has a record of operational losses that exceeds the average of other, similarly situated corporate credit unions; has management deficiencies, including failure to adequately monitor and control financial and operating risks, particularly the risks presented by concentrations of credit and nontraditional activities; or has a poor record of supervisory compliance.

(3) *Standards for determination of appropriate individual minimum capital requirements.* The appropriate minimum capital levels for an individual corporate credit union cannot be determined solely through the application of a rigid mathematical formula or wholly objective criteria. The decision is necessarily based, in part, on subjective judgment grounded in agency expertise. The factors to be considered in NCUA's determination will vary in each case and may include, for example:

(i) The conditions or circumstances leading to the determination that a higher minimum capital requirement is appropriate or necessary for the corporate credit union;

(ii) The exigency of those circumstances or potential problems;

(iii) The overall condition, management strength, and future prospects of the corporate credit union and, if applicable, its subsidiaries, affiliates, and business partners;

(iv) The corporate credit union's liquidity, capital and other indicators of financial stability, particularly as compared with those of similarly situated corporate credit unions; and

(v) The policies and practices of the corporate credit union's directors, officers, and senior management as well as the internal control and internal audit systems for implementation of such adopted policies and practices.

(4) Procedures—(i) In the case of a state chartered corporate credit union, NCUA will consult with the appropriate state regulator when considering imposing a new minimum capital requirement.

(ii) When the NCUA determines that a minimum capital requirement is necessary or appropriate for a particular corporate credit union, it will notify the corporate credit union in writing of its proposed individual minimum capital requirement; the schedule for compliance with the new requirement; and the specific causes for determining that the higher individual minimum capital requirement is necessary or appropriate for the corporate credit union. The NCUA shall forward the notifying letter to the appropriate state supervisory authority (SSA) if a state-chartered corporate credit union would be subject to an individual minimum capital requirement.

(iii) The corporate credit union's response must include any information that the credit union wants the NCUA to consider in deciding whether to establish or to amend an individual minimum capital requirement for the corporate credit union, what the individual capital requirement should be, and, if applicable, what compliance schedule is appropriate for achieving the required capital level. The responses of the corporate credit union

§ 704.3

and SSA must be in writing and must be delivered to the NCUA within 30 days after the date on which the notification was received. The NCUA may extend the time period for good cause, and the time period for response by the insured corporate credit union may be shortened for good cause:

(A) When, in the opinion of the NCUA, the condition of the corporate credit union so requires, and the NCUA informs the corporate credit union of the shortened response period in the notice;

(B) With the consent of the corporate credit union; or

(C) When the corporate credit union already has advised the NCUA that it cannot or will not achieve its applicable minimum capital requirement.

(iv) Failure by the corporate credit union to respond within 30 days, or such other time period as may be specified by the NCUA, may constitute a waiver of any objections to the proposed individual minimum capital requirement or to the schedule for complying with it, unless the NCUA has provided an extension of the response period for good cause.

(v) After expiration of the response period, the NCUA will decide whether or not the proposed individual minimum capital requirement should be established for the corporate credit union, or whether that proposed requirement should be adopted in modified form, based on a review of the corporate credit union's response and other relevant information. The NCUA's decision will address comments received within the response period from the corporate credit union and the appropriate state supervisory authority (SSA) (if a state-chartered corporate credit union is involved) and will state the level of capital required, the schedule for compliance with this requirement, and any specific remedial action the corporate credit union could take to eliminate the need for continued applicability of the individual minimum capital requirement. The NCUA will provide the corporate credit union and the appropriate SSA (if a state-chartered corporate credit union is involved) with a written decision on the individual minimum capital requirement, addressing the substantive comments made by the corporate credit union and setting forth the decision and the basis for that decision. Upon receipt of this decision by the corporate credit union, the individual minimum capital requirement becomes effective and binding upon the corporate credit union. This decision represents final agency action.

(vi) In lieu of the procedures established above, a corporate credit union may request an informal hearing. The corporate credit union must make the request for a hearing in writing, and NCUA must receive the request no later than 10 days following the date of the notice described in paragraph (d)(4)(ii) of this section. Upon receipt of the request for hearing, NCUA will conduct an informal hearing and render a decision using the procedures described in paragraphs (d), (e), and (f) of § 747.3003 of this chapter.

(5) *Failure to comply.* Failure to satisfy any individual minimum capital requirement, or to meet any required incremental additions to capital under a schedule for compliance with such an individual minimum capital requirement, will constitute a basis to take action as described in § 704.4.

(6) *Change in circumstances.* If, after a decision is made under paragraph (b)(3)(iv) of this section, there is a change in the circumstances affecting the corporate credit union's capital adequacy or its ability to reach its required minimum capital level by the specified date, the NCUA may amend the individual minimum capital requirement or the corporate credit union's schedule for such compliance. The NCUA may decline to consider a corporate credit union's request for such changes that are not based on a significant change in circumstances or that are repetitive or frivolous. Pending the NCUA's reexamination of the original decision, that original decision and any compliance schedule established in that decision will continue in full force and effect.

(e) *Reservation of authority.*

(1) *Transactions for purposes of evasion.* The NCUA may disregard any transaction entered into primarily for the purpose of reducing the minimum required amount of regulatory capital

National Credit Union Administration § 704.3

or otherwise evading the requirements of this section.

(2) *Period-end versus average figures.* The NCUA reserves the right to require a corporate credit union to compute its capital ratios on the basis of period-end assets rather than average assets when the NCUA determines this requirement is appropriate to carry out the purposes of this part.

(3) *Reservation of authority.* (i) Notwithstanding the definitions of core and supplementary capital in paragraph (d) of this section, the NCUA may find that a particular asset or core or supplementary capital component has characteristics or terms that diminish its contribution to a corporate credit union's ability to absorb losses, and the NCUA may require the discounting or deduction of such asset or component from the computation of core, supplementary, or total capital.

(ii) Notwithstanding Appendix C to this Part, the NCUA will look to the substance of a transaction and may find that the assigned risk-weight for any asset, or credit equivalent amount or credit conversion factor for any off-balance sheet item does not appropriately reflect the risks imposed on the corporate credit union. The NCUA may require the corporate credit union to apply another risk-weight, credit equivalent amount, or credit conversion factor that NCUA deems appropriate.

(iii) If Appendix C to this part does not specifically assign a risk-weight, credit equivalent amount, or credit conversion factor to a particular asset or activity of the corporate credit union, the NCUA may assign any risk-weight, credit equivalent amount, or credit conversion factor that it deems appropriate. In making this determination, NCUA will consider the risks associated with the asset or off-balance sheet item as well as other relevant factors.

(4) Where practicable, the NCUA will consult with the appropriate state regulator before taking any action under this paragraph (e) that involves a state chartered corporate credit union.

(5) Before taking any action under this paragraph (e), NCUA will provide the corporate credit union with written notice of the intended action and the reasons for such action. The corporate credit union will have seven days to provide the NCUA with a written response, and the NCUA will consider the response before taking the action. Upon the timely request of the corporate credit union, and for good cause, NCUA may extend the seven day response period.

(f) *Former capital accounts.* This paragraph addresses membership capital accounts (MCAs) that qualified as corporate capital prior to October 20, 2011 but which no longer satisfy the definitions of capital because the accounts have not been converted by the member to nonperpetual capital accounts (NCAs) or to perpetual contributed capital (PCC).

(1) For MCAs structured as adjustable balance accounts, the corporate will immediately place the account on notice of withdrawal if the member has not already done so. The corporate will continue to adjust the balance of the MCA account in accordance with the original terms of the account until the entire notice period has run and then return the remaining balance, less any losses, to the member. Until the expiration of the notice period the entire adjusted balance will be available to cover losses at the corporate credit union that exceed retained earnings and PCC (excluding, if a corporate credit union exercises the capital prioritization option under Part I of Appendix A to this Part, any PCC with priority under that option).

(2) For term MCAs, the corporate credit union will return the balance of the MCA account to the member at the expiration of the term. Until the expiration of term, the entire account balance will be available to cover losses that exceed retained earnings and PCC (excluding, if a corporate credit union exercises the capital prioritization option under part I of Appendix A to this part, any PCC with priority under that option).

(3) A corporate credit union may count a portion of unconverted MCAs as Tier 2 capital. Beginning on the date of issuance (for term MCAs) or the date of notice of withdrawal (for other MCAs), the corporate may count the entire account balance as Tier 2 capital, but will then reduce the amount

§ 704.4.

of the account that can be considered as Tier 2 capital by a constant monthly amortization that ensures the capital is fully amortized one year before the date of maturity or one year before the end of the notice period. For adjustable balance account MCAs where the adjustment is determined based on some impermanent measure, such as shares on deposit with the corporate, the corporate credit union may not treat any part of the account as capital.

(4) A corporate credit union must, on or before December 20, 2011, provide any members that hold unconverted MCAs a one-time written disclosure about the status of their MCA accounts as described in this paragraph (f).

[75 FR 64829, Oct. 20, 2010]

§ 704.4   Prompt corrective action.

(a) *Purpose.* The principal purpose of this section is to define, for corporate credit unions that are not adequately capitalized, the capital measures and capital levels that are used for determining appropriate supervisory actions. This section establishes procedures for submission and review of capital restoration plans and for issuance and review of capital directives, orders, and other supervisory directives.

(b) *Scope.* This section applies to corporate credit unions, including officers, directors, and employees.

(1) This section does not limit the authority of NCUA in any way to take supervisory actions to address unsafe or unsound practices, deficient capital levels, violations of law, unsafe or unsound conditions, or other practices. The NCUA may take action under this section independently of, in conjunction with, or in addition to any other enforcement action available to the NCUA, including issuance of cease and desist orders, approval or denial of applications or notices, assessment of civil money penalties, or any other actions authorized by law.

(2) Unless permitted by the NCUA or otherwise required by law, no corporate credit union may state in any advertisement or promotional material its capital category under this part or that the NCUA has assigned the corporate credit union to a particular category.

(3) Any group of credit unions applying for a new corporate credit union charter will submit, as part of the charter application, a detailed draft plan for soliciting contributed capital and building retained earnings. The draft plan will include specific levels of contributed capital and retained earnings and the anticipated timeframes for achieving those levels. The Board will review the draft plan and modify it as necessary. If the Board approves the plan, the Board will include any necessary waivers of this section or part.

(c) *Notice of capital category.* (1) Effective date of determination of capital category. A corporate credit union will be deemed to be within a given capital category as of the most recent date:

(i) A 5310 Financial Report is required to be filed with the NCUA;

(ii) A final NCUA report of examination is delivered to the corporate credit union; or

(iii) Written notice is provided by the NCUA to the corporate credit union that its capital category has changed as provided in paragraphs (c)(2) or (d)(3) of this section.

(2) Adjustments to reported capital levels and category—

(i) Notice of adjustment by corporate credit union. A corporate credit union must provide the NCUA with written notice that an adjustment to the corporate credit union's capital category may have occurred no later than 15 calendar days following the date that any material event has occurred that would cause the corporate credit union to be placed in a lower capital category from the category assigned to the corporate credit union for purposes of this section on the basis of the corporate credit union's most recent call report or report of examination.

(ii) Determination by the NCUA to change capital category. After receiving notice pursuant to paragraph (c)(1) of this section, or on its own initiative, the NCUA will determine whether to change the capital category of the corporate credit union and will notify the corporate credit union of the NCUA's determination.

(d) *Capital measures and capital category definitions.* (1) Capital measures. For purposes of this section, the relevant capital measures are:

National Credit Union Administration
§ 704.4.

(i) The total risk-based capital ratio;
(ii) The Tier 1 risk-based capital ratio; and
(iii) The leverage ratio.

(2) *Capital categories.* For purposes of this section, a corporate credit union is:

(i) Well capitalized if the corporate credit union:

(A) Has a total risk-based capital ratio of 10.0 percent or greater; and

(B) Has a Tier 1 risk-based capital ratio of 6.0 percent or greater; and

(C) Has a leverage ratio of 5.0 percent or greater; and

(D) Is not subject to any written agreement, order, capital directive, or prompt corrective action directive issued by NCUA to meet and maintain a specific capital level for any capital measure.

(ii) Adequately capitalized if the corporate credit union:

(A) Has a total risk-based capital ratio of 8.0 percent or greater; and

(B) Has a Tier 1 risk-based capital ratio of 4.0 percent or greater; and

(C) Has:

(*1*) A leverage ratio of 4.0 percent or greater; and

(*2*) Does not meet the definition of a well capitalized corporate credit union.

(iii) Undercapitalized if the corporate credit union:

(A) Has a total risk-based capital ratio that is less than 8.0 percent; or

(B) Has a Tier 1 risk-based capital ratio that is less than 4.0 percent; or

(C) Has a leverage ratio that is less than 4.0 percent.

(iv) Significantly undercapitalized if the corporate credit union has:

(A) A total risk-based capital ratio that is less than 6.0 percent; or

(B) A Tier 1 risk-based capital ratio that is less than 3.0 percent; or

(C) A leverage ratio that is less than 3.0 percent.

(v) Critically undercapitalized if the corporate credit union has:

(A) A total risk-based capital ratio that is less than 4.0 percent; or

(B) A Tier 1 risk-based capital ratio that is less than 2.0 percent; or

(C) A leverage ratio that is less than 2.0 percent.

(3) *Reclassification based on supervisory criteria other than capital.* Notwithstanding the elements of paragraph (d)(2) of this section, the NCUA may reclassify a well capitalized corporate credit union as adequately capitalized, and may require an adequately capitalized or undercapitalized corporate credit union to comply with certain mandatory or discretionary supervisory actions as if the corporate credit union were in the next lower capital category, in the following circumstances:

(i) Unsafe or unsound condition. The NCUA has determined, after notice and opportunity for hearing pursuant to paragraph (h)(1) of this section, that the corporate credit union is in an unsafe or unsound condition; or

(ii) Unsafe or unsound practice. The NCUA has determined, after notice and an opportunity for hearing pursuant to paragraph (h)(1) of this section, that the corporate credit union received a less-than-satisfactory rating (*i.e.*, three or lower) for any rating category (other than in a rating category specifically addressing capital adequacy) under the Corporate Risk Information System (CRIS) rating system and has not corrected the conditions that served as the basis for the less than satisfactory rating. Ratings under this paragraph (d)(3)(ii) refer to the most recent ratings (as determined either on-site or off-site by the most recent examination) of which the corporate credit union has been notified in writing.

(4) The NCUA may, for good cause, modify any of the percentages in paragraph (d)(2) of this section as described in § 704.3(d).

(e) *Capital restoration plans.* (1) Schedule for filing plan—

(i) *In general.* A corporate credit union must file a written capital restoration plan with the NCUA within 45 days of the date that the corporate credit union receives notice or is deemed to have notice that the corporate credit union is undercapitalized, significantly undercapitalized, or critically undercapitalized, unless the NCUA notifies the corporate credit union in writing that the plan is to be filed within a different period. An adequately capitalized corporate credit union that has been required pursuant to paragraph (d)(3) of this section to comply with supervisory actions as if

§ 704.4.

the corporate credit union were undercapitalized is not required to submit a capital restoration plan solely by virtue of the reclassification.

(ii) *Additional capital restoration plans.* Notwithstanding paragraph (e)(1)(i) of this section, a corporate credit union that has already submitted and is operating under a capital restoration plan approved under this section is not required to submit an additional capital restoration plan based on a revised calculation of its capital measures or a reclassification of the institution under paragraph (d)(3) of this section unless the NCUA notifies the corporate credit union that it must submit a new or revised capital plan. A corporate credit union that is notified that it must submit a new or revised capital restoration plan must file the plan in writing with the NCUA within 45 days of receiving such notice, unless the NCUA notifies the corporate credit union in writing that the plan is to be filed within a different period.

(2) *Contents of plan.* All financial data submitted in connection with a capital restoration plan must be prepared in accordance with the instructions provided on the call report, unless the NCUA instructs otherwise. The capital restoration plan must include all of the information required to be filed under paragraph (k)(2)(ii) of this section. A corporate credit union required to submit a capital restoration plan as the result of a reclassification of the corporate credit union pursuant to paragraph (d)(3) of this section must include a description of the steps the corporate credit union will take to correct the unsafe or unsound condition or practice.

(3) *Failure to submit a capital restoration plan.* A corporate credit union that is undercapitalized and that fails to submit a written capital restoration plan within the period provided in this section will, upon the expiration of that period, be subject to all of the provisions of this section applicable to significantly undercapitalized credit unions.

(4) *Review of capital restoration plans.* Within 60 days after receiving a capital restoration plan under this section, the NCUA will provide written notice to the corporate credit union of whether it has approved the plan. The NCUA may extend this time period.

(5) *Disapproval of capital plan.* If the NCUA does not approve a capital restoration plan, the corporate credit union must submit a revised capital restoration plan, when directed to do so, within the time specified by the NCUA. An undercapitalized corporate credit union is subject to the provisions applicable to significantly undercapitalized credit unions until it has submitted, and NCUA has approved, a capital restoration plan. If the NCUA directs that the corporate submit a revised plan, it must do so in time frame specified by the NCUA.

(6) *Failure to implement a capital restoration plan.* Any undercapitalized corporate credit union that fails in any material respect to implement a capital restoration plan will be subject to all of the provisions of this section applicable to significantly undercapitalized institutions.

(7) *Amendment of capital plan.* A corporate credit union that has filed an approved capital restoration plan may, after prior written notice to and approval by the NCUA, amend the plan to reflect a change in circumstance. Until such time as NCUA has approved a proposed amendment, the corporate credit union must implement the capital restoration plan as approved prior to the proposed amendment.

(f) *Mandatory and discretionary supervisory actions.* (1) Mandatory supervisory actions.—

(i) *Provisions applicable to all corporate credit unions.* All corporate credit unions are subject to the restrictions contained in paragraph (k)(1) of this section on capital distributions.

(ii) *Provisions applicable to undercapitalized, significantly undercapitalized, and critically undercapitalized corporate credit unions.* Immediately upon receiving notice or being deemed to have notice, as provided in paragraph (c) or (e) of this section, that the corporate credit union is undercapitalized, significantly undercapitalized, or critically undercapitalized, the corporate credit union will be subject to the following provisions of paragraph (k) of this section:

(A) Restricting capital distributions (paragraph (k)(1));

National Credit Union Administration § 704.4.

(B) NCUA monitoring of the condition of the corporate credit union (paragraph (k)(2)(i));

(C) Requiring submission of a capital restoration plan (paragraph (k)(2)(ii));

(D) Restricting the growth of the corporate credit union's assets (paragraph (k)(2)(iii)); and

(E) Requiring prior approval of certain expansion proposals (paragraph (k)(2)(iv)).

(iii) Additional provisions applicable to significantly undercapitalized, and critically undercapitalized corporate credit unions. In addition to the mandatory requirements described in paragraph (f)(1) of this section, immediately upon receiving notice or being deemed to have notice that the corporate credit union is significantly undercapitalized, or critically undercapitalized, or that the corporate credit union is subject to the provisions applicable to corporate credit unions that are significantly undercapitalized because the credit union failed to submit or implement in any material respect an acceptable capital restoration plan, the corporate credit union will become subject to the provisions of paragraph (k)(3)(iii) of this section that restrict compensation paid to senior executive officers of the institution.

(iv) Additional provisions applicable to critically undercapitalized corporate credit unions. In addition to the provisions described in paragraphs (f)(1)(ii) and (f)(1)(iii) of this section, immediately upon receiving notice or being deemed to have notice that the corporate credit union is critically undercapitalized, the corporate credit union will become subject to these additional provisions of paragraph (k) of this section:

(A) Restricting the activities of the corporate credit union ((k)(5)(i)); and

(B) Restricting payments on subordinated debt of the corporate credit union ((k)(5)(ii)).

(2) Discretionary supervisory actions.

(i) All PCA actions listed in paragraph (k) of this section that are not discussed in paragraph (f)(1) of this section are discretionary.

(ii) All discretionary actions available to NCUA in the case of an undercapitalized corporate credit union are available to NCUA in the case of a significantly undercapitalized credit union. All discretionary actions available to NCUA in the case of an undercapitalized corporate credit union or a significantly undercapitalized corporate credit union are available to NCUA in the case of a critically undercapitalized corporate credit union.

(iii) In taking any discretionary PCA actions with a corporate credit union that is deemed to be undercapitalized, significantly undercapitalized or critically undercapitalized, or has been reclassified as undercapitalized, or significantly undercapitalized; or an action in connection with an officer or director of such corporate credit union; the NCUA will follow the procedures for issuing directives under paragraphs (g) and (i) of this section.

(iv) NCUA will consult and seek to work cooperatively with the appropriate state supervisory authority (SSA) before taking any discretionary supervisory action with respect to a state-chartered corporate credit union; will provide notice of its decision to the SSA; and will allow the appropriate SSA an opportunity to take the proposed action independently or jointly with NCUA.

(g) *Directives to take prompt corrective action.* The NCUA will provide an undercapitalized, significantly undercapitalized, or critically undercapitalized corporate credit union prior written notice of the NCUA's intention to issue a directive requiring such corporate credit union to take actions or to follow proscriptions described in this part. Section 747.3002 of this chapter prescribes the notice content and associated process.

(h) *Procedures for reclassifying a corporate credit union based on criteria other than capital.* When the NCUA intends to reclassify a corporate credit union or subject it to the supervisory actions applicable to the next lower capitalization category based on an unsafe or unsound condition or practice, the NCUA will provide the credit union with prior written notice of such intent. Section 747.3003 of this chapter prescribes the notice content and associated process.

(i) *Order to dismiss a Director or senior executive officer.* When the NCUA issues and serves a directive on a corporate credit union requiring it to dismiss

§ 704.4.

from office any director or senior executive officer under paragraphs (k)(3) of this section, the NCUA will also serve upon the person the corporate credit union is directed to dismiss (Respondent) a copy of the directive (or the relevant portions, where appropriate) and notice of the Respondent's right to seek reinstatement. Section 747.3004 of this chapter prescribes the content of the notice of right to seek reinstatement and the associated process.

(j) *Enforcement of directives.* Section 747.3005 of this chapter prescribes the process for enforcement of directives.

(k) *Remedial actions towards undercapitalized, significantly undercapitalized, and critically undercapitalized corporate credit unions.* (1) Provision applicable to all corporate credit unions. A corporate credit union is prohibited from making any capital distribution, including payment of dividends on perpetual and nonperpetual capital accounts, if, after making the distribution, the credit union would be undercapitalized.

(2) Provisions applicable to undercapitalized corporate credit unions.

(i) Monitoring required. The NCUA will—

(A) Closely monitor the condition of any undercapitalized corporate credit union;

(B) Closely monitor compliance with capital restoration plans, restrictions, and requirements imposed under this section; and

(C) Periodically review the plan, restrictions, and requirements applicable to any undercapitalized corporate credit union to determine whether the plan, restrictions, and requirements are achieving the purpose of this section.

(ii) Capital restoration plan required.

(A) Any undercapitalized corporate credit union must submit an acceptable capital restoration plan to the NCUA.

(B) The capital restoration plan will—

(*1*) Specify—

(*i*) The steps the corporate credit union will take to become adequately capitalized;

(*ii*) The levels of capital to be attained during each year in which the plan will be in effect;

(*iii*) How the corporate credit union will comply with the restrictions or requirements then in effect under this section; and

(*iv*) The types and levels of activities in which the corporate credit union will engage; and

(*2*) Contain such other information as the NCUA may require.

(C) The NCUA will not accept a capital restoration plan unless the NCUA determines that the plan—

(*1*) Complies with paragraph (k)(2)(ii)(B) of this section;

(*2*) Is based on realistic assumptions, and is likely to succeed in restoring the corporate credit union's capital; and

(*3*) Would not appreciably increase the risk (including credit risk, interest-rate risk, and other types of risk) to which the corporate credit union is exposed.

(iii) Asset growth restricted. An undercapitalized corporate credit union must not permit its daily average net assets during any calendar month to exceed its moving daily average net assets unless—

(A) The NCUA has accepted the corporate credit union's capital restoration plan; and

(B) Any increase in total assets is consistent with the plan.

(iv) Prior approval required for acquisitions, branching, and new lines of business. An undercapitalized corporate credit union must not, directly or indirectly, acquire any interest in any entity, establish or acquire any additional branch office, or engage in any new line of business unless the NCUA has accepted the corporate credit union's capital restoration plan, the corporate credit union is implementing the plan, and the NCUA determines that the proposed action is consistent with and will further the achievement of the plan.

(3) Provisions applicable to significantly undercapitalized corporate credit unions and undercapitalized corporate credit unions that fail to submit and implement capital restoration plans.

(i) In general. This paragraph applies with respect to any corporate credit union that—

(A) Is significantly undercapitalized; or

(B) Is undercapitalized and—

(1) Fails to submit an acceptable capital restoration plan within the time allowed by the NCUA under paragraph (e)(1) of this section; or

(2) Fails in any material respect to implement a plan accepted by the NCUA.

(ii) Specific actions authorized. The NCUA may take one or more of the following actions:

(A) Requiring recapitalization.

(1) Requiring the corporate credit union to seek and obtain additional contributed capital.

(2) Requiring the corporate credit union to increase its rate of earnings retention.

(3) Requiring the corporate credit union to combine, in whole or part, with another insured depository institution, if one or more grounds exist under this section or the Federal Credit Union Act for appointing a conservator or liquidating agent.

(B) Restricting any ongoing or future transactions with affiliates.

(C) Restricting interest rates paid.

(1) In general. Restricting the rates of dividends and interest that the corporate credit union pays on shares and deposits to the prevailing rates on shares and deposits of comparable amounts and maturities in the region where the institution is located, as determined by the NCUA.

(2) Retroactive restrictions prohibited. Paragraph (k)(3)(ii)(c) of this section does not authorize the NCUA to restrict interest rates paid on time deposits or shares made before (and not renewed or renegotiated after) the date the NCUA announced this restriction.

(D) Restricting asset growth. Restricting the corporate credit union's asset growth more stringently than in paragraph (k)(2)(iii) of this section, or requiring the corporate credit union to reduce its total assets.

(E) Restricting activities. Requiring the corporate credit union or any of its CUSOs to alter, reduce, or terminate any activity that the NCUA determines poses excessive risk to the corporate credit union.

(F) Improving management. Doing one or more of the following:

(1) New election of directors. Ordering a new election for the corporate credit union's board of directors.

(2) Dismissing directors or senior executive officers. Requiring the corporate credit union to dismiss from office any director or senior executive officer who had held office for more than 180 days immediately before the corporate credit union became undercapitalized.

(3) Employing qualified senior executive officers. Requiring the corporate credit union to employ qualified senior executive officers (who, if the NCUA so specifies, will be subject to approval by the NCUA).

(G) Requiring divestiture. Requiring the corporate credit union to divest itself of or liquidate any interest in any entity if the NCUA determines that the entity is in danger of becoming insolvent or otherwise poses a significant risk to the corporate credit union;

(H) Conserve or liquidate the corporate credit union if NCUA determines the credit union has no reasonable prospect of becoming adequately capitalized; and

(I) Requiring other action. Requiring the corporate credit union to take any other action that the NCUA determines will better carry out the purpose of this section than any of the actions described in this paragraph.

(iii) Senior executive officers' compensation restricted.

(A) In general. The corporate credit union is prohibited from doing any of the following without the prior written approval of the NCUA:

(1) Pay any bonus or profit-sharing to any senior executive officer.

(2) Provide compensation to any senior executive officer at a rate exceeding that officer's average rate of compensation (excluding bonuses and profit-sharing) during the 12 calendar months preceding the calendar month in which the corporate credit union became undercapitalized.

(B) Failing to submit plan. The NCUA will not grant approval with respect to a corporate credit union that has failed to submit an acceptable capital restoration plan.

(iv) Discretion to impose certain additional restrictions. The NCUA may

§ 704.4.

impose one or more of the restrictions prescribed by regulation under paragraph (k)(5) of this section if the NCUA determines that those restrictions are necessary to carry out the purpose of this section.

(4) More stringent treatment based on other supervisory criteria.

(i) In general. If the NCUA determines, after notice and an opportunity for hearing as described in subpart M of part 747 of this chapter, that a corporate credit union is in an unsafe or unsound condition or deems the corporate credit union to be engaging in an unsafe or unsound practice, the NCUA may—

(A) If the corporate credit union is well capitalized, reclassify the corporate credit union as adequately capitalized;

(B) If the corporate credit union is adequately capitalized (but not well capitalized), require the corporate credit union to comply with one or more provisions of paragraphs (k)(1) and (k)(2) of this section, as if the corporate credit union were undercapitalized; or

(C) If the corporate credit union is undercapitalized, take any one or more actions authorized under paragraph (k)(3)(ii) of this section as if the corporate credit union were significantly undercapitalized.

(ii) Contents of plan. Any plan required under paragraph (k)(4)(i) of this section will specify the steps that the corporate credit union will take to correct the unsafe or unsound condition or practice. Capital restoration plans, however, will not be required under paragraph (k)(4)(i)(B) of this section.

(5) Provisions applicable to critically undercapitalized corporate credit unions.

(i) Activities restricted. Any critically undercapitalized corporate credit union must comply with restrictions prescribed by the NCUA under paragraph (k)(6) of this section.

(ii) Payments on contributed capital and subordinated debt prohibited. A critically undercapitalized corporate credit union must not, beginning no later than 60 days after becoming critically undercapitalized, make any payment of dividends on contributed capital or any payment of principal or interest on the corporate credit union's subordinated debt unless the NCUA determines that an exception would further the purpose of this section. Interest, although not payable, may continue to accrue under the terms of any subordinated debt to the extent otherwise permitted by law. Dividends on contributed capital do not, however, continue to accrue.

(iii) Conservatorship, liquidation, or other action. The NCUA may, at any time, conserve or liquidate any critically undercapitalized corporate credit union or require the credit union to combine, in whole or part, with another institution. NCUA will consider, not later than 90 days after a corporate credit union becomes critically undercapitalized, whether NCUA should liquidate, conserve, or combine the institution.

(6) Restricting activities of critically undercapitalized corporate credit unions. To carry out the purpose of this section, the NCUA will, by order—

(i) Restrict the activities of any critically undercapitalized corporate credit union; and

(ii) At a minimum, prohibit any such corporate credit union from doing any of the following without the NCUA's prior written approval:

(A) Entering into any material transaction other than in the usual course of business, including any investment, expansion, acquisition, sale of assets, or other similar action.

(B) Extending credit for any transaction NCUA determines to be highly leveraged.

(C) Amending the corporate credit union's charter or bylaws, except to the extent necessary to carry out any other requirement of any law, regulation, or order.

(D) Making any material change in accounting methods.

(E) Paying compensation or bonuses NCUA determines to be excessive.

(F) Paying interest on new or renewed liabilities at a rate that would increase the corporate credit union's weighted average cost of funds to a level significantly exceeding the prevailing rates of interest on insured deposits in the corporate credit union's normal market areas.

[75 FR 64836, Oct. 20, 2010]

§ 704.5 Investments.

(a) *Policies.* A corporate credit union must operate according to an investment policy that is consistent with its other risk management policies, including, but not limited to, those related to credit risk management, asset and liability management, and liquidity management. The policy must address, at a minimum:

(1) Appropriate tests and criteria for evaluating investments and investment transactions before purchase; and

(2) Reasonable and supportable concentration limits for limited liquidity investments in relation to capital.

(b) *General.* All investments must be U.S. dollar-denominated and subject to the credit policy restrictions set forth in § 704.6.

(c) *Authorized activities.* A corporate credit union may invest in:

(1) Securities, deposits, and obligations set forth in Sections 107(7), 107(8), and 107(15) of the Federal Credit Union Act, 12 U.S.C. 1757(7), 1757(8), and 1757(15), except as provided in this section;

(2) Deposits in, the sale of federal funds to, and debt obligations of corporate credit unions, Section 107(8) institutions, and state banks, trust companies, and mutual savings banks not domiciled in the state in which the corporate credit union does business;

(3) Corporate CUSOs, as defined in and subject to the limitations of § 704.11;

(4) Marketable debt obligations of corporations chartered in the United States. This authority does not apply to debt obligations that are convertible into the stock of the corporation; and

(5) Domestically-issued asset-backed securities.

(d) *Repurchase agreements.* A corporate credit union may enter into a repurchase agreement provided that:

(1) The corporate credit union, directly or through its agent, receives written confirmation of the transaction, and either takes physical possession or control of the repurchase securities or is recorded as owner of the repurchase securities through the Federal Reserve Book-Entry Securities Transfer System;

(2) The repurchase securities are legal investments for that corporate credit union;

(3) The corporate credit union, directly or through its agent, receives daily assessment of the market value of the repurchase securities and maintains adequate margin that reflects a risk assessment of the repurchase securities and the term of the transaction; and

(4) The corporate credit union has entered into signed contracts with all approved counterparties and agents, and ensures compliance with the contracts. Such contracts must address any supplemental terms and conditions necessary to meet the specific requirements of this part. Third party arrangements must be supported by tri-party contracts in which the repurchase securities are priced and reported daily and the tri-party agent ensures compliance; and

(e) *Securities Lending.* A corporate credit union may enter into a securities lending transaction provided that:

(1) The corporate credit union, directly or through its agent, receives written confirmation of the loan, obtains a first priority security interest in the collateral by taking physical possession or control of the collateral, or is recorded as owner of the collateral through the Federal Reserve Book-Entry Securities Transfer System;

(2) The collateral is a legal investment for that corporate credit union;

(3) The corporate credit union, directly or through its agent, receives daily assessment of the market value of collateral and maintains adequate margin that reflects a risk assessment of the collateral and terms of the loan; and

(4) The corporate credit union has entered into signed contracts with all agents and, directly or through its agent, has executed a written loan and security agreement with the borrower. The corporate or its agent ensures compliance with the agreements.

(f) *Investment companies.* A corporate credit union may invest in an investment company registered with the Securities and Exchange Commission under the Investment Company Act of

§ 704.5

1940 (15 U.S.C. 80a), or a collective investment fund maintained by a national bank under 12 CFR 9.18 or a mutual savings bank under 12 CFR 550.260, provided that the company or fund prospectus restricts the investment portfolio to investments and investment transactions that are permissible for that corporate credit union.

(g) *Investment settlement.* A corporate credit union may only contract for the purchase or sale of an investment if the transaction is settled on a delivery versus payment basis within 60 days for mortgage-backed securities, within 30 days for new issues (other than mortgage-backed securities), and within three days for all other securities.

(h) *Prohibitions.* A corporate credit union is prohibited from:

(1) Purchasing or selling derivatives, except for embedded options not required under GAAP to be accounted for separately from the host contract or forward sales commitments on loans to be purchased by the corporate credit union;

(2) Engaging in trading securities unless accounted for on a trade date basis;

(3) Engaging in adjusted trading or short sales;

(4) Purchasing mortgage servicing rights, small business related securities, residual interests in collateralized mortgage obligations, residual interests in real estate mortgage investment conduits, or residual interests in asset-backed securities;

(5) Purchasing net interest margin securities;

(6) Purchasing collateralized debt obligations;

(7) Purchasing private label residential mortgage-backed securities;

(8) Purchasing subordinated securities; and

(9) Purchasing stripped mortgage-backed securities (SMBS), or securities that represent interests in SMBS, except as described in subparagraphs (i) and (iii) below.

(i) A corporate credit union may invest in exchangeable collateralized mortgage obligations (exchangeable CMOs) representing beneficial ownership interests in one or more interest-only classes of a CMO (IO CMOs) or principal-only classes of a CMO (PO CMOs), but only if:

(A) At the time of purchase, the ratio of the market price to the remaining principal balance is between .8 and 1.2, meaning that the discount or premium of the market price to par must be less than 20 points;

(B) The offering circular or other official information available at the time of purchase indicates that the notional principal on each underlying IO CMO should decline at the same rate as the principal on one or more of the underlying non-IO CMOs, and that the principal on each underlying PO CMO should decline at the same rate as the principal, or notional principal, on one or more of the underlying non-PO CMOs; and

(C) The credit union investment staff has the expertise dealing with exchangeable CMOs to apply the conditions in paragraphs (h)(5)(i)(A) and (B) of this section.

(ii) A corporate credit union that invests in an exchangeable CMO may exercise the exchange option only if all of the underlying CMOs are permissible investments for that credit union.

(iii) A corporate credit union may accept an exchangeable CMO representing beneficial ownership interests in one or more IO CMOs or PO CMOs as an asset associated with an investment repurchase transaction or as collateral in a securities lending transaction. When the exchangeable CMO is associated with one of these two transactions, it need not conform to the conditions in paragraphs (h)(5)(i)(A) or (B) of this section.

(i) *Conflicts of interest.* A corporate credit union's officials, employees, and immediate family members of such individuals, may not receive pecuniary consideration in connection with the making of an investment or deposit by the corporate credit union. Employee compensation is exempt from this prohibition. All transactions not specifically prohibited by this paragraph must be conducted at arm's length and in the interest of the corporate credit union.

(j) *Grandfathering.* A corporate credit union's authority to hold an investment is governed by the regulation in

National Credit Union Administration

§ 704.6

effect at the time of purchase. However, all grandfathered investments are subject to the requirements of §§ 704.8 and 704.9.

[75 FR 64839, Oct. 20, 2010]

§ 704.6 Credit risk management.

(a) *Policies.* A corporate credit union must operate according to a credit risk management policy that is commensurate with the investment risks and activities it undertakes. The policy must address at a minimum:

(1) The approval process associated with credit limits;

(2) Due diligence analysis requirements;

(3) Maximum credit limits with each obligor and transaction counterparty, set as a percentage of capital. In addition to addressing deposits and securities, limits with transaction counterparties must address aggregate exposures of all transactions including, but not limited to, repurchase agreements, securities lending, and forward settlement of purchases or sales of investments; and

(4) Concentrations of credit risk (*e.g.*, originator of receivables, servicer of receivables, insurer, industry type, sector type, geographic, collateral type, and tranche priority).

(b) *Exemption.* The limitations and requirements of this section do not apply to certain assets, whether or not considered investments under this part, including fixed assets, individual loans and loan participation interests, investments in CUSOs, investments that are issued or fully guaranteed as to principal and interest by the U.S. government or its agencies or its sponsored enterprises (but not exempting, for purposes of paragraph (d) of this section, mortgage backed securities), investments that are fully insured or guaranteed (including accumulated dividends and interest) by the NCUSIF or the Federal Deposit Insurance Corporation, and settlement funds in federally insured depository institutions.

(c) *Issuer concentration limits*—(1) General rule. The aggregate of all investments in any single obligor is limited to 25 percent of capital or $5 million, whichever is greater.

(2) Exceptions.

(i) Investments in one obligor where the remaining maturity of all obligations is less than 30 days are limited to 50 percent of capital;

(ii) Investments in credit card master trust asset-backed securities are limited to 50 percent of capital in any single obligor;

(iii) Aggregate investments in repurchase and securities lending agreements with any one counterparty are limited to 200 percent of capital;

(iv) Investments in non-money market registered investment companies are limited to of 50 percent of capital in any single obligor;

(v) Investments in money market registered investment companies are limited to 100 percent of capital in any single obligor; and

(vi) Investments in corporate CUSOs are subject to the limitations of § 704.11.

(3) For purposes of measurement, each new credit transaction must be evaluated in terms of the corporate credit union's capital at the time of the transaction. An investment that fails a requirement of this section because of a subsequent reduction in capital will be deemed non-conforming. A corporate credit union is required to exercise reasonable efforts to bring nonconforming investments into conformity within 90 calendar days. Investments that remain nonconforming for 90 calendar days will be deemed to fail a requirement of this section and the corporate credit union will have to comply with § 704.10.

(d) *Sector concentration limits.* (1) A corporate credit union must establish sector limits that do not exceed the following maximums:

(i) Mortgage-backed securities (Inclusive of commercial mortgage-backed securities)—the lower of 1000 percent of capital or 50 percent of assets;

(ii) Commercial mortgage-backed securities—the lower of 300 percent of capital or 15 percent of assets;

(iii) FFELP student loan asset-backed securities—the lower of 1000 percent of capital or 50 percent of assets;

(iv) Private student loan asset-backed securities—the lower of 500 percent of capital or 25 percent of assets;

(v) Auto loan/lease asset-backed securities—the lower of 500 percent of capital or 25 percent of assets;
(vi) Credit card asset-backed securities—the lower of 500 percent of capital or 25 percent of assets;
(vii) Other asset-backed securities not listed in paragraphs (ii) through (vi)—the lower of 500 percent of capital or 25 percent of assets;
(viii) Corporate debt obligations—the lower of 1000 percent of capital or 50 percent of assets; and
(ix) Municipal securities—the lower of 1000 percent of capital or 50 percent of assets.
(2) Registered investment companies—A corporate credit union must limit its investment in registered investment companies to the lower of 1000 percent of capital or 50 percent of assets. In addition to applying the limit in this paragraph (d)(2), a corporate credit union must also include the underlying assets in each registered investment company in the relevant sectors described in paragraph (d)(1) of this section when calculating those sector limits.
(3) A corporate credit union will limit its aggregate holdings in any investments not described in paragraphs (d)(1) or (d)(2) of this section to the lower of 100 percent of capital or 5 percent of assets. The NCUA may approve a higher percentage in appropriate cases.
(4) Investments in other federally insured credit unions, deposits and federal funds investments in other federally insured depository institutions, and investment repurchase agreements are excluded from the concentration limits in paragraphs (d)(1), (d)(2), and (d)(3) of this section.
(e) *Corporate debt obligation subsector limits.* In addition to the limitations in paragraph (d)(1)(viii) of this section, a corporate credit union must not exceed the lower of 200 percent of capital or 10 percent of assets in any single North American Industry Classification System (NAICS) industry sector. If the corporation does not have a readily ascertainable NAICS classification, a corporate credit union will use its reasonable judgment in assigning such a classification. NCUA may direct, however, that the corporate change the classification.
(f) *Credit ratings.*—(1) All investments, other than in another depository institution, must have an applicable credit rating from at least one NRSRO. At a minimum, 90 percent of all such investments, by book value, must have a rating by at least two NRSROs. Corporate credit unions may use either public or nonpublic NRSRO ratings to satisfy this requirement.
(2) At the time of purchase, investments with long-term ratings must be rated no lower than AA– (or equivalent) by every NRSRO that provides a publicly available long-term rating on that investment, and investments with short-term ratings must be rated no lower than A–1 (or equivalent) by every NRSRO that provides a publicly available short-term rating on that investment. If the corporate credit union obtains a nonpublic NRSRO rating, that rating must also be no lower than AA–, or A–1, for long-term and short-term ratings, respectively.
(3) All rating(s) relied upon to meet the requirements of this part must be identified at the time of purchase and must be monitored for as long as the corporate owns the investment. Corporate credit unions must identify and monitor any new post-purchase NRSRO ratings on investments they hold.
(4) Investments are subject to the requirements of §704.10 if:
(i) An NRSRO that rates the investment downgrades that rating, after purchase, below the minimum rating requirements of this part; or
(ii) The investment is part of an asset class or group of investments that exceeds the sector or obligor concentration limits of this section.
(g) *Reporting and documentation.* (1) At least annually, a written evaluation of each credit limit with each obligor or transaction counterparty must be prepared and formally approved by the board or an appropriate committee. At least monthly, the board or an appropriate committee must receive an investment watch list of existing and/or potential credit problems and summary credit exposure reports, which demonstrate compliance with the corporate credit union's risk management policies.

(2) At a minimum, the corporate credit union must maintain:

(i) A justification for each approved credit limit;

(ii) Disclosure documents, if any, for all instruments held in portfolio. Documents for an instrument that has been sold must be retained until completion of the next NCUA examination; and

(iii) The latest available financial reports, industry analyses, internal and external analyst evaluations, and rating agency information sufficient to support each approved credit limit.

[75 FR 64841, Oct. 20, 2010, as amended at 75 FR 71528, Nov. 24, 2010]

EFFECTIVE DATE NOTE: At 76 FR 79533, Dec. 22, 2011, § 704.6 was amended by removing paragraphs (c)(3) and (f)(4) and adding paragraph (h), effective Jan. 23, 2012. For the convenience of the user, the added text is set forth as follows:

§ 704.6   Credit risk management.

* * * * *

(h) Requirements for investment action plans. An investment is subject to the requirements of § 704.10 of this part if:

(1) An NRSRO that rates the investment downgrades that rating, after purchase, below the minimum rating requirements of this part; or

(2) The investment is part of an asset class or group of investments that exceeds the issuer, sector, or subsector concentration limits of this section. For purposes of measurement, each new credit transaction must be evaluated in terms of the corporate credit union's capital at the time of the transaction. An investment that fails a requirement of this section because of a subsequent reduction in capital will be deemed nonconforming. A corporate credit union is required to exercise reasonable efforts to bring nonconforming investments into conformity within 90 calendar days. Investments that remain nonconforming for more than 90 calendar days will be deemed to fail a requirement of this section and the corporate credit union will have to comply with § 704.10 of this part.

§ 704.7   Lending.

(a) *Policies.* A corporate credit union must operate according to a lending policy which addresses, at a minimum:

(1) Loan types and limits;

(2) Required documentation and collateral; and

(3) Analysis and monitoring standards.

(b) *General.* Each loan or line of credit limit will be determined after analyzing the financial and operational soundness of the borrower and the ability of the borrower to repay the loan.

(c) *Loans to members*—(1) *Credit unions.* (i) The maximum aggregate amount in unsecured loans and lines of credit to any one member credit union, excluding pass-through and guaranteed loans from the CLF and the NCUSIF, must not exceed 50 percent of capital.

(ii) The maximum aggregate amount in secured loans and lines of credit to any one member credit union, excluding those secured by shares or marketable securities and member reverse repurchase transactions, must not exceed 100 percent of capital.

(2) *Corporate CUSOs.* Any loan or line of credit must comply with § 704.11.

(3) *Other members.* The maximum aggregate amount of loans and lines of credit to any other one member must not exceed 15 percent of the corporate credit union's capital plus pledged shares.

(d) *Loans to nonmembers*—(1) *Credit unions.* A loan to a nonmember credit union, other than through a loan participation with another corporate credit union, is only permissible if the loan is for an overdraft related to the providing of correspondent services pursuant to § 704.12. Generally, such a loan will have a maturity of one business day.

(2) *Corporate CUSOs.* Any loan or line of credit must comply with § 704.11.

(e) *Member business loan rule.* Loans, lines of credit and letters of credit to:

(1) Member credit unions are exempt from part 723 of this chapter;

(2) Corporate CUSOs are not subject to part 723 of this chapter.

(3) Other members not excluded under § 723.1(b) of this chapter must comply with part 723 of this chapter unless the loan or line of credit is fully guaranteed by a credit union or fully secured by U.S. Treasury or agency securities. Those guaranteed and secured loans must comply with the aggregate limits of § 723.16 but are exempt from the other requirements of part 723.

(f) *Participation loans with other corporate credit unions.* A corporate credit union is permitted to participate in a loan with another corporate credit

§ 704.8

union provided the corporate retains an interest of at least 5 percent of the face amount of the loan and a master participation loan agreement is in place before the purchase or the sale of a participation. A participating corporate credit union must exercise the same due diligence as if it were the originating corporate credit union.

(g) *Prepayment penalties.* If provided for in the loan contract, a corporate credit union is authorized to assess prepayment penalties on loans.

[62 FR 12938, Mar. 19, 1997, as amended at 64 FR 57365, Oct. 25, 1999; 67 FR 65655, Oct. 25, 2002; 68 FR 56550, Oct. 1, 2003; 75 FR 34621, June 18, 2010]

§ 704.8 Asset and liability management.

(a) *Policies.* A corporate credit union must operate according to a written asset and liability management policy which addresses, at a minimum:

(1) The purpose and objectives of the corporate credit union's asset and liability activities;

(2) The maximum allowable percentage decline in net economic value (NEV), compared to base case NEV;

(3) The minimum allowable NEV ratio;

(4) Policy limits and specific test parameters for the NEV sensitivity analysis requirements set forth in paragraphs (d), (e), and (f) of this section;

(5) The modeling of indexes that serve as references in financial instrument coupon formulas; and

(6) The tests that will be used, prior to purchase, to estimate the impact of investments on the percentage decline in NEV compared to base case NEV. The most recent NEV analysis, as determined under paragraph (d)(1)(i) of this section may be used as a basis of estimation.

(b) *Asset and liability management committee (ALCO).* A corporate credit union's ALCO must have at least one member who is also a member of the board of directors. The ALCO must review asset and liability management reports on at least a monthly basis. These reports must address compliance with Federal Credit Union Act, NCUA Rules and Regulations (12 CFR chapter VII), and all related risk management policies.

(c) *Penalty for early withdrawals.* A corporate credit union that permits early certificate/share withdrawals must assess market-based penalties sufficient to cover the estimated replacement cost of the certificate redeemed. This means the minimum penalty must be reasonably related to the rate that the corporate credit union would be required to offer to attract funds for a similar term with similar characteristics.

(d) *Interest rate sensitivity analysis.* (1) A corporate credit union must:

(i) Evaluate the risk in its balance sheet by measuring, at least quarterly, including once on the last day of the calendar quarter, the impact of an instantaneous, permanent, and parallel shock in the yield curve of plus and minus 100, 200, and 300 BP on its NEV and NEV ratio. If the base case NEV ratio falls below 3 percent at the last testing date, these tests must be calculated at least monthly, including once on the last day of the month, until the base case NEV ratio again exceeds 3 percent;

(ii) Limit its risk exposure to levels that do not result in a base case NEV ratio or any NEV ratio resulting from the tests set forth in paragraph (d)(1)(i) of this section below 2 percent; and

(iii) Limit its risk exposures to levels that do not result in a decline in NEV of more than 15 percent.

(2) A corporate credit union must assess annually if it should conduct periodic additional tests to address market factors that may materially impact that corporate credit union's NEV. These factors should include, but are not limited to, the following:

(i) Changes in the shape of the Treasury yield curve;

(ii) Adjustments to prepayment projections used for amortizing securities to consider the impact of significantly faster/slower prepayment speeds; and

(iii) Adjustments to volatility assumptions to consider the impact that changing volatilities have on embedded option values.

(e) *Net interest income modeling.* A corporate credit union must perform net interest income (NII) modeling to project earnings in multiple interest rate environments for a period of no less than 2 years. NII modeling must,

National Credit Union Administration § 704.8

at minimum, be performed at least quarterly, including once on the last day of the calendar quarter.

(f) *Weighted average asset life.* The weighted average life (WAL) of a corporate credit union's loan and investment portfolio, excluding derivative contracts and equity investments, may not exceed 2 years. A corporate credit union must test its assets at least quarterly, including once on the last day of the calendar quarter, for compliance with this WAL limitation. When calculating its WAL, a corporate credit union must assume that no issuer or market options will be exercised. If the WAL of a corporate credit union's assets exceeds 2 years on the testing date, this test must be calculated at least monthly, including once on the last day of the month, until the WAL is below 2 years.

(g) *Weighted average asset life with 50 percent slowdown in prepayment speeds.* The weighted average life (WAL) of a corporate credit union's loan and investment portfolio, excluding derivative contracts and equity investments, may not exceed 2.25 years when prepayment speeds are reduced by 50 percent. A corporate credit union must test its investments at least quarterly, including once on the last day of the calendar quarter, for compliance with this WAL limitation. When calculating its WAL, a corporate credit union must assume that no issuer or market options will be exercised. If the WAL of a corporate credit union's assets exceeds 2.25 years, this test must be calculated at least monthly, including once on the last day of the month, until the WAL with the 50 slowdown in prepayment speeds is below 2.25 years.

(h) *Government issued or guaranteed securities.* The WAL of investments that are issued or fully guaranteed as to principal and interest by the U.S. government, its agencies or sponsored enterprises, including investments that are fully insured or guaranteed (including accumulated dividends and interest) by the NCUSIF or the Federal Deposit Insurance Corporation, will be multiplied by a factor of 0.50 for purposes of the WAL tests of paragraphs (f) and (g) of this section.

(i) *Effective and spread durations.* A corporate credit union must measure at least once a quarter, including once on the last day of the calendar quarter, the effective duration and spread durations of each of its assets and liabilities, where the values of these are affected by changes in interest rates or credit spreads.

(j) *Regulatory violations.* (1)(i) If a corporate credit union's decline in NEV, base case NEV ratio or any NEV ratio resulting from the test set forth in paragraph (d) of this section violates the limits established in that paragraph, or the corporate credit union is unable to satisfy the tests in paragraphs (f) or (g) of this section; and

(ii) The corporate cannot adjust its balance sheet so as to satisfy the requirements of paragraphs (d), (f), or (g) of this section within 10 calendar days after detecting the violation, then:

(iii) The operating management of the corporate credit union must immediately report this information to its board of directors, supervisory committee, and the NCUA.

(2) If any violation described in paragraph (j)(1)(i) persists for 30 or more calendar days, the corporate credit union:

(i) Must immediately submit a detailed, written action plan to the NCUA that sets forth the time needed and means by which it intends to correct the violation and, if the NCUA determines that the plan is unacceptable, the corporate credit union must immediately restructure its balance sheet to bring the exposure back within compliance or adhere to an alternative course of action determined by the NCUA; and

(ii) If presently categorized as adequately capitalized or well capitalized for PCA purposes, immediately be recategorized as undercapitalized until the violation is corrected, and

(iii) If presently less than adequately capitalized, immediately be downgraded one additional capital category.

(k) *Overall limit on business generated from individual credit unions.* On or after April 22, 2013, a corporate credit union is prohibited from accepting from any member, or any nonmember credit union, any investment, including shares, loans, PCC, or NCAs if, following that investment, the aggregate of all investments from that entity in the corporate would exceed 15 percent

§ 704.9

of the corporate credit union's moving daily average net assets.

[75 FR 64842, Oct. 20, 2010]

EFFECTIVE DATE NOTE: At 76 FR 79533, Dec. 22, 2011, §704.8 was amended by revising the first two sentences in paragraphs (f) and (g); and revising (j)(2)(ii) and (iii), effective Jan. 23, 2012. For the convenience of the user, the revised text is set forth as follows:

§ 704.8 Asset and liability management.

* * * * *

(f) * * * The weighted average life (WAL) of a corporate credit union's financial assets, consisting of cash, investments, and loans, but excluding derivative contracts and equity investments, may not exceed 2 years. A corporate credit union must test its financial assets at least quarterly, including once on the last day of the calendar quarter, for compliance with this WAL limitation. * * *

(g) * * * The weighted average life (WAL) of a corporate credit union's financial assets, consisting of cash, investments, and loans, but excluding derivative contracts and equity investments, may not exceed 2.25 years when prepayment speeds are reduced by 50 percent. A corporate credit union must test its financial assets at least quarterly, including once on the last day of the calendar quarter, for compliance with this WAL limitation. * * *

* * * * *

(j) * * *
(2) * * *

(ii) If presently categorized as adequately capitalized or well capitalized for prompt corrective action purposes, and the violation was of paragraph (d) of this section, immediately be recategorized as undercapitalized until the violation is corrected, and

(iii) If presently categorized as less than adequately capitalized, and the violation was of paragraph (d) of this section, immediately be downgraded one additional capital category.

* * * * *

§ 704.9 Liquidity management.

(a) *General.* In the management of liquidity, a corporate credit union must:

(1) Evaluate the potential liquidity needs of its membership in a variety of economic scenarios;

(2) Regularly monitor and demonstrate accessibility to sources of internal and external liquidity;

(3) Keep a sufficient amount of cash and cash equivalents on hand to support its payment system obligations;

(4) Demonstrate that the accounting classification of investment securities is consistent with its ability to meet potential liquidity demands; and

(5) Develop a contingency funding plan that addresses alternative funding strategies in successively deteriorating liquidity scenarios. The plan must:

(i) List all sources of liquidity, by category and amount, that are available to service an immediate outflow of funds in various liquidity scenarios;

(ii) Analyze the impact that potential changes in fair value will have on the disposition of assets in a variety of interest rate scenarios; and

(iii) Be reviewed by the board or an appropriate committee no less frequently than annually or as market or business conditions dictate.

(b) *Borrowing limits.* A corporate credit union may borrow up to the lower of 10 times capital or 50 percent of capital and shares (excluding shares created by the use of member reverse repurchase agreements).

(1) *Secured borrowings.* A corporate credit union may borrow on a secured basis for liquidity purposes, but the maturity of the borrowing may not exceed 30 days. Only a credit union with core capital in excess of five percent of its moving DANA may borrow on a secured basis for nonliquidity purposes, and the outstanding amount of secured borrowing for nonliquidity purposes may not exceed an amount equal to the difference between core capital and five percent of moving DANA.

(2) *Exclusions.* CLF borrowings and borrowed funds created by the use of member reverse repurchase agreements are excluded from this limit.

[75 FR 64843, Oct. 20, 2010]

§ 704.10 Investment action plan.

(a) Any corporate credit union in possession of an investment, including a derivative, that fails to meet a requirement of this part must, within 30 calendar days of the failure, report the failed investment to its board of directors, supervisory committee and the OCCU Director. If the corporate credit union does not sell the failed investment, and the investment continues to

National Credit Union Administration §704.11

fail to meet a requirement of this part, the corporate credit union must, within 30 calendar days of the failure, provide to the OCCU Director a written action plan that addresses:

(1) The investment's characteristics and risks;

(2) The process to obtain and adequately evaluate the investment's market pricing, cash flows, and risk;

(3) How the investment fits into the credit union's asset and liability management strategy;

(4) The impact that either holding or selling the investment will have on the corporate credit union's earnings, liquidity, and capital in different interest rate environments; and

(5) The likelihood that the investment may again pass the requirements of this part.

(b) The OCCU Director may require, for safety and soundness reasons, a shorter time period for plan development than that set forth in paragraph (a) of this section.

(c) If the plan described in paragraph (a) of this section is not approved by the OCCU Director, the credit union must adhere to the OCCU Director's directed course of action.

[62 FR 12938, Mar. 19, 1997, as amended at 67 FR 65656, 65659, Oct. 25, 2002]

§704.11 Corporate Credit Union Service Organizations (Corporate CUSOs).

(a) A corporate CUSO is an entity that:

(1) Is at least partly owned by a corporate credit union;

(2) Primarily serves credit unions;

(3) Restricts its services to those related to the normal course of business of credit unions as specified in paragraph (e) of this section; and

(4) Is structured as a corporation, limited liability company, or limited partnership under state law.

(b) *Investment and loan limitations.* (1) The aggregate of all investments in member and non-member corporate CUSOs must not exceed 15 percent of a corporate credit union's capital.

(2) The aggregate of all investments in and loans to member and non-member corporate CUSOs must not exceed 30 percent of a corporate credit union's capital. A corporate credit union may lend to member and non-member corporate CUSOs an additional 15 percent of capital if the loan is collateralized by assets in which the corporate has a perfected security interest under state law.

(3) If the limitations in paragraphs (b)(1) and (b)(2) of this section are reached or exceeded because of the profitability of the CUSO and the related GAAP valuation of the investment under the equity method without an additional cash outlay by the corporate, divestiture is not required. A corporate credit union may continue to invest up to the regulatory limit without regard to the increase in the GAAP valuation resulting from the corporate CUSO's profitability.

(c) *Due diligence.* A corporate credit union must comply with the due diligence requirements of §§723.5 and 723.6(f) through (j) of this chapter for all loans to corporate CUSOs. This requirement does not apply to loans excluded under §723.1(b).

(d) *Separate entity.* (1) A corporate CUSO must be operated as an entity separate from a corporate credit union.

(2) A corporate credit union investing in or lending to a corporate CUSO must obtain a written legal opinion that concludes the corporate CUSO is organized and operated in a manner that the corporate credit union will not reasonably be held liable for the obligations of the corporate CUSO. This opinion must address factors that have led courts to "pierce the corporate veil," such as inadequate capitalization, lack of corporate identity, common boards of directors and employees, control of one entity over another, and lack of separate books and records.

(e). *Permissible activities.* (1) Beginning on April 18, 2011, a corporate CUSO must agree to limit its activities to:

(i) Brokerage services,

(ii) Investment advisory services, and

(iii) Other categories of activities as approved in writing by NCUA and published on NCUA's Web site.

(2) A corporate credit union must divest from any CUSO that is engaged in activities not approved by NCUA under paragraph (e)(1) of this section. A corporate credit union may take until October 20, 2011 to divest itself from a

CUSO engaging in one or more unapproved activities, but only if the CUSO was engaging in those activities before October 20, 2010 and the corporate credit union can establish that those activities satisfied the requirements of this section as it existed before October 20, 2010.

(3) Once NCUA has approved an activity and published that activity on its Web site as provided for in paragraph (e)(1)(iii) of this section, NCUA will not remove that particular activity the approved list, or make substantial changes to the content or description of that approved activity, except through the formal rulemaking process.

(f) An official of a corporate credit union which has invested in or loaned to a corporate CUSO may not receive, either directly or indirectly, any salary, commission, investment income, or other income, compensation, or consideration from the corporate CUSO. This prohibition also extends to immediate family members of officials.

(g) Prior to making an investment in or loan to a corporate CUSO, a corporate credit union must obtain a written agreement that the CUSO:

(1) Will follow GAAP;

(2) Will provide financial statements to the corporate credit union at least quarterly;

(3) Will obtain an annual CPA opinion audit and provide a copy to the corporate credit union. A wholly owned or majority owned CUSO is not required to obtain a separate annual audit if it is included in the corporate credit union's annual consolidated audit;

(4) Will not acquire control, directly or indirectly, of another depository financial institution or to invest in shares, stocks, or obligations of an insurance company, trade association, liquidity facility, or similar organization;

(5) Will allow the auditor, board of directors, and NCUA complete access to the CUSO's personnel, facilities, equipment, books, records, and any other documentation that the auditor, directors, or NCUA deem pertinent;

(6) Will inform the corporate, at least quarterly, of all the compensation paid by the CUSO to its employees who are also employees of the corporate credit union; and

(7) Will comply with all the requirements of this section.

(h) Corporate credit union authority to invest in or loan to a CUSO is limited to that provided in this section. A corporate credit union is not authorized to invest in or loan to a CUSO under part 712 of this chapter.

[75 FR 64843, Oct. 20, 2010, as amended at 76 FR 23868, Apr. 29, 2011]

§ 704.12 **Permissible services.**

(a) *Preapproved services.* A corporate credit union may provide to members the preapproved services set out in this section. NCUA may at any time, based upon supervisory, legal, or safety and soundness reasons, limit or prohibit any preapproved service. The specific activities listed within each preapproved category are provided as illustrations of activities permissible under the particular category, not as an exclusive or exhaustive list.

(1) *Correspondent services agreement.* A corporate credit union may only provide financial services to nonmembers through a correspondent services agreement. A correspondent services agreement is an agreement between two corporate credit unions, whereby one of the corporate credit unions agrees to provide services to the other corporate credit union or its members.

(2) *Credit and investment services.* Credit and investment services are advisory and consulting activities that assist the member in lending or investment management. These services may include loan reviews, investment portfolio reviews and investment advisory services.

(3) *Electronic financial services.* Electronic financial services are any services, products, functions, or activities that a corporate credit union is otherwise authorized to perform, provide or deliver to its members but performed through electronic means. Electronic services may include automated teller machines, online transaction processing through a website, website hosting services, account aggregation services, and internet access services to perform or deliver products or services to members.

National Credit Union Administration

§ 704.13

(4) *Excess capacity.* Excess capacity is the excess use or capacity remaining in facilities, equipment or services that: a corporate credit union properly invested in or established, in good faith, with the intent of serving its members; and it reasonably anticipates will be taken up by the future expansion of services to its members. A corporate credit union may sell or lease the excess capacity in facilities, equipment or services, such as office space, employees and data processing.

(5) *Liquidity and asset and liability management.* Liquidity and asset and liability management services are any services, functions or activities that assist the member in liquidity and balance sheet management. These services may include liquidity planning and balance sheet modeling and analysis.

(6) *Operational services.* Operational services are services established to deliver financial products and services that enhance member service and promote safe and sound operations. Operational services may include tax payment, electronic fund transfers and providing coin and currency service.

(7) *Payment systems.* Payment systems are any methods used to facilitate the movement of funds for transactional purposes. Payment systems may include Automated Clearing House, wire transfer, item processing and settlement services.

(8) *Trustee or custodial services.* Trustee services are services in which the corporate credit union is authorized to act under a written trust agreement to the extent permitted under part 724 of this chapter. Custodial and safekeeping services are services a corporate credit union performs on behalf of its member to act as custodian or safekeeper of investments.

(b) *Procedure for adding services that are not preapproved.* To provide a service to its members that is not preapproved by NCUA:

(1) A federal corporate credit union must request approval from NCUA. The request must include a full explanation and complete documentation of the service and how the service relates to a corporate credit union's authority to provide services to its members. The request must be submitted jointly to the OCCU Director and the Secretary of the Board. The request will be treated as a petition to amend § 704.12 and NCUA will request public comment or otherwise act on the petition within a reasonable period of time. Before engaging in the formal approval process, a corporate credit union should seek an advisory opinion from NCUA's Office of General Counsel as to whether a proposed service is already covered by one of the authorized categories without filing a petition to amend the regulation; and

(2) A state-chartered corporate credit union must submit a request for a waiver that complies with § 704.1(b) to the OCCU Director.

(c) *Prohibition.* A corporate credit union is prohibited from purchasing loan servicing rights.

[67 FR 65656, Oct. 25, 2002]

§ 704.13 Board responsibilities.

(a) *General.* A corporate credit union's board of directors must approve comprehensive written strategic plans and policies, review them annually, and provide them upon request to the auditors, supervisory committee, and NCUA.

(b) *Policies.* A corporate credit union's policies must be commensurate with the scope and complexity of the corporate credit union.

(c) *Other requirements.* The board of directors of a corporate credit union must ensure:

(1) Senior managers have an in-depth, working knowledge of their direct areas of responsibility and are capable of identifying, hiring, and retaining qualified staff;

(2) Qualified personnel are employed or under contract for all line support and audit areas, and designated back-up personnel or resources with adequate cross-training are in place;

(3) GAAP is followed, except where law or regulation has provided for a departure from GAAP;

(4) Accurate balance sheets, income statements, and internal risk assessments (*e.g.*, risk management measures of liquidity, market, and credit risk associated with current activities) are produced timely in accordance with §§ 704.6, 704.8, and 704.9;

(5) Systems are audited periodically in accordance with industry-established standards;

(6) Financial performance is evaluated to ensure that the objectives of the corporate credit union and the responsibilities of management are met;

(7) Planning addresses the retention of external consultants, as appropriate, to review the adequacy of technical, human, and financial resources dedicated to support major risk areas; and

(8) For each item before the board, the meeting minutes list the names of directors and their votes, as well as the names of any directors who did not vote, except that if the minutes include a complete list of directors attending the meeting, the vote tally need only list the names of directors who voted against the item or who abstained.

[62 FR 12938, Mar. 19, 1997, as amended at 67 FR 65654, Oct. 25, 2002. Redesignated at 75 FR 64836, Oct. 20, 2010; 76 FR 23868, Apr. 29, 2011]

§ 704.14 Representation.

(a) *Board representation.* The board will be determined as stipulated in its bylaws governing election procedures, provided that:

(1) At least a majority of directors, including the chair of the board, must serve on the board as representatives of member credit unions;

(2) On or after February 17, 2011, only individuals who currently hold the position of chief executive officer, chief financial officer, chief operating officer, or treasurer/manager at a member may seek election or re-election to the board;

(3) No individual may be elected or appointed to serve on the board if, after such election or appointment, the individual would be a director at more than one corporate credit union;

(4) No individual may be elected or appointed to serve on the board if, after such election or appointment, any member of the corporate credit union would have more than one representative on the board of the corporate;

(5) The chair of the board may not serve simultaneously as an officer, director, or employee of a credit union trade association;

(6) A majority of directors may not serve simultaneously as officers, directors, or employees of the same credit union trade association or its affiliates (not including chapters or other subunits of a state trade association);

(7) For purposes of meeting the requirements of paragraphs (a)(5) and (a)(6) of this section, an individual may not serve as a director or chair of the board if that individual holds a subordinate employment relationship to another employee who serves as an officer, director, or employee of a credit union trade association;

(8) In the case of a corporate credit union whose membership is composed of more than 25 percent non credit unions, the majority of directors serving as representatives of member credit unions, including the chair, must be elected only by member credit unions, and

(9) After October 21, 2013, at least a majority of directors of every corporate credit union, including the chair of the board, must serve on the board as representatives of natural person credit union members.

(b) *Credit union trade association.* As used in this section, a credit union trade association includes but is not limited to, state credit union leagues and league service corporations and national credit union trade associations.

(c) *Representatives of organizational members.* (1) An organizational member of a corporate credit union is a member that is not a natural person. An organizational member may appoint one of its members or officials as a representative to the corporate credit union. The representative shall be empowered to attend membership meetings, to vote, and to stand for election on behalf of the member. No individual may serve as the representative of more than one organizational member in the same corporate credit union.

(2) Any vacancy on the board of a corporate credit union caused by a representative being unable to complete his or her term shall be filled by the board of the corporate credit union according to its bylaws governing the filling of board vacancies.

(d) *Recusal provision.* (1) No director, committee member, officer, or employee of a corporate credit union shall in any manner, directly or indirectly, participate in the deliberation upon or

National Credit Union Administration
§ 704.15

the determination of any question affecting his or her pecuniary interest or the pecuniary interest of any entity (other than the corporate credit union) in which he or she is interested, except if the matter involves general policy applicable to all members, such as setting dividend or loan rates or fees for services.

(2) An individual is "interested" in an entity if he or she:

(i) Serves as a director, officer, or employee of the entity;

(ii) Has a business, ownership, or deposit relationship with the entity; or

(iii) Has a business, financial, or familial relationship with an individual whom he or she knows has a pecuniary interest in the entity.

(3) In the event of the disqualification of any directors, by operation of paragraph (c)(1) of this section, the remaining qualified directors present at the meeting, if constituting a quorum with the disqualified directors, may exercise, by majority vote, all the powers of the board with respect to the matter under consideration. Where all of the directors are disqualified, the matter must be decided by the members of the corporate credit union.

(4) In the event of the disqualification of any committee member by operation of paragraph (c)(1) of this section, the remaining qualified committee members, if constituting a quorum with the disqualified committee members, may exercise, by majority vote, all the powers of the committee with respect to the matter under consideration. Where all of the committee members are disqualified, the matter shall be decided by the board of directors.

(e) *Administration.* (1) A corporate credit union shall be under the direction and control of its board of directors. While the board may delegate the performance of administrative duties, the board is not relieved of its responsibility for their performance. The board may employ a chief executive officer who shall have such authority and such powers as delegated by the board to conduct business from day to day. Such chief executive officer must answer solely to the board of the corporate credit union, and may not be an employee of a credit union trade association.

(2) The provisions of § 701.14 of this chapter apply to corporate credit unions, except that where "Regional Director" is used, read "NCUA Board."

[62 FR 12938, Mar. 19, 1997, as amended at 67 FR 65657, Oct. 25, 2002; 75 FR 64844, Oct. 20, 2010]

§ 704.15 Audit and reporting requirements.

(a) *Annual reporting requirements*—(1) *Audited financial statements.* A corporate credit union must prepare annual financial statements in accordance with generally accepted accounting principles (GAAP), which must be audited by an independent public accountant in accordance with generally accepted auditing standards. The annual financial statements and regulatory reports must reflect all material correcting adjustments necessary to conform with GAAP that were identified by the corporate credit union's independent public accountant.

(2) *Management report.* Each corporate credit union must prepare, as of the end of the previous calendar year, an annual management report that contains the following:

(i) A statement of management's responsibilities for preparing the corporate credit union's annual financial statements, for establishing and maintaining an adequate internal control structure and procedures for financial reporting, and for complying with laws and regulations relating to safety and soundness in the following areas: affiliate transactions, legal lending limits, loans to insiders, restrictions on capital and share dividends, and regulatory reporting that meets full and fair disclosure;

(ii) An assessment by management of the corporate credit union's compliance with such laws and regulations during the past calendar year. The assessment must state management's conclusion as to whether the corporate credit union has complied with the designated safety and soundness laws and regulations during the calendar year and disclose any noncompliance with the laws and regulations; and

(iii) Beginning on and after January 1, 2013, an assessment by management

§ 704.15

of the effectiveness of the corporate credit union's internal control structure and procedures as of the end of the past calendar year that must include the following:

(A) A statement identifying the internal control framework used by management to evaluate the effectiveness of the corporate credit union's internal control over financial reporting;

(B) A statement that the assessment included controls over the preparation of regulatory financial statements in accordance with regulatory reporting instructions including identification of such regulatory reporting instructions; and

(C) A statement expressing management's conclusion as to whether the corporate credit union's internal control over financial reporting is effective as of the end of the previous calendar year. Management must disclose all material weaknesses in internal control over financial reporting, if any, that it has identified that have not been remediated prior to the calendar year-end. Management may not conclude that the corporate credit union's internal control over financial reporting is effective if there are one or more material weaknesses.

(3) *Management report signatures.* The chief executive officer and either the chief accounting officer or chief financial officer of the corporate credit union must sign the management report.

(b) *Independent public accountant*—(1) *Annual audit of financial statements.* Each corporate credit union must engage an independent public accountant to audit and report on its annual financial statements in accordance with generally accepted auditing standards. The scope of the audit engagement must be sufficient to permit such accountant to determine and report whether the financial statements are presented fairly and in accordance with GAAP. A corporate credit union must provide its independent public accountant with a copy of its most recent Call Report and NCUA examination report. It must also provide its independent public accountant with copies of any notice that its capital category is being changed or reclassified and any correspondence from NCUA regarding compliance with this section.

(2) *Internal control over financial reporting.* Beginning on and after January 1, 2014, the independent public accountant who audits the corporate credit union's financial statements must examine, attest to, and report separately on the assertion of management concerning the effectiveness of the corporate credit union's internal control structure and procedures for financial reporting. The attestation and report must be made in accordance with generally accepted standards for attestation engagements. The accountant's report must not be dated prior to the date of the management report and management's assessment of the effectiveness of internal control over financial reporting. Notwithstanding the requirements set forth in applicable professional standards, the accountant's report must include the following:

(i) A statement identifying the internal control framework used by the independent public accountant, which must be the same as the internal control framework used by management, to evaluate the effectiveness of the corporate credit union's internal control over financial reporting;

(ii) A statement that the independent public accountant's evaluation included controls over the preparation of regulatory financial statements in accordance with regulatory reporting instructions including identification of such regulatory reporting instructions; and

(iii) A statement expressing the independent public accountant's conclusion as to whether the corporate credit union's internal control over financial reporting is effective as of the end of the previous calendar year. The report must disclose all material weaknesses in internal control over financial reporting that the independent public accountant has identified that have not been remediated prior to the calendar year-end. The independent public accountant may not conclude that the corporate credit union's internal control over financial reporting is effective if there are one or more material weaknesses.

National Credit Union Administration
§ 704.15

(3) *Notice by accountant of termination of services.* An independent public accountant performing an audit under this part who ceases to be the accountant for a corporate credit union must notify NCUA in writing of such termination within 15 days after the occurrence of such event and set forth in reasonable detail the reasons for such termination.

(4) *Communications with supervisory committee.* In addition to the requirements for communications with audit committees set forth in applicable professional standards, the independent public accountant must report the following on a timely basis to the supervisory committee:

(i) All critical accounting policies and practices to be used by the corporate credit union;

(ii) All alternative accounting treatments within GAAP for policies and practices related to material items that the independent public accountant has discussed with management, including the ramifications of the use of such alternative disclosures and treatments, and the treatment preferred by the independent public accountant; and

(iii) Other written communications the independent public accountant has provided to management, such as a management letter or schedule of unadjusted differences.

(5) *Retention of working papers.* The independent public accountant must retain the working papers related to the audit of the corporate credit union's financial statements and, if applicable, the evaluation of the corporate credit union's internal control over financial reporting for seven years from the report release date, unless a longer period of time is required by law.

(6) *Independence.* The independent public accountant must comply with the independence standards and interpretations of the American Institute of Certified Public Accountants (AICPA).

(7) *Peer reviews and inspection reports.* (i) Prior to commencing any services for a corporate credit union under this section, the independent public accountant must have received a peer review, or be enrolled in a peer review program, that meets acceptable guidelines. Acceptable peer reviews include peer reviews performed in accordance with the AICPA's Peer Review Standards and inspections conducted by the Public Company Accounting Oversight Board (PCAOB).

(ii) Within 15 days of receiving notification that the AICPA has accepted a peer review or the PCAOB has issued an inspection report, or before commencing any audit under this section, whichever is earlier, the independent public accountant must file a copy of the most recent peer review report and the public portion of the most recent PCAOB inspection report, if any, accompanied by any letters of comments, response, and acceptance, with NCUA if the report has not already been filed.

(iii) Within 15 days of the PCAOB making public a previously nonpublic portion of an inspection report, the independent public accountant must file a copy of the previously nonpublic portion of the inspection report with NCUA.

(c) *Filing and notice requirements*—(1) *Annual Report.* Each corporate credit union must, no later than 180 days after the end of the calendar year, file an Annual Report with NCUA consisting of the following documents:

(i) The audited comparative annual financial statements;

(ii) The independent public accountant's report on the audited financial statements;

(iii) The management report; and

(iv) The independent public accountant's attestation report on management's assessment concerning the corporate credit union's internal control structure and procedures for financial reporting.

(2) *Public availability.* The annual report in paragraph (c)(1) of this section will be made available by NCUA for public inspection.

(3) *Independent public accountant's letters and reports.* Each corporate credit union must file with NCUA a copy of any management letter or other report issued by its independent public accountant with respect to such corporate credit union and the services provided by such accountant pursuant to this part (except for the independent public accountant's reports that are included in the Annual Report) within 15 days after receipt by the corporate

§ 704.15

credit union. Such reports include, but are not limited to:

(i) Any written communication regarding matters that are required to be communicated to the supervisory committee (for example, critical accounting policies, alternative accounting treatments discussed with management, and any schedule of unadjusted differences); and

(ii) Any written communication of significant deficiencies and material weaknesses in internal control required by the AICPA's auditing standards.

(4) *Notice of engagement or change of accountants.* Each corporate credit union that engages an independent public accountant, or that loses an independent public accountant through dismissal or resignation, must notify NCUA within 15 days after the engagement, dismissal, or resignation. The corporate credit union must include with the notice a reasonably detailed statement of the reasons for any dismissal or resignation. The corporate credit union must also provide a copy of the notice to the independent public accountant at the same time the notice is filed with NCUA.

(5) *Notification of late filing.* A corporate credit union that is unable to timely file any part of its Annual Report or any other report or notice required by this paragraph (c) must submit a written notice of late filing to NCUA. The notice must disclose the corporate credit union's inability to timely file all or specified portions of its Annual Report or other report or notice and the reasons therefore in reasonable detail. The late filing notice must also state the date by which the report or notice will be filed. The written notice must be filed with NCUA before the deadline for filing the Annual Report or any other report or notice, as appropriate. NCUA may take appropriate enforcement action for failure to timely file any report, or notice of late filing, required by this section.

(6) *Report to Members.* A corporate credit union must submit a preliminary Annual Report to the membership at the next calendar year's annual meeting.

(d) *Supervisory committee.*—(1) *Composition.* Each corporate credit union must establish a supervisory committee, all of whose members must independent. A committee member is independent if:

(i) Neither the committee member, nor any immediate family member of the committee member, is supervised by, or has any material business or professional relationship with, the chief executive officer (CEO) of the corporate credit union, or anyone directly or indirectly supervised by the CEO, and

(ii) Neither the committee member, nor any immediate family member of the committee member, has had any of the relationships described in paragraph (d)(1)(i) for at least the past three years.

(2) *Duties.* In addition to any duties specified under the corporate credit union's bylaws and these regulations, the duties of the credit union's supervisory committee include the appointment, compensation, and oversight of the independent public accountant who performs services required under this section and reviewing with management and the independent public accountant the basis for all the reports prepared and issued under this section. The supervisory committee must submit the audited comparative annual financial statements and the independent public accountant's report on those statements to the corporate credit union's board of directors.

(3) *Independent public accountant engagement letters.* (i) In performing its duties with respect to the appointment of the corporate credit union's independent public accountant, the supervisory committee must ensure that engagement letters and/or any related agreements with the independent public accountant for services to be performed under this section:

(A) Obligate the independent public accountant to comply with the requirements of paragraph (b) of this section (including, but not limited to, the notice of termination of services, communications with the supervisory committee, and notifications of peer reviews and inspection reports); and

(B) Do not contain any limitation of liability provisions that:

(*1*) Indemnify the independent public accountant against claims made by third parties;

(2) Hold harmless or release the independent public accountant from liability for claims or potential claims that might be asserted by the client corporate credit union, other than claims for punitive damages; or

(3) Limit the remedies available to the client corporate credit union.

(ii) Engagement letters may include alternative dispute resolution agreements and jury trial waiver provisions provided that the letters do not incorporate any limitation of liability provisions set forth in paragraph (d)(3)(i)(B) of this section.

(4) *Outside counsel.* The supervisory committee of any corporate credit union must, when deemed necessary by the committee, have access to its own outside counsel.

(e) *Internal audit.* A corporate credit union with average daily assets in excess of $400 million for the preceding calendar year, or as ordered by NCUA, must employ or contract, on a full- or part-time basis, the services of an internal auditor. The internal auditor's responsibilities will, at a minimum, comply with the Standards and Professional Practices of Internal Auditing, as established by the Institute of Internal Auditors. The internal auditor will report directly to the chair of the corporate credit union's supervisory committee, who may delegate supervision of the internal auditor's daily activities to the chief executive officer of the corporate credit union. The internal auditor's reports, findings, and recommendations will be in writing and presented to the supervisory committee no less than quarterly, and will be provided upon request to the IPA and NCUA.

[76 FR 23868, Apr. 29, 2011]

§ 704.16 Contracts/written agreements.

Services, facilities, personnel, or equipment shared with any party shall be supported by a written contract, with the duties and responsibilities of each party specified and the allocation of service fee/expenses fully supported and documented.

§ 704.17 State-chartered corporate credit unions.

(a) This part does not expand the powers and authorities of any state-chartered corporate credit union, beyond those powers and authorities provided under the laws of the state in which it was chartered.

(b) A state-chartered corporate credit union that is not insured by the NCUSIF, but that receives funds from federally insured credit unions, is considered an "institution-affiliated party" within the meaning of Section 206(r) of the Federal Credit Union Act, 12 U.S.C. 1786(r).

(c) NCUA will notify, consult with, and provide explanation to the appropriate state supervisory authority before taking administrative action against a state-chartered corporate credit union.

§ 704.18 Fidelity bond coverage.

(a) *Scope.* This section provides the fidelity bond requirements for employees and officials in corporate credit unions.

(b) *Review of coverage.* The board of directors of each corporate credit union shall, at least annually, carefully review the bond coverage in force to determine its adequacy in relation to risk exposure and to the minimum requirements in this section.

(c) *Minimum coverage; approved forms.* Every corporate credit union will maintain bond coverage with a company holding a certificate of authority from the Secretary of the Treasury. All bond forms, and any riders and endorsements which limit the coverage provided by approved bond forms, must receive the prior written approval of NCUA. Fidelity bonds must provide coverage for the fraud and dishonesty of all employees, directors, officers, and supervisory and credit committee members. Notwithstanding the foregoing, all bonds must include a provision, in a form approved by NCUA, requiring written notification by surety to NCUA:

(1) When the bond of a credit union is terminated in its entirety;

(2) When bond coverage is terminated, by issuance of a written notice, on an employee, director, officer, supervisory or credit committee member; or

(3) When a deductible is increased above permissible limits. Said notification shall be sent to NCUA and shall

§ 704.19

include a brief statement of cause for termination or increase.

(d) *Minimum coverage amounts.* (1) The minimum amount of bond coverage will be computed based on the corporate credit union's daily average net assets for the preceding calendar year. The following table lists the minimum requirements:

Daily average net assets	Minimum bond (million)
Less than $50 million	$1.0
$50–$99 million	2.0
$100–$499 million	4.0
$500–$999 million	6.0
$1.0–$1.999 billion	8.0
$2.0–$4.999 billion	10.0
$5.0–$9.999 billion	15.0
$10.0–$24.999 billion	20.0
$25.0 billion plus	25.0

(2) It is the duty of the board of directors of each corporate credit union to provide adequate protection to meet its unique circumstances by obtaining, when necessary, bond coverage in excess of the minimums in the table in paragraph (d)(1) of this section.

(e) *Deductibles.* (1) The maximum amount of deductibles allowed are based on the corporate credit union's core capital ratio. The following table sets out the maximum deductibles, except that in each category the maximum deductible shall be $5 million:

Core capital ratio	Maximum deductible
Less than 1.0 percent	7.5 percent of the sum of retained earnings and paid-in capital.
1.0–1.74 percent	10.0 percent of the sum of retained earnings and paid-in capital
1.75–2.24 percent	12.0 percent of the sum of retained earnings and paid-in capital.
Greater than 2.25 percent	15.0 percent of the sum of retained earnings and paid-in capital.

(2) A deductible may be applied separately to one or more insuring clauses in a blanket bond. Deductibles in excess of those showing in this section must have the written approval of NCUA at least 30 calendar days prior to the effective date of the deductibles.

(f) *Additional coverage.* NCUA may require additional coverage for any corporate credit union when, in the opinion of NCUA, current coverage is insufficient. The board of directors of the corporate credit union must obtain additional coverage within 30 calendar days after the date of written notice from NCUA.

[62 FR 12938, Mar. 19, 1997, as amended at 67 FR 65657, Oct. 25, 2002]

EFFECTIVE DATE NOTE: At 76 FR 79533, Dec. 22, 2011, § 704.18 was amended by revising the table in paragraph (e)(1), effective Jan. 23, 2012. For the convenience of the user, the revised text is set forth as follows:

§ 704.18 Fidelity bond coverage.

* * * * *

(e) * * *
(1) * * *

Core capital ratio	Maximum deductible
Less than 1.0 percent	7.5 percent of core capital.
1.0–1.74 percent	10.0 percent of core capital.
1.75–2.24 percent	12.0 percent of core capital.
Greater than 2.25 percent	15.0 percent of core capital.

* * * * *

§ 704.19 Disclosure of executive and director compensation.

(a) *Annual disclosure.* A corporate credit union must annually prepare and maintain a disclosure of the dollar amount of compensation paid to its most highly compensated employees, including compensation from any corporate CUSO in which the corporate has invested or made a loan, in accordance with the following schedule:

(1) For corporate credit unions with forty-one or more full time employees, disclosure is required of the compensation paid to the five most highly compensated employees;

(2) For corporate credit unions with between thirty and forty-one full time employees, disclosure is required of the compensation paid to the four most highly compensated employees;

(3) For corporate credit unions with thirty or fewer full time employees, disclosure is required of the compensation paid to the three most highly compensated employees; and

(4) In all cases, compensation paid to the corporate credit union's chief executive officer must also be disclosed, if the chief executive officer is not already included among the most highly compensated employees described in paragraphs (a)(1) through (a)(3) of this section.

(b) *Availability of disclosure.* Any member may obtain a copy of the most current disclosure, and all disclosures for the previous three years, on request made in person or in writing. The corporate credit union must provide the disclosure(s), at no cost to the member, within five business days of receiving the request. In addition, the corporate must distribute the most current disclosure to all its members at least once a year, either in the annual report or in some other manner of the corporate's choosing.

(c) *Supplemental information.* In providing the disclosure required by this section, a corporate credit union may also provide supplementary information to put the disclosure in context, for example, salary surveys, a discussion of compensation in relation to other credit union expenses, or compensation information from similarly sized credit unions or financial institutions.

(d) *Special rule for mergers.* With respect to any merger involving a corporate credit union that would result in a material increase in compensation, *i.e.*, an increase of more than 15 percent or $10,000, whichever is greater, for any senior executive officer or director of the merging corporate, the corporate must:

(1) Describe the compensation arrangement in the merger plan documents submitted to NCUA for approval of the merger, pursuant to § 708b of this part; and

(2) In the case of any federally chartered corporate credit union, describe the compensation arrangement in the materials provided to the membership of the merging credit union before the member vote on approving the merger.

[75 FR 64844, Oct. 20, 2010, as amended at 76 FR 23871, Apr. 29, 2011]

EFFECTIVE DATE NOTE: At 76 FR 79534, Dec. 22, 2011, § 704.19 was amended by revising the section heading, effective Jan. 23, 2012. For the convenience of the user, the revised text is set forth as follows:

§ 704.19 Disclosure of executive compensation.

* * * * *

APPENDIX A TO PART 704—CAPITAL PRIORITIZATION AND MODEL FORMS

PART I—OPTIONAL CAPITAL PRIORITIZATION

Notwithstanding any other provision in this chapter, a corporate credit union, at its option, may determine that capital contributed to the corporate on or after January 18, 2011 will have priority, for purposes of availability to absorb losses and payout in liquidation, over capital contributed to the corporate before that date. The board of directors at a corporate credit union that desires to make this determination must:

(a) On or before January 18, 2011, adopt a resolution implementing its determination.

(b) Inform the credit union's members and NCUA, in writing and as soon as practicable after adoption of the resolution, of the contents of the board resolution.

(c) Ensure the credit union uses the appropriate initial and periodic Model Form disclosures in Part II below.

PART II—MODEL FORMS

Part II contains model forms intended for use by corporate credit unions to aid in compliance with the capital disclosure requirements of § 704.3 and Part I of this Appendix.

Model Form A

Terms and Conditions of Membership Capital Account

NOTE: This form is for use before October 20, 2011 in the circumstances where the credit union has determined NOT to give newly issued capital priority over older capital as described in Part I of this Appendix.

(1) A membership capital account is not subject to share insurance coverage by the NCUSIF or other deposit insurer.

(2) A membership capital account is not releasable due solely to the merger, charter conversion or liquidation of the member credit union. In the event of a merger, the

membership capital account transfers to the continuing credit union. In the event of a charter conversion, the membership capital account transfers to the new institution. In the event of liquidation, the membership capital account may be released to facilitate the payout of shares with the prior written approval of NCUA.

(3) A member credit union may withdraw membership capital with three years' notice.

(4) Membership capital cannot be used to pledge borrowings.

(5) Membership capital is available to cover losses that exceed retained earnings and paid-in capital.

(6) Where the corporate credit union is liquidated, membership capital accounts are payable only after satisfaction of all liabilities of the liquidation estate including uninsured obligations to shareholders and the NCUSIF.

(7) Where the corporate credit union is merged into another corporate credit union, the membership capital account will transfer to the continuing corporate credit union. The three-year notice period for withdrawal of the membership capital account will remain in effect.

(8) If an adjusted balance account—: The membership capital balance will be adjusted—(1 or 2)—time(s) annually in relation to the member credit union's—(assets or other measure)—as of—(date(s))—. If a term certificate—: The membership capital account is a term certificate that will mature on—(date)—.

I have read the above terms and conditions and I understand them.

I further agree to maintain in the credit union's files the annual notice of terms and conditions of the membership capital account.

The notice form must be signed by either all of the directors of the member credit union or, if authorized by board resolution, the chair and secretary of the board of the credit union.

The annual disclosure notice form must be signed by the chair of the corporate credit union. The chair must then sign a statement that certifies that the notice has been sent to member credit unions with membership capital accounts. The certification must be maintained in the corporate credit union's files and be available for examiner review.

Model Form B

Terms and Conditions of Membership Capital Account

NOTE: This form is for use before October 20, 2011 in the circumstances where the credit union has determined THAT IT WILL give newly issued capital priority over older capital as described in Part I of this Appendix.

(1) A membership capital account is not subject to share insurance coverage by the NCUSIF or other deposit insurer.

(2) A membership capital account is not releasable due solely to the merger, charter conversion or liquidation of the member credit union. In the event of a merger, the membership capital account transfers to the continuing credit union. In the event of a charter conversion, the membership capital account transfers to the new institution. In the event of liquidation, the membership capital account may be released to facilitate the payout of shares with the prior written approval of NCUA.

(3) A member credit union may withdraw membership capital with three years' notice.

(4) Membership capital cannot be used to pledge borrowings.

(5)(a) Membership capital that is issued on or after January 18, 2011, is available to cover losses that exceed retained earnings, contributed capital issued before January 18, 2011, and perpetual capital issued on or after January 18, 2011. Any such losses will be distributed *pro rata*, at the time the loss is realized, among membership capital account holders with accounts issued on or after January 18, 2011. To the extent that NCA funds are used to cover losses, the corporate credit union is prohibited from restoring or replenishing the affected accounts under any circumstances.

(b) Membership capital that is issued before January 18, 2011 is available to cover losses that exceed retained earnings and perpetual capital issued before January 18, 2011. Any such losses will be distributed *pro rata*, at the time the loss is realized, among membership capital account holders with accounts issued before January 18, 2011. To the extent that NCA funds are used to cover losses, the corporate credit union is prohibited from restoring or replenishing the affected accounts under any circumstances.

(c) Attached to this disclosure is a statement that describes the amount of NCA the credit union has with the corporate credit union in each of the categories described in paragraphs (5)(a) and (5)(b) above.

(6) If the corporate credit union is liquidated:

(a) Membership capital accounts issued on or after January 18, 2011 are payable only after satisfaction of all liabilities of the liquidation estate including uninsured obligations to shareholders and the NCUSIF, but not including contributed capital accounts issued before January 18, 2011 and perpetual capital accounts issued on or after January 18, 2011. However, membership capital that is used to cover losses in a calendar year previous to the year of liquidation has no claim against the liquidation estate.

(b) Membership capital accounts issued before January 18, 2011, are payable only after

National Credit Union Administration

satisfaction of all liabilities of the liquidation estate including uninsured obligations to shareholders and the NCUSIF, but not including perpetual capital accounts issued before January 18, 2011. However, membership capital that is used to cover losses in a calendar year previous to the year of liquidation has no claim against the liquidation estate.

(7) Where the corporate credit union is merged into another corporate credit union, the membership capital account will transfer to the continuing corporate credit union. The three-year notice period for withdrawal of the membership capital account will remain in effect.

(8) If an adjusted balance account—: The membership capital balance will be adjusted—(1 or 2)—time(s) annually in relation to the member credit union's—(assets or other measure)—as of—(date(s))—. If a term certificate—: The membership capital account is a term certificate that will mature on—(date)—.

I have read the above terms and conditions and I understand them.

I further agree to maintain in the credit union's files the annual notice of terms and conditions of the membership capital account.

The notice form must be signed by either all of the directors of the member credit union or, if authorized by board resolution, the chair and secretary of the board of the credit union.

The annual disclosure notice form must be signed by the chair of the corporate credit union. The chair must then sign a statement that certifies that the notice has been sent to member credit unions with membership capital accounts. The certification must be maintained in the corporate credit union's files and be available for examiner review.

Model Form C

Terms and Conditions of Nonperpetual Capital

NOTE: This form is for use on and after October 20, 2011 in the circumstances where the credit union has determined NOT to give newly issued capital priority over older capital as described in Part I of this Appendix. Also, corporate credit unions should ensure that existing membership capital accounts that do not meet the qualifying conditions for nonperpetual capital are modified so as to meet those conditions.

Terms and Conditions of Nonperpetual Capital Account

(1) A nonperpetual capital account is not subject to share insurance coverage by the NCUSIF or other deposit insurer.

(2) A nonperpetual capital account is not releasable due solely to the merger, charter conversion or liquidation of the member credit union. In the event of a merger, the nonperpetual capital account transfers to the continuing credit union. In the event of a charter conversion, the nonperpetual capital account transfers to the new institution. In the event of liquidation, the nonperpetual capital account may be released to facilitate the payout of shares with the prior written approval of NCUA.

(3) If the nonperpetual capital account is a notice account, a member credit union may withdraw the nonperpetual capital with a minimum of five years' notice. If the nonperpetual capital account is a term instrument it may be redeemed only at maturity. The corporate credit union may not redeem any account prior to the expiration of the notice period, or maturity, without the prior written approval of the NCUA.

(4) Nonperpetual capital cannot be used to pledge borrowings.

(5) Nonperpetual capital is available to cover losses that exceed retained earnings and perpetual contributed capital. Any such losses will be distributed *pro rata* among nonperpetual capital account holders at the time the loss is realized. To the extent that NCA funds are used to cover losses, the corporate credit union is prohibited from restoring or replenishing the affected accounts under any circumstances.

(6) Where the corporate credit union is liquidated, nonperpetual capital accounts are payable only after satisfaction of all liabilities of the liquidation estate including uninsured obligations to shareholders and the NCUSIF. However, nonperpetual capital that is used to cover losses in a calendar year previous to the year of liquidation has no claim against the liquidation estate.

(7) Where the corporate credit union is merged into another corporate credit union, the nonperpetual capital account will transfer to the continuing corporate credit union. For notice accounts, the five-year notice period for withdrawal of the nonperpetual capital account will remain in effect. For term accounts, the original term will remain in effect.

(8) If a term certificate—: The nonperpetual capital account is a term certificate that will mature on—(date)—(insert date with a minimum five-year original maturity).

I have read the above terms and conditions and I understand them.

I further agree to maintain in the credit union's files the annual notice of terms and conditions of the nonperpetual capital account.

The notice form must be signed by either all of the directors of the member credit union or, if authorized by board resolution, the chair and secretary of the board of the credit union.

The annual disclosure notice form must be signed by the chair of the corporate credit union. The chair must then sign a statement that certifies that the notice has been sent to member credit unions with nonperpetual capital accounts. The certification must be maintained in the corporate credit union's files and be available for examiner review.

Model Form D

Terms and Conditions of Nonperpetual Capital

NOTE: This form is for use before October 20, 2011 in the circumstances where the credit union has determined THAT IT WILL give newly issued capital priority over older capital as described in Part I of this Appendix. Also, corporate credit unions should ensure that existing membership capital accounts that do not meet the qualifying conditions for nonperpetual capital are modified so as to meet those conditions.

Terms and Conditions of Nonperpetual Capital Account

(1) A nonperpetual capital account is not subject to share insurance coverage by the NCUSIF or other deposit insurer.

(2) A nonperpetual capital account is not releasable due solely to the merger, charter conversion or liquidation of the member credit union. In the event of a merger, the nonperpetual capital account transfers to the continuing credit union. In the event of a charter conversion, the nonperpetual capital account transfers to the new institution. In the event of liquidation, the nonperpetual capital account may be released to facilitate the payout of shares with the prior written approval of NCUA.

(3) If the nonperpetual capital account is a notice account, a member credit union may withdraw the nonperpetual capital with a minimum of five years' notice. If the nonperpetual capital account is a term instrument it may be redeemed only at maturity. The corporate credit union may not redeem any account prior to the expiration of the notice period, or maturity, without the prior written approval of the NCUA.

(4) Nonperpetual capital cannot be used to pledge borrowings.

(5)(a) Nonperpetual capital that is issued on or after January 18, 2011 is available to cover losses that exceed retained earnings, all contributed capital issued before January 18, 2011, and perpetual capital issued on or after January 18, 2011. Any such losses will be distributed *pro rata*, at the time the loss is realized, among nonperpetual capital account holders with accounts issued on or after January 18, 2011. To the extent that NCA funds are used to cover losses, the corporate credit union is prohibited from restoring or replenishing the affected accounts under any circumstances.

(b) Nonperpetual capital that is issued before January 18, 2011, is available to cover losses that exceed retained earnings and perpetual capital issued before January 18, 2011. Any such losses will be distributed *pro rata*, at the time the loss is realized, among nonperpetual capital account holders with accounts issued before January 18, 2011. To the extent that NCA funds are used to cover losses, the corporate credit union is prohibited from restoring or replenishing the affected accounts under any circumstances.

(c) Attached to this disclosure is a statement that describes the amount of NCA the credit union has with the corporate credit union in each of the categories described in paragraphs (5)(a) and (5)(b) above.

(6) If the corporate credit union is liquidated:

(a) Nonperpetual capital accounts issued on or after January 18, 2011 are payable only after satisfaction of all liabilities of the liquidation estate including uninsured obligations to shareholders and the NCUSIF, but not including contributed capital accounts issued before January 18, 2011 or perpetual capital accounts issued on or after January 18, 2011. However, nonperpetual capital that is used to cover losses in a calendar year previous to the year of liquidation has no claim against the liquidation estate.

(b) Nonperpetual capital accounts issued before January 18, 2011 are payable only after satisfaction of all liabilities of the liquidation estate including uninsured obligations to shareholders and the NCUSIF, but not including perpetual capital accounts issued before January 18, 2011. However, nonperpetual capital that is used to cover losses in a calendar year previous to the year of liquidation has no claim against the liquidation estate.

(7) Where the corporate credit union is merged into another corporate credit union, the nonperpetual capital account will transfer to the continuing corporate credit union. For notice accounts, the five-year notice period for withdrawal of the nonperpetual capital account will remain in effect. For term accounts, the original term will remain in effect.

(8) If a term certificate—: The nonperpetual capital account is a term certificate that will mature on—(date)—(insert date with a minimum five-year original maturity).

I have read the above terms and conditions and I understand them.

I further agree to maintain in the credit union's files the annual notice of terms and conditions of the nonperpetual capital account.

The notice form must be signed by either all of the directors of the member credit union or, if authorized by board resolution, the chair and secretary of the board of the credit union.

The annual disclosure notice form must be signed by the chair of the corporate credit

National Credit Union Administration

union. The chair must then sign a statement that certifies that the notice has been sent to member credit unions with nonperpetual capital accounts. The certification must be maintained in the corporate credit union's files and be available for examiner review.

Model Form E

Terms and Conditions of Paid-In Capital

NOTE: This form is for use before October 20, 2011 in the circumstances where the credit union has determined NOT to give newly issued capital priority over older capital as described in Part I of this Appendix.

Terms and Conditions of Paid-In Capital

(1) A paid-in capital account is not subject to share insurance coverage by the NCUSIF or other deposit insurer.

(2) A paid-in capital account is not releasable due solely to the merger, charter conversion or liquidation of the member credit union. In the event of a merger, the paid-in capital account transfers to the continuing credit union. In the event of a charter conversion, the paid-in capital account transfers to the new institution. In the event of liquidation, the paid-in capital account may be released to facilitate the payout of shares with the prior written approval of NCUA.

(3) The funds are callable only at the option of the corporate credit union and only if the corporate credit union meets its minimum required capital and NEV ratios after the funds are called. The corporate must also obtain NCUA's approval before the corporate calls any paid-in capital.

(4) Paid-in capital cannot be used to pledge borrowings.

(5) Paid-in capital is available to cover losses that exceed retained earnings.

(6) Where the corporate credit union is liquidated, paid-in capital accounts are payable only after satisfaction of all liabilities of the liquidation estate including uninsured obligations to shareholders and the NCUSIF, and membership capital holders.

(7) Where the corporate credit union is merged into another corporate credit union, the paid-in capital account will transfer to the continuing corporate credit union.

(8) Paid-in capital is perpetual maturity and noncumulative dividend.

I have read the above terms and conditions and I understand them. I further agree to maintain in the credit union's files the annual notice of terms and conditions of the paid-in capital instrument.

The notice form must be signed by either all of the directors of the credit union or, if authorized by board resolution, the chair and secretary of the board of the credit union.

Pt. 704, App. A

Model Form F

Terms and Conditions of Paid-In Capital

NOTE: This form is for use before October 20, 2011 in the circumstances where the credit union has determined THAT IT WILL give newly issued capital priority over older capital as described in Part I of this Appendix.

Terms and Conditions of Paid-In Capital

(1) A paid-in capital account is not subject to share insurance coverage by the NCUSIF or other deposit insurer.

(2) A paid-in capital account is not releasable due solely to the merger, charter conversion or liquidation of the member credit union. In the event of a merger, the paid-in capital account transfers to the continuing credit union. In the event of a charter conversion, the paid-in capital account transfers to the new institution. In the event of liquidation, the paid-in capital account may be released to facilitate the payout of shares with the prior written approval of NCUA.

(3) The funds are callable only at the option of the corporate credit union and only if the corporate credit union meets its minimum required capital and NEV ratios after the funds are called. The corporate must also obtain NCUA's approval before the corporate calls any paid-in capital.

(4) Paid-in capital cannot be used to pledge borrowings.

(5) Availability to cover losses.

(a) Paid-in capital issued before January 18, 2011 is available to cover losses that exceed retained earnings. Any such losses must be distributed *pro rata*, at the time the loss is realized, among holders of paid-in capital issued before January 18, 2011. To the extent that paid-in capital funds are used to cover losses, the corporate credit union is prohibited from restoring or replenishing the affected accounts under any circumstances.

(b) Paid-in capital issued on or after January 18, 2011 is available to cover losses that exceed retained earnings and any contributed capital issued before January 18, 2011. Any such losses must be distributed *pro rata*, at the time the loss is realized, among holders of paid-in capital issued on or after January 18, 2011. To the extent that paid-in capital funds are used to cover losses, the corporate credit union is prohibited from restoring or replenishing the affected accounts under any circumstances.

(c) Attached to this disclosure is a statement that describes the amount of perpetual capital the credit union has with the corporate credit union in each of the categories described in paragraphs (5)(a) and (5)(b) above.

(6) Where the corporate credit union is liquidated:

(a) Paid-in capital accounts issued on or after January 18, 2011 are payable only after satisfaction of all liabilities of the liquidation estate including uninsured obligations to shareholders and the NCUSIF, but not including contributed capital accounts issued before January 18, 2011. However, paid-in capital that is used to cover losses in a calendar year previous to the year of liquidation has no claim against the liquidation estate.

(b) Paid-in capital accounts issued before January 18, 2011 are payable only after satisfaction of all liabilities of the liquidation estate including uninsured obligations to shareholders and the NCUSIF, nonperpetual accounts issued before January 18, 2011 and contributed capital accounts issued on or after January 18, 2011. However, paid-in capital that is used to cover losses in a calendar year previous to the year of liquidation has no claim against the liquidation estate.

(7) Where the corporate credit union is merged into another corporate credit union, the paid-in capital account will transfer to the continuing corporate credit union.

(8) Paid-in capital is perpetual maturity and noncumulative dividend.

I have read the above terms and conditions and I understand them. I further agree to maintain in the credit union's files the annual notice of terms and conditions of the paid-in capital instrument.

The notice form must be signed by either all of the directors of the credit union or, if authorized by board resolution, the chair and secretary of the board of the credit union.

Model Form G

Terms and Conditions of Perpetual Contributed Capital

NOTE: This form is for use on and after October 20, 2011 in the circumstances where the credit union has determined NOT to give newly issued capital priority over older capital as described in Part I of this Appendix. Also, capital previously issued under the nomenclature "paid-in capital" is considered perpetual contributed capital.

(1) A perpetual contributed capital account is not subject to share insurance coverage by the NCUSIF or other deposit insurer.

(2) A perpetual contributed capital account is not releasable due solely to the merger, charter conversion or liquidation of the member credit union. In the event of a merger, the perpetual contributed capital account transfers to the continuing credit union. In the event of a charter conversion, the perpetual contributed capital account transfers to the new institution. In the event of liquidation, the perpetual contributed capital account may be released to facilitate the payout of shares with the prior written approval of NCUA.

(3) The funds are callable only at the option of the corporate credit union and only if the corporate credit union meets its minimum required capital and NEV ratios after the funds are called. The corporate must also obtain the prior, written approval of the NCUA before releasing any perpetual contributed capital funds.

(4) Perpetual contributed capital cannot be used to pledge borrowings.

(5) Perpetual contributed capital is perpetual maturity and noncumulative dividend.

(6) Perpetual contributed capital is available to cover losses that exceed retained earnings. Any such losses must be distributed *pro rata* among perpetual contributed capital holders at the time the loss is realized. To the extent that perpetual contributed capital funds are used to cover losses, the corporate credit union is prohibited from restoring or replenishing the affected accounts under any circumstances.

(7) Where the corporate credit union is liquidated, perpetual contributed capital accounts are payable only after satisfaction of all liabilities of the liquidation estate including uninsured obligations to shareholders and the NCUSIF, and nonperpetual capital holders. However, perpetual contributed capital that is used to cover losses in a calendar year previous to the year of liquidation has no claim against the liquidation estate.

I have read the above terms and conditions and I understand them. I further agree to maintain in the credit union's files the annual notice of terms and conditions of the perpetual contributed capital instrument.

The notice form must be signed by either all of the directors of the credit union or, if authorized by board resolution, the chair and secretary of the board of the credit union.

Model Form H

Terms and Conditions of Perpetual Contributed Capital

NOTE: This form is for use on or after October 20, 2011 in the circumstances where the credit union has determined that it will give newly issued capital priority over older capital as described in Part I of this Appendix. Also, capital previously issued under the nomenclature "paid-in capital" is considered perpetual contributed capital.

(1) A perpetual contributed capital account is not subject to share insurance coverage by the NCUSIF or other deposit insurer.

(2) A perpetual contributed capital account is not releasable due solely to the merger, charter conversion or liquidation of the member credit union. In the event of a merger, the perpetual contributed capital account transfers to the continuing credit union. In the event of a charter conversion, the perpetual contributed capital account transfers to the new institution. In the event of liquidation, the perpetual contributed capital account may be released to facilitate the

payout of shares with the prior written approval of NCUA.

(3) The funds are callable only at the option of the corporate credit union and only if the corporate credit union meets its minimum required capital and NEV ratios after the funds are called. The corporate must also obtain the prior, written approval of the NCUA before releasing any perpetual contributed capital funds.

(4) Perpetual contributed capital cannot be used to pledge borrowings.

(5) Perpetual contributed capital is perpetual maturity and noncumulative dividend.

(6) Availability to cover losses.

(a) Perpetual contributed capital issued before January 18, 2011 is available to cover losses that exceed retained earnings. Any such losses must be distributed *pro rata*, at the time the loss is realized, among holders of perpetual contributed capital issued before January 18, 2011. To the extent that perpetual contributed capital funds are used to cover losses, the corporate credit union is prohibited from restoring or replenishing the affected accounts under any circumstances.

(b) Perpetual contributed capital issued on or after January 18, 2011 is available to cover losses that exceed retained earnings and any contributed capital issued before January 18, 2011. Any such losses must be distributed *pro rata*, at the time the loss is realized, among holders of perpetual contributed capital issued on or after January 18, 2011. To the extent that perpetual contributed capital funds are used to cover losses, the corporate credit union is prohibited from restoring or replenishing the affected accounts under any circumstances.

(c) Attached to this disclosure is a statement that describes the amount of perpetual capital the credit union has with the corporate credit union in each of the categories described in paragraphs (6)(a) and (6)(b) above.

(7) Where the corporate credit union is liquidated:

(a) Perpetual contributed capital accounts issued on or after January 18, 2011 are payable only after satisfaction of all liabilities of the liquidation estate including uninsured obligations to shareholders and the NCUSIF, but not including contributed capital accounts issued before January 18, 2011. However, perpetual contributed capital that is used to cover losses in a calendar year previous to the year of liquidation has no claim against the liquidation estate.

(b) Perpetual contributed capital accounts issued before January 18, 2011 are payable only after satisfaction of all liabilities of the liquidation estate including uninsured obligations to shareholders and the NCUSIF, nonperpetual capital accounts issued before January 18, 2011, and all contributed capital accounts issued on or after January 18, 2011. However, perpetual contributed capital that is used to cover losses in a calendar year previous to the year of liquidation has no claim against the liquidation estate.

I have read the above terms and conditions and I understand them. I further agree to maintain in the credit union's files the annual notice of terms and conditions of the perpetual contributed capital instrument.

The notice form must be signed by either all of the directors of the credit union or, if authorized by board resolution, the chair and secretary of the board of the credit union.

[75 FR 64848, Oct. 20, 2010, as amended at 75 FR 71528, Nov. 24, 2010]

EFFECTIVE DATE NOTES: 1. At 75 FR 71528, Nov. 24, 2010, appendix A to part 704 was amended by revising the introductory note in Model Form H, appendix A, effective Jan. 18, 2011. For the convenience of the user, the revised text is set forth as follows:

APPENDIX A TO PART 704—CAPITAL PRIORITIZATION AND MODEL FORMS

* * * * *

Model Form H

NOTE: This form is for use on or after October 20, 2011 in the circumstances where the credit union has determined that it will give newly issued capital priority over older capital as described in Part I of this Appendix. Also, capital previously issued under the nomenclature "paid-in capital" is considered perpetual contributed capital.

* * * * *

2. At 75 FR 71528, Nov. 24, 2010, appendix A to part 704 was amended by revising the introductory note in Model Form D, appendix A, effective Jan. 23, 2011. For the convenience of the user, the revised text is set forth as follows:

APPENDIX A TO PART 704—CAPITAL PRIORITIZATION AND MODEL FORMS

* * * * *

Model Form D

* * * * *

NOTE: This form is for use on and after October 20, 2011, in the circumstances where the corporate credit union has determined that it will give newly issued capital priority over older capital as described in Part I of this Appendix.

* * * * *

APPENDIX B TO PART 704—EXPANDED AUTHORITIES AND REQUIREMENTS

A corporate credit union may obtain all or part of the expanded authorities contained in this Appendix if it meets the applicable requirements of Part 704 and Appendix B, fulfills additional management, infrastructure, and asset and liability requirements, and receives NCUA's written approval. Additional guidance is set forth in the NCUA publication Guidelines for Submission of Requests for Expanded Authority.

A corporate credit union seeking expanded authorities must submit to NCUA a self-assessment plan supporting its request. A corporate credit union may adopt expanded authorities when NCUA has provided final approval. If NCUA denies a request for expanded authorities, it will advise the corporate credit union of the reason(s) for the denial and what it must do to resubmit its request. NCUA may revoke these expanded authorities at any time if an analysis indicates a significant deficiency. NCUA will notify the corporate credit union in writing of the identified deficiency. A corporate credit union may request, in writing, reinstatement of the revoked authorities by providing a self-assessment plan detailing how it has corrected the deficiency.

A state chartered corporate credit union may not exercise any expanded authority that exceeds the powers and authorities provided for under its state laws. Accordingly, requests by state chartered corporate credit unions for expansions under this part must be approved by the state regulator before being submitted to NCUA.

Minimum Requirement

In order to participate in any of the authorities set forth in Base-Plus, Part I, Part II, Part III, or Part IV of this Appendix, a corporate credit union must evaluate monthly, including once on the last day of the month, the changes in NEV, NEV ratio, NII, WAL, and duration as required by paragraphs (d)(1)(i), (e), (f), (g), and (i) of §704.8.

Base-Plus

A corporate that has met the requirements for this Base-plus authority may, in performing the rate stress tests set forth in 704.8(d)(1)(i), allow its NEV to decline as much as 20 percent.

Part I

(a) A corporate credit union that has met all the requirements established by NCUA for this Part I, including a minimum capital ratio of at least six percent, may:
(1) Purchase investments with long-term ratings no lower than A− (or equivalent);
(2) Purchase investments with short-term ratings no lower than A−2 (or equivalent), provided that the issuer has a long-term rating no lower than A− (or equivalent) or the investment is a domestically-issued asset-backed security;
(3) Engage in short sales of permissible investments to reduce interest rate risk;
(4) Purchase principal only (PO) stripped mortgage-backed securities to reduce interest rate risk; and
(5) Enter into a dollar roll transaction.
(b) In performing the rate stress tests set forth in §704.8(d), the NEV of a corporate credit union that has met the requirements of this Part I may decline as much as:
(1) 20 percent;
(2) 28 percent if the corporate credit union has a seven percent minimum capital ratio and is specifically approved by NCUA; or
(3) 35 percent if the corporate credit union has an eight percent minimum capital ratio and is specifically approved by NCUA.
(c) The maximum aggregate amount in unsecured loans and lines of credit to any one member credit union, excluding pass-through and guaranteed loans from the CLF and the NCUSIF, must not exceed 100 percent of the corporate credit union's capital. The board of directors must establish the limit, as a percent of the corporate credit union's capital plus pledged shares, for secured loans and lines of credit.
(d) The aggregate total of investments purchased under the authority of Part I (a)(1) and Part I (a)(2) may not exceed the lower of 500 percent of the corporate credit union's capital or 25 percent of assets.
(e) On or after October 20, 2011, corporate credit unions will substitute "leverage ratio" for "capital ratio" wherever it appears in Part I.

Part II

(a) A corporate credit union that has met the requirements of Part I of this Appendix and the additional requirements established by NCUA for Part II may invest in:
(1) Debt obligations of a foreign country;
(2) Deposits and debt obligations of foreign banks or obligations guaranteed by these banks;
(3) Marketable debt obligations of foreign corporations. This authority does not apply to debt obligations that are convertible into the stock of the corporation; and
(4) Foreign issued asset-backed securities.
(b) All foreign investments are subject to the following requirements:
(1) Investments must be rated no lower than the minimum permissible domestic rating under the corporate credit union's Part I authority;
(2) A sovereign issuer, and/or the country in which an obligor is organized, must have a long-term foreign currency (non-local currency) debt rating no lower than AA− (or equivalent);

National Credit Union Administration

(3) For each approved foreign bank line, the corporate credit union must identify the specific banking centers and branches to which it will lend funds;

(4) Obligations of any single foreign obligor may not exceed 25 percent of capital or $5 million, whichever is greater; and

(5) Obligations in any single foreign country may not exceed 250 percent of capital.

Part III

(a) A corporate credit union that has met the requirements established by NCUA for this Part III may enter into derivative transactions specifically approved by NCUA to:

(1) Create structured products;

(2) Mitigate interest rate risk and credit risk on its own balance sheet; and

(3) Hedge the balance sheets of its members.

(b) Credit Ratings:

(1) All derivative transactions are subject to the following requirements:

(i) If the intended counterparty is domestic, the counterparty rating must be no lower than A− (or equivalent) by every NRSRO that provides a publicly available long-term rating on the counterparty;

(ii) If the intended counterparty is foreign, the corporate must have Part II expanded authority and the counterparty rating must be no lower than the minimum permissible rating for a comparable term investment under Part II Authority;

(iii) The corporate must identify the rating(s) relied upon to meet the requirements of this part at the time the transaction is entered into and monitor those ratings for as long as the contract remains open; and

(iv) The corporate credit unions must comply with § 704.10 of this part if any rating relied upon to meet the requirements of paragraphs (b)(1)(i) or (ii) of this part is downgraded below the minimum rating requirements.

(2) Exceptions. Credit ratings are not required for derivative transactions with:

(i) Domestically chartered credit unions;

(ii) U.S. government sponsored enterprises; or

(iii) Counterparties where the transaction is fully guaranteed by an entity with a minimum permissible rating for comparable term investments.

Part IV

A corporate credit union that has met all the requirements established by NCUA for this Part IV may participate in loans with member natural person credit unions as approved by the NCUA and subject to the following:

(a) The maximum aggregate amount of participation loans with any one member credit union must not exceed 25 percent of capital; and

(b) The maximum aggregate amount of participation loans with all member credit unions will be determined on a case-by-case basis by the NCUA.

[75 FR 64851, Oct. 20, 2010]

APPENDIX C TO PART 704—RISK-BASED CAPITAL CREDIT RISK-WEIGHT CATEGORIES

TABLE OF CONTENTS

I. Introduction
(a) Scope
(b) Definitions
II. Risk-Weightings
(a) On-balance sheet assets
(b) Off-balance sheet activities
(c) Recourse obligations, direct credit substitutes, and certain other positions
(d) Collateral

PART I: INTRODUCTION

(a) Scope

(1) This Appendix explains how a corporate credit union must compute its risk-weighted assets for purposes of determining its capital ratios.

(2) Risk-weighted assets equal risk-weighted on-balance sheet assets (computed under Section II(a) of this Appendix), plus risk-weighted off-balance sheet activities (computed under Section II(b) of this Appendix), plus risk-weighted recourse obligations, direct credit substitutes, and certain other positions (computed under Section II(c) of this Appendix).

(3) Assets not included (*i.e.,* deducted from capital) for purposes of calculating capital under part 704 are not included in calculating risk-weighted assets.

(4) Although this Appendix describes risk-weightings for various assets and activities, this Appendix does not provide authority for corporate credit unions to invest in or purchase any particular type of asset or to engage in any particular type of activity. A corporate credit union *must have other identifiable authority* for any investment it makes or activity it engages in. So, for example, this Appendix describes risk weightings for subordinated securities. Section 704.5, however, prohibits corporate credit unions from investing in subordinated securities, and so a corporate credit union cannot invest in subordinated securities.

(b) Definitions

The following definitions apply to this Appendix. Additional definitions, applicable to this entire Part, are located in § 704.2 of this Part.

Cash items in the process of collection means checks or drafts in the process of collection that are drawn on another depository institution, including a central bank, and that are payable immediately upon presentation; U.S. Government checks that are drawn on the United States Treasury or any other U.S. Government or Government-sponsored agency and that are payable immediately upon presentation; broker's security drafts and commodity or bill-of-lading drafts payable immediately upon presentation; and unposted debits.

Commitment means any arrangement that obligates a corporate credit union to:

(1) Purchase loans or securities;

(2) Extend credit in the form of loans or leases, participations in loans or leases, overdraft facilities, revolving credit facilities, home equity lines of credit, eligible ABCP liquidity facilities, or similar transactions.

Depository institution means a financial institution that engages in the business of providing financial services; that is recognized as a bank or a credit union by the supervisory or monetary authorities of the country of its incorporation and the country of its principal banking operations; that receives deposits to a substantial extent in the regular course of business; and that has the power to accept demand deposits. In the United States, this definition encompasses all federally insured offices of commercial banks, mutual and stock savings banks, savings or building and loan associations (stock and mutual), cooperative banks, credit unions, and international banking facilities of domestic depository institutions.

Bank holding companies and savings and loan holding companies are excluded from this definition. For the purposes of assigning risk-weights, the differentiation between OECD depository institutions and non-OECD depository institutions is based on the country of incorporation. Claims on branches and agencies of foreign banks located in the United States are to be categorized on the basis of the parent bank's country of incorporation.

Direct credit substitute means an arrangement in which a corporate credit union assumes, in form or in substance, credit risk associated with an on-balance sheet or off-balance sheet asset or exposure that was not previously owned by the corporate credit union (third-party asset) and the risk assumed by the corporate credit union exceeds the *pro rata* share of the corporate credit union's interest in the third-party asset. If a corporate credit union has no claim on the third-party asset, then the corporate credit union's assumption of any credit risk is a direct credit substitute. Direct credit substitutes include:

(1) Financial standby letters of credit that support financial claims on a third party that exceed a corporate credit union's *pro rata* share in the financial claim;

(2) Guarantees, surety arrangements, credit derivatives, and similar instruments backing financial claims that exceed a corporate credit union's *pro rata* share in the financial claim;

(3) Purchased subordinated interests that absorb more than their *pro rata* share of losses from the underlying assets, including any tranche of asset-backed securities that is not the most senior tranche;

(4) Credit derivative contracts under which the corporate credit union assumes more than its *pro rata* share of credit risk on a third-party asset or exposure;

(5) Loans or lines of credit that provide credit enhancement for the financial obligations of a third party;

(6) Purchased loan servicing assets if the servicer is responsible for credit losses or if the servicer makes or assumes credit-enhancing representations and warranties with respect to the loans serviced. Servicer cash advances as defined in this section are not direct credit substitutes;

(7) Clean-up calls on third-party assets. However, clean-up calls that are 10 percent or less of the original pool balance and that are exercisable at the option of the corporate credit union are not direct credit substitutes; and

(8) Liquidity facilities that provide support to asset-backed commercial paper (other than eligible ABCP liquidity facilities).

Exchange rate contracts means cross-currency interest rate swaps; forward foreign exchange rate contracts; currency options purchased; and any similar instrument that, in the opinion of the NCUA, may give rise to similar risks.

Face amount means the notational principal, or face value, amount of an off-balance sheet item or the amortized cost of an on-balance sheet asset.

Financial asset means cash or other monetary instrument, evidence of debt, evidence of an ownership interest in an entity, or a contract that conveys a right to receive or exchange cash or another financial instrument from another party.

Financial standby letter of credit means a letter of credit or similar arrangement that represents an irrevocable obligation to a third-party beneficiary:

(1) To repay money borrowed by, or advanced to, or for the account of, a second party (the account party); or

(2) To make payment on behalf of the account party, in the event that the account party fails to fulfill its obligation to the beneficiary.

OECD-based country means a member of that grouping of countries that are full members of the Organization for Economic Cooperation and Development (OECD) plus countries that have concluded special lending arrangements with the International Monetary Fund (IMF) associated with the IMF's General Arrangements To Borrow. This term excludes any country that has rescheduled its external sovereign debt within the previous five years. A rescheduling of external sovereign debt generally would include any renegotiation of terms arising from a country's inability or unwillingness to meet its external debt service obligations, but generally would not include renegotiations of debt in the normal course of business, such as a renegotiation to allow the borrower to take advantage of a decline in interest rates or other change in market conditions.

Original maturity means, with respect to a commitment, the earliest date after a commitment is made on which the commitment is scheduled to expire (*i.e.*, it will reach its stated maturity and cease to be binding on either party), provided that either:

(1) The commitment is not subject to extension or renewal and will actually expire on its stated expiration date; or

(2) If the commitment is subject to extension or renewal beyond its stated expiration date, the stated expiration date will be deemed the original maturity only if the extension or renewal must be based upon terms and conditions independently negotiated in good faith with the member at the time of the extension or renewal and upon a new, bona fide credit analysis utilizing current information on financial condition and trends.

Performance-based standby letter of credit means any letter of credit, or similar arrangement, however named or described, which represents an irrevocable obligation to the beneficiary on the part of the issuer to make payment on account of any default by a third party in the performance of a nonfinancial or commercial obligation. Such letters of credit include arrangements backing subcontractors' and suppliers' performance, labor and materials contracts, and construction bids.

Prorated assets means the total assets (as determined in the most recently available GAAP report but in no event more than one year old) of a consolidated CUSO multiplied by the corporate credit union's percentage of ownership of that consolidated CUSO.

Qualifying mortgage loan means a loan that:

(1) Is fully secured by a first lien on a one- to four-family residential property;

(2) Is underwritten in accordance with prudent underwriting standards, including standards relating the ratio of the loan amount to the value of the property (LTV ratio), as presented in the *Interagency Guidelines for Real Estate Lending Policies*, 57 FR 62890 (December 31, 1992). A nonqualifying mortgage loan that is paid down to an appropriate LTV ratio (calculated using value at origination, appraisal obtained within the prior six months, or updated value using an automated valuation model) may become a qualifying loan if it meets all other requirements of this definition;

(3) Maintains an appropriate LTV ratio based on the amortized principal balance of the loan; and

(4) Is performing and is not more than 90 days past due.

If a corporate credit union holds the first and junior lien(s) on a residential property and no other party holds an intervening lien, the transaction is treated as a single loan secured by a first lien for the purposes of determining the LTV ratio and the appropriate risk-weight under Appendix C. Also, a loan to an individual borrower for the construction of the borrower's home may be included as a qualifying mortgage loan.

Qualifying multifamily mortgage loan. (1) *Qualifying multifamily mortgage loan* means a loan secured by a first lien on multifamily residential properties consisting of 5 or more dwelling units, provided that:

(i) The amortization of principal and interest occurs over a period of not more than 30 years;

(ii) The original minimum maturity for repayment of principal on the loan is not less than seven years;

(iii) When considering the loan for placement in a lower risk-weight category, all principal and interest payments have been made on a timely basis in accordance with its terms for the preceding year;

(iv) The loan is performing and not 90 days or more past due;

(v) The loan is made in accordance with prudent underwriting standards; and

(vi) If the interest rate on the loan does not change over the term of the loan, the current loan balance amount does not exceed 80 percent of the value of the property securing the loan, and for the property's most recent calendar year, the ratio of annual net operating income generated by the property (before payment of any debt service on the loan) to annual debt service on the loan is not less than 120 percent, or in the case of cooperative or other not-for-profit housing projects, the property generates sufficient cash flows to provide comparable protection to the institution; or

(vii) If the interest rate on the loan changes over the term of the loan, the current loan balance amount does not exceed 75 percent of the value of the property securing the loan, and for the property's most recent calendar year, the ratio of annual net operating income generated by the property (before payment of any debt service on the loan) to annual debt service on the loan is not less than 115 percent, or in the case of cooperative or other not-for-profit housing projects, the property generates sufficient cash flows to provide comparable protection to the institution.

(2) For purposes of paragraphs (1)(vi) and (1)(vii) of this definition, the term value of the property means, at origination of a loan to purchase a multifamily property, the lower of the purchase price or the amount of the initial appraisal, or if appropriate, the initial evaluation. In cases not involving purchase of a multifamily loan, the value of the property is determined by the most current appraisal, or if appropriate, the most current evaluation. In cases where a borrower refinances a loan on an existing property, as an alternative to paragraphs (1)(iii), (1)(vi), and (1)(vii) of this definition:

(i) All principal and interest payments on the loan being refinanced have been made on a timely basis in accordance with the terms of that loan for the preceding year; and

(ii) The net income on the property for the preceding year would support timely principal and interest payments on the new loan in accordance with the applicable debt service requirement.

Qualifying residential construction loan, also referred to as a residential bridge loan, means a loan made in accordance with sound lending principles satisfying the following criteria:

(1) The builder must have substantial project equity in the home construction project;

(2) The residence being constructed must be a 1–4 family residence sold to a home purchaser;

(3) The lending entity must obtain sufficient documentation from a permanent lender (which may be the construction lender) demonstrating that the home buyer intends to purchase the residence and has the ability to obtain a permanent qualifying mortgage loan sufficient to purchase the residence;

(4) The home purchaser must have made a substantial earnest money deposit;

(5) The construction loan must not exceed 80 percent of the sales price of the residence;

(6) The construction loan must be secured by a first lien on the lot, residence under construction, and other improvements;

(7) The lending credit union must retain sufficient undisbursed loan funds throughout the construction period to ensure project completion;

(8) The builder must incur a significant percentage of direct costs (*i.e.,* the actual costs of land, labor, and material) before any drawdown on the loan;

(9) If at any time during the life of the construction loan any of the criteria of this rule are no longer satisfied, the corporate must immediately recategorize the loan at a 100 percent risk-weight and must accurately report the loan in the corporate's next quarterly call report;

(10) The home purchaser must intend that the home will be owner-occupied;

(11) The home purchaser(s) must be an individual(s), not a partnership, joint venture, trust corporation, or any other entity (including an entity acting as a sole proprietorship) that is purchasing the home(s) for speculative purposes; and

(12) The loan must be performing and not more than 90 days past due.

The NCUA retains the discretion to determine that any loans not meeting sound lending principles must be placed in a higher risk-weight category. The NCUA also reserves the discretion to modify these criteria on a case-by-case basis provided that any such modifications are not inconsistent with the safety and soundness objectives of this definition.

Qualifying securities firm means:

(1) A securities firm incorporated in the United States that is a broker-dealer that is registered with the Securities and Exchange Commission (SEC) and that complies with the SEC's net capital regulations (17 CFR 240.15c3(1)); and

(2) A securities firm incorporated in any other OECD-based country, if the corporate credit union is able to demonstrate that the securities firm is subject to consolidated supervision and regulation (covering its subsidiaries, but not necessarily its parent organizations) comparable to that imposed on depository institutions in OECD countries. Such regulation must include risk-based capital requirements comparable to those imposed on depository institutions under the Accord on International Convergence of Capital Measurement and Capital Standards (1988, as amended in 1998).

Recourse means a corporate credit union's retention, in form or in substance, of any credit risk directly or indirectly associated with an asset it has sold (in accordance with Generally Accepted Accounting Principles) that exceeds a *pro rata* share of that corporate credit union's claim on the asset. If a corporate credit union has no claim on an asset it has sold, then the retention of any credit risk is recourse. A recourse obligation typically arises when a corporate credit union transfers assets in a sale and retains an explicit obligation to repurchase assets or to absorb losses due to a default on the payment of principal or interest or any other deficiency in the performance of the underlying obligor or some other party. Recourse may also exist implicitly if a corporate credit union provides credit enhancement beyond any contractual obligation to support assets it has sold. Recourse obligations include:

(1) Credit-enhancing representations and warranties made on transferred assets;

(2) Loan servicing assets retained pursuant to an agreement under which the corporate credit union will be responsible for losses associated with the loans serviced. Servicer cash advances as defined in this section are not recourse obligations;

(3) Retained subordinated interests that absorb more than their *pro rata* share of losses from the underlying assets;

(4) Assets sold under an agreement to repurchase, if the assets are not already included on the balance sheet;

(5) Loan strips sold without contractual recourse where the maturity of the transferred portion of the loan is shorter than the maturity of the commitment under which the loan is drawn;

(6) Credit derivatives that absorb more than the corporate credit union's *pro rata* share of losses from the transferred assets;

(7) Clean-up calls on assets the corporate credit union has sold. However, clean-up calls that are 10 percent or less of the original pool balance and that are exercisable at the option of the corporate credit union are not recourse arrangements; and

(8) Liquidity facilities that provide support to asset-backed commercial paper (other than eligible ABCP liquidity facilities).

Replacement cost means, with respect to interest rate and exchange-rate contracts, the loss that would be incurred in the event of a counterparty default, as measured by the net cost of replacing the contract at the current market value. If default would result in a theoretical profit, the replacement value is considered to be zero. This mark-to-market process must incorporate changes in both interest rates and counterparty credit quality.

Residential properties means houses, condominiums, cooperative units, and manufactured homes. This definition does not include boats or motor homes, even if used as a primary residence, or timeshare properties.

Residual interest. (1) *Residual interest* means any on-balance sheet asset that:

(i) Represents an interest (including a beneficial interest) created by a transfer that qualifies as a sale (in accordance with Generally Accepted Accounting Principles) of financial assets, whether through a securitization or otherwise; and

(ii) Exposes a corporate credit union to credit risk directly or indirectly associated with the transferred asset that exceeds a *pro rata* share of that corporate credit union's claim on the asset, whether through subordination provisions or other credit enhancement techniques.

(2) Residual interests generally include credit-enhancing interest-only strips, spread accounts, cash collateral accounts, retained subordinated interests (and other forms of overcollateralization), and similar assets that function as a credit enhancement. Residual interests further include those exposures that, in substance, cause the corporate credit union to retain the credit risk of an asset or exposure that had qualified as a residual interest before it was sold. Residual interests generally do not include assets purchased from a third party, but a credit-enhancing interest-only strip that is acquired in any asset transfer is a residual interest.

(3) Corporate credit unions will use this definition of the term "residual interests," and not the definition in §704.2, for purposes of applying this Appendix.

Risk participation means a participation in which the originating party remains liable to the beneficiary for the full amount of an obligation (*e.g.*, a direct credit substitute), notwithstanding that another party has acquired a participation in that obligation.

Risk-weighted assets means the sum total of risk-weighted on-balance sheet assets, as calculated under Section II(a) of this Appendix, and the total of risk-weighted off-balance sheet credit equivalent amounts. The total of risk-weighted off-balance sheet credit equivalent amounts equals the risk-weighted off-balance sheet activities as calculated under Section II(b) of this Appendix plus the risk-weighted recourse obligations, risk-weighted direct credit substitutes, and certain other risk-weighted positions as calculated under Section II(c) of this Appendix.

Servicer cash advance means funds that a residential mortgage servicer advances to ensure an uninterrupted flow of payments, including advances made to cover foreclosure costs or other expenses to facilitate the timely collection of the loan. A servicer cash advance is not a recourse obligation or a direct credit substitute if:

(1) The servicer is entitled to full reimbursement and this right is not subordinated to other claims on the cash flows from the underlying asset pool; or

(2) For any one loan, the servicer's obligation to make nonreimbursable advances is contractually limited to an insignificant amount of the outstanding principal amount on that loan.

Structured financing program means a program where receivable interests and asset-or mortgage-backed securities issued by multiple participants are purchased by a special purpose entity that repackages those exposures into securities that can be sold to investors. Structured financing programs allocate credit risk, generally, between the participants and credit enhancement provided to the program.

Traded position means a position retained, assumed, or issued in connection with a securitization that is rated by a NRSRO, where there is a reasonable expectation that, in the near future, the rating will be relied upon by:

(1) Unaffiliated investors to purchase the security; or

(2) An unaffiliated third party to enter into a transaction involving the position, such as a purchase, loan, or repurchase agreement.

Unconditionally cancelable means, with respect to a commitment-type lending arrangement, that the corporate credit union may, at any time, with or without cause, refuse to advance funds or extend credit under the facility.

United States Government or its agencies means an instrumentality of the U.S. Government whose debt obligations are fully and explicitly guaranteed as to the timely payment of principal and interest by the full faith and credit of the United States Government.

United States Government-sponsored agency or corporation means an agency or corporation originally established or chartered to serve public purposes specified by the United States Congress but whose obligations are not explicitly guaranteed by the full faith and credit of the United States Government.

PART II: RISK-WEIGHTINGS

(a) On-Balance Sheet Assets

Except as provided in Section II(b) of this Appendix, risk-weighted on-balance sheet assets are computed by multiplying the on-balance sheet asset amounts times the appropriate risk-weight categories. The risk-weight categories are:

(1) Zero percent Risk-Weight (Category 1).

(i) Cash, including domestic and foreign currency owned and held in all offices of a corporate credit union or in transit. Any foreign currency held by a corporate credit union must be converted into U.S. dollar equivalents;

(ii) Securities issued by and other direct claims on the U.S. Government or its agencies (to the extent such securities or claims are unconditionally backed by the full faith and credit of the United States Government) or the central government of an OECD country;

(iii) Notes and obligations issued or guaranteed by the Federal Deposit Insurance Corporation or the National Credit Union Share Insurance Fund and backed by the full faith and credit of the United States Government;

(iv) Deposit reserves at, claims on, and balances due from Federal Reserve Banks;

(v) The book value of paid-in Federal Reserve Bank stock;

(vi) That portion of assets directly and unconditionally guaranteed by the United States Government or its agencies, or the central government of an OECD country.

(viii) Claims on, and claims guaranteed by, a qualifying securities firm that are collateralized by cash on deposit in the corporate credit union or by securities issued or guaranteed by the United States Government or its agencies, or the central government of an OECD country. To be eligible for this risk-weight, the corporate credit union must maintain a positive margin of collateral on the claim on a daily basis, taking into account any change in a corporate credit union's exposure to the obligor or counterparty under the claim in relation to the market value of the collateral held in support of the claim.

(2) 20 percent Risk-Weight (Category 2).

(i) Cash items in the process of collection;

(ii) That portion of assets conditionally guaranteed by the United States Government or its agencies, or the central government of an OECD country;

(iii) That portion of assets collateralized by the current market value of securities issued or guaranteed by the United States government or its agencies, or the central government of an OECD country;

(iv) Securities (not including equity securities) issued by and other claims on the U.S. Government or its agencies which are not backed by the full faith and credit of the United States Government;

(v) Securities (not including equity securities) issued by, or other direct claims on, United States Government-sponsored agencies;

(vi) That portion of assets guaranteed by United States Government-sponsored agencies;

(vii) That portion of assets collateralized by the current market value of securities issued or guaranteed by United States Government-sponsored agencies;

(viii) Claims on, and claims guaranteed by, a qualifying securities firm, subject to the following conditions:

(A) A qualifying securities firm must have a long-term issuer credit rating, or a rating on at least one issue of long-term unsecured debt, from a NRSRO. The rating must be in one of the three highest investment grade categories used by the NRSRO. If two or more NRSROs assign ratings to the qualifying securities firm, the corporate credit union must use the lowest rating to determine whether the rating requirement of this paragraph is met. A qualifying securities firm may rely on the rating of its parent consolidated company, if the parent consolidated company guarantees the claim.

(B) A collateralized claim on a qualifying securities firm does not have to comply with the rating requirements under paragraph (a) if the claim arises under a contract that:

(*1*) Is a reverse repurchase/repurchase agreement or securities lending/borrowing transaction executed using standard industry documentation;

(*2*) Is collateralized by debt or equity securities that are liquid and readily marketable;

(*3*) Is marked-to-market daily;

(*4*) Is subject to a daily margin maintenance requirement under the standard industry documentation; and

(*5*) Can be liquidated, terminated or accelerated immediately in bankruptcy or similar proceeding, and the security or collateral agreement will not be stayed or avoided under applicable law of the relevant jurisdiction. For example, a claim is exempt from the automatic stay in bankruptcy in the

National Credit Union Administration

Pt. 704, App. C

United States if it arises under a securities contract or a repurchase agreement subject to Section 555 or 559 of the Bankruptcy Code (11 U.S.C. 555 or 559), a qualified financial contract under Section 207(c)(8) of the Federal Credit Union Act (12 U.S.C. 1787(c)(8)) or Section 11(e)(8) of the Federal Deposit Insurance Act (12 U.S.C. 1821(e)(8)), or a netting contract between or among financial institutions under Sections 401–407 of the Federal Deposit Insurance Corporation Improvement Act of 1991 (12 U.S.C. 4401–4407), or Regulation EE (12 CFR part 231).

(C) If the securities firm uses the claim to satisfy its applicable capital requirements, the claim is not eligible for a risk-weight under this paragraph II(a)(2)(viii);

(ix) Claims representing general obligations of any public-sector entity in an OECD country, and that portion of any claims guaranteed by any such public-sector entity;

(x) Balances due from and all claims on domestic depository institutions. This includes demand deposits and other transaction accounts, savings deposits and time certificates of deposit, federal funds sold, loans to other depository institutions, including overdrafts and term federal funds, holdings of the corporate credit union's own discounted acceptances for which the account party is a depository institution, holdings of bankers acceptances of other institutions and securities issued by depository institutions, except those that qualify as capital;

(xi) The book value of paid-in Federal Home Loan Bank stock;

(xii) Deposit reserves at, claims on and balances due from the Federal Home Loan Banks;

(xiii) Assets collateralized by cash held in a segregated deposit account by the reporting corporate credit union;

(xiv) Claims on, or guaranteed by, official multilateral lending institutions or regional development institutions in which the United States Government is a shareholder or contributing member;[1]

(xv) That portion of assets collateralized by the current market value of securities issued by official multilateral lending institutions or regional development institutions in which the United States Government is a shareholder or contributing member.

(xvi) All claims on depository institutions incorporated in an OECD country, and all assets backed by the full faith and credit of depository institutions incorporated in an OECD country. This includes the credit equivalent amount of participations in commitments and standby letters of credit sold to other depository institutions incorporated in an OECD country, but only if the originating bank remains liable to the member or beneficiary for the full amount of the commitment or standby letter of credit. Also included in this category are the credit equivalent amounts of risk participations in bankers' acceptances conveyed to other depository institutions incorporated in an OECD country. However, bank-issued securities that qualify as capital of the issuing bank are not included in this risk category;

(xvii) Claims on, or guaranteed by depository institutions other than the central bank, incorporated in a non-OECD country, with a remaining maturity of one year or less;

(xviii) That portion of local currency claims conditionally guaranteed by central governments of non-OECD countries, to the extent the corporate credit union has local currency liabilities in that country.

(3) 50 percent Risk-Weight (Category 3).

(i) Revenue bonds issued by any public-sector entity in an OECD country for which the underlying obligor is a public-sector entity, but which are repayable solely from the revenues generated from the project financed through the issuance of the obligations;

(ii) Qualifying mortgage loans and qualifying multifamily mortgage loans;

(iii) Privately-issued mortgage-backed securities (i.e., those that do not carry the guarantee of the U.S. Government, a U.S. government agency, or a U.S. government sponsored enterprise) representing an interest in qualifying mortgage loans or qualifying multifamily mortgage loans. If the security is backed by qualifying multifamily mortgage loans, the corporate credit union must receive timely payments of principal and interest in accordance with the terms of the security. Payments will generally be considered timely if they are not 30 days past due; and

(iv) Qualifying residential construction loans.

(4) 100 percent Risk-Weight (Category 4).

All assets not specified above or deducted from calculations of capital pursuant to §704.2 and §704.3 of this part, including, but not limited to:

(i) Consumer loans;
(ii) Commercial loans;
(iii) Home equity loans;
(iv) Non-qualifying mortgage loans;
(v) Non-qualifying multifamily mortgage loans;
(vi) Residential construction loans;
(vii) Land loans;
(viii) Nonresidential construction loans;
(ix) Obligations issued by any state or any political subdivision thereof for the benefit of a private party or enterprise where that

---

[1] These institutions include, but are not limited to, the International Bank for Reconstruction and Development (World Bank), the Inter-American Development Bank, the Asian Development Bank, the African Development Bank, the European Investments Bank, the International Monetary Fund and the Bank for International Settlements.

party or enterprise, rather than the issuing state or political subdivision, is responsible for the timely payment of principal and interest on the obligations, *e.g.*, industrial development bonds;

(x) Debt securities not specifically risk-weighted in another category;

(xi) Investments in fixed assets and premises;

(xii) Servicing assets;

(xiii) Interest-only strips receivable, other than credit-enhancing interest-only strips;

(xiv) Equity investments;

(xv) The prorated assets of subsidiaries (except for the assets of consolidated CUSOs) to the extent such assets are included in adjusted total assets;

(xvi) All repossessed assets or assets that are more than 90 days past due; and

(xvii) Intangible assets not specifically weighted in some other category.

(5) Indirect ownership interests in pools of assets. Assets representing an indirect holding of a pool of assets, *e.g.*, mutual funds, are assigned to risk-weight categories under this section based upon the risk-weight that would be assigned to the assets in the portfolio of the pool. An investment in shares of a mutual fund whose portfolio consists primarily of various securities or money market instruments that, if held separately, would be assigned to different risk-weight categories, generally is assigned to the risk-weight category appropriate to the highest risk-weighted asset that the fund is permitted to hold in accordance with the investment objectives set forth in its prospectus. The corporate credit union may, at its option, assign the investment on a *pro rata* basis to different risk-weight categories according to the investment limits in its prospectus. In no case will an investment in shares in any such fund be assigned to a total risk-weight less than 20 percent. If the corporate credit union chooses to assign investments on a *pro rata* basis, and the sum of the investment limits of assets in the fund's prospectus exceeds 100 percent, the corporate credit union must assign the highest *pro rata* amounts of its total investment to the higher risk categories. If, in order to maintain a necessary degree of short-term liquidity, a fund is permitted to hold an insignificant amount of its assets in short-term, highly liquid securities of superior credit quality that do not qualify for a preferential risk-weight, such securities will generally be disregarded in determining the risk-weight category into which the corporate credit union's holding in the overall fund should be assigned. The prudent use of hedging instruments by a mutual fund to reduce the risk of its assets will not increase the risk-weighting of the mutual fund investment. For example, the use of hedging instruments by a mutual fund to reduce the interest rate risk of its government bond portfolio will not increase the risk-weight of that fund above the 20 percent category. Nonetheless, if the fund engages in any activities that appear speculative in nature or has any other characteristics that are inconsistent with the preferential risk-weighting assigned to the fund's assets, holdings in the fund will be assigned to the 100 percent risk-weight category.

(6) Derivatives. Certain transactions or activities, such as derivatives transactions, may appear on a corporate's balance sheet but are not specifically described in the Section II(a) on-balance sheet risk-weight categories. These items will be assigned risk-weights as described in Section II(b) or II(c) below.

(b) Off-Balance Sheet Items

Except as provided in Section II(c) of this Appendix, risk-weighted off-balance sheet items are determined by the following two-step process. First, the face amount of the off-balance sheet item must be multiplied by the appropriate credit conversion factor listed in this Section II(b). This calculation translates the face amount of an off-balance sheet exposure into an on-balance sheet credit-equivalent amount. Second, the credit-equivalent amount must be assigned to the appropriate risk-weight category using the criteria regarding obligors, guarantors, and collateral listed in Section II(a) of this Appendix.[2] The following are the credit conversion factors and the off-balance sheet items to which they apply.

(1) 100 percent credit conversion factor (Group A).

(i) Risk participations purchased in bankers' acceptances;

(ii) Forward agreements and other contingent obligations with a certain draw down, *e.g.*, legally binding agreements to purchase assets at a specified future date. On the date a corporate credit union enters into a forward agreement or similar obligation, it should convert the principal amount of the assets to be purchased at 100 percent as of that date and then assign this amount to the risk-weight category appropriate to the obligor or guarantor of the item, or the nature of the collateral;

(iii) Indemnification of members whose securities the corporate credit union has lent

---

[2] The sufficiency of collateral and guarantees for off-balance sheet items is determined by the market value of the collateral or the amount of the guarantee in relation to the face amount of the item, except for derivative contracts, for which this determination is generally made in relation to the credit equivalent amount. Collateral and guarantees are subject to the same provisions noted under paragraph II(d) of this Appendix C.

as agent. If the member is not indemnified against loss by the corporate credit union, the transaction is excluded from the risk-based capital calculation. When a corporate credit union lends its own securities, the transaction is treated as a loan. When a corporate credit union lends its own securities or is acting as agent, agrees to indemnify a member, the transaction is assigned to the risk-weight appropriate to the obligor or collateral that is delivered to the lending or indemnifying institution or to an independent custodian acting on their behalf; and

(iv) Unused portions of ABCP liquidity facilities that do not meet the definition of an eligible ABCP liquidity facility. The resulting credit equivalent amount is assigned to the risk category appropriate to the assets to be funded by the liquidity facility based on the assets or the obligor, after considering any collateral or guarantees, or external credit ratings under paragraph II(c)(3) of this Appendix, if applicable.

(2) 50 percent credit conversion factor (Group B).

(i) Transaction-related contingencies, including, among other things, performance bonds and performance-based standby letters of credit related to a particular transaction;

(ii) Unused portions of commitments (including home equity lines of credit and eligible ABCP liquidity facilities) with an original maturity exceeding one year except those listed in paragraph II(b)(5) of this Appendix. For eligible ABCP liquidity facilities, the resulting credit equivalent amount is assigned to the risk category appropriate to the assets to be funded by the liquidity facility based on the assets or the obligor, after considering any collateral or guarantees, or external credit ratings under paragraph II(c)(3) of this Appendix, if applicable; and

(iii) Revolving underwriting facilities, note issuance facilities, and similar arrangements pursuant to which the corporate credit union's CUSO or member can issue short-term debt obligations in its own name, but for which the corporate credit union has a legally binding commitment to either:

(A) Purchase the obligations the member is unable to sell by a stated date; or

(B) Advance funds to its member, if the obligations cannot be sold.

(3) 20 percent credit conversion factor (Group C). Trade-related contingencies, i.e., short-term, self-liquidating instruments used to finance the movement of goods and collateralized by the underlying shipment. A commercial letter of credit is an example of such an instrument.

(4) 10 percent credit conversion factor (Group D). Unused portions of eligible ABCP liquidity facilities with an original maturity of one year or less. The resulting credit equivalent amount is assigned to the risk category appropriate to the assets to be funded by the liquidity facility based on the assets or the obligor, after considering any collateral or guarantees, or external credit ratings under paragraph II(c)(3) of this Appendix, if applicable;

(5) Zero percent credit conversion factor (Group E). (i) Unused portions of commitments with an original maturity of one year or less, except for eligible ABCP liquidity facilities;

(ii) Unused commitments with an original maturity greater than one year, if they are unconditionally cancelable at any time at the option of the corporate credit union and the corporate credit union has the contractual right to make, and in fact does make, either:

(A) A separate credit decision based upon the borrower's current financial condition before each drawing under the lending facility; or

(B) An annual (or more frequent) credit review based upon the borrower's current financial condition to determine whether or not the lending facility should be continued; and

(iii) The unused portion of retail credit card lines or other related plans that are unconditionally cancelable by the corporate credit union in accordance with applicable law.

(6) Off-balance sheet derivative contracts; interest rate and foreign exchange rate contracts (Group F).

(i) Calculation of credit equivalent amounts. The credit equivalent amount of an off-balance sheet derivative contract that is not subject to a qualifying bilateral netting contract in accordance with paragraph II(b)(6)(ii) of this Appendix is equal to the sum of the current credit exposure, i.e., the replacement cost of the contract, and the potential future credit exposure of the contract. The calculation of credit equivalent amounts is measured in U.S. dollars, regardless of the currency or currencies specified in the contract.

(A) Current credit exposure. The current credit exposure of an off-balance sheet derivative contract is determined by the mark-to-market value of the contract. If the mark-to-market value is positive, then the current credit exposure equals that mark-to-market value. If the mark-to-market value is zero or negative, then the current exposure is zero. In determining its current credit exposure for multiple off-balance sheet derivative contracts executed with a single counterparty, a corporate credit union may net positive and negative mark-to-market values of off-balance sheet derivative contracts if subject to a bilateral netting contract as provided in paragraph II(b)(6)(ii) of this Appendix.

(B) Potential future credit exposure. The potential future credit exposure of an off-balance sheet derivative contract, including a contract with a negative mark-to-market value, is estimated by multiplying the notional principal by a credit conversion factor.[3] Corporate credit unions, subject to examiner review, should use the effective rather than the apparent or stated notional amount in this calculation. The conversion factors are:[4]

Remaining maturity	Interest rate contracts (percent)	Foreign exchange rate contracts (percent)	Other derivative contracts (percent)
One year or less	0.0	1.0	10.0
Over one year but less than five years	0.50	5.0	12.0
Over five years	0.50	5.0	15.0

(ii) Off-balance sheet derivative contracts subject to bilateral netting contracts. In determining its current credit exposure for multiple off-balance sheet derivative contracts executed with a single counterparty, a corporate credit union may net off-balance sheet derivative contracts subject to a bilateral netting contract by offsetting positive and negative mark-to-market values, provided that:

(A) The bilateral netting contract is in writing;

(B) The bilateral netting contract creates a single legal obligation for all individual off-balance sheet derivative contracts covered by the bilateral netting contract. In effect, the bilateral netting contract provides that the corporate credit union has a single claim or obligation either to receive or pay only the net amount of the sum of the positive and negative mark-to-market values on the individual off-balance sheet derivative contracts covered by the bilateral netting contract. The single legal obligation for the net amount is operative in the event that a counterparty, or a counterparty to whom the bilateral netting contract has been validly assigned, fails to perform due to any of the following events: Default, insolvency, bankruptcy, or other similar circumstances;

(C) The corporate credit union obtains a written and reasoned legal opinion(s) representing, with a high degree of certainty, that in the event of a legal challenge, including one resulting from default, insolvency, bankruptcy or similar circumstances, the relevant court and administrative authorities would find the corporate credit union's exposure to be the net amount under:

(1) The law of the jurisdiction in which the counterparty is chartered or the equivalent location in the case of noncorporate entities, and if a branch of the counterparty is involved, then also under the law of the jurisdiction in which the branch is located;

(2) The law that governs the individual off-balance sheet derivative contracts covered by the bilateral netting contract; and

(3) The law that governs the bilateral netting contract;

(D) The corporate credit union establishes and maintains procedures to monitor possible changes in relevant law and to ensure that the bilateral netting contract continues to satisfy the requirements of this section; and

(E) The corporate credit union maintains in its files documentation adequate to support the netting of an off-balance sheet derivative contract.[5]

---

[3] For purposes of calculating potential future credit exposure for foreign exchange contracts and other similar contracts, in which notional principal is equivalent to cash flows, total notional principal is defined as the net receipts to each party falling due on each value date in each currency.

[4] No potential future credit exposure is calculated for single currency interest rate swaps in which payments are made based upon two floating rate indices, so-called floating/floating or basis swaps; the credit equivalent amount is measured solely on the basis of the current credit exposure.

[5] By netting individual off-balance sheet derivative contracts for the purpose of calculating its credit equivalent amount, a corporate credit union represents that documentation adequate to support the netting of an off-balance sheet derivative contract is in the corporate credit union's files and available for inspection by the NCUA. Upon determination by the NCUA that a corporate credit union's files are inadequate or that a

(iii) *Walkaway clause*. A bilateral netting contract that contains a walkaway clause is not eligible for netting for purposes of calculating the current credit exposure amount. The term "walkaway clause" means a provision in a bilateral netting contract that permits a nondefaulting counterparty to make a lower payment than it would make otherwise under the bilateral netting contract, or no payment at all, to a defaulter or the estate of a defaulter, even if the defaulter or the estate of the defaulter is a net creditor under the bilateral netting contract.

(iv) *Risk-weighting*. Once the corporate credit union determines the credit equivalent amount for an off-balance sheet derivative contract, that amount is assigned to the risk-weight category appropriate to the counterparty, or, if relevant, to the nature of any collateral or guarantee. Collateral held against a netting contract is not recognized for capital purposes unless it is legally available for all contracts included in the netting contract. However, the maximum risk-weight for the credit equivalent amount of such off-balance sheet derivative contracts is 50 percent.

(v) *Exceptions*. The following off-balance sheet derivative contracts are not subject to the above calculation, and therefore, are not part of the denominator of a corporate credit union's risk-based capital ratio:

(A) A foreign exchange rate contract with an original maturity of 14 calendar days or less; and

(B) Any interest rate or foreign exchange rate contract that is traded on an exchange requiring the daily payment of any variations in the market value of the contract.

(C) Asset-backed commercial paper programs.

(*1*) A corporate credit union that qualifies as a primary beneficiary and must consolidate an ABCP program that is a variable interest entity under Generally Accepted Accounting Principles may exclude the consolidated ABCP program assets from risk-weighted assets if the corporate credit union is the sponsor of the ABCP program.

(*2*) If a corporate credit union excludes such consolidated ABCP program assets from risk-weighted assets, the corporate credit union must assess the appropriate risk-based capital requirement against any exposures of the corporate credit union arising in connection with such ABCP programs, including direct credit substitutes, recourse obligations, residual interests, liquidity facilities, and loans, in accordance with Sections II(a), II(b), and II(c) of this Appendix.

(*3*) If a corporate credit union has multiple overlapping exposures (such as a program-wide credit enhancement and a liquidity facility) to an ABCP program that is not consolidated for risk-based capital purposes, the corporate credit union is not required to hold duplicative risk-based capital under this part against the overlapping position. Instead, the corporate credit union should apply to the overlapping position the applicable risk-based capital treatment that results in the highest capital charge.

(c) Recourse Obligations, Direct Credit Substitutes, and Certain Other Positions

(1) *In general*. Except as otherwise permitted in this Section II(c), to determine the risk-weighted asset amount for a recourse obligation or a direct credit substitute (but not a residual interest):

(i) Multiply the full amount of the credit-enhanced assets for which the corporate credit union directly or indirectly retains or assumes credit risk by a 100 percent conversion factor (For a direct credit substitute that is an on-balance sheet asset (*e.g.*, a purchased subordinated security), a corporate credit union must use the amount of the direct credit substitute and the full amount of the asset it supports, *i.e.*, all the more senior positions in the structure); and

(ii) Assign this credit equivalent amount to the risk-weight category appropriate to the obligor in the underlying transaction, after considering any associated guarantees or collateral. Section II(a) lists the risk-weight categories.

(2) *Residual interests*. Except as otherwise permitted under this Section II(c), a corporate credit union must maintain risk-based capital for residual interests as follows:

---

bilateral netting contract may not be legally enforceable under any one of the bodies of law described in paragraphs II(b)(5)(ii) of this Appendix, the underlying individual off-balance sheet derivative contracts may not be netted for the purposes of this section.

(i) Credit-enhancing interest-only strips. A corporate credit union must maintain risk-based capital for a credit-enhancing interest-only strip equal to the remaining amount of the strip even if the amount of risk-based capital that must be maintained exceeds the full risk-based capital requirement for the assets transferred.

(ii) Other residual interests. A corporate credit union must maintain risk-based capital for a residual interest (excluding a credit-enhancing interest-only strip) equal to the face amount of the residual interest, even if the amount of risk-based capital that must be maintained exceeds the full risk-based capital requirement for the assets transferred.

(iii) Residual interests and other recourse obligations. Where a corporate credit union holds a residual interest (including a credit-enhancing interest-only strip) and another recourse obligation in connection with the same transfer of assets, the corporate credit union must maintain risk-based capital equal to the greater of:

(A) The risk-based capital requirement for the residual interest as calculated under Section II(c)(2)(i) through (ii) of this Appendix; or

(B) The full risk-based capital requirement for the assets transferred, subject to the low-level recourse rules under Section II(c)(5) of this Appendix.

(3) Ratings-based approach—(i) Calculation. A corporate credit union may calculate the risk-weighted asset amount for an eligible position described in Section II(c)(3)(ii) of this section by multiplying the face amount of the position by the appropriate risk-weight determined in accordance with Table A or B of this section.

TABLE A

Long term rating category	Risk-weight (in percent)
Highest or second highest investment grade	20
Third highest investment grade	50
Lowest investment grade	100
One category below investment grade	200

TABLE B

Short term rating category	Risk-weight (in percent)
Highest investment grade	20
Second highest investment grade	50
Lowest investment grade	100

(ii) Eligibility.

(A) Traded positions. A position is eligible for the treatment described in paragraph II(c)(3)(i) of this Appendix if:

(1) The position is a corporate debt obligation with a remaining maturity of 120 days or less, a recourse obligation, a direct credit substitute, a residual interest, or an asset- or mortgage-backed security and is not a credit-enhancing interest-only strip;

(2) The position is a traded position; and

(3) The NRSRO has rated a long term position as one grade below investment grade or better or a short term position as investment grade. If two or more NRSROs assign ratings to a traded position, the corporate credit union must use the lowest rating to determine the appropriate risk-weight category under paragraph (3)(i).

(B) Non-traded positions. A position that is not traded is eligible for the treatment described in paragraph(3)(i) if:

(1) The position is a recourse obligation, a direct credit substitute, a residual interest, or an asset- or mortgage-backed security extended in connection with a securitization and is not a credit-enhancing interest-only strip;

(2) More than one NRSRO rate the position;

(3) All of the NRSROs that rate the position rate it as no lower than one grade below investment grade (for long term position) or no lower than investment grade (for short term investments). If the NRSROs assign different ratings to the position, the corporate credit union must use the lowest rating to determine the appropriate risk-weight category under paragraph (3)(i);

(4) The NRSROs base their ratings on the same criteria that they use to rate securities that are traded positions; and

(5) The ratings are publicly available.

(C) Unrated senior positions. If a recourse obligation, direct credit substitute, residual interest, or asset- or mortgage-backed security is not rated by an NRSRO, but is senior or preferred in all features to a traded position (including collateralization and maturity), the corporate credit union may risk-weight the face amount of the senior position under paragraph (3)(i) of this section, based on the rating of the traded position, subject to supervisory guidance. The corporate credit union must satisfy NCUA that this treatment is appropriate. This paragraph (3)(i)(c) applies only if the traded position provides substantive credit support to the unrated position until the unrated position matures.

(iii) Consistent use of Ratings Based Approach. A corporate credit union that determines to use the ratings based approach must do so in a consistent manner. For example, if the corporate credit union employs the ratings based approach on at least one security or position on a given call report, the credit union must use the ratings based approach on that call report for every security and position that is eligible for the ratings based approach.

(4) Certain positions that are not rated by NRSROs. (i) Calculation. A corporate credit union may calculate the risk-weighted asset amount for eligible position described in paragraph II(c)(4)(ii) of this section based on the corporate credit union's determination of the credit rating of the position. To risk-weight the asset, the corporate credit union must multiply the face amount of the position by the appropriate risk-weight determined in accordance with Table C of this section.

TABLE C

Rating category	Risk-weight (in percent)
Investment grade	100
One category below investment grade	200

(ii) Eligibility. A position extended in connection with a securitization is eligible for the treatment described in paragraph II(c)(4)(i) of this section if it is not rated by an NRSRO, is not a residual interest, and meets the one of the three alternative standards described in paragraphs (A), (B), or (C) below:

(A) Position rated internally. A direct credit substitute, but not a purchased credit-enhancing interest-only strip, is eligible for the treatment described under paragraph II(c)(4)(i) of this Appendix, if the position is assumed in connection with an asset-backed commercial paper program sponsored by the corporate credit union. Before it may rely on an internal credit risk rating system, the corporate must demonstrate to NCUA's satisfaction that the system is adequate. Acceptable internal credit risk rating systems typically:

(1) Are an integral part of the corporate credit union's risk management system that explicitly incorporates the full range of risks arising from the corporate credit union's participation in securitization activities;

(2) Link internal credit ratings to measurable outcomes, such as the probability that the position will experience any loss, the expected loss on the position in the event of default, and the degree of variance in losses in the event of default on that position;

(3) Separately consider the risk associated with the underlying loans or borrowers, and the risk associated with the structure of the particular securitization transaction;

(4) Identify gradations of risk among "pass" assets and other risk positions;

(5) Use clear, explicit criteria to classify assets into each internal rating grade, including subjective factors;

(6) Employ independent credit risk management or loan review personnel to assign or review the credit risk ratings;

(7) Include an internal audit procedure to periodically verify that internal risk ratings are assigned in accordance with the corporate credit union's established criteria;

(8) Monitor the performance of the assigned internal credit risk ratings over time to determine the appropriateness of the initial credit risk rating assignment, and adjust individual credit risk ratings or the overall internal credit risk rating system, as needed; and

(9) Make credit risk rating assumptions that are consistent with, or more conservative than, the credit risk rating assumptions and methodologies of NRSROs.

(B) Program ratings.

(1) A recourse obligation or direct credit substitute, but not a residual interest, is eligible for the treatment described in paragraph II(c)(4)(i) of this Appendix, if the position is retained or assumed in connection with a structured finance program and an NRSRO has reviewed the terms of the program and stated a rating for positions associated with the program. If the program has options for different combinations

of assets, standards, internal or external credit enhancements and other relevant factors, and the NRSRO specifies ranges of rating categories to them, the corporate credit union may apply the rating category applicable to the option that corresponds to the corporate credit union's position.

(2) To rely on a program rating, the corporate credit union must demonstrate to NCUA's satisfaction that that the credit risk rating assigned to the program meets the same standards generally used by NRSROs for rating traded positions. The corporate credit union must also demonstrate to NCUA's satisfaction that the criteria underlying the assignments for the program are satisfied by the particular position.

(3) If a corporate credit union participates in a securitization sponsored by another party, NCUA may authorize the corporate credit union to use this approach based on a program rating obtained by the sponsor of the program.

(C) Computer program. A recourse obligation or direct credit substitute, but not a residual interest, is eligible for the treatment described in paragraph II(c)(4)(i) of this Appendix, if the position is extended in connection with a structured financing program and the corporate credit union uses an acceptable credit assessment computer program to determine the rating of the position. An NRSRO must have developed the computer program and the corporate credit union must demonstrate to NCUA's satisfaction that the ratings under the program correspond credibly and reliably with the rating of traded positions.

(5) Limitations on risk-based capital requirements—

(i) Low-level exposure rule. If the maximum contractual exposure to loss retained or assumed by a corporate credit union is less than the effective risk-based capital requirement, as determined in accordance with this Section II(c), for the assets supported by the corporate credit union's position, the risk-based capital requirement is limited to the corporate credit union's contractual exposure less any recourse liability account established in accordance with Generally Accepted Accounting Principles. This limitation does not apply when a corporate credit union provides credit enhancement beyond any contractual obligation to support assets it has sold.

(ii) Mortgage-related securities or participation certificates retained in a mortgage loan swap. If a corporate credit union holds a mortgage-related security or a participation certificate as a result of a mortgage loan swap with recourse, it must hold risk-based capital to support the recourse obligation and that percentage of the mortgage-related security or participation certificate that is not covered by the recourse obligation. The total amount of risk-based capital required for the security (or certificate) and the recourse obligation is limited to the risk-based capital requirement for the underlying loans, calculated as if the corporate credit union continued to hold these loans as an on-balance sheet asset.

(iii) Related on-balance sheet assets. If an asset is included in the calculation of the risk-based capital requirement under this Section II(c) and also appears as an asset on the corporate credit union's balance sheet, the corporate credit union must risk-weight the asset only under this Section II(c), except in the case of loan servicing assets and similar arrangements with embedded recourse obligations or direct credit substitutes. In that case, the corporate credit union must separately risk-weight the on-balance sheet servicing asset and the related recourse obligations and direct credit substitutes under this section, and incorporate these amounts into the risk-based capital calculation.

(6) Obligations of CUSOs. All recourse obligations and direct credit substitutes retained or assumed by a corporate credit union on the obligations of CUSOs in which the corporate credit union has an equity investment are risk-weighted in accordance with this Section II(c), unless the corporate credit union's equity investment is deducted from the credit union's capital and assets under §704.2 and §704.3.

(d) *Collateral.* The only forms of collateral that are recognized for risk-weighting purposes are cash on deposit in the corporate credit union; Treasuries, U.S. Government agency securities, and U.S. Government-sponsored enterprise securities; and securities issued by multilateral lending institutions or regional development banks. Claims secured by cash on deposit are assigned to the zero percent risk-weight category (to the extent of the cash amount). Claims secured by securities are assigned to the twenty percent risk-weight category (to the extent of the fair market value of the securities).

[75 FR 64852, Oct. 20, 2010]

§ 704.21 Enterprise risk management.

(a) A corporate credit union must develop and follow an enterprise risk management policy.

(b) The board of directors of a corporate credit union must establish an enterprise risk management committee (ERMC) responsible for reviewing the enterprise-wide risk management practices of the corporate credit union. The ERMC must report at least quarterly to the board of directors.

(c) The ERMC must include at least one independent risk management expert. The risk management expert will have post-graduate education; an actuarial, accounting, economics, financial, or legal background; and at least five years experience in identifying, assessing, and managing risk exposures. The risk management expert's experience must also be commensurate with the size of the corporate credit union and the complexity of its operations. The board of directors may hire the independent risk management expert to work full-time or part-time for the ERMC or as a consultant for the ERMC.

(d) A risk management expert qualifies as independent if:

(1) The expert reports to the ERMC and to the corporate credit union's board of directors;

(2) Neither the expert, nor any immediate family member of the expert, is supervised by, or has any material business or professional relationship with, the chief executive officer (CEO) of the corporate credit union, or any one directly or indirectly supervised by the CEO; and

(3) Neither the expert, nor any immediate family member of the expert, has had any of the relationships described in paragraph (d)(2) of this section for at least the past three years.

(e) The risk management expert is not required to be a director of the corporate credit union.

[76 FR 23871, Apr. 29, 2011]

EFFECTIVE DATE NOTE: At 76 FR 23871, Apr. 29, 2011, § 704.21 was added, effective April 29, 2013.

§ 704.22 Membership fees.

(a) A corporate credit union may charge its members a membership fee. The fee may be one-time or periodic.

(b) The corporate credit union must calculate the fee uniformly for all members as a percentage of each member's assets, except that the corporate credit union may reduce the amount of the fee for members that have contributed capital to the corporate. Any reduction must be proportional to the amount of the member's nondepleted contributed capital.

(c) The corporate credit union must give its members at least six months advance notice of any initial or new fee, including terms and conditions, before invoicing the fee. For a recurring fee, the corporate credit union must also give six months notice of any material change to the terms and conditions of the fee.

(d) The corporate credit union may terminate the membership of any credit union that fails to pay the fee in full within 60 days of the invoice date.

[76 FR 23871, Apr. 29, 2011]

PART 705—COMMUNITY DEVELOPMENT REVOLVING LOAN FUND ACCESS FOR CREDIT UNIONS

Sec.
705.1 Authority, purpose, and scope
705.2 Definitions
705.3 Eligibility requirements
705.4 Permissible uses of loan funds
705.5 Terms and conditions
705.6 Application and award processes
705.7 Urgency
705.8 Qualifying state-chartered credit unions
705.9 Reporting and monitoring
705.10 Technical assistance grants

§ 705.1

AUTHORITY: 12 U.S.C. 1756, 1757(5)(D), and (7)(I), 1766, 1782, 1784, 1785 and 1786.

SOURCE: 76 FR 67587, Nov. 2, 2011, unless otherwise noted.

§ 705.1 Authority, purpose, and scope.

(a) This part 705 is issued by the National Credit Union Administration (NCUA) under section 130 of the Federal Credit Union Act, 12 U.S.C. 1772c–1, which implements the Community Development Credit Union Revolving Loan Fund Transfer Act (Pub. L. 99–609, 100 Stat. 3475 (Nov. 6, 1986)).

(b) This Part describes how NCUA makes money available to credit unions from its Community Development Revolving Loan Fund (Fund). NCUA administers the Fund and makes both loans and technical assistance grants to credit unions in accordance with the eligibility criteria and other qualifications, subject to the terms and conditions set out in this Part. All loans and technical assistance grants made under this Part are subject to funds availability and NCUA's discretion.

(c) The Fund is intended to support the efforts of credit unions through loans and technical assistance grants needed for:

(1) Providing basic financial and related services to members in their communities;

(2) Enhancing their capacity to better serve their members and the communities in which they operate; and

(3) Responding to emergencies.

(d) The policy of NCUA is to revolve funds to credit unions as often as practical in order to achieve maximum economic impact on as many credit unions as possible. NCUA anticipates the financial awards provided to credit unions through the Fund will better enable them to support the communities in which they operate. With these awards, credit unions will be able to provide basic financial services to low-income members of these communities, resulting in more opportunities for these members to improve their financial circumstances.

(e) This Part generally establishes the following:

(1) Definitions;

(2) The application process and requirements for qualifying for a loan from the Fund;

(3) The evaluation process;

(4) How loan funds are to be made available and their repayment; and

(5) Technical assistance grants to be provided to credit unions.

§ 705.2 Definitions.

For purposes of this Part, the following terms shall have the meanings assigned to them in this section.

Application means a form supplied by the NCUA by which a Qualifying Credit Union may apply for a loan or a technical assistance grant from the Fund.

Board refers to the National Credit Union Administration Board.

Credit Union means a credit union chartered under the Federal Credit Union Act or under the laws of any state of the United States.

Fund means the Community Development Revolving Loan Fund.

Loan is an award in the form of an extension of credit from the Fund to a Participating Credit Union that must be repaid, with interest.

Low-income Members are those members defined in § 701.34 of this chapter.

Notice of Funding Opportunity, as more fully described in § 705.6 of this part, means the notice NCUA publishes describing one or more loan or technical assistance grant programs or initiatives currently being supported by the Fund and inviting interested Qualifying Credit Unions to submit applications to participate in the program(s) or initiative(s).

Participating Credit Union refers to a Qualifying Credit Union that has submitted an application for a loan or a technical assistance grant from the Fund which has been approved by NCUA. A Participating Credit Union shall not be deemed to be an agency, department, or instrumentality of the United States because of its receipt of a financial award from the Fund.

Program means the Community Development Revolving Loan Fund Program under which NCUA makes loans and technical assistance grants available to credit unions.

Qualifying Credit Union means a credit union that may be, or has agreed to be, examined by NCUA, with a current

National Credit Union Administration § 705.5

low-income designation pursuant to § 701.34(a)(1) or § 741.204 of this chapter or, in the case of a non-federally insured, state-chartered credit union, a low-income designation from a state regulator, made under appropriate state standards with the concurrence of NCUA. Services to low-income members must include, at a minimum, offering share accounts and loans.

Technical Assistance Grant means an award of money from the Fund to a Participating Credit Union that does not have to be repaid.

§ 705.3 Eligibility requirements.

To be eligible to receive a CDRLF award, in the form of either a loan or a technical assistance grant, a Qualifying Credit Union must, within the timeframes specified in any Notice of Funding Opportunity:

(a) Complete and submit an Application; and

(b) Meet the underwriting standards established by NCUA, including those pertaining to financial viability, as set forth in the Application and any related materials developed by NCUA.

§ 705.4 Permissible uses of loan funds.

NCUA may make loans from the Fund to Participating Credit Unions for various uses. The following is a non-exhaustive list of permissible uses or projects:

(a) Development of new products or services for members, including new or expanded share draft or credit card programs;

(b) Partnership arrangements with community-based service organizations or government agencies;

(c) Loan programs, including, but not limited to, microbusiness loans, payday loan alternatives, education loans, and real estate loans;

(d) Acquisition, expansion, or improvement of office space or equipment, including branch facilities, ATMs, and electronic banking facilities; and

(e) Operational programs such as security or disaster recovery.

§ 705.5 Terms and conditions.

(a) NCUA may make loans, in such amounts and subject to such terms and conditions as it may determine, from the Fund to Participating Credit Unions.

(b) *Funding Limits.* Loans may be granted in amounts up to $300,000 in the aggregate, depending on the creditworthiness of the Qualifying Credit Union, its financial need, and its demonstrated capability to provide financial and related services to its members. NCUA may, however, make loans that exceed $300,000 in certain circumstances. NCUA will include in the related Notice of Funding Opportunity the particular criteria used to evaluate an Application for a loan that exceeds $300,000.

(c) *Recording of a loan.* At the discretion of NCUA, a loan will be recorded by a Participating Credit Union as either a note payable or a nonmember deposit.

(d) *Interest rate.* The rate of interest on loans is governed by the CDRLF Loan Interest Rate Policy, which can be found on NCUA's Web site or by contacting NCUA's Office of Small Credit Union Initiatives. The specific interest rate for a particular funding will be announced in the related Notice of Funding Opportunity. The Board will announce changes, if any, to the CDRLF Loan Interest Rate Policy and those changes will apply to loans made under future Notices of Funding Opportunities.

(e) *Repayment and maturity.* (1) Awards made available through loans, whether recorded as a note payable or nonmember deposit, must be repaid to NCUA. All loans will be scheduled for repayment consistent with sound business practices and the objectives of the Program, but in no case will the term exceed five years.

(2) Interest payments will be required semiannually beginning six months after the initial distribution of a loan.

(3) NCUA may allow flexible repayment of loan principal. Details and specific provisions will be addressed in the Notice of Funding Opportunity and other program materials.

(f) *Acceleration.* The terms of each loan agreement will provide for the immediate acceleration of the unpaid balance for breach or default in performance by the Participating Credit Union of the terms or conditions of the loan.

§ 705.6

Default and breach include misrepresentation; failure to make interest or principal payments when due; failure to file required reports; insolvency of the Participating Credit Union; and, if required by NCUA, failure to maintain adequate matching funds for the duration of the loan. Other specific causes of default and breach will be identified in the loan documents between the Participating Credit Union and NCUA. The unpaid balance will also be accelerated and immediately due if any part of the loan funds are improperly used or if uninvested loan proceeds remain unused for an unreasonable or unjustified period of time.

(g) *Matching requirements.* At its discretion, NCUA may require a Participating Credit Union to develop and implement a plan to match all or a portion of the funds represented by loan proceeds. Such requirement will be based on the financial condition of the Participating Credit Union, which will be evaluated under criteria contained in the related Notice of Funding Opportunity. Matching funds must be from non-governmental member or non-member share deposits. Participating Credit Unions required to provide matching funds are subject to the following general provisions and any other conditions in the related Notice of Funding Opportunity and agreements between the Participating Credit Union and NCUA:

(1) Loan monies made available generally must be matched by the Participating Credit Union in an amount equal to the loan amount. Any loan monies matched by nonmember share deposits are not subject to the 20% limitation on nonmember deposits under § 701.32 of this chapter. Participating Credit Unions must maintain the increase in the total amount of share deposits for the duration of the loan. Once the loan is repaid, nonmember share deposits accepted to meet the matching requirement are subject to § 701.32 of this chapter.

(2) Upon approval of its loan application, and before it meets its matching, if required, a Participating Credit Union may receive the entire loan commitment in a single payment. If, at NCUA's discretion, any funds are withheld, the remainder of the funds committed will be available to the Participating Credit Union only after it has documented that it has met the match requirement.

(3) Failure of a Participating Credit Union to generate the required match within the time specified in the loan documents may result in the reduction of the loan proportionate to the amount of match actually generated. Payment of any additional funds initially approved may be limited as appropriate to reflect the revised amount of the loan approved. Any funds already advanced to the Participating Credit Union in excess of the revised amount of loan approval must be repaid immediately to NCUA. Failure to repay such funds to NCUA upon demand may result in the default of the entire loan.

(h) *Other terms and conditions.* Other terms and conditions pertaining to loans, including but not necessarily limited to duration, repayment obligations, and covenants, will be specified in the related Notice of Funding Opportunity or applicable loan documents to be signed by the Participating Credit Union.

§ 705.6 Application and award processes.

(a) *Notice of Funding Opportunity.* NCUA will publish a Notice of Funding Opportunity in the FEDERAL REGISTER, on applicable government Web sites, and its own Web site. The Notice of Funding Opportunity will describe the loan and technical assistance grant programs for the period in which funds are available. It also will announce special initiatives, the amount of funds available, funding priorities, permissible uses of funds, funding limits, deadlines, and other pertinent details. The Notice of Funding Opportunity will also advise potential applicants on how to obtain an Application and related materials. NCUA may supplement the information contained in the Notice of Funding Opportunity through such other media as it determines appropriate, including Letters to Credit Unions, direct notices to Qualifying Credit Unions, and announcements on its Web site.

(b) *Application requirements.* A Qualifying Credit Union must demonstrate a sound financial position and ability to manage its day-to-day business affairs. It also must show that its planned use of proceeds is consistent with the purpose of the Program, the requirements of this Part, and the related Notice of Funding Opportunity. The related Notice of Funding Opportunity may include additional details and requirements.

(1) Applications to participate and qualify for a loan or technical assistance grant under the Program may be obtained from the National Credit Union Administration as outlined in the related Notice of Funding Opportunity.

(2) With respect to loans, NCUA will also require a Qualifying Credit Union to develop and submit a narrative describing how the Qualifying Credit Union intends to use the money obtained from the Fund to enhance the products or services it provides to its membership and how those enhanced products or services support the membership and community served by the Qualifying Credit Union.

(3) In addition to those items required in this section, a Qualifying Credit Union that is a non-federally insured state-chartered credit union must also include the following:

(i) A copy of its most recent external audit report;

(ii) Proof of deposit and surety bond insurance which states the maximum insurance levels permitted by the policies;

(iii) A balance sheet, an income and expense statement, and a schedule of delinquent loans, for each of the four most recent quarter-ends;

(iv) Documentation of the credit union's status as a low-income credit union by the appropriate state supervisory agency consistent with NCUA Rules and Regulations at §§ 701.34(a) and 741.204(b); and

(v) An agreement to be subject to examination by NCUA.

(c) *Evaluation and selection of Qualifying Credit Unions.* NCUA will generally evaluate applications submitted by Qualifying Credit Unions in accordance with the criteria described in this section. Nothing in this section, however, precludes NCUA from considering other criteria included in the related Notice of Funding Opportunity that NCUA determines to be necessary based on the type of funding initiative, economic environment, or other factors or conditions that warrant the evaluation of additional or alternative criteria. Generally, NCUA will evaluate complete applications to determine if the Qualifying Credit Union satisfies the following:

(1) *Financial and Performance.* The Qualifying Credit Union must exhibit a safe and sound financial condition, including a demonstrated ability to perform the requirements associated with the type of award being sought and compliance with NCUA's underwriting standards. In this respect, NCUA will consider the Qualifying Credit Union's long-term financial viability, including absence of indicators suggesting the Qualifying Credit Union is a candidate for merger, a purchase and assumption transaction, or conservatorship. NCUA will also consider the Qualifying Credit Union's compliance with the provisions of any previous loan or technical assistance grant received. NCUA may also consider information concerning the Qualifying Credit Union to which it already has access, including information obtained through the examination process and data contained in Call Reports.

(2) *Compatibility.* NCUA will evaluate whether the stated objectives to be accomplished through the use of the loan or technical assistance grant proceeds conform to the broad purposes and rationale underlying the Fund. Specifically, NCUA will consider whether the award will enable the Qualifying Credit Union to provide basic financial products and related services to its members or enhance its capacity to better serve its members and the community in which it operates. NCUA will also consider whether the use of the financial award will conform to any applicable funding priority, special initiative, or special instruction announced in the related Notice of Funding Opportunity.

(3) *Feasibility.* NCUA will consider the likelihood of the Qualifying Credit Union's success in accomplishing its stated objectives, based on its Application and the factors NCUA determines are relevant.

§ 705.7

(4) *Examination Information and Concurrence from Regional Director for Qualifying Federal Credit Unions.* In evaluating the Qualifying Credit Union, NCUA will consider information and statements provided by NCUA staff or State Supervisory Authority staff that performed the Qualifying Credit Union's most recent examination. NCUA will only provide a loan or a technical assistance grant to a Qualifying Credit Union with the concurrence of that credit union's supervising Regional Director. Examination information for a Qualifying Credit Union that is a state-chartered credit union is discussed in § 705.8 of this Part.

(d) *Requests for additional information.* NCUA will make its funding determinations among the several qualified Applications based on its discretion and consideration of which best meet the priorities and initiatives established and announced by NCUA. During its evaluation process, however, NCUA may request a Qualifying Credit Union to provide additional clarifying or technical information to support its application. NCUA may determine not to provide further consideration of any Application failing to provide additional required information.

(e) *Timing.* NCUA will announce, in the related Notice of Funding Opportunity, the deadline for Qualifying Credit Unions to submit all required documentation, including the Application. Failure to submit all of the requested information or to submit the information within the timeframe specified in the Notice of Funding Opportunity, or in the case of requests for additional clarifying or technical information, within the time specified by NCUA, may result in rejection of the Application without further consideration.

(f) *Notice of Award and Appeals.* NCUA will determine whether an application meets NCUA's standards established by this Part and the related Notice of Funding Opportunity. NCUA will provide written notice to a Qualifying Credit Union as to whether or not it has qualified for a loan or technical assistance grant under this Part. A Qualifying Credit Union whose application has been denied for failure of a qualification may appeal that decision to the NCUA Board in accordance with the following:

(1) Within thirty days of its receipt of a notice of non-qualification, a credit union may appeal the decision to the NCUA Board. The scope of the NCUA Board's review is limited to the threshold question of qualification and not the issue of whether, among qualified applicants, a particular loan or technical assistance grant is funded.

(2) The foregoing procedure shall apply only with respect to Applications received by NCUA during an open period in which funds are available and NCUA has called for Applications. Any Application submitted by an applicant during a period in which NCUA has not called for Applications will be rejected, except for those Applications submitted under § 705.7 of this section. Any such rejection shall not be subject to appeal or review by the NCUA Board.

(g) *Disbursement.* Before NCUA will disburse a loan, the Participating Credit Union must sign the loan agreement, promissory note, and any other loan related documents. NCUA may, in its discretion, choose not to disburse the entire amount of the loan at once.

§ 705.7 Urgency.

On an emergency basis, subject to funds availability, NCUA may consider a funding request from a Qualifying Credit Union experiencing an unplanned or unexpected expense that the Qualifying Credit Union is unable to meet with its own resources. The Qualifying Credit Union must demonstrate a compelling need for immediate assistance without which its continued operations would be threatened or severely disrupted. NCUA, in its discretion, will determine whether the situation constitutes an emergency and if the Qualifying Credit Union is required to submit any additional information to show why the funds are needed on an emergency basis. NCUA will determine and substantiate any reason to expedite funding in such case. Requests for loans or technical assistance grants under this section will be addressed on an ongoing basis and are outside the scope of the related Notice of Funding Opportunity. Technical assistance grants and loans provided on this basis must still demonstrate a purpose consistent with the goals of the Fund. Loans and technical assistance grants made under this section are not anticipated to be a regular source of funding for any Qualifying Credit Unions.

§ 705.8 Qualifying state-chartered credit unions.

A Qualifying Credit Union that is a state-chartered credit union and has submitted an Application to NCUA for participation must obtain written concurrence from its respective state regulatory authority before NCUA will approve its Application. A Qualifying Credit Union that is a state-chartered credit union must also make copies of its state examination reports available to NCUA and must agree to examination by NCUA.

§ 705.9 Reporting and monitoring.

(a) *General.* NCUA's policy is to monitor Participating Credit Unions to assure that loan and technical assistance grant funds awarded under this Part have been used in accordance with their intended purposes and to determine whether anticipated outcomes have been achieved. Particular emphasis will be placed on reviewing loan funds earmarked for programs or initiatives proposed by the Participating Credit Union to determine if the funds have been used as represented and whether the program or initiative has had the impact anticipated by the Participating Credit Union.

(b) *Reporting.* A Participating Credit Union must complete and submit all required reports, at such times and in such formats as NCUA will direct. Such reports must describe how the Participating Credit Union has used the loan or technical assistance grant proceeds and the results it has obtained, in relation to the programs, policies, or initiatives identified by the Participating Credit Union in its application. In addition, the participating Credit Union's board of directors must report on the progress of providing needed community services to the Participating Credit Union's members once a year, either at the annual meeting or in a written report sent to all members. The Participating Credit Union must also submit to NCUA the written report or a summary of the report given at the annual meeting. NCUA may request additional information as it determines appropriate.

(c) *Monitoring.* At its discretion, for verification purposes and as part of its evaluation of the effectiveness of the loan and technical assistance grant programs, NCUA may elect to review information concerning Participating Credit Unions to which it already has access, including information obtained through the examination process and data contained in Call Reports.

§ 705.10 Technical assistance grants.

Technical assistance grants may be funded in such amounts, and in accordance with such terms and conditions, as NCUA may establish. In general, technical assistance grants are provided on a reimbursement basis, to cover expenditures approved in advance by NCUA and supported by receipts evidencing payment by the Participating Credit Union.

(a) *Permissible uses of technical assistance grant funds.* Section 705.4(a) and (b) of this part also apply to technical assistance grants made under this section. Those sections provide examples and other information with respect to the permissible use of CDRLF funds. In addition, technical assistance grants generally should enhance and support the Participating Credit Union's internal capacity to serve its members and better enable it to provide financial services to the community in which the Participating Credit Union is located.

(b) *Appeals of technical assistance grant reimbursement denials.* Pursuant to NCUA Interpretative Ruling and Policy Statement 11-1, any Participating Credit Union may appeal a denial of a technical assistance grant reimbursement to NCUA's Supervisory Review Committee. All appeals of technical assistance grant reimbursements must be submitted to the Supervisory Review Committee within 30 days from the date of the denial. The decisions of the Supervisory Review Committee are final and may not be appealed to the NCUA Board.

PART 706—UNFAIR OR DECEPTIVE ACTS OR PRACTICES

Sec.
706.0 Purpose and scope.
706.1 Definitions.
706.2 Unfair credit practices.
706.3 Unfair or deceptive cosigner practices.
706.4 Late charges.

AUTHORITY: 15 U.S.C. 57a(f).

SOURCE: 75 FR 6559, July 1, 2010, unless otherwise indicated.

§ 706.0 Purpose and scope.

(a) *Purpose.* The purpose of this part is to prohibit unfair or deceptive acts or practices in violation of section 5(a)(1) of the Federal Trade Commission Act, 15 U.S.C. 45(a)(1). The prohibitions in this part do not limit NCUA's authority to enforce the Federal Trade Commission Act with respect to any other unfair or deceptive acts or practices.

(b) *Scope.* This part applies to Federal credit unions.

§ 706.1 Definitions.

(a) *Person.* An individual, corporation, or other business organization.

(b) *Consumer.* A natural person member who seeks or acquires goods, services, or money for personal, family, or household use.

(c) *Obligation.* An agreement between a consumer and a Federal credit union.

(d) *Debt.* Money that is due or alleged to be due from one to another.

(e) *Earnings.* Compensation paid or payable to an individual or for his or her account for personal services rendered or to be rendered by him or her, whether denominated as wages, salary, commission, bonus, or otherwise, including periodic payments pursuant to a pension, retirement, or disability program.

(f) *Household goods.* Clothing, furniture, appliances, one radio and one television, linens, china, crockery, kitchenware, and personal effects (including wedding rings) of the consumer and his or her dependents, provided that the following are not included within the scope of the term "household goods":

(1) Works of art;

(2) Electronic entertainment equipment (except one television and one radio);

(3) Items acquired as antiques; and

(4) Jewelry (except wedding rings).

(g) *Antique.* Any item over one hundred years of age, including such items that have been repaired or renovated without changing their original form or character.

(h) *Cosigner.* A natural person who renders himself or herself liable for the obligation of another person without receiving goods, services, or money in return for the credit obligation, or, in the case of an open-end credit obligation, without receiving the contractual right to obtain extensions of credit under the obligation. The term includes any person whose signature is requested as a condition to granting credit to a consumer, or as a condition for forbearance on collection of a consumer's obligation that is in default. The term does not include a spouse whose signature is required on a credit obligation to perfect a security interest pursuant to State law. A person is a cosigner within the meaning of this definition whether or not he or she is designated as such on a credit obligation.

§ 706.2 Unfair credit practices.

In connection with the extension of credit to consumers, it is an unfair act or practice for a Federal credit union, directly or indirectly, to take or receive from a consumer an obligation that:

(a) Constitutes or contains a cognovit or confession of judgment (for purposes other than executory process in the State of Louisiana), warrant of attorney, or other waiver of the right to notice and the opportunity to be heard in the event of suit or process thereon.

(b) Constitutes or contains an executory waiver or a limitation of exemption from attachment, execution, or other process on real or personal property held, owned by, or due to the consumer, unless the waiver applies solely to property subject to a security interest executed in connection with the obligation.

(c) Constitutes or contains an assignment of wages or other earnings unless:

(1) The assignment by its terms is revocable at the will of the debtor, or

(2) The assignment is a payroll deduction plan or preauthorized payment plan, commencing at the time of the transaction, in which the consumer authorizes a series of wage deductions as a method of making each payment, or

(3) The assignment applies only to wages or other earnings already earned at the time of the assignment.

(d) Constitutes or contains a nonpossessory security interest in household goods other than a purchase money security interest.

§ 706.3 Unfair or deceptive cosigner practices.

(a) *Prohibited practices.* In connection with the extension of credit to consumers, it is:

(1) A deceptive act or practice for a Federal credit union, directly or indirectly, to misrepresent the nature or extent of cosigner liability to any person.

(2) An unfair act or practice for a Federal credit union, directly or indirectly, to obligate a cosigner unless the cosigner is informed prior to becoming obligated, which in the case of open-end credit means prior to the time that the agreement creating the cosigner's liability for future charges is executed, of the nature of his or her liability as cosigner.

(b) *Disclosure requirement.* (1) To comply with the cosigner information requirement of paragraph (a)(2) of this section, a clear and conspicuous disclosure statement shall be of this section given in writing to the cosigner prior to becoming obligated. The disclosure statement will contain only the following statement, or one which is substantially equivalent, and shall either be a separate document or included in the documents evidencing the consumer credit obligation.

NOTICE TO COSIGNER

You are being asked to guarantee this debt. Think carefully before you do. If the borrower doesn't pay the debt, you will have to. Be sure you can afford to pay if you have to, and that you want to accept this responsibility.

You may have to pay up to the full amount of the debt if the borrower does not pay. You may also have to pay late fees or collection costs, which increase this amount.

The creditor can collect this debt from you without first trying to collect from the borrower. The creditor can use the same collection methods against you that can be used against the borrower, such as suing you, garnishing your wages, etc. If this debt is ever in default, that fact may become a part of your credit record.

This notice is not the contract that makes you liable for the debt.

(2) If the notice to cosigner is a separate document, nothing other than the following items may appear with the notice. The following paragraphs (b)(2)(i) through (v) may not be part of the narrative portion of the notice to cosigner.

(i) The name and address of the Federal credit union;

(ii) An identification of the debt to be cosigned (*e.g.*, a loan identification number);

(iii) The amount of the loan;

(iv) The date of the loan;

(v) A signature line for a cosigner to acknowledge receipt of the notice; and

(vi) To the extent permitted by State law, a cosigner notice required by State law may be included in the notice in paragraph (b)(1) of this section.

(3) To the extent the notice to cosigner specified in paragraph (b)(1) of this section refers to an action against a cosigner that is not permitted by State law, the notice to cosigner may be modified.

§ 706.4 Late charges.

(a) In connection with collecting a debt arising out of an extension of credit to a consumer, it is an unfair act or practice for a Federal credit union, directly or indirectly, to levy or collect any delinquency charge on a payment, which payment is otherwise a full payment for the applicable period and is paid on its due date or within an applicable grace period, when the only delinquency is attributable to late fee(s) or delinquency charge(s) assessed on earlier installment(s).

(b) For purposes of this section, "collecting a debt" means any activity other than the use of judicial process that is intended to bring about or does bring about repayment of all or part of a consumer debt.

PART 707—TRUTH IN SAVINGS

Sec.
707.1 Authority, purpose, coverage and effect on State laws.
707.2 Definitions.
707.3 General disclosure requirements.
707.4 Account disclosures.
707.5 Subsequent disclosures.
707.6 Periodic statement disclosures.
707.7 Payment of dividends.
707.8 Advertising.
707.9 Enforcement and record retention.
707.10 [Reserved]
707.11 Additional disclosure requirements for overdraft services.

APPENDIX A TO PART 707—ANNUAL PERCENTAGE YIELD CALCULATION
APPENDIX B TO PART 707—MODEL CLAUSES AND SAMPLE FORMS
APPENDIX C TO PART 707—OFFICIAL STAFF INTERPRETATIONS

AUTHORITY: 12 U.S.C. 4311.

SOURCE: 58 FR 50445, Sept. 27, 1993, unless otherwise noted.

§ 707.1 Authority, purpose, coverage and effect on State laws.

(a) *Authority.* This regulation is issued by the National Credit Union Administration to implement the Truth in Savings Act of 1991 (TISA), contained in the Federal Deposit Insurance Corporation Improvement Act of 1991, 12 U.S.C. 3201 *et seq.,* Pub. L. 102–242, 105 Stat. 2236. Information collection requirements in this regulation have been approved by the Office of Management and Budget under the provisions of 44 U.S.C. 3501 *et seq.* and have been assigned OMB No. 3133–0134.

(b) *Purpose.* The purpose of this part is to enable credit union members and potential members to make informed decisions about accounts at credit unions. This part requires credit unions to provide disclosures so that members and potential members can make meaningful comparisons among credit unions and depository institutions.

(c) *Coverage.* This part applies to all credit unions whose accounts are either insured by, or eligible to be insured by, the National Credit Union Share Insurance Fund, except for any credit union that has been designated as a corporate credit union by the National Credit Union Administration and any credit union that has $2 million or less in assets, after subtracting any nonmember deposits, and is determined to be nonautomated by the National Credit Union Administration. In addition, the advertising rules in § 707.8 apply to any person who advertises an account offered by a credit union, including any person who solicits any amount from any other person for placement in a credit union.

(d) *Effect on state laws.* State law requirements that are inconsistent with the requirements of the TISA and this part are preempted to the extent of the inconsistency.

[58 FR 50445, Sept. 27, 1993, as amended at 61 FR 68129, Dec. 27, 1996; 74 FR 36103, July 22, 2009]

§ 707.2 Definitions.

For purposes of this part, the following definitions apply:

(a) *Account* means a share or deposit account at a credit union held by or offered to a member or potential member. It includes, but is not limited to, accounts such as share, share draft, checking and term share accounts. For purposes of the advertising regulations in § 707.8, the term also includes an account at a credit union that is held by or offered by a share or deposit broker.

(b) *Advertisement* means a commercial message, appearing in any medium, that promotes directly or indirectly:

(1) The availability or terms of, or a deposit in, a new account; and

(2) For purposes of § 707.8(a) and § 707.11 of this part, the terms of, or a deposit in, a new or existing account.

(c) *Annual percentage yield* means a percentage rate reflecting the total amount of dividends paid on an account, based on the dividend rate and the frequency of compounding for a 365-day period and calculated according to the rules in appendix A of this part.

(d) *Average daily balance method* means the application of a periodic rate to the average daily balance in the account for the period. The average daily balance is determined by adding the full amount of principal in the account for each day of the period and dividing that figure by the number of days in the period.

(e) *Board* means the National Credit Union Administration Board.

(f) *Bonus* means a premium, gift, award, or other consideration worth more than $10 (whether in the form of cash, credit, merchandise, or any equivalent) given or offered to a member during a year in exchange for opening, maintaining, or renewing an account, or increasing an account balance. The term does not include dividends, other consideration worth $10 or less given during a year, the waiver or reduction of a fee, the absorption of expenses, non-dividend membership benefits, or extraordinary dividends.

(g) *Credit union* means a federal or state-chartered credit union that is either insured by, or is eligible to apply for insurance from, the National Credit Union Share Insurance Fund.

(h) *Daily balance method* means the application of a daily periodic rate to the full amount of principal in the account each day.

(i) *Dividend* and *dividends* mean any declared or prospective earnings on a member's shares in a credit union to be paid to a member or to the member's account. For purposes of this part, the term does not include the payment of a bonus or other consideration worth $10 or less given during a year, the waiver or reduction of a fee, the absorption of expenses, non-dividend membership benefits, or extraordinary dividends.

(j) *Dividend declaration date* means the date that the board of directors of a credit union declares a dividend for the preceding dividend period.

(k) *Dividend period* means the span of time established by the board of directors of a credit union by the end of which shares in a member account earn dividend credit. The dividend period may be different for each type of account.

(l) *Dividend rate* means the declared or prospective annual dividend rate paid on an account, which does not reflect compounding. For purposes of the account disclosures in § 707.4(b)(1)(i), the rate may, but need not, be referred to as the "annual percentage rate" in addition to being referred to as the "dividend rate."

(m) *Extraordinary dividends* means a nonrepetitive dividend paid at an irregular time from funds legally available for such distribution.

(n) *Fixed-rate account* means an account that is not a variable rate account as defined in paragraph (z) of this section.

(o) *Grace period* means a period following the maturity of an automatically renewing term share account during which the member may withdraw funds without being assessed a penalty.

(p) *Interest* means any payment to a member or to a member's account for the use of funds in a nondividend-bearing account at a state-chartered credit union offered pursuant to state law, calculated by application of a periodic rate to the balance. For purposes of this regulation, the term does not include the payment of a bonus or other consideration worth $10 or less given during a year, the waiver or reduction of a fee, the absorption of expenses, non-dividend membership benefits, or extraordinary dividends. Except as is specifically otherwise provided in this part, in the case of an interest-bearing account held in or offered by a state-chartered credit union pursuant to state law, the word "interest" shall be substituted for all references to "dividend" or "dividends" in this part.

(q) *Member* means:

(1) A natural person member of the credit union who holds an account primarily for personal, family, or household purposes;

(2) A natural person nonmember who holds an account primarily for personal, family, or household purposes, either jointly with a natural person member or in a credit union designated as a low-income credit union, or to whom such an account is offered; and

(3) A natural person nonmember who holds a deposit account in a state-chartered credit union pursuant to state law, or to whom such deposit account is offered.

The term does not include a natural person who holds an account for another in a professional capacity or an unincorporated nonbusiness association of natural person members.

(r) *Non-dividend membership benefits* means any property or service provided by a credit union to its members, the nature of which makes its valuation unreasonable and administratively impracticable.

§ 707.3

(s) *Passbook account* means an account in which the member retains a book or other document in which the credit union records transactions on the account.

(t) *Periodic statement* means a statement setting forth information about an account (other than a term share account or passbook account) that is provided to a member on a regular basis four or more times a year.

(u) *Potential member* means a natural person within the credit union's field of membership (or an unincorporated non-business association of such persons) or otherwise eligible to become a member as defined in paragraph (q) of this section.

(v) *State* means a state, the District of Columbia, the Commonwealth of Puerto Rico, and any territory or possession of the United States.

(w) *Stepped-rate account* means an account that has two or more dividend rates that take effect in succeeding periods and are known when the account is opened.

(x) *Term share account* means any share certificate, interest-bearing certificate of deposit account, or other account with a maturity of at least seven days in which the member generally does not have a right to make withdrawals for six days after the account is opened, unless the account is subject to an early withdrawal penalty of at least seven days' dividends on amounts withdrawn, offered by a credit union to a member or potential member.

(y) *Tiered-rate account* means an account that has two or more dividend rates that are applicable to specified balance levels.

(z) *Variable-rate account* means a share, share draft, checking, or term share account in which the simple dividend rate may change after the account is opened, unless the credit union contracts to give at least thirty days advance written notice of rate decreases.

[58 FR 50445, Sept. 27, 1993, as amended at 59 FR 13436, Mar. 22, 1994; 59 FR 59899, Nov. 21, 1994; 70 FR 72898, Dec. 8, 2005]

§ 707.3 General disclosure requirements.

(a) *Form.* Credit unions must make the disclosures required by §§ 707.4 through 707.6 of this part, as applicable, clearly and conspicuously, in writing, and in a form the member or potential member may keep. Credit unions may provide the disclosures required by this part to a member or potential member in electronic form, subject to compliance with the consent and other applicable provisions of the Electronic Signatures in Global and National Commerce Act (E–Sign Act), 15 U.S.C. 7001 *et seq.* Credit unions may provide the disclosures required by §§ 707.4(a)(2) and 707.8 to a member or potential member in electronic form without regard to the consent or other provisions of the E–Sign Act in the circumstances set forth in those sections. Disclosures for each account offered by a credit union may be presented separately or combined with disclosures for the credit union's other accounts, as long as it is clear which disclosures are applicable to the member or potential member's account.

(b) *General.* The disclosures shall reflect the terms of the legal obligation between the member and the credit union. Disclosures may be made in languages other than English, provided the disclosures are available in English upon request.

(c) *Relation to Regulation E (12 CFR part 205).* Disclosures required by and provided in accordance with the Electronic Fund Transfer Act (15 U.S.C. 1601) and its implementing Regulation E (12 CFR part 205) that are also required by this part may be substituted for the disclosures required by this part.

(d) *Multiple members.* If an account is held by more than one member, disclosures may be made to any one of the members.

(e) *Oral responses to inquiries.* In an oral response to a member or potential member's inquiry about dividend rates payable on its accounts, the credit union shall state the annual percentage yield. The dividend rate may be stated in addition to the annual percentage yield. No other rate may be stated. In stating a dividend rate and annual percentage yield, a credit union shall:

National Credit Union Administration § 707.4

(1) For dividend-bearing accounts other than term share accounts, specify a dividend rate and annual percentage yield as of the last dividend declaration date. In the event that disclosures of a dividend rate and annual percentage yield as of the last dividend declaration date might be inaccurate because of known or contemplated dividend rate changes, the credit union may disclose the prospective dividend rate and prospective annual percentage yield. Such prospective dividend rate and prospective annual percentage yield may be disclosed either in lieu of, or in addition to, the dividend rate and annual percentage yield as of the last dividend declaration date.

(2) For interest-bearing accounts and for dividend-bearing term share accounts, specify an interest (dividend) rate and annual percentage yield that were offered within the most recent seven calendar days; state that the rate and yield are accurate as of an identified date; and provide a telephone number members may call to obtain current rate information.

(f) *Rounding and accuracy rules for rates and yields*—(1) *Rounding.* The annual percentage yield, the annual percentage yield earned, and the dividend rate shall be rounded to the nearest one-hundredth of one percentage point (.01%) and expressed to two decimal places. For account disclosures, the dividend rate may be expressed to more than two decimal places.

(2) *Accuracy.* The annual percentage yield (and the annual percentage yield earned) will be considered accurate if not more than one-twentieth of one percentage point (.05%) above or below the annual percentage yield (and the annual percentage yield earned) determined in accordance with the rules in appendix A of this part.

(Approved by the Office of Management and Budget under control number 3133–0134)

[58 FR 50445, Sept. 27, 1993, as amended at 61 FR 114, Jan. 3, 1996; 66 FR 33162, June 21, 2001; 74 FR 36104, July 22, 2009]

§ 707.4 Account disclosures.

(a) *Delivery of account disclosures*—(1) *Account opening.* (i) *General.* A credit union must provide account disclosures to a member or potential member before an account is opened or a service is provided, whichever is earlier. A credit union is deemed to have provided a service when a fee required to be disclosed is assessed. Except as provided in paragraph (a)(1)(ii) of this section, if a member or potential member is not present at the credit union when the account is opened or the service is provided and has not already received the disclosures, the credit union must mail or deliver the disclosures no later than 10 business days after the account is opened or the service is provided, whichever is earlier.

(ii) *Timing of electronic disclosures.* If a member or potential member who is not present at the credit union uses electronic means, for example, an internet Web site, to open an account or request a service, the disclosures required under paragraph (a)(1) of this section must be provided before the account is opened or the service is provided.

(2) *Requests.* (i) A credit union must provide account disclosures to a member or potential member upon request. If a member or potential member who is not present at the credit union makes a request, the credit union must mail or deliver the disclosures within a reasonable time after it receives the request and may provide the disclosures in paper form or electronically if the member or potential member agrees.

(ii) In providing disclosures upon request, the credit union may:

(A) Specify rates as follows:

(*1*) For dividend-bearing accounts other than term share accounts, specify a dividend rate and annual percentage yield as of the last dividend declaration date. In the event that disclosures of a dividend rate and annual percentage yield as of the last dividend declaration date might be inaccurate because of known or contemplated dividend rate changes, the credit union may disclose the prospective dividend rate and prospective annual percentage yield. Such prospective dividend rate and prospective annual percentage yield may be disclosed either in lieu of, or in addition to, the dividend rate and annual percentage yield as of the last dividend declaration date.

§ 707.4

(2) For interest bearing accounts and for dividend-bearing term share accounts, specify an interest rate and annual percentage yield that were offered within the most recent seven calendar days; state that the rate and yield are accurate as of an identified date; and provide a telephone number members may call to obtain current rate information; and

(B) State the maturity of a term share account as either a term or a date.

(b) *Content of account disclosures.* Account disclosures shall include the following, as applicable:

(1) *Rate information*—(i) *Annual percentage yield and dividend rate.* (A) For interest-bearing accounts and for dividend-bearing term share accounts, the "annual percentage yield" and the "interest rate" ("dividend rate"), using those terms, and for fixed-rate accounts the period of time the interest (dividend) rate will be in effect.

(B) For dividend-bearing accounts other than term share accounts, a credit union shall specify a dividend rate and annual percentage yield (using those terms) as of the last dividend declaration date. In the event that disclosures of a dividend rate and annual percentage yield as of the last dividend declaration date might be inaccurate because of known or contemplated dividend rate changes, the credit union may disclose the prospective dividend rate and prospective annual percentage yield. Such prospective dividend rate and prospective annual percentage yield may be disclosed either in lieu of, or in addition to, the dividend rate and annual percentage yield as of the last dividend declaration date.

(ii) *Variable rates.* For variable-rate accounts:

(A) The fact that the dividend rate and annual percentage yield may change;

(B) How the dividend rate is determined;

(C) The frequency with which the dividend rate may change; and

(D) Any limitation on the amount the dividend rate may change.

(2) *Compounding and crediting*—(i) *Frequency.* The frequency with which dividends are compounded and credited, and the dividend period for dividend-bearing accounts.

(ii) *Effect of closing an account.* If members will forfeit dividends if they close an account before accrued dividends are credited, a statement that the dividends will not be paid in such cases.

(3) *Balance information*—(i) *Minimum balance requirements.* Any minimum balance required to:

(A) Open the account;
(B) Avoid the imposition of a fee; or
(C) Obtain the annual percentage yield disclosed.

Except for the balance to open the account, the disclosure shall state how the balance is determined for these purposes.

(ii) *Balance computation method.* An explanation of the balance computation method specified in § 707.7, used to calculate dividends on the account.

(iii) *When dividends begin to accrue.* A statement of when dividends begin to accrue on noncash deposits.

(4) *Fees.* The amount of any fee that may be imposed in connection with the account (or an explanation of how the fee will be determined) and the conditions under which the fee may be imposed.

(5) *Transaction limitations.* Any limitations on the number or dollar amount of withdrawals or deposits.

(6) *Features of term share accounts.* For term share accounts:

(i) *Time requirements.* The maturity date.

(ii) *Early withdrawal penalties.* A statement that a penalty will be imposed for early withdrawal, how it is calculated, and the conditions for its assessment.

(iii) *Withdrawal of dividends prior to maturity.* If compounding occurs and dividends may be withdrawn prior to maturity, a statement that the annual percentage yield assumes dividends remain in the account until maturity and that a withdrawal will reduce earnings. For accounts with a stated maturity greater than 1 year that do not compound dividends on an annual or more frequent basis, that require dividend payouts at least annually, and that disclose an APY determined in accordance with section E of appendix A of this part, a statement that dividends cannot remain on account and that payout of dividends is mandatory.

(iv) *Renewal policies.* A statement of whether or not the account will renew automatically at maturity. If it will, a statement of whether or not a grace period will be provided and, if so, the length of that period must be stated. If the account will not renew automatically, a statement of whether dividends will be paid after maturity if the member does not renew the account must be stated.

(7) *Bonuses.* The amount or type of any bonus, when the bonus will be provided, and any minimum balance and time requirements to obtain the bonus.

(8) *Nature of dividends.* For accounts earning dividends, other than term share accounts, a statement that dividends are paid from current income and available earnings, after required transfers to reserves at the end of a dividend period.

(c) *Notice to existing account holders*—(1) *Notice of availability of disclosures.* Credit unions shall provide a notice to members who receive periodic statements and who hold existing accounts of the type offered by the credit union on January 1, 1995. The notice shall be included on or with the first periodic statement sent after January 1, 1995 (or on or with the first periodic statement for a statement cycle beginning on or after that date). The notice shall state that the members may request account disclosures containing terms, fees, and rate information for the account. In responding to such a request, credit unions shall provide disclosures in accordance with paragraph (a)(2) of this section.

(2) *Alternative to notice.* As an alternative to the notice described in paragraph (c)(1) of this section, credit unions may provide account disclosures to members. The disclosures may be provided either with a periodic statement or separately, but must be sent no later than when the periodic statement described in paragraph (c)(1) of this section is sent.

(Approved by the Office of Management and Budget under control number 3133–0134)

[58 FR 50445, Sept. 27, 1993, as amended at 61 FR 114, Jan. 3, 1996; 63 FR 71574, Dec. 29, 1998; 66 FR 33163, June 21, 2001; 74 FR 36104, July 22, 2009]

§ 707.5 **Subsequent disclosures.**

(a) *Change in terms*—(1) *Advance notice required.* A credit union shall give advance notice to affected members of any change in a term required to be disclosed under § 707.4(b), if the change may reduce the annual percentage yield or adversely affect the member. The notice shall include the effective date of the change. The notice shall be mailed or delivered at least 30 calendar days before the effective date of the change.

(2) *No notice required.* No notice under this section is required for:

(i) *Variable-rate changes.* Changes in the dividend rate and corresponding changes in the annual percentage yield in variable-rate accounts.

(ii) *Share draft and check printing fees.* Changes in fees for check printing.

(iii) *Short-term term share accounts.* Changes in any term for term share accounts with maturities of one month or less.

(b) *Notice before maturity for term share accounts longer than one month that renew automatically.* For term share accounts with a maturity longer than one month that renew automatically at maturity, credit unions shall provide the disclosures described below before maturity. The disclosures shall be mailed or delivered at least 30 calendar days before maturity of the existing account. Alternatively, the disclosures may be mailed or delivered at least 20 calendar days before the end of the grace period on the existing account, provided a grace period of at least five calendar days is allowed.

(1) *Maturities of longer than one year.* If the maturity is longer than one year, the credit union shall provide account disclosures set forth in § 707.4(b) for the new account, along with the date the existing account matures. If the dividend rate and annual percentage yield that will be paid for the new account are unknown when disclosures are provided, the credit union shall state that those rates have not yet been determined, the date when they will be determined, and a telephone number members may call to obtain the dividend rate and the annual percentage yield that will be paid for the new account.

§ 707.6

(2) *Maturities of one year or less but longer than one month.* If the maturity is one year or less but longer than one month, the credit union shall either:

(i) Provide disclosures as set forth in paragraph (b)(1) of this section; or

(ii) Disclose to the member:

(A) The date the existing account matures and the new maturity date if the account is renewed;

(B) The dividend rate and the annual percentage yield for the new account if they are known (or that those rates have not yet been determined, the date when they will be determined, and a telephone number the member may call to obtain the dividend rate and the annual percentage yield that will be paid for the new account); and

(C) Any difference in the terms of the new account as compared to the terms required to be disclosed under § 707.4(b) for the existing account.

(c) *Notice before maturity for term share accounts longer than one year that do not renew automatically.* For term share accounts with a maturity longer than one year that do not renew automatically at maturity, credit unions shall disclose to members the maturity date and whether dividends will be paid after maturity. The disclosures shall be mailed or delivered at least 10 calendar days before maturity of the existing account.

(Approved by the Office of Management and Budget under control number 3133–0134)

[58 FR 50445, Sept. 27, 1993, as amended at 61 FR 114, Jan. 3, 1996; 63 FR 71574, Dec. 29, 1998]

§ 707.6 Periodic statement disclosures.

(a) *Rule when statement and crediting periods vary.* In making the disclosures described in paragraph (b) of this section, credit unions that calculate and credit dividends for a period other than the statement period, such as the dividend period, may calculate and disclose the annual percentage yield earned and amount of dividends earned based on that period rather than the statement period. The information in paragraph (b)(4) shall be stated for that period as well as for the statement period.

(b) *Statement disclosures.* If a credit union mails or delivers a periodic statement, the statement shall include the following disclosures:

(1) *Annual percentage yield earned.* The "annual percentage yield earned," using that term as calculated according to the rules in appendix A of this part.

(2) *Amount of dividends.* The dollar amount of dividends earned (accrued or paid and credited) on the account. The dollar amount of any extraordinary dividends earned during the statement period shall be shown as a separate figure.

(3) *Fees imposed.* Fees required to be disclosed under § 707.4(b)(4) of this part that were debited from the account during the statement period. The fees must be itemized by type and dollar amounts. Except as provided in § 707.11(a)(1) of this part, when fees of the same type are imposed more than once in a statement period, a credit union may itemize each fee separately or group the fees together and disclose a total dollar amount for all fees of that type.

(4) *Length of period.* The total number of days in the statement period, or the beginning and ending dates of the period.

(Approved by the Office of Management and Budget under control number 3133–0134)

(5) *Aggregate fee disclosure.* If applicable, the total overdraft and returned item fees required to be disclosed by § 707.11(a).

[58 FR 50445, Sept. 27, 1993, as amended at 59 FR 59899, Nov. 21, 1994; 61 FR 114, Jan. 3, 1996; 64 FR 66356, Nov. 26, 1999; 66 FR 33163, June 21, 2001; 70 FR 72898, Dec. 8, 2005; 75 FR 47175, Aug. 5, 2010]

§ 707.7 Payment of dividends.

(a) *Permissible methods*—(1) *Balance on which dividends are calculated.* Credit unions shall calculate dividends on the full amount of principal in an account for each day by use of either the daily balance method or the average daily balance method. Credit unions shall calculate dividends by use of a daily rate of at least $1/365$ of the dividend rate. In a leap year a daily rate of $1/366$ of the dividend rate may be used.

(2) *Determination of minimum balance to earn dividends.* A credit union shall use the same method to determine any minimum balance required to earn dividends as it uses to determine the

National Credit Union Administration § 707.8

balance on which dividends are calculated. A credit union may use an additional method that is unequivocally beneficial to the member.

(b) *Compounding and crediting policies.* This section does not require credit unions to compound or credit dividends at any particular frequency.

(c) *Date dividends begin to accrue.* Dividends shall begin to accrue not later than the day specified in section 606 of the Expedited Funds Availability Act (12 U.S.C. 4005) and implementing Regulation CC (12 CFR part 229). Dividends shall accrue on funds until the day funds are withdrawn.

(Approved by the Office of Management and Budget under control number 3133–0134)

[58 FR 50445, Sept. 27, 1993, as amended at 61 FR 114, Jan. 3, 1996]

§ 707.8 Advertising.

(a) *Misleading or inaccurate advertisements.* An advertisement must not:

(1) Be misleading or inaccurate or misrepresent a credit union's account agreement; or

(2) Refer to or describe an account as "free" or "no cost" or contain a similar term if any maintenance or activity fee may be imposed on the account. The word "profit" must not be used in referring to dividends or interest paid on an account.

(b) *Permissible rates.* If an advertisement states a rate of return, it shall state the rate as an "annual percentage yield," using that term. (The abbreviation "APY" may be used provided the term "annual percentage yield" is stated at least once in the advertisement.) The advertisement shall not state any other rate, except that the "dividend rate," using that term, may be stated in conjunction with, but not more conspicuously than, the annual percentage yield to which it relates.

(c) *When additional disclosures are required.* Except as provided in paragraph (e) of this section, if the annual percentage yield is stated in an advertisement, the advertisement shall state the following information, to the extent applicable, clearly and conspicuously:

(1) *Variable rates.* For variable-rate accounts, a statement that the rate may change after the account is opened.

(2) *Time annual percentage yield is offered.* For interest-bearing accounts and dividend-bearing term share accounts, the period of time the annual percentage yield will be offered, or a statement that the annual percentage yield is accurate as of a specified date. For dividend-bearing accounts other than term share accounts, a statement that the annual percentage yield is accurate as of the last dividend declaration date. In the event that disclosure of an annual percentage yield as of the last dividend declaration date might be inaccurate because of known or contemplated dividend rate changes, the credit union may disclose the prospective annual percentage yield. Such prospective annual percentage yield may be disclosed either in lieu of, or in addition to, the dividend rate and annual percentage yield as of the last dividend declaration date.

(3) *Minimum balance.* The minimum balance required to earn the advertised annual percentage yield. For tiered-rate accounts, the minimum balance required for each tier shall be stated in close proximity and with equal prominence to the applicable annual percentage yield.

(4) *Minimum opening deposit.* The minimum deposit required to open the account, if it is greater than the minimum balance necessary to earn the advertised annual percentage yield.

(5) *Effect of fees.* A statement that fees could reduce the earnings on the account.

(6) *Features of term share accounts.* For term share accounts:

(i) *Time requirements.* The term of the account.

(ii) *Early withdrawal penalties.* A statement that a penalty will or may be imposed for early withdrawal.

(iii) *Required dividend payouts.* For noncompounding term share accounts with a stated maturity greater than one year that do not compound dividends on an annual or more frequent basis, that require dividend payouts at least annually, and that disclose an APY determined in accordance with section E of appendix A of this part, a

§ 707.9

statement that dividends cannot remain on account and that payout of dividends is mandatory.

(d) *Bonuses.* Except as provided in paragraph (e) of this section, if a bonus is stated in an advertisement, the advertisement shall state the following information, to the extent applicable, clearly and conspicuously:

(1) The "annual percentage yield," using that term;

(2) The time requirements to obtain the bonus;

(3) The minimum balance required to obtain the bonus;

(4) The minimum balance required to open the account, if it is greater than the minimum balance necessary to obtain the bonus; and

(5) When the bonus will be provided.

(e) *Exemption for certain advertisements*—(1) *Certain media.* If an advertisement is made through one of the following media, it need not contain the information in paragraphs (c)(1), (c)(2), (c)(4), (c)(5), (c)(6)(ii), (d)(4) and (d)(5) of this section:

(i) Broadcast or electronic media, such as television or radio;

(ii) Outdoor media, such as billboards; or

(iii) Telephone response machines.

(2) *Indoors signs.* (i) Signs inside the premises of a credit union (or the premises of a share or deposit broker) are not subject to paragraphs (b), (c), (d) or (e)(1) of this section.

(ii) If a sign exempted by paragraph (e)(2) of this section states a rate of return, it shall:

(A) State the rate as an "annual percentage yield," using that term or the term "APY." The sign shall not state any other rate, except that the dividend rate may be stated in conjunction with the annual percentage yield to which it relates.

(B) Contain a statement advising members to contact an employee for further information about applicable fees and terms.

(3) *Newsletters.* (i) Newsletters sent by a credit union to existing members only are not subject to paragraphs (b), (c), (d) or (e)(1) of this section.

(ii) If a newsletter exempted by paragraph (e)(3) of this section states a rate of return, it shall:

(A) State the rate as an "annual percentage yield," using that term or the term "APY." The newsletter shall not state any other rate, except that the dividend rate may be stated in conjunction with the annual percentage yield to which it relates.

(B) Contain a statement advising members to contact an employee for further information about applicable fees and terms.

(f) *Additional disclosures in connection with the payment of overdrafts.* Credit unions that promote the payment of overdrafts in an advertisement must include in the advertisement the disclosures required by § 707.11(b) of this part.

(Approved by the Office of Management and Budget under control number 3133–0134)

[58 FR 50445, Sept. 27, 1993, as amended at 59 FR 13436, Mar. 22, 1994; 61 FR 114, Jan. 3, 1996; 63 FR 71575, Dec. 29, 1998; 70 FR 72898, Dec. 8, 2005; 73 FR 30477, May 28, 2008]

§ 707.9 Enforcement and record retention.

(a) *Administrative enforcement.* Section 270 of TISA (12 U.S.C. 4309) contains the provisions relating to administrative sanctions for failure to comply with the requirements of TISA and this part.

(b) *Civil liability.* Section 271 of TISA (12 U.S.C. 4310) contains the provisions relating to civil liability for failure to comply with the requirements of TISA and this part; Section 271 is repealed effective September 30, 2001.

(c) *Record retention.* A credit union shall retain evidence of compliance with this regulation for a minimum of two years after the date disclosures are required to be made or action is required to be taken.

(Approved by the Office of Management and Budget under control number 3133–0134)

[58 FR 50445, Sept. 27, 1993, as amended at 59 FR 13436, Mar. 22, 1994; 61 FR 114, Jan. 3, 1996; 63 FR 71575, Dec. 29, 1998]

§ 707.10 [Reserved]

§ 707.11 Additional disclosure requirements for overdraft services.

(a) *Disclosure of total fees on periodic statements*—(1) *General.* A credit union must separately disclose on each periodic statement, as applicable:

National Credit Union Administration § 707.11

(i) The total dollar amount for all fees or charges imposed on the account for paying checks or other items when there are insufficient or unavailable funds and the account becomes overdrawn, using the term "Total Overdraft Fees;" and

(ii) The total dollar amount for all fees or charges imposed on the account for returning items unpaid.

(2) *Totals required.* The disclosures required by paragraph (a)(1) of this section must be provided for the statement period and for the calendar year-to-date.

(3) *Format requirements.* The aggregate fee disclosures required by paragraph (a) of this section must be disclosed in close proximity to fees identified under § 707.6(a)(3), using a format substantially similar to Sample Form B-10 in appendix B.

(b) *Advertising disclosures for overdraft services*—(1) *Disclosures.* Except as provided in paragraphs (b)(2),(b)(3), and (b)(4) of this section, any advertisement promoting the payment of overdrafts must disclose in a clear and conspicuous manner:

(i) The fee or fees for the payment of each overdraft;

(ii) The categories of transactions for which a fee for paying an overdraft may be imposed;

(iii) The time period by which the member must repay or cover any overdraft; and

(iv) The circumstances under which the credit union will not pay an overdraft.

(2) *Communications about the payment of overdrafts not subject to additional advertising disclosures.* Paragraph (b)(1) of this section does not apply to:

(i) An advertisement promoting a service where the credit union's payment of overdrafts will be agreed upon in writing and subject to part 226 of this title (Regulation Z);

(ii) A communication by a credit union about the payment of overdrafts in response to a member-initiated inquiry about share accounts or overdrafts. Providing information about the payment of overdrafts in response to a balance inquiry made through an automated system, such as a telephone response machine, ATM, or a credit union's Internet site, is not a response to a member-initiated inquiry for purposes of this paragraph;

(iii) An advertisement made through broadcast or electronic media, such as television or radio;

(iv) An advertisement made on outdoor media, such as billboards;

(v) An ATM receipt;

(vi) An in-person discussion with a member;

(vii) Disclosures required by Federal or other applicable law;

(viii) Information included on a periodic statement or a notice informing a member about a specific overdrawn item or the amount the account is overdrawn;

(ix) A term in a share account agreement discussing the credit union's right to pay overdrafts;

(x) A notice provided to a member, such as at an ATM, that completing a requested transaction may trigger a fee for overdrawing an account, or a general notice that items overdrawing an account may trigger a fee;

(xi) Informational or educational materials concerning the payment of overdrafts if the materials do not specifically describe the credit union's overdraft service; or

(xii) An opt-out or opt-in notice regarding the credit union's payment of overdrafts or provision of discretionary overdraft services.

(3) *Exception for ATM screens and telephone response machines.* The disclosures described in paragraphs (b)(1)(ii) and (b)(1)(iv) of this section are not required in connection with any advertisement made on an ATM screen or using a telephone response machine.

(4) *Exception for indoor signs.* Paragraph (b)(1) of this section does not apply to advertisements for the payment of overdrafts on indoor signs as described by § 707.8(e)(2) of this part, provided that the sign contains a clear and conspicuous statement that fees may apply and that members should contact an employee for further information about applicable fees and terms. For purposes of this paragraph (b)(4), an indoor sign does not include an ATM screen.

Pt. 707, App. A

(c) *Disclosure of account balances.* If a credit union discloses balance information to a member through an automated system, the balance may not include additional amounts that the credit union may provide to cover an item when there are insufficient or unavailable funds in the member's account, whether under a service provided in its discretion, a service subject to part 226 of this title (Regulation Z), or a service to transfer funds from another member account. The credit union may, at its option, disclose additional account balances that include such additional amounts, if the credit union prominently states that any such balance includes such additional amounts and, if applicable, that additional amounts are not available for all transactions.

[70 FR 72898, Dec. 8, 2005, as amended at 74 FR 36104, July 22, 2009; 75 FR 47175, Aug. 5, 2010]

APPENDIX A TO PART 707—ANNUAL PERCENTAGE YIELD CALCULATION

The annual percentage yield (APY) measures the total amount of dividends a credit union pays on an account based on the dividend rate and the frequency of compounding. The annual percentage yield is expressed as an annualized rate, based on a 365-day year. (Credit unions may calculate the annual percentage yield based on a 365-day or a 366-day year in a leap year.) Part I of this appendix discusses the annual percentage yield calculations for account disclosures and advertisements, while Part II discusses annual percentage yield earned calculations for statements. The annual percentage yield reflects only dividends and does not include the value of any bonus, as that term is defined in part 707, that may be provided to the member to open, maintain, increase or renew an account. Dividends, interest or other earnings are not to be included in the annual percentage yield if such amounts are determined by circumstances that may or may not occur in the future. These formulas apply to both dividend-bearing and interest-bearing accounts held by credit unions.

PART I. ANNUAL PERCENTAGE YIELD FOR ACCOUNT DISCLOSURES AND ADVERTISING PURPOSES

In general, the annual percentage yield for account disclosures under §§ 707.4 and 707.5 and for advertising under § 707.8 is an annualized rate that reflects the relationship between the amount of dividends that would be earned by the member for the term of the account and the amount of principal used to calculate those dividends. The amount of dividends that would be earned may be projected based on the most recent past declared rate or an anticipated future rate, whichever the credit union judges to most reasonably approximate the dividends to be earned. Special rules apply to accounts with tiered and stepped dividend rates, and to certain term share accounts with a stated maturity greater than 1 year.

A. General Rules

Except as provided in Part I. E. of this appendix, the annual percentage yield shall be calculated by the formula shown below. Credit unions may calculate the annual percentage yield using projected dividends based on either the rate at the last dividend declaration date or the rate anticipated at a future date. The credit union must disclose whichever option it uses to members. Credit unions shall calculate the annual percentage yield based on the actual number of days for the term of the account. For accounts without a stated maturity date (such as a typical share or share draft account), the calculation shall be based on an assumed term of 365 days. In determining the total dividends figure to be used in the formula, credit unions shall assume that all principal and dividends remain on deposit for the entire term, and that no other transactions (deposits or withdrawals) occur during the term. (This assumption shall not be used if a credit union requires, as a condition of the account, that members withdraw dividends during the term. In such a case, the dividends (and annual percentage yield calculation) shall reflect that requirement.) For term share accounts that are offered in multiples of months, credit unions may base the number of days on either the actual number of days during the applicable period, or the number of days that would occur for any actual sequence of that many calendar months. If credit unions choose to use this permissive rule, they must use the same number of days to calculate the dollar amount of dividends that will be earned on the account in the annual percentage yield formula (where "Dividends" are divided by "Principal".)

The annual percentage yield is to be calculated by use of the following general formula (("APY") is used for convenience in the formulas):

APY=100 [(1 + Dividends/Principal) $^{(365/\text{Days in term})}$ − 1].

"Principal" is the amount of funds assumed to have been deposited at the beginning of the account.

"Dividends" is the total dollar amount of dividends earned on the Principal for the term of the account.

"Days in term" is the actual number of days in the term of the account.

634

National Credit Union Administration

When the "days in term" is 365 (that is, where the stated maturity is 365 days or where the account does not have a stated maturity), the APY can be calculated by use of the following simple formula:

APY=100 (Dividends/Principal).

Examples:

(1) If a credit union would pay $61.68 in dividends for a 365-day year on $1,000 deposited into a share draft account, the APY is 6.17%:

APY=100 [(1 + 61.68/1,000)$^{(365/365)}$ − 1]
APY=6.17%.

Or, using the simple formula above (since the term is deemed to be 365 days):

APY=100 (61.68/1,000)
APY=6.17%.

(2) If a credit union pays $30.37 in dividends on a $1,000 six-month term share certificate account (where the six-month period used by the credit union contains 182 days), using the general formula above, the APY is 6.18%:

APY=100 [(1+30.37/1,000)$^{(365/182)}$ − 1]
APY=6.18%.

The APY is affected by the frequency of compounding, i.e., the amount of dividends will be greater the more frequently dividends are compounded for a given nominal rate. When two credit unions are offering the same dividend rate on, for example, a share account, the APY disclosed may be different if the credit unions use a different frequency of compounding.

Examples:

(1) If a credit union pays $1,268.25 in dividends for a 365-day year on $10,000 deposited into a regular share account earning 12%, and the dividends are compounded monthly, the APY will be 12.68%.

APY=100 ($1,268.25/10,000)
APY=12.68%

(2) However, if a credit union is compounding dividends on a quarterly basis on an account which otherwise has the same terms, the dividends will be $1,255.09 and the APY will be 12.55%.

APY=100 ($1,255.09/10,000)
APY=12.55%

B. Stepped-Rate Accounts (Different Rates Apply in Succeeding Periods)

For accounts with two or more dividend rates applied in succeeding periods (where the rates are known at the time the account is opened), a credit union shall assume each dividend rate is in effect for the length of time provided for in any share agreement.

Examples:

(1) If a credit union offers a $1,000 6-month term share (certificate) account on which it pays a 5% dividend rate, compounded daily, for the first three months (which contain 91 days), and a 5.5% dividend rate, compounded daily, for the next three months (which contain 92 days), the total dividends for six months is $26.68, and, using the general formula above, the APY is 5.39%:

APY=100 [(1+26.68/1,000)$^{(365/183)}$ − 1]
APY=5.39%.

(2) If a credit union offers a $1,000 2-year share certificate on which it pays a 6% dividend rate, compounded daily, for the first year, and a 6.5% dividend rate, compounded daily, for the next year, the total dividends for two years is $133.13, and, using the general formula above, the APY is 6.45%:

APY=100 [(1+133.13/1,000)$^{(365/730)}$ − 1]
APY=6.45%.

C. Variable-Rate Accounts

For variable-rate accounts without an introductory premium or discounted rate, a credit union must base the calculation only on the initial dividend rate in effect when the account is opened (or advertised), and assume that this rate will not change during the year.

Variable-rate accounts with an introductory premium or discount rate must be treated like stepped-rate accounts. Thus, a credit union shall assume that: (1) The introductory simple dividend rate is in effect for the length of time provided for in the account contract; and (2) the variable dividend rate that would have been in effect when the account is opened or advertised (but for the introductory rate) is in effect for the remainder of the year. If the variable rate is tied to an index, the index-based rate in effect at the time of disclosure must be used for the remainder of the year. If the rate is not tied to an index, the rate in effect for existing members holding the same account (who are not receiving the introductory dividend rate) must be used for the remainder of the year.

For example, if a credit union offers an account on which it pays a 7% dividend rate, compounded daily, for the first three months (which, for example, contains 91 days), while the variable dividend rate that would have been in effect when the account was opened was 5%, the total dividends for a 365-day year for a $1,000 account balance is $56.52, (based on 91 days at 7% followed by 274 days at 5%). Using the simple formula, the APY is 5.65%:

APY=100 (56.52/1,000)
APY=5.65%.

D. Accounts With Tiered Rates (Different Rates Apply to Specified Balance Level)

For accounts in which two or more dividend rates paid on the account are applicable to specified balance levels, the credit union must calculate the annual percentage yield in accordance with the method described below that it uses to calculate dividends. In all cases, an annual percentage yield (or a range of annual percentage yields, if appropriate) must be disclosed for each balance tier.

Pt. 707, App. A

For purposes of the examples discussed below, assume the following:

Simple dividend rate (Percent)	Share balance required to earn rate
5.25	Up to but not exceeding $2,500.
5.50	Above $2,500, but not exceeding $15,000.
5.75	Above $15,000.

Tiering Method A

Under this method, a credit union pays on the full balance in the account the stated dividend rate that corresponds to the applicable share balance tier. For example, if a member deposits $8,000, the credit union pays the 5.50% dividend rate on the entire $8,000. This is also known as a "hybrid" or "plateau" tiered rate account.

When this method is used to determine dividends, only one annual percentage yield will apply to each tier. Within each tier, the annual percentage yield will not vary with the amount of principal assumed to have been deposited.

For the dividend rates and account balances assumed above, the credit union will state three annual percentage yields—one corresponding to each balance tier. Calculation of each annual percentage yield is similar for this type of account as for accounts with a single fixed dividend rate. Thus, the calculation is based on the total amount of dividends that would be received by the member for each tier of the account for a year and the principal assumed to have been deposited to earn that amount of dividends.

First tier. Assuming daily compounding, the credit union will pay $53.90 in dividends on a $1,000 account balance. Using the general formula for the first tier, the APY is 5.39%:

APY=100 [(1+53.90/1,000)$^{(365/365)}$ – 1]
APY=5.39%.

Using the simple formula:

APY=100 (53.90/1,000)
APY=5.39%.

Second tier. The credit union will pay $452.29 in dividends on an $8,000 deposit. Thus, using the simple formula, the annual percentage yield for the second tier is 5.65%:

APY=100 (452.29/8,000)
APY=5.65%.

Third tier. The credit union will pay $1,183.61 in dividends on a $20,000 account balance. Thus, using the simple formula, the annual percentage yield for the third tier is 5.92%:

APY=100 (1,183.61/20,000)
APY=5.92%.

Tiering Method B

Under this method, a credit union pays the stated dividend rate only on that portion of the balance within the specified tier. For example, if a member deposits $8,000, the credit union pays 5.25% on only $2,500 and 5.50% on $5,500 (the difference between $8,000 and the first tier cutoff of $2,500). This is also known as a "pure" tiered rate account.

The credit union that computes dividends in this manner must provide a range that shows the lowest and the highest annual percentage yields for each tier (other than for the first tier, which, like the tiers in Method A, has the same annual percentage yield throughout). The low figure for an annual percentage yield is calculated based on the total amount of dividends earned for a year assuming the *minimum* principal required to earn the dividend rate for that tier. The high figure for an annual percentage yield is based on the amount of dividends the credit union would pay on the *highest* principal that could be deposited to earn that same dividend rate. If the account does not have a limit on the amount that can be deposited, the credit union may assume any amount.

For the tiering structure assumed above, the credit union would state a total of five annual percentage yields—one figure for the first tier and two figures stated as a range for the other two tiers.

First tier. Assuming daily compounding, the credit union could pay $53.90 in dividends on a $1,000 account balance. For this first tier, using the simple formula, the annual percentage yield is 5.39%:

APY=100 (53.90/1,000)
APY=5.39%.

Second tier. For the second tier the credit union would pay between $134.75 and $841.45 in dividends, based on assumed balances of $2,500.01 and $15,000, respectively. For $2,500.01, dividends would be figured on $2,500 at 5.25% dividend rate plus dividends on $.01 at 5.50%. For the low end of the second tier, therefore, the annual percentage yield is 5.39%. Using the simple formula:

APY=100 (134.75/2,500)
APY=5.39%.

For $15,000, dividends are figured on $2,500 at 5.25% dividend rate plus dividends on $12,500 at 5.50% dividend rate. For the high end of the second tier, the annual percentage yield, using the simple formula, is 5.61%:

APY=100 (841.45/15,000)
APY=5.61%.

Thus, the annual percentage yield range that would be stated for the second tier is 5.39% to 5.61%.

Third tier. For the third tier, the credit union would pay $841.45 and $5,871.78 in dividends on the low end of the third tier (a balance of $15,000.01). For $15,000.01, dividends would be figured on $2,500 at 5.25% dividend rate, plus dividends on $12,500 at 5.50% dividend rate, plus dividends on $.01 at 5.75% dividend rate. For the low end of the third tier, therefore, the annual percentage yield, using the simple formula, is 5.61%:

APY=100 (841.45/15,000)

National Credit Union Administration

APY=5.61%.

Assuming the credit union does not limit the account balance, it may assume any maximum amount for the purposes of computing the annual percentage yield for the high end of the third tier. For an assumed maximum balance amount of $100,000, dividends would be figured on $2,500 at 5.25% dividend rate, plus dividends on $12,500 at 5.50% dividend rate, plus dividends on $85,000 at 5.75% dividend rate. For the high end of the third tier, therefore, the annual percentage yield, using the simple formula, is 5.87%:

APY=100 (5,871.78/100,000)
APY=5.87%.

Thus, the annual percentage yield that would be stated for the third tier is 5.61% to 5.87%. If the assumed maximum balance amount is $1,000,000, credit unions would use $985,000 rather than $85,000 in the last calculation. In that case for the high end of the third tier, the annual percentage yield, using the simple formula, is 5.91%:

APY=100 (59,134.22/1,000,000)
APY=5.91%

Thus, the annual percentage yield range that would be stated for the third tier is 5.61% to 5.91%.

E. Term Share Accounts with a Stated Maturity Greater than One Year that Pay Dividends At Least Annually

1. For term share accounts with a stated maturity greater than one year, that do not compound dividends on an annual or more frequent basis, and that require the member to withdraw dividends at least annually, the annual percentage yield may be disclosed as equal to the dividend rate.

Example:

If a credit union offers a $1,000 two-year term share account that does not compound and that pays out dividends semi-annually by check or transfer at a 6.00% dividend rate, the annual percentage yield may be disclosed as 6.00%.

2. For term share accounts covered by this paragraph that are also stepped-rate accounts, the annual percentage yield may be disclosed as equal to the composite dividend rate.

Example:

(1) If a credit union offers a $1,000 three-year term share account that does not compound and that pays out dividends annually by check or transfer at a 5.00% dividend rate for the first year, 6.00% dividend rate for the second year, and 7.00% dividend rate for the third year, the credit union may compute the composite dividend rate and APY as follows:

(a) Multiply each dividend rate by the number of days it will be in effect;
(b) Add these figures together; and
(c) Divide by the total number of days in the term.

(2) Applied to the example, the products of the dividend rates and days the rates are in effect are (5.00%×365 days) 1825, (6.00%×365 days) 2190, and (7.00%×365) 2555, respectively. The sum of these products, 6570, is divided by 1095, the total number of days in the term. The composite dividend rate and APY are both 6.00%.

PART II. ANNUAL PERCENTAGE YIELD EARNED FOR STATEMENTS

The annual percentage yield earned for statements under § 707.6 is an annualized rate that reflects the relationship between the amount of dividends actually earned (accrued or paid and credited) to the member's account during the period and the average daily balance in the account for the period over which the dividends were earned.

Pursuant to § 707.6(a), when dividends are paid less frequently than statements are sent, the APY Earned may reflect the number of days over which dividends were earned rather than the number of days in the statement period, e.g., if a credit union uses the average daily balance method and calculates dividends for a period other than the statement period, the annual percentage yield earned shall reflect the relationship between the amount of dividends earned and the average daily balance in the account for the other period, such as a crediting or dividend period.

The annual percentage yield shall be calculated by using the following formulas ("APY Earned" is used for convenience in the formulas):

A. General Formula

APY Earned=100 [(1+Dividends earned/Balance)$^{(365/\text{Days in period})}$ − 1].

"Balance" is the average daily balance in the account for the period.

"Dividends earned" is the actual amount of dividends accrued or paid and credited to the account for the period.

"Days in period" is the actual number of days over which the dividends disclosed on the statement were earned.

Examples:

(1) If a credit union calculates dividends for the statement period (and uses either the daily balance or the average daily balance method), and the account had a balance of $1,500 for 15 days and a balance of $500 for the remaining 15 days of a 30-day statement period, the average daily balance for the period is $1,000. Assume that $5.25 in dividends was earned during the period. The annual percentage yield earned (using the formula above) is 6.58%:

APY Earned=100 [(1+5.25/1,000)$^{(365/30)}$ − 1]
APY Earned=6.58%.

(2) Assume a credit union calculates dividends on the average daily balance for the

calendar month and provides periodic statements that cover the period from the 16th of one month to the 15th of the next month. The account has a balance of $2,000 September 1 through September 15 and a balance of $1,000 for the remaining 15 days of September. The average daily balance for the month of September is $1,500, which results in $6.50 in dividends earned for the month. The annual percentage yield earned for the month of September would be shown on the periodic statement covering September 16 through October 15. The annual percentage yield earned (using the formula above) is 5.40%:

APY Earned=100 [(1+6.50/1,500)$^{(365/30)}$ − 1]
APY Earned = 5.40%.

(3) Assume a credit union calculates dividends on the average daily balance for a quarter (for example, the calendar months of September through November), and provides monthly periodic statements covering calendar months. The account has a balance of $1,000 throughout the 30 days of September, a balance of $2,000 throughout the 31 days of October, and a balance of $3,000 throughout the 30 days of November. The average daily balance for the quarter is $2,000, which results in $21 in dividends earned for the quarter. The annual percentage yield earned would be shown on the periodic statement for November. The annual percentage yield earned (using the formula above) is 4.28%:

APY Earned=100 [(1+21/2,000)$^{(365/91)}$ − 1]
APY Earned=4.28%.

B. SPECIAL FORMULA FOR USE WHERE PERIODIC STATEMENT IS SENT MORE OFTEN THAN THE PERIOD FOR WHICH DIVIDENDS ARE COMPOUNDED.

Credit unions that use the daily balance method to accrue dividends and that issue periodic statements more often than the period for which dividends are compounded shall use the following special formula:

$$\text{APY Earned} = 100\left[\left\{1 + \frac{(\text{Dividends earned/Balance})}{\text{Days in period (Compounding)}}\right\}^{(365/\text{Compounding})} - 1\right]$$

The following definition applies for use in this formula (all other terms are defined under Part II):

"Compounding" is the number of days in each compounding period.

Assume a credit union calculates dividends for the statement period using the daily balance method, pays a 5.00% dividend rate, compounded annually, and provides periodic statements for each monthly cycle. The account has a daily balance of $1000.00 for a 30-day statement period. The dividend earned of $4.11 for the period, and the annual percentage yield earned (using the special formula above) is 5.00%:

$$\text{APY Earned} = 100\left[\left\{1 + \frac{(\$4.11/1,000)}{30}(365)\right\}^{(365/365)} - 1\right]$$

APY Earned = 5.00%.

[58 FR 50445, Sept. 27, 1993, as amended at 63 FR 71575, Dec. 29, 1998]

APPENDIX B TO PART 707—MODEL CLAUSES AND SAMPLE FORMS

Table of Contents

B-1—Model Clauses for Account Disclosures (§ 707.4(b))
B-2—Model Clauses for Changes in Terms (§ 707.5(a))
B-3—Model Clauses for Pre-Maturity Notices for Term Share Accounts (§ 707.5(b-d))
B-4—Sample Form (Signature Card/ Application for Membership)
B-5—Sample Form (Term Share (Certificate) Account)
B-6—Sample Form (Regular Share Account Disclosures)
B-7—Sample Form (Share Draft Account Disclosures)

National Credit Union Administration   **Pt. 707, App. B**

B-8—Sample Form (Money Market Share Account Disclosures)

B-9—Sample Form (Term Share (Certificate) Account Disclosures)

B-10—Sample Form (Periodic Statement)

B-11—Sample Form (Rate and Fee Schedule)

B-12 Aggregate Overdraft and Returned Item Fees Sample Form

GENERAL NOTE: Appendix B contains model clauses and sample forms intended for optional use by credit unions to aid in compliance with the disclosure requirements of §§ 707.4 (account disclosures), 707.5 (subsequent disclosures), 707.6 (statement disclosures), and 707.8 (advertisements). Section 269(b) of TISA provides that credit unions that use these clauses and forms will be in compliance with TISA's disclosure provisions.

As discussed in the supplementary information to § 707.3(a), this final rule provides for flexibility in designing the format of the disclosures. Credit unions can choose to prepare a single document or brochure that incorporates disclosures for all accounts offered, or to prepare different documents for each type of account. Credit unions may also use inserts to a document, or fill in blanks to show current rates, fees and other terms.

In the model clauses, words in parentheses indicate the type of disclosure a credit union should insert in the space provided (for example, a credit union might insert "July 23, 1995" in the blank for a "(date)" disclosure). Brackets and "/" indicate that a credit union must choose the alternative that best describes its practice (for example, "[daily balance/ average daily balance]"). It should be noted that only in sections B-6 through B-10 of this appendix have specific examples of disclosures been given, with dates and figures. Sections B-1 through B-5, and section B-11 provide only unspecific model clauses or blank forms. The Board felt, as did the FRB in the appendix A to Regulation DD, that a mix of blank clauses and forms and application of the model clauses to real specific situations would benefit those who must comply with TISA.

Any references to NCUA Rules and Regulations, the *NCUA Standard FCU Bylaws*, or the *NCUA Accounting Manual for FCUs*, are provided for guidance and as a point of reference for credit unions. Citations to these sources does not indicate that their application is required for those credit unions who need not follow them.

B-1 MODEL CLAUSES FOR ACCOUNT DISCLOSURES (§ 707.4(B))

(A) *Rate Information (Sec. 707.4(b)(1))*

(I) *Fixed-Rate Accounts (§ 707.4(b)(1)(i)(A–B))*

1. Interest-bearing Accounts

The interest rate on your deposit account is ____% with an annual percentage yield (APY) of ____%. [For purposes of this disclosure, this is a rate and APY that were offered within the most recent seven calendar days and were accurate as of (date). Please call (credit union telephone number) to obtain current rate information.] You will be paid this rate [for (time period)/until (date)/for at least 30 calendar days].

NOTE: This provision reflects an accurate statement for an interest-bearing account authorized by state law for state-chartered credit unions. While the definition of the term "interest" permits its substitution for the term "dividends," separate disclosures should be made for interest-bearing accounts. Since account opening disclosures may be provided to potential members requesting account information before opening an account, and members opening new accounts, information is provided indicating that the rate may not be current, but that the potential member or member may call the credit union to obtain up-to-date information. When opening a new account, of course, a credit union could provide the contractual rate alone, and delete the sentences in brackets. Given the definition of fixed-rate account in § 707.2(n), credit unions offering fixed-rate accounts must contract to hold rates steady for at least a 30-day period. Thus, if the 30-day option of the last sentence is not chosen, the period chosen must be longer than 30 days.

2. Dividend-bearing Term Share Accounts

The dividend rate on your term share account is ____% with an annual percentage yield (APY) of ____%. [For purposes of this disclosure, this is a rate and APY that were offered within the most recent seven calendar days and were accurate as of (date). Please call (credit union telephone number) to obtain current rate information.] You will be paid this rate [for (time period)/until (date)/for at least 30 calendar days].

NOTE: This provision reflects an accurate statement for a fixed-rate, dividend-bearing term share account. Interest-bearing term share accounts would use the disclosure in § 1, above. Since account opening disclosures may be provided to potential members requesting account information before opening an account, and members opening new accounts, information is provided indicating that the rate may not be current, but that the potential member or member may call the credit union to obtain up-to-date information. When opening a new account, of course, a credit union could provide the contractual rate alone, and delete the sentences in brackets. Given the definition of fixed-rate account in §707.2(n), credit unions offering fixed-rate accounts must contract to hold rates steady for at least a 30-day period. Thus, if the 30-day option of the last sentence is not chosen, the period chosen must be longer than 30 days.

3. Other Dividend-bearing Accounts

[As of [the last dividend declaration date/(date)], the dividend rate was ____% with an annual percentage yield (APY) of ____% on your account. /or The prospective dividend rate on your account is ____% with a prospective APY of ____% for the current dividend period.] You will be paid this rate for [(time period)/at least 30 calendar days].

or

[As of [the last dividend declaration date/(date)], the dividend rate was ____% with an annual percentage yield (APY) of ____% on your account. /or The prospective dividend rate on your account is ____% with an annual percentage yield (APY) of ____% for this dividend period.] This rate will not change unless the credit union notifies you at least 30 calendar days prior to any change.

NOTE: Credit unions may disclose the dividend rate and annual percentage yield on accounts as of the last dividend declaration date. This necessitates inclusion of a disclosure of the actual calendar date of the last dividend declaration date. Additionally or alternatively (if the last dividend rate could be inaccurate), credit unions may disclose a prospective dividend rate and a prospective annual percentage yield. Such prospective rates and yields must be estimated in good faith, and must be declared at the proper time if it is at all possible to do so. As for the last sentence in these disclosures, this provision reflects a credit union policy to set prospective dividend rates for the next month (or at least 30 days), quarter or other period. Many credit unions, at their mid-monthly board meeting, set prospective dividend rates for the next month beginning on the 1st day of the month and continuing to the last day of the month. These rates must be formalized or ratified at the end of a dividend period. Given the timing of the board meetings, the time to prepare and mail notices and the 30 day period, it will often take credit unions 45 to 60 days to effectively change rates. For these reasons, the Board strongly suggests that credit unions do not offer fixed-rate, dividend-bearing accounts.

(II) *Variable-Rate Accounts (§707.4(b)(1)(ii))*

1. Interest-bearing Accounts

The interest rate on your deposit account is ____%, with an annual percentage yield (APY) of ____%. [For purposes of this disclosure, this is a rate and APY that were offered within the most recent seven calendar days and were accurate as of (date). Please call (credit union telephone number) to obtain current rate information.] The interest rate and annual percentage yield may change every (time period) based on [(name of index)/the determination of the credit union board of directors]. The interest rate for your account will [never change by more than ____% each (time period)/never be less/more than ____%/never exceed ____% above or fall more than ____% below the initial interest rate].

NOTE: This disclosure combines the requirements of §707.4(b)(1)(i) with §707.4(b)(1)(ii) for interest-bearing accounts. The variable nature of a deposit account usually is based on an external index or is set at the discretion of the board. If another means of rate setting is used, that, instead of the proposed language, must be disclosed. Since account opening disclosures may be provided to potential members requesting account information before opening an account, and members opening new accounts, information is provided indicating that the rate may not be current, but that the potential member or member may call the credit union to obtain up-to-date information. When opening a new account, of course, a credit union could provide the contractual rate alone, and delete the sentences in brackets. Rarely would there be limitations on rate changes, but language is provided for this situation in the last sentence. Of course, it is only to be used if it applies to an account.

2. Dividend-bearing Term Share Accounts

The dividend rate on your term share account is ____%, with an annual percentage yield (APY) of ____%. [For purposes of this disclosure, this is a rate and APY that were offered within the most recent seven calendar days and were accurate as of (date). Please call (credit union telephone number) to obtain current rate information.] The dividend rate and annual percentage yield may change every (time period) based on [(name of index)/the determination of the credit union board of directors]. The dividend rate for your account will [never change by more than ____% each (time period)/never be less/more than ____% /never exceed ____% above or fall more than ____% below the initial dividend rate].

NOTE: This disclosure combines the requirements of §707.4(b)(1)(i) with §707.4(b)(1)(ii) for dividend-bearing, variable-

National Credit Union Administration

rate term share accounts. The variable nature of a deposit account usually is based on an external index or is set at the discretion of the board. If another means of rate setting is used, that, instead of the model language, must be disclosed. Since account opening disclosures may be provided to potential members requesting account information before opening an account, and members opening new accounts, information is provided indicating that the rate may not be current, but that the potential member or member may call the credit union to obtain up-to-date information. When opening a new account, of course, a credit union could provide the contractual rate alone, and delete the sentences in brackets. Rarely would there be limitations on rate changes, but language is provided for this situation in the last sentence. Of course, it is only to be used if it applies to an account.

3. Other Dividend-bearing Accounts

[As of [the last dividend declaration date/(date)], the dividend rate was ____% with an annual percentage yield (APY) of ____% on your account. /or The prospective dividend rate on your account is ____% with an anticipated annual percentage yield (APY) of ____% for the current dividend period.] The dividend rate and annual percentage yield may change every (dividend period) as determined by the credit union board of directors.

NOTE: This language combines the requirements of §707.4(b)(1)(i) with §707.4(b)(1)(ii). Credit unions may disclose the dividend rate and annual percentage yield on accounts as of the last dividend declaration date. This necessitates inclusion of a disclosure of the actual calendar date of the last dividend declaration date or use of the phrase "last dividend declaration date". Additionally or alternatively, credit unions may disclose a prospective dividend rate and a prospective annual percentage yield. Such prospective rates and yields must be estimated in good faith, and must be declared at the proper time if it is at all possible to do so. As for the last sentence in these disclosures, this provision reflects the variable nature of the account. Generally, there is only one variable-rate feature for share accounts: the frequency of dividend period rate changes (e.g., daily, weekly, monthly, quarterly, semi-annually, annually). Normally, there are no contractual limitations on share account earnings (unless imposed by a regulator), nor are earnings based on any internal or external index. If contractual limitations or an index are involved, however, those factors would need to be disclosed (unless a regulator orders otherwise).

Pt. 707, App. B

(III) *Stepped-Rate Accounts (§ 707.4(b)(1)(i))*

1. Interest-bearing Accounts

The initial interest rate on your deposit account is ____%. You will be paid that rate [for (time period)/ until (date)]. After that time, the interest rate for your deposit account will be ____% and you will be paid that rate [for (time period)/ until (date)]. The annual percentage yield (APY) for your account is ____%. [For purposes of this disclosure, this is a rate and APY that were offered within the most recent seven calendar days and were accurate as of (date). Please call (credit union telephone number) to obtain current rate information.] You will be paid this rate [for (time period)/until (date)/for at least 30 calendar days].

2. Dividend-bearing Term Share Accounts

The initial dividend rate on your term share account is ____%. You will be paid that rate [for (time period)/ until (date)]. After that time, the dividend rate for your term share account will be ____% and you will be paid that rate [for (time period)/ until (date)]. The annual percentage yield (APY) for your account is ____%. [For purposes of this disclosure, this is a rate and APY that were offered within the most recent seven calendar days and were accurate as of (date). Please call (credit union telephone number) to obtain current rate information.] You will be paid this rate [for (time period)/until (date)/for at least 30 calendar days].

3. Other Dividend-bearing Accounts

[As of [the last dividend declaration date/(date)], the initial dividend rate on your account was ____%. /or The prospective dividend rate on your account is ____%.] You will be paid that rate [for (time period)/ until (date)]. After that time, the prospective dividend rate for your share account will be ____% and you will be paid such rate [for (time period)/ until (date)]. The annual percentage yield (APY) for your account is ____%. You will be paid this rate for [(time period)/at least 30 calendar days].

NOTE: Stepped-rate accounts are accounts with two or more rates that take effect in succeeding periods. The applicable rates and time periods *are known* when the account is opened. By nature these are fixed-rate accounts and are usually associated with term share (certificate) accounts. Accordingly, a contract provision (for share accounts) to change rates should be included.

(IV) *Tiered-Rate Accounts (§ 707.4(b)(1)(i))*

1. Interest-bearing Accounts

Tiering Method A

1* If your [daily balance/average daily balance] is $____ or more, the interest rate paid on the entire balance in your account will be ____%, with an annual percentage yield (APY) of ____%.

2* If your [daily balance/average daily balance] is more than $____, but less than $____, the interest rate paid on the entire balance in your account will be ____%, with an APY of ____%.

3* If your [daily balance/average daily balance] is $____ or less, the interest rate paid on the entire balance will be ____% with an APY of ____%.

[For purposes of this disclosure, this is a rate and APY that were offered within the most recent seven calendar days and were accurate as of (date). Please call (credit union telephone number) to obtain current rate information.]

[*Fixed-rate*—You will be paid this rate [for (time period)/until (date)/for at least 30 calendar days]./ *Variable-rate*—The interest rate and APY may change every (time period) based on [(name of index)/ the determination of the credit union board of directors.]

NOTE: Tiering Method A pays the stated interest rate that corresponds to the applicable deposit tier on the full balance in the account. This example contemplates a two-tier system. The option (1, 2 or 3) most closely matching the terms of the account should be chosen as the appropriate disclosure. For tiered-rate accounts, a disclosure may be added about the currency of the rate, as is provided in the first set of brackets. A disclosure regarding the fixed-rate or variable-rate nature of the account must be added, as is provided in the last set of brackets.

Tiering Method B

1* An interest rate of ____% will be paid only on the portion of your [daily balance/ average daily balance] that is greater than $____. The annual percentage yield (APY) for this tier will range from ____% to ____%, depending on the balance in the account.

2* An interest rate of ____% will be paid only on the portion of your [daily balance/ average daily balance] that is greater than $____, but less than $____. The annual percentage yield (APY) for this tier will range from ____% to ____%, depending on the balance in the account.

3* If your [daily balance/average daily balance] is $____ or less, the interest rate paid on the entire balance will be ____%, with an annual percentage yield (APY) of ____%.

[For purposes of this disclosure, this is a rate and APY that were offered within the most recent seven calendar days and were accurate as of (date). Please call (credit union telephone number) to obtain current rate information.]

[*Fixed-rate*—You will be paid this rate [for (time period)/until (date)/for at least 30 calendar days]./ *Variable-rate*—The interest rate and APY may change every (time period) based on [(name of index)/ the determination of the credit union board of directors.]

NOTE: Tiering Method B pays different stated interest rates corresponding to applicable deposit tiers, on the applicable balance in each tier of the account. For example, a credit union might pay 3% interest on account funds of $500 or below, and pay 4% interest on the portion of the same account that exceeds $500. The example contemplates an account with two tiers, but additional tiers are possible. The option (1, 2 or 3) most closely matching the terms of the account should be chosen as the appropriate disclosure. For tiered-rate accounts, a disclosure may be added about the currency of the rate, as is provided in the first set of brackets.

Tiered-rate accounts can be either fixed-rate or variable-rate accounts. The last sentence offers an option of either fixed-rate or variable-rate disclosure. Thus, the disclosures outlined above will be made in addition to either: (i) Disclosure of the period the fixed-rates are in effect or (ii) the variable-rate disclosures. Tiered-rate accounts are also subject to the requirement for disclosure of the balance computation method, *see* paragraph (e) to this appendix.

2. Dividend-bearing Term Share Accounts

Tiering Method A

1* If your [daily balance/average daily balance] is $____ or more, the dividend rate paid on the entire balance in your account will be ____%, with an annual percentage yield (APY) of ____%.

2* If your [daily balance/average daily balance] is more than $____, but less than $____, the dividend rate paid on the entire balance in your account will be ____%, with an APY of ____%.

3* If your [daily balance/average daily balance] is $____ or less, the dividend rate paid on the entire balance will be ____% with an APY of ____%.

[For purposes of this disclosure, this is a rate and APY that were offered within the most recent seven calendar days and were accurate as of (date). Please call (credit union telephone number) to obtain current rate information.]

[*Fixed-rate*—You will be paid this rate [for (time period)/until (date)/for at least 30 calendar days]./ *Variable-rate*—The interest rate and APY may change every (time period) based on [(name of index)/ the determination of the credit union board of directors.]

NOTE: Tiering Method A pays the stated dividend rate that corresponds to the applicable account balance tier on the full balance in the account. This example contemplates a two-tier system. The option (1, 2 or 3) most closely matching the terms of the

National Credit Union Administration

account should be chosen as the appropriate disclosure. For tiered-rate accounts, a disclosure may be added about the currency of the rate, as is provided in the first set of brackets. A disclosure regarding the fixed-rate or variable-rate nature of the account must be added, as is provided in the last set of brackets.

Tiering Method B

1* A dividend rate of _____% will be paid only on the portion of your [daily balance/average daily balance] that is greater than $_____. The annual percentage yield (APY) for this tier will range from _____% to _____%, depending on the balance in the account.

2* A dividend rate of _____% will be paid only on the portion of your [daily balance/average daily balance] that is greater than $_____, but less than $_____. The annual percentage yield (APY) for this tier will range from _____% to _____%, depending on the balance in the account.

3* If your [daily balance/average daily balance] is $_____ or less, the dividend rate paid on the entire balance will be _____%, with an annual percentage yield (APY) of _____%.

[For purposes of this disclosure, this is a rate and APY that were offered within the most recent seven calendar days and were accurate as of (date). Please call (credit union telephone number) to obtain current rate information.]

[*Fixed-rate*—You will be paid this rate [for (time period)/until (date)/for at least 30 calendar days]./ *Variable-rate*—The interest rate and APY may change every (time period) based on [(name of index)/ the determination of the credit union board of directors.]

NOTE: Tiering Method B pays different stated dividend rates corresponding to applicable account balance tiers, on the applicable balance in each tier of the account. For example, a credit union might pay 3% dividend on account funds of $500 or below, and pay 4% dividend on the portion of the same account that exceeds $500. The example contemplates an account with two tiers, but additional tiers are possible. The option (1, 2 or 3) most closely matching the terms of the account should be chosen as the appropriate disclosure. For tiered-rate accounts, a disclosure may be added about the currentness of the rate, as is provided in the first set of brackets.

Tiered-rate accounts can be either fixed-rate or variable-rate accounts. The last sentence offers an option of either fixed-rate or variable-rate disclosure. Thus, the disclosures outlined above will be made in addition to either: (i) Disclosure of the period the fixed-rates are in effect or (ii) the variable-rate disclosures. Tiered-rate accounts are also subject to the requirement for disclo-

Pt. 707, App. B

sure of the balance computation method, *see* paragraph (e) to this appendix.

3. Other Dividend-bearing Accounts

Tiering Method A

1* [As of [the last dividend declaration date/ (date)], if your [daily balance/average daily balance] was $_____ or more, the dividend rate paid on the entire balance in your account was _____%, with an annual percentage yield (APY) of _____%. /or If your [daily balance/average daily balance] is $_____ or more, a prospective dividend rate of _____% will be paid on the entire balance in your account with a prospective annual percentage yield (APY) of _____% for this dividend period.]

2* [As of [the last dividend declaration date/ (date)], if your [daily balance/average daily balance] was more than $_____, but was less than $_____, the dividend rate paid on the entire balance in your account was _____%, with an annual percentage yield (APY) of _____%. /or If your [daily balance/average daily balance] is more than $_____, but is less than $_____, a prospective dividend rate of _____% will be paid on the entire balance in your account with a prospective annual percentage yield (APY) of _____% for this dividend period.]

3* [As of the last dividend declaration date/ (date)], if your [daily balance/average daily balance] was $_____ or less, the dividend rate paid on the entire balance in your account will be _____% with an annual percentage yield (APY) of _____%. /or If your [daily balance/average daily balance] is $_____ or less, the prospective dividend rate of _____% will be paid on the entire balance in your account with a prospective annual percentage yield (APY) of _____% for this dividend period.

[*Fixed-rate*—You will be paid this rate for [(time period)/at least 30 calendar days]./ *Variable-rate*—The dividend rate and APY may change every (dividend period) as determined by the credit union board of directors.]

NOTE: Tiering Method A pays the stated dividend rate that corresponds to the applicable deposit tier on the full balance in the account. This example contemplates a two-tier system. The option (1, 2 or 3) most closely matching the terms of the account should be chosen as the appropriate disclosure. For tiered-rate accounts, a disclosure may be added about the prospective rate. Note that the prospective rate disclosure options match the required tiered-rate disclosures based on the previous dividend declaration date. A disclosure regarding the fixed-rate or variable-rate nature of the account must be added, as is provided in the last set of brackets.

643

Tiering Method B

1* [As of [the last dividend declaration date/ (date)], a dividend rate of ____ % was paid only on the portion of your [daily balance/average daily balance] that was greater than $____. The annual percentage yield (APY) for this tier ranged from ____ % to ____ %, depending on the balance in the account. /or A prospective dividend rate of ____ % will be paid only on the portion of your [daily balance/average daily balance] that is greater than $____ with a prospective annual percentage yield (APY) ranging from ____ % to ____ %, depending on the balance in the account, for this dividend period.]

2* [As of [the last dividend declaration date/ (date)], a dividend rate of ____ % was paid only on the portion of your [daily balance/average daily balance] that was greater than $____ but less than $____. The annual percentage yield (APY) for this tier ranged from ____ % to ____ %, depending on the balance in the account. /or A prospective dividend rate of ____ % will be paid only on the portion of your [daily balance/average daily balance] that is greater than $____, but less than $____] with a prospective annual percentage yield (APY) ranging from ____ % to ____ %, depending on the balance in the account, for this dividend period.]

3* [As of [the last dividend declaration date/ (date)], if your [daily balance/average daily balance] was $____ or less, the dividend rate paid on the entire balance was ____ %, with an annual percentage yield (APY) of ____ %. /or If your [daily balance/average daily balance] was $____ or less, the prospective dividend rate paid on the entire balance in your account will be ____ % with a prospective annual percentage yield (APY) of ____ % for this dividend period.

NOTE: Tiering Method B pays different stated dividend rates corresponding to applicable account tiers, on the applicable balance in each tier of the account. For example, a credit union might pay a 3% dividend on account funds of $500 or below, and pay a 4% dividend on the portion of the same account that exceeds $500. The example contemplates an account with two tiers, but additional tiers are possible. The option (1, 2 or 3) most closely matching the terms of the account should be chosen as the appropriate disclosure. Note that the prospective rate disclosure options match the required tiered-rate disclosures based on the previous dividend declaration date.

Tiered-rate accounts can be either fixed-rate or variable-rate accounts. The last sentence offers an option of either fixed-rate or variable-rate disclosures. Thus, the disclosures outlined above must be made in addition to either: (i) Disclosure of the period the fixed-rates are in effect or (ii) the variable-rate disclosures. Tiered-rate accounts are also subject to the requirement for disclosure of the balance computation method, see paragraph (e) to this appendix.

(B) *Nature of Dividends (§ 707.4(b)(8))*

Dividends are paid from current income and available earnings, after required transfers to reserves at the end of a dividend period.

NOTE: The Board of Directors declares dividends based on current income and available earnings of the credit union after providing for the required reserves at the end of the month. The dividend rate and annual percentage yield shown may reflect either the last dividend declaration date on the account or the earnings the credit union anticipates having available for distribution. This disclosure only applies to share and share draft (as opposed to deposit) accounts and should be grouped with the Rate Information to make the disclosures more meaningful. This disclosure also does not apply to term share accounts for reasons discussed in the supplementary information regarding §§ 707.3(e) and 707.4(b)(8).

(C) *Compounding and Crediting (§ 707.4(b)(2))*

[Dividends/Interest] will be compounded (frequency) and will be credited (frequency).

and, if applicable:

If you close your [share/deposit] account before [dividends/interest] [are/is] paid, you will not receive the accrued [dividends/interest].

and, if applicable (for dividend-bearing accounts):

For this account type, the dividend period is (frequency), for example, the beginning date of the first dividend period of the calendar year is (date) and the ending date of such dividend period is (date). All other dividend periods follow this same pattern of dates. The dividend declaration date follows the ending date of a dividend period, and for the example is (date).

NOTE: Where the word "(frequency)" appears, time periods must be inserted to coincide with those specified in board resolutions of each credit union's board of directors. A disclosure of dividend period was added to § 707.4(b)(2)(i) in the final rule to assist members in knowing when dividend rate and APY disclosures would be given by a credit union using the optional statement rule of § 707.6(a). The dividend declaration date is important for purposes of § 707.4(a)(2)(ii), request disclosures, § 707.4(b)(2), account opening disclosures, and § 707.8(c)(2), advertising disclosures. The Board believes that this is critical information for dividend-bearing accounts, but that provision by an example (whether of the first dividend period of the

National Credit Union Administration

year, or of any randomly chosen dividend period) is favorable to providing a list of such dates for the entire year or for a period of years (although these methods would also be permissible). As noted in the supplementary information to § 707.2(j), dividend declaration date, the dividend period and actual dividend distribution date may vary. Thus, it is possible for crediting periods and dividend periods not to coincide, though the Board believes that credit unions should make every effort to attempt to coordinate the two periods.

(D) *Minimum Balance Requirements (§ 707.4(b)(3)(i))*

(i) *To open the account*
The minimum balance required to open this account is $_____.
or, for first share account at a credit union
The minimum required to open this account is the purchase of a (par value of a share) share in the credit union.

(ii) *To avoid imposition of fees*
You must maintain a minimum daily balance of $_____ in your account to avoid a service fee. If, during any (time period), your account balance falls below the required minimum daily balance, your account will be subject to a service fee of $_____ for that (time period).
or
You must maintain a minimum average daily balance of $_____ in your account to avoid a service fee. If, during any (time period), your average daily balance is below the required minimum, your account will be subject to a service fee of $_____ for that (time period).

(iii) *To obtain the annual percentage yield disclosed*
You must maintain a minimum daily balance of $_____ in your account each day to obtain the disclosed annual percentage yield.
or
You must maintain a minimum average daily balance of $_____ in your account to obtain the disclosed annual percentage yield.

(iv) *Absence of minimum balance requirements*
No minimum balance requirements apply to this account.

(v) *Par value*
The par value of a share in this credit union is $_____.

NOTE: Where the words "(time period)" appear, time periods should be inserted to coincide with those specified in board resolutions of each credit union's board of directors. As the supplementary information to § 707.4(b)(3)(i) explains, the par value of a share to establish membership is a critical disclosure to be made to potential members of credit unions. The par value disclosure is required by § 707.4(b)(3)(i) as being analogous to a minimum balance account opening requirement.

(E) *Balance Computation Method (§ 707.4(b)(3)(ii))*

(i) *Daily Balance Method*
[Dividends/Interest] [are/is] calculated by the daily balance method which applies a daily periodic rate to the balance in the account each day.

(ii) *Average Daily Balance Method*
[Dividends/Interest] [are/is] calculated by the average daily balance method which applies a periodic rate to the average daily balance in the account for the period. The average daily balance is calculated by adding the balance in the account for each day of the period and dividing that figure by the number of days in the period.

NOTE: Any explanation of balance computation method must contain enough information for members to grasp the means by which dividends or interest will be calculated on their accounts. Using a shorthand form, such as "day in/day out" for the daily balance method or "average balance" for the average daily balance method, without more information, is insufficient. In addition, any disclosure based on the equivalency of the two allowable methods, such as stating that the average daily balance method was the same as the daily balance method, is impermissible and misleading.

(F) *Accrual of Dividends/Interest on Noncash Deposits (§ 704.4(b)(3)(iii))*

[Dividends/Interest] will begin to accrue on the business day you [place/deposit] noncash items (e.g. checks) to your account.
or
[Dividends/Interest] will begin to accrue no later than the business day we receive provisional credit for the [placement/deposit] of noncash items (e.g. checks) to your account.

NOTE: Accrual information is not included in the explanation of balance computation method required by § 707.4(b)(4)(ii). In addition, the disclosures required by TISA do not affect the substantive requirements of the EFAA and Regulation CC.

The EFAA and Regulation CC control, and any modifications to them should occasion credit unions to revisit this disclosure with a view to revising it to reflect current law.

(G) *Fees and Charges (§ 707.4(b)(4))*

The following fees and charges may be assessed against your account:
(Service/explanation)—$_____.
(Service/explanation)—$_____.

NOTE: Fees and charges may be disclosed in an account disclosure, or separately in a Rate and Fee Schedule (see section B-11 of

Pt. 707, App. B

this appendix). In either event, the disclosure should also specify when the fee will be assessed by using phrases such as "per item," "per month," or "per inquiry."

(H) *Transaction Limitations (§ 707.4(b)(5))*

The minimum amount you may [withdraw/write a draft for] is $_____

During any statement period, you may not make more than six withdrawals or transfers to another credit union account of yours or to a third party by means of a preauthorized or automatic transfer or telephonic order or instruction. No more than three of the six transfers may be made by check, draft, debit card, if applicable, or similar order to a third party. If you exceed the transfer limitations set forth above in any statement period, your account will be subject to [closure by the credit union/a fee of $_____.

NOTE: This paragraph satisfies the requirements of § 707.4(b)(6) with respect to Regulation D limitations on share accounts and money market accounts. These are some of the more common limitations applicable.

The credit union reserves the right to require a member intending to make a withdrawal from any account (except a share draft account) to give written notice of such intent not less than seven days and up to 60 days before such withdrawal.

NOTE: This disclosure is limited to federal credit unions with Bylaws containing this limitation. See *Standard Federal Credit Union Bylaws*, Art. III, section 5(a). Similar disclosures are required of any state-chartered credit unions having similar limitations in their bylaws, or under state law. This limitation does not directly relate to the "number" or "amount" of transactions, and accordingly, may not be necessary under § 707.4(b)(5), but would, if applicable, be required by § 707.3(b).

(I) *Disclosures Related to Term Share Accounts (§ 707.4(b)(6))*

(i) *Time requirements*
Your account will mature on (date).
or
Your account will mature after (time period).

(ii) *Early withdrawal penalties*
We [will/may] impose a penalty if you withdraw [any/all] of the [funds/principal] in your account before the maturity date. The penalty will equal [_____ [days'/weeks'/months'] [dividends/interest] on your account.
or
We [will/may] impose a penalty of $_____ if you withdraw [any/all] of the [funds/principal] before the maturity date.

If you withdraw some of your funds before maturity, the [dividend/interest] rate for the

12 CFR Ch. VII (1-1-12 Edition)

remaining funds in your account will be _____%, with an annual percentage yield of _____%.

NOTE: In most cases, the dividend rate and annual percentage yield on the funds remaining in the account after early withdrawal are the same as before the withdrawal. Accordingly, the disclosure of dividend rate and annual percentage yield after withdrawal is required only if the dividend rate and APY will change.

(iii) *Withdrawal of Dividends/Interest Prior to Maturity*

The annual percentage yield is based on an assumption that [dividends/interest] will remain in the account until maturity. A withdrawal will reduce earnings.

NOTE: This disclosure may be used if the credit union compounds dividends/interest and allows withdrawal of accrued dividends/interest before maturity. This disclosure alerts members that the annual percentage yield is based on an assumption that the dividends/interest remain on deposit until maturity.

(iv) *Renewal Policies*

1. *Automatically Renewable Term Share Accounts*

Your term share account will automatically renew at maturity. You will have a grace period of _____ [calendar/business] days after the maturity date to withdraw the funds in the account without being charged an early withdrawal penalty.

or

Your term share account will automatically renew at maturity. There is no grace period following the maturity of this account.

2. *Non-Automatically Renewable Term Share Accounts*

This account will not renew automatically at maturity. If you do not renew the account, your account will [continue to earn/no longer earn] [dividends/interest] after the maturity date.

NOTE: These disclosures should agree with the necessary pre-maturity notices for term share accounts in B-3 of this appendix.

(v) *Required dividend distribution.*
This account requires the distribution of dividends and does not allow dividends to remain in the account.

(J) *Bonuses (§ 704.4(b)(7))*

You will [be paid/receive] [$_____/(description of item)] as a bonus [when you open the account/on (date)].

You must maintain a minimum [daily balance/average daily balance] of $_____ to obtain the bonus.

646

National Credit Union Administration

To earn the bonus, [$_____/your entire principal] must remain on deposit [for (time period)/until (date)].

NOTE: These disclosures follow the requirements of § 707.4(b)(7) and should be used as applicable. Further information may also be added, especially if it clarifies the conditions and timing of receiving the bonus, or better informs the member about the bonus.

B-2 MODEL CLAUSES FOR CHANGES IN TERMS (§ 707.5(A))

On (date), the (type of fee) will increase to $_____.

On (date), the [dividend/interest] rate on your account will decrease to _____%, with an annual percentage yield (APY) of _____%.

On (date), the [minimum daily balance/average daily balance] required to avoid imposition of a fee will increase to $_____.

NOTE: These examples apply to the more common changes necessitating a change in terms notice. However, any change, amendment or modification reducing the APY or adversely affecting the members holding such accounts must be disclosed. For such changes not contemplated by the model clauses, the Board recommends the use of as simple language as possible to convey the change, along with cross-referencing to the particular sections or paragraph numbers of the account opening disclosures, when to do so will assist members in reviewing and understanding the change.

B-3 MODEL CLAUSES FOR PRE-MATURITY NOTICES FOR TERM SHARE ACCOUNTS (§ 707.5(B-C))

(A) *Maturity Date*

Your term share account will mature on _____.

(B) *Nonrenewal*

Unless your term share account is renewed, it will not accrue further [dividends/interest] after the maturity date.

(C) *Rate Information*

The [dividend/interest] rate and annual percentage yield that will apply to your term share account if it is renewed have not yet been determined. That information will be available on _____. After that date, you may call the credit union during regular business hours at (telephone number) to find out the [dividend/interest] rate and annual percentage yield (APY) that will apply to your term share account if it is renewed.

NOTE: Pre-maturity notices should follow the requirements of § 707.5(b-d) as closely as possible. Care should be taken to explain any grace periods used. See discussion of use of

Pt. 707, App. B

alternative timing in supplementary information to § 707.2(o) and § 707.5(b-d).

B-4 SAMPLE FORM (SIGNATURE CARD/APPLICATION FOR MEMBERSHIP)

Application for Membership/Account Signature Card

ACCOUNT NUMBER _____

_____
(last name)(first name)(middle name)

_____
(street address) (apartment number)

_____
(city)(state)(zip code)

_____
(home telephone number)(business telephone number)

_____
(Social Security # or TIN)(date of birth)

_____
(mother's maiden name)(employer, occupation)

I hereby make application for membership in and agree to conform to the Bylaws, as amended, of _____ Credit Union (the "Credit Union"). I certify that: I am within the field of membership of this Credit Union; the information provided on this application is true and correct; and my signature on this card applies to all accounts under my name at this Credit Union. I also agree to be bound to the terms and conditions of any account that I have in the Credit Union now or in the future.

_____
(signature of applicant)

This application approved _____ (date) by the (Check one)

( ) Board   ( ) Exec. Committee
( ) Membership Officer

Signed: _____
(Secretary; Exec. Cmte. Member, or Membership Officer)

NOTE: This form is modeled on NCUA Form FCU 150, Application for Membership, as discussed in the *Accounting Manual for FCUs*, §§ 5030.1, 5150.3. It is noted that other information can also be requested on the signature card, as long as it is in accordance with federal and state laws. For example, information identifying the member, such as a state driver's license number, could be added. The types of accounts that the signature applies to could be specified. Furthermore, the Board notes that this card contains much identification information that may not be necessary for all credit unions; common sense should guide credit union boards of directors in designing their applications for membership/signature cards. However, the Board believes that the information solicited on this form is reasonable

Pt. 707, App. B

and prudent for many credit unions. Payable on death designations, joint account language required under state law, life savings beneficiary designations, and other like variations and designations may be added to the card if so desired. The proposed signature card/application for membership form contained taxpayer certification language. One commenter noted that the IRS may always change its requirements in this area, which are beyond the authority of the Board. Therefore, the Board has deleted reference to the IRS taxpayer certification required by 26 USC 3406, but notes that such certification must be made in accordance with applicable law and IRS rules. The information may be included on the front and back of a standard size signature card, or on the front of a large size signature card. However, no account terms may be included on a signature card unless a copy of the signature card is provided to the member at the time of account opening. The Board recommends that credit unions refrain from this practice, and instead use standard account disclosures. One reason for this is that if laws, regulations or credit union policies change, discrepancies may result between them and the earlier signature card terms. Given the longevity of credit union membership, signature cards may well be in use for up to or over a century. In addition, as signature cards are relatively small, they probably will not contain enough space to make all desired and required disclosures. Fragmentation of terms, some on signature cards, some on separate disclosures, could easily lead to member confusion. As terms are usually construed against the drafter, credit unions should be very careful in their use of account terms and conditions varying from those provided as model clauses and sample forms in this appendix.

B-5 SAMPLE FORM (TERM SHARE (CERTIFICATE) ACCOUNT)

Term Share Certificate

Date Issued _____

Account Number _____

Certificate Number _____

Social Security Number
 This is to certify that (name(s)) _____ [is/ are] the owner(s) of a term share certificate account in the _____ Credit Union (the "Credit Union") in the amount of _____ Dollars ($_____). This term share certificate account may be redeemed on (maturity date) _____ only upon presentation of the certificate to the Credit Union. The dividend rate of this certificate account is ____% with an annual percentage yield of ____%. The annual percentage yield and dividend rate assume that dividends are to be [check one] ( ) added to principal/( ) paid to regular share account number _____/ ( ) mailed to owner(s). This account is subject to all terms and conditions stated in the Term Share Certificate Account Disclosures, as they may be amended from time to time, and incorporates the same by reference into this agreement.

_____
Authorized signature

_____
Authorized signature

NOTE: This form is modeled on NCUA Form FCU 107SCP, Credit Union Share Certificate, as discussed in the *Accounting Manual for FCUs*, §§ 5030.1, 5150.6. It is simplified to reflect the term share (certificate) account agreement, the parties involved, the maturity term and the annual percentage yield and dividend rate. All other terms are incorporated by reference. This should allow the credit union maximum flexibility in fashioning certificate, and other term share account, products. If a credit union so desired, other terms and conditions could be incorporated into the term share certificate itself, as long as a copy is presented to the member at the account opening. Care should also be taken to ensure that the term share certificate format addresses any necessary state law concerns. As the FRB's Regulation D on reserve requirements permits all term share accounts to be represented by a transferable or nontransferable, or a negotiable or nonnegotiable, certificate, instrument, passbook, statement or otherwise, and still be considered a "time deposit", the Board has made no entry on this sample form regarding such terms, leaving the decision instead to each credit union's board of directors. 12 CFR 202.4(c)(2).

B-6 SAMPLE FORM (REGULAR SHARE ACCOUNT DISCLOSURES)

Regular Share Account Disclosures

1. *Rate information.* As of April 1, 1995, the dividend rate was 5.00% and the annual percentage yield (APY) was 5.13% on your regular share account. In addition, the credit union estimates a prospective dividend rate of 5.25% and a prospective APY of 5.39% on your share account for this dividend period. The dividend rate and annual percentage yield may change every quarter as determined by the credit union board of directors.

2. *Compounding and crediting.* Dividends will be compounded daily and will be credited quarterly. For this account type, the dividend period is quarterly, for example, the beginning date of the first dividend period of the calendar year is January 1 and the ending date of such dividend period is March 31.

All other dividend periods follow this same pattern of dates. The dividend declaration date follows the ending date of a dividend period, and for the example is April 1. If you close your regular share account before dividends are credited, you will not receive accrued dividends.

3. *Minimum balance requirements.* The minimum balance to open this account is the purchase of a $5 share in the Credit Union. You must maintain a minimum daily balance of $500 in your account to avoid a service fee. If, during any day during a quarter, your account balance falls below the required minimum daily balance, your account will be subject to a service fee of $5 for that quarter.

4. *Balance computation method.* Dividends are calculated by the daily balance method which applies a daily periodic rate to the principal in your account each day.

5. *Accrual of dividends.* Dividends will begin to accrue on the business day you deposit noncash items (e.g., checks) to your account.

6. *Fees and charges.* The following fees and charges may be assessed against your account.
   a. Statement copies—$5.00 per statement.
   b. Account inquiries—$3.00 per inquiry.
   c. Dormant account fee—$10.00 per month.
   d. Wire transfers—$8.00 per transfer.
   e. Minimum balance service fee—$5.00 per quarter.
   f. Share transfer—$1.00 per transfer.
   g. Excessive share withdrawals $1.00 per item.

7. *Transaction limitations.* During any statement period, you may not make more than six withdrawals or transfers to another credit union account of yours or to a third party by means of a preauthorized or automatic transfer or telephonic order or instruction. No more than three of the six transfers may be made by check, draft, debit card, if applicable, or similar order to a third party. If you exceed the transfer limitations set forth above in any statement period, your account will be subject to closure by the credit union or to a fee of $1.00 per item.

8. *Nature of dividends.* Dividends are paid from current income and available earnings, after required transfers to reserves at the end of a dividend period.

9. *Bylaw Requirements.* A member who fails to complete payment of one share within _____ of his admission to membership, or within _____ from the increase in the par value in shares, or a member who reduces his share balance below the par value of one share and does not increase the balance to at least the par value of one share within _____ of the reduction may be terminated from membership at the end of a dividend period. [All blanks should be filled with time chosen by credit union board of directors.] Shares may be transferred only from one member to another, by written instrument in such form as the Credit Union may prescribe. The Credit Union reserves the right, at any time, to require members to give, in writing, not more than 60 days notice of intention to withdraw the whole or any part of the amounts so paid in by them. No member may withdraw shareholdings that are pledged as required on security on loans without the written approval of the credit committee or a loan officer, except to the extent that such shares exceed the member's total primary and contingent liability to the Credit Union. No member may withdraw any shareholdings below the amount of his/her primary or contingent liability to the Credit Union if he/she is delinquent as a borrower, or if borrowers for whom he/she is comaker, endorser, or guarantor are delinquent, without the written approval of the credit committee or loan officer.

10. *Par value of shares; Dividend period.* The par value of a regular share in this Credit Union is $5. The dividend period of the Credit Union is quarterly.

11. *National Credit Union Share Insurance Fund.* Member accounts in this Credit Union are federally insured by the National Credit Union Share Insurance Fund.

12. *Other Terms and Conditions.* [In this item, which may be titled or subdivided in any manner by each credit union, NCUA suggests that the following issues be covered or handled: Statutory lien or setoff; expenses (garnishments and bankruptcy orders and holds on account); joint ownership accounts; trust accounts; payable-on-death accounts; retirement accounts; Uniform Transfer to Minor Act accounts; sole proprietorship accounts; escrow and custodial accounts; corporation accounts; not-for-profit corporation accounts; voluntary association accounts; partnership accounts; public unit accounts; powers of attorney (guardianship orders); tax disclosures and certifications; Uniform Commercial Code variances; amendments; reliance on signature card; change of address; incorporations of other documents by reference, such as expedited funds availability policies, service charges schedules or electronic banking disclosures; ability to suspend services; and operational matters (stop payment orders—verbal and written, satisfactory identification, refusal of deposits not in proper form, wire transfers, stale check deposits, availability of periodic statements or passbook feature.)]

NOTE: This form is modeled on the share account disclosures in the *Accounting Manual for FCUs*, §5150.7. The disclosures are for a variable-rate, daily balance method dividend calculation regular share account in an FCU with a $500 minimum balance to avoid service fees. For the example, the account was opened on May 1, 1995. Other terms are self-explanatory. The dividend rate paid and annual percentage yield disclosures will reflect the prospective dividend rate for a given dividend period. Item nos. 1–8 reflect standard TISA and part 707 disclosures discussed in sections B–1 through B–3 of this appendix. Note that if the credit union limits the maximum amount of shares which may be held by one member under *NCUA Standard FCU Bylaws*, Art. III, section 2, that this should be stated in item no. 7, transaction limitations. Item no. 9 reflects various terms provided in Art. III, sections 3–6 of the *NCUA Standard FCU Bylaws*. Item no. 10 reflects the par value amount of regular shares in a federal credit union, pursuant to section 117 of the FCU Act, 12 U.S.C. 117. It also states the dividend period of the credit union, which is set by the board of directors. Item no. 11 addresses the requirements of 12 CFR part 740. Nonfederally insured credit unions (NICUs) would be expected to disclose information required by section 151 of the Federal Deposit Insurance Corporation Improvement Act of 1991. 12 USC 1831t. By December 19, 1992, all NICUs were required to include conspicuously on all periodic statements of account, signature cards, passbooks, share certificates and other similar instruments of deposit and in all advertising a notice that the credit union is not federally insured. Additional disclosures will be required of NICUs by June 19, 1994. Item no. 12 is inserted to ensure that credit unions add other account terms and conditions not covered by the proposed regulation. These sorts of terms are contemplated by proposed § 707.3(b), requiring that the disclosures reflect the terms of the legal obligation between the member and the credit union. This list is not meant to be exhaustive, but to give a general idea of other topics often covered in share account contracts. Item no. 12 is not expressly required by either TISA or part 707, but any of these terms that are disclosed must be accurate and not misleading. Also the Board strongly recommends that such terms are included in account opening disclosures to inform the membership and to clearly set forth the legal relationship between the members and their credit union.

B–7 SAMPLE FORM (SHARE DRAFT ACCOUNT DISCLOSURES)

Share Draft Account Disclosures

1. *Rate information.* As of January 1, 1995, the dividend rate was 3.00% and the annual percentage yield (APY) was 3.04% on your share account. In addition, the prospective dividend rate on your account is 3.15% with a prospective annual percentage yield (APY) of 3.20% for the current dividend period. The dividend rate and APY may change every dividend period as determined by the credit union board of directors.

2. *Compounding and crediting.* Dividends will be compounded monthly and will be credited monthly. For this account type, the dividend period is monthly, for example, the beginning date of the first dividend period of the calendar year is January 1 and the ending date of such dividend period is January 31. All other dividend periods follow this same pattern of dates. The dividend declaration date follows the ending date of a dividend period, and for the example above is February 1. If you close your share draft account before dividends are credited, you will not receive accrued dividends.

3. *No Minimum balance requirements apply to this account.*

4. *Balance computation method.* Dividends are calculated by the average daily balance method which applies a periodic rate to the average daily balance in the account for the period. The average daily balance is calculated by adding the balance in the account for each day of the period and dividing that figure by the number of days in the period.

5. *Accrual of dividends.* Dividends will begin to accrue no later than the business day we receive provisional credit for the placement of noncash items (e.g. checks) to your account.

6. *Fees and charges.* The following fees and charges may be assessed against your account.

a. Statement copies—$5.00 per statement.
b. Account inquiries—$3.00 per inquiry.
c. Dormant account fee—$10.00 per month.
d. Wire transfers—$8.00 per transfer.
e. Overdrafts/Returned Items—$5.00 per draft.
f. Share transfer—$1.00 per transfer.
g. Excessive share withdrawals—$1.00 per item.
h. Certified checks—$5.00 per check.
i. Stop Payment Order—$5.00 per order.
j. Check Printing Fee—$12.00 per 200 checks (varies depending on style of check ordered).

7. *No transaction limitations apply to this account.*

8. *Nature of dividends.* Dividends are paid from current income and available earnings, after required transfers to reserves at the end of a dividend period.

9. *Bylaw Requirements.* A member who fails to complete payment of one share within _____ of his admission to membership, or within _____ from the increase in the par value in shares, or a member who reduces his share balance below the par value of one share and does not increase the balance to at least the par value of one share within _____ of the reduction may be terminated from membership at the end of a dividend period. [All blanks should be filled with time chosen by credit union board of directors.] Shares may be transferred only from one member to another, by written instrument in such form as the Credit Union may prescribe. The Credit Union reserves the right, at any time, to require members to give, in writing, not more than 60 days notice of intention to withdraw the whole or

National Credit Union Administration Pt. 707, App. B

any part of the amounts so paid in by them. Shares paid in under an accumulated payroll deduction plan may not be withdrawn until credited to a member's account. No member may withdraw shareholdings that are pledged as required on security on loans without the written approval of the credit committee or a loan officer, except to the extent that such shares exceed the member's total primary and contingent liability to the Credit Union. No member may withdraw any shareholdings below the amount of his/her primary or contingent liability to the Credit Union if he/she is delinquent as a borrower, or if borrowers for whom he/she is comaker, endorser, or guarantor are delinquent, without the written approval of the credit committee or loan officer.

10. *Par value of shares; Dividend period.* The par value of a regular share in this Credit Union is $5. The dividend period of the Credit Union is monthly, beginning on the first of a month and ending on the last day of the month.

11. *National Credit Union Share Insurance Fund.* Member accounts in this Credit Union are federally insured by the National Credit Union Share Insurance Fund.

12. *Other Terms and Conditions.* [See section B–6, item 12, of this appendix].

NOTE: This form is modeled on the share account disclosures in the *Accounting Manual for FCUs,* §5150.7. The disclosures are for a variable-rate, average daily balance method dividend calculation share draft account in an FCU with no minimum balance requirement. For purposes of this example, the account was opened on January 15, 1995. The Credit Union has monthly dividend periods. Other terms are self-explanatory. The dividend rate paid and annual percentage yield disclosures will reflect the prospective dividend rate for a given dividend period. The disclosures are very similar to the ones in section B–6 of appendix B, except for the rollback and par value disclosures, which have been removed from the final rule and appendices.

B–8 SAMPLE FORM (MONEY MARKET SHARE ACCOUNT DISCLOSURES)

Money Market Share Account Disclosures

1. *Rate information.* As of January 1, 1995, if your average daily balance was $500 or more, the dividend rate paid on the entire balance in your account was 4.75%, with an annual percentage yield (APY) of 4.85%. If your average daily balance is $500 or more, a prospective dividend rate of 4.95% will be paid on the entire balance in your account with a prospective APY of 5.00% for this dividend period on your account. The dividend rate and APY may change every dividend period as determined by the credit union board of directors.

2. *Compounding and crediting.* Dividends will be compounded monthly and will be credited quarterly. If you close your share money market account before dividends are credited, you will not receive accrued dividends.

3. *Minimum balance requirements.* The minimum balance required to open this account is $500. You must maintain a minimum daily balance of $500 in your account to avoid a service fee. If, during any (time period), your account falls below the required minimum daily balance, your account will be subject to a service fee of $5 for that (time period).

4. *Balance computation method.* Dividends are calculated by the average daily balance method which applies a periodic rate to the average daily balance in your account for the period. The average daily balance is calculated by adding the principal in the account for each day of the period and dividing that figure by the number of days in the period.

5. *Accrual of dividends.* Dividends will begin to accrue on the business day you deposit noncash items (e.g., checks) to your account.

6. *Fees and charges.* The following fees and charges may be assessed against your account.

  a. Statement copies—$5.00 per statement.
  b. Account inquiries—$3.00 per inquiry.
  c. Dormant account fee—$10.00 per month.
  d. Wire transfers—$8.00 per transfer.
  e. Minimum balance service fee—$5.00 per (time period).
  f. Share transfer—$1.00 per transfer.
  g. Excessive share withdrawals—$1.00 per item.
  h. Certified checks—$5.00 per check.
  i. Stop Payment Order—$5.00 per order.
  j. Check Printing Fee—$12.00 per 200 checks (varies depending on style of check ordered).

7. *Transaction limitations.* During any statement period, you may not make more than six withdrawals or transfers to another credit union account of yours or to a third party by means of a preauthorized or automatic transfer or telephonic order or instruction. No more than three of the six transfers may be made by check, draft, debit card, if applicable, or similar order to a third party. If you exceed the transfer limitations set forth above in any statement period, your account will be subject to closure by the credit union or to a fee of $1.00 per item.

8. *Nature of dividends.* Dividends are paid from current income and available earnings, after required transfers to reserves at the end of a dividend period.

9. *Bylaw Requirements.* [This section should reflect any requirements concerning share accounts in the FISCU's bylaws or charter.]

10. *Par value of shares; Dividend period.* The par value of a regular share in this Credit Union is $50. The dividend period of the Credit Union is monthly, beginning on the first of

a month and ending on the last day of the month.

11. *National Credit Union Share Insurance Fund.* Member accounts in this Credit Union are federally insured by the National Credit Union Share Insurance Fund.

12. *Other Terms and Conditions.* [See section B-6, item 12, of this appendix.]

NOTE: This form is modeled on the share account disclosures in the Accounting Manual for FCUs, §5150.7 and on the share draft account disclosures in section B-7 of this appendix. The disclosures are for a variable-rate, tiered-rate (method A, option 1), average daily balance method dividend calculation, money market share account in a FISCU with a $500 minimum balance to open the account and to avoid service fees. For purposes of this example, the account was opened on January 29, 1995. Other terms are self-explanatory. The dividend rate paid and annual percentage yield disclosures will reflect the prospective dividend rate for a given dividend period. Note that the contents of Item 9, Bylaw requirements, must be tailored to the specific bylaws of a FISCU or NICU. Also note the high par value amount in Item 10.

B-9 SAMPLE FORM (TERM SHARE (CERTIFICATE) ACCOUNT DISCLOSURES)

Term Share (Certificate) Account Disclosures

1. *Rate information.* [Repeat rates disclosed on face of term share certificate, *see* §B-5, Sample Form (Term Share (Certificate) Account)].

2. *Compounding and crediting.* Dividends will be compounded monthly and will be credited annually. If you close your certificate account before dividends are credited, you will not receive accrued dividends.

3. *Minimum balance requirements.* The minium balance required to open this account is $500.

4. *Balance computation method.* Dividends are calculated by the daily balance method, which applies a daily periodic rate to the principal in your account each day.

5. *Accrual of dividends.* Dividends will begin to accrue on the business day you deposit noncash items (e.g., checks) to your account.

6. *Fees and charges.* The following fees and charges may be assessed against your account.

    a. Statement copies—$5.00 per statement.
    b. Account inquiries—$3.00 per inquiry.
    c. Share transfer—$1.00 per transfer.

7. *Transaction limitations.* After the account is opened, you may not make deposits into the account until the maturity date stated on the certificate.

8. *Maturity date.* Your account will mature on January 1, 1996.

9. *Early withdrawal penalties.* We may impose a penalty if you withdraw any of the funds before the maturity date. The penalty will equal three months' dividends on your deposit.

10. *Renewal policies.* Your certificate account will automatically renew at maturity. You will have a grace period of 10 business days after the maturity date to withdraw the funds in the account without being charged an early withdrawal penalty.

11. *Bonus.* You will receive a new (insert brand name) toaster-oven as a bonus when you open the account after December 31, 1994, and before June 30, 1995. You must maintain your entire principal on deposit until the maturity date of your certificate account to obtain the bonus.

12. [Reserved]

13. *Bylaw Requirements.* [This section should reflect any requirements concerning share accounts in the FISCU's bylaws or charter.]

14. *Par value of shares; Dividend period.* The par value of a regular share in this Credit Union is $25. The dividend period of the Credit Union on this type of account is annual, beginning on the date the account is opened, and ending on the stated maturity date, unless renewed.

15. *National Credit Union Share Insurance Fund.* Member accounts in this Credit Union are federally insured by the National Credit Union Share Insurance Fund.

16. *Other Terms and Conditions.* [See section B-6, item 12, of this appendix.]

NOTE: Even though this disclosure if for an account at a FISCU, this form is modeled on the share account disclosures in the *Accounting Manual for FCUs*, §5150.7 and upon the regular share account disclosures in section B-6 of this appendix. The disclosures are for a fixed-rate, daily balance method dividend calculation, automatically renewing term share certificate account in a FISCU with a $500 minimum balance to open the account and a ten day grace period. For the example, the account is opened on January 1, 1995 and matures on January 1, 1996. Other terms are self-explanatory. The dividend rate paid and annual percentage yield disclosures reflect the contracted, prospective dividend rate for a given dividend period. Note the special disclosures for term share certificate accounts, items nos. 8–10. Note also the bonus disclosure, item no. 11.

B-10 SAMPLE FORM (PERIODIC STATEMENT)

Periodic Statement

Member Name

Account Number

[Transaction account activity by date.]
[Average daily balance of $1,500 for the month, daily compounding.]

National Credit Union Administration
Pt. 707, App. B

Your account earned $6.72, with an annual percentage yield earned of 5.40%, for the statement period from May 1 through and including May 31. In addition, your account earned $15 in extraordinary dividends for this period. Any fees assessed against your account are shown in the body of the periodic statement and are identified by the code at the bottom margin of this statement.

Service Charge Codes

SC-1   Stop Payment Order Fee
SC-2   Statement Copy Fee
SC-3   Draft Return Fee
SC-4   Transfer from Shares
SC-5   Microfilm Copy
SC-6   Share Draft Printing Fee
SC-7   Dormant Account Fee
SC-8   Wire Transfer Fee
SC-9   Excessive Share Withdrawal Fee
SC-10   _____

Other Transactions

D   Dividends
EC   Error Correction
OR   Overdraft Returned
OL   Overdraft Loan
OS   Overdraft Share Transfer

NOTE: This form is modeled on the share draft statement of account, Form FCU 107G-SD, in the *Accounting Manual for FCUs*, §5150.4. All information is self-explanatory. Codes of transactions are not required, but are a common credit union practice. The information regarding fees could also be included on the line of the periodic statement showing when the fees were debited from the account. Alternatively, a credit union could show all fees debited against the account for the statement period in a special area of the periodic statement. Clarity to the member of the required information—annual percentage yield earned; amount of dividends; fees imposed and length of period—is the important goal. An additional disclosure regarding the dollar value of any extraordinary dividends earned must be added to those statements showing the payment of such extraordinary dividends to the member.

B-11 SAMPLE FORM (RATE AND FEE SCHEDULE)

Rate and Fee Schedule

This Rate and Fee Schedule for all Accounts sets forth certain conditions, rates, fees and charges applicable to your regular share, share draft, and money market accounts at the _____ Federal Credit Union as of _____ [insert date of delivery to member]. This schedule is incorporated as part of your account agreement with the _____ Federal Credit Union.

Regular Share

Dividend Rate as of Last Dividend Declaration Date ____%.
Annual Percentage Yield as of Last Dividend Declaration Date ____%.
Prospective Dividend Rate ____%.
Prospective Annual Percentage Yield ____%.
Dividends Compounded [Annually, Semiannually, Quarterly, Monthly, Weekly, Daily].
Dividends Credited—At close of a dividend period.
Dividend Period [Annually, Semiannually, Quarterly, Monthly, Weekly, Daily].
Minimum Opening Deposit $5.00 par value share.
Minimum Monthly Balance [None, $ amount].

Share Draft

Dividend Rate as of Last Dividend Declaration Date ____%.
Annual Percentage Yield as of Last Dividend Declaration Date ____%.
Prospective Dividend Rate ____%.
Prospective Annual Percentage Yield ____%.
Dividends Compounded [Annually, Semiannually, Quarterly, Monthly, Weekly, Daily].
Dividends Credited—At close of a dividend period.
Dividend Period [Annually, Semiannually, Quarterly, Monthly, Weekly, Daily].
Minimum Opening Deposit [None, $ amount].
Minimum Monthly Balance [None, $ amount].

Money Market

Dividend Rate as of Last Dividend Declaration Date ____%.
Annual Percentage Yield as of Last Dividend Declaration Date ____%.
Prospective Dividend Rate ____%.
Prospective Annual Percentage Yield ____%.
Dividends Compounded [Annually, Semiannually, Quarterly, Monthly, Weekly, Daily].
Dividends Credited—At close of a dividend period.
Dividend Period [Annually, Semiannually, Quarterly, Monthly, Weekly, Daily].
Minimum Opening Deposit [None, $ amount].
Minimum Monthly Balance [None, $ amount].
The following fees may be assessed in connection with your accounts:

FEES APPLICABLE TO ALL ACCOUNTS

Returned item fee—$____.00 per item.
Account reconciliation fee—$____.00 per hour.

Pt. 707, App. C

Statement copies fee—$____.00 per statement.
Certified draft fee—$____.00 per draft.
Wire transfer fee—$____.00 per transfer.
Account inquiry fee—$____.00 per inquiry.
Dormant account fee—$____.00 per month.
Minimum balance service fee—$____.00 per day.
Share transfer fee—$____.00 per transfer.
Excessive share withdrawals fee—$____.00 per item.

SHARE DRAFT ACCOUNT FEES

Monthly service fee—$____.00 per month.
Overdraft transfers fee—$____.00 per overdraft.
Drafts returned insufficient funds fee—$____.00 per draft.
Stop payment order fee—$____.00 per order.
Draft copy fee—$____.00 per copy.
Check printing fee—$____.00 per 200 drafts.

MONEY MARKET SHARE ACCOUNT FEES

Monthly service fee—$____.00 per month.
Check printing fee—$____.00 per 200 drafts.

NOTE: This illustration is for use of an FCU. The information provided on a Rate and Fee Schedule can be presented in any format. To ensure that it is a part of the account agreement, if used, it should be incorporated by reference into the appropriate share account disclosures. The figures used are illustrative only.

B–12 AGGREGATE OVERDRAFT AND RETURNED ITEM FEES SAMPLE FORM

	Total for this period	Total year-to-date
Total overdraft fees	$60.00	$150.00
Total returned item fees	$0.00	$30.00

[58 FR 50445, Sept. 27, 1993, as amended at 59 FR 13436, 13437, Mar. 22, 1994; 63 FR 71575, Dec. 29, 1998; 72 FR 30246, May 31, 2007; 74 FR 36104, July 22, 2009; 75 FR 47175, Aug. 5, 2010]

APPENDIX C TO PART 707—OFFICIAL STAFF INTERPRETATIONS

Introduction

1. *Official status.* This commentary is the means by which the staff of the Office of General Counsel of the National Credit Union Administration issues official staff interpretations of Part 707 of the NCUA Rules and Regulations. Good faith compliance with this commentary affords protection from liability under section 271(f) of the Truth in Savings Act (TISA), 12 U.S.C. 4311.

Section 707.1—Authority, Purpose, Coverage, and Effect on State Laws

(c) Coverage

1. *Foreign applicability.* Part 707 applies to all credit unions that offer share and deposit accounts to residents (including resident aliens) of any state as defined in §707.2(v) and that offer accounts insurable by the National Credit Union Share Insurance Fund (NCUSIF) whether or not such accounts are insured by the NCUSIF. Corporate credit unions designated as such by NCUA under 12 CFR 704.2 (definition of "corporate credit union") are exempt from part 707.

2. *Persons who advertise accounts.* Persons who advertise accounts are subject to the advertising rules. This includes agent and agented accounts, such as a member who subdivides interests in a jumbo term share certificate account for sale to other parties or among members who form a certificate account investment club. For example, if an agent places an advertisement that offers members an interest in an account at a credit union, the advertising rules apply to the advertisement, whether the account is held by the agent or directly by the member.

3. *Nonautomated credit unions.* Nonautomated credit unions with an asset size of $2 million or less, after subtracting any nonmember deposits, are exempt from TISA and part 707. NCUA defines a "nonautomated credit union" as a credit union without sufficient data processing capability and capacity to establish, operate and maintain a share and loan software system to timely and accurately process all account transactions of all members. The nonautomated credit union exemption is available to all credit unions meeting the asset size and automation standards of this comment, including newly chartered credit unions. If any of the credit unions eligible for this exemption grow to have more than $2 million in assets as of December 31 of any year, the NCUA Board will require such credit unions to comply with TISA and part 707 on January 1 of one year after such credit union loses its exemption eligibility. Similarly, if a credit union becomes sufficiently automated to operate a complete share and loan system, such credit union will be entitled to the same compliance phase-in period.

(d) Effect on State Laws

1. *Preemption of state laws/Inconsistent requirements.* State law requirements that are inconsistent with the requirements of TISA and part 707 are preempted to the extent of the inconsistency. A state law is inconsistent if it requires a credit union to make disclosures or take actions that contradict the requirements of the federal law. A state law is also contradictory if it requires the use of the same term to represent a different

National Credit Union Administration

amount or a different meaning than the federal law, requires the use of a term different from that required in the federal law to describe the same item, or permits a method of calculating dividends or interest on an account different from that required in the federal law.

2. *Preemption determinations.* A credit union, state, or other interested party may request the Board to determine whether a state law requirement is inconsistent with the federal requirements. A request for a determination should be addressed to NCUA's Office of General Counsel, 1775 Duke Street, Alexandria, VA 22314. Written preemption requests should cite (or include a copy of) the allegedly inconsistent state law, demonstrate the inconsistency with TISA and part 707 and the burden on credit unions, and formally request a preemption determination. The Office of General Counsel may provide other interested parties, particularly affected states, an informal opportunity to comment on any request for a preemption determination, unless it finds that such notice and opportunity for comment would be impracticable, unnecessary, or contrary to the public interest. NCUA will publicize any preemption determinations using any means readily at its disposal.

3. *Effect of preemption determinations.* After the Board, through its Office of General Counsel, determines that a state law is inconsistent, a credit union may not make disclosures using the inconsistent term or take actions relying on the inconsistent law.

4. *Reversal of determination.* The Board reserves the right to reverse a determination for any reason bearing on the coverage or effect of state or federal law.

Section 707.2—Definitions

(a) Account

1. *Covered accounts.* Examples of accounts subject to the regulation are:
   i. Dividend-bearing and interest-bearing accounts.
   ii. Non-dividend-bearing and non-interest-bearing accounts.
   iii. Accounts opened as a condition of obtaining a credit card.
   iv. Escrow accounts with a consumer purpose, such as an account established by a member to escrow rental payments, pending resolution of a dispute with the member's landlord.
   v. Accounts held by a parent or custodian for a minor under a state's Uniform Gift to Minors Act (or Uniform Transfers to Minors Act).
   vi. Individual retirement accounts (IRAs) and simplified employee pension (SEP) accounts.
   vii. Payable-on-Death (POD) or "Totten trust" accounts.

2. *Other accounts.* Examples of accounts *not* subject to the regulation are:
   i. Mortgage escrow accounts for collecting taxes and property insurance premiums.
   ii. Accounts established to make periodic disbursements on construction loans.
   iii. Trust accounts opened by a trustee pursuant to a formal written trust agreement (not merely declarations of trust on a signature card such as a "Totten trust," or an IRA or SEP account).
   iv. Accounts opened by an executor in the name of decedent's estate.
   v. Accounts of individuals operating businesses as sole proprietors.
   vi. Certificates of indebtedness. Some credit unions borrow funds from their members through a certificate of indebtedness that sets forth the terms and conditions of the repayment of the borrowing, such as federal credit unions do through 12 CFR 701.38. Such an account does not represent an account in a credit union and is not covered by part 707.
   vii. Unincorporated nonbusiness association accounts.

3. *Other investments.* The term "account" does not apply to these products. Examples of products not covered are:
   i. Government securities.
   ii. Mutual funds.
   iii. Annuities.
   iv. Securities or obligations of a credit union.
   v. Contractual arrangements such as repurchase agreements, interest rate swaps, and bankers acceptances.
   vi. Purchases of U.S. Savings Bonds through a credit union.
   vii. Services offered through a group purchasing plan or a credit union service organization (CUSO).

4. *Options.* All dividend-bearing and interest-bearing accounts are either fixed-rate or variable-rate accounts.

5. *Use of synonyms.* Generally, it is not the purpose of part 707 to prohibit specific descriptive terms for accounts. For example, credit unions can use adjectives and trade names to describe accounts such as "Best Share Draft Account," or "Ultra Money Market Share Account." Synonyms for share, share draft, money market share, and term share accounts may be used to describe various types of credit union share and deposit accounts as long as the synonym is accurate and not misleading and, for account disclosures, is used in conjunction with the correct legal term. For example, the following synonyms may be used:
   i. The term "checking account" may be used to describe share draft accounts.
   ii. The term "money market account" may be used to describe money market share accounts.
   iii. The term "savings account" may be used to describe regular share and share accounts.

iv. The terms "share certificate," "certificate account," or "certificate" may be used to describe share certificates and other dividend-bearing term share accounts.

v. However, under no circumstances may a credit union describe a share account as a deposit account, or vice versa. For example, the term "certificate of deposit" or "CD" may not be used to describe share certificates and other dividend-bearing term share accounts. Similarly, the terms "time account" (used in Regulation DD, 12 CFR 230.2(u)) and "time deposit" (used in Regulation D, 12 CFR 204.2(c)) may not be used to describe term share accounts.

(b) Advertisement

1. *Covered messages.* Advertisements include commercial messages in visual, oral, or print media that invite, offer, or otherwise announce generally to members and potential members the availability of member accounts such as:

i. Telephone solicitations.

ii. Messages on automated teller machine (ATM) screens (including any printout).

iii. Messages on a computer screen in a credit union's lobby (including any printout) other than a screen viewed solely by the credit union's employee.

iv. Messages in a newspaper, magazine, or promotional flyer or on radio or television.

v. Messages promoting an account that are provided along with information about the member's existing account at a credit union and that promote another account at the credit union (such as account promotional messages on the periodic statement).

2. *Other messages.* Examples of messages that are *not* advertisements are:

i. Rate sheets published in newspapers, periodicals, or trade journals (unless the credit union or share and deposit broker that offers accounts at the credit union pays a fee to have the information included or otherwise controls publication).

ii. Telephone conversations initiated by a member or potential member about an account.

iii. An in-person discussion with a member about the terms for a specific account.

iv. For purposes of §707.8(b) of this part through §707.8(e) of this part, information given to members about existing accounts, such as current rates recorded on a voice-response machine or notices for automatically renewable time account sent before renewal.

v. Information about a particular transaction in an existing account.

vi. Disclosures required by Federal or other applicable law.

vii. A share account agreement.

(c) Annual Percentage Yield.

1. *General.* The annual percentage yield (APY) is required for disclosures for new accounts, oral responses to inquiries about rates; disclosures provided upon request; initial disclosures (if the credit union chooses to provide full disclosures instead of the abbreviated notice); notices prior to the renewal of a term share account, if known at the time the notice is sent, and in advertising. The annual percentage yield shows the total amount of dividends for a 365 day period (or a 366 day period for a leap year) on an assumed principal amount based on the dividend rate and frequency of compounding as a percentage of the assumed principal (for accounts such as share or share draft accounts) or for the total amount of dividends over the term of the account for term share accounts. The annual percentage yield assumes the principal amount remains in the account for 365 days (366 days for leap year) or for the term of the account.

2. *How Annual Percentage Yield Differs from Annual Percentage Yield Earned.* The annual percentage yield (APY) differs from the annual percentage yield earned (APYE). The annual percentage yield earned is required for periodic statements only. The annual percentage yield earned shows the total amount of dividends earned for the dividend or statement period as a percent of the actual average daily balance in the member's account. Unlike the annual percentage yield, the annual percentage yield earned is affected by additions and withdrawals during the period. The annual percentage yield and the annual percentage yield earned must be calculated according to the formulas provided in appendix A to this rule.

(d) Average Daily Balance Method

1. *General.* One of the two required methods (the daily balance is the other) of determining the balance upon which dividends must be accrued and paid. The average daily balance method requires the application of a periodic rate to the average daily balance in the account for the average daily balance calculation period. The average daily balance is determined by adding the full amount of principal in the account for each day of the period and dividing that figure by the number of days in the period.

(e) Board.

1. *General.* The NCUA Board.

(f) Bonus

1. *General.* Bonuses include items of value offered as incentives to members, such as an offer to pay the final installment deposit for a holiday club account if the final installment is over $10. Bonuses do not include the payment of dividends (including extraordinary dividends), the waiver or reduction of a fee, the absorption of expenses, non-dividend membership benefits, or other consideration aggregating $10 or less per year.

National Credit Union Administration

Pt. 707, App. C

2. *Examples.* The following are examples of bonuses.

i. A credit union offers $25 to potential members for becoming a member and opening an account. The $25 could be provided by check, cash, or direct deposit.

ii. A credit union offers $25 to a member with only a regular share account to open a share draft account. The $25 could be provided by check, cash, or direct deposit.

iii. A credit union offers a portable radio with a value of $20 to members and potential members for opening a share draft account.

iv. A credit union pays the final installment deposit for a holiday club account if over $10.

3. *Examples not comprising bonuses.* The following are examples of items that are *not* bonuses:

i. Discount coupons distributed by credit unions for use at restaurants or stores.

ii. A credit union offers $20 to any member if the member is responsible for encouraging a potential member to open an account. The $20 is not a bonus because the $20 is not paid to the individual opening the account. Any item, including cash, given or offered to a third party (that is not a joint member or joint owner in an account being opened) in exchange for a member or potential member opening (or a member renewing or adding to) an account is not a bonus.

iii. A credit union offers $25 to a member if the member can locate his name in the body of a newsletter.

iv. Life savings benefits. Many credit unions offer life savings benefits to beneficiaries of deceased members. Because the benefit accrues to a third party, such life savings plans offered are not bonuses.

v. A credit union offers to pay annual membership dues in a benevolent organization for a class of members.

4. *De minimis rule.* Items with a *de minimis* value of $10 or less are not bonuses. Credit unions may rely on the valuation standard used by the Internal Revenue Service (IRS) to determine if the value of the item is *de minimis*. Items required to be reported by the credit union under IRS rules are bonuses under this regulation. Examples of items of *de minimis* values are:

i. Disability insurance premiums on a share account valued at an amount of $10 or less per year.

ii. Coffee mugs, T-shirts or other merchandise with a market value of $10 or less per year.

5. *Aggregation.* In determining if an item valued at $10 or less is a bonus, credit unions must aggregate per account per calendar year items that may be given to members. In making this determination, credit unions aggregate per account only the market value of items that may be given for a specific promotion. To illustrate, assume a credit union offers in January to give members an item valued at $7 for each calendar quarter during the year that the average account balance in a share draft account exceeds $10,000. The bonus rules are triggered, since members are eligible under the promotion to receive up to $28 during the year. However, the bonus rules are not triggered if an item valued at $7 is offered to members opening a share draft account during the month of January, even though in November the credit union introduces a new promotion that includes, for example, an offer to existing share draft accountholders for an item valued at $8 for maintaining an average balance of $5,000 for the month.

6. *Waiver or reduction of a fee or absorption of expenses.* Bonuses do not include value received by members through the waiver or reduction of fees for credit union-related services (even if the fees waived exceed $10), such as the following:

i. Waiving a safe deposit box rental fee for one year for members who open a new account.

ii. Waiving fees for travelers checks for members, and waiving check and share draft printing fees.

iii. Nondiscriminatorily waiving all fees for a particular class of members, such as seniors or minors.

iv. Discounts on interest rates charged for loans at the credit union.

v. Rebates of loan interest already paid by a member.

vi. Discounts on application fees charged for loans at the credit union.

vii. Packaged, linked, or tied-account services.

7. *Non-dividend membership benefits.* Such benefits are not bonuses because they are sporadic in nature, often difficult to value, and providing non-dividend membership benefits is a long-standing unique credit union practice. (See commentary to §707.2(r) for examples of such benefits.)

(g) Credit Union

1. *General.* Includes credit unions in the United States, Puerto Rico, Guam, U.S. Virgin Islands, and U.S. territories. Applies to credit unions whether or not the accounts in the credit union are federally, state, privately insured, or uninsured.

(h) Daily Balance Method

1. *General.* One of the two required methods (the average daily balance is the other) of determining the balance upon which dividends must be accrued and paid. The daily balance method requires the application of a daily periodic rate to the full amount of principal in the account each day.

657

(i) Dividend and Dividends

1. *General.* Member savings placed in share accounts are equity investments, and the returns earned on these accounts are dividends. Federal credit unions may only offer dividend-bearing and non-dividend-bearing share accounts. State-chartered credit unions may offer both share and deposit accounts if permitted by state law. State law, including without limitation regulations and official interpretations, will determine if returns earned in accounts in state-chartered credit unions are dividends. Dividends exclude the payment of a bonus or other consideration worth $10 or less given during a year, the waiver or reduction of a fee, the absorption of expenses, non-dividend membership benefits and extraordinary dividends. Dividend-bearing accounts must be either fixed-rate or variable-rate accounts.

2. *Procedure.* Credit unions must follow appropriate law (state law for state-chartered credit unions and federal law for federal credit unions) in determining dividend policies and declaring dividends. Generally, dividends may be viewed as a portion of the available account and undivided earnings of the credit union which is set apart, after required transfer to reserves, by valid act of the board of directors, for distribution among the members. As a matter of legal procedure, members are usually not entitled to dividends until the following steps are completed: (1) The board of the credit union develops a nondiscriminatory dividend policy, by establishing dividend periods, dividend credit determination dates dividend distribution dates, any associated penalties (if applicable), and the method of dividend computation for each type of share account; (2) the provisions for required transfers to reserves are made; (3) sufficient and available prior and/or current earnings are available at the end of the dividend period; (4) the board formally makes a dividend declaration in accordance with the credit union's dividend policy; and (5) dividends must be paid to members by a credit to the appropriate share account, payment by check or share draft, or by a combination of the two methods.

3. *When available.* Credit unions must follow the law of their primary chartering authority to determine when dividends are available. Generally, it is the declaration of the dividend itself which creates the dividend and the member has no right to receive a dividend until it is so declared. The decision of when to declare dividends lies within the official discretion of each credit union's board of directors and cannot be abrogated by contract. An agreement to pay dividends on a share account is generally interpreted not as an obligation to pay the stipulated dividends absolutely and unconditionally, but as an undertaking to pay them out of the earnings when sufficiently accumulated from which dividends in general are properly payable. Generally, "prospective rates" are rates set in good faith in advance of the close of a dividend period, that may be altered if sufficient funds are not available, or in the event of a superseding event, such as a strike, plant closure, significant fluctuation in market rates and/or a significant change in financial structure, natural disaster or emergency that alters the assumptions under which the "prospective rates" were made. It is the intent of TISA that all disclosure be accurate when made, and credit unions are urged to make every effort to ratify disclosed "prospective rates." "Prospective rates" may also be referred to as "projected rates" or similar wording, but not as "estimated rates." (See comment 3(b)–2, prohibiting use of estimates).

4. *Sample dividend resolutions.* (i) The following resolution may be used where the dividend rates are set after the close of a dividend period.

RESOLUTION OF BOARD OF DIRECTORS FOR THE DECLARATION OF DIVIDENDS

A. I, _____, certify that I am Secretary of _____ Credit Union Board of Directors, and that the following is a correct copy of the resolution for declaring dividend adopted by the _____ Credit Union at a meeting of the Board of Directors duly and properly held on _____, 19____. This resolution appears in the minutes of this meeting and has not been rescinded or modified.

B. Resolved, that

(1) The Board of Directors has developed a nondiscriminatory dividend policy, by establishing dividend periods, dividend credit determination dates, dividend distribution dates, any associated penalties (if applicable), and the method of dividend computation for each type of share account;

(2) The required transfers to reserves have been made; and

(3) Sufficient and available prior and/or current earnings are available at the end of this dividend period.

C. Resolved, further, that the Board of Directors now formally makes a dividend declaration in accordance with the Credit Union's dividend policy and authorizes that on _____, 19____, dividends must be paid to members by a credit to the appropriate share account, payment by share draft or by a combination of the two methods.

D. I further certify that the Board of Directors of this Credit Union has, and the time of adoption of this resolution had, full power and lawful authority to adopt the foregoing resolutions and that this resolution revokes any prior resolution.

In witness whereof, this is my signature and the date on which I signed this Resolution.

National Credit Union Administration

Pt. 707, App. C

Signature

Date

[Attach list of accounts with dividend rates for each type of account.]

(ii) The following resolution may be used where the dividend rates are set before the close of a dividend period.

RESOLUTION OF BOARD OF DIRECTORS FOR THE DECLARATION OF DIVIDENDS

A. I, _____, certify that I am the Secretary of _____ Credit Union, and that the following is a correct copy of the resolution for declaring dividends adopted by the _____ Credit Union at a meeting of the Board of Directors duly and properly held on _____, 19___. This resolution appears in the minutes of that meeting and has not been rescinded or modified.

B. Resolved, that the Board of Directors has adopted a nondiscriminatory dividend policy, by establishing dividend periods, dividend credit determination dates, dividend distribution dates, any associated penalties (if applicable) and the method of dividend computation for each type of share account.

C. Resolved, that it is the policy and practice of the Board of Directors to meet periodically to establish prospective dividend rates for each type of dividend-bearing share account.

D. Resolved, that if the required transfers to reserves have been made and there are sufficient and available prior and/or current earnings available at the end of a dividend period, the officers of the Credit Union are authorized to pay dividends at the rate prospectively established by the Board of Directors for each account for the dividend period. The officers may pay the dividends without any further action of the Board of Directors. The act of paying the dividends shall constitute the declaration of the dividends and shall be a ratification of the prospective dividend rate.

In witness whereof, this is my signature and the date on which I signed this Resolution.

Signature

Date

[Attach list of accounts with prospective dividend rates for each type of account.]

5. *Referencing.* Except where specifically stated otherwise, use of the term "share" in part 707, as in "share account," also refers to "deposit," as in "deposit account," where appropriate (for interest-bearing or non-interest-bearing deposit accounts at some state-chartered credit unions).

(j) Dividend Declaration Date

1. *General.* The importance of the dividend declaration date is to tie the last paid dividend to a certain period of time to place members and potential members on notice that the last paid dividend is different from the next dividend to be paid. In order to achieve this purpose, a credit union may use any of the following methods:

i. "As of 3/15/95" (the date the board of directors last met and declared the last paid dividend).

ii. "As of 3/31/95" (the last day of the last dividend period upon which a dividend has been paid).

iii. "For the period 1/1/95 to 3/31/95" (the last dividend period upon which a dividend has been paid).

iv. "For the first quarter of 1995" (the last dividend period upon which a dividend has been paid).

v. "For April 1995" (the last dividend period upon which a dividend has been paid).

vi. "As of the last dividend declaration date" (the last dividend period upon which a dividend has been paid).

(k) Dividend Period

1. *General.* The dividend period is to be set by a credit union's board of directors for each account type, e.g., regular share, share draft, money market share, and term share. The most common dividend periods are weekly, monthly, quarterly, semi-annually, and annually. Dividend periods need not agree with calendar months, e.g., a monthly dividend period could begin March 15 and end April 14.

(l) Dividend Rate

1. *General.* The dividend rate does not reflect compounding. Compounding is reflected in the "annual percentage yield" definition.

2. *Referencing.* Except where specifically stated otherwise, use of the term "dividend rate" in part 707 also refers to "interest rate," where appropriate (for interest-bearing and non-interest-bearing deposit accounts at some state-chartered credit unions).

(m) Extraordinary Dividends

1. *General.* The definition encompasses all irregularly scheduled and declared dividends, and as dividends, extraordinary dividends are exempt from the "bonus" disclosure requirements. Extraordinary dividends do not have to be disclosed on account disclosures, but the dollar amount of an extraordinary dividend credited to the account during the statement period does have to be separately disclosed on the periodic statement for the dividend period during which the extraordinary dividends are earned. Extraordinary

dividends, like ordinary dividends, do not include the payment of a bonus or other consideration worth $10 or less given during a year, the waiver or reduction of a fee, the absorption of expenses or non-dividend membership benefits. See comments 2(f) 1 through 7 and 2(i) 1 through 4. Extraordinary dividends may be calculated by any means determined by the board of directors of a credit union and may not be used in the annual percentage yield earned calculation.

2. *Use of synonym.* Extraordinary dividends may be described as "bonus dividends."

(n) Fixed-Rate Account

1. *General.* Includes all accounts in which the credit union, by contract, agrees to give at least 30 days advance written notice of decreases in the dividend rate. Thus, credit unions can decrease rates only after providing advance written notice of rate decreases, e.g., a "change-in-terms notice."

(o) Grace Period

1. *General.* A period after maturity of an automatically renewing term share account during which the member may withdraw funds without being assessed a penalty. Use of a "grace period" is discretionary, not mandatory. This definition does not refer to the "grace period" account, which is a synonym for "federal rollback method" or "in by the 10th" accounts, which are prohibited by TISA and part 707.

(p) Interest

1. *General.* Member savings placed in deposit accounts are debt investments, and the return earned on these accounts is interest. Federal credit unions are not authorized to offer any interest-bearing deposit accounts. State-chartered credit unions may offer both share and deposit accounts if permitted by state law. State law, including without limitation regulations and official interpretations, will determine if returns earned in accounts in state-chartered credit unions are interest. Interest excludes the payment of a bonus or other consideration worth $10 or less given during a year, the waiver of reduction of a fee, the absorption of expenses, non-dividend membership benefits, and extraordinary dividends.

2. *Differences between dividends and interest.* Generally, dividends are returns on an equity investment (shares); interest is return on a debt investment (deposits). Dividends, in general, are not properly payable until declared at the close of a dividend period; interest, in general, is properly payable daily according to the deposit contract. Dividend rates are prospective until actually declared; interest rates are set according to contract in advance and are earned on that basis. Share accounts establish a member (owner)/credit union (cooperative) relationship; deposit accounts establish a depositor (creditor)/depository (debtor) relationship.

3. *Referencing.* Except where specifically stated otherwise, use of the terms "dividend" or "dividends" in part 707 also refers to "interest" where appropriate (for interest-bearing and non-interest-bearing deposit accounts at some state-chartered credit unions).

(q) Member

1. *Professional capacity.* Examples of accounts held by a natural person in a professional capacity for another are:
   i. Attorney-client trust accounts.
   ii. Trust, estate and court-ordered accounts.
   iii. Landlord-tenant security accounts.

2. *Other accounts.* Examples of accounts *not* held in a professional capacity include accounts held by parents for a child under the Uniform Gifts to Minors Act (or Uniform Transfers to Minors Act).

3. *Retirement plans.* IRAs and SEP accounts are member accounts to the extent that funds are invested in accounts subject to the regulation. Keogh accounts, like sole proprietor accounts, are not subject to the regulation.

(r) Non-Dividend Membership Benefits

1. *General.* Term reflects unique credit union practices that are difficult to value, encourage community spirit, and are not granted in such quantity as to be includable as calculable dividends.

2. *Examples.* Examples include:
   i Food, refreshments, and drawings and raffles at annual meetings, member functions, and branch openings.
   ii. Travel club benefits.
   iii. Prizes offered at annual meetings, such as U.S. Savings Bonds, a deposit of funds into the winner's account, trips, and other gifts. Such prizes are not bonuses because they are offered as an incentive to increase attendance at the annual meeting, and not to entice members to open, maintain, or renew accounts or increase an account balance.
   iv. Life savings benefits.

(s) Passbook Account

1. *Relation to Regulation E.* Passbook accounts include accounts accessed by preauthorized electronic fund transfers to the account (as defined in 12 CFR §205.2(j)), such as an account credited by direct share and deposit of social security payments. Accounts that permit access by other electronic means are not "passbook accounts," and any statements that are sent four or more times a year must comply with the requirements of §707.6.

National Credit Union Administration

(t) Periodic Statement

1. *General.* Periodic statements are not required by part 707. Passbook and term share accounts are exempt from periodic statement requirements.

2. *Examples.* Periodic statements do not include:
   i. Additional statements provided solely upon request.
   ii. General service information such as a quarterly newsletter or other correspondence that describes available services and products.

(u) Potential Member

1. *General.* A potential member is a natural person eligible for membership in a credit union, who has not yet taken the steps necessary to become a member. The term also includes natural person nonmembers eligible to hold accounts in a credit union pursuant to relevant federal or state law.

2. *Verification of eligibility.* It is recommended that credit unions have sound written procedures in place to identify those eligible for membership. If these procedures include verification measures, such as an application process, verification telephone call or letter to an employer or association within the field of membership, witnessing by an existing member, or similar procedure, then the credit union may first verify the membership eligibility of a potential member before providing account disclosures or other information to the potential member. This process of verifying a member's eligibility status, making a recommendation for membership, and providing account disclosures should be completed within 20 calendar days. This period also applies when potential members not on credit union premises request disclosures.

3. *Nonmembers.* Within its sole discretion, the board of directors of a credit union may provide TISA disclosures to nonmembers who are ineligible for membership or to hold an account at the credit union. If disclosures are made to such nonmembers, it is the position of the Board that no civil liability can accrue to the credit union for any errors in such disclosures. (See commentary to § 707.3(d)).

(v) State

1. *General.* Territories and possessions include American Samoa, Guam, the Mariana Islands, and the Marshall Islands.

(w) Stepped-Rate Account

1. *General.* Stepped-rate accounts are those accounts in which two or more dividend rates (known at the time the account is opened) will take effect in succeeding periods.

2. *Example.* An example of a stepped-rate account is a one-year term share certificate account in which a 5.00% dividend rate is paid for the first six months, and 5.50% for the second six months.

(x) Term Share Account

1. *Relation to Regulation D.* Regulation D permits, in limited circumstances, the withdrawal of funds without penalty during the first six days after a "time deposit" is opened. (See 12 CFR 204.2(c)(1)(i).) But the fact that a member makes a withdrawal as permitted by Regulation D does not disqualify the account from being a term share account for purposes of this regulation (such as withdrawals upon the death of the member, or within a "grace period" for automatically renewable term share accounts).

2. *Club accounts.* Club accounts, including Christmas club, holiday club, and vacation club accounts may be either term share or regular share accounts, depending on the terms of the account. Although club accounts typically have a maturity date, they are not term share accounts unless they also require a penalty of at least seven days' dividends for withdrawals during the first six days after the account is opened.

(y) Tiered-Rate Account

1. *General.* Tiered-rate accounts are those accounts in which two or more dividend rates are paid on the account and are determined by reference to a specified balance level. Tiered-rate accounts are of two types: Tiering Method A and Tiering Method B. In Tiering Method A accounts, the credit union pays the applicable tiered dividends rate on the entire amount in the account. This method is also known as the "hybrid" or "plateau" tiered-rate account. In Tiering Method B accounts, the credit union does not pay the applicable tiered dividends rate on the entire amount in the account, but only on the portion of the share account balance that falls within each specified tier. This method is also known as the "pure" or "split-rate" tiered-rate account. (See appendix A, part I, D.)

2. *Example.* An example of a tiered-rate account is one in which a credit union pays a 5.00% dividend rate on balances below $1,000, and 5.50% on balances $1,000 and above.

3. *Term share accounts.* Term share accounts that pay different rates based solely on the amount of the initial share and deposit are not tiered-rate accounts.

4. *Minimum balance accounts.* A requirement to maintain a minimum balance to earn dividends does not make an account a tiered-rate account. If dividends are not paid on amounts below a specified balance level, then the account has a minimum balance requirement (required to be disclosed under § 707.4(b)(3)(i)), but the account does not constitute a tiered-rate account. A zero rate

(0%) cannot constitute a tier. Minimum balance accounts are single rate accounts with a minimum balance requirement.

(z) Variable-Rate Account

1. *General.* Includes accounts in which the credit union does not contract to give at least 30 days advance written notice of decreases in the dividend rate. An account meets this definition whether the rate change is determined by reference to an index, by use of a formula, or merely at the discretion of the credit union's board of directors. An account that permits one or more rate adjustments prior to maturity at the member's option, such as a rate relock option, is a variable-rate account.

2. *Differences between fixed-rate and variable-rate accounts.* All ccounts must either be fixed-rate or variable-rate accounts. Classifying an account as variable-rate affects credit unions three ways:

i. Additional account disclosures are required (§ 707.4(b)(1)(ii));

ii. Rate decreases are exempted from change-in-terms requirements (§ 707.5(a)(2)(i)); and

iii. Advertising notice required (§ 707.8(c)(1)).

Fixed-rate accounts require a contract term obligating the credit union to a 30-day advance, written notice to members before decreasing the dividend rate on the account. Term changes adversely affecting the member and rate decreases cannot take effect until 30 days after such fixed-rate change-in-terms notices are mailed or delivered to members (§ 707.5(a)).

Section 707.3—General Disclosure Requirements

(a) Form

1. *General.* All required disclosures (e.g., account disclosures, change-in-terms notices, term share renewal/maturity notices, statement disclosures and advertising disclosures) must be made clearly and conspicuously, in a form the member may retain. Disclosures need be made only as applicable (e.g., disclosures for a non-dividend-bearing account would not include disclosure of annual percentage yield, dividend rate, or other disclosures pertaining to dividend calculations).

2. *Design requirements.* Disclosures must be presented in a format that allows members and potential members to readily understand the terms of their account. Credit unions are not required to use a particular type size or typeface, nor are credit unions required to state any term more conspicuously than any other term. Disclosures may be made:

i. In any order.

ii. In combination with other disclosures or account terms.

iii. In combination with disclosures for other types of accounts, as long as it is clear to members and potential members which disclosures apply to their account.

iv. On more than one page and on the front and reverse sides.

v. By using inserts to a document or filling in blanks.

vi. On more than one document, as long as the documents are provided at the same time.

3. *Consistent terminology.* A credit union must use the same terminology to describe terms or features that are required to be disclosed. For example, if a credit union describes a monthly fee (regardless of account activity), as a "monthly service fee" in account opening disclosures, the periodic statements and change-in-terms notices must use the same terminology so that members and potential members can readily identify the fee.

(b) General

1. *Terms and conditions.* Credit unions are required to have disclosures reflect the terms of the legal obligation between the credit union and a member at the time the member opens the account. This provision does not impose any contract terms or supersede state or other laws that define how the legal obligations between a credit union and its membership are determined.

2. *Specificity of legal obligation.* Credit unions may refer to the calendar month or to roughly equivalent intervals during a calendar year as a "month." Use of estimates is prohibited in TISA disclosures.

3. *Foreign language.* Disclosures may be made in any foreign language, if desired by the board of directors of a credit union. However, disclosures must also be provided in English, upon request.

(c) Relation to Regulation E

1. *General rule.* Compliance with Regulation E (12 CFR part 205) is deemed to satisfy the disclosure requirements of this regulation, such as when:

i. A credit union changes a term that triggers a notice under Regulation E, and the timing and disclosure rules of Regulation E for sending change-in-terms notices.

ii. A member adds an ATM access feature to an account, and the credit union provides disclosures pursuant to Regulation E, including disclosure of fees before the member receives ATM access. (See 12 CFR 205.7.)

iii. A credit union complying with the timing rules of Regulation E discloses at the same time fees for electronic services (such as balance inquiry fees imposed if the inquiry is made at an ATM) that are required to be disclosed by this regulation, but not by Regulation E.

iv. A credit union relies on Regulation E's rules regarding disclosures of limitations on the frequency and amount of electronic fund

National Credit Union Administration

transfers, including security-related exceptions. But any limitation on the number of "intra-institutional transfers" to or from the member's other accounts at the credit union during a given time period must be disclosed, even though intra-institutional transfers are exempt from Regulation E.

(d) Multiple Members

1. *General.* When an account has multiple natural person member accountholders, delivery of disclosures to any member accountholder or agent authorized by the accountholder satisfies the disclosure requirements of part 707.

(e) Oral Response to Inquiries

1. *Application of rule.* Credit unions need not provide rate information orally. Disclosures need be made only as appropriate. For example, the requirement to give a telephone number for a member to call about rates for interest-bearing accounts and dividend-bearing term share accounts, would not be necessary for members calling the credit union for information. Also, the disclosure requirements are applicable only to credit union employees and volunteers acting in the ordinary course of credit union business.

2. *Relation to advertising.* The advertising rules do not cover an oral response to a question about rates.

3. *Existing accounts.* This paragraph does not apply to oral responses about rate information for existing term share accounts or accounts not currently offered. For example, if a member holding a one-year term share account requests dividend rate information about the account during the term, the credit union need not disclose the annual percentage yield, unless the member is calling for rate information under a maturity notice.

(f) Rounding and Accuracy Rules for Rates and Yields

(f)(1) Rounding

1. *Permissible rounding.* The annual percentage yield, annual percentage yield earned and dividend rate must be rounded to the nearest one-hundredth of one percentage point (.01%) when disclosed. Examples of permissible rounding are an annual percentage yield calculated to be 5.644%, rounded down and shown as 5.64%; 5.645% would be rounded up and disclosed as 5.65%. For account disclosures, the dividend rate may be expressed to more than two decimal places.

(f)(2) Accuracy

1. *Annual percentage yield and annual percentage yield earned.* The tolerance for annual percentage yield and annual percentage yield earned calculations is designed to accommodate inadvertent errors. Credit unions may not purposely incorporate the one-twentieth of one percentage point (.05%) tolerance into their calculation of yields.

2. *Dividend rate.* There is no tolerance for an inaccuracy in the dividend rate.

Section 707.4—Account Disclosures

(a) Delivery of Account Disclosures

(a)(1) Account Opening

1. *New accounts.* New account disclosures must be provided when:

i. A term share account that does not automatically rollover is renewed by a member.

ii. A member changes the term for a renewable term share account (from a one-year term share account to a six-month term share account, for instance) (see comment 5(b)–5 regarding disclosure alternatives).

iii. A credit union transfers funds from an account to open a new account not at the member's request, unless the credit union previously gave account disclosures and any change-in-terms notices for the new account (e.g., funds in a money market share account are transferred by a credit union to open a new account for the member, such as a share draft account, because the member exceeded transaction limitations on the money market share account).

iv. A credit union accepts a deposit from a member to an account that the credit union had previously deemed to be "closed," under applicable federal or state law, for the purpose of treating accrued, but uncredited, dividends as forfeited dividends. New account numbers are not required by this requirement.

2. *Acquired accounts.* New account disclosures need not be given when a credit union acquires an account through an acquisition of, or merger with, another credit union (but see §707.5(a) regarding advance notice requirements if terms are changed).

3. *Combination disclosures.* New account disclosures need not be given when a member has already received disclosures covering several accounts, and opens a new account properly disclosed by the already received combination disclosures, if the new account is opened within a reasonable amount of time after receipt of the combination disclosures and if the received disclosures and terms are accurate at the time the new account is opened.

(a)(2) Requests

(a)(2)(i)

1. *Inquiries versus requests.* A response to an oral inquiry (by telephone or in person) about rates and yields or fees does not trigger the duty to provide account disclosures. But, when a member asks for written information about an account (whether by telephone, in person, or by other means), the

credit union must provide disclosures unless the account is no longer offered to the public.

2. *General requests.* When member's or potential member's request discloses about a type of account (a share draft account, for example), a credit union that offers several variations may provide disclosures for any one of them. No disclosures need be made to nonmembers, though a credit union may provide disclosures to nonmembers within its sole discretion.

3. *Timing for response.* Ten business days is a reasonable time for responding to requests for account information that members or potential members do not make in person, including requests made by electronic means, such as by electronic mail.

4. *Use of electronic means.* If a member or potential member who is not present at the credit union makes a request for account disclosures, including a request made by telephone, e-mail, or via the credit union's Web site, the credit union may send the disclosures in paper form or, if the member or potential member agrees, may provide the disclosures electronically, such as to an e-mail address that the member or potential member provides for that purpose, or on the credit union's Web site, without regard to the consent or other provisions of the E-Sign Act. The regulation does not require a credit union to provide, nor a member or potential member to agree to receive, the disclosures required by § 707.4(a)(2) in electronic form.

(a)(2)(ii)(A)(2)

1. *Recent rates.* Credit unions comply with this paragraph if they disclose an interest rate (or dividend rate on a dividend-bearing term share account) and annual percentage yield accurate within the seven calendar days preceding the date they send the disclosures.

(a)(2)(ii)(B)

1. *Term.* Describing the maturity of a term share account as "1 year" or "6 months," for example, illustrates a response stating the maturity of a term share account as a term rather than a date (e.g., "June 1, 1995").

(b) Content of Account Disclosures

(b)(1) Rate Information

(b)(1)(i) Annual Percentage Yield and Dividend Rate

1. *Rate disclosures.* In addition to the dividend rate and annual percentage yield, credit unions may disclose a periodic rate corresponding to the dividend rate. No other rate or yield (such as "tax effective yield") is permitted. If the annual percentage yield is the same as the dividend rate, credit unions may disclose a single figure but must use both terms.

2. *Fixed-rate accounts.* For fixed-rate term share accounts paying the opening rate until maturity, credit unions may disclose the period of time the dividend rate will be in effect by stating, or cross-referencing, the maturity date. For other fixed-rate accounts, credit unions may use a date (such as "This rate will be in effect through June 30, 1995") or a period (such as "This rate will be in effect for at least 30 days").

3. *Tiered-rate accounts.* Each dividend rate, along with the corresponding annual percentage yield for each specified balance level (or range of annual percentage yields, if appropriate), must be disclosed for tiered-rate accounts. (See appendix A, Part I, Paragraph D.)

4. *Stepped-rate accounts.* A single composite annual percentage yield must be disclosed for stepped-rate accounts. (See appendix A, Part I, Paragraph B.) The dividend rates and the period of time each will be in effect also must be provided. When the initial rate offered for a specified time on a variable-rate account is higher or lower than the rate that would otherwise be paid on the account, the calculation of the annual percentage yield must be made as if for a stepped-rate account. (See appendix A, Part I, Paragraph C.)

5. *Minimum balance accounts.* If a credit union sets a minimum balance to earn dividends, the credit union may, but need not, state that the annual percentage yield is 0% for those days the balance in the account drops below the minimum balance level when using the daily balance method. Nor is a disclosure of 0% required for credit unions using the average daily balance method, if the member fails to meet the minimum balance required for the average daily balance period.

(b)(1)(ii) Variable Rates

(b)(1)(ii)(B)

1. *Determining dividend rates.* To disclose how the dividend rate is determined, credit unions must:

i. Identify the index and specific margin, if the dividend rate is tied to an index.

ii. State that rate changes are within the credit union's discretion, if the credit union does not tie changes to an index.

(b)(1)(ii)(C)

1. *Frequency of rate changes.* A credit union reserving the right to change rates at its discretion must state the fact that rates may change at any time.

(b)(1)(ii)(D)

1. *Limitations.* A floor or ceiling on rates or on the amount the rate may decrease or increase during any time period must be disclosed. Credit unions need not disclose the absence of limitations on rate changes.

National Credit Union Administration

(b)(2) Compounding and Crediting

(b)(2)(i) Frequency

1. *General.* Descriptions such as "quarterly" or "monthly" are sufficient. Irregular crediting and compounding periods, such as if a cycle is out short at year end for tax reporting purposes, need not be disclosed.

2. *Dividend period.* For dividend-bearing accounts, the dividend period must be disclosed. (A specific example must also be given, see appendix B, §B–1(c).) The dividend period for term share accounts generally may be disclosed as the account's term (e.g., two years).

(b)(2)(ii) Effect of Closing an Account

1. *Deeming an account closed.* A credit union may, subject to state or other law, provide in account contracts the actions by members that will be treated as closing the account and that will result in the forfeiture of accrued but uncredited dividends. An example is the withdrawal of all funds from the account prior to the date dividends are credited. Credit unions are cautioned that bylaw requirements may prevent a credit union from deeming a member's account closed until certain time periods are extinguished if funds remain in a member's account. *NCUA Standard FCU Bylaws*, Art. III, §3. Such bylaw requirements may not be overridden without proper agency approval.

(b)(3) Balance Information

(b)(3)(i) Minimum Balance Requirements

1. *Par value.* Credit unions must disclose any minimum balance required to open the account, to avoid the imposition of a fee, or to obtain the annual percentage yield. Since members cannot generally maintain any accounts until the par value of the membership share is paid in full, this section requires that credit unions disclose the par value of a share necessary to become a member and maintain accounts at the credit union. The par value of a share and the minimum balance requirement do not have to be the same amount (e.g., a credit union may have a $5 par value for a membership share, in order for accounts to be opened and maintained, and a $100 minimum balance requirement, in order for the account to earn dividends).

2. *Disclosures.* The explanation of minimum balance computation methods may be combined with the balance computation method disclosures (§707.4(b)(3)(ii)) if they are the same. If a credit union uses different cycles for determining minimum balance requirements for purposes of assessing fees and for paying dividends, the credit union must disclose the specific cycle or time period used for each purpose (e.g., use of a midmonth statement cycle for determining dividends, and use of a calendar month cycle for determining fees). Credit unions may assess fees by using any method. If fees on one account are tied to the balance in another account, such provision must be explained (e.g., if share draft fees are tied to a minimum balance in the regular share account (or a combination of the share draft and regular share accounts), the share draft account must explain that fact and how the balance in the regular share account (or both accounts) is determined). The fee need not be disclosed in the account disclosures if the fee is not imposed on that account.

(b)(3)(ii) Balance Computation Method

1. *Methods and periods.* Credit unions may use different methods or periods to calculate minimum balances for purposes of imposing a fee (the daily balance for a calendar month, for example) and accruing dividends (the average daily balance for a statement period, for example). Each method and corresponding period must be disclosed.

(b)(3)(iii) When dividends begin to accrue

1. *Additional information.* Credit unions must include a statement as to when dividends begin to accrue for noncash deposits. Credit unions may disclose additional information such as the time of day after which deposits are treated as having been received the following business day, and may use additional descriptive terms such as "ledger" or "collected" balances to disclose when dividends begin to accrue. Under the ledger balance method, dividends begin to accrue on the day of deposit. Under the collected balance methods, dividends begin to accrue when provisional credit is received for the item deposited.

(b)(4) Fees

1. *Types of fees.* Fees related to the routine use of an account must be disclosed. The following are types of fees that must be disclosed in connection with an account:

i. Maintenance fees, such as monthly service fees.

ii. Fees related to share deposits or withdrawals.

iii. Fees for special services, such as stop payment fees, fees for balance inquiries or verification of share and deposits, fees associated with checks returned unpaid, fees for regularly sending to members share drafts that otherwise would be held by the credit union, and overdraft line of credit access fees (if charged against the share account).

iv. Fees to open or to close an account.

v. Fees imposed upon dormant or inactive accounts.

2. *Other fees.* Credit unions need not disclose fees such as the following:

i. Fees for services offered to members and nonmembers alike, such as fees for certain travelers checks, for wire transfers and automated clearinghouse (ACH) transfers, to process credit card cash advances, or to handle U.S. Savings Bond Redemption (even if different amounts are charged to members and nonmembers).

ii. Incidental fees, such as fees associated with state escheat laws, garnishment or attorneys fees, to change names on an account, to generate a midcycle periodic statement, to wrap loose coins, for photocopying, for statements returned to the credit union because of a wrong address, and locator fees.

3. *Amount of fees.* Credit unions are cautioned that merely providing fee information in an account disclosure may not be sufficient to gain the legal right to impose the fee involved under applicable law. Credit unions must state the amount and conditions under which a fee may be imposed. Naming and describing the fee typically satisfies this requirement. Some examples are:

i. "$4.00 monthly service fee".

ii. "$7.00 and up" or "fee depends on style of checks ordered" for check printing fees.

4. *Tied-accounts.* Credit unions must state if fees that may be assessed against an account are tied to other accounts at the credit union. For example, if a credit union ties the fees payable on a share draft account to balances held in the share draft account and in a regular share account, the share draft account disclosures must state that fact and explain how the fee is determined.

5. *Regulation E statements.* Some fees are required to be disclosed under both Regulation E (12 CFR 205.7) and part 707. If such fees, such as ATM transaction fees, are disclosed on a Regulation E statement, they need not be disclosed again on a periodic statement required under part 707.

6. *Fees for overdrawing an account.* Under §707.4(b)(4) of this part, credit unions must disclose the conditions under which a fee may be imposed. In satisfying this requirement credit unions must specify the categories of transactions for which an overdraft fee may be imposed. An exhaustive list of transactions is not required. It is sufficient for a credit union to state that the fee applies to overdrafts "created by check, in-person withdrawal, ATM withdrawal, or other electronic means." Disclosing a fee "for overdraft items" would not be sufficient.

(b)(5) Transaction Limitations

1. *General rule.* Examples of limitations on the number of dollar amount of share deposits or withdrawals that credit unions must disclose are:

i. Limits on the number of share drafts or checks that may be written on an account for a given time period.

ii. Limits on withdrawals or share deposits during the term of a term share account.

iii. Limitations required by Regulation D, such as the number of withdrawals permitted from money market share accounts by check to third parties each month (credit unions need not disclose reservation of right to require a notice for withdrawals from accounts required by federal or state law).

(b)(6) Features of Term Share Accounts

(b)(6)(i) Time Requirements

1. *"Callable" term share accounts.* In addition to the maturity date, credit unions must state the date or the circumstances under which the credit union may redeem a term share account at the credit union's option (a "callable" term share account).

(b)(6)(ii) Early Withdrawal Penalties

1. *General.* The term "penalty" may, but need not, be used to describe the loss that may be incurred by members for early withdrawal of funds from term share accounts.

2. *Examples.* Examples of early withdrawal penalties are:

i. Monetary penalties, such a specific dollar amount (e.g., "$10.00") or a specific days' worth of dividends (e.g., "seven days' dividends plus accrued but uncredited dividends, but only if the account is closed").

ii. Adverse changes to terms such as the lowering of the dividend rate, annual percentage yield, or reducing the compounding or crediting frequency for funds remaining in shares or on deposit.

iii. Reclamation of bonuses.

3. *Relation to rules for IRAs or similar plans.* Penalties imposed by the Internal Revenue Code for certain withdrawals from IRAs or similar pension or savings plans are not early withdrawal penalties for purposes of this regulation.

4. *Disclosing penalties.* Penalties may be stated in months, whether credit unions assess the penalty using the actual number of days during the period or using another method such as a number of days that occurs in any actual sequence of the total calendar months involved. For example, stating "one month's dividends" is permissible, whether the credit union assesses 30 days' dividends during the month of April, or selects a time period between 28 and 31 days for calculating the dividends for all early withdrawals regardless of when the penalty is assessed.

(b)(6)(iv) Renewal Policies

1. *Rollover term share accounts.* Credit unions are not required to provide a grace period, to pay dividends during the grace period, or to disclose whether or not dividends will be paid during the grace period. Credit unions offering a grace period on term share accounts must give the length of the grace period. Commentary, appendix B, Model Clauses, §B–1(i)(iv).

National Credit Union Administration

2. *Nonrollover term share accounts.* Credit unions that pay dividends on funds following the maturity of term share accounts that do not renew automatically need not state the rate (or annual percentage yield) that may be paid.

(b)(7) Bonuses

1. *General.* Credit unions are required to state the amount and type of bonus, and disclose any minimum balance or time requirement to obtain the bonus and when the bonus will be provided. If the minimum balance or time requirement is otherwise required to be disclosed, credit unions need not duplicate the disclosure for purposes of this paragraph.

(b)(8) Nature of Dividends

1. *General.* Dividends are not payable until declared and unless sufficient current and undivided earnings are available after required transfers to reserves at the close of a dividend period. A disclosure explaining dividends educates members and protects credit unions in the event that a prospective dividend cannot be paid, or is not properly payable. This disclosure is required for all dividend-bearing share accounts. Term share accounts need not include a statement regarding the nature of dividends.

2. *State-chartered credit unions with interest-bearing deposit accounts.* State law controls the nature of accounts (i.e., whether an account is a share account or a deposit account). If a member of a state-chartered credit union is opening only an interest-bearing deposit account, or is requesting account disclosures only for an interest-bearing deposit account (if state law requires the depositor to hold a share account), the disclosures must generally include the following information on any dividend-bearing share portion of the account (e.g., membership share): the par value of a share; a statement that the portion of the deposit that represents the par value of the membership share will earn dividends, and that dividends are paid from current income and available earnings after required transfers to reserves. Further additional disclosures, such as a separate dividend rate and annual percentage yield for the membership share, are not required (if the additional disclosures would agree with the remainder of the account which is invested in an interest-bearing deposit).

(c) Notice to Existing Accountholders

1. *General.* Only members who receive periodic statements (provided regularly at least four times per year) and who hold accounts of the type offered by the credit union as of the compliance date of part 707 (generally January 1, 1995) must receive the notice. If following receipt of the notice members request disclosures, credit unions have twenty calendar days from receipt of the request to provide the disclosures. Rate and annual percentage yield information in such disclosures must conform to that required for disclosures upon request. As an alternative to including the notice in or on the periodic statement, the final rule permits credit unions to send the account disclosures themselves, as long as they are sent at the same time as the periodic statement (the disclosures may be mailed either with the periodic statement or separately).

2. *Form of the notice.* The notice may be included on the periodic statement, in a member newsletter, or on a statement stuffer or other insert, if it is clear and conspicuous. The notice cannot be sent in a separate mailing from the periodic statement.

3. *Timing.* The notice may accompany the first periodic statement after the compliance date for part 707, or the periodic statement for the first cycle beginning after that date. For example, a credit union's statement cycle is December 15, 1994-January 14, 1995. The statement is mailed on January 15, The next cycle is January 15, 1995 through February 14, 1995, and the statement for that cycle is mailed on February 15. The credit union may provide the notice either on or with the January 15 statement or on or with the February 15 statement, as it covers the first cycle after January 1, 1995.

4. *Early compliance.* Credit unions that provide the notice to existing members prior to the compliance date of part 707, must be prepared to provide accurate and timely disclosures when, following receipt of the notice, members ask for account disclosures. Such disclosures must be provided even if they are requested before the compliance date of part 707. Credit unions who provide early notice to existing members need to comply with other aspects of part 707, but need not provide disclosures already provided in compliance with part 707.

Section 707.5—Subsequent Disclosures

(a) Change in Terms

(a)(1) Advance Notice required

1. *Form of notice.* Credit unions may provide a change-in-term notice on or with a regular periodic statement or in another mailing (such as a highlighted portion of a newsletter or statement stuffer insert). If a credit union provides notice through revised account disclosures, the changed term must be highlighted in some manner. For example, credit unions may state that a particular fee has been changed (also specifying the new amount) or use an accompanying letter that refers to the changed term. Credit unions are cautioned that unless credit unions have reserved the right to change terms in the account agreement or disclosures, a change-in-

terms notice may not be sufficient to amend the terms under applicable law.

2. *Effective date.* An example of a language for disclosing the effective date of a change is: "As of May 11, 1995".

3. *Terms that change upon the occurrence of an event.* A credit union offering terms that will automatically change upon the occurrence of a stated event need not send an advance notice of the change provided the credit union fully describes the conditions of the change in the account opening disclosures (and sends any change-in-term notices regardless of whether the changed term affects that member's account at that time).

4. *Examples.* Examples of changes not requiring an advance change-in-terms notice are:

i. The termination of employment for employee-members for whom account maintenance or activity fees were waived during their employment by the credit union.

ii. The expiration of one year in a promotion described in the account opening disclosures to "waive $4.00 monthly service charges for one year".

(a)(2) No Notice Required

(a)(2)(ii) Check Printing Fees

1. *Increase in fees.* A notice is not required for an increase in fees for printing share drafts (or deposit and withdrawal slips) even if the credit union adds some amount to the price charged by the vendor.

(b) Notice Before Maturity for Term Share Accounts Longer Than One Month That Renew Automatically.

1. *Maturity dates on nonbusiness days.* In determining the term of a term share account, credit unions may disregard the fact that the term will be extended beyond the disclosed number of days if the maturity date falls on a nonbusiness day. For example, a holiday or weekend may cause a "one-year" term share account to extend beyond 365 days (or 366, in a leap year), or a "one-month" term share account to extend beyond 31 days.

2. *Disclosing when rates will be determined.* Ways to disclose when the annual percentage yield will be available include the use of:

i. A specific date, such as "October 28".

ii. A date that is easily discernible, such as "the Tuesday prior to the maturity date stated on the notice" or "as of the maturity date stated on this notice".

3. *Alternative timing rule.* Under the alternative timing rule, a credit union that offers a 10-day grace period would have to provide the disclosures at least 10 calendar days prior to the scheduled maturity date.

4. *Club accounts.* If members have agreed to the transfer of payments from another account to a club term share account for the next club period, the credit union must comply with the requirements for automatically renewable term share accounts—even though members may withdraw funds from the club account at the end of the current club period.

5. *Renewal of a term share account.* In the case of a change-in-terms that becomes effective if a rollover term share account is subsequently renewed:

i. If the change is initiated by the credit union, the disclosure requirements of this paragraph apply. (Section 707.5(a) applies if the change becomes effective prior to the maturity of the existing term share account.)

ii. If the change is initiated by the member, the account opening disclosure requirements of §707.4(b) apply. (If the notice required by this paragraph has been provided, credit unions may give new account disclosures or disclosures that reflect the new term.)

6. *Example.* If a member receives a notice prior to maturity on a one-year term share account and requests a rollover to a six-month account, the credit union must provide either account opening disclosures including the new maturity date or, if all other terms previously disclosed in the prematurity notice remain the same, only the new maturity date.

(b)(1) Maturities of Longer Than One Year

1. *Highlighting changed terms.* Credit unions need not highlight terms that have changed since the last account disclosures were provided.

(c) Notice Before Maturity for Term Share Accounts Longer Than One Year That Do not Renew Automatically

1. *Subsequent account.* When funds are transferred following maturity of a nonrollover term share account, credit unions need not provide account disclosures unless a new account is established.

Section 707.6—Periodic Statement Disclosures

(a) Rule When Statement and Crediting Periods Vary

1. *General.* Credit unions are not required to provide periodic statements. If they provide periodic statements, disclosures need only be furnished to the extent applicable. For example, if no dividends are earned for a statement period, credit unions need not state that fact. Or, credit unions may disclose "$0" dividends earned and "0%" annual percentage yield earned.

2. *Regulation E interim statements.* When a credit union provides regular quarterly statements, and in addition provides a monthly interim statement to comply with Regulation E, the interim statement need not comply with this section unless it states

dividend or rate information. (See 12 CFR 205.9). For credit unions that choose not to treat Regulation E activity statements as part 707 periodic statements, the quarterly periodic statement must reflect the annual percentage yield earned and dividends earned for the full quarter. However, credit unions choosing this option need not redisclose fees already disclosed on an interim Regulation E activity statement on the quarterly periodic statement. For credit unions that choose to treat Regulation E activity statements as part 707 periodic statements, the Regulation E statement must meet all part 707 requirements.

3. *Combined statements.* Credit unions may provide certain information about an account (such as a money market share account or regular share account) on the periodic statement for another account (such as a share draft account) without triggering the disclosures required by this section, as long as:

i. The information is limited to information such as the account number, the type of account, balance information, accountholders' names, and social security or tax identification number; and

ii. The credit union also provides members a periodic statement complying with this section for the account (the money market share account or regular share account, in the example).

4. *Other information.* Additional information that may be given on or with a periodic statement, includes:

i. Dividend rates and corresponding periodic rates to the dividend rate applied to balances during the statement period.

ii. The dollar amount of dividends earned year-to-date.

iii. Bonuses paid (or any *de minimis* consideration of $10 or less).

iv. Fees for other products, such as safe deposit boxes.

v. Accounts not covered by the periodic statement disclosure requirements (passbook and term share accounts) may disclose any information on the statement related to such accounts, so long as such information is accurate and not misleading.

5. *When statement and crediting periods vary.* This rule permits credit unions, on dividend-bearing share accounts, to report the annual percentage yield earned and the amount of dividends earned on a statement other than on each periodic statement when the dividend period does not agree with, varies from, or is different than, the statement period. For dividend-bearing share accounts, credit unions may disclose the required information either upon each periodic statement, or on the statement on which dividends are actually earned (credited or posted) to the member's account. In addition, for accounts using the average daily balance method of calculating dividends, when the average daily balance period and the statement periods do not agree, vary or are different, credit unions may also report annual percentage yield earned and the dollar amount of dividends earned on the periodic statement on which the dividends or interest is earned. For example, if a credit union has quarterly dividend periods, or uses a quarterly average daily balance on an account, the first two monthly statements may not state annual percentage yield earned and dividends earned figures; the third "monthly" statement will reflect the dividends earned and the annual percentage yield earned for the entire quarter. The fees imposed disclosure must be given on the periodic statement on which they are imposed.

6. *Length of the period.* Credit unions must disclose the length of both the dividend period (or average daily balance calculation period) and the statement period. For example, a statement could disclose a statement period of April 16 through May 15 and further state that "the dividends earned and the annual percentage yield earned are based on your dividend period (or average daily balance) for the period April 1 through April 30."

7. *Dividend period more frequent than statement period.* Credit unions that calculate dividends on a monthly basis, but send statements on a quarterly basis, may disclose a single dividend (and annual percentage yield earned) figure. Alternatively, a credit union may disclose three dividends earned and three annual percentage yield earned figures, one of each month in the quarter, as long as the credit union states the number of days (or beginning and ending date) in each dividend period if it varies from the statement period.

8. *Additional voluntary disclosures.* For credit unions not disclosing the annual percentage yield earned and dividends earned on all periodic statements, credit unions may place a notice on statements without dividends and annual percentage yield earned figures, that the annual percentage yield earned and dollar amount of dividends earned will appear on the first statement at the close of the dividend (or average daily balance) period, or similar wording. Credit unions may also choose to include a telephone number to call for interim information, if desired by a member.

(b) Statement Disclosures

(b)(1) Annual Percentage Yield Earned

1. *Ledger and collected balances.* Credit unions that accrue interest using the collected balance method may use either the ledger or collected balance methods to determine the balance used to determine the annual percentage yield earned. Ledger balance means the record of the balance in a member's account, as per the credit union's

records. (The ledger balance may reflect additions and deposits for which the credit union has not yet received final payment). Collected balance means the record of balance in a member's account reflecting collected funds, that is, cash or checks deposited in the credit union which have been presented for payment and for which payment has actually been received. (See Regulation CC, 12 CFR 229.14).

(b)(2) Amount of Dividends or Interest

1. *Definition of earned.* The term "earned" is defined to include dividends and interest either "accrued" or "paid and credited." Credit unions may use either the "ledger" or the "collected" balance for either option. (See 707.6(b)(1)1. and 707.7(c)2. of this appendix.)

2. *Accrued interest.* Credit unions must state the amount of interest that accrued during the statement period, even if it was not credited.

3. *Terminology.* In disclosing dividends earned for the period, credit unions must use the term "dividends" or terminology such as: "Dividends paid," to describe dividends that have been credited; "Dividends accrued," to indicate that dividends are not yet credited.

4. *Closed accounts.* If a member closes an account between crediting periods and forfeits accrued dividends, the credit union may not show any figures for "dividends earned" or annual percentage yield earned for the period (other than zero, at the credit union's option).

5. *Extraordinary dividends.* Extraordinary dividends are not a component of the annual percentage yield earned or the dividend rate, but are an addition to the member's account. The dollar amount of the extraordinary dividends paid, denoted as a separate, identified figure, must be disclosed on the periodic statement on which the extraordinary dividends are earned. A credit union may also disclose information regarding the calculation of the extraordinary dividends, and additional annual percentage yield earned and dividend rate figures taking into account the extraordinary dividend, so long as such information is accurate and not misleading.

(b)(3) Fees Imposed

1. *General.* Periodic statements must state fees disclosed under §707.4(b) that were debited to the account during the statement period, even if assessed for an earlier period.

2. *Itemizing fees by type.* In itemizing fees imposed more than once in the period, credit unions may group fees if they are the same type. (*See* §707.11(a)(1) of this part regarding certain fees that are required to be grouped.) When fees of the same type are grouped together, the description must make clear that the dollar figure represents more than a single fee, for example, "total fees for checks written this period." Examples of fees that may not be grouped together are—

i. Monthly maintenance and excess-activity fees.

ii. "Transfer" fees, if different dollar amounts are imposed, such as $.50 for deposits and $1.00 for withdrawals.

iii. Fees for electronic fund transfers and fees for other services, such as balance-inquiry or maintenance fees.

iv. Fees for paying overdrafts and fees for returning checks or other items unpaid.

3. *Identifying fees.* Statement details must enable the member to identify the specific fee. For example:

i. Credit unions may use a code to identify a particular fee if the code is explained on the periodic statement or in documents accompanying the statement.

ii. Credit unions using debit slips may disclose the date the fee was debited on the periodic statement and show the amount and type of fee on the dated debit slip.

4. *Relation to Regulation E.* Disclosure of fees in compliance with Regulation E complies with this section for fees related to electronic fund transfers (for example, totaling all electronic funds transfer fees in a single figure).

(b)(4) Length of Period

1. *General.* Credit unions providing the beginning and ending dates of the period must make clear whether both dates are included in the period. For example, stating "April 1 through April 30" would clearly indicate that both April 1 and April 30 are included in the period.

2. *Opening or closing an account mid-cycle.* If an account is opened or closed during the period for which a statement is sent, credit unions must calculate the annual percentage yield earned based on account balances for each day the account was open.

Section 707.7—Payment of Dividends

(a) Permissible Methods

1. *Prohibited calculation methods.* Calculation methods that do not comply with the requirement to pay dividends on the full amount of principal in the account each day include:

i. The "rollback" method, also known as the "grace period" or "in by the 10th" method, where credit unions pay dividends on the lowest balance in the account for the period.

ii. The "increments of par value" method, where credit unions only pay dividends on full shares in an account, e.g., a credit union with $5 par value shares pays dividends on $20 of a $24 account balance.

iii. The "ending balance" method, where credit unions pay dividends on the balance in the account at the end of the period.

iv. The "investable balance" method, where credit unions pay dividends on a percentage of the balance, excluding an amount credit unions set aside for reserve requirements.

v. The "low balance" method, where credit unions pay dividends on the lowest balance in the account for any day in that period.

2. *Use of 365-day basis.* Credit unions may apply a daily periodic rate that is greater than 1/365 of the dividend rate—such as 1/360 of the dividend rate—as long as it is applied 365 days a year.

3. *Periodic dividend payments.* A credit union can pay dividends each day on the account and still make uniform dividend payments. For example, for a one-year term share account, a credit union could make monthly dividend payments that are equal to 1/12 of the amount of dividends that will be earned for a 365-day period (or 11 uniform monthly payments—each equal to roughly 1/12 of the total amount of dividends—and one payment that accounts to the remainder of the total amount of dividends earned for the period).

4. *Leap year.* Credit unions may apply a daily rate of 1/366 or 1/365 of the dividend rate for 366 days in a leap year, if the account will earn dividends for February 29.

5. *Maturity of term share accounts.* Credit unions are not required to pay dividends after term share accounts mature. Examples include:

i. During any grace period offered by a credit union for an automatically renewable term share account, if the member decides during that period not to renew the account.

ii. Following the maturity of nonrollover term share accounts.

iii. When the maturity date falls on a holiday, and the member must wait until the next business day to obtain the funds.

6. *Dormant accounts.* Credit unions must pay dividends on funds in an account, even if inactivity or the infrequency of transactions would permit the credit union to consider the account to be "inactive" or "dormant" (or similar status) as defined by state or other law or the account contract.

7. *Insufficient funds.* Credit unions are not required to pay dividends on checks or share drafts deposited to a member's account that are returned for insufficient funds. If a credit union accrues dividends on a check that it later determines is not good, it may deduct from the accrued dividends any dividends attributed to the proceeds of the returned check. If dividends have already been credited before the credit union determines the item has insufficient funds, the credit union may deduct the amount of the check and associated dividends from the account balance. The amount deducted will not be reflected in the dividend amount and annual percentage yield earned reported for the next period.

8. *Account drawn below par value of a share.* If a member draws his or her account below the par value of a share, dividends would continue to accrue on the account so long as any minimum balance requirement is met. However, under the *NCUA Standard FCU Bylaws*, if a member who reduces his or her share balance below the value of a par value share and does not increase the balance within at least six months, the credit union may terminate the member's membership. State-chartered credit unions may have similar termination provisions.

(a)(2) Determination of Minimum Balance To Earn Dividends

1. *General.* Credit unions may set minimum balance requirements that must be met in order to earn dividends. However, credit unions must use the same method to determine a minimum balance required to earn dividends as they use to determine the balance upon which dividends will accrue and pay. For example, a credit union that calculates dividends on the daily balance method must use the daily balance method to determine if the minimum balance to earn dividends has been met. Similarly, a credit union that calculates dividends on the average daily balance method must use the average daily balance method to determine if the minimum to earn dividends has been met. Credit unions may have a par value of a share that is different from the minimum balance requirement to earn dividends. (See commentary to § 707.4(b)(3)(i)).

2. *Daily balance accounts.* Credit unions that require a minimum balance to earn dividends may choose not to pay dividends for days when the balance drops below the required minimum balance if they use the daily balance method to calculate dividends. For example, a credit union could set a minimum daily balance level of $200 and pay dividends only those days the $200 daily balance is maintained.

3. *Average daily balance accounts.* Credit unions that require a minimum balance to earn dividends may choose not to pay dividends for the average daily balance calculation period in which the average daily balance drops below the required minimum, if they use the average daily balance method to calculate dividends. For example, a credit union could set a minimum average daily balance level of $200 and pay dividends only if the $200 average daily balance is met for the calculation period.

4. *Beneficial method.* Credit unions may not require members to maintain both a minimum daily balance and a minimum average daily balance to earn dividends, such as by requiring the member to maintain a $500 daily balance and a prescribed average daily balance (whether higher or lower). But a credit union could offer a minimum balance to earn dividends that includes an additional

method that is "unequivocally beneficial" to the member such as the following:

i. A credit union using the daily balance method to calculate dividends and requiring a $500 minimum daily balance could choose to pay dividends on the account (for those days the minimum balance is not met) as long as the member maintained an average daily balance throughout the month of $400.

ii. A credit union using the average daily balance method to calculate dividends and requiring a $400 minimum average daily balance could choose to pay dividends on the account as long as the member maintained a daily balance of $500 for at least half of the days in the period.

iii. A credit union using either the daily balance method or average daily balance method to calculate dividends that requires: (A) a $500 daily balance; or (B) a $400 average daily balance to pay dividends on the account.

5. *Paying on full balance.* Credit unions must pay dividends on the full balance in the account that meets the required minimum balance. For example, if $300 is the minimum daily balance required to earn dividends, and a member deposits $500, the credit union must pay the stated dividend rate on the full $500 and not just on the $200.

6. *Negative balances prohibited.* Credit unions must treat a negative account balance as zero to determine:

i. The daily or average daily balance on which dividends will be paid.

ii. Whether any minimum balance to earn dividends is met. (See commentary to appendix A, Part II, which prohibits credit unions from using negative balances in calculating the dividends figure for the annual percentage yield earned.)

7. *Club accounts.* Credit unions offering club accounts (such as a "holiday" or "vacation" club accounts) cannot impose a minimum balance requirement for dividends based on the total number or dollar amount of payments required under the club plan. For example, if a plan calls for $10 weekly payments for 50 weeks, the credit union cannot set a $500 minimum balance and then pay only if the member makes all 50 payments.

8. *Minimum balances not affecting dividends.* Credit unions may use the daily balance, average daily balance, or other computation method to calculate minimum balance requirements not involving the payment of dividends—such as to compute minimum balances for assessing fees.

(b) Compounding and Crediting Policies

1. *General.* Credit unions choosing to compound dividends may compound or credit dividends annually, semi-annually, quarterly, monthly, daily, continuously, or on any other basis.

2. *Withdrawals prior to crediting date.* If members withdraw funds (without closing the account), prior to a scheduled crediting date, credit unions may delay paying the accrued dividends on the withdrawn amount until the scheduled crediting date, but may not avoid paying dividends.

3. *Closed accounts.* Subject to state or other law, a credit union may choose not to pay accrued dividends if members close an account prior to the date accrued dividends are credited, as long as the credit union has disclosed that fact. If accrued dividends are paid, accrued dividends must be paid on funds up until the account is closed or the account is deemed closed. For example, if an account is closed on a Tuesday, accrued dividends on the funds through Monday would be paid. Whether (and the conditions under which) credit unions are permitted to deem an account closed by a member is determined by state or other law, if any. Credit unions are cautioned that bylaw requirements may prevent a credit union from deeming a member's account closed until certain time periods are extinguished. (See NCUA Standard FCU Bylaws, Art. III, §3. Such bylaw requirements may not be overridden without proper agency approval.)

(c) Date Dividends Begin To Accrue

1. *Relation to Regulation CC.* Credit unions may rely on the Expedited Funds Availability Act (EFAA) and Regulation CC (12 CFR part 229) to determine, for example, when a deposit is considered made for purposes of dividend accrual, or when dividends need not be paid on funds because a deposited check is later returned unpaid.

2. *Ledger and collected balances.* Credit unions may calculate dividends by using a "ledger" balance or "collected" balance method, as long as the crediting requirements of the EFAA are met (12 CFR 229.14).

3. *Withdrawal of principal.* Credit unions must accrue dividends on funds until the funds are withdrawn from the account. For example, if a check is debited to an account on a Tuesday, the credit union must accrue dividends on those funds through Monday.

Section 707.8—Advertising

(a) Misleading or Inaccurate Advertisements

1. *General.* All advertisements are subject to the rule against misleading or inaccurate advertisements, even though the disclosure applicable to various media differ. The word "profit" may be used when referring to dividend-bearing share accounts, as it reflects the nature of dividends. The word "profit" may not be used when referring to interest-bearing deposit accounts.

2. *Indoor signs.* An indoor sign advertising an annual percentage yield is not misleading or inaccurate if:

i. For a tiered-rate account, it also provides the upper and lower dollar amounts of the tier corresponding to the advertised annual percentage yield.

ii. For a term share account, it also provides the term required to obtain the advertised annual percentage yield.

3. *"Free" or "no cost" accounts.* For purposes of determining whether an account can be advertised as "free" or "no cost," maintenance and activity fees include:

i. Any fee imposed if a minimum balance requirement is not met, or if the member exceeds a specified number of transactions.

ii. Transaction and service fees that members reasonably expect to be imposed on an account on a regular basis (see comments 4(b)(4)–1 and 2).

iii. A flat fee, such as a monthly service fee.

iv. Fees imposed to deposit, withdraw or transfer funds, including per-check or per-transaction charges (for example, $.25 for each withdrawal, whether by check, in person).

4. *Other fees.* Examples of fees that are *not* maintenance or activity fees include:

i. Fees that are not required to be disclosed under § 707.4(b)(4).

ii. Check printing fees of any type.

iii. Fees for obtaining copies of checks, whether or not the original checks have been truncated or returned to the member periodically.

iv. Balance inquiry fees.

v. Fees assessed against a dormant account.

vi. Fees for using an ATM.

vii. Fees for electronic transfer services that are not required to obtain an account, such as preauthorized transfers or home electronic credit union services.

viii. Stop payment fees and fees for share drafts or checks returned unpaid.

5. *Similar terms.* An advertisement may not use a term such as "fees waived" if a maintenance or activity fee may be imposed because it is similar to the terms "free" or "no cost."

6. *Specific account services.* Credit unions may advertise a specific account service or feature as free as long as no fee is imposed for that service or feature. For example, credit unions offering an account that is free of deposit or withdrawal fees could advertise that fact, as long as the advertisement does not mislead members by implying that the account is free and that no other fee (a monthly service fee, for example) may be charged.

7. *Free for limited time.* If an account (or a specific account service) is free only for a limited period of time—for example, for one year following the account opening—the account (or service) may be advertised as free as long as the time period is stated.

8. *Conditions not related to share accounts.* Credit unions may advertise accounts as "free" for members that meet conditions not related to share accounts, such as the member's age. For example, credit unions may advertise a share draft account as "free for persons over 65 years old," even though a maintenance or activity fee may be assessed on accounts held by members that are 65 or younger.

9. *Electronic advertising.* If an electronic advertisement, such as an advertisement appearing on an internet Web site, displays a triggering term, such as a bonus or annual percentage yield, the advertisement must clearly refer the member to the location where the additional required information begins. For example, an advertisement that includes a bonus or annual percentage yield may be accompanied by a link that directly takes the member to the additional information.

10. *Examples.* Examples of advertisements that would ordinarily be misleading, inaccurate, or misrepresent the deposit contract are:

i. Representing an overdraft service as a "line of credit," unless the service is subject to 12 CFR part 226 (Regulation Z).

ii. Representing that the credit union will honor all checks or authorize payment of all transactions that overdraw an account, with or without a specified dollar limit, when the credit union retains discretion at any time not to honor checks or authorize transactions.

iii. Representing that members with an overdrawn account can maintain a negative balance when the terms of the account's overdraft service require members promptly to return the share account to a positive balance.

iv. Describing a credit union's overdraft service solely as protection against bounced checks when the credit union also permits overdrafts for a fee for overdrawing their accounts by other means, such as ATM withdrawals, debit card transactions, or other electronic fund transfers.

v. Advertising an account-related service for which the credit union charges a fee in an advertisement that also uses the word "free" or "no cost" or a similar term to describe the account, unless the advertisement clearly and conspicuously indicates that there is a cost associated with the service. If the fee is a maintenance or activity fee under § 707.8(a)(2) of this part, however, an advertisement may not describe the account as "free" or "no cost" or contain a similar term even if the fee is disclosed in the advertisement.

11. *Additional disclosures in connection with the payment of overdrafts.* The rule in § 707.3(a), providing that disclosures required by § 707.8 may be provided to the member in electronic form without regard to E–Sign Act requirements, applies to the disclosures described in § 707.11(b), which are incorporated by reference in § 707.8(f).

(b) Permissible Rates

1. *Tiered-rate accounts.* An advertisement for a tiered-rate account that states an annual percentage yield must also state the annual percentage yield for each tier, along with corresponding minimum balance requirements. Any dividend rates stated must appear in conjunction with the annual percentage yields for each tier.

2. *Stepped-rate accounts.* An advertisement that states a dividend rate for a stepped-rate account must state all the dividend rates and the time period that each rate is in effect.

3. *Representative examples.* An advertisement that states an annual percentage yield for a type of account (such as a term share account for a specified term) need not state the annual percentage yield applicable to every variation offered by the credit union or indicate that other maturity terms are available. In an advertisement stating that rates for an account may vary depending on the amount of the initial deposit or the term of a term share account, credit unions need not list each balance level and term offered. Instead, the advertisement may:

i. Provide a representative example of the annual percentage yields offered, clearly described as such. For example, if a credit union offers a $25 bonus on all term share accounts and the annual percentage yield will vary depending on the term selected, the credit union may provide a disclosure of the annual percentage yield as follows: "For example, our 6-month share certificate currently pays a 3.15% annual percentage yield."

ii. Indicate that various rates are available, such as by stating short-term and longer-term maturities along with the applicable annual percentage yields: "We offer share certificates with annual percentage yields that depend on the maturity you choose. For example, our one-month share certificate earns a 2.75% APY. Or, earn a 5.25% APY for a three-year share certificate."

(c) When Additional Disclosures are Required

1. *Trigger terms.* The following are examples of information stated in advertisements that are not "trigger" terms:

i. "One, three, and five year share certificates available".

ii. "Bonus rates available".

iii. "1% over our current rate," so long as the rates are not determinable from the advertisement.

(c)(2) Time Annual Percentage Yield is Offered

1. *Specified recent date.* If an advertisement discloses an annual percentage yield as of a specified date, that date must be recent in relation to the publication or broadcast frequency of the media used. For example, the printing date of a brochure printed once for an account promotion that will be in effect for six months would be considered "recent," even though rates change during the six-month period. Dividend rates published in a daily newspaper or on television must be a rate offered shortly before (or on) the date the rates are published or broadcast. Similarly, dividend rates published in a daily newspaper or on television must be a rate reflecting either the preceding dividend period, or a prospective rate, and the option chosen should be noted.

2. *Reference to date of publication.* An advertisement may refer to the annual percentage yield as being accurate as of the date of publication, if the date is on the publication itself. For instance, an advertisement in a periodical may state that a rate is "current through the date of this issue," if the periodical shows the date.

(c)(5) Effect of Fees

1. *Scope.* This requirement applies only to maintenance or activity fees as described in paragraph 8(a).

(c)(6) Features of Term Share Accounts

(c)(6)(i) Time Requirements

1. *Club accounts.* If a club account has a maturity date, but the term may vary depending on when the account is opened, credit unions may use a phrase such as: "The maturity date of this club account is November 15; its term varies depending on when the account is opened."

(c)(6)(ii) Early Withdrawal Penalties

1. *Discretionary penalties.* Credit unions imposing early withdrawal penalties on a case-by-case basis may disclose that they "may" (rather than "will") impose a penalty if that accurately describes the account terms.

(d) Bonuses

1. *General reference to "bonus."* General statements such as "bonus checking" or "get a bonus when you open a checking account" do not trigger the bonus disclosures.

(e) Exemption for Certain Advertisements

(e)(1) Certain Media

(e)(1)(i)

1. *Internet advertisements.* The exemption for advertisements made through broadcast or electronic media does not extend to advertisements posted on the internet or sent by e-mail.

2. *Internet advertisements.* The exemption for advertisements made through broadcast

National Credit Union Administration

or electronic media does not extend to advertisements made by electronic communication, such as advertisements posted on the Internet or sent by e-mail.

(e)(1)(iii)

1. *Tiered-rate accounts.* Solicitations for tiered-rate accounts made through telephone response machines must provide all annual percentage yields and the balance requirements applicable to each tier.

(e)(2) Indoor Signs

(e)(2)(i)

1. *General.* Indoor signs include advertisements displayed on computer screens, banners, preprinted posters, and chalk or peg boards. Any advertisement inside the premises that can be retained by a member (such as a brochure or a printout from a computer) is not an indoor sign.

(e)(3) Newsletters

1. *General.* The partial exemption applies to all credit union newsletters, whether instituted before or after the compliance date of part 707. Nor must a newsletter be of any particular circulation frequency (e.g., weekly, monthly, quarterly, biannually, annually, or irregularly) or of any certain format (e.g. magazine, bulletin, broadside, circular, mimeograph, letter, or pamphlet) in order to be eligible for the partial advertising exemption.

2. *Permissible Distribution.* In order for newsletters to retain the partial advertising exemption, newsletters can be sent to existing credit union members only. Any distribution reasonably calculated to reach only members is also acceptable, such as:

i. Mailing newsletters to existing members.

ii. Distributing newsletters at a function reasonably limited to members, such as an annual meeting or member picnic.

iii. Displaying or offering newsletters at a credit union lobby, branch, or office.

3. *Impermissible Distribution.* Distributing a newsletter in a place open to nonmembers, such as a sponsor's lunch room, is not reasonably calculated to reach only members, and such newsletter would be subject to all applicable advertising rules.

Section 707.9—Enforcement and Record Retention

(c) Record Retention

1. *Evidence of required actions.* Credit unions comply with the regulation by demonstrating they have done the following:

i. Established and maintained procedures for paying dividends and providing timely disclosures as required by the regulation, and

ii. Retained sample disclosures for each type account offered to members, such as account-opening disclosures, copies of advertisements, and change-in-term notices; and information regarding the dividend rates and annual percentage yields offered.

2. *Methods of retaining evidence.* Credit unions must be able to reconstruct the required disclosures or other actions. They need not keep disclosures or other business records in hard copy. Records evidencing compliance may be retained on microfilm, microfiche, or by other methods that reproduce records accurately (including computer files). Credit unions must retain copies of all printed advertisements and the text of all advertisements conveyed by electronic or broadcast media, and newsletters.

3. *Payment of dividends.* Credit unions must retain sufficient rate and balance information to permit the verification of dividends paid on an account, including the payment of dividends on the full principal balance.

Section 707.10 [Reserved]

Section 707.11—Additional Disclosures Regarding the Payment of Overdrafts

(a) Disclosure of total fees on periodic statements

(a)(1) General.

1. *Transfer services.* The overdraft services covered by §707.11(a)(1) of this part do not include a service providing for the transfer of funds from another share account of the member to permit the payment of items without creating an overdraft, even if a fee is charged for the transfer.

1. *Examples of credit unions advertising the payment of overdrafts.* A credit union would trigger the periodic statement disclosures if it:

i. Promotes the credit union's policy or practice of paying some overdrafts, unless the service would be subject to 12 CFR part 226 (Regulation Z), in advertisements using broadcast media, brochures, telephone solicitations ,or electronic mail, or on Internet sites, ATM screens or receipts, billboards, or indoor signs. But see, Sec. 707.11(a)(2) of this part regarding communications about the payment of overdrafts that would not trigger periodic statement disclosures;

ii. Includes a message on a periodic statement informing the member of an overdraft limit or the amount of funds available for overdrafts. For example, a credit union that includes a message on a periodic statement informing the member of a $500 overdraft limit or that the member has $300 remaining on the overdraft limit, is promoting an overdraft service;

iii. Discloses an overdraft limit or includes the dollar amount of an overdraft limit in a balance disclosed by any means, including on an ATM receipt or on an automated system, such as a telephone response machine, ATM screen, or the credit union's Internet site.

2. *Fees for paying overdrafts.* Credit unions must disclose on periodic statements a total dollar amount for all fees or charges imposed on the account for paying overdrafts. The credit union must disclose separate totals for the statement period and for the calendar year-to-date. The total dollar amount for each of these periods includes per-item fees as well as interest charges, daily or other periodic fees, or fees charged for maintaining an account in overdraft status, whether the overdraft is by check, debit card transaction, or by any other transaction type. It also includes fees charged when there are insufficient funds because previously deposited funds are subject to a hold or are uncollected. It does not include fees for transferring funds from another account of the member to avoid an overdraft, or fees charged under a service subject to the Federal Reserve Board's Regulation Z (12 CFR part 226). *See also* comment 11(c)–2. Under §707.11(a)(1)(i), the disclosure must describe the total dollar amount for all fees or charges imposed on the account for the statement period and calendar year-to-date for paying overdrafts using the term "Total Overdraft Fees." This requirement applies notwithstanding comment 3(a)–2.

3. *Fees for returning items unpaid.* The total dollar amount for all fees for returning items unpaid must include all fees charged to the account for dishonoring or returning checks or other items drawn on the account. The credit union must disclose separate totals for the statement period and for the calendar year-to-date. Fees imposed when deposited items are returned are not included. Credit unions may use terminology such as "returned item fee" or "NSF fee" to describe fees for returning items unpaid.

4. *Waived fees.* In some cases, a credit union may provide a statement for the current period reflecting that fees imposed during a previous period were waived and credited to the account. Credit unions may, but are not required to, reflect the adjustment in the total for the calendar year-to-date and in the applicable statement period. For example, if a credit union assesses a fee in January and refunds the fee in February, the credit union could disclose a year-to-date total reflecting the amount credited, but it should not affect the total disclosed for the February statement period, because the fee was not assessed in the February statement period. If a credit union assesses and then waives and credits a fee within the same cycle, the credit union may, at its option, reflect the adjustment in the total disclosed for fees imposed during the current statement period and for the total for the calendar year-to-date. Thus, if the credit union assesses and waives the fee in the February statement period, the February fee total could reflect a total net of the waived fee.

5. *Totals for the calendar year to date.* Some credit unions' statement periods do not coincide with the calendar month. In such cases, the credit union may disclose a calendar year-to-date total by aggregating fees for 12 monthly cycles, starting with the period that begins during January and finishing with the period that begins during December. For example, if statement periods begin on the 10th day of each month, the statement covering December 10, 2006 through January 9, 2007 may disclose the year-to-date total for fees imposed from January 10, 2006 through January 9, 2007. Alternatively, the credit union could provide a statement for the cycle ending January 9, 2007, showing the year-to-date total for fees imposed January 1, 2006 through December 31, 2006.

6. *Itemization of fees.* A credit union may itemize each fee in addition to providing the disclosures required by §707.11(a)(1) of this part.

(a)(3) Time period covered by disclosures

1. *Periodic statement disclosures.* The disclosures under §707.11(a) must be included on periodic statements provided by a credit union starting with the first statement period that begins after January 1, 2010. For example, if a member's statement period typically closes on the 15th of each month, a credit union must provide the disclosures required by §707.11(a)(1) on subsequent periodic statements for that member beginning with the statement reflecting the period from January 16, 2010 to February 15, 2010.

(a)(5) Acquired accounts

(b) Advertising disclosures in connection with overdraft services

1. *Examples of credit unions promoting the payment of overdrafts.* A credit union must include the advertising disclosures in §707.11(b)(1) of this part if the credit union:

i. Promotes the credit union's policy or practice of paying overdrafts, unless the service would be subject to 12 CFR part 226 (Regulation Z). This includes advertisements using print media such as newspapers or brochures, telephone solicitations, electronic mail, or messages posted on an Internet site. But see, §707.11(b)(2) of this part for communications that are not subject to the additional advertising disclosures;

ii. Includes a message on a periodic statement informing the member of an overdraft limit or the amount of funds available for overdrafts. For example, a credit union that includes a message on a periodic statement informing the member of a $500 overdraft limit or that the member has $300 remaining on the overdraft limit, is promoting an overdraft service.

National Credit Union Administration

iii. Discloses an overdraft limit or includes the dollar amount of an overdraft limit in a balance disclosed on an automated system, such as a telephone response machine, ATM screen, or the credit union's Internet site. See, however, §707.11(b)(3) of this part.

2. *Transfer services.* The overdraft services covered by §707.11(b)(1) of this part do not include a service providing for the transfer of funds from another share account of the member to permit the payment of items without creating an overdraft, even if a fee is charged for the transfer.

3. *Electronic media.* The exception for advertisements made through broadcast or electronic media, such as television or radio, does not apply to advertisements posted on a credit union's Internet site, on an ATM screen, provided on telephone response machines, or sent by electronic mail.

4. *Fees.* The fees that must be disclosed under §707.11(b)(1) of this part include per-item fees as well as interest charges, daily or other periodic fees, and fees charged for maintaining an account in overdraft status, whether the overdraft is by check or by other means. The fees also include fees charged when there are insufficient funds because previously deposited funds are subject to a hold or are uncollected. The fees do not include fees for transferring funds from another account to avoid an overdraft or fees charged when the credit union has previously agreed in writing to pay items that overdraw the account and the service is subject to 12 CFR part 226 (Regulation Z).

5. *Categories of transactions.* An exhaustive list of transactions is not required. Disclosing that a fee may be imposed for covering overdrafts created by check, in-person withdrawal, ATM withdrawal, or other electronic means would satisfy the requirements of §707.11(b)(1)(ii) of this part where the fee may be imposed in these circumstances. See comment 4(b)(4)-5 of this part.

6. *Time period to repay.* If a credit union reserves the right to require a member to pay an overdraft immediately or on demand instead of affording members a specific time period to establish a positive balance in the account, a credit union may comply with §707.11(b)(1)(iii) of this part by disclosing this fact.

7. *Circumstances for nonpayment.* A credit union must describe the circumstances under which it will not pay an overdraft. It is sufficient to state, as applicable: "Whether your overdrafts will be paid is discretionary and we reserve the right not to pay. For example, we typically do not pay overdrafts if your account is not in good standing, or you are not making regular deposits, or you have too many overdrafts."

8. *Advertising an account as "free."* If the advertised account-related service is an overdraft service subject to the requirements of §707.11(b)(1) of this part, credit unions must disclose the fee or fees for the payment of each overdraft, not merely that a cost is associated with the overdraft service, as well as other required information. Compliance with comment 8(a)—10.v is not sufficient.

(c) Disclosure of account balances

1. *Balance that does not include additional amounts.* For purposes of the balance disclosure requirement in §707.11(c), if a credit union discloses balance information to a member through an automated system, it must disclose a balance that excludes any funds the credit union may provide to cover an overdraft pursuant to a discretionary overdraft service that will be paid by the credit union under a service subject to part 226 of this title (Regulation Z) or that will be transferred from another account held individually or jointly by a member. The balance may, but need not, include funds that are deposited in the member's account, such as from a check, that are not yet made available for withdrawal in accordance with the funds availability rules under part 229 of the title (Regulation CC). In addition, the balance may, but need not, include funds that are held by the credit union to satisfy a prior obligation of the member, for example, to cover a hold for an ATM or debit card transaction that has been authorized but for which the credit union has not settled.

2. *Retail sweep programs.* In a retail sweep program, a credit union establishes two legally distinct subaccounts, a share draft subaccount and a share savings subaccount, which together make up the member's account. The credit union allocates and transfers funds between the two subaccounts in order to maximize the balance in the share savings account while complying with the monthly limitations on transfers out of savings accounts under the Federal Reserve Board's Regulation D, 12 CFR 204.2(d)(2). Retail sweep programs are generally not established for the purpose of covering overdrafts. Rather, credit unions typically establish retail sweep programs by agreement with the member in order for the credit union to minimize its transaction account reserve requirements and, in some cases, to provide a higher interest rate than the member would earn on a share draft account alone. Section 707.11(c) does not require a credit union to exclude funds from the member's balance that may be transferred from another account pursuant to a retail sweep program that is established for such purposes and that has the following characteristics:

i. The account involved complies with the Federal Reserve Board's Regulation D, 12 CFR 204.2(d)(2),

ii. The member does not have direct access to the share savings subaccount that is part of the retail sweep program, and

Pt. 707, App. C

iii. The member's periodic statements show the account balance as the combined balance in the subaccounts.

3. *Additional balance.* The credit union may disclose additional balances supplemented by funds that may be provided by the credit union to cover an overdraft, whether pursuant to a discretionary overdraft service, a service subject to the Federal Reserve Board's Regulation Z (12 CFR part 226), or a service that transfers funds from another account held individually or jointly by the member, so long as the credit union prominently states that any additional balance includes these additional overdraft amounts. The credit union may not simply state, for instance, that the second balance is the members "available balance," or contains "available funds." Rather, the credit union should provide enough information to convey that the second balance includes these amounts. For example, the credit union may state that the balance includes "overdraft funds." Where a member has not opted into, or as applicable, has opted out of the credit union's discretionary overdraft service, any additional balance disclosed should not include funds that otherwise might be available under that service. Where a member has not opted into, or as applicable, has opted out of, the credit union's discretionary overdraft service for some, but not all transactions (*e.g.,* the member has not opted into overdraft services for ATM and one-time debit card transactions), a credit union that includes these additional overdraft funds in the second balance should convey that the overdraft funds are not available for all transactions. For example, the credit union could state that overdraft funds are not available for ATM and one-time (or everyday) debit card transactions. Similarly, if funds are not available for all transactions pursuant to a service subject to the Federal Reserve Board's Regulation Z (12 CFR part 226) or a service that transfers funds from another account, a second balance that includes such funds should also indicate this fact.

4. *Automated systems.* The balance disclosure requirement in §707.11(c) applies to any automated system through which the member requests a balance, including, but not limited to, a telephone response system, the credit union's Internet site, or an ATM. The requirement applies whether the credit union discloses a balance through an ATM owned or operated by the credit union or through an ATM not owned or operated by the credit union, including an ATM operated by an entity that is not a financial institution. If the balance is obtained at an ATM, the requirement also applies whether the balance is disclosed on the ATM screen or on a paper receipt.

12 CFR Ch. VII (1-1-12 Edition)

Appendix A to Part 707—Annual Percentage Yield Calculation

Part I. Annual Percentage Yield for Account Disclosures and Advertising Purposes

1. *Rounding for calculations.* The following are examples of permissible rounding rules for calculating dividends and the annual percentage yield:

i. The daily rate applied to a balance carried to five or more decimals. For example: .008219178%, 3.00% for a 365 day year, would be rounded to no less than .00822%.

ii. The daily dividends or interest earned carried to five or more decimals. For example; $.08219178082, daily dividends on $1,000 at 3% for a 365 day year, would be rounded to no less than $.08219.

2. *Exponents in a leap year.* The annual percentage yield formula's exponent numerator will remain 365 in leap years. The "days in term" figure used in the denominator should be consistent with the length of term used in the dividends calculation.

3. *First tier of a tiered-rate account.* When credit unions use a rate table, the first tier of a tiered rate account is to be disclosed and advertised; "Up to but not exceeding * * *", "$.01 to * * *", or similar language.

4. *Term Share Accounts Opened in Midterm.* For club accounts that meet the definition of a term share account, the annual percentage yield is based on the maximum number of days in the term not to exceed 365 days (or 366 days in a leap year).

Part II. Annual Percentage Yield Earned for Periodic Statements

1. *Balance method.* The dividend or interest figure used in the calculation of the annual percentage yield earned may be derived from the daily balance method or the average daily balance method. Regardless of the dividend calculation method, the balance used in the annual percentage yield earned formula is the average daily balance. The average daily balance calculation is the sum of the balances for each day in the period divided by the number of days in the period. The balance for each day is based on a point in time; i.e. beginning of day balance, end of day balance, closing of day balance, etc. Each day's balance, for dividend accrual and payment purposes, must be based on the same point in time and cannot be based on the day's low balance.

2. *Negative balances prohibited.* Credit unions must treat a negative account balance as zero to determine the balance on which the annual percentage yield earned is calculated. (See commentary to §707.7(a)(2).)

A. General Formula

1. *Accrued but uncredited dividends.* To calculate the annual percentage yield earned, accrued but uncredited dividends:

National Credit Union Administration

i. May not be included in the balance for statements that are issued at the same time or less frequently than the account's compounding and crediting frequency. For example, if monthly statements are sent for an account that compounds dividends daily and credits dividends monthly, the balance may not be increased each day to reflect the effect of daily compounding. Assume a credit union will pay $13.70 in dividends on $100,000 for the first day, $6.85 in dividends on $50,013.70 for the second day, and $3.43 in dividends on $25,020.55 for the third day. The sum of each days balance is $175,000 (does not include accrued, but uncredited, dividends amounts $13.70, $6.85, and $3.43), thereby resulting in an average daily balance for the three days of $58,333.33.

ii. Must be included in the balance for succeeding statements if a statement is issued more frequently than compounded dividends is credited on an account. For example, if monthly statements are sent for an account that compounds dividends daily and credits dividends quarterly, the balance for the second monthly statement would include dividends that had accrued for the prior month. Assume a credit union will pay $411.78 in dividends on 30 days of $100,000, $427.28 in dividends on 31 days of $100,411.78, and $415.23 in dividends on 30 days of $100,839.06. The balance (average daily balance in the account for the period) for the second 31 days is $100,411.78.

2. *Rounding.* The dividends earned figure used to calculate the annual percentage yield earned must be rounded to two decimals to reflect the amount actually paid. For example, if the dividends earned for a statement period is $20.074 and the credit union pays the member $20.07, the credit union must use $20.07 (not $20.074) to calculate the annual percentage yield earned. For accounts that pay dividends based on the daily balance method, compound and credit dividends or interest quarterly, and send monthly statements, the credit union may, but need not, round accrued dividends to two decimals for calculating the "projected" or "anticipated" annual percentage yield earned on the first two monthly statements issued during the quarter. However, on the quarterly statement the dividends earned figure must reflect the amount actually paid.

3. *Compounding frequency using the average daily balance method.* Any compounding frequency, including daily compounding, can be used when calculating dividends using the average daily balance method. (See comment 707.7(b), which does not require credit unions to compound or credit dividends at any particular frequency).

Pt. 707, App. C

B. *Special Formula for Use Where Periodic Statement is Sent More Often Than the Period for Which Dividends are Compounded*

1. *Statements triggered by Regulation E.* Credit unions may, but need not, use this formula to calculate the annual percentage yield earned for accounts that receive quarterly statements and that are subject to Regulation E's rule calling for monthly statements when an electronic fund transfer has occurred. They may do so even though no monthly statement was issued during a specific quarter. This formula must be used for accounts that compound and credit dividends quarterly and that receive monthly statements, triggered by Regulation E, which comply with the provisions of §707.6.

2. *Days in compounding period.* Credit unions using the special annual percentage yield earned formula must use the actual number of days in the compounding period.

Appendix B to Part 707—Model Clauses and Sample Forms

1. *Modifications.* Credit unions that modify the model clauses will be deemed in compliance as long as they do not delete information required by TISA or regulation or rearrange the format so as to affect the substance or clarity of the disclosures.

2. *Format.* Credit unions may use inserts to a document (see Sample Form B–11) or fill-in blanks (see Sample Forms B–4 and B–5, which use double underlining to indicate terms that have been filled in) to show current rates, fees or other terms.

3. *Disclosures for opening accounts.* The sample forms illustrate the information that must be provided to a member when an account is opened, as required by §707.4(a)(1). (See §707.4(a)(2), which states the requirements for disclosing the annual percentage yield, the dividend rate, and the maturity of a term share account in responding to a member's request.)

4. *Compliance with Regulation E.* Credit unions may satisfy certain requirements under Part 707 with disclosures that meet the requirements of Regulation E. (See §707.3(c).) The model clauses and sample forms do not give examples of disclosures that would be covered by both this regulation and Regulation E (such as disclosing the amount of a fee for ATM usage). Credit unions should consult appendix A to Regulation E for appropriate model clauses.

5. *Duplicate disclosures.* If a requirement such as a minimum balance applies to more than one account term (to obtain a bonus and determine the annual percentage yield, for example), credit unions need not repeat the requirement for each term, as long as it is clear which terms the requirement applies to.

6. *Guide to model clauses.* In the model clauses, italicized words indicate the type of

disclosure a credit union should insert in the space provided (for example, a credit union might insert "March 25, 1995" in the blank for "(date)" disclosure). Brackets and diagonals ("/") indicate a credit union must choose the alternative that describes its practice (for example, [daily balance/average daily balance]).

7. *Sample forms.* The sample forms (B-4 through B-11) serve a purpose different from the model clauses. They illustrate various ways of adapting the model clauses to specific accounts. The clauses shown relate only to the specific transactions described.

[59 FR 59899, Nov. 21, 1994, as amended at 60 FR 21699, May 3, 1995; 61 FR 68129, Dec. 27, 1996; 63 FR 71575, Dec. 29, 1998; 66 FR 33163, June 21, 2001; 70 FR 72899, Dec. 8, 2005; 72 FR 30246, May 31, 2007; 74 FR 36105, July 22, 2009; 75 FR 47175, Aug. 5, 2010]

EDITORIAL NOTE: At 74 FR 36105, July 22, 2009, part 707, appendix C was amended by redesignating (a)(1)-3 through (a)(1)-8 as (a)(1)1 through (a)(1)-6 however (a)(1)7ndash;1 already existed.

PART 708a—BANK CONVERSIONS AND MERGERS

Sec.

Subpart A—Conversion of Insured Credit Unions to Mutual Savings Banks

708a.101 Definitions.
708a.102 Authority to convert.
708a.103 Board of directors' approval and members' opportunity to comment.
708a.104 Disclosures and communications to members.
708a.105 Notice to NCUA.
708a.106 Membership approval of a proposal to convert.
708a.107 Certification of vote on conversion proposal.
708a.108 NCUA oversight of methods and procedures of membership vote.
708a.109 Other regulatory oversight of methods and procedures of membership vote.
708a.110 Completion of conversion.
708a.111 Limit on compensation of officials.
708a.112 Voting incentives.
708a.113 Voting guidelines.

Subpart B—[Reserved]

Subpart C—Merger of Insured Credit Unions Into Banks

708a.301 Definitions.
708a.302 Authority to merge.
708a.303 Board of directors' approval and members' opportunity to comment.
708a.304 Notice to NCUA and request to proceed with member vote.
708a.305 Disclosures and communications to members.
708a.306 Membership approval of a proposal to merge.
708a.307 Certification of vote on merger proposal.
708a.308 NCUA approval of the merger.
708a.309 Completion of merger.
708a.310 Limits on compensation of officials.
708a.311 Voting incentives.
708a.312 Voting guidelines.

AUTHORITY: 12 U.S.C. 1766, 1785(b), and 1785(c).

SOURCE: 71 FR 77167, Dec 22, 2006, unless otherwise noted.

Subpart A—Conversion of Insured Credit Unions to Mutual Savings Banks

§ 708a.101 Definitions.

As used in this part:

Clear and conspicuous means text in bold type in a font size at least one size larger than any other text used in the document (exclusive of headings), but in no event smaller than 12 point.

Conducted by an independent entity means:

(1) The independent entity will receive the ballots directly from voting members.

(2) After the conclusion of the special meeting that ends the ballot period, the independent entity will open all the ballots in its possession and tabulate the results. The entity must not open or tabulate any ballots before the conclusion of the special meeting.

(3) The independent entity will certify the final vote tally in writing to the credit union and provide a copy to the NCUA Regional Director. The certification will include, at a minimum, the number of members who voted, the number of affirmative votes, and the number of negative votes. During the course of the voting period the independent entity may provide the credit union with the names of members who have not yet voted, but may not provide any voting results to the credit union prior to certifying the final vote tally.

Credit union has the same meaning as insured credit union in section 101 of the Federal Credit Union Act.

National Credit Union Administration

§ 708a.103

Federal banking agencies have the same meaning as in section 3 of the Federal Deposit Insurance Act.

Independent entity means a company with experience in conducting corporate elections. No official or senior management official of the credit union, or the immediate family member of any official or senior management official, may have any ownership interest in, or be employed by, the entity.

Mutual savings bank and *savings association* have the same meaning as in section 3 of the Federal Deposit Insurance Act.

Regional director means either the director of the NCUA regional office for the region where a natural person credit union's main office is located or the director of the NCUA's Office of Consumer Protection. For corporate credit unions, *regional director* means the director of NCUA's Office of Corporate Credit Unions.

Secret ballot means no credit union employee or official can determine how a particular member voted. Credit union employees and officials are prohibited from assisting members in completing ballots or handling completed ballots.

Senior management official means a chief executive officer, an assistant chief executive officer, a chief financial officer, and any other senior executive officer as defined by the appropriate federal banking agencies pursuant to section 32(f) of the Federal Deposit Insurance Act.

[71 FR 77167, Dec 22, 2006. Redesignated and amended at 75 FR 81386, Dec. 28, 2010; 76 FR 13505, Mar. 14, 2011]

§ 708a.102 Authority to convert.

A credit union, with the approval of its members, may convert to a mutual savings bank or a savings association that is in mutual form without the prior approval of the NCUA, subject to applicable law governing mutual savings banks and savings associations and the other requirements of this part.

[71 FR 77167, Dec 22, 2006. Redesignated at 75 FR 81386, Dec. 28, 2010]

§ 708a.103 Board of directors' approval and members' opportunity to comment.

(a) A credit union's board of directors must comply with the following notice requirements before voting on a proposal to convert.

(1) No later than 30 days before a board of directors votes on a proposal to convert, it must publish a notice in a general circulation newspaper, or in multiple newspapers if necessary, serving all areas where the credit union has an office, branch, or service center. It must also post the notice in a clear and conspicuous fashion in the lobby of the credit union's home office and branch offices and on the credit union's Web site, if it has one. If the notice is not on the home page of the Web site, the home page must have a clear and conspicuous link, visible on a standard monitor without scrolling, to the notice.

(2) The public notice must include the following:

(i) The name and address of the credit union;

(ii) The type of institution to which the credit union's board is considering a proposal to convert;

(iii) A brief statement of why the board is considering the conversion and the major positive and negative effects of the proposed conversion;

(iv) A statement that directs members to submit any comments on the proposal to the credit union's board of directors by regular mail, electronic mail, or facsimile;

(v) The date on which the board plans to vote on the proposal and the date by which members must submit their comments for consideration, which may not be more than 5 days before the board vote;

(vi) The street address, electronic mail address, and facsimile number of the credit union where members may submit comments; and

(vii) A statement that, in the event the board approves the proposal to convert, the proposal will be submitted to the membership of the credit union for a vote following a notice period that is no shorter than 90 days.

(3) The board of directors must approve publication of the notice.

681

§ 708a.104

(b) The credit union must collect member comments and retain copies at the credit union's main office until the conversion process is completed.

(c) The board of directors may vote on the conversion proposal only after reviewing and considering all member comments. The conversion proposal may only be approved by an affirmative vote of a majority of board members who have determined the conversion is in the best interests of the members. If approved, the board of directors must set a date for a vote on the proposal by the members of the credit union.

[71 FR 77167, Dec 22, 2006. Redesignated at 75 FR 81386, Dec. 28, 2010]

§ 708a.104 Disclosures and communications to members.

(a) After the board of directors has complied with § 708a.3 and approves a conversion proposal, the credit union must provide written notice of its intent to convert to each member who is eligible to vote on the conversion. The notice to members must be submitted 90 calendar days, 60 calendar days, and 30 calendar days before the date of the membership vote on the conversion. A ballot must be included in the same envelope as the 30-day notice and only in the 30-day notice. A converting credit union may not distribute ballots with either the 90-day or 60-day notice, in any other written communications, or in person before the 30-day notice is sent.

(b)(1) The notice to members must adequately describe the purpose and subject matter of the vote to be taken at the special meeting or by submission of the written ballot. The notice must clearly inform members that they may vote at the special meeting or by submitting the written ballot. The notice must state the date, time, and place of the meeting.

(2) The notices that are submitted 90 and 60 days before the membership vote on the conversion must state in a clear and conspicuous fashion that a written ballot will be mailed together with another notice 30 days before the date of the membership vote on conversion. The notice submitted 30 days before the membership vote on the conversion must state in a clear and conspicuous fashion that a written ballot is included in the same envelope as the 30-day notice materials.

(3) For purposes of facilitating the member-to-member contact described in paragraph (f) of this section, the 90-day notice must indicate the number of credit union members eligible to vote on the conversion proposal and state how many members have agreed to accept communications from the credit union in electronic form. The 90-day notice must also include the information listed in paragraph (f)(9) of this section.

(4) The member ballot must include:

(i) A brief description of the proposal (e.g., "Proposal: Approval of the Plan of Charter Conversion by which (insert name of credit union) will convert its charter to that of a federal mutual savings bank.");

(ii) Two blocks marked respectively as "FOR" and "AGAINST;" and

(iii) The following language: "A vote FOR the proposal means that you want your credit union to become a mutual savings bank. A vote AGAINST the proposal means that you want your credit union to remain a credit union." This language must be displayed in a clear and conspicuous fashion immediately beneath the FOR and AGAINST blocks.

(5) The ballot may also include voting instructions and the recommendation of the board of directors (i.e., "Your Board of Directors recommends a vote FOR the Plan of Conversion") but may not include any further information without the prior written approval of the Regional Director.

(c) An adequate description of the purpose and subject matter of the member vote on conversion, as required by paragraph (b) of this section, must include:

(1) A clear and conspicuous disclosure that the conversion from a credit union to a mutual savings bank could lead to members losing their ownership interests in the credit union if the mutual savings bank subsequently converts to a stock institution and the members do not become stockholders;

(2) A clear and conspicuous disclosure of how a conversion from a credit union to a mutual savings bank will affect members' voting rights and if the

National Credit Union Administration § 708a.104

mutual savings bank intends to base voting rights on account balances;

(3) A clear and conspicuous disclosure of any conversion-related economic benefit a director or senior management official will or may receive including receipt of or an increase in compensation and an explanation of any foreseeable stock-related benefits associated with a subsequent conversion to a stock institution or mutual holding company structure. The explanation of stock-related benefits must include a comparison of the opportunities to acquire stock available to officials and employees with those opportunities available to the general membership;

(4) An affirmative statement that, at the time of conversion to a mutual savings bank, the credit union does or does not intend to convert to a stock institution or a mutual holding company structure;

(5) A clear and conspicuous disclosure of the estimated, itemized cost of the proposed conversion, including printing fees, postage fees, advertising, consulting and professional fees, legal fees, staff time, the cost of holding a special meeting, other costs of conducting the vote, and any other conversion-related expenses;

(6) A clear and conspicuous disclosure of how the conversion from a credit union to a mutual savings bank will affect the institution's ability to make non-housing-related consumer loans because of a mutual savings bank's obligations to satisfy certain lending requirements as a mutual savings bank. This disclosure should specify possible reductions in some kinds of loans to members;

(7) A clear and conspicuous disclosure that the National Credit Union Administration does not approve or disapprove of the conversion proposal or the reasons advanced in support of and the reasons against the proposal; and

(8) A clear and conspicuous disclosure of how the conversion from a credit union to a mutual savings bank is likely to affect the availability of facilities and services. At a minimum, this disclosure should include the name and location of any branches, including shared branches, and automatic teller networks, to which members may lose access as a result of the conversion. This disclosure must be based on research and analysis completed before the date the board of directors votes to adopt the conversion proposal.

(d)(1) A converting credit union must provide the following disclosures in a clear and conspicuous fashion with the 90-, 60-, and 30-day notices it sends to its members regarding the conversion:

IMPORTANT REGULATORY DISCLOSURE ABOUT YOUR VOTE
The National Credit Union Administration, the federal government agency that supervises credit unions, requires [insert name of credit union] to provide the following disclosures:
1. LOSS OF CREDIT UNION MEMBERSHIP. A vote "FOR" the proposed conversion means you want your credit union to become a mutual savings bank. A vote "AGAINST" the proposed conversion means you want your credit union to remain a credit union.
2. RATES ON LOANS AND SAVINGS. If your credit union converts to a bank, you may experience changes in your loan and savings rates. Available historic data indicates that, for most loan products, credit unions on average charge lower rates than banks. For most savings products, credit unions on average pay higher rates than banks.
3. POTENTIAL PROFITS BY OFFICERS AND DIRECTORS. Conversion to a mutual savings bank is often the first step in a two-step process to convert to a stock-issuing bank or holding company structure. In such a scenario, the officers and directors of the institution often profit by obtaining stock in excess of that available to other members.

---

(2) This text must be placed in a box, must be the only text on the front side of a single piece of paper, and must be placed so that the member will see the text after reading the credit union's cover letter but before reading any other part of the member notice. The back side of the paper must be blank. A converting credit union may modify this text only with the prior written consent of the Regional Director and, in the case of a state-chartered credit

683

§ 708a.104

union, the appropriate state regulatory agency.

(e) All written communications from a converting credit union to its members regarding the conversion must be written in a manner that is simple and easy to understand. Simple and easy to understand means the communications are written in plain language designed to be understood by ordinary consumers and use clear and concise sentences, paragraphs, and sections. For purposes of this part, examples of factors to be considered in determining whether a communication is in plain language and uses clear and concise sentences, paragraphs and sections include the use of short explanatory sentences; use of definite, concrete, everyday words; use of active voice; avoidance of multiple negatives; avoidance of legal and technical business terminology; avoidance of explanations that are imprecise and reasonably subject to different interpretations; and use of language that is not misleading.

(f)(1) A converting credit union must mail or e-mail a requesting member's proper conversion-related materials to other members eligible to vote if:

(i) A credit union's board of directors has adopted a proposal to convert;

(ii) A member makes a written request that the credit union mail or e-mail materials for the member;

(iii) The request is received by the credit union no later than 35 days after it sends out the 90-day member notice; and

(iv) The requesting member agrees to reimburse the credit union for the reasonable expenses, excluding overhead, of mailing or e-mailing the materials and also provides the credit union with an appropriate advance payment.

(2) A member's request must indicate if the member wants the materials mailed or e-mailed. If a member requests that the materials be mailed, the credit union will mail the materials to all eligible voters. If a member requests the materials be e-mailed, the credit union will e-mail the materials to all members who have agreed to accept communications electronically from the credit union. The subject line of the credit union's e-mail will be "Proposed Credit Union Conversion to a Bank—Views of Member (insert member name)."

(3) (i) A converting credit union may, at its option, include the following statement with a member's material:

On (date), the board of directors of (name of converting credit union) adopted a proposal to convert from a credit union to a mutual savings bank. Credit union members who wish to express their opinions about the proposed conversion to other members may provide those opinions to (name of credit union). By law, the credit union, at the requesting members' expense, must then send those opinions to the other members. The attached document represents the opinion of a member of this credit union. This opinion is a personal opinion and does not necessarily reflect the views of the management or directors of the credit union.

(ii) A converting credit union may not add anything other than this statement to a member's material without the prior approval of the Regional Director.

(4) The term "proper conversion-related materials" does not include materials that:

(i) Due to size or similar reasons are impracticable to mail or e-mail;

(ii) Are false or misleading with respect to any material fact;

(iii) Omit a material fact necessary to make the statements in the material not false or misleading;

(iv) Relate to a personal claim or a personal grievance, or solicit personal gain or business advantage by or on behalf of any party;

(v) Relate to any matter, including a general economic, political, racial, religious, social, or similar cause, that is not significantly related to the proposed conversion;

(vi) Directly or indirectly and without expressed factual foundation impugn a person's character, integrity, or reputation;

(vii) Directly or indirectly and without expressed factual foundation make charges concerning improper, illegal, or immoral conduct; or

(viii) Directly or indirectly and without expressed factual foundation make statements impugning the stability and soundness of the credit union.

(5) If a converting credit union believes some or all of a member's request is not proper it must submit the

National Credit Union Administration

§ 708a.105

member materials to the Regional Director within seven days of receipt. The credit union must include with its transmittal letter a specific statement of why the materials are not proper and a specific recommendation for how the materials should be modified, if possible, to make them proper. The Regional Director will review the communication, communicate with the requesting member, and respond to the credit union within seven days with a determination on the propriety of the materials. The credit union must then immediately mail or e-mail the material to the members if so directed by NCUA.

(6) A credit union must ensure that its members receive all materials that meet the requirements of § 708a.4(f) on or before the date the members receive the 30-day notice and associated ballot. If a credit union cannot meet this delivery requirement, it must postpone mailing the 30-day notice until it can deliver the member materials. If a credit union postpones the mailing of the 30-day notice, it must also postpone the special meeting by the same number of days. When the credit union has completed the delivery, it must inform the requesting member that the delivery was completed and provide the number of recipients.

(7) The term "appropriate advance payment" means:

(i) For requests to mail materials to all eligible voters, a payment in the amount of 150% of the first class postage rate times the number of mailings, and

(ii) For requests to e-mail materials only to members that have agreed to accept electronic communications, a payment in the amount of 200 dollars.

(8) If a credit union posts conversion-related information or material on its Web site, then it must simultaneously make a portion of its Web site available free of charge to its members to post and share their opinions on the conversion. A link to the portion of the Web site available to members to post their views on the conversion must be marked "Members: Share your views on the proposed conversion and see other members views" and the link must also be visible on all pages on which the credit union posts its own conversion-related information or material, as well as on the credit union's homepage. If a credit union believes a particular member submission is not proper for posting, it will provide that submission to the Regional Director for review as described in paragraph (f)(5) of this section. The credit union may also post a content-neutral disclaimer using language similar to the language in paragraph (f)(3)(i) of this section.

(9) A converting credit union must inform members with the 90-day notice that if they wish to provide their opinions about the proposed conversion to other members they can submit their opinions in writing to the credit union no later than 35 days from the date of the notice and the credit union will forward those opinions to other members. The 90-day notice will provide a contact at the credit union for delivery of communications, will explain that members must agree to reimburse the credit union's costs of transmitting the communication including providing an advance payment, and will refer members to this section of NCUA's rules for further information about the communication process. The credit union, at its option, may include additional factual information about the communication process with its 90-day notice.

(10) A group of members may make a joint request that the credit union send its materials to other members. For purposes of paragraphs (f)(2) and (f)(3) of this section, the credit union will use the group name provided by the group.

[71 FR 77167, Dec 22, 2006, as amended at 75 FR 34621, June 18, 2010]

[71 FR 77167, Dec 22, 2006. Redesignated and amended at 75 FR 81386, Dec. 28, 2010]

§ 708a.105 Notice to NCUA.

(a) If a converting credit union's board of directors approves a proposal to convert, it must provide the Regional Director with notice of its intent to convert during the 90 calendar day period preceding the date of the membership vote on the conversion.

(1) A credit union must give notice to the Regional Director of its intent to convert by providing a letter describing the material features of the conversion or a copy of the filing the credit

§ 708a.105

union has made or intends to make with another federal or state regulatory agency in which the credit union seeks that agency's approval of the conversion. A credit union must include with the notice to the Regional Director copies of the notices the credit union has provided or intends to provide to members under §§ 708a.3 and 708a.4. The credit union must also include a copy of the ballot form and all written materials the credit union has distributed or intends to distribute to members. The term "written materials" includes written documentation or information of any sort, including electronic communications posted on a Web site or transmitted by electronic mail.

(2) As part of its notice to NCUA of intent to convert, the credit union's board of directors must provide the Regional Director with a certification of its support for the conversion proposal and plan. Each director who voted in favor of the conversion proposal must sign the certification. The certification must contain the following:

(i) A statement that each director signing the certification supports the proposed conversion and believes the proposed conversion is in the best interests of the members of the credit union;

(ii) A description of all materials submitted to the Regional Director with the notice and certification;

(iii) A statement that each board member signing the certification has examined all these materials carefully and these materials are true, correct, current, and complete as of the date of submission; and

(iv) An acknowledgement that federal law (18 U.S.C. 1001) prohibits any misrepresentations or omissions of material facts, or false, fictitious or fraudulent statements or representations made with respect to the certification or the materials provided to the Regional Director or any other documents or information provided to the members of the credit union or NCUA in connection with the conversion.

(3) A state-chartered credit union must state as part of the notice required by § 708a.5(a) if its state chartering law permits it to convert to a mutual savings bank and provide the specific legal citation. A state-chartered credit union will remain subject to any state law requirements for conversion that are more stringent than those this part imposes, including any internal governance requirements, such as the requisite membership vote for conversion and the determination of a member's eligibility to vote. If a state-chartered credit union relies for its authority to convert to a mutual savings bank on a state law parity provision, meaning a provision in state law permitting a state-chartered credit union to operate with the same or similar authority as a federal credit union, it must:

(i) Include in its notice a statement that its state regulatory authority agrees that it may rely on the state law parity provision as authority to convert; and

(ii) Indicate its state regulatory authority's position as to whether federal law and regulations or state law will control internal governance issues in the conversion such as the requisite membership vote for conversion and the determination of a member's eligibility to vote.

(b) If it chooses, a credit union may seek a preliminary determination from the Regional Director regarding any of the notices required under this part and its proposed methods and procedures applicable to the membership conversion vote. The Regional Director will make a preliminary determination regarding the notices and methods and procedures applicable to the membership vote within 30 calendar days of receipt of a credit union's request for review unless the Regional Director extends the period as necessary to request additional information or review a credit union's submission. A credit union's prior submission of any notice or proposed voting procedures does not relieve the credit union of its obligation to certify the results of the membership vote required by § 708a.6 or eliminate the right of the Regional Director to disapprove the actual methods and procedures applicable to the membership vote if the credit union fails to conduct the membership vote in a fair and legal manner consistent with the Federal Credit Union Act and these rules.

(c) After receiving the notice described in paragraph (a)(3) of this section, the Regional Director will contact and consult with the appropriate State Supervisory Authority.

[71 FR 77167, Dec 22, 2006. Redesignated at 75 FR 81386, Dec. 28, 2010]

§ 708a.106 Membership approval of a proposal to convert.

(a) A proposal for conversion approved by a board of directors requires approval by a majority of the members who vote on the proposal.

(b) The board of directors must set a voting record date to determine member voting eligibility that is at least one day before the publication of notice required in § 708a.3.

(c) A member may vote on a proposal to convert in person at a special meeting held on the date set for the vote or by written ballot filed by the member. The vote on the conversion proposal must be by secret ballot and conducted by an independent entity. The independent entity must be a company with experience in conducting corporate elections. No official or senior management official of the credit union or the immediate family members of any official or senior management official may have any ownership interest in or be employed by the independent entity.

[71 FR 77167, Dec 22, 2006. Redesignated at 75 FR 81386, Dec. 28, 2010]

§ 708a.107 Certification of vote on conversion proposal.

(a) The board of directors of the converting credit union must certify the results of the membership vote to the Regional Director within 14 calendar days after the vote is taken.

(b) The certification must also include a statement that the notice, ballot and other written materials provided to members were identical to those submitted to NCUA pursuant to § 708a.5. If the board cannot certify this, the board must provide copies of any new or revised materials and an explanation of the reasons for any changes.

(c) The certification must be accompanied by copies of all correspondence between the credit union and any Federal banking agency whose approval is required for the conversion.

[71 FR 77167, Dec 22, 2006. Redesignated at 75 FR 81386, Dec. 28, 2010. Amended at 75 FR 81387, Dec. 28, 2010]

§ 708a.108 NCUA oversight of methods and procedures of membership vote.

(a) The Regional Director will review the methods by which the membership vote was taken and the procedures applicable to the membership vote. The Regional Director will determine: if the notices and other communications to members were accurate, not misleading, and timely; the membership vote was conducted in a fair and legal manner; and the credit union has otherwise complied with part 708a.

(b) After completion of this review, the Regional Director will issue a determination that the methods and procedures applicable to the membership vote are approved or disapproved. The Regional Director will issue this determination within 30 calendar days of receipt from the credit union of the certification of the result of the membership vote required under § 708a.7 unless the Regional Director extends the period as necessary to request additional information or review the credit union's submission. Approval of the methods and procedures under this paragraph remains subject to a credit union fulfilling the requirements in § 708a.10 for timely completion of the conversion.

(c) If the Regional Director disapproves the methods by which the membership vote was taken or the procedures applicable to the membership vote, the Regional Director may direct that a new vote be taken.

(d) A converting credit union may appeal the Regional Director's determination to the NCUA Board. The credit union must file the appeal within 30 days after receipt of the Regional Director's determination. The NCUA Board will act on the appeal within 90 days of receipt.

[71 FR 77167, Dec 22, 2006. Redesignated at 75 FR 81386, Dec. 28, 2010]

§ 708a.109 Other regulatory oversight of methods and procedures of membership vote.

The federal or state regulatory agency that will have jurisdiction over the financial institution after conversion must verify the membership vote and may direct that a new vote be taken, if it disapproves of the methods by which the membership vote was taken or the procedures applicable to the membership vote.

[71 FR 77167, Dec 22, 2006. Redesignated at 75 FR 81386, Dec. 28, 2010]

§ 708a.110 Completion of conversion.

(a) After receipt of the approvals under § 708a.8 and § 708a.9 the credit union may complete the conversion.

(b) The credit union must complete the conversion within one year of the date of receipt of NCUA approval under § 708a.8. If a credit union fails to complete the conversion within one year the Regional Director will disapprove of the methods and procedures. The credit union's board of directors must then adopt a new conversion proposal and solicit another member vote if it still desires to convert.

(c) The Regional Director may, upon timely request and for good cause, extend the one year completion period for an additional six months.

(d) After notification by the board of directors of the mutual savings bank or mutual savings association that the conversion has been completed, the NCUA will cancel the insurance certificate of the credit union and, if applicable, the charter of a federal credit union.

[71 FR 77167, Dec 22, 2006. Redesignated at 75 FR 81386, Dec. 28, 2010]

§ 708a.111 Limit on compensation of officials.

No director or senior management official of an insured credit union may receive any economic benefit in connection with the conversion of a credit union other than compensation and other benefits paid to directors or senior management officials of the converted institution in the ordinary course of business.

[71 FR 77167, Dec 22, 2006. Redesignated at 75 FR 81386, Dec. 28, 2010]

§ 708a.112 Voting incentives.

If a converting credit union offers an incentive to encourage members to participate in the vote, including a prize raffle, every reference to such incentive made by the credit union in a written communication to its members must also state that members are eligible for the incentive regardless of whether they vote for or against the proposed conversion.

[71 FR 77167, Dec 22, 2006. Redesignated at 75 FR 81386, Dec. 28, 2010]

§ 708a.113 Voting guidelines.

A converting credit union must conduct its member vote on conversion in a fair and legal manner. NCUA provides the following guidelines as suggestions to help a credit union obtain a fair and legal vote and otherwise fulfill its regulatory obligations. These guidelines are not an exhaustive checklist and do not by themselves guarantee a fair and legal vote.

(a) *Applicability of state law.* While NCUA's conversion rule applies to all conversions of federally insured credit unions, federally insured state-chartered credit unions (FISCUs) are also subject to state law on conversions. NCUA's position is that a state legislature or state supervisory authority may impose conversion requirements more stringent or restrictive than NCUA's. States that permit this kind of conversion may have substantive and procedural requirements that vary from federal law. For example, there may be different voting standards for approving a vote. While the Federal Credit Union Act requires a simple majority of those who vote to approve a conversion, some states have higher voting standards requiring two-thirds or more of those who vote. A FISCU should be careful to understand both federal and state law to navigate the conversion process and conduct a proper vote.

(b) *Eligibility to vote.* (1) Determining who is eligible to cast a ballot is fundamental to any vote. No conversion vote can be fair and legal if some members are improperly excluded. A converting credit union should be cautious to identify all eligible members and make certain they are included on its voting

National Credit Union Administration

§ 708a.113

list. NCUA recommends that a converting credit union establish internal procedures to manage this task.

(2) A converting credit union should be careful to make certain its member list is accurate and complete. For example, when a credit union converts from paper recordkeeping to computer recordkeeping, some member names may not transfer unless the credit union is careful in this regard. This same problem can arise when a credit union converts from one computer system to another where the software is not completely compatible.

(3) Problems with keeping track of who is eligible to vote can also arise when a credit union converts from a federal charter to a state charter or vice versa. NCUA is aware of an instance where a federal credit union used membership materials allowing two or more individuals to open a joint account and also allowed each to become a member. The federal credit union later converted to a state-chartered credit union that, like most other state-chartered credit unions in its state, used membership materials allowing two or more individuals to open a joint account but only allowed the first person listed on the account to become a member. The other individuals did not become members as a result of their joint account, but were required to open another account where they were the first or only person listed on the account. Over time, some individuals who became members of the federal credit union as the second person listed on a joint account were treated like those individuals who were listed as the second person on a joint account opened directly with the state-chartered credit union. Specifically, both of those groups were treated as non-members not entitled to vote. This example makes the point that a credit union must be diligent in maintaining a reliable membership list.

(c) *Scheduling the special meeting.* NCUA's conversion rule requires a converting credit union to permit members to vote by written mail ballot or in person at a special meeting held for the purpose of voting on the conversion. Although most members may choose to vote by mail, a significant number may choose to vote in person. As a result, a converting credit union should be careful to conduct its special meeting in a manner conducive to accommodating all members wishing to attend, including selecting a meeting location that can accommodate the anticipated number of attendees and is conveniently located. The meeting should also be held on a day and time suitable to most members' schedules. A credit union should conduct its meeting in accordance with applicable federal and state law, its bylaws, Robert's Rules of Order or other appropriate parliamentary procedures, and determine before the meeting the nature and scope of any discussion to be permitted.

(d) *Voting incentives.* Some credit unions may wish to offer incentives to members, such as entry to a prize raffle, to encourage participation in the conversion vote. The credit union must exercise care in the design and execution of such incentives.

(1) The credit union should ensure that the incentive complies with all applicable state, federal, and local laws.

(2) The incentive should not be unreasonable in size. The cost of the incentive should have a negligible impact on the credit union's net worth ratio and the incentive should not be so large that it distracts the member from the purpose of the vote. If the board desires to use such incentives, the cost of the incentive should be included in the directors' deliberation and determination that the conversion is in the best interests of the credit union's members.

(3) The credit union should ensure that the incentive is available to every member that votes regardless of how or when he or she votes. All of the credit union's written materials promoting the incentive to the membership must disclose to the members, as required by § 708a.12 of this part, that they have an equal opportunity to participate in the incentive program regardless of whether they vote for or against the conversion. The credit union should also design its incentives so that they are available equally to all members who vote, regardless of whether they vote

§ 708a.301

by mail or in person at the special meeting.

(e) *Solicitation of votes.* Some credit unions may wish to contact members who have not voted and encourage them to vote on the conversion proposal. NCUA believes, however, that using credit union employees to solicit votes is problematic. Employees directed to solicit votes could easily neglect everyday duties critical to the credit union's safe and sound operation. Also, employees may very well feel pressured to solicit votes for the conversion, regardless of whether or not they support the conversion. Accordingly, NCUA strongly encourages converting credit unions to use an independent third party to solicit votes rather than diverting credit union employees from their usual duties.

[71 FR 77167, Dec 22, 2006. Redesignated at 75 FR 81386, Dec. 28, 2010. Amended at 75 FR 81387, Dec. 28, 2010]

Subpart B[Reserved]

Subpart C—Merger of Insured Credit Unions Into Banks

SOURCE: 75 FR 81387, Dec. 28, 2010, unless otherwise noted.

§ 708a.301 Definitions.

As used in this part:

Bank has the same meaning as in section 3(a) of the Federal Deposit Insurance Act, 12 U.S.C. 1813(a).

Clear and conspicuous means text in bold type in a font size at least one size larger than any other text used in the document (exclusive of headings), but in no event smaller than 12 point.

Conducted by an independent entity means:

(1) The independent entity will receive the ballots directly from voting members.

(2) After the conclusion of the special meeting that ends the ballot period, the independent entity will open all the ballots in its possession and tabulate the results. The entity must not open or tabulate any ballots before the conclusion of the special meeting.

(3) The independent entity will certify the final vote tally in writing to the credit union and provide a copy to the NCUA Regional Director. The certification will include, at a minimum, the number of members who voted, the number of affirmative votes, and the number of negative votes. During the course of the voting period the independent entity may provide the credit union with the names of members who have not yet voted, but may not provide any voting results to the credit union prior to certifying the final vote tally.

Credit union has the same meaning as insured credit union in section 101 of the Federal Credit Union Act.

Distribution formula is the formula the bank will use to determine each member's portion of that payment to be received upon completion of the merger.

Federal banking agencies have the same meaning as in section 3 of the Federal Deposit Insurance Act.

Merger means any transaction in which a credit union transfers all, or substantially all, of its assets to a bank. The term *merger* includes any purported conversion of a credit union to a bank if the purported conversion is conducted pursuant to an agreement between a preexisting bank and the credit union that provides—

(1) The credit union will not conduct business as a stand-alone bank, and

(2) The purported conversion will be followed by the transfer of all, or substantially all, of the credit union's assets to the preexisting bank.

Merger value or *merger valuation* is the amount that a stock bank would pay in an arm's-length transaction to purchase the credit union's assets and assume its liabilities and shares (deposits).

Qualified appraisal entity means entity that has significant experience in the valuation of depository institutions and that has no past financial relationship with the merging credit union; the continuing bank, the continuing bank's owners, affiliates, or holding companies; or any law firm representing the credit union or the bank in connection with the merger.

Regional director means the director of the NCUA regional office for the region where a natural person credit union's main office is located. For corporate credit unions, *regional director*

National Credit Union Administration § 708a.303

means the director of NCUA's Office of Corporate Credit Unions.

Secret ballot means no credit union employee or official can determine how a particular member voted. Credit union employees and officials are prohibited from assisting members in completing ballots or handling completed ballots.

Senior management official means a chief executive officer, an assistant chief executive officer, a chief financial officer, and any other senior executive officer as defined by the appropriate Federal banking agencies pursuant to section 32(f) of the Federal Deposit Insurance Act.

§ 708a.302 Authority to merge.

A credit union, with the approval of its members, may merge into a bank only with the prior approval of NCUA, the Federal Deposit Insurance Corporation, and the regulator of the bank. If the credit union is State chartered, it also needs the prior approval of its State regulator.

§ 708a.303 Board of directors' approval and members' opportunity to comment.

(a) *Merger valuation.* Before selecting a bank merger partner and voting on a proposal to merge, a credit union's board of directors must determine, as part of its due diligence, the merger value of the credit union. In making its determination of the merger value of the credit union, the credit union must either:

(1) Conduct a well-publicized merger auction and obtain purchase quotations from at least three banks, two or more of which must be stock banks; or

(2) Retain a qualified appraisal entity to analyze and estimate the merger value of the credit union.

(b) *Advance notice.* A credit union that does not conduct a public auction as described in paragraph (a)(1) of this section must comply with the following notice requirements before voting on a proposal to merge.

(1) No later than 30 days before a board of directors votes on a proposal to merge, it must publish a notice in a general circulation newspaper, or in multiple newspapers if necessary, serving all areas where the credit union has an office, branch, or service center. It must also post the notice in a clear and conspicuous fashion in the lobby of the credit union's home office and branch offices and on the credit union's Web site, if it has one. If the notice is not on the home page of the Web site, the home page must have a clear and conspicuous link, visible on a standard monitor without scrolling, to the notice.

(2) The public notice must include the following:

(i) The name and address of the credit union;

(ii) The name and type of institution into which the credit union's board is considering a proposal to merge;

(iii) A brief statement of why the board is considering the merger and the major positive and negative effects of the proposed merger;

(iv) A statement that directs members to submit any comments on the proposal to the credit union's board of directors by regular mail, electronic mail, or facsimile;

(v) The date on which the board plans to vote on the proposal and the date by which members must submit their comments for consideration; which submission date may not be more than 5 days before the board vote;

(vi) The street address, electronic mail address, and facsimile number of the credit union where members may submit comments; and

(vii) A statement that, in the event the board approves the proposal to merge, the proposal will be submitted to the membership of the credit union for a vote following a notice period that is no shorter than 90 days.

(3) The board of directors must approve publication of the notice.

(c) *Member comments.* A credit union must collect and review any member comments about the merger received during the merger process. The credit union must retain the comments until the merger is consummated.

(d) *Approval of proposal to merge.* The merger proposal may only be approved by an affirmative vote of a majority of board members who have determined:

(1) A merger with a bank is in the best interests of the members, and

691

§ 708a.304

(2) The merger partner selected by the directors is the best choice for the members, taking into account the merger value of the credit union and the amount that the selected merger partner is willing to pay the credit union's members to effect the merger.

§ 708a.304 Notice to NCUA and request to proceed with member vote.

(a) *NIMRA.* If a credit union's board of directors adopts a proposal to merge, it must, within 30 days of the adoption, provide the Regional Director with a Notice of its Intent to Merge and Request for NCUA Authorization (NIMRA) to conduct a member vote. The NIMRA must include the following:

(1) The merger plan (as described below in paragraph (b) of this section);

(2) Resolutions of the boards of directors of both institutions;

(3) Certification of the board of directors (as described below);

(4) Proposed Merger Agreement;

(5) Proposed Notice of Special Meeting of the Members and any other communications about the merger that the credit union intends to send to its members, including electronic communications posted on a Web site or transmitted by electronic mail;

(6) Proposed ballot to be sent to the members;

(7) For State chartered credit unions, evidence that the proposed merger is authorized under State law (as described below);

(8) A copy of the bank's last two examination reports;

(9) A statement of the merger valuation of the credit union;

(10) A statement of whether any merger payment will be made to the members and how such a payment will be distributed among the members;

(11) Information about the due diligence of the directors in locating a merger partner and determining that the merger is in best interests of the members of the credit union (as described below);

(12) Copies of all contracts reflecting any merger-related compensation or other benefit to be received by any director or senior management official of the credit union;

(13) If the merging credit union's assets on its latest call report are equal to or greater than the threshold amount established annually by the Federal Trade Commission under 15 U.S.C. 18a(a)(2)(B)(i), currently $63.4 million, a statement about whether the two institutions intend to make a Hart-Scott-Rodino Act premerger notification filing with the Federal Trade Commission and, if not, an explanation why not;

(14) Copies of any filings the credit union or bank intends to make with another Federal or State regulatory agency in which the credit union or bank seeks that agency's approval of the merger; and

(15) Proof that the accounts of the credit union will be accepted for coverage by the Federal Deposit Insurance Corporation.

(b) *Merger plan.* The merger plan must include:

(1) Current financial statements for both institutions;

(2) Current delinquent loan summaries and analyses of the adequacy of the Allowance for Loan and Lease Losses account for both institutions;

(3) Consolidated financial statements of the continuing institution after the merger;

(4) Explanation of any provisions for reserves, undivided earnings or dividends;

(5) Provisions with respect to notification and payment of creditors; and

(6) Explanation of any changes relative to insurance such as life savings and loan protection insurance and insurance of member accounts.

(c) *Director certification.* The NIMRA must include a certification by the credit union's board of directors of their support for the merger proposal and plan. Each director who voted in favor of the merger proposal must sign the certification. The certification must contain the following:

(1) A statement that each director signing the certification supports the proposed merger and believes the proposed merger, and the selected bank merger partner, are both in the best interests of the members of the credit union;

(2) A description of all materials submitted to the Regional Director with the notice and certification;

(3) A statement that each board member signing the certification has examined all these materials carefully and these materials are true, correct, current, and complete as of the date of submission; and

(4) An acknowledgement that Federal law (18 U.S.C. 1001) prohibits any misrepresentations or omissions of material facts, or false, fictitious or fraudulent statements or representations made with respect to the certification or the materials provided to the Regional Director or any other documents or information provided to the members of the credit union or NCUA in connection with the merger.

(d) *Due diligence.* The NIMRA must include a description of all the credit union's due diligence in determining that the merger satisfies the factors contained in section 205(c) of the Act. In particular, the NIMRA must describe how the board located the merger partner, how the board negotiated the merger agreement, and how the board determined that this merger was in the best interests of the credit union's members. The description must include all information relied upon by the credit union in determining the merger value of the credit union, the amount of any payment to be made by the bank to the credit union's members (the "merger payment"), and, if that merger payment is less than the merger value of the credit union, an explanation why the merger and the merger partner selected is in the best interests of the members. The description must include an explanation of the distribution formula by which the merger payment will be distributed among the credit union's members.

(e) *State chartered credit unions.* A State chartered credit union must state as part of its NIMRA if its State chartering law permits it to merge into a bank and provide the specific legal citation. A State chartered credit union will remain subject to any State law requirements for merger that are more stringent than those this part imposes, including any internal governance requirements, such as the requisite membership vote for merger and the determination of a member's eligibility to vote. If a State chartered credit union relies for its authority to merge into a bank on a State law parity provision, meaning a provision in State law permitting a State chartered credit union to operate with the same or similar authority as a Federal credit union, it must:

(1) Include in its notice a statement that its State regulatory authority agrees that it may rely on the State law parity provision as authority to merge; and

(2) Indicate its State regulatory authority's position as to whether Federal law and regulations or State law will control internal governance issues in the merger such as the requisite membership vote for merger and the determination of a member's eligibility to vote.

(f) *Consultation with State authorities.* After receiving a NIMRA from a State chartered credit union, the Regional Director will consult with the appropriate State supervisory authority.

(g) *Regional Director approval.* After receiving a NIMRA, the Regional Director will either disapprove the proposed merger or authorize the credit union to proceed with its membership vote.

(1) The Regional Director will disapprove the proposed merger if the NIMRA either lacks the documentation required by this section or lacks substantial evidence to support each of the factors in section 205(c) of the Act. As part of this determination, the Regional Director must disapprove the proposed merger if:

(i) The merger payment offered by the bank to the members is less than the merger valuation, absent some additional, quantifiable benefit to the members from the selected merger partner; or

(ii) The NIMRA fails to adequately explain the nature and amount of any compensation to be received by the credit union's directors or senior management officials in connection with the merger or to justify that compensation.

(2) NCUA's authorization to proceed with the member vote does not mean NCUA has approved of the merger proposal.

§ 708a.305

(h) *Appeal of adverse decision.* If the Regional Director disapproves a merger proposal, the credit union may appeal the Regional Director's determination to the Board. The credit union must file the appeal within 30 days after receipt of the Regional Director's determination. The Board will act on the appeal within 120 days of receipt.

§ 708a.305 Disclosures and communications to members.

(a) After the board of directors approves a merger proposal and receives NCUA's authorization as described in §§ 708a.303 and 708a.304, the credit union must provide written notice of its intent to merge to each member who is eligible to vote on the merger. The notice to members must be mailed 90 calendar days and 30 calendar days before the date of the membership vote on the merger. A ballot must be included in the same envelope as the 30-day notice and only with the 30-day notice. A merging credit union may not distribute ballots with the 90-day notice, in any other written communications, or in person before the 30-day notice is sent.

(b)(1) The notice to members must adequately describe the purpose and subject matter of the vote and clearly inform members that they may vote at the special meeting or by submitting the written ballot. The notice must state the date, time, and place of the meeting.

(2) The 90-day notice must state in a clear and conspicuous fashion that a written ballot will be mailed together with another notice 30 days before the date of the membership vote on merger. The 30-day notice must state in a clear and conspicuous fashion that a written ballot is included in the same envelope as the 30-day notice materials.

(3) For purposes of facilitating the member-to-member contact described in paragraph (f) of this section, the 90-day notice must indicate the number of credit union members eligible to vote on the merger proposal and state how many members have agreed to accept communications from the credit union in electronic form. The 90-day notice must also include the information listed in paragraph (g)(9) of this section.

(4) The member ballot must include:

(i) A brief description of the proposal (*e.g.*, "Proposal: Approval of the Plan of Merger by which [insert name of credit union] will merge with a bank");

(ii) Two blocks marked respectively as "FOR" and "AGAINST;" and

(iii) The following language: "A vote FOR the proposal means that you want your credit union to merge with and become a bank. A vote AGAINST the proposal means that you want your credit union to remain a credit union." This language must be displayed in a clear and conspicuous fashion immediately beneath the FOR and AGAINST blocks.

(5) The ballot may also include voting instructions and the recommendation of the board of directors (*i.e.*, "Your Board of Directors recommends a vote FOR the Plan of Merger") but may not include any further information without the prior written approval of the Regional Director.

(c) For mergers into stock banks, an adequate description of the purpose and subject matter of the member vote on merger, as required by paragraph (b) of this section, must include:

(1) A clear and conspicuous disclosure that if the merger is approved the members will lose all of their ownership interests in the institution, including the right to vote, the right to share in the value of the institution should it be liquidated, the right to share in any extraordinary dividends, and the right to have the net worth of the institution managed in their best interests;

(2) A clear and conspicuous disclosure of any post-merger employment or consulting relationships offered by the bank to any of the credit union's directors and senior management officials and the amount of the associated compensation;

(3) A clear and conspicuous disclosure of how the merger of the credit union will affect the members' ability to obtain non-housing-related consumer loans from the bank because of because of the bank's obligations to satisfy statutory or regulatory lending requirements (if any). This disclosure should specify possible reductions in some kinds of loans to members;

National Credit Union Administration § 708a.305

(4) A clear and conspicuous statement of the merger value of the credit union, the total dollar amount the selected bank merger partner has agreed to pay to effect the merger, and the distribution formula the bank will use to determine each member's portion of that payment to be received upon completion of the merger; and

(d) For mergers into mutual banks, an adequate description of the purpose and subject matter of the member vote on merger, as required by paragraph (b) of this section, must include:

(1) A clear and conspicuous disclosure of how the merger will affect members' voting rights including whether the bank bases voting rights on account balances;

(2) A clear and conspicuous disclosure that the merger could lead to members losing all of their ownership interests in the credit union if the bank subsequently converts to a stock institution and the members do not purchase stock;

(3) A clear and conspicuous disclosure of any post-merger employment or consulting relationships offered by the bank to the credit union's directors and senior management officials and the associated compensation for each;

(4) A clear and conspicuous disclosure of how the merger of the credit union will affect the members' ability to obtain non-housing-related consumer loans from the bank because of the bank's obligations to satisfy statutory or regulatory lending requirements (if any). This disclosure should specify possible reductions in some kinds of loans to members;

(5) A clear and conspicuous statement that, at the time of merger, the bank does or does not intend to convert to a stock institution or a mutual holding company structure;

(6) A clear and conspicuous statement of the merger value of the credit union, the total dollar amount the selected bank merger partner has agreed to pay to effect the merger, and the distribution formula the bank will use to determine each member's portion of that payment to be received upon completion of the merger; and

(7) If the bank plans to add one or more of the credit union's directors to its board or employ one or more senior officials of the credit union, a clear and conspicuous statement that bank could convert to a stock bank in the future and a comparison of the opportunities available to those officials and employees to obtain stock with the opportunities available to the depositors of the bank.

(e)(1) A merging credit union must provide the following disclosures in a clear and conspicuous fashion with the 90-day and 30-day notices it sends to its members regarding the merger:

IMPORTANT REGULATORY DISCLOSURE ABOUT YOUR VOTE

The National Credit Union Administration, the Federal government agency that supervises credit unions, requires [insert name of credit union] to provide the following disclosures:

1. LOSS OF CREDIT UNION MEMBERSHIP. A vote "FOR" the proposed merger means you want your credit union to merge with and become a bank. A vote "AGAINST" the proposed merger means you want your credit union to remain a credit union.

2. [For Mergers into Stock Banks Only]. LOSS OF OWNERSHIP INTERESTS. If your credit union merges into the bank, you will lose all the ownership interests you currently have in the credit union and you will become a customer of the bank. The bank's stockholders own the bank, and the directors of the bank have a fiduciary responsibility to run the bank in the best interests of the stockholders, not the customers.

2. [For Mergers into Mutual Banks Only]. POTENTIAL PROFITS BY OFFICERS AND DIRECTORS. Merger into a mutual savings bank is often the first step in a two-step process to convert to a stock-issuing bank or holding company structure. In such a scenario, the officers and directors of the bank often profit by obtaining stock in excess of that available to other members.

3. RATES ON LOANS AND SAVINGS. If your credit union merges into the bank, you may experience changes in your loan and savings rates. Available historic data indicates that, for most loan products, credit unions on average charge lower rates than banks. For most savings products, credit unions on average pay higher rates than banks.

695

§ 708a.305

(2) This text must be placed in a box, must be the only text on the front side of a single piece of paper, and must be placed so that the member will see the text after reading the credit union's cover letter but before reading any other part of the member notice. The back side of the paper must be blank. A merging credit union may modify this text only with the prior written consent of the Regional Director and, in the case of a State chartered credit union, the appropriate State regulatory agency.

(f) All written communications from a merging credit union to its members regarding the merger must be written in a manner that is simple and easy to understand. Simple and easy to understand means the communications are written in plain language designed to be understood by ordinary consumers and use clear and concise sentences, paragraphs, and sections. For purposes of this part, examples of factors to be considered in determining whether a communication is in plain language and uses clear and concise sentences, paragraphs and sections include the use of short explanatory sentences; use of definite, concrete, everyday words; use of active voice; avoidance of multiple negatives; avoidance of legal and technical business terminology; avoidance of explanations that are imprecise and reasonably subject to different interpretations; and use of language that is not misleading.

(g)(1) A merging credit union must mail or e-mail a requesting member's proper merger-related materials to other members eligible to vote if:

(i) A credit union's board of directors has adopted a proposal to merge;

(ii) A member makes a written request that the credit union mail or e-mail materials for the member;

(iii) The request is received by the credit union no later than 35 days after it sends out the 90-day member notice; and

(iv) The requesting member agrees to reimburse the credit union for the reasonable expenses, excluding overhead, of mailing or e-mailing the materials and also provides the credit union with an appropriate advance payment.

(2) A member's request must indicate if the member wants the materials mailed or e-mailed. If a member requests that the materials be mailed, the credit union will mail the materials to all eligible voters. If a member requests the materials be e-mailed, the credit union will e-mail the materials to all members who have agreed to accept communications electronically from the credit union. The subject line of the credit union's e-mail will be "Proposed Credit Union Merger—Views of Member (insert member name)."

(3)(i) A merging credit union may, at its option, include the following statement with a member's material:

On (date), the board of directors of (name of merging credit union) adopted a proposal to merge the credit union into a bank. Credit union members who wish to express their opinions about the proposed merger to other members may provide those opinions to (name of credit union). By law, the credit union, at the requesting members' expense, must then send those opinions to the other members. The attached document represents the opinion of a member (or group of members) of this credit union. This opinion is a personal opinion and does not necessarily reflect the views of the management or directors of the credit union.

(ii) A merging credit union may not add anything other than this statement to a member's material without the prior approval of the Regional Director.

(4) The term "proper merger-related materials" does not include materials that:

(i) Due to size or similar reasons are impracticable to mail or e-mail;

(ii) Are false or misleading with respect to any material fact;

(iii) Omit a material fact necessary to make the statements in the material not false or misleading;

(iv) Relate to a personal claim or a personal grievance, or solicit personal gain or business advantage by or on behalf of any party;

(v) Relate to any matter, including a general economic, political, racial, religious, social, or similar cause, that is not significantly related to the proposed merger;

(vi) Directly or indirectly and without expressed factual foundation impugn a person's character, integrity, or reputation;

(vii) Directly or indirectly and without expressed factual foundation make

National Credit Union Administration

§ 708a.305

charges concerning improper, illegal, or immoral conduct; or

(viii) Directly or indirectly and without expressed factual foundation make statements impugning the stability and soundness of the credit union.

(5) If a merging credit union believes some or all of a member's request is not proper it must submit the member materials to the Regional Director within seven days of receipt. The credit union must include with its transmittal letter a specific statement of why the materials are not proper and a specific recommendation for how the materials should be modified, if possible, to make them proper. The Regional Director will review the communication, communicate with the requesting member, and respond to the credit union within seven days with a determination on the propriety of the materials. The credit union must then mail or e-mail the material to the members if so directed by NCUA.

(6) A credit union must ensure that its members receive all materials that meet the requirements of § 708a.305(g) on or before the date the members receive the 30-day notice and associated ballot. If a credit union cannot meet this delivery requirement, it must postpone mailing the 30-day notice until it can deliver the member materials. If a credit union postpones the mailing of the 30-day notice, it must also postpone the special meeting by the same number of days. When the credit union has completed the delivery, it must inform the requesting member that the delivery was completed and provide the number of recipients.

(7) The term "appropriate advance payment" means:

(i) For requests to mail materials to all eligible voters, a payment in the amount of 150 percent of the first class postage rate times the number of mailings, and

(ii) For requests to e-mail materials only to members that have agreed to accept electronic communications, a payment in the amount of 200 dollars.

(8) If a credit union posts merger-related information or material on its Web site, then it must simultaneously make a portion of its Web site available free of charge to its members to post and share their opinions on the merger. A link to the portion of the Web site available to members to post their views on the merger must be marked "Members: Share your views on the proposed merger and see other members' views" and the link must also be visible on all pages on which the credit union posts its own merger-related information or material, as well as on the credit union's homepage. If a credit union believes a particular member submission is not proper for posting, it will provide that submission to the Regional Director for review as described in paragraph (g)(5) of this section. The credit union may also post a content-neutral disclaimer using language similar to the language in paragraph (g)(3)(i) of this section.

(9) A merging credit union must inform members with the 90-day notice that if they wish to provide their opinions about the proposed merger to other members they can submit their opinions in writing to the credit union no later than 35 days from the date of the notice and the credit union will forward those opinions to other members. The 90-day notice will provide a contact at the credit union for delivery of communications, will explain that members must agree to reimburse the credit union's costs of transmitting the communication including providing an advance payment, and will refer members to this section of NCUA's rules for further information about the communication process. The credit union, at its option, may include additional factual information about the communication process with its 90-day notice.

(10) A group of members may make a joint request that the credit union send its materials to other members. For purposes of paragraphs (g)(2) and (g)(3) of this section, the credit union will use the group name provided by the group.

(h) If it chooses, a credit union may seek a preliminary determination from the Regional Director regarding any of the notices required under this subchapter and its proposed methods and procedures applicable to the membership merger vote. The Regional Director will make a preliminary determination regarding the notices and methods and procedures applicable to the membership vote within 30 calendar days of receipt of a credit union's request for review unless the Regional Director extends the period as necessary to request additional information or review a credit union's submission. A credit union's prior submission of any notice or proposed voting procedures does not relieve the credit union of its obligation to certify the results of the membership vote required by § 708a.307 or eliminate the right of the Regional Director to disapprove the merger if the credit union fails to conduct the membership vote in a fair and legal manner consistent with the Federal Credit Union Act and these rules.

§ 708a.306 Membership approval of a proposal to merge.

(a) A proposal for merger approved by a board of directors also requires approval by a majority of the members who vote on the proposal. At least 20 percent of the members eligible to vote must participate in the vote. The credit union must also have NCUA's written authorization to proceed with the member vote.

(b) The board of directors must set a voting record date to determine member voting eligibility. The record date must be at least one day before the publication of notice required in § 708a.303.

(c) A member may vote on a proposal to merge in person at a special meeting held on the date set for the vote or by written ballot delivered by mail or otherwise. The vote on the merger proposal must be by secret ballot and conducted by an independent entity. The independent entity must be a company with experience in conducting corporate elections. No official or senior management official of the credit union or the immediate family members of any official or senior management official may have any ownership interest in or be employed by the independent entity.

§ 708a.307 Certification of vote on merger proposal.

(a) The board of directors of the merging credit union must certify the results of the membership vote to the Regional Director within 14 calendar days after the vote is taken.

(b) The certification must also include a statement that the notice, ballot, and other written materials provided to members were identical to those submitted to NCUA pursuant to § 708a.305. If the board cannot certify this, the board must provide copies of any new or revised materials and an explanation of the reasons for any changes.

(c) The certification must include copies of any correspondence between the credit union and other regulators related to the pending merger.

§ 708a.308 NCUA approval of the merger.

(a) The Regional Director will review the methods by which the membership vote was taken and the procedures applicable to the membership vote. The Regional Director will determine if the notices and other communications to members were accurate, not misleading, and timely; if the membership vote was conducted in a fair and legal manner; and if the credit union has otherwise met the requirements of this subpart, including whether there is substantial evidence that the factors in section 205(c) of the Act are satisfied.

(b) After completion of this review, the Regional Director will approve or disapprove the proposed merger. The Regional Director will issue the approval or disapproval within 30 calendar days of receipt from the credit union of the certification of the result of the membership vote required under § 708a.307, unless the Regional Director extends the period as necessary to request additional information or review the credit union's submission. The Regional Director's approval is conditional on the credit union completing the merger in the timeframes required by § 708a.309.

(c) If the Regional Director disapproves the methods by which the membership vote was taken or the procedures applicable to the membership vote, the Regional Director may direct that a new vote be taken.

(d) A merging credit union may appeal a Regional Director's disapproval to the NCUA Board. The credit union must file the appeal within 30 days

National Credit Union Administration § 708a.312

after receipt of the Regional Director's determination. The NCUA Board will act on the appeal within 120 days of receipt.

§ 708a.309 Completion of merger.

(a) After receipt of the approvals under §§ 708a.302 and 708a.308 a credit union may complete the merger.

(b) The credit union must complete the merger within one year of the date of NCUA approval under § 708a.308. If a credit union fails to complete the merger within one year the Regional Director will disapprove the merger. The credit union's board of directors must then adopt a new merger proposal and solicit another member vote if it still desires to merge.

(c) The Regional Director may, upon timely request and for good cause, extend the one year completion period for an additional six months.

(d) After notification by the board of directors of the bank that the merger has been completed, the NCUA will cancel the insurance certificate of the credit union and, if applicable, the charter of a Federal credit union.

§ 708a.310 Limits on compensation of officials.

No director or senior management official of an insured credit union may receive any economic benefit in connection with the merger of a credit union other than reasonable compensation and other benefits paid in the ordinary course of business.

§ 708a.311 Voting incentives.

If a merging credit union offers an incentive to encourage members to participate in the vote, including a prize raffle, every reference to such incentive made by the credit union in a written communication to its members must also state that members are eligible for the incentive regardless of whether they vote for or against the proposed merger.

§ 708a.312 Voting guidelines.

A merging credit union must conduct its member vote on merger in a fair and legal manner. NCUA provides the following guidelines as suggestions to help a credit union obtain a fair and legal vote and otherwise fulfill its regulatory obligations. These guidelines are not an exhaustive checklist and do not by themselves guarantee a fair and legal vote.

(a) *Applicability of State law.* While NCUA's merger rules apply to all mergers of Federally insured credit unions, Federally insured State chartered credit unions (FISCUs) are also subject to State law on mergers. NCUA's position is that no merger of a State chartered credit union is authorized unless permitted by State law, and also that a State legislature or State supervisory authority may impose merger requirements more stringent or restrictive than NCUA's. States that permit mergers may have substantive and procedural requirements that vary from Federal law. For example, there may be different voting standards for approving a vote. While the Federal Credit Union Act requires a simple majority of those who vote to approve a merger, some States have higher voting standards requiring two-thirds or more of those who vote. A FISCU should be careful to understand both Federal and State law to navigate the merger process and conduct a proper vote.

(b) *Eligibility to vote.* (1) Determining who is eligible to cast a ballot is fundamental to any vote. No merger vote can be fair and legal if some members are improperly excluded. A merging credit union should be cautious to identify all eligible members and make certain they are included on its voting list. NCUA recommends that a merging credit union establish internal procedures to manage this task.

(2) A merging credit union should be careful to make certain its member list is accurate and complete. For example, when a credit union converts from paper record keeping to computer record keeping, some member names may not transfer unless the credit union is careful in this regard. This same problem can arise when a credit union merges from one computer system to another where the software is not completely compatible.

(3) Problems with keeping track of who is eligible to vote can also arise when a credit union merges from a Federal charter to a State charter or

§ 708a.312

vice versa. NCUA is aware of an instance where a Federal credit union used membership materials allowing two or more individuals to open a joint account and also allowed each to become a member. The Federal credit union later converted to a State chartered credit union that, like most other State chartered credit unions in its State, used membership materials allowing two or more individuals to open a joint account but only allowed the first person listed on the account to become a member. The other individuals did not become members as a result of their joint account, but were required to open another account where they were the first or only person listed on the account. Over time, some individuals who became members of the Federal credit union as the second person listed on a joint account were treated like those individuals who were listed as the second person on a joint account opened directly with the State chartered credit union. Specifically, both of those groups were treated as non-members not entitled to vote. This example makes the point that a credit union must be diligent in maintaining a reliable membership list.

(c) *Scheduling the special meeting.* NCUA's merger rule requires a merging credit union to permit members to vote by written mail ballot or in person at a special meeting held for the purpose of voting on the merger. Although most members may choose to vote by mail, a significant number may choose to vote in person. As a result, a merging credit union should be careful to conduct its special meeting in a manner conducive to accommodating all members wishing to attend, including selecting a meeting location that can accommodate the anticipated number of attendees and is conveniently located. The meeting should also be held on a day and time suitable to most members' schedules. A credit union should conduct its meeting in accordance with applicable Federal and State law, its bylaws, Robert's Rules of Order or other appropriate parliamentary procedures, and determine before the meeting the nature and scope of any discussion to be permitted.

(d) *Voting incentives.* Some credit unions may wish to offer incentives to members, such as entry to a prize raffle, to encourage participation in the merger vote. The credit union must exercise care in the design and execution of such incentives.

(1) The credit union should ensure that the incentive complies with all applicable State, Federal, and local laws.

(2) The incentive should not be unreasonable in size. The cost of the incentive should have a negligible impact on the credit union's net worth ratio and the incentive should not be so large that it distracts the member from the purpose of the vote. If the board desires to use such incentives, the cost of the incentive should be included in the directors' deliberation and determination that the merger is in the best interests of the credit union's members.

(3) The credit union should ensure that the incentive is available to every member that votes regardless of how or when he or she votes. All of the credit union's written materials promoting the incentive to the membership must disclose to the members, as required by § 708a.311 of this part, that they have an equal opportunity to participate in the incentive program regardless of whether they vote for or against the merger. The credit union should also design its incentives so that they are available equally to all members who vote, regardless of whether they vote by mail or in person at the special meeting.

(e) *Solicitation of votes.* Some credit unions may wish to contact members who have not voted and encourage them to vote on the merger proposal. NCUA believes, however, that using credit union employees to solicit votes is problematic. Employees directed to solicit votes could easily neglect everyday duties critical to the credit union's safe and sound operation. Also, employees may very well feel pressured to solicit votes for the merger, regardless of whether or not they support the merger. Accordingly, NCUA strongly encourages credit unions to use an independent third party to solicit votes rather than diverting credit union employees from their usual duties.

PART 708b—MERGERS OF FEDERALLY-INSURED CREDIT UNIONS; VOLUNTARY TERMINATION OR CONVERSION OF INSURED STATUS

Sec.
708b.1 Scope.
708b.2 Definitions.

Subpart A—Mergers

708b.101 Mergers generally.
708b.102 Special provisions for federal insurance.
708b.103 Preparation of merger plan.
708b.104 Submission of merger proposal to the NCUA.
708b.105 Approval of merger proposal by the NCUA.
708b.106 Approval of the merger proposal by members.
708b.107 Certification of vote on merger proposal.
708b.108 Completion of merger.

Subpart B—Voluntary Termination or Conversion of Insured Status

708b.201 Termination of insurance.
708b.202 Notice to members of proposal to terminate insurance.
708b.203 Conversion of insurance.
708b.204 Notice to members of proposal to convert insurance.
708b.205 Modifications to notice and ballot.
708b.206 Share insurance communications to members.

Subpart C—Forms

708b.301 Conversion of insurance (State Chartered Credit Union)
708b.302 Conversion of insurance (Federal Credit Union).
708b.303 Conversion of insurance through merger.

AUTHORITY: 12 U.S.C. 1752(7), 1766, 1785, 1786, 1789.

SOURCE: 70 FR 3288, Jan. 24, 2005, unless otherwise noted.

§ 708b.1 Scope.

(a) Subpart A of this part prescribes the procedures for merging one or more credit unions with a continuing credit union where at least one of the credit unions is federally-insured.

(b) Subpart B of this part prescribes the procedures and notice requirements for termination of federal insurance or conversion of federal insurance to nonfederal insurance, including termination or conversion resulting from a merger.

(c) Subpart C prescribes required forms for use in conversion of federal insurance to nonfederal insurance.

(d) Nothing in this part restricts or otherwise impairs the authority of the NCUA to approve a merger pursuant to section 205(h) of the Act.

(e) This part does not address procedures or requirements that may be applicable under state law for a state credit union.

§ 708b.2 Definitions.

Conducted by an independent entity means:

(1) The independent entity will receive the ballots directly from voting members.

(2) After the conclusion of the special meeting that ends the ballot period, the independent entity will open all the ballots in its possession and tabulate the results. The entity must not open or tabulate any ballots before the conclusion of the special meeting.

(3) The independent entity will certify the final vote tally in writing to the credit union and provide a copy to the NCUA Regional Director. The certification will include, at a minimum, the number of members who voted, the number of affirmative votes, and the number of negative votes. During the course of the voting period the independent entity may provide the credit union with the names of members who have not yet voted, but may not provide any voting results to the credit union prior to certifying the final vote tally.

Continuing credit union means the credit union that will continue in operation after the merger.

Convert, conversion, and *converting,* when used in connection with insurance, refer to the act of canceling federal insurance and simultaneously obtaining insurance from another insurance carrier. They mean that after cancellation of federal insurance the credit union will be nonfederally-insured.

Federally-insured means insured by the National Credit Union Administration (NCUA) through the National Credit Union Share Insurance Fund (NCUSIF).

§ 708b.101

Independent entity means a company with experience in conducting corporate elections. No official or senior manager of the credit union, or the immediate family members of any official or senior manager, may have any ownership interest in, or be employed by, the entity.

Insurance and *insured* refer to primary share or deposit insurance. These terms do not include excess share or deposit insurance as referred to in part 740 of this chapter.

Merger-related financial arrangement means a material increase in compensation (including indirect compensation, for example, bonuses, deferred compensation, or other financial rewards) or benefits that any board member or senior management official of a merging credit union may receive in connection with a merger transaction. For purposes of this definition, a material increase is an increase that exceeds the greater of 15 percent or $10,000.

Merging credit union means the credit union that will cease to exist as an operating credit union at the time of the merger.

Nonfederally-insured means insured by a private or cooperative insurance fund or guaranty corporation organized or chartered under state or territorial law.

Regional director means either the director of the NCUA regional office for the region where a natural person credit union's main office is located or the director of the NCUA's Office of Consumer Protection. For corporate credit unions, *regional director* means the director of NCUA's Office of Corporate Credit Unions.

Secret ballot means no credit union employee or official can determine how a particular member voted. Credit union employees and officials are prohibited from assisting members in completing ballots or handling completed ballots.

Senior management official means the chief executive officer (who may hold the title of president or treasurer/manager), any assistant chief executive officer, and the chief financial officer.

Share insurance communication means any written communication, excluding the forms in Subpart C of this Part, that is made by or on behalf of a federally-insured credit union that is intended to be read by two or more credit union members and that mentions share insurance conversion or termination. The term:

(1) Includes communications delivered or made available before, during, and after the credit union's board of directors decides to seek conversion or termination.

(2) Includes, but is not limited to, communications delivered or made available by mail, e-mail, and internet website posting.

(3) Does not include communications intended to be read only by the credit union's own employees or officials.

State credit union means any credit union organized and operated according to the laws of any state, the several territories and possessions of the United States, or the Commonwealth of Puerto Rico. Accordingly, *state authority* means the appropriate state or territorial regulatory or supervisory authority for any such credit union.

Terminate, termination, and *terminating,* when used in reference to insurance, refer to the act of canceling federal insurance and mean that the credit union will become uninsured.

Uninsured means there is no share or deposit insurance available on the credit union accounts.

[70 FR 3288, Jan. 24, 2005, as amended at 75 FR 80680, Dec. 23, 2010; 75 FR 81393, Dec. 28, 2010]

Subpart A—Mergers

§ 708b.101 Mergers generally.

(a) In any case where a merger will result in the termination of federal insurance or conversion to nonfederal insurance, the merging credit union must comply with the provisions of subparts B and C of this part in addition to this subpart A.

(b) A federally-insured credit union must have the prior written approval of the NCUA before merging with any other credit union.

(c) Where the continuing credit union is a federal credit union, it must be in compliance with the chartering policies of the NCUA.

(d) Where the continuing or merging credit union is a state credit union, the merger must be permitted by state law or authorized by the state authority.

(e) Where both the merging and continuing credit unions are federally-insured and the two credit unions have overlapping fields of membership, the continuing credit union must, within three months after completion of the merger, either:

(1) Notify all members of the continuing credit union of the potential loss of insurance coverage if they had overlapping membership,

(2) Notify all individuals and entities that were actually members of both credit unions of the potential loss of insurance coverage, or

(3) Determine which members of both credit unions may actually have uninsured funds six months after the merger and notify those members of the potential loss of insurance coverage.

§ 708b.102 Special provisions for federal insurance.

(a) Where the continuing credit union is federally-insured, the NCUSIF will assess a deposit and a prorated insurance premium (unless waived in whole or in part for all insured credit unions during that year) on the additional share accounts insured as a result of the merger of a nonfederally-insured or uninsured credit union with a federally-insured credit union.

(b) Where the continuing credit union is nonfederally-insured or uninsured but desires to be federally-insured as of the date of the merger, it must submit an application to the appropriate Regional Director when the merging credit union requests approval of the merger proposal. If the Regional Director approves the merger, the NCUSIF will assess a deposit and a prorated insurance premium (unless waived in whole or in part for all insured credit unions during that year) on any additional share accounts insured as a result of the merger.

(c) Where the continuing credit union is nonfederally-insured or uninsured and does not make application for insurance, but the merging credit union is federally-insured, the continuing credit union is entitled to a refund of the merging credit union's NCUSIF deposit and to a refund of the unused portion of the NCUSIF share insurance premium (if any). If the continuing credit union is uninsured, the NCUSIF will make the refund only after expiration of the one-year period of continued insurance coverage noted in paragraph (e) of this section.

(d) Where the continuing credit union is nonfederally-insured, NCUSIF insurance of the member accounts of a merging federally-insured credit union ceases as of the effective date of the merger.

(e) Where the continuing credit union is uninsured, NCUSIF insurance of the member accounts of the merging federally-insured credit union will continue for a period of one year, subject to the restrictions in section 206(d)(1) of the Act.

§ 708b.103 Preparation of merger plan.

(a) Upon the approval of a proposition for merger by the boards of directors of the credit unions, the two credit unions must prepare a plan for the proposed merger that includes:

(1) Current financial statements for both credit unions;

(2) Current delinquent loan summaries and analyses of the adequacy of the Allowance for Loan and Lease Losses account;

(3) Consolidated financial statements, including an assessment of the generally accepted accounting principles (GAAP) net worth of each credit union before the merger and the GAAP net worth of the continuing credit union after the merger;

(4) Analyses of share values;

(5) Explanation of any proposed share adjustments, and where the net worth ratio of the merging credit union is more than 500 basis points higher than the net worth ratio of the continuing credit union, an explanation of the factors considered in establishing the amount of any proposed adjustment or in determining no adjustment is necessary;

(6) Explanation of any provisions for reserves, undivided earnings or dividends;

(7) Description of any merger-related financial arrangement, as defined in § 708b.2;

(8) Provisions with respect to notification and payment of creditors;

§ 708b.104

(9) Explanation of any changes relative to insurance such as life savings and loan protection insurance and insurance of member accounts;

(10) Provisions for determining that all assets and liabilities of the continuing credit union will conform with the requirements of the Act (where the continuing credit union is a federal credit union); and

(11) Proposed charter amendments (where the continuing credit union is a federal credit union). These amendments, if any, will usually pertain to the name of the credit union and the definition of its field of membership.

(b) [Reserved]

[70 FR 3288, Jan. 24, 2005, as amended at 75 FR 81394, Dec. 28, 2010]

§ 708b.104 Submission of merger proposal to the NCUA.

(a) Upon approval of the merger plan by the boards of directors of the credit unions, the credit unions must submit the following information to the Regional Director:

(1) The merger plan, as described in this part;

(2) Resolutions of the boards of directors;

(3) Proposed Merger Agreement;

(4) Proposed Notice of Special Meeting of the Members (for merging federal credit unions);

(5) Copy of the form of Ballot to be sent to the members (for merging federal credit unions);

(6) Evidence that the state's supervisory authority approves the merger proposal (for states that require such agreement before NCUA approval);

(7) Application and Agreement for Insurance of Member Accounts (for continuing state credit unions desiring to become federally-insured);

(8) If the merging credit union's assets on its latest call report are equal to or greater than the threshold amount established annually by the Federal Trade Commission under 15 U.S.C. 18a(a)(2)(B)(i), currently $63.4 million, a statement about whether the two credit unions intend to make a Hart-Scott-Rodino Act premerger notification filing with the Federal Trade Commission and, if not, an explanation why not; and

(9) For mergers where the continuing credit union is not federally-insured and will not apply for federal insurance:

(i) A written statement from the continuing credit union that it "is aware of the requirements of 12 U.S.C. 1831t(b), including all notification and acknowledgment requirements"; and

(ii) Proof that the accounts of the credit union will be accepted for coverage by the nonfederal insurer (if the credit union will have nonfederal insurance).

(b) [Reserved]

[70 FR 3288, Jan. 24, 2005, as amended at 75 FR 81394, Dec. 28, 2010]

§ 708b.105 Approval of merger proposal by the NCUA.

(a) In any case where the continuing credit union is federally-insured and the merging credit union is nonfederally-insured or uninsured, the NCUA will determine the potential risk to the NCUSIF.

(b) If the NCUA finds that the merger proposal complies with the provisions of this part and does not present an undue risk to the NCUSIF, it may approve the proposal subject to any other specific requirements as it may prescribe to fulfill the intended purposes of the proposed merger. For mergers of federal credit unions into federally-insured credit unions, if the NCUA determines that the merging credit union is in danger of insolvency and that the proposed merger would reduce the risk or avoid a threatened loss to the NCUSIF, the NCUA may permit the merger to become effective without an affirmative vote of the membership of the merging credit union otherwise required by § 708b.106 of this part.

(c) NCUA may approve any proposed charter amendments for a continuing federal credit union contingent upon the completion of the merger. All charter amendments must be consistent with NCUA chartering policy.

[70 FR 3288, Jan. 24, 2005, as amended at 73 FR 30477, May 28, 2008]

§ 708b.106 Approval of the merger proposal by members.

(a) When the merging credit union is a federal credit union, the members must:

(1) Have the right to vote on the merger proposal in person at the annual meeting, if within 60 days after NCUA approval, or at a special meeting to be called within 60 days of NCUA approval, or by mail ballot, received no later than the date and time announced for the annual meeting or the special meeting called for that purpose.

(2) Be given advance notice of the meeting in accordance with the provisions of Article IV, Meetings of Members, Federal Credit Union Bylaws. The notice must:

(i) Specify the purpose of the meeting and the time and place;

(ii) Contain a summary of the merger plan, including, but not necessarily limited to, current financial statements for each credit union, a consolidated financial statement for the continuing credit union, analyses of share values, explanation of any proposed share adjustments, explanation of any changes relative to insurance such as life savings and loan protection insurance and insurance of member accounts, and a detailed description of any merger related financial arrangement, as defined in §708b.2. The description must include the name and title of each individual recipient and an explanation of the financial impact of each element of the arrangement, including direct salary increases and any indirect compensation, such as any bonus, deferred compensation or other financial reward;

(iii) State reasons for the proposed merger;

(iv) Provide name and location, including branches, of the continuing credit union;

(v) Inform the members that they have the right to vote on the merger proposal in person at the meeting or by written ballot to be received no later than the date and time announced for the annual meeting or the special meeting called for that purpose; and

(vi) Be accompanied by a Ballot for Merger Proposal.

(b) Approval of a proposal to merge a federal credit union into a federally-insured credit union requires the affirmative vote of a majority of the members of the merging credit union who vote on the proposal. If the continuing credit union is uninsured or nonfederally-insured, the voting requirements of subpart B apply. If the continuing credit union is nonfederally-insured, the merging credit union must use the form notice and ballot in subpart C of this part unless the Regional Director approves the use of different forms.

[70 FR 3288, Jan. 24, 2005, as amended at 75 FR 81394, Dec. 28, 2010]

§ 708b.107 Certification of vote on merger proposal.

The board of directors of the merging federal credit union must certify the results of the membership vote to the Regional Director within 10 days after the vote is taken. The certification must include the total number of members of record of the credit union, the number who voted on the merger, the number who voted in favor, and the number who voted against. If the continuing credit union is nonfederally-insured, the merging credit union must use the certification form in subpart C of this part unless the Regional Director approves the use of a different form.

[70 FR 3288, Jan. 24, 2005, as amended at 75 FR 81394, Dec. 28, 2010]

§ 708b.108 Completion of merger.

(a) Upon approval of the merger proposal by the NCUA and by the state supervisory authority (where the continuing or merging credit union is a state credit union) and by the members of each credit union where required, the credit unions may complete the merger.

(b) Upon completion of the merger, the board of directors of the continuing credit union must certify the completion of the merger to the Regional Director within 30 days after the effective date of the merger.

(c) Upon the NCUA's receipt of certification that the merger has been completed, the NCUA will cancel the charter of the merging federal credit union (if applicable) and the insurance certificate of any merging federally-insured credit union.

Subpart B—Voluntary Termination or Conversion of Insured Status

§ 708b.201 Termination of insurance.

(a) A state credit union may terminate federal insurance, if permitted by state law, either on its own or by merging into an uninsured credit union.

(b) A federal credit union may terminate federal insurance only by merging into, or converting its charter to, an uninsured state credit union.

(c) A majority of the credit union's members must approve a termination of insurance by affirmative vote. The vote must be taken by secret ballot and conducted by an independent entity.

(d) Termination of federal insurance requires the NCUA's prior written approval. A credit union must notify the NCUA and request approval of the termination through the Regional Director in writing at least 90 days before the proposed termination date and within one year after obtaining the membership vote. The notice to the NCUA must include:

(1) A written statement from the credit union that it "is aware of the requirements of 12 U.S.C. 1831t(b), including all notification and acknowledgment requirements;" and

(2) A certification of the member vote that must include the total number of members of record of the credit union, the number who voted in favor of the termination, and the number who voted against.

(e) The NCUA will approve or disapprove the termination in writing within 90 days after being notified by the credit union.

[70 FR 3288, Jan. 24, 2005, as amended at 75 FR 81394, Dec. 28, 2010]

§ 708b.202 Notice to members of proposal to terminate insurance.

(a) When the board of directors of a federally-insured credit union adopts a resolution proposing to terminate federal insurance, including termination due to a merger or conversion of charter, it must provide its members with written notice of the proposal to terminate and of the date set for the membership vote. The first written communication following the resolution that is made by or on behalf of the credit union and that informs the members that the credit union will seek termination is the notice of the proposal to terminate. This notice must:

(1) Inform the members of the requirement for a membership vote and the date for the vote;

(2) Explain that the insurance provided by the NCUA is federal insurance and is backed by the full faith and credit of the United States government; and

(3) Include a conspicuous statement that if the termination or merger is approved, and the credit union, or the continuing credit union in the case of a merger, subsequently fails, the federal government does not guarantee the member will get his or her money back.

(b) The credit union must deliver the notice in person to each member, or mail it to each member at the address for the member as it appears on the records of the credit union, not more than 30 nor less than 7 days before the date of the vote. The membership must be given the opportunity to vote by mail ballot. The credit union may provide the notice of the proposal and the ballot to members at the same time.

(c) If the membership and the NCUA approve the proposition for termination of insurance, the credit union must give the members prompt and reasonable notice of termination.

§ 708b.203 Conversion of insurance.

(a) A federally-insured state credit union may convert to nonfederal insurance, if permitted by state law, either on its own or by merging into a nonfederally-insured credit union.

(b) A federal credit union may convert to nonfederal insurance only by merging into, or converting its charter to, a nonfederally-insured state credit union.

(c) Conversion to nonfederal insurance requires the prior written approval of the NCUA. After the credit union board of directors resolves to seek a conversion, the credit union must notify the Regional Director promptly, in writing, of the desired conversion and request NCUA approval of the conversion. The notification must be in the form specified in subpart C of this part, unless the Regional Director approves a different form. The credit union must provide this notification and request for approval to the Regional Director at least 14 days before the credit union notifies its members and seeks their vote and at least 90 days before the proposed conversion date. NCUA will approve or disapprove the conversion as described in paragraph (g) of this section.

(d) Approval of a conversion of Federal to nonfederal insurance requires the affirmative vote of a majority of the credit union's members who vote on the proposition, provided at least 20 percent of the total membership participates in the voting. The vote must be taken by secret ballot and conducted by an independent entity.

(e) For all conversions, the notice to the NCUA must include:

(1) A written statement from the credit union that "it is aware of the requirements of 12 U.S.C. 1831t(b), including all notification and acknowledgment requirements;" and

(2) Proof that the nonfederal insurer is authorized to issue share insurance in the state where the credit union is located and that the insurer will insure the credit union.

(f) The board of directors of the credit union and the independent entity that conducts the membership vote must certify the results of the membership vote to the NCUA within 14 calendar days after the deadline for receipt of votes. The certification must include the total number of members of record of the credit union, the number who voted on the conversion, the number who voted in favor of the conversion, and the number who voted against. The certification must be in the form specified in subpart C of this part.

(g) Generally, the NCUA will conditionally approve or disapprove the conversion in writing within 14 days after receiving the certification of the vote. The credit union must complete the conversion within six months of the date of conditional approval. If a credit union fails to complete the conversion within six months the Regional Director will disapprove the conversion. The credit union's board of directors, if it still wishes to convert, must then adopt a new conversion proposal and solicit another member vote.

(h) For conversions by merger, the merging credit unions must follow the procedures specified in subparts A and B of this part and use the forms specified in subpart C of this part. In the event the procedures of Subpart A and B conflict, the credit union must follow subpart B.

[70 FR 3288, Jan. 24, 2005, as amended at 73 FR 30477, May 28, 2008; 75 FR 81394, Dec. 28, 2010]

§ 708b.204 Notice to members of proposal to convert insurance.

(a) When the board of directors of a federally-insured credit union adopts a resolution proposing to convert from federal to nonfederal insurance, including an insurance conversion associated with a merger or conversion of charter, it must provide its members with written notice of the proposal to convert insurance and of the date set for the membership vote. The first written communication following this resolution that is made by or on behalf of the credit union and that informs the members that the credit union will seek conversion of insurance is the notice of the proposal to convert. This notice must:

(1) Inform the members of the requirement for a membership vote and the date for the vote;

(2) Explain that the insurance provided by the NCUA is federal insurance and is backed by the full faith and credit of the United States government, while the insurance provided by the nonfederal insurer is not guaranteed by the federal or any state government;

(3) Include a conspicuous statement that if the conversion or merger is approved, and the credit union, or the continuing credit union in the case of a merger, subsequently fails, the federal government does not guarantee the member will get his or her money back; and

(4) Be in the form set forth in subpart C of this part, unless the Regional Director approves a different form.

(b) The credit union must deliver the notice in person to each member or mail it to each member at the address for the member as it appears on the records of the credit union, not more than 30 nor less than 7 days before the date for the vote. The credit union must give the membership the opportunity to vote by mail ballot. The form of the ballot must be as set forth in subpart C of this part, unless the Regional Director approves the use of a different form. The notice of the proposal and the ballot may be provided to the members at the same time.

(c) If the membership and the NCUA approve the proposition for conversion of insurance, the credit union will give prompt and reasonable notice to the membership. The credit union must deliver the notice at least 30 days before the effective date of the conversion. The notice must identify the effective date of the conversion, and the first page must also include a conspicuous statement (*i.e.*, in bold and no smaller than any other font size used in the notice) that:

(1) The conversion will result in the loss of federal share insurance, and

(2) The credit union will, at any time before the effective date of conversion, permit all members who have share certificates or other term accounts to close the federally-insured portion of those accounts without an early withdrawal penalty.

§ 708b.205 Modifications to notice and ballot.

(a) Converting credit unions will use the form notice and ballot as provided in subpart C of this part unless the Regional Director approves the use of a different form.

(b) A converting credit union will provide the Regional Director with a copy of the notice and ballot, including any reasons for conversion and estimated costs of conversion, on or before the date the notice and ballot are mailed to the members.

(c) Federally-insured state credit unions may include additional language in the notice and ballot regarding state requirements for mergers, where appropriate.

§ 708b.206 Share insurance communications to members.

(a) Every share insurance communication must comply with § 740.2 of this chapter, which, in part, prohibits federally-insured credit unions from making any representation that is inaccurate or deceptive in any particular.

(b) Every share insurance communication must contain the following conspicuous statement: "IF YOU ARE A MEMBER OF THIS CREDIT UNION, YOUR ACCOUNTS ARE CURRENTLY INSURED BY THE NATIONAL CREDIT UNION ADMINISTRATION, A FEDERAL AGENCY. THIS FEDERAL INSURANCE IS BACKED BY THE FULL FAITH AND CREDIT OF THE UNITED STATES GOVERNMENT. IF THE CREDIT UNION CONVERTS TO PRIVATE INSURANCE WITH [insert name of private share insurer] AND THE CREDIT UNION FAILS, THE FEDERAL GOVERNMENT DOES NOT GUARANTEE THAT YOU WILL GET YOUR MONEY BACK." The statement must:

(1) Appear on the first page of the communication where conversion is discussed and, if the communication is on an Internet Web site posting, the credit union must make reasonable efforts to make it visible without scrolling; and (2) Must be in capital letters, bolded, offset from the other text by use of a border, and at least one font size larger than any other text (exclusive of headings) used in the communication.

(c) Every share insurance communication about share insurance termination must contain the following conspicuous statement: "IF YOU ARE A MEMBER OF THIS CREDIT UNION, YOUR ACCOUNTS ARE CURRENTLY INSURED BY THE NATIONAL CREDIT UNION ADMINISTRATION, A FEDERAL AGENCY. THIS FEDERAL INSURANCE IS BACKED BY THE FULL FAITH AND CREDIT OF THE UNITED STATES GOVERNMENT. IF THE CREDIT UNION TERMINATES ITS FEDERAL INSURANCE AND THE CREDIT UNION FAILS, THE FEDERAL GOVERNMENT DOES NOT GUARANTEE THAT YOU WILL GET YOUR MONEY BACK." The statement must:

(1) Appear on the first page of the communication where termination is discussed and, if the communication is on an internet website posting, the

credit union must make reasonable efforts to make it visible without scrolling; and

(2) Must be in capital letters, bolded, offset from the other text by use of a border, and at least one font size larger than any other text (exclusive of headings) used in the communication.

(d) A converting credit union must provide the Regional Director with a copy of any share insurance communication that the credit union will make during the voting period. The Regional Director must receive the copy at or before the time the credit union makes it available to members. The converting credit union must inform the Regional Director when the communication is to be made, to which members it will be directed, and how it will be disseminated. For purposes of this section, the voting period begins on the date of the board of director's resolution to seek conversion or termination and ends on the date the member voting closes.

(e) The Regional Director may take appropriate action, including disapproving a conversion, if he or she determines that a converting credit union, by inclusion or omission of information in a share insurance communication, materially mislead or misinformed its membership. For example, the Regional Director will treat any share insurance communication that compares the relative strength, safety, or claims paying ability of a private insurer with that of the National Credit Union Share Insurance Fund as materially misleading if the comparison fails to mention that the federal insurance provided by the NCUA is backed by the full faith and credit of the United States government.

[70 FR 3288, Jan. 24, 2005, as amended at 75 FR 81394, Dec. 28, 2010]

Subpart C—Forms

§ 708b.301 Conversion of insurance (State Chartered Credit Union).

Unless the Regional Director approves the use of different forms, a state chartered credit union must use the forms in this section in connection with a conversion to nonfederal insurance.

(a) Form letter notifying NCUA of intent to convert:

(insert name), NCUA Regional Director

(insert address of NCUA Regional Director)

Re: Notice of Intent to Convert to Private Share Insurance

Dear Director (insert name):

In accordance with federal law at Title 12, United States Code Section 1785(b)(1)(D), I request the National Credit Union Administration approve the conversion of (insert name of credit union) from federal share insurance to private primary share insurance with (insert name of private insurance company).

On (insert date), the board of directors of (insert name of credit union) resolved to pursue the conversion from federal insurance to private insurance. A copy of the resolution is enclosed.

On (insert date), the credit union plans to solicit the vote of our members on the conversion. The credit union will employ (insert name, address, and telephone number of independent entity) to conduct the member vote. The credit union will use the form notice and ballot required by NCUA regulations, and will certify the results to NCUA as required by NCUA regulations.

Aside from the notice and ballot, the credit union (does)(does not) intend to provide its members with additional written information about the conversion. I understand that NCUA regulations forbid any communications to members, including communications about NCUA insurance or private insurance, that are inaccurate or deceptive.

(Insert name of State) allows credit unions to obtain primary share insurance from (insert name of private insurance company). I have enclosed a copy of a letter from (insert name and title of state regulator) establishing that (insert name of private insurer) has the authority to provide (insert name of credit union) with primary share insurance.

I have enclosed a copy of a letter from (insert name of private insurer) indicating it has accepted (insert name of credit union) for primary share insurance and will insure the credit union immediately upon the date that it loses its federal share insurance.

I am aware of the requirements of 12 U.S.C. 1831t(b), including all notification and acknowledgment requirements.

The point of contact for conversion matters is (insert name and title of credit union employee), who can be reached at (insert telephone number).

Sincerely,

(signature)

Chief Executive Officer.

Enclosures

§ 708b.301

(b) Form notice to members of intent to convert and special meeting of members:

NOTICE OF PROPOSAL TO CONVERT TO NONFEDERALLY-INSURED STATUS AND SPECIAL MEETING OF MEMBERS

(INSERT NAME OF CONVERTING CREDIT UNION)

On (insert date), the board of directors of your credit union approved a proposition to convert from federal share (deposit) insurance to private insurance. You are encouraged to attend a special meeting of our credit union at (insert address) on (insert time and date) to address this proposition.

PURPOSE OF MEETING

The meeting has two purposes:
1. To consider and act upon a proposal to convert your account insurance from federal insurance to private insurance.
2. To approve the action of the Board of Directors in authorizing the officers of the credit union to carry out the proposed conversion.

INSURANCE CONVERSION

Currently, your accounts have share insurance provided by the National Credit Union Administration, an agency of the federal government. The basic federal coverage is up to $100,000, but accounts may be structured in different ways, such as joint accounts, payable-on-death accounts, or IRA accounts, to achieve federal coverage of much more than $100,000. If the conversion is approved, your federal insurance will terminate on the effective date of the conversion. Instead, your accounts in the credit union will be insured up to $(insert dollar amount) by (insert name of insurer), a corporation chartered by the State of (insert name of State). The federal insurance provided by the National Credit Union Administration is backed by the full faith and credit of the United States government. The private insurance you will receive from (insert name of insurer), however, is not guaranteed by the federal or any state or local government.

IF THIS CONVERSION IS APPROVED, AND THE (insert name of credit union) FAILS, THE FEDERAL GOVERNMENT DOES NOT GUARANTEE YOU WILL GET YOUR MONEY BACK.

Also, because this conversion, if approved, would result in the loss of federal share insurance, the credit union will, at any time between the approval of the conversion and the effective date of conversion and upon request by the member, permit all members who have share certificates or other term accounts to close the federally-insured portion of those accounts without an early withdrawal penalty. (This is an optional sentence. It may be deleted without the approval of the Regional Director. The members must be informed about this right, however, as described in 12 CFR 708b.204(c).)

The board of directors has concluded that the proposed conversion is desirable for the following reasons: (insert reasons). (This is an optional paragraph. It may be deleted without the prior approval of the Regional Director.)

The proposed conversion will result in the following one-time cost associated with the conversion: (List the total estimated dollar amount, including (1) the cost of conducting the vote, (2) the cost of changing the credit union's name and insurance logo, and (3) attorney and consultant fees.)

The conversion must have the approval of a majority of members who vote on the proposal, provided at least 20 percent of the total membership participates in the voting.

Enclosed with this Notice of Special Meeting is a ballot. If you cannot attend the meeting, please complete the ballot and return it to (insert name and address of independent entity conducting the vote) by no later than (insert time and date). To be counted, your ballot must reach us by that date and time.

By order of the board of directors.
(signature of Board Presiding Officer)
(insert title and date)

(c) Form ballot:

BALLOT FOR CONVERSION TO NONFEDERALLY-INSURED STATUS

(INSERT NAME OF CONVERTING CREDIT UNION)

Name of Member: (insert name)
Account Number: (insert account number)

The credit union must receive this ballot by (insert date and time for vote). Please mail or bring it to: (Insert name of independent entity and address).

I understand if the conversion of the (insert name of credit union) is approved, the National Credit Union Administration share

National Credit Union Administration § 708b.302

(deposit) insurance I now have, up to $100,000, or possibly more if I use different account structures, will terminate upon the effective date of the conversion. Instead, my shares in the (insert name of credit union) will be insured up to $(insert dollar amount) by (insert name of insurer), a corporation chartered by the State of (insert name of state). The federal insurance provided by the National Credit Union Administration is backed by the full faith and credit of the United States Government. The private insurance provided by (insert name of insurer) is not.

I FURTHER UNDERSTAND THAT IF THIS CONVERSION IS APPROVED AND THE (insert name of credit union) FAILS, THE FEDERAL GOVERNMENT DOES NOT GUARANTEE THAT I WILL GET MY MONEY BACK.

I vote on the proposal as follows (check one box):

[ ] Approve the conversion to private insurance and authorize the Board of Directors to take all necessary action to accomplish the conversion.

[ ] Do not approve the conversion to private insurance.

Signed: _____
(Insert printed member's name)

Date: _____

(d) Form certification of member vote to NCUA:

CERTIFICATION OF VOTE ON CONVERSION TO NONFEDERALLY-INSURED STATUS

We, the undersigned officers of the (insert name of converting credit union), certify the completion of the following actions:

1. At a meeting on (insert date), the Board of Directors adopted a resolution to seek the conversion of our primary share insurance coverage from NCUA to (insert name of private insurer).

2. Not more than 30 nor less than 7 days before the date of the vote, copies of the notice of special meeting and the ballot, as approved by the National Credit Union Administration, were mailed to our members.

3. The credit union arranged for the conduct of a special meeting of our members at the time and place announced in the Notice to consider and act upon the proposed conversion.

4. At the special meeting, the credit union arranged for an explanation of the conversion to the members present at the special meeting.

5. The (insert name), an entity independent of the credit union, conducted the membership vote at the special meeting. The members voted as follows:

(insert) Number of total members
(insert) Number of members present at the special meeting
(insert) Number of members present who voted in favor of the conversion
(insert) Number of members present who voted against the conversion
(insert) Number of additional written ballots in favor of the conversion
(insert) Number of additional written ballots opposed to the conversion
(insert "20% or more") OR (insert "Less than 20%") of the total membership voted. Of those who voted, a majority voted (insert "in favor of") OR ("against") conversion.

The action of the members at the special meeting was recorded in the minutes.

This certification signed the (insert date).
(signature of Board Presiding Officer)
(insert typed name and title)
(signature of Board Secretary)
(insert typed name and title)

I (insert name), an officer of the (insert name of independent entity that conducted the vote), hereby certify that the information recorded in paragraph 5 above is accurate.

This certification signed the (insert date):
(signature of officer of independent entity)
(typed name, title, and phone number)

[70 FR 3288, Jan. 24, 2005, as amended at 73 FR 30477, May 28, 2008]

§ 708b.302 Conversion of insurance (Federal Credit Union).

Unless the Regional Director approves the use of different forms, a federal credit union must use the following forms in this section in connection with a conversion to a nonfederally-insured state charter.

(a) Form letter notifying NCUA of intent to convert:

(insert name), NCUA Regional Director
(insert address of NCUA Regional Director)

§ 708b.302

Re: Notice of Intent To Convert to State Charter and to Private Share Insurance

Dear Director (insert name):

In accordance with federal law at Title 12, United States Code Section 1785(b)(1)(D), I request the National Credit Union Administration approve the conversion of (insert name of federal credit union) to a state charter in (insert name of state) and from federal share insurance to private primary share insurance with (insert name of private insurance company).

On (insert date), the board of directors of (insert name of credit union) resolved to pursue the charter conversion and the conversion from federal insurance to private insurance. A copy of the resolution is enclosed.

On (insert date), the credit union plans to solicit the vote of our members on the conversion. The credit union will employ (insert name, address, and telephone number of independent entity) to conduct the vote. The credit union will use the form notice and ballot required by NCUA regulations, and will certify the results to NCUA as required by NCUA regulations.

Aside from the notice and ballot, the credit union (does)(does not) intend to provide our members with additional written information about the conversion. I understand that NCUA regulations forbid any communications to members, including communications about NCUA insurance or private insurance, that are inaccurate or deceptive.

I have enclosed a copy of a letter from (insert name and title of state regulator) indicating approval of our conversion to a state charter.

(Insert name of State) allows credit unions to obtain primary share insurance from (insert name of private insurance company). I have enclosed a copy of a letter from (insert name and title of state regulator) establishing that (insert name of private insurer) has the authority to provide (insert name of credit union), after conversion to a state charter, with primary share insurance.

I have enclosed a copy of a letter from (insert name of private insurer) indicating it has accepted (insert name of credit union) for primary share insurance and will insure the credit union immediately upon the date that it loses its federal share insurance.

I am aware of the requirements of 12 U.S.C. 1831t(b), including all notification and acknowledgment requirements.

Enclosed you will also find other information required by NCUA's Chartering and Field of Membership Manual, Chapter 4, § III.C.

The point of contact for conversion matters is (insert name and title of credit union employee), who can be reached at (insert telephone number).

Sincerely,

(signature),
Chief Executive Officer.

Enclosures

(b) Form notice to members of intent to convert and special meeting of members:

NOTICE OF PROPOSAL TO CONVERT TO A STATE CHARTER AND TO NONFEDERALLY-INSURED STATUS AND SPECIAL MEETING OF MEMBERS

(INSERT NAME OF CONVERTING CREDIT UNION)

On (insert date), the board of directors of your credit union approved a proposition to convert from federal share (deposit) insurance to private insurance and to convert from a federal credit union to a state-chartered credit union. You are encouraged to attend a special meeting of our credit union at (insert address) on (insert time and date) to address this proposition.

PURPOSE OF MEETING

The meeting has two purposes:

1. To consider and act upon a proposal to convert your credit union from a federal charter to a state charter and your account insurance from federal insurance to private insurance.

2. To approve the action of the Board of Directors in authorizing the officers of the credit union to carry out the proposed conversion.

INSURANCE CONVERSION

Currently, your accounts have share insurance provided by the National Credit Union Administration, an agency of the federal government. The basic federal coverage is up to $100,000, but accounts may be structured in different ways, such as joint accounts, payable-on-death accounts, or IRA accounts, to achieve federal coverage of much more than $100,000. If the conversion is approved, your federal insurance will terminate on the effective date of the conversion. Instead, your accounts in the credit union will be insured up to $(insert dollar amount) by (insert name of insurer), a corporation chartered by the State of (insert name of State). The federal insurance provided by the National Credit Union Administration is backed by the full faith and credit of the United States government. The private insurance you will receive from (insert name of insurer), however, is not guaranteed by the federal or any state or local government.

National Credit Union Administration § 708b.302

> **IF THIS CONVERSION IS APPROVED, AND THE (insert name of credit union) FAILS, THE FEDERAL GOVERNMENT DOES NOT GUARANTEE YOU WILL GET YOUR MONEY BACK.**

Also, because this conversion, if approved, would result in the loss of federal share insurance, the credit union will, at any time between the approval of the conversion and the effective date of conversion and upon request of the member, permit all members who have share certificates or other term accounts to close the federally-insured portion of those accounts without an early withdrawal penalty. (This is an optional sentence. It may be deleted without the approval of the Regional Director. The members must be informed about this right, however, as described in 12 CFR 708b.204(c).)

The board of directors has concluded that the proposed conversion is desirable for the following reasons: (Insert reasons). (This is an optional paragraph. It may be deleted without the approval of the Regional Director.).

The proposed conversion will result in the following one-time cost associated with the conversion: (List the total estimated dollar amount, including (1) the cost of conducting the vote, (2) the cost of changing the credit union's name and insurance logo, and (3) attorney and consultant fees.)

The conversion must have the approval of a majority of members who vote on the proposal, provided at least 20 percent of the total membership participates in the voting.

Enclosed with this Notice of Special Meeting is a ballot. If you cannot attend the meeting, please complete the ballot and return it to (insert name and address of independent entity conducting the vote) by no later than (insert time and date). To be counted, your ballot must reach us by that date and time.

By order of the board of directors.

(signature of Board Presiding Officer)

(insert title and date)

(c) Form ballot:

BALLOT FOR CONVERSION TO STATE CHARTER AND NONFEDERALLY-INSURED STATUS

(INSERT NAME OF CONVERTING CREDIT UNION)

Name of Member: (insert name)

Account Number: (insert account number)

The credit union must receive this ballot by (insert date and time for vote). Please mail or bring it to: (Insert name of independent entity and address).

I understand if the conversion of the (insert name of credit union) is approved, the National Credit Union Administration share (deposit) insurance I now have, up to $100,000, or possibly more if I use different accounts structures, will terminate upon the effective date of the conversion. Instead, my shares in the (insert name of credit union) will be insured up to $(insert dollar amount) by (insert name of insurer), a corporation chartered by the State of (insert name of state). The federal insurance provided by the National Credit Union Administration is backed by the full faith and credit of the United States Government. The private insurance provided by (insert name of insurer) is not.

> **I FURTHER UNDERSTAND THAT, IF THIS CONVERSION IS APPROVED AND THE (insert name of credit union) FAILS, THE FEDERAL GOVERNMENT DOES NOT GUARANTEE THAT I WILL GET MY MONEY BACK.**

I vote on the proposal as follows (check one box):

[ ] Approve the conversion of charter and conversion to private insurance and authorize the Board of Directors to take all necessary action to accomplish the conversion.

[ ] Do not approve the conversion of charter and the conversion to private insurance.

Signed: _____
(Insert printed member's name)

Date: _____

§ 708b.303

(d) Form certification to NCUA of member vote:

CERTIFICATION OF VOTE ON CONVERSION TO STATE CHARTER AND NONFEDERALLY-INSURED STATUS

We, the undersigned officers of the (insert name of converting credit union), certify the completion of the following actions:

1. At a meeting on (insert date), the Board of Directors adopted a resolution to seek the conversion of our credit union to a state charter and the conversion of our primary share insurance coverage from NCUA to (insert name of private insurer).

2. Not more than 30 nor less than 7 days before the date of the vote, copies of the notice of special meeting and ballot, as approved by the National Credit Union Administration, were mailed to our members.

3. The credit union arranged for the conduct of a special meeting of our members at the time and place announced in the Notice to consider and act upon the proposed conversion.

4. At the special meeting, the credit union arranged for an explanation of the conversion to the members present at the special meeting.

5. The (insert name), an entity independent of the credit union, conducted the membership vote at the special meeting. The members voted as follows:

(insert) Number of total members

(insert) Number of members present at the special meeting

(insert) Number of members present who voted in favor of the conversion

(insert) Number of members present who voted against the conversion

(insert) Number of additional written ballots in favor of the conversion

(insert) Number of additional written ballots opposed to the conversion

(insert "20% or more") OR (insert "Less than 20%") of the total membership voted. Of those who voted, a majority voted (inset "in favor of") OR ("against") conversion.

The action of the members at the special meeting was recorded in the minutes.

This certification signed the (insert date).

(signature of Board Presiding Officer)
(insert typed name and title)
(signature of Board Secretary)
(insert typed name and title)

I (insert name), an officer of the (insert name of independent entity that conducted the vote), hereby certify that the information recorded in paragraph 5 above is accurate.

This certification signed the (insert date):

(signature of officer of independent entity)

(typed name, title, and phone number)

[70 FR 3288, Jan. 24, 2005, as amended at 73 FR 30477, May 28, 2008; 75 FR 34621, June 18, 2010]

§ 708b.303 Conversion of insurance through merger.

Unless the Regional Director approves the use of different forms, a federally-insured credit union that is merging into a nonfederally-insured credit union must use the forms in this section.

(a) Form notice to members of intent to merge and convert and special meeting of members:

NOTICE OF SPECIAL MEETING ON PROPOSAL TO MERGE AND CONVERT TO NONFEDERALLY-INSURED STATUS

(INSERT NAME OF MERGING CREDIT UNION)

On (insert date), the Board of Directors of your credit union approved a proposition to merge with (insert name of continuing credit union) and to convert from federal share (deposit) insurance to private insurance. You are encouraged to attend a special meeting of our credit union at (insert address) on (insert time and date).

PURPOSE OF MEETING

The meeting has two purposes:

1. To consider and act upon a proposal to merge our credit union with (insert name of continuing credit union), the continuing credit union.

2. To approve the action of the Board of Directors of our credit union in authorizing the officers of the credit union, subject to member approval, to carry out the proposed merger.

If this merger is approved, our credit union will transfer all its assets and liabilities to the continuing credit union. As a member of our credit union, you will become a member of the continuing credit union. On the effective date of the merger, you will receive shares in the continuing credit union for the shares you own now in our credit union.

INSURANCE CONVERSION

Currently, your accounts have share insurance provided by the National Credit Union Administration, an agency of the federal government. The basic federal coverage is up to $100,000, but accounts may be structured in different ways, such as joint accounts, payable-on-death accounts, or IRA accounts, to achieve federal coverage of much more than $100,000. If the merger is approved, your federal insurance will terminate on the effective date of the merger. Instead, your accounts in the credit union will be insured up

National Credit Union Administration § 708b.303

to $(insert dollar amount) by (insert name of insurer), a corporation chartered by the State of (insert name of State). The federal insurance provided by the National Credit Union Administration is backed by the full faith and credit of the United States government. The private insurance you will receive from (insert name of insurer), however, is not guaranteed by the federal or any state or local government.

IF THIS MERGER IS APPROVED AND THE (insert name of continuing credit union) FAILS, THE FEDERAL GOVERNMENT DOES NOT GUARANTEE YOU WILL GET YOUR MONEY BACK.

Also, because this merger, if approved, would result in the loss of federal share insurance, the (insert name of merging credit union) will, at any time between the approval of the merger and the effective date of merger and upon request of the member, permit all members who have share certificates or other term accounts to close the federally-insured portion of those accounts without an early withdrawal penalty. (This is an optional sentence. It may be deleted without the approval of the Regional Director. The members must be informed about this right, however, as described in 12 CFR 708b.204(c).)

OTHER INFORMATION RELATED TO THE PROPOSED MERGER

The directors of the participating credit unions carefully analyzed the assets and liabilities of the participating credit unions and appraised each credit union's share values. The appraisal of the share values appears on the attached individual and consolidated financial statements of the participating credit unions.

The directors of the participating credit unions have concluded that the proposed merger is desirable for the following reasons: (insert reasons)

The Board of Directors of our credit union believes the merger should include/not include an adjustment in shares for the following reasons: (insert reasons)

The main office of the continuing credit union will be as follows: (insert location)

The branch office(s) of the continuing credit union will be as follows: (insert locations)

The merger must have the approval of a majority of members who vote on the proposal, provided at least 20 percent of the total membership participates in the voting.

Enclosed with this Notice of Special Meeting is a Ballot for Merger Proposal and Conversion to Nonfederally-insured Status. If you cannot attend the meeting, please complete the ballot and return it to (insert name of independent entity conducting vote) at (insert mailing address) by no later than (insert date and time). To be counted, your ballot must reach (insert name of independent entity conducting vote) by the date and time announced for the meeting.

By order of the board of directors.

(signature of Board Presiding Officer)
(insert name and title of Board Presiding Officer) (insert date)

(b) Form ballot:

BALLOT FOR MERGER PROPOSAL AND CONVERSION TO NONFEDERALLY-INSURED STATUS

Name of Member: (insert name)
Account Number: (insert account number)

The credit union must receive this ballot by (insert date and time for vote). Please mail or bring it to: (Insert name of independent entity and address)

I understand if the merger or conversion of the (insert name of merging credit union) into the (insert name of continuing credit union) is approved, the National Credit Union Administration share (deposit) insurance I now have, up to $100,000, or possibly more if I use different account structures, will terminate upon the effective date of the conversion. Instead, my shares in the (insert name of credit union) will be insured up to $(insert dollar amount) by (insert name of insurer), a corporation chartered by the State of (insert name of state). The federal insurance provided by the National Credit Union Administration is backed by the full faith and credit of the United States Government. The private insurance provided by (insert name of insurer) is not.

> I FURTHER UNDERSTAND THAT, IF THIS MERGER IS APPROVED AND THE (insert name of continuing credit union) FAILS, THE FEDERAL GOVERNMENT DOES NOT GUARANTEE THAT I WILL GET MY MONEY BACK.

I vote on the proposal as follows (check one box):

[ ] Approve the merger and the conversion to private insurance and authorize the Board of Directors to take all necessary action to accomplish the merger and conversion.

[ ] Do not approve the merger and the conversion to private insurance.

Signed: _____
(Insert printed member's name)

Date:

(c) Form certification of vote:

CERTIFICATION OF VOTE ON MERGER PROPOSAL AND CONVERSION TO NONFEDERALLY-INSURED STATUS OF THE (INSERT NAME OF MERGING CREDIT UNION)

We, the undersigned officers of the (insert name of merging credit union), certify the completion of the following actions:

1. At a meeting on (insert date), the Board of Directors adopted a resolution approving the merger of our credit union with (insert name of continuing credit union).

2. Not more than 30 nor less than 7 days before the date of the vote, copies of the notice of special meeting and the ballot, as approved by the National Credit Union Administration, and a copy of the merger plan announced in the notice, were mailed to our members.

3. The credit union arranged for the conduct of a special meeting of our members at the time and place announced in the Notice to consider and act upon the proposed merger.

4. At the special meeting, the credit union arranged for an explanation of the merger proposal and any changes in federally-insured status to the members present at the special meeting.

5. The (insert name), and entity independent of the credit union, conducted the membership vote at the special meeting. At least 20 percent of our total membership voted and a majority of voting members favor the merger as follows:

(insert) Number of total members

(insert) Number of members present at the special meeting

(insert) Number of members present who voted in favor of the merger

(insert) Number of members present who voted against the merger

(insert) Number of additional written ballots in favor of the merger

(insert) Number of additional written ballots opposed to the merger

6. The action of the members at the special meeting was recorded in the minutes.

This certification signed the (insert date):

(signature of Board Presiding Officer)
(insert typed name and title)
(signature of Board Secretary)
(insert typed name and title)

I (insert name), an officer of the (insert name of independent entity that conducted the vote), hereby certify that the information recorded in paragraph 5 above is accurate.

This certification signed the (insert date):

(signature of officer of independent entity)
(typed name, title, and phone number)

[70 FR 3288, Jan. 24, 2005, as amended at 73 FR 30477, May 28, 2008]

PART 709—INVOLUNTARY LIQUIDATION OF FEDERAL CREDIT UNIONS AND ADJUDICATION OF CREDITOR CLAIMS INVOLVING FEDERALLY INSURED CREDIT UNIONS IN LIQUIDATION

Sec.
709.0 Scope.
709.1 Definitions.
709.2 NCUA Board as liquidating agent.
709.3 Challenge to revocation of charter and involuntary liquidation.
709.4 Powers and duties of liquidating agent.
709.5 Payout priorities in involuntary liquidation.
709.6 Initial determination of creditor claims by the liquidating agent.
709.7 Procedures for appeal of initial determination.
709.8 Administrative appeal of the initial determination.
709.9 Expedited determination of creditor claims.
709.10 Treatment by conservator or liquidating agent of financial assets transferred in connection with a securitization or participation.

National Credit Union Administration § 709.3

709.11 Treatment by conservator or liquidating agent of collateralized public funds.
709.12 Prepayment fees to Federal Home Loan Bank.
709.13 Treatment of swap agreements in liquidation or conservatorship.

AUTHORITY: 12 U.S.C. 1757, 1766, 1767, 1786(h), 1787, 1788, 1789, 1789a.

SOURCE: 56 FR 56925, Nov. 7, 1991, unless otherwise noted.

§ 709.0 Scope.

The rules and procedures in this part apply to charter revocations of federal credit unions under 12 U.S.C. 1787(a)(1)(A), (B), the involuntary liquidation and adjudication of creditor claims in all cases involving federally-insured credit unions, the treatment by the Board as conservator or liquidating agent of financial assets transferred in connection with a securitization or participation or of public funds held by a federally-insured credit union, and the allowance of prepayment fees to Federal Home Loan Banks under specified conditions. Remaining sections of this part are applicable to all federally insured credit unions. This part does not apply to share insurance claims arising out of the liquidation of a federally insured credit union. Insurance claims are decided pursuant to part 745 of this chapter.

[56 FR 56925, Nov. 7, 1991, as amended at 65 FR 55442, Sept. 14, 2000; 66 FR 11230, Feb. 23, 2001; 66 FR 40575, Aug. 3, 2001]

§ 709.1 Definitions.

For the purposes of this part, the following definitions apply:

(a) *General Counsel* means the General Counsel of the National Credit Union Administration or any attorney assigned to the General Counsel's staff.

(b) *Liquidating Agent* means the NCUA Board or person(s) appointed by it with delegated authority to carry out the liquidation of the credit union.

(c) *Insolvent* means insolvent as that term is defined in § 700.1(e)(1) of this chapter.

(d) *Claim* means a creditor's claim against the credit union in liquidation. This term does not include insurance claims arising out of the liquidation of a federally insured credit union. Insurance claims are decided pursuant to part 745 of this chapter.

(e) *Shareholder* means members, nonmembers, accountholders or any other party or entity that is the owner of a share, share certificate or share draft account or the equivalent of such accounts under state law.

[56 FR 56925, Nov. 7, 1991, as amended at 69 FR 27828, May 17, 2004]

§ 709.2 NCUA Board as liquidating agent.

(a) The Board, as liquidating agent, by operation of law and without any conveyance or other instrument, act or deed, shall succeed to all the rights, titles, powers, and privileges of the credit union, and of its shareholders, officers, and directors, with respect to the credit union and its assets, and such shareholders, officers, or directors, shall not thereafter have or exercise any such rights, powers, or privileges or act in connection with any assets or property of any nature of the credit union.

(b) The Board, as liquidating agent, shall take possession of and title to books, records, and assets of every description of such credit union to which such credit union has rights of possession and title to all offices and other facilities of such credit union.

§ 709.3 Challenge to revocation of charter and involuntary liquidation.

If a Federal credit union is determined to be insolvent and placed into liquidation pursuant to 12 U.S.C. 1787, the Federal credit union may, not later than 10 days after the date on which the Board closes the credit union for liquidation, apply to the United States District Court for the Judicial district in which the principal office of the credit union is located or the United States District Court for the District of Columbia for an order requiring the Board to show cause why it should not be prohibited from continuing such liquidation. Notwithstanding other provisions of this part, the board of directors of the credit union may meet following the placing of the institution into liquidation for the sole purpose of considering and authorizing the filing of this action in the name of the credit

§ 709.4

union. No such action in the name of the credit union may be instituted without the authorization of the board of directors of the institution pursuant to a valid board of directors resolution. No credit union funds shall be available to pay expenses incurred in bringing a legal action to challenge the Board's liquidation action.

§ 709.4 Powers and duties of liquidating agent.

(a) *Inventory of assets.* As soon as practicable after taking possession, the liquidating agent shall inventory the assets of such credit union as of the date of taking possession, showing the value as carried on the books of the credit union, and the security therefore, if any, a brief description of the assets and any security, and a record of the credit union's creditor and accounts liabilities.

(b) *Notice to creditors.* The liquidating agent shall promptly publish a notice to the credit union's creditors to present their claims, together with proof, to the liquidating agent by a date specified in the notice. This date shall be not less than 90 days after the publication of the notice. The liquidating agent shall republish such notice approximately one and two months, respectively, after the initial publication. At the time of initial publication, the liquidating agent shall mail a notice similar to the published notice to any creditor shown on the credit union's books at the last address appearing therein. If the liquidating agent discovers the name of a creditor whose name does not appear on the credit union's books, a notice similar to the published notice shall be mailed to such creditor within 30 days after the discovery of the name and address.

(c) *General.* The liquidating agent shall collect all obligations and money due such credit union and may, to the extent consistent with its appointment, do all things desirable or expedient in its discretion to wind up the affairs of the credit union including, but not limited to, the following:

(1) Exercise all rights and powers of the credit union including, but not limited to, any rights and powers under any mortgage, deed of trust, chose in action, option, collateral note, con-

12 CFR Ch. VII (1-1-12 Edition)

tract, judgment or decree, or instrument of any nature;

(2) Institute, prosecute, maintain, defend, intervene, and otherwise participate in any and all actions, suits, or other legal proceedings by and against the liquidating agent or the credit union or in which the liquidating agent, the credit union, or its creditors or shareholders, or any of them, shall have an interest, and in every way to represent the credit union, its shareholders and creditors, subject to the direction of General Counsel;

(3) Employ on a salary or fee basis such persons as in the judgment of the liquidating agent are necessary or desirable to carry out its responsibilities and functions, including, but not limited to, appraisers and Certified Public Accountants, and pay the costs out of the assets of the liquidated credit union;

(4) Employ or retain any attorney or attorneys designated by, or acceptable to, the General Counsel in connection with litigation or for legal advice and assistance, for the liquidation generally or in particular instances, and pay compensation and retainers of such attorney or attorneys, together with all expenses, including, but not limited to, the costs and expenses of any litigation, as approved by the General Counsel, out of the assets of the liquidated credit union;

(5) Execute, acknowledge, and deliver any and all deeds, contracts, leases, assignments, bills of sale, releases, extensions, satisfactions, and other instruments necessary or proper for any purposes, including, but not limited to, the effectuation, termination, or transfer of real, personal or mixed property, or that shall be necessary or proper to liquidate the credit union, and any deed or other instrument executed pursuant to the authority hereby given shall be as valid and effective for all purposes as if the same had been executed as the act and deed of the credit union;

(6) With concurrence of General Counsel, disaffirm or repudiate any contract or lease to which the credit union is a party, the performance of which the liquidating agent, in his sole

National Credit Union Administration §709.5

discretion, determines to be burdensome, and which disaffirmance or repudiation in the liquidating agent's sole discretion will promote the orderly administration of the credit union's affairs;

(7) Deposit, withdraw, or transfer funds, and otherwise exercise complete control over all investment or depository accounts maintained by or for the credit union at financial dispository or similar institutions;

(8) Do such things, and have such rights, powers, privileges, immunities, and duties, whether or not otherwise granted in this part 709, as shall be authorized, directed, conferred, or imposed from time to time by the Board, or as shall be conferred by the Federal Credit Union Act;

(9) Exercise such other authority as is conferred by the Federal Credit Union Act; and

(10) Where acting as liquidating agent for a state-chartered federally insured credit union, exercise all the rights, powers, and privileges granted by state law to such a liquidating agent.

(d) *Expenditure of funds of the liquidation.* The liquidating agent shall have power to:

(1) Pay all costs and expenses of the liquidation as determined by the liquidating agent;

(2) Pay off and discharge taxes and liens;

(3) Pay out and expend such sums as are deemed necessary or advisable for or in connection with the preservation, maintenance, conservation, protection, remodeling, repair, rehabilitation, or improvement of any asset or property of any nature of the credit union or the liquidating agent;

(4) Pay off and discharge any assessments, liens, claims, or charges of any kind against any asset or property of any nature on which the credit union or the liquidating agent has a lien by way of mortgage, deed of trust, pledge, or otherwise, or in which the credit union or liquidating agent has any interest;

(5) Settle, compromise, or obtain the release of, for cash or other consideration, claims and demands against the credit union or the liquidating agent; and

(6) Indemnify its employees and agents from the assets of the credit union against liabilities incurred in the good faith performance of their duties.

(e) *Assets, claims, and contracts.* The liquidating agent shall have power to:

(1) Sell for cash or on terms, exchange, assign, or otherwise dispose of, in whole or in part, any or all of the assets and property of the credit union, real, personal and mixed, tangible and intangible, of any nature, including any mortgage, deed of trust, chose in action, bond, note, contract, judgment, or decree, share or certificate of share of stock or debt, owing to the credit union or the liquidating agent; and

(2) Surrender, abandon, and release any chose in action, or other assets or property of any nature, whether the subject of pending litigation or not, and settle, compromise, modify, or release, for cash or other consideration, claims and demands in favor of the credit union or the liquidating agent.

[56 FR 56925, Nov. 7, 1991, as amended at 75 FR 34621, June 18, 2010]

§709.5 Payout priorities in involuntary liquidation.

(a) Claimants whose claims are secured shall receive their security. To the extent their respective claims exceed the value of the security for those claims, as determined to the satisfaction of the liquidating agent, they shall each have an unsecured claim against the credit union having priority as provided in paragraph (b) of this section.

(b) Unsecured claims against the liquidation estate that are proved to the satisfaction of the liquidating agent shall have priority in the following order:

(1) Administrative costs and expenses of liquidation;

(2) Claims for wages and salaries, including vacation, severance, and sick leave pay;

(3) Taxes legally due and owing to the United States or any state or subdivision thereof;

(4) Debts due and owing the United States, including the National Credit Union Administration;

§ 709.6

(5) General creditors, and secured creditors (to the extent that their respective claims exceed the value of the security for those claims);

(6) Shareholders to the extent of their respective uninsured shares and the National Credit Union Share Insurance Fund to the extent of its payment of share insurance;

(7) in a case involving liquidation of a corporate credit union, holders of then-outstanding membership capital accounts and nonperpetual capital accounts or instruments to the extent not depleted in a calendar year prior to the date of liquidation and also subject to the capital priority option described in Appendix A of part 704 of this chapter;

(8) In a case involving liquidation of a low-income designated credit union, any outstanding secondary capital accounts issued pursuant to the authority of §§ 701.34 or 741.204(c) of this chapter; and

(9) in a case involving liquidation of a corporate credit union, holders of then-outstanding paid in capital or perpetual contributed capital instruments to the extent not depleted in a calendar year prior to the date of liquidation and also subject to the capital priority option described in Appendix A of Part 704 of this chapter;

(c) Priorities are to be based on the circumstances that exist on the date of liquidation.

(d) If the repudiation or disaffirmance of any contract or lease gives rise to a claim for damages, such claim shall be considered a general creditor claim under paragraph (b)(5) of this section and not a cost or expense of liquidation under paragraph (b)(1) of this section.

(e) All unsecured claims of any category or class or priority described in paragraphs (b)(1) through (b)(7) of this section shall be paid in full, or provisions made for such payment, before any claims of lesser priority are paid. If there are insufficient funds to pay all claims of a category or class, payment shall be made pro rata. Notwithstanding anything to the contrary herein, the liquidating agent may, at any time, and from time to time, prior to the payment in full of all claims of a category or class with higher priority, make such distributions to claimants in priority categories described in paragraphs (b)(1), (b)(2), (b)(3), (b)(4), and (b)(5) of this section as the liquidating agent believes are reasonably necessary to conduct the liquidation, provided that the liquidating agent determines that adequate funds exist or will be recovered during the liquidation to pay in full all claims of any higher priority. If a surplus remains after making distribution in full on all allowed claims described in paragraphs (b)(1) through (b)(9) of this section, such surplus shall be distributed pro rata to the credit union's shareholders.

[56 FR 56825, Nov. 7, 1991, as amended at 61 FR 3791, Feb. 2, 1996; 62 FR 12949, Mar. 19, 1997; 64 FR 57365, Oct. 25, 1999; 75 FR 64859, Oct. 20, 2010]

§ 709.6 Initial determination of creditor claims by the liquidating agent.

(a)(1) Any party wishing to submit a claim against the liquidated credit union must submit a written proof of claim in accordance with the requirements set forth in the notice to creditors. A failure to submit a written claim within the time provided in the notice to creditors shall be deemed a waiver of said claim and claimant shall have no further rights or remedies with respect to such claim.

(2) Notwithstanding paragraph (a)(1) of this section, the liquidating agent may, at his discretion, consider an untimely claim provide the following two criteria are present:

(i) The claimant did not receive notice of the appointment of the liquidating agent in time to file a claim before the date provided for in the notice; and

(ii) The claim is filed in time to permit payment of the claim.

(b) The liquidating agent may require submission of supplemental evidence by the claimant and by interested parties in the event of a dispute concerning a claim against any asset of the liquidated credit union. In requiring the submission of supplemental evidence, the liquidating agent may set such limitations of time, scope, and size as the liquidating agent deems reasonable in the circumstances, and may refuse to include in the record submissions or portions of submissions not in compliance with such limitations or requirements. The liquidating agent shall compile such written record of a claim or dispute as, in its discretion, is deemed sufficient to provide a reasonable basis for allowing or disallowing a claim or resolving a dispute. This written record shall be considered the administrative record.

(c) The liquidating agent shall determine whether to allow or disallow a claim and shall notify the claimant within 180 days from the date a claim against a credit union is filed pursuant to paragraph (a)(1) of the section. This 180-day period may be extended by written agreement between the claimant and the liquidating agent. Failure by the liquidating agent to determine a claim and notify the claimant within the 180-day period or, if the period is extended, within the extended period, shall be deemed a denial of the claim.

(d) If a claim or any portion thereof is disallowed, the notice to the claimant shall contain a statement of the reasons for the disallowance and an explanation of appeal rights pursuant to §709.7 of this part.

(e) Notice of any determination with respect to a claim shall be sufficient if mailed to the most recent address of the claimant which appears:

(1) On the credit union's books;
(2) In the claim filed by the claimant; or
(3) In the documents submitted in the proof of claim.

(f) In the event the liquidating agent disallows all or part of a claim, the liquidating agent shall file with the Board, or its designated agent, a report of its determination. This report shall become part of the record and shall include the notice to the claimant and findings on all issues raised and decided by the liquidating agent.

§709.7 Procedures for appeal of initial determination.

In order to appeal all or part of an initial decision which disallows a claim, in whole or in part, a claimant must, within 60 days of the mailing of the initial determination, file an administrative appeal pursuant to §709.8 of this part, or file suit against the liquidated credit union in the United States District Court for the District of Columbia or in the United States district court having jurisdiction over the place where the credit union's principal place of business is located, or continue an action commenced before the appointment of the liquidating agent. If the claimant does not appeal or file or continue a suit, any disallowance shall be final and the claimant shall have no further rights or remedies with respect to such claim.

§709.8 Administrative appeal of the initial determination.

(a) *General.* A claimant requesting an administrative appeal may request review pursuant to any of the procedures listed in paragraph (b) or (c) of this section. Any appeal of the initial determination must be in writing and must specify what type of appeal the claimant requests. The determination of whether to agree to a request for administrative appeal shall rest solely with the Board, which shall notify the claimant of its decision in writing. The 60 day period for filing a lawsuit in United States district court, provided for in §709.7 of this part, shall be tolled from the date of claimant's request for an administrative appeal to the date of the Board's decision regarding that request.

(b) *Hearing on the record.* Except as provided herein, any hearing requested pursuant to this section shall be conducted in accordance with the provisions of subpart A, part 747, of this chapter. The Board shall render a final decision with respect to such claim after consideration of the hearing record and recommended decision. The Board's determination shall be subject to judicial review under chapter 7 of title 5, United States Code. Any claimant seeking judicial review of the Board's final decision under this paragraph must file a petition in the court of appeals for the circuit in which the principal office of the credit union is located, or in the United States Court of Appeals for the District of Columbia Circuit, within 30 days of the date of the Board's final decision. If a claimant does not file a petition before the end of the 30-day period, the Board's

§ 709.8

decision shall be final, and the claimant shall have no further rights or remedies with respect to such claim.

(1) *Burden of proof.* In any hearing on the record, the burden of proof to establish entitlement to any modification of the initial determination shall rest solely upon the claimant.

(2) *Order of procedure.* In any hearing on the record, at the time for opening arguments, counsel for the claimant shall argue first, and at the time for closing arguments, counsel for the claimant shall argue last.

(c) *Alternative dispute resolution.* Paragraphs (c) (1) and (2) of this section list alternatives for dispute resolution which may be available at the discretion of the Board. From time to time, the NCUA Board may authorize additional alternative dispute resolution processes.

(1) *Appeal to the Board.* Pursuant to this paragraph (c)(1), the claimant may file an appeal with the NCUA Board within the time provided for in § 709.7. The appeal must be in writing and filed with the Secretary of the Board, National Credit Union Administration, 1775 Duke Street, Alexandria, VA 22314–3428. There shall be no personal appearance before the Board in connection with an appeal under this paragraph (c)(1).

(i) *Content of appeal.* Any appeal must include:

(A) A statement of the facts on which the appeal is based;

(B) A statement of the basis for the initial determination to which the claimant objects and the alleged error in such determination, including citations to applicable statutes and regulations;

(C) Any other evidence relied upon by the claimant which was not previously provided to the liquidating agent.

(ii) *Procedures for review of the appeal.* (A) Within 60 days of the date of the Board's receipt of an appeal, pursuant to paragraph (c)(1) of this section, the Board may request in writing that the claimant submit supplemental evidence in support of its appeal. If additional evidence is requested, the claimant shall have 45 days from the date of issuance of such request to provide such additional information. Failure by the claimant to provide such additional information may, as determined solely by the Board, result in denial of the claimant's appeal.

(B) Within 60 days from the date of the Board's receipt of an appeal, pursuant to paragraph (c)(1) of this section, the claimant may amend or supplement the appeal in writing. In the event the claimant does amend or supplement the appeal, the provisions of paragraph (c)(1)(ii)(A) of this section, with respect to requests for additional information and responses to such requests, shall apply with equal force to any such amendment or supplement to an appeal.

(iii) *Determination on appeal.* (A) Within 180 days from the date of receipt of an appeal by the Board, the Board shall issue a decision allowing or disallowing claimant's appeal.

(B) The decision by the Board on appeal shall be provided to the claimant in writing, stating the reasons for the decision, and shall constitute a final agency decision regarding the claimant's claim.

(C) Failure by the Board to issue a decision on appeal of the claimant's claim within the 180-day period provided for under paragraph (c)(1)(iii)(A) of this section shall be deemed to be a denial of such appeal for the purposes of paragraph (c)(1)(iv) of this section.

(iv) *Judicial review.* (A) For the purposes of seeking judicial review of actions taken pursuant to paragraph (c)(1) of this section, only a determination on appeal issued by the NCUA Board pursuant to this section shall constitute a final determination regarding a claim.

(B) A final determination by the Board is reviewable in accordance with the provisions of chapter 7, title 5, United States Code, by the United States Court of Appeals for the District of Columbia or the court of appeals for the Federal judicial circuit where the credit union's principal place of business is located. Any request for judicial review under this paragraph must be filed within 60 days of the date of the Board's final decision. If any claimant fails to file before the end of the 60-day period, the Board's decision shall be final, and the claimant shall have no further rights or remedies with respect to such claim.

National Credit Union Administration § 709.9

(2) The following additional procedures for dispute resolution may be made available at the sole discretion of the Board: mediation; nonbinding arbitration; and neutral fact finding.

[56 FR 56925, Nov. 7, 1991, as amended at 59 FR 36041, July 15, 1994]

§ 709.9 Expedited determination of creditor claims.

(a) *General.* The provisions of this section establish procedures under which claimants may request expedited relief in lieu of the procedures set forth in § 709.6 of this part. A claimant shall be entitled to expedited determination of a claim only upon a showing that there exists a legally valid and enforceable or perfected security interest in assets of the liquidated credit union and that irreparable injury will occur if the routine claims procedure is followed.

(b) *Filing of request for expedited relief.* All requests for expedited relief must be filed within 30 days from the date of mailing, by the liquidating agent, of the notice to the creditor concerned. The request shall be deemed to be filed when received by the Secretary of the Board, National Credit Union Administration, 1775 Duke Street, Alexandria, VA 22314–3428. A copy of the request must be simultaneously served upon the liquidating agent for the credit union concerned. There shall be no right of personal appearance before the Board in connection with any claim submitted under this paragraph.

(c) *Content of request for expedited relief.* Any Request for Expedited Relief must contain the following:

(1) A clear and concise statement of the facts and issues on which the request is based;

(2) A clear and concise statement describing the nature of any security interests in any assets of the credit union;

(3) A clear and concise statement of the probable, imminent and irreparable harm likely to occur if expedited relief is not granted;

(4) An assessment of the likelihood of success on the merits of the underlying claim, including statutory citations and relevant documentation supporting the merits of the claim;

(5) Any other relevant documentation that supports the request;

(6) Citations to applicable statutes, regulations, or other legal authority; and

(7) A signed statement certifying that a copy of the request has been mailed or hand delivered to the liquidating agent on or before the day that the request was filed with the Board.

(d) *Burden of proof.* The burden of proving entitlement to expedited relief rests at all times with the requester.

(e) *Additional information.* The Board may order the filing of additional information and or documentation in order to make its determination. Such filing shall be on a date certain, and failure to provide the additional documentation or information may constitute the sole grounds for denial of the request.

(f) *Decision.* Before the end of the 90-day period beginning on the date a request filed, the Board shall render its decision and provide it to the requester. The Board will determine whether to grant expedited review and allow or disallow the claim or whether such claim should be resolved pursuant to the claims process described in § 709.6 of this part.

(1) *Expedited review denied.* A decision by the Board that expedited review is not appropriate shall be final and the claim shall be decided pursuant to the claims adjudication process set forth in § 709.6 of this part.

(2) *Expedited review granted.* If expedited review is granted, the Board shall decide the claim. If the claim is disallowed, in whole or part, the decision shall contain a statement of each reason for the disallowance and the procedure for obtaining judicial review.

(g) *Period for filing or renewing suit.* Any claimant who files a request for expedited relief shall be permitted to file a suit, or to continue a suit filed before the appointment of the liquidating agent, seeking a determination of the claimant's rights with respect to its security interest after the earlier of:

(1) The end of the 90-day period beginning on the date of the filing of a request for expedited relief; or

(2) The date the Board denies all or part of the claim.

§ 709.10

(h) *Statute of limitations.* If an action described in paragraph (g) of this section is not filed, or the motion to renew a previously filed suit is not made, before the end of the 30-day period beginning on the date on which such action or motion may be filed in accordance with paragraph (g) of this section, the claim shall be deemed to be disallowed as of the end of such period (other than any portion of such claim that was allowed by the Board). Such disallowance shall be final and the claimant shall have no further rights or remedies with respect to such claim.

[56 FR 56925, Nov. 7, 1991, as amended at 59 FR 36041, July 15, 1994; 75 FR 34621, June 18, 2010]

§ 709.10 **Treatment by conservator or liquidating agent of financial assets transferred in connection with a securitization or participation.**

(a) *Definitions.* (1) *Beneficial interest* means debt or equity (or mixed) interests or obligations of any type issued by a special purpose entity that entitle their holders to receive payments that depend primarily on the cash flow from financial assets owned by the special purpose entity.

(2) *Financial asset* means cash or a contract or instrument that conveys to one entity a contractual right to receive cash or another financial instrument from another entity.

(3) *Legal isolation* means that transferred financial assets have been put presumptively beyond the reach of the transferor, its creditors, a trustee in bankruptcy, or a receiver, either by a single transaction or a series of transactions taken as a whole.

(4) *Participation* means the transfer or assignment of an undivided interest in all or part of a loan or a lease from a seller, known as the "lead," to a buyer, known as the "participant," without recourse to the lead, under an agreement between the lead and the participant. *Without recourse* means that the participation is not subject to any agreement that requires the lead to repurchase the participant's interest or to otherwise compensate the participant due to a default on the underlying obligation.

(5) *Securitization* means the issuance by a special purpose entity of beneficial interests:

(i) The most senior class of which at time of issuance is rated in one of the four highest categories assigned to long-term debt or in an equivalent short-term category (within either of which there may be sub-categories or gradations indicating relative standing) by one or more nationally recognized statistical rating organizations; or

(ii) Which are sold in transactions by an issuer not involving any public offering for purposes of section 4 of the Securities Act of 1933, as amended, or in transactions exempt from registration under such Act under 17 CFR 230.91 through 230.905 (Regulation S) thereunder (or any successor regulation).

(6) *Special purpose entity* means a trust, corporation, or other entity demonstrably distinct from the federally-insured credit union that is primarily engaged in acquiring and holding (or transferring to another special purpose entity) financial assets, and in activities related or incidental thereto, in connection with the issuance by such special purpose entity (or by another special purpose entity that acquires financial assets directly or indirectly from such special purpose entity) of beneficial interests.

(b) The Board, by exercise of its authority to disaffirm or repudiate contracts under 12 U.S.C. 1787(c), will not reclaim, recover, or recharacterize as property of the credit union or the liquidation estate any financial assets transferred to another party by a federally-insured credit union in connection with a securitization or participation, provided that a transfer meets all conditions for sale accounting treatment under generally accepted accounting principles, other than the "legal isolation" condition addressed by this section.

(c) Paragraph (b) of this section will not apply unless the federally-insured credit union received adequate consideration for the transfer of financial assets at the time of the transfer, and the documentation effecting the transfer of financial assets reflects the intent of the parties to treat the transaction as a sale, and not as a secured borrowing, for accounting purposes.

(d) Paragraph (b) of this section will not be construed as waiving, limiting, or otherwise affecting the power of the Board, as conservator or liquidating agent, to disaffirm or repudiate any agreement imposing continuing obligations or duties upon the federally-insured credit union in conservatorship or the liquidation estate.

(e) Paragraph (b) of this section will not be construed as waiving, limiting or otherwise affecting the rights or powers of the Board to take any action or to exercise any power not specifically limited by this section, including, but not limited to, any rights, powers or remedies of the Board regarding transfers taken in contemplation of the credit union's insolvency or with the intent to hinder, delay, or defraud the credit union or the creditors of such credit union, or that is a fraudulent transfer under applicable law.

(f) The Board will not seek to avoid an otherwise legally enforceable securitization agreement or participation agreement executed by a federally-insured credit union solely because such agreement does not meet the "contemporaneous" requirement of sections 207(b)(9) and 208(a)(3) of the Federal Credit Union Act.

(g) This section may be repealed by the NCUA upon 30 days notice and opportunity for comment provided in the FEDERAL REGISTER, but any such repeal or amendment will not apply to any transfers of financial assets made in connection with a securitization or participation that was in effect before such repeal or modification. For purposes of this paragraph, a securitization would be in effect on the earliest date that the most senior level of beneficial interests is issued, and a participation would be in effect on the date that the parties executed the participation agreement.

[65 FR 55442, Sept. 14, 2000]

§ 709.11 Treatment by conservator or liquidating agent of collateralized public funds.

An agreement to provide for the lawful collateralization of funds of a federal, state, or local governmental entity or of any depositor or member referred to in section 207(k)(2)(A) of the Act will not be deemed to be invalid under sections 207(b)(9) and 208(a)(3) of the Act solely because such agreement was not executed contemporaneously with the acquisition of collateral or with any changes, increases, or substitutions in the collateral made in accordance with such agreement, provided the following conditions are met:

(a) The agreement was undertaken in the ordinary course of business, not in contemplation of insolvency, and with no intent to hinder, delay or defraud the credit union or its creditors;

(b) The secured obligation represents a bona fide and arm's length transaction;

(c) The secured party or parties are not insiders or affiliates of the credit union;

(d) The grant or creation of the security interest was for adequate consideration; and,

(e) The security agreement evidencing the security interest is in writing, was approved by the credit union's board of directors, and has been continuously an official record of the credit union from the time of its execution.

[65 FR 55443, Sept. 14, 2000]

§ 709.12 Prepayment fees to Federal Home Loan Bank.

The Board as conservator or liquidating agent of a federally-insured credit union in receipt of any extension of credit from a Federal Home Loan Bank will allow a claim for a prepayment fee by the Bank if:

(a) The claim is made pursuant to a written contract that provides for a prepayment fee but the prepayment fee allowed by the Board will not exceed the present value of the loss attributable to the difference between the contract rate of the secured borrowing and the reinvestment rate then available to the Bank; and

(b) The indebtedness owed to the Bank is secured by sufficient collateral in which a perfected security interest in favor of the Bank exists or as to which the Bank's security interest is entitled to priority under section 306(d) of the Competitive Equality Banking

Act of 1987, 12 U.S.C. 1430(e), or otherwise so that the aggregate of the outstanding principal on the advances secured by the collateral, the accrued but unpaid interest on the outstanding principal and the prepayment fee applicable to the advances can be paid in full from the amounts realized from the collateral. For purposes of this paragraph, the adequacy of the collateral will be determined as of the date the prepayment fees are due and payable under the terms of the written contract.

[66 FR 40575, Aug. 3, 2001]

§ 709.13 Treatment of swap agreements in liquidation or conservatorship.

The Board has determined that a swap agreement, as defined in the Federal Deposit Insurance Act at 12 U.S.C. 1821(e)(8)(D)(vi), is a qualified financial contract for purposes of the special treatment for qualified financial contracts provided in 12 U.S.C. 1787(c). Any master agreement for any swap agreement, together with all supplements to such master agreement, will be treated as one swap agreement.

[68 FR 32356, May 30, 2003]

PART 710—VOLUNTARY LIQUIDATION

Sec.
710.0 Scope.
710.1 Definitions.
710.2 Responsibility for conducting voluntary liquidation.
710.3 Approval of the liquidation proposal by members.
710.4 Transaction of business during liquidation.
710.5 Notice of liquidation to creditors.
710.6 Distribution of assets.
710.7 Retention of records.
710.8 Certificate of dissolution and liquidation.
710.9 Federally insured state credit unions.

AUTHORITY: 12 U.S.C. 1766(a), 1786, and 1787.

SOURCE: 58 FR 35365, July 1, 1993, unless otherwise noted.

§ 710.0 Scope.

This part describes the requirements that must be followed to accomplish the voluntary liquidation of a Federal credit union. Federally insured state credit unions are only subject to the notification requirement provided in § 710.9; voluntary liquidation is to be accomplished in accordance with state law or procedures established by the state regulatory authority.

§ 710.1 Definitions.

For the purpose of this part, the following definitions apply:

(a) *Voluntary liquidation* means the dissolution of a solvent Federal credit union with the assets being sold or collected, liabilities paid, and shares distributed under the direction of the board of directors or its duly appointed liquidating agent.

(b) *Liquidation date* means the date the members vote to approve liquidation.

(c) *Liquidating agent* means the person or persons, including any legally recognized entity, appointed by the board of directors to liquidate the Federal credit union.

§ 710.2 Responsibility for conducting voluntary liquidation.

(a) The board of directors shall be responsible for conserving the assets, for expediting the liquidation, and for equitable distribution of the assets to the members.

(b) After voting to present the question of liquidation to the members, the board of directors may appoint a liquidating agent and delegate all or part of the board's responsibility to such agent and authorize reasonable compensation for the services provided.

(c) The board of directors shall determine that the liquidating agent and all persons who handle or have access to funds of the Federal credit union are adequately covered by surety bond and that either such coverage remains in effect, or the discovery period is extended, for at least four months after final distribution of assets.

(d) Within three days after the decision of the board of directors to submit the question of liquidation to the members, the Regional Director will be notified in writing, setting forth in detail the reasons for the proposed action. A balance sheet and income statement as of the previous month-end will be included with the notification. During the liquidation process, financial statements will be submitted to the Regional Director as requested.

(e) Promptly after the decision to present the question of liquidation to the members, the board of directors or liquidating agency shall develop a written plan for the liquidation of the assets and payment of shares (liquidation plan). The plan should provide for the liquidation of assets and payment of creditors and shareholders within one year of the liquidation date. If the liquidation period is projected to exceed one year, an explanation must be provided in the liquidation plan. A copy of the liquidation plan will be mailed to the Regional Director within 30 days of the date the board of directors votes to present the question of liquidation to the members.

§ 710.3 Approval of the liquidation proposal by members.

(a) When the board of directors decides to present the question of liquidation to the members, it shall act promptly to obtain the members' approval. The members shall be given advance notice of the membership meeting at which the liquidation proposal is to be submitted. The notice shall:

(1) Inform members that they have the right to vote on the liquidation proposal in person at the membership meeting called for that purpose or by written ballot to be received no later than the time and date indicated on the notice.

(2) Include or be accompanied by a ballot for the liquidation proposal.

(b) The liquidation proposal must be approved by the affirmative vote of a majority of the Federal credit union members who vote on the proposal.

(c) If the members do not approve the liquidation, the board of directors, or if delegated the authority, the liquidating agent, must decide within seven days whether the Federal credit union should resume operations or, if good cause exists, to resubmit the question of liquidation to the members.

(d) If the members approve the liquidation, neither the members nor the board of directors may rescind the decision to liquidate unless the Regional Director concurs in the recision.

(e) The Regional Director will be notified in writing of the results of the membership vote on the voluntary liquidation proposal within three days of the date of the vote.

[58 FR 35365, July 1, 1993, as amended at 72 FR 30246, May 31, 2007]

§ 710.4 Transaction of business during liquidation.

(a) Immediately upon decision by the board of directors to present the question of liquidation to the members, payments on shares, withdrawal of shares (except for transfer of shares to loans and interest), transfer of shares to another share account, granting of loans, and making of investments other than short-term investments shall be suspended pending action by the members on the proposal to liquidate. Collection of loans and interest, payment of necessary expenses, clearing of share drafts and credit card charges will continue.

(b) Upon approval of the members, payments on shares, withdrawal of shares (except for transfer of shares to loans and interest), transfer of shares to another share account, granting of loans, and making of investments other than short-term investments shall be discontinued permanently. Collection of loans and interest and payment of necessary expenses will continue during the period of liquidation. Members will be notified to discontinue the use of share drafts and credit cards, and items will not be cleared 15 days from the liquidation date.

(c) Approval of the Regional Director must be obtained prior to consummating any sale of assets which would not provide sufficient funds to pay shareholders at par.

§ 710.5 Notice of liquidation to creditors.

(a) When approval for liquidation is obtained from the members, the board of directors or the liquidating agent shall cause notice to be given to creditors to present their claims.

(1) Federal credit unions with assets in excess of $5 million as of the month end prior to the liquidation date shall publish the notice once a week in each

§ 710.6

of three successive weeks, in a newspaper of general circulation, in each county in which the Federal credit union maintains an office or branch for the transaction of business on the liquidation date. The first notice shall be published within seven days of the liquidation date.

(2) Federal credit unions with assets in excess of $500,000 but less than $5 million as of the month end prior to the liquidation date shall publish the notice once, in a newspaper of general circulation, in each county in which the Federal credit union maintains an office or branch for the transaction of business on the liquidation date. The notice shall be published within seven days of the liquidation date.

(3) Federal credit unions with assets less than $500,000 as of the month end prior to the liquidation date shall not be required to publish the notice.

(b) Within 10 days of the liquidation date, a copy of the notice of liquidation shall be mailed to all creditors reflected on the records of the Federal credit union.

(c) Creditors shall be provided 30 days from the liquidation date to submit their claims.

§ 710.6 Distribution of assets.

(a) With the approval of the regional director, a partial pro rata distribution of the Federal credit union's assets may be made to its members from cash funds available on authorization by the board of directors or liquidating agent. Payment of a partial distribution may exclude member accounts of less than $25.00.

(b) After all assets of the Federal credit union have been converted to cash or found to be worthless and all loans and debts owing to it have been collected or found to be uncollectible and all obligations of the Federal credit union have been paid, with the exception of shares due its members, the books shall be closed and the pro rata distribution to the members shall be computed. The computation shall be based on the total amount in each share account.

(c) Promptly after the pro rata distribution to members has been computed, checks shall be drawn for the amounts to be distributed to each member. The checks shall be mailed to the members at their last known address or handed to them in person.

(d) Unclaimed share accounts, unpaid claims, and unpaid claims of members or creditors who failed to cash their final distribution checks shall be trusteed or escheated in accordance with the laws of the state in which the member or creditor resides.

(e) The Regional Director will be notified in writing within three days when the final distribution of assets to the members is started.

§ 710.7 Retention of records.

(a) The board of directors or liquidating agent shall appoint a custodian for the Federal credit union's records which are to be retained after the final distribution of assets.

(b) All records of the liquidated Federal credit union necessary to establish that creditors were paid and that assets were equitably distributed to the members shall be retained by the custodian for a period of five years following the date of charter cancellation.

§ 710.8 Certificate of dissolution and liquidation.

Within 120 days after the final distribution of assets to members is started, a duly executed Certificate of Dissolution and Liquidation shall be filed with the Regional Director.

§ 710.9 Federally insured state credit unions.

A federal insured state credit union will notify the Regional Director in writing within three days after the board of directors' decision to liquidate is made. A balance sheet and income statement as of the previous month-end and a copy of any liquidation plan will be included with the notification to the Regional Director.

PART 711—MANAGEMENT OFFICIAL INTERLOCKS

Sec.
711.1 Authority, purpose, and scope.
711.2 Definitions.
711.3 Prohibitions.
711.4 Interlocking relationships permitted by statute.
711.5 Small market share exemption.
711.6 General exemption.

711.7 Change in circumstances.
711.8 Enforcement.

AUTHORITY: 12 U.S.C. 1757 and 3201–3208.

SOURCE: 61 FR 50702, Sept. 27, 1996, unless otherwise noted.

§ 711.1 Authority, purpose, and scope.

(a) *Authority*. This part is issued under the provisions of the Depository Institution Management Interlocks Act (Interlocks Act) (12 U.S.C. 3201 *et seq*).

(b) *Purpose*. The purpose of the Interlocks Act and this part is to foster competition by generally prohibiting a management official from serving two nonaffiliated depository organizations in situations where the management interlock likely would have an anticompetitive effect.

(c) *Scope*. This part applies to management officials of federally insured credit unions. Section 711.4(c) exempts a management official of a credit union from the prohibitions of the Interlocks Act when the individual serves as a management official of another credit union. Therefore, the Interlocks Act prohibitions contained in this part only apply to a management official of a credit union when that individual also serves as a management official of another type of depository organization (usually a bank or thrift).

§ 711.2 Definitions.

For purposes of this part, the following definitions apply:

(a) *Affiliate*. (1) The term *affiliate* has the meaning given in section 202 of the Interlocks Act (12 U.S.C. 3201). For purposes of that section 202, shares held by an individual include shares held by members of his or her immediate family. "Immediate family" means spouse, mother, father, child, grandchild, sister, brother, or any of their spouses, whether or not any of their shares are held in trust.

(2) For purposes of section 202(3)(B) of the Interlocks Act (12 U.S.C. 3201(3)(B)), an affiliate relationship involving a depository institution based on common ownership does not exist if the appropriate federal supervisory agency determines, after giving the affected persons the opportunity to respond, that the asserted affiliation was established in order to avoid the prohibitions of the Interlocks Act and does not represent a true commonality of interest between the depository organizations. In making this determination, the appropriate Federal supervisory agency considers, among other things, whether a person, including members of his or her immediate family, whose shares are necessary to constitute the group owns a nominal percentage of the shares of one of the organizations and the percentage is substantially disproportionate to that person's ownership of shares in the other organization.

(b) *Area median income* means:

(1) The median family income for the metropolitan statistical area (MSA), if a depository organization is located in an MSA; or

(2) The statewide nonmetropolitan median family income, if a depository organization is located outside an MSA.

(c) *Community* means a city, town, or village, and contiguous or adjacent cities, towns, or villages.

(d) *Contiguous or adjacent cities, towns, or villages* means cities, towns, or villages whose borders touch each other or whose borders are within 10 road miles of each other at their closest points. The property line of an office located in an unincorporated city, town, or village is the boundary line of that city, town, or village for the purpose of this definition.

(e) *Depository holding company* means a bank holding company or a savings and loan holding company (as more fully defined in section 202 of the Interlocks Act (12 U.S.C. 3201)) having its principal office located in the United States.

(f) *Depository institution* means a commercial bank (including a private bank), a savings bank, a trust company, a savings and loan association, a building and loan association, a homestead association, a cooperative bank, an industrial bank, or a credit union, chartered under the laws of the United States and having a principal office located in the United States. Additionally, a United States office, including a branch or agency, of a foreign commercial bank is a depository institution.

(g) *Depository institution affiliate* means a depository institution that is an affiliate of a depository organization.

(h) *Depository organization* means a depository institution or a depository holding company.

(i) *District bank* means any State bank operating under the Code of Law of the District of Columbia.

(j) *Low and moderate-income areas* means census tracts (or, if an area is not in a census tract, block numbering areas delineated by the United States Bureau of the Census) where the median family income is less than 100 percent of the area median income.

(k) *Management official.* (1) The term *management official* means:

(i) A director;

(ii) An advisory or honorary director of a depository institution with total assets of $100 million or more;

(iii) A senior executive officer as that term is defined in 12 CFR 701.14(b)(2), or a person holding an equivalent position regardless of title;

(iv) A branch manager;

(v) A trustee of a depository organization under the control of trustees; and

(vi) Any person who has a representative or nominee serving in any of the capacities in this paragraph (m)(1).

(2) The term *management official* does not include:

(i) A person whose management functions relate exclusively to the business of retail merchandising or manufacturing;

(ii) A person whose management functions relate principally to the business outside the United States of a foreign commercial bank; or

(iii) A person described in the provisions of section 202(4) of the Interlocks Act (12 U.S.C. 3201(4)) (referring to an officer of a State-chartered savings bank, cooperative bank, or trust company that neither makes real estate mortgage loans nor accepts savings).

(l) *Office* means a principal or branch office of a depository institution located in the United States. *Office* does not include a representative office of a foreign commercial bank, an electronic terminal, or a loan production office.

(m) *Person* means a natural person, corporation, or other business entity.

(n) *Relevant metropolitan statistical area (RMSA)* means an MSA, a primary MSA, or a consolidated MSA that is not comprised of designated primary MSAs to the extent that these terms are defined and applied by the Office of Management and Budget.

(o) *Representative or nominee* means a natural person who serves as a management official and has an obligation to act on behalf of another person with respect to management responsibilities. NCUA will find that a person has an obligation to act on behalf of another person only if the first person has an agreement, express or implied, to act on behalf of the second person with respect to management responsibilities. NCUA will determine, after giving the affected persons an opportunity to respond, whether a person is a *representative or nominee*.

(p) *Total assets.* (1) The term *total assets* means assets measured on a consolidated basis and reported in the most recent fiscal year-end Consolidated Report of Condition and Income.

(2) The term *total assets* does not include:

(i) Assets of a diversified savings and loan holding company as defined by section 10(a)(1)(F) of the Home Owners' Loan Act (12 U.S.C. 1467a(a)(1)(F)) other than the assets of its depository institution affiliate;

(ii) Assets of a bank holding company that is exempt from the prohibitions of section 4 of the Bank Holding Company Act of 1956 pursuant to an order issued under section 4(d) of that Act (12 U.S.C. 1843(d)) other than the assets of its depository institution affiliate; or

(iii) Assets of offices of a foreign commercial bank other than the assets of its United States branch or agency.

(q) *United States* includes any State or territory of the United States of America, the District of Columbia, Puerto Rico, Guam, American Samoa, and the Virgin Islands.

[61 FR 50702, Sept. 27, 1996, as amended at 64 FR 66360, Nov. 26, 1999; 73 FR 30477, May 28, 2008; 75 FR 34621, June 18, 2010]

§ 711.3 Prohibitions.

(a) *Community.* A management official of a depository organization may not serve at the same time as a management official of an unaffiliated depository organization if the depository organizations in question (or a depository institution affiliate thereof) have offices in the same community.

(b) *RMSA.* A management official of a depository organization may not serve at the same time as a management official of an unaffiliated depository organization if the depository organizations in question (or a depository institution affiliate thereof) have offices in the same RMSA and each depository organization has total assets of $50 million or more.

(c) *Major assets.* A management official of a depository organization with total assets exceeding $2.5 billion (or any affiliate thereof) may not serve at the same time as a management official of an unaffiliated depository organization with total assets exceeding $1.5 billion (or any affiliate thereof), regardless of the location of the two depository organizations. The NCUA will adjust these thresholds, as necessary, based on year-to-year change in the average of the Consumer Price Index for the Urban Wage Earners and Clerical Workers, not seasonally adjusted, with rounding to the nearest $100 million. The NCUA will announce the revised thresholds by publishing a notice in the FEDERAL REGISTER.

[61 FR 50702, Sept. 27, 1996, as amended at 64 FR 66360, Nov. 26, 1999; 72 FR 58249, Oct. 15, 2007]

§ 711.4 Interlocking relationships permitted by statute.

The prohibitions of § 711.3 do not apply in the case of any one or more of the following organizations or to a subsidiary thereof:

(a) A depository organization that has been placed formally in liquidation, or which is in the hands of a receiver, conservator, or other official exercising a similar function;

(b) A corporation operating under section 25 or section 25A of the Federal Reserve Act (12 U.S.C. 601 *et seq.* and 12 U.S.C. 611 *et seq.*, respectively) (Edge Corporations and Agreement Corporations);

(c) A credit union being served by a management official of another credit union;

(d) A depository organization that does not do business within the United States except as an incident to its activities outside the United States;

(e) A State-chartered savings and loan guaranty corporation;

(f) A Federal Home Loan Bank or any other bank organized solely to serve depository institutions (a bankers' bank) or solely for the purpose of providing securities clearing services and services related thereto for depository institutions and securities companies;

(g) A depository organization that is closed or is in danger of closing as determined by the appropriate Federal depository institutions regulatory agency and is acquired by another depository organization. This exemption lasts for five years, beginning on the date the depository organization is acquired; and

(h)(1) A diversified savings and loan holding company (as defined in section 10(a)(1)(F) of the Home Owners' Loan Act (12 U.S.C. 1467a(a)(1)(F)) with respect to the service of a director of such company who also is a director of an unaffiliated depository organization if:

(i) Both the diversified savings and loan holding company and the unaffiliated depository organization notify their appropriate Federal depository institutions regulatory agency at least 60 days before the dual service is proposed to begin; and

(ii) The appropriate regulatory agency does not disapprove the dual service before the end of the 60-day period.

(2) The NCUA Board or its designee may disapprove a notice of proposed service if it finds that:

(i) The service cannot be structured or limited so as to preclude an anticompetitive effect in financial services in any part of the United States;

(ii) The service would lead to substantial conflicts of interest or unsafe or unsound practices; or

(iii) The notificant failed to furnish all the information required by NCUA.

(3) The NCUA Board or its designee may require that any interlock permitted under this paragraph (h) be terminated if a change in circumstances occurs with respect to one of the interlocked depository organizations that would have provided a basis for disapproval of the interlock during the notice period.

§ 711.5 Small market share exemption.

(a) *Exemption.* A management interlock that is prohibited by § 711.3(a) or § 711.3(b) is permissible, provided:

(1) The interlock is not prohibited by § 711.3(c); and

(2) The depository organizations (and their depository institution affiliates) hold, in the aggregate, no more than 20% of the deposits, in each RMSA or community in which the depository organizations (or their depository institution affiliates) are located. The amount of deposits will be determined by reference to the most recent annual Summary of Deposits published by the FDIC. This information is available on the Internet at *http://www.fdic.gov.*

(b) *Confirmation and records.* Each depository organization must maintain records sufficient to support its determination of eligibility for the exemption under paragraph (a) of this section, and must reconfirm that determination on an annual basis.

[64 FR 66360, Nov. 26, 1999]

§ 711.6 General exemption.

(a) *Exemption.* NCUA may, by agency order issued following receipt of an application, exempt an interlock from the prohibitions in § 711.3, if NCUA finds that the interlock would not result in a monopoly or substantial lessening of competition, and would not present other safety and soundness concerns.

(b) *Presumptions.* In reviewing applications for an exemption under this section, NCUA will apply a rebuttable presumption that an interlock will not result in a monopoly or substantial lessening of competition if the depository organization seeking to add a management official:

(1) Primarily serves, low- and moderate-income areas;

(2) Is controlled or managed by persons who are members of a minority group or women;

(3) Is a depository institution that has been chartered for less than two years; or

(4) Is deemed to be in "troubled condition" as defined in § 701.14(b)(3) of this chapter.

(c) *Duration.* Unless a shorter expiration period is provided in the NCUA approval, an exemption permitted by paragraph (a) of this section may continue so long as it would not result in a monopoly or substantial lessening of competition, or be unsafe or unsound. If the NCUA grants an interlock exemption in reliance upon a presumption under paragraph (b) of this section, the interlock may continue for three years, unless otherwise provided in the approval.

[64 FR 66360, Nov. 26, 1999]

§ 711.7 Change in circumstances.

(a) *Termination.* A management official shall terminate his or her service if a change in circumstances causes the service to become prohibited. A change in circumstances may include, but is not limited to, an increase in asset size of an organization, a change in the delineation of the RMSA or community, the establishment of an office, an increase in the aggregate deposits of the depository organization, or an acquisition, merger, consolidation, or reorganization of the ownership structure of a depository organization that causes a previously permissible interlock to become prohibited.

(b) *Transition period.* A management official described in paragraph (a) of this section may continue to serve the depository organization involved in the interlock for 15 months following the date of the change in circumstances. NCUA may shorten this period under appropriate circumstances.

[61 FR 50702, Sept. 27, 1996, as amended at 64 FR 66360, Nov. 26, 1999]

§ 711.8 Enforcement.

Except as provided in this section, NCUA administers and enforces the Interlocks Act with respect to federally insured credit unions, and may refer any case of a prohibited interlocking relationship involving these entities to the Attorney General of the United States to enforce compliance with the Interlocks Act and this part.

PART 712—CREDIT UNION SERVICE ORGANIZATIONS (CUSOs)

Sec.
712.1 What does this part cover?

National Credit Union Administration

§ 712.3

712.2 How much can an FCU invest in or loan to CUSOs, and what parties may participate?
712.3 What are the characteristics of and what requirements apply to CUSOs?
712.4 What must an FCU and a CUSO do to maintain separate corporate identities?
712.5 What activities and services are preapproved for CUSOs?
712.6 What activities and services are prohibited for CUSOs?
712.8 What transaction and compensation limits might apply to individuals related to both an FCU and a CUSO?
712.9 When must an FCU comply with this part?
712.10 How can a state supervisory authority obtain an exemption for state chartered credit unions from compliance with § 712.3(d)(3)?

AUTHORITY: 12 U.S.C. 1756, 1757(5)(D) and (7)(I), 1766, 1782, 1784, 1785, and 1786.

SOURCE: 63 FR 10756, Mar. 5, 1998, unless otherwise noted.

§ 712.1 What does this part cover?

This part establishes when a Federal credit union (FCU) can invest in and make loans to CUSOs. CUSOs are subject to review by NCUA. This part does not apply to corporate credit unions that have CUSOs subject to § 704.11 of this title. Sections 712.3(d)(3) and 712.4 of this part apply to state-chartered credit unions and their subsidiaries, as provided in § 741.222 of this chapter.

[63 FR 10756, Mar. 5, 1998, as amended at 73 FR 79311, Dec. 29, 2008]

§ 712.2 How much can an FCU invest in or loan to CUSOs, and what parties may participate?

(a) *Investments.* An FCU's total investments in CUSOs must not exceed, in the aggregate, 1% of its paid-in and unimpaired capital and surplus as of its last calendar year-end financial report.

(b) *Loans.* An FCU's total loans to CUSOs must not exceed, in the aggregate, 1% of its paid-in and unimpaired capital and surplus as of its last calendar year-end financial report. Loan authority is independent and separate from the 1% investment authority of subsection (a) of this section.

(c) *Parties.* An FCU may invest in or loan to a CUSO by itself, with other credit unions, or with non-credit union parties.

(d) *Measurement for calculating regulatory limitation.* For purposes of paragraphs (a) and (b) of this section:

(1) *Paid-in and unimpaired capital and surplus* means shares plus post-closing, undivided earnings (this does not include regular reserves or special reserves required by law, regulation or special agreement between the credit union and its regulator or share insurer); and

(2) Total investments in and total loans to CUSOs will be measured consistent with GAAP.

(3) *Special rule in the case of less than adequately capitalized FCUs.* This paragraph (d)(3) applies in the case of either an FCU that is currently less than adequately capitalized, as determined under part 702, or where the making of an investment in a CUSO would render the FCU less than adequately capitalized under part 702. Before making an investment in a CUSO, the FCU must obtain prior written approval from the appropriate NCUA regional office if the making of the investment would result in an aggregate cash outlay, measured on a cumulative basis (regardless of how the investment is valued for accounting purposes) in an amount in excess of one percent of the credit union's paid in and unimpaired capital and surplus.

(e) *Divestiture.* If the limitations in paragraph (a) of this section are reached or exceeded because of the profitability of the CUSO and the related GAAP valuation of the investment under the equity method, without an additional cash outlay by the FCU, divestiture is not required. An FCU may continue to invest up to 1% without regard to the increase in the GAAP valuation resulting from a CUSO's profitability.

[63 FR 10756, Mar. 5, 1998, as amended at 64 FR 33187, June 22, 1999; 66 FR 65624, Dec. 20, 2001; 73 FR 79312, Dec. 29, 2008]

§ 712.3 What are the characteristics of and what requirements apply to CUSOs?

(a) *Structure.* An FCU can invest in or loan to a CUSO only if the CUSO is structured as a corporation, limited liability company, or limited partnership. An FCU may only participate in a

§ 712.4

limited partnership as a limited partner. For purposes of this part, "corporation" means a legally incorporated corporation as established and maintained under relevant federal or state law. For purposes of this part, "limited partnership" means a legally established limited partnership as established and maintained under relevant state law. For purposes of this part, "limited liability company" means a legally established limited liability company as established and maintained under relevant state law, provided that the FCU obtains written legal advice that the limited liability company is a recognized legal entity under the applicable laws of the state of formation and that the limited liability company is established in a manner that will limit potential exposure of the FCU to no more than the amount of funds invested in, or loaned to, the CUSO.

(b) *Customer base.* An FCU can invest in or loan to a CUSO only if the CUSO primarily serves credit unions, its membership, or the membership of credit unions contracting with the CUSO *provided, however,* that with respect to any approved CUSO service, as set out in § 712.5, that also meets the description of services set out in § 701.30 of this chapter, this requirement is met if the CUSO primarily provides such services to persons who are eligible for membership in the FCU or are eligible for membership in credit unions contracting with the CUSO.

(c) *Federal credit union accounting for financial reporting purposes.* An FCU must account for its investments in or loans to a CUSO in conformity with "generally accepted accounting principles" (GAAP).

(d) *CUSO accounting; audits and financial statements; NCUA access to information.* An FCU must obtain written agreements from a CUSO, prior to investing in or lending to the CUSO, that the CUSO will:

(1) Account for all its transactions in accordance with GAAP;

(2) Prepare quarterly financial statements and obtain an annual financial statement audit of its financial statements by a licensed certified public accountant in accordance with generally accepted auditing standards. A wholly owned CUSO is not required to obtain a separate annual financial statement audit if it is included in the annual consolidated financial statement audit of the credit union that is its parent; and

(3)(i) Provide NCUA, its representatives, and the state credit union regulatory authority having jurisdiction over any federally insured, state-chartered credit union with an outstanding loan to, investment in or contractual agreement for products or services with the CUSO with complete access to any books and records of the CUSO and the ability to review CUSO internal controls, as deemed necessary by NCUA or the state credit union regulatory authority in carrying out their respective responsibilities under the Act and the relevant state credit union statute.

(ii) The effective date for compliance with this section is June 29, 2009.

(e) *Other laws.* A CUSO must comply with applicable Federal, state and local laws.

[63 FR 10756, Mar. 5, 1998, as amended at 64 FR 33187, June 22, 1999; 64 FR 57365, Oct. 25, 1999; 66 FR 40578, Aug. 3, 2001; 70 FR 55228, Sept. 21, 2005; 73 FR 79312, Dec. 29, 2008]

§ 712.4 **What must an FCU and a CUSO do to maintain separate corporate identities?**

(a) *Corporate separateness.* An FCU and a CUSO must be operated in a manner that demonstrates to the public the separate corporate existence of the FCU and the CUSO. Good business practices dictate that each must operate so that:

(1) Its respective business transactions, accounts, and records are not intermingled;

(2) Each observes the formalities of its separate corporate procedures;

(3) Each is adequately financed as a separate unit in the light of normal obligations reasonably foreseeable in a business of its size and character;

(4) Each is held out to the public as a separate enterprise;

(5) The FCU does not dominate the CUSO to the extent that the CUSO is treated as a department of the FCU; and

(6) Unless the FCU has guaranteed a loan obtained by the CUSO, all borrowings by the CUSO indicate that the FCU is not liable.

(b) *Legal opinion.* Prior to an FCU investing in a CUSO, the FCU must obtain written legal advice as to whether the CUSO is established in a manner that will limit potential exposure of the FCU to no more than the loss of funds invested in, or lent to, the CUSO. In addition, if a CUSO in which an FCU has an investment plans to change its structure under § 712.3(a), an FCU must also obtain prior, written legal advice that the CUSO will remain established in a manner that will limit potential exposure of the FCU to no more than the loss of funds invested in, or loaned to, the CUSO. The legal advice must address factors that have led courts to "pierce the corporate veil" such as inadequate capitalization, lack of separate corporate identity, common boards of directors and employees, control of one entity over another, and lack of separate books and records. The legal advice may be provided by independent legal counsel of the investing FCU or the CUSO.

§ 712.5 What activities and services are preapproved for CUSOs?

NCUA may at any time, based upon supervisory, legal, or safety and soundness reasons, limit any CUSO activities or services, or refuse to permit any CUSO activities or services. Otherwise, an FCU may invest in, loan to, and/or contract with only those CUSOs that are sufficiently bonded or insured for their specific operations and engaged in the preapproved activities and services related to the routine daily operations of credit unions. The specific activities listed within each preapproved category are provided in this section as illustrations of activities permissible under the particular category, not as an exclusive or exhaustive list.

(a) *Checking and currency services:*
(1) Check cashing;
(2) Coin and currency services;
(3) Money order, savings bonds, travelers checks, and purchase and sale of U.S. Mint commemorative coins services; and
(4) Stored value products

(b) *Clerical, professional and management services:*
(1) Accounting services;
(2) Courier services;
(3) Credit analysis;
(4) Facsimile transmissions and copying services;
(5) Internal audits for credit unions;
(6) Locator services;
(7) Management and personnel training and support;
(8) Marketing services;
(9) Research services;
(10) Supervisory committee audits; and
(11) Employee leasing services.

(c) *Business loan origination,* including the authority to buy and sell participation interests in such loans;

(d) *Consumer mortgage loan origination,* including the authority to buy and sell participation interests in such loans;

(e) *Electronic transaction services:*
(1) Automated teller machine (ATM) services;
(2) Credit card and debit card services;
(3) Data processing;
(4) Electronic fund transfer (EFT) services;
(5) Electronic income tax filing;
(6) Payment item processing;
(7) Wire transfer services; and
(8) Cyber financial services;

(f) *Financial counseling services:*
(1) Developing and administering Individual Retirement Accounts (IRA), Keogh, deferred compensation, and other personnel benefit plans;
(2) Estate planning;
(3) Financial planning and counseling;
(4) Income tax preparation;
(5) Investment counseling;
(6) Retirement counseling; and
(7) Business counseling and consultant services;

(g) *Fixed asset services:*
(1) Management, development, sale, or lease of fixed assets; and
(2) Sale, lease, or servicing of computer hardware or software;

(h) *Insurance brokerage or agency:*
(1) Agency for sale of insurance;
(2) Provision of vehicle warranty programs;
(3) Provision of group purchasing programs; and

§ 712.6

(4) Real estate settlement services;
(i) *Leasing:*
(1) Personal property; and
(2) Real estate leasing of excess CUSO property;
(j) *Loan support services:*
(1) Debt collection services;
(2) Loan processing, servicing, and sales;
(3) Sale of repossessed collateral; and
(4) Real estate settlement services;
(5) Purchase and servicing of non-performing loans; and
(6) Referral and processing of loan applications for members whose loan applications have been denied by the credit union;
(k) *Record retention, security and disaster recovery services:*
(1) Alarm-monitoring and other security services;
(2) Disaster recovery services;
(3) Microfilm, microfiche, optical and electronic imaging, CD-ROM data storage and retrieval services;
(4) Provision of forms and supplies; and
(5) Record retention and storage;
(1) *Securities brokerage services;*
(m) *Shared credit union branch (service center) operations;*
(n) *Student loan origination*, including the authority to buy and sell participation interests in such loans;
(o) *Travel agency services; and*
(p) *Trust and trust-related services:*
(1) Acting as administrator for prepaid legal service plans;
(2) Acting as trustee, guardian, conservator, estate administrator, or in any other fiduciary capacity; and
(3) Trust services.
(q) *Real estate brokerage services.*
(r) *CUSO investments in non-CUSO service providers:* In connection with providing a permissible service, a CUSO may invest in a non-CUSO service provider. The amount of the CUSO's investment is limited to the amount necessary to participate in the service provider, or a greater amount if necessary to receive a reduced price for goods or services.
(s) Credit card loan origination;
(t) Payroll processing services.

[63 FR 10756, Mar. 5, 1998, as amended at 64 FR 33187, June 22, 1999; 64 FR 66361, Nov. 26, 1999; 66 FR 40578, Aug. 3, 2001; 68 FR 56551, Oct. 1, 2003; 73 FR 79312, Dec. 29, 2008; 75 FR 34621, June 18, 2010]

§ 712.6 What activities and services are prohibited for CUSOs?

General. CUSOs must not acquire control of, either directly or indirectly, another depository financial institution, nor invest in shares, stocks, or obligations of an insurance company, trade association, liquidity facility or similar organization, corporation, or association.

[63 FR 10756, Mar. 5, 1998, as amended at 64 FR 66361, Nov. 26, 1999]

§ 712.8 What transaction and compensation limits might apply to individuals related to both an FCU and a CUSO?

(a) *Officials and Senior Management Employees.* The officials, senior management employees, and their immediate family members of an FCU that has outstanding loans or investments in a CUSO must not receive any salary, commission, investment income, or other income or compensation from the CUSO either directly or indirectly, or from any person being served through the CUSO. This provision does not prohibit such FCU officials or senior management employees from assisting in the operation of a CUSO, provided the officials or senior management employees are not compensated by the CUSO. Further, the CUSO may reimburse the FCU for the services provided by such FCU officials and senior management employees only if the account receivable of the FCU due from the CUSO is paid in full at least every 120 days. For purposes of this paragraph (a), "official" means affiliated credit union directors or committee members. For purposes of this paragraph (a), "senior management employee" means affiliated credit union chief executive officer (typically this individual holds the title of President or Treasurer/Manager), any assistant chief executive officers (e.g. Assistant President, Vice President, or Assistant

Treasurer/Manager) and the chief financial officer (Comptroller). For purposes of this paragraph (a), "immediate family member" means a spouse or other family members living in the same household.

(b) *Employees.* The prohibition contained in paragraph (a) of this section also applies to FCU employees not otherwise covered if the employees are directly involved in dealing with the CUSO unless the FCU's board of directors determines that the FCU employees' positions do not present a conflict of interest.

(c) *Others.* All transactions with business associates or family members of FCU officials, senior management employees, and their immediate family members, not specifically prohibited by paragraphs (a) and (b) of this section must be conducted at arm's length and in the interest of the FCU.

§ 712.9 When must an FCU comply with this part?

(a) *Investments.* An FCU's investments in CUSOs in existence prior to April 1, 1998, must conform with this part not later than April 1, 2001, unless the Board grants prior approval to continue such investment for a stated period.

(b) *Loans.* An FCU's loans to CUSOs in existence prior to April 1, 1998, must conform with this part not later than April 1, 2001, unless:

(1) The Board grants prior approval to continue the FCU's loan for a stated period; or

(2) Under the terms of its loan agreement, the FCU cannot require accelerated repayment without breaching the agreement.

§ 712.10 How can a state supervisory authority obtain an exemption for state chartered credit unions from compliance with § 712.3(d)(3)?

(a) The NCUA Board may exempt federally insured credit unions in a given state from compliance with § 712.3(d)(3) if the NCUA Board determines the laws and procedures available to the supervisory authority in that state are sufficient to provide NCUA with the degree of access to CUSO books and records it believes is necessary to evaluate the safety and soundness of credit unions having business relationships with CUSOs owned by credit union(s) chartered in that state.

(b) To obtain the exemption, the state supervisory authority must submit a copy of the legal authority pursuant to which it secures access to CUSO books and records to NCUA's regional office having responsibility for that state, along with all procedural and operational documentation supporting and describing the actual practices by which it implements and exercises the authority.

(c) The state supervisory authority must also provide the regional director with an assurance that NCUA examiners will be provided with co-extensive authority and will be allowed direct access to CUSO books and records at such times as NCUA, in its sole discretion, may determine necessary or appropriate. For purposes of this section, access includes the right to make and retain copies of any CUSO record, as to which NCUA will accord the same level of control and confidentiality that it uses with respect to all other examination-related materials it obtains in the course of its duties.

(d) The regional director will review the applicable authority, procedures and assurances and forward the exemption request, along with the regional director's recommendation, to the NCUA Board for a final determination.

(e) For purposes of this section, whether an entity is a CUSO shall be determined in accordance with the definition set out in § 741.222 of this chapter.

[73 FR 79312, Dec. 29, 2008]

PART 713—FIDELITY BOND AND INSURANCE COVERAGE FOR FEDERAL CREDIT UNIONS

Sec.
713.1 What is the scope of this section?
713.2 What are the responsibilities of a credit union's board of directors under this section?
713.3 What bond coverage must a credit union have?
713.4 What bond forms may be used?
713.5 What is the required minimum dollar amount of coverage?
713.6 What is the permissible deductible?

§ 713.1

713.7 May the NCUA Board require a credit union to secure additional insurance coverage?

AUTHORITY: 12 U.S.C. 1761a, 1761b, 1766(a), 1766(h), 1789(a)(11).

SOURCE: 64 FR 28720, May 27, 1999, unless otherwise noted.

§ 713.1 What is the scope of this section?

This section provides the requirements for fidelity bonds for Federal credit union employees and officials and for other insurance coverage for losses such as theft, holdup, vandalism, etc., caused by persons outside the credit union.

§ 713.2 What are the responsibilities of a credit union's board of directors under this section?

The board of directors of each Federal credit union must at least annually review its fidelity and other insurance coverage to ensure that it is adequate in relation to the potential risks facing the credit union and the minimum requirements set by the Board.

[64 FR 28720, May 27, 1999, as amended at 64 FR 57365, Oct. 25, 1999]

§ 713.3 What bond coverage must a credit union have?

At a minimum, your bond coverage must:

(a) Be purchased in an individual policy from a company holding a certificate of authority from the Secretary of the Treasury; and

(b) Include fidelity bonds that cover fraud and dishonesty by all employees, directors, officers, supervisory committee members, and credit committee members.

§ 713.4 What bond forms may be used?

(a) A current listing of basic bond forms that may be used without prior NCUA Board approval is on NCUA's Web site, *http://www.ncua.gov*. If you are unable to access the NCUA website, you can get a current listing of approved bond forms by contacting NCUA's Public and Congressional Affairs Office, at (703) 518–6330.

(b) To use any of the following, you need prior written approval from the Board:

(1) Any other basic bond form; or

(2) Any rider or endorsement that limits coverage of approved basic bond forms.

[64 FR 28720, May 27, 1999, as amended at 70 FR 61716, Oct. 26, 2005; 73 FR 30478, May 28, 2008]

§ 713.5 What is the required minimum dollar amount of coverage?

(a) The minimum required amount of fidelity bond coverage for any single loss is computed based on a federal credit union's total assets.

Assets	Minimum bond
$0 to $4,000,000	Lesser of total assets or $250,000.
$4,000,001 to $50,000,000	$100,000 plus $50,000 for each million or fraction thereof over $1,000,000.
$50,000,000 to $500,000,000	$2,550,000 plus $10,000 for each million or fraction thereof over $50,000,000, to a maximum of $5,000,000.
Over $500,000,000	One percent of assets, rounded to the nearest hundred million, to a maximum of $9,000,000.

(b) This is the minimum coverage required, but a federal credit union's board of directors should purchase additional or enhanced coverage when its circumstances warrant. In making this determination, a board of directors should consider its own internal risk assessment, its fraud trends and loss experience, and factors such as its cash on hand, cash in transit, and the nature and risks inherent in any expanded services it offers such as wire transfer and remittance services.

(c) While the above is the required minimum amount of bond coverage, credit unions should maintain increased coverage equal to the greater of either of the following amounts within thirty days of discovery of the need for such increase:

(1) The amount of the daily cash fund, i.e. daily cash plus anticipated

daily money receipts on the credit union's premises, or

(2) The total amount of the credit union's money in transit in any one shipment.

(3) Increased coverage is not required pursuant to paragraph (c) of this section, however, when the credit union temporarily increased its cash fund because of unusual events which cannot reasonably be expected to recur.

(d) Any aggregate limit of liability provided for in a fidelity bond policy must be at least twice the single loss limit of liability. This requirement does not apply to optional insurance coverage.

(e) Any proposal to reduce your required bond coverage must be approved in writing by the NCUA Board at least twenty days in advance of the proposed effective date of the reduction.

[64 FR 28720, May 27, 1999, as amended at 70 FR 61716, Oct. 26, 2005]

§ 713.6 What is the permissible deductible?

(a)(1) The maximum amount of allowable deductible is computed based on a federal credit union's asset size and capital level, as follows:

Assets	Maximum deductible
$0 to $100,000	No deductible allowed.
$100,001 to $250,000	$1,000.
$250,000 to $1,000,000	$2,000.
Over $1,000,000	$2,000 plus 1/1000 of total assets up to a maximum of $200,000; for credit unions over $1 million in assets that qualify for NCUA's Regulatory Flexibility Program in Part 742, the maximum deductible is $1,000,000.

(2) The deductibles may apply to one or more insurance clauses in a policy. Any deductibles in excess of the above amounts must receive the prior written permission of the NCUA Board.

(b) A deductible may not exceed 10 percent of a credit union's Regular Reserve unless a separate Contingency Reserve is set up for the excess. In computing the maximum deductible, valuation accounts such as the allowance for loan losses cannot be considered.

(c) A credit union's eligibility to qualify for a deductible in excess of $200,000 is determined based on it having assets in excess of $1 million as reflected in its most recent year-end 5300 call report and, as of that same year-end, qualifying for NCUA's Regulatory Flexibility Program under part 742 of this title as determined by its most recent examination report. A credit union that previously qualified for a deductible in excess of $200,000, but that subsequently fails to qualify based on its most recent year-end 5300 call report because either its assets have decreased or it no longer meets the net worth requirements of part 742 of this title or fails to meet the CAMEL rating requirements of part 742 of this title as determined by its most recent examination report, must obtain the coverage otherwise required by paragraph (b) of this section within 30 days of filing its year-end call report and must notify the appropriate NCUA regional office in writing of its changed status and confirm that it has obtained the required coverage.

[64 FR 28720, May 27, 1999, as amended at 70 FR 61716, Oct. 26, 2005]

§ 713.7 May the NCUA Board require a credit union to secure additional insurance coverage?

The NCUA Board may require additional coverage when the Board determines that a credit union's current coverage is inadequate. The credit union must purchase this additional coverage within 30 days.

PART 714—LEASING

Sec.
714.1 What does this part cover?
714.2 What are the permissible leasing arrangements?
714.3 Must you own the leased property in an indirect leasing arrangement?
714.4 What are the lease requirements?

§ 714.1

714.5 What is required if you rely on an estimated residual value greater than 25% of the original cost of the leased property?
714.6 Are you required to retain salvage powers over the leased property?
714.7 What are the insurance requirements applicable to leasing?
714.8 Are the early payment provisions, or interest rate provisions, applicable in leasing arrangements?
714.9 Are indirect leasing arrangements subject to the purchase of eligible obligation limit set forth in § 701.23 of this chapter?
714.10 What other laws must you comply with when engaged in leasing?

AUTHORITY: 12 U.S.C. 1756, 1757, 1766, 1785, 1789.

SOURCE: 65 FR 34585, May 31, 2000, unless otherwise noted.

§ 714.1 What does this part cover?

This part covers the standards and requirements that you, a federal credit union, must follow when engaged in the leasing of personal property.

§ 714.2 What are the permissible leasing arrangements?

(a) You may engage in direct leasing. In direct leasing, you purchase personal property from a vendor, becoming the owner of the property at the request of your member, and then lease the property to that member.

(b) You may engage in indirect leasing. In indirect leasing, a third party leases property to your member and you then purchase that lease from the third party for the purpose of leasing the property to your member. You do not have to purchase the leased property if you comply with the requirements of § 714.3.

(c) You may engage in open-end leasing. In an open-end lease, your member assumes the risk and responsibility for any difference in the estimated residual value and the actual value of the property at lease end.

(d) You may engage in closed-end leasing. In a closed-end lease, you assume the risk and responsibility for any difference in the estimated residual value and the actual value of the property at lease end. However, your member is always responsible for any excess wear and tear and excess mileage charges as established under the lease.

§ 714.3 Must you own the leased property in an indirect leasing arrangement?

You do not have to own the leased property in an indirect leasing arrangement if:

(a) You obtain a full assignment of the lease. A full assignment is the assignment of all the rights, interests, obligations, and title in a lease to you, that is, you become the owner of the lease;

(b) You are named as the sole lienholder of the leased property;

(c) You receive a security agreement, signed by the leasing company, granting you a sole lien in the leased property and the right to take possession and dispose of the leased property in the event of a default by the lessee, a default in the leasing company's obligations to you, or a material adverse change in the leasing company's financial condition; and

(d) You take all necessary steps to record and perfect your security interest in the leased property. Your state's Commercial Code may treat the automobiles as inventory, and require a filing with the Secretary of State.

§ 714.4 What are the lease requirements?

(a) Your lease must be a net lease. In a net lease, your member assumes all the burdens of ownership including maintenance and repair, licensing and registration, taxes, and insurance;

(b) Your lease must be a full payout lease. In a full payout lease, you must reasonably expect to recoup your entire investment in the leased property, plus the estimated cost of financing, from the lessee's payments and the estimated residual value of the leased property at the expiration of the lease term; and

(c) The amount of the estimated residual value you rely upon to satisfy the full payout lease requirement may not exceed 25% of the original cost of the leased property unless the amount above 25% is guaranteed. Estimated residual value is the projected value of the leased property at lease end. Estimated residual value must be reasonable in light of the nature of the leased property and all circumstances relevant to the leasing arrangement.

§ 714.5 What is required if you rely on an estimated residual value greater than 25% of the original cost of the leased property?

If the amount of the estimated residual value you rely upon to satisfy the full payout lease requirement of § 714.4(b) exceeds 25% of the original cost of the leased property, a financially capable party must guarantee the excess. The guarantor may be the manufacturer. The guarantor may also be an insurance company with an A.M. Best rating of at least a B+, or with at least the equivalent of an A.M. Best B+ rating from another major rating company. You must obtain or have on file financial documentation demonstrating that the guarantor has the resources to meet the guarantee.

§ 714.6 Are you required to retain salvage powers over the leased property?

You must retain salvage powers over the leased property. Salvage powers protect you from a loss and provide you with the power to take action if there is an unanticipated change in conditions that threatens your financial position by significantly increasing your exposure to risk. Salvage powers allow you:

(a) As the owner and lessor, to take reasonable and appropriate action to salvage or protect the value of the property or your interests arising under the lease; or

(b) As the assignee of a lease, to become the owner and lessor of the leased property pursuant to your contractual rights, or take any reasonable and appropriate action to salvage or protect the value of the property or your interests arising under the lease.

§ 714.7 What are the insurance requirements applicable to leasing?

(a) You must maintain a contingent liability insurance policy with an endorsement for leasing or be named as the co-insured if you do not own the leased property. Contingent liability insurance protects you should you be sued as the owner of the leased property. You must use an insurance company with a nationally recognized industry rating of at least a B+.

(b) Your member must carry the normal liability and property insurance on the leased property. You must be named as an additional insured on the liability insurance policy and as the loss payee on the property insurance policy.

§ 714.8 Are the early payment provisions, or interest rate provisions, applicable in leasing arrangements?

You are not subject to the early payment provisions set forth in § 701.21(c)(6) of this chapter. You are also not subject to the interest rate provisions in § 701.21(c)(7).

§ 714.9 Are indirect leasing arrangements subject to the purchase of eligible obligation limit set forth in § 701.23 of this chapter?

Your indirect leasing arrangements are not subject to the eligible obligation limit if they satisfy the provisions of § 701.23(b)(3)(iv) that require that you make the final underwriting decision and that the lease contract is assigned to you very soon after it is signed by the member and the dealer or leasing company.

§ 714.10 What other laws must you comply with when engaged in leasing?

You must comply with the Consumer Leasing Act, 15 U.S.C. 1667–67f, and its implementing regulation, Regulation M, 12 CFR part 213. You must comply with state laws on consumer leasing, but only to the extent that the state leasing laws are consistent with the Consumer Leasing Act, 15 U.S.C. 1667e, or provide the member with greater protections or benefits than the Consumer Leasing Act. You are also subject to the lending rules set forth in § 701.21 of this chapter, except as provided in § 714.8 and § 714.9 of this part. The lending rules in § 701.21 address the preemption of other state and federal laws that impact on credit transactions.

PART 715—SUPERVISORY COMMITTEE AUDITS AND VERIFICATIONS

Sec.
715.1 Scope of this part.

§ 715.1

715.2 Definitions used in this part.
715.3 General responsibilities of the Supervisory Committee.
715.4 Audit responsibility of the Supervisory Committee.
715.5 Audit of Federal Credit Unions.
715.6 Audit of Federally-insured State-chartered credit unions.
715.7 Supervisory Committee audit alternatives to a financial statement audit.
715.8 Requirements for verification of accounts and passbooks.
715.9 Assistance from outside, compensated person.
715.10 Audit report and working paper maintenance and access.
715.11 Sanctions for failure to comply with this part.
715.12 Statutory audit remedies for Federal credit unions.

AUTHORITY: 12 U.S.C. 1761(b), 1761d, 1782(a)(6).

SOURCE: 64 FR 41035, July 29, 1999, unless otherwise noted.

§ 715.1 Scope of this part.

This part implements section 202(a)(6)(D) of the Federal Credit Union Act, 12 U.S.C. 1782(a)(6)(D), as added by section 201(a) of the Credit Union Membership Access Act, Pub. L. No. 105–219, 112 Stat. 918 (1998). This part prescribes the responsibilities of the Supervisory Committee to obtain an annual audit of the credit union according to its charter type and asset size, and to conduct a verification of members' accounts.

§ 715.2 Definitions used in this part.

As used in this part:

(a) *Balance sheet audit* refers to the examination of a credit union's assets, liabilities, and equity under generally accepted auditing standards (GAAS) by an independent public accountant for the purpose of opining on the fairness of the presentation on the balance sheet. Credit unions required to file call reports consistent with GAAP should ensure the audited balance sheet is likewise prepared on a GAAP basis. The opinion under this type of engagement would not address the fairness of the presentation of the credit union's income statement, statement of changes in equity (including comprehensive income), or statement of cash flows.

(b) *Compensated person* refers to any accounting/auditing professional, excluding a credit union employee, who is compensated for performing more than one supervisory committee audit and/or verification of members' accounts per calendar year.

(c) *Financial statements* refers to a presentation of financial data, including accompanying notes, derived from accounting records of the credit union, and intended to disclose a credit union's economic resources or obligations at a point in time, or the changes therein for a period of time, in conformity with GAAP, as defined herein, or regulatory accounting procedures. Each of the following is considered to be a financial statement: a balance sheet or statement of financial condition; statement of income or statement of operations; statement of undivided earnings; statement of cash flows; statement of changes in members' equity; statement of revenue and expenses; and statement of cash receipts and disbursements.

(d) *Financial statement audit* (also known as an "opinion audit") refers to an audit of the financial statements of a credit union performed in accordance with GAAS by an independent person who is licensed by the appropriate State or jurisdiction. The objective of a financial statement audit is to express an opinion as to whether those financial statements of the credit union present fairly, in all material respects, the financial position and the results of its operations and its cash flows in conformity with GAAP, as defined herein, or regulatory accounting practices.

(e) *GAAP* is an acronym for "generally accepted accounting principles" which refers to the conventions, rules, and procedures which define accepted accounting practice. GAAP includes both broad general guidelines and detailed practices and procedures, provides a standard by which to measure financial statement presentations, and encompasses not only accounting principles and practices but also the methods of applying them.

(f) *GAAS* is an acronym for "generally accepted auditing standards" which refers to the standards approved and adopted by the American Institute of Certified Public Accountants which apply when an "independent, licensed certified public accountant" audits financial statements. Auditing standards differ from auditing procedures in that "procedures" address acts to be performed, whereas "standards" measure the quality of the performance of those acts and the objectives to be achieved by use of the procedures undertaken. In addition, auditing standards address the auditor's professional qualifications as well as the judgment exercised in performing the audit and in preparing the report of the audit.

(g) *Independent* means the impartiality necessary for the dependability of the compensated auditor's findings. Independence requires the exercise of fairness toward credit union officials, members, creditors and others who may rely upon the report of a supervisory committee audit report.

(h) *Internal control* refers to the process, established by the credit union's board of directors, officers and employees, designed to provide reasonable assurance of reliable financial reporting and safeguarding of assets against unauthorized acquisition, use, or disposition. A credit union's internal control structure consists of five components: control environment; risk assessment; control activities; information and communication; and monitoring. Reliable financial reporting refers to preparation of Call Reports (NCUA Forms 5300 and 5310) that meet management's financial reporting objectives. Internal control over safeguarding of assets against unauthorized acquisition, use, or disposition refers to prevention or timely detection of transactions involving such unauthorized access, use, or disposition of assets which could result in a loss that is material to the financial statements.

(i) *Reportable conditions* refers to a matter coming to the attention of the independent, compensated auditor which, in his or her judgment, represents a significant deficiency in the design or operation of the internal control structure of the credit union, which could adversely affect its ability to record, process, summarize, and report financial data consistent with the representations of management in the financial statements.

(j) *Report on Examination of Internal Control over Call Reporting* refers to an engagement in which an independent, licensed, certified public accountant or public accountant, consistent with attestation standards, examines and reports on management's written assertions concerning the effectiveness of its internal control over financial reporting in its most recently filed semiannual or year-end Call Report, with a concentration in high risk areas. For credit unions, such high risk areas most often include: lending activity; investing activity; and cash handling and deposit-taking activity.

(k) *State-licensed person* refers to a certified public accountant or public accountant who is licensed by the State or jurisdiction where the credit union is principally located to perform accounting or auditing services for that credit union.

(l) *Supervisory committee* refers to a supervisory committee as defined in Section 111(b) of the Federal Credit Union Act, 12 U.S.C. 1761(b). For some federally-insured state chartered credit unions, the "audit committee" designated by state statute or regulation is the equivalent of a supervisory committee.

(m) *Supervisory committee audit* refers to an engagement under either §715.5 or §715.6 of this part.

(n) *Working papers* refers to the principal record, in any form, of the work performed by the auditor and/or supervisory committee to support its findings and/or conclusions concerning significant matters. Examples include the written record of procedures applied, tests performed, information obtained, and pertinent conclusions reached in the engagement, proprietary audit programs, analyses, memoranda, letters of confirmation and representation, abstracts of credit union documents, reviewer's notes, if retained, and schedules or commentaries prepared or obtained in the course of the engagement.

[64 FR 41035, July 29, 1999, as amended at 66 FR 65624, Dec. 20, 2001]

§ 715.3 General responsibilities of the Supervisory Committee.

(a) *Basic.* The supervisory committee is responsible for ensuring that the board of directors and management of the credit union—

§ 715.4

(1) Meet required financial reporting objectives and

(2) Establish practices and procedures sufficient to safeguard members' assets.

(b) *Specific.* To carry out the responsibilities set forth in paragraph (a) of this section, the supervisory committee must determine whether:

(1) Internal controls are established and effectively maintained to achieve the credit union's financial reporting objectives which must be sufficient to satisfy the requirements of the supervisory committee audit, verification of members' accounts and its additional responsibilities;

(2) The credit union's accounting records and financial reports are promptly prepared and accurately reflect operations and results;

(3) The relevant plans, policies, and control procedures established by the board of directors are properly administered; and

(4) Policies and control procedures are sufficient to safeguard against error, conflict of interest, self-dealing and fraud.

(c) *Mandates.* In carrying out the responsibilities set forth in paragraphs (a) and (b) of this section, the Supervisory Committee must:

(1) Ensure that the credit union adheres to the measurement and filing requirements for reports filed with the NCUA Board under § 741.6 of this chapter;

(2) Perform or obtain a supervisory committee audit, as prescribed in § 715.4 of this part;

(3) Verify or cause the verification of members' passbooks and accounts against the records of the credit union, as prescribed in § 715.8 of this part;

(4) Act to avoid imposition of sanctions for failure to comply with the requirements of this part, as prescribed in §§ 715.11 and 715.12 of this part.

[64 FR 41035, July 29, 1999, as amended at 69 FR 27828, May 17, 2004]

§ 715.4 Audit responsibility of the Supervisory Committee.

(a) *Annual audit requirement.* A federally-insured credit union is required to obtain an annual supervisory committee audit which occurs at least once every calendar year (period of performance) and must cover the period elapsed since the last audit period (period effectively covered).

(b) *Financial statement audit option.* Any federally-insured credit union, whether Federally- or State-chartered and regardless of asset size, may choose to fulfill its Supervisory Committee audit responsibility by obtaining an annual audit of its financial statements performed in accordance with GAAS by an independent person who is licensed to do so by the State or jurisdiction in which the credit union is principally located. (A "financial statement audit" is distinct from a "supervisory committee audit," although a financial statement audit is included among the options for fulfilling the supervisory committee audit requirement. *Compare* § 715.2(c) and (j).)

(c) *Other audit options.* A federally insured credit union which does not choose to obtain a financial statement audit as permitted by subsection (b) must fulfill its supervisory audit responsibility under either of § 715.5 or § 715.6 of this part, whichever is applicable. *See* Table 1. For purposes of this part, a credit union's asset size is the amount of total assets reported in the year-end Call Report (NCUA form 5300) filed for the calendar year-end immediately preceding the period under audit.

Type of Charter	Asset Size	Minimum Audit Required to Fulfill Supervisory Committee Audit Responsibility[1]	Part 715 section
Federal charter	$500 Million or more	Financial statement audit per GAAS by independent, State-licensed person	§ 715.5
	Less than $500 Million but greater than $10 Million	Either financial statement audit or other supervisory committee audit options	
	$10 Million or less	Either of three supervisory committee audit options	
State charter	$500 Million or more	Financial statement audit per GAAS by independent, State-licensed person	§ 715.6
	Less than $500 Million	Either of three supervisory committee audit options unless audit prescribed by State law is more stringent.	

[1] The Supervisory Committee audit responsibility under Part 715 can always be fulfilled by obtaining a financial statement audit. § 715.4(b).

§ 715.5 Audit of Federal Credit Unions.

(a) *Total assets of $500 million or greater.* To fulfill its Supervisory Committee audit responsibility, a federal credit union having total assets of $500 million or greater must obtain an annual audit of its financial statements performed in accordance with GAAS by an independent person who is licensed to do so by the State or jurisdiction in which the credit union is principally located.

(b) *Total assets of less than $500 million but more than $10 million.* To fulfill its Supervisory Committee audit responsibility, a Federally-chartered credit union having total assets of less than $500 million but more than $10 million which does not choose to obtain an audit under § 715.5(a), must obtain an annual supervisory committee audit as prescribed in § 715.7.

(c) *Total assets of $10 million or less.* To fulfill its Supervisory Committee audit responsibility, a Federally-chartered credit union having total assets of $10 million or less must obtain an annual Supervisory Committee audit as prescribed in § 715.7.

(d) *Other requirements.* A federally chartered credit union, regardless of which audit it is required to obtain under this section, must meet other applicable requirements of this part.

[64 FR 41035, July 29, 1999, as amended at 75 FR 34621, June 18, 2010]

§ 715.6 Audit of Federally-insured State-chartered credit unions.

(a) *Total assets of $500 million or greater.* To fulfill its Supervisory Committee audit responsibility, a federally-insured State-chartered credit union having total assets of $500 million or greater must obtain an annual audit of its financial statements performed in accordance with GAAS by an independent person who is licensed to do so by the State or jurisdiction in which the credit union is principally located.

(b) *Total assets of less than $500 million.* To fulfill its Supervisory Committee audit responsibility, a federally-insured State-chartered credit union having total assets of less than $500 million must obtain either an annual supervisory committee audit as prescribed under either § 715.6(a) or § 715.7, or an audit as prescribed by the State

§ 715.7

or jurisdiction in which the credit union is principally located, whichever audit is more stringent.

(c) *Other requirements.* A federally-insured, state-chartered credit union, regardless of which audit it is required to obtain under this section, must meet other applicable requirements of this part except §§ 715.5 and 715.12.

§ 715.7 Supervisory Committee audit alternatives to a financial statement audit.

A credit union which is not required to obtain a financial statement audit may fulfill its supervisory committee responsibility by any one of the following engagements:

(a) *Balance sheet audit.* A balance sheet audit, as defined in § 715.2(a), performed by a person who is licensed to do so by the State or jurisdiction in which the credit union is principally located; or

(b) *Report on Examination of Internal Control over Call Reporting.* An engagement and report on management's written assertions concerning the effectiveness of internal control over financial reporting in the credit union's most recently filed semiannual or year-end call report (NCUA Form 5300), as defined in § 715.2(j), performed by a person who is licensed to do so by the State or jurisdiction in which the credit union is principally located, and in which management specifies the criteria on which it based its evaluation of internal control; or

(c) *Audit per Supervisory Committee Guide.* An audit performed by the supervisory committee, its internal auditor, or any other qualified person (such as a certified public accountant, public accountant, league auditor, credit union auditor consultant, retired financial institutions examiner, etc.) in accordance with the procedures prescribed in NCUA's *Supervisory Committee Guide.* Qualified persons who are not State-licensed cannot provide assurance services under this subsection.

§ 715.8 Requirements for verification of accounts and passbooks.

(a) *Verification obligation.* The Supervisory Committee shall, at least once every two years, cause the passbooks (including any book, statements of account, or other record approved by the NCUA Board) and accounts of the members to be verified against the records of the treasurer of the credit union.

(b) *Methods.* Any of the following methods may be used to verify members' passbooks and accounts, as appropriate:

(1) *Controlled verification.* A controlled verification of 100 percent of members' share and loan accounts;

(2) *Statistical method.* A sampling method which provides for:

(i) Random selection:

(ii) A sample which is representative of the population from which it was selected;

(iii) An equal chance of selecting each dollar in the population;

(iv) Sufficient accounts in both number and scope on which to base conclusions concerning management's financial reporting objectives; and

(v) Additional procedures to be performed if evidence provided by confirmations alone is not sufficient.

(3) *Non-statistical method.* When the verification is performed by an Independent person licensed by the State or jurisdiction in which the credit union is principally located, the auditor may choose among the sampling methods set forth in paragraphs (b)(1) and (2) of this section and non-statistical sampling methods consistent with GAAS if such methods provide for:

(i) Sufficient accounts in both number and scope on which to base conclusions concerning management's financial reporting objectives to provide assurance that the General Ledger accounts are fairly stated in relation to the financial statements taken as a whole;

(ii) Additional procedures to be performed by the auditor if evidence provided by confirmations alone is not sufficient; and

(iii) Documentation of the sampling procedures used and of their consistency with GAAS (to be provided to the NCUA Board upon request).

(c) *Retention of records.* The supervisory committee must retain the records of each verification of members' passbooks and accounts until it completes the next verification of members' passbooks and accounts.

National Credit Union Administration

§ 715.9 Assistance from outside, compensated person.

(a) *Unrelated to officials.* A compensated auditor who performs a Supervisory Committee audit on behalf of a credit union shall not be related by blood or marriage to any management employee, member of either the board of directors, the Supervisory Committee or the credit committee, or loan officer of that credit union.

(b) *Engagement letter.* The engagement of a compensated auditor to perform all or a portion of the scope of a financial statement audit or supervisory committee audit shall be evidenced by an engagement letter. In all cases, the engagement must be contracted directly with the Supervisory Committee. The engagement letter must be signed by the compensated auditor and acknowledged therein by the Supervisory Committee prior to commencement of the engagement.

(c) *Contents of letter.* The engagement letter shall:

(1) Specify the terms, conditions, and objectives of the engagement;

(2) Identify the basis of accounting to be used;

(3) If a Supervisory Committee Guide audit, include an appendix setting forth the procedures to be performed;

(4) Specify the rate of, or total, compensation to be paid for the audit;

(5) Provide that the auditor shall, upon completion of the engagement, deliver to the Supervisory Committee a written report of the audit and notice in writing, either within the report or communicated separately, of any internal control reportable conditions and/or irregularities or illegal acts, if any, which come to the auditor's attention during the normal course of the audit (i.e., no notice required if none noted);

(6) Specify a target date of delivery of the written reports, such target date not to exceed 120 days from date of calendar or fiscal year-end under audit (period covered), unless the supervisory committee obtains a waiver from the supervising NCUA Regional Director;

(7) Certify that NCUA staff and/or the State credit union supervisor, or designated representatives of each, will be provided unconditional access to the complete set of original working papers, either at the offices of the credit union or at a mutually agreed upon location, for purposes of inspection; and

(8) Acknowledge that working papers shall be retained for a minimum of three years from the date of the written audit report.

(d) *Complete scope.* If the engagement is to perform a *Supervisory Committee Guide* audit intended to fully meet the requirements of § 715.7(c), the engagement letter shall certify that the audit will address the complete scope of that engagement;

(e) *Exclusions from scope.* If the engagement is to perform a *Supervisory Committee Guide* audit which will exclude any item required by the applicable section, the engagement letter shall:

(1) Identify the excluded items;

(2) State that, because of the exclusion(s), the resulting audit will not, by itself, fulfill the scope of a supervisory committee audit; and

(3) Caution that the supervisory committee will remain responsible for fulfilling the scope of a supervisory committee audit with respect to the excluded items.

§ 715.10 Audit report and working paper maintenance and access.

(a) *Audit report.* Upon completion and/or receipt of the written report of a financial statement audit or a supervisory committee audit, the Supervisory Committee must verify that the audit was performed and reported in accordance with the terms of the engagement letter prescribed herein. The Supervisory Committee must submit the report(s) to the board of directors, and provide a summary of the results of the audit to the members of the credit union orally or in writing at the next annual meeting of the credit union. If a member so requests, the Supervisory Committee shall provide the member access to the full audit report. If the National Credit Union Administration ("NCUA") so requests, the Supervisory Committee shall provide NCUA a copy of each of the audit reports it receives or produces.

(b) *Working papers.* The supervisory committee shall be responsible for preparing and maintaining, or making available, a complete set of original

§ 715.11

working papers supporting each supervisory committee audit. The supervisory committee shall, upon request, provide NCUA staff unconditional access to such working papers, either at the offices of the credit union or at a mutually agreeable location, for purposes of inspecting such working papers.

§ 715.11 Sanctions for failure to comply with this part.

(a) *Sanctions.* Failure of a supervisory committee and/or its independent compensated auditor or other person to comply with the requirements of this section, or the terms of an engagement letter required by this section, is grounds for:

(1) The regional director to reject the supervisory committee audit and provide a reasonable opportunity to correct deficiencies;

(2) The regional director to impose the remedies available in § 715.12, provided any of the conditions specified therein is present; and

(3) The NCUA Board to seek formal administrative sanctions against the supervisory committee and/or its independent, compensated auditor pursuant to section 206(r) of the Federal Credit Union Act, 12 U.S.C. 1786(r).

(b) *State Charters.* In the case of a federally-insured state chartered credit union, NCUA shall provide the state regulator an opportunity to timely impose a remedy satisfactory to NCUA before exercising it authority under § 741.202 of this chapter to impose a sanction permitted under paragraph (a) of this section.

§ 715.12 Statutory audit remedies for Federal credit unions.

(a) *Audit by alternative licensed person.* The NCUA Board may compel a federal credit union to obtain a supervisory committee audit which meets the minimum requirements of § 715.5 or § 715.7, and which is performed by an independent person who is licensed by the State or jurisdiction in which the credit union is principally located, for any fiscal year in which any of the following three conditions is present:

(1) The Supervisory Committee has not obtained an annual financial statement audit or performed a supervisory committee audit; or

(2) The Supervisory Committee has obtained a financial statement audit or performed a supervisory committee audit which does not meet the requirements of part 715 including those in § 715.8.

(3) The credit union has experienced serious and persistent recordkeeping deficiencies as defined in paragraph (c) of this section.

(b) *Financial statement audit required.* The NCUA Board may compel a federal credit union to obtain a financial statement audit performed in accordance with GAAS by an independent person who is licensed by the State or jurisdiction in which the credit union is principally located (even if such audit is not required by § 715.5), for any fiscal year in which the credit union has experienced serious and persistent recordkeeping deficiencies as defined in paragraph (c) of this section. The objective of a financial statement audit performed under this paragraph is to reconstruct the records of the credit union sufficient to allow an unqualified or, if necessary, a qualified opinion on the credit union's financial statements. An adverse opinion or disclaimer of opinion should be the exception rather than the norm.

(c) *"Serious and persistent recordkeeping deficiencies."* A record-keeping deficiency is "serious" if the NCUA Board reasonably believes that the board of directors and management of the credit union have not timely met financial reporting objectives and established practices and procedures sufficient to safeguard members' assets. A serious recordkeeping deficiency is "persistent" when it continues beyond a usual, expected or reasonable period of time.

PART 716—PRIVACY OF CONSUMER FINANCIAL INFORMATION

Sec.
716.1 Purpose and scope.
716.2 Model privacy form and examples.
716.3 Definitions.

National Credit Union Administration § 716.3

Subpart A—Privacy and Opt Out Notices

716.4 Initial privacy notice to consumers required.
716.5 Annual privacy notice to members required.
716.6 Information to be included in initial and annual privacy notices.
716.7 Form of opt-out notice to consumers; opt-out methods.
716.8 Revised privacy notices.
716.9 Delivering privacy and opt out notices.

Subpart B—Limits on Disclosures

716.10 Limits on disclosure of nonpublic personal information to nonaffiliated third parties.
716.11 Limits on redisclosure and reuse of information.
716.12 Limits on sharing of account number information for marketing purposes.

Subpart C—Exceptions

716.13 Exception to opt out requirements for service providers and joint marketing.
716.14 Exceptions to notice and opt out requirements for processing and servicing transactions.
716.15 Other exceptions to notice and opt out requirements.

Subpart D—Relation to Other Laws; Effective Date

716.16 Protection of Fair Credit Reporting Act.
716.17 Relation to state laws.
716.18 Effective date; transition rule.
APPENDIX A TO PART 716—MODEL PRIVACY FORM

AUTHORITY: 15 U.S.C. 6801 et seq., 12 U.S.C. 1751 et seq.

SOURCE: 65 FR 31740, May 18, 2000, unless otherwise noted.

§ 716.1 Purpose and scope.

(a) *Purpose.* This part governs the treatment of nonpublic personal information about consumers by the credit unions listed in paragraph (b) of this section. This part:

(1) Requires a credit union to provide notice to members about its privacy policies and practices;

(2) Describes the conditions under which a credit union may disclose nonpublic personal information about consumers to nonaffiliated third parties; and

(3) Provides a method for consumers to prevent a credit union from disclosing that information to most nonaffiliated third parties by "opting out" of that disclosure, subject to the exceptions in §§ 716.13, 716.14, and 716.15.

(b) *Scope.* (1) This part applies only to nonpublic personal information about individuals who obtain financial products or services for personal, family or household purposes. This part does not apply to information about companies or about individuals who obtain financial products or services for business, commercial or agricultural purposes. This part applies to federally-insured credit unions. This part refers to a federally-insured credit union as "you" or "the credit union."

(2) Nothing in this part modifies, limits, or supersedes the standards governing individually identifiable financial information promulgated by the Secretary of Health and Human Services under the authority of §§ 262 and 264 of the Health Insurance Portability and Accountability Act of 1996 (42 U.S.C. 1320d–1320d–8).

§ 716.2 Model privacy form and examples.

(a) *Model privacy form.* Use of the model privacy form in Appendix A of this part, consistent with the instructions in Appendix A, constitutes compliance with the notice content requirements of §§ 716.6 and 716.7 of this part, although use of the model privacy form is not required.

(b) *Examples.* The examples in this part are not exclusive. Compliance with an example, to the extent applicable, constitutes compliance with this part.

[74 FR 62955, Dec. 1, 2009]

§ 716.3 Definitions.

As used in this part, unless the context requires otherwise:

(a)(1) *Affiliate* means any company that controls, is controlled by, or is under common control with another company.

(2) *Examples.* (i) An affiliate of a federal credit union is a credit union service organization (CUSO), as provided in 12 CFR part 712, that is controlled by the federal credit union.

§716.3

(ii) An affiliate of a federally-insured, state-chartered credit union is a company that is controlled by the credit union.

(b)(1) *Clear and conspicuous* means that a notice is reasonably understandable and designed to call attention to the nature and significance of the information in the notice.

(2) *Examples.* (i) *Reasonably understandable.* You make your notice reasonably understandable if you:

(A) Present the information contained in the notice in clear, concise sentences, paragraphs and sections;

(B) Use short, explanatory sentences or bullet lists whenever possible;

(C) Use definite, concrete, everyday words and active voice whenever possible;

(D) Avoid multiple negatives;

(E) Avoid legal and highly technical business terminology wherever possible; and

(F) Avoid explanations that are imprecise and readily subject to different interpretations.

(ii) *Designed to call attention.* You design your notice to call attention to the nature and significance of the information in it if you:

(A) Use a plain-language heading to call attention to the notice;

(B) Use a typeface and type size that are easy to read;

(C) Provide wide margins and ample line spacing;

(D) Use boldface or italics for key words; and

(E) In a form that combines your notice with other information, use distinctive type size, style, and graphic devices, such as shading or sidebars.

(iii) *Notices on websites.* If you provide notices on a web page, you design your notice to call attention to the nature and significance of the information in it if you use text or visual cues to encourage scrolling down the page if necessary to view the entire notice and ensure that other elements on the website (such as text, graphics, hyperlinks or sound) do not distract attention from the notice, and you either:

(A) Place the notice on a screen frequently accessed by consumers, such as a home page or a page on which transactions are conducted; or

(B) Place a link on a screen frequently accessed by consumers, such as a home page or a page on which transactions are conducted, that connects directly to the notice and is labeled appropriately to convey the importance, nature and relevance of the notice.

(c) *Collect* means to obtain information that you organize or can retrieve by the name of an individual or by identifying number, symbol, or other identifying particular assigned to the individual, irrespective of the source of the underlying information.

(d) *Company* means any corporation, limited liability company, business trust, general or limited partnership, association or similar organization.

(e)(1) *Consumer* means an individual who obtains or has obtained a financial product or service from you, that is to be used primarily for personal, family or household purposes, or that individual's legal representative.

(2) *Examples.* (i) An individual who provides nonpublic personal information to you in connection with obtaining or seeking to obtain credit union membership is your consumer regardless of whether you establish a member relationship.

(ii) An individual who provides nonpublic personal information to you in connection with using your ATM is your consumer.

(iii) If you hold ownership or servicing rights to an individual's loan, the individual is your consumer, even if you hold those rights in conjunction with one or more financial institutions. The individual is also a consumer with respect to the other financial institutions involved. This applies, even if you, or another financial institution with those rights, hire an agent to collect on the loan or to provide processing or other services.

(iv) An individual who is a consumer of another financial institution is not your consumer solely because you act as agent for, or provide processing or other services to, that financial institution.

(v) An individual is not your consumer solely because he or she is a participant or a beneficiary of an employee benefit plan that you sponsor or for which you act as a trustee or fiduciary.

(f) *Consumer reporting agency* has the same meaning as in section 603(f) of the Fair Credit Reporting Act (15 U.S.C. 1681a(f)).

(g) *Control* of a company means:

(1) Ownership, control, or power to vote 25 percent or more of the outstanding shares of any class of voting security of the company, directly or indirectly, or acting through one or more other persons;

(2) Control in any manner over the election of a majority of the directors, trustees or general partners (or individuals exercising similar functions) of the company; or

(3) The power to exercise, directly or indirectly, a controlling influence over the management or policies of the company, as the NCUA determines. With respect to state-chartered credit unions, NCUA will consult with the appropriate state regulator prior to making its determination.

(4) *Example.* NCUA will presume a credit union has a controlling influence over the management or policies of a CUSO, if the CUSO is 67% owned by credit unions.

(h) *Credit union* means a federal or state-chartered credit union that the National Credit Union Share Insurance Fund insures.

(i) *Customer* means a consumer who has a customer relationship with a financial institution other than a credit union.

(j) *Customer relationship* means a continuing relationship between a consumer and a financial institution other than a credit union.

(k) *Federal functional regulator* means—

(1) The National Credit Union Administration Board;

(2) The Board of Governors of the Federal Reserve System;

(3) The Office of the Comptroller of the Currency;

(4) The Board of Directors of the Federal Deposit Insurance Corporation;

(5) The Director of the Office of Thrift Supervision; and

(6) The Securities and Exchange Commission.

(l)(1) *Financial institution* means any institution the business of which is engaging in activities that are financial in nature or incidental to such financial activity as described in section 4(k) of the Bank Holding Company Act of 1956 (12 U.S.C. 1843(k)).

(2) Examples of financial institutions may include, but are not limited to: credit unions; banks; insurance companies; securities brokers, dealers, and underwriters; loan brokers and servicers; tax planners and preparation services; personal property appraisers; real estate appraisers; career counselors for employees in financial occupations; digital signature services; courier services; real estate settlement services; manufacturers of computer software and hardware; and travel agencies operated in connection with financial services.

(3) *Financial institution* does not include:

(i) Any person or entity with respect to any financial activity that is subject to the jurisdiction of the Commodity Futures Trading Commission under the Commodity Exchange Act (7 U.S.C. 1 *et seq.*);

(ii) The Federal Agricultural Mortgage Corporation or any entity chartered and operating under the Farm Credit Act of 1971 (12 U.S.C. 2001 *et seq.*); or

(iii) Institutions chartered by Congress specifically to engage in securitizations, secondary market sales (including sales of servicing rights) or similar transactions related to a transaction of a consumer, as long as such institutions do not sell or transfer nonpublic personal information to a nonaffiliated third party.

(m) (1) *Financial product or service* means any product or service that a financial holding company could offer by engaging in an activity that is financial in nature or incidental to such a financial activity under section 4(k) of the Bank Holding Company Act of 1956 (12 U.S.C. 1843(k)).

(2) *Financial service* includes your evaluation or brokerage of information that you collect in connection with a request or an application from a consumer for a financial product or service.

(n) *Member* means a consumer who has a member relationship with you. For purposes of this part only, it will include certain nonmembers.

§ 716.3

(o)(1) *Member relationship* means a continuing relationship between a consumer and you under which you provide one or more financial products or services to the consumer that are to be used primarily for personal, family or household purposes. As noted in the examples, this will include certain consumers that are not your members.

(2) *Examples.* (i) A consumer has a continuing relationship with you if the consumer:

(A) Is your member as defined in your bylaws;

(B) Is a nonmember who has a share, share draft, or credit card account with you jointly with a member;

(C) Is a nonmember who has a loan that you service;

(D) Is a nonmember who has an account with you and you are a credit union that has been designated as a low-income credit union; or

(E) Is a nonmember who has an account in a federally-insured, state-chartered credit union pursuant to state law.

(ii) A consumer does not, however, have a member relationship with you if the consumer is a nonmember and:

(A) The consumer only obtains a financial product or service in isolated transactions, such as using your ATM to withdraw cash from an account maintained at another financial institution or purchasing travelers checks; or

(B) You sell the consumer's loan and do not retain the rights to service that loan.

(p)(1) *Nonaffiliated third party* means any person except:

(i) Your affiliate; or

(ii) A person employed jointly by you and any company that is not your affiliate (but nonaffiliated third party includes the other company that jointly employs the person).

(q)(1) *Nonpublic personal information* means:

(i) Personally identifiable financial information; and

(ii) Any list, description or other grouping of consumers (and publicly available information pertaining to them) that is derived using any personally identifiable financial information.

(2) *Nonpublic personal information* does not include:

(i) Publicly available information, except as included on a list described in paragraph (q)(1)(ii) of this section; or

(ii) Any list, description, or other grouping of consumers (and publicly available information pertaining to them) that is derived without using any personally identifiable financial information, other than publicly available information.

(3) *Examples of lists.* (i) Nonpublic personal information includes any list of individuals' names and street addresses that is derived in whole or in part using personally identifiable financial information, other than publicly available information, such as account numbers.

(ii) Nonpublic personal information does not include any list of individuals' names and addresses that contains only publicly available information, is not derived using personally identifiable financial information, other than publicly available information, either in whole or in part, and is not disclosed in a manner that indicates that any of the individuals on the list is a consumer of a credit union, other than publicly available information.

(r)(1) *Personally identifiable financial information* means any information:

(i) A consumer provides to you to obtain a financial product or service from you;

(ii) About a consumer resulting from any transaction involving a financial product or service between you and a consumer; or

(iii) You otherwise obtain about a consumer in connection with providing a financial product or service to that consumer.

(2) Personally identifiable financial information does not include publicly available information.

(3) *Examples.* (i) *Information included.* Personally identifiable financial information includes:

(A) Information a consumer provides to you on an application to obtain membership, a loan, credit card or other financial product or service;

(B) Account balance information, payment history, overdraft history, and credit or debit card purchase information;

(C) The fact that an individual is or has been one of your members or has

National Credit Union Administration

§ 716.4

obtained a financial product or service from you;

(D) Any information about your consumer if it is disclosed in a manner that indicates that the individual is or has been your consumer;

(E) Any information that a consumer provides to you or that you or your agent otherwise obtain in connection with collecting on a loan or servicing a loan;

(F) Any information you collect through an Internet "cookie" (an information collecting device from a web server); and

(G) Information from a consumer report.

(ii) *Information not included.* Personally identifiable financial information does not include:

(A) A list of names and addresses of customers of an entity that is not a financial institution; and

(B) Information that does not identify a consumer, such as aggregate information or blind data that does not contain personal identifiers such as account numbers, names, or addresses.

(s)(1) *Publicly available information* means any information that you have a reasonable basis to believe is lawfully made available to the general public from:

(i) Federal, state or local government records;

(ii) Widely distributed media; or

(iii) Disclosures to the general public that are required to be made by federal, state or local law.

(2) *Reasonable basis.* You have a reasonable basis to believe that information is lawfully made available to the general public if you have taken steps to determine:

(i) That the information is of the type that is available to the general public; and

(ii) Whether an individual can direct that the information not be made available to the general public and, if so, that your member or consumer has not done so.

(3) *Examples.* (i) *Government records.* Publicly available information in government records includes information in government real estate records and security interest filings.

(ii) *Widely distributed media.* Publicly available information from widely distributed media includes information from a telephone book, a television or radio program, a newspaper or a web site that is available to the general public on an unrestricted basis. A web site is not restricted merely because an Internet service provider or site operator requires a fee or a password, so long as access is available to the general public.

(iii) *Reasonable basis.* (1) You have a reasonable basis to believe that mortgage information is lawfully made available to the general public if you have determined that the information is of the type included on the public record in the jurisdiction where the mortgage would be recorded.

(2) You have a reasonable basis to believe that an individual's telephone number is lawfully made available to the general public if you have located the telephone number in the telephone book or have been informed by the consumer that the telephone number is not unlisted.

(t) *You* means a federally-insured credit union.

[65 FR 31740, May 18, 2000, as amended at 73 FR 30478, May 28, 2008]

Subpart A—Privacy and Opt Out Notices

§ 716.4 Initial privacy notice to consumers required.

(a) *Initial notice requirement.* You must provide a clear and conspicuous notice that accurately reflects your privacy policies and practices to a:

(1) *Member,* not later than when you establish a member relationship, except as provided in paragraph (e) of this section; and

(2) *Consumer,* before you disclose any nonpublic personal information about the consumer to any nonaffiliated third party, if you make such a disclosure other than as authorized by §§ 716.14 and 716.15.

(b) *When initial notice to a consumer is not required.* You are not required to provide an initial notice to a consumer under paragraph (a) of this section if:

(1) You do not disclose any nonpublic personal information about the consumer to any nonaffiliated third party, other than as authorized by §§ 716.14 and 716.15; and

§716.4

(2) You do not have a member relationship with the consumer.

(c) *When you establish a member relationship*—(1) *General rule.* You establish a member relationship when you and the consumer enter into a continuing relationship.

(2) *Special rule for loans.* You establish a member relationship with a consumer when you originate, or acquire the servicing rights to a loan to the consumer for personal, household or family purposes and that is the only basis for the member relationship. If you subsequently transfer the servicing rights to that loan to another financial institution, the member relationship transfers with the servicing rights.

(3)(i) *Examples of establishing member relationship.* You establish a member relationship when the consumer:

(A) Becomes your member under your bylaws;

(B) Is a nonmember and opens a credit card account with you jointly with a member under your procedures;

(C) Is a nonmember and executes the contract to open a share or share draft account with you or obtains credit from you jointly with a member, including an individual acting as a guarantor;

(D) Is a nonmember and opens an account with you and you are a credit union designated as a low-income credit union;

(E) Is a nonmember and opens an account with you pursuant to state law and you are a state-chartered credit union.

(ii) *Examples of loan rule.* You establish a member relationship with a consumer who obtains a loan for personal, family, or household purposes when you:

(A) Originate the loan to the consumer and retain the servicing rights; or

(B) Purchase the servicing rights to the consumer's loan.

(d) *Existing members.* When an existing member obtains a new financial product or service that is to be used primarily for personal, family, or household purposes, you satisfy the initial notice requirements of paragraph (a) of this section as follows:

(1) You may provide a revised policy notice, under §716.8, that covers the member's new financial product or service; or

(2) If the initial, revised, or annual notice that you most recently provided to that member was accurate with respect to the new financial product or service, you do not need to provide a new privacy notice under paragraph (a) of this section.

(e) *Exceptions to allow subsequent delivery of notice.* (1) You may provide the initial notice required by paragraph (a)(1) of this section within a reasonable time after you establish a member relationship if:

(i) Establishing the member relationship is not at the member's election;

(ii) Providing notice not later than when you establish a member relationship would substantially delay the member's transaction and the member agrees to receive the notice at a later time.

(2) *Examples of exceptions.* (i) *Not at member's election.* Establishing a member relationship is not at the member's election if you acquire a member's deposit liability from another financial institution and the member does not have a choice about your acquisition.

(ii) *Substantial delay of member's transaction.* Providing notice not later than when you establish a member relationship would substantially delay the member's transaction when:

(A) You and the individual agree over the telephone to enter into a member relationship involving prompt delivery of the financial product or service; or

(B) You establish a member relationship with an individual under a program authorized by Title IV of the Higher Education Act of 1965 (20 U.S.C. 1070 *et seq.*) or similar student loan programs where loan proceeds are disbursed promptly without prior communication between you and the member.

(iii) *No substantial delay of member's transaction.* Providing notice not later than when you establish a member relationship would not substantially delay the member's transaction when the relationship is initiated in person at your office or through other means by which the member may view the notice, such as on a web site.

(f)(1) *Joint relationships.* If two or more consumers jointly obtain a financial product or service, other than a

National Credit Union Administration § 716.6

loan, from you, you may satisfy the requirements of paragraph (a) of this section by providing one initial notice to those consumers jointly.

(2) *Special rule for loans.* (i) You are required to provide an initial notice to a borrower or guarantor on a loan if you share his or her nonpublic personal information with nonaffiliated third parties other than for purposes under §§ 716.13, 716.14 and 716.15. (ii) You may satisfy the annual notice requirements of § 716.5 by providing one notice to those borrowers and guarantors jointly.

(g) *Delivery.* When you are required to deliver an initial privacy notice by this section, you must deliver it according to the methods in § 716.9. If you use a short-form initial notice for non-member consumers according to § 716.6(c), you may deliver your privacy notice according to § 716.6(c)(3).

[65 FR 31740, May 18, 2000, as amended at 65 FR 36783, June 12, 2000; 75 FR 34621, June 18, 2010]

§ 716.5 Annual privacy notice to members required.

(a)(1) *General rule.* You must provide a clear and conspicuous notice to members that accurately reflects your privacy policies and practices not less than annually during the continuation of the member relationship. *Annually* means at least once in any period of 12 consecutive months during which that relationship exists. You may define the 12-consecutive-month period, but you must apply it to the member on a consistent basis.

(2) *Example.* You provide a notice annually if you define the 12-consecutive-month period as a calendar year and provide the annual notice to the member once in each calendar year following the calendar year in which you provide the initial notice. For example, if a member opens an account on any day of year one, you must provide an annual notice to that member by December 31 of year two.

(b) (1) *Termination of member relationship.* You are not required to provide an annual notice to a former member.

(2) *Examples.* Your member becomes your former member when:

(i) An individual is no longer your member as defined in your bylaws;

(ii) In the case of a nonmember's share or share draft account, the account is inactive under the credit union's policies;

(iii) In the case of a nonmember's closed-end loan, the loan is paid in full, you charge off the loan, or you sell the loan without retaining servicing rights;

(iv) In the case of a credit card relationship or other open-end credit relationship with a nonmember, you no longer provide any statements or notices to the nonmember concerning that relationship or you sell the credit card receivables without retaining servicing rights; or

(v) You have not communicated with the nonmember about the relationship for a period of twelve consecutive months, other than to provide annual privacy notices or promotional material.

(c) *Delivery.* When you are required to deliver an annual privacy notice by this section, you must deliver it according to the methods in § 716.9.

§ 716.6 Information to be included in initial and annual privacy notices.

(a) *General rule.* The initial and annual privacy notices under §§ 716.4 and 716.5 must include each of the following items of information that applies to you or to the consumers to whom you send your privacy notice, in addition to any other information you wish to provide:

(1) The categories of nonpublic personal information that you collect;

(2) The categories of nonpublic personal information that you disclose;

(3) The categories of affiliates and nonaffiliated third parties to whom you disclose nonpublic personal information, other than those parties to whom you disclose information under §§ 716.14 and 716.15;

(4) The categories of nonpublic personal information about your former members that you disclose and the categories of affiliates and nonaffiliated third parties to whom you disclose it, other than those parties to whom you disclose information under §§ 716.14 and 716.15;

(5) If you disclose nonpublic personal information to a nonaffiliated third

755

§ 716.6

party under § 716.13 (and no other exception applies to that disclosure), a separate statement of the categories of information you disclose and the categories of third parties with whom you have contracted;

(6) An explanation of the consumer's right under § 716.10(a) to opt out of the disclosure of nonpublic personal information to nonaffiliated third parties, including the methods by which the consumer may exercise that right at that time;

(7) Any disclosures that you make under section 603(d)(2)(A)(iii) of the Fair Credit Reporting Act (15 U.S.C. 1681a(d)(2)(A)(iii)) (that is, notices regarding the ability to opt out of disclosure of information among affiliates);

(8) Your policies and practices with respect to protecting the confidentiality and security of nonpublic personal information; and

(9) Any disclosures you make under paragraph (b) of this section.

(b) *Description of nonaffiliated third parties subject to exceptions.* If you disclose nonpublic personal information to third parties as authorized under §§ 716.14 and 716.15, you are not required to list those exceptions in the initial or annual privacy notices required by §§ 716.4 and 716.5. When describing the categories with respect to those parties, you are required to state only that you make disclosures to other nonaffiliated third parties as permitted by law.

(c) *Short-form initial notice with opt out notice for nonmember consumers.* (1) You may satisfy the initial notice requirements in §§ 716.4(a)(2), 716.7(b), and 716.7(c) for a consumer who is not a member by providing a short-form initial notice at the same time as you deliver an opt out notice as required in § 716.7.

(2) A short-form initial notice must:

(i) Be clear and conspicuous;

(ii) State that your privacy notice is available upon request; and

(iii) Explain a reasonable means by which the consumer may obtain that notice.

(3) You must deliver your short-form initial notice according to § 716.9. You are not required to deliver your privacy notice with your short form initial notice. You instead may simply provide the consumer a reasonable means to obtain your privacy notice. If a consumer who receives your short-form notice requests your privacy notice, you must deliver your privacy notice according to § 716.9.

(4) *Examples of obtaining privacy notice.* You provide a reasonable means by which a consumer may obtain a copy of your privacy notice if you:

(i) Provide a toll-free telephone number that the consumer may call to request the notice; or

(ii) For a consumer who conducts business in person at your office, maintain copies of the notice on hand that you provide to a consumer immediately upon request.

(d) *Future disclosures.* Your notice may include:

(1) Categories of nonpublic personal information that you reserve the right to disclose in the future, but do not currently disclose; and

(2) Categories of affiliates or nonaffiliated third parties to whom you reserve the right in the future to disclose, but to whom you do not currently disclose, nonpublic personal information.

(e) *Examples*—(1) *Categories of nonpublic personal information that you collect.* You satisfy the requirement to categorize the nonpublic personal information that you collect if you list the following categories, as applicable:

(i) Information from the consumer;

(ii) Information about the consumer's transactions with you or your affiliates;

(iii) Information about the consumer's transactions with nonaffiliated third parties; and

(iv) Information from a consumer reporting agency.

(2) *Categories of nonpublic personal information you disclose.* (i) You satisfy the requirement to categorize the nonpublic personal information that you disclose if you list the categories described in paragraph (e)(1) of this section, as applicable, and a few examples to illustrate the types of information in each category.

(ii) If you reserve the right to disclose all of the nonpublic personal information about consumers that you collect, you may simply state that fact without describing the categories or

National Credit Union Administration § 716.7

examples of the nonpublic personal information you disclose.

(3) *Categories of affiliates and nonaffiliated third parties to whom you disclose.* You satisfy the requirement to categorize the affiliates and nonaffiliated third parties to whom you disclose nonpublic personal information if you list the following categories, as applicable, and a few examples to illustrate the types of third parties in each category.

(i) Financial service providers;
(ii) Non-financial companies; and
(iii) Others.

(4) *Disclosures under exception for service providers and joint marketers.* If you disclose nonpublic personal information under the exception in § 716.13 to a nonaffiliated third party to market products or services that you offer alone or jointly with another financial institution, you satisfy the disclosure requirement of paragraph (a)(5) of this section if you:

(i) List the categories of nonpublic personal information you disclose, using the same categories and examples you used to meet the requirements of paragraphs (a)(2) of this section, as applicable; and

(ii) State whether the third party is:
(A) A service provider that performs marketing services on your behalf or on behalf of you and another financial institution; or
(B) A financial institution with whom you have a joint marketing agreement.

(5) *Simplified notices.* If you do not disclose, and do not intend to disclose, nonpublic personal information about members or former members to affiliates or nonaffiliated third parties except as authorized under §§ 716.14 and 716.15, you may simply state that fact, in addition to the information you must provide under paragraphs (a)(1), (a)(8), (a)(9) and (c) of this section.

(6) *Confidentiality and security.* You describe your policies and practices with respect to protecting the confidentiality and security of nonpublic personal information if you do both of the following:

(i) Describe in general terms who is authorized to have access to the information.

(ii) State whether you have security practices and procedures in place to ensure the confidentiality of the information in accordance with your policy. You are not required to describe technical information about the safeguards you use.

(7) *Joint notice with affiliates.* You may provide a joint notice from you and one or more of your affiliates or other financial institutions, as specified in the notice, as long as the notice is accurate with respect to you and the other institution.

[65 FR 31740, May 18, 2000, as amended at 74 FR 62955, Dec. 1, 2009; 75 FR 34621, June 18, 2010]

§ 716.7 Form of opt out notice to consumers and opt out methods.

(a)(1) *Form of opt out notice.* If you are required to provide an opt out notice under § 716.10(a)(1), you must provide a clear and conspicuous notice to each of your consumers that accurately explains the right to opt out under that section. The notice must state:

(i) That you disclose or reserve the right to disclose nonpublic personal information about your consumer to a nonaffiliated third party;

(ii) That the consumer has the right to opt out of that disclosure; and

(iii) A reasonable means by which the consumer may exercise the opt out right.

(2) *Examples.* (i) *Adequate opt out notice.* You provide adequate notice that the consumer can opt out of the disclosure of nonpublic personal information to a nonaffiliated third party if you:

(A) Identify all of the categories of nonpublic personal information that you disclose or reserve the right to disclose and all of the categories of nonaffiliated third parties to whom you disclose the information, as described in § 716.6(a)(2) and (3) and state that the consumer can opt out of the disclosure of that information; and

(B) Identify the financial products or services that the consumer obtains from you, either singly or jointly, to which the opt out direction would apply.

(ii) *Reasonable opt out means.* You provide a reasonable means to exercise an opt out right if you:

(A) Designate check-off boxes in a prominent position on the relevant forms with the opt out notice;

(B) Include a reply form together with the opt out notice;

(C) Provide an electronic means to opt out, such as a form that can be sent via electronic mail or a process at your web site, if the consumer agrees to the electronic delivery of information; or

(D) Provide a toll-free telephone number that consumers may call to opt out.

(iii) *Unreasonable opt out means.* You *do not* provide a reasonable means of opting out if:

(A) The only means of opting out is for the consumer to write his or her own letter to exercise that opt out right; or

(B) The only means of opting out as described in any notice subsequent to the initial notice is to use a check-off box that was provided with the initial notice but not included with the subsequent notice.

(iv) *Specific opt out means.* You may require each consumer to opt out through a specific means, as long as that means is reasonable for that consumer.

(b) *Same form as initial notice permitted.* You may provide the opt out notice together with or on the same written or electronic form as the initial notice you provide in accordance with §716.4.

(c) *Initial notice required when opt out notice delivered subsequent to initial notice.* If you provide the opt out notice later than required for the initial notice in accordance with §716.4, you must also include a copy of the initial notice in writing or, if the consumer agrees, electronically.

(d) *Joint relationships.* (1) If two or more consumers jointly obtain a financial product or service, other than a loan, from you, you may provide only a single opt out notice. Your opt out notice must explain how you will treat an opt out direction by a joint consumer as explained in the examples in paragraph (d)(5) of this section.

(2) Any of the joint consumers may exercise the right to opt out. You may either:

(i) Treat an opt out direction by a joint consumer to apply to all of the associated joint consumers; or

(ii) Permit each joint consumer to opt out separately.

(3) If you permit each joint consumer to opt out separately, you must permit one of the joint consumers to opt out on behalf of all of the joint consumers.

(4) You may not require all joint consumers to opt out before you implement any opt out direction.

(5) *Example.* If John and Mary have a joint share account with you and arrange for you to send statements to John's address, you may do any of the following, but you must explain in your opt out notice which opt out policy you will follow:

(i) Send a single opt out notice to John's address, but you must accept an opt out direction from either John or Mary.

(ii) Treat an opt out direction by either John or Mary as applying to the entire account. If you do so, and John opts out, you may not require Mary to opt out as well before implementing John's opt out direction.

(iii) Permit John and Mary to make different opt out directions. If you do so, and if John and Mary both opt out, you must permit one or both of them to notify you in a single response (such as on a form or through a telephone call).

(6) *Special rule for loans.* (i) You are required to provide an initial opt out notice to a borrower or guarantor on a loan if you share his or her nonpublic personal information with non-affiliated third parties other than for purposes under §§716.13, 716.14 and 716.15.

(ii) You may satisfy your annual opt out notice requirement by providing one notice to those borrowers and guarantors jointly.

(e) *Time to comply with opt out.* You must comply with the consumer's opt out direction as soon as reasonably practicable after you receive it.

(f) *Continuing right to opt out.* A consumer may exercise the right to opt out at any time.

(g) *Duration of consumer's opt out direction.* (1) A consumer's direction to opt out under this section is effective

National Credit Union Administration § 716.9

until the consumer revokes it in writing or, if the consumer agrees, electronically.

(2) When a member relationship terminates, the member's opt out direction continues to apply to the nonpublic personal information that you collected during or related to the relationship. If the individual subsequently establishes a new member relationship with you, the opt out direction that applied to the former relationship does not apply to the new relationship.

(h) *Delivery.* When you are required to deliver an opt out notice by this section, you must deliver it according to the methods in § 716.9.

(i) *Model privacy form.* Pursuant to § 716.2(a) of this part, a model privacy form that meets the notice content requirements of this section is included in Appendix A of this part.

[65 FR 31740, May 18, 2000, as amended at 65 FR 36783, June 12, 2000; 74 FR 62956, Dec. 1, 2009]

§ 716.8 Revised privacy notices.

(a) *General rule.* Except as otherwise authorized in this part, you must not, directly or through any affiliate, disclose any nonpublic personal information about a consumer to a nonaffiliated third party other than as described in the initial notice that you provided to that consumer under § 716.4, unless:

(1) You have provided to the consumer a revised notice that accurately describes your policies and practices;

(2) You have provided to the consumer a new opt out notice;

(3) You have given the consumer a reasonable opportunity, before you disclose the information to the nonaffiliated third party, to opt out of the disclosure; and

(4) The consumer does not opt out.

(b) *Examples.* (1) Except as otherwise permitted by §§ 716.13, 716.14 and 716.15, you must provide a revised notice if you—

(i) Disclose a new category of nonpublic personal information to any nonaffiliated third party;

(ii) Disclose nonpublic personal information to a new category of nonaffiliated third party; or

(iii) Disclose nonpublic personal information about a former member to a nonaffiliated third party, and that former member has not had the opportunity to exercise an opt out right regarding that disclosure.

(2) A revised notice is not required if you disclose nonpublic personal information to a new nonaffiliated third party that you adequately described in your prior notice.

(c) *Delivery.* When you are required to deliver a revised privacy notice by this section, you must deliver it according to the methods in § 716.9.

§ 716.9 Delivering privacy and opt out notices.

(a) *How to provide notices.* You must provide any privacy notices and opt out notices, including short-form initial notices, that this part requires so that each consumer can reasonably be expected to receive actual notice in writing or, if the consumer agrees, electronically.

(b) (1) *Examples of reasonable expectation of actual notice.* You may reasonably expect that a consumer will receive actual notice if you:

(i) Hand-deliver a printed copy of the notice to the consumer;

(ii) Mail a printed copy of the notice to the last known address of the consumer;

(iii) For the consumer who conducts transactions electronically, post the notice on the electronic site and require the consumer to acknowledge receipt of the notice as a necessary step to obtaining a particular financial product or service;

(iv) For an isolated transaction with the consumer, such as an ATM transaction, post the notice on the ATM screen and require the consumer to acknowledge receipt of the notice as a necessary step to obtaining the particular financial product or service.

(2) *Examples of unreasonable expectations of actual notice.* You may not, however, reasonably expect that a consumer will receive actual notice if you:

(i) Only post a sign in your branch or office or generally publish advertisements of your privacy policies and practices;

(ii) Send the notice via electronic mail to a consumer who does not obtain a financial product or service from you electronically.

§ 716.10

(c) *Annual notices only.* You may reasonably expect that a member will receive actual notice of your annual privacy notice if:

(1) The member uses your web site to access financial products and services electronically and agrees to receive notices at your web site and you post your current privacy notice continuously in a clear and conspicuous manner on your web site; or

(2) The member has requested that you refrain from sending any information regarding the member relationship, and your current privacy notice remains available to the member upon request.

(d) *Oral description of notice insufficient.* You may not provide any notice required by this part solely by orally explaining the notice, either in person or over the telephone.

(e) *Retention or accessibility of notices for members.* (1) For members only, you must provide the initial notice required by § 716.4 (a)(1), the annual notice required by § 716.5(a) and the revised notice required by § 716.8 so that the member can retain them or obtain them later in writing or, if the member agrees, electronically.

(2) *Examples of retention or accessibility.* You provide the privacy notice to the member so that the member can retain it or obtain it later if you:

(i) Hand-deliver a printed copy of the notice to the member;

(ii) Mail a printed copy of the notice to the last known address of the member upon request of the member; or

(iii) Make your current privacy notice available on a web site (or a link to another web site) for the member who obtains a financial product or service electronically and agrees to receive the notice at the web site.

Subpart B—Limits on Disclosures

§ 716.10 Limits on disclosure of nonpublic personal information to nonaffiliated third parties.

(a) (1) *Conditions for disclosure.* Except as otherwise authorized in this part, you may not, directly or through any affiliate, disclose any nonpublic personal information about a consumer to a nonaffiliated third party unless:

(i) You have provided to the consumer an initial notice as required under § 716.4;

(ii) You have provided to the consumer an opt out notice as required in § 716.7;

(iii) You have given the consumer a reasonable opportunity, before you disclose the information to the nonaffiliated third party, to opt out of the disclosure; and

(iv) The consumer does not opt out.

(2) *Opt out definition.* Opt out means a direction by the consumer that you not disclose nonpublic personal information about that consumer to a nonaffiliated third party, other than as permitted by §§ 716.13, 716.14 and 716.15.

(3) *Examples of reasonable opportunity to opt out.* You provide a consumer with a reasonable opportunity to opt out if:

(i) *By mail.* You mail the notices required in paragraph (a)(1) of this section to the consumer and allow the consumer to opt out by mailing a form, calling a toll-free telephone number, or any other reasonable means within 30 days from the date you mailed the notices.

(ii) *By electronic means.* A member opens an on-line account with you and agrees to receive the notices required in paragraph (a)(1) of this section electronically, and you make the notices available to the member on your web site and allow the member to opt out by any reasonable means within 30 days after the date that the member acknowledges receipt of the notices.

(iii) *Isolated transaction with consumer.* For an isolated transaction, such as the purchase of a traveler's check by a consumer, you provide the consumer with a reasonable opportunity to opt out if you provide the notices required in paragraph (a)(1) of this section at the time of the transaction and request that the consumer decide, as a necessary part of the transaction, whether to opt out before completing the transaction.

(b) *Application of opt out to all consumers and all nonpublic personal information.* (1) You must comply with this section, regardless of whether you and the consumer have established a member relationship.

(2) Unless you comply with this section, you may not, directly or through

National Credit Union Administration § 716.11

an affiliate, disclose any nonpublic personal information about a consumer that you have collected, regardless of whether you collected it before or after receiving the direction to opt out from the consumer.

(c) *Partial opt out.* You may allow a consumer to select certain nonpublic personal information or certain nonaffiliated third parties with respect to which the consumer wishes to opt out.

§ 716.11 Limits on redisclosure and reuse of information.

(a)(1) *Information you receive under an exception.* If you receive nonpublic personal information from a nonaffiliated financial institution under an exception in § 716.14 or 716.15 of this part, your disclosure and use of that information is limited as follows:

(i) You may disclose the information to the affiliates of the financial institution from which you received the information; and

(ii) You may disclose the information to your affiliates, but your affiliates may, in turn, disclose and use the information only to the extent that you may disclose and use the information; and

(iii) You may disclose and use the information pursuant to an exception in § 716.14 or 716.15 in the ordinary course of business to carry out the activity covered by the exception under which you received the information.

(2) *Example.* If you receive a member list from a credit union in order to provide correspondent services under the exception in § 716.14(a), you may disclose that information under any exception in § 716.14 or 716.15 in order to provide those services. For example, you could disclose the information in response to a properly authorized subpoena or to your attorneys, accountants, and auditors. You could not disclose that information to a third party for marketing purposes or use that information for your own marketing purposes.

(b)(1) *Information you receive outside of an exception.* If you receive nonpublic personal information from a nonaffiliated financial institution other than under an exception in § 716.14 or 716.15 of this part, you may disclose the information only:

(i) To the affiliates of the financial institution from which you received the information;

(ii) To your affiliates, but your affiliates may, in turn, disclose the information only to the extent that you can disclose the information;

(iii) To any other person, if the disclosure would be lawful if made directly to that person by the financial institution from which you received the information; and

(iv) Pursuant to an exception in § 716.14 or 716.15.

(2) *Example.* If you obtain a customer list from a nonaffiliated financial institution outside of the exceptions in §§ 716.14 and 716.15,

(i) You may use the list for your own purposes;

(ii) You may disclose that list to another non-affiliated third party only if the financial institution from which you purchased the list could have disclosed the list to that third party, that is you may disclose the list in accordance with the privacy policy of the financial institution from which you received the list, as limited by the opt out direction of each consumer whose nonpublic personal information you intend to disclose; and

(iii) You may disclose that list as permitted by § 716.14 or 716.15, such as to your attorneys or accountants.

(c) *Information you disclose under an exception.* If you disclose nonpublic personal information to a nonaffiliated third party under an exception in § 716.14 or 716.15 of this part, the disclosure and use of that information by the third party is limited as follows:

(1) The third party may disclose the information to your affiliates;

(2) The third party may disclose the information to its affiliates, but its affiliates may, in turn, disclose and use the information only to the extent that the third party may disclose and use the information; and

(3) The third party may disclose and use the information pursuant to an exception in § 716.14 or 716.15 in the ordinary course of business to carry out the activity covered by the exception under which it received the information.

(d) *Information you disclose outside of an exception.* If you disclose nonpublic personal information to a nonaffiliated third party other than under an exception in §716.14 or 716.15 of this part, the third party may disclose the information only:

(1) To your affiliates;

(2) To its affiliates, but its affiliates, in turn, may disclose the information only to the extent the third party can disclose the information;

(3) To any other person, if the disclosure would be lawful if made directly to that person by you; and

(4) Pursuant to an exception in §716.14 or 716.15.

§716.12 Limits on sharing of account number information for marketing purposes.

(a) *General prohibition on disclosure of account numbers.* You must not, directly or through an affiliate, disclose, other than to a consumer reporting agency, an account number or similar form of access number or access code for a consumer's credit card account, share account or transaction account to any nonaffiliated third party for use in telemarketing, direct mail marketing or other marketing through electronic mail to the consumer.

(b) *Exceptions.* Paragraph (a) of this section does not apply if you disclose an account number or similar form of access number or access code:

(1) To your agent or service provider solely in order to perform marketing for your own products or services, as long as the agent or service provider cannot directly initiate charges to the account; or

(2) To a participant in a private label credit card program or an affinity or similar program where the participants in the program are identified to the member when the member enters into the program.

(c) *Examples*—(1) *Account number.* An account number, or similar form of access number or access code, does not include a number or code in an encrypted form, as long as you do not provide the recipient with a means to decode the number or code.

(2) *Transaction account.* A transaction account is an account other than a share or credit card account. A transaction account does not include an account to which a third party cannot initiate a charge.

Subpart C—Exceptions

§716.13 Exception to opt out requirements for service providers and joint marketing.

(a) *General rule.* (1) The opt out requirements in §§716.7 and 716.10 do not apply when you provide nonpublic personal information to a nonaffiliated third party to perform services for you or functions on your behalf, if you:

(i) Provide the initial notice in accordance with §716.4; and

(ii) Enter into a contractual agreement with the third party that prohibits the third party from disclosing or using the information other than to carry out the purposes for which you disclosed the information, including use under an exception in §716.14 or 716.15 in the ordinary course of business to carry out those purposes.

(2) *Example.* If you disclose nonpublic personal information under this section to a financial institution with which you perform joint marketing, your contractual agreement with that institution meets the requirements of paragraph (a)(1)(ii) of this section if it prohibits the institution from disclosing or using the nonpublic personal information except as necessary to carry out the joint marketing or under an exception in §716.14 or 716.15 in the ordinary course of business to carry out that joint marketing.

(b) *Service may include joint marketing.* The services that a nonaffiliated third party performs for you under paragraph (a) of this section may include marketing of your own products or services or marketing of financial products or services offered pursuant to joint agreements between you and one or more financial institutions.

(c) *Definition of joint agreement.* For purposes of this section, *joint agreement* means a written contract pursuant to which you and one or more financial institutions jointly offer, endorse, or sponsor a financial product or service.

§ 716.14 Exceptions to notice and opt out requirements for processing and servicing transactions.

(a) *Exceptions for processing transactions at consumer's request.* The requirements for initial notice in § 716.4(a)(2), the opt out in §§ 716.7 and 716.10 and service providers and joint marketing in § 716.13 do not apply if you disclose nonpublic personal information as necessary to effect, administer, or enforce a transaction that a consumer requests or authorizes, or in connection with:

(1) Servicing or processing a financial product or service that a consumer requests or authorizes;

(2) Maintaining or servicing the consumer's account with you, or with another entity as part of a private label credit card program or other extension of credit on behalf of such entity; or

(3) A proposed or actual securitization, secondary market sale (including sales of servicing rights) or similar transaction related to a transaction of the consumer.

(b) *Necessary to effect, administer, or enforce a transaction* means that the disclosure is:

(1) Required, or is one of the lawful or appropriate methods, to enforce your rights or the rights of other persons engaged in carrying out the financial transaction or providing the product or service; or

(2) Required, or is a usual, appropriate or acceptable method:

(i) To carry out the transaction or the product or service business of which the transaction is a part, and record, service or maintain the consumer's account in the ordinary course of providing the financial service or financial product;

(ii) To administer or service benefits or claims relating to the transaction or the product or service business of which it is a part;

(iii) To provide a confirmation, statement or other record of the transaction, or information on the status or value of the financial service or financial product to the consumer or the consumer's agent or broker;

(iv) To accrue or recognize incentives or bonuses associated with the transaction that are provided by you or any other party;

(v) In connection with:

(A) The authorization, settlement, billing, processing, clearing, transferring, reconciling or collection of amounts charged, debited, or otherwise paid using a debit, credit or other payment card, check or account number, or by other payment means;

(B) The transfer of receivables, accounts or interests therein; or

(C) The audit of debit, credit or other payment information.

§ 716.15 Other exceptions to notice and opt out requirements.

(a) *Exceptions to opt out requirements.* The requirements for initial notice to consumers in § 716.4(a)(2), the opt out in §§ 716.7 and 716.10 and service providers and joint marketing in § 716.13 do not apply when you disclose nonpublic personal information:

(1) With the consent or at the direction of the consumer, provided that the consumer has not revoked the consent or direction;

(2)(i) To protect the confidentiality or security of your records pertaining to the consumer, service, product or transaction;

(ii) To protect against or prevent actual or potential fraud, unauthorized transactions, claims or other liability;

(iii) For required institutional risk control or for resolving consumer disputes or inquiries;

(iv) To persons holding a legal or beneficial interest relating to the consumer; or

(v) To persons acting in a fiduciary or representative capacity on behalf of the consumer;

(3) To provide information to insurance rate advisory organizations, guaranty funds or agencies, agencies that are rating you, persons that are assessing your compliance with industry standards, and your attorneys, accountants, and auditors;

(4) To the extent specifically permitted or required under other provisions of law and in accordance with the Right to Financial Privacy Act of 1978 (12 U.S.C. 3401 *et seq.*), to law enforcement agencies (including a federal functional regulator, the Secretary of the Treasury, with respect to 31 U.S.C. Chapter 53, Subchapter II (Records and Reports on Monetary Instruments and

§716.16

Transactions) and 12 U.S.C. Chapter 21 (Financial Recordkeeping), a state insurance authority, with respect to any person domiciled in that insurance authority's state that is engaged in providing insurance, and the Federal Trade Commission), self-regulatory organizations, or for an investigation on a matter related to public safety;

(5)(i) To a consumer reporting agency in accordance with the Fair Credit Reporting Act (15 U.S.C. 1681 et seq.), or

(ii) From a consumer report reported by a consumer reporting agency;

(6) In connection with a proposed or actual sale, merger, transfer, or exchange of all or a portion of a business or operating unit if the disclosure of nonpublic personal information concerns solely consumers of such business or unit; or

(7)(i) To comply with federal, state or local laws, rules and other applicable legal requirements;

(ii) To comply with a properly authorized civil, criminal or regulatory investigation, or subpoena or summons by federal, state or local authorities; or

(iii) To respond to judicial process or government regulatory authorities having jurisdiction over you for examination, compliance or other purposes as authorized by law.

(b) *Examples of consent and revocation of consent.* (1) A consumer may specifically consent to your disclosure to a nonaffiliated insurance company of the fact that the consumer has applied to you for a mortgage so that the insurance company can offer homeowner's insurance to the consumer.

(2) A consumer may revoke consent by subsequently exercising the right to opt out of future disclosures of nonpublic personal information as permitted under §716.7(f).

Subpart D—Relation to Other Laws; Effective Date

§716.16 **Protection of Fair Credit Reporting Act.**

Nothing in this part shall be construed to modify, limit, or supersede the operation of the Fair Credit Reporting Act (15 U.S.C. 1681 et seq.), and no inference shall be drawn on the basis of the provisions of this part regarding whether information is trans-action or experience information under section 603 of that Act.

§716.17 **Relation to state laws.**

(a) *In general.* This part shall not be construed as superseding, altering, or affecting any statute, regulation, order or interpretation in effect in any state, except to the extent that such state statute, regulation, order or interpretation is inconsistent with the provisions of this part, and then only to the extent of the inconsistency.

(b) *Greater protection under state law.* For purposes of this section, a state statute, regulation, order or interpretation is not inconsistent with the provisions of this part if the protection such statute, regulation, order or interpretation affords any consumer is greater than the protection provided under this part, as determined by the Federal Trade Commission, after consultation with the National Credit Union Administration, on the Federal Trade Commission's own motion or upon the petition of any interested party.

§716.18 **Effective date; transition rule.**

(a) *Effective date.* This part is effective November 13, 2000. In order to provide sufficient time for you to establish policies and systems to comply with the requirements of this part, the National Credit Union Administration Board has extended the time for compliance with this part until July 1, 2001.

(b)(1) *Notice requirement for consumers who were your members on the compliance date.* By July 1, 2001, you must provide an initial notice, as required by §716.4, to consumers who are your members on July 1, 2001.

(2) *Example.* You provide an initial notice to consumers who are your members on July 1, 2001, if, by that date, you have established a system for providing an initial notice to all new members and have mailed the initial notice to all your existing members.

(c) *Two-year grandfathering of service agreements.* Until July 1, 2002, a contract that you have entered into with a nonaffiliated third party to perform services for you or functions on your behalf satisfies the provisions of §716.13(a)(2) of this part, even if the

National Credit Union Administration   **Pt. 716, App. A**

contract does not include a requirement that the third party maintain the confidentiality of nonpublic personal information, as long as the agreement was entered into on or before July 1, 2000.

APPENDIX A TO PART 716—MODEL PRIVACY FORM

A. The Model Privacy Form

Version 1: Model Form With No Opt-Out.

Rev. [insert date]

FACTS	WHAT DOES [NAME OF FINANCIAL INSTITUTION] DO WITH YOUR PERSONAL INFORMATION?
Why?	Financial companies choose how they share your personal information. Federal law gives consumers the right to limit some but not all sharing. Federal law also requires us to tell you how we collect, share, and protect your personal information. Please read this notice carefully to understand what we do.
What?	The types of personal information we collect and share depend on the product or service you have with us. This information can include: ■ Social Security number and [income] ■ [account balances] and [payment history] ■ [credit history] and [credit scores] When you are *no longer* our customer, we continue to share your information as described in this notice.
How?	All financial companies need to share customers' personal information to run their everyday business. In the section below, we list the reasons financial companies can share their customers' personal information; the reasons [name of financial institution] chooses to share; and whether you can limit this sharing.

Reasons we can share your personal information	Does [name of financial institution] share?	Can you limit this sharing?
For our everyday business purposes— such as to process your transactions, maintain your account(s), respond to court orders and legal investigations, or report to credit bureaus		
For our marketing purposes— to offer our products and services to you		
For joint marketing with other financial companies		
For our affiliates' everyday business purposes— information about your transactions and experiences		
For our affiliates' everyday business purposes— information about your creditworthiness		
For our affiliates to market to you		
For nonaffiliates to market to you		

Questions?	Call [phone number] or go to [website]

Pt. 716, App. A   12 CFR Ch. VII (1-1-12 Edition)

Page 2

Who we are	
Who is providing this notice?	[insert]

What we do	
How does [name of financial institution] protect my personal information?	To protect your personal information from unauthorized access and use, we use security measures that comply with federal law. These measures include computer safeguards and secured files and buildings. [insert]
How does [name of financial institution] collect my personal information?	We collect your personal information, for example, when you ■ [open an account] or [deposit money] ■ [pay your bills] or [apply for a loan] ■ [use your credit or debit card] [We also collect your personal information from other companies.] OR [We also collect your personal information from others, such as credit bureaus, affiliates, or other companies.]
Why can't I limit all sharing?	Federal law gives you the right to limit only ■ sharing for affiliates' everyday business purposes—information about your creditworthiness ■ affiliates from using your information to market to you ■ sharing for nonaffiliates to market to you State laws and individual companies may give you additional rights to limit sharing. [See below for more on your rights under state law.]

Definitions	
Affiliates	Companies related by common ownership or control. They can be financial and nonfinancial companies. ■ [affiliate information]
Nonaffiliates	Companies not related by common ownership or control. They can be financial and nonfinancial companies. ■ [nonaffiliate information]
Joint marketing	A formal agreement between nonaffiliated financial companies that together market financial products or services to you. ■ [joint marketing information]

Other important information
[insert other important information]

766

National Credit Union Administration   **Pt. 716, App. A**

Version 2: Model Form with Opt-Out by Telephone and/or Online.

Rev. [insert date]

FACTS	**WHAT DOES [NAME OF FINANCIAL INSTITUTION] DO WITH YOUR PERSONAL INFORMATION?**
Why?	Financial companies choose how they share your personal information. Federal law gives consumers the right to limit some but not all sharing. Federal law also requires us to tell you how we collect, share, and protect your personal information. Please read this notice carefully to understand what we do.
What?	The types of personal information we collect and share depend on the product or service you have with us. This information can include: ■ Social Security number and [income] ■ [account balances] and [payment history] ■ [credit history] and [credit scores]
How?	All financial companies need to share customers' personal information to run their everyday business. In the section below, we list the reasons financial companies can share their customers' personal information; the reasons [name of financial institution] chooses to share; and whether you can limit this sharing.

Reasons we can share your personal information	Does [name of financial institution] share?	Can you limit this sharing?
For our everyday business purposes—such as to process your transactions, maintain your account(s), respond to court orders and legal investigations, or report to credit bureaus		
For our marketing purposes—to offer our products and services to you		
For joint marketing with other financial companies		
For our affiliates' everyday business purposes—information about your transactions and experiences		
For our affiliates' everyday business purposes—information about your creditworthiness		
For our affiliates to market to you		
For nonaffiliates to market to you		

To limit our sharing	■ Call [phone number]—our menu will prompt you through your choice(s) or ■ Visit us online: [website] **Please note:** If you are a *new* customer, we can begin sharing your information [30] days from the date we sent this notice. When you are *no longer* our customer, we continue to share your information as described in this notice. However, you can contact us at any time to limit our sharing.
Questions?	Call [phone number] or go to [website]

767

Page 2

Who we are	
Who is providing this notice?	[insert]

What we do	
How does [name of financial institution] protect my personal information?	To protect your personal information from unauthorized access and use, we use security measures that comply with federal law. These measures include computer safeguards and secured files and buildings. [insert]
How does [name of financial institution] collect my personal information?	We collect your personal information, for example, when you - [open an account] or [deposit money] - [pay your bills] or [apply for a loan] - [use your credit or debit card] [We also collect your personal information from other companies.] OR [We also collect your personal information from others, such as credit bureaus, affiliates, or other companies.]
Why can't I limit all sharing?	Federal law gives you the right to limit only - sharing for affiliates' everyday business purposes—information about your creditworthiness - affiliates from using your information to market to you - sharing for nonaffiliates to market to you State laws and individual companies may give you additional rights to limit sharing. [See below for more on your rights under state law.]
What happens when I limit sharing for an account I hold jointly with someone else?	[Your choices will apply to everyone on your account.] OR [Your choices will apply to everyone on your account—unless you tell us otherwise.]

Definitions	
Affiliates	Companies related by common ownership or control. They can be financial and nonfinancial companies. - [affiliate information]
Nonaffiliates	Companies not related by common ownership or control. They can be financial and nonfinancial companies. - [nonaffiliate information]
Joint marketing	A formal agreement between nonaffiliated financial companies that together market financial products or services to you. - [joint marketing information]

Other important information	
[insert other important information]	

National Credit Union Administration

Pt. 716, App. A

Version 3: Model Form with Mail-In Opt-Out Form.

Rev. [insert date]

FACTS	WHAT DOES [NAME OF FINANCIAL INSTITUTION] DO WITH YOUR PERSONAL INFORMATION?
Why?	Financial companies choose how they share your personal information. Federal law gives consumers the right to limit some but not all sharing. Federal law also requires us to tell you how we collect, share, and protect your personal information. Please read this notice carefully to understand what we do.
What?	The types of personal information we collect and share depend on the product or service you have with us. This information can include: ■ Social Security number and [income] ■ [account balances] and [payment history] ■ [credit history] and [credit scores]
How?	All financial companies need to share customers' personal information to run their everyday business. In the section below, we list the reasons financial companies can share their customers' personal information; the reasons [name of financial institution] chooses to share; and whether you can limit this sharing.

Reasons we can share your personal information	Does [name of financial institution] share?	Can you limit this sharing?
For our everyday business purposes— such as to process your transactions, maintain your account(s), respond to court orders and legal investigations, or report to credit bureaus		
For our marketing purposes— to offer our products and services to you		
For joint marketing with other financial companies		
For our affiliates' everyday business purposes— information about your transactions and experiences		
For our affiliates' everyday business purposes— information about your creditworthiness		
For our affiliates to market to you		
For nonaffiliates to market to you		

To limit our sharing	■ Call [phone number]—our menu will prompt you through your choice(s) ■ Visit us online: [website] or ■ Mail the form below **Please note:** If you are a *new* customer, we can begin sharing your information [30] days from the date we sent this notice. When you are *no longer* our customer, we continue to share your information as described in this notice. However, you can contact us at any time to limit our sharing.
Questions?	Call [phone number] or go to [website]

✂- -

Mail-in Form		
Leave Blank OR [If you have a joint account, your choice(s) will apply to everyone on your account unless you mark below. ☐ Apply my choices only to me]	Mark any/all you want to limit: ☐ Do not share information about my creditworthiness with your affiliates for their everyday business purposes. ☐ Do not allow your affiliates to use my personal information to market to me. ☐ Do not share my personal information with nonaffiliates to market their products and services to me.	
	Name _____	
	Address _____	Mail to: [Name of Financial Institution] [Address 1] [Address 2] [City], [ST] [ZIP]
	City, State, Zip _____	

Pt. 716, App. A   12 CFR Ch. VII (1–1–12 Edition)

Page 2

Who we are	
Who is providing this notice?	[insert]

What we do	
How does [name of financial institution] protect my personal information?	To protect your personal information from unauthorized access and use, we use security measures that comply with federal law. These measures include computer safeguards and secured files and buildings. [insert]
How does [name of financial institution] collect my personal information?	We collect your personal information, for example, when you • [open an account] or [deposit money] • [pay your bills] or [apply for a loan] • [use your credit or debit card] [We also collect your personal information from other companies.] OR [We also collect your personal information from others, such as credit bureaus, affiliates, or other companies.]
Why can't I limit all sharing?	Federal law gives you the right to limit only • sharing for affiliates' everyday business purposes—information about your creditworthiness • affiliates from using your information to market to you • sharing for nonaffiliates to market to you State laws and individual companies may give you additional rights to limit sharing. [See below for more on your rights under state law.]
What happens when I limit sharing for an account I hold jointly with someone else?	[Your choices will apply to everyone on your account.] OR [Your choices will apply to everyone on your account—unless you tell us otherwise.]

Definitions	
Affiliates	Companies related by common ownership or control. They can be financial and nonfinancial companies. • [affiliate information]
Nonaffiliates	Companies not related by common ownership or control. They can be financial and nonfinancial companies. • [nonaffiliate information]
Joint marketing	A formal agreement between nonaffiliated financial companies that together market financial products or services to you. • [joint marketing information]

Other important information	
[insert other important information]	

Version 4. Optional Mail-in Form.

Mail-in Form		
Leave Blank OR [If you have a joint account, your choice(s) will apply to everyone on your account unless you mark below. ☐ Apply my choices only to me]	Mark any/all you want to limit: ☐ Do not share information about my creditworthiness with your affiliates for their everyday business purposes. ☐ Do not allow your affiliates to use my personal information to market to me. ☐ Do not share my personal information with nonaffiliates to market their products and services to me.	
	Name	
	Address	
	City, State, Zip	

Mail To: [Name of Financial Institution], [Address1] [Address2], [City], [ST] [ZIP]

1. How the Model Privacy Form Is Used

(a) The model form may be used, at the option of a financial institution, including a group of financial institutions that use a common privacy notice, to meet the content requirements of the privacy notice and opt-out notice set forth in §§ 716.6 and 716.7 of this part.

(b) The model form is a standardized form, including page layout, content, format, style, pagination, and shading. Institutions seeking to obtain the safe harbor through use of the model form may modify it only as described in these Instructions.

(c) Note that disclosure of certain information, such as assets, income, and information from a consumer reporting agency, may give rise to obligations under the Fair Credit Reporting Act [15 U.S.C. 1681—1681x] (FCRA), such as a requirement to permit a consumer to opt out of disclosures to affiliates or designation as a consumer reporting agency if disclosures are made to nonaffiliated third parties.

(d) The word "customer" may be replaced by the word "member" whenever it appears in the model form, as appropriate.

2. The Contents of the Model Privacy Form

The model form consists of two pages, which may be printed on both sides of a single sheet of paper, or may appear on two separate pages. Where an institution provides a long list of institutions at the end of the model form in accordance with Instruction C.3(a)(1), or provides additional information in accordance with Instruction C.3(c), and such list or additional information exceeds the space available on page two of the model form, such list or additional information may extend to a third page.

(a) *Page One*. The first page consists of the following components:

(1) Date last revised (upper right-hand corner).

(2) Title.

(3) Key frame (Why?, What?, How?).

(4) Disclosure table ("Reasons we can share your personal information").

(5) "To limit our sharing" box, as needed, for the financial institution's opt-out information.

(6) "Questions" box, for customer service contact information.

(7) Mail-in opt-out form, as needed.

(b) *Page Two*. The second page consists of the following components:

(1) Heading (Page 2).

(2) Frequently Asked Questions ("Who we are" and "What we do").

(3) Definitions.

(4) "Other important information" box, as needed.

3. The Format of the Model Privacy Form

The format of the model form may be modified only as described below.

(a) *Easily readable type font*. Financial institutions that use the model form must use an easily readable type font. While a number of factors together produce easily readable type font, institutions are required to use a minimum of 10-point font (unless otherwise expressly permitted in these Instructions) and sufficient spacing between the lines of type.

(b) *Logo*. A financial institution may include a corporate logo on any page of the notice, so long as it does not interfere with the readability of the model form or the space constraints of each page.

Pt. 716, App. A

(c) *Page size and orientation.* Each page of the model form must be printed on paper in portrait orientation, the size of which must be sufficient to meet the layout and minimum font size requirements, with sufficient white space on the top, bottom, and sides of the content.

(d) *Color.* The model form must be printed on white or light color paper (such as cream) with black or other contrasting ink color. Spot color may be used to achieve visual interest, so long as the color contrast is distinctive and the color does not detract from the readability of the model form. Logos may also be printed in color.

(e) *Languages.* The model form may be translated into languages other than English.

C. Information Required in the Model Privacy Form

The information in the model form may be modified only as described below:

1. Name of the Institution or Group of Affiliated Institutions Providing the Notice

Insert the name of the financial institution providing the notice or a common identity of affiliated institutions jointly providing the notice on the form wherever [name of financial institution] appears.

2. Page One

(a) *Last revised date.* The financial institution must insert in the upper right-hand corner the date on which the notice was last revised. The information shall appear in minimum 8-point font as "rev. [month/year]" using either the name or number of the month, such as "rev. July 2009" or "rev. 7/09".

(b) *General instructions for the "What?" box.*

(1) The bulleted list identifies the types of personal information that the institution collects and shares. All institutions must use the term "Social Security number" in the first bullet.

(2) Institutions must use five (5) of the following terms to complete the bulleted list: income; account balances; payment history; transaction history; transaction or loss history; credit history; credit scores; assets; investment experience; credit-based insurance scores; insurance claim history; medical information; overdraft history; purchase history; account transactions; risk tolerance; medical-related debts; credit card or other debt; mortgage rates and payments; retirement assets; checking account information; employment information; wire transfer instructions.

(c) *General instructions for the disclosure table.* The left column lists reasons for sharing or using personal information. Each reason correlates to a specific legal provision described in paragraph C.2(d) of this Instruction. In the middle column, each institution must provide a "Yes" or "No" response that accurately reflects its information sharing policies and practices with respect to the reason listed on the left. In the right column, each institution must provide in each box one of the following three (3) responses, as applicable, that reflects whether a consumer can limit such sharing: "Yes" if it is required to or voluntarily provides an opt-out; "No" if it does not provide an opt-out; or "We don't share" if it answers "No" in the middle column. Only the sixth row ("For our affiliates to market to you") may be omitted at the option of the institution. *See* paragraph C.2(d)(6) of this Instruction.

(d) *Specific disclosures and corresponding legal provisions.*

(1) *For our everyday business purposes.* This reason incorporates sharing information under §§716.14 and 716.15 and with service providers pursuant to §716.13 of this part other than the purposes specified in paragraphs C.2(d)(2) or C.2(d)(3) of these Instructions.

(2) *For our marketing purposes.* This reason incorporates sharing information with service providers by an institution for its own marketing pursuant to §716.13 of this part. An institution that shares for this reason may choose to provide an opt-out.

(3) *For joint marketing with other financial companies.* This reason incorporates sharing information under joint marketing agreements between two or more financial institutions and with any service provider used in connection with such agreements pursuant to §716.13 of this part. An institution that shares for this reason may choose to provide an opt-out.

(4) *For our affiliates' everyday business purposes—information about transactions and experiences.* This reason incorporates sharing information specified in sections 603(d)(2)(A)(i) and (ii) of the FCRA. An institution that shares for this reason may choose to provide an opt-out.

(5) *For our affiliates' everyday business purposes—information about creditworthiness.* This reason incorporates sharing information pursuant to section 603(d)(2)(A)(iii) of the FCRA. An institution that shares for this reason must provide an opt-out.

(6) *For our affiliates to market to you.* This reason incorporates sharing information specified in section 624 of the FCRA. This reason may be omitted from the disclosure table when: the institution does not have affiliates (or does not disclose personal information to its affiliates); the institution's affiliates do not use personal information in a manner that requires an opt-out; or the institution provides the affiliate marketing notice separately. Institutions that include this reason must provide an opt-out of indefinite duration. An institution that is required to provide an affiliate marketing opt-

out, but does not include that opt-out in the model form under this part, must comply with section 624 of the FCRA and 12 CFR part 717, subpart C, with respect to the initial notice and opt-out and any subsequent renewal notice and opt-out. An institution not required to provide an opt-out under this subparagraph may elect to include this reason in the model form.

(7) *For nonaffiliates to market to you.* This reason incorporates sharing described in §§ 716.7 and 716.10(a) of this part. An institution that shares personal information for this reason must provide an opt-out.

(e) *To limit our sharing:* A financial institution must include this section of the model form *only* if it provides an opt-out. The word "choice" may be written in either the singular or plural, as appropriate. Institutions must select one or more of the applicable opt-out methods described: telephone, such as by a toll-free number; a Web site; or use of a mail-in opt-out form. Institutions may include the words "toll-free" before telephone, as appropriate. An institution that allows consumers to opt out online must provide either a specific Web address that takes consumers directly to the opt-out page or a general Web address that provides a clear and conspicuous direct link to the opt-out page. The opt-out choices made available to the consumer who contacts the institution through these methods must correspond accurately to the "Yes" responses in the third column of the disclosure table. In the part titled "Please note" institutions may insert a number that is 30 or greater in the space marked "[30]." Instructions on voluntary or state privacy law opt-out information are in paragraph C.2(g)(5) of these Instructions.

(f) *Questions box.* Customer service contact information must be inserted as appropriate, where [phone number] or [Web site] appear. Institutions may elect to provide either a phone number, such as a toll-free number, or a Web address, or both. Institutions may include the words "toll-free" before the telephone number, as appropriate.

(g) *Mail-in opt-out form.* Financial institutions must include this mail-in form *only* if they state in the "To limit our sharing" box that consumers can opt out by mail. The mail-in form must provide opt-out options that correspond accurately to the "Yes" responses in the third column in the disclosure table. Institutions that require customers to provide only name and address may omit the section identified as "[account #]." Institutions that require additional or different information, such as a random opt-out number or a truncated account number, to implement an opt-out election should modify the "[account #]" reference accordingly. This includes institutions that require customers with multiple accounts to identify each account to which the opt-out should apply. An institution must enter its opt-out mailing address: in the far right of this form (*see* version 3); or below the form (*see* version 4). The reverse side of the mail-in opt-out form must not include any content of the model form.

(1) *Joint accountholder.* Only institutions that provide their joint accountholders the choice to opt out for only one accountholder, in accordance with paragraph C.3(a)(5) of these Instructions, must include in the far left column of the mail-in form the following statement: "If you have a joint account, your choice(s) will apply to everyone on your account unless you mark below. ☐ Apply my choice(s) only to me." The word "choice" may be written in either the singular or plural, as appropriate. Financial institutions that provide insurance products or services, provide this option, and elect to use the model form may substitute the word "policy" for "account" in this statement. Institutions that do not provide this option may eliminate this left column from the mail-in form.

(2) *FCRA Section 603(d)(2)(A)(iii) opt-out.* If the institution shares personal information pursuant to section 603(d)(2)(A)(iii) of the FCRA, it must include in the mail-in opt-out form the following statement: "☐ Do not share information about my creditworthiness with your affiliates for their everyday business purposes."

(3) *FCRA Section 624 opt-out.* If the institution incorporates section 624 of the FCRA in accord with paragraph C.2(d)(6) of these Instructions, it must include in the mail-in opt-out form the following statement: "☐ Do not allow your affiliates to use my personal information to market to me."

(4) *Nonaffiliate opt-out.* If the financial institution shares personal information pursuant to § 716.10(a) of this part, it must include in the mail-in opt-out form the following statement: "☐ Do not share my personal information with nonaffiliates to market their products and services to me."

(5) *Additional opt-outs.* Financial institutions that use the disclosure table to provide opt-out options beyond those required by Federal law must provide those opt-outs in this section of the model form. A financial institution that chooses to offer an opt-out for its own marketing in the mail-in opt-out form must include one of the two following statements: "☐ Do not share my personal information to market to me." *or* "☐ Do not use my personal information to market to me." A financial institution that chooses to offer an opt-out for joint marketing must include the following statement: "☐ Do not share my personal information with other financial institutions to jointly market to me."

(h) *Barcodes.* A financial institution may elect to include a barcode and/or "tagline" (an internal identifier) in 6-point font at the bottom of page one, as needed for information internal to the institution, so long as these do not interfere with the clarity or text of the form.

3. Page Two

(a) *General Instructions for the Questions.* Certain of the Questions may be customized as follows:

(1) *"Who is providing this notice?"* This question may be omitted where only one financial institution provides the model form and that institution is clearly identified in the title on page one. Two or more financial institutions that jointly provide the model form must use this question to identify themselves as required by § 716.9(f) of this part. Where the list of institutions exceeds four (4) lines, the institution must describe in the response to this question the general types of institutions jointly providing the notice and must separately identify those institutions, in minimum 8-point font, directly following the "Other important information" box, or, if that box is not included in the institution's form, directly following the "Definitions." The list may appear in a multi-column format.

(2) *"How does [name of financial institution] protect my personal information?"* The financial institution may only provide additional information pertaining to its safeguards practices following the designated response to this question. Such information may include information about the institution's use of cookies or other measures it uses to safeguard personal information. Institutions are limited to a maximum of 30 additional words.

(3) *"How does [name of financial institution] collect my personal information?"* Institutions must use five (5) of the following terms to complete the bulleted list for this question: open an account; deposit money; pay your bills; apply for a loan; use your credit or debit card; seek financial or tax advice; apply for insurance; pay insurance premiums; file an insurance claim; seek advice about your investments; buy securities from us; sell securities to us; direct us to buy securities; direct us to sell your securities; make deposits or withdrawals from your account; enter into an investment advisory contract; give us your income information; provide employment information; give us your employment history; tell us about your investment or retirement portfolio; tell us about your investment or retirement earnings; apply for financing; apply for a lease; provide account information; give us your contact information; pay us by check; give us your wage statements; provide your mortgage information; make a wire transfer; tell us who receives the money; tell us where to send the money; show your government-issued ID; show your driver's license; order a commodity futures or option trade. Institutions that collect personal information from their affiliates and/or credit bureaus must include after the bulleted list the following statement: "We also collect your personal information from others, such as credit bureaus, affiliates, or other companies." Institutions that do not collect personal information from their affiliates or credit bureaus but do collect information from other companies must include the following statement instead: "We also collect your personal information from other companies." Only institutions that do not collect any personal information from affiliates, credit bureaus, or other companies can omit both statements.

(4) *"Why can't I limit all sharing?"* Institutions that describe state privacy law provisions in the *"Other important information"* box must use the bracketed sentence: "See below for more on your rights under state law." Other institutions must omit this sentence.

(5) *"What happens when I limit sharing for an account I hold jointly with someone else?"* Only financial institutions that provide opt-out options must use this question. Other institutions must omit this question. Institutions must choose one of the following two statements to respond to this question: "Your choices will apply to everyone on your account." or "Your choices will apply to everyone on your account—unless you tell us otherwise." Financial institutions that provide insurance products or services and elect to use the model form may substitute the word "policy" for "account" in these statements.

(b) *General Instructions for the Definitions.* The financial institution must customize the space below the responses to the three definitions in this section. This specific information must be in italicized lettering to set off the information from the standardized definitions.

(1) *Affiliates.* As required by § 716.6(a)(3) of this part, where *[affiliate information]* appears, the financial institution must:

(i) If it has no affiliates, state: "*[name of financial institution] has no affiliates*";

(ii) If it has affiliates but does not share personal information, state: "*[name of financial institution] does not share with our affiliates*; or

(iii) If it shares with its affiliates, state, as applicable: "*Our affiliates include companies with a [common corporate identity of financial institution] name; financial companies such as [insert illustrative list of companies]; nonfinancial companies, such as [insert illustrative list of companies;] and others, such as [insert illustrative list].*"

(2) *Nonaffiliates.* As required by § 716.6(c)(3) of this part, where *[nonaffiliate information]* appears, the financial institution must:

National Credit Union Administration

(i) If it does not share with nonaffiliated third parties, state: *"[name of financial institution] does not share with nonaffiliates so they can market to you"*; or

(ii) If it shares with nonaffiliated third parties, state, as applicable: *"Nonaffiliates we share with can include [list categories of companies such as mortgage companies, insurance companies, direct marketing companies, and nonprofit organizations]."*

(3) *Joint Marketing.* As required by §716.13 of this part, where *[joint marketing]* appears, the financial institution must:

(i) If it does not engage in joint marketing, state: *"[name of financial institution] doesn't jointly market "*; or

(ii) If it shares personal information for joint marketing, state, as applicable: *"Our joint marketing partners include [list categories of companies such as credit card companies]."*

(c) *General instructions for the "Other important information" box.* This box is optional. The space provided for information in this box is not limited. Only the following types of information can appear in this box.

(1) State and/or international privacy law information; and/or

(2) Acknowledgment of receipt form.

[74 FR 62956, 62965, Dec. 1, 2009]

PART 717—FAIR CREDIT REPORTING

Subpart A—General Provisions

Sec.
717.1 Purpose, scope, and effective dates.
717.2 Examples.
717.3 Definitions.

Subpart B [Reserved]

Subpart C—Affiliate Marketing

717.20 Coverage and definitions.
717.21 Affiliate marketing opt-out and exceptions.
717.22 Scope and duration of opt-out.
717.23 Contents of opt-out notice; consolidated and equivalent notices.
717.24 Reasonable opportunity to opt out.
717.25 Reasonable and simple methods of opting out.
717.26 Delivery of opt-out notices.
717.27 Renewal of opt-out.
717.28 Effective date, compliance date, and prospective application.

Subpart D—Medical Information

717.30 Obtaining or using medical information in connection with a determination of eligibility for credit.
717.31 Limits on redisclosure of information.
717.32 Sharing medical information with affiliates.

Subpart E—Duties of Furnishers of Information

717.40 Scope.
717.41 Definitions.
717.42 Reasonable policies and procedures concerning the accuracy and integrity of furnished information.
717.43 Direct disputes.

Subparts F–H [Reserved]

Subpart Subpart I—Duties of Users of Consumer Reports Regarding Address Discrepancies and Records Disposal

717.80–717.81 [Reserved]
717.82 Duties of users regarding address discrepancies.
717.83 Disposal of consumer information.

Subpart J—Identity Theft Red Flags

717.90 Duties regarding the detection, prevention, and mitigation of identity theft.
717.91 Duties of card issuers regarding changes of address.

APPENDICES A–B TO PART 717 [RESERVED]
APPENDIX C TO PART 717—MODEL FORMS FOR OPT-OUT NOTICES
APPENDIX D TO PART 717 [RESERVED]
APPENDIX E TO PART 717—INTERAGENCY GUIDELINES CONCERNING THE ACCURACY AND INTEGRITY OF INFORMATION FURNISHED TO CONSUMER REPORTING AGENCIES
APPENDICES F–I TO PART 717 [RESERVED]
APPENDIX J TO PART 717—INTERAGENCY GUIDELINES ON IDENTITY THEFT DETECTION, PREVENTION, AND MITIGATION

AUTHORITY: 12 U.S.C. 1751 *et seq.*; 15 U.S.C. 1681a, 1681b, 1681c, 1681m, 1681s, 1681s–1, 1681t, 1681w, 6801 and 6805, Public Law 108–159, 117 Stat. 1952.

SOURCE: 69 FR 69273, Nov. 29, 2004, unless otherwise noted.

Subpart A—General Provisions

SOURCE: 70 FR 70692, Nov. 22, 2005, unless otherwise noted.

§ 717.1 Purpose, scope, and effective dates.

(a) *Purpose.* The purpose of this part is to implement the provisions of the Fair Credit Reporting Act. This part generally applies to federal credit unions that obtain and use information about consumers to determine the consumer's eligibility for products, services, or employment, share such information among affiliates, and furnish

§ 717.2

information to consumer reporting agencies.

(b) *Scope.* (1) [Reserved]

(2) *Institutions covered.* (i) Except as otherwise provided in this part, the regulations in this part apply to federal credit unions.

[72 FR 62981, Nov. 7, 2007]

§ 717.2 Examples.

The examples in this part are not exclusive. Compliance with an example, to the extent applicable, constitutes compliance with this part. Examples in a paragraph illustrate only the issue described in the paragraph and do not illustrate any other issue that may arise in this part.

§ 717.3 Definitions.

For purposes of this part, unless explicitly stated otherwise:

(a) *Act* means the Fair Credit Reporting Act (15 U.S.C. 1681 *et seq.*).

(b) *Affiliate* means any company that is related by common ownership or common corporate control with another company. For example, an affiliate of a Federal credit union is a credit union service corporation (CUSO), as provided in 12 CFR part 712, that is controlled by the Federal credit union.

(c) [Reserved]

(d) *Company* means any corporation, limited liability company, business trust, general or limited partnership, association, or similar organization.

(e) *Consumer* means an individual.

(f)–(h) [Reserved]

(i) *Common ownership or common corporate control* means a relationship between two companies under which:

(1) One company has, with respect to the other company:

(i) Ownership, control, or power to vote 25 percent or more of the outstanding shares of any class of voting security of a company, directly or indirectly, or acting through one or more other persons;

(ii) Control in any manner over the election of a majority of the directors, trustees, or general partners (or individuals exercising similar functions) of a company; or

(iii) The power to exercise, directly or indirectly, a controlling influence over the management or policies of a company, as the NCUA determines; or

(iv) *Example.* NCUA will presume a credit union has a controlling influence over the management or policies of a CUSO, if the CUSO is 67% owned by credit unions.

(2) Any other person has, with respect to both companies, a relationship described in paragraphs (i)(1)(i) through (i)(1)(iii) of this section.

(j) [Reserved]

(k) *Medical information* means:

(1) Information or data, whether oral or recorded, in any form or medium, created by or derived from a health care provider or the consumer, that relates to:

(i) The past, present, or future physical, mental, or behavioral health or condition of an individual;

(ii) The provision of health care to an individual; or

(iii) The payment for the provision of health care to an individual.

(2) The term does not include:

(i) The age or gender of a consumer;

(ii) Demographic information about the consumer, including a consumer's residence address or e-mail address;

(iii) Any other information about a consumer that does not relate to the physical, mental, or behavioral health or condition of a consumer, including the existence or value of any insurance policy; or

(iv) Information that does not identify a specific consumer.

(l) *Person* means any individual, partnership, corporation, trust, estate, cooperative, association, government or governmental subdivision or agency, or other entity.

[70 FR 70692, Nov. 22, 2005, as amended at 72 FR 63768, Nov. 9, 2007; 75 FR 34621, June 18, 2010]

Subpart B [Reserved]

Subpart C—Affiliate Marketing

SOURCE: 72 FR 62981, Nov. 7, 2007, unless otherwise noted.

§ 717.20 Coverage and definitions.

(a) *Coverage.* Subpart C of this part applies to federal credit unions and their affiliates as defined in § 717.3(a) of Subpart A.

(b) *Definitions.* For purposes of this subpart:

(1) *Clear and conspicuous.* The term "clear and conspicuous" means reasonably understandable and designed to call attention to the nature and significance of the information presented.

(2) *Concise.* (i) In general. The term "concise" means a reasonably brief expression or statement.

(ii) *Combination with other required disclosures.* A notice required by this subpart may be concise even if it is combined with other disclosures required or authorized by federal or state law.

(3) *Eligibility information.* The term "eligibility information" means any information the communication of which would be a consumer report if the exclusions from the definition of "consumer report" in section 603(d)(2)(A) of the Act did not apply. Eligibility information does not include aggregate or blind data that does not contain personal identifiers such as account numbers, names, or addresses.

(4) *Pre-existing business relationship.* (i) *In general.* The term "pre-existing business relationship" means a relationship between a person, or a person's licensed agent, and a consumer based on—

(A) A financial contract between the person and the consumer which is in force on the date on which the consumer is sent a solicitation covered by this subpart;

(B) The purchase, rental, or lease by the consumer of the person's goods or services, or a financial transaction (including holding an active account or a policy in force or having another continuing relationship) between the consumer and the person, during the 18-month period immediately preceding the date on which the consumer is sent a solicitation covered by this subpart; or

(C) An inquiry or application by the consumer regarding a product or service offered by that person during the three-month period immediately preceding the date on which the consumer is sent a solicitation covered by this subpart.

(ii) *Examples of pre-existing business relationships.* (A) If a consumer has a time deposit account, such as a share certificate, at a federal credit union that is currently in force, the federal credit union has a pre-existing business relationship with the consumer and can use eligibility information it receives from its affiliates to make solicitations to the consumer about its products or services.

(B) If a consumer obtained a share certificate from a federal credit union, but did not renew the certificate at maturity, the federal credit union has a pre-existing business relationship with the consumer and can use eligibility information it receives from its affiliates to make solicitations to the consumer about its products or services for 18 months after the date of maturity of the share certificate.

(C) If a consumer obtains a mortgage, the mortgage lender has a pre-existing business relationship with the consumer. If the mortgage lender sells the consumer's entire loan to an investor, the mortgage lender has a pre-existing business relationship with the consumer and can use eligibility information it receives from its affiliates to make solicitations to the consumer about its products or services for 18 months after the date it sells the loan, and the investor has a pre-existing business relationship with the consumer upon purchasing the loan. If, however, the mortgage lender sells a fractional interest in the consumer's loan to an investor but also retains an ownership interest in the loan, the mortgage lender continues to have a pre-existing business relationship with the consumer, but the investor does not have a pre-existing business relationship with the consumer. If the mortgage lender retains ownership of the loan, but sells ownership of the servicing rights to the consumer's loan, the mortgage lender continues to have a pre-existing business relationship with the consumer. The purchaser of the servicing rights also has a pre-existing business relationship with the consumer as of the date it purchases ownership of the servicing rights, but only if it collects payments from or otherwise deals directly with the consumer on a continuing basis.

(D) If a consumer applies to a federal credit union for a product or service that it offers, but does not obtain a product or service from or enter into a financial contract or transaction with the institution, the federal credit union has a pre-existing business relationship with the consumer and can therefore use eligibility information it receives from an affiliate to make solicitations to the consumer about its products or services for three months after the date of the application.

(E) If a consumer makes a telephone inquiry to a federal credit union about its products or services and provides contact information to the institution, but does not obtain a product or service from or enter into a financial contract or transaction with the institution, the federal credit union has a pre-existing business relationship with the consumer and can therefore use eligibility information it receives from an affiliate to make solicitations to the consumer about its products or services for three months after the date of the inquiry.

(F) If a consumer makes an inquiry to a federal credit union by e-mail about its products or services, but does not obtain a product or service from or enter into a financial contract or transaction with the institution, the federal credit union has a pre-existing business relationship with the consumer and can therefore use eligibility information it receives from an affiliate to make solicitations to the consumer about its products or services for three months after the date of the inquiry.

(G) If a consumer has an existing relationship with a federal credit union that is part of a group of affiliated companies, makes a telephone call to the centralized call center for the group of affiliated companies to inquire about products or services offered by the insurance brokerage affiliate, and provides contact information to the call center, the call constitutes an inquiry to the insurance brokerage affiliate that offers those products or services. The insurance brokerage affiliate has a pre-existing business relationship with the consumer and can therefore use eligibility information it receives from its affiliated federal credit union to make solicitations to the consumer about its products or services for three months after the date of the inquiry.

(iii) *Examples where no pre-existing business relationship is created.* (A) If a consumer makes a telephone call to a centralized call center for a group of affiliated companies to inquire about the consumer's existing account at a federal credit union, the call does not constitute an inquiry to any affiliate other than the federal credit union that holds the consumer's account and does not establish a pre-existing business relationship between the consumer and any affiliate of the account-holding federal credit union.

(B) If a consumer who has a deposit account with a federal credit union makes a telephone call to an affiliate of the institution to ask about the affiliate's retail locations and hours, but does not make an inquiry about the affiliate's products or services, the call does not constitute an inquiry and does not establish a pre-existing business relationship between the consumer and the affiliate. Also, the affiliate's capture of the consumer's telephone number does not constitute an inquiry and does not establish a pre-existing business relationship between the consumer and the affiliate.

(C) If a consumer makes a telephone call to a federal credit union in response to an advertisement that offers a free promotional item to consumers who call a toll-free number, but the advertisement does not indicate that the federal credit union's products or services will be marketed to consumers who call in response, the call does not create a pre-existing business relationship between the consumer and the federal credit union because the consumer has not made an inquiry about a product or service offered by the institution, but has merely responded to an offer for a free promotional item.

(5) *Solicitation.* (i) *In general.* The term "solicitation" means the marketing of a product or service initiated by a person to a particular consumer that is—

(A) Based on eligibility information communicated to that person by its affiliate as described in this subpart; and

(B) Intended to encourage the consumer to purchase or obtain such product or service.

(ii) *Exclusion of marketing directed at the general public.* A solicitation does not include marketing communications that are directed at the general public. For example, television, general circulation magazine, and billboard advertisements do not constitute solicitations, even if those communications are intended to encourage consumers to purchase products and services from the person initiating the communications.

(iii) *Examples of solicitations.* A solicitation would include, for example, a telemarketing call, direct mail, e-mail, or other form of marketing communication directed to a particular consumer that is based on eligibility information received from an affiliate.

(6) You means a person described in paragraph (a) of this section.

[70 FR 70692, Nov. 22, 2005, as amended at 75 FR 34621, June 18, 2010]

§ 717.21 Affiliate marketing opt-out and exceptions.

(a) *Initial notice and opt-out requirement.* (1) *In general.* You may not use eligibility information about a consumer that you receive from an affiliate to make a solicitation for marketing purposes to the consumer, unless—

(i) It is clearly and conspicuously disclosed to the consumer in writing or, if the consumer agrees, electronically, in a concise notice that you may use eligibility information about that consumer received from an affiliate to make solicitations for marketing purposes to the consumer;

(ii) The consumer is provided a reasonable opportunity and a reasonable and simple method to "opt out," or prohibit you from using eligibility information to make solicitations for marketing purposes to the consumer; and

(iii) The consumer has not opted out.

(2) *Example.* A consumer has a homeowner's insurance policy obtained through an insurance brokerage. The insurance brokerage furnishes eligibility information about the consumer to its affiliated federal credit union. Based on that eligibility information, the federal credit union wants to make a solicitation to the consumer about its home equity loan products. The federal credit union does not have a pre-existing business relationship with the consumer and none of the other exceptions apply. The federal credit union is prohibited from using eligibility information received from its insurance brokerage affiliate to make solicitations to the consumer about its home equity loan products unless the consumer is given a notice and opportunity to opt out and the consumer does not opt out.

(3) *Affiliates who may provide the notice.* The notice required by this paragraph must be provided:

(i) By an affiliate that has or has previously had a pre-existing business relationship with the consumer; or

(ii) As part of a joint notice from two or more members of an affiliated group of companies, provided that at least one of the affiliates on the joint notice has or has previously had a pre-existing business relationship with the consumer.

(b) *Making solicitations.* (1) *In general.* For purposes of this subpart, you make a solicitation for marketing purposes if—

(i) You receive eligibility information from an affiliate;

(ii) You use that eligibility information to do one or more of the following:

(A) Identify the consumer or type of consumer to receive a solicitation;

(B) Establish criteria used to select the consumer to receive a solicitation; or

(C) Decide which of your products or services to market to the consumer or tailor your solicitation to that consumer; and

(iii) As a result of your use of the eligibility information, the consumer is provided a solicitation.

(2) *Receiving eligibility information from an affiliate, including through a common database.* You may receive eligibility information from an affiliate in various ways, including when the affiliate places that information into a common database that you may access.

(3) *Receipt or use of eligibility information by your service provider.* Except as provided in paragraph (b)(5) of this section, you receive or use an affiliate's eligibility information if a service provider acting on your behalf (whether an affiliate or a nonaffiliated third party)

§ 717.21

receives or uses that information in the manner described in paragraphs (b)(1)(i) or (b)(1)(ii) of this section. All relevant facts and circumstances will determine whether a person is acting as your service provider when it receives or uses an affiliate's eligibility information in connection with marketing your products and services.

(4) *Use by an affiliate of its own eligibility information.* Unless you have used eligibility information that you receive from an affiliate in the manner described in paragraph (b)(1)(ii) of this section, you do not make a solicitation subject to this subpart if your affiliate:

(i) Uses its own eligibility information that it obtained in connection with a pre-existing business relationship it has or had with the consumer to market your products or services to the consumer; or

(ii) Directs its service provider to use the affiliate's own eligibility information that it obtained in connection with a pre-existing business relationship it has or had with the consumer to market your products or services to the consumer, and you do not communicate directly with the service provider regarding that use.

(5) *Use of eligibility information by a service provider.* (i) *In general.* You do not make a solicitation subject to Subpart C of this part if a service provider (including an affiliated or third-party service provider that maintains or accesses a common database that you may access) receives eligibility information from your affiliate that your affiliate obtained in connection with a pre-existing business relationship it has or had with the consumer and uses that eligibility information to market your products or services to the consumer, so long as—

(A) Your affiliate controls access to and use of its eligibility information by the service provider (including the right to establish the specific terms and conditions under which the service provider may use such information to market your products or services);

(B) Your affiliate establishes specific terms and conditions under which the service provider may access and use the affiliate's eligibility information to market your products and services (or those of affiliates generally) to the consumer, such as the identity of the affiliated companies whose products or services may be marketed to the consumer by the service provider, the types of products or services of affiliated companies that may be marketed, and the number of times the consumer may receive marketing materials, and periodically evaluates the service provider's compliance with those terms and conditions;

(C) Your affiliate requires the service provider to implement reasonable policies and procedures designed to ensure that the service provider uses the affiliate's eligibility information in accordance with the terms and conditions established by the affiliate relating to the marketing of your products or services;

(D) Your affiliate is identified on or with the marketing materials provided to the consumer; and

(E) You do not directly use your affiliate's eligibility information in the manner described in paragraph (b)(1)(ii) of this section.

(ii) *Writing requirements.* (A) The requirements of paragraphs (b)(5)(i)(A) and (C) of this section must be set forth in a written agreement between your affiliate and the service provider; and

(B) The specific terms and conditions established by your affiliate as provided in paragraph (b)(5)(i)(B) of this section must be set forth in writing.

(6) *Examples of making solicitations.* (i) A consumer has a deposit account with a federal credit union, which is affiliated with an insurance brokerage. The insurance brokerage receives eligibility information about the consumer from the federal credit union. The insurance brokerage uses that eligibility information to identify the consumer to receive a solicitation about insurance brokerage services, and, as a result, the insurance brokerage provides a solicitation to the consumer about its services. Pursuant to paragraph (b)(1) of this section, the insurance brokerage has made a solicitation to the consumer.

(ii) The same facts as in the example in paragraph (b)(6)(i) of this section, except that after using the eligibility information to identify the consumer

National Credit Union Administration § 717.21

to receive a solicitation about insurance brokerage services, the insurance brokerage asks the federal credit union to send the solicitation to the consumer and the federal credit union does so. Pursuant to paragraph (b)(1) of this section, the insurance brokerage has made a solicitation to the consumer because it used eligibility information about the consumer that it received from an affiliate to identify the consumer to receive a solicitation about its products or services, and, as a result, a solicitation was provided to the consumer about the insurance brokerage's services.

(iii) The same facts as in the example in paragraph (b)(6)(i) of this section, except that eligibility information about consumers that have deposit accounts with the federal credit union is placed into a common database that all members of the affiliated group of companies may independently access and use. Without using the federal credit union's eligibility information, the insurance brokerage develops selection criteria and provides those criteria, marketing materials, and related instructions to the federal credit union. The federal credit union reviews eligibility information about its own consumers using the selection criteria provided by the insurance brokerage to determine which consumers should receive the insurance brokerage's marketing materials and sends marketing materials about the insurance brokerage's services to those consumers. Even though the insurance brokerage has received eligibility information through the common database as provided in paragraph (b)(2) of this section, it did not use that information to identify consumers or establish selection criteria; instead, the federal credit union used its own eligibility information. Therefore, pursuant to paragraph (b)(4)(i) of this section, the insurance brokerage has not made a solicitation to the consumer.

(iv) The same facts as in the example in paragraph (b)(6)(iii) of this section, except that the federal credit union provides the insurance brokerage's criteria to the federal credit union's service provider and directs the service provider to use the federal credit union's eligibility information to identify federal credit union consumers who meet the criteria and to send the insurance brokerage's marketing materials to those consumers. The insurance brokerage does not communicate directly with the service provider regarding the use of the federal credit union's information to market its services to the federal credit union's consumers. Pursuant to paragraph (b)(4)(ii) of this section, the insurance brokerage has not made a solicitation to the consumer.

(v) An affiliated group of companies includes a federal credit union, an insurance brokerage, and a service provider. Each affiliate in the group places information about its consumers into a common database. The service provider has access to all information in the common database. The federal credit union controls access to and use of its eligibility information by the service provider. This control is set forth in a written agreement between the federal credit union and the service provider. The written agreement also requires the service provider to establish reasonable policies and procedures designed to ensure that the service provider uses the federal credit union's eligibility information in accordance with specific terms and conditions established by the federal credit union relating to the marketing of the products and services of all affiliates, including the insurance brokerage. In a separate written communication, the federal credit union specifies the terms and conditions under which the service provider may use the federal credit union's eligibility information to market the insurance brokerage's products and services to the federal credit union's consumers. The specific terms and conditions are: a list of affiliated companies (including the insurance brokerage) whose products or services may be marketed to the federal credit union's consumers by the service provider; the specific products or types of products that may be marketed to the federal credit union's consumers by the service provider; the categories of eligibility information that may be used by the service provider in marketing products or services to the federal credit union's consumers; the types or categories of the federal credit union's

§717.21

consumers to whom the service provider may market products or services of federal credit union affiliates; the number and/or types of marketing communications that the service provider may send to the federal credit union's consumers; and the length of time during which the service provider may market the products or services of the federal credit union's affiliates to its consumers. The federal credit union periodically evaluates the service provider's compliance with these terms and conditions. The insurance brokerage asks the service provider to market insurance products to certain consumers who have deposit accounts with the federal credit union. Without using the federal credit union's eligibility information, the insurance brokerage develops selection criteria and provides those criteria, marketing materials, and related instructions to the service provider. The service provider uses the federal credit union's eligibility information from the common database to identify the federal credit union's consumers to whom insurance brokerage services will be marketed. When the insurance brokerage's marketing materials are provided to the identified consumers, the name of the federal credit union is displayed on the brokerage marketing materials, an introductory letter that accompanies the marketing materials, an account statement that accompanies the marketing materials, or the envelope containing the marketing materials. The requirements of paragraph (b)(5) of this section have been satisfied, and the insurance brokerage has not made a solicitation to the consumer.

(vi) The same facts as in the example in paragraph (b)(6)(v) of this section, except that the terms and conditions permit the service provider to use the federal credit union's eligibility information to market the products and services of other affiliates to the federal credit union's consumers whenever the service provider deems it appropriate to do so. The service provider uses the federal credit union's eligibility information in accordance with the discretion afforded to it by the terms and conditions. Because the terms and conditions are not specific, the requirements of paragraph (b)(5) of this section have not been satisfied.

(c) *Exceptions.* The provisions of this subpart do not apply to you if you use eligibility information that you receive from an affiliate:

(1) To make a solicitation for marketing purposes to a consumer with whom you have a pre-existing business relationship;

(2) To facilitate communications to an individual for whose benefit you provide employee benefit or other services pursuant to a contract with an employer related to and arising out of the current employment relationship or status of the individual as a participant or beneficiary of an employee benefit plan;

(3) To perform services on behalf of an affiliate, except that this subparagraph shall not be construed as permitting you to send solicitations on behalf of an affiliate if the affiliate would not be permitted to send the solicitation as a result of the election of the consumer to opt out under this subpart;

(4) In response to a communication about your products or services initiated by the consumer;

(5) In response to an authorization or request by the consumer to receive solicitations; or

(6) If your compliance with this subpart would prevent you from complying with any provision of State insurance laws pertaining to unfair discrimination in any State in which you are lawfully doing business.

(d) *Examples of exceptions.* (1) *Example of the pre-existing business relationship exception.* A consumer has a deposit account with a federal credit union. The consumer also has a relationship with the federal credit union's securities brokerage affiliate. The federal credit union receives eligibility information about the consumer from its securities brokerage affiliate and uses that information to make a solicitation to the consumer about the federal credit union's wealth management services. The federal credit union may make this solicitation even if the consumer has not been given a notice and opportunity to opt out because the federal credit union has a pre-existing business relationship with the consumer.

(2) *Examples of service provider exception.* (i) A consumer has an insurance policy obtained through an insurance brokerage. The insurance brokerage furnishes eligibility information about the consumer to its affiliated federal credit union. Based on that eligibility information, the federal credit union wants to make a solicitation to the consumer about membership and its deposit products. The federal credit union does not have a pre-existing business relationship with the consumer and none of the other exceptions in paragraph (c) of this section apply. The consumer has been given an opt-out notice and has elected to opt out of receiving such solicitations. The federal credit union asks a service provider to send the solicitation to the consumer on its behalf. The service provider may not send the solicitation on behalf of the federal credit union because, as a result of the consumer's opt-out election, the federal credit union is not permitted to make the solicitation.

(ii) The same facts as in paragraph (d)(2)(i) of this section, except the consumer has been given an opt-out notice, but has not elected to opt out. The federal credit union asks a service provider to send the solicitation to the consumer on its behalf. The service provider may send the solicitation on behalf of the federal credit union because, as a result of the consumer's not opting out, the federal credit union is permitted to make the solicitation.

(3) *Examples of consumer-initiated communications.* (i) A consumer who has a deposit account with a federal credit union initiates a communication with the federal credit union's credit card affiliate to request information about a credit card. The credit card affiliate may use eligibility information about the consumer it obtains from the federal credit union or any other affiliate to make solicitations regarding credit card products in response to the consumer-initiated communication.

(ii) A consumer who has a deposit account with a federal credit union contacts the institution to request information about how to save and invest for a child's college education without specifying the type of product in which the consumer may be interested. Information about a range of different products or services offered by the federal credit union and one or more affiliates of the institution may be responsive to that communication. Such products or services may include the following: Mutual funds offered by the institution; section 529 plans offered by the institution or its securities brokerage affiliate; or trust services offered by the institution or its trust services affiliate. Any affiliate offering investment counseling services that would be responsive to the consumer's request for information about saving and investing for a child's college education may use eligibility information to make solicitations to the consumer in response to this communication.

(iii) A credit card issuer makes a marketing call to the consumer without using eligibility information received from an affiliate. The issuer leaves a voice-mail message that invites the consumer to call a toll-free number to apply for the issuer's credit card. If the consumer calls the toll-free number to inquire about the credit card, the call is a consumer-initiated communication about a product or service and the credit card issuer may now use eligibility information it receives from its affiliates to make solicitations to the consumer.

(iv) A consumer calls a federal credit union to ask about retail locations and hours, but does not request information about products or services. The institution may not use eligibility information it receives from an affiliate to make solicitations to the consumer about its products or services because the consumer-initiated communication does not relate to the federal credit union's products or services. Thus, the use of eligibility information received from an affiliate would not be responsive to the communication and the exception does not apply.

(v) A consumer calls a federal credit union to ask about retail locations and hours. The customer service representative asks the consumer if there is a particular product or service about which the consumer is seeking information. The consumer responds that the consumer wants to stop in and find out about share certificates. The customer service representative offers to

§ 717.22

provide that information by telephone and mail additional information and application materials to the consumer. The consumer agrees and provides or confirms contact information for receipt of the materials to be mailed. The federal credit union may use eligibility information it receives from an affiliate to make solicitations to the consumer about share certificates because such solicitations would respond to the consumer-initiated communication about products or services.

(4) *Examples of consumer authorization or request for solicitations.* (i) A consumer who obtains a mortgage from a federal credit union authorizes or requests information about obtaining homeowner's insurance through the federal credit union's insurance brokerage affiliate. Such authorization or request, whether given to the federal credit union or to the insurance brokerage affiliate, would permit the insurance brokerage to use eligibility information about the consumer it obtains from the federal credit union or any other affiliate to make solicitations to the consumer about its homeowner's insurance services.

(ii) A consumer completes an online application to apply for a credit card from a credit card issuer. The issuer's online application contains a blank check box that the consumer may check to authorize or request information from the credit card issuer's affiliates. The consumer checks the box. The consumer has authorized or requested solicitations from the card issuer's affiliates.

(iii) A consumer completes an online application to apply for a credit card from a credit card issuer. The issuer's online application contains a pre-selected check box indicating that the consumer authorizes or requests information from the issuer's affiliates. The consumer does not deselect the check box. The consumer has not authorized or requested solicitations from the card issuer's affiliates.

(iv) The terms and conditions of a credit card account agreement contain preprinted boilerplate language stating that by applying to open an account the consumer authorizes or requests to receive solicitations from the credit card issuer's affiliates. The consumer has not authorized or requested solicitations from the card issuer's affiliates.

(e) *Relation to affiliate-sharing notice and opt-out.* Nothing in this subpart limits the responsibility of a person to comply with the notice and opt-out provisions of section 603(d)(2)(A)(iii) of the Act where applicable.

§ 717.22 Scope and duration of opt-out.

(a) *Scope of opt-out.* (1) *In general.* Except as otherwise provided in this section, the consumer's election to opt out prohibits any affiliate covered by the opt-out notice from using eligibility information received from another affiliate as described in the notice to make solicitations to the consumer.

(2) *Continuing relationship.* (i) *In general.* If the consumer establishes a continuing relationship with you or your affiliate, an opt-out notice may apply to eligibility information obtained in connection with—

(A) A single continuing relationship or multiple continuing relationships that the consumer establishes with you or your affiliates, including continuing relationships established subsequent to delivery of the opt-out notice, so long as the notice adequately describes the continuing relationships covered by the opt-out; or

(B) Any other transaction between the consumer and you or your affiliates as described in the notice.

(ii) *Examples of continuing relationships.* A consumer has a continuing relationship with you or your affiliate if the consumer—

(A) Opens a deposit or investment account with you or your affiliate;

(B) Obtains a loan for which you or your affiliate owns the servicing rights;

(C) Purchases an insurance product from you or your affiliate;

(D) Holds an investment product through you or your affiliate, such as when you act or your affiliate acts as a custodian for securities or for assets in an individual retirement arrangement;

(E) Enters into an agreement or understanding with you or your affiliate whereby you or your affiliate undertakes to arrange or broker a home mortgage loan for the consumer;

(F) Enters into a lease of personal property with you or your affiliate; or

(G) Obtains financial, investment, or economic advisory services from you or your affiliate for a fee.

(3) *No continuing relationship.* (i) *In general.* If there is no continuing relationship between a consumer and you or your affiliate, and you or your affiliate obtain eligibility information about a consumer in connection with a transaction with the consumer, such as an isolated transaction or a credit application that is denied, an opt-out notice provided to the consumer only applies to eligibility information obtained in connection with that transaction.

(ii) *Examples of isolated transactions.* An isolated transaction occurs if—

(A) The consumer uses your or your affiliate's ATM to withdraw cash from an account at another financial institution; or

(B) You or your affiliate sells the consumer a cashier's check or money order, airline tickets, travel insurance, or traveler's checks in isolated transactions.

(4) *Menu of alternatives.* A consumer may be given the opportunity to choose from a menu of alternatives when electing to prohibit solicitations, such as by electing to prohibit solicitations from certain types of affiliates covered by the opt-out notice but not other types of affiliates covered by the notice, electing to prohibit solicitations based on certain types of eligibility information but not other types of eligibility information, or electing to prohibit solicitations by certain methods of delivery but not other methods of delivery. However, one of the alternatives must allow the consumer to prohibit all solicitations from all of the affiliates that are covered by the notice.

(5) *Special rule for a notice following termination of all continuing relationships.* (i) *In general.* A consumer must be given a new opt-out notice if, after all continuing relationships with you or your affiliate(s) are terminated, the consumer subsequently establishes another continuing relationship with you or your affiliate(s) and the consumer's eligibility information is to be used to make a solicitation. The new opt-out notice must apply, at a minimum, to eligibility information obtained in connection with the new continuing relationship. Consistent with paragraph (b) of this section, the consumer's decision not to opt out after receiving the new opt-out notice would not override a prior opt-out election by the consumer that applies to eligibility information obtained in connection with a terminated relationship, regardless of whether the new opt-out notice applies to eligibility information obtained in connection with the terminated relationship.

(ii) *Example.* A consumer is a member of a federal credit union that is part of an affiliated group. The consumer terminates his membership. One year later, the consumer rejoins and opens a savings account with the same federal credit union. The consumer must be given a new notice and opportunity to opt out before the federal credit union's affiliates may make solicitations to the consumer using eligibility information obtained by the federal credit union in connection with the newly established account relationship, regardless of whether the consumer opted out in connection with accounts held during the previous member relationship.

(b) *Duration of opt-out.* The election of a consumer to opt out must be effective for a period of at least five years (the "opt-out period") beginning when the consumer's opt-out election is received and implemented, unless the consumer subsequently revokes the opt-out in writing or, if the consumer agrees, electronically. An opt-out period of more than five years may be established, including an opt-out period that does not expire unless revoked by the consumer.

(c) *Time of opt-out.* A consumer may opt out at any time.

§ 717.23 Contents of opt-out notice; consolidated and equivalent notices.

(a) *Contents of opt-out notice.* (1) *In general.* A notice must be clear, conspicuous, and concise, and must accurately disclose:

(i) The name of the affiliate(s) providing the notice. If the notice is provided jointly by multiple affiliates and

§717.23

each affiliate shares a common name, such as "ABC," then the notice may indicate that it is being provided by multiple companies with the ABC name or multiple companies in the ABC group or family of companies, for example, by stating that the notice is provided by "all of the ABC companies," "the ABC federal credit union, credit card, insurance brokerage, and securities brokerage companies," or by listing the name of each affiliate providing the notice. But if the affiliates providing the joint notice do not all share a common name, then the notice must either separately identify each affiliate by name or identify each of the common names used by those affiliates, for example, by stating that the notice is provided by "all of the ABC and XYZ companies" or by "the ABC federal credit union and credit card companies and the XYZ insurance brokerage company"

(ii) A list of the affiliates or types of affiliates whose use of eligibility information is covered by the notice, which may include companies that become affiliates after the notice is provided to the consumer. If each affiliate covered by the notice shares a common name, such as "ABC," then the notice may indicate that it applies to multiple companies with the ABC name or multiple companies in the ABC group or family of companies, for example, by stating that the notice is provided by "all of the ABC companies," "the ABC federal credit union, credit card, insurance brokerage, and securities brokerage companies," or by listing the name of each affiliate providing the notice. But if the affiliates covered by the notice do not all share a common name, then the notice must either separately identify each covered affiliate by name or identify each of the common names used by those affiliates, for example, by stating that the notice applies to "all of the ABC and XYZ companies" or to "the ABC federal credit union and credit card companies and the XYZ insurance brokerage company"

(iii) A general description of the types of eligibility information that may be used to make solicitations to the consumer;

(iv) That the consumer may elect to limit the use of eligibility information to make solicitations to the consumer;

(v) That the consumer's election will apply for the specified period of time stated in the notice and, if applicable, that the consumer will be allowed to renew the election once that period expires;

(vi) If the notice is provided to consumers who may have previously opted out, such as if a notice is provided to consumers annually, that the consumer who has chosen to limit solicitations does not need to act again until the consumer receives a renewal notice; and

(vii) A reasonable and simple method for the consumer to opt out.

(2) *Joint relationships.* (i) If two or more consumers jointly obtain a product or service, a single opt-out notice may be provided to the joint consumers. Any of the joint consumers may exercise the right to opt out.

(ii) The opt-out notice must explain how an opt-out direction by a joint consumer will be treated. An opt-out direction by a joint consumer may be treated as applying to all of the associated joint consumers, or each joint consumer may be permitted to opt-out separately. If each joint consumer is permitted to opt out separately, one of the joint consumers must be permitted to opt out on behalf of all of the joint consumers and the joint consumers must be permitted to exercise their separate rights to opt out in a single response.

(iii) It is impermissible to require all joint consumers to opt out before implementing any opt-out direction.

(3) *Alternative contents.* If the consumer is afforded a broader right to opt out of receiving marketing than is required by this subpart, the requirements of this section may be satisfied by providing the consumer with a clear, conspicuous, and concise notice that accurately discloses the consumer's opt-out rights.

(4) *Model notices.* Model notices are provided in appendix C of this part.

(b) *Coordinated and consolidated notices.* A notice required by this subpart may be coordinated and consolidated with any other notice or disclosure required to be issued under any other provision of law by the entity providing the notice, including but not limited to the notice described in section 603(d)(2)(A)(iii) of the Act and the Gramm-Leach-Bliley Act privacy notice.

(c) *Equivalent notices.* A notice or other disclosure that is equivalent to the notice required by this subpart, and that is provided to a consumer together with disclosures required by any other provision of law, satisfies the requirements of this section.

§ 717.24 Reasonable opportunity to opt out.

(a) *In general.* You must not use eligibility information about a consumer that you receive from an affiliate to make a solicitation to the consumer about your products or services, unless the consumer is provided a reasonable opportunity to opt out, as required by § 717.21(a)(1)(ii) of this part.

(b) *Examples of a reasonable opportunity to opt out.* The consumer is given a reasonable opportunity to opt out if:

(1) *By mail.* The opt-out notice is mailed to the consumer. The consumer is given 30 days from the date the notice is mailed to elect to opt out by any reasonable means.

(2) *By electronic means.* (i) The opt-out notice is provided electronically to the consumer, such as by posting the notice at an Internet Web site at which the consumer has obtained a product or service. The consumer acknowledges receipt of the electronic notice. The consumer is given 30 days after the date the consumer acknowledges receipt to elect to opt out by any reasonable means.

(ii) The opt-out notice is provided to the consumer by e-mail where the consumer has agreed to receive disclosures by e-mail from the person sending the notice. The consumer is given 30 days after the e-mail is sent to elect to opt out by any reasonable means.

(3) *At the time of an electronic transaction.* The opt-out notice is provided to the consumer at the time of an electronic transaction, such as a transaction conducted on an Internet Web site. The consumer is required to decide, as a necessary part of proceeding with the transaction, whether to opt out before completing the transaction.

There is a simple process that the consumer may use to opt out at that time using the same mechanism through which the transaction is conducted.

(4) *At the time of an in-person transaction.* The opt-out notice is provided to the consumer in writing at the time of an in-person transaction. The consumer is required to decide, as a necessary part of proceeding with the transaction, whether to opt out before completing the transaction, and is not permitted to complete the transaction without making a choice. There is a simple process that the consumer may use during the course of the in-person transaction to opt out, such as completing a form that requires consumers to write a "yes" or "no" to indicate their opt-out preference or that requires the consumer to check one of two blank check boxes—one that allows consumers to indicate that they want to opt out and one that allows consumers to indicate that they do not want to opt out.

(5) *By including in a privacy notice.* The opt-out notice is included in a Gramm-Leach-Bliley Act privacy notice. The consumer is allowed to exercise the opt-out within a reasonable period of time and in the same manner as the opt-out under that privacy notice.

§ 717.25 Reasonable and simple methods of opting out.

(a) *In general.* You must not use eligibility information about a consumer that you receive from an affiliate to make a solicitation to the consumer about your products or services, unless the consumer is provided a reasonable and simple method to opt out, as required by § 717.21(a)(1)(ii) of this part.

(b) *Examples.* (1) *Reasonable and simple opt-out methods.* Reasonable and simple methods for exercising the opt-out right include—

(i) Designating a check-off box in a prominent position on the opt-out form;

(ii) Including a reply form and a self-addressed envelope together with the opt-out notice;

(iii) Providing an electronic means to opt out, such as a form that can be electronically mailed or processed at an Internet Web site, if the consumer

§ 717.26

agrees to the electronic delivery of information;

(iv) Providing a toll-free telephone number that consumers may call to opt out; or

(v) Allowing consumers to exercise all of their opt-out rights described in a consolidated opt-out notice that includes the privacy opt-out under the Gramm-Leach-Bliley Act, 15 U.S.C. 6801 et seq., the affiliate sharing opt-out under the Act, and the affiliate marketing opt-out under the Act, by a single method, such as by calling a single toll-free telephone number.

(2) *Opt-out methods that are not reasonable and simple.* Reasonable and simple methods for exercising an opt-out right do not include—

(i) Requiring the consumer to write his or her own letter;

(ii) Requiring the consumer to call or write to obtain a form for opting out, rather than including the form with the opt-out notice;

(iii) Requiring the consumer who receives the opt-out notice in electronic form only, such as through posting at an Internet Web site, to opt out solely by paper mail or by visiting a different Web site without providing a link to that site.

(c) *Specific opt-out means.* Each consumer may be required to opt out through a specific means, as long as that means is reasonable and simple for that consumer.

[70 FR 70692, Nov. 22, 2005, as amended at 75 FR 34621, June 18, 2010]

§ 717.26 Delivery of opt-out notices.

(a) *In general.* The opt-out notice must be provided so that each consumer can reasonably be expected to receive actual notice. For opt-out notices provided electronically, the notice may be provided in compliance with either the electronic disclosure provisions in this subpart or the provisions in section 101 of the Electronic Signatures in Global and National Commerce Act, 15 U.S.C. 7001 *et seq.*

(b) *Examples of reasonable expectation of actual notice.* A consumer may reasonably be expected to receive actual notice if the affiliate providing the notice:

(1) Hand-delivers a printed copy of the notice to the consumer;

12 CFR Ch. VII (1-1-12 Edition)

(2) Mails a printed copy of the notice to the last known mailing address of the consumer;

(3) Provides a notice by e-mail to a consumer who has agreed to receive electronic disclosures by e-mail from the affiliate providing the notice; or

(4) Posts the notice on the Internet Web site at which the consumer obtained a product or service electronically and requires the consumer to acknowledge receipt of the notice.

(c) *Examples of no reasonable expectation of actual notice.* A consumer may not reasonably be expected to receive actual notice if the affiliate providing the notice:

(1) Only posts the notice on a sign in a branch or office or generally publishes the notice in a newspaper;

(2) Sends the notice via e-mail to a consumer who has not agreed to receive electronic disclosures by e-mail from the affiliate providing the notice; or

(3) Posts the notice on an Internet Web site without requiring the consumer to acknowledge receipt of the notice.

§ 717.27 Renewal of opt-out.

(a) *Renewal notice and opt-out requirement.* (1) *In general.* After the opt-out period expires, you may not make solicitations based on eligibility information you receive from an affiliate to a consumer who previously opted out, unless:

(i) The consumer has been given a renewal notice that complies with the requirements of this section and §§ 717.24 through 717.26 of this part, and a reasonable opportunity and a reasonable and simple method to renew the opt-out, and the consumer does not renew the opt-out; or

(ii) An exception in § 717.21(c) of this part applies.

(2) *Renewal period.* Each opt-out renewal must be effective for a period of at least five years as provided in § 717.22(b) of this part.

(3) *Affiliates who may provide the notice.* The notice required by this paragraph must be provided:

(i) By the affiliate that provided the previous opt-out notice, or its successor; or

National Credit Union Administration § 717.27

(ii) As part of a joint renewal notice from two or more members of an affiliated group of companies, or their successors, that jointly provided the previous opt-out notice.

(b) *Contents of renewal notice.* The renewal notice must be clear, conspicuous, and concise, and must accurately disclose:

(1) The name of the affiliate(s) providing the notice. If the notice is provided jointly by multiple affiliates and each affiliate shares a common name, such as "ABC," then the notice may indicate that it is being provided by multiple companies with the ABC name or multiple companies in the ABC group or family of companies, for example, by stating that the notice is provided by "all of the ABC companies," "the ABC federal credit union, credit card, insurance brokerage, and securities brokerage companies," or by listing the name of each affiliate providing the notice. But if the affiliates providing the joint notice do not all share a common name, then the notice must either separately identify each affiliate by name or identify each of the common names used by those affiliates, for example, by stating that the notice is provided by "all of the ABC and XYZ companies" or by "the ABC federal credit union and credit card companies and the XYZ insurance brokerage company";

(2) A list of the affiliates or types of affiliates whose use of eligibility information is covered by the notice, which may include companies that become affiliates after the notice is provided to the consumer. If each affiliate covered by the notice shares a common name, such as "ABC," then the notice may indicate that it applies to multiple companies with the ABC name or multiple companies in the ABC group or family of companies, for example, by stating that the notice is provided by "all of the ABC companies," "the ABC federal credit union, credit card, insurance brokerage, and securities brokerage companies," or by listing the name of each affiliate providing the notice. But if the affiliates covered by the notice do not all share a common name, then the notice must either separately identify each covered affiliate by name or identify each of the common names used by those affiliates, for example, by stating that the notice applies to "all of the ABC and XYZ companies" or to "the ABC federal credit union and credit card companies and the XYZ insurance brokerage company";

(3) A general description of the types of eligibility information that may be used to make solicitations to the consumer;

(4) That the consumer previously elected to limit the use of certain information to make solicitations to the consumer;

(5) That the consumer's election has expired or is about to expire;

(6) That the consumer may elect to renew the consumer's previous election;

(7) If applicable, that the consumer's election to renew will apply for the specified period of time stated in the notice and that the consumer will be allowed to renew the election once that period expires; and

(8) A reasonable and simple method for the consumer to opt out.

(c) *Timing of the renewal notice.* (1) *In general.* A renewal notice may be provided to the consumer either—

(i) A reasonable period of time before the expiration of the opt-out period; or

(ii) Any time after the expiration of the opt-out period but before solicitations that would have been prohibited by the expired opt-out are made to the consumer.

(2) *Combination with annual privacy notice.* If you provide an annual privacy notice under the Gramm-Leach-Bliley Act, 15 U.S.C. 6801 et seq., providing a renewal notice with the last annual privacy notice provided to the consumer before expiration of the opt-out period is a reasonable period of time before expiration of the opt-out in all cases.

(d) *No effect on opt-out period.* An opt-out period may not be shortened by sending a renewal notice to the consumer before expiration of the opt-out period, even if the consumer does not renew the opt out.

[70 FR 70692, Nov. 22, 2005, as amended at 75 FR 34621, June 18, 2010]

§ 717.28 Effective date, compliance date, and prospective application.

(a) *Effective date.* This subpart is effective January 1, 2008.

(b) *Mandatory compliance date.* Compliance with this subpart is required not later than October 1, 2008.

(c) *Prospective application.* The provisions of this subpart shall not prohibit you from using eligibility information that you receive from an affiliate to make solicitations to a consumer if you receive such information prior to October 1, 2008. For purposes of this section, you are deemed to receive eligibility information when such information is placed into a common database and is accessible by you.

Subpart D—Medical Information

SOURCE: 70 FR 70693, Nov. 22, 2005 and 70 FR 75931, Dec. 22, 2005 unless otherwise noted.

§ 717.30 Obtaining or using medical information in connection with a determination of eligibility for credit.

(a) *Scope.* This section applies to:

(1) A Federal credit union that participates as a creditor in a transaction; or

(2) Any other person that participates as a creditor in a transaction involving a person described in paragraph (a)(1) of this section.

(b) *General prohibition on obtaining or using medical information*—(1) *In general.* A creditor may not obtain or use medical information pertaining to a consumer in connection with any determination of the consumer's eligibility, or continued eligibility, for credit, except as provided in this section.

(2) *Definitions.* (i) *Credit* has the same meaning as in section 702 of the Equal Credit Opportunity Act, 15 U.S.C. 1691a.

(ii) *Creditor* has the same meaning as in section 702 of the Equal Credit Opportunity Act, 15 U.S.C. 1691a.

(iii) *Eligibility, or continued eligibility, for credit* means the consumer's qualification or fitness to receive, or continue to receive, credit, including the terms on which credit is offered. The term does not include:

(A) Any determination of the consumer's qualification or fitness for employment, insurance (other than a credit insurance product), or other non-credit products or services;

(B) Authorizing, processing, or documenting a payment or transaction on behalf of the consumer in a manner that does not involve a determination of the consumer's eligibility, or continued eligibility, for credit; or

(C) Maintaining or servicing the consumer's account in a manner that does not involve a determination of the consumer's eligibility, or continued eligibility, for credit.

(c) *Rule of construction for obtaining and using unsolicited medical information*—(1) *In general.* A creditor does not obtain medical information in violation of the prohibition if it receives medical information pertaining to a consumer in connection with any determination of the consumer's eligibility, or continued eligibility, for credit without specifically requesting medical information.

(2) *Use of unsolicited medical information.* A creditor that receives unsolicited medical information in the manner described in paragraph (c)(1) of this section may use that information in connection with any determination of the consumer's eligibility, or continued eligibility, for credit to the extent the creditor can rely on at least one of the exceptions in § 717.30(d) or (e).

(3) *Examples.* A creditor does not obtain medical information in violation of the prohibition if, for example:

(i) In response to a general question regarding a consumer's debts or expenses, the creditor receives information that the consumer owes a debt to a hospital.

(ii) In a conversation with the creditor's loan officer, the consumer informs the creditor that the consumer has a particular medical condition.

(iii) In connection with a consumer's application for an extension of credit, the creditor requests a consumer report from a consumer reporting agency and receives medical information in the consumer report furnished by the agency even though the creditor did not specifically request medical information from the consumer reporting agency.

(d) *Financial information exception for obtaining and using medical information*—(1) *In general.* A creditor may obtain and use medical information pertaining to a consumer in connection with any determination of the consumer's eligibility, or continued eligibility, for credit so long as:

(i) The information is the type of information routinely used in making credit eligibility determinations, such as information relating to debts, expenses, income, benefits, assets, collateral, or the purpose of the loan, including the use of proceeds;

(ii) The creditor uses the medical information in a manner and to an extent that is no less favorable than it would use comparable information that is not medical information in a credit transaction; and

(iii) The creditor does not take the consumer's physical, mental, or behavioral health, condition or history, type of treatment, or prognosis into account as part of any such determination.

(2) *Examples.* (i) *Examples of the types of information routinely used in making credit eligibility determinations.* Paragraph (d)(1)(i) of this section permits a creditor, for example, to obtain and use information about:

(A) The dollar amount, repayment terms, repayment history, and similar information regarding medical debts to calculate, measure, or verify the repayment ability of the consumer, the use of proceeds, or the terms for granting credit;

(B) The value, condition, and lien status of a medical device that may serve as collateral to secure a loan;

(C) The dollar amount and continued eligibility for disability income, workers' compensation income, or other benefits related to health or a medical condition that is relied on as a source of repayment; or

(D) The identity of creditors to whom outstanding medical debts are owed in connection with an application for credit, including but not limited to, a transaction involving the consolidation of medical debts.

(ii) *Examples of uses of medical information consistent with the exception.* (A) A consumer includes on an application for credit information about two $20,000 debts. One debt is to a hospital; the other debt is to a retailer. The creditor contacts the hospital and the retailer to verify the amount and payment status of the debts. The creditor learns that both debts are more than 90 days past due. Any two debts of this size that are more than 90 days past due would disqualify the consumer under the creditor's established underwriting criteria. The creditor denies the application on the basis that the consumer has a poor repayment history on outstanding debts. The creditor has used medical information in a manner and to an extent no less favorable than it would use comparable non-medical information.

(B) A consumer indicates on an application for a $200,000 mortgage loan that she receives $15,000 in long-term disability income each year from her former employer and has no other income. Annual income of $15,000, regardless of source, would not be sufficient to support the requested amount of credit. The creditor denies the application on the basis that the projected debt-to-income ratio of the consumer does not meet the creditor's underwriting criteria. The creditor has used medical information in a manner and to an extent that is no less favorable than it would use comparable non-medical information.

(C) A consumer includes on an application for a $10,000 home equity loan that he has a $50,000 debt to a medical facility that specializes in treating a potentially terminal disease. The creditor contacts the medical facility to verify the debt and obtain the repayment history and current status of the loan. The creditor learns that the debt is current. The applicant meets the income and other requirements of the creditor's underwriting guidelines. The creditor grants the application. The creditor has used medical information in accordance with the exception.

(iii) *Examples of uses of medical information inconsistent with the exception.* (A) A consumer applies for $25,000 of credit and includes on the application information about a $50,000 debt to a hospital. The creditor contacts the hospital to verify the amount and payment status of the debt, and learns that the debt is current and that the consumer has no delinquencies in her repayment history. If the existing debt were instead owed to a retail department store, the creditor would approve the application and extend credit based on the amount and repayment history of the outstanding debt. The creditor, however, denies the application because the consumer is indebted to a hospital. The creditor has used medical information, here the identity of the medical creditor, in a manner and to an extent that is less favorable than it would use comparable non-medical information.

(B) A consumer meets with a loan officer of a creditor to apply for a mortgage loan. While filling out the loan application, the consumer informs the loan officer orally that she has a potentially terminal disease. The consumer meets the creditor's established requirements for the requested mortgage loan. The loan officer recommends to the credit committee that the consumer be denied credit because the consumer has that disease. The credit committee follows the loan officer's recommendation and denies the application because the consumer has a potentially terminal disease. The creditor has used medical information in a manner inconsistent with the exception by taking into account the consumer's physical, mental, or behavioral health, condition, or history, type of treatment, or prognosis as part of a determination of eligibility or continued eligibility for credit.

(C) A consumer who has an apparent medical condition, such as a consumer who uses a wheelchair or an oxygen tank, meets with a loan officer to apply for a home equity loan. The consumer meets the creditor's established requirements for the requested home equity loan and the creditor typically does not require consumers to obtain a debt cancellation contract, debt suspension agreement, or credit insurance product in connection with such loans. However, based on the consumer's apparent medical condition, the loan officer recommends to the credit committee that credit be extended to the consumer only if the consumer obtains a debt cancellation contract, debt suspension agreement, or credit insurance product from a nonaffiliated third party. The credit committee agrees with the loan officer's recommendation. The loan officer informs the consumer that the consumer must obtain a debt cancellation contract, debt suspension agreement, or credit insurance product from a nonaffiliated third party to qualify for the loan. The consumer obtains one of these products and the creditor approves the loan. The creditor has used medical information in a manner inconsistent with the exception by taking into account the consumer's physical, mental, or behavioral health, condition, or history, type of treatment, or prognosis in setting conditions on the consumer's eligibility for credit.

(e) *Specific exceptions for obtaining and using medical information*—(1) *In general.* A creditor may obtain and use medical information pertaining to a consumer in connection with any determination of the consumer's eligibility, or continued eligibility, for credit:

(i) To determine whether the use of a power of attorney or legal representative that is triggered by a medical condition or event is necessary and appropriate or whether the consumer has the legal capacity to contract when a person seeks to exercise a power of attorney or act as legal representative for a consumer based on an asserted medical condition or event;

(ii) To comply with applicable requirements of local, state, or Federal laws;

(iii) To determine, at the consumer's request, whether the consumer qualifies for a legally permissible special credit program or credit-related assistance program that is:

(A) Designed to meet the special needs of consumers with medical conditions; and

(B) Established and administered pursuant to a written plan that:

(*1*) Identifies the class of persons that the program is designed to benefit; and

(*2*) Sets forth the procedures and standards for extending credit or providing other credit-related assistance under the program;

(iv) To the extent necessary for purposes of fraud prevention or detection;

(v) In the case of credit for the purpose of financing medical products or services, to determine and verify the

National Credit Union Administration §717.30

medical purpose of a loan and the use of proceeds;

(vi) Consistent with safe and sound practices, if the consumer or the consumer's legal representative specifically requests that the creditor use medical information in determining the consumer's eligibility, or continued eligibility, for credit, to accommodate the consumer's particular circumstances, and such request is documented by the creditor;

(vii) Consistent with safe and sound practices, to determine whether the provisions of a forbearance practice or program that is triggered by a medical condition or event apply to a consumer;

(viii) To determine the consumer's eligibility for, the triggering of, or the reactivation of a debt cancellation contract or debt suspension agreement if a medical condition or event is a triggering event for the provision of benefits under the contract or agreement; or

(ix) To determine the consumer's eligibility for, the triggering of, or the reactivation of a credit insurance product if a medical condition or event is a triggering event for the provision of benefits under the product.

(2) *Example of determining eligibility for a special credit program or credit assistance program.* A not-for-profit organization establishes a credit assistance program pursuant to a written plan that is designed to assist disabled veterans in purchasing homes by subsidizing the down payment for the home purchase mortgage loans of qualifying veterans. The organization works through mortgage lenders and requires mortgage lenders to obtain medical information about the disability of any consumer that seeks to qualify for the program, use that information to verify the consumer's eligibility for the program, and forward that information to the organization. A consumer who is a veteran applies to a creditor for a home purchase mortgage loan. The creditor informs the consumer about the credit assistance program for disabled veterans and the consumer seeks to qualify for the program. Assuming that the program complies with all applicable law, including applicable fair lending laws, the creditor may obtain and use medical information about the medical condition and disability, if any, of the consumer to determine whether the consumer qualifies for the credit assistance program.

(3) *Examples of verifying the medical purpose of the loan or the use of proceeds.* (i) If a consumer applies for $10,000 of credit for the purpose of financing vision correction surgery, the creditor may verify with the surgeon that the procedure will be performed. If the surgeon reports that surgery will not be performed on the consumer, the creditor may use that medical information to deny the consumer's application for credit, because the loan would not be used for the stated purpose.

(ii) If a consumer applies for $10,000 of credit for the purpose of financing cosmetic surgery, the creditor may confirm the cost of the procedure with the surgeon. If the surgeon reports that the cost of the procedure is $5,000, the creditor may use that medical information to offer the consumer only $5,000 of credit.

(iii) A creditor has an established medical loan program for financing particular elective surgical procedures. The creditor receives a loan application from a consumer requesting $10,000 of credit under the established loan program for an elective surgical procedure. The consumer indicates on the application that the purpose of the loan is to finance an elective surgical procedure not eligible for funding under the guidelines of the established loan program. The creditor may deny the consumer's application because the purpose of the loan is not for a particular procedure funded by the established loan program.

(4) *Examples of obtaining and using medical information at the request of the consumer.* (i) If a consumer applies for a loan and specifically requests that the creditor consider the consumer's medical disability at the relevant time as an explanation for adverse payment history information in his credit report, the creditor may consider such medical information in evaluating the consumer's willingness and ability to repay the requested loan to accommodate the consumer's particular circumstances, consistent with safe and sound practices. The creditor may also

793

decline to consider such medical information to accommodate the consumer, but may evaluate the consumer's application in accordance with its otherwise applicable underwriting criteria. The creditor may not deny the consumer's application or otherwise treat the consumer less favorably because the consumer specifically requested a medical accommodation, if the creditor would have extended the credit or treated the consumer more favorably under the creditor's otherwise applicable underwriting criteria.

(ii) If a consumer applies for a loan by telephone and explains that his income has been and will continue to be interrupted on account of a medical condition and that he expects to repay the loan by liquidating assets, the creditor may, but is not required to, evaluate the application using the sale of assets as the primary source of repayment, consistent with safe and sound practices, provided that the creditor documents the consumer's request by recording the oral conversation or making a notation of the request in the consumer's file.

(iii) If a consumer applies for a loan and the application form provides a space where the consumer may provide any other information or special circumstances, whether medical or non-medical, that the consumer would like the creditor to consider in evaluating the consumer's application, the creditor may use medical information provided by the consumer in that space on that application to accommodate the consumer's application for credit, consistent with safe and sound practices, or may disregard that information.

(iv) If a consumer specifically requests that the creditor use medical information in determining the consumer's eligibility, or continued eligibility, for credit and provides the creditor with medical information for that purpose, and the creditor determines that it needs additional information regarding the consumer's circumstances, the creditor may request, obtain, and use additional medical information about the consumer as necessary to verify the information provided by the consumer or to determine whether to make an accommodation for the consumer. The consumer may decline to provide additional information, withdraw the request for an accommodation, and have the application considered under the creditor's otherwise applicable underwriting criteria.

(v) If a consumer completes and signs a credit application that is not for medical purpose credit and the application contains boilerplate language that routinely requests medical information from the consumer or that indicates that by applying for credit the consumer authorizes or consents to the creditor obtaining and using medical information in connection with a determination of the consumer's eligibility, or continued eligibility, for credit, the consumer has not specifically requested that the creditor obtain and use medical information to accommodate the consumer's particular circumstances.

(5) *Example of a forbearance practice or program.* After an appropriate safety and soundness review, a creditor institutes a program that allows consumers who are or will be hospitalized to defer payments as needed for up to three months, without penalty, if the credit account has been open for more than one year and has not previously been in default, and the consumer provides confirming documentation at an appropriate time. A consumer is hospitalized and does not pay her bill for a particular month. This consumer has had a credit account with the creditor for more than one year and has not previously been in default. The creditor attempts to contact the consumer and speaks with the consumer's adult child, who is not the consumer's legal representative. The adult child informs the creditor that the consumer is hospitalized and is unable to pay the bill at that time. The creditor defers payments for up to three months, without penalty, for the hospitalized consumer and sends the consumer a letter confirming this practice and the date on which the next payment will be due. The creditor has obtained and used medical information to determine whether the provisions of a medically-triggered forbearance practice or program apply to a consumer.

National Credit Union Administration

§ 717.31 Limits on redisclosure of information

(a) *Scope.* This section applies to Federal credit unions.

(b) *Limits on redisclosure.* If a Federal credit union receives medical information about a consumer from a consumer reporting agency or its affiliate, the person must not disclose that information to any other person, except as necessary to carry out the purpose for which the information was initially disclosed, or as otherwise permitted by statute, regulation, or order.

§ 717.32 Sharing medical information with affiliates.

(a) *Scope.* This section applies to Federal credit unions.

(b) *In general.* The exclusions from the term "consumer report" in section 603(d)(2) of the Act that allow the sharing of information with affiliates do not apply if a Federal credit union communicates to an affiliate:

(1) Medical information;

(2) An individualized list or description based on the payment transactions of the consumer for medical products or services; or

(3) An aggregate list of identified consumers based on payment transactions for medical products or services.

(c) *Exceptions.* A Federal credit union may rely on the exclusions from the term "consumer report" in section 603(d)(2) of the Act to communicate the information in paragraph (b) to an affiliate:

(1) In connection with the business of insurance or annuities (including the activities described in section 18B of the model Privacy of Consumer Financial and Health Information Regulation issued by the National Association of Insurance Commissioners, as in effect on January 1, 2003);

(2) For any purpose permitted without authorization under the regulations promulgated by the Department of Health and Human Services pursuant to the Health Insurance Portability and Accountability Act of 1996 (HIPAA);

(3) For any purpose referred to in section 1179 of HIPAA;

§ 717.41

(4) For any purpose described in section 502(e) of the Gramm-Leach-Bliley Act;

(5) In connection with a determination of the consumer's eligibility, or continued eligibility, for credit consistent with § 717.30; or

(6) As otherwise permitted by order of the NCUA.

Subpart E—Duties of Furnishers of Information

SOURCE: 74 FR 31522, July 1, 2009, unless otherwise noted.

§ 717.40 Scope.

This subpart applies to a Federal credit union that furnishes information to a consumer reporting agency.

§ 717.41 Definitions.

For purposes of this subpart and Appendix E of this part, the following definitions apply:

(a) *Accuracy* means that information that a furnisher provides to a consumer reporting agency about an account or other relationship with the consumer correctly:

(1) Reflects the terms of and liability for the account or other relationship;

(2) Reflects the consumer's performance and other conduct with respect to the account or other relationship; and

(3) Identifies the appropriate consumer.

(b) *Direct dispute* means a dispute submitted directly to a furnisher (including a furnisher that is a debt collector) by a consumer concerning the accuracy of any information contained in a consumer report and pertaining to an account or other relationship that the furnisher has or had with the consumer.

(c) *Furnisher* means an entity that furnishes information relating to consumers to one or more consumer reporting agencies for inclusion in a consumer report. An entity is not a furnisher when it:

(1) Provides information to a consumer reporting agency solely to obtain a consumer report in accordance with sections 604(a) and (f) of the Fair Credit Reporting Act;

§ 717.42

(2) Is acting as a "consumer reporting agency" as defined in section 603(f) of the Fair Credit Reporting Act;

(3) Is a consumer to whom the furnished information pertains; or

(4) Is a neighbor, friend, or associate of the consumer, or another individual with whom the consumer is acquainted or who may have knowledge about the consumer, and who provides information about the consumer's character, general reputation, personal characteristics, or mode of living in response to a specific request from a consumer reporting agency.

(d) *Identity theft* has the same meaning as in 16 CFR 603.2(a).

(e) *Integrity* means that information that a furnisher provides to a consumer reporting agency about an account or other relationship with the consumer:

(1) Is substantiated by the furnisher's records at the time it is furnished;

(2) Is furnished in a form and manner that is designed to minimize the likelihood that the information may be incorrectly reflected in a consumer report; and

(3) Includes the information in the furnisher's possession about the account or other relationship that the NCUA has:

(i) Determined that the absence of which would likely be materially misleading in evaluating a consumer's creditworthiness, credit standing, credit capacity, character, general reputation, personal characteristics, or mode of living; and

(ii) Listed in section I.(b)(2)(iii) of Appendix E of this part.

§ 717.42 **Reasonable policies and procedures concerning the accuracy and integrity of furnished information.**

(a) *Policies and procedures.* Each furnisher must establish and implement reasonable written policies and procedures regarding the accuracy and integrity of the information relating to consumers that it furnishes to a consumer reporting agency. The policies and procedures must be appropriate to the nature, size, complexity, and scope of each furnisher's activities.

(b) *Guidelines.* Each furnisher must consider the guidelines in Appendix E of this part in developing its policies and procedures required by this section, and incorporate those guidelines that are appropriate.

(c) *Reviewing and updating policies and procedures.* Each furnisher must review its policies and procedures required by this section periodically and update them as necessary to ensure their continued effectiveness.

§ 717.43 **Direct disputes.**

(a) *General rule.* Except as otherwise provided in this section, a furnisher must conduct a reasonable investigation of a direct dispute if it relates to:

(1) The consumer's liability for a credit account or other debt with the furnisher, such as direct disputes relating to whether there is or has been identity theft or fraud against the consumer, whether there is individual or joint liability on an account, or whether the consumer is an authorized user of a credit account;

(2) The terms of a credit account or other debt with the furnisher, such as direct disputes relating to the type of account, principal balance, scheduled payment amount on an account, or the amount of the credit limit on an open-end account;

(3) The consumer's performance or other conduct concerning an account or other relationship with the furnisher, such as direct disputes relating to the current payment status, high balance, date a payment was made, the amount of a payment made, or the date an account was opened or closed; or

(4) Any other information contained in a consumer report regarding an account or other relationship with the furnisher that bears on the consumer's creditworthiness, credit standing, credit capacity, character, general reputation, personal characteristics, or mode of living.

(b) *Exceptions.* The requirements of paragraph (a) of this section do not apply to a furnisher if:

(1) The direct dispute relates to:

(i) The consumer's identifying information (other than a direct dispute relating to a consumer's liability for a credit account or other debt with the furnisher, as provided in paragraph (a)(1) of this section) such as name(s), date of birth, Social Security number, telephone number(s), or address(es);

(ii) The identity of past or present employers;

(iii) Inquiries or requests for a consumer report;

(iv) Information derived from public records, such as judgments, bankruptcies, liens, and other legal matters (unless provided by a furnisher with an account or other relationship with the consumer);

(v) Information related to fraud alerts or active duty alerts; or

(vi) Information provided to a consumer reporting agency by another furnisher; or

(2) The furnisher has a reasonable belief that the direct dispute is submitted by, is prepared on behalf of the consumer by, or is submitted on a form supplied to the consumer by, a credit repair organization, as defined in 15 U.S.C. 1679a(3), or an entity that would be a credit repair organization, but for 15 U.S.C. 1679a(3)(B)(i).

(c) *Direct dispute address.* A furnisher is required to investigate a direct dispute only if a consumer submits a dispute notice to the furnisher at:

(1) The address of a furnisher provided by a furnisher and set forth on a consumer report relating to the consumer;

(2) An address clearly and conspicuously specified by the furnisher for submitting direct disputes that is provided to the consumer in writing or electronically (if the consumer has agreed to the electronic delivery of information from the furnisher); or

(3) Any business address of the furnisher if the furnisher has not so specified and provided an address for submitting direct disputes under paragraphs (c)(1) or (2) of this section.

(d) *Direct dispute notice contents.* A dispute notice must include:

(1) Sufficient information to identify the account or other relationship that is in dispute, such as an account number and the name, address, and telephone number of the consumer, if applicable;

(2) The specific information that the consumer is disputing and an explanation of the basis for the dispute; and

(3) All supporting documentation or other information reasonably required by the furnisher to substantiate the basis of the dispute. This documentation may include, for example: a copy of the relevant portion of the consumer report that contains the allegedly inaccurate information; a police report; a fraud or identity theft affidavit; a court order; or account statements.

(e) *Duty of furnisher after receiving a direct dispute notice.* After receiving a dispute notice from a consumer pursuant to paragraphs (c) and (d) of this section, the furnisher must:

(1) Conduct a reasonable investigation with respect to the disputed information;

(2) Review all relevant information provided by the consumer with the dispute notice;

(3) Complete its investigation of the dispute and report the results of the investigation to the consumer before the expiration of the period under section 611(a)(1) of the Fair Credit Reporting Act (15 U.S.C. 1681i(a)(1)) within which a consumer reporting agency would be required to complete its action if the consumer had elected to dispute the information under that section; and

(4) If the investigation finds that the information reported was inaccurate, promptly notify each consumer reporting agency to which the furnisher provided inaccurate information of that determination and provide to the consumer reporting agency any correction to that information that is necessary to make the information provided by the furnisher accurate.

(f) *Frivolous or irrelevant disputes.* (1) A furnisher is not required to investigate a direct dispute if the furnisher has reasonably determined that the dispute is frivolous or irrelevant. A dispute qualifies as frivolous or irrelevant if:

(i) The consumer did not provide sufficient information to investigate the disputed information as required by paragraph (d) of this section;

(ii) The direct dispute is substantially the same as a dispute previously submitted by or on behalf of the consumer, either directly to the furnisher or through a consumer reporting agency, with respect to which the furnisher has already satisfied the applicable requirements of the Act or this section; provided, however, that a direct dispute is not substantially the same as a

§§ 717.80–717.81

dispute previously submitted if the dispute includes information listed in paragraph (d) of this section that had not previously been provided to the furnisher; or

(iii) The furnisher is not required to investigate the direct dispute because one or more of the exceptions listed in paragraph (b) of this section applies.

(2) *Notice of determination.* Upon making a determination that a dispute is frivolous or irrelevant, the furnisher must notify the consumer of the determination not later than five business days after making the determination, by mail or, if authorized by the consumer for that purpose, by any other means available to the furnisher.

(3) *Contents of notice of determination that a dispute is frivolous or irrelevant.* A notice of determination that a dispute is frivolous or irrelevant must include the reasons for such determination and identify any information required to investigate the disputed information, which notice may consist of a standardized form describing the general nature of such information.

Subparts F–H [Reserved]

Subpart I—Duties of Users of Consumer Reports Regarding Address Discrepancies and Records Disposal

§§ 717.80–717.81 [Reserved]

§ 717.82 Duties of users regarding address discrepancies.

(a) *Scope.* This section applies to a user of consumer reports (user) that receives a notice of address discrepancy from a consumer reporting agency described in 15 U.S.C. 1681a(p), and that is federal credit union.

(b) *Definition.* For purposes of this section, a *notice of address discrepancy* means a notice sent to a user by a consumer reporting agency described in 15 U.S.C. 1681a(p) pursuant to 15 U.S.C. 1681c(h)(1), that informs the user of a substantial difference between the address for the consumer that the user provided to request the consumer report and the address(es) in the agency's file for the consumer.

(c) *Reasonable belief*—(1) *Requirement to form a reasonable belief.* A user must develop and implement reasonable policies and procedures designed to enable the user to form a reasonable belief that a consumer report relates to the consumer about whom it has requested the report, when the user receives a notice of address discrepancy.

(2) *Examples of reasonable policies and procedures.* (i) Comparing the information in the consumer report provided by the consumer reporting agency with information the user:

(A) Obtains and uses to verify the consumer's identity in accordance with the requirements of the Customer Identification Program (CIP) rules implementing 31 U.S.C. 5318(l) (31 CFR 1020.220);

(B) Maintains in its own records, such as applications, change of address notifications, other member account records, or retained CIP documentation; or

(C) Obtains from third-party sources; or

(ii) Verifying the information in the consumer report provided by the consumer reporting agency with the consumer.

(d) *Consumer's address*—(1) *Requirement to furnish consumer's address to a consumer reporting agency.* A user must develop and implement reasonable policies and procedures for furnishing an address for the consumer that the user has reasonably confirmed is accurate to the consumer reporting agency described in 15 U.S.C. 1681a(p) from whom it received the notice of address discrepancy when the user:

(i) Can form a reasonable belief that the consumer report relates to the consumer about whom the user requested the report;

(ii) Establishes a continuing relationship with the consumer; and

(iii) Regularly and in the ordinary course of business furnishes information to the consumer reporting agency from which the notice of address discrepancy relating to the consumer was obtained.

(2) *Examples of confirmation methods.* The user may reasonably confirm an address is accurate by:

(i) Verifying the address with the consumer about whom it has requested the report;

(ii) Reviewing its own records to verify the address of the consumer;
(iii) Verifying the address through third-party sources; or
(iv) Using other reasonable means.
(3) *Timing.* The policies and procedures developed in accordance with paragraph (d)(1) of this section must provide that the user will furnish the consumer's address that the user has reasonably confirmed is accurate to the consumer reporting agency described in 15 U.S.C. 1681a(p) as part of the information it regularly furnishes for the reporting period in which it establishes a relationship with the consumer.

[72 FR 63768, Nov. 9, 2007, as amended at 74 FR 22644, May 14, 2009; 76 FR 18365, Apr. 4, 2011]

§ 717.83 Disposal of consumer information.

(a) *In general.* You must properly dispose of any consumer information that you maintain or otherwise possess in a manner consistent with the Guidelines for Safeguarding Member Information, in appendix A to part 748 of this chapter.

(b) *Examples.* Appropriate measures to properly dispose of consumer information include the following examples. These examples are illustrative only and are not exclusive or exhaustive methods for complying with this section.

(1) Burning, pulverizing, or shredding papers containing consumer information so that the information cannot practically be read or reconstructed.

(2) Destroying or erasing electronic media containing consumer information so that the information cannot practically be read or reconstructed.

(c) *Rule of construction.* This section does not:

(1) Require you to maintain or destroy any record pertaining to a consumer that is not imposed under any other law; or

(2) Alter or affect any requirement imposed under any other provision of law to maintain or destroy such a record.

(d) *Definitions.* As used in this section:

(1) *Consumer information* means any record about an individual, whether in paper, electronic, or other form, that is a consumer report or is derived from a consumer report and that is maintained or otherwise possessed by or on behalf of the credit union for a business purpose. Consumer information also means a compilation of such records. The term does not include any record that does not identify an individual.

(i) *Consumer information* includes:

(A) A consumer report that you obtain;

(B) Information from a consumer report that you obtain from your affiliate after the consumer has been given a notice and has elected not to opt out of that sharing;

(C) Information from a consumer report that you obtain about an individual who applies for but does not receive a loan, including any loan sought by an individual for a business purpose;

(D) Information from a consumer report that you obtain about an individual who guarantees a loan (including a loan to a business entity); or

(E) Information from a consumer report that you obtain about an employee or prospective employee.

(ii) *Consumer information* does not include:

(A) Aggregate information, such as the mean credit score, derived from a group of consumer reports; or

(B) Blind data, such as payment history on accounts that are not personally identifiable, you use for developing credit scoring models or for other purposes.

(2) *Consumer report* has the same meaning as set forth in the Fair Credit Reporting Act, 15 U.S.C. 1681a(d). The meaning of consumer report is broad and subject to various definitions, conditions and exceptions in the Fair Credit Reporting Act. It includes written or oral communications from a consumer reporting agency to a third party of information used or collected for use in establishing eligibility for credit or insurance used primarily for personal, family or household purposes, and eligibility for employment purposes. Examples include credit reports, bad check lists, and tenant screening reports.

Subpart J—Identity Theft Red Flags

SOURCE: 72 FR 63768, Nov. 9, 2007, unless otherwise noted.

§ 717.90 Duties regarding the detection, prevention, and mitigation of identity theft.

(a) *Scope.* This section applies to a financial institution or creditor that is a federal credit union.

(b) *Definitions.* For purposes of this section and appendix J, the following definitions apply:

(1) *Account* means a continuing relationship established by a person with a federal credit union to obtain a product or service for personal, family, household or business purposes. Account includes:

(i) An extension of credit, such as the purchase of property or services involving a deferred payment; and

(ii) A share or deposit account.

(2) The term *board of directors* refers to a federal credit union's board of directors.

(3) *Covered account* means:

(i) An account that a federal credit union offers or maintains, primarily for personal, family, or household purposes, that involves or is designed to permit multiple payments or transactions, such as a credit card account, mortgage loan, automobile loan, checking account, or share account; and

(ii) Any other account that the federal credit union offers or maintains for which there is a reasonably foreseeable risk to members or to the safety and soundness of the federal credit union from identity theft, including financial, operational, compliance, reputation, or litigation risks.

(4) *Credit* has the same meaning as in 15 U.S.C. 1681a(r)(5).

(5) *Creditor* has the same meaning as in 15 U.S.C. 1681a(r)(5).

(6) *Customer* means a member that has a covered account with a federal credit union.

(7) *Financial institution* has the same meaning as in 15 U.S.C. 1681a(t).

(8) *Identity theft* has the same meaning as in 16 CFR 603.2(a).

(9) *Red Flag* means a pattern, practice, or specific activity that indicates the possible existence of identity theft.

(10) *Service provider* means a person that provides a service directly to the federal credit union.

(c) *Periodic Identification of Covered Accounts.* Each federal credit union must periodically determine whether it offers or maintains covered accounts. As a part of this determination, a federal credit union must conduct a risk assessment to determine whether it offers or maintains covered accounts described in paragraph (b)(3)(ii) of this section, taking into consideration:

(1) The methods it provides to open its accounts;

(2) The methods it provides to access its accounts; and

(3) Its previous experiences with identity theft.

(d) *Establishment of an Identity Theft Prevention Program.* (1) *Program requirement.* Each federal credit union that offers or maintains one or more covered accounts must develop and implement a written Identity Theft Prevention Program (Program) that is designed to detect, prevent, and mitigate identity theft in connection with the opening of a covered account or any existing covered account. The Program must be appropriate to the size and complexity of the federal credit union and the nature and scope of its activities.

(2) *Elements of the Program.* The Program must include reasonable policies and procedures to:

(i) Identify relevant Red Flags for the covered accounts that the federal credit union offers or maintains, and incorporate those Red Flags into its Program;

(ii) Detect Red Flags that have been incorporated into the Program of the federal credit union;

(iii) Respond appropriately to any Red Flags that are detected pursuant to paragraph (d)(2)(ii) of this section to prevent and mitigate identity theft; and

(iv) Ensure the Program (including the Red Flags determined to be relevant) is updated periodically, to reflect changes in risks to members and to the safety and soundness of the federal credit union from identity theft.

(e) *Administration of the Program.* Each federal credit union that is required to implement a Program must provide for the continued administration of the Program and must:

(1) Obtain approval of the initial written Program from either its board of directors or an appropriate committee of the board of directors;

(2) Involve the board of directors, an appropriate committee thereof, or a designated employee at the level of senior management in the oversight, development, implementation and administration of the Program;

(3) Train staff, as necessary, to effectively implement the Program; and

(4) Exercise appropriate and effective oversight of service provider arrangements.

(f) *Guidelines.* Each federal credit union that is required to implement a Program must consider the guidelines in appendix J of this part and include in its Program those guidelines that are appropriate.

§ 717.91 Duties of card issuers regarding changes of address.

(a) *Scope.* This section applies to an issuer of a debit or credit card (card issuer) that is a federal credit union.

(b) *Definitions.* For purposes of this section:

(1) *Cardholder* means a member who has been issued a credit or debit card.

(2) *Clear and conspicuous* means reasonably understandable and designed to call attention to the nature and significance of the information presented.

(c) *Address validation requirements.* A card issuer must establish and implement reasonable policies and procedures to assess the validity of a change of address if it receives notification of a change of address for a member's debit or credit card account and, within a short period of time afterwards (during at least the first 30 days after it receives such notification), the card issuer receives a request for an additional or replacement card for the same account. Under these circumstances, the card issuer may not issue an additional or replacement card, until, in accordance with its reasonable policies and procedures and for the purpose of assessing the validity of the change of address, the card issuer:

(1)(i) Notifies the cardholder of the request:

(A) At the cardholder's former address; or

(B) By any other means of communication that the card issuer and the cardholder have previously agreed to use; and

(ii) Provides to the cardholder a reasonable means of promptly reporting incorrect address changes; or

(2) Otherwise assesses the validity of the change of address in accordance with the policies and procedures the card issuer has established pursuant to § 717.90 of this part.

(d) *Alternative timing of address validation.* A card issuer may satisfy the requirements of paragraph (c) of this section if it validates an address pursuant to the methods in paragraph (c)(1) or (c)(2) of this section when it receives an address change notification, before it receives a request for an additional or replacement card.

(e) *Form of notice.* Any written or electronic notice that the card issuer provides under this paragraph must be clear and conspicuous and provided separately from its regular correspondence with the cardholder.

APPENDICES A–B TO PART 717
[RESERVED]

APPENDIX C TO PART 717—MODEL FORMS FOR OPT-OUT NOTICES

a. Although use of the model forms is not required, use of the model forms in this appendix (as applicable) complies with the requirement in section 624 of the Act for clear, conspicuous, and concise notices.

b. Certain changes may be made to the language or format of the model forms without losing the protection from liability afforded by use of the model forms. These changes may not be so extensive as to affect the substance, clarity, or meaningful sequence of the language in the model forms. Persons making such extensive revisions will lose the safe harbor that this appendix provides. Acceptable changes include, for example:

1. Rearranging the order of the references to ''your income,'' ''your account history,'' and ''your credit score.''

2. Substituting other types of information for ''income,'' ''account history,'' or ''credit score'' for accuracy, such as ''payment history,'' ''credit history,'' ''payoff status,'' or ''claims history.''

3. Substituting a clearer and more accurate description of the affiliates providing or covered by the notice for phrases such as ''the [ABC] group of companies,'' including

without limitation a statement that the entity providing the notice recently purchased the consumer's account.

4. Substituting other types of affiliates covered by the notice for "credit card," "insurance brokerage," or "securities brokerage" affiliates.

5. Omitting items that are not accurate or applicable. For example, if a person does not limit the duration of the opt-out period, the notice may omit information about the renewal notice.

6. Adding a statement informing consumers how much time they have to opt out before shared eligibility information may be used to make solicitations to them.

7. Adding a statement that the consumer may exercise the right to opt out at any time.

8. Adding the following statement, if accurate: "If you previously opted out, you do not need to do so again."

9. Providing a place on the form for the consumer to fill in identifying information, such as his or her name and address:

10. Adding disclosures regarding the treatment of opt-outs by joint consumers to comply with § 717.23(a)(2) of this part.

C-1 Model Form for Initial Opt-out Notice (Single-Affiliate Notice)
C-2 Model Form for Initial Opt-out Notice (Joint Notice)
C-3 Model Form for Renewal Notice (Single-Affiliate Notice)
C-4 Model Form for Renewal Notice (Joint Notice)
C-5 Model Form for Voluntary "No Marketing" Notice

C–1—Model Form for Initial Opt-out Notice (Single-Affiliate Notice)—[Your Choice To Limit Marketing]/[Marketing Opt-out]

• [Name of Affiliate] is providing this notice.

• [Optional: Federal law gives you the right to limit some but not all marketing from our affiliates. Federal law also requires us to give you this notice to tell you about your choice to limit marketing from our affiliates.]

• You may limit our affiliates in the [ABC group of companies], such as our [credit card, insurance brokerage, and securities brokerage] affiliates, from marketing their products or services to you based on your personal information that we collect and share with them. This information includes your [income], your [account history with us], and your [credit score].

• Your choice to limit marketing offers from our affiliates will apply [until you tell us to change your choice]/[for x years from when you tell us your choice]/[for at least 5 years from when you tell us your choice]. [Include if the opt-out period expires.] Once that period expires, you will receive a renewal notice that will allow you to continue to limit marketing offers from our affiliates for [another x years]/[at least another 5 years].

• [Include, if applicable, in a subsequent notice, including an annual notice, for consumers who may have previously opted out.] If you have already made a choice to limit marketing offers from our affiliates, you do not need to act again until you receive the renewal notice.

To limit marketing offers, contact us [include all that apply]:

• By telephone: 1-877-###-####
• On the Web: *www.---.com*
• By mail: Check the box and complete the form below, and send the form to:

[Company name]
[Company address]

__ Do not allow your affiliates to use my personal information to market to me.

C–2—Model Form for Initial Opt-out Notice (Joint Notice)—[Your Choice To Limit Marketing]/[Marketing Opt-out]

• The [ABC group of companies] is providing this notice.

• [Optional: Federal law gives you the right to limit some but not all marketing from the [ABC] companies. Federal law also requires us to give you this notice to tell you about your choice to limit marketing from the [ABC] companies.]

• You may limit the [ABC] companies, such as the [ABC credit card, insurance brokerage, and securities brokerage] affiliates, from marketing their products or services to you based on your personal information that they receive from other [ABC] companies. This information includes your [income], your [account history], and your [credit score].

• Your choice to limit marketing offers from the [ABC] companies will apply [until you tell us to change your choice]/[for x years from when you tell us your choice]/[for at least 5 years from when you tell us your choice]. [Include if the opt-out period expires.] Once that period expires, you will receive a renewal notice that will allow you to continue to limit marketing offers from the [ABC] companies for [another x years]/[at least another 5 years].

• [Include, if applicable, in a subsequent notice, including an annual notice, for consumers who may have previously opted out.] If you have already made a choice to limit marketing offers from the [ABC] companies, you do not need to act again until you receive the renewal notice.

To limit marketing offers, contact us [include all that apply]:

• By telephone: 1-877-###-####
• On the *Web: www.---.com*
• By mail: Check the box and complete the form below, and send the form to:

National Credit Union Administration

Pt. 717, App. E

[Company name]
[Company address]

__Do not allow any company [in the ABC group of companies] to use my personal information to market to me.

C-3—Model Form for Renewal Notice (Single-Affiliate Notice)—[Renewing Your Choice To Limit Marketing]/[Renewing Your Marketing Opt-out]

• [Name of Affiliate] is providing this notice.

• [Optional: Federal law gives you the right to limit some but not all marketing from our affiliates. Federal law also requires us to give you this notice to tell you about your choice to limit marketing from our affiliates.]

• You previously chose to limit our affiliates in the [ABC] group of companies, such as our [credit card, insurance brokerage, and securities brokerage] affiliates, from marketing their products or services to you based on your personal information that we share with them. This information includes your [income], your [account history with us], and your [credit score].

• Your choice has expired or is about to expire.

To renew your choice to limit marketing for [x] more years, contact us [include all that apply]:
• By telephone: 1-877-###-####
• On the Web: *www.---.com*
• By mail: Check the box and complete the form below, and send the form to:

[Company name]
[Company address]

__Renew my choice to limit marketing for [x] more years.

C-4—Model Form for Renewal Notice (Joint Notice)—[Renewing Your Choice To Limit Marketing]/[Renewing Your Marketing Opt-out]

• The [ABC group of companies] is providing this notice.

• [Optional: Federal law gives you the right to limit some but not all marketing from the [ABC] companies. Federal law also requires us to give you this notice to tell you about your choice to limit marketing from the [ABC] companies.]

• You previously chose to limit the [ABC] companies, such as the [ABC credit card, insurance brokerage, and securities brokerage] affiliates, from marketing their products or services to you based on your personal information that they receive from other ABC companies. This information includes your [income], your [account history], and your [credit score].

• Your choice has expired or is about to expire.

To renew your choice to limit marketing for [x] more years, contact us [include all that apply]:
• By telephone: 1-877-###-####
• On the Web: *www.---.com*
• By mail: Check the box and complete the form below, and send the form to:

[Company name]
[Company address]

__Renew my choice to limit marketing for [x] more years.

C-5—MODEL FORM FOR VOLUNTARY "NO MARKETING" NOTICE

YOUR CHOICE TO STOP MARKETING

• [Name of Affiliate] is providing this notice.

• You may choose to stop all marketing from us and our affiliates.

• [Your choice to stop marketing from us and our affiliates will apply until you tell us to change your choice.]

To stop all marketing, contact us [include all that apply]:
• By telephone: 1-877-###-####
• On the Web: www.—.com
• By mail: Check the box and complete the form below, and send the form to:

[Company name]
[Company address]

__Do not market to me.

[72 FR 62989, Nov. 7, 2007, as amended at 74 FR 22644, May 14, 2009]

APPENDIX D TO PART 717 [RESERVED]

APPENDIX E TO PART 717—INTERAGENCY GUIDELINES CONCERNING THE ACCURACY AND INTEGRITY OF INFORMATION FURNISHED TO CONSUMER REPORTING AGENCIES

The NCUA encourages voluntary furnishing of information to consumer reporting agencies. Section 717.42 of this part requires each furnisher to establish and implement reasonable written policies and procedures concerning the accuracy and integrity of the information it furnishes to consumer reporting agencies. Under §717.42(b), a furnisher must consider the guidelines set forth below in developing its policies and procedures. In establishing these policies and procedures, a furnisher may include any of its existing policies and procedures that are relevant and appropriate. Section 717.42(c) requires each furnisher to review its policies and procedures periodically and update them as necessary to ensure their continued effectiveness.

I. NATURE, SCOPE, AND OBJECTIVES OF POLICIES AND PROCEDURES

(a) *Nature and Scope.* Section 717.42(a) of this part requires that a furnisher's policies and procedures be appropriate to the nature, size, complexity, and scope of the furnisher's activities. In developing its policies and procedures, a furnisher should consider, for example:

(1) The types of business activities in which the furnisher engages;

(2) The nature and frequency of the information the furnisher provides to consumer reporting agencies; and

(3) The technology used by the furnisher to furnish information to consumer reporting agencies.

(b) *Objectives.* A furnisher's policies and procedures should be reasonably designed to promote the following objectives:

(1) To furnish information about accounts or other relationships with a consumer that is accurate, such that the furnished information:

(i) Identifies the appropriate consumer;

(ii) Reflects the terms of and liability for those accounts or other relationships; and

(iii) Reflects the consumer's performance and other conduct with respect to the account or other relationship;

(2) To furnish information about accounts or other relationships with a consumer that has integrity, such that the furnished information:

(i) Is substantiated by the furnisher's records at the time it is furnished;

(ii) Is furnished in a form and manner that is designed to minimize the likelihood that the information may be incorrectly reflected in a consumer report; thus, the furnished information should:

(A) Include appropriate identifying information about the consumer to whom it pertains; and

(B) Be furnished in a standardized and clearly understandable form and manner and with a date specifying the time period to which the information pertains; and

(iii) Includes the credit limit, if applicable and in the furnisher's possession;

(3) To conduct reasonable investigations of consumer disputes and take appropriate actions based on the outcome of such investigations; and

(4) To update the information it furnishes as necessary to reflect the current status of the consumer's account or other relationship, including, for example:

(i) Any transfer of an account (*e.g.,* by sale or assignment for collection) to a third party; and

(ii) Any cure of the consumer's failure to abide by the terms of the account or other relationship.

II. ESTABLISHING AND IMPLEMENTING POLICIES AND PROCEDURES

In establishing and implementing its policies and procedures, a furnisher should:

(a) Identify practices or activities of the furnisher that can compromise the accuracy or integrity of information furnished to consumer reporting agencies, such as by:

(1) Reviewing its existing practices and activities, including the technological means and other methods it uses to furnish information to consumer reporting agencies and the frequency and timing of its furnishing of information;

(2) Reviewing its historical records relating to accuracy or integrity or to disputes; reviewing other information relating to the accuracy or integrity of information provided by the furnisher to consumer reporting agencies; and considering the types of errors, omissions, or other problems that may have affected the accuracy or integrity of information it has furnished about consumers to consumer reporting agencies;

(3) Considering any feedback received from consumer reporting agencies, consumers, or other appropriate parties;

(4) Obtaining feedback from the furnisher's staff; and

(5) Considering the potential impact of the furnisher's policies and procedures on consumers.

(b) Evaluate the effectiveness of existing policies and procedures of the furnisher regarding the accuracy and integrity of information furnished to consumer reporting agencies; consider whether new, additional, or different policies and procedures are necessary; and consider whether implementation of existing policies and procedures should be modified to enhance the accuracy and integrity of information about consumers furnished to consumer reporting agencies.

(c) Evaluate the effectiveness of specific methods (including technological means) the furnisher uses to provide information to consumer reporting agencies; how those methods may affect the accuracy and integrity of the information it provides to consumer reporting agencies; and whether new, additional, or different methods (including technological means) should be used to provide information to consumer reporting agencies to enhance the accuracy and integrity of that information.

III. SPECIFIC COMPONENTS OF POLICIES AND PROCEDURES

In developing its policies and procedures, a furnisher should address the following, as appropriate:

(a) Establishing and implementing a system for furnishing information about consumers to consumer reporting agencies that is appropriate to the nature, size, complexity, and scope of the furnisher's business operations.

(b) Using standard data reporting formats and standard procedures for compiling and furnishing data, where feasible, such as the electronic transmission of information about consumers to consumer reporting agencies.

(c) Maintaining records for a reasonable period of time, not less than any applicable recordkeeping requirement, in order to substantiate the accuracy of any information about consumers it furnishes that is subject to a direct dispute.

(d) Establishing and implementing appropriate internal controls regarding the accuracy and integrity of information about consumers furnished to consumer reporting agencies, such as by implementing standard procedures and verifying random samples of information provided to consumer reporting agencies.

(e) Training staff that participates in activities related to the furnishing of information about consumers to consumer reporting agencies to implement the policies and procedures.

(f) Providing for appropriate and effective oversight of relevant service providers whose activities may affect the accuracy or integrity of information about consumers furnished to consumer reporting agencies to ensure compliance with the policies and procedures.

(g) Furnishing information about consumers to consumer reporting agencies following mergers, portfolio acquisitions or sales, or other acquisitions or transfers of accounts or other obligations in a manner that prevents re-aging of information, duplicative reporting, or other problems that may similarly affect the accuracy or integrity of the information furnished.

(h) Deleting, updating, and correcting information in the furnisher's records, as appropriate, to avoid furnishing inaccurate information.

(i) Conducting reasonable investigations of disputes.

(j) Designing technological and other means of communication with consumer reporting agencies to prevent duplicative reporting of accounts, erroneous association of information with the wrong consumer(s), and other occurrences that may compromise the accuracy or integrity of information provided to consumer reporting agencies.

(k) Providing consumer reporting agencies with sufficient identifying information in the furnisher's possession about each consumer about whom information is furnished to enable the consumer reporting agency properly to identify the consumer.

(l) Conducting a periodic evaluation of its own practices, consumer reporting agency practices of which the furnisher is aware, investigations of disputed information, corrections of inaccurate information, means of communication, and other factors that may affect the accuracy or integrity of information furnished to consumer reporting agencies.

(m) Complying with applicable requirements under the Fair Credit Reporting Act and its implementing regulations.

[74 FR 31524, July 1, 2009]

APPENDICES F–I TO PART 717 [RESERVED]

APPENDIX J TO PART 717—INTERAGENCY GUIDELINES ON IDENTITY THEFT DETECTION, PREVENTION, AND MITIGATION

Section 717.90 of this part requires each federal credit union that offers or maintains one or more covered accounts, as defined in § 717.90(b)(3) of this part, to develop and provide for the continued administration of a written Program to detect, prevent, and mitigate identity theft in connection with the opening of a covered account or any existing covered account. These guidelines are intended to assist federal credit unions in the formulation and maintenance of a Program that satisfies the requirements of § 717.90 of this part.

I. The Program

In designing its Program, a federal credit union may incorporate, as appropriate, its existing policies, procedures, and other arrangements that control reasonably foreseeable risks to members or to the safety and soundness of the federal credit union from identity theft.

II. Identifying Relevant Red Flags

(a) *Risk Factors.* A federal credit union should consider the following factors in identifying relevant Red Flags for covered accounts, as appropriate:

(1) The types of covered accounts it offers or maintains;

(2) The methods it provides to open its covered accounts;

(3) The methods it provides to access its covered accounts; and

(4) Its previous experiences with identity theft.

(b) *Sources of Red Flags.* Federal credit unions should incorporate relevant Red Flags from sources such as:

(1) Incidents of identity theft that the federal credit union has experienced;

(2) Methods of identity theft that the federal credit union has identified that reflect changes in identity theft risks; and

(3) Applicable supervisory guidance.

(c) *Categories of Red Flags.* The Program should include relevant Red Flags from the following categories, as appropriate. Examples of Red Flags from each of these categories are appended as Supplement A to this appendix J.

(1) Alerts, notifications, or other warnings received from consumer reporting agencies or service providers, such as fraud detection services;

(2) The presentation of suspicious documents;

(3) The presentation of suspicious personal identifying information, such as a suspicious address change;

(4) The unusual use of, or other suspicious activity related to, a covered account; and

(5) Notice from members, victims of identity theft, law enforcement authorities, or other persons regarding possible identity theft in connection with covered accounts held by the federal credit union.

III. Detecting Red Flags

The Program's policies and procedures should address the detection of Red Flags in connection with the opening of covered accounts and existing covered accounts, such as by:

(a) Obtaining identifying information about, and verifying the identity of, a person opening a covered account; for example, using the policies and procedures regarding identification and verification set forth in the Customer Identification Program rules implementing 31 U.S.C. 5318(l) (31 CFR 1020.220); and

(b) Authenticating members, monitoring transactions, and verifying the validity of change of address requests, in the case of existing covered accounts.

IV. Preventing and Mitigating Identity Theft

The Program's policies and procedures should provide for appropriate responses to the Red Flags the federal credit union has detected that are commensurate with the degree of risk posed. In determining an appropriate response, a federal credit union should consider aggravating factors that may heighten the risk of identity theft, such as a data security incident that results in unauthorized access to a member's account records held by the federal credit union or a third party, or notice that a member has provided information related to a covered account held by the federal credit union to someone fraudulently claiming to represent the federal credit union or to a fraudulent website. Appropriate responses may include the following:

(a) Monitoring a covered account for evidence of identity theft;

(b) Contacting the member;

(c) Changing any passwords, security codes, or other security devices that permit access to a covered account;

(d) Reopening a covered account with a new account number;

(e) Not opening a new covered account;

(f) Closing an existing covered account;

(g) Not attempting to collect on a covered account or not selling a covered account to a debt collector;

(h) Notifying law enforcement; or

(i) Determining that no response is warranted under the particular circumstances.

V. Updating the Program

Federal credit unions should update the Program (including the Red Flags determined to be relevant) periodically, to reflect changes in risks to members or to the safety and soundness of the federal credit union from identity theft, based on factors such as:

(a) The experiences of the federal credit union with identity theft;

(b) Changes in methods of identity theft;

(c) Changes in methods to detect, prevent, and mitigate identity theft;

(d) Changes in the types of accounts that the federal credit union offers or maintains; and

(e) Changes in the business arrangements of the federal credit union, including mergers, acquisitions, alliances, joint ventures, and service provider arrangements.

VI. Methods for Administering the Program

(a) *Oversight of Program.* Oversight by the board of directors, an appropriate committee of the board, or a designated employee at the level of senior management should include:

(1) Assigning specific responsibility for the Program's implementation;

(2) Reviewing reports prepared by staff regarding compliance by the federal credit union with §717.90 of this part; and

(3) Approving material changes to the Program as necessary to address changing identity theft risks.

(b) *Reports.* (1) *In general.* Staff of the federal credit union responsible for development, implementation, and administration of its Program should report to the board of directors, an appropriate committee of the board, or a designated employee at the level of senior management, at least annually, on compliance by the federal credit union with §717.90 of this part.

(2) *Contents of report.* The report should address material matters related to the Program and evaluate issues such as: the effectiveness of the policies and procedures of the federal credit union in addressing the risk of identity theft in connection with the opening of covered accounts and with respect to existing covered accounts; service provider arrangements; significant incidents involving identity theft and management's response; and recommendations for material changes to the Program.

(c) *Oversight of service provider arrangements.* Whenever a federal credit union engages a service provider to perform an activity in connection with one or more covered accounts the federal credit union should take steps to ensure that the activity of the service provider is conducted in accordance with reasonable policies and procedures designed to detect, prevent, and mitigate the

National Credit Union Administration

risk of identity theft. For example, a federal credit union could require the service provider by contract to have policies and procedures to detect relevant Red Flags that may arise in the performance of the service provider's activities, and either report the Red Flags to the federal credit union, or to take appropriate steps to prevent or mitigate identity theft.

VII. Other Applicable Legal Requirements

Federal credit unions should be mindful of other related legal requirements that may be applicable, such as:

(a) Filing a Suspicious Activity Report under 31 U.S.C. 5318(g) and 12 CFR 748.1(c);

(b) Implementing any requirements under 15 U.S.C. 1681c–1(h) regarding the circumstances under which credit may be extended when the federal credit union detects a fraud or active duty alert;

(c) Implementing any requirements for furnishers of information to consumer reporting agencies under 15 U.S.C. 1681s–2, for example, to correct or update inaccurate or incomplete information, and to not report information that the furnisher has reasonable cause to believe is inaccurate; and

(d) Complying with the prohibitions in 15 U.S.C. 1681m on the sale, transfer, and placement for collection of certain debts resulting from identity theft.

Supplement A to Appendix J

In addition to incorporating Red Flags from the sources recommended in section II.b. of the Guidelines in appendix J of this part, each federal credit union may consider incorporating into its Program, whether singly or in combination, Red Flags from the following illustrative examples in connection with covered accounts:

Alerts, Notifications or Warnings From a Consumer Reporting Agency

1. A fraud or active duty alert is included with a consumer report.

2. A consumer reporting agency provides a notice of credit freeze in response to a request for a consumer report.

3. A consumer reporting agency provides a notice of address discrepancy, as defined in §717.82(b) of this part.

4. A consumer report indicates a pattern of activity that is inconsistent with the history and usual pattern of activity of an applicant or member, such as:

a. A recent and significant increase in the volume of inquiries;

b. An unusual number of recently established credit relationships;

c. A material change in the use of credit, especially with respect to recently established credit relationships; or

d. An account that was closed for cause or identified for abuse of account privileges by a financial institution or creditor.

Suspicious Documents

5. Documents provided for identification appear to have been altered or forged.

6. The photograph or physical description on the identification is not consistent with the appearance of the applicant or member presenting the identification.

7. Other information on the identification is not consistent with information provided by the person opening a new covered account or member presenting the identification.

8. Other information on the identification is not consistent with readily accessible information that is on file with the federal credit union, such as a signature card or a recent check.

9. An application appears to have been altered or forged, or gives the appearance of having been destroyed and reassembled.

Suspicious Personal Identifying Information

10. Personal identifying information provided is inconsistent when compared against external information sources used by the federal credit union. For example:

a. The address does not match any address in the consumer report; or

b. The Social Security Number (SSN) has not been issued, or is listed on the Social Security Administration's Death Master File.

11. Personal identifying information provided by the member is not consistent with other personal identifying information provided by the member. For example, there is a lack of correlation between the SSN range and date of birth.

12. Personal identifying information provided is associated with known fraudulent activity as indicated by internal or third-party sources used by the federal credit union. For example:

a. The address on an application is the same as the address provided on a fraudulent application; or

b. The phone number on an application is the same as the number provided on a fraudulent application.

13. Personal identifying information provided is of a type commonly associated with fraudulent activity as indicated by internal or third-party sources used by the federal credit union. For example:

a. The address on an application is fictitious, a mail drop, or prison; or

b. The phone number is invalid, or is associated with a pager or answering service.

14. The SSN provided is the same as that submitted by other persons opening an account or other members.

15. The address or telephone number provided is the same as or similar to the address

or telephone number submitted by an unusually large number of other persons opening accounts or by other members.

16. The person opening the covered account or the member fails to provide all required personal identifying information on an application or in response to notification that the application is incomplete.

17. Personal identifying information provided is not consistent with personal identifying information that is on file with the federal credit union.

18. For federal credit unions that use challenge questions, the person opening the covered account or the member cannot provide authenticating information beyond that which generally would be available from a wallet or consumer report.

Unusual Use of, or Suspicious Activity Related to, the Covered Account

19. Shortly following the notice of a change of address for a covered account, the institution or creditor receives a request for a new, additional, or replacement card or a cell phone, or for the addition of authorized users on the account.

20. A new revolving credit account is used in a manner commonly associated with known patterns of fraud. For example:

a. The majority of available credit is used for cash advances or merchandise that is easily convertible to cash (e.g., electronics equipment or jewelry); or

b. The member fails to make the first payment or makes an initial payment but no subsequent payments.

21. A covered account is used in a manner that is not consistent with established patterns of activity on the account. There is, for example:

a. Nonpayment when there is no history of late or missed payments;

b. A material increase in the use of available credit;

c. A material change in purchasing or spending patterns;

d. A material change in electronic fund transfer patterns in connection with a deposit account; or

e. A material change in telephone call patterns in connection with a cellular phone account.

22. A covered account that has been inactive for a reasonably lengthy period of time is used (taking into consideration the type of account, the expected pattern of usage and other relevant factors).

23. Mail sent to the member is returned repeatedly as undeliverable although transactions continue to be conducted in connection with the member's covered account.

24. The federal credit union is notified that the member is not receiving paper account statements.

25. The federal credit union is notified of unauthorized charges or transactions in connection with a member's covered account.

Notice From Members, Victims of Identity Theft, Law Enforcement Authorities, or Other Persons Regarding Possible Identity Theft in Connection With Covered Accounts Held by the Federal Credit Union

26. The federal credit union is notified by a member, a victim of identity theft, a law enforcement authority, or any other person that it has opened a fraudulent account for a person engaged in identity theft.

[72 FR 63769, Nov. 9, 2007, as amended at 74 FR 22644, May 14, 2009; 76 FR 18365, Apr. 4, 2011]

PART 721—INCIDENTAL POWERS

Sec.
721.1 What does this part cover?
721.2 What is an incidental powers activity?
721.3 What categories of activities are preapproved as incidental powers necessary or requisite to carry on a credit union's business?
721.4 How may a credit union apply to engage in an activity that is not preapproved as within a credit union's incidental powers?
721.5 What limitations apply to a credit union engaging in activities approved under this part?
721.6 May a credit union derive income from activities approved under this part?
721.7 What are the potential conflicts of interest for officials and employees when credit unions engage in activities approved under this part?

AUTHORITY: 12 U.S.C. 1757(17), 1766 and 1789.

SOURCE: 66 FR 40857, Aug. 6, 2001, unless otherwise noted.

§ 721.1 What does this part cover?

This part authorizes a federal credit union (you) to engage in activities incidental to your business as set out in this part. This part also describes how interested parties may request a legal opinion on whether an activity is within a federal credit union's incidental powers or apply to add new activities or categories to the regulation. An activity approved in a legal opinion to an interested party or as a result of an application by an interested party to add new activities or categories is recognized as an incidental powers activity for all federal credit unions. This part does not apply to the activities of corporate credit unions.

National Credit Union Administration

§ 721.2 What is an incidental powers activity?

An incidental powers activity is one that is necessary or requisite to enable you to carry on effectively the business for which you are incorporated. An activity meets the definition of an incidental power activity if the activity:

(a) Is convenient or useful in carrying out the mission or business of credit unions consistent with the Federal Credit Union Act;

(b) Is the functional equivalent or logical outgrowth of activities that are part of the mission or business of credit unions; and

(c) Involves risks similar in nature to those already assumed as part of the business of credit unions.

§ 721.3 What categories of activities are preapproved as incidental powers necessary or requisite to carry on a credit union's business?

The categories of activities in this section are preapproved as incidental to carrying on your business under § 721.2. The examples of incidental powers activities within each category are provided in this section as illustrations of activities permissible under the particular category, not as an exclusive or exhaustive list.

(a) *Certification services.* Certification services are services whereby you attest or authenticate a fact for your members' use. Certification services may include such services as notary services, signature guarantees, certification of electronic signatures, and share draft certifications.

(b) *Correspondent services.* Correspondent services are services you provide to other credit unions including foreign credit unions that you are authorized to perform for your members or as part of your operation. These services may include loan processing, loan servicing, member check cashing services, disbursing share withdrawals and loan proceeds, cashing and selling money orders, performing internal audits, and automated teller machine deposit services.

(c) *Electronic financial services.* Electronic financial services are any services, products, functions, or activities that you are otherwise authorized to perform, provide, or deliver to your members but performed through electronic means. Electronic services may include automated teller machines, electronic fund transfers, online transaction processing through a web site, web site hosting services, account aggregation services, and Internet access services to perform or deliver products or services to members.

(d) *Excess capacity.* Excess capacity is the excess use or capacity remaining in facilities, equipment, or services that: You properly invested in or established, in good faith, with the intent of serving your members; and you reasonably anticipate will be taken up by the future expansion of services to your members. You may sell or lease the excess capacity in facilities, equipment or services such as office space, employees and data processing.

(e) *Financial counseling services.* Financial counseling services means advice, guidance or services that you offer to your members to promote thrift or to otherwise assist members on financial matters. Financial counseling services may include income tax preparation service, electronic tax filing for your members, counseling regarding estate and retirement planning, investment counseling, and debt and budget counseling.

(f) *Finder activities.* Finder activities are activities in which you introduce or otherwise bring together outside vendors with your members so that the two parties may negotiate and consummate transactions and include vendors of non-financial products, vendors that are other financial institutions, and vendors of financial products such as insurance and securities. Finder activities may include endorsing a product or service, negotiating group discounts on behalf of your members, offering third party products and services to members through the sale of advertising space on your website, account statements and receipts, and selling statistical or consumer financial information to outside vendors to facilitate the sale of their products to your members. You may perform administrative functions on behalf of vendors to facilitate transactions between your members and another institution.

§ 721.4

(g) *Loan-related products.* Loan-related products are the products, activities or services you provide to your members in a lending transaction that protect you against credit-related risks or are otherwise incidental to your lending authority. These products or activities may include debt cancellation agreements, debt suspension agreements, letters of credit and leases.

(h) *Marketing activities.* Marketing activities are the activities or means you use to promote membership in your credit union and the products and services you offer to your members. Marketing activities may include advertising and other promotional activities such as raffles, membership referral drives, and the purchase or use of advertising.

(i) *Monetary instrument services.* Monetary instrument services are services that enable your members to purchase, sell, or exchange various currencies. These services may include the sale and exchange of foreign currency and U.S. commemorative coins. You may also use accounts you have in foreign financial institutions to facilitate your members' transfer and negotiation of checks denominated in foreign currency or engage in monetary transfer services for your members.

(j) *Operational programs.* Operational programs are programs that you establish within your business to establish or deliver products and services that enhance member service and promote safe and sound operation. Operational programs may include electronic funds transfers, remote tellers, point of purchase terminals, debit cards, payroll deduction, payroll services, pre-authorized member transactions, direct deposit, check clearing services, savings bond purchases and redemptions, tax payment services, wire transfers, safe deposit boxes, loan collection services, and service fees.

(k) *Stored value products.* Stored value products are alternate media to currency in which you transfer monetary value to the product and create a medium of exchange for your members' use. Examples of stored value products include stored value cards, public transportation tickets, event and attraction tickets, gift certificates, prepaid phone cards, postage stamps, electronic benefits transfer script, and similar media.

(l) *Trustee or custodial services.* Trustee or custodial services are services in which you are authorized to act under any written trust instrument or custodial agreement created or organized in the United States and forming part of a tax-advantaged savings plan, as authorized under the Internal Revenue Code. These services may include acting as a trustee or custodian for member retirement, education and health savings accounts.

[66 FR 40857, Aug. 6, 2001, as amended at 69 FR 45238, July 29, 2004; 73 FR 62856, Oct. 22, 2008; 75 FR 34621, June 18, 2010]

§ 721.4 How may a credit union apply to engage in an activity that is not preapproved as within a credit union's incidental powers?

(a) *Application contents.* To engage in an activity that may be within an FCU's incidental powers but that does not fall within a preapproved category listed in § 721.3, you may submit an application by certified mail, return receipt requested, to the NCUA Board. Your application must describe the activity, your explanation, consistent with the test provided in paragraph (c) of this section, of why this activity is within your incidental powers, your plan for implementing the proposed activity, any state licenses you must obtain to conduct the activity, and any other information necessary to describe the proposed activity adequately. Before you engage in the petition process you should seek an advisory opinion from NCUA's Office of General Counsel, as to whether a proposed activity fits into one of the authorized categories or is otherwise within your incidental powers without filing a petition to amend the regulation.

(b) *Processing of application.* Your application must be filed with the Secretary of the NCUA Board. NCUA will review your application for completeness and will notify you whether additional information is required or whether the activity requested is permissible under one of the categories listed in § 721.3. If the activity falls within a category provided in § 721.3,

NCUA will notify you that the activity is permissible and treat the application as withdrawn. If the activity does not fall within a category provided in §721.3, NCUA staff will consider whether the proposed activity is legally permissible. Upon a recommendation by NCUA staff that the activity is within a credit union's incidental powers, the NCUA Board may amend §721.3 and will request public comment on the establishment of a new category of activities within §721.3. If the activity proposed in your application fails to meet the criteria established in paragraph (c) of this section, NCUA will notify you within a reasonable period of time.

(c) *Decision on application.* In determining whether an activity is authorized as an appropriate exercise of a federal credit union's incidental powers, the Board will consider:

(1) Whether the activity is convenient or useful in carrying out the mission or business of credit unions consistent with the Act;

(2) Whether the activity is the functional equivalent or logical outgrowth of activities that are part of the mission or business of credit unions; and

(3) Whether the activity involves risks similar in nature to those already assumed as part of the business of credit unions.

§721.5 What limitations apply to a credit union engaging in activities approved under this part?

You must comply with any applicable NCUA regulations, policies, and legal opinions, as well as applicable state and federal law, if an activity authorized under this part is otherwise regulated or conditioned.

§721.6 May a credit union derive income from activities approved under this part?

You may earn income for those activities determined to be incidental to your business.

§721.7 What are the potential conflicts of interest for officials and employees when credit unions engage in activities approved under this part?

(a) *Conflicts.* No official, employee, or their immediate family member may receive any compensation or benefit, directly or indirectly, in connection with your engagement in an activity authorized under this part, except as otherwise provided in paragraph (b) of this section. This section does not apply if a conflicts of interest provision within another section of this chapter applies to a particular activity; in such case, the more specific conflicts of interest provision controls. For example: An official or employee that refers loan-related products offered by a third-party to a member, in connection with a loan made by you, is subject to the conflicts of interest provision in §701.21(c)(8) of this chapter.

(b) *Permissible payments.* This section does not prohibit:

(1) Payment, by you, of salary to your employees;

(2) Payment, by you, of an incentive or bonus to an employee based on your overall financial performance;

(3) Payment, by you, of an incentive or bonus to an employee, other than a senior management employee or paid official, in connection with an activity authorized by this part, provided that your board of directors establishes written policies and internal controls for the incentive program and monitors compliance with such policies and controls at least annually; and

(4) Payment, by a person other than you, of any compensation or benefit to an employee, other than a senior management employee or paid official, in connection with an activity authorized by this part, provided that your board of directors establishes written policies and internal controls regarding third-party compensation and determines that the employee's involvement does not present a conflict of interest.

(c) *Business associates and family members.* All transactions with business associates or family members not specifically prohibited by paragraph (a) of this section must be conducted at arm's length and in the interest of the credit union.

(d) *Definitions.* For purposes of this part, the following definitions apply.

(1) *Senior management employee* means your chief executive officer (typically,

this individual holds the title of President or Treasurer/Manager), any assistant chief executive officers (e.g. Assistant President, Vice President, or Assistant Treasurer/Manager), and the chief financial officer (Comptroller).

(2) *Official* means any member of your board of directors, credit committee or supervisory committee.

(3) *Immediate family member* means a spouse or other family member living in the same household.

PART 722—APPRAISALS

Sec.
722.1 Authority, purpose, and scope.
722.2 Definitions.
722.3 Appraisals required; transactions requiring a State certified or licensed appraiser.
722.4 Minimum appraisal standards.
722.5 Appraiser independence.
722.6 Professional association membership; competency.
722.7 Enforcement.

AUTHORITY: 12 U.S.C. 1766, 1789 and 3339.

SOURCE: 55 FR 30207, July 25, 1990, unless otherwise noted.

§ 722.1 Authority, purpose, and scope.

(a) *Authority.* Part 722 is issued by the National Credit Union Administration ("NCUA") under title XI of the Financial Institutions Reform, Recovery, and Enforcement Act of 1989 ("FIRREA") (Pub. L. 101–73, 103 Stat. 183, 1989) and 12 U.S.C. 1757 and 1766.

(b) *Purpose and scope.* (1) Title XI provides protection for federal financial and public policy interests in real estate-related transactions by requiring real estate appraisals used in connection with federally related transactions to be performed in writing, in accordance with uniform standards, by appraisers whose competency has been demonstrated and whose professional conduct will be subject to effective supervision. This part implements the requirements of title XI and applies to all federally related transactions entered into by the National Credit Union Administration or by federally insured credit unions ("regulated institutions").

(2) This part: (i) Identifies which real estate-related financial transactions require the services of an appraiser;

(ii) Prescribes which categories of federally related transactions shall be appraised by a state-certified appraiser and which by a state-licensed appraiser; and

(iii) Prescribes minimum standards for the performance of real estate appraisals in connection with federally related transactions under the jurisdiction of the National Credit Union Administration.

§ 722.2 Definitions.

(a) *Appraisal* means a written statement independently and impartially prepared by a qualified appraiser setting forth an opinion as to the market value of an adequately-described property as of a specific date(s), supported by the presentation and analysis of relevant market information.

(b) *Appraisal Foundation* means the Appraisal Foundation established on November 30, 1987, as a not-for-profit corporation under the laws of Illinois.

(c) *Appraisal Subcommittee* means the Appraisal Subcommittee of the Federal Financial Institutions Examination Council.

(d) *Complex 1- to 4-family residential property appraisal* means one in which the property to be appraised, the form of ownership or market conditions are atypical.

(e) *Federally related transaction* means any real estate-related financial transaction entered into on or after August 9, 1990 that:

(1) The National Credit Union Administration, or any federally insured credit union, engages in or contracts for; and

(2) Requires the services of an appraiser.

(f) *Market value* means the most probable price which a property should bring in a competitive and open market under all conditions requisite to a fair sale, the buyer and seller each acting prudently and knowledgeably and assuming the price is not affected by undue stimulus. Implicit in this definition is the consummation of a sale as of a specified date and the passing of title from seller to buyer under conditions whereby:

(1) Buyer and seller are typically motivated;

(2) Both parties are well informed or well advised, and acting in what they consider their own best interests;

(3) A reasonable time is allowed for exposure in the open market;

(4) Payment is made in terms of cash in U.S. dollars or in terms of financial arrangements comparable thereto; and

(5) The price represents the normal consideration for the property sold unaffected by special or creative financing or sales concessions granted by anyone associated with the sale.

(g) *Real estate or real property* means an identified parcel or tract of land, including easements, rights of way, undivided or future interests and similar rights in a parcel or tract of land, but does not include mineral rights, timber rights, and growing crops, water rights and similar interests severable from the land when the transaction does not involve the associated parcel or tract of land.

(h) *Real estate-related financial transaction* means any transaction involving:

(1) The sale, lease, purchase, investment in or exchange of real property, including interests in property, or the financing thereof; or

(2) The refinancing of real property or interests in real property; or

(3) The use of real property or interests in property as security for a loan or investment, including mortgage-backed securities.

(i) *State-certified appraiser* means any individual who has satisfied the requirements for certification in a state or territory whose criteria for certification as a real estate appraiser currently meet the minimum criteria for certification issued by the Appraiser Qualification Board of the Appraisal Foundation. No individual shall be a state-certified appraiser unless such individual has achieved a passing grade upon a suitable examination administered by a state or territory that is consistent with and equivalent to the Uniform State Certification Examination issued or endorsed by the Appraiser Qualification Board. In addition, the Appraisal Subcommittee must not have issued a finding that the policies, practices, or procedures of a state or territory are inconsistent with title XI of FIRREA. The National Credit Union Administration may, from time to time, impose additional qualification criteria for certified appraisers performing appraisals in connection with federally related transactions within its jurisdiction.

(j) *State-licensed appraiser* means any individual who has satisfied the requirements for licensing in a state or territory where the licensing procedures comply with title XI of FIRREA and where the Appraisal Subcommittee has not issued a finding that the policies, practices, or procedures of the State or territory are inconsistent with title XI. The NCUA may, from time to time, impose additional qualification criteria for licensed appraisers performing appraisals in connection with federally related transactions within its jurisdiction.

(k) *Tract development* means a project of five units or more that is constructed or is to be constructed as a single development.

(l) *Transaction value means:* (1) For loans or other extensions of credit, the amount of the loan or extension of credit; and

(2) For sales, leases, purchases, and investments in or exchanges of real property, the market value of the real property interest involved; and

(3) For the pooling of loans or interests in real property for resale or purchase, the amount of the loan or market value of the real property calculated with respect to each such loan or interest in real property.

[55 FR 30207, July 25, 1990, as amended at 57 FR 28998, June 30, 1992; 75 FR 34622, June 18, 2010]

§ 722.3 Appraisals required; transactions requiring a State certified or licensed appraiser.

(a) *Appraisals required.* An appraisal performed by a State certified or licensed appraiser is required for all real estate-related financial transactions except those in which:

(1) The transaction value is $250,000 or less;

(2) A lien on real property has been taken as collateral through an abundance of caution and where the terms of the transaction as a consequence have not been made more favorable

§ 722.3

than they would have been in the absence of a lien;

(3) A lien on real estate has been taken for purposes other than the real estate's value;

(4) A lease of real estate is entered into, unless the lease is the economic equivalent of a purchase or sale of the leased real estate;

(5) The transaction involves an existing extension of credit at the credit union, provided that:

(i) There is no advancement of new monies, other than funds necessary to cover reasonable closing costs; and

(ii) There has been no obvious and material change in market conditions or physical aspects of the property that threatens the adequacy of the credit union's real estate collateral protection after the transaction;

(6) The transaction involves the purchase, sale, investment in, exchange of, or extension of credit secured by, a loan or interest in a loan, pooled loans, or interests in real property, including mortgage-backed securities, and each loan or interest in a loan, pooled loan, or real property interest met the requirements of this regulation, if applicable, at the time of origination;

(7) The transaction is wholly or partially insured or guaranteed by a United States government agency or United States government sponsored agency;

(8) The transaction either:

(i) Qualifies for sale to a United States government agency or United States government sponsored agency; or

(ii) Involves a residential real estate transaction in which the appraisal conforms to the Federal National Mortgage Association or Federal Home Loan Mortgage Corporation appraisal standards applicable to that category of real estate; or

(9) The regional director has granted a waiver from the appraisal requirement for a category of loans meeting the definition of a member business loan.

(b) *Transactions requiring a State-certified appraiser.* (1) (All transactions of $1,000,000 or more) All federally related transactions having a transaction value of $1,000,000 or more shall require an appraisal prepared by a state-certified appraiser.

(2) (Nonresidential transactions) All federally related transactions having a transaction value of more than $250,000, other than those involving appraisals of 1- to 4-family residential properties, shall require an appraisal prepared by a state-certified appraiser.

(3) (Complex residential transactions of $250,000 or more) All complex 1- to 4-family residential property appraisals rendered in connection with federally related transactions shall require a state-certified appraiser if the transaction value is $250,000 or more. A regulated institution may presume that appraisals of 1- to 4-family residential properties are not complex unless the institution has readily available information that a given appraisal will be complex. The regulated institution shall be responsible for making the final determination of whether the appraisal is complex. If, during the course of the appraisal, a licensed appraiser identifies factors that would result in the property, form of ownership, or market conditions being considered atypical, then either:

(i) The regulated institution may ask the licensed appraiser to complete the appraisal and have a certified appraiser approve and cosign the appraisal; or

(ii) The institution may engage a certified appraiser to complete the appraisal.

(c) *Transactions requiring either a State-certified or -licensed appraiser.* All appraisals for federally related transactions not requiring the services of a state-certified appraiser shall be prepared by either a state-certified appraiser or a state-licensed appraiser.

(d) *Valuation requirement.* Secured transactions exempted from appraisal requirements pursuant to paragraphs (a)(1) and (a)(5) of this section and not otherwise exempted from this regulation or fully insured shall be supported by a written estimate of market value, as defined in this regulation, performed by an individual having no direct or indirect interest in the property, and qualified and experienced to perform such estimates of value for the type and amount of credit being considered.

(e) *Appraisals to address safety and soundness concerns.* NCUA reserves the right to require an appraisal under this subpart whenever the agency believes it is necessary to address safety and soundness concerns.

[55 FR 30207, July 25, 1990, as amended at 60 FR 51894, Oct. 4, 1995; 63 FR 51799, Sept. 29, 1998; 67 FR 67102, Nov. 4, 2002; 72 FR 30247, May 31, 2007]

§ 722.4 Minimum appraisal standards.

For federally related transactions, all appraisals shall, at a minimum:

(a) Conform to generally accepted appraisal standards as evidenced by the Uniform Standards of Professional Appraisal Practice (USPAP) promulgated by the Appraisal Standards Board of the Appraisal Foundation, 1029 Vermont Ave., NW., Washington, DC 20005;

(b) Be written and contain sufficient information and analysis to support the institution's decision to engage in the transaction;

(c) Analyze and report appropriate deductions and discounts for proposed construction or renovation, partially leased buildings, non-market lease terms, and tract developments with unsold units;

(d) Be based upon the definition of market value as set forth in § 722.2(f); and

(e) Be performed by State licensed or certified appraisers in accordance with requirements set forth in this subpart.

[60 FR 51894, Oct. 4, 1995]

§ 722.5 Appraiser independence.

(a) *Staff appraiser.* If an appraisal is prepared by a staff appraiser, that appraiser must be independent of the lending, investment, and collection functions and not involved, except as an appraiser, in the federally related transaction, and have no direct or indirect interest, financial or otherwise, in the property. If the only qualified persons available to perform an appraisal are involved in the lending, investment, or collection functions of the credit union, the credit union shall take appropriate steps to ensure that the appraisers exercise independent judgment. Such steps include, but are not limited to, prohibiting an individual from performing an appraisal in connection with federally related transactions in which the appraiser is otherwise involved.

(b) *Fee Appraisers.* (1) If an appraisal is prepared by a fee appraiser, the appraiser shall be engaged directly by the credit union or its agent and have no direct or indirect interest, financial or otherwise, in the property or the transaction.

(2) A credit union also may accept an appraisal that was prepared by an appraiser engaged directly by another financial services institution; if:

(i) The appraiser has no direct or indirect interest, financial or otherwise, in the property or transaction; and

(ii) The credit union determines that the appraisal conforms to the requirement of this regulation and is otherwise acceptable.

[55 FR 30207, July 25, 1990, as amended at 60 FR 51895, Oct. 4, 1995]

§ 722.6 Professional association membership; competency.

(a) *Membership in appraisal organization.* A state-certified appraiser or a state-licensed appraiser may not be excluded from consideration for an assignment for a federally related transaction solely by virtue of membership or lack of membership in any particular appraisal organization.

(b) *Competency.* All staff and fee appraisers performing appraisals in connection with federally related transactions must be state-certified or -licensed as appropriate. However, a state-certified or -licensed appraiser may not be considered competent solely by virtue of being certified or licensed. Any determination of competency shall be based upon the individual's experience and educational background as they relate to the particular appraisal assignment for which he or she is being considered.

§ 722.7 Enforcement.

Credit unions and institution-affiliated parties, including staff appraisers and fee appraisers, may be subject to removal and/or prohibition orders, cease-and-desist orders, and the imposition of civil money penalties pursuant to section 1786 of the Federal Credit Union Act, or any other applicable law.

PART 723—MEMBER BUSINESS LOANS

Sec.
723.1 What is a member business loan?
723.2 What are the prohibited activities?
723.3 What are the requirements for construction and development lending?
723.4 What other regulations apply to member business lending?
723.5 How do you implement a member business loan program?
723.6 What must your member business loan policy address?
723.7 What are the collateral and security requirements?
723.8 How much may one member or a group of associated members borrow?
723.9 [Reserved]
723.10 What waivers are available?
723.11 How do you obtain a waiver?
723.12 What will NCUA do with my waiver request?
723.13 What options are available if the NCUA Regional Director denies my waiver request, or a portion of it?
723.14–723.15 [Reserved]
723.16 What is the aggregate member business loan limit for a credit union?
723.17 Are there any exceptions to the aggregate loan limit?
723.18 How do I obtain an exception?
723.19 What are the recordkeeping requirements?
723.20 How can a state supervisory authority develop and enforce a member business loan regulation?
723.21 Definitions.

AUTHORITY: 12 U.S.C. 1756, 1757, 1757A, 1766, 1785, 1789.

SOURCE: 64 FR 28729, May 27, 1999, unless otherwise noted.

§ 723.1 What is a member business loan?

(a) *General rule.* A member business loan includes any loan, line of credit, or letter of credit (including any unfunded commitments) where the borrower uses the proceeds for the following purposes:

(1) Commercial;
(2) Corporate;
(3) Other business investment property or venture; or
(4) Agricultural.

(b) *Exceptions to the general rule.* The following are not member business loans:

(1) A loan fully secured by a lien on a 1 to 4 family dwelling that is the member's primary residence;

(2) A loan fully secured by shares in the credit union making the extension of credit or deposits in other financial institutions;

(3) Loan(s) to a member or an associated member which, when the net member business loan balances are added together, are equal to less than $50,000;

(4) A loan where a federal or state agency (or its political subdivision) fully insures repayment, or fully guarantees repayment, or provides an advance commitment to purchase in full; or

(5) A loan granted by a corporate credit union to another credit union.

(c) *Loans to credit unions and credit union service organizations.* This part does not apply to loans made by federal credit unions to credit unions and credit union service organizations. This part does not apply to loans made by a federally insured, state-chartered credit union to credit unions and credit union service organizations if the credit union's supervisory authority determines that state law grants authority to lend to these entities other than the general authority to grant loans to members.

(d) *Purchase of member loans and member loan participations.* Any interest a credit union obtains in a loan that was made by another lender to the credit union's member is a member business loan, for purposes of this rule and the risk weighting standards of part 702 of this chapter to the same extent as if made directly by the credit union to its member.

(e) *Purchases of nonmember loans and nonmember loan participations.* Any interest a credit union obtains in a nonmember loan, pursuant to § 701.22 or part 742 of this chapter or other authority, is treated the same as a member business loan for purposes of this rule and the risk weighting standards under part 702 of this chapter, except that the effect of such interest on a credit union's aggregate member business loan limit will be as set forth in § 723.16(b) of this part.

[64 FR 28729, May 27, 1999, as amended at 64 FR 57365, Oct. 25, 1999; 68 FR 56551, Oct. 1, 2003]

§723.2 What are the prohibited activities?

(a) *Who is ineligible to receive a member business loan?* You may not grant a member business loan to the following:

(1) Your chief executive officer (typically this individual holds the title of President or Treasurer/Manager);

(2) Any assistant chief executive officers (e.g., Assistant President, Vice President, or Assistant Treasurer/Manager);

(3) Your chief financial officer (Comptroller); or

(4) Any associated member or immediate family member of anyone listed in paragraphs (a) (1) through (3) of this section.

(b) *Equity agreements/joint ventures.* You may not grant a member business loan if any additional income received by the credit union or senior management employees is tied to the profit or sale of the business or commercial endeavor for which the loan is made.

(c) *Loans to compensated directors.* A credit union may not grant a member business loan to a compensated director unless the board of directors approves granting the loan and the compensated director is recused from the decision making process.

§723.3 What are the requirements for construction and development lending?

Except as provided in §723.4 or unless your Regional Director grants a waiver, loans granted for the construction or development of commercial or residential property are subject to the following additional requirements.

(a) The aggregate of the net member business loan balances for all construction and development loans must not exceed 15% of net worth. In determining the aggregate balances for purposes of this limitation, a credit union may exclude any loan made to finance the construction of a single-family residence if a prospective homeowner has contracted to purchase the property and may also exclude a loan to finance the construction of one single-family residence per member-borrower or group of associated member-borrowers, irrespective of the existence of a contractual commitment from a prospective homeowner to purchase the property.

(b) The borrower must have a minimum of 25% equity interest in the project being financed, the value of which is determined by the market value of the project at the time the loan is made, except that this requirement will not apply in the case of a loan made to finance the construction of a single-family residence if a prospective homeowner has contracted to purchase the property and in the case of one loan to a member-borrower or group of associated member-borrowers to finance the construction of a single-family residence, irrespective of the existence of a contractual commitment from a prospective homeowner to purchase the property. Instead, the collateral requirements of §723.7 will apply; and

(c) The funds may be released only after on-site, written inspections by qualified personnel and according to a preapproved draw schedule and any other conditions as set forth in the loan documentation.

[64 FR 28729, May 27, 1999, as amended at 68 FR 56551, Oct. 1, 2003; 69 FR 62565, Oct. 27, 2004]

§723.4 What other regulations apply to member business lending?

(a) The provisions of §701.21(a) through (g) and part 702 of this chapter apply to member business loans granted by credit unions to the extent they are consistent with this part. Except as required by part 741 of this chapter, federally insured State-chartered credit unions are not required to comply with the provisions of §701.21(a) through (g) of this chapter.

(b) If a federal credit union makes a member business loan as part of a Small Business Administration guaranteed loan program with loan requirements that are less restrictive than those required by NCUA, then the federal credit union may follow the loan requirements of the relevant Small Business Administration guaranteed loan program to the extent they are consistent with this part. A federally insured State-chartered credit union that is subject to this part and makes a member business loan as part of a

§ 723.5

Small Business Administration guaranteed loan program with loan requirements that are less restrictive than those required by NCUA may follow the loan requirements of the relevant Small Business Administration guaranteed loan program to the extent they are consistent with this part if its state supervisory authority has determined that the credit union has authority to do so under State law.

(c) The collateral and security requirements of § 723.3 and § 723.7 do not apply to member business loans made as part of a Small Business Administration guaranteed loan program.

[69 FR 62565, Oct. 27, 2004]

§ 723.5 How do you implement a member business loan program?

(a) *Generally.* The board of directors must adopt specific business loan policies and review them at least annually. The board must also use the services of an individual with at least two years direct experience with the type of lending the credit union will be engaging in. The experience must provide the credit union sufficient expertise given the complexity and risk exposure of the loans in which the credit union intends to engage. Credit unions do not have to hire staff to meet the requirements of this section but must ensure that the expertise is available. A credit union can meet the experience requirement through various approaches. For example, a credit union can use the services of a credit union service organization (CUSO), an employee of another credit union, an independent contractor, or other third parties. However, the actual decision to grant a loan must reside with the credit union.

(b) *Conflicts of Interest.* Any third party used by a credit union to meet the requirements of paragraph (a) of this section must be independent from the transaction and is prohibited from having a participation in the loan or an interest in the collateral securing the loan that the third party is responsible for reviewing, with the following exceptions:

(1) The third party may provide a service to the credit union related to the transaction, such as loan servicing;

(2) The third party may provide the requisite experience to the credit union

and purchase a loan or a participation interest in a loan originated by the credit union that the third party reviewed; or

(3) A credit union may use the services of a CUSO that otherwise meets the requirements of paragraph (a) of this section even though the CUSO is not independent from the transaction, provided the credit union has a controlling financial interest in the CUSO as determined under Generally Accepted Accounting Principles.

[68 FR 56551, Oct. 1, 2003]

§ 723.6 What must your member business loan policy address?

At a minimum, your policy must address the following:

(a) The types of business loans you will make;

(b) Your trade area;

(c) The maximum amount of your assets, in relation to net worth, that you will invest in secured and unsecured business loans;

(d) The maximum amount of your assets, in relation to net worth, that you will invest in a given category or type of business loan;

(e) The maximum amount of your assets, in relation to net worth, that you will loan to any one member or group of associated members, subject to § 723.7(c)(2) and § 723.8;

(f) The qualifications and experience of personnel (minimum of 2 years) involved in making and administering business loans;

(g) A requirement to analyze and document the ability of the borrower to repay the loan consistent with appropriate underwriting and due diligence standards, which also addresses the need for periodic financial statements, credit reports, and other data when necessary to analyze future loans and lines of credit, such as, borrower's history and experience, balance sheet, cash flow analysis, income statements, tax data, environmental impact assessment, and comparison with industry averages, depending upon the loan purpose;

(h) The collateral requirements must include:

(1) Loan-to-value ratios;

(2) Determination of value;

(3) Determination of ownership;

National Credit Union Administration § 723.10

(4) Steps to secure various types of collateral; and

(5) How often the credit union will re-evaluate the value and marketability of collateral;

(i) The interest rates and maturities of business loans;

(j) General loan procedures which include:

(1) Loan monitoring;

(2) Servicing and follow-up; and

(3) Collection;

(k) Identification of those individuals prohibited from receiving member business loans.

[64 FR 28729, May 27, 1999, as amended at 68 FR 56551, Oct. 1, 2003]

§ 723.7 What are the collateral and security requirements?

(a) Except as provided in § 723.3 or unless your Regional Director grants a waiver, all member business loans, except those made under paragraphs (c), (d), and (e) of this section, must be secured by collateral as follows:

(1) The maximum loan-to-value ratio for all liens must not exceed 80% unless the value in excess of 80% is covered through private mortgage insurance or equivalent type of insurance, or insured, guaranteed, or subject to advance commitment to purchase by an agency of the federal government, an agency of a state or any of its political subdivisions, but in no case may the ratio exceed 95%;

(2) A borrower may not substitute any insurance, guarantee, or advance commitment to purchase by any agency of the federal government, a state or any political subdivision of such state for the collateral requirements of this paragraph.

(b) Principals, other than a not for profit organization as defined by the Internal Revenue Service Code (26 U.S.C. 501) or those where the Regional Director grants a waiver, must provide their personal liability and guarantee.

(c) You may make unsecured member business loans under the following conditions:

(1) You are a natural person credit union that is well capitalized as defined by § 702.102(a)(1) of this chapter or you are a corporate credit union that maintains a minimum capital ratio as required by § 704.3(d) of this chapter or a different ratio as permitted under § 704.3(e) of this chapter;

(2) The aggregate of the unsecured outstanding member business loans to any one member or group of associated members does not exceed the lesser of $100,000 or 2.5% of your net worth; and

(3) The aggregate of all unsecured outstanding member business loans does not exceed 10% of your net worth.

(d) You are exempt from the provisions of paragraphs (a), (b), and (c) of this section with respect to credit card line of credit programs offered to non-natural person members that are limited to routine purposes normally made available under those programs.

(e) You may make vehicle loans under this part without complying with the loan-to-value ratios in this section, provided that the vehicle is a car, van, pick-up truck, or sports utility vehicle and not part of a fleet of vehicles.

[68 FR 56551, Oct. 1, 2003, as amended at 69 FR 62565, Oct. 27, 2004; 70 FR 75722, Dec. 21, 2005; 72 FR 30247, May 31, 2007; 75 FR 66298, Oct. 28, 2010]

§ 723.8 How much may one member or a group of associated members borrow?

Unless your Regional Director grants a waiver for a higher amount, the aggregate amount of net member business loan balances to any one member or group of associated members must not exceed the greater of:

(a) 15% of the credit union's net worth; or

(b) $100,000.

[68 FR 56552, Oct. 1, 2003]

§ 723.9 [Reserved]

§ 723.10 What waivers are available?

You may seek a waiver for a category of loans in any of the following areas:

(a) Appraisal requirements under § 722.3;

(b) Aggregate construction and development loans limits under § 723.3(a);

(c) Minimum borrower equity requirements for construction and development loans under § 723.3(b);

(d) Loan-to-value ratio requirements for business loans under § 723.7(a);

(e) Requirement for personal liability and guarantee under § 723.7(b);

§ 723.11

(f) Maximum unsecured business loans to one member or group of associated members under § 723.7(c)(2);

(g) Maximum aggregate unsecured member business loan limit under § 723.7(c)(3); and

(h) Maximum aggregate net member business loan balance to any one member or group of associated members under § 723.8.

[68 FR 56552, Oct. 1, 2003, as amended at 69 FR 62565, Oct. 27, 2004]

§ 723.11 How do you obtain a waiver?

To obtain a waiver, a federal credit union must submit a request to the Regional Director (a corporate federal credit union submits the waiver request to the Director of the Office of Corporate Credit Unions). A state chartered federally insured credit union must submit the request to its state supervisory authority. If the state supervisory authority approves the request, the state regulator will forward the request to the Regional Director (or if appropriate the Director of the Office of Corporate Credit Unions). A waiver is not effective until it is approved by the Regional Director (or in the case of a corporate federal credit union the Director of the Office of Corporate Credit Unions). The waiver request must contain the following:

(a) A copy of your business lending policy;

(b) The higher limit sought (if applicable);

(c) An explanation of the need to raise the limit (if applicable);

(d) Documentation supporting your ability to manage this activity; and

(e) An analysis of the credit union's prior experience making member business loans, including as a minimum:

(1) The history of loan losses and loan delinquency;

(2) Volume and cyclical or seasonal patterns;

(3) Diversification;

(4) Concentrations of credit to one borrower or group of associated borrowers in excess of 15% of net worth;

(5) Underwriting standards and practices;

(6) Types of loans grouped by purpose and collateral; and

(7) The qualifications of personnel responsible for underwriting and administering member business loans.

§ 723.12 What will NCUA do with my waiver request?

Your Regional Director (or the Director of the Office of Corporate Credit Unions) will:

(a) Review the information you provided in your request;

(b) Evaluate the level of risk to your credit union;

(c) Consider your credit union's historical CAMEL composite and component ratings when evaluating your request; and

(d) Notify you whenever your waiver request is deemed complete. Notify you of the action taken within 45 calendar days of receiving a complete request from the federal credit union or the state supervisory authority. If you do not receive notification within 45 calendar days of the date the complete request was received by the regional office, the credit union may assume approval of the waiver request.

§ 723.13 What options are available if the NCUA Regional Director denies my waiver request, or a portion of it?

You may appeal the Regional Director's (or the Director of the Office of Corporate Credit Unions) decision in writing to the NCUA Board. Your appeal must include all information requested in § 723.11 and why you disagree with your Regional Director's (or the Office of Corporate Credit Union Director's) decision.

§§ 723.14–723.15 [Reserved]

§ 723.16 What is the aggregate member business loan limit for a credit union?

(a) *General.* The aggregate limit on a credit union's net member business loan balances is the lesser of 1.75 times the credit union's net worth or 12.25% of the credit union's total assets. Loans that are exempt from the definition of member business loans are not counted for the purpose of the aggregate loan limit.

(b) *Effect of nonmember loans and nonmember participations.* If a credit union

National Credit Union Administration

§ 723.18

holds any nonmember loans or nonmember loan participation interests that would constitute a member business loan if made to a member, those loans will affect the credit union's aggregate limit on net member business loan balances as follows:

(1) The total of the credit union's net member business loan balances and the nonmember loan balances must not exceed the lesser of 1.75 times the credit union's net worth or 12.25% of the credit union's total assets, unless the credit union has first received approval from the NCUA regional director.

(2) To request approval from the NCUA regional director, a credit union must submit an application that:

(i) Includes a current copy of the credit union's member business loan policies;

(ii) Confirms that the credit union is in compliance with all other aspects of this rule;

(iii) States the credit union's proposed limit on the total amount of nonmember loans and participation interests that the credit union may acquire if the application is granted; and

(iv) Attests that the acquisition of nonmember loans and participations is not being used, in conjunction with one or more other credit unions, to have the effect of trading member business loans that would otherwise exceed the aggregate limit.

(3) A federal credit union must submit its request for approval to the regional director (a corporate federal credit union submits its request to the Director of the Office of Corporate Credit Unions). A state chartered federally insured credit union must submit the request to its state supervisory authority. If the state supervisory authority approves the request, the state regulator will forward the application and its decision to the regional director (or if appropriate, the Director of the Office of Corporate Credit Unions). An approved application is not effective until it is approved by the regional director (or in the case of a corporate federal credit union the Director of the Office of Corporate Credit Unions). The regional director will issue a decision within 30 days of receipt of a federal credit union's completed application or within 30 days of receipt of a completed application and the state supervisory authority's approval for a state chartered federally insured credit union.

[68 FR 56552, Oct. 1, 2003, as amended at 70 FR 75722, Dec. 21, 2005]

§ 723.17 Are there any exceptions to the aggregate loan limit?

There are three circumstances where a credit union qualifies for an exception from the aggregate limit. Loans that are excepted from the definition of member business loans are not counted for the purpose of the exceptions. The three exceptions are:

(a) Credit unions that have a low-income designation or participate in the Community Development Financial Institutions program;

(b) Credit unions that were chartered for the purpose of making member business loans and can provide documentary evidence (such evidence includes but is not limited to the original charter, original bylaws, original business plan, original field of membership, board minutes and loan portfolio);

(c) Credit unions that have a history of primarily making member business loans, meaning that either member business loans comprise at least 25% of the credit union's outstanding loans (as evidenced in any call report filed between January 1995 and September 1998 or any equivalent documentation including financial statements) or member business loans comprise the largest portion of the credit union's loan portfolio (as evidenced in any call report filed between January 1995 and September 1998 or any equivalent documentation including financial statements). For example, if a credit union makes 23% member business loans, 22% first mortgage loans, 22% new automobile loans, 20% credit card loans, and 13% total other real estate loans, then the credit union meets this exception.

§ 723.18 How do I obtain an exception?

To obtain the exception, a federal credit union must submit documentation to the Regional Director, demonstrating that it meets the criteria of one of the exceptions. A state chartered federally insured credit union must submit documentation to its state supervisory authority. The state

§ 723.19

supervisory authority will forward its decision to NCUA. The exception does not expire unless revoked by the state supervisory authority for a state chartered federally insured credit union or the Regional Director for a federal credit union. If an exception request is denied for a federal credit union, it may be appealed to the NCUA Board within 60 days of the denial by the Regional Director. Until the NCUA Board acts on the appeal, the credit union can continue to make new member business loans.

§ 723.19 What are the recordkeeping requirements?

You must separately identify member business loans in your records and in the aggregate on your financial reports.

§ 723.20 How can a state supervisory authority develop and enforce a member business loan regulation?

(a) The NCUA Board may exempt federally insured state chartered credit unions in a given state from NCUA's member business loan rule if NCUA approves the state's rule for use for state chartered federally insured credit unions. In making this determination, the Board is guided by safety and soundness considerations and reviews whether the state regulation minimizes the risk and accomplishes the overall objectives of NCUA's member business loan rule in this part. Specifically, the Board will focus its review on:

(1) The definition of a member business loan;

(2) Loan to one borrower limits;

(3) Written loan policies;

(4) Collateral and security requirements;

(5) Construction and development lending; and

(6) Loans to senior management.

(b) To receive NCUA's approval of a state's member business loan rule, the state supervisory authority must submit its rule to the NCUA regional office. After reviewing the rule, the region will forward the request to the NCUA Board for a final determination.

(c) A state supervisory authority that administers a state member business loans rule, approved by NCUA under §§ 723.20(a) and (b), may rescind its rule without NCUA approval. A state supervisory authority should notify NCUA if it anticipates rescinding its rule to foster regulatory continuity and cooperation.

[64 FR 28729, May 27, 1999, as amended at 69 FR 27828, May 17, 2004; 70 FR 75722, Dec. 21, 2005]

§ 723.21 Definitions.

For purposes of this part, the following definitions apply:

Associated member is any member with a shared ownership, investment, or other pecuniary interest in a business or commercial endeavor with the borrower.

Construction or development loan is a financing arrangement for acquiring property or rights to property, including land or structures, with the intent to convert it to income-producing property such as residential housing for rental or sale; commercial use; industrial use; or similar uses. Construction or development loan includes a financing arrangement for the major renovation or development of property already owned by the borrower that will convert the property to income producing property or convert the use of income producing property to a different use from its use before the major renovation or development or is a major expansion of its current use. Construction or development loan does not include loans to finance maintenance, repairs, or improvements to an existing income producing property that do not change its use. Examples to illustrate when a loan is or is not a construction or development loan follow.

Example 1. If a member borrows money to repair a roof on a barn on an existing farming operation, this is a member business loan but is not a construction or development loan. A construction or development loan does not include a loan for routine maintenance of a borrower's existing business or a loan to enhance or expand a borrower's existing business unless those renovations convert the property to a different use or are so major as to be considered the equivalent of converting the use of the property.

Example 2. A loan to convert a movie theater into a restaurant is a construction or development loan. A loan to convert a large Victorian home used for residential purposes into a six-room inn also would be a construction or development loan. In both instances, the loans are for the purpose of converting the use of the properties. By contrast, a loan to repair the roof or replace the carpet and wallpaper of an operating inn would not be a construction or development loan as it neither converts the use of the property, nor is so major a renovation to be considered the equivalent of converting the use of the property.

Example 3. A loan to expand the parking lot of a small strip shopping center would not be a construction or development loan, but a loan to renovate the small strip shopping center into a mega-mall would be a construction or development loan as it would be viewed as a major renovation that converts the use of the property.

Example 4. A hotel with a fair market value of $10 million borrows $1 million to build an exercise facility in the hotel to enhance the property. The loan amount is 10% of the fair market value of the property. This is not a construction or development loan. It is a member business loan to improve or renovate an existing income producing property, but it is not so major a renovation as to be considered the equivalent of converting the use of the property. In another scenario, a hotel with a fair market value of $10 million borrows $5 million to build a luxury health spa on the hotel grounds. The loan amount is 50% of the fair market value of the property. This is a construction or development loan, even if the use of the property has not been converted, as the renovation is so major as to be considered the equivalent of converting the use of the property.

Immediate family member is a spouse or other family member living in the same household.

Loan-to-value ratio is the aggregate amount of all sums borrowed including outstanding balances plus any unfunded commitment or line of credit from all sources on an item of collateral divided by the market value of the collateral used to secure the loan.

Net member business loan balance means the outstanding loan balance plus any unfunded commitments, reduced by any portion of the loan that is secured by shares in the credit union, or by shares or deposits in other financial institutions, or by a lien on the member's primary residence, or insured or guaranteed by any agency of the federal government, a state or any political subdivision of such state, or subject to an advance commitment to purchase by any agency of the federal government, a state or any political subdivision of such state, or sold as a participation interest without recourse and qualifying for true sales accounting under generally accepted accounting principles.

Net worth means the retained earnings balance of the credit union at quarter end as determined under generally accepted accounting principles. Retained earnings consists of undivided earnings, regular reserves, and any other appropriations designated by management or regulatory authorities. This means that only undivided earnings and appropriations of undivided earnings are included in net worth. For low-income designated credit unions, net worth also includes secondary capital accounts that are uninsured and subordinate to all other claims, including claims of creditors, shareholders and the NCUSIF. For any credit union, net worth does not include the allowance for loan and lease losses account.

[64 FR 28729, May 27, 1999, as amended at 68 FR 56552, Oct. 1, 2003; 69 FR 27828, May 17, 2004; 70 FR 75722, Dec. 21, 2005; 73 FR 30478, May 28, 2008]

PART 724—TRUSTEES AND CUSTODIANS OF CERTAIN TAX-ADVANTAGED SAVINGS PLANS

Sec.
724.1 Federal credit unions acting as trustees and custodians of certain tax-advantaged savings plans.
724.2 Self-directed plans.
724.3 Appointment of successor trustee or custodian.

AUTHORITY: 12 U.S.C. 1757, 1765, 1766 and 1787.

SOURCE: 55 FR 30211, July 25, 1990, unless otherwise noted.

§ 724.1 Federal credit unions acting as trustees and custodians of certain tax-advantaged savings plans.

A federal credit union is authorized to act as trustee or custodian, and may receive reasonable compensation for so acting, under any written trust instrument or custodial agreement created or organized in the United States and forming part of a tax-advantaged savings plan which qualifies or qualified for specific tax treatment under sections 223, 401(d), 408, 408A and 530 of the Internal Revenue Code (26 U.S.C. 223,

§ 724.2

401(d), 408, 408A and 530), for its members or groups of its members, provided the funds of such plans are invested in share accounts or share certificate accounts of the Federal credit union. Federal credit unions located in a territory, including the trust territories, or a possession of the United States, or the Commonwealth of Puerto Rico, are also authorized to act as trustee or custodian for such plans, if authorized under sections 223, 401(d), 408, 408A and 530 of the Internal Revenue Code as applied to the territory or possession under similar provisions of territorial law. All funds held in a trustee or custodial capacity must be maintained in accordance with applicable laws and rules and regulations as may be promulgated by the Secretary of Labor, the Secretary of the Treasury, or any other authority exercising jurisdiction over such trust or custodial accounts. The federal credit union shall maintain individual records for each participant which show in detail all transactions relating to the funds of each participant or beneficiary.

[55 FR 30211, July 25, 1990, as amended at 63 FR 14026, Mar. 24, 1998; 65 FR 10934, Mar. 1, 2000; 69 FR 45238, July 29, 2004]

§ 724.2 Self-directed plans.

A federal credit union may facilitate transfers of plan funds to assets other than share and share certificates of the credit union, provided the conditions of § 724.1 are met and the following additional conditions are met:

(a) All contributions of funds are initially made to a share or share certificate account in the Federal credit union;

(b) Any subsequent transfer of funds to other assets is solely at the direction of the member and the Federal credit union exercises no investment discretion and provides no investment advice with respect to plan assets (i.e., the credit union performs only custodial duties); and

(c) The member is clearly notified of the fact that National Credit Union Share Insurance Fund coverage is limited to funds held in share or share certificate accounts of NCUSIF-insured credit unions.

[55 FR 30211, July 25, 1990, as amended at 69 FR 45139, July 29, 2004]

§ 724.3 Appointment of successor trustee or custodian.

Any plan operated pursuant to this part shall provide for the appointment of a successor trustee or custodian by a person, committee, corporation or organization other than the Federal credit union or any person acting in his capacity as a director, employee or agent of the Federal credit union upon notice from the Federal credit union or the Board that the Federal credit union is unwilling or unable to continue to act as trustee or custodian.

PART 725—NATIONAL CREDIT UNION ADMINISTRATION CENTRAL LIQUIDITY FACILITY

Sec.
725.1 Scope.
725.2 Definitions.
725.3 Regular membership.
725.4 Agent membership.
725.5 Capital stock.
725.6 Termination of membership.
725.7 Special share accounts in federally chartered agent members.
725.8–725.16 [Reserved]
725.17 Applications for extensions of credit.
725.18 Creditworthiness.
725.19 Collateral requirements.
725.20 Repayment, security and credit reporting agreements; other terms and conditions.
725.21 Modification of agreements.
725.22 Advances to insurance organizations.
725.23 Other advances.

AUTHORITY: Secs. 301–307 Federal Credit Union Act, 92 Stat. 3719–3722 (12 U.S.C. 1795–1795f).

SOURCE: 44 FR 49437, Aug. 23, 1979, unless otherwise noted.

§ 725.1 Scope.

This part contains the regulations implementing the National Credit Union Central Liquidity Facility Act, subchapter III of the Federal Credit Union Act. The National Credit Union Administration Central Liquidity Facility is a mixed-ownership Government corporation within the National Credit Union Administration. It is managed by the National Credit Union Administration Board and is owned by its member credit unions. The purpose of the Facility is to improve the general financial stability of credit unions by meeting their liquidity needs and

National Credit Union Administration § 725.2

thereby encourage savings, support consumer and mortgage lending and provide basic financial resources to all segments of the economy.

§ 725.2 Definitions.

As used in this part:

(a) *Agent* means an Agent member of the Facility.

(b) *Agent group* means an Agent member of the Facility consisting of a group of central credit unions, one of which is designated as the group's *Agent group representative* and authorized to transact business with the Facility on behalf of the group or any member of the group.

(c) *Agent loan* means an advance of funds by an Agent to a member natural person credit union to meet liquidity needs which have been the basis for a Facility advance.

(d) *Central credit union* means a Federal or state-chartered credit union primarily serving other credit unions. A credit union is primarily serving other credit unions when the total dollar amount of the shares and deposits received from other credit unions plus loans to other credit unions exceeds 50 percent of the total dollar amount of all shares and deposits plus loans during the qualifying period, as defined in paragraph (o) of this section.

(e) *Facility* or *Central Liquidity Facility* means the National Credit Union Administration Central Liquidity Facility.

(f) *Facility advance* means an advance of funds by the Facility to a Regular or Agent member.

(g) *Facility lending officer* means any employee of the Facility or the National Credit Union Administration who has been designated by the NCUA Board as a Facility lending officer.

(h) *Liquid assets* means the following unpledged assets:

(1) Cash on hand;

(2) Share or deposit accounts with remaining maturities of one year or less maintained in central credit unions or institutions insured by the Federal Deposit Insurance Corporation or Federal Savings and Loan Insurance Corporation;

(3) Investments in obligations of the United States or any agency thereof, or securities fully guaranteed as to principal and interest thereby, which are authorized under 12 U.S.C. 1757(7) and which have a remaining maturity of one year or less;

(4) Common trust investments and similar investments in funds or securities authorized for Federal credit unions, the objectives of which are to provide daily liquidity for participating credit unions;

(5) Shares in the National Credit Union Administration Central Liquidity Facility or in special share accounts authorized by § 725.7 of this part;

(6) In the case of a federally-insured state-chartered credit union, any asset held in satisfaction of liquidity requirements imposed by applicable state law or regulation; and

(7) Balances maintained by federally-insured credit unions in a Federal Reserve bank, or in a pass-through account to a Federal Reserve bank, pursuant to the requirements of section 19(b) of the Federal Reserve Act (12 U.S.C. 461(b)).

(i) *Liquidity needs* means the needs of credit unions primarily serving natural persons for:

(1) Short-term adjustment credit available to assist in meeting temporary requirements for funds or to cushion more persistent outflows of funds pending an orderly adjustment of credit union assets and liabilities;

(2) Seasonal credit available for longer periods to assist in meeting seasonal needs for funds arising from a combination of expected patterns of movement in share and deposit accounts and loans; and

(3) Protracted adjustment credit available in the event of unusual or emergency circumstances of a longer term nature resulting from national, regional or local difficulties.

(j) *Management policies* means policies of a credit union with respect to membership, shares, deposits, dividends, interest rates, lending, investing, borrowing, safeguarding of assets, hiring, training and supervision of employees, and general operating and control practices and procedures.

(k) *Member* means a Regular or Agent member of the Facility, unless the context indicates otherwise.

(l) *Member natural person credit union* means a natural person credit union

§ 725.3

which is a member of an Agent or of any central credit union in an Agent group. Member natural person credit unions are not members of the Facility unless they are also Regular members of the Facility.

(m) *Natural person credit union* means a Federal or state-chartered credit union primarily serving natural persons. A credit union is primarily serving natural persons if it is not a central credit union as defined in paragraph (d) of this section.

(n) *NCUA Board* or *Board* means the National Credit Union Administration Board.

(o) *Paid-in and unimpaired capital and surplus* means shares and deposits plus post-closing, undivided earnings. This does not include regular reserves or special reserves required by law, regulation or special agreement between the credit union and its regulator or share insurer.

(p) *Qualifying Period* means:

(1) For initial qualification, any 7 months out of the 12 months immediately preceding the month in which application is made to become a member of the Facility; and

(2) For qualification during each subsequent calendar year, any 7 months out of the previous calendar year.

(q) *Stock subscription* means the stock subscription required for membership in the Facility. "Total subscribed Facility stock" is the sum of all members' stock subscriptions.

[44 FR 49437, Aug. 23, 1979, as amended at 53 FR 22472, June 16, 1988; 66 FR 65624, Dec. 20, 2001]

§ 725.3 Regular membership.

(a) A natural person credit union may become a Regular member of the Facility by:

(1) Making application on a form approved by the Facility;

(2) Subscribing to capital stock of the Facility in an amount equal to one-half of 1 percent of the credit union's paid-in and unimpaired capital and surplus, as determined in accordance with § 725.5(b) of this part, and forwarding with its completed application funds equal to one-half of this stock subscription;[1] and

(3) Furnishing the following reports and documents with the completed membership application:

(i) A copy of the credit union's financial and statistical report for the most recent calendar month; and

(ii) Copies of the credit union's charter and bylaws, unless the credit union is federally chartered.

(b) A credit union which becomes a Regular member of the Facility after February 23, 1980, may not receive Facility advances without approval of the NCUA Board for a period of six months after becoming a member. This subsection shall not apply to any credit union which becomes a Regular member of the Facility within six months after such credit union is chartered, or which has had access to Facility funds through an Agent member of the Facility at any time within six months prior to becoming a Regular member of the Facility.

[44 FR 49437, Aug. 23, 1979, as amended at 47 FR 1371, Jan. 13, 1982]

§ 725.4 Agent membership.

(a) A central credit union or a group of central credit unions may become an Agent member of the Facility by (in the case of a group of central credit unions, each central credit union in the group must do each of the following except for paragraph (a)(2) of this section, which shall be done by the Agent group representative):

(1) Making application on a form approved by the Facility;

(2) Subscribing to the capital stock of the Facility in an amount equal to one-half of 1 percent of the paid-in and unimpaired capital and surplus (as determined in accordance with § 725.5(b) of this part) of all the central credit union's or central credit union group's member natural person credit unions, except those which are Regular members of the Facility or which have access to the Facility through, and are included in the stock subscription of,

---

[1] A credit union which submits its application for membership prior to October 1, 1979, is not required to forward these funds to the Facility until October 1, 1979.

National Credit Union Administration § 725.4

another Agent.[2] Upon approval of the application, the Agent shall forward funds equal to one-half of this initial stock subscription to the Facility.[3]

(3) Furnishing the following reports and documents with the completed membership application:

(i) A copy of the central credit union's financial and statistical report for the most recent calendar month;

(ii) Copies of the central credit union's charter and bylaws, unless such credit union is federally chartered; and

(iii) A list of all the central credit union's member natural person credit unions.

(4) Agreeing to submit to the supervision of the NCUA Board and to comply with all regulations and reporting requirements which the NCUA Board shall prescribe for Agent members;

(5) Agreeing to submit to periodic unrestricted examinations by the NCUA Board or its designee; and

(6) Obtaining the written approval of the NCUA Board.

(b) The NCUA Board may approve a central credit union or group of central credit unions as an Agent member of the Facility, provided the NCUA Board is satisfied that such credit union or credit union group meets certain criteria, including but not limited to the following (in the case of a group of central credit unions, each central credit union in the group must meet these criteria):

(1) The management policies are in writing, approved by the central credit union's board of directors, and reviewed annually by such board;

(2) Adequate internal controls are in place to assure accurate and timely reporting of transactions and the safeguarding of assets;

(3) The financial condition of the central credit union is sound with adequate reserves for losses;

(4) Surety bond coverage provides protection for the central credit union while the central credit union is performing the duties of an Agent member of Facility;

(5) Management has demonstrated its ability to use such techniques as cash flow analysis, budgeting, and projections of sources and uses of funds to manage the affairs of the central credit union efficiently and in conformity with sound business practices; and

(6) There are no practices, procedures, policies, or other factors that would result in discrimination by the central credit union among natural person credit unions or inhibit its ability to act independently in its role as an Agent member of the Facility.

(c) Each Agent, or in the case of an Agent group, each central credit union in the group, must:

(1) Maintain records related to Facility activity in conformity with requirements prescribed by the NCUA Board from time to time; and

(2) Submit such reports as may be required by the Facility to determine financial soundness, quality and level of service, and conformity with established guidelines and procedures.

(d) Each Agent, or in the case of an Agent group, each central credit union in the group, must have on an annual basis a third party independent audit of its books and records and provide the Facility with copies of the report of such audit. The auditor selected must be recognized by a State or territorial licensing authority as possessing the requisite knowledge and experience to perform audits.

(e) Within 30 days after a natural person credit union becomes a member of a central credit union which is an Agent or a member of an Agent group, the agent, or in the case of an Agent group, the Agent group representative, shall subscribe to additional capital stock of the Facility in an amount equal to one-half of 1 percent of such credit union's paid-in and unimpaired capital and surplus, and shall forward funds equal to one-half of this stock subscription to the Facility. This subsection shall not apply if the natural

---

[2] A natural person credit union which is a member of more than one Agent member of the Facility must designate through which Agent it will deal with the Facility, and the designated Agent will be responsible for including the capital and surplus of such credit union in the calculation of its stock subscription.

[3] If the application is approved prior to October 1, 1979, these funds are not required to be forwarded to the Facility until October 1, 1979.

§ 725.5

person credit union is a Regular member of the Facility or has access to the Facility through, and is included in the stock subscription of, another Agent.

(f) A central credit union or group of central credit unions which becomes an Agent member of the Facility after February 23, 1980, may not receive a Facility advance without approval of the NCUA Board for a period of six months after becoming a member. This subsection shall not apply to any credit union which becomes an Agent member or a member of an Agent group within six months after such credit union is chartered within six months after such credit union has been an Agent or a member of another Agent group.

(g) Agent members will be compensated for the services they perform for the Facility in a manner to be specified by the NCUA Board.

§ 725.5 Capital stock.

(a) The capital stock of the Facility is divided into nonvoting shares having a par value of $50 each. The Facility issues whole and fractional shares. Shares are issued in book entry form upon receipt of payment for such shares, and cannot be transferred or hypothecated except to the Facility.

(b) The capital stock subscriptions provided for in §§ 725.3 and 725.4 shall be:

(1) Based on an arithmetic average of paid-in and unimpaired capital and surplus over the six months preceding application for membership, and

(2) Adjusted at the close of each calendar year in accordance with an arithmetic average of paid-in and unimpaired capital and surplus over the twelve months in such calendar year. Payments for adjustments to the capital stock subscription must be received by the Facility no later than March 31 of the following year.

(c) That part of a member's stock subscription which is not paid-in shall be held by the member on call of the NCUA Board and shall be invested in liquid assets.

(d) Any member may at any time purchase additional shares of capital stock in the Facility. Any shares in excess of the member's required paid-in portion of its stock subscription can be redeemed by the member as long as the member maintains investments in other assets sufficient to meet the requirement of paragraph (c) of this section. The member's required paid-in portion of its stock subscription includes one-half of its stock subscription plus any "calls" that may have been issued by the NCUA Board against the "on-call" portion of such stock subscription.

(e) Dividends will be paid on capital stock at such times and rates as are determined by the NCUA Board. The NCUA Board shall declare such dividends no less frequently than annually. All issued (paid for) capital stock shall share in dividend distributions without preference. Payment of dividends will be made by the issuance of capital stock to the member in the amount of the dividend.

[44 FR 49437, Aug. 23, 1979, as amended at 45 FR 47122, July 14, 1980; 47 FR 1371, Jan. 13, 1982; 53 FR 22472, June 16, 1988]

§ 725.6 Termination of membership.

(a) A member of the Facility whose stock subscription constitutes less than 5 percent of total subscribed Facility stock may withdraw from membership in the Facility six months after notifying the NCUA Board in writing of its intention to do so.

(b) A member of the Facility whose stock subscription constitutes 5 percent or more of total subscribed Facility stock may withdraw from membership in the Facility twenty-four months after notifying the NCUA Board in writing of its intention to do so.

(c) The NCUA Board may terminate membership in the Facility if, after the opportunity for a hearing, the NCUA Board determines the member has failed to comply with any provision of the National Credit Union Central Liquidity Facility Act or any regulation issued pursuant thereto. If membership is terminated under this subsection, the credit union will be required to obtain the approval of the NCUA Board before becoming a member of the Facility again. Such approval will be granted only if the NCUA Board is satisfied that the credit union will comply with such Act and regulations.

(d)(1) If membership is terminated under any provision of this section, the terminated member's stock shall be redeemed upon termination. In such event, the Facility may retain any amount owed to the Facility by the member.

(2) When a member natural person credit union withdraws from membership in a central credit union which is an Agent or a member of an Agent group, the stock subscription of the Agent, or in the case of an Agent group, the stock subscription of the Agent group representative, will be adjusted after the waiting period which would apply under paragraph (a) or (b) of this section if the withdrawing credit union were a member of the Facility.

§ 725.7 Special share accounts in federally chartered agent members.

(a) A federally chartered Agent member of the Facility may require its member natural person credit unions to establish and maintain special share accounts in the Agent member to reimburse it for the portion of the Agent's Facility stock subscription which is attributable to the paid-in and unimpaired capital and surplus of each such natural person credit union.

(b) The amount which the Agent member requires each member natural person credit union to maintain in such special share accounts shall be based on a uniform percentage of the paid-in and unimpaired capital and surplus of such credit unions, and shall not exceed the amount of the Agent's stock subscription which is attributable to the capital and surplus of each such credit union. An Agent shall not permit a member to maintain in a special share account any amounts in excess of the required amount.

(c) A natural person credit union that withdraws from membership in an Agent member or that becomes a Regular member of the Facility, shall be entitled to the return of all amounts in its special share account upon withdrawal from membership in the Agent or upon becoming a Regular member, as applicable.

[45 FR 47122, July 14, 1980]

§§ 725.8–725.16 [Reserved]

§ 725.17 Applications for extensions of credit.

(a) A Regular member may apply for a Facility advance to meet its liquidity needs by filing an application on a Facility-approved form, or by any other method approved by the Facility.

(b)(1) An Agent member may apply for a Facility advance by filing an application on a Facility-approved form, or by any other method approved by the Facility.[4]

(2) The Agent's application shall be based on the following:

(i) Approved applications to the Agent by its member natural person credit unions for pending loans to meet liquidity needs; or

(ii) Outstanding loans previously made by the Agent to meet liquidity needs of its member natural person credit unions; or

(iii) Such other demonstrable liquidity needs as the NCUA Board may specify.

(3) An Agent shall not submit an application to the Facility based on the liquidity needs of any member natural person credit union which has not agreed to the repayment, security and credit reporting terms prescribed by the Facility for Agent loans;

(4) Any loan to meet liquidity needs which have been or will be the basis for an application by the Agent for a Facility advance must be applied for on an application form approved by the Facility.

(5) Unless approved by the Facility, an Agent shall not submit an application to the Facility based on the liquidity needs of any credit union which became a member natural person credit union of the Agent after February 2, 1980, unless such credit union has been a member natural person credit union of the Agent for six months, was chartered within six months before becoming a member natural person credit union of the Agent, or had access to the Facility either as a Regular member or through another Agent within

---

[4] If the Agent is an Agent group, the application must be filed by the Agent group representative, and any Facility advance will be made to the Agent group representative.

§ 725.18

six months before becoming a member natural person credit union of the Agent.

(c) In emergency circumstances, the applications for extensions of credit required under paragraph (a) and paragraphs (b)(1) and (b)(4) of this section may be verbal, but must be confirmed within five working days by an application as required by such subsection or paragraphs.

(d) Applications of Regular and Agent members shall be filed with a Facility lending officer. Each application for credit which is completed and properly filed will be approved or denied within five working days after the day of receipt.

[44 FR 49437, Aug. 23, 1979, as amended at 47 FR 1371, Jan. 13, 1982]

§ 725.18 Creditworthiness.

(a) Prior to Facility approval of each application of a Regular member for a Facility advance, the Facility shall consider the creditworthiness of such member.

(b) Prior to an Agent's approval of each application of a member natural person credit union for an extension of credit on which an application by the Agent to the Facility will be based, an Agent shall consider the creditworthiness of such member natural person credit union.

(c) Specific characteristics of an uncreditworthy credit union include, but are not limited to, insolvency as defined in paragraph (1) to the definition of "insolvency in § 700.2 of this chapter, unsatisfactory practices in extending credit, lower than desirable reserve levels, high expense ratio, failure to repay previous Facility advances as agreed, excessive dependence on borrowed funds, inadequate cash management policies and planning, or any other relevant characteristics creating a less than satisfactory condition. The presence of one or more of these characteristics will not necessarily mean that a credit union will be considered uncreditworthy.

(d) A natural person credit union (whether a Regular member of the Facility or a member natural person credit union) which does not meet the Facility's creditworthiness standards may be limited in or denied the use of advances for its liquidity needs.

[44 FR 49437, Aug. 23, 1979, as amended at 69 FR 27829, May 17, 2004; 76 FR 60367, Sept. 29, 2011]

§ 725.19 Collateral requirements.

(a) Each Facility advance and each Agent loan shall be secured by a first priority security interest in collateral of the credit union with a net book value at least equal to 110% of all amounts due under the applicable Facility advance or Agent loan, or by guarantee of the National Credit Union Share Insurance Fund.

(b) The Facility may accept as collateral for each Facility advance to a Regular member, a security interest in all assets of the Regular member; provided however, that the value of any assets in which any third party has a perfected security interest that is superior to the security interest of the Facility shall be excluded for purposes of complying with the requirements of paragraph (a) of this section.

(c) The Facility may accept as collateral for each Facility advance to an Agent member, a security interest in the Agent loans for which the Facility advance was made; provided however, that the collateral for such Agent loan meets the requirements of paragraph (a) of this section.

[62 FR 67550, Dec. 29, 1997]

§ 725.20 Repayment, security and credit reporting agreements; other terms and conditions.

(a) Regular and Agent members, or in the case of an Agent group, the Agent group representative, shall sign the repayment, security and credit reporting agreements prescribed by the Facility, and all Facility advances to Regular and Agent members shall be governed by the terms and conditions of such agreements.

(b) All Agent loans shall be made subject to the repayment, security and credit reporting terms prescribed by the Facility for Agent loans.

(c) Other terms and conditions applicable to Facility advances and Agent loans will be specified in confirmations of credit provided in connection with such advances and loans, and/or in operating circulars of the Facility.

National Credit Union Administration

§ 725.21 Modification of agreements.

The repayment, security, and credit reporting terms under which Facility advances and Agent loans will be made, as provided in § 725.20 of this part, shall be subject to modification from time to time as the NCUA Board may determine. Any change in such terms shall be published in the FEDERAL REGISTER and shall apply to all advances disbursed by the Facility after the effective date of the change.

§ 725.22 Advances to insurance organizations.

(a) In accordance with policies established by the NCUA Board, the Facility may advance funds to a State credit union share or deposit insurance corporation, guaranty credit union, guaranty association, or similar organization. Requests for such advances shall be supported by an application which sets forth and supports the need for the advance.

(b) Advances under paragraph (a) shall be subject to the approval of the NCUA Board and shall be made subject to the following terms:

(1) The advance shall be fully secured,

(2) The maturity of the advance shall not exceed 12 months,

(3) The advance shall not be renewable at maturity, and

(4) The funds advanced shall not be relent at an interest rate exceeding that imposed by the Facility.

§ 725.23 Other advances.

(a) The NCUA Board may authorize extensions of credit to members of the Facility for purposes other than liquidity needs if the NCUA Board, the Board of Governors of the Federal Reserve System, and the Secretary of the Treasury concur in a determination that such extensions of credit are in the national economic interest.

(b) Extensions of credit approved under the conditions of paragraph (a) of this section shall be subject to such terms and conditions as shall be established by the NCUA Board.

§ 740.1

PART 740—ACCURACY OF ADVERTISING AND NOTICE OF INSURED STATUS

Sec.
740.0 Scope.
740.1 Definitions.
740.2 Accuracy of advertising.
740.3 Advertising of excess insurance.
740.4 Requirements for the official sign.
740.5 Requirements for the official advertising statement.

AUTHORITY: 12 U.S.C. 1766, 1781, 1785, and 1789.

SOURCE: 68 FR 23382, May 2, 2003, unless otherwise noted.

§ 740.0 Scope.

This part applies to all federally insured credit unions. It prescribes the requirements for the official sign insured credit unions must display and the requirements with regard to the official advertising statement insured credit unions must include in their advertisements. It requires that all other kinds of advertisements be accurate. It also establishes requirements for advertisements of excess insurance.

§ 740.1 Definitions.

(a) *Account* or *accounts* as used in this part means share, share certificate or share draft accounts (or their equivalent under state law, as determined by the Board in the case of insured state credit unions) of a member (which includes other credit unions, public units, and nonmembers where permitted under the Act) in a credit union of a type approved by the Board which evidences money or its equivalent received or held by a credit union in the usual course of business and for which it has given or is obligated to give credit to the account of the member.

(b) *Advertisement* as used in this part means a commercial message, in any medium, that is designed to attract public attention or patronage to a product or business.

(c) *Insured credit union and federally insured credit union* as used in this part mean a credit union with National Credit Union Administration share insurance.

(d) *Nonfederally insured credit union* as used in this part means a credit union with either no account insurance or

§ 740.2

with primary account insurance provided by some entity other than the National Credit Union Administration.

[68 FR 23382, May 2, 2003, as amended at 74 FR 9348, Mar. 4, 2009; 76 FR 30523, May 26, 2011]

§ 740.2 Accuracy of advertising.

No insured credit union may use any advertising (which includes print, electronic, or broadcast media, displays and signs, stationery, and other promotional material) or make any representation which is inaccurate or deceptive in any particular, or which in any way misrepresents its services, contracts, or financial condition, or which violates the requirements of § 707.8 of this subchapter, if applicable. This provision does not prohibit an insured credit union from using a trade name or a name other than its official charter name in advertising or signage, so long as it uses its official charter name in communications with NCUA and for share certificates or certificates of deposit, signature cards, loan agreements, account statements, checks, drafts and other legal documents.

§ 740.3 Advertising of excess insurance.

Any advertising that mentions share or savings account insurance provided by a party other than the NCUA must clearly explain the type and amount of such insurance and the identity of the carrier and must avoid any statement or implication that the carrier is affiliated with the NCUA or the federal government.

§ 740.4 Requirements for the official sign.

(a) Each insured credit union must continuously display the official sign described in paragraph (b) of this section at each station or window where insured account funds or deposits are normally received in its principal place of business and in all its branches, 30 days after its first day of operation as an insured credit union. Each insured credit union must also display the official sign on its Internet page, if any, where it accepts deposits or open accounts, but it may vary the font sizes from that depicted in paragraph (b) of this section to ensure its legibility.

(b) The official sign shall be as depicted below:

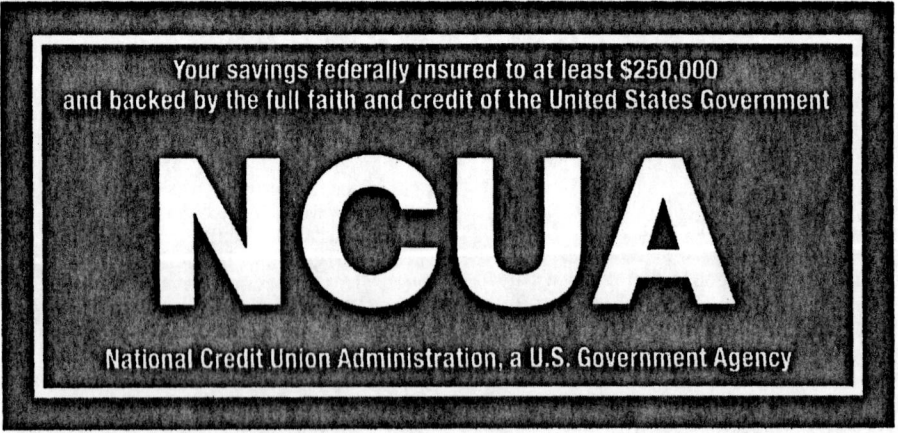

(1) NCUA will automatically supply all insured credit unions an initial supply of official signs with a blue background and white lettering at no cost for compliance with paragraph (a) of this section. If the initial supply is not adequate, the insured credit unions must immediately request additional signs from NCUA. Any credit union that does not have an adequate supply

but requests additional signs from NCUA will not be considered to have violated paragraph (a) of this section unless the credit union fails to display the signs after receiving them.

(2) An insured credit union may purchase signs from commercial suppliers or develop its own in any color scheme so long as they are legible and otherwise comply with this part. A credit union may alter the font size of the official sign to make it legible on its Internet page and on documents it provides to its members including advertisements, but it may not do so on signs to be placed at each station or window where the credit union normally receives insured funds or deposits in its principal place of business and all of its branches.

(c) To avoid any member confusion from the use of the official NCUA sign, federally insured credit unions are prohibited from receiving account funds at any teller station or window where any nonfederally insured credit union also receives account funds. As exceptions to this prohibition:

(1) A teller in a branch of a federally insured credit union may accept account funds for nonfederally insured credit unions, but only if the teller displays a conspicuous sign next to the official sign that states "This credit union participates in a shared branch network with other credit unions and accepts share deposits for members of those other credit unions. While this credit union is federally insured, not all of these other credit unions are federally insured. If you need information on the insurance status of your credit union, please contact your credit union directly." This sign must be similar to the official sign in terms of design, color, and font.

(2) A teller in a facility operated by a non-credit union entity may accept account funds for both federally insured credit unions and nonfederally insured credit unions, but only if the teller displays a conspicuous sign next to the official sign stating "This facility accepts share deposits for multiple credit unions. Not all of these credit unions are federally insured. If you need information on the insurance status of your credit union, please contact your credit union directly." This sign must be similar to the official sign in terms of design, color, and font.

(3) A teller in a branch of a nonfederally insured credit union may accept account funds for federally insured credit unions. No teller in a nonfederally insured credit union may display the official NCUA sign.

(d) The Board may require any insured credit union, upon at least 30 days' written notice, to change the wording of its official signs in a manner deemed necessary for the protection of shareholders or others.

(e) For purposes of this section, the terms "branch," "station," "teller station," and "window" do not include automated teller machines or point of sale terminals.

(f) An insured credit union that fails to comply with Section 205(a) of the Federal Credit Union Act regarding the official sign, 12 U.S.C. 1785(a), or any requirement in this part is subject to a penalty of up to $100 per day.

[68 FR 23382, May 2, 2003, as amended at 71 FR 67438, Nov. 22, 2006; 73 FR 62858, Oct. 22, 2008; 74 FR 9348, Mar. 4, 2009; 74 FR 55749, Oct. 29, 2009; 75 FR 53843, Sept. 2, 2010]

§ 740.5 Requirements for the official advertising statement.

(a) Each insured credit union must include the official advertising statement, prescribed in paragraph (b) of this section, in all of its advertisements including, but not limited to, annual reports and statements of condition required to be published by law, and on its main Internet page, except as provided in paragraph (c) of this section. For annual reports and statements of condition required to be published by law, an insured credit union must place the official advertising statement in a prominent position on the cover page of such documents or on the first page a reader sees if there is no cover page.

(b) The official advertising statement is in substance as follows: "This credit union is federally insured by the National Credit Union Administration." Insured credit unions, at their option, may use the short title "Federally insured by NCUA" or a reproduction of the official sign, as described in § 740.4(b), as the official advertising statement. The official advertising statement must be in a size and print that is clearly legible and may be no smaller than the smallest font size used in other portions of the advertisement intended to convey information to the consumer. If the official sign is used as the official advertising statement, an insured credit union may alter the font size to ensure its legibility as provided in § 740.4(b)(2).

(c) The following advertisements need not include the official advertising statement:

(1) Credit union supplies such as stationery (except when used for circular letters), envelopes, deposit slips, checks, drafts, signature cards, account passbooks, and noninsurable certificates;

(2) Signs or plates in the credit union office or attached to the building or buildings in which the offices are located;

(3) Listings in directories;

(4) Advertisements not setting forth the name of the insured credit union;

(5) Display advertisements in credit union directories, provided the name of the credit union is listed on any page in the directory with a symbol or other descriptive matter indicating it is insured;

(6) Joint or group advertisements of credit union services where the names of insured credit unions and noninsured credit unions are listed and form a part of such advertisement;

(7) Advertisements by radio that are less than fifteen (15) seconds in time;

(8) Advertisements by television, other than display advertisements, that are less than fifteen (15) seconds in time;

(9) Advertisements that because of their type or character would be impractical to include the official advertising statement, including but not limited to, promotional items such as calendars, matchbooks, pens, pencils, and key chains;

(10) Advertisements that contain a statement to the effect that the credit union is insured by the National Credit Union Administration, or that its accounts and shares or members are insured by the Administration to the maximum insurance amount for each member or shareholder;

(11) Advertisements that do not relate to member accounts, including but not limited to advertisements relating to loans by the credit union, safekeeping box business or services, traveler's checks on which the credit union is not primarily liable, and credit life or disability insurance.

(d) The non-English equivalent of the official advertising statement may be used in any advertisement provided that the Regional Director gives prior approval to the translation.

[68 FR 23382, May 2, 2003, as amended at 71 FR 67439, Nov. 22, 2006; 73 FR 56936, Oct. 1, 2008; 76 FR 30523, May 26, 2011]

PART 741—REQUIREMENTS FOR INSURANCE

Sec.
741.0 Scope.

Subpart A—Regulations That Apply to Both Federal Credit Unions and Federally Insured State-Chartered Credit Unions and That Are Not Codified Elsewhere in NCUA's Regulations

741.1 Examination.
741.2 Maximum borrowing authority.
741.3 Criteria.
741.4 Insurance premium and one percent deposit.
741.5 Notice of termination of excess insurance coverage.
741.6 Financial and statistical and other reports.
741.7 Conversion to a state-chartered credit union.
741.8 Purchase of assets and assumption of liabilities.
741.9 Uninsured membership shares.
741.10 Disclosure of share insurance.
741.11 Foreign branching.

Subpart B—Regulations Codified Elsewhere in NCUA's Regulations as Applying to Federal Credit Unions That Also Apply to Federally Insured State-Chartered Credit Unions

741.201 Minimum fidelity bond requirements.
741.202 Audit and verification requirements.
741.203 Minimum loan policy requirements.
741.204 Maximum public unit and nonmember accounts, and low-income designation.
741.205 Reporting requirements for credit unions that are newly chartered or in troubled condition.
741.206 Corporate credit unions.

National Credit Union Administration § 741.2

741.207 Community development revolving loan program for credit unions.
741.208 Mergers of federally insured credit unions: voluntary termination or conversion of insured status.
741.209 Management official interlocks.
741.210 Central liquidity facility.
741.211 Advertising.
741.212 Share insurance.
741.213 Administrative actions, adjudicative hearings, rules of practice and procedure.
741.214 Report of crime or catastrophic act and Bank Secrecy Act compliance.
741.215 Records preservation program.
741.216 Flood insurance.
741.217 Truth in savings.
741.218 Involuntary liquidation and creditor claims.
741.219 Investment requirements.
741.220 Privacy of consumer financial information.
741.221 Suretyship and guaranty requirements.
741.222 Credit union service organizations.
741.223 Registration of residential mortgage loan originators.
741.224 Golden parachute and indemnification payments.

APPENDIX A TO PART 741—EXAMPLES OF PARTIAL-YEAR NCUSIF ASSESSMENT AND DISTRIBUTION CALCULATIONS UNDER § 741.4

AUTHORITY: 12 U.S.C. 1757, 1766(a), 1781–1790, and 1790d; 31 U.S.C. 3717.

SOURCE: 60 FR 58504, Nov. 28, 1995, unless otherwise noted.

§ 741.0 Scope.

The provisions of this part apply to federal credit unions, federally insured state-chartered credit unions, and credit unions making application for insurance of accounts pursuant to Title II of the Act, unless the context of a provision indicates its application is otherwise limited. This part prescribes various requirements for obtaining and maintaining federal insurance and the payment of insurance premiums and capitalization deposit. Subpart A of this part contains substantive requirements that are not codified elsewhere in this chapter. Subpart B of this part lists additional regulations, set forth elsewhere in this chapter as applying to federal credit unions, that also apply to federally insured state-chartered credit unions. As used in this part, "insured credit union" means a credit union whose accounts are insured by the National Credit Union Share Insurance Fund (NCUSIF).

Subpart A—Regulations That Apply to Both Federal Credit Unions and Federally Insured State-Chartered Credit Unions and That Are Not Codified Elsewhere in NCUA's Regulations

§ 741.1 Examination.

As provided in Sections 201 and 204 of the Act (12 U.S.C. 1781 and 1784), the NCUA Board is authorized to examine any insured credit union or any credit union making application for insurance of its accounts. Such examination may require access to all records, reports, contracts to which the credit union is a party, and information concerning the affairs of the credit union. Upon request, such documentation must be provided to the NCUA Board or its representative. Any credit union which makes application for insurance will be required to pay the cost of such examination and processing. To the maximum extent feasible, the NCUA Board will utilize examinations conducted by state regulatory agencies.

§ 741.2 Maximum borrowing authority.

(a) Any credit union which makes application for insurance of its accounts pursuant to Title II of the Act, or any insured credit union, must not borrow, from any source, an aggregate amount in excess of 50 per centum of its paid-in and unimpaired capital and surplus (shares and undivided earnings, plus net income or minus net loss).

(b) A federally insured state-chartered credit union may apply to the regional director for a waiver of paragraph (a) of this section up to the amount permitted under the applicable state law or by the state regulator. The waiver request must include:

(1) Written approval from the state regulator;

(2) A detailed analysis of the safety and soundness implications of the proposed waiver;

(3) A proposed aggregate dollar amount or percentage of paid-in and unimpaired capital and surplus limitation; and

(4) An explanation demonstrating the need to raise the limit.

§ 741.3

(c) The regional director will approve the waiver request if the proposed borrowing limit will not adversely affect the safety and soundness of the federally insured state-chartered credit union.

[60 FR 58504, Nov. 28, 1995, as amended at 69 FR 8547, Feb. 25, 2004]

§ 741.3 Criteria.

In determining the insurability of a credit union which makes application for insurance and in continuing the insurability of its accounts pursuant to Title II of the Act, the following criteria shall be applied:

(a) *Reserves*—(1) *General rule.* State-chartered credit unions are subject to section 216 of the Act, 12 U.S.C. 1790d, and to part 702 and subpart L of part 747 of this chapter.

(2) *Special reserve for nonconforming investments.* State-chartered credit unions (except state-chartered corporate credit unions) are required to establish an additional special reserve for investments if those credit unions are permitted by their respective state laws to make investments beyond those authorized in the Act or the NCUA Rules and Regulations. For any investment other than loans to members and obligations or securities expressly authorized in Title I of the Act and part 703 of this chapter, as amended, state-chartered credit unions (except state-chartered corporate credit unions) are required to establish and maintain at the end of each accounting period and prior to payment of any dividend, an Appropriation for Non-conforming Investments in an amount at least equal to the net excess of book value over current market value of the investments. If the market value cannot be determined, an amount equal to the full book value will be established. When at the end of any dividend period, the amount in the Appropriation for Non-conforming Investments exceeds the difference between book value and market value, the board of directors may authorize the transfer of the excess to Undivided Earnings.

(b) *Financial condition and policies.* The following factors are to be considered in determining whether the credit union's financial condition and policies are both safe and sound:

(1) The existence of unfavorable trends which may include excessive losses on loans (i.e., losses which exceed the regular reserve or its equivalent [in the case of state-chartered credit unions] plus other irrevocable reserves established as a contingency against losses on loans), the presence of special reserve accounts used specifically for charging off loan balances of deceased borrowers, and an expense ratio so high that the required transfers to reserves create a net operating loss for the period or that the net gain after these transfers is not sufficient to permit the payment of a nominal dividend;

(2) The existence of written lending policies, including adequate documentation of secured loans and the protection of security interests by recording, bond, insurance, or other adequate means, adequate determination of the financial capacity of borrowers and co-makers for repayment of the loan, and adequate determination of value of security on loans to ascertain that said security is adequate to repay the loan in the event of default;

(3) Investment policies which are within the provisions of applicable law and regulations, i.e., the Act and part 703 of this chapter for federal credit unions and the laws of the state in which the credit union operates for state-chartered credit unions, except state-chartered corporate credit unions. State-chartered corporate credit unions are permitted to make only those investments that are in conformance with part 704 of this chapter and applicable state laws and regulations;

(4) The presence of any account or security, the form of which has not been approved by the Board, except for accounts authorized by state law for state-chartered credit unions.

(c) *Fitness of management.* The officers, directors, and committee members of the credit union must have conducted its operations in accordance with provisions of applicable law, regulations, its charter and bylaws. No person shall serve as a director, officer, committee member, or employee of an

National Credit Union Administration §741.4

insured credit union who has been convicted of any criminal offense involving dishonesty or breach of trust, except with the written consent of the Board.

(d) *Insurance of member accounts would not otherwise involve undue risk to the NCUSIF.* The credit union must maintain adequate fidelity bond coverage as specified in §741.201. Any circumstances which may be unique to the particular credit union concerned shall also be considered in arriving at the determination of whether or not an undue risk to the NCUSIF is or may be present. For purposes of this section, the term "undue risk to the NCUSIF" is defined as a condition which creates a probability of loss in excess of that normally found in a credit union and which indicates a reasonably foreseeable probability of the credit union becoming insolvent because of such condition, with a resultant claim against the NCUSIF.

(e) *Powers and purposes.* The credit union must not perform services other than those which are consistent with the promotion of thrift and the creation of a source of credit for its members, except as otherwise permitted by law or regulation.

(f) *Letter of disapproval.* A credit union whose application for share insurance is disapproved shall receive a letter indicating the reasons for such disapproval, a citation of the authority for such disapproval, and suggested methods by which the applying credit union may correct its deficiencies and thereby qualify for share insurance.

(g) Nothing in this section shall preclude the NCUA Board from imposing additional terms or conditions pursuant to the insurance agreement.

[60 FR 58504, Nov. 28, 1995, as amended at 64 FR 41040, July 29, 1999; 65 FR 8593, Feb. 18, 2000; 67 FR 71094, Nov. 29, 2002]

§741.4 Insurance premium and one percent deposit.

(a) *Scope.* This section implements the requirements of Section 202 of the Act (12 U.S.C. 1782) providing for capitalization of the NCUSIF through the maintenance of a deposit by each insured credit union in an amount equaling one percent of its insured shares and payment of an insurance premium.

(b) *Definitions.* For purposes of this section:

Available assets ratio means the ratio of:

(i) The amount determined by subtracting all liabilities of the NCUSIF, including contingent liabilities for which no provision for losses has been made, from the sum of cash and the market value of unencumbered investments authorized under Section 203(c) of the Act (12 U.S.C. 1783(c)), to:

(ii) The aggregate amount of the insured shares in all insured credit unions.

(iii) Shown as an abbreviated mathematical formula, the available assets ratio is:

$$\frac{(\text{cash} + \text{market value of unencumbered investments}) - (\text{liabilities} + \text{contingent liabilities for which no provision for losses has been made})}{\text{aggregate amount of all insured shares from final reporting period of calendar year}}$$

Equity ratio which shall be calculated using the financial statements of the NCUSIF alone, without any consolidation or combination with the financial statements of any other fund or entity, means the ratio of:

(i) The amount of NCUSIF's capitalization, meaning insured credit unions' one percent capitalization deposits plus the retained earnings balance of the NCUSIF (less contingent liabilities for which no provision for losses has been made) to:

(ii) The aggregate amount of the insured shares in all insured credit unions.

(iii) Shown as an abbreviated mathematical formula, the equity ratio is:

$$\frac{\text{(insured credit unions' 1.0\% capitalization deposits} + \text{(NCUSIF's retained earnings} - \text{contingent liabilities for which no provision for losses has been made)}}{\text{aggregate amount of all insured shares}}$$

Insured shares means the total amount of a federally-insured credit union's share, share draft and share certificate accounts, or their equivalent under state law (which may include deposit accounts), authorized to be issued to members, other credit unions, public units, or nonmembers (where permitted under the Act or equivalent state law), but does not include amounts in excess of insurance coverage as provided in part 745 of this chapter. For a credit union or other entity that is not federally insured, "insured shares" means, for purposes of this section only, the amount of deposits or shares that would have been insured by the NCUSIF under part 745 had the institution been federally insured on the date of measurement.

Modified premium/distribution ratio means one minus the premium/distribution ratio.

Normal operating level means an equity ratio not less than 1.2 percent and not more than 1.5 percent, as established by action of the NCUA Board.

Premium/distribution ratio means the number of full remaining months in the calendar year following the date of the institution's conversion or merger divided by 12.

Reporting period means calendar year for credit unions with total assets of less than $50,000,000 and means semiannual period for credit union with total assets of $50,000,000 or more.

(c) *One percent deposit.* Each insured credit union must maintain with the NCUSIF during each reporting period a deposit in an amount equaling one percent of the total of the credit union's insured shares at the close of the preceding reporting period. For credit unions with total assets of less than $50,000,000, insured shares will be measured and adjusted annually based on the insured shares reported in the credit union's 5300 report for December 31 of each year. For credit unions with total assets of $50,000,000 or more, insured shares will be measured and adjusted semiannually based on the insured shares reported in the credit union's 5300 reports for December 31 and June 30 of each year.

(d) *Insurance premium charges*—(1) *In general.* Each insured credit union will pay to the NCUSIF, on dates the NCUA Board determines, but not more than twice in any calendar year, an insurance premium in an amount stated as a percentage of insured shares, which will be the same percentage for all insured credit unions.

(2) *Relation of premium charge to equity ratio of NCUSIF.* (i) The NCUA Board may assess a premium charge only if the NCUSIF's equity ratio is less than 1.3 percent and the premium charge does not exceed the amount necessary to restore the equity ratio to 1.3 percent.

(ii) If the equity ratio of the NCUSIF falls to between 1.0 and 1.2 percent, the NCUA Board is required to assess a premium in an amount it determines is necessary to restore the equity ratio to at least 1.2 percent, as provided for in the restoration plan adopted under Section 202(c)(2)(D) of the Act (12 U.S.C. 1782(c)(20)(D)). If the equity ratio of the NCUSIF falls below 1.0 percent, the NCUA Board is required to assess a deposit replenishment charge in an amount it determines is necessary to restore the equity ratio to 1.0 percent and to assess a premium charge in an amount it determines is necessary to restore the equity ratio to, at least 1.2 percent, as provided for in the restoration plan adopted under Section 202(c)(2)(D) of the Act (12 U.S.C. 1782(c)(20)(D)).

(e) *Distribution of NCUSIF equity.* If, as of the end of a calendar year, the NCUSIF exceeds its normal operating level and its available assets ratio exceeds 1.0 percent, the NCUA Board will make a proportionate distribution of NCUSIF equity to insured credit unions. The distribution will be the maximum amount possible that does not reduce the NCUSIF's equity ratio

National Credit Union Administration § 741.4

below its normal operating level and does not reduce its available assets ratio below 1.0 percent. The distribution will be after the calendar year and in the form determined by the NCUA Board. The form of the distribution may include a waiver of insurance premiums, premium rebates, or distributions from NCUSIF equity in the form of dividends. The NCUA Board will use the aggregate amount of the insured shares from all insured credit unions from the final reporting period of the calendar year in calculating the NCUSIF's equity ratio and available assets ratio for purposes of this paragraph.

(f) *Invoices.* The NCUA provides invoices to all federally insured credit unions stating any change in the amount of a credit union's one percent deposit and the computation and funding of any NCUSIF premium or deposit replenishment assessments due. Invoices for federal credit unions also include any annual operating fees that are due. Invoices are calculated based on a credit union's insured shares as of the most recently ended reporting period. The invoices may also provide for any distribution the NCUA Board declares in accordance with paragraph (e) of this section, resulting in a single net transfer of funds between a credit union and the NCUA.

(g) *New charters.* A newly-chartered credit union that obtains share insurance coverage from the NCUSIF during the calendar year in which it has obtained its charter will not be required to pay an insurance premium for that calendar year. The credit union will fund its one percent deposit on a date to be determined by the NCUA Board in the following calendar year, but will not participate in any distribution from NCUSIF equity related to the period prior to the credit union's funding of its deposit.

(h) *Depletion of one percent deposit.* All or part of the one percent deposit may be used by the NCUSIF if necessary to meet its expenses. The NCUSIF may invoice credit unions in an amount necessary to replenish the one percent deposit at any time following the effective date of the depletion.

(i) *Conversion to Federal insurance.*

(1) A credit union or other institution that converts to insurance coverage with the NCUSIF will:

(i) Immediately fund its one percent deposit based on the total of its insured shares as of the last day of the most recently ended reporting period prior to the date of conversion;

(ii) If the NCUSIF assesses a premium in the calendar year of conversion, pay a premium based on the institution's insured shares as of the last day of the most recently ended reporting period preceding the invoice date times the institution's premium/distribution ratio;

(iii) If the NCUSIF declares, in the calendar year of conversion on or before the date of conversion, an assessment to replenish the one-percent deposit, pay nothing related to that assessment;

(iv) If the NCUSIF declares, at any time after the date of conversion through the end of that calendar year, an assessment to replenish the one-percent deposit, pay a replenishment amount based on the institution's insured shares as of the last day of the most recently ended reporting period preceding the invoice date; and

(v) If the NCUSIF declares a distribution in the year following conversion based the NCUSIF's equity at the end of the year of conversion, receive a distribution based on the institution's insured shares as of the end of the year of conversion times the institution's premium/distribution ratio. With regard to distributions declared in the calendar year of conversion but based on the NCUSIF's equity from the end of the preceding year, the converting institution will receive no distribution.

(2) A federally-insured credit union that merges with a nonfederally insured credit union or other nonfederally insured institution (the "merging institution"), where the federally insured credit union is the continuing institution, will:

(i) Immediately on the date of merger increase the amount of its NCUSIF deposit by an amount equal to one percent of the merging institution's insured shares as of the last day of the merging institution's most recently ended reporting period preceding the date of merger;

§ 741.4

(ii) With regard to any NCUSIF premiums assessed in the calendar year of merger, pay a two-part premium, with one part calculated on the merging institution's insured shares as described in paragraph (i)(1)(ii) of this section, and the other part calculated on the continuing institution's insured shares as of the last day of its most recently ended reporting period preceding the date of merger; and

(iii) If the NCUSIF declares a distribution in the year following the merger based the NCUSIF's equity at the end of the year of merger, receive a distribution based on the continuing institution's insured shares as of the end of the year of merger. With regard to distributions declared in the calendar year of merger but based on the NCUSIF's equity from the end of the preceding year, the institution will receive a distribution based on its insured shares as of the end of the preceding year.

(j) *Conversion from, or termination of, Federal share insurance.*

(1) A federally insured credit union whose insurance coverage with the NCUSIF terminates, including through a conversion to, or merger into, a nonfederally insured credit union or a noncredit union entity, will:

(i) Receive the full amount of its NCUSIF deposit paid, less any amounts applied to cover NCUSIF losses that exceed NCUSIF retained earnings, immediately after the final date on which any shares of the credit union are NCUSIF-insured;

(ii) If the NCUSIF declares a distribution at the end of the calendar year of conversion, receive a distribution based on the institution's insured shares as of the last day of the most recently ended reporting period preceding the date of conversion times the institution's modified premium/distribution ratio; and

(iii) If the NCUSIF assesses a premium in the calendar year of conversion or merger on or before the day in which the conversion or merger is completed, pay a premium based on the institution's insured shares as of the last day of the most recently ended reporting period preceding the conversion or merger date times the institution's modified premium/distribution ratio. If the institution has previously paid a premium based on this same assessment that exceeds this amount, the institution will receive a refund of the difference following completion of the conversion or merger.

(2) Notwithstanding the requirements of paragraph (j)(1) of this section:

(i) Any insolvent credit union that is closed for involuntary liquidation will not be entitled to a return of its deposit;

(ii) Any solvent credit union that is closed due to voluntary or involuntary liquidation will be entitled to a return of its deposit paid, less any amounts applied to cover NCUSIF losses that exceed NCUSIF retained earnings, prior to final distribution of member shares; and

(iii) The Board reserves the right to delay return of the deposit to any credit union converting from or terminating its federal insurance, or voluntarily liquidating, for up to one year if the Board determines that immediate repayment would jeopardize the NCUSIF.

(k) *Assessment of administrative fee and interest for delinquent payment.* Each federally insured credit union must pay to the NCUA an administrative fee, the costs of collection, and interest on any delinquent payment of its capitalization deposit or insurance premium. A payment will be considered delinquent if it is postmarked or electronically posted later than the date stated in the invoice provided to the credit union. The NCUA may waive or abate charges or collection of interest, if circumstances warrant.

(1) The administrative fee for a delinquent payment shall be an amount as fixed from time to time by the NCUA Board based upon the administrative costs of such delinquent payments to the NCUA in the preceding year.

(2) The costs of collection shall be calculated as the actual hours expended by NCUA personnel multiplied by the average hourly cost of the salaries and benefits of such personnel.

(3) The interest rate charged on any delinquent payment shall be the U.S. Department of the Treasury Tax and loan Rate in effect on the date when the loan payment is due as provided in 31 U.S.C. 3717.

National Credit Union Administration § 741.7

(4) The Act contains specific penalties and other consequences for delinquent payments, including, but not limited to:

(i) Section 202(d)(2)(B) of the Act (12 U.S.C. 1782(d)(2)(B)) provides that the Board may assess and collect a penalty from an insured credit union of not more than $20,000 for each day the credit union fails or refuses to pay any deposit or premium due to the fund; and

(ii) Section 202(d)(3) of the Act (12 U.S.C. 1782(d)(3)) provides, generally, that no insured credit union shall pay any dividends on its insured shares or distribute any of its assets while it remains in default in the payment of its deposit or any premium charge due to the fund. Section 202(d)(3) further provides that any director or officer of any insured credit union who knowingly participates in the declaration or payment of any such dividend or in any such distribution shall, upon conviction, be fined not more than $1,000 or imprisoned more than one year, or both.

[74 FR 63279, Jan. 4, 2010, as amended at 76 FR 60367, Sept. 29, 2011]

§ 741.5 Notice of termination of excess insurance coverage.

In the event of a credit union's termination of share insurance coverage other than that provided by the NCUSIF, the credit union must notify all members in writing of such termination at least thirty days prior to the effective date of termination.

§ 741.6 Financial and statistical and other reports.

(a) Upon written notice from the Board, Regional Director, or Director of the Office of Corporate Credit Unions, insured credit unions must file financial and other reports in accordance with the instructions in the notice. Credit unions with the capacity to do so must use NCUA's information management system to submit their data online. If a credit union is unable to use the information system, it must file written reports in accordance with the instructions.

(1) *Credit Union Profile.* Insured credit unions must submit to NCUA a Credit Union Profile, NCUA Form 4501 or its equivalent, within 10 days after an election or appointment of senior management or volunteer officials or within 30 days of any change of the information in the profile.

(2) *Financial and statistical report.* Natural person credit unions must file a Call Report with NCUA quarterly in accordance with the instructions in the NCUA Form 5300. Corporate credit unions must file a Corporate Credit Union Call Report with NCUA monthly in accordance with the instructions in the NCUA Form 5310. Credit unions must submit a corrected Call Report upon notification or the discovery of a need for correction.

(b) *Consistency with GAAP.* The accounts of financial statements and reports required to be filed quarterly under paragraph (a) of this section must reflect GAAP if the credit union has total assets of $10 million or greater, but may reflect regulatory accounting principles other than GAAP if the credit union has total assets of less than $10 million (except that a Federally-insured State-chartered credit union may be required by its state credit union supervisor to follow GAAP regardless of asset size).

(c) *GAAP sources.* GAAP means generally accepted accounting principles, as defined in § 715.2(e) of this chapter. GAAP is distinct from GAAS, which means generally accepted auditing standards, as defined in § 715.2(f) of this chapter. Authoritative sources of GAAP include, but are not limited to, pronouncements of the Financial Accounting Standards Board (FASB) and its predecessor organizations, the Accounting Standards Executive Committee (AcSEC) of the American Institute of Certified Public Accountants (AICPA), the FASB's Emerging Issues Task Force (EITF), and the applicable AICPA Audit and Accounting Guide.

[60 FR 58504, Nov. 28, 1995, as amended at 64 FR 41040, July 29, 1999; 67 FR 12464, Mar. 19, 2002; 71 FR 4034, Jan. 25, 2006; 74 FR 35769, July 21, 2009]

§ 741.7 Conversion to a state-chartered credit union.

Any federal credit union that petitions to convert to a state-chartered

§ 741.8

federally insured credit union is required to apply to the Regional Director for continued insurance of its accounts and meet the requirements as stated in the Act and this part. If the application for continued insurance is not approved, such insurance will terminate subject to the conditions set forth in section 206(d) of the Act.

§ 741.8 Purchase of assets and assumption of liabilities.

(a) Any credit union insured by the National Credit Union Share Insurance Fund (NCUSIF) must receive approval from the NCUA before purchasing loans or assuming an assignment of deposits, shares, or liabilities from:

(1) Any credit union that is not insured by the NCUSIF;

(2) Any other financial-type institution (including depository institutions, mortgage banks, consumer finance companies, insurance companies, loan brokers, and other loan sellers or liability traders); or

(3) Any successor in interest to any institution identified in paragraph (a)(1) or (a)(2) of this section.

(b) Approval is not required for:

(1) Purchases of student loans or real estate secured loans to facilitate the packaging of a pool of loans to be sold or pledged on the secondary market under § 701.23(b)(1)(iii) or (iv) of this chapter or comparable state law for state-chartered credit unions, or purchases of member loans under § 701.23(b)(1)(i) of this chapter or comparable state law for state-chartered credit unions;

(2) Assumption of deposits, shares or liabilities as rollovers or transfers of member retirement accounts or in which a federally-insured credit union perfects a security interest in connection with an extension of credit to any member; or

(3) Purchases of assets, including loans, or assumptions of deposits, shares, or liabilities by any credit union insured by the NCUSIF from another credit union insured by the NCUSIF, except a purchase or assumption as a part of a merger under Part 708b.

(c) A credit union seeking approval under paragraph (a) of this section must submit a letter to the regional office with jurisdiction for the state where the credit union is headquartered. A corporate credit union seeking approval under paragraph (a) of this section must submit a letter to the Office of Corporate Credit Unions. The letter must request approval and state the nature of the transaction and include copies of relevant transaction documents. The NCUA will make a decision to approve or disapprove the request as soon as possible depending on the complexity of the proposed transaction. Credit unions should submit a request for approval in sufficient time to close the transaction.

[70 FR 75725, Dec. 21, 2005, as amended at 75 FR 34622, June 18, 2010]

§ 741.9 Uninsured membership shares.

Any credit union that is insured pursuant to Title II of the Act may not offer membership shares that, due to the terms and conditions of the account, are not eligible for insurance coverage. This prohibition does not apply to shares that are uninsured solely because the amount is in excess of the maximum insurance coverage provided pursuant to part 745 of this chapter.

§ 741.10 Disclosure of share insurance.

Any credit union which is insured pursuant to Title II of the Act and is permitted by state law to accept nonmember shares or deposits from sources other than other credit unions and public units (or, for low-income designated credit unions, any nonmembers), shall identify such nonmember accounts as nonmember shares or deposits on any statement or report required by the NCUA Board for insurance purposes. Immediately after a state-chartered credit union receives notice from NCUA that its member accounts are federally insured, the credit union shall advise any present nonmember share and deposit holders by letter that their accounts are not insured by the NCUSIF. Also, future nonmember share and deposit fund holders will be so advised by letter as they open accounts.

§ 741.11 Foreign branching.

(a) *Application and Prior NCUA Approval Required.* Any credit union insured under Title II of the Act must apply for and receive approval from the regional director before establishing a credit union branch outside the United States unless the foreign branch is located on a United States military instillation or embassy outside the United States. The regional director will have 60 days to approve or deny the request.

(b) *Contents of Application.* The application must include a business plan, written approval by the state supervisory agency if the applicant is a state-chartered credit union, and documentation evidencing written permission from the host country to establish the branch that explicitly recognizes NCUA's authority to examine and take any enforcement action, including conservatorship and liquidation actions.

(c) *Contents of Business Plan.* The written business plan must address the following:

(1) Analysis of market conditions in the area where the branch is to be established;

(2) The credit union's plan for addressing foreign currency risk;

(3) Operating facilities, including office space/equipment and supplies;

(4) Safeguarding of assets, bond coverage, insurance coverage, and records preservation;

(5) Written policies regarding the branch (shares, lending, capital, charge-offs, collections);

(6) The field of membership or portion of the field of membership to be served through the foreign branch and the financial needs of the members to be served and services and products to be provided;

(7) Detailed *pro forma* financial statements for branch operations (balance sheet and income and expense projections) for the first and second year including assumptions;

(8) Internal controls including cash disbursal procedures for shares and loans at the branch;

(9) Accounting procedures used to identify branch activity and performance; and

(10) Foreign income taxation and employment law.

(d) *Revocation of Approval.* A state regulator that revokes approval of the branch office must notify NCUA of the action once it issues the notice of revocation. The regional director may revoke approval of the branch office for failure to follow the business plan in a material respect or for substantive and documented safety and soundness reasons. If the regional director revokes the approval, the credit union will have six months from the date of the revocation letter to terminate the operations of the branch. The credit union can appeal this revocation directly to the NCUA Board within 30 days of the date of the revocation letter.

(e) *Insurance Coverage.* Accounts at foreign branches are insured by the NCUSIF only if denominated in U.S. dollars and only if payable, by the terms of the account agreement, at a U.S. office of the credit union. If the host country requires insurance from its own system, accounts will not be insured by the National Credit Union Share Insurance Fund.

[68 FR 23030, Apr. 30, 2003]

Subpart B—Regulations Codified Elsewhere in NCUA's Regulations as Applying to Federal Credit Unions That Also Apply to Federally Insured State-Chartered Credit Unions

§ 741.201 Minimum fidelity bond requirements.

(a) Any credit union which makes application for insurance of its accounts pursuant to Title II of the Act must possess the minimum fidelity bond coverage stated in part 713 of this chapter in order for its application for such insurance to be approved and for such insurance coverage to continue. A federally insured credit union whose fidelity bond coverage is terminated shall mail notice of such termination to the Regional Director not less than 35 days prior to the effective date of such termination.

(b) Corporate credit unions must comply with § 704.18 of this chapter in lieu of part 713 of this chapter.

[60 FR 58504, Nov. 28, 1995, as amended at 64 FR 28721, May 27, 1999; 70 FR 61716, Oct. 26, 2005]

§ 741.202 Audit and verification requirements.

(a) The supervisory committee of each credit union insured pursuant to Title II of the Act shall make or cause to be made an audit of the credit union at least once every calendar year covering the period elapsed since the last audit. The audit must fully meet the applicable requirements set forth in part 715 of this chapter or applicable state law, whichever requirement is more stringent.

(b) Each credit union which is insured pursuant to Title II of the Act shall verify or cause to be verified, under controlled conditions, all passbooks and accounts with the records of the financial officer not less frequently than once every 2 years. The verification must fully meet the requirements set forth in §715.8 of this chapter.

[60 FR 58504, Nov. 28, 1995, as amended at 64 FR 41040, July 29, 1999]

§ 741.203 Minimum loan policy requirements.

Any credit union which is insured pursuant to Title II of the Act must:

(a) Adhere to the requirements stated in part 723 of this chapter concerning member business loans, §701.21(c)(8) of this chapter concerning prohibited fees, and §701.21(d)(5) of this chapter concerning nonpreferential loans. State-chartered, NCUSIF-insured credit unions in a given state are exempt from these requirements if the state supervisory authority for that state adopts substantially equivalent regulations as determined by the NCUA Board or, in the case of the member business loan requirements, if the state supervisory authority adopts member business loan regulations that are approved by the NCUA Board pursuant to §723.20. In nonexempt states, all required NCUA reviews and approvals will be handled in coordination with the state credit union supervisory authority; and

(b) Adhere to the requirements stated in part 722 of this chapter concerning appraisals.

(c) Adhere to the requirements stated in §701.21(h) of this chapter concerning third-party servicing of indirect vehicle loans. Before a state-chartered credit union applies to a regional director for a waiver under §701.21(h)(2), it must first notify its state supervisory authority. The regional director will not grant a waiver unless the appropriate state official concurs in the waiver. The 45-day period for the regional director to act on a waiver request, as described §701.21(h)(3), will not begin until the regional director has received the state official's concurrence and any other necessary information.

[60 FR 58504, Nov. 28, 1995, as amended at 63 FR 51802, Sept. 29, 1998; 64 FR 28733, May 27, 1999; 71 FR 36667, June 28, 2006]

§ 741.204 Maximum public unit and nonmember accounts, and low-income designation.

Any credit union that is insured, or that makes application for insurance, pursuant to Title II of the Act must:

(a) Adhere to the requirements of §701.32 of this chapter regarding public unit and nonmember accounts, provided it has the authority to accept such accounts. Requests by federally insured state-chartered credit unions for an exemption from the limitation of §701.32 of this chapter will be made and reviewed on the same basis as that provided in §701.32 of this chapter for federal credit unions, provided, however that NCUA will not grant an exemption without the concurrence of the appropriate state regulator.

(b) Obtain a low-income designation in order to accept nonmember accounts, other than from public units or other credit unions, provided it has the authority to accept such accounts under state law. The state regulator shall make the low-income designation with the concurrence of the appropriate regional director. The designation will be made and reviewed by the state regulator on the same basis as that provided in §701.34(a) of this chapter for federal credit unions. Removal of the designation by the state regulator for such credit unions shall be with the concurrence of NCUA.

(c) Receive secondary capital accounts only if the credit has a low-income designation pursuant to paragraph (b) of this section, and then only in accordance with the terms and conditions authorized for Federal credit

National Credit Union Administration § 741.211

unions pursuant to § 701.34(b)(1) of this chapter and to the extent not inconsistent with applicable state law and regulation. State chartered federally insured credit unions offering secondary capital accounts must submit the plan required by § 701.34(b)(1) to both the state supervisory authority and the NCUA Regional Director for approval. The state supervisory authority must approve or disapprove the plan with the concurrence of the appropriate NCUA Regional Director.

(d) Redeem secondary capital accounts only in accordance with the terms and conditions authorized for federal credit unions pursuant to § 701.34(d) of this chapter and to the extent not inconsistent with applicable state law and regulation. State chartered federally insured credit unions seeking to redeem secondary capital accounts must submit the request required by § 701.34(d)(1) to both the state supervisory authority and the NCUA Regional Director. The state supervisory authority must grant or deny the request with the concurrence of the appropriate NCUA Regional Director.

[60 FR 58504, Nov. 28, 1995, as amended at 61 FR 3792, Feb. 2, 1996; 71 FR 4240, Jan. 26, 2006]

§ 741.205 Reporting requirements for credit unions that are newly chartered or in troubled condition.

Any federally insured credit union chartered for less than 2 years or any credit union defined to be in troubled condition as set forth in § 701.14(b)(3) of this chapter must adhere to the requirements stated in § 701.14(c) of this chapter concerning the prior notice and NCUA review. Federally insured state-chartered credit unions must submit required information to both the appropriate NCUA Regional Director and their state supervisor. NCUA will consult with the state supervisor before making its determination pursuant to § 701.14 (d)(2) and (f) of this chapter. NCUA will notify the state supervisor of its approval/disapproval no later than the time that it notifies the affected individual pursuant to § 701.14(d)(1) of this chapter.

§ 741.206 Corporate credit unions.

Any corporate credit union insured pursuant to Title II of the Act shall adhere to the requirements of part 704 of this chapter.

§ 741.207 Community development revolving loan program for credit unions.

Any credit union which is insured pursuant to Title II of the Act and is a "participating credit union," as defined in § 705.2 of this chapter, shall adhere to the requirements stated in part 705 of this chapter.

[60 FR 58504, Nov. 28, 1995, as amended at 76 FR 67591, Nov. 2, 2011]

§ 741.208 Mergers of federally insured credit unions: voluntary termination or conversion of insured status.

Any credit union which is insured pursuant to Title II of the Act and which merges with another credit union or non-credit union institution, and any state-chartered credit union which voluntarily terminates its status as a federally-insured credit union, or converts from federal insurance to other insurance from a government or private source authorized to insure member accounts, shall adhere to the applicable requirements stated in section 206 of the Act and parts 708a and 708b of this chapter concerning mergers and voluntary termination or conversion of insured status.

§ 741.209 Management official interlocks.

Any credit union which is insured pursuant to Title II of the Act shall adhere to the requirements stated in part 711 of this chapter concerning management official interlocks, issued under the provisions of the Depository Institution Management Interlocks Act (12 U.S.C. 3201 et seq.).

§ 741.210 Central liquidity facility.

Any credit union which is insured pursuant to Title II of the Act and is a member of the Central Liquidity Facility, shall adhere to the requirements stated in part 725 of this chapter.

§ 741.211 Advertising.

Any credit union which is insured pursuant to Title II of the Act shall adhere to the requirements prescribed by part 740 of this chapter.

§ 741.212 Share insurance.

(a) Member share accounts received by any credit union which is insured pursuant to Title II of the Act in its usual course of business, including regular shares, share certificates, and share draft accounts, are insured subject to the limitations and rules in subpart A of part 745 of this chapter.

(b) The payment of share insurance and the appeal process applicable to any credit union which is insured pursuant to Title II of the Act are addressed in subpart B of part 745 of this chapter.

§ 741.213 Administrative actions, adjudicative hearings, rules of practice and procedure.

Any credit union which is insured pursuant to Title II of the Act shall adhere to the applicable rules of practice and procedures for administrative actions and adjudicative hearings prescribed by part 747 of this chapter. Subpart E of part 747 of this chapter applies only to federal credit unions.

§ 741.214 Report of crime or catastrophic act and Bank Secrecy Act compliance.

Any credit union which is insured pursuant to Title II of the Act shall adhere to the requirements stated in part 748 of this chapter.

§ 741.215 Records preservation program.

Any credit union which is insured pursuant to Title II of the Act shall maintain a records preservation program as prescribed by part 749 of this chapter.

§ 741.216 Flood insurance.

Any credit union which is insured pursuant to Title II of the Act shall adhere to the requirements stated in part 760 of this chapter.

§ 741.217 Truth in savings.

Any credit union which is insured pursuant to Title II of the Act shall adhere to the requirements stated in part 707 of this chapter.

§ 741.218 Involuntary liquidation and creditor claims.

Any credit union which is insured pursuant to Title II of the Act shall adhere to the applicable provisions in part 709 of this chapter. Section 709.3 of this chapter applies only to federal credit unions.

§ 741.219 Investment requirements.

Any credit union which is insured pursuant to Title II of the Act must adhere to the requirements stated in part 703 of this chapter concerning transacting business with corporate credit unions.

[62 FR 12949, Mar. 19, 1997]

§ 741.220 Privacy of consumer financial information.

Any credit union which is insured pursuant to Title II of the Act must adhere to the requirements stated in part 716 of this chapter.

[65 FR 31750, May 18, 2000]

§ 741.221 Suretyship and guaranty requirements.

Any credit union, which is insured pursuant to Title II of the Act, must adhere to the requirements in § 701.20 of this chapter. State-chartered, NCUSIF-insured credit unions may only enter into suretyship and guaranty agreements to the extent authorized under state law.

[69 FR 8548, Feb. 25, 2004]

§ 741.222 Credit union service organizations.

(a) Any credit union that is insured pursuant to Title II of the Act must adhere to the requirements in §§ 712.3(d)(3) and 712.4 of this chapter concerning agreements between credit unions and their credit union service organizations (CUSOs) and the requirement to maintain separate corporate identities. For purposes of this section, a CUSO is any entity in which a credit union has an ownership interest or to which a credit union has extended a loan and that is engaged primarily in providing products or services to credit unions or credit union members, or, in the case of checking and currency services, including check cashing services, sale of negotiable checks, money orders, and electronic transaction services, including international and domestic electronic fund transfers, to persons eligible for membership in any credit union having a loan, investment or contract with the entity.

(b) This section shall have no preemptive effect with respect to the laws or rules of any state providing for access to CUSO books and records or CUSO examination by credit union regulatory authorities.

(c) The effective date for compliance with this section is June 29, 2009.

[73 FR 79313, Dec. 29, 2008]

§ 741.223 Registration of residential mortgage loan originators.

Any credit union which is insured pursuant to Title II of the Act must adhere to the requirements stated in part 761 of this chapter.

[75 FR 44704, July 28, 2010]

§ 741.224 Golden parachute and indemnification payments.

Any credit union insured pursuant to Title II of the Act must adhere to the requirements stated in part 750 of this chapter.

[76 FR 30517, May 26, 2011]

APPENDIX A TO PART 741—EXAMPLES OF PARTIAL-YEAR NCUSIF ASSESSMENT AND DISTRIBUTION CALCULATIONS UNDER § 741.4

The following examples illustrate the calculation of deposit and premium assessments under each circumstance addressed in paragraphs (i) and (j) of § 741.4.

A. *Direct Conversion to NCUSIF Insurance*

1. Paragraph (i)(1)(i) provides that a credit union or other institution that converts to insurance coverage with the NCUSIF will immediately fund its one percent deposit based on the total of its insured shares as of the last day of the most recently ended reporting period prior to the date of conversion.

i. The following hypothetical illustrates the application of this provision. Assume Main Street Credit Union completes its conversion from nonfederal to federal insurance on May 15 of Year One. Assume further that Main Street credit union had 1,000 insured shares for the end of month in December of the previous year (Year zero), 1,100 insured shares for at the end of May, the month of conversion, and 1,200 insured shares at the end of June. This information is presented in this Table A:[1]

TABLE A

	End of month, December, year zero	End of month, May, year one (month conversion completed)	End of month, June, year one
Main Street Credit Union's Federally Insured Shares	1,000	1,100	1,200

ii. Paragraph (i)(1)(i) requires that on the date of its conversion, Main Street fund its one percent deposit based on "the total of its insured shares as of the last day of the most recently ended reporting period prior to the date of conversion." Since Main Street has less than $50,000,000 in assets, its reporting period is annual, and ends on December 31. 12 CFR 741.4(b)(6) (definition of "reporting period"). Main Street had $1,000 in insured shares on that date, and one percent of that is $10, and so that is the amount Main Street must immediately remit to the NCUSIF to establish its one percent deposit.

2. Paragraph (i)(1)(ii) provides that a credit union or other institution that converts to insurance coverage with the NCUSIF will, if the NCUSIF assesses a premium in the calendar year of conversion, pay a premium based on the institution's insured shares as of the last day of the most recently ended reporting period preceding the invoice date times the institution's premium/distribution ratio * * *.

i. To illustrate the application of paragraph (i)(1)(ii), take the same facts in hypothetical A related to the conversion of Main Street from nonfederal to federal insurance.

---

[1] Although Main Street Credit Union was not federally insured as of December 31 of Year Zero, proposed § 741.4(b)(3) provides that "For a credit union or other entity that is not federally insured, 'insured shares' means, for purposes of this section only, the amount of deposits or shares that would have been insured by the NCUSIF under part 745 had the institution been federally insured on the date of measurement."

Pt. 741, App. A

Now, further assume that on the previous March 15, NCUA had declared a premium assessment, and on September 15 following the conversion NCUA sent out the invoices for the March 15 assessment. Also assume that Main Street had grown to 1,300 insured shares at the end of September, the month the invoices were sent to Main Street and other credit unions. This information is presented in this Table B:

TABLE B

	End of month, December, year zero	End of month, May, year one (month conversion completed)	End of month, June, year one	End of month, September, year one (month invoice sent)
Main Street Credit Union's Federally Insured Shares	1,000	1,100	1,200	1,300

ii. Paragraph (i)(1)(ii) requires Main Street pay a premium based on the institution's "insured shares as of the last day of the most recently ended reporting period preceding the invoice date times the institution's premium/distribution ratio." Again, because Main Street is under $50 million in assets, the most recently ended reporting period preceding the September 15 invoice date is all the way back to December of Year Zero, when Main Street had $1,000 in shares. Main Street's "premium/distribution ratio," as defined in § 741.4(b)(5), is "the number of full remaining months in the calendar year following the date of the institution's conversion or merger divided by 12." Since Main Street completed its conversion in May, there are seven full months remaining in the calendar year (June through December), and Main Street's premium/distribution ratio is seven divided by 12. Accordingly, Main Street's premium will be assessed on $1,000 times seven divided by 12, or about $583.[2] Note that if Main Street's assets had exceeded $50 million as of June 30, it would have had semiannual reporting periods under § 741.4(b)(6), and its "insured shares as of the last day of the most recently ended reporting period preceding the invoice date" would have been its insured shares as of June 30, Year One, and not as of December 31, Year Zero.

3. Paragraphs (i)(1)(iii) and (iv) describe the responsibility of a credit union or other entity converting to federal insurance to replenish a depleted NCUSIF deposit, as follows: A credit union or other institution that converts to insurance coverage with the NCUSIF will, if the NCUSIF declares, in the calendar year of conversion but on or before the date of conversion, an assessment to replenish the one-percent deposit, pay nothing related to that assessment; if the NCUSIF declares, at any time after the date of conversion through the end of that calendar year, an assessment to replenish the one-percent deposit, pay a replenishment amount based on the institution's insured shares as of the last day of the most recently ended reporting period preceding the invoice date.

i. Paragraph (i)(1)(iii) clarifies that a converting credit union has no responsibility to pay anything toward the replenishment of a depleted deposit that is declared on or before the date of conversion, even if NCUA sends out invoices related to the depletion after the date of conversion. Paragraph (i)(1)(iv) requires that a converting credit union replenish its deposit with regard to a depletion declared after the date of conversion through the end of the calendar year. Again, assume the same facts for Main Street as in Table B, but that the deposit depletion was announced in June, after Main Street converted, and that NCUA sent the invoices in September.

TABLE B

	End of month, December, year zero	End of month, May, year one (month conversion completed)	End of month, June, year one	End of month, September, year one (month invoice sent)
Main Street Credit Union's Federally Insured Shares	1,000	1,100	1,200	1,300

---

[2] Main Street's actual premium charge will be this $583 divided by the aggregate insured shares of all federally insured credit unions times the aggregate premium for all federally insured credit unions.

ii. Main Street would receive an invoice amount "based on the [Main Street's] insured shares as of the last day of the most recently ended reporting period preceding the invoice date." Since Main Street has less than $50 million in shares, the most recently ended reporting period preceding the September invoice date was December 31, Year Zero, and it would pay for the replenishment based on $1,000 in insured shares. If Main Street, however, had had $50 million or more in assets on June 30, its most recently ended reporting period preceding the invoice date would have been the semiannual period ending on June 30, and Main Street would have used its insured shares as of June 30 to calculate the replenishment amount due to the NCUSIF.

4. Under the Federal Credit Union Act, distributions, if any, are declared once a year, early in the year, based on excess funds in the NCUSIF as of the prior December 31. Paragraph (i)(1)(v) describes the right of a credit union or other entity converting to federal insurance to receive a distribution from the NCUSIF, specifically: A credit union or other institution that converts to insurance coverage with the NCUSIF will, if the NCUSIF declares a distribution in the year following conversion based the NCUSIF's equity at the end of the year of conversion, receive a distribution based on the institution's insured shares as of the end of the year of conversion times the institution's premium/distribution ratio. With regard to distributions declared in the calendar year of conversion but based on the NCUSIF's equity at the end of the preceding year, the converting institution will receive no distribution.

i. To illustrate how paragraph (i)(1)(v) works, assume that Main Street Credit Union converts to federal insurance in May of Year One, and that the NCUA declares a distribution in January of Year Two based on the NCUSIF equity as of December 31 of Year One. Then Main Street will be entitled to a pro rata portion of the distribution, calculated on its insured shares as of December 31 of Year One times its premium/distribution ratio. Since it converted in May of Year One, and there were seven full months remaining in Year One at on the date of conversion, Main Street's premium/distribution ratio under §741.4(b)(6) equals seven divided by 12.

ii. On the other hand, if the NCUA declared a distribution a year earlier, that is, in January of Year One based on the NCUSIF's equity ratio as of December 31 in Year Zero, then under paragraph (i)(1)(v) Main Street would receive no part of this distribution. Main Street is not entitled to any part of this distribution because Main Street, which completed its conversion in Year One, did not contribute in any way to the excess funds in the NCUSIF as of the end of Year Zero.

B. *Conversion to NCUSIF Coverage Through Merger with a Federally Insured Credit Union.*

Paragraph (i)(2) addresses the NCUSIF premiums, deposit replenishments, and distribution calculations when a nonfederally insured credit union or entity converts to NCUSIF coverage by merging with a federally insured credit union.

1. Paragraph (i)(2)(i) provides that a federally-insured credit union that merges with a nonfederally-insured credit union or other non-federally insured institution (the "merging institution"), where the federally-insured credit union is the continuing institution, will immediately on the date of merger increase the amount of its NCUSIF deposit by an amount equal to one percent of the merging institution's insured shares as of the last day of the merging institution's most recently ended reporting period preceding the date of merger.

i. To illustrate this provision, and the other provisions of paragraph (i)(2) related to mergers of nonfederally insured entities into federally-insured credit unions, consider the following hypothetical. Nonfederally-insured Credit Union A merges into federally-insured Credit Union B on August 15 of Year One. The relevant insured shares of Credit Union A and Credit Union B at various dates before and after the merger are reflected in Table D:

TABLE D

	End of month December, year zero	End of month June, year one	End of month August, year one (month merger completed)	End of Month September, year one (month invoice sent)
Credit Union A Insured shares	1,000	1,100	N/A	N/A
Credit Union B Insured shares	9,000	9,900	12,900	14,000

ii. Paragraph (i)(2)(i) requires that Credit Union B, the continuing credit union, immediately increase the amount of its deposit with the NCUSIF in an amount "equal to one percent of the merging institution's insured shares as of the last day of the merging institution's most recently ended reporting period preceding the date of merger." Since

Credit Union A, the merging institution, has less than $50 million in assets, its reporting period is the calendar year, and its most recently ended reporting period preceding the August merger date is December 31 in Year Zero. Credit Union A had $1,000 in insured shares on that date. Accordingly, Credit Union B, the continuing credit union, must immediately increase the amount of its deposit with the NCUSIF by one percent of $1,000, or $10. Note that if Credit Union A had been a larger credit union, with $50 million or more in assets on June 30 in Year One, then Credit Union B would have used Credit Union A's insured shares as of June 30 in this calculation.

2. Paragraph (i)(2)(ii), relating to NCUSIF premium assessments, provides that the continuing institution will, with regard to any NCUSIF premiums assessed in the calendar year of merger, pay a two-part premium, with one part calculated on the merging institution's insured shares as described in subparagraph (1)(ii) above, and the other part calculated on the continuing institution's insured shares as of the last day of its most recently ended reporting period preceding the date of merger.

i. Paragraph (i)(2)(ii) provides for a two-part calculation, with the first part relating to the merging credit union and the second part relating to the continuing credit union. Assuming the facts as in Table D, and assuming the premium is assessed sometime in Year One, calculate the insured shares of Credit Union A, the merging credit union, as in the example for paragraph (i)(1)(ii). Once again, because Credit Union A is under $50 million in assets, the most recently ended reporting period preceding the invoice date is December of Year Zero, when Credit Union A had $1,000 in shares. The merger was completed in August, leaving four full months in the calendar year, so the premium/distribution ratio is four divided by 12. Accordingly, this part of the premium will be assessed on $1,000 times four divided by 12, or about $333. Then calculate the insured shares of Credit Union B, the continuing credit union, "as of the last day of its most recently ended reporting period preceding the merger date." Since Credit Union B is also under $50 million in assets, "the last day of the most recently ended reporting period" is also December 31 of Year Zero. Credit Union B's insured shares on that date were $9,000, and so the combined insured shares for purposes of the premium assessment is $9,333. Note that if Credit Union B had $50 million or more in assets on June 30 of Year One, then Credit Union B's "most recently ended reporting period preceding the merger date" would have been June 30 of Year One, and not December 31 of Year Zero. The Board is aware that the NCUA might declare a NCUSIF premium, invoice it, and receive the premiums in Year One from the continuing institution before the continuing institution consummates its merger. In that case, the Board would invoice the continuing credit union again after the merger, but only for the difference between the amount previously invoiced and the amount calculated under paragraph (i)(2)(ii).

3. Paragraph (i)(2)(iii) prescribes the procedures for calculating the NCUSIF distribution when a nonfederally insured credit union or entity merges into a federally insured credit union. Paragraph (i)(2)(iii) provides that the federally insured credit union will, if the NCUSIF declares a distribution in the year following the merger based on the NCUSIF's equity at the end of the year of merger, receive a distribution based on the continuing institution's insured shares as of the end of the year of merger. With regard to distributions declared in the calendar year of merger but based on the NCUSIF's equity from the end of the preceding year, the institution will receive a distribution based on its insured shares as of the end of the preceding year.

i. This formula recognizes that the merging institution did not contribute to the NCUSIF equity as of the end of the year preceding the merger and so no distribution is allotted against the merging institution's shares. As for distributions based on the NCUSIF equity at the end of the year of merger, this formula does not include any pro rata reduction for the merging institution's contribution. The Board determined that a pro rata reduction was unnecessary, given the generally small relative size of merging institutions to continuing institutions, and the fact that the Federal Credit Union Act does not require any sort of pro rata reduction or other pro rata calculation with regard to distributions.

C. *Conversion from, or termination of, Federal share insurance.*

Paragraph (j)(1) addresses direct insurance conversions and conversions by merger. Paragraph (j)(2) addresses liquidations and insurance termination.

1. Paragraph (j)(1)(i) provides that a federally insured credit union whose insurance coverage with the NCUSIF terminates, including through a conversion to, or merger into, a nonfederally insured credit union or a noncredit union entity, will receive the full amount of its NCUSIF deposit paid, less any amounts applied to cover NCUSIF losses that exceed NCUSIF retained earnings, immediately after the final date on which any shares of the credit union are NCUSIF-insured.

i. To illustrate the application of this paragraph (j)(1)(i), consider the following hypothetical. Assume Anytown Credit Union, a credit union with $30 million in assets, converts from federal to nonfederal insurance on November 15. Also assume Anytown Credit Union had $20 million in insured shares as of the previous December 31, the end of its most recent reporting period. 12 CFR 741.4(b)(5), (c). The NCUSIF would return one-percent of $20 million, or $200,000 to Anytown Credit Union immediately following the effective date of its conversion. Note that, if Anytown Credit Union had reported $50 million or more in assets on June 30, then June 30 would have been the end of its most recent reporting period. Now further assume that, on July 15 of that same year, the NCUSIF had announced an expense that reduced the equity ratio from 1.3 to .75, which would have included a write-off (depletion) of 25%, or 25 basis points, of the one-percent deposit. The amount of the deposit returned to Anytown would be reduced by 25%, from $200,000 to $150,000. If the NCUSIF had announced expenses reducing the equity ratio to .75 after the November 15 conversion date, this announcement would have no effect on Anytown and it would still receive the full $200,000 from the NCUSIF.

2. Paragraph (j)(1)(ii) provides that a federally insured credit union whose insurance coverage with the NCUSIF terminates, including through a conversion to, or merger into, a nonfederally insured credit union or a noncredit union entity, will, if the NCUSIF declares a distribution at the end of the calendar year of conversion, receive a distribution based on the institution's insured shares as of the last day of the most recently ended reporting period preceding the date of conversion times the institution's modified premium/distribution ratio.

i. To illustrate the application of this paragraph (j)(1)(ii), again assume Anytown Credit Union converts to nonfederal insurance on November 15, and in January of the following year, the NCUSIF declares a distribution based on the NCUSIF's equity ratio as of December 31. Anytown would receive a pro rata distribution calculated as its $20 million in insured shares multiplied by the modified premium/distribution ratio. Anytown's modified premium/distribution ratio, from the definition in § 741.4(b)(5), is one minus Anytown's premium/distribution ratio, which is one minus the ratio of the full number of months remaining in the year divided by twelve, which is one minus (one divided by twelve), which is eleven divided by twelve. So Anytown would receive a pro rata distribution based on $20 million of insured shares times eleven-twelfths, or based on about $18.33 million in shares.[3]

3. Paragraph (j)(1)(iii) provides that a federally insured credit union whose insurance coverage with the NCUSIF terminates, including through a conversion to, or merger into, a nonfederally insured credit union or a noncredit union entity, will, if the NCUSIF assesses a premium in the calendar year of conversion or merger on or before the day in which the conversion or merger is completed, pay a premium based on the institution's insured shares as of the last day of the most recently ended reporting period preceding the conversion or merger date times the institution's modified premium/distribution ratio. If the institution has previously paid a premium based on this same assessment that exceeds this amount, the institution will receive a refund of the difference following completion of the conversion or merger.

i. To illustrate these premium provisions, again assume Anytown Credit Union is a credit union with $30 million in assets that converts from federal to nonfederal insurance on November 15 of Year One, and that Anytown Credit Union had $20 million in insured shares as of the previous December 31 (of Year Zero), the end of its most recent reporting period. Further assume that NCUA declares a premium on February 12 of Year One and invoices the premium on November 15. Since the premium was declared "on or before the day in which [Anytown's] conversion [was] completed," § 741.4(j)(1)(iii) applies. Anytown would then pay a premium based on $20 million (its "insured shares as of the last day of the most recently ended reporting period preceding the conversion or merger date") times eleven-twelfths (its "modified premium/distribution ratio"), or based on about $18.33 million. Note that NCUA might have already have invoiced Anytown for the premium sometime between February 12 and Anytown's merger on November 15. If so, Anytown will likely receive a refund of some of this earlier premium, as provided in the last sentence of § 741.1(j)(1)(iii), since it may have overpaid the earlier premium.

[74 FR 63281, Dec. 3, 2009]

PART 742—REGULATORY FLEXIBILITY PROGRAM

Sec.
742.1 Regulatory Flexibility Program.
742.2 Criteria to qualify for RegFlex designation.
742.3 Loss and revocation of RegFlex designation.
742.4 RegFlex relief.

AUTHORITY: 12 U.S.C. 1756, 1766.

SOURCE: 71 FR 4039, Jan. 25, 2006, unless otherwise noted.

---

[3] Anytown's actual distribution would be $18.33 million times the aggregate amount of the distribution divided by the aggregate amount of all insured shares at all federally insured credit unions.

§ 742.1 Regulatory Flexibility Program.

NCUA's Regulatory Flexibility Program (RegFlex) exempts from all or part of the NCUA regulatory restrictions identified elsewhere in this part credit unions that demonstrate sustained superior performance as measured by CAMEL rating and net worth classification. RegFlex credit unions also are authorized to purchase and hold an expanded range of obligations.

§ 742.2 Criteria to qualify for RegFlex designation.

(a) *Automatic qualification.* A credit union automatically qualifies for RegFlex designation, without formal notification, when it has:

(1) *CAMEL.* Received a composite CAMEL rating of "1" or "2" for the two (2) preceding examinations; and

(2) *Net worth.* Maintained a net worth classification of "well capitalized" under part 702 of this chapter for six (6) consecutive preceding quarters or, if subject to a risk-based net worth (RBNW) requirement under part 702 of this chapter, has remained "well capitalized" for six (6) consecutive preceding quarters after applying the applicable RBNW requirement.

(b) *Application for designation.* A credit union that does not automatically qualify under paragraph (a) of this section may apply for a RegFlex designation, which may be granted in whole or in part upon notification by the appropriate Regional Director, provided the credit union has either:

(1) *CAMEL.* Received a composite CAMEL rating of "3" or better for the preceding examination; or

(2) *Net worth.* Maintained a net worth classification of "well capitalized" under part 702 of this chapter for less than six (6) consecutive quarters or, if subject to an RBNW requirement under part 702 of this chapter, has remained "well capitalized" for less than six (6) consecutive preceding quarters after applying the applicable RBNW requirement.

§ 742.3 Loss and revocation of RegFlex designation.

(a) *Loss of authority.* RegFlex authority is lost when a credit union that qualified automatically under the CAMEL and net worth criteria in § 742.2(a) no longer meets either of those criteria. Once the authority is lost, the credit union may no longer claim the exemptions and authority set forth in § 742.4.

(b) *Revocation of authority.* The Regional Director may revoke a credit union's RegFlex authority under § 742.2, in whole or in part, for substantive, documented safety and soundness reasons. When revoking RegFlex authority, the regional director must give written notice to the credit union stating the reasons for the revocation. The revocation is effective upon the credit union's receipt of notice from the Regional Director.

(c) *Appeal of revocation.* A credit union has 60 days from the date of the regional director's determination to revoke RegFlex authority to appeal the action, in whole or in part, to NCUA's Supervisory Review Committee. The Regional Director's determination will remain in effect unless and until the Supervisory Review Committee issues a different determination. If the credit union is dissatisfied with the decision of the Supervisory Review Committee, the credit union has 60 days from the date of the Committee's decision to appeal to the NCUA Board.

(d) *Grandfathering of past actions.* Any action duly taken in reliance upon RegFlex authority will not be affected or undone by subsequent loss or revocation of that authority. Any actions exercised after RegFlex authority is lost or revoked must comply with all applicable regulatory requirements and restrictions. Nothing in this part shall affect NCUA's authority to require a credit union to divest its investments or assets for substantive safety and soundness reasons.

§ 742.4 RegFlex relief.

(a) *Exemptions.* RegFlex credit unions are exempt from the following regulatory restrictions:

(1) *Charitable contributions.* Section 701.25 of this chapter concerning charitable contributions;

(2) *Nonmember deposits.* Section 701.32(b) and (c) of this chapter concerning the maximum amount of nonmember deposits a credit union can accept; and

National Credit Union Administration

(3) *Fixed assets.* Section 701.36(b)(2) of this chapter concerning the three-year partial occupancy requirement when acquiring unimproved land for future expansion; RegFlex credit unions are instead subject to a six-year partial occupancy requirement when acquiring unimproved land but remain subject to all other provisions of that section including the waiver provision;

(4) *Zero-coupon securities.* Section 703.16(b) of this chapter concerning the maximum maturity length of zero-coupon securities;

(5) *Borrowing repurchase transactions.* Section 703.13(d)(3) of this chapter, concerning the maturity of investments a credit union purchases with the proceeds received in a borrowing repurchase transaction, provided the value of the investments that mature later than the borrowing repurchase transaction does not exceed 100 percent of the federal credit union's net worth;

(6) *Commercial mortgage related security.* Section 703.16(d) of this chapter prohibiting the purchase of a commercial mortgage related security of an issuer other than a government-sponsored enterprise enumerated in 12 U.S.C. 1757(7)(E), provided:

(i) The security is rated in one of the two highest rating categories by at least one nationally-recognized statistical rating organization;

(ii) The security meets the definition of mortgage related security as defined in 15 U.S.C. 78c(a)(41) and the definition of commercial mortgage related security as defined in §703.2 of this chapter;

(iii) The security's underlying pool of loans contains more than 50 loans with no one loan representing more than 10 percent of the pool; and

(iv) The aggregate total of commercial mortgage related securities purchased by the Federal credit union does not exceed 50 percent of its net worth.

(b) *Purchase of obligations from a FICU.* A RegFlex credit union is authorized to purchase and hold the following obligations, provided that it would be empowered to grant them:

(1) *Eligible obligations.* Eligible obligations pursuant to §701.23(b)(1)(i) of this chapter without regard to whether they are obligations of its members, provided they are purchased from a federally-insured credit union only;

(2) *Student loans.* Student loans pursuant to §701.23(b)(1)(iii) of this chapter, provided they are purchased from a federally-insured credit union only;

(3) *Mortgage loans.* Real-state secured loans pursuant to 701.23(b)(1)(iv) of this chapter, provided they are purchased from a federally-insured credit union only;

(4) *Eligible obligations of a liquidating credit union.* Eligible obligations of a liquidating credit union pursuant to §701.23(b)(1)(ii) of this chapter without regard to whether they are obligations of the liquidating credit union's members, provided that such purchases do not exceed 5 percent (5%) of the unimpaired capital and surplus of the purchasing credit union.

[71 FR 4039, Jan. 25, 2006, as amended at 72 FR 30247, May 31, 2007; 74 FR 13083, Mar. 26, 2009; 75 FR 34622, June 18, 2010; 75 FR 66298, Oct. 28, 2010]

PART 745—SHARE INSURANCE AND APPENDIX

Subpart A—Clarification and Definition of Account Insurance Coverage

Sec.
745.0 Scope.
745.1 Definitions.
745.2 General principles applicable in determining insurance of accounts.
745.3 Single ownership accounts.
745.4 Revocable trust accounts.
745.5 Accounts held by executors or administrators.
745.6 Accounts held by a corporation, partnership, or unincorporated association.
745.7 Shares accepted in a foreign currency.
745.8 Joint ownership accounts.
745.9–1 Trust accounts.
745.9–2 Retirement and other employee benefit plan accounts.
745.10 Accounts held by government depositors.
745.11 Accounts evidenced by negotiable instruments.
745.12 Account obligations for payment of items forwarded for collection by depository institution acting as agent.
745.13 Notification to members/shareholders.
745.14 Noninterest-bearing transaction accounts.

Subpart B—Payment of Share Insurance and Appeals

745.200 General.
745.201 Processing of insurance claims.

§ 745.0

745.202 Appeal.
745.203 Judicial review.
APPENDIX TO PART 745—EXAMPLES OF INSURANCE COVERAGE AFFORDED ACCOUNTS IN CREDIT UNIONS INSURED BY THE NATIONAL CREDIT UNION SHARE INSURANCE FUND

AUTHORITY: 12 U.S.C. 1752(5), 1757, 1765, 1766, 1781, 1782, 1787, 1789; Title V, Pub. L. 109-351;120 Stat. 1966.

SOURCE: 51 FR 37560, Oct. 23, 1986, unless otherwise noted.

Subpart A—Clarification and Definition of Account Insurance Coverage

§ 745.0 Scope.

The regulation and appendix contained in this part describe the insurance coverage of various types of member accounts. In general, all types of member share accounts received by the credit union in its usual course of business, including regular shares, share certificates, and share draft accounts, represent equity and are insured. For the purposes of applying the rules in this part, it is presumed that the owner of funds in an account is an insured credit union member or otherwise eligible to maintain an insured account in a credit union. These rules do not extend insurance coverage to persons not entitled to maintain an insured account or to account relationships that have not been approved by the Board as an insured account. Where there are multiple owners of a single account, generally only that part which is allocable to the member(s) is insured.

§ 745.1 Definitions.

(a) The terms *account* or *accounts* as used in this part mean share, share certificate or share draft accounts (or their equivalent under state law, as determined by the Board in the case of insured state credit unions) of a member (which includes other credit unions, public units and nonmembers where permitted under the Act) in a credit union of a type approved by the Board which evidences money or its equivalent received or held by a credit union in the usual course of business and for which it has given or is obligated to give credit to the account of the member.

(b) The terms *member* or *members* as used in this part mean those persons enumerated in the credit union's field of membership who have been elected to membership in accordance with the Act or state law in the case of state credit unions. It also includes those nonmembers permitted under the Act to maintain accounts in an insured credit union, including nonmember credit unions and nonmember public units and political subdivisions.

(c) The term *public unit* means the United States, any state of the United States, the District of Columbia, the Commonwealth of Puerto Rico, the Panama Canal Zone, any territory or possession of the United States, any county, municipality, or political subdivision thereof, or any Indian tribe as defined in section 3(c) of the Indian Financing Act of 1974.

(d) The term *political subdivision* includes any subdivision of a public unit, as defined in paragraph (c) of this section, or any principal department of such public unit, (1) the creation of which subdivision or department has been expressly authorized by state statute, (2) to which some functions of government have been delegated by state statute, and (3) to which funds have been allocated by statute or ordinance for its exclusive use and control. It also includes drainage, irrigation, navigation improvement, levee, sanitary, school or power districts and bridge or port authorities, and other special districts created by state statute or compacts between the states. Excluded from the term are subordinate or nonautonomous divisions, agencies, or boards within principal departments.

(e) The term "standard maximum share insurance amount," referred to as the "SMSIA" hereafter, means $250,000 adjusted pursuant to subparagraph (F) of section 11(a)(1) of the Federal Deposit Insurance Act (12 U.S.C. 1821(a)(1)(F)).

(f) The term *noninterest-bearing transaction account* means an account or deposit maintained at an insured credit union—

(1) With respect to which either interest or dividends are neither accrued nor paid;

(2) On which the account holder or depositor is permitted to make withdrawals by negotiable or transferable instrument, payment orders of withdrawal, telephone or other electronic media transfers, or other similar items for the purpose of making payments or transfers to third parties or others; and

(3) On which the insured credit union does not reserve the right to require advance notice of an intended withdrawal.

[51 FR 37560, Oct. 23, 1986, as amended at 71 FR 14635, Mar. 23, 2006; 73 FR 62858, Oct. 22, 2008; 74 FR 55749, Oct. 29, 2009; 75 FR 53843, Sept. 2, 2010; 76 FR 30253, May 25, 2011]

§ 745.2 General principles applicable in determining insurance of accounts.

(a) *General.* This part provides for determination by the Board of the amount of members' insured accounts. The rules for determining the insurance coverage of accounts maintained by members in the same or different rights and capacities in the same insured credit union are set forth in the following provisions of this part. The appendix provides examples of the application of these rules to various factual situations. While the provisions of this part govern in determining share insurance coverage, to the extent local law enters into a share insurance determination, the local law of the jurisdiction in which the insured credit union's principal office is located will control over the local law of other jurisdictions where the insured credit union has offices or service facilities.

(b) The regulations in this part in no way are to be interpreted to authorize any type of account that is not authorized by Federal law or regulation or State law or regulation or by the bylaws of a particular credit union. The purpose is to be as inclusive as possible of all situations.

(c) *Records.* (1) The account records of the insured credit union shall be conclusive as to the existence of any relationship pursuant to which the funds in the account are deposited and on which a claim for insurance coverage is founded. Examples would be trustee, agent, custodian, or executor. No claim for insurance based on such a relationship will be recognized in the absence of such disclosure.

(2) If the account records of an insured credit union disclose the existence of a relationship which may provide a basis for additional insurance, the details of the relationship and the interest of other parties in the account must be ascertainable either from the records of the credit union or the records of the member maintained in good faith and in the regular course of business.

(3) The account records of an insured credit union in connection with a trust account shall disclose the name of both the settlor (grantor) and the trustee of the trust and shall contain an account signature card executed by the trustee.

(4) The interests of the co-owners of a joint account shall be deemed equal, unless otherwise stated on the insured credit union's records in the case of a tenancy in common.

(d) *Valuation of trust interests.* (1) Trust interests in the same trust deposited in the same account will be separately insured if the value of the trust interest is capable of determination, without evaluation of contingencies, except for those covered by the present worth tables and rules of calculation for their use set forth in § 20.2031-7 of the Federal Estate Tax Regulations (26 CFR 20.2031-7).

(2) In connection with any trust in which certain trust interests are not capable of evaluation in accordance with the foregoing rule, payment by the Board to the trustee with respect to all such trust interests shall not exceed the SMSIA.

(3) Each trust interest in any trust established by two or more settlors shall be deemed to be derived from each settlor pro rata to his contribution to the trust.

(4) The term "trust interest" means the interest of a beneficiary in an irrevocable express trust, whether created by trust instrument or statute, but does not include any interest retained by the settlor.

(e) *Continuation of insurance coverage following the death of a member.* The death of a member will not affect the member's share insurance coverage for a period of six months following death unless the member's share accounts are restructured in that time period. If the accounts are restructured during the six-month grace period, or upon the expiration of the six months if not restructured, the share insurance coverage will be provided on the basis of actual ownership of the accounts in accordance with the provisions of this part. The operation of this grace period, however, will not result in a reduction of coverage.

(f) *Continuation of separate share insurance coverage after merger of insured credit unions.* Whenever the liability to pay the member accounts of one or more insured credit unions is assumed by another insured credit union, whether by merger, consolidation, other statutory assumption or contract: The insured status of the credit unions whose member account liability has been assumed terminates, for purposes of this section, on the date of receipt by NCUA of satisfactory evidence of the assumption; and the separate insurance of member accounts assumed continues for six months from the date the assumption takes effect or, in the case of a share certificate, the earliest maturity date after the six-month period. In the case of a share certificate that matures within the six-month grace period that is renewed at the same dollar amount, either with or without accrued dividends having been added to the principal amount, and for the same term as the original share certificate, the separate insurance applies to the renewed share certificate until the first maturity date after the six-month period. A share certificate that matures within the six-month grace period that is renewed on any other basis, or that is not renewed, is separately insured only until the end of the six-month grace period.

[51 FR 37560, Oct. 23, 1986, as amended at 65 FR 34924, June 1, 2000; 68 FR 75114, Dec. 30, 2003; 71 FR 14635, Mar. 23, 2006]

§ 745.3 Single ownership accounts.

(a) Funds owned by an individual and deposited in the manner set forth below shall be added together and insured up to the SMSIA in the aggregate.

(1) *Individual accounts.* Funds owned by an individual (or by the husband-wife community of which the individual is a member) and deposited in one or more accounts in the individual's own name shall be insured up to the SMSIA in the aggregate.

(2) *Accounts held by agents or nominees.* Funds owned by a principal and deposited in one or more accounts in the name or names of agents or nominees shall be added to any individual account of the principal and insured up to the SMSIA in the aggregate. This applies to interests created in qualified tuition savings programs established in connection with section 529 of the Internal Revenue Code (26 U.S.C. 529).

(3) *Mortgage servicing accounts.* Accounts maintained by a mortgage servicer, in a custodial or other fiduciary capacity, which are comprised of payments by mortgagors of principal and interest, shall be insured for the cumulative balance paid into the account by the mortgagors, up to the limit of the SMSIA per mortgagor. Accounts maintained by a mortgage servicer, in a custodial or other fiduciary capacity, which are comprised of payments by mortgagors of taxes and insurance premiums shall be added together and insured in accordance with paragraph (a)(2) of this section for the ownership interest of each mortgagor in such accounts. This provision is effective as of October 22, 2008, for all existing and future mortgage servicing accounts.

(b) Funds held by a guardian, custodian, or conservator for the benefit of his ward or for the benefit of a minor under a Uniform Gifts to Minors Act and deposited in one or more accounts in the name of the guardian, custodian, or conservator are insured up to the SMSIA in the aggregate, separately from any other accounts of the guardian, custodian, conservator, ward, or minor.

[51 FR 37560, Oct. 23, 1986, as amended at 71 FR 14635, Mar. 23, 2006; 73 FR 62858, Oct. 22, 2008; 74 FR 55749, Oct. 29, 2009]

§ 745.4 Revocable trust accounts.

(a) *General rule.* Except as provided in paragraph (e) of this section, the funds owned by an individual and deposited into one or more accounts with respect to which the owner evidences an intention that upon his or her death the

National Credit Union Administration § 745.4

funds shall belong to one or more beneficiaries shall be separately insured (from other types of accounts the owner has at the same insured credit union) in an amount equal to the total number of different beneficiaries named in the account(s) multiplied by the SMSIA. This section applies to all accounts held in connection with informal and formal testamentary revocable trusts. Such informal trusts are commonly referred to as payable-on-death accounts, in-trust-for accounts or Totten Trust accounts, and such formal trusts are commonly referred to as living trusts or family trusts. (EXAMPLE 1: Account Owner "A" has a living trust account with four different beneficiaries named in the trust. A has no other revocable trust accounts at the same NCUA-insured credit union. The maximum insurance coverage would be $1,000,000, determined by multiplying 4 times $250,000 (the number of beneficiaries times the SMSIA). (EXAMPLE 2: Account Owner "A" has a payable-on-death account naming his niece and cousin as beneficiaries, and A also has, at the same NCUA-insured credit union, another payable-on-death account naming the same niece and a friend as beneficiaries. The maximum coverage available to the account owner would be $750,000. This is because the account owner has named only three different beneficiaries in the revocable trust accounts—his niece and cousin in the first, and the same niece and a friend in the second. The naming of the same beneficiary in more than one revocable trust account, whether it be a payable-on-death account or living trust account, does not increase the total coverage amount.) (EXAMPLE 3: Account Owner "A" establishes a living trust account with a balance of $300,000, naming his two children "B" and "C" as beneficiaries. A also establishes, at the same NCUA-insured credit union, a payable-on-death account, with a balance of $300,000, also naming his children B and C as beneficiaries. The maximum coverage available to A is $500,000, determined by multiplying 2 times $250,000 (the number of different beneficiaries times the SMSIA). A is uninsured in the amount of $100,000. This is because all funds that an owner holds in both living trust accounts and payable-on-death accounts, at the same NCUA-insured credit union and naming the same beneficiaries, are aggregated for insurance purposes and insured to the applicable coverage limits.)

(b) *Required intention and naming of beneficiaries.* The required intention in paragraph (a) of this section that upon the owner's death the funds shall belong to one or more beneficiaries must be manifested in the title of the account or elsewhere in the account records of the credit union using commonly accepted terms such as, but not limited to, *in trust for, as trustee for, payable-on-death to,* or any acronym therefore, or by listing one or more beneficiaries in the account records of the credit union. In addition, for informal revocable trust accounts, the beneficiaries must be specifically named in the account records of the insured credit union. The settlor of a revocable trust shall be presumed to own the funds deposited into the account.

(c) *Definition of beneficiary.* For purposes of this section, a beneficiary includes a natural person as well as a charitable organization and other nonprofit entity recognized as such under the Internal Revenue Code of 1986, as amended.

(d) *Interests of beneficiaries outside the definition of beneficiary in this section.* If a beneficiary named in a trust covered by this section does not meet the definition of beneficiary in paragraph (c) of this section, the funds corresponding to that beneficiary shall be treated as the individually owned (single ownership) funds of the owner(s). As such, they shall be aggregated with any other single ownership accounts of such owner(s) and insured up to the SMSIA per owner. (EXAMPLE: Account Owner "A" establishes a payable-on-death account naming a pet as beneficiary with a balance of $100,000. A also has an individual account at the same NCUA-insured credit union with a balance of $175,000. Because the pet is not a "beneficiary," the two accounts are aggregated and treated as a single ownership account. As a result, A is insured in the amount of $250,000, but is uninsured for the remaining $25,000.)

(e) *Revocable trust accounts with aggregate balances exceeding five times the*

§ 745.4

SMSIA and naming more than five different beneficiaries. Notwithstanding the general coverage provisions in paragraph (a) of this section, for funds owned by an individual in one or more revocable trust accounts naming more than five different beneficiaries and whose aggregate balance is more than five times the SMSIA, the maximum revocable trust account coverage for the account owner shall be the greater of either: five times the SMSIA or the aggregate amount of the interests of each different beneficiary named in the trusts, to a limit of the SMSIA per different beneficiary. (EXAMPLE 1: Account Owner "A" has a living trust with a balance of $1 million and names two friends, "B" and "C" as beneficiaries. At the same NCUA-insured credit union, A establishes a payable-on-death account, with a balance of $1 million naming his two cousins, "D" and "E" as beneficiaries. Coverage is determined under the general coverage provisions in paragraph (a) of this section, and not this paragraph (e). This is because all funds that A holds in both living trust accounts and payable-on-death accounts, at the same NCUA-insured credit union, are aggregated for insurance purposes. Although A's aggregated balance of $2 million is more than five times the SMDIA, A names only four different beneficiaries, and coverage under this paragraph (e) applies only if there are more than five different beneficiaries. A is insured in the amount of $1 million (4 beneficiaries times the SMSIA), and uninsured for the remaining $1 million.) (EXAMPLE 2: Account Owner "A" has a living trust account with a balance of $1,500,000. Under the terms of the trust, upon A's death, A's three children are each entitled to $125,000, A's friend is entitled to $15,000, and a designated charity is entitled to $175,000. The trust also provides that the remainder of the trust assets shall belong to A's spouse. In this case, because the balance of the account exceeds $1,250,000 (5 times the SMSIA) and there are more than five different beneficiaries named in the trust, the maximum coverage available to A would be the greater of: $1,250,000 or the aggregate of each different beneficiary's interest to a limit of $250,000 per beneficiary. The beneficial interests in the trust for purposes of determining coverage are: $125,000 for each of the children (totaling $375,000), $15,000 for the friend, $175,000 for the charity, and $250,000 for the spouse (because the spouse's $935,000 is subject to the $250,000 per-beneficiary limitation). The aggregate beneficial interests total $815,000. Thus, the maximum coverage afforded to the account owner would be $1,250,000, the greater of $1,250,000 or $815,000.)

(f) *Co-owned revocable trust accounts.* (1) Where an account described in paragraph (a) of this section is established by more than one owner, the respective interest of each account owner (which shall be deemed equal) shall be insured separately, per different beneficiary, up to the SMSIA, subject to the limitation imposed in paragraph (e) of this section. (EXAMPLE 1: A and B, two individuals, establish a payable-on-death account naming their three nieces as beneficiaries. Neither A nor B has any other revocable trust accounts at the same NCUA-insured credit union. The maximum coverage afforded to A and B would be $1,500,000, determined by multiplying the number of owners (2) times the SMSIA ($250,000) times the number of different beneficiaries (3). In this example, A would be entitled to revocable trust coverage of $750,000 and B would be entitled to revocable trust coverage of $750,000.) (EXAMPLE 2: A and B, two individuals, establish a payable-on-death account naming their two children, two cousins, and a charity as beneficiaries. The balance in the account is $1,750,000. Neither A nor B has any other revocable trust accounts at the same NCUA-insured credit union. The maximum coverage would be determined under paragraph (a) of this section by multiplying the number of account owners (2) times the number of different beneficiaries (5) times $250,000, totaling $2,500,000. Because the account balance ($1,750,000) is less than the maximum coverage amount ($2,500,000), the account would be fully insured.) (EXAMPLE 3: A and B, two individuals, establish a living trust account with a balance of $3.75 million. Under the terms of the trust, upon the death of both A and B, each of their three children is entitled to $600,000, B's cousin is entitled to $380,000, A's

National Credit Union Administration §745.4

friend is entitled to $70,000, and the remaining amount ($1,500,000) goes to a charity. Under paragraph (e) of this section, the maximum coverage, as to each co-owned account owner, would be the greater of $1,250,000 or the aggregate amount (as to each co-owner) of the interest of each different beneficiary named in the trust, to a limit of $250,000 per account owner per beneficiary. The beneficial interests in the trust considered for purposes of determining coverage for account owner A are: $750,000 for the children (each child's interest attributable to A, $300,000, is subject to the $250,000-per-beneficiary limitation), $190,000 for the cousin, $35,000 for the friend, and $250,000 for the charity (the charity's interest attributable to A, $750,000, is subject to the $250,000 per-beneficiary limitation). As to A, the aggregate amount of the beneficial interests eligible for deposit insurance coverage totals $1,225,000. Thus, the maximum coverage afforded to account co-owner A would be $1,250,000, which is the greater of $1,250,000 or the aggregate of all the beneficial interests attributable to A (limited to $250,000 per beneficiary), which totaled slightly less at $1,225,000. Because B has equal ownership interest in the trust, the same analysis and coverage determination also would apply to B. Thus, of the total account balance of $3.75 million, $2.5 million would be insured and $1.25 million would be uninsured.)

(2) Notwithstanding paragraph (f)(1) of this section, where the owners of a co-owned revocable trust account are themselves the sole beneficiaries of the corresponding trust, the account shall be insured as a joint account under section 745.8 and shall not be insured under the provisions of this section. (EXAMPLE: If A and B establish a payable-on-death account naming themselves as the sole beneficiaries of the account, the account will be insured as a joint account because the account does not satisfy the intent requirement (under paragraph (a) of this section) that the funds in the account belong to the named beneficiaries upon the owners' death. The beneficiaries are in fact the actual owners of the funds during the account owners' lifetimes.)

(g) For deposit accounts held in connection with a living trust that provides for a life estate interest for designated beneficiaries, NCUA shall value each such life estate interest as the SMSIA for purposes of determining the insurance coverage available to the account owner under paragraph (e) of this section. (EXAMPLE: Account Owner "A" has a living trust account with a balance of $1,500,000. Under the terms of the trust, A provides a life estate interest for his spouse. Moreover, A's three children are each entitled to $275,000, A's friend is entitled to $15,000, and a designated charity is entitled to $175,000. The trust also provides that the remainder of the trust assets shall belong to A's granddaughter. In this case, because the balance of the account exceeds $1,250,000 (5 five times the SMSIA) and there are more than five different beneficiaries named in the trust, the maximum coverage available to A would be the greater of: $1,250,000 or the aggregate of each different beneficiary's interest to a limit of $250,000 per beneficiary. The beneficial interests in the trust considered for purposes of determining coverage are: $250,000 for the spouse's life estate, $750,000 for the children (because each child's $275,000 is subject to the $250,000 per-beneficiary limitation), $15,000 for the friend, $175,000 for the charity, and $250,000 for the granddaughter (because the granddaughter's $310,000 remainder is limited by the $250,000 per-beneficiary limitation). The aggregate beneficial interests total $1,440,000. Thus, the maximum coverage afforded to the account owner would be $1,440,000, the greater of $1,250,000 or $1,440,000.)

(h) *Revocable trusts that become irrevocable trusts.* Notwithstanding the provisions in section 745.9–1 on the insurance coverage of irrevocable trust accounts, if a revocable trust account converts in part or entirely to an irrevocable trust upon the death of one or more of the trust's owners, the trust account shall continue to be insured under the provisions of this section. (EXAMPLE: Assume A and B have a trust account in connection with a living trust, of which they are joint grantors. If upon the death of either A or B the trust transforms into an irrevocable trust as to the deceased

§ 745.5

grantor's ownership in the trust, the account will continue to be insured under the provisions of this section.)

(i) This section shall apply to all existing and future revocable trust accounts and all existing and future irrevocable trust accounts resulting from formal revocable trust accounts.

[74 FR 55749, Oct. 29, 2009]

§ 745.5 Accounts held by executors or administrators.

Funds of a decedent held in the name of the decedent or in the name of the executor or administrator of the decedent's estate and deposited in one or more accounts shall be insured up to the SMSIA in the aggregate for all such accounts, separately from the individual accounts of the beneficiaries of the estate or of the executor or administrator.

[51 FR 37560, Oct. 23, 1986, as amended at 71 FR 14635, Mar. 23, 2006]

§ 745.6 Accounts held by a corporation, partnership, or unincorporated association.

Accounts of a corporation, partnership, or unincorporated association engaged in any independent activity shall be insured up to the SMSIA in the aggregate. The account of a corporation, partnership, or unincorporated association not engaged in an independent activity shall be deemed to be owned by the person or persons owning such corporation or comprising such partnership or unincorporated association and, for account insurance purposes, the interest of each person in such an account shall be added to any other account individually owned by such person and insured up to the SMSIA in the aggregate. For purposes of this section, "independent activity" means an activity other than one directed solely at increasing insurance coverage.

[51 FR 37560, Oct. 23, 1986, as amended at 71 FR 14635, Mar. 23, 2006]

§ 745.7 Shares accepted in a foreign currency.

An insured credit union may accept shares denominated in a foreign currency. Shares denominated in a foreign currency will be insured in accordance with this part to the same extent as shares denominated in U.S. dollars. Insurance for shares denominated in foreign currency will be determined and paid in the amount of United States dollars that is equivalent in value to the amount of the shares denominated in the foreign currency as of close of business on the date of default of the insured credit union. The exchange rates to be used for such conversions are the 12 p.m. rates (the "noon buying rates for cable transfers") quoted for major currencies by the Federal Reserve Bank of New York on the date of default of the insured credit union, unless the share agreement provides that some other widely recognized exchange rates are to be used for all purposes under that agreement.

[71 FR 14635, Mar. 23, 2006]

§ 745.8 Joint ownership accounts.

(a) *Separate insurance coverage.* Qualifying joint accounts, whether owned as joint tenants with right of survivorship, as tenants by the entireties, as tenants in common, or by husband and wife as community property, shall be insured separately from accounts individually owned by any of the co-owners. The interest of a co-owner in all qualifying joint accounts shall be added together and the total for that co-owner shall be insured up to the SMSIA.

(b) *Determination of insurance coverage.* The interests of each co-owner in all qualifying joint accounts shall be added together and the total shall be insured up to the SMSIA. (EXAMPLE: "A&B" have a qualifying joint account with a balance of $150,000; "A&C" have a qualifying joint account with a balance of $200,000; and "A&B&C" have a qualifying joint account with a balance of $375,000. A's combined ownership interest in all qualifying joint accounts would be $300,000 ($75,000 plus $100,000 plus $125,000); therefore, A's interest would be insured in the amount of $250,000 and uninsured in the amount of $50,000. B's combined ownership interest in all qualifying joint accounts would be $200,000 ($75,000 plus $125,000); therefore, B's interest would be fully insured. C's combined ownership interest in all qualifying joint accounts would be $225,000 ($100,000 plus $125,000);

therefore, C's interest would be fully insured.

(c) *Qualifying joint accounts.* A joint account is a qualifying joint account if each of the co-owners has personally signed a membership or account signature card and has a right of withdrawal on the same basis as the other co-owners. The signature requirement does not apply to share certificates, or to any accounts maintained by an agent, nominee, guardian, custodian or conservator on behalf of two or more persons if the records of the credit union properly reflect that the account is so maintained.

(d) *Failure to qualify.* A joint account that does not meet the requirements for a qualifying joint account shall be treated as owned by the named persons as individuals and the actual ownership interest of each such person in such account shall be added to any other accounts individually owned by such person and insured up to the SMSIA in the aggregate. An account will not fail to qualify as a joint account if a joint owner is a minor and applicable state law limits or restricts a minor's withdrawal rights.

(e) *Nonmember joint owners.* A nonmember may become a joint owner with a member on a joint account with right of survivorship. The nonmember's interest in such accounts will be insured in the same manner as the member joint-owner's interest.

[64 FR 19687, Apr. 22, 1999, as amended at 71 FR 14636, Mar. 23, 2006; 74 FR 55751, Oct. 29, 2009]

§ 745.9-1 Trust accounts.

(a) For purposes of this section, "trust" refers to an irrevocable trust.

(b) All trust interests (as defined in § 745.2(d)(4)), for the same beneficiary, deposited in an account and established pursuant to valid trust agreements created by the same settlor (grantor) shall be added together and insured up to the SMSIA in the aggregate, separately from other accounts of the trustee of such trust funds or the settlor or beneficiary of such trust arrangements.

(c) This section applies to trust interests created in Coverdell Education Savings Accounts, formerly Education IRAs, established in connection with section 530 of the Internal Revenue Code (26 U.S.C. 530).

[51 FR 37560, Oct. 23, 1986, as amended at 65 FR 34924, June 1, 2000; 68 FR 75114, Dec. 30, 2003; 71 FR 14636, Mar. 23, 2006]

§ 745.9-2 Retirement and other employee benefit plan accounts.

(a) *Pass-through share insurance.* Any shares of an employee benefit plan in an insured credit union shall be insured on a "pass-through" basis, in the amount of up to the SMSIA for the non-contingent interest of each plan participant, in accordance with § 745.2 of this part. An insured credit union that is not "well capitalized" or "adequately capitalized," as those terms are defined in 12 U.S.C. 1790d(c), may not accept employee benefit plan deposits. The terms "employee benefit plan" and "pass-through share insurance" are given the same meaning in this section as in 12 U.S.C. 1787(k)(4).

(b) *Treatment of contingent interests.* In the event that participants' interests in an employee benefit plan are not capable of evaluation in accordance with the provisions of this section, or an account established for any such plan includes amounts for future participants in the plan, payment by the NCUA with respect to all such interests shall not exceed the SMSIA in the aggregate.

(c)(1) *Certain retirement accounts.* Shares in an insured credit union made in connection with the following types of retirement plans shall be aggregated and insured in the amount of up to $250,000 (which amount shall be subject to inflation adjustments as provided under section 11(a)(1)(F) of the Federal Deposit Insurance Act, except that $250,000 shall be substituted for $100,000 wherever such term appears in such section) per account:

(i) Any individual retirement account described in section 408(a) (IRA) of the Internal Revenue Code (26 U.S.C. 408(a)) or similar provisions of law applicable to a U.S. territory or possession;

(ii) Any individual retirement account described in section 408A (Roth IRA) of the Internal Revenue Code (26 U.S.C. 408A) or similar provisions of law applicable to a U.S. territory or possession; and

(iii) Any plan described in section 401(d) (Keogh account) of the Internal

§ 745.10

Revenue Code (26 U.S.C. 401(d)) or similar provisions of law applicable to a U.S. territory or possession.

(2) Insurance coverage for the accounts enumerated in paragraph (c)(1) of this section is based on the present vested ascertainable interest of a participant or designated beneficiary. For insurance purposes, IRA and Roth IRA accounts will be combined together and insured in the aggregate up to $250,000 (which amount shall be subject to inflation adjustments as provided under section 11(a)(1)(F) of the Federal Deposit Insurance Act, except that $250,000 shall be substituted for $100,000 wherever such term appears in such section). A Keogh account will be separately insured from an IRA account, Roth IRA account or, where applicable, aggregated IRA and Roth IRA accounts.

[71 FR 14636, Mar. 23, 2006, as amended at 75 FR 34622, June 18, 2010]

§ 745.10 Accounts held by government depositors.

(a) Public funds invested in Federal credit unions and federally-insured state credit unions authorized to accept such investments shall be insured as follows:

(1) Each official custodian of funds of the United States lawfully investing the same in a federally-insured credit union will be separately insured in the amount of:

(i) Up to the SMSIA in the aggregate for all share draft accounts; and

(ii) Up to the SMSIA in the aggregate for all share certificate and regular share accounts;

(2) Each official custodian of funds of any state of the United States or any county, municipality, or political subdivision thereof lawfully investing the same in a federally-insured credit union in the same state will be separately insured in the amount of:

(i) Up to the SMSIA in the aggregate for all share draft accounts; and

(ii) Up to the SMSIA in the aggregate for all share certificate and regular share accounts;

(3) Each official custodian of funds of the District of Columbia lawfully investing the same in a federally-insured credit union in the District of Columbia will be separately insured in the amount of:

(i) Up to the SMSIA in the aggregate for all share draft accounts; and

(ii) Up to the SMSIA in the aggregate for all share certificate and regular share accounts;

(4) Each official custodian of funds of the Commonwealth of Puerto Rico, the Panama Canal Zone, or any territory or possession of the United States, or any county, municipality, or political subdivision thereof lawfully investing the same in a federally-insured credit union in Puerto Rico, the Panama Canal Zone, or any such territory or possession, respectively, will be separately insured in the amount of:

(i) Up to the SMSIA in the aggregate for all share draft accounts; and

(ii) Up to the SMSIA in the aggregate for all share certificate and regular share accounts;

(5) Each official custodian of tribal funds of any Indian tribe (as defined in section 3(c) of the Indian Financing Act of 1974) or agency thereof lawfully investing the same in a federally-insured credit union will be separately insured in the amount of:

(i) Up to the SMSIA in the aggregate for all share draft accounts; and

(ii) Up to the SMSIA in the aggregate for all share certificate and regular share accounts;

(b) Each official custodian referred to in paragraphs (a)(2), (3), and (4) of this section lawfully investing such funds in share accounts in a federally-insured credit union outside of their respective jurisdictions shall be separately insured up to the SMSIA in the aggregate for all such accounts regardless of whether they are share draft, share certificate or regular share accounts.

(c) For purposes of this section, if the same person is an official custodian of more than one public unit, he shall be separately insured with respect to the public funds held by him for each such unit, but he shall not be separately insured with respect to all public funds of the same public unit by virtue of holding different offices in such unit or by holding such funds for different purposes. Where an officer, agent or employee of a public unit has custody of certain funds which by law or under a bond indenture are required to be set aside to discharge a debt owed to the holders of notes or bonds issued by the public unit, any investment of such funds in an account in a federally-insured credit union will be deemed to be a share account established by a trustee of trust funds of which the noteholders or bondholders are pro rata beneficiaries, and the beneficial interest of each noteholder or bondholder in the share account will be separately insured up to the SMSIA.

(d) For purposes of this section, "lawfully investing" means pursuant to the statutory or regulatory authority of the custodian or public unit.

[51 FR 37560, Oct. 23, 1986, as amended at 65 FR 34925, June 1, 2000; 71 FR 14636, Mar. 23, 2006]

§ 745.11 Accounts evidenced by negotiable instruments.

If any insured account obligation of a credit union is evidenced by a negotiable certificate account, negotiable draft, negotiable cashier's or officer's check, negotiable certified check, or negotiable traveler's check or letter of credit, the owner of such account obligation will be recognized for all purposes of a claim for insured accounts to the same extent as if his name and interest were disclosed on the records of the credit union provided the instrument was in fact negotiated to such owner prior to the date of the closing of the credit union. Affirmative proof of such negotiation must be offered in all cases to substantiate the claim.

§ 745.12 Account obligations for payment of items forwarded for collection by depository institution acting as agent.

Where a closed credit union has become obligated for the payment of items forwarded for collection by a depository institution acting solely as agent, the owner of such items will be recognized for all purposes of a claim for insured accounts to the same extent as if his name and interest were disclosed on the records of the credit union when such claim for insured accounts, if otherwise payable, has been established by the execution and delivery of prescribed forms. Such depository institution forwarding such items for the owners thereof will be recognized as agent for such owners for the purpose of making an assignment of the rights of such owners against the closed insured credit union to the Board and for the purpose of receiving payment on behalf of such owners.

§ 745.13 Notification to members/shareholders.

Each insured credit union shall provide notice to its members concerning NCUA insurance coverage of member accounts. This may be accomplished by placing either a copy of part 745 of these rules, the appendix, or one or more copies of the NCUA brochure "Your Insured Funds" in each branch office and main office of the credit union. Copies of these materials shall also be made available to members upon request. For purposes of this section, an automated teller machine or point of sale terminal is not a branch office.

Subpart B—Payment of Share Insurance and Appeals

SOURCE: 55 FR 5586, Feb. 16, 1990, unless otherwise noted.

§ 745.14 Noninterest-bearing transaction accounts.

(a) *Separate insurance coverage.* Through December 31, 2012, a member's funds in a "noninterest-bearing transaction account" (as defined in § 745.1(f) of this part) are fully insured, irrespective of the SMSIA. Such insurance coverage shall be separate from the coverage provided for other accounts maintained at the same insured credit union.

(b) *Certain swept funds.* NCUA will treat funds swept from a noninterest-bearing transaction account to a noninterest-bearing savings deposit account as being in a noninterest-bearing transaction account.

(c) *Disclosure and notice requirements.* (1) Each insured credit union that offers noninterest-bearing transaction accounts must post prominently the following notice in the lobby of its main office, in each branch and, if it offers internet deposit services, on its Web site:

§ 745.200

NOTICE OF CHANGES IN TEMPORARY NCUA INSURANCE COVERAGE FOR TRANSACTION ACCOUNTS

All funds in a "noninterest-bearing transaction account" are insured in full by the National Credit Union Administration through December 31, 2012. This temporary unlimited coverage is in addition to, and separate from, the coverage of at least $250,000 available to members under the NCUA's general share insurance rules.

The term "noninterest-bearing transaction account" includes a traditional share draft account (or demand deposit account) on which the insured credit union pays no interest or dividend. It does *not* include any transaction account that may earn interest or dividends, a negotiable order of withdrawal ("NOW") account, money-market deposit account, and Interest on Lawyers Trust Account ("IOLTA"), even if share drafts may be drawn on the account. For more information about temporary NCUA insurance coverage of transaction accounts, visit *www.ncua.gov*.

(2) If an insured credit union uses sweep arrangements, modifies the terms of an account, or takes other actions that result in funds no longer being eligible for full coverage under this section, the insured credit union must notify affected members and clearly advise them, in writing, that such actions will affect their share insurance coverage.

[76 FR 30253, May 25, 2011]

§ 745.200 General.

(a) *Payment.* In the event of the liquidation of an insured credit union, the Board will promptly determine the insured accountholders thereof and the amount of the insured account or accounts of each such accountholder. Payment may be in cash, or its equivalent, or may be made by making available to each accountholder a transferred account in a new federally-insured credit union in the same community or in another federally-insured credit union or institution in an amount equal to the accountholder's insured account. Notwithstanding the foregoing, the Board may withhold payment of such portion of the insured account of any member as may be required to provide for payment of any direct or indirect liability to the closed credit union or the liquidating agent, which is not offset against a claim due from such credit union, pending the determination and payment of such liability by the member of or any person liable therefor.

(b) *Amount of insurance.* The amount of insurance on an insured account shall be determined in accordance with the provisions of Subpart A of this part and the Federal Credit Union Act. For the purpose of determining insurance coverage, dividends earned in the ordinary course of business and posted to share accounts for any prior accounting or dividend period shall be deemed to be principal under this part. Dividends earned or accrued in the ordinary course of business, but not posted to share accounts, may be paid at the discretion of the liquidating agent. In making such determination, the liquidating agent will take into consideration whether the failure to post dividends earned or accrued was due to the fraud, embezzlement or accounting errors of credit union personnel. The liquidating agent may require an accountholder to submit documentation supporting any claim for unposted dividends not otherwise evidenced in the credit union records. However, in no event will dividend amounts be considered as principal for insurance purposes pursuant to this section if not consistent with the amounts paid on similar classes of shares.

(c) *Multiple accounts.* In the event an insured member holds more than one insured account in the same capacity, and the aggregate amount of such accounts (including share draft accounts held in such capacity) exceeds the amount of insurance afforded thereon, the insurance coverage will be prorated among the member's interest in all accounts held in the same capacity. In the case of individual accounts, the insurance proceeds shall be paid to the holder of the account, whether or not the holder is the beneficial owner. In the case of accounts which are owned jointly, the insurance proceeds shall be paid to the owners jointly. In the case of trust estates, the insurance proceeds shall be paid to the indicated trustee unless otherwise provided for in the trust instrument or under state law. In the case of corporations, partnerships and unincorporated associations engaged in an independent activity, the insurance proceeds shall be paid to the indicated holder of the account. Where insurance payment is in the form of a transferred account to another insured institution, the same rules shall be applied.

(d) *Computing time.* In computing any period of time prescribed by this subpart, the provisions of § 747.12(a) shall apply.

[55 FR 5586, Feb. 16, 1990, as amended at 61 FR 60186, Nov. 27, 1996]

§ 745.201 Processing of insurance claims.

(a) *Delegations of authority.* The Agent for the Liquidating Agent ("Liquidating Agent") or his or her designee is authorized to make initial determinations with respect to insurance claims pursuant to the principles set forth in this part, and to act on requests for reconsideration of the initial determination.

(b) *Initial determination.* In the event the Liquidating Agent determines that all or a portion of an accountholder's account is uninsured, the Liquidating Agent shall so notify the accountholder in writing, stating the reason(s) for such initial determination, and shall provide the accountholder with a certificate of claim in liquidation in the amount of the uninsured account from the Board in its capacity as Liquidating Agent for the insured credit union to enable the accountholder to share in the proceeds of the liquidation of the credit union, if any, up to the amount of the uninsured account.

(c) *Request for reconsideration.* An accountholder may, at his or her option, request reconsideration from the Liquidating Agent of the initial determination within 30 days of the date of the initial determination, or directly appeal the initial determination to the Board pursuant to § 745.202 of this subpart. The Liquidating Agent shall act on the request for reconsideration within 30 days from its receipt.

§ 745.202 Appeal.

(a) *Time for filing.* Within 60 days after issuance of an initial determination, or of the determination on a request for reconsideration by the liquidating agent, the accountholder may appeal by filing with the Board a written request for appeal. The appeal may be filed with the Secretary of the Board, National Credit Union Administration, 1775 Duke Street, Alexandria, VA 22314–3428.

(b) *Content of request.* Any appeal must include:

(1) A statement of the facts on which the claim for insurance is based;

(2) A statement of the basis for the initial determination or determination on the request for reconsideration to which the accountholder objects and the alleged error in such determination, including citations to applicable statutes and regulations;

(3) Any other evidence relied upon by the accountholder which was not previously provided to the Liquidating Agent.

(c) *Procedures for review of request.* (1) Within 60 days of the date of the Board's receipt of an appeal, the Board may request in writing that the accountholder submit additional facts and records in support of its request. The accountholder shall have 45 days from the date of issuance of such written request to provide such additional information. Failure by the accountholder to provide additional information may, as determined solely by the Board, result in denial of the accountholder's appeal.

(2) Within 60 days from the date of the Board's receipt of an appeal, the accountholder may amend or supplement the request in writing. In the event that the accountholder does amend or supplement the request, the provisons of paragraph (c)(1) of this section with respect to requests for additional information and responses to such requests shall apply with equal force to any such amendment or supplement to a request.

(d) *Determination on appeal.* (1) Within 180 days from the date of the receipt of an appeal by the Board, the Board shall issue a decision determining the extent of the accountholder's insurance pursuant to the rules of this part.

§ 745.203

(2) The determination by the Board on appeal shall be provided to the accountholder in writing, stating the reason(s) for the determination, and shall constitute a final Agency order regarding the accountholder's claim for insurance.

(3) If the Board determines that the accountholder is entitled to the amount of insurance claimed or a portion thereof, upon payment of such insurance the accountholder shall promptly surrender to the Board the certificate of claim in liquidation provided in connection with the initial determination. In the event that the Board determines that the accountholder is only entitled to a portion of the amount of insurance claimed, upon the accountholder's surrender of such certificate a new certificate of claim in liquidation will be provided which reflects the revised amount of the uninsured account.

(4) Failure by the Board to issue a determination on appeal of the accountholder's claim for insurance within the 180-day period provided for under paragraph (d)(1) of this section, shall be deemed to be a denial of such claim for purposes of § 745.203 of this subpart.

[55 FR 5586, Feb. 16, 1990, as amended at 59 FR 36041, July 15, 1994]

§ 745.203 Judicial review.

(a) For purposes of seeking judicial review of actions taken pursuant to this subpart, only a determination on appeal issued by the Board pursuant to § 745.202 of this subpart shall constitute a final determination regarding an accountholder's claim for insurance.

(b) Failure to file an appeal with regard to an initial determination, or a decision rendered on a request for reconsideration with the applicable time periods shall constitute a failure by the accountholder to exhaust available administrative remedies and, due to such failure, any objections to the initial determination or request for reconsideration shall be deemed to be waived and such determination shall be deemed to have been accepted by, and binding upon, the accountholder.

(c) Final determination by the Board is reviewable in accordance with the provisions of chapter 7, title 5, United States Code, by the United States district court for the Federal judicial district where the credit union's principal place of business is located. Such action must be filed not later than 60 days after such final determination is ordered.

[51 FR 37560, Oct. 23, 1986, as amended at 71 FR 67440, Nov. 22, 2006]

APPENDIX TO PART 745—EXAMPLES OF INSURANCE COVERAGE AFFORDED ACCOUNTS IN CREDIT UNIONS INSURED BY THE NATIONAL CREDIT UNION SHARE INSURANCE FUND

WHAT IS THE PURPOSE OF THIS APPENDIX?

The following examples illustrate insurance coverage on accounts maintained in the same federally-insured credit union. They are intended to cover various types of ownership interests and combinations of accounts which may occur in connection with funds invested in insured credit unions. These examples interpret the rules for insurance of accounts contained in 12 CFR part 745 and focus on those accounts for which examples are not provided in the regulatory text.

The examples, as well as the rules which they interpret, are predicated upon the assumption that: (1) Invested funds are actually owned in the manner indicated on the credit union's records and (2) the owner of funds in an account is a credit union member or otherwise eligible to maintain an insured account in a credit union. If available evidence shows that ownership is different from that on the institution's records, the National Credit Union Share Insurance Fund may pay claims for insured accounts on the basis of actual rather than ostensible ownership. Further, the examples and the rules which they interpret do not extend insurance coverage to persons otherwise not entitled to maintain an insured account or to account relationships that have not been approved by the NCUA Board as an insured account.

A. How Are Single Ownership Accounts Insured?

All funds owned by an individual member (or, in a community property state, by the husband-wife community of which the individual is a member) and invested in one or more individual accounts are added together and insured to the $250,000 maximum. This is true whether the accounts are maintained in the name of the individual member owning the funds or in the name of the member's agent or nominee. (§ 745.3(a)(1) and (2).) All such accounts are added together and insured as one individual account. Funds held in one or more accounts in the name of a guardian, custodian, or conservator for the

National Credit Union Administration

benefit of a ward or minor are added together and insured up to $250,000. However, such an account or accounts will not be added to any other individual accounts of the guardian, custodian, conservator, ward, or minor for purposes of determining insurance coverage. (§ 745.3(b).) A mortgage servicing account maintained by a mortgage servicer, in a custodial or other fiduciary capacity, comprised of payments by a mortgagor of principal and interest is insured for the cumulative balance paid into the account by the mortgagor, up to $250,000 for the mortgagor separately from other individual accounts of the mortgagor. A mortgage servicing account maintained by a mortgage servicer, in a custodial or other fiduciary capacity, comprised of payments by a mortgagor of taxes and insurance premiums shall be added together with the mortgagor's other individual accounts and insured up to $250,000. (§ 745.3(a)(3).)

Example 1. Question: Members A and B, husband and wife, each maintain an individual account containing $250,000. What is the insurance coverage?

Answer: Each account is separately insured up to $250,000, for a total coverage of $500,000. The coverage would be the same whether the individual accounts contain funds owned as community property or as individual property of the spouses (§ 745.3(a)(1)).

Example 2. Question: Members H and W, husband and wife, reside in a community property state. H maintains a $250,000 account consisting of his separately-owned funds and invests $250,000 of community property funds in another account, both of which are in his name alone. What is the insurance coverage?

Answer: The two accounts are added together and insured for a total of $250,000. $250,000 is uninsured (§ 745.3(a)(1)).

Example 3. Question: Member A has $192,500 invested in an individual account, and his agent, Member B, invests $125,000 of A's funds in a properly designated agency account. B also holds a $250,000 individual account. What is the insurance coverage?

Answer: A's individual account and the agency account are added together and insured to the $250,000 maximum, leaving $67,500 uninsured. The investment of funds through an agent does not result in additional insurance coverage for the principal (§ 745.3(a)(2)). B's individual account is insured separately from the agency account (§ 745.3(a)(1)). However, if the account records of the credit union do not show the agency relationship under which the funds in the $125,000 account are held, the $250,000 in B's name could, at the option of the NCUSIF, be added to his individual account and insured to $250,000 in the aggregate, leaving $125,000 uninsured (§ 745.2(c)).

Pt. 745, App.

Example 4. Question: Member A holds a $250,000 individual account. Member B holds two accounts in his own name, the first containing $125,000 and the second containing $192,500. In processing the claims for payment of insurance on these accounts, the NCUSIF discovers that the funds in the $125,000 account actually belong to A and that B had invested these funds as agent for A, his undisclosed principal. What is the insurance coverage?

Answer: Since the available evidence shows that A is the actual owner of the funds in the $125,000 account, those funds would be added to the $250,000 individual account held by A (rather than to B's $192,500 account) and insured to the $250,000 maximum, leaving $125,000 uninsured. (§ 745.3(a)(2).) B's $192,500 individual account would be separately insured.

Example 5. Question: Member C, a minor, maintains an individual account of $750. C's grandfather makes a gift to him of $250,000, which is invested in another account by C's father, designated on the credit union's records as custodian under a Uniform Gift to Minors Act. C's father, also a member, maintains an individual account of $250,000. What is the insurance coverage?

Answer: C's individual account and the custodian account held for him by his father are each separately insured: The $250,000 maximum on the custodian account, and $750 on his individual account. The individual account held by C's father is also separately insured to the $250,000 maximum. (§ 745.3 (a)(1) and (b).)

Example 6. Question: Member G, a court-appointed guardian, invests in a properly designated account $250,000 of funds in his custody which belong to member W, his ward. W and G each maintain $25,000 individual accounts. What is the insurance coverage?

Answer: W's individual account and the guardianship account in G's name are each insured to $250,000 providing W with $275,000 in insured funds. G's individual account is also separately insured. (§ 745.3 (a)(1) and (b).)

Example 7. Question: Member A has three individual accounts at the same NCUA-insured credit union. Account #1 is a $250,000 individual account. Account #2 is a mortgage servicing account maintained by a mortgage servicer, in a custodial or other fiduciary capacity, comprised of payments by Member A of principal and interest in the amount of $3,000. Account #3 is a mortgage servicing account maintained by a mortgage servicer, in a custodial or other fiduciary capacity, comprised of payments by Member A of taxes and insurance premiums in the amount of $1,500. What is the insurance coverage?

Answer: Accounts # 1 and #3 are added together and insured up to $250,000, leaving

$1,500 uninsured. Account #2 is separately insured up to $250,000.

B. How Are Accounts Held by Executors or Administrators Insured?

All funds belonging to a decedent and invested in one or more accounts, whether held in the name of the decedent or in the name of his executor or administrator, are added together and insured to the $250,000 maximum. Such funds are insured separately from the individual accounts of any of the beneficiaries of the estate or of the executor or administrator.

Example 1. Question: Member A, administrator of Member D's estate, sells D's automobile and invests the proceeds of $12,500 in an account entitled "A Administrator of the estate of D." A has an individual account in that same credit union containing $250,000. Prior to his death, D had opened an individual account of $250,000. What is the insurance coverage?

Answer: The $12,500 is added to D's individual account and insured to $250,000, leaving $12,500 uninsured. A's individual account is separately insured for $250,000 (§ 745.5).

C. How Are Accounts Held by a Corporation, Partnership or Unincorporated Association Insured?

All funds invested in an account or accounts by a corporation, a partnership or an unincorporated association engaged in any independent activity are added together and insured to the $250,000 maximum. The term "independent activity" means any activity other than the one directed solely at increasing coverage. If the corporation, partnership or unincorporated association is not engaged in an independent activity, any account held by the entity is insured as if owned by the persons owning or comprising the entity, and the imputed interest of each such person is added for insurance purposes to any individual account which he maintains.

Example 1. Question: Member X Corporation maintains a $250,000 account. The stock of the corporation is owned by members A, B, C, and D in equal shares. Each of these stockholders also maintains an individual account of $250,000 with the same credit union. What is the insurance coverage?

Answer: Each of the five accounts would be separately insured to $250,000 if the corporation is engaged in an independent activity and has not been established merely for the purpose of increasing insurance coverage. The same would be true if the business were operated as a bona fide partnership instead of as a corporation (§ 745.6). However, if X corporation was not engaged in an independent activity, then $62,500 (¼ interest) would be added to each account of A, B, C, and D. The accounts of A, B, C, and D would then each be insured to $250,000, leaving $62,500 in each account uninsured.

Example 2. Question: Member C College maintains three separate accounts with the same credit union under the titles: "General Operating Fund," "Teachers Salaries," and "Building Fund." What is the insurance coverage?

Answer: Since all of the funds are the property of the college, the three accounts are added together and insured only to the $250,000 maximum (§ 745.6).

Example 3. Question: The men's club of X Church carries on various social activities in addition to holding several fund-raising campaigns for the church each year. The club is supported by membership dues. Both the club and X Church maintain member accounts in the same credit union. What is the insurance coverage?

Answer: The men's club is an unincorporated association engaged in an independent activity. If the club funds are, in fact, legally owned by the club itself and not the church, each account is separately insured to the $250,000 maximum (§ 745.6).

Example 4. Question: The PQR Union, a member of the ABC Federal Credit Union, has three locals in a certain city. Each of the locals maintains an account containing funds belonging to the parent organization. All three accounts are in the same insured credit union. What is the insurance coverage?

Answer: The three accounts are added together and insured up to the $250,000 maximum (§ 745.6).

D. How Are Accounts Held by Government Depositors Insured?

For insurance purposes, the official custodian of funds belonging to a public unit, rather than the public unit itself, is insured as the account holder. All funds belonging to a public unit and invested by the same custodian in a federally-insured credit union are categorized as either share draft accounts or share certificate and regular share accounts. If these accounts are invested in a federally-insured credit union located in the jurisdiction from which the official custodian derives his authority, then the share draft accounts will be insured separately from the share certificate and regular share accounts. Under this circumstance, all share draft accounts are added together and insured to the $250,000 maximum and all share certificate and regular share accounts are also added together and separately insured up to the $250,000 maximum. If, however, these accounts are invested in a federally-insured credit union located outside of the jurisdiction from which the official custodian derives his authority, then insurance coverage

National Credit Union Administration

is limited to $250,000 for all accounts regardless of whether they are share draft, share certificate or regular share accounts. If there is more than one official custodian for the same public unit, the funds invested by each custodian are separately insured. If the same person is custodian of funds for more than one public unit, he is separately insured with respect to the funds of each unit held by him in properly designated accounts.

For insurance purposes, a "political subdivision" is entitled to the same insurance coverage as any other public unit. "Political subdivision" includes any subdivision of a public unit or any principal department of such unit: (1) The creation of which has been expressly authorized by state statute, (2) to which some functions of government have been allocated by state statute, and (3) to which funds have been allocated by statute or ordinance for its exclusive use and control.

Example 1. Question: As Comptroller of Y Consolidated School District, A maintains a $275,000 account in the credit union containing school district funds. He also maintains his own $250,000 member account in the same credit union. What is the insurance coverage?

Answer: The two accounts will be separately insured, assuming the credit union's records indicate that the account containing the school district funds is held by A in a fiduciary capacity. Thus, $250,000 of the school's funds and the entire $250,000 in A's personal account will be insured (§§ 745.10(a)(2) and 754.3).

Example 2. Question: A, as city treasurer, and B, as chief of the city police department, each have $250,000 in city funds invested in custodial accounts. What is the insurance coverage?

Answer: Assuming that both A and B have official custody of the city funds, each account is separately insured to the $250,000 maximum (§ 745.10(a)(2)).

Example 3. Question: A is Treasurer of X County and collects certain tax assessments, a portion of which must be paid to the state under statutory requirement. A maintains an account for general funds of the county and establishes a separate account for the funds which belong to the State Treasurer. The credit union's records indicate that the separate account contains funds held for the State. What is the insurance coverage?

Answer: Since two public units own the funds held by A, the accounts would each be separately insured to the $250,000 maximum (§ 745.10(a)(2)).

Example 4. Question: A city treasurer invests city funds in each of the following accounts: "General Operating Account," "School Transportation Fund," "Local Maintenance Fund," and "Payroll Fund." Each account is available to the custodian upon demand. By administrative direction, the city treasurer has allocated the funds for the use of and control by separate departments of the city. What is the insurance coverage?

Answer: All of the accounts are added together and insured in the aggregate to $250,000. Because the allocation of the city's funds is not by statute or ordinance for the specific use of and control by separate departments of the city, separate insurance coverage to the maximum of $250,000 is not afforded to each account (§§ 745.1(d) and 745.10(a)(2)).

Example 5. Question: A, the custodian of retirement funds of a military exchange, invests $2,500,000 in an account in an insured credit union. The military exchange, a nonappropriated fund instrumentality of the United States, is deemed to be a public unit. The employees of the exchange are the beneficiaries of the retirement funds but are not members of the credit union. What is the insurance coverage?

Answer: Because A invested the funds on behalf of a public unit, in his capacity as custodian, those funds qualify for $250,000 share insurance even though A and the public unit are not within the credit union's field of membership. Since the beneficiaries are neither public units nor members of the credit union they are not entitled to separate share insurance. Therefore, $2,250,000 is uninsured (§ 745.10(a)(1)).

Example 6. Question: A is the custodian of the County's employee retirement funds. He deposits $2,500,000 in retirement funds in an account in an insured credit union. The "beneficiaries" of the retirement fund are not themselves public units nor are they within the credit union's field of membership. What is the insurance coverage?

Answer: Because A invested the funds on behalf of a public unit, in his capacity as custodian, those funds qualify for $250,000 share insurance even though A and the public unit are not within the credit union's field of membership. Since the beneficiaries are neither public units nor members of the credit union they are not entitled to separate share insurance. Therefore, $2,250,000 is uninsured (§ 745.10(a)(2)).

Example 7. Question: A county treasurer establishes the following share draft accounts in an insured credit union each with $250,000:
"General Operating Fund"
"County Roads Department Fund"
"County Water District Fund"
"County Public Improvement District Fund"
"County Emergency Fund"
What is the insurance coverage?

Answer: The "County Roads Department," "County Water District" and "County Public Improvement District" accounts would each be separately insured to $250,000 if the funds in each such account have been allocated by law for the exclusive use of a separate county department or subdivision expressly authorized by State statute. Funds in the "General Operating" and "Emergency Fund" accounts would be added together and insured in the aggregate to $250,000, if such funds are for countywide use and not for the exclusive use of any subdivision or principal department of the county, expressly authorized by State statute (§§ 745.1(d) and 745.10(a)(2)).

Example 8. Question: A, the custodian of Indian tribal funds, lawfully invests $2,500,000 in an account in an insured credit union on behalf of 15 different tribes; the records of the credit union show that no tribe's interest exceeds $250,000. A, as official custodian, also invests $2,500,000 in the same credit union on behalf of 100 individual Indians, who are not members; each Indian's interest is $10,000. What is the insurance coverage?

Answer: Because each tribe is considered a separate public unit, the custodian of each tribe, even though the same person, is entitled to separate insurance for each tribe (§ 745.10(a)(5)). Since the credit union's records indicate no tribe has more than $250,000 in the account, the $2,500,000 would be fully insured as 15 separate tribal accounts. If anyone tribe had more than a $250,000 interest in the funds, it would be insured only to $250,000 and any excess would be uninsured.

However, the $2,500,000 invested on behalf of the individual Indians would not be insured since the individual Indians are neither public units nor, in the example, members of the credit union. If A is the custodian of the funds in his capacity as an official of a governmental body that qualified as a public unit, then the account would be insured for $250,000, leaving $2,250,000 uninsured.

Example 9. Question: A, an official custodian of funds of a state of the United States, lawfully invests $500,000 of state funds in a federally-insured credit union located in the state from which he derives his authority as an official custodian. What is the insurance coverage?

Answer: If A invested the entire $500,000 in a share draft account, then $250,000 would be insured and $250,000 would be uninsured. If A invested $250,000 in share draft accounts and another $250,000 in share certificate and regular share accounts, then A would be insured for $250,000 for the share draft accounts and $250,000 for the share certificate and regular share accounts leaving nothing uninsured (§ 745.10(a)(2)). If A had invested the $500,000 in a federally-insured credit union located outside the state from which he derives his authority as an official custodian, then $250,000 would be insured for all accounts regardless of whether they were share draft, share certificate or regular share accounts, leaving $250,000 uninsured (§ 745.10(b)).

E. How Are Trust Accounts and Retirement Accounts Insured?

A trust estate is the interest of a beneficiary in an irrevocable express trust, whether created by trust instrument or statute, which is valid under state law. Thus, funds invested in an account by a trustee under an irrevocable express trust are insured on the basis of the beneficial interests under such trust. The interest of each beneficiary in an account (or accounts) established under such a trust arrangement is insured to $250,000 separately from other accounts held by the trustee, the settlor (grantor), or the beneficiary. However, in cases where a beneficiary has an interest in more than one trust arrangement created by the same settlor, the interests of the beneficiary in all accounts established under such trusts are added together for insurance purposes, and the beneficiary's aggregate interest derived from the same settlor is separately insured to the $250,000 maximum.

A beneficiary's interest in an account established pursuant to an irrevocable express trust arrangement is insured separately from other beneficial interests (trust estates) invested in the same account if the value of the beneficiary's interest (trust estate) can be determined (as of the date of a credit union's insolvency) without evaluation of contingencies except for those covered by the present worth tables and rules of calculation for their use set forth in § 20.2031–10 of the Federal Estate Tax Regulations (26 CFR 20.2031-10). If any trust estates in such an account cannot be so determined, the insurance with respect to all such trust estates together shall not exceed $250,000.

In order for insurance coverage of trust accounts to be effective in accordance with the foregoing rules, certain recordkeeping requirements must be met. In connection with each trust account, the credit union's records must indicate the name of both the settlor and the trustee of the trust and must contain an account signature card executed by the trustee indicating the fiduciary capacity of the trustee. In addition, the interests of the beneficiaries under the trust must be ascertainable from the records of either the credit union or the trustee, and the settlor or beneficiary must be a member of the credit union. If there are two or more settlors or beneficiaries, then either all the settlors or all the beneficiaries must be members of the credit union.

Although each ascertainable trust estate is separately insured, it should be noted that in short-term trusts the insurable interest or interests may be very small, since the interests are computed only for the duration of the trust. Thus, if a trust is made irrevocable for a specified period of time, the beneficial interest will be calculated in terms of the length of time stated. A reversionary interest retained by the settlor is treated in the same manner as an individual account of the settlor.

As stated, the trust must be valid under local law. A trust which does not meet local requirements, such as one imposing no duties on the trustee or conveying no interest to the beneficiary, is of no effect for insurance purposes. An account in which such funds are invested is considered to be an individual account.

IRA and Keogh accounts are separately insured, each up to $250,000. Although credit unions may serve as trustees or custodians for self-directed IRA, Roth IRA and Keogh accounts, once the funds in those accounts are taken out of the credit union, they are no longer insured.

In the case of an employee retirement fund where only a portion of the fund is placed in a credit union account, the amount of insurance available to an individual participant on his interest in the account will be in proportion to his interest in the entire employee retirement fund. If, for example, the member's interest represents 10% of the entire plan funds, then he is presumed to have only a 10% interest in the plan account. Said another way, if a member has a vested interest of $10,000 in a municipal employees retirement plan and the trustee invests 25% of the total plan funds in a credit union, the member would be insured for only $2,500 on that credit union account. There is an exception, however. The member would be insured for $10,000 if the trustee can document, through records maintained in the ordinary course of business, that individual beneficiary's interests are segregated and the total vested interest of the member was, in fact, invested in that account.

Example 1. Question: Member S invests $250,000 in trust for B, the beneficiary. S also has an individual account containing $250,000 in the same credit union. What is the insurance coverage?

Answer: Both accounts are fully insured. The trust account is separately insured from the individual account of S (§§ 745.3(a)(1) and 745.9–1).

Example 2. Question: S invests funds in trust for A, B, C, D, and E. A, B, and C are members of the credit union, D, E and S are not. What is the insurance coverage?

Answer: This is an uninsurable account. Where there is more than one settlor or more than one beneficiary, all the settlors or all the beneficiaries must be members to establish this type of account. Since D, E and S are not members, this account cannot legally be established or insured.

Example 3(a). Question: Member T invests $5,000,000 in trust for ABC Employees Retirement Fund. Some of the participants are members and some are not. What is the insurance coverage?

Answer: The account is insured as to the determinable interests of each participant to a maximum of $250,000 per participant regardless of credit union member status. T's member status is also irrelevant. Participant interests not capable of evaluation shall be added together and insured to a maximum of $250,000 in the aggregate (§ 745.9–2).

Example 3(b). Question: T is trustee for the ABC Employees Retirement Fund containing $1,000,000. Fund participant A has a determinable interest of $90,000 in the Fund (9% of the total). T invests $500,000 of the Fund in an insured credit union and the remaining $500,000 elsewhere. Some of the participants of the Fund are members of the credit union and some are not. T does not segregate each participant's interest in the Fund. What is the insurance coverage?

Answer: The account is insured as to the determinable interest of each participant, adjusted in proportion to the Fund's investment in the credit union, regardless of the membership status of the participants or trustee. A's insured interest in the account is $45,000, or 9% of $500,000. This reflects the fact that only 50% of the Fund is in the account and A's interest in the account is in the same proportion as his interest in the overall plan. All other participants would be similarly insured. Participants' interests not capable of evaluation are added together and insured to a maximum of $250,000 in the aggregate (§ 745.9–2).

Example 4. Question: Member A has an individual account of $250,000 and establishes an IRA account and accumulates $250,000 in that account. Subsequently, A becomes self-employed and establishes a Keogh account in the same credit union and accumulates $250,000 in that account. What is the insurance coverage?

Answer: Each of A's accounts would be separately insured as follows: the individual account for $250,000, the maximum for that type of account; the IRA account for $250,000, the maximum for that type of account; and the Keogh account for $250,000, the maximum for that type of account. (§§ 745.3(a)(1) and 745.9–2).

Example 5. Question: Member A has a self-directed IRA account with $70,000 in it. The FCU is the trustee of the account. Member transfers $40,000 into a blue chip stock; $30,000 remains in the FCU. What is the insurance coverage?

Answer: Originally, the full $70,000 in A's IRA account is insured. The $40,000 is no longer insured once it is moved out of the FCU. The $30,000 remaining in the FCU is insured (§ 745.9–2).

[74 FR 55751, Oct. 29, 2009, as amended at 75 FR 34622, June 18, 2010]

PART 747—ADMINISTRATIVE ACTIONS, ADJUDICATIVE HEARINGS, RULES OF PRACTICE AND PROCEDURE, AND INVESTIGATIONS

Sec.
747.0 Scope of part 747.

Subpart A—Uniform Rules of Practice and Procedure

747.1 Scope.
747.2 Rules of construction.
747.3 Definitions.
747.4 Authority of NCUA Board.
747.5 Authority of the administrative law judge.
747.6 Appearance and practice in adjudicatory proceedings.
747.7 Good faith certification.
747.8 Conflicts of interest.
747.9 Ex parte communications.
747.10 Filing of papers.
747.11 Service of papers.
747.12 Construction of time limits.
747.13 Change of time limits.
747.14 Witness fees and expenses.
747.15 Opportunity for informal settlement.
747.16 NCUA's right to conduct examination.
747.17 Collateral attacks on adjudicatory proceeding.
747.18 Commencement of proceeding and contents of notice.
747.19 Answer.
747.20 Amended pleadings.
747.21 Failure to appear.
747.22 Consolidation and severance of actions.
747.23 Motions.
747.24 Scope of document discovery.
747.25 Request for document discovery from parties.
747.26 Document subpoenas to nonparties.
747.27 Deposition of witness unavailable for hearing.
747.28 Interlocutory review.
747.29 Summary disposition.
747.30 Partial summary disposition.
747.31 Scheduling and prehearing conferences.
747.32 Prehearing submissions.
747.33 Public hearings.
747.34 Hearing subpoenas.
747.35 Conduct of hearings.
747.36 Evidence.
747.37 Post-hearing filings.
747.38 Recommended decision and filing of record.
747.39 Exceptions to recommended decision.
747.40 Review by the NCUA Board.
747.41 Stays pending judicial review.

Subpart B—Local Rules of Practice and Procedure

747.100 Discovery limitations.

Subpart C—Local Rules and Procedures Applicable to Proceedings for the Involuntary Termination of Insured Status

747.201 Scope.
747.202 Grounds for termination of insurance.
747.203 Notice of charges.
747.204 Notice of intention to terminate insured status.
747.205 Order terminating insured status.
747.206 Consent to termination of insured status.
747.207 Notice of termination of insured status.
747.208 Duties after termination.

Subpart D—Local Rules and Procedures Applicable to Suspensions and Prohibitions Where Felony Charged

747.301 Scope.
747.302 Rules of practice; remainder of board of directors.
747.303 Notice of suspension or prohibition.
747.304 Removal or permanent prohibition.
747.305 Effectiveness of suspension or removal until completion of hearing.
747.306 Notice of opportunity for hearing.
747.307 Hearing.
747.308 Waiver of hearing; failure to request hearing or review based on written submissions; failure to appear.
747.309 Decision of the NCUA Board.
747.310 Reconsideration by the NCUA Board.
747.311 Relevant considerations.

Subpart E—Local Rules and Procedures Applicable to Proceedings Relating to the Suspension or Revocation of Charters and to Involuntary Liquidations Under Title I

747.401 Scope.
747.402 Grounds for suspension or revocation of charter and for involuntary liquidation.
747.403 Notice of intent to suspend or revoke charter; notice of suspension.
747.404 Notice of hearing.
747.405 Issuance of order.
747.406 Cancellation of charter.

Subpart F—Local Rules and Procedures Applicable to Proceedings Relating to

National Credit Union Administration

§ 747.0

the Termination of Membership in the Central Liquidity Facility [Reserved]

Subpart G—Local Rules and Procedures Applicable to Recovery of Attorneys Fees and Other Expenses Under the Equal Access to Justice Act in NCUA Board Adjudications

747.601 Purpose and scope.
747.602 Eligibility of applicants.
747.603 Prevailing party.
747.604 Standards for award.
747.605 Allowable fees and expenses.
747.606 Contents of application.
747.607 Statement of net worth.
747.608 Documentation of fees and expenses.
747.609 Filing and service of applications.
747.610 Answer to application.
747.611 Comments by other parties.
747.612 Settlement.
747.613 Further proceedings.
747.614 Recommended decision.
747.615 Decision of the NCUA Board.
747.616 Payment of award.

Subpart H—Local Rules and Procedures Applicable to Investigations

747.701 Applicability.
747.702 Information obtained in investigations.
747.703 Authority to conduct investigations.

Subpart I—Local Rules Applicable to Formal Investigative Proceedings

747.801 Applicability.
747.802 Non-public formal investigative proceedings.
747.803 Subpoenas.
747.804 Oath; false statements.
747.805 Self-incrimination; immunity.
747.806 Transcripts.
747.807 Rights of witnesses.

Subpart J—Local Procedures and Standards Applicable to a Notice of Change in Senior Executive Officers, Directors or Committee Members Pursuant to Section 212 of the Act

747.901 Scope.
747.902 Grounds for disapproval of notice.
747.903 Procedures where notice of disapproval issued; reconsideration.
747.904 Appeal.
747.905 Judicial review.

Subpart K—Inflation Adjustment of Civil Monetary Penalties

747.1001 Adjustment of civil money penalties by the rate of inflation.

Subpart L—Issuance, Review and Enforcement of Orders Imposing Prompt Corrective Action

747.2001 Scope.
747.2002 Review of order imposing discretionary supervisory action.
747.2003 Review of order reclassifying a credit union on safety and soundness criteria.
747.2004 Review of order to dismiss a director or senior executive officer.
747.2005 Enforcement of orders.

Subpart M—Issuance, Review and Enforcement of Orders Imposing Prompt Corrective Action on Corporate Credit Unions

Sec.
747.3001. Scope.
747.3002. Review of orders imposing discretionary supervisory action.
747.3003. Review of order reclassifying a corporate credit union on safety and soundness criteria.
747.3004. Review of order to dismiss a director or senior executive officer.
747.3005. Enforcement of directives.
747.3006. Conservatorship or liquidation of critically undercapitalized corporate credit union.

AUTHORITY: 12 U.S.C. 1766, 1782, 1784, 1785, 1786, 1787, 1790a, 1790d; 42 U.S.C. 4012a; Pub. L. 101–410; Pub. L. 104–134; Pub. L. 109–351; 120 Stat. 1966.

SOURCE: 56 FR 37767, Aug. 8, 1991, unless otherwise noted.

§ 747.0 Scope of part 747.

(a) This part describes the various formal and informal adjudicative actions and non-adjudicative proceedings available to the National Credit Union Administration Board ("NCUA Board"), the grounds for those actions and proceedings, and the procedures used in formal and informal hearings related to each available action. As mandated by section 916 of the Financial Institutions Reform, Recovery, and Enforcement Act of 1989 ("FIRREA") (12 U.S.C. 1818 note), this part incorporates uniform rules of practice and procedure governing formal adjudications generally, as well as proceedings involving cease-and-desist

§ 747.1

actions, assessment of civil money penalties, and removal, prohibition and suspension actions. In addition, the Uniform Rules are incorporated in other subparts of this part which provide for formal adjudications. The administrative actions and proceedings described herein, as well as the grounds and hearing procedures for each, are controlled by sections 120(b) (except where the Federal credit union is closed due to insolvency), 202(a)(3) and 206 of the Federal Credit Union Act ("the Act"), 12 U.S.C. 1766(b), 1782(a)(3), 1786. Should any provision of this part be inconsistent with these or any other provisions of the Act, as amended, the Act shall control. Judicial enforcement of any action or order described in this part, as well as judicial review thereof, shall be as prescribed under the Act (12 U.S.C. 1751 et seq.) and the Administrative Procedure Act (5 U.S.C. 500 et seq.).

(b) As used in this part, the term insured credit union means any Federal credit union or any state chartered credit union insured under subchapter II of the Act unless the context indicates otherwise.

[56 FR 37767, Aug. 8, 1991; 57 FR 523, Jan. 7, 1992]

Subpart A—Uniform Rules of Practice and Procedure

§ 747.1 Scope.

This subpart prescribes uniform rules of practice and procedure applicable to adjudicatory proceedings required to be conducted on the record after opportunity for a hearing under the following statutory provisions:

(a) Cease-and-desist proceedings under section 206(e) of the Act (12 U.S.C. 1786(e));

(b) Removal and prohibition proceedings under section 206(g) of the Act (12 U.S.C. 1786(g));

(c) Assessment of civil money penalties by the NCUA Board against institutions and institution-affiliated parties for any violation of:

(1) Section 202 of the Act (12 U.S.C. 1782);

(2) Section 1120 of FIRREA (12 U.S.C. 3349), or any order or regulation issued thereunder;

(3) The terms of any final or temporary order issued under section 206 of the Act or any written agreement executed by the National Credit Union Administration ("NCUA"), any condition imposed in writing by the NCUA in connection with any action on any application, notice, or other request by the credit union or institution-affiliated party, certain unsafe or unsound practices or breaches of fiduciary duty, or any law or regulation not otherwise provided herein, pursuant to 12 U.S.C. 1786(k); and

(4) Any provision of law referenced in section 102(f) of the Flood Disaster Protection Act of 1973 (42 U.S.C. 4012a(f)) or any order or regulation issued thereunder;

(d) Remedial action under section 102(g) of the Flood Disaster Protection Act of 1973 (42 U.S.C. 4012a(g)); and

(e) This subpart also applies to all other adjudications required by statute to be determined on the record after opportunity for an agency hearing, unless otherwise specifically provided for in subparts B through J of this part.

[56 FR 37767, Aug. 8, 1991; 57 FR 523, Jan. 7, 1992, as amended at 61 FR 28025, June 4, 1996; 71 FR 67440, Nov. 22, 2006]

§ 747.2 Rules of construction.

For purposes of this subpart:

(a) Any term in the singular includes the plural, and the plural includes the singular, if such use would be appropriate;

(b) Any use of a masculine, feminine, or neuter gender encompasses all three, if such use would be appropriate;

(c) The term *counsel* includes a non-attorney representative; and

(d) Unless the context requires otherwise, a party's counsel of record, if any, may, on behalf of that party, take any action required to be taken by the party.

§ 747.3 Definitions.

For purposes of this subpart, unless explicitly stated to the contrary:

(a) *Administrative law judge* means one who presides at an administrative hearing under authority set forth at 5 U.S.C. 556.

(b) *Adjudicatory proceeding* means a proceeding conducted pursuant to this subpart and leading to the formulation of a final order other than a regulation.

(c) *Decisional employee* means any member of the NCUA's or administrative law judge's staff who has not engaged in an investigative or prosecutorial role in a proceeding and who may assist the Agency or the administrative law judge, respectively, in preparing orders, recommended decisions, decisions, and other documents under the Uniform Rules.

(d) *Enforcement Counsel* means any individual who files a notice of appearance as counsel on behalf of the NCUA in an adjudicatory proceeding.

(e) *Final order* means an order issued by the NCUA with or without the consent of the affected institution or the institution-affiliated party, that has become final, without regard to the pendency of any petition for reconsideration or review.

(f) *Institution* includes: (1) Any Federal credit union as that term is defined in section 101(1) of the Act (12 U.S.C. 1752(1)); and

(2) Any insured state credit union as that term is defined in section 101(7) of the FCUA (12 U.S.C. 1752(7)).

(g) *Institution-affiliated party* means any institution-affiliated party as that term is defined in section 206(r) of the Act (12 U.S.C. 1786(r)).

(h) *Local Rules* means those rules promulgated by the NCUA in the subparts of this part other than subpart A of this part.

(i) *OFIA* means the Office of Financial Institution Adjudication, which is the executive body charged with overseeing the administration of administrative enforcement proceedings for the NCUA, the Office of the Comptroller of the Currency ("OCC"), the Board of Governors of the Federal Reserve System ("Board"), the Federal Deposit Insurance Corporation ("FDIC"), and the Office of Thrift Supervision ("OTS").

(j) *Party* means the NCUA and any person named as a party in any notice.

(k) *Person* means an individual, sole proprietor, partnership, corporation, unincorporated association, trust, joint venture, pool, syndicate, agency or other entity or organization, including an institution as defined in paragraph (f) of this section.

(l) *Respondent* means any party other than the NCUA.

(m) *Uniform Rules* means those rules in subpart A of this part that are common to the NCUA, the OCC, the Board, the FDIC and the OTS.

(n) *Violation* includes any action (alone or with another or others) for or toward causing, bringing about, participating in, counseling, or aiding or abetting a violation.

[56 FR 37767, Aug. 8, 1991; 57 FR 523, Jan. 7, 1992]

§ 747.4 Authority of the NCUA Board.

The NCUA Board may, at any time during the pendency of a proceeding perform, direct the performance of, or waive performance of, any act which could be done or ordered by the administrative law judge.

§ 747.5 Authority of the administrative law judge.

(a) *General rule.* All proceedings governed by this part shall be conducted in accordance with the provisions of chapter 5 of title 5 of the United States Code. The administrative law judge shall have all powers necessary to conduct a proceeding in a fair and impartial manner and to avoid unnecessary delay.

(b) *Powers.* The administrative law judge shall have all powers necessary to conduct the proceeding in accordance with paragraph (a) of this section, including the following powers:

(1) To administer oaths and affirmations;

(2) To issue subpoenas, subpoenas duces tecum, and protective orders, as authorized by this part, and to quash or modify any such subpoenas and orders;

(3) To receive relevant evidence and to rule upon the admission of evidence and offers of proof;

(4) To take or cause depositions to be taken as authorized by this subpart;

(5) To regulate the course of the hearing and the conduct of the parties and their counsel;

(6) To hold scheduling and/or prehearing conferences as set forth in § 747.31;

(7) To consider and rule upon all procedural and other motions appropriate

§ 747.6

in an adjudicatory proceeding, provided that only the NCUA Board shall have the power to grant any motion to dismiss the proceeding or to decide any other motion that results in a final determination of the merits of the proceeding;

(8) To prepare and present to the NCUA Board a recommended decision as provided herein;

(9) To recuse himself or herself by motion made by a party or on his or her own motion;

(10) To establish time, place and manner limitations on the attendance of the public and the media for any public hearing; and

(11) To do all other things necessary and appropriate to discharge the duties of a presiding officer.

§ 747.6 Appearance and practice in adjudicatory proceedings.

(a) *Appearance before the NCUA or an administrative law judge*—(1) *By attorneys.* Any member in good standing of the bar of the highest court of any state, commonwealth, possession, territory of the United States, or the District of Columbia may represent others before the NCUA if such attorney is not currently suspended or debarred from practice before the NCUA.

(2) *By non-attorneys.* An individual may appear on his or her own behalf; a member of a partnership may represent the partnership; a duly authorized officer, director, or employee of any government unit, agency, institution, corporation or authority may represent that unit, agency, institution, corporation or authority if such officer, director, or employee is not currently suspended or debarred from practice before the NCUA.

(3) *Notice of appearance.* Any individual acting as counsel on behalf of a party, including the NCUA Board, shall file a notice of appearance with OFIA at or before the time that the individual submits papers or otherwise appears on behalf of a party in the adjudicatory proceeding. The notice of appearance must include a written declaration that the individual is currently qualified as provided in paragraph (a)(1) or (a)(2) of this section and is authorized to represent the particular party. By filing a notice of appearance on behalf of a party in an adjudicatory proceeding, the counsel agrees and represents that he or she is authorized to accept service on behalf of the represented party and that, in the event of withdrawal from representation, he or she will, if required by the administrative law judge, continue to accept service until new counsel has filed a notice of appearance or until the represented party indicates that he or she will proceed on a *pro se* basis.

(b) *Sanctions.* Dilatory, obstructionist, egregious, contemptuous or contumacious conduct at any phase of any adjudicatory proceeding may be grounds for exclusion or suspension of counsel from the proceeding.

[56 FR 37767, Aug. 8, 1991, as amended at 61 FR 28025, June 4, 1996]

§ 747.7 Good faith certification.

(a) *General requirement.* Every filing or submission of record following the issuance of a notice shall be signed by at least one counsel of record in his or her individual name and shall state that counsel's address and telephone number. A party who acts as his or her own counsel shall sign his or her individual name and state his or her address and telephone number on every filing or submission of record.

(b) *Effect of signature.* (1) The signature of counsel or a party shall constitute a certification that: the counsel or party has read the filing or submission of record; to the best of his or her knowledge, information, and belief formed after reasonable inquiry, the filing or submission of record is well-grounded in fact and is warranted by existing law or a good faith argument for the extension, modification, or reversal of existing law; and the filing or submission of record is not made for any improper purpose, such as to harass or to cause unnecessary delay or needless increase in the cost of litigation.

(2) If a filing or submission of record is not signed, the administrative law judge shall strike the filing or submission of record, unless it is signed promptly after the omission is called to the attention of the pleader or movant.

(c) *Effect of making oral motion or argument.* The act of making any oral motion or oral argument by any counsel or party constitutes a certification that to the best of his or her knowledge, information, and belief formed after reasonable inquiry, his or her statements are well-grounded in fact and are warranted by existing law or a good faith argument for the extension, modification, or reversal of existing law, and are not made for any improper purpose, such as to harass or to cause unnecessary delay or needless increase in the cost of litigation.

[56 FR 37767, Aug. 8, 1991, as amended at 75 FR 34622, June 18, 2010]

§ 747.8 Conflicts of interest.

(a) *Conflict of interest in representation.* No person shall appear as counsel for another person in an adjudicatory proceeding if it reasonably appears that such representation may be materially limited by that counsel's responsibilities to a third person or by the counsel's own interests. The administrative law judge may take corrective measures at any stage of a proceeding to cure a conflict of interest in representation, including the issuance of an order limiting the scope of representation or disqualifying an individual from appearing in a representative capacity for the duration of the proceeding.

(b) *Certification and waiver.* If any person appearing as counsel represents two or more parties to an adjudicatory proceeding or also represents a nonparty on a matter relevant to an issue in the proceeding, counsel must certify in writing at the time of filing the notice of appearance required by § 747.6(a):

(1) That the counsel has personally and fully discussed the possibility of conflicts of interest with each such party and non-party; and

(2) That each such party and non-party waives any right it might otherwise have had to assert any known conflicts of interest or to assert any nonmaterial conflicts of interest during the course of the proceeding.

[56 FR 37767, Aug. 8, 1991, as amended at 61 FR 28025, June 4, 1996]

§ 747.9 Ex parte communications.

(a) *Definition*—(1) *Ex parte communication* means any material oral or written communication relevant to the merits of an adjudicatory proceeding that was neither on the record nor on reasonable prior notice to all parties that takes place between—

(i) An interested person outside the NCUA (including such person's counsel); and

(ii) The administrative law judge handling that proceeding, the NCUA Board, or a decisional employee.

(2) *Exception.* A request for status of the proceeding does not constitute an ex parte communication.

(b) *Prohibition of ex parte communications.* From the time the notice is issued by the NCUA Board until the date that the NCUA Board issues its final decision pursuant to § 747.40(c):

(1) No interested person outside the NCUA shall make or knowingly cause to be made an ex parte communication to any member of the NCUA Board, the administrative law judge, or a decisional employee; and

(2) No member of the NCUA Board, administrative law judge, or decisional employee shall make or knowingly cause to be made to any interested person outside the NCUA any ex parte communication.

(c) *Procedure upon occurrence of ex parte communication.* If an ex parte communication is received by the administrative law judge, a member of the NCUA Board or any other person identified in paragraph (a) of this section, that person shall cause all such written communications (or, if the communication is oral, a memorandum stating the substance of the communication) to be placed on the record of the proceeding and served on all parties. All other parties to the proceeding shall have an opportunity, within ten days of receipt of service of the ex parte communication, to file responses thereto and to recommend any sanctions, in accordance with paragraph (d) of this section, that they believe to be appropriate under the circumstances.

(d) *Sanctions.* Any party or his or her counsel who makes a prohibited ex parte communication, or who encourages or solicits another to make any such communication, may be subject to any appropriate sanction or sanctions imposed by the NCUA Board or the administrative law judge including,

§ 747.10

but not limited to, exclusion from the proceedings and an adverse ruling on the issue which is the subject of the prohibited communication.

(e) *Separation of functions.* Except to the extent required for the disposition of ex parte matters as authorized by law, the administrative law judge may not consult a person or party on any matter relevant to the merits of the adjudication, unless on notice and opportunity for all parties to participate. An employee or agent engaged in the performance of investigative or prosecuting functions for the NCUA in a case may not, in that or a factually related case, participate or advise in the decision, recommended decision, or agency review of the recommended decision under section 747.40, except as witness or counsel in public proceedings.

[56 FR 37767, Aug. 8, 1991; 57 FR 523, Jan. 7, 1992, as amended at 61 FR 28025, June 4, 1996]

§ 747.10 Filing of papers.

(a) *Filing.* Any papers required to be filed, excluding documents produced in response to a discovery request pursuant to §§ 747.25 and 747.26, shall be filed with the OFIA, except as otherwise provided.

(b) *Manner of filing.* Unless otherwise specified by the NCUA Board or the administrative law judge, filing may be accomplished by:

(1) Personal service;

(2) Delivering the papers to a reliable commercial courier service, overnight delivery service, or to the U.S. Post Office for Express Mail delivery;

(3) Mailing the papers by first class, registered, or certified mail; or

(4) Transmission by electronic media, only if expressly authorized, and upon any conditions specified, by the NCUA Board or the administative law judge. All papers filed by electronic media shall also concurrently be filed in accordance with paragraph (c) of this section.

(c) *Formal requirements as to papers filed*—(1) *Form.* All papers filed must set forth the name, address, and telephone number of the counsel or party making the filing and must be accompanied by a certification setting forth when and how service has been made on all other parties. All papers filed must be double-spaced and printed or typewritten on 8½×11 inch paper, and must be clear and legible.

(2) *Signature.* All papers must be dated and signed as provided in § 747.7.

(3) *Caption.* All papers filed must include at the head thereof, or on a title page, the name of the NCUA and of the filing party, the title and docket number of the proceeding, and the subject of the particular paper.

(4) *Number of copies.* Unless otherwise specified by the NCUA Board, or the administrative law judge, an original and one copy of all documents and papers shall be filed, except that only one copy of transcripts of testimony and exhibits shall be filed.

[56 FR 37767, Aug. 8, 1991, as amended at 75 FR 34622, June 18, 2010]

§ 747.11 Service of papers.

(a) *By the parties.* Except as otherwise provided, a party filing papers shall serve a copy upon the counsel of record for all other parties to the proceeding so represented, and upon any party not so represented.

(b) *Method of service.* Except as provided in paragraphs (c)(2) and (d) of this section, a serving party shall use one or more of the following methods of service:

(1) Personal service;

(2) Delivering the papers to a reliable commercial courier service, overnight delivery service, or to the U.S. Post Office for Express Mail delivery;

(3) Mailing the papers by first class, registered, or certified mail; or

(4) Transmission by electronic media, only if the parties mutually agree. Any papers served by electronic media shall also concurrently be served in accordance with the requirements of § 747.10(c).

(c) *By the NCUA Board or the administrative law judge.* (1) All papers required to be served by the NCUA Board or the administrative law judge upon a party who has appeared in the proceeding in accordance with § 747.6, shall be served by any means specified in paragraph (b) of this section.

(2) If a party has not appeared in the proceeding in accordance with § 747.6, the NCUA Board or the administrative law judge shall make service by any of the following methods:

National Credit Union Administration

§ 747.12

(i) By personal service;

(ii) If the person to be served is an individual, by delivery to a person of suitable age and discretion at the physical location where the individual resides or works;

(iii) If the person to be served is a corporation or other association, by delivery to an officer, managing or general agent, or to any other agent authorized by appointment or by law to receive service and, if the agent is one authorized by statute to receive service and the statute so requires, by also mailing a copy to the party;

(iv) By registered or certified mail addressed to the person's last known address; or

(v) By any other method reasonably calculated to give actual notice.

(d) *Subpoenas.* Service of a subpoena may be made:

(1) By personal service;

(2) If the person to be served is an individual, by delivery to a person of suitable age and discretion at the physical location where the individual resides or works;

(3) By delivery to an agent, which, in the case of a corporation or other association, is delivery to an officer, managing or general agent, or to any other agent authorized by appointment or by law to receive service and, if the agent is one authorized by statute to receive service and the statute so requires, by also mailing a copy to the party;

(4) By registered or certified mail addressed to the person's last known address; or

(5) By any other method reasonably calculated to give actual notice.

(e) *Area of service.* Service in any state, territory, possession of the United States, or the District of Columbia, on any person or company doing business in any state, territory, possession of the United States, or the District of Columbia, or on any person as otherwise provided by law, is effective without regard to the place where the hearing is held, provided that if service is made on a foreign bank in connection with an action or proceeding involving one or more of its branches or agencies located in any state, territory, possession of the United States, or the District of Columbia, service shall be made on at least one branch or agency so involved.

[56 FR 37767, Aug. 8, 1991, as amended at 61 FR 28025, June 4, 1996]

§ 747.12 Construction of time limits.

(a) *General rule.* In computing any period of time prescribed by this subpart, the date of the act or event that commences the designated period of time is not included. The last day so computed is included unless it is a Saturday, Sunday, or Federal holiday. When the last day is a Saturday, Sunday, or Federal holiday, the period runs until the end of the next day that is not a Saturday, Sunday, or Federal holiday. Intermediate Saturdays, Sundays, and Federal holidays are included in the computation of time. However, when the time period within which an act is to be performed is ten days or less, not including any additional time allowed for in § 747.12(c), intermediate Saturdays, Sundays, and Federal holidays are not included.

(b) *When papers are deemed to be filed or served.* (1) Filing and service are deemed to be effective:

(i) In the case of personal service or same day commercial courier delivery, upon actual service;

(ii) In the case of overnight commercial delivery service, U.S. Express Mail delivery, or first class, registered, or certified mail, upon deposit in or delivery to an appropriate point of collection;

(iii) In the case of transmission by electronic media, as specified by the authority receiving the filing, in the case of filing, and as agreed among the parties, in the case of service.

(2) The effective filing and service dates specified in paragraph (b)(1) of this section may be modified by the NCUA Board or administrative law judge in the case of filing or by agreement of the parties in the case of service.

(c) *Calculation of time for service and filing of responsive papers.* Whenever a time limit is measured by a prescribed period from the service of any notice or paper, the applicable time limits are calculated as follows:

(1) If service is made by first class, registered, or certified mail, add three calendar days to the prescribed period;

§ 747.13

(2) If service is made by express mail or overnight delivery service, add one calendar day to the prescribed period; or

(3) If service is made by electronic media transmission, add one calendar day to the prescribed period, unless otherwise determined by the NCUA Board or the administrative law judge in the case of filing, or by agreement among the parties in the case of service.

[56 FR 37767, Aug. 8, 1991, as amended at 61 FR 28026, June 4, 1996]

§ 747.13 Change of time limits.

Except as otherwise provided by law, the administrative law judge may, for good cause shown, extend the time limits prescribed by the Uniform Rules or by any notice or order issued in the proceedings. After the referral of the case to the NCUA Board pursuant to § 747.38, the NCUA Board may grant extensions of the time limits for good cause shown. Extensions may be granted upon the motion of a party after notice and opportunity to respond is afforded all non-moving parties, or upon the NCUA Board's or the administrative law judge's own motion.

§ 747.14 Witness fees and expenses.

Witnesses subpoenaed for testimony or depositions shall be paid the same fees for attendance and mileage as are paid in the United States district courts in proceedings in which the United States is a party, provided that, in the case of a discovery subpoena addressed to a party, no witness fees or mileage need be paid. Fees for witnesses shall be tendered in advance by the party requesting the subpoena, except that fees and mileage need not be tendered in advance where the NCUA is the party requesting the subpoena. The NCUA shall not be required to pay any fees to, or expenses of, any witness not subpoenaed by the NCUA.

§ 747.15 Opportunity for informal settlement.

Any respondent may, at any time in the proceeding, unilaterally submit to Enforcement Counsel written offers or proposals for settlement of a proceeding, without prejudice to the rights of any of the parties. No such offer or proposal shall be made to any NCUA representative other than Enforcement Counsel. Submission of a written settlement offer does not provide a basis for adjourning or otherwise delaying all or any portion of a proceeding under this part. No settlement offer or proposal, or any subsequent negotiation or resolution, is admissible as evidence in any proceeding.

§ 747.16 NCUA's right to conduct examination.

Nothing contained in this subpart limits in any manner the right of the NCUA to conduct any examination, inspection, or visitation of any institution or institution-affiliated party, or the right of the NCUA to conduct or continue any form of investigation authorized by law.

[56 FR 37767, Aug. 8, 1991; 57 FR 523, Jan. 7, 1992]

§ 747.17 Collateral attacks on adjudicatory proceeding.

If an interlocutory appeal or collateral attack is brought in any court concerning all or any part of an adjudicatory proceeding, the challenged adjudicatory proceeding shall continue without regard to the pendency of that court proceeding. No default or other failure to act as directed in the adjudicatory proceeding within the times prescribed in this subpart shall be excused based on the pendency before any court of any interlocutory appeal or collateral attack.

§ 747.18 Commencement of proceeding and contents of notice.

(a) *Commencement of proceeding.* (1) A proceeding governed by this subpart is commenced by issuance of a notice by the NCUA Board.

(2) The notice must be served by the NCUA Board upon the respondent and given to any other appropriate financial institution supervisory authority where required by law.

(3) The notice must be filed with the OFIA.

(b) *Contents of notice.* The notice must set forth:

(1) The legal authority for the proceeding and for the NCUA's jurisdiction over the proceeding;

National Credit Union Administration § 747.21

(2) A statement of the matters of fact or law showing that the NCUA is entitled to relief;

(3) A proposed order or prayer for an order granting the requested relief;

(4) The time, place, and nature of the hearing as required by law or regulation;

(5) The time within which to file an answer as required by law or regulation;

(6) The time within which to request a hearing as required by law or regulation; and

(7) That the answer and/or request for a hearing shall be filed with OFIA.

§ 747.19 Answer.

(a) *When.* Within 20 days of service of the notice, respondent shall file an answer as designated in the notice. In a civil money penalty proceeding, respondent shall also file a request for a hearing within 20 days of service of the notice.

(b) *Content of answer.* An answer must specifically respond to each paragraph or allegation of fact contained in the notice and must admit, deny, or state that the party lacks sufficient information to admit or deny each allegation of fact. A statement of lack of information has the effect of a denial. Denials must fairly meet the substance of each allegation of fact denied; general denials are not permitted. When a respondent denies part of an allegation, that part must be denied and the remainder specifically admitted. Any allegation of fact in the notice which is not denied in the answer must be deemed admitted for purposes of the proceeding. A respondent is not required to respond to the portion of a notice that constitutes the prayer for relief or proposed order. The answer must set forth affirmative defenses, if any, asserted by the respondent.

(c) *Default*—(1) *Effect of failure to answer.* Failure of a respondent to file an answer required by this section within the time provided constitutes a waiver of his or her right to appear and contest the allegations in the notice. If no timely answer is filed, the administrative law judge, upon motion of the Enforcement Counsel, shall file with the NCUA Board a recommended decision containing the findings and the relief sought in the notice. Any final order issued by the NCUA Board based upon a respondent's failure to answer is deemed to be an order issued upon consent.

(2) *Effect of failure to request a hearing in civil money penalty proceedings.* If respondent fails to request a hearing as required by law within the time provided, the notice of assessment constitutes a final and unappealable order.

§ 747.20 Amended pleadings.

(a) *Amendments.* The notice or answer may be amended or supplemented at any stage of the proceeding. The respondent must answer an amended notice within the time remaining for the respondent's answer to the original notice, or within ten days after service of the amended notice, whichever period is longer, unless the NCUA Board or administrative law judge orders otherwise for good cause.

(b) *Amendments to conform to the evidence.* When issues not raised in the notice or answer are tried at the hearing by express or implied consent of the parties, they will be treated in all respects as if they had been raised in the notice or answer, and no formal amendments are required. If evidence is objected to at the hearing on the ground that it is not within the issues raised by the notice or answer, the administrative law judge may admit the evidence when admission is likely to assist in adjudicating the merits of the action and the objecting party fails to satisfy the administrative law judge that the admission of such evidence would unfairly prejudice that party's action or defense upon the merits. The administrative law judge may grant a continuance to enable the objecting party to meet such evidence.

[61 FR 28026, June 4, 1996]

§ 747.21 Failure to appear.

Failure of a respondent to appear in person at the hearing or by a duly authorized counsel constitutes a waiver of respondent's right to a hearing and is deemed an admission of the facts as alleged and consent to the relief sought in the notice. Without further proceedings or notice to the respondent, the administrative law judge shall file with the NCUA Board a recommended

§ 747.22

decision containing the findings and the relief sought in the notice.

§ 747.22 **Consolidation and severance of actions.**

(a) *Consolidation.* (1) On the motion of any party, or on the administrative law judge's own motion, the administrative law judge may consolidate, for some or all purposes, any two or more proceedings, if each such proceeding involves or arises out of the same transaction, occurrence or series of transactions or occurrences, or involves at least one common respondent and a material common question of law or fact, unless such consolidation would cause unreasonable delay or injustice.

(2) In the event of consolidation under paragraph (a)(1) of this section, appropriate adjustment to the prehearing schedule must be made to avoid unnecessary expense, inconvenience, or delay.

(b) *Severance.* The administrative law judge may, upon the motion of any party, sever the proceeding for separate resolution of the matter as to any respondent only if the administrative law judge finds that:

(1) Undue prejudice or injustice to the moving party would result from not severing the proceeding; and

(2) Such undue prejudice or injustice would outweigh the interests of judicial economy and expedition in the complete and final resolution of the proceeding.

§ 747.23 **Motions.**

(a) *In writing.* (1) Except as otherwise provided herein, an application or request for an order or ruling must be made by written motion.

(2) All written motions must state with particularity the relief sought and must be accompanied by a proposed order.

(3) No oral argument may be held on written motions except as otherwise directed by the administrative law judge. Written memorandum, briefs, affidavits or other relevant material or documents may be filed in support of or in opposition to a motion.

(b) *Oral motions.* A motion may be made orally on the record unless the administrative law judge directs that such motion be reduced to writing.

(c) *Filing of motions.* Motions must be filed with the administrative law judge, except that upon the filing of the recommended decision, motions must be filed with the NCUA Board.

(d) *Responses.* (1) Except as otherwise provided herein, within ten days after service of any written motion, or within such other period of time as may be established by the administrative law judge or the NCUA Board, any party may file a written response to a motion. The administrative law judge shall not rule on any oral or written motion before each party has had an opportunity to file a response.

(2) The failure of a party to oppose a written motion or an oral motion made on the record is deemed a consent by that party to the entry of an order substantially in the form of the order accompanying the motion.

(e) *Dilatory motions.* Frivolous, dilatory or repetitive motions are prohibited. The filing of such motions may form the basis for sanctions.

(f) *Dispositive motions.* Dispositive motions are governed by §§ 747.29 and 747.30.

§ 747.24 **Scope of document discovery.**

(a) *Limits on discovery.* (1) Subject to the limitations set out in paragraphs (b), (c), and (d) of this section, a party to a proceeding under this subpart may obtain document discovery by serving a written request to produce documents. For purposes of a request to produce documents, the term "documents" may be defined to include drawings, graphs, charts, photographs, recordings, data stored in electronic form, and other data compilations from which information can be obtained, or translated, if necessary, by the parties through detection devices into reasonably usable form, as well as written material of all kinds.

(2) Discovery by use of deposition is governed by subpart I of this part.

(3) Discovery by use of interrogatories is not permitted.

(b) *Relevance.* A party may obtain document discovery regarding any matter, not privileged, that has material relevance to the merits of the pending action. Any request to produce documents that calls for irrelevant material, that is unreasonable, oppressive, excessive in scope, unduly burdensome, or repetitive of previous requests, or that seeks to obtain privileged documents will be denied or modified. A request is unreasonable, oppressive, excessive in scope, or unduly burdensome if, among other things, it fails to include justifiable limitations on the time period covered and the geographic locations to be searched, the time provided to respond in the request is inadequate, or the request calls for copies of documents to be delivered to the requesting party and fails to include the requester's written agreement to pay in advance for the copying, in accordance with § 747.25.

(c) *Privileged matter.* Privileged documents are not discoverable. Privileges include the attorney-client privilege, work-product privilege, any government's or government agency's deliberative-process privilege, and any other privileges the Constitution, any applicable act of Congress, or the principles of common law provide.

(d) *Time limits.* All discovery, including all responses to discovery requests, shall be completed at least 20 days prior to the date scheduled for the commencement of the hearing, except as provided in the Local Rules. No exceptions to this time limit shall be permitted, unless the administrative law judge finds on the record that good cause exists for waiving the requirements of this paragraph.

[56 FR 37767, Aug. 8, 1991, as amended at 61 FR 28026, June 4, 1996]

§ 747.25 Request for document discovery from parties.

(a) *General rule.* Any party may serve on any other party a request to produce for inspection any discoverable documents that are in the possession, custody, or control of the party upon whom the request is served. The request must identify the documents to be produced either by individual item or by category, and must describe each item and category with reasonable particularity. Documents must be produced as they are kept in the usual course of business or must be organized to correspond with the categories in the request.

(b) *Production or copying.* The request must specify a reasonable time, place, and manner for production and performing any related acts. In lieu of inspecting the documents, the requesting party may specify that all or some of the responsive documents be copied and the copies delivered to the requesting party. If copying of fewer than 250 pages is requested, the party to whom the request is addressed shall bear the cost of copying and shipping charges. If a party requests 250 pages or more of copying, the requesting party shall pay for the copying and shipping charges. Copying charges are the current per-page copying rate imposed by 12 CFR 792.5(b) implementing the Freedom of Information Act (5 U.S.C. 552). The party to whom the request is addressed may require payment in advance before producing the documents.

(c) *Obligation to update responses.* A party who has responded to a discovery request with a response that was complete when made is not required to supplement the response to include documents thereafter acquired, unless the responding party learns that:

(1) The response was materially incorrect when made; or

(2) The response, though correct when made, is no longer true and a failure to amend the response is, in substance, a knowing concealment.

(d) *Motions to limit discovery.* (1) Any party that objects to a discovery request may, within ten days of being served with such request, file a motion in accordance with the provisions of § 747.23 to strike or otherwise limit the request. If an objection is made to only a portion of an item or category in a request, the portion objected to shall be specified. Any objections not made in accordance with this paragraph and § 747.23 are waived.

(2) The party who served the request that is the subject of a motion to strike or limit may file a written response within five days of service of the motion. No other party may file a response.

(e) *Privilege.* At the time other documents are produced, the producing party must reasonably identify all documents withheld on the grounds of privilege and must produce a statement of the basis for the assertion of privilege. When similar documents

§ 747.26

that are protected by deliberative process, attorney work-product, or attorney-client privilege are voluminous, these documents may be identified by category instead of by individual document. The administrative law judge retains discretion to determine when the identification by category is insufficient.

(f) *Motions to compel production.* (1) If a party withholds any documents as privileged or fails to comply fully with a discovery request, the requesting party may, within ten days of the assertion of privilege or of the time the failure to comply becomes known to the requesting party, file a motion in accordance with the provisions of § 747.23 for the issuance of a subpoena compelling production.

(2) The party who asserted the privilege or failed to comply with the request may file a written response to a motion to compel within five days of service of the motion. No other party may file a response.

(g) *Ruling on motions.* After the time for filing responses pursuant to this section has expired, the administrative law judge shall rule promptly on all motions filed pursuant to this section. If the administrative law judge determines that a discovery request, or any of its terms, calls for irrelevant material, is unreasonable, oppressive, excessive in scope, unduly burdensome, or repetitive of previous requests, or seeks to obtain privileged documents, he or she may deny or modify the request, and may issue appropriate protective orders, upon such conditions as justice may require. The pendency of a motion to strike or limit discovery or to compel production is not a basis for staying or continuing the proceeding, unless otherwise ordered by the administrative law judge. Notwithstanding any other provision in this part, the administrative law judge may not release, or order a party to produce, documents withheld on grounds of privilege if the party has stated to the administrative law judge its intention to file a timely motion for interlocutory review of the administrative law judge's order to produce the documents, and until the motion for interlocutory review has been decided.

(h) *Enforcing discovery subpoenas.* If the administrative law judge issues a subpoena compelling production of documents by a party, the subpoenaing party may, in the event of noncompliance and to the extent authorized by applicable law, apply to any appropriate United States district court for an order requiring compliance with the subpoena. A party's right to seek court enforcement of a subpoena shall not in any manner limit the sanctions that may be imposed by the administrative law judge against a party who fails to produce subpoenaed documents.

[56 FR 37767, Aug. 8, 1991, as amended at 61 FR 28026, June 4, 1996; 61 FR 45876, Aug. 30, 1996]

§ 747.26 Document subpoenas to nonparties.

(a) *General rules.* (1) Any party may apply to the administrative law judge for the issuance of a document discovery subpoena addressed to any person who is not a party to the proceeding. The application must contain a proposed document subpoena and a brief statement showing the general relevance and reasonableness of the scope of documents sought. The subpoenaing party shall specify a reasonable time, place, and manner for making production in response to the document subpoena.

(2) A party shall only apply for a document subpoena under this section within the time period during which such party could serve a discovery request under § 747.24(d). The party obtaining the document subpoena is responsible for serving it on the subpoenaed person and for serving copies on all parties. Document subpoenas may be served in any state, territory, or possession of the United States, the District of Columbia, or as otherwise provided by law.

(3) The administrative law judge shall promptly issue any document subpoena requested pursuant to this section. If the administrative law judge determines that the application does not set forth a valid basis for the issuance of the subpoena, or that any of its terms are unreasonable, oppressive, excessive in scope, or unduly burdensome, he or she may refuse to issue

National Credit Union Administration § 747.27

the subpoena or may issue it in a modified form upon such conditions as may be consistent with the Uniform Rules.

(b) *Motion to quash or modify.* (1) Any person to whom a document subpoena is directed may file a motion to quash or modify such subpoena, accompanied by a statement of the basis for quashing or modifying the subpoena. The movant shall serve the motion on all parties, and any party may respond to such motion within ten days of service of the motion.

(2) Any motion to quash or modify a document subpoena must be filed on the same basis, including the assertion of privilege, upon which a party could object to a discovery request under § 747.25(d), and during the same time limits during which such an objection could be filed.

(c) *Enforcing document subpoenas.* If a subpoenaed person fails to comply with any subpoena issued pursuant to this section or any order of the administrative law judge which directs compliance with all or any portion of a document subpoena, the subpoenaing party or any other aggrieved party may, to the extent authorized by applicable law, apply to an appropriate United States district court for an order requiring compliance with so much of the document subpoena as the administrative law judge has not quashed or modified. A party's right to seek court enforcement of a document subpoena shall in no way limit the sanctions that may be imposed by the administrative law judge on a party who induces a failure to comply with subpoenas issued under this section.

§ 747.27 Deposition of witness unavailable for hearing.

(a) *General rules.* (1) If a witness will not be available for the hearing, a party desiring that witness' testimony for the record may apply in accordance with the procedures set forth in paragraph (a)(2) of this section, to the administrative law judge for the issuance of a subpoena, including a subpoena duces tecum, requiring the attendance of the witness at a deposition. The administrative law judge may issue a deposition subpoena under this section upon showing that:

(i) The witness will be unable to attend or may be prevented from attending the hearing because of age, sickness or infirmity, or will otherwise be unavailable;

(ii) The witness' unavailability was not procured or caused by the subpoenaing party;

(iii) The testimony is reasonably expected to be material; and

(iv) Taking the deposition will not result in any undue burden to any other party and will not cause undue delay of the proceeding.

(2) The application must contain a proposed deposition subpoena and a brief statement of the reasons for the issuance of the subpoena. The subpoena must name the witness whose deposition is to be taken and specify the time and place for taking the deposition. A deposition subpoena may require the witness to be deposed at any place within the country in which that witness resides or has a regular place of employment or such other convenient place as the administrative law judge shall fix.

(3) Any requested subpoena that sets forth a valid basis for its issuance must be promptly issued, unless the administrative law judge on his or her own motion, requires a written response or requires attendance at a conference concerning whether the requested subpoena should be issued.

(4) The party obtaining a deposition subpoena is responsible for serving it on the witness and for serving copies on all parties. Unless the administrative law judge orders otherwise, no deposition under this section shall be taken on fewer than ten days' notice to the witness and all parties. Deposition subpoenas may be served in any state, territory, possession of the United States, or the District of Columbia, on any person or company doing business in any state, territory, possession of the United States, or the District of Columbia, or as otherwise permitted by law.

(b) *Objections to deposition subpoenas.* (1) The witness and any party who has not had an opportunity to oppose a deposition subpoena issued under this section may file a motion with the administrative law judge to quash or modify the subpoena prior to the time

§ 747.28

for compliance specified in the subpoena, but not more than ten days after service of the subpoena.

(2) A statement of the basis for the motion to quash or modify a subpoena issued under this section must accompany the motion. The motion must be served on all parties.

(c) *Procedure upon deposition.* (1) Each witness testifying pursuant to a deposition subpoena must be duly sworn, and each party shall have the right to examine the witness. Objections to questions or documents must be in short form, stating the grounds for the objection. Failure to object to questions or documents is not deemed a waiver except where the ground for the objection might have been avoided if the objection had been timely presented. All questions, answers, and objections must be recorded.

(2) Any party may move before the administrative law judge for an order compelling the witness to answer any questions the witness has refused to answer or submit any evidence the witness has refused to submit during the deposition.

(3) The deposition must be subscribed by the witness, unless the parties and the witness, by stipulation, have waived the signing, or the witness is ill, cannot be found, or has refused to sign. If the deposition is not subscribed by the witness, the court reporter taking the deposition shall certify that the transcript is a true and complete transcript of the deposition.

(d) *Enforcing subpoenas.* If a subpoenaed person fails to comply with any order of the administrative law judge which directs compliance with all or any portion of a deposition subpoena under paragraph (b) or (c)(3) of this section, the subpoenaing party or other aggrieved party may, to the extent authorized by applicable law, apply to an appropriate United States district court for an order requiring compliance with the portions of the subpoena that the administrative law judge has ordered enforced. A party's right to seek court enforcement of a deposition subpoena in no way limits the sanctions that may be imposed by the administrative law judge on a party who fails to comply with, or procures a failure to comply with, a subpoena issued under this section.

§ 747.28 **Interlocutory review.**

(a) *General rule.* The NCUA Board may review a ruling of the administrative law judge prior to the certification of the record to the NCUA Board only in accordance with the procedures set forth in this section and § 747.23.

(b) *Scope of review.* The NCUA Board may exercise interlocutory review of a ruling of the administrative law judge if the NCUA Board finds that:

(1) The ruling involves a controlling question of law or policy as to which substantial grounds exist for a difference of opinion;

(2) Immediate review of the ruling may materially advance the ultimate termination of the proceeding;

(3) Subsequent modification of the ruling at the conclusion of the proceeding would be an inadequate remedy; or

(4) Subsequent modification of the ruling would cause unusual delay or expense.

(c) *Procedure.* Any request for interlocutory review shall be filed by a party with the administrative law judge within ten days of his or her ruling and shall otherwise comply with § 747.23. Any party may file a response to a request for interlocutory review in accordance with § 747.23(d). Upon the expiration of the time for filing all responses, the administrative law judge shall refer the matter to the NCUA Board for final disposition.

(d) *Suspension of proceeding.* Neither a request for interlocutory review nor any disposition of such a request by the NCUA Board under this section suspends or stays the proceeding unless otherwise ordered by the administrative law judge or the NCUA Board.

§ 747.29 **Summary disposition.**

(a) *In general.* The administrative law judge shall recommend that the NCUA Board issue a final order granting a motion for summary disposition if the undisputed pleaded facts, admissions, affidavits, stipulations, documentary evidence, matters as to which official notice may be taken, and any other evidentiary materials properly submitted in connection with a motion for summary disposition show that:

(1) There is no genuine issue as to any material fact; and

(2) The moving part is entitled to a decision in its favor as a matter of law.

(b) *Filing of motions and responses.* (1) Any party who believes that there is no genuine issue of material fact to be determined and that he or she is entitled to a decision as a matter of law may move at any time for summary disposition in its favor of all or any part of the proceeding. Any party, within 20 days after service of such a motion, or within such time period as allowed by the administrative law judge, may file a response to such motion.

(2) A motion for summary disposition must be accompanied by a statement of the material facts as to which the moving party contends there is no genuine issue. Such motion must be supported by documentary evidence, which may take the form of admissions in pleadings, stipulations, depositions, investigatory depositions, transcripts, affidavits and any other evidentiary materials that the moving party contends support his or her position. The motion must also be accompanied by a brief containing the points and authorities in support of the contention of the moving party. Any party opposing a motion for summary disposition must file a statement setting forth those material facts as to which he or she contends a genuine dispute exists. Such opposition must be supported by evidence of the same type as that submitted with the motion for summary disposition and a brief containing the points and authorities in support of the contention that summary disposition would be inappropriate.

(c) *Hearing on motion.* At the request of any party or on his or her own motion, the administrative law judge may hear oral argument on the motion for summary disposition.

(d) *Decision on motion.* Following receipt of a motion for summary disposition and all responses thereto, the administrative law judge shall determine whether the moving party is entitled to summary disposition. If the administrative law judge determines that summary disposition is warranted, the administrative law judge shall submit a recommended decision to that effect to the NCUA Board. If the administrative law judge finds that no party is entitled to summary disposition, he or she shall make a ruling denying the motion.

§ 747.30 **Partial summary disposition.**

If the administrative law judge determines that a party is entitled to summary disposition as to certain claims only, he or she shall defer submitting a recommended decision as to those claims. A hearing on the remaining issues must be ordered. Those claims for which the administrative law judge has determined that summary disposition is warranted will be addressed in the recommended decision filed at the conclusion of the hearing.

§ 747.31 **Scheduling and prehearing conferences.**

(a) *Scheduling conference.* Within 30 days of service of the notice or order commencing a proceeding or such other time as parties may agree, the administrative law judge shall direct counsel for all parties to meet with him or her in person at a specified time and place prior to the hearing or to confer by telephone for the purpose of scheduling the recourse and conduct of the proceeding. This meeting or telephone conference is called a "scheduling conference." The identification of potential witnesses, the time for and manner of discovery, and the exchange of any prehearing materials including witness lists, statements of issues, stipulations, exhibits and any other materials may also be determined at the scheduling conference.

(b) *Prehearing conferences.* The administrative law judge may, in addition to the scheduling conference, on his or her own motion or at the request of any party, direct counsel for the parties to meet with him or her (in person or by telephone) at a prehearing conference to address any or all of the following:

(1) Simplification and clarification of the issues;

(2) Stipulations, admissions of fact, and the contents, authenticity and admissibility into evidence of documents;

§ 747.32

(3) Matters of which official notice may be taken;
(4) Limitation of the number of witnesses;
(5) Summary disposition of any or all issues;
(6) Resolution of discovery issues or disputes;
(7) Amendments to pleadings; and
(8) Such other matters as may aid in the orderly disposition of the proceeding.

(c) *Transcript.* The administrative law judge, in his or her discretion, may require that a scheduling or prehearing conference be recorded by a court reporter. A transcript of the conference and any materials filed, including orders, becomes part of the record of the proceeding. A party may obtain a copy of the transcript at its expense.

(d) *Scheduling or prehearing orders.* At or within a reasonable time following the conclusion of the scheduling conference or any prehearing conference, the administrative law judge shall serve on each party an order setting forth any agreements reached and any procedural determinations made.

[56 FR 37767, Aug. 8, 1991, as amended at 75 FR 34622, June 18, 2010]

§ 747.32 Prehearing submissions.

(a) Within the time set by the administrative law judge, but in no case later than 14 days before the start of the hearing, each party shall serve on every other party, his or her:
(1) Prehearing statement;
(2) Final list of witnesses to be called to testify at the hearing, including name and address of each witness and a short summary of the expected testimony of each witness;
(3) List of the exhibits to be introduced at the hearing along with a copy of each exhibit; and
(4) Stipulations of fact, if any.

(b) *Effect of failure to comply.* No witness may testify and no exhibits may be introduced at the hearing if such witness or exhibit is not listed in the prehearing submissions pursuant to paragraph (a) of this section, except for good cause shown.

§ 747.33 Public hearings.

(a) *General rule.* All hearings shall be open to the public, unless the NCUA Board, in its discretion, determines that holding an open hearing would be contrary to the public interest. Within 20 days of service of the notice, any respondent may file with the NCUA Board a request for a private hearing, and any party may file a reply to such a request. A party must serve on the administrative law judge a copy of any request or reply the party files with the NCUA Board. The form of, and procedure for, these requests and replies are governed by § 747.23. A party's failure to file a request or a reply constitutes a waiver of any objections regarding whether the hearing will be public or private.

(b) *Filing document under seal.* Enforcement Counsel, in his or her discretion, may file any document or part of a document under seal if disclosure of the document would be contrary to the public interest. The administrative law judge shall take all appropriate steps to preserve the confidentiality of such documents or parts thereof, including closing portions of the hearing to the public.

[56 FR 37767, Aug. 8, 1991; 57 FR 523, Jan. 7, 1992, as amended at 61 FR 28027, June 4, 1996]

§ 747.34 Hearing subpoenas.

(a) *Issuance.* (1) Upon application of a party showing general relevance and reasonableness of scope of the testimony or other evidence sought, the administrative law judge may issue a subpoena or a subpoena *duces tecum* requiring the attendance of a witness at the hearing or the production of documentary or physical evidence at the hearing. The application for a hearing subpoena must also contain a proposed subpoena specifying the attendance of a witness or the production of evidence from any state, territory, or possession of the United States, the District of Columbia, or as otherwise provided by law at any designated place where the hearing is being conducted. The party making the application shall serve a copy of the application and the proposed subpoena on every other party.

(2) A party may apply for a hearing subpoena at any time before the commencement of a hearing. During a hearing, a party may make an application for a subpoena orally on the

record before the administrative law judge.

(3) The administrative law judge shall promptly issue any hearing subpoena requested pursuant to this section. If the administrative law judge determines that the application does not set forth a valid basis for the issuance of the subpoena, or that any of its terms are unreasonable, oppressive, excessive in scope, or unduly burdensome, he or she may refuse to issue the subpoena or may issue it in a modified form upon any conditions consistent with this subpart. Upon issuance by the administrative law judge, the party making the application shall serve the subpoena on the person named in the subpoena and on each party.

(b) *Motion to quash or modify.* (1) Any person to whom a hearing subpoena is directed or any party may file a motion to quash or modify the subpoena, accompanied by a statement of the basis for quashing or modifying the subpoena. The movant must serve the motion on each party and on the person named in the subpoena. Any party may respond to the motion within ten days of service of the motion.

(2) Any motion to quash or modify a hearing subpoena must be filed prior to the time specified in the subpoena for compliance, but not more than ten days after the date of service of the subpoena upon the movant.

(c) *Enforcing subpoenas.* If a subpoenaed person fails to comply with any subpoena issued pursuant to this section or any order of the administrative law judge which directs compliance with all or any portion of a document subpoena, the subpoenaing party or any other aggrieved party may seek enforcement of the subpoena pursuant to § 747.26(c).

[56 FR 37767, Aug. 8, 1991, as amended at 61 FR 28027, June 4, 1996]

§ 747.35 Conduct of hearings.

(a) *General rules.* (1) Hearings shall be conducted so as to provide a fair and expeditious presentation of the relevant disputed issues. Each party has the right to present its case or defense by oral and documentary evidence and to conduct such cross examination as may be required for full disclosure of the facts.

(2) *Order of hearing.* Enforcement Counsel shall present its case-in-chief first, unless otherwise ordered by the administrative law judge, or unless otherwise expressly specified by law or regulation. Enforcement Counsel shall be the first party to present an opening statement and a closing statement, and may make a rebuttal statement after the respondent's closing statement. If there are multiple respondents, respondents may agree among themselves as to their order of presentation of their cases, but if they do not agree the administrative law judge shall fix the order.

(3) *Examination of witnesses.* Only one counsel for each party may conduct an examination of a witness, except that in the case of extensive direct examination, the administrative law judge may permit more than one counsel for the party presenting the witness to conduct the examination. A party may have one counsel conduct the direct examination and another counsel conduct re-direct examination of a witness, or may have one counsel conduct the cross examination of a witness and another counsel conduct the re-cross examination of a witness.

(4) *Stipulations.* Unless the administrative law judge directs otherwise, all stipulations of fact and law previously agreed upon by the parties, and all documents, the admissibility of which have been previously stipulated, will be admitted into evidence upon commencement of the hearing.

(b) *Transcript.* The hearing must be recorded and transcribed. The reporter will make the transcript available to any party upon payment by that party to the reporter of the cost of the transcript. The administrative law judge may order the record corrected, either upon motion to correct, upon stipulation of the parties, or following notice to the parties upon the administrative law judge's own motion.

[56 FR 37767, Aug. 8, 1991, as amended at 61 FR 28027, June 4, 1996]

§ 747.36 Evidence.

(a) *Admissibility.* (1) Except as is otherwise set forth in this section, relevant, material, and reliable evidence

§ 747.37

that is not unduly repetitive is admissible to the fullest extent authorized by the Administrative Procedure Act and other applicable law.

(2) Evidence that would be admissible under the Federal Rules of Evidence is admissible in a proceeding conducted pursuant to this subpart.

(3) Evidence that would be inadmissible under the Federal Rules of Evidence may not be deemed or ruled to be inadmissible in a proceeding conducted pursuant to this subpart if such evidence is relevant, material, reliable and not unduly repetitive.

(b) *Official notice.* (1) Official notice may be taken of any material fact which may be judicially noticed by a United States district court and any material information in the official public records of any Federal or state government agency.

(2) All matters officially noticed by the administrative law judge or NCUA Board shall appear on the record.

(3) If official notice is requested or taken of any material fact, the parties, upon timely request, shall be afforded an opportunity to object.

(c) *Documents.* (1) A duplicate copy of a document is admissible to the same extent as the original, unless a genuine issue is raised as to whether the copy is in some material respect not a true and legible copy of the original.

(2) Subject to the requirements of paragraph (a) of this section, any document, including a report of examination, supervisory activity, inspection or visitation, prepared by an appropriate Federal financial institution regulatory agency or by a state regulatory agency, is admissible either with or without a sponsoring witness.

(3) Witnesses may use existing or newly created charts, exhibits, calendars, calculations, outlines or other graphic material to summarize, illustrate, or simplify the presentation of testimony. Such materials may, subject to the administrative law judge's discretion, be used with or without being admitted into evidence.

(d) *Objections.* (1) Objections to the admissibility of evidence must be timely made and rulings on all objections must appear on the record.

(2) When an objection to a question or line of questioning propounded to a witness is sustained, the examining counsel may make a specific proffer on the record of what he or she expected to prove by the expected testimony of the witness, either by representation of counsel or by direct interrogation of the witness.

(3) The administrative law judge shall retain rejected exhibits, adequately marked for identification, for the record, and transmit such exhibits to the NCUA Board.

(4) Failure to object to admission of evidence or to any ruling constitutes a waiver of the objection.

(e) *Stipulations.* The parties may stipulate as to any relevant matters of fact or the authentication of any relevant documents. Such stipulations must be received in evidence at a hearing, and are binding on the parties with respect to the matters therein stipulated.

(f) *Depositions of unavailable witnesses.* (1) If a witness is unavailable to testify at a hearing, and that witness has testified in a deposition to which all parties in a proceeding had notice and an opportunity to participate, a party may offer as evidence all or any part of the transcript of the deposition, including deposition exhibits, if any.

(2) Such deposition transcript is admissible to the same extent that testimony would have been admissible had that person testified at the hearing, provided that if a witness refused to answer proper questions during the depositions, the administrative law judge may, on that basis, limit the admissibility of the deposition in any manner that justice requires.

(3) Only those portions of a deposition received in evidence at the hearing constitute a part of the record.

§ 747.37 Post-hearing filings.

(a) *Proposed findings and conclusions and supporting briefs.* (1) Using the same method of service for each party, the administrative law judge shall serve notice upon each party that the certified transcript, together with all hearing exhibits and exhibits introduced but not admitted into evidence at the hearing, has been filed. Any party may file with the administrative law judge proposed findings of fact, proposed conclusions of law, and a proposed order within 30 days following

National Credit Union Administration § 747.39

service of this notice by the administrative law judge or within such longer period as may be ordered by the administrative law judge.

(2) Proposed findings and conclusions must be supported by citation to any relevant portions of the record. A posthearing brief may be filed in support of proposed findings and conclusions, either as part of the same document or in a separate document. Any party who fails to file timely with the administrative law judge any proposed finding or conclusion is deemed to have waived the right to raise in any subsequent filing or submission any issue not addressed in such party's proposed finding or conclusion.

(b) *Reply briefs.* Reply briefs may be filed within 15 days after the date on which the parties' proposed findings, conclusions, and order are due. Reply briefs must be strictly limited to responding to new matters, issues, or arguments raised in another party's papers. A party who has not filed proposed findings of fact and conclusions of law or a post-hearing brief may not file a reply brief.

(c) *Simultaneous filing required.* The administrative law judge shall not order the filing by any party of any brief or reply brief in advance of the other party's filing of its brief.

[56 FR 37767, Aug. 8, 1991, as amended at 61 FR 28027, June 4, 1996]

§ 747.38 Recommended decision and filing of record.

(a) *Filing of recommended decision and record.* Within 45 days after expiration of the time allowed for filing reply briefs under § 747.37(b), the administrative law judge shall file with and certify to the NCUA Board, for decision, the record of the proceeding. The record must include the administrative law judge's recommended decision, recommended findings of fact, recommended conclusions of law, and proposed order; all prehearing and hearing transcripts, exhibits, and rulings; and the motions, briefs, memoranda, and other supporting papers filed in connection with the hearing. The administrative law judge shall serve upon each party the recommended decision, findings, conclusions, and proposed order.

(b) *Filing of index.* At the same time the administrative law judge files with and certifies to the NCUA Board for final determination the record of the proceeding, the administrative law judge shall furnish to the NCUA Board a certified index of the entire record of the proceeding. The certified index shall include, at a minimum, an entry for each paper, document or motion filed with the administrative law judge in the proceeding, the date of the filing, and the identity of the filer. The certified index shall also include an exhibit index containing, at a minimum, an entry consisting of exhibit number and title or description for: Each exhibit introduced and admitted into evidence at the hearing; each exhibit introduced but not admitted into evidence at the hearing; each exhibit introduced and admitted into evidence after the completion of the hearing; and each exhibit introduced but not admitted into evidence after the completion of the hearing.

[61 FR 28027, June 4, 1996]

§ 747.39 Exceptions to recommended decision.

(a) *Filing exceptions.* Within 30 days after service of the recommended decision, findings, conclusions, and proposed order under § 747.38, a party may file with the NCUA Board written exceptions to the administrative law judge's recommended decision, findings, conclusions or proposed order, to the admission or exclusion of evidence, or to the failure of the administrative law judge to make a ruling proposed by a party. A supporting brief may be filed at the time the exceptions are filed, either as part of the same document or in a separate document.

(b) *Effect of failure to file or raise exceptions.* (1) Failure of a party to file exceptions to those matters specified in paragraph (a) of this section within the time prescribed is deemed a waiver of objection thereto.

(2) No exception need be considered by the NCUA Board if the party taking exception had an opportunity to raise the same objection, issue, or argument before the administrative law judge and failed to do so.

(c) *Contents.* (1) All exceptions and briefs in support of such exceptions

§ 747.40

must be confined to the particular matters in, or omissions from, the administrative law judge's recommendations to which that party takes exception.

(2) All exceptions and briefs in support of exceptions must set forth page or paragraph references to the specific parts of the administrative law judge's recommendations to which exception is taken, the page or paragraph references to those portions of the record relied upon to support each exception, and the legal authority relied upon to support each exception.

[56 FR 37767, Aug. 8, 1991, as amended at 75 FR 34622, June 18, 2010]

§ 747.40 Review by the NCUA Board.

(a) *Notice of submission to NCUA Board.* When the NCUA Board determines that the record in the proceeding is complete, the NCUA Board shall serve notice upon the parties that the proceeding has been submitted to the NCUA Board for final decision.

(b) *Oral argument before NCUA Board.* Upon the initiative of the NCUA Board or on the written request of any party filed with the NCUA Board within the time for filing exceptions, the NCUA Board may order and hear oral argument on the recommended findings, conclusions, decision, and order of the administrative law judge. A written request by a party must show good cause for oral argument and state reasons why arguments cannot be presented adequately in writing. A denial of a request for oral argument may be set forth in the NCUA Board's final decision. Oral argument before the NCUA Board must be on the record.

(c) *Final Decision of NCUA Board.* (1) Decisional employees may advise and assist the NCUA Board in the consideration and disposition of the case. The final decision of the NCUA Board will be based upon review of the entire record of the proceeding, except that the NCUA Board may limit the issues to be reviewed to those findings and conclusions to which opposing arguments or exceptions have been filed by the parties.

(2) The NCUA Board shall render a final decision within 90 days after notification of the parties that the case has been submitted for final decision, or 90 days after oral argument, whichever is later, unless the NCUA Board orders that the action or any aspect thereof be remanded to the administrative law judge for further proceedings. Copies of the final decision and order of the NCUA Board shall be served upon each party to the proceeding, upon other persons required by statute, and, if directed by the NCUA Board or required by statute, upon any appropriate state or Federal supervisory authority.

[56 FR 37767, Aug. 8, 1991, as amended at 75 FR 34622, June 18, 2010]

§ 747.41 Stays pending judicial review.

The commencement of proceedings for judicial review of a final decision and order of the NCUA Board may not, unless specifically ordered by the NCUA Board or a reviewing court, operate as a stay of any order issued by the NCUA Board. The NCUA Board may, in its discretion, and on such terms as it finds just, stay the effectiveness of all or any part of its order pending a final decision on a petition for review of that order.

Subpart B—Local Rules of Practice and Procedure

§ 747.100 Discovery limitations.

(a) Parties to a proceeding set forth either at § 747.1 of subpart A or in subpart C, E or G of this part may obtain discovery only through the production of documents. No other form of discovery shall be allowed.

(b) In the event that a person producing documents pursuant to a document subpoena is permitted to be deposed, all questioning shall be strictly limited to the identification of documents produced by that person and a reasonable examination to determine whether the subpoenaed person made an adequate search for, and has produced, all subpoenaed documents.

Subpart C—Local Rules and Procedures Applicable to Proceedings for the Involuntary Termination of Insured Status

§ 747.201 Scope.

Under the authority of section 206(b) of the Act (12 U.S.C. 1786(b)), the NCUA

Board may terminate the insured status of an insured credit union upon the grounds set forth therein and enumerated in § 747.202. The procedure for terminating the insured status of an insured credit union as therein prescribed will be followed and hearings required thereunder will be conducted in accordance with the rules and procedures set forth in this subpart and subpart A of this part. To the extent any rule or procedure of subpart A is inconsistent with a rule or procedure prescribed in this subpart C, subpart C shall control.

[56 FR 37767, Aug. 8, 1991; 57 FR 523, Jan. 7, 1992]

§ 747.202 Grounds for termination of insurance.

The NCUA Board may institute proceedings to terminate the insured status of an insured credit union whenever it determines that an insured credit union is:

(a) Engaging or has engaged in unsafe or unsound practices in conducting its business;

(b) In unsafe or unsound condition to continue as an insured credit union; or

(c) Violating or has violated any applicable law, rule, regulation, order, written condition imposed by the NCUA Board in response to any action on any application, notice, or other request by the credit union or institution-affiliated party, or any written agreement entered into with the NCUA Board.

[56 FR 37767, Aug. 8, 1991, as amended at 71 FR 67440, Nov. 22, 2006]

§ 747.203 Notice of charges.

(a) Whenever the NCUA Board determines that grounds for termination of insured status exists, it will, for the purpose of securing correction of errant or illegal conditions, serve a Notice of Charges upon the concerned credit union. This notice will contain a statement describing the unsafe or unsound practices, condition or the relevant violations.

(b) In the case of an insured State-chartered credit union, the NCUA Board shall send a copy of the Notice of Charges to the appropriate State authority, if any, having supervision over the credit union.

[56 FR 37767, Aug. 8, 1991, as amended at 75 FR 34622, June 18, 2010]

§ 747.204 Notice of intention to terminate insured status.

Unless correction of the practices, condition, or violations set forth in the Notice of Charges is made within 120 days after service of such statement, or within a shorter period of not less than 20 days after such service as the NCUA Board may require in any case where it determines that the insurance risk with respect to such credit union could be unduly jeopardized by further delay or as the appropriate State supervisory authority shall require in the case of an insured State-chartered credit union, the Board, if it determines to proceed further, shall give to the credit union not less than 30 days written notice of its intent to terminate the status of the credit union as an insured credit union. The notice shall contain a statement of the facts constituting the alleged unsafe or unsound practices or conditions or violations on which a hearing will be held. Such hearing shall commence not earlier than 30 days nor later than 60 days after the date of service of such notice upon the credit union, unless an earlier or later date is set by the NCUA Board at the request of the credit union.

§ 747.205 Order terminating insured status.

If, upon the record of the hearing held pursuant to § 747.204, the NCUA Board finds that any unsafe or unsound practice or condition or violation specified in the notice has been established and has not been corrected within the time prescribed under § 747.204, the NCUA Board may issue and serve upon the credit union an order terminating its status as an insured credit union on a date subsequent to the date of such finding and subsequent to the expiration of the time specified in the Notice.

§ 747.206 Consent to termination of insured status.

Unless the credit union appears at the hearing designated in the notice of

§ 747.207

hearing by a duly authorized representative, it will be deemed to have consented to the termination of its status as an insured credit union. In the event the credit union fails to so appear at such hearing, the administrative law judge shall forthwith report the matter to the NCUA Board and the NCUA Board may thereupon issue an order terminating the credit union's insured status.

§ 747.207 Notice of termination of insured status.

Prior to the effective date of the termination of the insured status of an insured credit union under section 206(b) of the Act (12 U.S.C. 1786(b)) and at such time as the Board shall specify, the credit union shall mail to each member at his or her last address of record on the books of the credit union, and publish in not less than two issues of a local newspaper of general circulation, notices of the termination of its insured status, and the credit union shall furnish the NCUA Board with proof of publication of such notice. The notice shall be as follows:

NOTICE

(Date)

1. The status of the ____ as an insured credit union under the provisions of the Federal Credit Union Act, will terminate as of the close of business on the ___ day of ___;
2. Any deposits made by you after that date, either new deposits or additions to existing accounts, will not be insured by the National Credit Union Administration;
3. Accounts in the credit union on the ___ day of ___, ___ up to a maximum of $100,000 for each member, will continue to be insured, as provided by the Federal Credit Union Act, for one (1) year after the close of business on the ___ day of ___, ___: *Provided, however,* That any withdrawals after the close of business on the day of ___, ___; will reduce the insurance coverage by the amount of such withdrawals.

(Name of Credit Union)

(Address)

[56 FR 37767, Aug. 8, 1991; 57 FR 523, Jan. 7, 1992, as amended at 75 FR 34622, June 18, 2010]

§ 747.208 Duties after termination.

(a) After the termination of the insured status of any credit union under section 206(b) of the Act (12 U.S.C. 1786(b)), insurance of its member accounts to the extent they were insured on the effective date of such termination, less any amounts thereafter withdrawn which reduce the accounts below the amount covered by insurance on the effective date of such termination, shall continue for a period of one year, but no shares issued by the credit union or deposits made after the date of such termination shall be insured by the NCUA Board.

(b) The credit union shall continue to pay premiums to the NCUA Board during such period and the Board shall have the right to examine the credit union from time to time during the period. The credit union shall, in all other respects, be subject to the duties and obligations of an insured credit union during the one year period. If the credit union is closed for liquidation within this period, the Board shall have the same powers and rights with respect to such credit union as in the case of an insured credit union.

[56 FR 37767, Aug. 8, 1991; 57 FR 523, Jan. 7, 1992]

Subpart D—Local Rules and Procedures Applicable to Suspensions and Prohibitions Where Felony Charged

§ 747.301 Scope.

The rules and procedures set forth in this subpart are applicable to informal proceedings conducted by the NCUA Board, or a Presiding Officer designated by the Board, pursuant to section 206(i) of the Act (12 U.S.C. 1786(i)), to suspend, remove and/or prohibit from office or from further participation any institution-affiliated party of an insured credit union who:

(a) Is charged in a state, Federal or territorial information or indictment or complaint with committing or participating in a crime involving dishonesty or breach of trust, which crime is punishable by imprisonment for a term exceeding one year under state or Federal law; or

(b) Enters a pretrial diversion or other similar program as result of being charged in such information or indictment or complaint with participating or committing such crime; or

(c) Is convicted of such crime.

National Credit Union Administration § 747.302

Subpart A of this part does not apply to proceedings under this subpart.

[56 FR 37767, Aug. 8, 1991; 57 FR 523, Jan. 7, 1992]

§ 747.302 Rules of practice; remainder of board of directors.

Except as otherwise specifically provided in this subpart, the following provisions shall apply to proceedings conducted under this subpart:

(a)(1) *Power of attorney and notice of appearance.* Any person who is a member in good standing of the bar of the highest court of any State, possession, territory, Commonwealth, or the District of Columbia may represent others before the NCUA Board or Presiding Officer designated by the NCUA Board upon filing with the NCUA Board a written declaration that he or she is currently qualified as provided by this paragraph, and is authorized to represent the particular party on whose behalf he acts. Any other person desiring to appear before or transact business with the NCUA Board in a representative capacity may be required to file with the NCUA Board a power of attorney showing his or her authority to act in such capacity, and he or she may be required to show to the satisfaction of the NCUA Board that he or she has the requisite qualifications. Attorneys and representatives of parties to proceedings shall file a written notice of appearance with the NCUA Board or with the Presiding Officer designated by the NCUA Board.

(2) *Summary suspension.* Contemptuous conduct by any person at an argument before the NCUA Board or at the hearing before a Presiding Officer shall be grounds for exclusion therefrom and suspension for the duration of the argument or hearing.

(b)(1) *Notice of hearing.* Whenever a hearing within the scope of this subpart is ordered by the NCUA Board, a notice of hearing shall be given by the NCUA Board to the party afforded the hearing and to any appropriate state supervisory authority. The notice shall state the time, place, and nature of the hearing and the legal authority and jurisdiction under which the hearing is to be held, and shall contain a statement of the matters of fact or law constituting the grounds for the hearing. It shall be delivered by personal service, by registered or certified mail to the last known address, or by other appropriate means, not later than 30 nor earlier than 60 days before the hearing.

(2) *Party.* The term "party" means a person or agency named or admitted as a party, or any person or agency who has filed a written request and is entitled as of right to be admitted as a party; but a person or agency may be admitted for a limited purpose.

(c)(1) *Computation of time.* In computing any period of time prescribed or allowed by this subpart, the date of the act, event or default from which the designated period of time begins to run is not to be included. The last day so computed shall be included, unless it is a Saturday, Sunday or legal holiday in the District of Columbia, in which event the period shall run until the end of the next day which is neither a Saturday, Sunday, nor such legal holiday. Intermediate Saturdays, Sundays, and legal holidays shall be included in the computation unless the time within which the act is to be performed is ten days or less in which event Saturdays, Sundays, and legal holidays shall not be included.

(2) *Service by mail.* Whenever any party has the right or is required to do some act or take some proceeding, within a period of time prescribed in this subpart, after the service upon him of any document or other paper of any kind, and such service is made by mail, three days shall be added to the prescribed period from the date when the matter served is deposited in the U.S. mail.

(d) *Nonpublication of submissions.* Unless and until otherwise ordered by the NCUA Board, the notice of hearing, the transcript, written materials submitted during the hearing, the Presiding Officer's recommendation to the NCUA Board and any other papers filed in connection with a hearing under this subpart, shall not be made public, and shall be for the confidential use only of the NCUA Board, the Presiding Officer, the parties and appropriate authorities.

(e) *Remainder of board of directors.* (1) If at any time, because of the suspension of one or more directors pursuant to this subpart, there shall be on the

§ 747.303

board of directors of an insured credit union less than a quorum of directors not so suspended, all powers and functions vested in or exercisable by such board shall vest in and be exercisable by the director or directors on the board not so suspended, until such time as there shall be a quorum on the board of directors.

(2) In the event all of the directors of an insured credit union are suspended pursuant to this subpart, the NCUA Board shall appoint persons to serve temporarily as directors in their place pending the termination of such suspensions, or until such time as those who have been suspended cease to be directors of the credit union and their respective successors have been elected by the members at an annual or special meeting and have taken office.

(3) Directors appointed temporarily by the NCUA Board pursuant to paragraph (e)(2) of this section, shall, within 30 days following their appointment, call a special meeting for the election of new directors, unless during such 30-day period—

(i) The regular annual meeting is convened; or

(ii) The suspensions giving rise to the appointment of temporary directors are terminated.

[56 FR 37767, Aug. 8, 1991, as amended at 75 FR 34622, June 18, 2010]

§ 747.303 Notice of suspension or prohibition.

Whenever an institution-affiliated party of an insured credit union is charged in any state, Federal or territorial information or indictment or complaint with the commission of or participation in a crime involving dishonesty or breach of trust, which crime is punishable by imprisonment for a term exceeding one year under state or Federal law, the NCUA Board may, if continued service or participation by the concerned party may pose a threat to the interests of any credit union's members or may threaten to impair public confidence in any credit union, by written notice served upon such party, suspend him or her from office, or prohibit him or her from further participation in any manner in the affairs of any credit union, or both. A copy of the notice of suspension or prohibition shall also be served upon the credit union of which the subject of the order is, or most recently was, an institution-affiliated party.

[71 FR 67440, Nov. 22, 2006]

§ 747.304 Removal or permanent prohibition.

(a) In the event that a judgment of conviction or an agreement to enter a pretrial diversion or other similar program is entered against the institution-affiliated party, and at such time as the judgment, if any, is not subject to further appellate review, the NCUA Board may, if continued service or participation by such party may pose a threat to the interests of any credit union's members or may threaten to impair public confidence in any credit union, issue and serve upon the individual an order removing him or her from office or prohibiting him or her from further participation in any manner in the conduct of the affairs of any credit union except with the consent of the NCUA Board. A copy of such order will also be served upon the credit union of which the subject of the order is, or most recently was, an institution-affiliated party.

(b) The NCUA Board may issue such order with respect to an individual who is an institution-affiliated party at a credit union at the time of the offense without regard to whether such individual is an institution-affiliated party at any credit union at the time the order is considered or issued by the Board or whether the credit union at which the individual was an institution-affiliated party at the time of the offense remains in existence at the time the order is considered or issued by the board.

(c) A finding of not guilty or other disposition of the charge will not preclude the Board from thereafter instituting proceedings, pursuant to the provisions of section 206(g) of the Act (12 U.S.C. 1786(g)) and subpart A of this part, to remove such director, committee member, officer, or other person from office or to prohibit his or her further participation in the affairs of the credit union.

[71 FR 67441, Nov. 22, 2006]

§ 747.305 Effectiveness of suspension or removal until completion of hearing.

Any notice of suspension or prohibition issued under § 747.303 and any order of removal or prohibition issued under § 747.304 will be effective upon service on the concerned party and will remain effective and outstanding until the completion of any hearing or appeal authorized under section 206(i) of the Act (12 U.S.C. 1786(i)) and this subpart, unless such notice of suspension or order of removal is terminated by the NCUA Board.

[56 FR 37767, Aug. 8, 1991; 57 FR 523, Jan. 7, 1992]

§ 747.306 Notice of opportunity for hearing.

(a) Any notice of suspension or prohibition issued pursuant to § 747.303, and any order of removal or prohibition issued pursuant to § 747.304, shall be accompanied by a further notice to the concerned individual that he or she may, within 30 days of service of such notice, request in writing an informal hearing at which he or she may present evidence and argument that his or her continued service to or participation in the conduct of the affairs of the credit union does not, or is not likely to, pose a threat to the interests of the credit union's members or threaten to impair confidence in the credit union. Any notice of the opportunity for such a hearing shall be accompanied by a description of the hearing procedure and the criteria to be considered.

(b) A request for a hearing filed pursuant to paragraph (a) of this section shall state with state with particularity the relief desired, the grounds thereof, and shall include, when available, supporting evidence. The request and supporting evidence shall be filed in writing with the Secretary of the Board, National Credit Union Administration, 1775 Duke Street, Alexandria, VA 22314–3428.

[56 FR 37767, Aug. 8, 1991; 57 FR 523, Jan. 7, 1992, as amended at 59 FR 36041, July 15, 1994; 75 FR 34622, June 18, 2010]

§ 747.307 Hearing.

(a) Upon receipt of a request for a hearing which complies with § 747.306, the NCUA Board will order an informal hearing to commence within the following 30 days in the Washington, DC metropolitan area or at such other place as the NCUA Board designates before a Presiding Officer designated by the NCUA Board to conduct the hearing. At the request of the concerned party, the NCUA Board may order the hearing to commence at a time more than 30 days after the receipt of the request for such hearing.

(b) The notice of hearing shall be served by the NCUA Board upon the party or parties afforded the hearing and shall set forth the time and place of the hearing and the name and address of the Presiding Officer.

(c) The subject individual may appear at the hearing personally, through counsel, or personally with counsel. The individual shall have the right to introduce relevant and material written materials (or, at the discretion of the NCUA Board, oral testimony), and to present an oral argument before the Presiding Officer. A member of the enforcement staff of the Office of General Counsel of the NCUA may attend the hearing and may participate as a party. Neither the formal rules of evidence nor the adjudicative procedures of the Administrative Procedure Act (5 U.S.C. 554–557), nor subpart A of this part shall apply to the hearing. The proceedings shall be recorded and a transcript furnished to the individual upon request and after the payment of the cost thereof. The NCUA Board shall have the discretion to permit the presentation of witnesses, within specified time limits, so long as a list of such witnesses is furnished to the Presiding Officer at least ten days prior to the hearing. Witnesses shall not be sworn, unless specifically requested by either party or directed by the Presiding Officer. The Presiding Officer may examine any witnesses and each party shall have the opportunity to cross-examine any witness presented by an opposing party. Upon the request of either the subject individual or the representative of the Office of General Counsel, the record shall remain open for a period of five business days following the hearing, during which time the parties may make any additional submissions

§ 747.308

to the record. Thereafter, the record shall be closed.

(d) In the course of or in connection with any proceeding under this subpart, the NCUA Board and the Presiding Officer will have the power to administer oaths and affirmations, to take or cause depositions to be taken, and to issue, revoke, quash, or modify subpoenas and subpoenas duces tecum. If the NCUA Board permits the presentation of witnesses, the NCUA Board or the Presiding Officer may require the attendance of witnesses from any place in any state or in any territory or other place subject to the jurisdiction of the United States at any designated place where such proceeding is being conducted. Witnesses subpoenaed shall be paid the same fees and mileage as are paid witnesses in the District Courts of the United States. The NCUA Board or the Presiding Officer may require the production of documents from any place in any such state, territory, or other place.

(e) The Presiding Officer will make his or her recommendations to the Board, where possible, within ten business days following the close of the record.

[56 FR 37767, Aug. 8, 1991, as amended at 59 FR 36042, July 15, 1994]

§ 747.308 Waiver of hearing; failure to request hearing or review based on written submissions; failure to appear.

(a) The subject individual may, in writing, waive an oral hearing and instead elect to have the matter determined by the NCUA Board on the basis of written submissions alone.

(b) Should any concerned party fail to request in writing an oral hearing or consideration based on written submissions alone within 30 days of service of the notice described in § 747.306, he or she will be deemed to have consented to the NCUA Board's action.

(c) Unless the concerned party appears at the hearing personally or by duly appointed representative, he or she will be deemed to have consented to the NCUA Board's action.

§ 747.309 Decision of the NCUA Board.

Within 60 days following the hearing, or receipt of the subject individual's written submissions where hearing has been waived pursuant to § 747.308, the NCUA Board shall notify the institution-affiliated party whether the suspension or prohibition will be continued, terminated, or otherwise modified, or whether the order of removal or prohibition will be rescinded or otherwise modified. Such notification shall contain a statement of the basis for the decision of the NCUA Board, if that decision is adverse to the respondent party. In the case of a decision favorable to the respondent on the subject of a prior order of removal or prohibition, the NCUA Board shall take prompt action to rescind or otherwise modify the order of removal or prohibition.

§ 747.310 Reconsideration by the NCUA Board.

(a) The subject individual shall have ten business days following receipt of the decision of the NCUA Board in which to petition the NCUA Board for initial reconsideration.

(b) The subject individual also shall be entitled to petition the NCUA Board for reconsideration of its decision any time after the expiration of a 12-month period from the date of the NCUA Board's decision, but no petition for reconsideration may be made within 12 months of a previous petition.

(c) Any petition shall state with particularity the basis for reconsideration, the relief sought, and any exceptions the individual has to the NCUA Board's findings. An individual's petition may be accompanied by a memorandum of points and authorities in support of his or her petition and any supporting documentation the individual may wish to have considered.

(d) No hearing need be granted on such petition for reconsideration. Promptly following receipt of the petition, the Board shall render its decision.

§ 747.311 Relevant considerations.

In deciding the question of suspension, prohibition, or removal under this subpart, the NCUA Board will consider the following:

(a) Whether the alleged offense is a crime which is punishable by imprisonment for a term exceeding one year under state or Federal law, and which involves dishonesty or breach of trust;

(b) Whether the continued presence of the subject individual in his or her position may pose a threat to the interests of the credit union's members because of the nature and extent of the individual's participation in the affairs of the insured credit union and/or the nature of the offense with the commission of or participation in which the individual has been charged;

(c) Whether there is cause to believe that there may be an erosion of public confidence in the integrity, safety, or soundness of a particular credit union (either generally or in the particular locality in which the credit union is situated) if the subject individual is permitted to remain in his or her position in an insured credit union;

(d) Whether the individual is covered by the credit union's fidelity bond and, if so, whether the bond is likely to be revoked, or whether coverage under the bond will be affected adversely as a result of the information, indictment, complaint, judgment of conviction or entry into a pretrial diversion or other similar program; and

(e) The NCUA Board may consider any other factors which, in the specific case, appear relevant to the decision to continue in effect, rescind, terminate, or modify a suspension, prohibition, or removal order, except that it shall not consider the ultimate question of the guilt or innocence of the subject individual with regard to the crime with which he or she has been charged.

Subpart E—Local Rules and Procedures Applicable to Proceedings Relating to the Suspension or Revocation of Charters and to Involuntary Liquidations Under Title I

§ 747.401 Scope.

The rules and procedures set forth in this subpart and subpart A of this part are applicable to proceedings by the NCUA Board pursuant to section 120(b)(1) of the Act (12 U.S.C. 1766(b)(1)) to suspend or revoke the charter of a solvent Federal credit union, and to place a solvent Federal credit union into involuntary liquidation. To the extent a rule or procedure set forth in subpart A of this part is inconsistent with a rule or procedure set forth in this subpart E, subpart E shall control.

[56 FR 37767, Aug. 8, 1991; 57 FR 523, Jan. 7, 1992]

§ 747.402 Grounds for suspension or revocation of charter and for involuntary liquidation.

(a) *Grounds in general.* The NCUA Board may suspend or revoke the charter of any Federal credit union, and place such credit union into involuntary liquidation and appoint a liquidating agent therefor, upon its finding that the credit union has violated any provision of its charter or bylaws or of the FCUA or regulations issued thereunder.

(b) *Immediate suspension.* In any case where the Board determines that the grounds set forth in paragraph (a) of this section exist and that immediate action is necessary in order to prevent further dissipation or credit union assets or earnings, or further weakening of the credit union's condition, or to otherwise protect the interest of the credit union's insured members or the National Credit Union Share Insurance Fund, it may order without prior notice the immediate suspension of the charter of such credit union, and if the circumstances so warrant, may take possession of all books, records, assets, and property of every description of such credit union.

§ 747.403 Notice of intent to suspend or revoke charter; notice of suspension.

(a) Upon its determination that one or more of the grounds listed in § 747.402(a) exists, or that because of conditions described in § 747.402(b) immediate suspension of charter is necessary, the NCUA Board shall cause to be served upon that credit union a notice of intent to suspend or revoke charter and of intent to place into involuntary liquidation, or a notice of suspension. Such notice shall contain a statement of the facts which constitute the grounds for this action, a recitation of the options available to the credit union under paragraph (b) of this

§ 747.404

section, and an explanation of the results that will occur if the credit union fails to exercise said options.

(b) Not later than 40 days after the receipt of the notice provided for in paragraph (a) of this section, the Federal credit union may file with the NCUA Board a statement in writing setting forth the grounds and reasons why its charter should not be suspended or revoked and why it should not be placed into involuntary liquidation; or in lieu of a written statement, request an oral hearing which shall be conducted in accordance with the procedures set forth in this subpart. This statement or request shall be accompanied by a certified copy of a resolution of the board of directors of the Federal credit union concerned authorizing such statement or request, such certification to be made by the president and secretary of the board of directors.

(c) If the Federal credit union concerned does not exercise either alternative available in paragraph (b) of this section within the time required, it shall be deemed to have admitted the facts alleged in the notice and may be deemed to have consented to the relief sought.

§ 747.404 Notice of hearing.

(a) Upon receipt of a request for hearing which complies with § 747.403(b), the NCUA Board shall transmit the request to the Office of Financial Institution Adjudication ("OFIA"). Such hearing shall commence no earlier than 30 days nor later than 60 days after the date the OFIA receives the request for, a hearing, unless an earlier or later date is requested by the Federal credit union concerned and is granted by the NCUA Board in its discretion.

(b) Except as provided in § 747.405(b), the procedures of the Administrative Procedure Act (5 U.S.C. 554–557) and subpart A of this part will apply to the hearing.

(c) Unless the Federal credit union shall appear at such hearing by a duly authorized representative it shall be deemed to have consented to the suspension or revocation of its charter and to the placing of said credit union into involuntary liquidation.

§ 747.405 Issuance of order.

(a) In the event of such consent as referred to in § 747.403(c) or § 747.404(c), or if upon the record made at any such hearing as referred to in § 747.403(b), the NCUA Board finds that the charter of the Federal credit union concerned should be suspended or revoked and the credit union closed and placed into involuntary liquidation, it shall cause to be served on such credit union an order directing the suspension or revocation of its charter and directing that it be closed and placed into involuntary liquidation. Such order shall contain a statement of the findings upon which the order is based. Additionally, the NCUA Board shall appoint a liquidating agent or agents.

(b) The NCUA Board shall render its decision and cause such order to be served not later than 45 days after receipt of consent, or written submissions as the case may be, or in the case of a formal hearing after service or the notice of submission referred to in § 747.40(a).

(c) Upon the receipt of a copy of the order which provides that the Federal credit union concerned be placed into involuntary liquidation, the officers and directors of that Federal credit union shall immediately deliver to the agent for the liquidating agent possession and control of all books, records, assets, and property of every description of the Federal credit union, and the agent for the liquidating agent shall proceed to convert said assets to cash, collect all debts due to said Federal credit union and to wind up its affairs in accordance with the provisions of the Act.

[56 FR 37767, Aug. 8, 1991; 57 FR 523, Jan. 7, 1992]

§ 747.406 Cancellation of charter.

Upon the completion of the liquidation and certification by the agent for the liquidating agent that the distribution of the assets of the Federal credit union has been completed, the NCUA

Subpart F—Local Rules and Procedures Applicable to Proceedings Relating to the Termination of Membership in the Central Liquidity Facility [Reserved]

Subpart G—Local Rules and Procedures Applicable to Recovery of Attorneys Fees and Other Expenses Under the Equal Access to Justice Act in NCUA Board Adjudications

§ 747.601 Purpose and scope.

This subpart contains the regulations of the NCUA implementing the Equal Access to Justice Act (5 U.S.C. 504), as amended ("EAJA"). The EAJA provides for the award of attorneys fees and other expenses to eligible individuals and entities who are parties to proceedings conducted under this part. An eligible party may receive an award when it prevails over NCUA in a proceeding, or in a significant and discrete substantive portion of the proceeding, unless the position of the NCUA was substantially justified or special circumstances make an award unjust. The rules in this subpart describe the parties eligible for fee awards, explain how to apply for awards and the procedures and standards that NCUA will use to make them. To the extent a rule or procedure set forth in subpart A of this part is inconsistent with a rule or procedure set forth in this subpart G, subpart G will control.

§ 747.602 Eligibility of applicants.

(a) To be eligible for an award of attorneys fees and expenses, an applicant must be a prevailing party in the proceeding for which it seeks an award and must be:

(1) An individual with a net worth of not more than $2 million;

(2) The sole owner of an unincorporated business who has a net worth of not more than $7 million, including both personal and business interests and not more than 500 employees at the time the proceeding was commenced (an applicant who owns an unincorporated business will be considered as an "individual" rather than a "sole owner of an unincorporated business" if the issues on which the applicant prevails are related primarily to personal interests rather than to business interests);

(3) A charitable or other tax-exempt organization described in section 501(c)(3) of the Internal Revenue Code (26 U.S.C. 501(c)(3)) with not more than 500 employees;

(4) A cooperative association as defined in section 15(a) of the Agricultural Marketing Act (12 U.S.C. 1141j(a)) with not more than 500 employees; or

(5) Any other partnership, corporation, association, or public or private organization with a net worth of not more than $7 million and not more than 500 employees.

(b) For the purpose of determining eligibility, the net worth of an applicant and the number of employees of an applicant shall be determined as of the date the proceeding was initiated.

(c) The applicant's net worth includes the value of any assets disposed of for the purpose of meeting an eligibility standard and excludes any obligations incurred for this purpose. Transfers of assets or obligations incurred for less than reasonably equivalent value will be presumed to have been made for this purpose.

(d) The employees of an applicant include all persons who regularly perform services for remuneration for the applicant, under the applicant's direction and control; part-time employees shall be included on a proportional basis.

(e) The net worth and number of employees of the applicant and all of its affiliates shall be aggregated to determine eligibility. Any individual, corporation or other entity that directly or indirectly controls or owns a majority of the voting shares or other interest of the applicant, or any corporation or other entity of which the applicant directly or indirectly owns or controls a majority of the voting shares or other interest, will be considered an affiliate for purposes of this subpart, unless the NCUA Board determines that such treatment would be unjust and contrary to the purposes of the EAJA

§ 747.603

in light of the actual relationship between the affiliated entities. In addition, the NCUA Board may determine that financial relationships of the applicant other than those described in this paragraph constitute special circumstances that would make an award unjust.

(f) An applicant that participates in a proceeding primarily on behalf of one or more other persons or entities that would be ineligible is not itself eligible for an award.

[56 FR 37767, Aug. 8, 1991, as amended at 75 FR 34622, June 18, 2010]

§ 747.603 Prevailing party.

An eligible applicant may be a "prevailing party" if the applicant wins an action after a full hearing or trial on the merits, if a settlement of the proceeding was effected on terms favorable to it, or if the proceeding against it has been dismissed. In appropriate situations an applicant may also have prevailed if the outcome of the proceeding has substantially vindicated the applicant's position on the significant substantive matters at issue, even though the applicant has not totally avoided adverse final action.

§ 747.604 Standards for award.

(a) A prevailing party may receive an award for fees and expenses incurred in connection with a proceeding, or in a significant and discrete substantive portion of the proceeding, by or against NCUA unless the position of NCUA during the proceeding was substantially justified. The burden of proving that an award should not be made is on counsel for NCUA. To avoid an award, counsel for NCUA must show that its position was reasonable in law and in fact.

(b) An award will be reduced or denied if the applicant has unduly or unreasonably protracted the proceeding or if special circumstances make the award sought unjust.

(c) Where an applicant has prevailed on one or more discrete substantive issues in a proceeding, even though all the issues were not resolved in its favor, any award shall be based on the fees and expenses incurred in connection with the discrete significant substantive issue or issues on which the applicant's position has been upheld. If such segregation of costs is not practicable, the award may be based on a fair proration of those fees and expenses incurred in the entire proceeding which would be recoverable under this section if proration were not performed.

(d) Whether separate or prorated treatment under the preceding paragraph, including the applicable proration percentage, is appropriate shall be determined on the facts of the particular case. Attention shall be given to the significance and nature of the respective issues and their separability and interrelationship.

§ 747.605 Allowable fees and expenses.

(a) Except as provided by § 747.604(b), awards will be based on rates customarily charged by persons engaged in the business of acting as attorneys, agents and expert witnesses, even if the services were made available without charge or at a reduced rate.

(b) No award under this subpart for the fee of an attorney or agent may exceed $75.00 per hour. No award to compensate an expert witness may exceed the highest rate at which NCUA is permitted to pay expert witnesses. However, an award may also include the reasonable expenses of the attorney, agent or witness as a separate item, if the attorney, agent or witness ordinarily charges clients separately for such expenses.

(c) In determining the reasonableness of the fee sought for an attorney, agent, or expert witness, the NCUA Board shall consider the following:

(1) If the attorney, agent, or expert witness is in private practice, his or her customary fee for like services, or, if he or she is an employee of the applicant, the fully allocated cost of the services;

(2) The prevailing rate for similar services in the community in which the attorney, agent, or expert witness ordinarily performs services;

(3) The time actually spent in the representation of the applicant; and

(4) Such other factors as may bear on the value of the services provided.

(d) The reasonable cost of any study, analysis, report, test, project, or similar matter prepared on behalf of the party may be awarded to the extent

National Credit Union Administration

§ 747.607

that the charge for the service does not exceed the prevailing rate for similar services, and the study or other matter was necessary for preparation of the applicant's case.

[56 FR 37767, Aug. 8, 1991, as amended at 75 FR 34622, June 18, 2010]

§ 747.606 Contents of application.

(a) A prevailing eligible party, as defined in §§ 747.602, 747.603, and 747.604, seeking an award under this section, must file an application for an award of fees and expenses with the Secretary of the NCUA Board. The application shall include the following information:

(1) The identity of the applicant and the proceeding for which an award is sought;

(2) A showing that the applicant has prevailed and an identification of the issues in the proceeding on which the applicant believes that the position of NCUA was not substantially justified;

(3) A statement, with supporting documentation, that the applicant is an eligible party, as defined by § 747.602. If the applicant is an individual, he or she must state that his or her net worth does not exceed $2 million. If the applicant is not an individual, it shall state the number of its employees and that its net worth does not exceed $7 million as of the date the proceeding was initiated. However, an applicant may omit a statement of net worth if:

(i) It attaches a copy of a ruling by the Internal Revenue Service that it qualifies as an organization described in section 501(c)(3) of the Internal Revenue Code (26 U.S.C. 501(c)(3)) or, in the case of a tax-exempt organization not required to obtain a ruling from the Internal Revenue Service on its exempt status, a statement that describes the basis for the applicant's belief that it qualifies under such section; or

(ii) It states that it is a cooperative association as defined in section 15(a) of the Agricultural Marketing Act (12 U.S.C. 1141j(a)).

(4) A Statement of the amount of fees and expenses for which an award is sought; and

(5) Any other matters that the applicant believes may assist or wishes the NCUA Board to consider in determining whether and in what amount an award should be made.

(b) The application shall be signed by the applicant or an authorized officer or attorney of the applicant. It shall also contain or be accompanied by a written verification under oath or under penalty of perjury that the information provided in the application is true and correct.

(c) The application and documentation requirements of this subpart are required by law as a prerequisite to obtaining a benefit under the EAJA and this subpart.

[56 FR 37767, Aug. 8, 1991; 57 FR 523, Jan. 7, 1992, as amended at 75 FR 34622, June 18, 2010]

§ 747.607 Statement of net worth.

(a) Each applicant (other than a qualified tax-exempt organization or cooperative association) must provide a detailed statement showing the net worth of the applicant and any affiliates, as defined in § 747.602(a), when the proceeding was initiated. The exhibit may be in any form convenient to the applicant that provides full disclosure of the applicant's and its affiliates' assets and liabilities and is sufficient to determine whether the applicant is an eligible party. The administrative law judge or the NCUA Board may require additional information from the applicant to determine eligibility. Unless otherwise ordered by the Board or required by law, the statement shall be kept confidential and used by the NCUA Board only in making its determination of an award.

(b) If the applicant or any of its affiliates is a Federal credit union, the portion of the statement of net worth which relates to the Federal credit union shall consist of a copy of the Federal credit union's last Statement of Financial Condition filed before the initiation of the underlying proceeding.

(c) All statements of net worth shall describe any transfers of assets from or obligations incurred by the applicant or any affiliate, occurring in the six-month period prior to the date on which the proceeding was initiated,

903

§ 747.608

which reduced the net worth of the applicant and its affiliates below the applicable net-worth ceiling. If there were none, the applicant shall so state.

[56 FR 37767, Aug. 8, 1991, as amended at 75 FR 34622, June 18, 2010]

§ 747.608 Documentation of fees and expenses.

The application shall be accompanied by full documentation of the fees and expenses, including the cost of any study, analysis, audit, test, project or similar matter, for which an award is sought. A separate itemized statement shall be submitted for each professional firm or individual whose services are covered by the application, showing hours spent in connection with the proceeding by each individual, a description of the specific services performed, the rate at which each fee has been computed, any expenses for which reimbursement is sought, the total amount claimed, and the total amount paid or payable by the applicant or by any other person or entity for the services provided. The administrative law judge or the NCUA Board may require the applicant to provide vouchers, receipts, or other substantiation for any expenses claimed.

§ 747.609 Filing and service of applications.

(a) An application may be filed whenever the applicant has prevailed in the proceeding or in a significant and discrete substantive portion of the proceeding, but in no case later than 30 days after the Board's final disposition of the proceeding.

(b) If review or reconsideration is sought or taken of a decision on which an applicant believes it has prevailed, proceedings for the award of fees shall be stayed pending final disposition of the underlying controversy.

(c) As used in this subpart, final disposition means the issuance of a final order or any other final resolution of a proceeding, such as a settlement or voluntary dismissal.

(d) Any application for an award of fees and expenses shall be filed with the Secretary of the Board, National Credit Union Administration, 1775 Duke Street, Alexandria, VA 22314-3428. Any application for an award and any other pleading or document related to an application, shall be filed and served on all parties to the proceeding in the same manner as other pleadings in the proceeding, except as provided in § 747.607(a) for statements of net worth.

[56 FR 37767, Aug. 8, 1991, as amended at 59 FR 36041, July 15, 1994]

§ 747.610 Answer to application.

(a) Within 30 days after service of an application, counsel for NCUA may file an answer to the application. Unless counsel for NCUA requests and is granted an extension of time for filing or files a statement of intent to negotiate under paragraph (b) of this section, failure to file an answer within the 30-day period will be treated as a consent to the award requested.

(b) If counsel for NCUA and the applicant believe that the issues in the fee application can be settled, they may jointly file a statement of their intent to negotiate a settlement. The filing of this statement shall extend the time for filing an answer for an additional 30 days, and further extensions may be granted by the NCUA Board upon the joint request of counsel for NCUA and the applicant.

(c) The answer shall explain in detail any objections to the award requested and identify the facts relied on in support of counsel's position. If the answer is based on any alleged facts not already in the record of the proceeding, counsel shall include with the answer a request for further proceedings under § 747.613.

(d)(1) The applicant may file a reply if counsel for NCUA has addressed in his or her answer any of the following issues:

(i) That the position of NCUA in the proceeding was substantially justified;

(ii) That the applicant unduly protracted the proceedings; or

(iii) That special circumstances make an award unjust.

(2) The reply shall be filed within 15 days after service of the answer. If the reply is based on any alleged facts not already in the record of the proceeding, the applicant shall include with the reply a request for further proceedings under § 747.613.

§ 747.611 Comments by other parties.

Any party to a proceeding other than the applicant and counsel for NCUA may file comments on an application within 30 days after service of the application or on an answer within 15 days after service of the answer. A commenting party may not participate further in proceedings on the application unless the administrative law judge or the NCUA Board determines that the public interest requires such participation in order to permit full exploration of matters raised in the comments.

[56 FR 37767, Aug. 8, 1991, as amended at 75 FR 34622, June 18, 2010]

§ 747.612 Settlement.

The applicant and counsel for NCUA may agree on a proposed settlement of the award before final action on the application, either in connection with a settlement of the underlying proceeding, or after the underlying proceeding has been concluded, in accordance with NCUA's standard settlement procedure. If a prevailing party and counsel for NCUA agree on a proposed settlement of an award before an application has been filed, the application shall be filed with the proposed settlement.

§ 747.613 Further proceedings.

(a) After the expiration of the time allowed for the filing of all documents necessary for the determination of a recommended fee award, the NCUA Board shall transmit the entire record to the administrative law judge who presided at the underlying proceeding. Ordinarily, the determination of an award will be made on the basis of the written record. However, on request of either the applicant or counsel for NCUA, or on its own initiative, the administrative law judge or the NCUA Board may order further proceedings, such as an informal conference, oral argument, additional written submissions or an evidentiary hearing. Such further proceedings shall be held only when necessary for full and fair resolution of the issues arising from the application, and shall be conducted as promptly as possible.

(b) A request that the administrative law judge or the NCUA Board order further proceedings under this section shall specifically identify the information sought or the disputed issues and shall explain why the additional proceedings are necessary to resolve the issues.

§ 747.614 Recommended decision.

The administrative law judge shall file a recommended decision on the application with the NCUA Board within 60 days after completion of the proceedings on the application. The recommended decision shall include written findings and conclusions on the applicant's eligibility and status as a prevailing party, and an explanation of the reasons for any difference between the amount requested and the amount awarded. The recommended decision shall also include, if at issue, findings on whether NCUA's position was substantially justified, whether the applicant unduly protracted the proceedings, or whether special circumstances make an award unjust. If the applicant has sought an award against more than one agency, the recommended decision shall allocate responsibility for payment of any award made among the agencies, and shall explain the reasons for the allocation made. The administrative law judge shall file with and certify to the NCUA Board the record of the proceeding on the fee application, the recommended decision and proposed order. Promptly upon such filing, the NCUA Board shall serve upon each party to the proceeding a copy of the administrative law judge's recommended decision, findings, conclusions and proposed order. The provisions of this section and § 747.613 shall not apply, however, in any case where the hearing was held before the NCUA Board.

§ 747.615 Decision of the NCUA Board.

Within 15 days after service of the recommended decision, findings, conclusions, and proposed order, the applicant or counsel for NCUA may file with the NCUA Board written exceptions thereto. A supporting brief may also be filed. The NCUA Board shall render its decision within 60 days after the matter is submitted to it. The NCUA Board

§ 747.616 Payment of award.

An applicant seeking payment of an award granted by the NCUA Board shall submit to the NCUA's Office of Chief Financial Officer a copy of the NCUA Board's Final Decision and Order granting the award, accompanied by a statement that it will not seek review of the decision and order in the United States court. All submissions shall be addressed to the Office of the Controller, National Credit Union Administration, 1775 Duke Street, Alexandria, VA 22314-3428. The NCUA will pay the amount awarded within 60 days after receiving the applicant's statement, unless judicial review of the award or of the underlying decision of the adversary adjudication has been sought by the applicant or any other party to the proceeding.

[56 FR 37767, Aug. 8, 1991, as amended at 59 FR 36041, July 15, 1994; June 18, 2010]

Subpart H—Local Rules and Procedures Applicable to Investigations

§ 747.701 Applicability.

The rules in this subpart apply only to informal and formal investigations conducted by the NCUA Board itself or its delegates. They do not apply to adjudicative or rulemaking proceedings or to routine, periodic or special examinations conducted by the NCUA Board's staff.

§ 747.702 Information obtained in investigations.

Information and documents obtained by the Board in the course of any investigation, unless made a matter of public record by the NCUA Board, shall be deemed non-public, but the NCUA Board approves the practice whereby the General Counsel may engage in, and may authorize any person acting on his or her behalf or at his or her direction to engage in, discussions with representatives of domestic or foreign governmental authorities, self-regulatory organizations, and with receivers, trustees, masters and special counsels or special agents appointed by and subject to the supervision of the courts of the United States, concerning information obtained in individual investigations, including investigations conducted pursuant to any order entered by the NCUA Board or its General Counsel pursuant to delegated authority.

§ 747.703 Authority to conduct investigations.

(a) The General Counsel and persons acting on his or her behalf and at his or her direction may conduct such investigations into the affairs of any insured credit union or institution-affiliated parties as deemed appropriate to determine whether such credit union or party has violated, is violating or is about to violate any provision of the Act, the NCUA Board's regulations or other relevant statutes or regulations that may bear on a party's fitness to participate in the affairs of a credit union. The General Counsel and persons acting on his or her behalf may investigate whether any party is unfit to participate in the affairs of a credit union, whether formal enforcement proceedings are warranted, or such other matters as the General Counsel or his or her designee, in his or her discretion, shall deem appropriate. Such investigations may be conducted either informally or formally.

(b) Formal investigations involve the exercise of the NCUA Board's subpoena power and are referred to here as formal investigative proceedings. In formal investigative proceedings, the General Counsel and those to whom he or she delegates authority to act on his or her behalf and at his or her direction have augmented investigatory powers and need not rely on the powers available to them in informal investigations, and they may gather evidence through the issuance of subpoenas compelling the production of documents or testimony as well. In informal investigations evidence may be gathered ordinarily through the use of investigatory procedures or credit union examinations and through voluntary statements and submissions.

(c) The NCUA Board has delegated authority to the General Counsel, or designee thereof, to institute formal investigative proceedings by the entry of an order indicating the purpose of the investigation and the designation of persons to conduct that investigation on his or her behalf and at his or her direction. This delegation also extends to the NCUA Board's role as liquidator and conservator of insured credit unions. The power to issue a subpoena may not be delegated outside the agency. The General Counsel may amend such order as he deems appropriate.

[56 FR 37767, Aug. 8, 1991; 57 FR 523, Jan. 7, 1992]

Subpart I—Local Rules Applicable to Formal Investigative Proceedings

§ 747.801 Applicability.

The rules in this subpart are applicable to a witness who is sworn in a formal investigative proceeding. Formal investigative proceedings may be held before the NCUA Board, before one or more of its members, or before any officer designated by the NCUA Board or its General Counsel, as described in subpart H of this part, and with or without the assistance of such other counsel as the NCUA Board deems appropriate, for the purpose of taking testimony of witnesses, conducting an investigation and receiving other evidence. The term "officer conducting the investigation" shall mean any of the foregoing.

§ 747.802 Non-public formal investigative proceedings.

Unless otherwise ordered by the NCUA Board, all formal investigative proceedings shall be non-public.

§ 747.803 Subpoenas.

(a) *Issuance.* In the course of a formal investigative proceeding the officer conducting the investigation may issue a subpoena directing the party named therein to appear before the officer conducting the investigation at a specified time and place to testify or to produce documentary evidence, or both, relating to any matter under investigation.

(b) *Service.* Service of subpoenas shall be effected in the following manner:

(1) *Service upon a natural party.* Delivery of a copy of a subpoena to a natural person may be effected by—

(i) Handing it to the person;

(ii) Leaving it at his or her office with the person in charge thereof or, if there is no one in charge, by leaving it at a conspicuous place there;

(iii) Leaving it at his or her dwelling place or usual place of abode with some person of suitable age and discretion who is found there; or

(iv) Mailing it by registered or certified mail to him or her at his or her last known address. In the event that personal service as described in this paragraph is impracticable, any other method whereby actual notice is given to the respondent may be employed.

(2) *Service upon other persons.* When the person to be served is not a natural person, delivery of a copy of the subpoena may be effected by—

(i) Handing it to a registered agent for service, or to any officer, director, or agent in charge of any office of such person;

(ii) Mailing it by registered or certified mail to any such representative at his or her last known address; or

(iii) Any other method whereby actual notice is given to any such representative.

(c) *Witness fees and mileage.* Witnesses appearing pursuant to subpoena shall be paid the same fees and mileage that are paid to witnesses in the United States district courts. Any such fees and mileage payments need be paid only upon submission of a properly completed application for reimbursement and in no event need they be paid sooner than 30 days after the appearance of the witness pursuant to subpoena.

(d) *Enforcement.* Whenever it appears to the General Counsel that any person upon whom a subpoena was properly served pursuant to these Rules is refusing to fully comply with the terms of that subpoena, then the General Counsel, in his or her discretion, may apply

§ 747.804 to the courts of the United States for enforcement of such subpoena.

[56 FR 37767, Aug. 8, 1991; 57 FR 523, Jan. 7, 1992; June 18, 2010]

§ 747.804 Oath; false statements.

At the discretion of the officer conducting the investigation, testimony of a witness may be taken under oath and administered by the officer. Any person making false statements under oath during the course of a formal investigative proceeding is subject to the criminal penalties for perjury in 18 U.S.C. 1621. Any person who knowingly and willfully makes false and fraudulent statements, whether under oath or otherwise, or who falsifies, conceals or covers up any material fact, or submits any false, fictitious or fraudulent information in connection with such a proceeding, is subject to the criminal penalties set forth in 18 U.S.C. 1001.

§ 747.805 Self-incrimination; immunity.

(a) *Self-incrimination.* Except as provided in paragraph (b) of this section, a witness testifying or otherwise giving information in a formal investigative proceeding may refuse to answer questions on the basis of his or her right against self-incrimination granted by the Fifth Amendment of the Constitution of the United States.

(b) *Immunity.* (1) No officer conducting any formal investigative proceeding (or any other informal investigation or examination) shall have the power to grant or promise any party any immunity from criminal prosecution under the laws of the United States or of any other jurisdiction.

(2) If the NCUA Board believes that the testimony or other information sought to be obtained from any party may be necessary to the public interest and that party has refused or is likely to refuse to testify or provide other information on the basis of his or her privilege against self-incrimination, the NCUA Board, with the approval of the Attorney General, may issue an order requiring the party to give testimony or provide other information that he or she has previously refused to provide on the basis of self-incrimination.

(3) Whenever a witness refuses, on the basis of his privilege against self-incrimination, to testify or provide other information in a formal investigative proceeding, and the officer conducting the investigation communicates to that person an order of the NCUA Board requiring him or her to testify or provide other information, the witness may not refuse to comply with the order on the basis of his or her privilege against self-incrimination; but no testimony or other information compelled under the order (or any information directly or indirectly derived from such testimony or other information) may be used against the witness in any criminal case, except a prosecution for perjury, giving a false statement, or otherwise failing to comply with the order.

§ 747.806 Transcripts.

Transcripts, if any, of formal investigative proceedings shall be recorded solely by the official reporter, or by any other person or means designated by the officer conducting the investigation. A party who has submitted documentary evidence or testimony in a formal investigative proceeding shall be entitled, upon written request, to procure a copy of his or her documentary evidence or a transcript of his or her testimony on payment of the appropriate fees; provided, however, that in a non-public formal investigative proceeding the NCUA Board may for good cause deny such request or the NCUA Board may place reasonable limitations upon the use of the documentary evidence and transcript. In any event, any witness, upon proper identification, shall have the right to inspect the official transcript of the witness's own testimony.

§ 747.807 Rights of witnesses.

(a) In the event that a formal investigative proceeding is conducted pursuant to a specific order entered by the NCUA Board or by its General Counsel, then any party who is compelled or requested to provide documentary evidence or testimony as part of such proceeding shall, upon request, be shown a copy of the NCUA Board's or its delegate's order. Copies of such orders shall not be provided for their retention to such persons requesting same except in the sole discretion of the General Counsel or his designee.

(b) Any party compelled to appear, or who appears by request or permission of the officer conducting the investigation, in person at a formal investigative proceeding may be accompanied, represented and advised by counsel who is a member of the bar of the highest court of any state; provided however, that all witnesses in such proceeding shall be sequestered, and unless permitted in the discretion of the officer conducting the investigation, no witness or the counsel accompanying any such witness shall be permitted to be present during the examination of any other witness called in such proceeding.

(c)(1) The right of a witness to be accompanied, represented and advised by counsel shall mean the right to have an attorney present during any formal investigative proceeding and to have the attorney—

(i) Advise such person before, during and after such testimony;

(ii) Question such person briefly at the conclusion of his testimony to clarify any answers such person has given; and

(iii) Make summary notes during such testimony solely for the use of such person.

(2) From time to time, in the discretion of the officer, it shall be necessary for persons other than the witness and his or her counsel to attend non-public investigative proceedings. For example, the officer may deem it appropriate that outside counsel to the NCUA Board attend and advise him or her concerning the proceeding including the examination of a particular witness. In these circumstances, outside counsel would not be an officer as that term is used. In other circumstances, it may be appropriate that a technical expert (such as an accountant) accompany the witness and his or her counsel in order to assist counsel in understanding technical issues. These latter circumstances should be rare, are left to the discretion of the officer conducting the investigation, and shall not in any event be allowed to serve as a ruse to coordinate testimony between witnesses, to oversee or supervise the testimony of any witnesses, or otherwise defeat the beneficial effects of the witness sequestration rule.

(d) The officer conducting the investigation may report to the NCUA Board any instances where any witness or counsel has been guilty of dilatory, obstructionist or contumacious conduct during the course of a formal investigative proceeding or any other instance of violations of these rules. The NCUA Board will thereupon take such further action as the circumstance may warrant including barring the offending person from further participation in the particular formal investigative proceeding or even from further practice before the Board.

Subpart J—Local Procedures and Standards Applicable to a Notice of Change in Senior Executive Officers, Directors or Committee Members Pursuant to Section 212 of the Act

§ 747.901 Scope.

The rules and procedures set forth in this subpart shall apply to the notice filed by a credit union pursuant to section 212 of the Act (12 U.S.C. 1790a) and § 701.14 of this chapter, for the consent of the NCUA to add to or replace an individual on the board of directors or supervisory or credit committee, or to employ any individual as a senior executive officer or change the responsibilities of any individual to a position of senior executive officer where the credit union either has been chartered less than 2 years; or is in "troubled condition," as defined in § 701.14 of this chapter. Subpart A of this part shall not apply to any proceeding under this subpart.

[56 FR 37767, Aug. 8, 1991; 57 FR 523, Jan. 7, 1992, as amended at 60 FR 31911, June 19, 1995]

§ 747.902 Grounds for disapproval of notice.

The NCUA Board or its designee may issue a notice of disapproval with respect to a notice submitted by a credit union pursuant to section 212 of the Act (12 U.S.C. 1790a) and § 701.14 of this

§ 747.903

chapter, where the competence, experience, character, or integrity of the individual with respect to whom such notice is submitted indicates that it would not be in the best interest of the members of the credit union or the public to permit the individual to be employed by or associated with, such credit union.

[56 FR 37767, Aug. 8, 1991; 57 FR 523, Jan. 7, 1992, as amended at 60 FR 31911, June 19, 1995; 75 FR 34623, June 18, 2010]

§ 747.903 Procedures where notice of disapproval issued; reconsideration.

(a) The notice of disapproval shall be served upon the federally insured credit union and the candidate for director, committee member or senior executive officer. The notice of disapproval shall:

(1) Summarize or cite the relevant consideration specified in § 747.902;

(2) Inform the individual and the credit union that, within 15 days of receipt of the notice of disapproval, they can request reconsideration by the Regional Director of the initial determination, or can appeal the determination directly to the NCUA Board;

(3) Specify what additional information, if any, must be considered in the reconsideration.

(b) The request for reconsideration by the Regional Director must be filed at the appropriate Regional Office.

(c) The Regional Director shall act on a request for reconsideration within 30 days of its receipt.

[56 FR 37767, Aug. 8, 1991; 57 FR 523, Jan. 7, 1992]

§ 747.904 Appeal.

(a) *Time for filing.* Within 15 days after issuance of a Notice of Disapproval or a determination on a request for reconsideration by the Regional Director, the individual or credit union (henceforth petitioner) may appeal by filing with the NCUA Board a written request for appeal.

(b) *Contents of request.* Any appeal must be in writing and include:

(1) The reasons why the NCUA Board should review the disapproval; and

(2) Relevant, substantive and material facts that for good cause were not previously set forth in the notice required to be filed pursuant to section 212 of the Act (12 U.S.C. 1790a) and § 701.14 of this chapter.

(c) *Procedures for review of request.* Within 30 days of the NCUA Board's receipt of an appeal, the NCUA Board may request in writing that the petitioner submit additional facts and records to support the appeal. The petitioner shall have 15 days from the date of issuance of such written request to provide such additional information. Failure by the petitioner to provide additional information may, as determined solely by the NCUA Board or its designee, result in denial of the petitioner's appeal.

(d) *Determination on appeal by NCUA Board or its designee.* (1) Within 90 days from the date of the receipt of an appeal by the NCUA Board or its designee or of its receipt of additional information requested under paragraph (c) of this section, the NCUA Board or its designee shall notify the petitioner whether the disapproval will be continued, terminated, or otherwise modified. The NCUA Board or its designee shall promptly rescind or modify the notice of disapproval where the decision is favorable to the petitioner.

(2) The determination by the NCUA Board on the appeal shall be provided to the petitioner in writing, stating the basis for any decision of the NCUA Board or its designee that is adverse to the petitioner, and shall constitute a final order of the NCUA Board.

(3) Failure by the NCUA Board to issue a determination on the petitioner's appeal within the 90-day period prescribed under paragraph (d)(1) of this section shall be deemed a denial of the appeal for purpose of § 747.905.

[56 FR 37767, Aug. 8, 1991; 57 FR 523, Jan. 7, 1992, as amended at 60 FR 31911, June 19, 1995]

§ 747.905 Judicial review.

(a) Failure to file an appeal within the applicable time periods, either to the initial determination or to the decision on a request for reconsideration, shall constitute a failure by the petitioner to exhaust available administrative remedies and, due to such failure, any objections to the initial determination or request for reconsideration shall be deemed to be waived and such determination shall be deemed to have been accepted by, and shall be binding upon, the petitioner.

(b) For purposes of seeking judicial review of actions taken pursuant to this section, suit may be filed in the United States District Court for the district where the requester resides, for the district where the credit union's principal place of business is located, or for the District of Columbia.

[56 FR 37767, Aug. 8, 1991; 57 FR 524, Jan. 7, 1992]

Subpart K—Inflation Adjustment of Civil Monetary Penalties

§ 747.1001 Adjustment of civil money penalties by the rate of inflation.

(a) NCUA is required by the Federal Civil Penalties Inflation Adjustment Act of 1990 (Pub. L. 101–410, 104 Stat. 890, as amended (28 U.S.C. 2461 note)) to adjust the maximum amount of each civil money penalty within its jurisdiction by the rate of inflation. The following chart displays those adjustments, as calculated pursuant to the statute:

U.S. code citation	CMP description	New maximum amount
(1) 12 U.S.C. 1782(a)(3).	Inadvertent failure to submit a report or the inadvertent submission of a false or misleading report.	$2,200.
(2) 12 U.S.C. 1782(a)(3).	Non-inadvertent failure to submit a report or the non-inadvertent submission of a false or misleading report.	$22,000.
(3) 12 U.S.C. 1782(a)(3).	Failure to submit a report or the submission of a false or misleading report done knowingly or with reckless disregard.	$1,300,000 or 1 percent of the total assets of the credit union, whichever is less.
(4) 12 U.S.C. 1782(d)(2)(A).	First tier	$2,200.
(5) 12 U.S.C. 1782(d)(2)(B).	Second tier	$22,000.
(6) 12 U.S.C. 1782(d)(2)(C).	Third tier	$1,300,000 or 1 percent of the total assets of the credit union, whichever is less.
(7) 12 U.S.C. 1785(e)(3).	Non-compliance with NCUA security regulations.	$110.
(8) 12 U.S.C. 1786(k)(2)(A).	First tier	$7,500.
(9) 12 U.S.C. 1786(k)(2)(B).	Second tier	$37,500.
(10) 12 U.S.C. 1786(k)(2)(C).	Third tier	For a person other than an insured credit union: $1,375,000; For an insured credit union: $1,375,000 or 1 percent of the total assets of the credit union, whichever is less.
(11) 42 U.S.C. 4012a(f).	Per violation	$385.
	Per calendar year	$130,000.

(b) The adjustments displayed in paragraph (a) of this section apply to acts occurring after the date of publication in the FEDERAL REGISTER.

[74 FR 9351, Mar. 4, 2009]

Subpart L—Issuance, Review and Enforcement of Orders Imposing Prompt Corrective Action

SOURCE: 65 FR 8594, Feb. 18, 2000, unless otherwise noted.

§ 747.2001 Scope.

(a) *Independent review process.* The rules and procedures set forth in this subpart apply to federally-insured credit unions, whether federally- or state-chartered (other than corporate credit unions), which are subject to discretionary supervisory actions under part 702 of this chapter, and to reclassification under §§ 702.102(b) and 702.302(d) of this chapter, to facilitate prompt corrective action under section 216 of the Federal Credit Union Act, 12 U.S.C. 1790d; and to senior executive officers and directors of such credit unions who are dismissed pursuant to a discretionary supervisory action imposed under part 702. NCUA staff decisions to impose discretionary supervisory actions under part 702 shall be considered material supervisory determinations for purposes of 12 U.S.C. 1790d(k). Section 747.2002 of this subpart provides an independent appellate process to challenge such decisions.

§ 747.2002

(b) *Notice to State officials.* With respect to a federally-insured State-chartered credit union under §§ 747.2002, 747.2003 and 747.2004 of this subpart, notices, directives and decisions on appeal served upon a credit union, or a dismissed director or officer thereof, by the NCUA Board shall also be served upon the appropriate State official. Responses, requests for a hearing and to present witnesses, requests to modify or rescind a discretionary supervisory action and requests for reinstatement served upon the NCUA Board by a credit union, or dismissed director or officer thereof, shall also be served upon the appropriate State official.

§ 747.2002 Review of orders imposing discretionary supervisory action.

(a) *Notice of intent to issue directive*—(1) *Generally.* Whenever the NCUA Board intends to issue a directive imposing a discretionary supervisory action under §§ 702.202(b), 702.203(b) and 702.204(b) of this chapter on a credit union classified "undercapitalized" or lower, or under §§ 702.304(b) or 702.305(b) of this chapter on a new credit union classified "moderately capitalized" or lower, it must give the credit union prior notice of the proposed action and an opportunity to respond.

(2) *Immediate issuance of directive without notice.* The NCUA Board may issue a directive to take effect immediately under paragraph (a)(1) of this section without notice to the credit union if the NCUA Board finds it necessary in order to carry out the purposes of part 702 of this chapter. A credit union that is subject to a directive which takes effect immediately may appeal the directive in writing to the NCUA Board. Such an appeal must be received by the NCUA Board within 14 calendar days after the directive was issued, unless the NCUA Board permits a longer period. Unless ordered by the NCUA Board, the directive shall remain in effect pending a decision on the appeal. The NCUA Board shall consider any such appeal, if timely filed, within 60 calendar days of receiving it.

(b) *Contents of notice.* The NCUA Board's notice to a credit union of its intention to issue a directive imposing a discretionary supervisory action must state:

(1) The credit union's net worth ratio and net worth category classification;

(2) The specific restrictions or requirements that the NCUA Board intends to impose, and the reasons therefor;

(3) The proposed date when the discretionary supervisory action would take effect and the proposed date for completing the required action or terminating the action; and

(4) That a credit union must file a written response to a notice within 14 calendar days from the date of the notice, or within such shorter period as the NCUA Board determines is appropriate in light of the financial condition of the credit union or other relevant circumstances.

(c) *Contents of response to notice.* A credit union's response to a notice under paragraph (b) of this section must:

(1) Explain why it contends that the proposed discretionary supervisory action is not an appropriate exercise of discretion under this part;

(2) Request the NCUA Board to modify or to not issue the proposed directive;

(3) Include other relevant information, mitigating circumstances, documentation, or other evidence in support of the credit union's position regarding the proposed directive; and

(4) If desired, request the recommendation of NCUA's ombudsman pursuant to paragraph (g) of this section.

(d) *NCUA Board consideration of response.* The NCUA Board, or an independent person designated by the NCUA Board to act on its behalf, after considering a response under paragraph (c) of this section, may:

(1) Issue the directive as originally proposed or as modified;

(2) Determine not to issue the directive and to so notify the credit union; or

(3) Seek additional information or clarification from the credit union or any other relevant source.

(e) *Failure to file response.* A credit union which fails to file a written response to a notice of the NCUA Board's intention to issue a directive imposing a discretionary supervisory action, within the specified time period, shall

National Credit Union Administration

§ 747.2003

be deemed to have waived the opportunity to respond, and to have consented to the issuance of the directive.

(f) *Request to modify or rescind directive.* A credit union that is subject to an existing directive imposing a discretionary supervisory action may request in writing that the NCUA Board reconsider the terms of the directive, or rescind or modify it, due to changed circumstances. Unless otherwise ordered by the NCUA Board, the directive shall remain in effect while such request is pending. A request under this paragraph which remains pending 60 days following receipt by the NCUA Board is deemed granted.

(g) *Ombudsman.* A credit union may request in writing the recommendation of NCUA's ombudsman to modify or to not issue a proposed directive under paragraph (b) of this section, or to modify or rescind an existing directive due to changed circumstances under paragraph (f) of this section. A credit union which fails to request the ombudsman's recommendation in a response under paragraph (c) of this section, or in a request under paragraph (f) of this section, shall be deemed to have waived the opportunity to do so. The ombudsman shall promptly notify the credit union and the NCUA Board of his or her recommendation.

§ 747.2003 Review of order reclassifying a credit union on safety and soundness criteria.

(a) *Notice of proposed reclassification based on unsafe or unsound condition or practice.* When the NCUA Board proposes to reclassify a credit union or subject it to the supervisory actions applicable to the next lower net worth category pursuant to §§ 702.102(b) and 702.302(d) of this chapter (each such action hereinafter referred to as "reclassification"), the NCUA Board shall issue and serve on the credit union reasonable prior notice of the proposed reclassification.

(b) *Contents of notice.* A notice of intention to reclassify a credit union based on unsafe or unsound condition or practice shall state:

(1) The credit union's net worth ratio, current net worth category classification, and the net worth category to which the credit union would be reclassified;

(2) The unsafe or unsound practice(s) and/or condition(s) justifying reasons for reclassification of the credit union;

(3) The date by which the credit union must file a written response to the notice (including a request for a hearing), which date shall be no less than 14 calendar days from the date of service of the notice unless the NCUA Board determines that a shorter period is appropriate in light of the financial condition of the credit union or other relevant circumstances; and

(4) That a credit union which fails to—

(i) File a written response to the notice of reclassification, within the specified time period, shall be deemed to have waived the opportunity to respond, and to have consented to reclassification;

(ii) Request a hearing shall be deemed to have waived any right to a hearing; and

(iii) Request the opportunity to present witness testimony shall be deemed to have waived any right to present such testimony.

(c) *Contents of response to notice.* A credit union's response to a notice under paragraph (b) of this section must:

(1) Explain why it contends that the credit union should not be reclassified;

(2) Include any relevant information, mitigating circumstances, documentation, or other evidence in support of the credit union's position;

(3) If desired, request an informal hearing before the NCUA Board under this section; and

(4) If a hearing is requested, identify any witness whose testimony the credit union wishes to present and the general nature of each witness's expected testimony.

(d) *Order to hold informal hearing.* Upon timely receipt of a written response that includes a request for a hearing, the NCUA Board shall issue an order commencing an informal hearing no later than 30 days after receipt of the request, unless the credit union requests a later date. The hearing shall be held in Alexandria, Virginia, or at such other place as may be designated by the NCUA Board, before a presiding

§ 747.2004

officer designated by the NCUA Board to conduct the hearing and to recommend a decision.

(e) *Procedures for informal hearing.* (1) The credit union may appear at the hearing through a representative or through counsel. The credit union shall have the right to introduce relevant documents and to present oral argument at the hearing. The credit union may introduce witness testimony only if expressly authorized by the NCUA Board or the presiding officer. Neither the provisions of the Administrative Procedure Act (5 U.S.C. 554–557) governing adjudications required by statute to be determined on the record nor the Uniform Rules of Practice and Procedure (12 CFR part 747) shall apply to an informal hearing under this section unless the NCUA Board orders otherwise.

(2) The informal hearing shall be recorded, and a transcript shall be furnished to the credit union upon request and payment of the cost thereof. Witnesses need not be sworn, unless specifically requested by a party or by the presiding officer. The presiding officer may ask questions of any witness.

(3) The presiding officer may order that the hearing be continued for a reasonable period following completion of witness testimony or oral argument to allow additional written submissions to the hearing record.

(4) Within 20 calendar days following the closing of the hearing and the record, the presiding officer shall make a recommendation to the NCUA Board on the proposed reclassification.

(f) *Time for final decision.* Not later than 60 calendar days after the date the record is closed, or the date of receipt of the credit union's response in a case where no hearing was requested, the NCUA Board will decide whether to reclassify the credit union, and will notify the credit union of its decision. The decision of the NCUA Board shall be final.

(g) *Request to rescind reclassification.* Any credit union that has been reclassified under this section may file a written request to the NCUA Board to reconsider or rescind the reclassification, or to modify, rescind or remove any directives issued as a result of the reclassification. Unless otherwise ordered by the NCUA Board, the credit union shall remain reclassified, and subject to any directives issued as a result, while such request is pending.

(h) *Non-delegation.* The NCUA Board may not delegate its authority to reclassify a credit union into a lower net worth category or to treat a credit union as if it were in a lower net worth category pursuant to §§ 702.102(b) or 702.302(d) of this chapter.

[65 FR 8594, Feb. 18, 2000, as amended at 75 FR 34623, June 18, 2010]

§ 747.2004 Review of order to dismiss a director or senior executive officer.

(a) *Service of directive to dismiss and notice.* When the NCUA Board issues and serves a directive on a credit union requiring it to dismiss from office any director or senior executive officer under §§ 702.202(b)(7), 702.203(b)(8), 702.204(b)(8), 702.304(b) or 702.305(b) of this chapter, the NCUA Board shall also serve upon the person the credit union is directed to dismiss (Respondent) a copy of the directive (or the relevant portions, where appropriate) and notice of the Respondent's right to seek reinstatement.

(b) *Contents of notice of right to seek reinstatement.* A notice of a Respondent's right to seek reinstatement shall state:

(1) That a request for reinstatement (including a request for a hearing) shall be filed with the NCUA Board within 14 calendar days after the Respondent receives the directive and notice under paragraph (a) of this section, unless the NCUA Board grants the Respondent's request for further time;

(2) The reasons for dismissal of the Respondent; and

(3) That the Respondent's failure to—

(i) Request reinstatement shall be deemed a waiver of any right to seek reinstatement;

(ii) Request a hearing shall be deemed a waiver of any right to a hearing; and

(iii) Request the opportunity to present witness testimony shall be deemed a waiver of the right to present such testimony.

(c) *Contents of request for reinstatement.* A request for reinstatement in response to a notice under paragraph (b) of this section must:

(1) Explain why the Respondent should be reinstated;

(2) Include any relevant information, mitigating circumstances, documentation, or other evidence in support of the Respondent's position;

(3) If desired, request an informal hearing before the NCUA Board under this section; and

(4) If a hearing is requested, identify any witness whose testimony the Respondent wishes to present and the general nature of each witness's expected testimony.

(d) *Order to hold informal hearing.* Upon receipt of a timely written request from a Respondent for an informal hearing on the portion of a directive requiring a credit union to dismiss from office any director or senior executive officer, the NCUA Board shall issue an order directing an informal hearing to commence no later than 30 days after receipt of the request, unless the Respondent requests a later date. The hearing shall be held in Alexandria, Virginia, or at such other place as may be designated by the NCUA Board, before a presiding officer designated by the NCUA Board to conduct the hearing and recommend a decision.

(e) *Procedures for informal hearing.* (1) A Respondent may appear at the hearing personally or through counsel. A Respondent shall have the right to introduce relevant documents and to present oral argument at the hearing. A Respondent may introduce witness testimony only if expressly authorized by the NCUA Board or by the presiding officer. Neither the provisions of the Administrative Procedure Act (5 U.S.C. 554–557) governing adjudications required by statute to be determined on the record nor the Uniform Rules of Practice and Procedure (12 CFR part 747) apply to an informal hearing under this section unless the NCUA Board orders otherwise.

(2) The informal hearing shall be recorded, and a transcript shall be furnished to the Respondent upon request and payment of the cost thereof. Witnesses need not be sworn, unless specifically requested by a party or the presiding officer. The presiding officer may ask questions of any witness.

(3) The presiding officer may order that the hearing be continued for a reasonable period following completion of witness testimony or oral argument to allow additional written submissions to the hearing record.

(4) A Respondent shall bear the burden of demonstrating that his or her continued employment by or service with the credit union would materially strengthen the credit union's ability to—

(i) Become "adequately capitalized," to the extent that the directive was issued as a result of the credit union's net worth category classification or its failure to submit or implement a net worth restoration plan or revised business plan; and

(ii) Correct the unsafe or unsound condition or unsafe or unsound practice, to the extent that the directive was issued as a result of reclassification of the credit union pursuant to §§ 702.102(b) and 702.302(d) of this chapter.

(5) Within 20 calendar days following the date of closing of the hearing and the record, the presiding officer shall make a recommendation to the NCUA Board concerning the Respondent's request for reinstatement with the credit union.

(f) *Time for final decision.* Not later than 60 calendar days after the date the record is closed, or the date of the response in a case where no hearing was requested, the NCUA Board shall grant or deny the request for reinstatement and shall notify the Respondent of its decision. If the NCUA Board denies the request for reinstatement, it shall set forth in the notification the reasons for its decision. The decision of the NCUA Board shall be final.

(g) *Effective date.* Unless otherwise ordered by the NCUA Board, the Respondent's dismissal shall take and remain in effect pending a final decision on the request for reinstatement.

§ 747.2005 Enforcement of orders.

(a) *Judicial remedies.* Whenever a credit union fails to comply with a directive imposing a discretionary supervisory action, or enforcing a mandatory supervisory action under part 702 of this chapter, the NCUA Board may seek enforcement of the directive in the appropriate United States District Court pursuant to 12 U.S.C. 1786(k)(1).

§ 747.3001

(b) *Administrative remedies*—(1) *Failure to comply with directive.* Pursuant to 12 U.S.C. 1786(k)(2)(A), the NCUA Board may assess a civil money penalty against any credit union that violates or otherwise fails to comply with any final directive issued under part 702 of this chapter, or against any institution-affiliated party of a credit union (per 12 U.S.C. 1786(r)) who participates in such violation or noncompliance.

(2) *Failure to implement plan.* Pursuant to 12 U.S.C. 1786(k)(2)(A), the NCUA Board may assess a civil money penalty against a credit union which fails to implement a net worth restoration plan under subpart B of part 702 of this chapter or a revised business plan under subpart C of part 702, regardless whether the plan was published.

(c) *Other enforcement action.* In addition to the actions described in paragraphs (a) and (b) of this section, the NCUA Board may seek enforcement of the directives issued under part 702 of this chapter through any other judicial or administrative proceeding authorized by law.

[65 FR 8594, Feb. 18, 2000, as amended at 67 FR 71094, Nov. 29, 2002]

Subpart M—Issuance, Review and Enforcement of Orders Imposing Prompt Corrective Action on Corporate Credit Unions

SOURCE: 75 FR 64860, Oct. 20, 2010, unless otherwise noted.

§ 747.3001 Scope.

(a) *Independent review process.* The rules and procedures set forth in this subpart apply to corporate credit unions which are subject to discretionary supervisory actions under § 704.4 of this chapter and to reclassification under § 704.4(d)(3) of this chapter to facilitate prompt corrective action, and to senior executive officers and directors of such corporate credit unions who are dismissed pursuant to a discretionary supervisory action imposed under § 704.4 of this chapter. Section 747.3002 of this subpart provides an independent appellate process to challenge such decisions.

(b) *Notice to State officials.* With respect to a State-chartered corporate credit union under §§ 747.3002, 747.3003 and 747.3004 of this subpart, any notices, directives and decisions on appeal served upon a corporate credit union, or a dismissed director or officer thereof, by the NCUA will also be served upon the appropriate State official. Responses, requests for a hearing and to present witnesses, requests to modify or rescind a discretionary supervisory action and requests for reinstatement served upon the NCUA by a corporate credit union, or any dismissed director or officer of a corporate credit union, will also be served upon the appropriate State official.

§ 747.3002 Review of orders imposing discretionary supervisory action.

(a) *Notice of intent to issue directive.*—(1) *Generally.* Whenever the NCUA intends to issue a directive imposing a discretionary supervisory action under §§ 704.4(k)(2)(v) and 704.4(k)(3) of this chapter on a corporate credit union classified "undercapitalized" or lower, the NCUA will give the corporate credit union prior notice of the proposed action and an opportunity to respond.

(2) *Immediate issuance of directive without notice.* The NCUA may issue a directive to take effect immediately under paragraph (a)(1) of this section without notice to the corporate credit union if the NCUA finds it necessary in order to carry out the purposes of § 704.4 of this chapter. A corporate credit union that is subject to a directive which takes effect immediately may appeal the directive in writing to the NCUA Board (Board). Such an appeal must be received by the Board within 14 calendar days after the directive was issued, unless the Board permits a longer period. Unless ordered by the NCUA, the directive will remain in effect pending a decision on the appeal. The Board will consider any such appeal, if timely filed, within 60 calendar days of receiving it.

(b) *Contents of notice.* The NCUA's notice to a corporate credit union of its intention to issue a directive imposing a discretionary supervisory action will state:

(1) The corporate credit union's capital measures and capital category classification;

National Credit Union Administration

§ 747.3003

(2) The specific restrictions or requirements that the Board intends to impose, and the reasons therefore;

(3) The proposed date when the discretionary supervisory action would take effect and the proposed date for completing the required action or terminating the action; and

(4) That a corporate credit union must file a written response to a notice within 14 calendar days from the date of the notice, or within such shorter period as the Board determines is appropriate in light of the financial condition of the corporate credit union or other relevant circumstances.

(c) *Contents of response to notice.* A corporate credit union's response to a notice under paragraph (b) of this section must:

(1) Explain why it contends that the proposed discretionary supervisory action is not an appropriate exercise of discretion under this section;

(2) Request the Board to modify or to not issue the proposed directive; and

(3) Include other relevant information, mitigating circumstances, documentation, or other evidence in support of the corporate credit union's position regarding the proposed directive.

(d) *NCUA Board consideration of response.* The Board, or an independent person designated by the Board to act on the Board's behalf, after considering a response under paragraph (c) of this section, may:

(1) Issue the directive as originally proposed or as modified;

(2) Determine not to issue the directive and to so notify the corporate credit union; or

(3) Seek additional information or clarification from the corporate credit union or any other relevant source.

(e) *Failure to file response.* A corporate credit union which fails to file a written response to a notice of the Board's intention to issue a directive imposing a discretionary supervisory action, within the specified time period, will be deemed to have waived the opportunity to respond, and to have consented to the issuance of the directive.

(f) *Request to modify or rescind directive.* A corporate credit union that is subject to an existing directive imposing a discretionary supervisory action may request in writing that the Board reconsider the terms of the directive, or rescind or modify it, due to changed circumstances. Unless otherwise ordered by the Board, the directive will remain in effect while such request is pending. A request under this paragraph which remains pending 60 days following receipt by the Board is deemed granted.

§ 747.3003 Review of order reclassifying a corporate credit union on safety and soundness criteria.

(a) *Notice of proposed reclassification based on unsafe or unsound condition or practice.* When the Board proposes to reclassify a corporate credit union or subject it to the supervisory actions applicable to the next lower capitalization category pursuant to § 704.4(d)(3) of this chapter (such action hereinafter referred to as "reclassification"), the Board will issue and serve on the corporate credit union reasonable prior notice of the proposed reclassification.

(b) *Contents of notice.* A notice of intention to reclassify a corporate credit union based on unsafe or unsound condition or practice will state:

(1) The corporate credit union's current capital ratios and the capital category to which the corporate credit union would be reclassified;

(2) The unsafe or unsound practice(s) and/or condition(s) justifying reasons for reclassification of the corporate credit union;

(3) The date by which the corporate credit union must file a written response to the notice (including a request for a hearing), which date will be no less than 14 calendar days from the date of service of the notice unless the Board determines that a shorter period is appropriate in light of the financial condition of the corporate credit union or other relevant circumstances; and

(4) That a corporate credit union which fails to —

(i) File a written response to the notice of reclassification, within the specified time period, will be deemed to have waived the opportunity to respond, and to have consented to reclassification;

(ii) Request a hearing will be deemed to have waived any right to a hearing; and

§ 747.3004

(iii) Request the opportunity to present witness testimony will be deemed to have waived any right to present such testimony.

(c) *Contents of response to notice.* A corporate credit union's response to a notice under paragraph (b) of this section must:

(1) Explain why it contends that the corporate credit union should not be reclassified;

(2) Include any relevant information, mitigating circumstances, documentation, or other evidence in support of the corporate credit union's position;

(3) If desired, request an informal hearing before the Board under this section; and

(4) If a hearing is requested, identify any witness whose testimony the corporate credit union wishes to present and the general nature of each witness's expected testimony.

(d) *Order to hold informal hearing.* Upon timely receipt of a written response that includes a request for a hearing, the Board will issue an order commencing an informal hearing no later than 30 days after receipt of the request, unless the corporate credit union requests a later date. The hearing will be held in Alexandria, Virginia, or at such other place as may be designated by the Board, before a presiding officer designated by the Board to conduct the hearing and to recommend a decision.

(e) *Procedures for informal hearing.*—(1) The corporate credit union may appear at the hearing through a representative or through counsel. The corporate credit union will have the right to introduce relevant documents and to present oral argument at the hearing. The corporate credit union may introduce witness testimony only if expressly authorized by the Board or the presiding officer. Neither the provisions of the Administrative Procedure Act (5 U.S.C. 554–557) governing adjudications required by statute to be determined on the record nor the Uniform Rules of Practice and Procedure (12 CFR part 747) will apply to an informal hearing under this section unless the Board orders otherwise.

(2) The informal hearing will be recorded, and a transcript will be furnished to the corporate credit union upon request and payment of the cost thereof. Witnesses need not be sworn, unless specifically requested by a party or by the presiding officer. The presiding officer may ask questions of any witness.

(3) The presiding officer may order that the hearing be continued for a reasonable period following completion of witness testimony or oral argument to allow additional written submissions to the hearing record.

(4) Within 20 calendar days following the closing of the hearing and the record, the presiding officer will make a recommendation to the Board on the proposed reclassification.

(f) *Time for final decision.* Not later than 60 calendar days after the date the record is closed, or the date of receipt of the corporate credit union's response in a case where no hearing was requested, the Board will decide whether to reclassify the corporate credit union, and will notify the corporate credit union of its decision. The decision of the Board will be final.

(g) *Request to rescind reclassification.* Any corporate credit union that has been reclassified under this section may file a written request to the Board to reconsider or rescind the reclassification, or to modify, rescind or remove any directives issued as a result of the reclassification. Unless otherwise ordered by the Board, the corporate credit union will remain reclassified, and subject to any directives issued as a result, while such request is pending.

§ 747.3004 Review of order to dismiss a director or senior executive officer.

(a) *Service of directive to dismiss and notice.* When the Board issues and serves a directive on a corporate credit union requiring it to dismiss from office any director or senior executive officer under §§ 704.4(g) and 704.4(k)(3) of this chapter, the Board will also serve upon the person the corporate credit union is directed to dismiss (Respondent) a copy of the directive (or the relevant portions, where appropriate) and notice of the Respondent's right to seek reinstatement.

National Credit Union Administration § 747.3004

(b) *Contents of notice of right to seek reinstatement.* A notice of a Respondent's right to seek reinstatement will state:

(1) That a request for reinstatement (including a request for a hearing) must be filed with the Board within 14 calendar days after the Respondent receives the directive and notice under paragraph (a) of this section, unless the Board grants the Respondent's request for further time;

(2) The reasons for dismissal of the Respondent; and

(3) That the Respondent's failure to—

(i) Request reinstatement will be deemed a waiver of any right to seek reinstatement;

(ii) Request a hearing will be deemed a waiver of any right to a hearing; and

(iii) Request the opportunity to present witness testimony will be deemed a waiver of the right to present such testimony.

(c) *Contents of request for reinstatement.* A request for reinstatement in response to a notice under paragraph (b) of this section must:

(1) Explain why the Respondent should be reinstated;

(2) Include any relevant information, mitigating circumstances, documentation, or other evidence in support of the Respondent's position;

(3) If desired, request an informal hearing before the Board under this section; and

(4) If a hearing is requested, identify any witness whose testimony the Respondent wishes to present and the general nature of each witness's expected testimony.

(d) *Order to hold informal hearing.* Upon receipt of a timely written request from a Respondent for an informal hearing on the portion of a directive requiring a corporate credit union to dismiss from office any director or senior executive officer, the Board will issue an order directing an informal hearing to commence no later than 30 days after receipt of the request, unless the Respondent requests a later date. The hearing will be held in Alexandria, Virginia, or at such other place as may be designated by the Board, before a presiding officer designated by the Board to conduct the hearing and recommend a decision.

(e) *Procedures for informal hearing.*—(1) A Respondent may appear at the hearing personally or through counsel. A Respondent will have the right to introduce relevant documents and to present oral argument at the hearing. A Respondent may introduce witness testimony only if expressly authorized by the Board or by the presiding officer. Neither the provisions of the Administrative Procedure Act (5 U.S.C. 554–557) governing adjudications required by statute to be determined on the record nor the Uniform Rules of Practice and Procedure (12 CFR part 747) apply to an informal hearing under this section unless the Board orders otherwise.

(2) The informal hearing will be recorded, and a transcript will be furnished to the Respondent upon request and payment of the cost thereof. Witnesses need not be sworn, unless specifically requested by a party or the presiding officer. The presiding officer may ask questions of any witness.

(3) The presiding officer may order that the hearing be continued for a reasonable period following completion of witness testimony or oral argument to allow additional written submissions to the hearing record.

(4) A Respondent will bear the burden of demonstrating that his or her continued employment by or service with the corporate credit union would materially strengthen the corporate credit union's ability to —

(i) Become "adequately capitalized," to the extent that the directive was issued as a result of the corporate credit union's capital classification category or its failure to submit or implement a capital restoration plan; and

(ii) Correct the unsafe or unsound condition or unsafe or unsound practice, to the extent that the directive was issued as a result of reclassification of the corporate credit union pursuant to § 704.4(d)(3) of this chapter.

(5) Within 20 calendar days following the date of closing of the hearing and the record, the presiding officer will make a recommendation to the Board concerning the Respondent's request for reinstatement with the corporate credit union.

(f) *Time for final decision.* Not later than 60 calendar days after the date

§ 747.3005

the record is closed, or the date of the response in a case where no hearing was requested, the Board will grant or deny the request for reinstatement and will notify the Respondent of its decision. If the Board denies the request for reinstatement, it will set forth in the notification the reasons for its decision. The decision of the Board will be final.

(g) *Effective date.* Unless otherwise ordered by the Board, the Respondent's dismissal will take and remain in effect pending a final decision on the request for reinstatement.

§ 747.3005 Enforcement of directives.

(a) *Judicial remedies.* Whenever a corporate credit union fails to comply with a directive imposing a discretionary supervisory action, or enforcing a mandatory supervisory action under § 704.4 of this chapter, the Board may seek enforcement of the directive in the appropriate United States District Court pursuant to 12 U.S.C. 1786(k)(1).

(b) *Administrative remedies*—(1) *Failure to comply with directive.* Pursuant to 12 U.S.C. 1786(k)(2)(A), the Board may assess a civil money penalty against any corporate credit union that violates or otherwise fails to comply with any final directive issued under § 704.4 of this chapter, or against any institution-affiliated party of a corporate credit union (per 12 U.S.C. 1786(r)) who participates in such violation or noncompliance.

(2) *Failure to implement plan.* Pursuant to 12 U.S.C. 1786(k)(2)(A), the Board may assess a civil money penalty against a corporate credit union which fails to implement a capital restoration plan under § 704.4(e) of this chapter, regardless whether the plan was published.

(c) *Other enforcement action.* In addition to the actions described in paragraphs (a) and (b) of this section, the Board may seek enforcement of the directives issued under Section 704.4 of this chapter through any other judicial or administrative proceeding authorized by law.

§ 747.3006 Conservatorship or liquidation of critically undercapitalized corporate credit union.

Notwithstanding any other provision of this title, the NCUA may, without any administrative due process, immediately place into conservatorship or liquidation any corporate credit union that has been categorized as critically undercapitalized.

PART 748—SECURITY PROGRAM, REPORT OF SUSPECTED CRIMES, SUSPICIOUS TRANSACTIONS, CATASTROPHIC ACTS AND BANK SECRECY ACT COMPLIANCE

Sec.
748.0 Security program.
748.1 Filing of reports.
748.2 Procedures for monitoring Bank Secrecy Act (BSA) compliance.
APPENDIX A TO PART 748—GUIDELINES FOR SAFEGUARDING MEMBER INFORMATION
APPENDIX B TO PART 748 GUIDANCE ON RESPONSE PROGRAMS FOR UNAUTHORIZED ACCESS TO MEMBER INFORMATION AND MEMBER NOTICE

AUTHORITY: 12 U.S.C. 1766(a), 1786(Q); 15 U.S.C. 6801 and 6805(b); 31 U.S.C. 5311 and 5318.

§ 748.0 Security program.

(a) Each federally insured credit union will develop a written security program within 90 days of the effective date of insurance.

(b) The security program will be designed to:

(1) Protect each credit union office from robberies, burglaries, larcenies, and embezzlement;

(2) Ensure the security and confidentiality of member records, protect against the anticipated threats or hazards to the security or integrity of such records, and protect against unauthorized access to or use of such records that could result in substantial harm or serious inconvenience to a member;

(3) Respond to incidents of unauthorized access to or use of member information that could result in substantial harm or serious inconvenience to a member;

(4) Assist in the identification of persons who commit or attempt such actions and crimes, and

National Credit Union Administration § 748.1

(5) Prevent destruction of vital records, as defined in 12 CFR part 749.

(c) Each Federal credit union, as part of its information security program, must properly dispose of any consumer information the Federal credit union maintains or otherwise possesses, as required under § 717.83 of this chapter.

[50 FR 53295, Dec. 31, 1985, as amended at 53 FR 4845, Feb. 18, 1988; 66 FR 8161, Jan. 30, 2001; 69 FR 69274, Nov. 29, 2004; 70 FR 22778, May 2, 2005]

§ 748.1 Filing of reports.

(a) The president or managing official of each federally-insured credit union must certify compliance with the requirements of this part in its Credit Union Profile annually. Credit unions that cannot update their profile online must certify compliance in writing in accordance with the instructions on NCUA Form 4501 or its equivalent. The credit union president or managing official must sign and date the written certification.

(b) *Catastrophic act report.* Each federally insured credit union will notify the regional director within 5 business days of any catastrophic act that occurs at its office(s). A catastrophic act is any disaster, natural or otherwise, resulting in physical destruction or damage to the credit union or causing an interruption in vital member services, as defined in § 749.1 of this chapter, projected to last more than two consecutive business days. Within a reasonable time after a catastrophic act occurs, the credit union shall ensure that a record of the incident is prepared and filed at its main office. In the preparation of such record, the credit union should include information sufficient to indicate the office where the catastrophic act occurred; when it took place; the amount of the loss, if any; whether any operational or mechanical deficiency(ies) might have contributed to the catastrophic act; and what has been done or is planned to be done to correct the deficiency(ies).

(c) *Suspicious Activity Report.* A credit union must file a report if it knows, suspects, or has reason to suspect that any crime or any suspicious transaction related to money laundering activity or a violation of the Bank Secrecy Act has occurred. For the purposes of this paragraph (c) *credit union* means a federally-insured credit union and *official* means any member of the board of directors or a volunteer committee.

(1) *Reportable activity.* Transaction for purposes of this paragraph means a deposit, withdrawal, transfer between accounts, exchange of currency, loan, extension of credit, purchase or sale of any stock, bond, share certificate, or other monetary instrument or investment security, or any other payment, transfer, or delivery by, through, or to a financial institution, by whatever means effected. A credit union must report any known or suspected crime or any suspicious transaction related to money laundering or other illegal activity, for example, terrorism financing, loan fraud, or embezzlement, or a violation of the Bank Secrecy Act by sending a completed suspicious activity report (SAR) to the Financial Crimes Enforcement Network (FinCEN) in the following circumstances:

(i) *Insider abuse involving any amount.* Whenever the credit union detects any known or suspected Federal criminal violations, or pattern of criminal violations, committed or attempted against the credit union or involving a transaction or transactions conducted through the credit union, where the credit union believes it was either an actual or potential victim of a criminal violation, or series of criminal violations, or that the credit union was used to facilitate a criminal transaction, and the credit union has a substantial basis for identifying one of the credit union's officials, employees, or agents as having committed or aided in the commission of the criminal violation, regardless of the amount involved in the violation;

(ii) *Transactions aggregating $5,000 or more where a suspect can be identified.* Whenever the credit union detects any known or suspected Federal criminal violation, or pattern of criminal violations, committed or attempted against the credit union or involving a transaction or transactions conducted through the credit union, and involving or aggregating $5,000 or more in funds or other assets, where the credit union

§ 748.1

believes it was either an actual or potential victim of a criminal violation, or series of criminal violations, or that the credit union was used to facilitate a criminal transaction, and the credit union has a substantial basis for identifying a possible suspect or group of suspects. If it is determined before filing this report that the identified suspect or group of suspects has used an alias, then information regarding the true identity of the suspect or group of suspects, as well as alias identifiers, such as drivers' licenses or social security numbers, addresses and telephone numbers, must be reported;

(iii) *Transactions aggregating $25,000 or more regardless of potential suspects.* Whenever the credit union detects any known or suspected Federal criminal violation, or pattern of criminal violations, committed or attempted against the credit union or involving a transaction or transactions conducted through the credit union, involving or aggregating $25,000 or more in funds or other assets, where the credit union believes it was either an actual or potential victim of a criminal violation, or series of criminal violations, or that the credit union was used to facilitate a criminal transaction, even though the credit union has no substantial basis for identifying a possible suspect or group of suspects; or

(iv) *Transactions aggregating $5,000 or more that involve potential money laundering or violations of the Bank Secrecy Act.* Any transaction conducted or attempted by, at or through the credit union and involving or aggregating $5,000 or more in funds or other assets, if the credit union knows, suspects, or has reason to suspect:

(A) The transaction involves funds derived from illegal activities or is intended or conducted in order to hide or disguise funds or assets derived from illegal activities (including, without limitation, the ownership, nature, source, location, or control of such funds or assets) as part of a plan to violate or evade any Federal law or regulation or to avoid any transaction reporting requirement under Federal law;

(B) The transaction is designed to evade any regulations promulgated under the Bank Secrecy Act; or

12 CFR Ch. VII (1–1–12 Edition)

(C) The transaction has no business or apparent lawful purpose or is not the sort of transaction in which the particular member would normally be expected to engage, and the credit union knows of no reasonable explanation for the transaction after examining the available facts, including the background and possible purpose of the transaction.

(v) *Exceptions.* A credit union is not required to file a SAR for a robbery or burglary committed or attempted that is reported to appropriate law enforcement authorities, or for lost, missing, counterfeit, or stolen securities and the credit union files a report pursuant to the reporting requirements of 17 CFR 240.17f–1.

(2) *Filing Procedures.* (i) *Timing.* A credit union must file a SAR with FinCEN no later than 30 calendar days from the date the suspicious activity is initially detected, unless there is no identified suspect on the date of detection. If no suspect is identified on the date of detection, a credit union may use an additional 30 calendar days to identify a suspect before filing a SAR. In no case may a credit union take more than 60 days from the date it initially detects a reportable transaction to file a SAR. In situations involving violations requiring immediate attention, such as ongoing money laundering schemes, a credit union must immediately notify, by telephone, an appropriate law enforcement authority and its supervisory authority, in addition to filing a SAR.

(ii) *Content.* A credit union must complete, fully and accurately, SAR form TDF 90–22.47, Suspicious Activity Report (also known as NCUA Form 2362) in accordance with the form's instructions and 31 CFR 1020.320. A copy of the SAR form may be obtained from the credit union resources section of NCUA's Web site, *http://www.ncua.gov*, or the regulatory section of FinCEN's Web site, *http://www.fincen.gov*. These sites include other useful guidance on SARs, for example, forms and filing instructions, Frequently Asked Questions, and the FFIEC Bank Secrecy Act/Anti-Money Laundering Examination Manual.

(iii) *Compliance.* Failure to file a SAR as required by the form's instructions and 31 CFR 1020.320 may subject the credit union, its officials, employees, and agents to the assessment of civil money penalties or other administrative actions.

(3) *Retention of Records.* A credit union must maintain a copy of any SAR that it files and the original or business record equivalent of all supporting documentation to the report for a period of five years from the date of the report. Supporting documentation must be identified and maintained by the credit union as such. Supporting documentation is considered a part of the filed report even though it should not be actually filed with the submitted report. A credit union must make all supporting documentation available to appropriate law enforcement authorities and its regulatory supervisory authority upon request.

(4) *Notification to board of directors.* (i) *Generally.* The management of the credit union must promptly notify its board of directors, or a committee designated by the board of directors to receive such notice, of any SAR filed.

(ii) *Suspect is a director or committee member.* If a credit union files a SAR and the suspect is a director or member of a committee designated by the board of directors to receive notice of SAR filings, the credit union may not notify the suspect, pursuant to 31 U.S.C. 5318(g)(2), but must notify the remaining directors, or designated committee members, who are not suspects.

(5) *Confidentiality of reports.* SARs are confidential. Any credit union, including its officials, employees, and agents, subpoenaed or otherwise requested to disclose a SAR or the information in a SAR must decline to produce the SAR or to provide any information that would disclose that a SAR was prepared or filed, citing this part, applicable law, for example, 31 U.S.C. 5318(g), or both, and notify NCUA of the request. A credit union must make the filed report and all supporting documentation available to appropriate law enforcement authorities and its regulatory supervisory authority upon request.

(6) *Safe Harbor.* Any credit union, including its officials, employees, and agents, that makes a report of suspected or known criminal violations and suspicious activities to law enforcement and financial institution supervisory authorities, including supporting documentation, are protected from liability for any disclosure in the report, or for failure to disclose the existence of the report, or both, to the full extent provided by 31 U.S.C. 5318(g)(3). This protection applies if the report is filed pursuant to this part or is filed on a voluntary basis.

[50 FR 53295, Dec. 31, 1985, as amended at 53 FR 26232, July 12, 1988; 58 FR 17492, Apr. 5, 1993; 61 FR 11527, Mar. 21, 1996; 71 FR 62878, Oct. 27, 2006; 72 FR 42273, Aug. 2, 2007; 74 FR 35769, July 21, 2009; 76 FR 18366, Apr. 4, 2011]

§ 748.2 Procedures for monitoring Bank Secrecy Act (BSA) compliance.

(a) *Purpose.* This section is issued to ensure that all federally insured credit unions establish and maintain procedures reasonably designed to assure and monitor compliance with the requirements of subchapter II of chapter 53 of title 31, United States Code, the Financial Recordkeeping and Reporting of Currency and Foreign Transactions Act, and the implementing regulations promulgated under it by the Department of Treasury, 31 CFR chapter X.

(b) *Establishment of a BSA compliance program*—(1) *Program requirement.* Each federally insured credit union shall develop and provide for the continued administration of a program reasonably designed to assure and monitor compliance with the recordkeeping and recording requirements in subchapter II of chapter 53 of title 31, United States Code and implementing regulations issued by the Department of Treasury at 31 CFR chapter X. The compliance program must be written, approved by the credit union's board of directors, and reflected in the credit union's minutes.

(2) *Customer identification program.* Each federally insured credit union is subject to the requirements of 31 U.S.C. 5318(l) and the implementing regulation jointly promulgated by the NCUA and Department of the Treasury at 31 CFR 1020.220, which require a customer identification program to be implemented as part of the BSA compliance program required under this section.

Pt. 748, App. A

(2) *Customer identification program.* Each federally-insured credit union is subject to the requirements of 31 U.S.C. 5318(l) and the implementing regulation jointly promulgated by the NCUA and the Department of the Treasury at 31 CFR 103.121, which require a customer identification program to be implemented as part of the BSA compliance program required under this section.

(c) *Contents of compliance program.* Such compliance program shall at a minimum—

(1) Provide for a system of internal controls to assure ongoing compliance;

(2) Provide for independent testing for compliance to be conducted by credit union personnel or outside parties;

(3) Designate an individual responsible for coordinating and monitoring day-to-day compliance; and

(4) Provide training for appropriate personnel.

(Approved by the Office of Management and Budget under control number 3133–0094)

[52 FR 2861, Jan. 27, 1987, as amended at 52 FR 8062, Mar. 16, 1987; 68 FR 25112, May 9, 2003; 76 FR 18366, Apr. 4, 2011]

APPENDIX A TO PART 748—GUIDELINES FOR SAFEGUARDING MEMBER INFORMATION

TABLE OF CONTENTS

I. Introduction
 A. Scope
 B. Definitions
II. Guidelines for Safeguarding Member Information
 A. Information Security Program
 B. Objectives
III. Development and Implementation of Member Information Security Program
 A. Involve the Board of Directors
 B. Assess Risk
 C. Manage and Control Risk
 D. Oversee Service Provider Arrangements
 E. Adjust the Program
 F. Report to the Board
 G. Implement the Standards

I. INTRODUCTION

The Guidelines for Safeguarding Member Information (Guidelines) set forth standards pursuant to sections 501 and 505(b), codified at 15 U.S.C. 6801 and 6805(b), of the Gramm-Leach-Bliley Act. These Guidelines provide guidance standards for developing and implementing administrative, technical, and physical safeguards to protect the security, confidentiality, and integrity of member information. These Guidelines also address standards with respect to the proper disposal of consumer information pursuant to sections 621(b) and 628 of the Fair Credit Reporting Act (15 U.S.C. 1681s(b) and 1681w).

A. *Scope.* The Guidelines apply to member information maintained by or on behalf of federally-insured credit unions. Such entities are referred to in this appendix as "the credit union." These Guidelines also apply to the proper disposal of consumer information by such entities.

B. *Definitions.* 1. *In general.* Except as modified in the Guidelines or unless the context otherwise requires, the terms used in these Guidelines have the same meanings as set forth in 12 CFR part 716.

2. For purposes of the Guidelines, the following definitions apply:

a. *Consumer information* means any record about an individual, whether in paper, electronic, or other form, that is a consumer report or is derived from a consumer report and that is maintained or otherwise possessed by or on behalf of the credit union for a business purpose. Consumer information also means a compilation of such records. The term does not include any record that does not identify an individual.

b. *Consumer report* has the same meaning as set forth in the Fair Credit Reporting Act, 15 U.S.C. 1681a(d). The meaning of consumer report is broad and subject to various definitions, conditions and exceptions in the Fair Credit Reporting Act. It includes written or oral communications from a consumer reporting agency to a third party of information used or collected for use in establishing eligibility for credit or insurance used primarily for personal, family or household purposes, and eligibility for employment purposes. Examples include credit reports, bad check lists, and tenant screening reports.

c. *Member* means any member of the credit union as defined in 12 CFR 716.3(n).

d. *Member information* means any records containing nonpublic personal information, as defined in 12 CFR 716.3(q), about a member, whether in paper, electronic, or other form, that is maintained by or on behalf of the credit union.

e. *Member information system* means any method used to access, collect, store, use, transmit, protect, or dispose of member information.

f. *Service provider* means any person or entity that maintains, processes, or otherwise is permitted access to member information through its provision of services directly to the credit union.

II. STANDARDS FOR SAFEGUARDING MEMBER INFORMATION

A. *Information Security Program.* A comprehensive written information security program includes administrative, technical, and physical safeguards appropriate to the size and complexity of the credit union and the nature and scope of its activities. While all parts of the credit union are not required to implement a uniform set of policies, all elements of the information security program must be coordinated.

B. *Objectives.* A credit union's information security program should be designed to: ensure the security and confidentiality of member information; protect against any anticipated threats or hazards to the security or integrity of such information; protect against unauthorized access to or use of such information that could result in substantial harm or inconvenience to any member; and ensure the proper disposal of member information and consumer information. Protecting confidentiality includes honoring members' requests to opt out of disclosures to nonaffiliated third parties, as described in 12 CFR 716.1(a)(3).

III. DEVELOPMENT AND IMPLEMENTATION OF MEMBER INFORMATION SECURITY PROGRAM

A. *Involve the Board of Directors.* The board of directors or an appropriate committee of the board of each credit union should:

1. Approve the credit union's written information security policy and program; and
2. Oversee the development, implementation, and maintenance of the credit union's information security program, including assigning specific responsibility for its implementation and reviewing reports from management.

B. *Assess Risk.* Each credit union should:

1. Identify reasonably foreseeable internal and external threats that could result in unauthorized disclosure, misuse, alteration, or destruction of member information or member information systems;
2. Assess the likelihood and potential damage of these threats, taking into consideration the sensitivity of member information; and
3. Assess the sufficiency of policies, procedures, member information systems, and other arrangements in place to control risks.

C. *Manage and Control Risk.* Each credit union should:

1. Design its information security program to control the identified risks, commensurate with the sensitivity of the information as well as the complexity and scope of the credit union's activities. Each credit union must consider whether the following security measures are appropriate for the credit union and, if so, adopt those measures the credit union concludes are appropriate:

a. Access controls on member information systems, including controls to authenticate and permit access only to authorized individuals and controls to prevent employees from providing member information to unauthorized individuals who may seek to obtain this information through fraudulent means;

b. Access restrictions at physical locations containing member information, such as buildings, computer facilities, and records storage facilities to permit access only to authorized individuals;

c. Encryption of electronic member information, including while in transit or in storage on networks or systems to which unauthorized individuals may have access;

d. Procedures designed to ensure that member information system modifications are consistent with the credit union's information security program;

e. Dual controls procedures, segregation of duties, and employee background checks for employees with responsibilities for or access to member information;

f. Monitoring systems and procedures to detect actual and attempted attacks on or intrusions into member information systems;

g. Response programs that specify actions to be taken when the credit union suspects or detects that unauthorized individuals have gained access to member information systems, including appropriate reports to regulatory and law enforcement agencies; and

h. Measures to protect against destruction, loss, or damage of member information due to potential environmental hazards, such as fire and water damage or technical failures.

2. Train staff to implement the credit union's information security program.

3. Regularly test the key controls, systems and procedures of the information security program. The frequency and nature of such tests should be determined by the credit union's risk assessment. Tests should be conducted or reviewed by independent third parties or staff independent of those that develop or maintain the security programs.

4. Develop, implement, and maintain, as part of its information security program, appropriate measures to properly dispose of member information and consumer information in accordance with the provisions in paragraph III.

D. *Oversee Service Provider Arrangements.* Each credit union should:

1. Exercise appropriate due diligence in selecting its service providers;
2. Require its service providers by contract to implement appropriate measures designed to meet the objectives of these guidelines; and
3. Where indicated by the credit union's risk assessment, monitor its service providers to confirm that they have satisfied their obligations as required by paragraph D.2. As part of this monitoring, a credit union should review audits, summaries of test results, or other equivalent evaluations of its service providers.

E. *Adjust the Program.* Each credit union should monitor, evaluate, and adjust, as appropriate, the information security program in light of any relevant changes in technology, the sensitivity of its member information, internal or external threats to information, and the credit union's own changing business arrangements, such as mergers and acquisitions, alliances and joint ventures, outsourcing arrangements, and changes to member information systems.

F. *Report to the Board.* Each credit union should report to its board or an appropriate committee of the board at least annually. This report should describe the overall status of the information security program and the credit union's compliance with these guidelines. The report should discuss material matters related to its program, addressing issues such as: risk assessment; risk management and control decisions; service provider arrangements; results of testing; security breaches or violations and management's responses; and recommendations for changes in the information security program.

G. *Implement the Standards.*

1. *Effective date.* Each credit union must implement an information security program pursuant to the objectives of these Guidelines by July 1, 2001.

2. *Two-year grandfathering of agreements with service providers.* Until July 1, 2003, a contract that a credit union has entered into with a service provider to perform services for it or functions on its behalf satisfies the provisions of paragraph III.D., even if the contract does not include a requirement that the servicer maintain the security and confidentiality of member information, as long as the credit union entered into the contract on or before March 1, 2001.

3. *Effective date for measures relating to the disposal of consumer information.* Each Federal credit union must properly dispose of consumer information in a manner consistent with these Guidelines by July 1, 2005.

4. *Exception for existing agreements with service providers relating to the disposal of consumer information.* Notwithstanding the requirement in paragraph III.G.3., a Federal credit union's existing contracts with its service providers with regard to any service involving the disposal of consumer information should implement the objectives of these Guidelines by July 1, 2006.

[66 FR 8161, Jan. 30, 2001, as amended at 69 FR 69274, Nov. 29, 2004]

APPENDIX B TO PART 748—GUIDANCE ON RESPONSE PROGRAMS FOR UNAUTHORIZED ACCESS TO MEMBER INFORMATION AND MEMBER NOTICE

I. BACKGROUND

This Guidance in the form of appendix B to NCUA's Security Program, Report of Crime and Catastrophic Act and Bank Secrecy Act Compliance regulation,[29] interprets section 501(b) of the Gramm-Leach-Bliley Act ("GLBA") and describes response programs, including member notification procedures, that a federally insured credit union should develop and implement to address unauthorized access to or use of member information that could result in substantial harm or inconvenience to a member. The scope of, and definitions of terms used in, this Guidance are identical to those of appendix A to Part 748 (appendix A). For example, the term "member information" is the same term used in appendix A, and means any record containing nonpublic personal information about a member, whether in paper, electronic, or other form, maintained by or on behalf of the credit union.

A. *Security Guidelines*

Section 501(b) of the GLBA required the NCUA to establish appropriate standards for credit unions subject to its jurisdiction that include administrative, technical, and physical safeguards to protect the security and confidentiality of member information. Accordingly, the NCUA amended Part 748 of its rules to require credit unions to develop appropriate security programs, and issued appendix A, reflecting its expectation that every federally insured credit union would develop an information security program designed to:

1. Ensure the security and confidentiality of member information;

2. Protect against any anticipated threats or hazards to the security or integrity of such information; and

3. Protect against unauthorized access to or use of such information that could result in substantial harm or inconvenience to any member.

B. *Risk Assessment and Controls*

1. Appendix A directs every credit union to assess the following risks, among others, when developing its information security program:

a. Reasonably foreseeable internal and external threats that could result in unauthorized disclosure, misuse, alteration, or destruction of member information or member information systems;

b. The likelihood and potential damage of threats, taking into consideration the sensitivity of member information; and

c. The sufficiency of policies, procedures, member information systems, and other arrangements in place to control risks.[30]

2. Following the assessment of these risks, appendix A directs a credit union to design a program to address the identified risks. The

---

[29] 12 CFR Part 748.

[30] *See* 12 CFR Part 748, appendix A, Paragraph III.B.

National Credit Union Administration

particular security measures a credit union should adopt will depend upon the risks presented by the complexity and scope of its business. At a minimum, the credit union should consider the specific security measures enumerated in appendix A,[31] and adopt those that are appropriate for the credit union, including:

a. Access controls on member information systems, including controls to authenticate and permit access only to authorized individuals and controls to prevent employees from providing member information to unauthorized individuals who may seek to obtain this information through fraudulent means;

b. Background checks for employees with responsibilities for access to member information; and

c. Response programs that specify actions to be taken when the credit union suspects or detects that unauthorized individuals have gained access to member information systems, including appropriate reports to regulatory and law enforcement agencies.[32]

C. Service Providers

Appendix A advises every credit union to require its service providers by contract to implement appropriate measures designed to protect against unauthorized access to or use of member information that could result in substantial harm or inconvenience to any member.[33]

II. RESPONSE PROGRAM

i. Millions of Americans, throughout the country, have been victims of identity theft.[34] Identity thieves misuse personal information they obtain from a number of sources, including credit unions, to perpetrate identity theft. Therefore, credit unions should take preventative measures to safeguard member information against such attempts to gain unauthorized access to the information. For example, credit unions should place access controls on member information systems and conduct background checks for employees who are authorized to access member information.[35] However, every credit union should also develop and implement a risk-based response program to address incidents of unauthorized access to member information in member information systems that occur nonetheless.[36] A response program should be a key part of a credit union's information security program.[37] The program should be appropriate to the size and complexity of the credit union and the nature and scope of its activities.

ii. In addition, each credit union should be able to address incidents of unauthorized access to member information in member information systems maintained by its domestic and foreign service providers. Therefore, consistent with the obligations in this Guidance that relate to these arrangements, and with existing guidance on this topic issued by the NCUA,[38] a credit union's contract with its service provider should require the service provider to take appropriate actions to address incidents of unauthorized access to or use of the credit union's member information, including notification of the credit union as soon as possible of any such incident, to enable the institution to expeditiously implement its response program.

A. Components of a Response Program

1. At a minimum, a credit union's response program should contain procedures for the following:

---

[31] See appendix A, paragraph III.C.

[32] See appendix A, Paragraph III.C.

[33] See appendix A, Paragraph III.B. and III.D. Further, the NCUA notes that, in addition to contractual obligations to a credit union, a service provider may be required to implement its own comprehensive information security program in accordance with the Safeguards Rule promulgated by the Federal Trade Commission ("FTC"), 12 CFR Part 314.

[34] The FTC estimates that nearly 10 million Americans discovered they were victims of some form of identify theft in 2002. *See* The Federal Trade Commission, *Identity Theft Survey Report*, (September 2003), available at http://www.ftc.gov/os/2003/09synovatereport.pdf.

[35] Credit unions should also conduct background checks of employees to ensure that the credit union does not violate 12 U.S.C. 1785(d), which prohibits a credit union from hiring an individual convicted of certain criminal offenses or who is subject to a prohibition order under 12 U.S.C. 1786(g).

[36] Under 12 CFR Part 748, appendix A, a credit union's *member information systems* consists of all of the methods used to access, collect, store, use, transmit, protect, or dispose of member information, including the systems maintained by its service providers. *See* 12 CFR Part 748, appendix A, Paragraph I.C.2.d.

[37] *See* FFIEC Information Technology Examination Handbook, Information Security Booklet, (December, 2002), available at http://www.ffiec.gov/ffiecinfobase/html_pages/it_01.html#infosec, for additional guidance on preventing, detecting, and responding to intrusions into financial institution computer systems.

[38] *See* FFIEC Information Technology Examination Handbook, Outsourcing Technology Services Booklet, (June 2004), available at http://www.ffiec.gov/ffiecinfobase/html_pages/it_01.html#outscouring for additional guidance on managing outsourced relationships.

a. Assessing the nature and scope of an incident, and identifying what member information systems and types of member information have been accessed or misused;

b. Notifying the appropriate NCUA Regional Director, and, in the case of state-chartered credit unions, its applicable state supervisory authority, as soon as possible when the credit union becomes aware of an incident involving unauthorized access to or use of sensitive member information as defined below.

c. Consistent with the NCUA's Suspicious Activity Report ("SAR") regulations,[39] notifying appropriate law enforcement authorities, in addition to filing a timely SAR in situations involving Federal criminal violations requiring immediate attention, such as when a reportable violation is ongoing;

d. Taking appropriate steps to contain and control the incident to prevent further unauthorized access to or use of member information, for example, by monitoring, freezing, or closing affected accounts, while preserving records and other evidence;[40] and

e. Notifying members when warranted.

2. Where an incident of unauthorized access to member information involves member information systems maintained by a credit union's service providers, it is the responsibility of the credit union to notify the credit union's members and regulator. However, a credit union may authorize or contract with its service provider to notify the credit union's members or regulators on its behalf.

III. MEMBER NOTICE

i. Credit unions have an affirmative duty to protect their members' information against unauthorized access or use. Notifying members of a security incident involving the unauthorized access or use of the member's information in accordance with the standard set forth below is a key part of that duty.

ii. Timely notification of members is important to manage a credit union's reputation risk. Effective notice also may reduce a credit union's legal risk, assist in maintaining good member relations, and enable the credit union's members to take steps to protect themselves against the consequences of identity theft. When member notification is warranted, a credit union may not forgo notifying its customers of an incident because the credit union believes that it may be potentially embarrassed or inconvenienced by doing so.

A. Standard for Providing Notice

When a credit union becomes aware of an incident of unauthorized access to sensitive member information, the credit union should conduct a reasonable investigation to promptly determine the likelihood that the information has been or will be misused. If the credit union determines that misuse of its information about a member has occurred or is reasonably possible, it should notify the affected member as soon as possible. Member notice may be delayed if an appropriate law enforcement agency determines that notification will interfere with a criminal investigation and provides the credit union with a written request for the delay. However, the credit union should notify its members as soon as notification will no longer interfere with the investigation.

1. Sensitive Member Information

Under Part 748.0, a credit union must protect against unauthorized access to or use of member information that could result in substantial harm or inconvenience to any member. Substantial harm or inconvenience is most likely to result from improper access to *sensitive member information* because this type of information is most likely to be misused, as in the commission of identity theft.

For purposes of this Guidance, sensitive member information means a member's name, address, or telephone number, in conjunction with the member's social security number, driver's license number, account number, credit or debit card number, or a personal identification number or password that would permit access to the member's account. *Sensitive member information* also includes any combination of components of member information that would allow someone to log onto or access the member's account, such as user name and password or password and account number.

2. Affected Members

If a credit union, based upon its investigation, can determine from its logs or other data precisely which members' information has been improperly accessed, it may limit notification to those members with regard to whom the credit union determines that misuse of their information has occurred or is reasonably possible. However, there may be situations where the credit union determines that a group of files has been accessed improperly, but is unable to identify which specific member's information has been

---

[39] A credit union's obligation to file a SAR is set out in the NCUA's SAR regulations and guidance. *See* 12 CFR Part 748.1(c); NCUA Letter to Credit Unions No. 04–CU–03, Suspiciouis Activity Reports, March 2004; NCUA Regulatory Alert No. 04–RA–01, The Suspicious Activity Report (SAR) Activity Review—Trends, Tips, & Isues, Issue 6, November 2003, February 2004.

[40] *See* FFIEC Information Technology Examination Handbook, Information Security Booklet, (December 2002), pp. 68–74.

accessed. If the circumstances of the unauthorized access lead the credit union to determine that misuse of the information is reasonably possible, it should notify all members in the group.

B. Content of Member Notice

1. Member notice should be given in a clear and conspicuous manner. The notice should describe the incident in general terms and the type of member information that was the subject of unauthorized access or use. It also should generally describe what the credit union has done to protect the members' information from further unauthorized access. In addition, it should include a telephone number that members can call for further information and assistance.[41] The notice also should remind members of the need to remain vigilant over the next twelve to twenty-four months, and to promptly report incidents of suspected identity theft to the credit union. The notice should include the following additional items, when appropriate:

a. A recommendation that the member review account statements and immediately report any suspicious activity to the credit union;

b. A description of fraud alerts and an explanation of how the member may place a fraud alert in the member's consumer reports to put the member's creditors on notice that the member may be a victim of fraud;

c. A recommendation that the member periodically obtain credit reports from each nationwide credit reporting agency and have information relating to fraudulent transactions deleted;

d. An explanation of how the member may obtain a credit report free of charge; and

e. Information about the availability of the FTC's online guidance regarding steps a consumer can take to protect against identity theft. The notice should encourage the member to report any incidents of identity theft to the FTC, and should provide the FTC's Web site address and toll-free telephone number that members may use to obtain the identity theft guidance and report suspected incidents of identity theft.[42]

---

[41] The credit union should, therefore, ensure that it has reasonable policies and procedures in place, including trained personnel, to respond appropriately to member inquiries and requests for assistance.

[42] Currently, the FTC Web site for the ID Theft brochure and the FTC Hotline phone number are *http://www.ftc.gov/idtheft* and 1-877-IDTHEFT. The credit union may also refer members to any materials developed pursuant to section 15(1)(b) of the FACT Act (educational materials developed by the FTC to teach the public how to prevent identity theft).

2. NCUA encourages credit unions to notify the nationwide consumer reporting agencies prior to sending notices to a large number of members that include contact information for the reporting agencies.

C. Delivery of Member Notice

Member notice should be delivered in any manner designed to ensure that a member can reasonably be expected to receive it. For example, the credit union may choose to contact all members affected by telephone or by mail, or by electronic mail for those members for whom it has a valid e-mail address and who have agreed to receive communications electronically.

[70 FR 22778, May 2, 2005]

PART 749—RECORDS PRESERVATION PROGRAM AND APPENDICES—RECORD RETENTION GUIDELINES; CATASTROPHIC ACT PREPAREDNESS GUIDELINES

Sec.
749.0 Purpose and scope.
749.1 Definitions.
749.2 Vital records preservation program.
749.3 Vital records center.
749.4 Format for vital records preservation.
749.5 Format for records required by other NCUA regulations.

APPENDIX A TO PART 749—RECORD RETENTION GUIDELINES

APPENDIX B TO PART 749—CATASTROPHIC ACT PREPAREDNESS GUIDELINES

AUTHORITY: 12 U.S.C. 1766, 1783 and 1789, 15 U.S.C. 7001(d).

SOURCE: 66 FR 40579, Aug. 3, 2001, unless otherwise noted.

§ 749.0 Purpose and scope.

(a) This part describes the obligations of all federally-insured credit unions to maintain a records preservation program to identify, store and reconstruct vital records in the event that the credit union's records are destroyed and provides recommendations for restoring vital member services. All credit unions must have a written program that includes plans for safeguarding records and reconstructing vital records. To complement these plans, it is recommended a credit union develop a method for restoring vital member services in the event of a catastrophic act as defined in § 748.1(b) of

§ 749.1

this chapter. Additionally, the regulation establishes flexibility in the format credit unions may use for maintaining writings, records or information required by other NCUA regulations.

(b) Appendix A to this part provides guidance concerning the appropriate length of time credit unions should retain various types of operational records. Appendix B to this part also provides guidance for developing a program for responding to a catastrophic act to ensure duplicate vital records can be used for restoration of vital member services.

[72 FR 42273, Aug. 2, 2007]

§ 749.1 Definitions.

For purposes of this part:

Vital member services mean informational account inquiries, share withdrawals and deposits, and loan payments and disbursements.

Vital records refer to the following records:

(a) A list of share, deposit, and loan balances for each member's account as of the close of the most recent business day that:

(1) Shows each balance individually identified by a name or number;

(2) Lists multiple loans of one account separately; and

(3) Contains information sufficient to enable the credit union to locate each member, such as address and telephone number.

(b) A financial report, which lists all of the credit union's asset and liability accounts and bank reconcilements, current as of the most recent month-end.

(c) A list of the credit union's accounts at financial institutions, insurance policies, and investments along with related contact information, current as of the most recent month-end.

(d) Emergency contact information for employees, officials, regulatory offices, and vendors used to support vital records.

[72 FR 42273, Aug. 2, 2007]

§ 749.2 Vital records preservation program.

The board of directors of a credit union is responsible for establishing a vital records preservation program within 6 months after its insurance certificate is issued. The program must be in writing and contain procedures for maintaining duplicate vital records at a vital records center. The procedures must include: designated staff responsible for vital records preservation, a schedule for the storage and destruction of records, and a records preservation log detailing for each record stored, its name, storage location, storage date, and name of the person sending the record for storage. It is recommended credit unions include in these procedures a method for using duplicate records to restore vital member services in the event of catastrophic act. Credit unions which have some or all of their records maintained by an off-site data processor are considered to be in compliance for the storage of those records if the service agreement specifies the data processor safeguards against the simultaneous destruction of production and back-up information.

[72 FR 42273, Aug. 2, 2007]

§ 749.3 Vital records center.

A vital records center is defined as a storage facility, which may include another federally-insured credit union, at any location far enough from the credit union's offices to avoid the simultaneous loss of both sets of records in the event of a catastrophic act. A credit union must maintain or contract with a third party to maintain any equipment or software for its vital records center necessary to access records.

[72 FR 42273, Aug. 2, 2007]

§ 749.4 Format for vital records preservation.

Preserved records may be in any format that can be used to reconstruct the credit union's records. The format used must accurately reflect the information in the record, remain accessible to all persons entitled to access by statute, regulation or rule of law, and be capable of reproduction by transmission, printing, or otherwise.

[72 FR 42273, Aug. 2, 2007]

National Credit Union Administration

§ 749.5 Format for records required by other NCUA regulations.

Where NCUA regulations require credit unions to retain certain writings, records or information, credit unions may use any format that accurately reflects the information in the record, is accessible to all persons entitled to access by statute, regulation or rule of law, and is capable of being reproduced by transmission, printing, or otherwise. The credit union must maintain the necessary equipment or software to permit an examiner to access the records during the examination process.

[72 FR 42273, Aug. 2, 2007]

APPENDIX A TO PART 749—RECORD RETENTION GUIDELINES

Credit unions often look to NCUA for guidance on the appropriate length of time to retain various types of operational records. NCUA does not regulate in this area, but as an aid to credit unions it is publishing this appendix of suggested guidelines for record retention. NCUA recognizes that credit unions must strike a balance between the competing demands of space, resource allocation and the desire to retain all the records that they may need to conduct their business successfully. Efficiency requires that all records that are no longer useful be discarded, just as both efficiency and safety require that useful records be preserved and kept readily available.

A. What Format Should the Credit Union Use for Retaining Records?

NCUA does not recommend a particular format for record retention. If the credit union stores records on microfilm, microfiche, or in an electronic format, the stored records must be accurate, reproducible and accessible to an NCUA examiner. If records are stored on the credit union premises, they should be immediately accessible upon the examiner's request; if records are stored by a third party or off-site, then they should be made available to the examiner within a reasonable time after the examiner's request. The credit union must maintain the necessary equipment or software to permit an examiner to review and reproduce stored records upon request. The credit union should also ensure that the reproduction is acceptable for submission as evidence in a legal proceeding.

B. Who Is Responsible for Establishing a System for Record Disposal?

The credit union's board of directors may approve a schedule authorizing the disposal of certain records on a continuing basis upon expiration of specified retention periods. A schedule provides a system for disposal of records and eliminates the need for board approval each time the credit union wants to dispose of the same types of records created at different times.

C. What Procedures Should a Credit Union Follow When Destroying Records?

The credit union should prepare an index of any records destroyed and retain the index permanently. Destruction of records should ordinarily be carried out by at least two persons whose signatures, attesting to the fact that records were actually destroyed, should be affixed to the listing.

D. What Are the Recommended Minimum Retention Times?

Record destruction may impact the credit union's legal standing to collect on loans or defend itself in court. Since each state can impose its own rules, it is prudent for a credit union to consider consulting with local counsel when setting minimum retention periods. A record pertaining to a member's account that is not considered a vital record may be destroyed once it is verified by the supervisory committee. Individual Share and Loan Ledgers should be retained permanently. Records, for a particular period, should not be destroyed until both a comprehensive annual audit by the supervisory committee and a supervisory examination by the NCUA have been made for that period.

E. What Records Should Be Retained Permanently?

1. Official records of the credit union that should be retained permanently are:

(a) Charter, bylaws, and amendments.

(b) Certificates or licenses to operate under programs of various government agencies, such as a certificate to act as issuing agent for the sale of U.S. savings bonds.

(c) Current manuals, circular letters and other official instructions of a permanent character received from the NCUA and other governmental agencies.

2. Key operational records that should be retained permanently are:

(a) Minutes of meetings of the membership, board of directors, credit committee, and supervisory committee.

(b) One copy of each financial report, NCUA Form 5300 or 5310, or their equivalent, and the Credit Union Profile report, NCUA Form 4501, or its equivalent as submitted to NCUA at the end of each quarter.

Pt. 749, App. B

(c) One copy of each supervisory committee comprehensive annual audit report and attachments.
(d) Supervisory committee records of account verification.
(e) Applications for membership and joint share account agreements.
(f) Journal and cash record.
(g) General ledger.
(h) Copies of the periodic statements of members, or the individual share and loan ledger. (A complete record of the account should be kept permanently.)
(i) Bank reconcilements.
(j) Listing of records destroyed.

F. What Records Should a Credit Union Designate for Periodic Destruction?

Any record not described above is appropriate for periodic destruction unless it must be retained to comply with the requirements of consumer protection regulations. Periodic destruction should be scheduled so that the most recent of the following records are available for the annual supervisory committee audit and the NCUA examination. Records that may be periodically destroyed include:
(a) Applications of paid off loans.
(b) Paid notes.
(c) Various consumer disclosure forms, unless retention is required by law.
(d) Cash received vouchers.
(e) Journal vouchers.
(f) Canceled checks.
(g) Bank statements.
(h) Outdated manuals, canceled instructions, and nonpayment correspondence from the NCUA and other governmental agencies.

[66 FR 40579, Aug. 3, 2001, as amended at 74 FR 35769, July 21, 2009]

APPENDIX B TO PART 749—CATASTROPHIC ACT PREPAREDNESS GUIDELINES

Credit unions often look to NCUA for guidance on preparing for a catastrophic act. While NCUA has minimal regulation in this area,[1] as an aid to credit unions it is publishing this appendix of suggested guidelines. It is recommended that all credit unions develop a program to prepare for a catastrophic act. The program should be developed with oversight and approval of the board of directors. It is recommended the program address the following five elements:

---
[1] See 12 CFR 748.1(b) concerning a FICU's reporting of any catastrophic act that occurs at its office to its regional director and 12 CFR 749.3 concerning the location of a FICU's vital records center to avoid the simultaneous loss of both sets of records in the event of disaster.

(1) A business impact analysis to evaluate potential threats;
(2) A risk assessment to determine critical systems and necessary resources;
(3) A written plan addressing:
i. Persons with authority to enact the plan;
ii. Preservation and ability to restore vital records;
iii. A method for restoring vital member services through identification of alternate operating location(s) or mediums to provide services, such as telephone centers, shared service centers, agreements with other credit unions, or other appropriate methods;
iv. Communication methods for employees and members;
v. Notification of regulators as addressed in 12 CFR 748.1(b);
vi. Training and documentation of training to ensure all employees and volunteer officials are aware of procedures to follow in the event of destruction of vital records or loss of vital member services; and
vii. Testing procedures, including a means for documenting the testing results.
(4) Internal controls for reviewing the plan at least annually and for revising the plan as circumstances warrant, for example, to address changes in the credit union's operations; and
(5) Annual testing.

[72 FR 42274, Aug. 2, 2007]

PART 750—GOLDEN PARACHUTE AND INDEMNIFICATION PAYMENTS

Sec.
750.0 Scope.
750.1 Definitions.
750.2 Golden parachute payments prohibited.
750.3 Prohibited indemnification payments.
750.4 Permissible golden parachute payments.
750.5 Permissible indemnification payments.
750.6 Filing instructions; appeal.
750.7 Applicability in the event of liquidation or conservatorship.

AUTHORITY: 12 U.S.C. 1786(t).

SOURCE: 76 FR 30517, May 26, 2011, unless otherwise noted.

§ 750.0 Scope.

(a) This part limits and prohibits, in certain circumstances, the ability of Federally insured credit unions, including Federally and state chartered natural person credit unions and Federally and state chartered corporate credit unions, to enter into contracts to pay

National Credit Union Administration § 750.1

and to make golden parachute and indemnification payments to institution-affiliated parties (IAPs).

(b) The limitations on golden parachute payments apply to troubled Federally insured credit unions that seek to enter into contracts to pay or to make golden parachute payments to their IAPs. A "golden parachute payment" is generally considered to be any payment to an IAP which is contingent on the termination of that person's employment and is received when the Federally insured credit union making the payment is troubled. The definition of golden parachute payment does not include payments pursuant to qualified retirement plans, non-qualified bona fide deferred compensation plans, nondiscriminatory severance pay plans, other types of common benefits plans, state statutes and death benefits. Certain limited exceptions to the golden parachute payment prohibition are provided for in cases involving unassisted mergers and the hiring of new management to help improve a troubled Federally insured credit union's financial condition. A procedure is also set forth to permit a Federally insured credit union to request permission to make what would otherwise be a prohibited golden parachute payment.

(c) The limitations on indemnification payments apply to all Federally insured credit unions, including state chartered credit unions, regardless of their financial health. Generally, this part prohibits Federally insured credit unions from indemnifying an IAP for that portion of the costs sustained with regard to an administrative proceeding or civil action commenced by NCUA or a state regulatory authority that results in a final order or settlement pursuant to which the IAP is assessed a civil money penalty, removed from office, prohibited from participating in the affairs of a Federally insured credit union or required to cease and desist from an action or take an affirmative action described in section 206 of the Federal Credit Union Act, 12 U.S.C. 1786. There are exceptions to this general prohibition. First, a Federally insured credit union may purchase commercial insurance to cover these expenses, except judgments and penalties. Second, the credit union may advance legal and other professional expenses to an IAP directly (except for judgments and penalties) if its board of directors makes certain specific findings and the IAP provides a written affirmation and agrees in writing to reimburse the credit union if it is ultimately determined that the IAP violated a law or regulation or has engaged in certain unsafe or unsound practices or breaches of fiduciary duty. For Federal credit unions, fiduciary duty is defined in 701.4 of this chapter. State chartered credit unions should look to applicable state law.

§ 750.1 Definitions.

As used in this part:

(a) *Act* means the Federal Credit Union Act.

(b) *Benefit plan* means any employee benefit plan, contract, agreement or other arrangement subject to the requirements in § 701.19 of this chapter; provided, however, that to the extent the plan exhibits characteristics of a deferred compensation plan or arrangement, or severance plan, it meets the criteria set forth in paragraph (c) or (i), respectively, of this section.

(c) *Bona fide deferred compensation plan or arrangement* means any plan, contract, agreement or other arrangement where:

(1) An IAP voluntarily elects to defer all or a portion of the reasonable compensation, wages or fees paid for services rendered that otherwise would have been paid to the IAP at the time the services were rendered, including a plan providing for crediting a reasonable investment return on the elective deferrals, and the Federally insured credit union either:

(i) Recognizes compensation expense and accrues a liability for the benefit payments according to generally accepted accounting principles (GAAP); or

(ii) Segregates or otherwise sets aside assets in a trust that may only be used to pay plan and other benefits, except that the assets of the trust may be available to satisfy claims of the Federally insured credit union's creditors in the case of insolvency; or

(2) A Federally insured credit union establishes a nonqualified deferred

compensation or supplemental retirement plan, other than an elective deferral plan described in paragraph (c)(1) of this section:

(i) Primarily for the purpose of providing benefits for certain IAPs in excess of the limitations on contributions and benefits imposed by sections 415, 401(a)(17), 402(g) or any other applicable provision of the Internal Revenue Code of 1986 (26 U.S.C. 415, 401(a)(17), 402(g)); or

(ii) Primarily for the purpose of providing supplemental retirement benefits or other deferred compensation for a select group of directors, management or highly compensated employees, excluding severance payments described in paragraph (e)(2)(v) of this section and permissible golden parachute payments described in § 750.4; and

(3) In the case of any nonqualified deferred compensation or supplemental retirement plans as described in paragraphs (c)(1) and (2) of this section, the following requirements apply:

(i) The plan was in effect at least one year before any of the events described in paragraph (e)(1)(ii) of this section;

(ii) Any payment made pursuant to the plan is made in accordance with the terms of the plan as in effect no later than one year before any of the events described in paragraph (e)(1)(ii) of this section and in accordance with any amendments to the plan during that one year period that do not increase the benefits payable under the plan;

(iii) The IAP has a vested right, as defined under the applicable plan document, at the time of termination of employment to payments under the plan;

(iv) Benefits under the plan are accrued each period only for current or prior service rendered to the employer, except that an allowance may be made for service with a predecessor employer;

(v) Any payment made pursuant to the plan is not based on any discretionary acceleration of vesting or accrual of benefits that occurs at any time later than one year before any of the events described in paragraph (e)(1)(ii) of this section;

(vi) The Federally insured credit union has previously recognized compensation expense and accrued a liability for the benefit payments according to GAAP or segregated or otherwise set aside assets in a trust that may only be used to pay plan benefits, except that the assets of the trust may be available to satisfy claims of the credit union's creditors in the case of insolvency; and

(vii) Payments pursuant to the plans must not exceed the accrued liability computed in accordance with GAAP.

(d) *Federally insured credit union* means a Federal credit union, state chartered credit union, or corporate credit union the member accounts of which are insured under the Act.

(e) *Golden parachute payment.*

(1) The term *golden parachute payment* means any payment or any agreement to make any payment in the nature of compensation by any Federally insured credit union for the benefit of any current or former IAP pursuant to an obligation of the credit union that:

(i) Is contingent on, or by its terms is payable on or after, the termination of the party's primary employment or affiliation with the credit union; and

(ii) Is received on or after, or is made in contemplation of, any of the following events:

(A) The insolvency of the Federally insured credit union that is making the payment; or

(B) The appointment of any conservator or liquidating agent for the Federally insured credit union; or

(C) A determination by NCUA or, in the case of a state chartered credit union, the appropriate state supervisory authority that the Federally insured credit union is in a troubled condition, as defined in § 701.14(b)(3) and (4) of this chapter; or

(D) The Federally insured credit union has been assigned:

(1) In the case of a Federal credit union, 4 or 5 CAMEL composite rating by NCUA; or

(2) In the case of a Federally insured state chartered credit union, an equivalent 4 or 5 CAMEL composite rating by the state supervisor; or

(3) In the case of a Federally insured state chartered credit union in a state that does not use the CAMEL system, a 4 or 5 CAMEL composite rating by NCUA based on core workpapers received from the state supervisor; or

National Credit Union Administration § 750.1

(4) In the case of a corporate credit union, the corporate credit union is undercapitalized as defined in §704.4, or has been assigned a 4 or 5 Corporate Risk Information System (CRIS) rating by NCUA in either the Financial Risk or Risk Management composites, or, in the case of a state chartered corporate credit union, assigned a rating equivalent to a 4 or 5 CRIS rating in either composite by the state supervisory authority (SSA) or by NCUA, based on core exam work papers received from the SSA (in states not using the CRIS or CAMEL rating systems); or

(E) The Federally insured credit union is subject to a proceeding to terminate or suspend its share insurance; and

(iii) Is payable to an IAP whose employment by or affiliation with a Federally insured credit union is terminated at a time when the Federally insured credit union by which the IAP is employed or with which the IAP is affiliated satisfies any of the conditions enumerated in paragraphs (e)(1)(ii) (A) through (E) of this section, or in contemplation of any of these conditions.

(2) *Exceptions.* The term *golden parachute payment* does not include:

(i) Any payment made pursuant to a deferred compensation plan under section 457(b) of the Internal Revenue Code of 1986, 26 U.S.C. 457(b), or a pension or retirement plan that is qualified or is intended within a reasonable period of time to be qualified under section 401 of the Internal Revenue Code of 1986, 26 U.S.C. 401; or

(ii) Any payment made pursuant to a benefit plan as that term is defined in paragraph (b) of this section; or

(iii) Any payment made pursuant to a *bona fide deferred compensation plan or arrangement* as defined in paragraph (c) of this section; or

(iv) Any payment made by reason of death or by reason of termination caused by the disability of an IAP; or

(v) Any payment made pursuant to a nondiscriminatory severance pay plan or arrangement that provides for payment of severance benefits to all eligible employees upon involuntary termination other than for cause, voluntary resignation, or early retirement; provided, however, that no employee will receive any payment that exceeds the base compensation paid to the employee during the twelve months, or a longer period or greater benefit as the NCUA will consent to, immediately preceding termination of employment, resignation or early retirement, and the severance pay plan or arrangement must not or cannot have been adopted or modified to increase the amount or scope of severance benefits at a time when the Federally insured credit union was in a condition specified in paragraph (e)(1)(ii) of this section or in contemplation of that condition without the prior written consent of NCUA; or

(vi) Any severance or similar payment required to be made pursuant to a state statute applicable to all employers within the appropriate jurisdiction, with the exception of employers that may be exempt due to their small number of employees or other similar criteria; or

(vii) Any other payment NCUA determines to be permissible in accordance with §750.4.

(f) *Institution-affiliated party (IAP)* means any individual meeting the criteria in section 206(r) of the Act, 12 U.S.C. 1786(r).

(g) *Liability or legal expense* means:

(1) Any legal or other professional fees and expenses incurred in connection with any claim, proceeding, or action;

(2) The amount of, and any cost incurred in connection with, any settlement of any claim, proceeding, or action; and

(3) The amount of, and any cost incurred in connection with, any judgment or penalty imposed with respect to any claim, proceeding, or action.

(h) *NCUA* means the National Credit Union Administration.

(i) *Nondiscriminatory* means that the plan, contract or arrangement applies to all employees of a Federally insured credit union who meet reasonable and customary eligibility requirements applicable to all employees, such as minimum length of service requirements. A nondiscriminatory plan, contract or arrangement may provide different benefits based only on objective criteria, such as salary, total compensation, length of service, job grade or classification, applied on a proportionate basis (with a variance in severance benefits relating to any criterion of plus or minus ten percent) to groups of employees consisting of not less than 33% of all employees.

(j) *Payment* means:

(1) Any direct or indirect transfer of any funds or any asset;

(2) Any forgiveness of any debt or other obligation;

(3) The conferring of any benefit; or

(4) Any segregation of any funds or assets, the establishment or funding of any trust or the purchase of or arrangement for any letter of credit or other instrument, for the purpose of making, or pursuant to any agreement to make, any payment on or after the date on which the funds or assets are segregated, or at the time of or after such trust is established or letter of credit or other instrument is made available, without regard to whether the obligation to make such payment is contingent on:

(i) The determination, after such date, of the liability for the payment of such amount; or

(ii) The liquidation, after such date, of the amount of such payment.

(k) *Prohibited indemnification payment.* (1) *Prohibited indemnification payment* means any payment or any agreement or arrangement to make any payment by any Federally insured credit union for the benefit of any person who is or was an IAP of the Federally insured credit union, to pay or reimburse such person for any civil money penalty, judgment, or other liability or legal expense resulting from any administrative or civil action instituted by NCUA or any appropriate state regulatory authority, in the case of a credit union or corporate credit union chartered by a state, that results in a final order or settlement pursuant to which such person:

(i) Is assessed a civil money penalty;

(ii) Is removed from office or prohibited from participating in the conduct of the affairs of the Federally insured credit union; or

(iii) Is required to cease and desist from an action or take any affirmative action described in section 206 of the Act (12 U.S.C.1786) with respect to the credit union.

(2) *Exceptions. Prohibited indemnification payment* does not include any reasonable payment that:

(i) Is used to purchase a commercial insurance policy or fidelity bond, provided that the insurance policy or bond must not be used to pay or reimburse an IAP for the cost of any judgment or civil money penalty assessed against the IAP in an administrative proceeding or civil action commenced by NCUA or the appropriate state supervisory authority, in the case of a credit union or corporate credit union chartered by a state, but may pay any legal or professional expenses incurred in connection with a proceeding or action or the amount of any restitution, to the Federally insured credit union or its conservator or liquidating agent; or

(ii) Represents partial indemnification for legal or professional expenses specifically attributable to particular charges for which there has been a formal and final adjudication or finding in connection with a settlement that the IAP has not violated certain laws or regulations or has not engaged in certain unsafe or unsound practices or breaches of fiduciary duty, unless the administrative action or civil proceeding has resulted in a final prohibition order against the IAP.

(l) *Troubled condition* means any Federally insured credit union that meets the criteria as described in §701.14(b)(3) and (4) of this chapter, or has been granted assistance described in sections 208 or 216 of the Act.

[76 FR 30517, May 26, 2011, as amended at 76 FR 36980, June 24, 2011]

§ 750.2 Golden parachute payments prohibited.

A Federally insured credit union must not make or agree to make any golden parachute payment, except as permitted by this part.

§ 750.3 Prohibited indemnification payments.

A Federally insured credit union must not make or agree to make any prohibited indemnification payment, except as permitted by this chapter.[1]

---

[1] The provisions in this part 750 control to the extent of any inconsistency with § 701.33 of this chapter.

§ 750.4 Permissible golden parachute payments.

(a) A Federally insured credit union may agree to make or may make a golden parachute payment if:

(1) NCUA, with written concurrence of the appropriate state supervisory authority in the case of a state chartered credit union or corporate credit union, determines the payment or agreement is permissible; or

(2) An agreement is made in order to hire a person to become an IAP at a time when the Federally insured credit union satisfies or in an effort to prevent it from imminently satisfying any of the criteria in § 750.1(e)(1)(ii), and NCUA, with written concurrence of the appropriate state supervisory authority in the case of a state chartered credit union or corporate credit union, consents in writing to the amount and terms of the golden parachute payment. NCUA's consent will not improve the IAP's position in the event of the insolvency of the credit union since NCUA's consent cannot bind a liquidating agent or affect the provability of claims in liquidation. In the event the credit union is placed into conservatorship or liquidation, the conservator or the liquidating agent will not be obligated to pay the promised golden parachute and the IAP will not be accorded preferential treatment on the basis of any prior approval; or

(3) A payment is made pursuant to an agreement that provides for a reasonable severance payment, not to exceed twelve months' salary, to an IAP in the event of a merger of the Federally insured credit union; provided, however, that a Federally insured credit union must obtain the consent of NCUA before making a payment and this paragraph (a)(3) does not apply to any merger of a Federally insured credit union resulting from an assisted transaction described in section 208 of the Act, 12 U.S.C. 1788, or the Federally insured credit union being placed into conservatorship or liquidation; and

(4) A Federally insured credit union or IAP making a request pursuant to paragraphs (a)(1) through (3) of this section must demonstrate it does not possess and is not aware of any information, evidence, documents or other materials indicating there is a reasonable basis to believe, at the time the payment is proposed to be made, that:

(i) The IAP has committed any fraudulent act or omission, breach of trust or fiduciary duty, or insider abuse with regard to the Federally insured credit union that has had or is likely to have a material adverse effect on the Federally insured credit union;

(ii) The IAP is substantially responsible for the insolvency of, the appointment of a conservator liquidating agent for, or the troubled condition, as defined by § 750.1(l), of the Federally insured credit union;

(iii) The IAP has materially violated any applicable Federal or state law or regulation that has had or is likely to have a material effect on the Federally insured credit union; or

(iv) The IAP has violated or conspired to violate sections 215, 656, 657, 1005, 1006, 1007, 1014, 1032, or 1344 of title 18 of the United States Code, or sections 1341 or 1343 of that title affecting a Federally insured financial institution, as defined in title 18 of the United States Code.

(b) In making a determination under paragraphs (a)(1) through (3) of this section, NCUA may consider:

(1) Whether, and to what degree, the IAP was in a position of managerial or fiduciary responsibility;

(2) The length of time the IAP was affiliated with the Federally insured credit union and the degree to which the proposed payment represents a reasonable payment for services rendered over the period of employment; and

(3) Any other factors or circumstances indicating the proposed payment would be contrary to the intent of section 206(t) of the Act or this part.

§ 750.5 Permissible indemnification payments.

(a) A Federally insured credit union may make or agree to make reasonable indemnification payments to an IAP, including advanced funds to pay or reimburse reasonable legal fees or other professional expenses incurred by an IAP in an administrative proceeding or civil action initiated by NCUA or a state regulatory authority if:

(1) The Federally insured credit union's board of directors, in good

§ 750.6

faith, determines in writing after due investigation and consideration that:

(i) The IAP acted in good faith and in a manner he or she believed to be consistent with his or her fiduciary duty;

(ii) The advancement or payment of the expenses will not materially adversely affect the credit union's safety and soundness; and

(iii) The IAP has the financial capability or has otherwise made appropriate financial arrangements sufficient to repay the advance if required in accordance with this rule; and

(2) The IAP provides:

(i) A written affirmation of his or her reasonable good faith belief that he or she acted in a manner believed to be consistent with his or her fiduciary duty; and

(ii) An agreement in writing to reimburse the Federally insured credit union, to the extent not covered by payments from insurance or bonds purchased pursuant to § 750.1(k)(2)(i), for that portion of any advanced indemnification payments which ultimately become prohibited indemnification payments as defined in § 750.1(k); and

(3) The indemnification payments do not ultimately constitute prohibited indemnification payments as defined in § 750.1(k).

(b) An IAP seeking indemnification payments must not participate in any way in the board of director's discussion and approval of such payments; however, the IAP may present his or her request to the board and respond to any inquiries from the board concerning his or her involvement in the circumstances giving rise to the administrative proceeding or civil action.

(c) In the event a majority of the members of the board of directors are named as respondents in an administrative proceeding or civil action and request indemnification, the remaining members of the board may authorize independent legal counsel to review the indemnification request and provide the remaining members of the board with a written opinion of counsel as to whether the conditions in paragraph (a)(1) through (3) of this section have been met. If independent legal counsel concludes that the conditions have been met, the remaining members of the board of directors may rely on the opinion in authorizing the requested indemnification.

(d) In the event all of the members of the board of directors are named as respondents in an administrative proceeding or civil action and request indemnification, the board will authorize independent legal counsel to review the indemnification request and provide the board with a written opinion of counsel as to whether the conditions in paragraph (a)(1) through (3) of this section have been met. If independent legal counsel concludes the conditions have been met, the board of directors may rely on the opinion in authorizing the requested indemnification.

§ 750.6 Filing instructions; appeal.

(a) Requests to make excess non-discriminatory severance plan payments pursuant to § 750.1(e)(2)(v) and golden parachute payments permitted by § 750.4 must be submitted in writing to NCUA. In the case of a Federal or state chartered natural person credit union, such written requests must be submitted to the NCUA regional director for the region in which the credit union is located. In the case of a Federal or state chartered corporate credit union, such written requests must be submitted to the Director of the Office of Corporate Credit Unions. The request must be in letter form and must contain all relevant factual information as well as the reasons why such approval should be granted. If written concurrence by the state supervisory authority is required, the requesting party must submit a copy of its written request to the state supervisory authority where the credit union is located.

(b) An FICU whose request for approval by NCUA in accordance with paragraph (a) of this section has been denied may file an appeal of that denial with the NCUA Board by following the procedures set out in this paragraph.

(1) The appeal must be in writing and filed with the Secretary of the Board, National Credit Union Administration, 1775 Duke Street, Alexandria, VA 22314–3428, and must be filed not later than sixty days after the initial determination denying the request.

(2) The Board shall make its determination concerning the appeal based on what is submitted in writing; there shall be no personal appearance before the Board in connection with an appeal under this paragraph.

(3) The Board shall make its determination concerning the appeal within 180 days from the date of its receipt of the appeal. The decision by the Board on appeal shall be provided to the appellant in writing, stating the reasons for the decision, and shall constitute a final agency decision. Failure by the Board to issue a decision on appeal within the 180-day period provided for under this section shall be deemed to be denial of such appeal.

(4) A final determination by the Board is reviewable in accordance with the provisions of chapter 7, title 5, United States Code, by the United States District Court for the Eastern District of Virginia or the U.S. District Court for the Federal judicial district where the FICU's principal place of business is located. Any request for judicial review under this section must be filed within 60 days of the date of the Board's final decision. If any appellant fails to file before the end of the 60-day period, the Board's decision shall be final, and the appellant shall have no further rights or remedies with respect to the request.

§ 750.7 Applicability in the event of liquidation or conservatorship.

The provisions of this part, or any consent or approval granted under the provisions of this part by NCUA, will not in any way bind any liquidating agent or conservator for a failed Federally insured credit union and will not in any way obligate the liquidating agent or conservator to pay any claim or obligation pursuant to any golden parachute, severance, indemnification or other agreement. Claims for employee welfare benefits or other benefits that are contingent, even if otherwise vested, when a liquidating agent or conservator is appointed for any Federally insured credit union, including any contingency for termination of employment, are not provable claims or actual, direct compensatory damage claims against such liquidating agent or conservator. Nothing in this part may be construed to permit the payment of salary or any liability or legal expense of any IAP contrary to 12 U.S.C. 1786(t)(3).

PART 760—LOANS IN AREAS HAVING SPECIAL FLOOD HAZARDS

Sec.
760.1 Authority, purpose, and scope.
760.2 Definitions.
760.3 Requirement to purchase flood insurance where available.
760.4 Exemptions.
760.5 Escrow requirement.
760.6 Required use of standard flood hazard determination form.
760.7 Forced placement of flood insurance.
760.8 Determination fees.
760.9 Notice of special flood hazards and availability of Federal disaster relief assistance.
760.10 Notice of servicer's identity.

APPENDIX TO PART 760—SAMPLE FORM OF NOTICE OF SPECIAL FLOOD HAZARDS AND AVAILABILITY OF FEDERAL DISASTER RELIEF ASSISTANCE

AUTHORITY: 12 U.S.C. 1757, 1789; 42 U.S.C. 4012a, 4104a, 4104b, 4106, and 4128.

SOURCE: 61 FR 45713, Aug. 29, 1996, unless otherwise noted.

§ 760.1 Authority, purpose, and scope.

(a) *Authority.* This part is issued pursuant to 12 U.S.C. 1757, 1789 and 42 U.S.C. 4012a, 4104a, 4104b, 4106, 4128.

(b) *Purpose.* The purpose of this part is to implement the requirements of the National Flood Insurance Act of 1968 and the Flood Disaster Protection Act of 1973, as amended (42 U.S.C. 4001–4129).

(c) *Scope.* This part, except for §§ 760.6 and 760.8, applies to loans secured by buildings or mobile homes located or to be located in areas determined by the Director of the Federal Emergency Management Agency to have special flood hazards. Sections 760.6 and 760.8 apply to loans secured by buildings or mobile homes, regardless of location.

§ 760.2 Definitions.

(a) *Act* means the National Flood Insurance Act of 1968, as amended (42 U.S.C. 4001–4129).

(b) *Credit union* means a Federal or State-chartered credit union that is insured by the National Credit Union Share Insurance Fund.

§ 760.3

(c) *Building* means a walled and roofed structure, other than a gas or liquid storage tank, that is principally above ground and affixed to a permanent site, and a walled and roofed structure while in the course of construction, alteration, or repair.

(d) *Community* means a State or a political subdivision of a State that has zoning and building code jurisdiction over a particular area having special flood hazards.

(e) *Designated loan* means a loan secured by a building or mobile home that is located or to be located in a special flood hazard area in which flood insurance is available under the Act.

(f) *Director of FEMA* means the Director of the Federal Emergency Management Agency.

(g) *Mobile home* means a structure, transportable in one or more sections, that is built on a permanent chassis and designed for use with or without a permanent foundation when attached to the required utilities. The term *mobile home* does not include a recreational vehicle. For purposes of this part, the term *mobile home* means a mobile home on a permanent foundation. The term *mobile home* means a manufactured home as that term is used in the NFIP.

(h) *NFIP* means the National Flood Insurance Program authorized under the Act.

(i) *Residential improved real estate* means real estate upon which a home or other residential building is located or to be located.

(j) *Servicer* means the person responsible for:

(1) Receiving any scheduled, periodic payments from a borrower under the terms of a loan, including amounts for taxes, insurance premiums, and other charges with respect to the property securing the loan; and

(2) Making payments of principal and interest and any other payments from the amounts received from the borrower as may be required under the terms of the loan.

(k) *Special flood hazard area* means the land in the flood plain within a community having at least a one percent chance of flooding in any given year, as designated by the Director of FEMA.

(l) *Table funding* means a settlement at which a loan is funded by a contemporaneous advance of loan funds and an assignment of the loan to the person advancing the funds.

§ 760.3 Requirement to purchase flood insurance where available.

(a) *In general.* A credit union shall not make, increase, extend, or renew any designated loan unless the building or mobile home and any personal property securing the loan is covered by flood insurance for the term of the loan. The amount of insurance must be at least equal to the lesser of the outstanding principal balance of the designated loan or the maximum limit of coverage available for the particular type of property under the Act. Flood insurance coverage under the Act is limited to the overall value of the property securing the designated loan minus the value of the land on which the property is located.

(b) *Table funded loan.* A credit union that acquires a loan from a mortgage broker or other entity through table funding shall be considered to be making a loan for the purposes of this part.

§ 760.4 Exemptions.

The flood insurance requirement prescribed by § 760.3 does not apply with respect to:

(a) Any State-owned property covered under a policy of self-insurance satisfactory to the Director of FEMA, who publishes and periodically revises the list of States falling within this exemption; or

(b) Property securing any loan with an original principal balance of $5,000 or less and a repayment term of one year or less.

§ 760.5 Escrow requirement.

If a credit union requires the escrow of taxes, insurance premiums, fees, or any other charges for a loan secured by *residential* improved real estate or a mobile home that is made, increased, extended, or renewed on or after November 1, 1996, the credit union shall also require the escrow of all premiums and fees for any flood insurance required under § 760.3. The credit union, or a servicer acting on behalf of the credit union, shall deposit the flood insurance premiums on behalf of the borrower in an escrow account. This escrow account will be subject to escrow requirements adopted pursuant to section 10 of the Real Estate Settlement Procedures Act of 1974 (12 U.S.C. 2609) (RESPA), which generally limits the amount that may be maintained in escrow accounts for certain types of loans and requires escrow account statements for those accounts, only if the loan is otherwise subject to RESPA. Following receipt of a notice from the Director of FEMA or other provider of flood insurance that premiums are due, the credit union, or a servicer acting on behalf of the credit union, shall pay the amount owed to the insurance provider from the escrow account by the date when such premiums are due.

§ 760.6 Required use of standard flood hazard determination form.

(a) *Use of form.* A credit union shall use the standard flood hazard determination form developed by the Director when determining whether the building or mobile home offered as collateral security for a loan is or will be located in a special flood hazard area in which flood insurance is available under the Act. The standard flood hazard determination form may be used in a printed, computerized, or electronic manner. A credit union may obtain the standard flood hazard determination form from FEMA, P.O. Box 2012, Jessup, MD 20794–2012.

(b) *Retention of form.* A credit union shall retain a copy of the completed standard flood hazard determination form, in either hard copy or electronic form, for the period of time the credit union owns the loan.

[61 FR 45713, Aug. 29, 1996, as amended at 64 FR 71274, Dec. 21, 1999]

§ 760.7 Forced placement of flood insurance.

If a credit union, or a servicer acting on behalf of the credit union, determines at any time during the term of a designated loan that the building or mobile home and any personal property securing the designated loan is not covered by flood insurance, or is covered by flood insurance in an amount less than the amount required under § 760.3, then the credit union or its servicer shall notify the borrower that the borrower should obtain flood insurance, at the borrower's expense, in an amount at least equal to the amount required under § 760.3, for the remaining term of the loan. If the borrower fails to obtain flood insurance within 45 days after notification, then the credit union or its servicer shall purchase insurance on the borrower's behalf. The credit union or its servicer may charge the borrower for the cost of premiums and fees incurred in purchasing the insurance.

[61 FR 45713, Aug. 29, 1996, as amended at 73 FR 30478, May 28, 2008]

§ 760.8 Determination fees.

(a) *General.* Notwithstanding any Federal or State law other than the Flood Disaster Protection Act of 1973, as amended (42 U.S.C. 4001–4129), any credit union, or a servicer acting on behalf of the credit union, may charge a reasonable fee for determining whether the building or mobile home securing the loan is located or will be located in a special flood hazard area. A determination fee may also include, but is not limited to, a fee for life-of-loan monitoring.

(b) *Borrower fee.* The determination fee authorized by paragraph (a) of this section may be charged to the borrower if the determination:

(1) Is made in connection with a making, increasing, extending, or renewing of the loan that is initiated by the borrower;

(2) Reflects the Director of FEMA's revision or updating of floodplain areas or flood-risk zones;

(3) Reflects the Director of FEMA's publication of a notice or compendium that:

(i) Affects the area in which the building or mobile home securing the loan is located; or

(ii) By determination of the Director of FEMA, may reasonably require a determination whether the building or mobile home securing the loan is located in a special flood hazard area; or

(4) Results in the purchase of flood insurance coverage by the credit union or its servicer on behalf of the borrower under § 760.7.

(c) *Purchaser or transferee fee.* The determination fee authorized by paragraph (a) of this section may be charged to the purchaser or transferee of a loan in the case of the sale or transfer of the loan.

§ 760.9 **Notice of special flood hazards and availability of Federal disaster relief assistance.**

(a) *Notice requirement.* When a credit union makes, increases, extends, or renews a loan secured by a building or a mobile home located or to be located in a special flood hazard area, the credit union shall mail or deliver a written notice to the borrower and to the servicer in all cases whether or not flood insurance is available under the Act for the collateral securing the loan.

(b) *Contents of notice.* The written notice must include the following information:

(1) A warning, in a form approved by the Director of FEMA, that the building or the mobile home is or will be located in a special flood hazard area;

(2) A description of the flood insurance purchase requirements set forth in section 102(b) of the Flood Disaster Protection Act of 1973, as amended (42 U.S.C. 4012a(b));

(3) A statement, where applicable, that flood insurance coverage is available under the NFIP and may also be available from private insurers; and

(4) A statement whether Federal disaster relief assistance may be available in the event of damage to the building or mobile home caused by flooding in a Federally-declared disaster.

(c) *Timing of notice.* The credit union shall provide the notice required by paragraph (a) of this section to the borrower within a reasonable time before the completion of the transaction and to the servicer as promptly as practicable after the credit union provides notice to the borrower and in any event no later than the time the credit union provides other similar notices to the servicer concerning hazard insurance and taxes. Notice to the servicer may be made electronically or may take the form of a copy of the notice to the borrower.

(d) *Record of receipt.* The credit union shall retain a record of the receipt of the notices by the borrower and the servicer for the period of time the credit union owns the loan.

(e) *Alternate method of notice.* Instead of providing the notice to the borrower required by paragraph (a) of this section, a credit union may obtain satisfactory written assurance from a seller or lessor that, within a reasonable time before the completion of the sale or lease transaction, the seller or lessor has provided such notice to the purchaser or lessee. The credit union shall retain a record of the written assurance from the seller or lessor for the period of time the credit union owns the loan.

(f) *Use of prescribed form of notice.* A credit union will be considered to be in compliance with the requirement for notice to the borrower of this section providing written notice to the borrower containing the language presented in the appendix to this part within a reasonable time before the completion of the transaction. The notice presented in the appendix to this part satisfies the borrower notice requirements of the Act.

§ 760.10 **Notice of servicer's identity.**

(a) *Notice requirement.* When a credit union makes, increases, extends, renews, sells, or transfers a loan secured by a building or mobile home located or to be located in a special flood hazard area, the credit union shall notify the Director of FEMA (or the Director's designee) in writing of the identity of the servicer of the loan. The Director of FEMA has designated the insurance provider to receive the credit union's notice of the servicer's identity. This notice may be provided electronically if electronic transmission is satisfactory to the Director of FEMA's designee.

(b) *Transfer of servicing rights.* The credit union shall notify the Director of FEMA (or the Director's designee) of any change in the servicer of a loan described in paragraph (a) of this section within 60 days after the effective date of the change. This notice may be provided electronically if electronic transmission is satisfactory to the Director of FEMA's designee. Upon any change in the servicing of a loan described in paragraph (a) of this section, the duty

National Credit Union Administration

§ 761.101

to provide notice under this paragraph (b) shall transfer to the transferee servicer.

APPENDIX TO PART 760—SAMPLE FORM OF NOTICE OF SPECIAL FLOOD HAZARDS AND AVAILABILITY OF FEDERAL DISASTER RELIEF ASSISTANCE

We are giving you this notice to inform you that:

The building or mobile home securing the loan for which you have applied is or will be located in an area with special flood hazards.

The area has been identified by the Director of the Federal Emergency Management Agency (FEMA) as a special flood hazard area using FEMA's *Flood Insurance Rate Map* or the *Flood Hazard Boundary Map* for the following community: _____. This area has at least a one percent (1%) chance of a flood equal to or exceeding the base flood elevation (a 100-year flood) in any given year. During the life of a 30-year mortgage loan, the risk of a 100-year flood in a special flood hazard area is 26 percent (26%).

Federal law allows a lender and borrower jointly to request the Director of FEMA to review the determination of whether the property securing the loan is located in a special flood hazard area. If you would like to make such a request, please contact us for further information.

_____ The community in which the property securing the loan is located participates in the National Flood Insurance Program (NFIP). Federal law will not allow us to make you the loan that you have applied for if you do not purchase flood insurance. The flood insurance must be maintained for the life of the loan. If you fail to purchase or renew flood insurance on the property, Federal law authorizes and requires us to purchase the flood insurance for you at your expense.

• Flood insurance coverage under the NFIP may be purchased through an insurance agent who will obtain the policy either directly through the NFIP or through an insurance company that participates in the NFIP. Flood insurance also may be available from private insurers that do not participate in the NFIP.

• At a minimum, flood insurance purchased must cover *the lesser of*:

(1) the outstanding principal balance of the loan; *or*

(2) the maximum amount of coverage allowed for the type of property under the NFIP.

Flood insurance coverage under the NFIP is limited to the overall value of the property securing the loan minus the value of the land on which the property is located.

• Federal disaster relief assistance (usually in the form of a low-interest loan) may be available for damages incurred in excess of your flood insurance if your community's participation in the NFIP is in accordance with NFIP requirements.

_____ Flood insurance coverage under the NFIP is not available for the property securing the loan because the community in which the property is located does not participate in the NFIP. In addition, if the non-participating community has been identified for at least one year as containing a special flood hazard area, properties located in the community will not be eligible for Federal disaster relief assistance in the event of a Federally-declared flood disaster.

PART 761—REGISTRATION OF RESIDENTIAL MORTGAGE LOAN ORIGINATORS

Sec.
761.101 Authority, purpose, and scope.
761.102 Definitions.
761.103 Registration of mortgage loan originators.
761.104 Policies and procedures.
761.105 Use of unique identifier.

APPENDIX A TO PART 761—EXAMPLES OF MORTGAGE LOAN ORIGINATOR ACTIVITIES.

AUTHORITY: 12 U.S.C. 1751 *et seq.* and 5101 *et seq.*

SOURCE: 75 FR 44704, July 28, 2010, unless otherwise noted.

§ 761.101 Authority, purpose, and scope.

(a) *Authority.* This part is issued pursuant to the Secure and Fair Enforcement for Mortgage Licensing Act of 2008, title V of the Housing and Economic Recovery Act of 2008 (S.A.F.E. Act) (Pub. L. 110–289, 122 Stat. 2654, 12 U.S.C. 5101 *et seq.*).

(b) *Purpose.* This part implements the S.A.F.E. Act's Federal registration requirement for mortgage loan originators. The S.A.F.E. Act provides that the objectives of this registration include aggregating and improving the flow of information to and between regulators; providing increased accountability and tracking of mortgage loan originators; enhancing member protections; reducing fraud in the residential mortgage loan origination process; and providing members with easily accessible information at no charge regarding the employment history of, and publicly adjudicated disciplinary and enforcement actions against, mortgage loan originators.

§ 761.102

(c) *Scope*—(1) *In general.* This part applies to any Federally insured credit union and its employees, including volunteers, who act as mortgage loan originators. This part also applies to non-Federally insured credit unions and their employees, including volunteers, who act as mortgage loan originators, subject to the conditions in paragraph (c)(3) of this section.

(2) *Exception.* (i) This part and the requirements of 12 U.S.C. 5104(a)(1)(A) and (2) of the S.A.F.E. Act do not apply to any employee of a credit union who has never been registered or licensed through the Registry as a mortgage loan originator if during the past 12 months the employee acted as a mortgage loan originator for 5 or fewer residential mortgage loans.

(ii) Prior to engaging in mortgage loan origination activity that exceeds the exception limit in paragraph (c)(2)(i) of this section, a credit union employee must register with the Registry pursuant to this part.

(iii) *Evasion.* Credit unions are prohibited from engaging in any act or practice to evade the limits of the *de minimis* exception set forth in paragraph (c)(2)(i) of this section.

(3) *For non-Federally insured credit unions.* Non-Federally insured credit unions and their employees who are mortgage loan originators may register under this rule only if:

(i) The appropriate State supervisory authorities where non-Federally insured credit unions are located enter into a Memorandum of Understanding (MOU) with the National Credit Union Administration on or before the date NCUA provides in a public notice that the Registry is accepting initial registrations.

(ii) The MOU may require non-Federally insured credit unions to pay various fees related to oversight costs and registration costs for the non-Federally insured credit unions' mortgage loan originators.

(iii) Any Nationwide Mortgage Licensing System and Registry listing of a non-Federally insured credit union and its employees must contain a clear and conspicuous statement that the non-Federally insured credit union is not insured by the National Credit Union Share Insurance Fund.

(iv) If any State supervisory authority where non-Federally insured credit unions are located fails to enter into or maintain an agreement with the National Credit Union Administration for this registration process and oversight, the non-Federally insured credit unions and their employees in that State cannot register or maintain registration under the Federal system. They instead must use the appropriate State licensing and registration system, or if the State does not have such a system, the licensing and registration system established by the Department of Housing and Urban Department ment (HUD) for mortgage loan originators and their employees.

§ 761.102 Definitions.

For purposes of this part, the following definitions apply:

(a) *Annual renewal period* means November 1 through December 31 of each year.

(b)(1) *Mortgage loan originator*[1] means an individual who:

(i) Takes a residential mortgage loan application; and

(ii) Offers or negotiates terms of a residential mortgage loan for compensation or gain.

(2) The term *mortgage loan originator* does not include:

(i) An individual who performs purely administrative or clerical tasks on behalf of an individual who is described in paragraph (b)(1) of this section;

(ii) An individual who only performs real estate brokerage activities (as defined in 12 U.S.C. 5102(3)(D)) and is licensed or registered as a real estate broker in accordance with applicable State law, unless the individual is compensated by a lender, a mortgage broker, or other mortgage loan originator or by any agent of such lender, mortgage broker, or other mortgage loan originator, and meets the definition of mortgage loan originator in paragraph (b)(1) of this section; or

(iii) An individual or entity solely involved in extensions of credit related

---

[1] Appendix A of this part provides examples of activities that would, and would not, cause an employee to fall within the definition of mortgage loan originator.

to timeshare plans, as that term is defined in 11 U.S.C. 101(53D).

(3) *Administrative or clerical tasks* means the receipt, collection, and distribution of information common for the processing or underwriting of a loan in the residential mortgage industry and communication with a member to obtain information necessary for the processing or underwriting of a residential mortgage loan.

(c) *Nationwide Mortgage Licensing System and Registry* or *Registry* means the system developed and maintained by the Conference of State Bank Supervisors and the American Association of Residential Mortgage Regulators for the State licensing and registration of State-licensed mortgage loan originators and the registration of mortgage loan originators pursuant to 12 U.S.C. 5107.

(d) *Registered mortgage loan originator* or *registrant* means any individual who:

(1) Meets the definition of mortgage loan originator and is an employee of a credit union; and

(2) Is registered pursuant to this part with, and maintains a unique identifier through, the Registry.

(e) *Residential mortgage loan* means any loan primarily for personal, family, or household use that is secured by a mortgage, deed of trust, or other equivalent consensual security interest on a dwelling (as defined in section 103(v) of the Truth in Lending Act, 15 U.S.C. 1602(v)) or residential real estate upon which is constructed or intended to be constructed a dwelling, and includes refinancings, reverse mortgages, home equity lines of credit and other first and additional lien loans that meet the qualifications listed in this definition.

(f) *Unique identifier* means a number or other identifier that:

(1) Permanently identifies a registered mortgage loan originator;

(2) Is assigned by protocols established by the Nationwide Mortgage Licensing System and Registry, the Federal banking agencies, and the Farm Credit Administration to facilitate:

(i) Electronic tracking of mortgage loan originators; and

(ii) Uniform identification of, and public access to, the employment history of and the publicly adjudicated disciplinary and enforcement actions against mortgage loan originators; and

(3) Must not be used for purposes other than those set forth under the S.A.F.E. Act.

§ 761.103 Registration of mortgage loan originators.

(a) *Registration requirement*—(1) *Employee registration.* Each employee of a credit union who acts as a mortgage loan originator must register with the Registry, obtain a unique identifier, and maintain this registration in accordance with the requirements of this part. Any such employee who is not in compliance with the registration and unique identifier requirements set forth in this part is in violation of the S.A.F.E. Act and this part.

(2) *Credit union requirement*—(i) *In general.* A credit union that employs one or more individuals who act as a residential mortgage loan originator must require each employee who is a mortgage loan originator to register with the Registry, maintain this registration, and obtain a unique identifier in accordance with the requirements of this part.

(ii) *Prohibition.* A credit union must not permit an employee of the credit union who is subject to the registration requirements of this part to act as a mortgage loan originator for the credit union unless such employee is registered with the Registry pursuant to this part.

(3) *Implementation period for initial registration.* An employee of a credit union who is a mortgage loan originator must complete an initial registration with the Registry pursuant to this part within 180 days from the date that the NCUA provides in a public notice that the Registry is accepting registrations.

(4) *Employees previously registered or licensed through the Registry*—(i) *In general.* If an employee of a credit union was registered or licensed through, and obtained a unique identifier from, the Registry and has maintained this registration or license before the employee becomes subject to this part at this credit union, then the registration requirements of the S.A.F.E. Act and this part are deemed to be met, provided that:

§ 761.103

(A) The employment information in paragraphs (d)(1)(i)(C) and (d)(1)(ii) of this section is updated and the requirements of paragraph (d)(2) of this section are met;

(B) New fingerprints of the employee are submitted to the Registry for a background check, as required by paragraph (d)(1)(ix) of this section, unless the employee has fingerprints on file with the Registry that are less than 3 years old;

(C) The credit union information required in paragraphs (e)(1)(i) (to the extent the credit union has not previously met these requirements) and (e)(2)(i) of this section is submitted to the Registry; and

(D) The registration is maintained pursuant to paragraphs (b) and (e)(1)(ii) of this section, as of the date that the employee is employed by the credit union.

(ii) *Rule for certain acquisitions, mergers, or reorganizations.* When registered or licensed mortgage loan originators become credit union employees as a result of an acquisition, merger, or reorganization, the requirements of paragraphs (a)(4)(i)(A), (C), and (D) of this section must be met within 60 days from the effective date of the acquisition, merger, or reorganization.

(b) *Maintaining registration.* (1) A mortgage loan originator who is registered with the Registry pursuant to paragraph (a) of this section must:

(i) Except as provided in paragraph (b)(3) of this section, renew the registration during the annual renewal period, confirming the responses set forth in paragraphs (d)(1)(i) through (viii) of this section remain accurate and complete, and updating this information, as appropriate; and

(ii) Update the registration within 30 days of any of the following events:

(A) A change in the name of the registrant;

(B) The registrant ceases to be an employee of the credit union; or

(C) The information required under paragraphs (d)(1)(iii) through (viii) of this section becomes inaccurate, incomplete, or out-of-date.

(2) A registered mortgage loan originator must maintain his or her registration, unless the individual is no longer engaged in the activity of a mortgage loan originator.

(3) The annual registration renewal requirement set forth in paragraph (b)(1) of this section does not apply to a registered mortgage loan originator who has completed his or her registration with the Registry pursuant to paragraph (a)(1) of this section less than 6 months prior to the end of the annual renewal period.

(c) *Effective dates*—(1) *Registration.* A registration pursuant to paragraph (a)(1) of this section is effective on the date the Registry transmits notification to the registrant that the registrant is registered.

(2) *Renewals or updates.* A renewal or update pursuant to paragraph (b) of this section is effective on the date the Registry transmits notification to the registrant that the registration has been renewed or updated.

(d) *Required employee information*—(1) *In general.* For purposes of the registration required by this section, a credit union must require each employee who is a mortgage loan originator to submit to the Registry, or must submit on behalf of the employee, the following categories of information, to the extent this information is collected by the Registry:

(i) Identifying information, including the employee's:

(A) Name and any other names used;

(B) Home address and contact information;

(C) Principal business location address and business contact information;

(D) Social security number;

(E) Gender; and

(F) Date and place of birth;

(ii) Financial services-related employment history for the 10 years prior to the date of registration or renewal, including the date the employee became an employee of the credit union;

(iii) Convictions of any criminal offense involving dishonesty, breach of trust, or money laundering against the employee or organizations controlled by the employee, or agreements to enter into a pretrial diversion or similar program in connection with the prosecution for such offense(s);

(iv) Civil judicial actions against the employee in connection with financial services-related activities, dismissals with settlements, or judicial findings that the employee violated financial services-related statutes or regulations, except for actions dismissed without a settlement agreement;

(v) Actions or orders by a State or Federal regulatory agency or foreign financial regulatory authority that:

(A) Found the employee to have made a false statement or omission or been dishonest, unfair or unethical; to have been involved in a violation of a financial services-related regulation or statute; or to have been a cause of a financial services-related business having its authorization to do business denied, suspended, revoked, or restricted;

(B) Are entered against the employee in connection with a financial services-related activity;

(C) Denied, suspended, or revoked the employee's registration or license to engage in a financial services-related activity; disciplined the employee or otherwise by order prevented the employee from associating with a financial services-related business or restricted the employee's activities; or

(D) Barred the employee from association with an entity or its officers regulated by the agency or authority or from engaging in a financial services-related business;

(vi) Final orders issued by a State or Federal regulatory agency or foreign financial regulatory authority based on violations of any law or regulation that prohibits fraudulent, manipulative, or deceptive conduct;

(vii) Revocation or suspension of the employee's authorization to act as an attorney, accountant, or State or Federal contractor;

(viii) Customer-initiated financial services-related arbitration or civil action against the employee that required action, including settlements, or which resulted in a judgment; and

(ix) Fingerprints of the employee, in digital form if practicable, and any appropriate identifying information for submission to the Federal Bureau of Investigation and any governmental agency or entity authorized to receive such information in connection with a State and national criminal history background check; however, fingerprints provided to the Registry that are less than 3 years old may be used to satisfy this requirement.

(2) *Employee authorization and attestation.* An employee registering as a mortgage loan originator or renewing or updating his or her registration under this part, and not the employing credit union or other employees of the credit union, must:

(i) Authorize the Registry and the employing institution to obtain information related to sanctions or findings in any administrative, civil, or criminal action, to which the employee is a party, made by any governmental jurisdiction;

(ii) Attest to the correctness of all information required by paragraph (d) of this section, whether submitted by the employee or on behalf of the employee by the employing credit union; and

(iii) Authorize the Registry to make available to the public information required by paragraphs (d)(1)(i)(A) and (C), and (d)(1)(ii) through (viii) of this section.

(3) *Submission of information.* A credit union may identify one or more employees of the credit union who may submit the information required by paragraph (d)(1) of this section to the Registry on behalf of the credit union's employees provided that this individual, and any employee delegated such authority, does not act as a mortgage loan originator, consistent with (e)(1)(i)(F) of this section. In addition, a credit union may submit to the Registry some or all of the information required by paragraphs (d)(1) and (e)(2) of this section for multiple employees in bulk through batch processing in a format to be specified by the Registry, to the extent such batch processing is made available by the Registry.

(e) *Required credit union information.* A credit union must submit the following categories of information to the Registry:

(1) *Credit union record.* (i) In connection with the registration of one or more mortgage loan originators:

(A) Name, main office address, and business contact information;

(B) Internal Revenue Service Employer Tax Identification Number (EIN);

§ 761.104

(C) Research Statistics Supervision and Discount (RSSD) number, as issued by the Board of Governors of the Federal Reserve System;

(D) Identification of its primary Federal regulator;

(E) Name(s) and contact information of the individual(s) with authority to act as the credit union's primary point of contact for the Registry;

(F) Name(s) and contact information of the individual(s) with authority to enter the information required by paragraphs (d)(1) and (e) of this section to the Registry and who may delegate this authority to other individuals. For the purpose of providing information required by paragraph (e) of this section, this individual and their delegates must not act as mortgage loan originators unless the credit union has 10 or fewer full time or equivalent employees.

(ii) *Attestation.* The individual(s) identified in paragraphs (e)(1)(i)(E) and (F) of this section must comply with Registry protocols to verify their identity and must attest that they have the authority to enter data on behalf of the credit union, that the information provided to the Registry pursuant to this paragraph (e) is correct, and that the credit union will keep the information required by this paragraph (e) current and will file accurate supplementary information on a timely basis.

(iii) A credit union must update the information required by this paragraph (e) of this section within 30 days of the date that this information becomes inaccurate.

(iv) A credit union must renew the information required by paragraph (e) of this section on an annual basis.

(2) *Employee information.* In connection with the registration of each employee who acts as a mortgage loan originator:

(i) After the information required by paragraph (d) of this section has been submitted to the Registry, confirmation that it employs the registrant; and

(ii) Within 30 days of the date the registrant ceases to be an employee of the credit union, notification that it no longer employs the registrant and the date the registrant ceased being an employee.

§ 761.104 Policies and procedures.

A credit union that employs one or more mortgage loan originators must adopt and follow written policies and procedures designed to assure compliance with this part. These policies and procedures must be appropriate to the nature, size, complexity, and scope of the mortgage lending activities of the credit union, and apply only to those employees acting within the scope of their employment at the credit union. At a minimum, these policies and procedures must:

(a) Establish a process for identifying which employees of the credit union are required to be registered mortgage loan originators;

(b) Require that all employees of the credit union who are mortgage loan originators be informed of the registration requirements of the S.A.F.E. Act and this part and be instructed on how to comply with such requirements and procedures;

(c) Establish procedures to comply with the unique identifier requirements in § 761.105;

(d) Establish reasonable procedures for confirming the adequacy and accuracy of employee registrations, including updates and renewals, by comparisons with its own records;

(e) Establish reasonable procedures and tracking systems for monitoring compliance with registration and renewal requirements and procedures;

(f) Provide for independent testing for compliance with this part to be conducted at least annually by credit union personnel or by an outside party;

(g) Provide for appropriate action in the case of any employee who fails to comply with the registration requirements of the S.A.F.E. Act, this part, or the credit union's related policies and procedures, including prohibiting such employees from acting as mortgage loan originators or other appropriate disciplinary actions;

(h) Establish a process for reviewing employee criminal history background reports received pursuant to this part, taking appropriate action consistent with applicable Federal law, including section 206 of the Federal Credit Union Act (12 U.S.C. 1786(i)) and implementing regulations with respect to these reports, and maintaining records of these reports and actions taken with respect to applicable employees; and

(i) Establish procedures designed to ensure that any third party with which the credit union has arrangements related to mortgage loan origination has policies and procedures to comply with the S.A.F.E. Act, including appropriate licensing and/or registration of individuals acting as mortgage loan originators.

§ 761.105 Use of unique identifier.

(a) The credit union shall make the unique identifier(s) of its registered mortgage loan originator(s) available to members in a manner and method practicable to the credit union.

(b) A registered mortgage loan originator shall provide his or her unique identifier to a member:

(1) Upon request;

(2) Before acting as a mortgage loan originator; and

(3) Through the originator's initial written communication with a member, if any, whether on paper or electronically.

APPENDIX A TO PART 761—EXAMPLES OF MORTGAGE LOAN ORIGINATOR ACTIVITIES

This Appendix provides examples to aid in the understanding of activities that would cause an employee of a credit union to fall within or outside the definition of mortgage loan originator. The examples in this Appendix are not all inclusive. They illustrate only the issue described and do not illustrate any other issues that may arise under this part. For the purposes of the examples below, the term "loan" refers to a residential mortgage loan.

(a) *Taking a loan application.* The following examples illustrate when an employee takes, or does not take, a loan application.

(1) Taking an application includes: receiving information provided in connection with a request for a loan to be used to determine whether the member qualifies for a loan, even if the employee:

(i) Has received the member's information indirectly in order to make an offer or negotiate a loan;

(ii) Is not responsible for further verification of information;

(iii) Is inputting information into an online application or other automated system on behalf of the member; or

(iv) Is not engaged in approval of the loan, including determining whether the member qualifies for the loan.

(2) Taking an application does not include any of the following activities performed solely or in combination:

(i) Contacting a member to verify the information in the loan application by obtaining documentation, such as tax returns or payroll receipts;

(ii) Receiving a loan application through the mail and forwarding it, without review, to loan approval personnel;

(iii) Assisting a member who is filling out an application by clarifying what type of information is necessary for the application or otherwise explaining the qualifications or criteria necessary to obtain a loan product;

(iv) Describing the steps that a member would need to take to provide information to be used to determine whether the member qualifies for a loan or otherwise explaining the loan application process;

(v) In response to an inquiry regarding a prequalified offer that a member has received from a credit union, collecting only basic identifying information about the member and forwarding the member to a loan originator; or

(vi) Receiving information in connection with a modification to the terms of an existing loan to a borrower as part of the credit union's loss mitigation efforts when the borrower is reasonably likely to default.

(b) *Offering or negotiating terms of a loan.* The following examples are designed to illustrate when an employee offers or negotiates terms of a loan, and conversely, what does not constitute offering or negotiating terms of a loan.

(1) Offering or negotiating the terms of a loan includes:

(i) Presenting a loan offer to a member for acceptance, either verbally or in writing, including, but not limited to, providing a disclosure of the loan terms after application under the Truth in Lending Act, even if:

(A) Further verification of information is necessary;

(B) The offer is conditional;

(C) Other individuals must complete the loan process; or

(D) Only the rate approved by the credit union's loan approval mechanism function for a specific loan product is communicated without authority to negotiate the rate.

(ii) Responding to a member's request for a lower rate or lower points on a pending loan application by presenting to the member a revised loan offer, either verbally or in writing, that includes a lower interest rate or lower points than the original offer.

(2) Offering or negotiating terms of a loan does not include solely or in combination:

(i) Providing general explanations or descriptions in response to member queries regarding qualification for a specific loan product, such as explaining loan terminology (*i.e.*, debt-to-income ratio); lending policies (*i.e.*, the loan-to-value ratio policy of the credit union); or product-related services;

(ii) In response to a member's request, informing a member of the loan rates that are publicly available, such as on the credit union's Web site, for specific types of loan products without communicating to the member whether qualifications are met for that loan product;

(iii) Collecting information about a member in order to provide the member with information on loan products for which the member generally may qualify, without presenting a specific loan offer to the member for acceptance, either verbally or in writing;

(iv) Arranging the loan closing or other aspects of the loan process, including communicating with a member about those arrangements, provided that communication with the member only verifies loan terms already offered or negotiated;

(v) Providing a member with information unrelated to loan terms, such as the best days of the month for scheduling loan closings at the credit union;

(vi) Making an underwriting decision about whether the member qualifies for a loan;

(vii) Explaining or describing the steps or process that a member would need to take in order to obtain a loan offer, including qualifications or criteria that would need to be met without providing guidance specific to that member's circumstances; or

(viii) Communicating on behalf of a mortgage loan originator that a written offer, including disclosures provided pursuant to the Truth in Lending Act, has been sent to a member without providing any details of that offer.

(c) *Offering or negotiating a loan for compensation or gain.* The following examples illustrate when an employee does or does not offer or negotiate terms of a loan "for compensation or gain."

(1) Offering or negotiating terms of a loan for compensation or gain includes engaging in any of the activities in paragraph (b)(1) of this Appendix in the course of carrying out employment duties, even if the employee does not receive a referral fee or commission or other special compensation for the loan.

(2) Offering or negotiating terms of a loan for compensation or gain does not include engaging in a seller-financed transaction for the employee's personal property that does not involve the credit union.

SUBCHAPTER B—REGULATIONS AFFECTING THE OPERATIONS OF THE NATIONAL CREDIT UNION ADMINISTRATION

PART 790—DESCRIPTION OF NCUA; REQUESTS FOR AGENCY ACTION

Sec.
790.1 Scope.
790.2 Central and regional office organization.
790.3 Requests for action.

AUTHORITY: 12 U.S.C. 1766, 1789, 1795f.

SOURCE: 58 FR 45431, Aug. 30, 1993, unless otherwise noted.

§ 790.1 Scope.

This part contains a description of NCUA's organization and the procedures for public requests for action by the Board. Part 790 pertains to the practices of the National Credit Union Administration (NCUA) only and does not apply to credit union operations.

§ 790.2 Central and regional office organization.

(a) *General organization.* NCUA is composed of the Board with a Central Office in Alexandria, Virginia, five Regional Offices, the Asset Management and Assistance Center, the Community Development Revolving Loan Program, and the NCUA Central Liquidity Facility (CLF).

(b) *Central Office.* The Central Office address is NCUA, 1775 Duke St., Alexandria, Virginia 22314-3428.

(1) *The NCUA Board.* NCUA is managed by its Board. The Board consists of three members appointed by the President, with the advice and consent of the Senate, for six-year terms. One Board member is designated by the President to be Chairman of the Board. The Chairman shall be the spokesman for the Board and shall represent the Board and the NCUA in its official relations with other branches of the government. A second member is designated by the Board to be Vice-Chairman. The Board is also responsible for management of the National Credit Union Share Insurance Fund (NCUSIF) and serves as the Board of Directors of the CLF.

(2) *Secretary of the Board.* The Secretary of the Board is responsible for the secretarial functions of the Board. The Secretary's responsibilities include preparing agendas for meetings of the Board, preparing and maintaining the minutes for all official actions taken by the Board, and executing and maintaining all documents adopted by the Board or under its direction. The Secretary also serves as the Secretary of the CLF.

(3) *Asset Management and Assistance Center.* The President of the Asset Management and Assistance Center (AMAC) is responsible for monitoring, evaluating, disposing, and/or managing major assets acquired by NCUA; responsible for managing involuntary liquidations for all federally insured credit unions placed into involuntary liquidation including the orderly processing of payments of share insurance, sale and/or collection of loan portfolios, liquidation of other assets and achieving other recoveries, payments to creditors, and distributions to any uninsured shareholders. The President, AMAC, serves as a primary consultant with regional offices on asset sales or purchases to restructure problem case credit unions, as technical expert to evaluate specific areas of credit union operations, and as instructor in training classes; responsible to prepare and negotiate bond claims; responsible to manage or assist in the management of conservatorships. The address of AMAC is 4807 Spicewood Springs Road, Suite 5100, Austin, Texas 78759-8490.

(4) *Office of Chief Financial Officer.* NCUA's chief financial officer is in charge of budgetary, accounting and financial matters for the NCUA, including responsibility for submitting annual budget and staffing requests for approval by the Board and, as required, by the Office of Management and Budget; for managing NCUA's budgetary resources; for managing the operations of the National Credit Union Share Insurance Fund (NCUSIF) to include accounting, financial reporting and the

§ 790.2

collection and payment of capitalization deposits, insurance premiums and insurance dividends; for collecting annual operating fees from federal credit unions, for maintaining NCUA's accounting system and accounting records; for processing payroll, travel, and accounts payable disbursements; and for preparing internal and external financial reports. The Director is also responsible for providing NCUA's executive offices and Regional Directors with administrative services, including: agency security; contracting and procurement; management of equipment and supplies; acquisition; printing; graphics; and warehousing and distribution.

(5) *Office of Examination and Insurance.* The Director of the Office of Examination and Insurance: Formulates standards and procedures for examination and supervision of the community of federally insured credit unions, and reports to the Board on the performance of the examination program; manages the risk to the NCUSIF, to include overseeing the NCUSIF Investment Committee, monitoring the adequacy of NCUSIF reserves, analyzing the reasons for NCUSIF losses, formulating policies and procedures regarding the supervision of financially troubled credit unions, and evaluating certain requests for special assistance pursuant to Section 208 of the Federal Credit Union Act and for certain proposed administrative actions regarding federally-insured credit unions; serves as the Board expert on accounting principles and standards and on auditing standards; represents NCUA at meetings with the American Institute of Certified Public Accountants (AICPA), Federal Financial Institutions Examination Council (FFIEC) and General Accounting Office (GAO); and collects data and provides statistical reports. The Director is also responsible for developing and conducting research in support of NCUA programs, and for preparing reports on research activities for the information and use of agency staff, credit union officials, state credit union supervisory authorities, and other governmental and private groups.

(6) *Office of the Executive Director.* The Executive Director reports to the entire NCUA Board. The Executive Director translates NCUA Board policy decisions into workable programs, delegates responsibility for these programs to appropriate staff members, and coordinates the activities of the senior executive staff, which includes: The General Counsel; the Regional Directors; and the Office Directors for Chief Financial Officer, Examination and Insurance, Human Resources, Chief Information Officer, and Public and Congressional Affairs. Because of the nature of the attorney/client relationship between the Board and General Counsel, the General Counsel may be directed by the Board not to disclose discussions and/or assignments with anyone, including the Executive Director. The Executive Director is otherwise to be privy to all matters within senior executive staff's responsibility. The Executive Director also serves as the agency's Director of Equal Employment Opportunity (EEO).

(7) *Office of General Counsel.* The General Counsel reports to the entire NCUA Board. The General Counsel has overall responsibility for all legal matters affecting NCUA and for liaison with the Department of Justice. The General Counsel represents NCUA in all litigation and administrative hearings when such direct representation is permitted by law and, in other instances, assists the attorneys responsible for the conduct of such litigation. The General Counsel also provides NCUA with legal advice and opinions on all matters of law, and the public with interpretations of the Federal Credit Union Act, the NCUA Rules and Regulations, and other NCUA Board directives. The Office has responsibility for processing Freedom of Information Act requests and appeals. The General Counsel has responsibility for the drafting, reviewing, and publication of all items which appear in the FEDERAL REGISTER, including rules, regulations, and notices required by law and carrying out the Board's responsibilities under the Privacy Act.

(8) *The Office of Human Resources.* The Office of Human Resources provides a comprehensive program for the management of NCUA's human resources. This is done in support of NCUA's goal

National Credit Union Administration § 790.2

to recruit, develop, and retain a quality and representative workforce. The Director is responsible for managing NCUA's compensation program, for facilitating good organization design, for staffing positions through recruitment and merit promotion programs, and for maintaining an automated personnel records system. The Director is also responsible for the Board's performance management, incentive awards, employee assistance, and benefit programs. These programs are geared to foster healthy employee/management relations and to provide employees with good working conditions. The Director is also responsible for providing a comprehensive program for the training and development of NCUA's staff, including developing policy consistent with the Government Employees Training Act; providing training opportunities equitably so that all employees have the skills necessary to help meet the agency's mission; evaluating the agency's training and development efforts; and ensuring that the agencies training monies are spent in a cost efficient manner and in accordance with the law.

(9) *Office of the Chief Information Officer.* The Chief Information Officer has responsibility for the management and administration of NCUA's information resources. This includes the development, maintenance, operation, and support of information systems which directly support the Agency's mission, maintaining and operating the Agency's information processing infrastructure, responding to requests for releasable Agency information, and insuring all related material security and integrity risks are recognized and controlled as much as possible. The Chief Information Officer is also responsible for carrying out the Board's responsibilities under the Paperwork Reduction Act and in directing NCUA responses to reporting requirements.

(10) *Office of the Inspector General.* The Inspector General reports directly to the Board and provides semi-annual reports regarding audit and investigation activities to the Board and the Congress. The Inspector General is responsible for: (a) Conducting independent audits and investigations of all NCUA programs and functions to promote efficiency; (b) reviewing policies and procedures to evaluate controls to prevent fraud, waste, and abuse; and (c) reviewing existing and proposed legislation and regulations to evaluate their impact on the economic and efficient administration of the Agency.

(11) *Office of Public and Congressional Affairs.* The Director of the Office of Public Congressional Affairs is responsible for maintaining NCUA's relationship with the public and the media; for liaison with the U.S. Congress, and with other Executive Branch agencies concerning legislative matters; and for the analysis and development of legislative proposals and public affairs programs.

(12) *Office of Small Credit Union Initiatives.* This Office is responsible for coordinating NCUA policy as it relates to community development credit unions, including those credit unions designated as "low-income." The Office administers the Community Development Revolving Loan Program for Credit Unions (Program). This Program was funded from a congressional appropriation and serves as a loan and technical assistance vehicle for low-income credit unions. The Office Director serves as Program Chairman and authorizes loans and technical assistance to participating credit unions. The Program is governed by part 705 of subchapter A of this chapter.

(13) *Office of Capital Markets.* This office is responsible for providing interest rate risk assessment, investment expertise and advice to the Board and agency staff and conducting research and development to assess risk areas of emerging products, delivery systems, infrastructure issues, and investments. The office provides leadership, vision and focus on the internal and external environment related to the development of the agency's long range planning and implementation of the Government Performance Act of 1993. The office provides a macro view of the industry in a way that can be integrated into the day-to-day program functions. A working relationship is maintained with the financial marketplace to develop resources available to the NCUA and keep abreast of product initiatives. The NCUA Investment Hotline housed in this office is a toll-free number that

§ 790.2

is available to examiners, credit unions and financial product vendors to ask investment related questions. The Hotline provides NCUA an opportunity to be aware of current investment issues as they arise in credit unions and has permitted NCUA to become proactive, rather than reactive, to such issues. In addition, investment officers advise agency management on the purchase of authorized investments for the NCUSIF and the CLF.

(14) *Office of Corporate Credit Unions.* The Director, Office of Corporate Credit Unions, manages NCUA's corporate credit union program in accordance with established policies and the corporate regulation. The Director's duties include directing chartering, examination and supervision programs to promote and assure safety and soundness; managing NCUA's corporate resources to meet program objectives in the most economical and practical manner; and maintaining good public relations with public, private and governmental organizations, corporate credit union officials, credit union organizations, and other groups which have an interest in corporate credit union matters.

(15) *NCUA Central Liquidity Facility (CLF).* The CLF was created to improve general financial stability by providing funds to meet the liquidity needs of credit unions. It is a mixed-ownership government corporation under the Government Corporation Control Act (31 U.S.C. 9101 *et seq.*). The CLF is managed by the President, under the general supervision of the NCUA Board which serves as the CLF Board of Directors. The Chairman of the NCUA Board serves as the Chairman of the CLF Board of Directors. The Secretary of the NCUA Board serves as the Secretary of the CLF Board of Directors. The NCUA Board shall appoint the CLF President and Vice President.

(16) *Office of Consumer Protection.* The Office of Consumer Protection contains two divisions, the Division of Consumer Protection and the Division of Consumer Access. The office provides consumer services, including consumer education and complaint resolution; establishes, consolidates, and coordinates consumer protections within the agency; acts as the central liaison on consumer protection with other federal agencies; nationalizes field of membership processing; absorbs centralized chartering activities; and assumes the activities of the agency's ombudsman. The ombudsman investigates complaints and recommends solutions on regulatory issues that cannot be resolved at the regional level.

(17) *The Office of Chief Economist.* The Office of Chief Economist is within the Office of the Executive Director and reports to the Deputy Executive Director. The office analyzes developments in key components of the economy and monitors trends and conditions in the domestic and international markets for money, credit, foreign exchange and commodities, and relates these trends to overall macroeconomic conditions and government monetary and fiscal policies for the purpose of evaluating effects on credit unions. The office provides advice and guidance to the NCUA Board, the Office of the Executive Director, and the Office of Capital Markets.

(c) *Regional offices.* (1) NCUA's programs are conducted through five Regional Offices:

Region No.	Area within region	Office address
I	Connecticut, Maine, Massachusetts, Michigan, New Hampshire, Michigan, New Hampshire, New York, Rhode Island, Vermont, Nevada.	9 Washington Square, Washington Avenue Extension, Albany, NY 12205–5512.
II	Delaware, District of Columbia, Maryland, New Jersey, Pennsylvania, Virginia, West Virginia, California.	1775 Duke Street, Suite 4206, Alexandria, VA 22314–3437.
III	Alabama, Florida, Georgia, Indiana, Kentucky, Mississippi, North Carolina, Ohio, Puerto Rico, South Carolina, Tennessee, Virgin Islands.	7000 Central Parkway, Suite 1600, Atlanta, GA 30328–4598.
IV	Arkansas, Illinois, Iowa, Kansas, Louisiana, Minnesota, Missouri, Nebraska, North Dakota, Oklahoma, South Dakota, Texas, Wisconsin.	4807 Spicewood Springs Road, Suite 5200, Austin, TX 78759–8490.
V	Alaska, Arizona, American Samoa, Colorado, Guam, Hawaii, Idaho, Montana , New Mexico, Oregon, Utah, Washington, Wyoming.	1230 W. Washington Street, Suite 301, Tempe, AZ 85281.

(2) A Regional Director is in charge of each Regional Office. The Regional Director manages NCUA's programs in the Region assigned in accordance with established policies. This person's duties include: Directing chartering, insurance, examination, and supervision programs to promote and assure safety and soundness; managing regional resources to meet program objectives in the most economical and practical manner; and maintaining good public relations with public, private, and governmental organizations, Federal credit union officials, credit union organizations, and other groups which have an interest in credit union matters in the assigned Region. The Director maintains liaison and cooperation with other regional offices of Federal departments and agencies, state agencies, city and county officials, and other governmental units that affect credit unions. The Regional Director is aided by an Associate Regional Director for Operations and Associate Regional Director for Programs. Staff working in the Regional Office report to the Associate Regional Director for Operations. Each region is divided into examiner districts, each assigned to a Supervisory Credit Union Examiner; groups of examiners are directed by a Supervisory Credit Union Examiner, each of whom in turn reports directly to the Associate Regional Director for Programs. Special Actions staff also report to the Associate Regional Director.

[58 FR 45431, Aug. 30, 1993, as amended at 59 FR 36042, July 15, 1994; 59 FR 47072, Sept. 14, 1994; 60 FR 31911, June 19, 1995; 61 FR 45876, Aug. 30, 1996; 62 FR 8155, Feb. 24, 1997; 62 FR 37126, July 11, 1997; 62 FR 65197, Dec. 11, 1997; 64 FR 17086, Apr. 8, 1999; 64 FR 57365, Oct. 25, 1999; 65 FR 25267, May 1, 2000; 66 FR 65624, Dec. 20, 2001; 67 FR 30773, May 8, 2002; 69 FR 9201, Feb. 27, 2004; 70 FR 55517, Sept. 22, 2005; 75 FR 34623, June 18, 2010]

§ 790.3 Requests for action.

Except as otherwise provided by NCUA regulation, all applications, requests, and submittals for action by the NCUA shall be in writing and addressed to the appropriate office described in § 790.2. This will usually be one of the Regional Offices. In instances where the appropriate office cannot be determined, requests should be sent to the Office of Public and Congressional Affairs.

PART 791—RULES OF NCUA BOARD PROCEDURE; PROMULGATION OF NCUA RULES AND REGULATIONS; PUBLIC OBSERVATION OF NCUA BOARD MEETINGS

Subpart A—Rules of NCUA Board Procedure

Sec.
791.1 Scope.
791.2 Number of votes required for board action.
791.3 Voting by proxy.
791.4 Methods of acting.
791.5 Scheduling of board meetings.
791.6 Subject matter of a meeting.

Subpart B—Promulgation of NCUA Rules and Regulations

791.7 Scope.
791.8 Promulgation of NCUA rules and regulations.

Subpart C—Public Observation of NCUA Board Meetings Under the Sunshine Act

791.9   Scope.
791.10 Definitions.
791.11 Open meetings.
791.12 Exemptions.
791.13 Public announcement of meetings.
791.14 Regular procedure for closing meeting discussions or limiting the disclosure of information.
791.15 Requests for open meeting.
791.16 General counsel certification.
791.17 Maintenance of meeting records.
791.18 Public availability of meeting records and other documents.

AUTHORITY: 12 U.S.C. 1766, 1789 and 5 U.S.C. 552b.

SOURCE: 53 FR 29647, Aug. 8, 1988, unless otherwise noted.

Subpart A—Rules of NCUA Board Procedure

§ 791.1 Scope.

The rules contained in this subpart are the rules of procedure governing how the Board conducts its business. These rules concern the Board's exercise of its authority to act on behalf of NCUA; the conduct, scheduling and subject matter of Board meetings; and the recording of Board action.

§ 791.2 Number of votes required for board action.

The agreement of at least two of the three Board members is required for any action by the Board.

§ 791.3 Voting by proxy.

Proxy voting shall not be allowed for any action by the Board.

§ 791.4 Methods of acting.

(a) *Board meetings*—(1) *Applicability of the Sunshine Act.* The Government in the Sunshine Act (5 U.S.C. 552b, "Sunshine Act") requires that joint deliberations of the Board be held in accordance with its open meetings provisions (5 U.S.C. 552b (b) through (f)). (Subpart C of this part contains NCUA's regulations implementing the Sunshine Act.)

(2) *Presiding officer.* The Chairman is the presiding officer, and in the Chairman's absence, the designated Vice Chairman shall preside. The presiding officer shall make procedural rulings. Any Board member may appeal a ruling made by the presiding officer. The appeal of a procedural ruling by the presiding officer shall be immediately considered by the Board, and a majority decision by the Board shall decide the procedural ruling.

(b) *Notation voting.* Notation voting is the circulation of written memoranda and voting sheets to the office of each Board member simultaneously and the tabulation of responses.

(1) *Matters that may be decided by notation voting.* Notation voting may be used only for administrative or time sensitive matters, for example, enforcement or interagency actions requiring prompt Board action matters.

(2) *Notation vote sheets.* Notation vote sheets will be used to record the vote tally on a notation vote. The Secretary of the Board has administrative responsibility over notation voting, including the authority to establish deadlines for voting, receive notation vote sheets, count votes, and determine whether further action is required.

(3) *Veto of notation voting.* In view of public policy for openness reflected in the Sunshine Act, each Board member is authorized to veto the use of notation voting for the consideration of any particular matter, and thus requires that the matter be placed on the agenda of the next regularly scheduled Board meeting that is held at least ten days after the date of the veto.

(4) *Disclosure of result.* A record is to be maintained of Board transactions by use of the notation voting procedure. Public disclosure of this record is determined by the provisions of the Freedom of Information Act (5 U.S.C. 552).

[53 FR 29647, Aug. 8, 1988, as amended at 62 FR 64267, Dec. 5, 1997; 70 FR 55517, Sept. 22, 2005; 75 FR 34623, June 18, 2010]

§ 791.5 Scheduling of board meetings.

(a) *Meeting calls*—(1) *Regular meetings.* The Board will hold regular meetings each month unless there is no business or a quorum is not available. The Secretary of the Board will coordinate the dates for meetings.

(2) *Special meetings.* The Chairman shall call special meetings either on the Chairman's own initiative or within fourteen days of a request from two Board members that is accompanied by an NCUA B-1 form and a Board Action Memorandum that states the specific issue(s) or action(s) to be considered by the Board.

(b) *Notice of meetings*—(1) *Notifying the public.* The Sunshine Act and subpart C set forth the procedures for notifying the public of Board meetings.

(2) *Notifying board members*—(i) *Special meetings.* Except in cases of emergency, as determined by a majority of the Board, each Board member is entitled to receive notice of any special meeting at least twenty-four hours in advance of such meeting. The notice shall set forth the place, day, hour, and nature of business to be transacted at the meeting. In cases of emergency a record of the vote, including a statement explaining the decision that an emergency exists, will be maintained.

(ii) *Regular meetings.* Each Board member is entitled to receive notice of the agenda and/or notice of any changes in the subject matter of such meetings concurrent with the public release of such notices under the Sunshine Act. Each Board member shall be entitled to at least twenty-four hours advance notice of the consideration of a particular subject matter, except in cases of emergency as determined by a majority of the Board. In cases of emergency, a record of the vote, including a statement explaining the decision that an emergency exists, will be maintained.

[53 FR 29647, Aug. 8, 1988, as amended at 62 FR 64267, Dec. 5, 1997; 63 FR 5859, Feb. 5, 1998; 75 FR 34623, June 18, 2010]

§ 791.6 Subject matter of a meeting.

(a) *Agenda.* The Chairman is responsible for the final order of each meeting agenda. Items shall be placed on the agenda by determination of the Chairman or, at the request of any Board Member, an item will be placed on the agenda of the next regularly scheduled meeting provided that the request is submitted at least ten days in advance of the next regularly scheduled meeting and is accompanied by an NCUA B–1 form and a Board Action Memorandum that states the specific issue(s) or action(s) to be considered by the Board.

(b) *Submission of recommended agenda items.* Recommended agenda items may be submitted to the Secretary of the Board by Board members, the Executive Staff (which includes all Office Directors and President of the Central Liquidity Facility), and Regional Directors.

[61 FR 55208, Oct. 25, 1996, as amended at 62 FR 64267, Dec. 5, 1997; 63 FR 5859, Feb. 5, 1998]

Subpart B—Promulgation of NCUA Rules and Regulations

§ 791.7 Scope.

The rules contained in this subpart B pertain to the promulgation of NCUA rules and regulations.

§ 791.8 Promulgation of NCUA rules and regulations.

(a) NCUA's procedures for developing regulations are governed by the Administrative Procedure Act (5 U.S.C. 551 *et seq.*), the Regulatory Flexibility Act (5 U.S.C. 601 *et seq.*), and NCUA's policies for the promulgation of rules and regulations as set forth in its Interpretive Ruling and Policy Statement 87–2 as amended by Interpretive Ruling and Policy Statement 03–2.

(b) *Proposed rulemaking.* Notices of proposed rulemaking are published in the FEDERAL REGISTER except as specified in paragraph (d) of this section or as otherwise provided by law. A notice of proposed rulemaking may also be identified as a "request for comments" or as a "proposed rule." The notice will include:

(1) A statement of the nature of the rulemaking proceedings;

(2) Reference to the authority under which the rule is proposed;

(3) Either the terms or substance of the proposed rule or a description of the subjects and issues involved; and

(4) A statement of the effect of the proposed rule on state-chartered federally-insured credit unions.

(c) *Public participation.* After publication of notice of proposed rulemaking, interested persons will be afforded the opportunity to participate in the making of the rule through the submission of written data, views, or arguments, delivered within the time prescribed in the notice of proposed rulemaking, to the Secretary, NCUA Board, 1775 Duke Street, Alexandria, VA 22314–3428. Interested persons may also petition the Board for the issuance, amendment, or repeal of any rule by mailing such petition to the Secretary of the Board at the address given in this section.

(d) *Exceptions to notice.* The following are not subject to the notice requirement contained in paragraph (b) of this section:

(1) Matters relating to agency management or personnel or to public property, loans, grants, benefits, or contracts;

(2) When persons subject to the proposed rule are named and either personally served or otherwise have actual notice thereof in accordance with law;

(3) Interpretive rules, general statements of policy, or rules of agency organization, procedure or practice, unless notice or hearing is required by statute; and

(4) If the Board, for good cause, finds (and incorporates the finding and a brief statement therefor in the rules issued) that notice and public procedure thereon are impracticable, unnecessary, or contrary to the public interest, unless notice or hearing is required by statute.

(e) *Effective dates.* No substantive rule issued by NCUA shall be effective less than 30 days after its publication in the

§ 791.9

FEDERAL REGISTER, except that this requirement may not apply to:

(1) Rules which grant or recognize an exemption or relieve a restriction;

(2) Interpretive rules and statements of policy; or

(3) Any substantive rule which the Board makes effective at an earlier date upon good cause found and published with such rule.

(f) NCUA has an Office of Management and Budget (OMB) control number for rulemakings containing an information collection within the meaning of the Paperwork Reduction Act (44 U.S.C. 3501). A list of OMB control numbers is available to the public for review online at *http://www.RegInfo.gov*.

[53 FR 29647, Aug. 8, 1988, as amended at 59 FR 36041, July 15, 1994; 68 FR 31952, May 29, 2003; 75 FR 34623, June 18, 2010]

Subpart C—Public Observation of NCUA Board Meetings Under the Sunshine Act

§ 791.9 Scope.

This subpart contains regulations implementing subsections (b) through (f) of the "Government in the Sunshine Act" (5 U.S.C. 552b). The primary purpose of these regulations is to provide the public with the fullest access authorized by law to the deliberations and decisions of the Board, while protecting the rights of individuals and preserving the ability of the agency to carry out its responsibilities.

§ 791.10 Definitions.

For the purpose of this subpart:

(a) *Agency* means the National Credit Union Administration;

(b) *Board* means the National Credit Union Administration Board, whose members were appointed by the President with the advice and consent of the Senate;

(c) *Subdivision of the Board* means a group composed of two Board members authorized by the Board to act on behalf of the agency;

(d) *Meeting* means any deliberations by two or more members of the Board or any subdivision of the Board that determine or result in the joint conduct or disposition of official agency business with the exception of: (1) Deliberations to determine whether a meeting or a portion thereof will be open or closed to public observation and whether information regarding closed meetings will be withheld from public disclosure; (2) deliberations to determine whether or when to schedule a meeting; and (3) infrequent dispositions of official agency business by sequential circulation of written recommendations to individual Board members ("notation voting procedure"), provided the votes of each Board member and the action taken are recorded for each matter and are publicly available, unless exempted from disclosure pursuant to 5 U.S.C. 552 (the Freedom of Information Act);

(e) *Public observation* means that a member or group of the public may listen to and observe any open meeting and may record in an unobtrusive manner any portion of that meeting by use of a camera or any other electronic device, but shall not participate in any meeting unless authorized by the Board;

(f) *Public announcement* or *publicly announce* means making reasonable efforts under the particular circumstances to fully inform the public, especially those individuals who have expressed interest in the subject matters to be discussed or the decisions of the agency;

(g) *Sunshine Act* means the open meeting provisions of the "Government in the Sunshine Act" (5 U.S.C. 552b.)

§ 791.11 Open meetings.

Except as provided in § 791.12(a), any portion of any meeting of the Board shall be open to public observation. The Board, and any subdivision of the Board, shall jointly conduct official agency business only in accordance with this subpart.

§ 791.12 Exemptions.

(a) Under the procedures specified in § 791.14, the Board may close a meeting or any portion of a meeting from public observation or may withhold information pertaining to such meetings provided the Board has properly determined that the public interest does not require otherwise and that the meeting (or any portion thereof) or the disclosure of meeting information is likely to:

(1) Disclose matters that are:

(i) Specifically authorized under criteria established by an Executive Order to be kept secret in the interests of national defense or foreign policy; and

(ii) In fact properly classified pursuant to such Executive Order;

(2) Relate solely to internal personnel rules and practices;

(3) Disclose matters specifically exempted from disclosure by statute (other than section 552 of title 5 of the United States Code, the Freedom of Information Act), provided that such statute:

(i) Requires that the matters be withheld from the public in such a manner as to leave no discretion on the issue, or

(ii) Establishes particular criteria for withholding or refers to particular types of matters to be withheld;

(4) Disclose trade secrets and commercial or financial information obtained from a person and privileged or confidential;

(5) Involve accusing any person of a crime, or formally censuring any person;

(6) Disclose information of a personal nature where disclosure would constitute a clearly unwarranted invasion of personal privacy;

(7) Disclose investigatory records compiled for enforcement purposes, or information which if written would be contained in such records, but only to the extent that the production of such records or information would:

(i) Interfere with enforcement proceedings,

(ii) Deprive a person of a right to a fair trial or an impartial adjudication,

(iii) Constitute an unwarranted invasion of personal privacy,

(iv) Disclose the identity of a confidential source and, in the case of a record compiled by a criminal law enforcement authority in the course of a criminal investigation, or by a Federal agency conducting a lawful national security intelligence investigation, confidential information furnished only by the confidential source,

(v) Disclose investigative techniques and procedures, or

(vi) Endanger the life or physical safety of law enforcement personnel;

(8) Disclose information contained in or related to examination, operating, or condition reports prepared by, on behalf of, or for the use of Federal agencies responsible for the regulation or supervision of financial institutions;

(9) Disclose information the premature disclosure of which would be likely to (i)(A) lead to significant speculation in currencies, securities, or commodities, or (B) significantly endanger the stability of any financial institution, or (ii) be likely to significantly frustrate implementation of a proposed action,

except that this paragraph (a)(9) shall not apply in any instance where the Board has already disclosed to the public the content or nature of its proposed action, or where the Board is required by law to make such disclosure on its own initiative prior to taking final action on such proposal; or

(10) Specifically concern the issuance of a subpoena, participation in a civil action or proceeding, an action in a foreign court or international tribunal, or an arbitration, or the initiation, conduct or disposition of a particular case of formal agency adjudication pursuant to the procedures in section 554 of title 5 of the United States Code or otherwise involving a determination on the record after opportunity for a hearing.

(b) Prior to closing a meeting whose discussions are likely to fall within the exemptions stated in paragraph (a) of this section, the Board will balance the public interest in observing the deliberations of an exemptible matter and the agency need for confidentiality of the exemptible matter. In weighing these interests, the Board is assisted by the General Counsel as provided in §791.16, by expressions of the public interest set forth in requests for open meetings as provided by §791.15(b), and by the brief staff analysis of public interest which will accompany each staff recommendation that an agenda item be considered in a closed meeting.

[53 FR 29647, Aug. 8, 1988, as amended at 75 FR 34623, June 18, 2010]

§ 791.13 Public announcement of meetings.

(a) Except as otherwise provided in this section, the Board shall, for each meeting, make a public announcement, at least one week in advance of the meeting, of the time, place and subject matter of the meeting, whether it will be open or closed to public observation, and the name and telephone number of the Secretary of the Board or the person designated by the Board to respond to requests for information about the meeting.

(b) Advance notice is required unless a majority of the members of the Board determine by a recorded vote that agency business requires that a meeting be called at an earlier date, in which case, the information to be announced in paragraph (a) of this section shall be publicly announced at the earliest practicable time.

(c) A change, including a postponement or a cancellation, in the time or place of a meeting after a published announcement may be made only if announced at the earliest practicable time.

(d) A change in or deletion of the subject matter of a meeting or any portion of a meeting or a redetermination to open or close a meeting or any portion of a meeting after a published announcement may be made only if:

(1) A majority of the Board determines by recorded vote that agency business so requires and that no earlier announcement of the change was possible and

(2) Public announcement of the change and of the vote of each member on such change shall be made at the earliest practicable time.

(e) Each meeting announcement or amendment thereof shall be posted on the Public Notice Bulletin Board in the reception area of the agency headquarters and may be made available by other means deemed desirable by the Board. Immediately following each public announcement required by this section, the stated information shall be submitted to the FEDERAL REGISTER for publication.

(f) No announcement shall contain information which is determined to be exempt from disclosure under § 791.12(a).

(g) The agency shall maintain a mailing list of names and addresses of all persons who wish to receive copies of agency announcements of meetings open to public observation and amendments to such announcements. Requests to be placed on the mailing list should be made by telephoning or by writing to the Secretary of the Board.

§ 791.14 Regular procedure for closing meeting discussions or limiting the disclosure of information.

(a) A decision to close any portion of a meeting and to withhold information about any portion of a meeting closed pursuant to § 791.12(a) will be taken only when a majority of the entire Board votes to take such action. In deciding whether to close a meeting or any portion of a meeting or to withhold information, the Board shall independently consider whether the public interest requires an open meeting. A separate vote of the Board will be taken and recorded for each portion of a meeting to be closed to public observation pursuant to § 791.12(a) or to withhold information from the public pursuant to § 791.12(a). A single vote may be taken and recorded with respect to a series of meetings, or any portions of meetings which are proposed to be closed to the public, or with respect to any information concerning the series of meetings, so long as each meeting in the series involves the same particular matters and is scheduled to be held no more than thirty days after the initial meeting in such series. No proxies shall be allowed.

(b) Any person whose interests may be directly affected by any portion of a meeting for any of the reasons stated in § 791.12(a) (5), (6) or (7) may request that the Board close such portion of the meeting. After receiving notice of a person's desire for any specified portion of a meeting to be closed, the Board, upon a request by one member, will decide by recorded vote whether to close the relevant portion or portions of the meeting. This procedure applies to requests received either prior or subsequent to the announcement of a decision to hold an open meeting.

(c) Within one day after any vote is taken pursuant to paragraph (a) or (b) of this section, the Board shall make publicly available a written copy of the vote taken indicating the vote of each Board member. Except to the extent that such information is withheld and exempt from disclosure, for each meeting or any portion of a meeting closed to the public, the Board shall make publicly available within one day after the required vote, a written explanation of its action, together with a list of all persons expected to attend the closed meeting and their affiliation. The list of persons to attend need not include the names of individual staff, but shall state the offices of the agency expected to participate in the meeting discussions.

§ 791.15 Requests for open meeting.

(a) Following any announcement that the Board intends to close a meeting or any portion of any meeting, any person may make a written request to the Secretary of the Board that the meeting or a portion of the meeting be open. The request shall be circulated to the members of the Board, and the Board, upon the request of one member, shall reconsider its action under § 791.14 before the meeting or before discussion of the matter at the meeting. If the Board decides to open a portion of a meeting proposed to be closed, the Board shall publicly announce its decision in accordance with § 791.13(e). If no request is received from a Board member to reconsider the decision to close a meeting or portion thereof prior to the meeting discussion, the Chairman of the Board shall certify that the Board did not receive a request to reconsider its decision to close the discussion of the matter.

(b) The request to open a portion of a meeting shall be submitted to the Secretary of the Board in advance of the meeting in question. The request shall set forth the requestor's interest in the matter to be discussed and the reasons why the requestor believes that the public interest requires that the meeting or portions thereof be open to public observation.

(c) The submission of a request to open a portion of a meeting shall not act to stay the effectiveness of Board action or to postpone or delay the meeting unless the Board decides otherwise.

(d) The Secretary of the Board shall advise the requestor of the Board's consideration of the request to open a portion of the meeting as soon as practicable.

§ 791.16 General counsel certification.

For each meeting or any portion of a meeting closed to public observation under § 791.14, the General Counsel shall publicly certify, whether in his or her opinion, the meeting or portion thereof may be closed to public observation and shall state each relevant exemption provision of law. A copy of the certification, together with a statement from the presiding officer of the meeting setting forth the time and place of the meeting and the persons present, shall be retained as a part of the permanent meeting records. As part of the certification, the General Counsel shall recommend to the Board whether the public interest requires that the meeting or portions thereof proposed to be closed to public observation be held in the open.

§ 791.17 Maintenance of meeting records.

(a) Except in those circumstances which are beyond the control of the agency, the Board shall maintain a complete transcript or electronic recording adequate to record fully the proceedings of each meeting, or any portion thereof, closed to public observation. However, for meetings closed under § 791.12(a) (8), (9)(i) or (10), the Board shall maintain either a transcript, a recording or a set of minutes. The Board shall maintain a complete electronic recording for each open meeting or any portion thereof. All records shall clearly identify each speaker.

(b) A set of minutes shall fully and clearly describe all matters discussed and shall provide a full and accurate summary of any actions taken, and the reasons for taking such action. Minutes shall also include a description of each of the views expressed by each person in attendance on any item and the record of any roll call vote, reflecting the vote of each member. All documents considered in connection with

§ 791.18

any action shall be identified in the minutes.

(c) The agency shall maintain a complete verbatim copy of the transcript, a complete copy of the minutes or a complete electronic recording of each meeting, or any portion of a meeting, closed to public observation, for at least two years after such meeting or for one year after the conclusion of any agency proceeding with respect to which the meeting or any portion was held, whichever occurs later. The agency shall maintain a complete electronic recording of each open meeting for at least three months after the meeting date. A complete set of minutes shall be maintained on a permanent basis for all meetings.

§ 791.18 Public availability of meeting records and other documents.

(a) The agency shall make promptly available to the public, in the Public Reference Room, the transcript, electronic recording, or minutes of any meeting, deleting any agenda item or any item of the testimony of a witness received at a closed meeting which the Board determined, pursuant to paragraph (c) of this section, was exempt from disclosure under § 791.12(a). The exemption or exemptions relied upon for any deleted information shall be reflected on any record or recording.

(b) Copies of any transcript, minutes or transcription of a recording, disclosing the identity of each speaker, shall be furnished to any person requesting such information in the form specified in paragraph (a) of this section. Copies shall be furnished at the actual cost of duplication or transcription unless waived by the Secretary of the Board.

(c) Following each meeting or any portion of a meeting closed pursuant to § 791.12(a), the General Counsel or his designee, after consultation with the Secretary of the Board, shall determine which, if any, portions of the meeting transcript, electronic recording or minutes not otherwise available under 5 U.S.C. 552a (the Privacy Act) contain information which should be withheld pursuant to § 791.12(a). If, at a later time, the Board determines that there is no further justification for withholding any meeting record or other item of information from the public which has previously been withheld, then such information shall be made available to the public.

(d) Except for information determined by the Board to be exempt from disclosure pursuant to paragraph (c) of this section, meeting records shall be promptly available to the public in the Public Reference Room. Meeting records include but are not limited to: The transcript, electronic recording or minutes of each meeting, as required by § 791.17(a); the notice requirements of §§ 791.13 and 791.14(c); and the General Counsel Certification along with the presiding officer's statement, as required by § 791.16.

(e) These provisions do not affect the procedures set forth in part 792, subpart A, governing the inspection and copying of agency records, except that the exemptions set forth in § 791.12(a) of this subpart and in 5 U.S.C. 552b(c) shall govern in the case of a request made pursuant to part 792, subpart A, to copy or inspect the meeting records described in this section. Any documents considered or mentioned at Board meetings may be obtained subject to the procedures set forth in part 792, subpart A.

[53 FR 29647, Aug. 8, 1988, as amended at 58 FR 17493, Apr. 5, 1993; 64 FR 57365, Oct. 25, 1999]

PART 792—REQUESTS FOR INFORMATION UNDER THE FREEDOM OF INFORMATION ACT AND PRIVACY ACT, AND BY SUBPOENA; SECURITY PROCEDURES FOR CLASSIFIED INFORMATION

Subpart A—The Freedom of Information Act

GENERAL PURPOSE

Sec.
792.01 What is the purpose of this subpart?

RECORDS PUBLICLY AVAILABLE

792.02 What records does NCUA make available to the public for inspection and copying?
792.03 How will I know which records to request?
792.04 How can I obtain these records?
792.05 What is the significance of records made available and indexed?

National Credit Union Administration

Pt. 792

RECORDS AVAILABLE UPON REQUEST

792.06 Can I obtain other records?
792.07 Where do I send my request?
792.08 What must I include in my request?
792.09 What if my request does not meet the requirements of this subpart?
792.10 What will NCUA do with my request?
792.11 What kind of records are exempt from public disclosure?
792.12 How will I know what records NCUA has determined to be exempt?
792.13 Can I get the records in different forms or formats?
792.14 Who is responsible for responding to my request?
792.15 How long will it take to process my request?
792.16 What unusual circumstances can delay NCUA's response?
792.17 What can I do if the time limit passes and I still have not received a response?

EXPEDITED PROCESSING

792.18 What if my request is urgent and I cannot wait for the records?

FEES

792.19 How does NCUA calculate the fees for processing my request?
792.20 What are the charges for each fee category?
792.21 Will NCUA provide a fee estimate?
792.22 What will NCUA charge for other services?
792.23 Can I avoid charges by sending multiple, small requests?
792.24 Can NCUA charge me interest if I fail to pay my bill?
792.25 Will NCUA charge me if the records are not found or are determined to be exempt?
792.26 Will I be asked to pay fees in advance?

FEE WAIVER OR REDUCTION

792.27 Can fees be reduced or waived?

APPEALS

792.28 What if I am not satisfied with the response I receive?

SUBMITTER NOTICE

792.29 If I send NCUA confidential commercial information, can it be disclosed under FOIA?

RELEASE OF EXEMPT RECORDS

792.30 Is there a prohibition against disclosure of exempt records?
792.31 Can exempt records be disclosed to credit unions, financial institutions and state or federal agencies?
792.32 Can exempt records be disclosed to investigatory agencies?

Subpart B [Reserved]

Subpart C—Production of Nonpublic Records and Testimony of NCUA Employees in Legal Proceedings

792.40 What does this subpart prohibit?
792.41 When does this subpart apply?
792.42 How do I request nonpublic records or testimony?
792.43 What must my written request contain?
792.44 When should I make a request?
792.45 Where do I send my request?
792.46 What will the NCUA do with my request?
792.47 If my request is granted, what fees apply?
792.48 If my request is granted, what restrictions apply?
792.49 Definitions.

Subpart D—Security Procedures for Classified Information

792.50 Program.
792.51 Procedures.

Subpart E—The Privacy Act

792.52 Scope.
792.53 Definitions.
792.54 Procedures for requests pertaining to individual records in a system of records.
792.55 Times, places, and requirements for identification of individuals making requests and identification of records requested.
792.56 Notice of existence of records, access decisions and disclosure of requested information; time limits.
792.57 Special procedures: Information furnished by other agencies; medical records.
792.58 Requests for correction or amendment to a record; administrative review of requests.
792.59 Appeal of initial determination.
792.60 Disclosure of record to person other than the individual to whom it pertains.
792.61 Accounting for disclosures.
792.62 Requests for accounting for disclosures.
792.63 Collection of information from individuals; information forms.
792.64 Contracting for the operation of a system of records.
792.65 Fees.
792.66 Exemptions.
792.67 Security of systems of records.
792.68 Use and collection of Social Security numbers.
792.69 Training and employee standards of conduct with regard to privacy.

AUTHORITY: 5 U.S.C. 301, 552, 552a, 552b; 12 U.S.C. 1752a(d), 1766, 1789, 1795f; E.O. 12600, 52

§ 792.01

FR 23781, 3 CFR, 1987 Comp., p. 235; E.O. 12958, 60 FR 19825, 3 CFR, 1995 Comp., p.333.

SOURCE: 54 FR 18476, May 1, 1989, unless otherwise noted.

Subpart A—The Freedom of Information Act

SOURCE: 63 FR 14338, Mar. 25, 1998, unless otherwise noted.

GENERAL PURPOSE

§ 792.01 What is the purpose of this subpart?

This subpart describes the procedures you must follow to obtain records from NCUA under the Freedom of Information Act (FOIA), (5 U.S.C. 552).

RECORDS PUBLICLY AVAILABLE

§ 792.02 What records does NCUA make available to the public for inspection and copying?

Except for records that are exempt from public disclosure under FOIA as amended (5 U.S.C. 552) or are promptly published and copies are available for purchase, NCUA routinely makes the following five types of records available for you to inspect and copy:

(a) Final opinions, including concurring and dissenting opinions, and orders made in the adjudication of cases;

(b) Statements of policy and interpretations which have been adopted by the agency but not published in the FEDERAL REGISTER;

(c) Administrative staff manuals and instructions to staff that affect a member of the public;

(d) Copies of all records, regardless of form or format, which have been released after March 31, 1997, in response to a FOIA request and which, because of the nature of their subject matter, NCUA determines have been or are likely to become the subject of subsequent requests; and

(e) Indices of the documents referred to in this paragraph.

§ 792.03 How will I know which records to request?

NCUA maintains current indices providing identifying information for the public for any matter referred to in § 792.02, issued, adopted, or promulgated after July 4, 1967. The listing of material in an index is for the convenience of possible users and does not constitute a determination that all of the items listed will be disclosed. NCUA has determined that publication of the indices is unnecessary and impractical. You may obtain copies of indices by making a request to the NCUA, Office of General Counsel, 1775 Duke Street, Alexandria, VA 22314-2387, *Attn:* FOIA Officer or as indicated on the NCUA Web site at *www.ncua.gov*. The indices are available for public inspection and copying and are provided at their duplication cost. The indices are:

(a) NCUA Publications List: Manuals relating to general and technical information, booklets published by NCUA, and the Credit Union Directory. The NCUA Publications list is available on the NCUA web site.

(b) Directives Control Index: A list of statements of policy, NCUA Instructions, Bulletins, Letters to Credit Unions, and certain internal manuals.

(c) Popular FOIA Index: Records released in response to a FOIA request, that NCUA determines are likely to be the subject of subsequent requests because of the nature of their subject matter. The Popular FOIA Index is available on the NCUA web site.

[63 FR 14338, Mar. 25, 1998, as amended at 73 FR 56937, Oct. 1, 2008]

§ 792.04 How can I obtain these records?

You may obtain these types of records or information in the following ways:

(a) You may obtain copies of the records referenced in § 792.02 by obtaining the index referred to in § 792.03 and following the ordering instructions it contains, or by making a written request to NCUA, Office of General Counsel, 1775 Duke Street, Alexandria, Virginia 22314-3428, *Attn:* FOIA Officer or as indicated on the NCUA Web site.

(b) If they were created by NCUA on or after November 1, 1996, records referenced in § 792.02 are available on the NCUA web site, found at *http://www.ncua.gov*.

[63 FR 14338, Mar. 25, 1998, as amended at 73 FR 56937, Oct. 1, 2008]

§ 792.05 What is the significance of records made available and indexed?

The records referred to in § 792.02 may be relied on, used, or cited as precedent by NCUA against a party, provided:

(a) The materials have been indexed and either made available or published; or

(b) The party has actual and timely notice of the materials' contents.

RECORDS AVAILABLE UPON REQUEST

§ 792.06 Can I obtain other records?

Except with respect to records routinely made available under § 792.02 or published in the FEDERAL REGISTER, or to the extent that records are exempt under the FOIA, if you make a request for records in accordance with this subpart, NCUA will make such records available to you, including records maintained in electronic format, as long as you agree to pay the actual, direct costs.

§ 792.07 Where do I send my request?

(a) You must send your written request to one of NCUA's Information Centers. The Central Office and Office of Inspector General are designated as Information Centers for the NCUA. The Freedom of Information Officer of the Office of General Counsel is responsible for the operation of the Information Center maintained at the Central Office. The Inspector General is responsible for the operation of the Inspector General Information Center.

(b) If you are seeking any NCUA record, other than those maintained by the Office of Inspector General, you should send your request to NCUA, Office of the General Counsel, 1775 Duke Street, Alexandria, Virginia 22314–3428, *Attn:* FOIA Officer or as indicated on the NCUA Web site at *http://www.ncua.gov*.

(c) If you are seeking a record you think may be maintained by the NCUA Office of Inspector General, then you should send your request to the Inspector General, NCUA, 1775 Duke Street, Alexandria, Virginia 22314–3428.

[68 FR 61737, Oct. 30, 2003; 73 FR 56937, Oct. 1, 2008]

§ 792.08 What must I include in my request?

Until an Information Center receives your FOIA request, it is not obligated to search for responsive records, meet time deadlines, or release any records. A request will not be considered received if it does not include all of the items in paragraphs (a) through (c) of this section.

(a) Your request must be in writing and include the words "FOIA REQUEST" on both the envelope and request letter. The request letter must also include your name, address and a telephone number where you can be reached during normal business hours. If you would like us to respond to your FOIA request by electronic mail (e-mail), you should include your e-mail address.

(b) A reasonable description of the records you seek. A reasonable description is one that enables an NCUA employee, who is familiar with the subject area of the request, to locate the record with a reasonable amount of effort.

(c) A statement agreeing to pay all applicable fees or to pay fees up to a certain maximum amount, or requesting a fee reduction or waiver in accordance with § 792.27. If the actual fees are expected to exceed the maximum amount you indicate in your request, NCUA will contact you to see if you are willing to pay the estimated fees. If you do not want to pay the estimated fees, your request will be closed and no bill will be sent.

(d) If other than paper copy, you must identify the form and format of responsive information you are requesting.

[63 FR 14338, Mar. 25, 1998, as amended at 68 FR 61737, Oct. 30, 2003; 73 FR 56937, Oct. 1, 2008]

§ 792.09 What if my request does not meet the requirements of this subpart?

NCUA need not accept or process your request if it does not comply with the requirements of this subpart. NCUA may return such a request to you with an explanation of the deficiency. You may then submit a corrected request, which will be treated as a new request.

§ 792.10 What will NCUA do with my request?

(a) On receipt of any request, the Information Center assigns it to the appropriate processing schedule, pursuant to paragraph (b) of this section. The date of receipt for any request, including one that is addressed incorrectly or is forwarded to NCUA by another agency, is the earlier of the date the appropriate Information Center actually receives the request or 10 working days after either of NCUA's Information Centers receives the request.

(b) NCUA has a multi-track processing system. Requests for records that are readily identifiable by the Information Center and have already been cleared for public release may qualify for fast track processing. Requests that meet the requirements of § 792.18 will be processed on the expedited track. All other requests will be handled under normal processing procedures in the order they were received.

(c) The Information Center will make the determination whether a request qualifies for fast track processing or expedited track processing. You may contact the Information Center to learn to which track your request has been assigned. If your request has not qualified for fast track processing, you will have an opportunity to limit the scope of material requested to qualify for fast track processing. Limitations of requests must be in writing. If your request for expedited processing is not granted, you will be advised of your right to appeal.

(d) The Information Center will normally process requests in the order they are received in the separate processing tracks. However, in NCUA's discretion, a particular request may be processed out of turn.

(e) Upon a determination by the appropriate Information Center to comply with your initial request for records, the records will be made promptly available to you. If we notify you of a denial of your request, we will include the reason for the denial.

(f) The Information Center will search for records responsive to your request and will generally include all records in existence at the time the search begins. If we use a different search cut-off date, we will inform you of that date.

[63 FR 14338, Mar. 25, 1998, as amended at 68 FR 61737, Oct. 30, 2003; 73 FR 30478, May 28, 2008; 73 FR 56937, Oct. 1, 2008]

§ 792.11 What kind of records are exempt from public disclosure?

(a) All records of NCUA or any officer, employee, or agent thereof, are confidential, privileged and exempt from disclosure, except as otherwise provided in this subpart, if they are:

(1) Records specifically authorized under criteria established by an Executive Order to be kept secret in the interest of national defense or foreign policy and are in fact properly classified pursuant to an Executive Order.

(2) Records related solely to NCUA internal personnel rules and practices. This exemption applies to internal rules or instructions which must be kept confidential in order to assure effective performance of the functions and activities for which NCUA is responsible and which do not materially affect members of the public. This exemption also applies to manuals and instructions to the extent that release of the information would permit circumvention of laws or regulations.

(3) Specifically exempted from disclosure by statute, where the statute either makes nondisclosure mandatory or establishes particular criteria for withholding information.

(4) Records which contain trade secrets and commercial or financial information which relate to the business, personal or financial affairs of any person or organization, are furnished to NCUA, and are confidential or privileged. This exemption includes, but is not limited to, various types of confidential sales and cost statistics, trade secrets, and names of key customers and personnel. Assurances of confidentiality given by staff are not binding on NCUA.

(5) Inter-agency or intra-agency memoranda or letters which would not be available by law to a private party in litigation with NCUA. This exemption preserves the existing freedom of NCUA officials and employees to engage in full and frank written or taped communications with each other and with officials and employees of other

agencies. It includes, but is not limited to, inter-agency and intra-agency reports, memoranda, letters, correspondence, work papers, and minutes of meetings, as well as staff papers prepared for use within NCUA or in concert with other governmental agencies.

(6) Personnel, medical, and similar files (including financial files) pertaining to another person, the disclosure of which would constitute a clearly unwarranted invasion of personal privacy without the subject person's written consent or proof of death. Written consent consists of a written statement by the subject person, authorizing the release of the information to you, and including either the subject person's notarized signature or a declaration made under penalty of perjury that the statement is true and correct. Proof of death consists of evidence that the subject of your request is deceased—such as a death certificate, a newspaper obituary, or some comparable proof of death. Files exempt from disclosure include, but are not limited to:

(i) The personnel records of the NCUA;

(ii) The personnel records voluntarily submitted by private parties in response to NCUA's requests for proposals; and

(iii) Files containing reports, records or other material pertaining to individual cases in which disciplinary or other administrative action has been or may be taken.

(7) Records or information compiled for law enforcement purposes, but only to the extent that the production of such law enforcement records or information:

(i) Could reasonably be expected to interfere with enforcement proceedings;

(ii) Would deprive a person of a right to a fair trial or an impartial adjudication;

(iii) Could reasonably be expected to constitute an unwarranted invasion of personal privacy;

(iv) Could reasonably be expected to disclose the identity of a confidential source, including a state, local, or foreign agency or authority or any private institution which furnished information on a confidential basis, and, in the case of a record or information compiled by a criminal law enforcement authority in the course of a criminal investigation on or by an agency conducting a lawful national security intelligence investigation, information furnished by the confidential source;

(v) Would disclose techniques and procedures for law enforcement investigation or prosecutions, or would disclose guidelines for law enforcement investigations or prosecutions if such disclosure could reasonably be expected to risk circumvention of the law; or

(vi) Could reasonably be expected to endanger the life or physical safety of any individual. This includes, but is not limited to, information relating to enforcement proceedings upon which NCUA has acted or will act in the future.

(8) Contained in or related to examination, operating or condition reports prepared by, or on behalf of, or for the use of NCUA or any agency responsible for the regulation or supervision of financial institutions. This includes all information, whether in formal or informal report form, the disclosure of which would harm the financial security of credit unions or would interfere with the relationship between NCUA and credit unions.

(b) We will provide any reasonably segregable portion of a requested record after deleting those portions that are exempt from disclosure under this section.

[63 FR 14338, Mar. 25, 1998, as amended at 73 FR 56937, Oct. 1, 2008]

§ 792.12 How will I know what records NCUA has determined to be exempt?

As long as it is technically feasible and does not threaten an interest protected by the FOIA, we will:

(a) Mark the place where we redacted information from documents released to you and note the exemption that protects the information from public disclosure; or

(b) Make reasonable efforts to include with our response to you an estimate of the volume of information withheld.

§ 792.13 Can I get the records in different forms or formats?

NCUA will provide a copy of the record in any form or format requested, such as computer disk, if the record is readily reproducible by us in that form or format, but we will not provide more than one copy of any record.

§ 792.14 Who is responsible for responding to my request?

The Freedom of Information Officer or designee is responsible for making the initial determination whether to grant or deny a request for information submitted to the Central Office Information Center. The Inspector General or designee is responsible for making the initial determination whether to grant or deny a request for information submitted to the Inspector General Information Center. This official may refer a request to an NCUA employee who is familiar with the subject area of the request. Other NCUA staff members may aid the official by providing information, advice, recommending a decision, or implementing a decision, but no NCUA employee other than an authorized official may make the initial determination. Referral of a request by the official to an employee will not affect the time limitation imposed in § 792.15 unless the request involves an unusual circumstance as provided in § 792.16.

[63 FR 14338, Mar. 25, 1998, as amended at 68 FR 61737, Oct. 30, 2003]

§ 792.15 How long will it take to process my request?

NCUA will respond to requests within 20 working days, except:

(a)(1) Where the running of such time is suspended while:

(i) The Information Center awaits additional information from the requester. A suspension of time for this purpose may occur only once during the processing period; and

(ii) The Information Center clarifies with the requester issues regarding the payment of fees pursuant to § 792.26.

(2) The Information Center's receipt of the requester's response to the request for additional information or clarification ends the tolling period;

(b) In unusual circumstances, as defined in 5 U.S.C. 552(a)(6)(B) and § 792.16, the time limit may be extended for:

(1) An additional 10 working days as provided by written notice to you, stating the reasons for the extension and the date on which a determination will be sent; or

(2) Such alternative time period as mutually agreed by you and the Information Office, when NCUA notifies you that the request cannot be processed in the specified time limit.

[63 FR 14338, Mar. 25, 1998, as amended at 73 FR 56938, Oct. 1, 2008]

§ 792.16 What unusual circumstances can delay NCUA's response?

(a) In unusual circumstances, the time limits for responding to your request (or your appeal) may be extended by NCUA. If NCUA extends the time, it will provide you with written notice setting forth the reasons for such extension and the date on which a determination is expected to be dispatched. Our notice will not specify a date that would result in an extension for more than 10 working days, except as set forth in paragraph (c) of this section. The unusual circumstances that can delay NCUA's response to your request are:

(1) The need to search for, and collect the requested records from field facilities or other establishments that are separate from the office processing the request;

(2) The need to search for, collect, and appropriately examine a voluminous amount of separate and distinct records which are demanded in a single request; or

(3) The need for consultation, which will be conducted with all practicable speed, with another agency having substantial interest in the determination of the request or among two or more components of NCUA having a substantial interest in the subject matter.

(b) If you, or you and a group of others acting in concert, submit multiple requests that NCUA believes actually constitute a single request, which would otherwise satisfy the unusual circumstances criteria specified in this

National Credit Union Administration § 792.19

section, and the requests involve related matters, then NCUA may aggregate those requests and the provisions of § 792.15(b) will apply.

(c) If NCUA sends you an extension notice, it will also advise you that you can either limit the scope of your request so that it can be processed within the statutory time limit or agree to an alternative time frame for processing your request.

[63 FR 14338, Mar. 25, 1998, as amended at 73 FR 30478, May 28, 2008]

§ 792.17 What can I do if the time limit passes and I still have not received a response?

If NCUA does not comply with the time limits under § 792.15, or as extended under § 792.16, you do not have to pay search fees; requesters qualifying for free search fees will not have to pay duplication fees. You also can file suit against NCUA because you will be deemed to have exhausted your administrative remedies if NCUA fails to comply with the time limit provisions of this subpart. If NCUA can show that exceptional circumstances exist and that it is exercising due diligence in responding to your request, the court may retain jurisdiction and allow NCUA to complete its review of the records. In determining whether exceptional circumstances exist, the court may consider your refusal to modify the scope of your request or arrange an alternative time frame for processing after being given the opportunity to do so by NCUA, when it notifies you of the existence of unusual circumstances as set forth in § 792.16.

[73 FR 56938, Oct. 1, 2008]

EXPEDITED PROCESSING

§ 792.18 What if my request is urgent and I cannot wait for the records?

You may request expedited processing of your request if you can show a compelling need for the records. In cases where your request for expedited processing is granted or if NCUA has determined to expedite the response, it will be processed as soon as practicable.

(a) To demonstrate a compelling need for expedited processing, you must provide a certified statement. The statement, certified by you to be true and correct to the best of your knowledge and belief, must demonstrate that:

(1) The failure to obtain the records on an expedited basis could reasonably be expected to pose an imminent threat to the life or physical safety of an individual; or

(2) The requester is a representative of the news media, as defined in § 792.20, and there is urgency to inform the public concerning actual or alleged NCUA activity.

(b) In response to a request for expedited processing, the Information Center will notify you of the determination within ten working days of receipt of the request. If the Information Center denies your request for expedited processing, you may file an appeal pursuant to the procedures set forth in § 792.28, and NCUA will expeditiously respond to the appeal.

(c) The Information Center will normally process requests in the order they are received in the separate processing tracks. However, in NCUA's discretion, a particular request may be processed out of turn.

[63 FR 14338, Mar. 25, 1998, as amended at 73 FR 56938, Oct. 1, 2008]

FEES

§ 792.19 How does NCUA calculate the fees for processing my request?

We will charge you our allowable direct costs, unless they are less than the cost of billing you. Direct costs means those expenditures that NCUA actually incurs in searching for, duplicating and reviewing documents to respond to a FOIA request. Search means all time spent looking for material that is responsive to a request, including page-by-page or line-by-line identification of material within documents. Searches may be done manually or by computer. Search does not include modification of an existing program or system that would significantly interfere with the operation of an automated information system. Review means examining documents to determine whether any portion should be withheld and preparing documents for disclosure. Fees are subject to change as costs increase. The current rate schedule is available on our web site at *http://www.ncua.gov*. We

§ 792.20

may contract with the private sector to locate, reproduce or disseminate records. NCUA will not contract out responsibilities that FOIA requires it to discharge, such as determining the applicability of an exemption, or determining whether to waive or reduce fees. The following labor and duplication rate calculations apply:

(a) NCUA will charge fees at the following rates for manual searches for and review of records:

(1) If search/review is done by clerical staff, the hourly rate for CU-5, plus 16% of that rate to cover benefits;

(2) If search/review is done by professional staff, the hourly rate for CU-13, plus 16% of that rate to cover benefits.

(b) NCUA will charge fees at the hourly rate for CU-13, plus 16% of that rate to cover benefits, plus the hourly cost of operating the computer for computer searches for records.

(c) NCUA will charge the following duplication fees:

(1) The per-page fee for paper copy reproduction of a document is $.10;

(2) The fee for documents generated by computer is the hourly fee for the computer operator, plus the cost of materials (computer paper, tapes, labels, etc.);

(3) If any other method of duplication is used, NCUA will charge the actual direct cost of duplication.

[63 FR 14338, Mar. 25, 1998, as amended at 73 FR 56938, Oct. 1, 2008]

§ 792.20 What are the charges for each fee category?

The fee category definitions are:

(a) *Commercial use request* means a request from or on behalf of one who seeks information for a use or purpose that furthers the commercial, trade, or profit interests of the requester or the person on whose behalf the request is made.

(b) *Educational institution* means a preschool, an elementary or secondary school, an institution of undergraduate higher education, an institution of graduate higher education, an institution of professional education, and an institution of vocational education operating a program or programs of scholarly research.

(c) *Noncommercial scientific institution* means an institution that is not operated for a "commercial" purpose as that term is used in paragraph (a) of this section and is operated solely for the purpose of conducting scientific research, the results of which are not intended to promote any particular product or industry.

(d) *Representative of the news media* means any person actively gathering news for an entity that is organized and operated to publish or broadcast news to the public. Included within the meaning of public is the credit union community. The term news means information that is about current events or that would be of current interest to the public. You may consult the following chart to find the fees applicable to your request:

If your fee category is	You'll receive	And you'll be charged
Commercial use	0 hours free search 0 hours free review 0 free pages	search time review time duplication
Educational institution, noncommercial scientific institution, newsmedia.	Unlimited free search hours Unlimited free review hours 100 free pages	duplication
All others	2 hours free search Unlimited free review hours. 100 free pages	search time duplication

§ 792.21 Will NCUA provide a fee estimate?

NCUA will notify you of the estimated amount if fees are likely to exceed $25, unless you have indicated in advance a willingness to pay fees as high as those anticipated. You will then have the opportunity to confer with NCUA personnel to reformulate the request to meet your needs at a lower cost.

§ 792.22 What will NCUA charge for other services?

Complying with requests for special services is entirely at the discretion of NCUA. NCUA will recover the full costs of providing such services to the extent it elects to provide them.

§ 792.23 Can I avoid charges by sending multiple, small requests?

You may not file multiple requests, each seeking portions of a document or similar documents, solely to avoid payment of fees. If this is done, NCUA may aggregate any such requests and charge you accordingly.

§ 792.24 Can NCUA charge me interest if I fail to pay my bill?

NCUA can assess interest charges on an unpaid bill starting on the 31st day following the date of the bill. If you fail to pay your bill within 30 days, interest will be at the rate prescribed in 31 U.S.C. 3717, and will accrue from the date of the billing.

§ 792.25 Will NCUA charge me if the records are not found or are determined to be exempt?

NCUA may assess fees for time spent searching and reviewing, even if it fails to locate the records or if records located are determined to be exempt from disclosure.

§ 792.26 Will I be asked to pay fees in advance?

NCUA will require you to give an assurance of payment or an advance payment only when:

(a) NCUA estimates or determines that allowable charges that you may be required to pay are likely to exceed $250. NCUA will notify you of the likely cost and obtain satisfactory assurance of full payment where you have a history of prompt payment of FOIA fees, or require an advance payment of an amount up to the full estimated charges in the case where you have no history of payment; or

(b) You have previously failed to pay a fee charged in a timely fashion. NCUA may require you to pay the full amount owed, plus any applicable interest, or demonstrate that you have, in fact, paid the fee, and to make an advance payment of the full amount of the estimated fee before we begin to process a new request or a pending request from you.

(c) If you are required to make an advance payment of fees, then the administrative time limits prescribed in § 792.16 will begin only after NCUA has received the fee payments described.

FEE WAIVER OR REDUCTION

§ 792.27 Can fees be reduced or waived?

You may request that NCUA waive or reduce fees if disclosure of the information you request is in the public interest because it is likely to contribute significantly to public understanding of the operations or activities of the government, and is not primarily in your commercial interest.

(a) NCUA will make a determination of whether the public interest requirement above is met based on the following factors:

(1) Whether the subject of the requested records concerns identifiable operations or activities of the government, with a connection that is direct and clear;

(2) Whether the disclosable portions of the requested records are meaningfully informative about government operations and activities in order to be likely to contribute to an understanding of government operations or activities. Information already in the public domain, either in a duplicate or substantially identical form where nothing new would be added to the public's understanding, would not be meaningfully informative;

(3) Whether disclosure of the requested information will contribute to public understanding, meaning a reasonably broad audience of persons interested in the subject, as opposed to the individual understanding of the requester. A requester's expertise in the subject area and ability and intention to effectively convey information to the public will be considered. Representatives of the news media are presumed to satisfy this consideration; and

(4) Whether the disclosure is likely to contribute significantly to public understanding of government operations

§ 792.28

or activities. The level of public understanding before disclosure must be enhanced by the disclosure to a significant extent.

(b) If the public interest requirement is met, NCUA will make a determination on the commercial interest requirement based upon the following factors:

(1) Whether you have a commercial interest that would be furthered by the requested disclosure; and if so

(2) Whether the magnitude of your commercial interest is sufficiently large in comparison with the public interest in disclosure, that disclosure is primarily in your commercial interest.

(c) If the required public interest exists and your commercial interest is not primary in comparison, NCUA will waive or reduce fees.

(d) If you are not satisfied with our determination on your fee waiver or reduction request, you may submit an appeal to the General Counsel in accordance with § 792.28.

[63 FR 14338, Mar. 25, 1998, as amended at 73 FR 56938, Oct. 1, 2008]

APPEALS

§ 792.28 What if I am not satisfied with the response I receive?

If you are not satisfied with NCUA's response to your request, you can file an administrative appeal. Your appeal must be in writing and must be filed within 30 days from receipt of the initial determination (in cases of denials of an entire request, or denial of a request for fee waiver or reduction), or from receipt of any records being made available pursuant to the initial determination (in cases of partial denials). In its response to your initial request, the Freedom of Information Act Officer or the Inspector General (or designee), will notify you that you may appeal any adverse determination to the Office of General Counsel. The General Counsel, or designee, as set forth in this paragraph, will:

(a) Make a determination with respect to any appeal within 20 working days after the receipt of such appeal. If, on appeal, the denial of the request for records is, in whole or in part, upheld, the Office of General Counsel will notify you of the provisions for judicial review of that determination under FOIA. Where you do not address your appeal to the General Counsel, the time limitations stated above will be computed from the date of receipt of the appeal by the General Counsel.

(b) The General Counsel is the official responsible for determining all appeals from initial determinations. In case of this person's absence, the appropriate officer acting in the General Counsel's stead will make the appellate determination, unless such officer was responsible for the initial determination, in which case the Vice-Chairman of the NCUA Board will make the appellate determination.

(c) All appeals should be addressed to the General Counsel in the Central Office and should be clearly identified as such on the envelope and in the letter of appeal by using the indicator "FOIA-APPEAL." Failure to address an appeal properly may delay commencement of the time limitation stated in paragraph (a)(1) of this section, to take account of the time reasonably required to forward the appeal to the Office of General Counsel.

[63 FR 14338, Mar. 25, 1998, as amended at 68 FR 61737, Oct. 30, 2003; 73 FR 30478, May 28, 2008; 73 FR 56938, Oct. 1, 2008]

SUBMITTER NOTICE

§ 792.29 If I send NCUA confidential commercial information, can it be disclosed under FOIA?

(a) If you submit confidential commercial information to NCUA, it may be disclosed in response to a FOIA request in accordance with this section.

(b) For purposes of this section:

(1) *Confidential commercial information* means commercial or financial information provided to NCUA by a submitter that arguably is protected from disclosure under § 792.11(a)(4) because disclosure could reasonably be expected to cause substantial competitive harm.

(2) *Submitter* means any person or entity who provides business information, directly or indirectly, to NCUA.

(c) Submitters of business information must use good faith efforts to designate, by appropriate markings, either at the time of submission or at a reasonable time thereafter, those portions of their submissions deemed to be protected from disclosure under §792.11(a)(4). Such a designation shall expire ten years after the date of submission.

(d) We will provide a submitter with written notice of a FOIA request or administrative appeal encompassing designated business information when:

(1) The information has been designated in good faith by the submitter as confidential commercial information deemed protected from disclosure under §792.11(a)(4); or

(2) NCUA has reason to believe that the information may be protected from disclosure under §792.11(a)(4).

(e) A copy of the notice to the submitter will also be provided to the FOIA requester.

(f) Through the notice described in paragraph (d) of this section, NCUA will afford the submitter a reasonable period of time within which to provide a detailed written statement of any objection to disclosure. The statement must describe why the information is confidential commercial information and why it should not be disclosed.

(g) Whenever we decide that we must disclose confidential commercial information over the objection of the submitter, we will send both the submitter and the FOIA requester, within a reasonable number of days prior to the specified disclosure date, a written notice which will include:

(1) A statement of the reasons for which the submitter's disclosure objection was not sustained; and

(2) A description of the information to be disclosed; and

(3) A specified disclosure date.

(h) If a requester brings suit to compel disclosure of confidential commercial information, we will promptly notify the submitter.

(i) The notice requirements of paragraph (d) of this section do not apply if:

(1) We determine that the information should not be disclosed;

(2) The information has been lawfully published or has been officially made available to the public;

(3) Disclosure of the information is required by law; or

(4) The designation made by the submitter in accordance with paragraph (c) of this section appears obviously frivolous; except that in such case, NCUA will provide the submitter with written notice of any final administrative decision to disclose the information within a reasonable number of days prior to the specified disclosure date.

RELEASE OF EXEMPT INFORMATION

§ 792.30 Is there a prohibition against disclosure of exempt records?

Except those authorized officials listed in §792.14, or as provided in §§792.31-792.32, and subpart C of this part, no officer, employee, or agent of NCUA or of any federally-insured credit union shall disclose or permit the disclosure of any exempt records of NCUA to any person other than those NCUA or credit union officers, employees, or agents properly entitled to such information for the performance of their official duties.

§ 792.31 Can exempt records be disclosed to credit unions, financial institutions and state or federal agencies?

The NCUA Board, in its sole discretion, or any person designated by it in writing, may make available to certain governmental agencies and insured financial institutions copies of reports of examination and other documents, papers or information for their use, when necessary, in the performance of their official duties or functions. All reports, documents and papers made available pursuant to this paragraph shall remain the property of NCUA. No person, agency or employee shall disclose the reports or exempt records without NCUA's express written authorization.

§ 792.32 Can exempt records be disclosed to investigatory agencies?

The NCUA Board, or any person designated by it in writing, in its discretion and in appropriate circumstances, may disclose to proper federal or state authorities copies of exempt records pertaining to irregularities discovered in credit unions which may constitute either unsafe or unsound practices or violations of federal or state, civil or criminal law.

Subpart B [Reserved]

Subpart C—Production of Nonpublic Records and Testimony of NCUA Employees in Legal Proceedings

SOURCE: 62 FR 56054, Oct. 29, 1997, unless otherwise noted.

§ 792.40 What does this subpart prohibit?

This subpart prohibits the release of nonpublic records or the appearance of an NCUA employee to testify in legal proceedings except as provided in this subpart. Any person possessing nonpublic records may release them or permit their disclosure only as provided in this subpart.

(a) *Duty of NCUA employees.* (1) If an NCUA employee is served with a subpoena requiring him or her to appear as a witness or produce records, the employee must promptly notify the Office of General Counsel. The General Counsel has the authority to instruct NCUA employees to refuse appearing as a witness or to withhold nonpublic records. The General Counsel may let an NCUA employee provide testimony, including expert or opinion testimony, if the General Counsel determines that the need for the testimony clearly outweighs contrary considerations.

(2) If a court or other appropriate authority orders or demands expert or opinion testimony or testimony beyond authorized subjects contrary to the General Counsel's instructions, an NCUA employee must immediately notify the General Counsel of the order and respectfully decline to comply. An NCUA employee must decline to answer questions on the grounds that this subpart forbids such disclosure and should produce a copy of this subpart, request an opportunity to consult with the Office of General Counsel, and explain that providing such testimony without approval may expose him or her to disciplinary or other adverse action.

(b) *Duty of persons who are not NCUA employees.* (1) If you are not an NCUA employee but have custody of nonpublic records and are served with a subpoena requiring you to appear as a witness or produce records, you must promptly notify the NCUA about the subpoena. Also, you must notify the issuing court or authority and the person or entity for whom the subpoena was issued of the contents of this subpart. Notice to the NCUA is made by sending a copy of the subpoena to the General Counsel of the NCUA, Office of General Counsel, 1775 Duke Street, Alexandria, Virginia 22314–3428. After receiving notice, the NCUA may advise the issuing court or authority and the person or entity for whom the subpoena was issued that this subpart applies and, in addition, may intervene, attempt to have the subpoena quashed or withdrawn, or register appropriate objections.

(2) After notifying the Office of General Counsel, you should respond to a subpoena by appearing at the time and place stated in the subpoena. Unless authorized by the General Counsel, you should decline to produce any records or give any testimony, basing your refusal on this subpart. If the issuing court or authority orders the disclosure of records or orders you to testify, you should continue to decline to produce records or testify and should advise the Office of General Counsel.

(c) *Penalties.* Anyone who discloses nonpublic records or gives testimony related to those records, except as expressly authorized by the NCUA or as ordered by a federal court after NCUA has had the opportunity to be heard, may face the penalties provided in 18 U.S.C. 641 and other applicable laws. Also, former NCUA employees, in addition to the prohibition contained in this subpart, are subject to the restrictions and penalties of 18 U.S.C. 207.

§ 792.41 When does this subpart apply?

This subpart applies if you want to obtain nonpublic records or testimony of an NCUA employee for legal proceedings. It doesn't apply to the release of records under the Freedom of Information Act (FOIA), 5 U.S.C. 552, or the Privacy Act, 5 U.S.C. 552a, or the release of records to federal or state investigatory agencies under § 792.32.

[62 FR 56054, Oct. 29, 1997, as amended at 65 FR 63589, Oct. 25, 2000]

§ 792.42 How do I request nonpublic records or testimony?

(a) To request nonpublic records or the testimony of an NCUA employee, you must submit a written request to the General Counsel of the NCUA. If you serve a subpoena on the NCUA or an NCUA employee before submitting a written request and receiving a final determination, the NCUA will oppose the subpoena on the grounds that you failed to follow the requirements of this subpart. You may serve a subpoena as long as it is accompanied by a written request that complies with this subpart.

(b) To request nonpublic records that are part of the records of the Office of the Inspector General or the testimony of an NCUA employee on matters within the knowledge of the NCUA employee as a result of his or her employment with the Office of the Inspector General, you must submit a written request to the Office of the Inspector General. Your request will be handled in accordance with the provisions of this subpart except that the Inspector General will be responsible for those determinations that would otherwise be made by the General Counsel.

§ 792.43 What must my written request contain?

Your written request for records or testimony must include:

(a) The caption of the legal proceeding, docket number, and name of the court or other authority involved.

(b) A copy of the complaint or equivalent document setting forth the assertions in the case and any other pleading or document necessary to show relevance.

(c) A list of categories of records sought, a detailed description of how the information sought is relevant to the issues in the legal proceeding, and a specific description of the substance of the testimony or records sought.

(d) A statement as to how the need for the information outweighs the need to maintain the confidentiality of the information and outweighs the burden on the NCUA to produce the records or provide testimony.

(e) A statement indicating that the information sought is not available from another source, such as a credit union's own books and records, other persons or entities, or the testimony of someone other than an NCUA employee, for example, retained experts.

(f) A description of all prior decisions, orders, or pending motions in the case that bear upon the relevance of the records or testimony you want.

(g) The name, address, and telephone number of counsel to each party in the case.

(h) An estimate of the amount of time you anticipate that you and other parties will need with each NCUA employee for interviews, depositions, or testifying.

§ 792.44 When should I make a request?

You should submit your request at least 45 days before the date that you need the records or testimony. If you want to have your request processed in less time, you must explain why you couldn't submit the request earlier and why you need expedited processing. If you are requesting the testimony of an NCUA employee, the NCUA expects you to anticipate your need for the testimony in sufficient time to obtain it by a deposition. The General Counsel may deny a request for testimony at a legal proceeding unless you explain why you could not use deposition testimony. The General Counsel will determine the location of a deposition taking into consideration the NCUA's interest in minimizing the disruption for an NCUA employee's work schedule and the costs and convenience of other persons attending the deposition.

§ 792.45 Where do I send my request?

You must send your request or subpoena for records or testimony to the attention of the General Counsel for the NCUA, Office of General Counsel, 1775 Duke Street, Alexandria, Virginia 22314–3428. You must send your request or subpoena for records or testimony from the Office of the Inspector General to the attention of the NCUA Inspector General, 1775 Duke Street, Alexandria, Virginia 22314–3428.

§ 792.46 What will the NCUA do with my request?

(a) *Factors the NCUA will consider.* The NCUA may consider various factors in reviewing a request for nonpublic records or testimony of NCUA employees, including:

§ 792.47

(1) Whether disclosure would assist or hinder the NCUA in performing its statutory duties or use NCUA resources unreasonably, including whether responding to the request will interfere with NCUA employees' ability to do their work.

(2) Whether disclosure is necessary to prevent the perpetration of a fraud or other injustice in the matter or if you can get the records or testimony you want from sources other than the NCUA.

(3) Whether the request is unduly burdensome.

(4) Whether disclosure would violate a statute, executive order, or regulation, for example, the Privacy Act, 5 U.S.C. 552a.

(5) Whether disclosure would reveal confidential, sensitive or privileged information, trade secrets or similar, confidential commercial or financial information, or would otherwise be inappropriate for release and, if so, whether a confidentiality agreement or protective order as provided in § 792.48(a) can adequately limit the disclosure.

(6) Whether the disclosure would interfere with law enforcement proceedings, compromise constitutional rights, or hamper NCUA research or investigatory activities.

(7) Whether the disclosure could result in NCUA appearing to favor one litigant over another.

(8) Any other factors the NCUA determines to be relevant to the interests of the NCUA.

(b) *Review of your request.* The NCUA will process your request in the order it is received. The NCUA will try to respond to your request within 45 days, but this may vary depending on the scope of your request.

(c) *Final determination.* The General Counsel makes the final determination on requests for nonpublic records or NCUA employee testimony. All final determinations are in the sole discretion of the General Counsel. The General Counsel will notify you and the court or other authority of the final determination of your request. In considering your request, the General Counsel may contact you to inform you of the requirements of this subpart, ask that the request or subpoena be modified or withdrawn, or may try to resolve the request or subpoena informally without issuing a final determination. You may seek judicial review of the final determination under the Administrative Procedure Act. 5 U.S.C. 702.

§ 792.47 If my request is granted, what fees apply?

(a) *Generally.* You must pay any fees associated with complying with your request, including copying fees for records and witness fees for testimony. The General Counsel may condition the production of records or appearance for testimony upon advance payment of a reasonable estimate of the fees.

(b) *Fees for records.* You must pay all fees for searching, reviewing and duplicating records produced in response to your request. The fees will be the same as those charged by the NCUA under its Freedom of Information Act regulations, § 792.19.

(c) *Witness fees.* You must pay the fees, expenses, and allowances prescribed by the court's rules for attendance by a witness. If no such fees are prescribed, the local federal district court rule concerning witness fees, for the federal district court closest to where the witness appears, will apply. For testimony by current NCUA employees, you must pay witness fees, allowances, and expenses to the General Counsel by check made payable to the "National Credit Union Administration" within 30 days from receipt of NCUA's billing statement. For the testimony of a former NCUA employee, you must pay witness fees, allowances, and expenses directly to the former employee, in accordance with 28 U.S.C. 1821 or other applicable statutes.

(d) *Certification of records.* The NCUA may authenticate or certify records to facilitate their use as evidence. If you require authenticated records, you must request certified copies at least 45 days before the date they will be needed. The request should be sent to the General Counsel. You will be charged a certification fee of $5.00 per document.

(e) *Waiver of fees.* A waiver or reduction of any fees in connection with the testimony, production, or certification or authentication of records may be granted in the discretion of the General Counsel. Waivers will not be granted routinely. If you request a waiver, your request for records or testimony must state the reasons why a waiver should be granted.

[62 FR 56054, Oct. 29, 1997, as amended at 65 FR 63789, Oct. 25, 2000]

§ 792.48 If my request is granted, what restrictions apply?

(a) *Records.* The General Counsel may impose conditions or restrictions on the release of nonpublic records, including a requirement that you obtain a protective order or execute a confidentiality agreement with the other parties in the legal proceeding that limits access to and any further disclosure of the nonpublic records. The terms of a confidentiality agreement or protective order must be acceptable to the General Counsel. In cases where protective orders or confidentiality agreements have already been executed, the NCUA may condition the release of nonpublic records on an amendment to the existing protective order or confidentiality agreement.

(b) *Testimony.* The General Counsel may impose conditions or restrictions on the testimony of NCUA employees, including, for example, limiting the areas of testimony or requiring you and the other parties to the legal proceeding to agree that the transcript of the testimony will be kept under seal or will only be used or made available in the particular legal proceeding for which you requested the testimony. The General Counsel may also require you to provide a copy of the transcript of the testimony to the NCUA at your expense.

§ 792.49 Definitions.

Legal proceedings means any matter before any federal, state or foreign administrative or judicial authority, including courts, agencies, commissions, boards or other tribunals, involving such proceedings as lawsuits, licensing matters, hearings, trials, discovery, investigations, mediation or arbitration. When the NCUA is a party to a legal proceeding, it will be subject to the applicable rules of civil procedure governing production of documents and witnesses, however, this subpart will still apply to the testimony of former NCUA employees.

NCUA employee means current and former officials, members of the Board, officers, directors, employees and agents of the National Credit Union Administration, including contract employees and consultants and their employees. This definition does not include persons who are no longer employed by the NCUA and are retained or hired as expert witnesses or agree to testify about general matters, matters available to the public, or matters with which they had no specific involvement or responsibility during their employment.

Nonpublic records means any NCUA records that are exempt from disclosure under § 792.11, the NCUA regulations implementing the provisions of the Freedom of Information Act. For example, this means records created in connection with NCUA's examination and supervision of insured credit unions, including examination reports, internal memoranda, and correspondence, and, also, records created in connection with NCUA's enforcement and investigatory responsibilities.

Subpoena means any order, subpoena for records or other tangible things or for testimony, summons, notice or legal process issued in a legal proceeding.

Testimony means any written or oral statements made by an individual in connection with a legal proceeding including personal appearances in court or at depositions, interviews in person or by telephone, responses to written interrogatories or other written statements such as reports, declarations, affidavits, or certifications or any response involving more than the delivery of records.

[62 FR 56054, Oct. 29, 1997, as amended at 65 FR 63789, Oct. 25, 2000]

Subpart D—Security Procedures for Classified Information

§ 792.50 Program.

(a) The NCUA's Chief Financial Officer is designated as the person responsible for implementation and oversight of NCUA's program for maintaining the

§ 792.51

security of confidential information regarding national defense and foreign relations. The Chief Financial Officer receives questions, suggestions and complaints regarding all elements of this program. The Chief Financial Officer is solely responsible for changes to the program and assures that the program is consistent with legal requirements.

(b) The Chief Financial Officer is the Agency's official contact for declassification requests regardless of the point of origin of such requests.

[54 FR 18476, May 1, 1989, as amended at 59 FR 36042, July 15, 1994; 67 FR 30774, May 8, 2002; 73 FR 30478, May 28, 2008]

§ 792.51 Procedures.

(a) *Mandatory review.* All declassification requests made by a member of the public, by a government employee or by an agency shall be handled by the Chief Financial Officer or the Chief Financial Officer's designee. Under no circumstances shall the Chief Financial Officer refuse to confirm the existence or nonexistence of a document under the Freedom of Information Act or the mandatory review provisions of other applicable law, unless the fact of its existence or nonexistence would itself be classifiable under applicable law. Although NCUA has no authority to classify or declassify information, it occasionally handles information classified by another agency. The Chief Financial Officer shall refer all declassification requests to the agency that originally classified the information. The Chief Financial Officer or the Chief Financial Officer's designee shall notify the requesting person or agency that the request has been referred to the originating agency and that all further inquiries and appeals must be made directly to the other agency.

(b) *Handling and safeguarding national security information.* All information classified "Top Secret," "Secret," and "Confidential" shall be delivered to the Chief Financial Officer or the Chief Financial Officer's designee immediately upon receipt. The Chief Financial Officer shall advise those who may come into possession of such information of the name of the current designee. If the Chief Financial Officer is unavailable, the designee shall lock the documents, unopened, in the combination safe located in the Office of Chief Financial Officer. If the Chief Financial Officer or the designee is unavailable to receive such documents, the documents shall be delivered to the Chief Financial Officer of the Office of Human Resources who shall lock them, unopened, in the combination safe in the Office of Human Resources. Under no circumstances shall classified materials that cannot be delivered to the Chief Financial Officer be stored other than in the two designated safes.

(c) *Storage.* All classified documents shall be stored in the combination safe located in the Chief Financial Officer's Office, except as provided in paragraph (b) of this section. The combination shall be known only to the Chief Financial Officer and the Chief Financial Officer's designee holding the proper security clearance.

(d) *Employee education.* The Chief Financial Officer shall send a memo to every NCUA employee who:

(1) Has a security clearance and

(2) May handle classified materials.

This memo shall describe NCUA procedures for handling, reproducing and storing classified documents. The Chief Financial Officer shall require each such employee to review Executive Order 12356.

(e) *Agency terminology.* The National Credit Union Administration's Central Office shall use the terms "Top Secret," "Secret" or "Confidential" only in relation to materials classified for national security purposes.

[63 FR 14338, Mar. 25, 1998, as amended at 67 FR 30774, May 8, 2002; 73 FR 30478, May 28, 2008]

Subpart E—The Privacy Act

SOURCE: 54 FR 18476, May 1, 1989, unless otherwise noted. Redesignated at 63 FR 14338, Mar. 25, 1998. Nomenclature change at 73 FR 56938, Oct. 1, 2008.

§ 792.52 Scope.

This subpart governs requests made of NCUA under the Privacy Act (5 U.S.C. 552a). The regulation applies to all records maintained by NCUA which contain personal information about an individual and some means of identifying the individual, and which are

National Credit Union Administration § 792.55

contained in a system of records from which information may be retrieved by use of an identifying particular; sets forth procedures whereby individuals may seek and gain access to records concerning themselves and request amendments of those records; and sets forth requirements applicable to NCUA employees' maintaining, collecting, using, or disseminating such records.

§ 792.53 Definitions.

For purposes of this subpart:

(a) *Individual* means a citizen of the United States or an alien lawfully admitted for permanent residence.

(b) *Maintain* includes maintain, collect, use, or disseminate.

(c) *Record* means any item, collection, or grouping of information about an individual that is maintained by NCUA, and that contains the name, or an identifying number, symbol, or other identifying particular assigned to the individual.

(d) *System of records* means a group of any records under NCUA's control from which information is retrieved by the name of the individual or by some identifying number, symbol, or other identifying particular assigned to the individual.

(e) *Routine use* means, with respect to the disclosure of a record, the use of such record for a purpose which is compatible with the purpose for which it was collected.

(f) *Statistical record* means a record in a system of records maintained for statistical research or reporting purposes only and not used in whole or in part in making any determination about an identifiable individual, except as provided by section 8 of title 13 of the United States Code.

(g) *Notice of Systems of Records* means the annual notice published by NCUA in the FEDERAL REGISTER informing the public of the existence and character of the systems of records it maintains. The Notice of Systems of Records also is available on NCUA's Web site at *http://www.ncua.gov*.

(h) *System manager* means the NCUA official responsible for the maintenance, collection, use or distribution of information contained in a system of records. The system manager for each system of records is provided in the FEDERAL REGISTER publication of NCUA's annual systems of records notice.

(i) *Working day* means Monday through Friday excluding legal public holidays.

[54 FR 18476, May 1, 1989, as amended at 73 FR 56938, Oct. 1, 2008]

§ 792.54 Procedures for requests pertaining to individual records in a system of records.

(a) Individuals desiring to know if a system of records contains records pertaining to them, and individuals requesting access to records in a system of records pertaining to them should submit a written request to the appropriate system manager as identified in the Notice of Systems of Records. An individual who does not have access to the FEDERAL REGISTER and who is unable to determine the appropriate system manager to whom to submit a request may submit a request to the Privacy Officer, Office of General Counsel, National Credit Union Administration, 1775 Duke Street, Alexandria, VA 22314–3428, in which case the request will be referred to the appropriate system manager.

(b) Individuals requesting notification of, or access to, records should include the words "PRIVACY ACT REQUEST" on both the letter and, as appropriate, the envelope, cover document or subject line; describe the record sought; the approximate dates covered by the record; and, the systems of record in which records are thought to be included. Individuals must also meet the identification requirements in § 792.55.

[73 FR 56938, Oct. 1, 2008]

§ 792.55 Times, places, and requirements for identification of individuals making requests and identification of records requested.

(a) The following standards are applicable to an individual submitting requests either in person or by mail under § 792.54:

(1) Individuals appearing in person, if not personally known to the system manager responding to the request, must present a single document bearing a photograph (such as a passport or identification badge) or two items of

§ 792.56

identification which do not bear a photograph but do bear both a name and address (such as a driver's license or voter registration card);

(2) Individuals submitting requests by mail or written electronic form, such as facsimile or e-mail, may establish identity by a signature, address, date of birth, employee identification number if any, and one other identifier such as a photocopy of driver's license or other document. If inadequate identifying information is provided, the system manager responding to the request may require further identifying information before any notification or responsive disclosure.

(3) Individuals appearing in person or submitting requests by mail or written electronic form, who cannot provide the required documentation or identification, may provide an unsworn declaration subscribed to as true under penalty of perjury.

(b) The parent or guardian of a minor or a person judicially determined to be incompetent shall, in addition to establishing identity of the minor or other person as required in paragraph (a) of this section, furnish a copy of a birth certificate showing parentage or a court order establishing guardianship.

(c) A record may be disclosed to a representative of an individual to whom the record pertains provided the system manager receives written authorization from the individual who is the subject of the record.

(d) An individual seeking to review records about that individual may be accompanied by another person of their own choosing. In such cases, the individual seeking access shall be required to furnish a written statement authorizing discussion of that individual's records in the accompanying person's presence.

(e) In addition to the requirements set forth in paragraphs (a), (b) and (c) of this section, the published "Notice of System of Records" for individual systems may include further requirements of identification where necessary to retrieve the individual records from the system.

[54 FR 18476, May 1, 1989. Redesignated at 63 FR 14338, Mar. 25, 1998, as amended at 64 FR 57365, Oct. 25, 1999; 65 FR 63790, Oct. 25, 2000; 73 FR 56939, Oct. 1, 2008]

§ 792.56 Notice of existence of records, access decisions and disclosure of requested information; time limits.

(a) The system manager identified in the record access procedure section of the "Notice of Systems of Records" and identified in accordance with § 792.54(a), by an individual seeking notification of, or access to, a record, shall be responsible:

(1) For determining whether access is available under the Privacy Act; (2) for notifying the requesting individual of that determination; and (3) for providing access to information determined to be available. In the case of an individual access request made in person, information determined to be available shall be provided by allowing a personal review of the record or portion of a record containing the information requested and determined to be available, and the individual shall be allowed to have a copy of all or any portion of available information made in a form comprehensible to him. In the case of an individual access request made by mail, information determined to be available shall be provided by mail, unless the individual has requested otherwise.

(b) The following time limits shall be applicable to the required determinations, notification and provisions of access set forth in paragraph (a) of this section:

(1) A request concerning a single system of records which does not require consultation with or requisition of records from another agency will be responded to within 20 working days after receipt of the request.

(2) A request requiring requisition of records from or consultation with another agency will be responded to within 30 working days of receipt of the request.

(3) If a request under paragraphs (b)(1) or (2) of this section presents unusual difficulties in determining whether the records involved are exempt from disclosure, the Privacy Act Officer, in the Office of General Counsel, may extend the time period established by the regulations by 10 working days.

(c) Nothing in this section shall be construed to allow an individual access

National Credit Union Administration § 792.59

to any information compiled in reasonable anticipation of a civil action or proceeding, or any information exempted from the access provisions of the Privacy Act.

[54 FR 18476, May 1, 1989, as amended at 59 FR 36042, July 15, 1994; 64 FR 57365, Oct. 25, 1999; 65 FR 63790, Oct. 25, 2000]

§ 792.57 Special procedures: Information furnished by other agencies; medical records.

(a) When a request for records or information from NCUA includes information furnished by other Federal agencies, the system manager responsible for action on the request shall consult with the appropriate agency prior to making a decision to disclose or refuse access to the record, but the decision whether to disclose the record shall be made in the first instance by the system manager.

(b) Medical records may be disclosed on request to the individuals to whom they pertain unless disclosing the medical information directly to the requesting individual could have an adverse effect on the individual. Where medical information is potentially adverse to the requesting individual, the system manager responsible may advise the requesting individual that the medical records will be transmitted only to a physician designated in writing by the individual.

[54 FR 18476, May 1, 1989. Redesignated at 63 FR 14338, Mar. 25, 1998, as amended at 65 FR 63790, Oct. 25, 2000; 73 FR 56939, Oct. 1, 2008]

§ 792.58 Requests for correction or amendment to a record; administrative review of requests.

(a) An individual may request amendment of a record concerning that individual by submitting a written request, either in person or by mail, to the system manager identified in the Notice of Systems of Records. The words "PRIVACY ACT—REQUEST TO AMEND RECORD" should be written on the letter and the envelope. The request must describe the system of records containing the record sought to be amended, indicate the particular record involved, the nature of the correction sought, and the justification for the correction or amendment. An individual who does not have access to NCUA's Notice of Systems of Records, and to whom the appropriate address is otherwise unavailable, may submit a request to the Privacy Act Officer, Office of General Counsel, National Credit Union Administration, 1775 Duke Street, Alexandria, Virginia 22314–3428, in which case the request will then be referred to the appropriate system manager. The date of receipt of the request will be determined as of the date of receipt by the system manager.

(b) Within 10 working days of receipt of the request, the appropriate system manager shall advise the individual that the request has been received. The appropriate system manager will promptly (under normal circumstances, not later than 30 working days after receipt of the request) advise the individual that the record will be amended or corrected, or inform the individual of rejection of the request to amend the record, the reason for the rejection, and the procedures established by § 792.59 for the individual to request a review of that rejection.

[54 FR 18476, May 1, 1989, as amended at 59 FR 36041, 36042, July 15, 1994; 65 FR 63790, Oct. 25, 2000; 73 FR 56939, Oct. 1, 2008]

§ 792.59 Appeal of initial determination.

(a) A rejection, in whole or in part, of a request to amend or correct a record may be appealed to the General Counsel within 30 working days of receipt of notice of the rejection. Appeals shall be in writing, and shall set forth the specific item of information sought to be corrected and the documentation justifying the correction. Appeals must be addressed to the Office of General Counsel, National Credit Union Administration, 1775 Duke Street, Alexandria, VA 22314–3428 with the words "PRIVACY ACT—APPEAL" written on the letter and the envelope. Appeals shall be decided within 30 working days of receipt unless the General Counsel, for good cause, extends such period for an additional 30 working days.

(b) Within the time limits set forth in paragraph (a) of this section, the General Counsel shall either advise the individual of a decision to amend or correct the record, or advise the individual of a determination that an

§ 792.60

amendment or correction is not warranted on the facts, in which case the individual shall be advised of the right to provide for the record a "Statement of Disagreement" and of the right to further appeal pursuant to the Privacy Act. For records under the jurisdiction of the Office of Personnel Management, appeals will be made pursuant to that agency's regulations.

(c) If an appeal under this section is denied in whole or in part, an individual may file a statement of disagreement concisely stating the reason(s) for disagreeing with the denial for amendment or correction, and clearly identifying each part of any record that is disputed. The statement must be sent within 30 working days of the date of receipt of the notice of General Counsel's refusal to authorize amendment or correction, to the General Counsel, National Credit Union Administration, 1775 Duke Street, Alexandria, VA 22314–3428. Upon receipt of a statement of disagreement in accordance with this section, the General Counsel shall take steps to ensure that the statement is included in the system of records containing the disputed item and that the original item is so marked to indicate that there is a statement of dispute and where, within the system of records, that statement may be found.

(d) When a record has been amended or corrected or a statement of disagreement has been furnished, the system manger for the system of records containing the record shall, within 30 days thereof, advise all prior recipients of information to which the amendment or statement of disagreement relates whose identity can be determined by an accounting made as required by the Privacy Act of 1974 or any other accounting previously made, of the amendment or statement of disagreement. When a statement of disagreement has been furnished, the system manager shall also provide any subsequent recipient of a disclosure containing information to which the statement relates with a copy of the statement and note the disputed portion of the information disclosed. A concise statement of the reasons for not making the requested amendment may also be provided if deemed appropriate.

(e) If access is denied because of an exemption, the individual will be notified of the right to appeal that determination to the General Counsel within 30 days after receipt. Appeals will be determined within 20 working days.

[54 FR 18476, May 1, 1989, as amended at 59 FR 36041, July 15, 1994; 65 FR 63790, Oct. 25, 2000; 73 FR 56939, Oct. 1, 2008]

§ 792.60 Disclosure of record to person other than the individual to whom it pertains.

No record or item of information concerning an individual which is contained in a system of records maintained by NCUA shall be disclosed by any means of communication to any person, or to another agency, without the prior written consent of the individual to whom the record or item of information pertains, unless the disclosure would be—

(a) To an employee of the NCUA who has need for the record in the performance of duty;

(b) Required by the Freedom of Information Act;

(c) For a routine use as described in the "Notice of Systems of Records," published in the FEDERAL REGISTER, which describes the system of records in which the record or item of information is contained;

(d) To the Bureau of the Census for purposes of planning or carrying out a census or survey or related activity pursuant to the provisions of title 13 of the United States Code;

(e) To a recipient who has provided the NCUA with advance adequate written assurance that the record or item will be used soley as a statistical research or reporting record, and the record is to be transferred in a form that is not individually identifiable;

(f) To the National Archives and Records Administration as a record or item which has sufficient historical or other value to warrant its continued preservation by the United States Government, or for evaluation by the Archivist of the United States or the designee of the Archivist to determine whether the record has such value;

(g) To another agency or to an instrumentality of any governmental jurisdiction within or under the control of the United States for a civil or criminal law enforcement activity if the activity is authorized by law, and if the head of the agency or instrumentality has made a written request to NCUA specifying the particular portion desired and the law enforcement activity for which the record or item is sought;

(h) To a person pursuant to a showing of compelling circumstances affecting the health or safety of an individual if, upon such disclosure, notification is transmitted to the last known address of such individual;

(i) To either House of Congress, or, to the extent of matter within its jurisdiction, any committee or subcommittee thereof, any joint committee of Congress or subcommittee of any such joint committee;

(j) To the Comptroller General, or any of his authorized representatives, in the course of the performance of the duties of the Government Accountability Office;

(k) Pursuant to the order of a court of competent jurisdiction; or

(l) To a consumer reporting agency in accordance with section 3711(f) of title 31 of the United States Code (31 U.S.C. 3711(f)).

[54 FR 18476, May 1, 1989, as amended at 73 FR 56939, Oct. 1, 2008]

§ 792.61 Accounting for disclosures.

(a) Each system manager identified in the "Notice of Systems of Records" must establish a system of accounting for all disclosures of information or records under the Privacy Act made outside NCUA. Accounting procedures may be established in the least expensive and most convenient form that will permit the system manager to advise individuals, promptly upon request, of the persons or agencies to which records concerning them have been disclosed.

(b) Accounting records, at a minimum, shall include the information disclosed, the name and address of the person or agency to whom disclosure was made, and the date of disclosure. When records are transferred to the National Archives and Records Administration for storage in records centers, the accounting pertaining to those records shall be transferred with the records themselves.

(c) Any accounting made under this section shall be retained for at least five years or the life of the record, whichever is longer, after the disclosure for which the accounting is made.

[54 FR 18476, May 1, 1989, as amended at 73 FR 56939, Oct. 1, 2008]

§ 792.62 Requests for accounting for disclosures.

At the time of the request for access or correction or at any other time, an individual may request an accounting of disclosures made of the individual's record outside the NCUA. Request for accounting shall be directed to the system manager. Any available accounting, whether kept in accordance with the requirements of the Privacy Act or under procedures established prior to September 27, 1975, shall be made available to the individual, except that an accounting need not be made available if it relates to:

(a) A disclosure made pursuant to the Freedom of Information Act (5 U.S.C. 552);

(b) A disclosure made within the NCUA;

(c) A disclosure made to a law enforcement agency pursuant to 5 U.S.C. 552a(b)(7);

(d) A disclosure which has been exempted from the provisions of 5 U.S.C. 552a(c)(3) pursuant to 5 U.S.C. 552a (j) or (k).

§ 792.63 Collection of information from individuals; information forms.

(a) The system manager for each system of records is responsible for reviewing all forms developed and used to collect information from or about individuals for incorporation into the system of records.

(b) The purpose of the review shall be to eliminate any requirement for information that is not relevant and necessary to carry out an NCUA function and to accomplish the following objectives:

(1) To ensure that no information concerning religion, political beliefs or activities, association memberships (other than those required for a professional license), or the exercise of other First Amendment rights is required to be disclosed unless such requirement of disclosure is expressly authorized by

§ 792.64

statute or by the individual about whom the record is maintained, or unless pertinent to and within the scope of any authorized law enforcement activity;

(2) To ensure that the form or accompanying statement makes clear to the individual which information by law must be disclosed and the authority for that requirement, and which information is voluntary;

(3) To ensure that the form or accompanying statement makes clear the principal purpose or purposes for which the information is being collected, and states concisely the routine uses that will be made of the information;

(4) To ensure that the form or accompanying statement clearly indicates to the individual the effects on him or her, if any, of refusing to provide some or all of the requested information; and

(5) To ensure that any form requesting disclosure of a social security number, or an accompanying statement, clearly advises the individual of the statute or regulation requiring disclosure of the number, or clearly advises the individual that disclosure is voluntary and that no consequence will flow from a refusal to disclose it, and the uses that will be made of the number whether disclosed mandatorily or voluntarily.

(c) Any form which does not meet the objectives specified in the Privacy Act and this section shall be revised to conform thereto.

[54 FR 18476, May 1, 1989, as amended at 73 FR 56939, Oct. 1, 2008]

§ 792.64 Contracting for the operation of a system of records.

(a) No NCUA component shall contract for the operation of a system of records by or on behalf of the Agency without the express approval of the NCUA Board.

(b) Any contract which is approved shall continue to ensure compliance with the requirements of the Privacy Act. The contracting component shall have the responsibility for ensuring that the contractor complies with the contract requirements relating to the Privacy Act.

§ 792.65 Fees.

(a) Fees pursuant to 5 U.S.C. 552a(f)(5) shall be assessed for actual copies of records provided to individuals on the following basis, unless the system manager determining access waives the fee because of the inability of the individual to pay or the cost of collecting the fee exceeds the fee:

(1) For copies of documents provided, copy fees as stated in NCUA's current FOIA fee schedule; and

(2) For copying information, if any, maintained in nondocument form, the direct cost to NCUA may be assessed.

(b) If it is determined that access fees chargeable under this section will amount to more than $25, and the individual has not indicated in advance willingness to pay fees as high as are anticipated, the individual shall be notified of the amount of the anticipated fees before copies are made, and the individual's access request shall not be considered to have been received until receipt by NCUA of written agreement to pay.

[54 FR 18476, May 1, 1989. Redesignated at 63 FR 14338, Mar. 25, 1998, as amended at 65 FR 63790, Oct. 25, 2000]

§ 792.66 Exemptions.

(a) NCUA maintains several systems of records that are exempted from some provisions of the Privacy Act. The system number and name, description of records contained in the system, exempted provisions and reasons for exemption are as follows:

(b)(1) System NCUA–1, entitled "Employee Suitability Security Investigations Containing Adverse Information," consists of adverse information about NCUA employees that had been obtained as a result of routine U.S. Office of Personnel Management (OPM) security investigations. To the extent that NCUA maintains records in this system pursuant to OPM guidelines that may require retrieval of information by use of individual identifiers, those records are encompassed by and included in the OPM Central system of records number Central–9 entitled, "Personnel Investigations Records," and thus are subject to the exemptions promulgated by OPM. Additionally, in order to ensure the protection of properly confidential sources, particularly as to those records which are not maintained pursuant to such Office of Personnel Management requirements, the records in these systems of records are exempted, pursuant to section k(5) of the Privacy Act (5 U.S.C. 552a(k)(5)), from section (d) of the Act (5 U.S.C. 552a(d)). To the extent that disclosure of a record would reveal the identity of a confidential source, NCUA need not grant access to that record by its subject. Information which would reveal a confidential source shall, however, whenever possible, be extracted or summarized in a manner which protects the source and the summary or extract shall be provided to the requesting individual.

(2) System NCUA-8, entitled, "Investigative Reports Involving Any Crime or Suspicious Activity Against a Credit Union, NCUA," consists of investigatory or enforcement records about individuals suspected of involvement in violations of laws or regulations, whether criminal or administrative. These records are maintained in an overall context of general investigative information concerning crimes against credit unions. To the extent that individually identifiable information is maintained for purposes of protecting the security of any investigations by appropriate law enforcement authorities and promoting the successful prosecution of all actual criminal activity, the records in this system are exempted, pursuant to section k(2) of the Privacy Act (5 U.S.C. 552a (k)(2)), from sections (c)(3), (d), (e)(1), (e)(2), (e)(4)(G), (e)(4)(H), (f), and (g). The records in this system are also exempted pursuant to section (j)(2) of the Privacy Act, 5 U.S.C. 552a(j)(2), from sections (c)(3), (d), (e)(1), (e)(2), (e)(4)(G), (e)(4)(H), (f), and (g). Where possible, information that would identify a confidential source will be extracted or summarized in a manner that protects the source and the summary or extract will be provided to the requesting individual.

(3) System NCUA-20, entitled, "Office of Inspector General (OIG) Investigative Records," consists of OIG records of closed and pending investigations of individuals alleged to have been involved in criminal violations. The records in this system are exempted pursuant to sections (k)(2) of the Privacy Act, 5 U.S.C. 552a(k)(2), from sections (c)(3), (d), (e)(1), (e)(4)(G), (e)(4)(H), (e)(4)(I), and (f). The records in this system are also exempted pursuant to section (j)(2) of the Privacy Act, 5 U.S.C. 552a(j)(2), from sections (c)(3), (c)(4), (d), (e)(1), (e)(2), (e)(3), and (g). NCUA need not make an accounting of previous disclosures of a record in this system of records available to its subject, and NCUA need not grant access to any records in this system of records by their subject. Further, whenever individuals request records about themselves and maintained in this system of records, the NCUA will advise the individuals only that no records available to them pursuant to the Privacy Act of 1974 have been identified. However, if review of the record reveals that the information contained therein has been used or is being used to deny the individuals any right, privilege or benefit for which they are eligible or to which they would otherwise be entitled under federal law, the individuals will be advised of the existence of the information and will be provided the information, except to the extent disclosure would identify a confidential source. Where possible, information which would identify a confidential source will be extracted or summarized in a manner which protects the source and the summary or extract will be provided to the requesting individual.

(4) System NCUA-13, entitled, "Litigation Case Files," consists of investigatory materials compiled for law enforcement purposes. Records in the Litigation Case Files system are used in connection with the execution of NCUA's legal and enforcement responsibilities. Because the system covers investigatory materials compiled for law enforcement purposes, it is eligible for exemption under subsection (k)(2) of the Privacy Act. 5 U.S.C. 552a(k)(2). The Litigation Case Files system is exempt from subsections (c)(3), (d), (e)(1), (e)(4)(G), (H), (I) and (f) of the Privacy Act. 5 U.S.C. 552a (c)(3), (d), (e)(1), (e)(4)(G), (H), (I) and (f). However, if an

individual is denied any right, privilege, or benefit to which he would otherwise be entitled by federal law, or for which he otherwise would be eligible, as a result of the maintenance of such records, the records or information will be made available to him, provided the identity of a confidential source is not disclosed. NCUA need not make an accounting of previous disclosures of a record in this system of records available to its subject, and NCUA need not grant access to any records in this system of records by their subject. Further, whenever individuals request records about themselves and maintained in this system of records, the NCUA will advise the individuals only that no records available to them pursuant to the Privacy Act of 1974 have been identified. However, if review of the record reveals that the information contained therein has been used or is being used to deny the individuals any right, privilege or benefit for which they are eligible or to which they would otherwise be entitled under federal law, the individuals will be advised of the existence of the information and will be provided the information, except to the extent disclosure would identify a confidential source. Where possible, information that would identify a confidential source will be extracted or summarized in a manner which protects the source and the summary or extract will be provided to the requesting individual.

(c) For purposes of this section, a "confidential source" means a source who furnished information to the Government under an express promise that the identity of the source would remain confidential, or, prior to September 27, 1976, under an implied promise that the identity of the source would be held in confidence.

[54 FR 18476, May 1, 1989, as amended at 60 FR 31912, June 19, 1995; 64 FR 57365, Oct. 25, 1999; 65 FR 63790, Oct. 25, 2000; 73 FR 56940, Oct. 1, 2008; 75 FR 34623, June 18, 2010]

§ 792.67 Security of systems of records.

(a) Each system manager, with the approval of the head of that Office, shall establish administrative and physical controls to insure the protection of a system of records from unauthorized access or disclosure and from physical damage or destruction. The controls instituted shall be proportional to the degree of sensitivity of the records, but at a minimum must insure: that records are enclosed in a manner to protect them from public view; that the area in which the records are stored is supervised during all business hours to prevent unauthorized personnel from entering the area or obtaining access to the records; and that the records are inaccessible during nonbusiness hours.

(b) Each system manager, with the approval of the head of that Office, shall adopt access restriction to insure that only those individuals within the agency who have a need to have access to the records for the performance of duty have access. Procedures shall also be adopted to prevent accidental access to or dissemination of records.

§ 792.68 Use and collection of Social Security numbers.

The head of each NCUA Office shall take such measures as are necessary to ensure that employees authorized to collect information from individuals are advised that individuals may not be required without statutory or regulatory authorization to furnish Social Security numbers, and that individuals who are requested to provide Social Security numbers voluntarily must be advised that furnishing the number is not required and that no penalty or denial of benefits will flow from the refusal to provide it.

§ 792.69 Training and employee standards of conduct with regard to privacy.

(a) The Director of the Office of Human Resources, with advice from the Senior Privacy Act Officer, is responsible for training NCUA employees in the obligations imposed by the Privacy Act and this subpart.

(b) The head of each NCUA Office shall be responsible for assuring that employees subject to that person's supervision are advised of the provisions of the Privacy Act, including the criminal penalties and civil liabilities provided therein, and that such employees are made aware of their responsibilities to protect the security of personal information, to assure its accuracy, relevance, timeliness, and completeness, to avoid unauthorized disclosure either orally or in writing, and to insure that no information system concerning individuals, no matter how small or specialized, is maintained without public notice.

(c) With respect to each system of records maintained by NCUA, Agency employees shall:

(1) Collect no information of a personal nature from individuals unless authorized to collect it to achieve a function or carry out an NCUA responsibility;

(2) Collect from individuals only that information which is necessary to NCUA functions or responsibilities;

(3) Collect information, wherever possible, directly from the individual to whom it relates;

(4) Inform individuals from whom information is collected of the authority for collection, the purposes thereof, the routine uses that will be made of the information, and the effects, both legal and practical of not furnishing the information;

(5) Not collect, maintain, use, or disseminate information concerning an individual's religious or political beliefs or activities or his membership in associations or organizations, unless:

(i) The individual has volunteered such information for his own benefit;

(ii) The information is expressly authorized by statute to be collected, maintained, used, or disseminated; or

(iii) Activities involved are pertinent to and within the scope of an authorized investigation or adjudication.

(6) Advise their supervisors of the existence or contemplated development of any record system which retrieves information about individuals by individual identifier.

(7) Maintain an accounting, in the prescribed form, of all dissemination of personal information outside NCUA, whether made orally or in writing;

(8) Disseminate no information concerning individuals outside NCUA except when authorized by 5 U.S.C. 552a or pursuant to a routine use as set forth in the "routine use" section of the "Notice of Systems of Records" published in the FEDERAL REGISTER.

(9) Maintain and process information concerning individuals with care in order to ensure that no inadvertent disclosure of the information is made either within or outside NCUA; and

(10) Call to the attention of the proper NCUA authorities any information in a system maintained by NCUA which is not authorized to be maintained under the provisions of the Privacy Act, including information on First Amendment activities, information that is inaccurate, irrelevant or so incomplete as to risk unfairness to the individuals concerned.

(c) Heads of offices within NCUA shall, at least annually, review the record systems subject to their supervision to ensure compliance with the provisions of the Privacy Act.

[54 FR 18476, May 1, 1989, as amended at 59 FR 36042, July 15, 1994; 65 FR 63790, Oct. 25, 2000; 67 FR 30774, May 8, 2002; 73 FR 56940, Oct. 1, 2008]

PART 793—TORT CLAIMS AGAINST THE GOVERNMENT

Subpart A—General

Sec.
793.1 Scope of regulations.

Subpart B—Procedures

793.2 Administrative claim; when presented; place of filing.
793.3 Administrative claim; who may file.
793.4 Administrative claims; evidence and information to be submitted.
793.5 Investigation, examination, and determination of claims.
793.6 Final denial of claim.
793.7 Payment of approved claims.
793.8 Release.
793.9 Penalties.
793.10 Limitation of National Credit Union Administration's authority.

AUTHORITY: 12 U.S.C. 1766.

SOURCE: 37 FR 5928, Mar. 23, 1972, unless otherwise noted. Redesignated at 49 FR 559, Jan. 5, 1984.

Subpart A—General

§ 793.1 Scope of regulations.

The regulation in this part shall apply only to claims asserted under the Federal Tort Claims Act, as amended,

28 U.S.C. 2671–2680, accruing on or after January 18, 1967, for money damages against the United States for damage to or loss of property or personal injury or death caused by the negligent or wrongful act or omission of any employee of the National Credit Union Administration while acting within the scope of his office of employment.

Subpart B—Procedures

§ 793.2 Administrative claim; when presented; place of filing.

(a) For purposes of the regulations in this part, a claim shall be deemed to have been presented when the National Credit Union Administration receives, at a place designated in paragraph (b) of this section, an executed Standard Form 95 or other written notification of an incident accompanied by a claim for money damages in a sum certain for damage to or loss of property, for personal injury, or for death, alleged to have occurred by reason of the incident. A claim which should have been presented to the National Credit Union Administration but which was mistakenly addressed to or filed with another Federal agency, shall be deemed to be presented to the National Credit Union Administration as of the date that the claim is received by the National Credit Union Administration. A claim mistakenly addressed to or filed with the National Credit Union Administration shall forthwith be transferred to the appropriate Federal agency, if ascertainable, or returned to the claimant.

(b) A claim presented in compliance with paragraph (a) of this section may be amended by the claimant at any time prior to final action by the Office of General Counsel, National Credit Union Administration or prior to the exercise of the claimant's option to bring suit under 28 U.S.C. 2675(a). Amendments shall be submitted in writing and signed by the claimant or his duly authorized agent or legal representative. Upon the timely filing of an amendment to a pending claim, the National Credit Union Administration shall have 6 months in which to make a final disposition of the claim as amended and the claimant's option under 28 U.S.C. 2675(a) shall not accrue until 6 months after the filing of an amendment.

(c) Forms may be obtained and claims may be filed with the regional office of the National Credit Union Administration having jurisdiction over the employee involved in the accident or incident, or with the Office of General Counsel, National Credit Union Administration, 1775 Duke Street, Alexandria, VA 22314–3428.

[37 FR 5928, Mar. 23, 1972. Redesignated at 49 FR 559, Jan. 5, 1984, and amended at 59 FR 36041, July 15, 1994]

§ 793.3 Administrative claim; who may file.

(a) A claim for injury to or loss of property may be presented by the owner of the property interest which is the subject matter of the claim, his duly authorized agent, or his legal representative.

(b) A claim for personal injury may be presented by the injured person, his duly authorized agent, or his legal representative.

(c) A claim based on death may be presented by the executor or administrator of the decedent's estate or by any other person legally entitled to assert such a claim under applicable State law.

(d) A claim for loss wholly compensated by an insurer with the rights of a subrogee may be presented by the insurer. A claim for loss partially compensated by an insurer with the rights of a subrogee may be presented by the insurer or the insured individually, as their respective interests appear, or jointly. Whenever an insurer presents a claim asserting the rights of a subrogee, he shall present with his claim appropriate evidence that he has the rights of a subrogee.

(e) A claim presented by an agent or legal representative shall be presented in the name of the claimant, be signed by the agent or legal representative, show the title or legal capacity of the person signing, and be accompanied by evidence of his authority to present a claim on behalf of the claimant as agent, executor, administrator, parent, guardian, or other representative.

§ 793.4 Administrative claims; evidence and information to be submitted.

(a) *Death.* In support of a claim based on death, the claimant may be required to submit the following evidence or information:

(1) An authenticated death certificate or other competent evidence showing the cause of death, date of death, and age of the decedent.

(2) Decedent's employment or occupation at the time of death, including his monthly or yearly salary or earnings (if any), and the duration of his last employment or occupation.

(3) Full names, addresses, birthdates, kinship, and marital status of the decedent's survivors, including those survivors who were dependent for support upon the decedent at the time of his death.

(4) Degree of support afforded by the decedent to each survivor dependent upon him for support at the time of his death.

(5) Decedent's general physical and mental condition before death.

(6) Itemized bills for medical and burial expenses incurred by reason of the incident causing death, or itemized receipts or payments for such expenses.

(7) If damages for pain and suffering before death are claimed, a physician's detailed statement specifying the injuries suffered, duration of pain and suffering, any drugs administered for pain and the decedent's physical condition in the interval between injury and death.

(8) Any other evidence or information which may have a bearing on the responsibility of the United States for the death or the damages claimed.

(b) *Personal injury.* In support of a claim based on personal injury, the claimant may be required to submit the following evidence or information:

(1) A written report by his attending physician or dentist setting forth the nature and extent of the injury, nature and extent of the treatment, any degree of temporary or permanent disability, the prognosis, period of hospitalization, and any diminished earning capacity. In addition, the claimant may be required to submit to a physical and/or mental examination by a physician employed or designated by the National Credit Union Administration. A copy or report of the examining physician shall be made available to the claimant upon the claimant's written request provided that claimant has, upon request, furnished the report referred to in the first sentence of this paragraph and has made or agrees to make available to the National Credit Union Administration any other physician's reports previously or thereafter made of the physical or mental condition which is the subject of his claim.

(2) Itemized bills for medical, dental, and hospital expenses incurred, or itemized receipts of payment for such expenses.

(3) If the prognosis reveals the necessity for future treatment, a statement of expected duration of and expenses for such treatment.

(4) If a claim is made for loss of time from employment, a written statement from his employer showing actual time lost from his employment, whether he is a full or part time employee, and wages or salary actually lost.

(5) If a claim is made for loss of income and the claimant is self-employed, documentary evidence showing the amount of earnings actually lost.

(6) Any other evidence or information which may have a bearing on the responsibility of the United States for the personal injury or the damages claimed.

(c) *Property damage.* In support of a claim for damages to or loss of property, real or personal, the claimant may be required to submit the following information or evidence:

(1) Proof of ownership.

(2) A detailed statement of the amount claimed with respect to each item of property.

(3) An itemized receipt of payment for necessary repairs or itemized written estimates of the cost of such repairs.

(4) A statement listing date of purchase, purchase price, market value of the property as of date of damage, and salvage value, where repair is not economical.

(5) Any other evidence or information which may have a bearing on the responsibility of the United States for the injury to or loss of property or the damages claimed.

§ 793.5

(d) *Time limit.* All evidence required to be submitted by this section shall be furnished by the claimant within a reasonable time. Failure of a claimant to furnish evidence necessary for a determination of his claim within 3 months after a request therefore has been mailed to his last known address may be deemed an abandonment of the claim. The claim may be thereupon disallowed.

[37 FR 5928, Mar. 23, 1972, as amended at 75 FR 34623, June 18, 2010]

§ 793.5 Investigation, examination, and determination of claims.

When a claim is received, the constituent agency out of whose activities the claim arose shall make such investigation as may be necessary or appropriate for a determination of the validity of the claim and thereafter shall forward the claim, together with all pertinent material, and a recommendation based on the merits of the case, with regard to the allowance or disallowance of the claim, to the Office of General Counsel, National Credit Union Administration to whom authority has been delegated to adjust, determine, compromise and settle all claims hereunder.

§ 793.6 Final denial of claim.

(a) Final denial of an administrative claim shall be in writing and sent to the claimant, his attorney, or legal representative by certified or registered mail. The notification of final denial may include a statement of the reasons for the denial and shall include a statement that, if the claimant is dissatisfied with the action of the National Credit Union Administration, he may file suit in an appropriate U.S. District Court not later than 6 months after the date of mailing the notification.

(b) Prior to the commencement of suit and prior to the expiration of the 6-month period after the date of mailing, by certified or registered mail of notice of final denial of the claim as provided in 28 U.S.C. 2401(b), a claimant, his duly authorized agent, or legal representative, may file a written request with the National Credit Union Administration for reconsideration of a final denial of a claim under paragraph (a) of this section. Upon the timely filing of a request for reconsideration the National Credit Union Administration shall have 6 months from the date of filing in which to make a final disposition of the claim and the claimant's option under 28 U.S.C. 2675(a) to bring suit shall not accrue until 6 months after the filing of a request for reconsideration. Final National Credit Union Administration action on a request for reconsideration shall be effected in accordance with the provisions of paragraph (a) of this section.

§ 793.7 Payment of approved claims.

(a) Upon allowance of his claim, claimant or his duly authorized agent shall sign the voucher for payment, Standard Form 1145, before payment is made.

(b) When the claimant is represented by an attorney, the voucher for payment (S.F. 1145) shall designate both the claimant and his attorney as "payees." The check shall be delivered to the attorney whose address shall appear on the voucher.

§ 793.8 Release.

Acceptance by the claimant, his agent or legal representative, of any award, compromise or settlement made hereunder, shall be final and conclusive on the claimant, his agent or legal representative and any other person on whose behalf or for whose benefit the claim has been presented, and shall constitute a complete release of any claim against the United States and any employee of the Government whose act or omission gave rise to the claim, by reason of the same subject matter.

§ 793.9 Penalties.

A person who files a false claim or makes a false or fraudulent statement in a claim against the United States may be liable to a fine of not more than $10,000 or to imprisonment of not more than 5 years, or both (18 U.S.C. 287–1001), and, in addition, to a forfeiture of $2,000 and a penalty of double the loss or damage sustained by the United States (31 U.S.C. 231).

§ 793.10 Limitation on National Credit Union Administration's authority.

(a) An award, compromise or settlement of a claim hereunder in excess of $25,000 shall be effected only with the prior written approval of the Attorney General or his designee. For purposes of this paragraph, a principal claim and any derivative or subrogated claim shall be treated as a single claim.

(b) An administrative claim may be adjusted, determined, compromised or settled hereunder only after consultation with the Department of Justice when, in the opinion of the National Credit Union Administration:

(1) A new precedent or a new point of law is involved; or

(2) A question of policy is or may be involved; or

(3) The United States is or may be entitled to indemnity or contribution from a third party and the National Credit Union Administration is unable to adjust the third party claim; or

(4) The compromise of a particular claim, as a practical matter, will or may control the disposition of a related claim in which the amount to be paid may exceed $25,000.

(c) An administrative claim may be adjusted, determined, compromised or settled only after consultation with the Department of Justice when it is learned that the United States or any employee, agent or cost-plus contractor of the United States is involved in litigation based on a claim arising out of the same incident or transaction.

PART 794—ENFORCEMENT OF NONDISCRIMINATION ON THE BASIS OF HANDICAP IN PROGRAMS OR ACTIVITIES CONDUCTED BY THE NATIONAL CREDIT UNION ADMINISTRATION

Sec.
794.101 Purpose.
794.102 Application.
794.103 Definitions.
794.104–794.109 [Reserved]
794.110 Self-evaluation.
794.111 Notice.
794.112–794.129 [Reserved]
794.130 General prohibitions against discrimination.
794.131–794.139 [Reserved]
794.140 Employment.
794.141–794.148 [Reserved]
794.149 Program accessibility: Discrimination prohibited.
794.150 Program accessibility: Existing facilities.
794.151 Program accessibility: New construction and alterations.
794.152–794.159 [Reserved]
794.160 Communications.
794.161–794.169 [Reserved]
794.170 Compliance procedures.
794.171–794.999 [Reserved]

AUTHORITY: 29 U.S.C. 794.

SOURCE: 51 FR 22889, 22896, June 23, 1986, unless otherwise noted.

§ 794.101 Purpose.

This part effectuates section 119 of the Rehabilitation, Comprehensive Services, and Developmental Disabilities Amendments of 1978, which amended section 504 of the Rehabilitation Act of 1973 to prohibit discrimination on the basis of handicap in programs or activities conducted by Executive agencies or the United States Postal Service.

§ 794.102 Application.

This part applies to all programs or activities conducted by the agency.

§ 794.103 Definitions.

For purposes of this part, the term—

Assistant Attorney General means the Assistant Attorney General, Civil Rights Division, United States Department of Justice.

Auxiliary aids means services or devices that enable persons with impaired sensory, manual, or speaking skills to have an equal opportunity to participate in, and enjoy the benefits of, programs or activities conducted by the agency. For example, auxiliary aids useful for persons with impaired vision include readers, brailled materials, audio recordings, telecommunications devices and other similar services and devices. Auxiliary aids useful for persons with impaired hearing include telephone handset amplifiers, telephones compatible with hearing aids, telecommunication devices for deaf persons (TDD's), interpreters, notetakers, written materials, and other similar services and devices.

§794.103

Complete complaint means a written statement that contains the complainant's name and address and describes the agency's alleged discriminatory action in sufficient detail to inform the agency of the nature and date of the alleged violation of section 504. It shall be signed by the complainant or by someone authorized to do so on his or her behalf. Complaints filed on behalf of classes or third parties shall describe or identify (by name, if possible) the alleged victims of discrimination.

Facility means all or any portion of buildings, structures, equipment, roads, walks, parking lots, rolling stock or other conveyances, or other real or personal property.

Handicapped person means any person who has a physical or mental impairment that substantially limits one or more major life activities, has a record of such an impairment, or is regarded as having such an impairment.

As used in this definition, the phrase:

(1) *Physical or mental impairment* includes—

(i) Any physiological disorder or condition, cosmetic disfigurement, or anatomical loss affecting one or more of the following body systems: Neurological; musculoskeletal; special sense organs; respiratory, including speech organs; cardiovascular; reproductive; digestive; genitourinary; hemic and lymphatic; skin; and endocrine; or

(ii) Any mental or psychological disorder, such as mental retardation, organic brain syndrome, emotional or mental illness, and specific learning disabilities. The term *physical or mental impairment* includes, but is not limited to, such diseases and conditions as orthopedic, visual, speech, and hearing impairments, cerebral palsy, epilepsy, muscular dystrophy, multiple sclerosis, cancer, heart disease, diabetes, mental retardation, emotional illness, and drug addiction and alcoholism.

(2) *Major life activities* includes functions such as caring for one's self, performing manual tasks, walking, seeing, hearing, speaking, breathing, learning, and working.

(3) *Has a record of such an impairment* means has a history of, or has been misclassified as having, a mental or physical impairment that substantially limits one or more major life activities.

(4) *Is regarded as having an impairment* means—

(i) Has a physical or mental impairment that does not substantially limit major life activities but is treated by the agency as constituting such a limitation;

(ii) Has a physical or mental impairment that substantially limits major life activities only as a result of the attitudes of others toward such impairment; or

(iii) Has none of the impairments defined in paragraph (1) of this definition but is treated by the agency as having such an impairment.

Historic preservation programs means programs conducted by the agency that have preservation of historic properties as a primary purpose.

Historic properties means those properties that are listed or eligible for listing in the National Register of Historic Places or properties designated as historic under a statute of the appropriate State or local government body.

Qualified handicapped person means—

(1) With respect to preschool, elementary, or secondary education services provided by the agency, a handicapped person who is a member of a class of persons otherwise entitled by statute, regulation, or agency policy to receive education services from the agency.

(2) With respect to any other agency program or activity under which a person is required to perform services or to achieve a level of accomplishment, a handicapped person who meets the essential eligibility requirements and who can acheive the purpose of the program or activity without modifications in the program or activity that the agency can demonstrate would result in a fundamental alteration in its nature;

(3) With respect to any other program or activity, a handicapped person who meets the essential eligibility requirements for participation in, or receipt of benefits from, that program or activity; and

(4) *Qualified handicapped person* is defined for purposes of employment in 29 CFR 1613.702(f), which is made applicable to this part by §794.140.

Section 504 means section 504 of the Rehabilitation Act of 1973 (Pub. L. 93-112, 87 Stat. 394 (29 U.S.C. 794)), as amended by the Rehabilitation Act Amendments of 1974 (Pub. L. 93-516, 88 Stat. 1617), and the Rehabilitation, Comprehensive Services, and Developmental Disabilities Amendments of 1978 (Pub. L. 95-602, 92 Stat. 2955). As used in this part, section 504 applies only to programs or activities conducted by Executive agencies and not to federally assisted programs.

Substantial impairment means a significant loss of the integrity of finished materials, design quality, or special character resulting from a permanent alteration.

§§ 794.104-794.109 [Reserved]

§ 794.110 Self-evaluation.

(a) The agency shall, by August 24, 1987, evaluate its current policies and practices, and the effects thereof, that do not or may not meet the requirements of this part, and, to the extent modification of any such policies and practices is required, the agency shall proceed to make the necessary modifications.

(b) The agency shall provide an opportunity to interested persons, including handicapped persons or organizations representing handicapped persons, to participate in the self-evaluation process by submitting comments (both oral and written).

(c) The agency shall, until three years following the completion of the self-evaluation, maintain on file and make available for public inspection:

(1) A description of areas examined and any problems identified, and

(2) A description of any modifications made.

§ 794.111 Notice.

The agency shall make available to employees, applicants, participants, beneficiaries, and other interested persons such information regarding the provisions of this part and its applicability to the programs or activities conducted by the agency, and make such information available to them in such manner as the head of the agency finds necessary to apprise such persons of the protections against discrimination assured them by section 504 and this regulation.

§§ 794.112-794.129 [Reserved]

§ 794.130 General prohibitions against discrimination.

(a) No qualified handicapped person shall, on the basis of handicap, be excluded from participation in, be denied the benefits of, or otherwise be subjected to discrimination under any program or activity conducted by the agency.

(b)(1) The agency, in providing any aid, benefit, or service, may not, directly or through contractual, licensing, or other arrangements, on the basis of handicap—

(i) Deny a qualified handicapped person the opportunity to participate in or benefit from the aid, benefit, or service;

(ii) Afford a qualified handicapped person an opportunity to participate in or benefit from the aid, benefit, or service that is not equal to that afforded others;

(iii) Provide a qualified handicapped person with an aid, benefit, or service that is not as effective in affording equal opportunity to obtain the same result, to gain the same benefit, or to reach the same level of achievement as that provided to others;

(iv) Provide different or separate aid, benefits, or services to handicapped persons or to any class of handicapped persons than is provided to others unless such action is necessary to provide qualified handicapped persons with aid, benefits, or services that are as effective as those provided to others;

(v) Deny a qualified handicapped person the opportunity to participate as a member of planning or advisory boards; or

(vi) Otherwise limit a qualified handicapped person in the enjoyment of any right, privilege, advantage, or opportunity enjoyed by others receiving the aid, benefit, or service.

(2) The agency may not deny a qualified handicapped person the opportunity to participate in programs or activities that are not separate or different, despite the existence of permissibly separate or different programs or activities.

(3) The agency may not, directly or through contractual or other arrangements, utilize criteria or methods of administration the purpose or effect of which would—

(i) Subject qualified handicapped persons to discrimination on the basis of handicap; or

(ii) Defeat or substantially impair accomplishment of the objectives of a program activity with respect to handicapped persons.

(4) The agency may not, in determining the site or location of a facility, make selections the purpose or effect of which would—

(i) Exclude handicapped persons from, deny them the benefits of, or otherwise subject them to discrimination under any program or activity conducted by the agency; or

(ii) Defeat or substantially impair the accomplishment of the objectives of a program or activity with respect to handicapped persons.

(5) The agency, in the selection of procurement contractors, may not use criteria that subject qualified handicapped persons to discrimination on the basis of handicap.

(6) The agency may not administer a licensing or certification program in a manner that subjects qualified handicapped persons to discrimination on the basis of handicap, nor may the agency establish requirements for the programs or activities of licensees or certified entities that subject qualified handicapped persons to discrimination on the basis of handicap. However, the programs or activities of entities that are licensed or certified by the agency are not, themselves, covered by this part.

(c) The exclusion of nonhandicapped persons from the benefits of a program limited by Federal statute or Executive order to handicapped persons or the exclusion of a specific class of handicapped persons from a program limited by Federal statute or Executive order to a different class of handicapped persons is not prohibited by this part.

(d) The agency shall administer programs and activities in the most integrated setting appropriate to the needs of qualified handicapped persons.

§§ 794.131–794.139 [Reserved]

§ 794.140 Employment.

No qualified handicapped person shall, on the basis of handicap, be subjected to discrimination in employment under any program or activity conducted by the agency. The definitions, requirements, and procedures of section 501 of the Rehabilitation Act of 1973 (29 U.S.C. 791), as established by the Equal Employment Opportunity Commission in 29 CFR part 1613, shall apply to employment in federally conducted programs or activities.

§§ 794.141–794.148 [Reserved]

§ 794.149 Program accessibility: Discrimination prohibited.

Except as otherwise provided in § 794.150, no qualified handicapped person shall, because the agency's facilities are inaccessible to or unusable by handicapped persons, be denied the benefits of, be excluded from participation in, or otherwise be subjected to discrimination under any program or activity conducted by the agency.

§ 794.150 Program accessibility: Existing facilities.

(a) *General.* The agency shall operate each program or activity so that the program or activity, when viewed in its entirety, is readily accessible to and usable by handicapped persons. This paragraph does not—

(1) Necessarily require the agency to make each of its existing facilities accessible to and usable by handicapped persons;

(2) In the case of historic preservation programs, require the agency to take any action that would result in a substantial impairment of significant historic features of an historic property; or

(3) Require the agency to take any action that it can demonstrate would result in a fundamental alteration in the nature of a program or activity or in undue financial and administrative burdens. In those circumstances where agency personnel believe that the proposed action would fundamentally alter the program or activity or would result in undue financial and administrative burdens, the agency has the

burden of proving that compliance with § 794.150(a) would result in such alteration or burdens. The decision that compliance would result in such alteration or burdens must be made by the agency head or his or her designee after considering all agency resources available for use in the funding and operation of the conducted program or activity, and must be accompanied by a written statement of the reasons for reaching that conclusion. If an action would result in such an alteration or such burdens, the agency shall take any other action that would not result in such an alteration or such burdens but would nevertheless ensure that handicapped persons receive the benefits and services of the program or activity.

(b) *Methods*—(1) *General.* The agency may comply with the requirements of this section through such means as redesign of equipment, reassignment of services to accessible buildings, assignment of aides to beneficiaries, home visits, delivery of services at alternate accessible sites, alteration of existing facilities and construction of new facilities, use of accessible rolling stock, or any other methods that result in making its programs or activities readily accessible to and usable by handicapped persons. The agency is not required to make structural changes in existing facilities where other methods are effective in achieving compliance with this section. The agency, in making alterations to existing buildings, shall meet accessibility requirements to the extent compelled by the Architectural Barriers Act of 1968, as amended (42 U.S.C. 4151–4157), and any regulations implementing it. In choosing among available methods for meeting the requirements of this section, the agency shall give priority to those methods that offer programs and activities to qualified handicapped persons in the most integrated setting appropriate.

(2) *Historic preservation programs.* In meeting the requirements of § 794.150(a) in historic preservation programs, the agency shall give priority to methods that provide physical access to handicapped persons. In cases where a physical alteration to an historic property is not required because of § 794.150(a)(2) or (a)(3), alternative methods of achieving program accessibility include—

(i) Using audio-visual materials and devices to depict those portions of an historic property that cannot otherwise be made accessible;

(ii) Assigning persons to guide handicapped persons into or through portions of historic properties that cannot otherwise be made accessible; or

(iii) Adopting other innovative methods.

(c) *Time period for compliance.* The agency shall comply with the obligations established under this section by October 21, 1986, except that where structural changes in facilities are undertaken, such changes shall be made by August 22, 1989, but in any event as expeditiously as possible.

(d) *Transition plan.* In the event that structural changes to facilities will be undertaken to achieve program accessibility, the agency shall develop, by February 23, 1987, a transition plan setting forth the steps necessary to complete such changes. The agency shall provide an opportunity to interested persons, including handicapped persons or organizations representing handicapped persons, to participate in the development of the transition plan by submitting comments (both oral and written). A copy of the transition plan shall be made available for public inspection. The plan shall, at a minimum—

(1) Identify physical obstacles in the agency's facilities that limit the accessibility of its programs or activities to handicapped persons;

(2) Describe in detail the methods that will be used to make the facilities accessible;

(3) Specify the schedule for taking the steps necessary to achieve compliance with this section and, if the time period of the transition plan is longer than one year, identify steps that will be taken during each year of the transition period; and

(4) Indicate the official responsible for implementation of the plan.

§ 794.151 Program accessibility: New construction and alterations.

Each building or part of a building that is constructed or altered by, on behalf of, or for the use of the agency shall be designed, constructed, or altered so as to be readily accessible to and usable by handicapped persons. The definitions, requirements, and standards of the Architectural Barriers Act (42 U.S.C. 4151–4157), as established in 41 CFR 101–19.600 to 101–19.607, apply to buildings covered by this section.

§§ 794.152–794.159 [Reserved]

§ 794.160 Communications.

(a) The agency shall take appropriate steps to ensure effective communication with applicants, participants, personnel of other Federal entities, and members of the public.

(1) The agency shall furnish appropriate auxiliary aids where necessary to afford a handicapped person an equal opportunity to participate in, and enjoy the benefits of, a program or activity conducted by the agency.

(i) In determining what type of auxiliary aid is necessary, the agency shall give primary consideration to the requests of the handicapped person.

(ii) The agency need not provide individually prescribed devices, readers for personal use or study, or other devices of a personal nature.

(2) Where the agency communicates with applicants and beneficiaries by telephone, telecommunication devices for deaf person (TDD's) or equally effective telecommunication systems shall be used.

(b) The agency shall ensure that interested persons, including persons with impaired vision or hearing, can obtain information as to the existence and location of accessible services, activities, and facilities.

(c) The agency shall provide signage at a primary entrance to each of its inaccessible facilities, directing users to a location at which they can obtain information about accessible facilities. The international symbol for accessibility shall be used at each primary entrance of an accessible facility.

(d) This section does not require the agency to take any action that it can demonstrate would result in a fundamental alteration in the nature of a program or activity or in undue financial and adminstrative burdens. In those circumstances where agency personnel believe that the proposed action would fundamentally alter the program or activity or would result in undue financial and administrative burdens, the agency has the burden of proving that compliance with § 794.160 would result in such alteration or burdens. The decision that compliance would result in such alteration or burdens must be made by the agency head or his or her designee after considering all agency resources available for use in the funding and operation of the conducted program or activity, and must be accompanied by a written statement of the reasons for reaching that conclusion. If an action required to comply with this section would result in such an alteration or such burdens, the agency shall take any other action that would not result in such an alteration or such burdens but would nevertheless ensure that, to the maximum extent possible, handicapped persons receive the benefits and services of the program or activity.

§§ 794.161–794.169 [Reserved]

§ 794.170 Compliance procedures.

(a) Except as provided in paragraph (b) of this section, this section applies to all allegations of discrimination on the basis of handicap in programs or activities conducted by the agency.

(b) The agency shall process complaints alleging violations of section 504 with respect to employment according to the procedures established by the Equal Employment Opportunity Commission in 29 CFR part 1613 pursuant to section 501 of the Rehabilitation Act of 1973 (29 U.S.C. 791).

(c) The Director, Office of Administration, shall be responsible for coordinating implementation of this section. Complaints may be sent to NCUA, 1776 G Street NW., Room 7261, Washington, DC 20456.

(d) The agency shall accept and investigate all complete complaints for which it has jurisdiction. All complete complaints must be filed within 180 days of the alleged act of discrimination. The agency may extend this time period for good cause.

(e) If the agency receives a complaint over which it does not have jurisdiction, it shall promptly notify the complainant and shall make reasonable efforts to refer the complaint to the appropriate government entity.

(f) The agency shall notify the Architectural and Transportation Barriers Compliance Board upon receipt of any complaint alleging that a building or facility that is subject to the Architectural Barriers Act of 1968, as amended (42 U.S.C. 4151–4157), or section 502 of the Rehabilitation Act of 1973, as amended (29 U.S.C. 792), is not readily accessible to and usable by handicapped persons.

(g) Within 180 days of the receipt of a complete complaint for which it has jurisdiction, the agency shall notify the complainant of the results of the investigation in a letter containing—

(1) Findings of fact and conclusions of law;

(2) A description of a remedy for each violation found; and

(3) A notice of the right to appeal.

(h) Appeals of the findings of fact and conclusions of law or remedies must be filed by the complainant within 90 days of receipt from the agency of the letter required by §794.170(g). The agency may extend this time for good cause.

(i) Timely appeals shall be accepted and processed by the head of the agency.

(j) The head of the agency shall notify the complainant of the results of the appeal within 60 days of the receipt of the request. If the head of the agency determines that additional information is needed from the complainant, he or she shall have 60 days from the date of receipt of the additional information to make his or her determination on the appeal.

(k) The time limits cited in paragraphs (g) and (j) of this section may be extended with the permission of the Assistant Attorney General.

(l) The agency may delegate its authority for conducting complaint investigations to other Federal agencies, except that the authority for making the final determination may not be delegated to another agency.

[51 FR 22889, 22896, June 23, 1986, as amended at 51 FR 22889, June 23, 1986; 59 FR 36042, July 15, 1994]

§§ 794.171–794.999 [Reserved]

PART 796—POST-EMPLOYMENT RESTRICTIONS FOR CERTAIN NCUA EXAMINERS

Sec.
796.1 What is the purpose and scope of this part?
796.2 Who is considered a senior examiner of the NCUA?
796.3 What special post-employment restrictions apply to senior examiners?
796.4 When do these special restrictions become effective and may they be waived?
796.5 What are the penalties for violating these special post-employment restrictions?
796.6 What other definitions and rules of construction apply for purposes of this part?

AUTHORITY: 12 U.S.C. 1786(w).

SOURCE: 70 FR 72703, Dec. 7, 2005, unless otherwise noted.

§ 796.1 What is the purpose and scope of this part?

This part identifies those National Credit Union Administration (NCUA) employees who are subject to the special, post-employment restrictions in section 1786(w) of the Act and implements those restrictions as they apply to NCUA employees.

§ 796.2 Who is considered a senior examiner of the NCUA?

For purposes of this part, an NCUA employee is considered to be the "senior examiner" for a federally insured credit union if the employee—

(a) Has been authorized by NCUA to conduct examinations or inspections of federally insured credit unions on behalf of NCUA;

(b) Has continuing, broad, and lead responsibility for examining or inspecting that federally insured credit union;

(c) Routinely interacts with officers or employees of that federally insured credit union; and

(d) Devotes a substantial portion of his or her time to supervising or examining that federally insured credit union.

§ 796.3 What special post-employment restrictions apply to senior examiners?

(a) *Senior examiners of federally insured credit unions.* An officer or employee of the NCUA who performs work (onsite or offsite) as the senior examiner of a federally insured credit union for a total of two or more months during the last 12 months of individual's employment with NCUA may not, within one year after leaving NCUA employment, knowingly accept compensation as an employee, officer, director, or consultant from that credit union.

(b) *Example.* An NCUA resident corporate credit union examiner assigned to work at a federally insured, corporate credit union for two or more months during the last 12 months of that individual's employment with NCUA will be subject to the one-year prohibition of this section.

§ 796.4 When do these special restrictions become effective and may they be waived?

The post-employment restrictions in section 1786(w) of the Act and § 796.3 do not apply to any current or former NCUA employee, if:

(a) The individual ceased to be an NCUA employee on or before December 17, 2005; or

(b) The Chairman of the NCUA Board certifies in writing and on a case-by-case basis that granting the senior examiner a waiver of the restrictions would not affect the integrity of the NCUA's supervisory program.

§ 796.5 What are the penalties for violating these special post-employment restrictions?

(a) *Penalties under section 1786(w)(5) of the Act.* An NCUA senior examiner who violates the post-employment restrictions set forth in § 796.3 can be:

(1) Removed from participating in the affairs of the relevant credit union and prohibited from participating in the affairs of any federally insured credit union for a period of up to five years; and, alternatively, or in addition,

(2) Assessed a civil monetary penalty of not more than $250,000.

(b) *Other penalties.* The penalties in paragraph (a) of this section are not exclusive, and a senior examiner who violates the restrictions in § 796.3 also may be subject to other administrative, civil, and criminal remedies and penalties as provided in law.

§ 796.6 What other definitions and rules of construction apply for purposes of this part?

For purposes of this part, a person shall be deemed to act as a "*consultant*" for a federally insured credit union or other company only if the person works directly on matters for, or on behalf of, such credit union.

PART 797—PROCEDURES FOR DEBT COLLECTION

Subpart A—Scope, Purpose, Definitions and Delegation of Authority

Sec.
797.1 Scope.
797.2 Purpose.
797.3 Definitions.
797.4 Delegation of authority.

Subpart B—Administrative Offset

797.5 Authority and scope.
797.6 Administrative offset prior to completion of procedures.
797.7 Procedures.
797.8 Right to agency review.
797.9 Review procedures.
797.10 Special review.
797.11 Interest, administrative costs, and penalties.
797.12 Refunds.
797.13 Requests for administrative offset where NCUA is the creditor agency.
797.14 Requests for administrative offset where NCUA is the paying agency.
797.15 Administrative offset against amounts payable from Civil Service Retirement and Disability Fund.
797.16 Stay of offset.

Subpart C—Salary Offset

797.17 Authority and scope.
797.18 Notice requirements where NCUA is the creditor agency.
797.19 Review of agency records related to the debt.
797.20 Procedures to request a hearing.
797.21 Hearing procedures.
797.22 Voluntary repayment agreement.
797.23 Certification where NCUA is the creditor agency.
797.24 Certification where NCUA is the paying agency.

National Credit Union Administration

797.25 Recovery from final check or other payments due a separated employee.

AUTHORITY: 12 U.S.C. 1752a; 5 U.S.C. 5514; 31 U.S.C. 3711, 3716, 3720A, 3720D.

SOURCE: 73 FR 11341, Mar. 3, 2008, unless otherwise noted.

Subpart A—Scope, Purpose, Definitions and Delegation of Authority

§ 797.1 Scope.

This part establishes NCUA procedures for the collection of certain debts owed to the United States.

(a) This part applies to collections by NCUA from:

(1) Federal employees who are indebted to NCUA;

(2) Employees of NCUA who are indebted to other agencies or NCUA; and

(3) Former federal employees who are indebted to NCUA.

(b) This part does not apply:

(1) To debts or claims arising under the Internal Revenue Code of 1986 (Title 26, U.S. Code), the Social Security Act (*42 U.S.C. 301 et seq.*), or the tariff laws of the United States;

(2) To a situation to which the Contract Disputes Act (*41 U.S.C. 601 et seq.*) applies;

(3) In any case where collection of a debt is explicitly provided for or prohibited by another statute;

(4) To debts owed to or payments made by NCUA in connection with NCUA's conservatorship, liquidation, supervision, enforcement, or insurance responsibilities pursuant to *12 U.S.C. 1786 and 1787*, nor does it limit or affect NCUA's authority with respect to debts and/or claims pursuant to *12 U.S.C. 1752(a) and 1766.*

(c) Nothing in this part precludes the compromise, suspension, or termination of collection actions, where appropriate, under standards implementing the Debt Collection Improvement Act (DCIA) (*31 U.S.C. 3711 et seq.*), the Federal Claims Collection Standards (FCCS) (31 CFR parts 900 through 904); or any other applicable law.

§ 797.2 Purpose.

(a) The purpose of this part is to implement federal statutes and regulatory standards authorizing NCUA to collect debts owed to the United States. This part is consistent with the following federal statutes and regulations:

(1) DCIA at *31 U.S.C. 3711* (collection and compromise of claims); section 3716 (administrative offset), and section 3717 (interest and penalty on claims);

(2) *5 U.S.C. 5514* (salary offset);

(3) *5 U.S.C. 5584* (waiver of claims for overpayment);

(4) 31 CFR parts 900 through 904 (FCCS);

(5) 5 CFR part 550, subpart K (salary offset);

(6) *31 U.S.C. 3720D*, 31 CFR 285.11 (administrative wage garnishment); and

(7) 5 CFR 831.1801 through 1808 (U.S. Office of Personnel Management (OPM) offset).

(b) Collectively, these statutes and regulations prescribe the manner in which federal agencies should proceed to establish the existence and validity of debts owed to the federal government and describe the remedies available to agencies to offset valid debts.

§ 797.3 Definitions.

Except where the context clearly indicates otherwise or where the term is defined elsewhere in this subpart, the following definitions shall apply to this subpart.

(a) *Administrative offset*, as defined in *31 U.S.C. 3701(a)(1)*, means withholding money payable by the United States government to, or held by the government for, a person to satisfy a debt the person owes the government.

(b) *Agency* means a department, agency, or instrumentality in the Executive, Judicial, or Legislative branch of the government.

(c) *Claim or debt* means money or property owed by a person or entity to an agency of the federal government. A "claim" or "debt" includes amounts due the government, fees, services, overpayments, penalties, damages, interest, fines and forfeitures. For purposes of this part, a debt owed to NCUA constitutes a debt owed to the federal government.

(d) *Claim certification* means a creditor agency's written request to a paying agency to effect an administrative or salary offset.

§ 797.4

(e) *Creditor agency* means an agency to which a claim or debt is owed.

(f) *Debtor* means the person or entity owing money to the federal government.

(g) *Disposable pay* means that part of current basic pay or other authorized pay remaining after the deduction of any amount required by law to be withheld. NCUA shall allow the deductions described in 5 CFR 581.105(b) through (f).

(h) *Employee* means a current employee of NCUA or another agency.

(i) *FCCS* means the Federal Claims Collection Standards published in 31 CFR part 900.

(j) *Hearing official* means an individual who is authorized to conduct a hearing with respect to the existence or amount of a debt claimed and issue a final decision on the basis of such hearing. A hearing official may not be under the supervision or control of NCUA when NCUA is the creditor agency.

(k) *NCUA* means the National Credit Union Administration.

(l) *Paying agency* means an agency of the federal government owing money to a debtor against which an administrative or salary offset can be effected.

(m) *Salary offset* means an administrative offset to collect a debt under *5 U.S.C. 5514* by deductions at one or more officially established pay intervals from the current pay account of a debtor.

(n) *Waiver* means the cancellation, remission, forgiveness, or nonrecovery of a debt allegedly owed by an employee to NCUA or another agency as permitted or required by *5 U.S.C. 5584* or any other law.

§ 797.4 Delegation of authority.

Authority to conduct the following activities is delegated to the Executive Director to:

(a) Initiate and carry out the debt collection process on behalf of NCUA, in accordance with the FCCS;

(b) Accept or reject compromise offers, suspend, terminate or waive collection actions to the full extent of NCUA's legal authority under *12 U.S.C. 1752(a)* and *1789; 31 U.S.C. 3711*, and any other applicable statute or regulation.

(c) Report to consumer reporting agencies certain data pertaining to delinquent debts, where appropriate;

(d) Use offset procedures, including administrative and salary offset, to collect debts; and

(e) Take any other action necessary to promptly and effectively collect debts owed to the government in accordance with the policies contained herein and as otherwise provided by law.

Subpart B—Administrative Offset

§ 797.5 Authority and scope.

NCUA may collect a debt owed to the federal government from a person, organization, or other entity by administrative offset, pursuant to 31 U.S.C. 3716, where:

(a) The debt is certain in amount;

(b) Administrative offset is feasible, desirable, and not otherwise prohibited;

(c) The applicable statute of limitations has not expired; and

(d) Administrative offset is in the best interest of the federal government.

§ 797.6 Administrative offset prior to completion of procedures.

Prior to the completion of the procedures described in § 797.7, NCUA may effect administrative offset if failure to offset would substantially prejudice its ability to collect the debt, and if the time before the payment is to be made does not reasonably permit completion of the procedures described in § 797.7. Such prior administrative offset shall be followed promptly by the completion of the procedures described in § 797.7.

§ 797.7 Procedures.

Prior to collecting any debt by administrative offset or referring such claim to another agency for collection through administrative offset, NCUA shall provide the debtor with a written Notice of Intent to Collect by Administrative Offset (the Notice) at least 30 calendar days before administrative offset is to commence.

The Notice shall provide the following information:

(a) The nature and amount of the debt, the intention of NCUA to collect the debt through administrative offset, and a statement of the rights of the debtor under this section, including the right to request a waiver under *5 U.S.C. 5584*;

(b) An opportunity to inspect and copy the records of NCUA related to the debt or receive copies if personal inspection is impractical;

(c) The payment due date, which shall be 30 calendar days from the date after receipt of the initial demand for payment;

(d) An opportunity for the debtor to obtain a review of the determination of indebtedness. Any request for review by the debtor shall be in writing and shall be submitted to NCUA within 15 calendar days after receipt of the Notice. NCUA may waive the time limits for requesting review for good cause shown by the debtor. NCUA shall provide the debtor with a reasonable opportunity for an oral hearing when:

(1) An applicable statute authorizes or requires NCUA to consider waiver of the indebtedness involved, the debtor requests waiver of the indebtedness, and the waiver determination turns on an issue of credibility or veracity; or

(2) The debtor requests reconsideration of the debt and NCUA determines that the question of the indebtedness cannot be resolved by review of the documentary evidence, as for example, when the validity of the debt turns on an issue of credibility or veracity. Unless otherwise required by law, an oral hearing under this subpart is not required to be a formal evidentiary hearing, although NCUA shall document all significant matters discussed at the hearing. In those cases where an oral hearing is not required by this subpart, NCUA shall make its determination on the request for waiver or reconsideration based upon a review of the written record.

(e) An opportunity to enter into a written agreement for the repayment of the amount of the claim at the discretion of NCUA;

(f) That charges for interest, penalties, and administrative costs will be assessed against the debtor, in accordance with *31 U.S.C. 3717*, if payment is not received by the payment due date, unless excused by the FCCS;

(g) That if the debtor has not entered into an agreement with NCUA to pay the debt, has not requested NCUA to review the debt, or has not paid the debt by the payment due date, NCUA intends to collect the debt by all legally available means;

(h) The name and address of the Executive Director whom the debtor shall send all correspondence relating to the debt; and

(i) Other information, as may be appropriate.

§ 797.8 Right to agency review.

(a) If the debtor disputes the claim, the debtor may request a review of NCUA's determination of the existence of the debt or of the amount of the debt. If only part of the claim is disputed, the undisputed portion should be paid by the payment due date.

(b) To obtain a review, the debtor shall submit a written request for review to the Executive Director within 15 calendar days after receipt of the Notice. The debtor's request for review shall state the basis on which the claim is disputed.

(c) The NCUA shall promptly notify the debtor, in writing, that the NCUA has received the request for review. The NCUA shall conduct its review of the claim in accordance with § 797.9.

§ 797.9 Review procedures.

(a) Unless an oral hearing is required by § 797.7(d), NCUA's review shall be a review of the written record of the claim.

(b) If an oral hearing is required, NCUA shall provide the debtor with a reasonable opportunity for such a hearing. The oral hearing, however, shall not be an adversarial adjudication and need not take the form of a formal evidentiary hearing. All significant matters discussed at the hearing, however, will be carefully documented.

(c) Any review required by this part, whether a review of the written record or an oral hearing, shall be conducted by a hearing official. When NCUA is the creditor agency and the debtor is an NCUA employee, NCUA shall contact any agency designated in appendix A to 5 CFR part 581 to arrange for a

§ 797.10

hearing official. When NCUA is the creditor agency and the debtor is not an NCUA employee (i.e., the debtor is employed by another federal agency, also known as the paying agency), and NCUA cannot provide a prompt and appropriate hearing, NCUA may contact an agent of the paying agency designated in appendix A to 5 CFR part 581 to arrange for a hearing official. The paying agency must cooperate with NCUA to provide a hearing official, as required by the FCCS.

(d) The hearing official shall issue a final written decision based on documentary evidence and, if applicable, information developed at an oral hearing. The written decision shall be issued as soon as practicable after the review but not later than 60 days after the date on which the request for review was received by NCUA, unless the debtor requests a delay in the proceedings. A delay in the proceedings shall be granted if the hearing official determines that there is good cause to grant the delay. If a delay is granted, the 60-day decision period shall be extended by the number of days by which the review was postponed.

(e) Upon issuance of the written opinion, NCUA shall promptly notify the debtor of the hearing official's decision. The notification shall include a copy of the written decision issued by the hearing official.

§ 797.10 Special review.

(a) An employee subject to offset, or a voluntary repayment agreement, may, at any time, request a special review by the Executive Director of the amount of the offset or voluntary repayment, based on materially changed circumstances, including, but not limited to, catastrophic illness, divorce, death, or disability.

(b) To determine whether an offset would prevent the employee from meeting essential subsistence expenses, the employee shall submit a detailed statement and supporting documents for the employee, the employee's spouse, and dependents indicating the employee's assets and liabilities.

(c) If the employee requests a special review under this section, the employee shall file an alternative proposed offset or payment schedule and a statement.

(d) The Executive Director shall evaluate the statement and supporting documents, and determine whether the original offset or repayment schedule imposes an undue financial hardship on the employee. The Executive Director shall notify the employee in writing within 30 calendar days of such determination, including, if appropriate, a revised offset or payment schedule. If the special review results in a revised offset or repayment schedule, NCUA shall provide a new certification to the paying agency.

§ 797.11 Interest, administrative costs, and penalties.

Where NCUA is the creditor agency, it shall assess interest, penalties and administrative costs pursuant to *31 U.S.C. 3717* and 31 CFR parts 900 through 904, unless excused in accordance with the FCCS.

§ 797.12 Refunds.

NCUA shall refund promptly those amounts recovered by offset but later found not to be owed to the federal government.

§ 797.13 Requests for administrative offset where NCUA is the creditor agency.

(a) NCUA may request that a debt owed to NCUA be collected by administrative offset against funds due and payable to a debtor by another agency.

(b) In requesting administrative offset, NCUA, as creditor, shall certify in writing to the agency holding funds of the debtor:

(1) That the debtor owes the debt;

(2) The amount and basis of the debt; and

(3) That NCUA has complied with the requirements of its own administrative offset regulations and the applicable provisions of the FCCS with respect to providing the debtor with due process.

§ 797.14 Requests for administrative offset from other federal agencies where NCUA is the paying agency.

(a) Any agency may request that funds due and payable to a debtor by NCUA be administratively offset in

National Credit Union Administration

§ 797.18

order to collect a debt owed to such agency by the debtor.

(b) NCUA shall initiate the requested administrative offset only upon receipt of a written certification from the creditor agency that:

(1) The debtor owes the debt, including the amount and basis of the debt;

(2) The agency has prescribed regulations for the exercise of administrative offset; and

(3) The agency has complied with its own administrative offset regulations and with the applicable provisions of the FCCS, with respect to providing the debtor with due process.

§ 797.15 Administrative offset against amounts payable from Civil Service Retirement and Disability Fund.

NCUA may request that monies payable to a debtor from the Civil Service Retirement and Disability Fund be administratively offset to collect debts owed to NCUA by the debtor. NCUA shall provide OPM with a written certification that states the debtor owes the debt, the amount of the debt, and that NCUA has complied with the agency's offset regulations, as well as, the requirements set forth in 31 CFR parts 900 through 904 and OPM's regulations.

§ 797.16 Stay of offset.

(a) When a creditor agency receives a debtor's request for inspection of agency records, the offset is stayed for 15 calendar days beyond the date set for the record inspection.

(b) When a creditor agency receives a debtor's offer to enter into a repayment agreement, the offset is stayed until the debtor is notified as to whether the proposed agreement is acceptable.

(c) When a review is conducted, the offset is stayed until the creditor agency issues a final written decision. The written decision must be issued within 60 days after receipt of the debtor's request for review.

Subpart C—Salary Offset

§ 797.17 Authority and scope.

(a) NCUA may collect debts owed by employees to the federal government by means of salary offset under the authority of 5 U.S.C. 5514, 5 CFR part 550, subpart K, and this subpart. The procedures set forth in this subpart apply to situations where NCUA is attempting to collect a debt by salary offset that is owed to it by an individual employed by NCUA or by another agency; or where NCUA employs an individual who owes a debt to another agency. Since salary offset is a type of administrative offset, this subpart supplements subpart B.

(b) The procedures set forth in this subpart do not apply to:

(1) Any routine intra-agency adjustment of pay that is attributable to clerical or administrative error or delay in processing pay documents that have occurred within the four pay periods preceding the adjustment, or any adjustment to collect a debt amounting to $50 or less. However, at the time of any such adjustment, or as soon thereafter as possible, NCUA or its designated payroll agent shall provide the employee with a written notice of the nature and the amount of the adjustment and a point of contact for contesting such adjustment.

(2) Any negative adjustment to pay that arises from an employee's election of coverage or a change in coverage under a federal benefits program that requires periodic deductions from pay, if the amount to be recovered was accumulated over four pay periods or less. However, at the time that such adjustment is made, NCUA shall provide the employee a statement that informs the employee of the previous overpayment.

§ 797.18 Notice requirements where NCUA is the creditor agency.

Where NCUA seeks salary offset under 5 U.S.C. 5514 as the creditor agency, NCUA shall first provide the employee with a written Notice of Intent to Collect by Salary Offset (the Notice) at least 30 calendar days before salary offset is to commence. The Notice shall provide the following information:

(a) That the Executive Director has determined that a debt is owed to NCUA and intends to collect the debt by means of deduction from the employee's current disposable pay account until the debt and all accumulated interest is paid in full or otherwise resolved;

(b) The amount of the debt and the factual basis for the debt;

(c) A salary offset schedule stating the frequency and amount of each deduction, stated as a fixed dollar amount or percentage of disposable pay not to exceed 15 percent;

(d) That in lieu of salary offset, the employee may propose a voluntary repayment plan to satisfy the debt on terms acceptable to NCUA, which must be documented in writing, signed by the employee and the Executive Director, and documented in NCUA's files;

(e) NCUA's policy concerning interest, penalties, and administrative costs, and a statement that such assessments must be made, unless excused in accordance with the FCCS;

(f) That the employee has the right to inspect and copy NCUA records related to the debt, or to receive copies of such records if personal inspection is impractical;

(g) That the employee has a right to request a hearing regarding the existence and amount of the debt claimed or the salary offset schedule proposed by NCUA, provided that the employee files a request for such a hearing with NCUA in accordance with §797.20, and that such a hearing will be conducted by a hearing official not under the supervision or control of NCUA;

(h) The procedure and deadline for requesting a hearing, including the name, address, and telephone number of the Executive Director or other designated individual to whom a request for a hearing must be sent;

(i) That a request for hearing must be received by NCUA on or before the 30th calendar day following receipt of the Notice, and that filing of a request for hearing will stay the collection proceedings;

(j) That NCUA will initiate salary offset procedures not less than 30 days from the date of the employee's receipt of the Notice, unless the employee files a timely request for a hearing;

(k) That if a hearing is held, the hearing official will issue a decision at the earliest practical date, but not later than 60 days after the filing of the request for the hearing, unless the employee requests a delay in the proceedings which is granted by the hearing official;

(l) That any knowingly false or frivolous statements, representations, or evidence may subject the employee to disciplinary procedures appropriate under *5 U.S.C. chapter 75,* 5 CFR part 752; penalties under the False Claims Act, *31 U.S.C. 3729* through *3731;* criminal penalties under *18 U.S.C. 286, 287, 1001, 1002;* or any other applicable statutory authority; and

(m) That the employee also has the right to request waiver of overpayment pursuant to *5 U.S.C. 5584,* and may exercise any other rights and remedies available under statutes or regulations governing the program for which the collection is being made.

§ 797.19 Review of NCUA records related to the debt.

(a) An employee who desires to inspect or copy NCUA records related to the employee's debt must send a written request to the Executive Director or the individual designated in the Notice. The letter must be received in the office of that individual within 15 calendar days after the employee's receipt of the Notice.

(b) In response to a timely request submitted by the employee, the employee shall be notified of the location and time when the employee may inspect and copy records related to the debt. If the employee is unable personally to inspect such records, NCUA shall arrange to send copies of such records to the employee.

§ 797.20 Procedures to request a hearing.

(a) To request a hearing, an employee must send a written request to the Executive Director within 15 calendar days after the employee's receipt of the Notice. If the employee files a request for a hearing after the expiration of the 15th calendar day, NCUA may accept the request if the employee can show that the delay was the result of circumstances beyond the employee's control or the employee failed to receive actual notice of the filing deadline.

(b) The request for a hearing must be signed by the employee and must fully identify and explain with reasonable specificity all the facts, evidence, and witnesses, if any, that support the employee's position. The request must also state whether the employee is requesting an oral or documentary hearing. If an oral hearing is requested, the request shall state why the matter cannot be resolved by a review of documentary evidence alone.

(c) The failure of an employee to request a hearing will be considered an admission by the employee that the debt exists in the amount specified in the Notice.

§ 797.21 Hearing procedures.

(a) *Obtaining the services of a hearing official.* When the debtor is not an NCUA employee and NCUA cannot provide a prompt and appropriate hearing before a hearing official, NCUA may request a hearing official from an agent of the paying agency, as designated in 5 CFR part 581, appendix A, or as otherwise designated by the paying agency. When the debtor is an NCUA employee, NCUA may contact any agent of another agency, as designated in 5 CFR part 581, appendix A.

(b) *Notice of hearing.* After the employee requests a hearing, the hearing official shall notify the employee of the form of the hearing to be provided. If the hearing will be oral, the notice shall set forth the date, time, and location of the hearing, which must occur no more than 30 calendar days after the request is received, unless the employee requests that the hearing be delayed. If the hearing will be conducted by an examination of documents, the employee, within 30 calendar days, shall submit any evidence or written arguments that should be considered by the hearing official.

(c) *Oral hearing.* (1) An employee who requests an oral hearing shall be provided an oral hearing if the hearing official determines that the matter cannot be resolved by an examination of the documents alone, as for example, when an issue of credibility or veracity is involved. The oral hearing need not be an adversarial adjudication and rules of evidence need not apply.

(2) Oral hearings may take the form of, but are not limited to:

(i) Informal conferences with the hearing official in which the employee and agency representative are given full opportunity to present evidence, witnesses, and argument;

(ii) Informal meetings in which the hearing examiner interviews the employee; or

(iii) Formal written submissions followed by an opportunity for oral presentation.

(d) *Hearing by examination of documents.* If the hearing official determines that an oral hearing is not necessary, the hearing official shall make the determination based upon an examination of the documents.

(e) *Record.* The hearing official shall maintain a summary record of any hearing conducted under this section.

(f) *Decision.* (1) The hearing official shall issue a written decision based upon evidence and information developed at the hearing or in the case of a documentary hearing the decision shall be based on the documents and written submissions. The decision shall be issued, as soon as practicable after the hearing, but not later than 60 calendar days after the hearing request was received by NCUA. If the hearing was delayed at the request of the employee, the 60-day decision period shall be extended by the number of days by which the hearing was postponed.

(2) The decision of the hearing official shall be final and is considered to be an official certification regarding the existence and the amount of the debt for purposes of executing salary offset under *5 U.S.C. 5514.* If the hearing official determines that a debt may not be collected by salary offset, but NCUA finds that the debt is still valid, NCUA may seek collection of the debt through other means in accordance with applicable law and regulations.

(g) *Content of decision.* The written decision shall include:

(1) A summary of the facts concerning the origin, nature, and amount of the debt;

(2) The hearing official's findings, analysis, and conclusions; and

(3) The terms of any repayment schedules, if applicable.

§ 797.22

(h) *Failure to appear.* If the employee or the NCUA representative fails to appear, the hearing official shall proceed with the hearing as scheduled, and issue the decision based upon the oral testimony presented and the documentation submitted by both parties. At the request of both parties, the hearing official may re-schedule the hearing date.

§ 797.22 Voluntary repayment agreement.

(a) In response to the Notice, an employee may propose to repay the debt voluntarily in lieu of salary offset by submitting a written proposed repayment schedule to NCUA. Any proposal under this section must be received by NCUA within 15 calendar days after receipt of the Notice.

(b) In response to a timely proposal by the employee, NCUA shall notify the employee whether the employee's proposed repayment schedule is acceptable. NCUA has the discretion to accept, reject, or propose to the employee a modification of the proposed repayment schedule.

(1) If NCUA decides that the proposed repayment schedule is unacceptable, the employee shall have 15 calendar days from the date of the decision in which to file a request for a hearing.

(2) If NCUA decides that the proposed repayment schedule is acceptable or the employee agrees to a modification proposed by NCUA, an agreement shall be put in writing and signed by both the employee and NCUA.

§ 797.23 Certification where NCUA is the creditor agency.

(a) NCUA shall issue a certification in all cases where the hearing official determines that a debt exists or the employee admits the existence and amount of the debt, as for example, by failing to request a hearing.

(b) The certification must be in writing and state:

(1) That the employee owes the debt;
(2) The amount and basis of the debt;
(3) The date the federal government's right to collect the debt first accrued;
(4) The date the employee was notified of the debt, the action(s) taken pursuant to NCUA's regulations, and the dates such actions were taken;

(5) If the collection is to be made by lump-sum payment, the amount and date such payment will be collected;

(6) If the collection is to be made in installments, the amount or percentage of disposable pay to be collected in each installment and, if NCUA wishes, the desired commencing date of the first installment, if a date other than the next officially established pay period; and

(7) A statement that NCUA's regulation on salary offset has been approved by OPM pursuant to 5 CFR part 550, subpart K.

§ 797.24 Certification where NCUA is the paying agency.

(a) Upon issuance of a proper certification by NCUA or upon receipt of a proper certification from another creditor agency, NCUA shall send the employee a written notice of salary offset.

(b) Such written notice of salary offset shall advise the employee of the:

(1) Certification that has been issued by NCUA or received from another creditor agency;
(2) Amount of the debt and of the deductions to be made; and
(3) Date and pay period when the salary offset will begin.

(c) If NCUA is not the creditor agency, NCUA shall provide a copy of the notice to the creditor agency and advise the creditor agency of the dollar amount to be offset and the pay period when the offset will begin.

§ 797.25 Recovery from final check or other payments due a separated employee.

(a) *Lump-sum deduction from final check.* In order liquidate a debt, a lump-sum deduction exceeding 15 percent of disposable pay may be made pursuant to *31 U.S.C. 3716* from any final salary payment due a former employee, whether the former employee was separated voluntarily or involuntarily.

(b) *Lump-sum deductions from other sources.* Whenever an employee subject to salary offset is separated from NCUA, and the balance of the debt cannot be liquidated by offset of the final salary payment, NCUA may offset any later payments of any kind to the former employee to collect the balance of the debt pursuant to *31 U.S.C. 3716*.

CHAPTER VIII—FEDERAL FINANCING BANK

Part		Page
810	Federal financing bank bills	1011
811	Book-entry procedure for Federal financing bank securities	1012

PART 810—FEDERAL FINANCING BANK BILLS

Sec.
810.0 Authority for issue and sale.
810.1 Description of Federal Financing Bank bills.
810.2 Public notice of offering.
810.3 Payment at maturity.
810.4 Acceptance of FFB bills for various purposes.
810.5 Taxation.
810.6 Exemption.
810.7 Federal Reserve Banks as fiscal agents.
810.8 Reservations as to terms of circular.

AUTHORITY: Secs. 9-11, 87 Stat. 939, 940; (12 U.S.C. 2288, 2289, 2290).

SOURCE: 39 FR 26397, July 19, 1974, unless otherwise noted.

§ 810.0 Authority for issue and sale.

The Federal Financing Bank is authorized under the Federal Financing Bank Act of 1973, to issue publicly, with the approval of the Secretary of the Treasury, obligations having such maturities and bearing such rate or rates of interest as may be determined by the Bank. Pursuant to this authority, Federal Financing Bank bills, referred to herein as "FFB bills," are offered for sale from time to time and tenders invited therefor, through the Federal Reserve Banks. The FFB bills so offered, the tenders made, and all subsequent transactions therein are subject to the terms and conditions of the public notice offering the bills for sale, this circular, and to the extent not inconsistent with such notice and circular, to Department of the Treasury Circular No. 418, current revision, the regulations governing United States Treasury bills, and all other regulations governing United States securities.

§ 810.1 Description of Federal Financing Bank bills.

(a) *General.* Federal Financing Bank bills are bearer obligations of the Federal Financing Bank, the terms of which provide for payment of a specified amount on a specified date. They are issued only by Federal Reserve Banks and Branches, pursuant to tenders accepted by the Federal Financing Bank, and are available in both definitive and book-entry form. Where issued as a definitive security, it shall not be valid unless the issue date, the maturity date and the CUSIP number are imprinted thereon.

(b) *Denominations.* Federal Financing Bank bills will be issued in denominations of $10,000, $15,000, $50,000, $100,000, $500,000 and $1,000,000 (maturity value).

§ 810.2 Public notice of offering.

On the occasion of an offering of FFB bills, tenders therefor will be invited through public notices issued by the Federal Financing Bank. Each notice will set forth the amount offered, the issue date, the date they will be due and payable, the place and the date of the closing hour for the receipt of tenders and the date on which payment for accepted tenders must be made or completed.

§ 810.3 Payment at maturity.

Each FFB bill will be paid in its face amount at maturity upon presentation and surrender to any Federal Reserve Bank or Branch or to the Department of the Treasury, Bureau of the Public Debt, Securities Transaction Branch, Washington, DC 20226. If a FFB bill is presented and surrendered for redemption after it has become overdue, the Federal Financing Bank may require satisfactory proof of ownership, as provided in § 306.25 of Department of the Treasury Circular No. 300, current revision.

§ 810.4 Acceptance of FFB bills for various purposes.

Federal Financing Bank bills are lawful investments and may be accepted as security for all fiduciary, trust, and public funds, the investment or deposit of which shall be under the authority or control of the United States, the District of Columbia, the Commonwealth of Puerto Rico or any territory or possession of the United States. They are eligible for purchase by national banks, and will be accepted at maturity value to secure public moneys.

§ 810.5 Taxation.

All FFB bills shall be subject to Federal taxation to the same extent as obligations of private corporations are taxed.

§ 810.6 Exemption.

Obligations of the Federal Financing Bank are deemed to be exempted securities within the meaning of section 3(a)(2) of the Securities Act of 1933 (15 U.S.C. 77c(a)(2), of section 3(a)(12) of the Securities Exchange Act of 1934 (15 U.S.C. 78(a)(12)), and of section 304(a)(4) of the Trust Indenture Act of 1939 (15 U.S.C. 77ddd(a)(4)).

§ 810.7 Federal Reserve Banks as fiscal agents.

The Federal Reserve Banks, as fiscal agents of the United States, have been authorized by the Department of the Treasury to perform all such acts as may be necessary to carry out the provisions of this and other circulars of the Department of the Treasury as may be applicable to FFB bills, and of any public notice or notices issued in connection with any offering of these securities.

§ 810.8 Reservations as to terms of circular.

The Federal Financing Bank reserves the right to amend, supplement, revise or withdraw all or any of the provisions of this circular at any time or from time to time.

PART 811—BOOK-ENTRY PROCEDURE FOR FEDERAL FINANCING BANK SECURITIES

Sec.
811.0 Definition of terms.
811.1 Authority of Reserve Banks.
811.2 Scope and effect of book-entry procedure.
811.3 Transfer or pledge.
811.4 Withdrawal of Federal Financing Bank securities.
811.5 Delivery of Federal Financing Bank securities.
811.6 Registered bonds and notes.
811.7 Servicing book-entry Federal Financing Bank securities; payment of interest; payment at maturity or upon call.

AUTHORITY: The Federal Financing Bank Act of 1973, sections 9–11, 87 Stat. 939, 940; 12 U.S.C. 2288, 2289, 2290.

SOURCE: 40 FR 5532, Feb. 6, 1975, unless otherwise noted.

§ 811.0 Definition of terms.

In this part, unless the context otherwise requires or indicates:

(a) *Reserve Bank* means the Federal Reserve Bank of New York (and any other Federal Reserve Bank which agrees to issue Federal Financing Bank securities in book-entry form) as fiscal agent of the United States acting on behalf of the Federal Financing Bank and, when indicated, acting in its individual capacity.

(b) *Federal Financing Bank security* means a Federal Financing Bank bond, note, certificate of indebtedness, or bill issued under the Federal Financing Bank Act of 1973, in the form of a definitive Federal Financing Bank security or a book-entry Federal Financing Bank security.

(c) *Definitive Federal Financing Bank security* means a Federal Financing Bank bond, note, certificate of indebtedness, or bill issued under the Federal Financing Bank Act of 1973, in engraved or printed form.

(d) *Book-entry Federal Financing Bank security* means a Federal Financing Bank bond, note, certificate of indebtedness, or bill issued under the Federal Financing Bank Act of 1973, in the form of an entry made as prescribed in this part on the records of a Reserve Bank.

(e) *Pledge* includes a pledge of, or any other security interest in, Federal Financing Bank securities as collateral for loans or advances or to secure deposits of public monies or the performance of an obligation.

(f) *Date of call* is the date fixed in the official notice of call published in the FEDERAL REGISTER on which the Federal Financing Bank will make payment of the security before maturity in accordance with its terms.

(g) *Member bank* means any national bank, State bank or bank or trust company which is a member of a Reserve Bank.

§ 811.1 Authority of Reserve Banks.

Each Reserve Bank is hereby authorized, in accordance with the provisions of this part, to: (a) Issue book-entry Federal Financing Bank securities by means of entries on its records which shall include the name of the depositor, the amount, the loan title (or series)

Federal Financing Bank   § 811.3

and maturity date; (b) effect conversions between book-entry Federal Financing Bank securities and definitive Federal Financing Bank securities; (c) otherwise service and maintain book-entry Federal Financing Bank securities; and (d) issue a confirmation of transaction in the form of a written advice (serially numbered or otherwise) which specifies the amount and description of any securities, that is, loan title (or series) and maturity date, sold or transferred and the date of the transaction.

§ 811.2 Scope and effect of book-entry procedure.

(a) A Reserve Bank, as fiscal agent of the United States acting on behalf of the Federal Financing Bank, may apply the book-entry procedure provided for in this part to any Federal Financing Bank securities which have been or are hereafter deposited for any purpose in accounts with it in its individual capacity under terms and conditions which indicate that the Reserve Bank will continue to maintain such deposit accounts in its individual capacity, notwithstanding application of the book-entry procedure to such securities. This paragraph is applicable, but not limited, to securities deposited:

(1) As collateral pledged to a Reserve Bank (in its individual capacity) for advances by it;

(2) By a member bank for its sole account;

(3) By a member bank held for the account of its customers;

(4) In connection with deposits in a member bank of funds of States, municipalities, or other political subdivisions; or,

(5) In connection with the performance of an obligation or duty under Federal, State, municipal, or local law, or judgments or decrees of courts.

The application of the book-entry procedure under this paragraph shall not derogate from or adversely affect the relationship that would otherwise exist between a Reserve Bank in its individual capacity and its depositors covering any deposits under this paragraph. Whenever the book-entry procedure is applied to such Federal Financing Bank securities, the Reserve Bank is authorized to take all action necessary in respect of the book-entry procedure to enable such Reserve Bank in its individual capacity to perform its obligations as depositary with respect to such Federal Financing Bank securities.

(b) A Reserve Bank, as fiscal agent of the United States acting on behalf of the Federal Financing Bank, shall apply the book-entry procedure to Federal Financing Bank securities deposited as collateral pledged to the United States under current revisions of Department of the Treasury Circulars Nos. 92 and 176 (31 CFR, parts 203 and 202), and may apply the book-entry procedure, with the approval of the Secretary of the Treasury, to any other Federal Financing Bank securities deposited with a Reserve Bank, as fiscal agent of the United States.

(c) Any person having an interest in Federal Financing Bank securities which are deposited with a Reserve Bank (in either its individual capacity or as fiscal agent of the United States) for any purpose shall be deemed to have consented to their conversion to book-entry Federal Financing Bank securities pursuant to the provisions of this part, and in the manner and under the procedures prescribed by the Reserve Bank.

(d) No deposits shall be accepted under this section on or after the date of maturity or call of the securities.

§ 811.3 Transfer or pledge.

(a) A transfer or a pledge of book-entry Federal Financing Bank securities to a Reserve Bank (in its individual capacity or as fiscal agent of the United States), or to the United States, or to any transferee or pledgee eligible to maintain an appropriate book-entry account in its name with a Reserve Bank under this part, is effected and perfected, notwithstanding any provision of law to the contrary, by a Reserve Bank making an appropriate entry in its records of the securities transferred or pledged. The making of such an entry in the records of a Reserve Bank shall:

(1) Have the effect of a delivery in bearer form of definitive Federal Financing Bank securities; (2) have the effect of a taking of delivery by the transferee or pledgee; (3) constitute the

§ 811.4

transferee or pledgee a holder; and (4) if a pledge, effect a perfected security interest therein in favor of the pledgee. A transfer or pledge of book-entry Federal Financing Bank securities effected under this paragraph shall have priority over any transfer, pledge, or other interest, theretofore or thereafter effected or perfected under paragraph (b) of this section or in any other manner.

(b) A transfer or a pledge of transferable Federal Financing Bank securities, or any interest therein, which is maintained by a Reserve Bank (in its individual capacity or as fiscal agent of the United States) in a book-entry account under this part, including securities in book-entry form under § 811.2(a)(3), is effected, and a pledge is perfected, by any means that would be effective under applicable law to effect a transfer or to effect and perfect a pledge of the Federal Financing Bank securities, or any interest therein, if the securities were maintained by the Reserve Bank in bearer definitive form. For purposes of transfer or pledge hereunder, book-entry Federal Financing Bank securities maintained by a Reserve Bank shall, notwithstanding any provision of law to the contrary, be deemed to be maintained in bearer definitive form. A Reserve Bank maintaining book-entry Federal Financing Bank securities either in its individual capacity or as fiscal agent of the United States is not a bailee for purposes of notification of pledges of those securities under this subsection, or a third person in possession for purposes of acknowledgement of transfers thereof under this subsection. Where transferable Federal Financing Bank securities are recorded on the books of a depositary (a bank, banking institution, financial firm, or a similar party, which regularly accepts in the course of its business Federal Financing Bank securities as a custodial service for customers, and maintains accounts in the names of such customers reflecting ownership of or interest in such securities) for account of the pledgor or transferor thereof and such securities are on deposit with a Reserve Bank in a book-entry account hereunder, such depositary shall, for purposes of perfecting a pledge of such securities or effecting delivery of such securities to a purchaser under applicable provisions of law, be the bailee to which notification of the pledge of the securities may be given or the third person in possession from which acknowledgment of the holding of the securities for the purchaser may be obtained. A Reserve Bank will not accept notice or advice of a transfer or pledge effected or perfected under this subsection, and any such notice or advice shall have no effect. A Reserve Bank may continue to deal with its depositor in accordance with the provisions of this part, notwithstanding any transfer or pledge effected or perfected under this subsection.

(c) No filing or recording with a public recording office or officer shall be necessary or effective with respect to any transfer or pledge of book-entry Federal Financing Bank securities or any interest therein.

(d) A Reserve Bank shall, upon receipt of appropriate instructions, convert book-entry Federal Financing Bank securities into definitive Federal Financing Bank securities and deliver them in accordance with such instructions; no such conversion shall affect existing interests in such Federal Financing Bank securities.

(e) A transfer of book-entry Federal Financing Bank securities within a Reserve Bank shall be made in accordance with procedures established by the Bank not inconsistent with this part. The transfer of book-entry Federal Financing Bank securities by a Reserve Bank may be made through a telegraphic transfer procedure.

(f) All requests for transfer or withdrawal must be made prior to the maturity or date of call of the securities.

§ 811.4 Withdrawal of Federal Financing Bank securities.

(a) A depositor of book-entry Federal Financing Bank securities may withdraw them from a Reserve Bank by requesting delivery of like definitive Federal Financing Bank securities to itself or on its order to a transferee.

(b) Federal Financing Bank securities which are actually to be delivered upon withdrawal may be issued either in registered or in bearer form, except

Federal Financing Bank

that Federal Financing Bank bills will be issued in bearer form only.

§ 811.5 Delivery of Federal Financing Bank securities.

A Reserve Bank which has received Federal Financing Bank securities and effected pledges, made entries regarding them, or transferred or delivered them according to the instructions of its depositor is not liable for conversion or for participation in breach of fiduciary duty even though the depositor had no right to dispose of or take other action in respect of the securities. A Reserve Bank shall be fully discharged of its obligations under this part by the delivery of Federal Financing Bank securities in definitive form to its depositor or upon the order of such depositor. Customers of a member bank or other depository (other than a Reserve Bank) may obtain Federal Financing Bank securities in definitive form only by causing the depositor of the Reserve Bank to order the withdrawal thereof from the Reserve Bank.

§ 811.6 Registered bonds and notes.

Registered Federal Financing Bank securities deposited with a Reserve Bank for any purpose specified in § 811.2 shall be assigned for conversion to book-entry Federal Financing Bank securities. The assignment, which shall be executed in accordance with the provisions of subpart F of 31 CFR, part 306, so far as applicable, shall be to—

Federal Reserve Bank of _____, as fiscal agent of the United States acting on behalf of the Federal Financing Bank for conversion to book-entry Federal Financing Bank securities.

§ 811.7 Servicing book-entry Federal Financing Bank securities; payment of interest; payment at maturity or upon call.

Interest becoming due on book-entry Federal Financing Bank securities shall be charged against the special agent account maintained by the Department of the Treasury for the Federal Financing Bank on the interest due date and remitted or credited in accordance with the depositor's instructions. Such securities shall be redeemed and charged against the above said account on the date of maturity or call, and the redemption proceeds, principal and interest, shall be disposed of in accordance with the depositor's instructions.

FINDING AIDS

A list of CFR titles, subtitles, chapters, subchapters and parts and an alphabetical list of agencies publishing in the CFR are included in the CFR Index and Finding Aids volume to the Code of Federal Regulations which is published separately and revised annually.

Table of CFR Titles and Chapters
Alphabetical List of Agencies Appearing in the CFR
List of CFR Sections Affected

Table of CFR Titles and Chapters
(Revised as of January 1, 2012)

Title 1—General Provisions

I	Administrative Committee of the Federal Register (Parts 1—49)
II	Office of the Federal Register (Parts 50—299)
III	Administrative Conference of the United States (Parts 300—399)
IV	Miscellaneous Agencies (Parts 400—500)

Title 2—Grants and Agreements

SUBTITLE A—OFFICE OF MANAGEMENT AND BUDGET GUIDANCE FOR GRANTS AND AGREEMENTS

I	Office of Management and Budget Governmentwide Guidance for Grants and Agreements (Parts 2—199)
II	Office of Management and Budget Circulars and Guidance (200—299)

SUBTITLE B—FEDERAL AGENCY REGULATIONS FOR GRANTS AND AGREEMENTS

III	Department of Health and Human Services (Parts 300— 399)
IV	Department of Agriculture (Parts 400—499)
VI	Department of State (Parts 600—699)
VII	Agency for International Development (Parts 700—799)
VIII	Department of Veterans Affairs (Parts 800—899)
IX	Department of Energy (Parts 900—999)
XI	Department of Defense (Parts 1100—1199)
XII	Department of Transportation (Parts 1200—1299)
XIII	Department of Commerce (Parts 1300—1399)
XIV	Department of the Interior (Parts 1400—1499)
XV	Environmental Protection Agency (Parts 1500—1599)
XVIII	National Aeronautics and Space Administration (Parts 1800—1899)
XX	United States Nuclear Regulatory Commission (Parts 2000—2099)
XXII	Corporation for National and Community Service (Parts 2200—2299)
XXIII	Social Security Administration (Parts 2300—2399)
XXIV	Housing and Urban Development (Parts 2400—2499)
XXV	National Science Foundation (Parts 2500—2599)
XXVI	National Archives and Records Administration (Parts 2600—2699)
XXVII	Small Business Administration (Parts 2700—2799)
XXVIII	Department of Justice (Parts 2800—2899)

Title 2—Grants and Agreements—Continued

Chap.
- XXX Department of Homeland Security (Parts 3000—3099)
- XXXI Institute of Museum and Library Services (Parts 3100—3199)
- XXXII National Endowment for the Arts (Parts 3200—3299)
- XXXIII National Endowment for the Humanities (Parts 3300—3399)
- XXXV Export-Import Bank of the United States (Parts 3500—3599)
- XXXVII Peace Corps (Parts 3700—3799)
- LVIII Election Assistance Commission (Parts 5800—5899)

Title 3—The President

- I Executive Office of the President (Parts 100—199)

Title 4—Accounts

- I Government Accountability Office (Parts 1—99)
- II Recovery Accountability and Transparency Board (Parts 200—299)

Title 5—Administrative Personnel

- I Office of Personnel Management (Parts 1—1199)
- II Merit Systems Protection Board (Parts 1200—1299)
- III Office of Management and Budget (Parts 1300—1399)
- V The International Organizations Employees Loyalty Board (Parts 1500—1599)
- VI Federal Retirement Thrift Investment Board (Parts 1600—1699)
- VIII Office of Special Counsel (Parts 1800—1899)
- IX Appalachian Regional Commission (Parts 1900—1999)
- XI Armed Forces Retirement Home (Parts 2100—2199)
- XIV Federal Labor Relations Authority, General Counsel of the Federal Labor Relations Authority and Federal Service Impasses Panel (Parts 2400—2499)
- XV Office of Administration, Executive Office of the President (Parts 2500—2599)
- XVI Office of Government Ethics (Parts 2600—2699)
- XXI Department of the Treasury (Parts 3100—3199)
- XXII Federal Deposit Insurance Corporation (Parts 3200—3299)
- XXIII Department of Energy (Parts 3300—3399)
- XXIV Federal Energy Regulatory Commission (Parts 3400—3499)
- XXV Department of the Interior (Parts 3500—3599)
- XXVI Department of Defense (Parts 3600— 3699)
- XXVIII Department of Justice (Parts 3800—3899)
- XXIX Federal Communications Commission (Parts 3900—3999)
- XXX Farm Credit System Insurance Corporation (Parts 4000—4099)
- XXXI Farm Credit Administration (Parts 4100—4199)
- XXXIII Overseas Private Investment Corporation (Parts 4300—4399)

Title 5—Administrative Personnel—Continued

Chap.	
XXXIV	Securities and Exchange Commission (Parts 4400—4499)
XXXV	Office of Personnel Management (Parts 4500—4599)
XXXVII	Federal Election Commission (Parts 4700—4799)
XL	Interstate Commerce Commission (Parts 5000—5099)
XLI	Commodity Futures Trading Commission (Parts 5100—5199)
XLII	Department of Labor (Parts 5200—5299)
XLIII	National Science Foundation (Parts 5300—5399)
XLV	Department of Health and Human Services (Parts 5500—5599)
XLVI	Postal Rate Commission (Parts 5600—5699)
XLVII	Federal Trade Commission (Parts 5700—5799)
XLVIII	Nuclear Regulatory Commission (Parts 5800—5899)
XLIX	Federal Labor Relations Authority (Parts 5900—5999)
L	Department of Transportation (Parts 6000—6099)
LII	Export-Import Bank of the United States (Parts 6200—6299)
LIII	Department of Education (Parts 6300—6399)
LIV	Environmental Protection Agency (Parts 6400—6499)
LV	National Endowment for the Arts (Parts 6500—6599)
LVI	National Endowment for the Humanities (Parts 6600—6699)
LVII	General Services Administration (Parts 6700—6799)
LVIII	Board of Governors of the Federal Reserve System (Parts 6800—6899)
LIX	National Aeronautics and Space Administration (Parts 6900—6999)
LX	United States Postal Service (Parts 7000—7099)
LXI	National Labor Relations Board (Parts 7100—7199)
LXII	Equal Employment Opportunity Commission (Parts 7200—7299)
LXIII	Inter-American Foundation (Parts 7300—7399)
LXIV	Merit Systems Protection Board (Parts 7400—7499)
LXV	Department of Housing and Urban Development (Parts 7500—7599)
LXVI	National Archives and Records Administration (Parts 7600—7699)
LXVII	Institute of Museum and Library Services (Parts 7700—7799)
LXVIII	Commission on Civil Rights (Parts 7800—7899)
LXIX	Tennessee Valley Authority (Parts 7900—7999)
LXX	Court Services and Offender Supervision Agency for the District of Columbia (Parts 8000—8099)
LXXI	Consumer Product Safety Commission (Parts 8100—8199)
LXXIII	Department of Agriculture (Parts 8300—8399)
LXXIV	Federal Mine Safety and Health Review Commission (Parts 8400—8499)
LXXVI	Federal Retirement Thrift Investment Board (Parts 8600—8699)
LXXVII	Office of Management and Budget (Parts 8700—8799)
LXXX	Federal Housing Finance Agency (Parts 9000—9099)
LXXXII	Special Inspector General for Iraq Reconstruction (Parts 9200—9299)

Title 5—Administrative Personnel—Continued

Chap.

XCVII   Department of Homeland Security Human Resources Management System (Department of Homeland Security—Office of Personnel Management) (Parts 9700—9799)

Title 6—Domestic Security

I   Department of Homeland Security, Office of the Secretary (Parts 1—99)

Title 7—Agriculture

SUBTITLE A—OFFICE OF THE SECRETARY OF AGRICULTURE (PARTS 0—26)

SUBTITLE B—REGULATIONS OF THE DEPARTMENT OF AGRICULTURE

I   Agricultural Marketing Service (Standards, Inspections, Marketing Practices), Department of Agriculture (Parts 27—209)

II   Food and Nutrition Service, Department of Agriculture (Parts 210—299)

III   Animal and Plant Health Inspection Service, Department of Agriculture (Parts 300—399)

IV   Federal Crop Insurance Corporation, Department of Agriculture (Parts 400—499)

V   Agricultural Research Service, Department of Agriculture (Parts 500—599)

VI   Natural Resources Conservation Service, Department of Agriculture (Parts 600—699)

VII   Farm Service Agency, Department of Agriculture (Parts 700—799)

VIII   Grain Inspection, Packers and Stockyards Administration (Federal Grain Inspection Service), Department of Agriculture (Parts 800—899)

IX   Agricultural Marketing Service (Marketing Agreements and Orders; Fruits, Vegetables, Nuts), Department of Agriculture (Parts 900—999)

X   Agricultural Marketing Service (Marketing Agreements and Orders; Milk), Department of Agriculture (Parts 1000—1199)

XI   Agricultural Marketing Service (Marketing Agreements and Orders; Miscellaneous Commodities), Department of Agriculture (Parts 1200—1299)

XIV   Commodity Credit Corporation, Department of Agriculture (Parts 1400—1499)

XV   Foreign Agricultural Service, Department of Agriculture (Parts 1500—1599)

XVI   Rural Telephone Bank, Department of Agriculture (Parts 1600—1699)

XVII   Rural Utilities Service, Department of Agriculture (Parts 1700—1799)

XVIII   Rural Housing Service, Rural Business-Cooperative Service, Rural Utilities Service, and Farm Service Agency, Department of Agriculture (Parts 1800—2099)

XX   Local Television Loan Guarantee Board (Parts 2200—2299)

Title 7—Agriculture—Continued

Chap.	
XXV	Office of Advocacy and Outreach, Department of Agriculture (Parts 2500—2599)
XXVI	Office of Inspector General, Department of Agriculture (Parts 2600—2699)
XXVII	Office of Information Resources Management, Department of Agriculture (Parts 2700—2799)
XXVIII	Office of Operations, Department of Agriculture (Parts 2800—2899)
XXIX	Office of Energy Policy and New Uses, Department of Agriculture (Parts 2900—2999)
XXX	Office of the Chief Financial Officer, Department of Agriculture (Parts 3000—3099)
XXXI	Office of Environmental Quality, Department of Agriculture (Parts 3100—3199)
XXXII	Office of Procurement and Property Management, Department of Agriculture (Parts 3200—3299)
XXXIII	Office of Transportation, Department of Agriculture (Parts 3300—3399)
XXXIV	National Institute of Food and Agriculture (Parts 3400—3499)
XXXV	Rural Housing Service, Department of Agriculture (Parts 3500—3599)
XXXVI	National Agricultural Statistics Service, Department of Agriculture (Parts 3600—3699)
XXXVII	Economic Research Service, Department of Agriculture (Parts 3700—3799)
XXXVIII	World Agricultural Outlook Board, Department of Agriculture (Parts 3800—3899)
XLI	[Reserved]
XLII	Rural Business-Cooperative Service and Rural Utilities Service, Department of Agriculture (Parts 4200—4299)

Title 8—Aliens and Nationality

I	Department of Homeland Security (Immigration and Naturalization) (Parts 1—499)
V	Executive Office for Immigration Review, Department of Justice (Parts 1000—1399)

Title 9—Animals and Animal Products

I	Animal and Plant Health Inspection Service, Department of Agriculture (Parts 1—199)
II	Grain Inspection, Packers and Stockyards Administration (Packers and Stockyards Programs), Department of Agriculture (Parts 200—299)
III	Food Safety and Inspection Service, Department of Agriculture (Parts 300—599)

Title 10—Energy

Chap.
- I Nuclear Regulatory Commission (Parts 0—199)
- II Department of Energy (Parts 200—699)
- III Department of Energy (Parts 700—999)
- X Department of Energy (General Provisions) (Parts 1000—1099)
- XIII Nuclear Waste Technical Review Board (Parts 1300—1399)
- XVII Defense Nuclear Facilities Safety Board (Parts 1700—1799)
- XVIII Northeast Interstate Low-Level Radioactive Waste Commission (Parts 1800—1899)

Title 11—Federal Elections

- I Federal Election Commission (Parts 1—9099)
- II Election Assistance Commission (Parts 9400—9499)

Title 12—Banks and Banking

- I Comptroller of the Currency, Department of the Treasury (Parts 1—199)
- II Federal Reserve System (Parts 200—299)
- III Federal Deposit Insurance Corporation (Parts 300—399)
- IV Export-Import Bank of the United States (Parts 400—499)
- V Office of Thrift Supervision, Department of the Treasury (Parts 500—599)
- VI Farm Credit Administration (Parts 600—699)
- VII National Credit Union Administration (Parts 700—799)
- VIII Federal Financing Bank (Parts 800—899)
- IX Federal Housing Finance Board (Parts 900—999)
- X Bureau of Consumer Financial Protection (Parts 1000—1099)
- XI Federal Financial Institutions Examination Council (Parts 1100—1199)
- XII Federal Housing Finance Agency (Parts 1200—1299)
- XIII Financial Stability Oversight Council (Parts 1300—1399)
- XIV Farm Credit System Insurance Corporation (Parts 1400—1499)
- XV Department of the Treasury (Parts 1500—1599)
- XVI Office of Financial Research (Parts 1600—1699)
- XVII Office of Federal Housing Enterprise Oversight, Department of Housing and Urban Development (Parts 1700—1799)
- XVIII Community Development Financial Institutions Fund, Department of the Treasury (Parts 1800—1899)

Title 13—Business Credit and Assistance

- I Small Business Administration (Parts 1—199)
- III Economic Development Administration, Department of Commerce (Parts 300—399)
- IV Emergency Steel Guarantee Loan Board (Parts 400—499)
- V Emergency Oil and Gas Guaranteed Loan Board (Parts 500—599)

Title 14—Aeronautics and Space

Chap.

I   Federal Aviation Administration, Department of Transportation (Parts 1—199)

II   Office of the Secretary, Department of Transportation (Aviation Proceedings) (Parts 200—399)

III   Commercial Space Transportation, Federal Aviation Administration, Department of Transportation (Parts 400—1199)

V   National Aeronautics and Space Administration (Parts 1200—1299)

VI   Air Transportation System Stabilization (Parts 1300—1399)

Title 15—Commerce and Foreign Trade

SUBTITLE A—OFFICE OF THE SECRETARY OF COMMERCE (PARTS 0—29)

SUBTITLE B—REGULATIONS RELATING TO COMMERCE AND FOREIGN TRADE

I   Bureau of the Census, Department of Commerce (Parts 30—199)

II   National Institute of Standards and Technology, Department of Commerce (Parts 200—299)

III   International Trade Administration, Department of Commerce (Parts 300—399)

IV   Foreign-Trade Zones Board, Department of Commerce (Parts 400—499)

VII   Bureau of Industry and Security, Department of Commerce (Parts 700—799)

VIII   Bureau of Economic Analysis, Department of Commerce (Parts 800—899)

IX   National Oceanic and Atmospheric Administration, Department of Commerce (Parts 900—999)

XI   Technology Administration, Department of Commerce (Parts 1100—1199)

XIII   East-West Foreign Trade Board (Parts 1300—1399)

XIV   Minority Business Development Agency (Parts 1400—1499)

SUBTITLE C—REGULATIONS RELATING TO FOREIGN TRADE AGREEMENTS

XX   Office of the United States Trade Representative (Parts 2000—2099)

SUBTITLE D—REGULATIONS RELATING TO TELECOMMUNICATIONS AND INFORMATION

XXIII   National Telecommunications and Information Administration, Department of Commerce (Parts 2300—2399)

Title 16—Commercial Practices

I   Federal Trade Commission (Parts 0—999)

II   Consumer Product Safety Commission (Parts 1000—1799)

Title 17—Commodity and Securities Exchanges

Chap.
- I Commodity Futures Trading Commission (Parts 1—199)
- II Securities and Exchange Commission (Parts 200—399)
- IV Department of the Treasury (Parts 400—499)

Title 18—Conservation of Power and Water Resources

- I Federal Energy Regulatory Commission, Department of Energy (Parts 1—399)
- III Delaware River Basin Commission (Parts 400—499)
- VI Water Resources Council (Parts 700—799)
- VIII Susquehanna River Basin Commission (Parts 800—899)
- XIII Tennessee Valley Authority (Parts 1300—1399)

Title 19—Customs Duties

- I U.S. Customs and Border Protection, Department of Homeland Security; Department of the Treasury (Parts 0—199)
- II United States International Trade Commission (Parts 200—299)
- III International Trade Administration, Department of Commerce (Parts 300—399)
- IV U.S. Immigration and Customs Enforcement, Department of Homeland Security (Parts 400—599)

Title 20—Employees' Benefits

- I Office of Workers' Compensation Programs, Department of Labor (Parts 1—199)
- II Railroad Retirement Board (Parts 200—399)
- III Social Security Administration (Parts 400—499)
- IV Employees' Compensation Appeals Board, Department of Labor (Parts 500—599)
- V Employment and Training Administration, Department of Labor (Parts 600—699)
- VI Office of Workers' Compensation Programs, Department of Labor (Parts 700—799)
- VII Benefits Review Board, Department of Labor (Parts 800—899)
- VIII Joint Board for the Enrollment of Actuaries (Parts 900—999)
- IX Office of the Assistant Secretary for Veterans' Employment and Training Service, Department of Labor (Parts 1000—1099)

Title 21—Food and Drugs

- I Food and Drug Administration, Department of Health and Human Services (Parts 1—1299)
- II Drug Enforcement Administration, Department of Justice (Parts 1300—1399)
- III Office of National Drug Control Policy (Parts 1400—1499)

Title 22—Foreign Relations

Chap.
- I Department of State (Parts 1—199)
- II Agency for International Development (Parts 200—299)
- III Peace Corps (Parts 300—399)
- IV International Joint Commission, United States and Canada (Parts 400—499)
- V Broadcasting Board of Governors (Parts 500—599)
- VII Overseas Private Investment Corporation (Parts 700—799)
- IX Foreign Service Grievance Board (Parts 900—999)
- X Inter-American Foundation (Parts 1000—1099)
- XI International Boundary and Water Commission, United States and Mexico, United States Section (Parts 1100—1199)
- XII United States International Development Cooperation Agency (Parts 1200—1299)
- XIII Millennium Challenge Corporation (Parts 1300—1399)
- XIV Foreign Service Labor Relations Board; Federal Labor Relations Authority; General Counsel of the Federal Labor Relations Authority; and the Foreign Service Impasse Disputes Panel (Parts 1400—1499)
- XV African Development Foundation (Parts 1500—1599)
- XVI Japan-United States Friendship Commission (Parts 1600—1699)
- XVII United States Institute of Peace (Parts 1700—1799)

Title 23—Highways

- I Federal Highway Administration, Department of Transportation (Parts 1—999)
- II National Highway Traffic Safety Administration and Federal Highway Administration, Department of Transportation (Parts 1200—1299)
- III National Highway Traffic Safety Administration, Department of Transportation (Parts 1300—1399)

Title 24—Housing and Urban Development

SUBTITLE A—OFFICE OF THE SECRETARY, DEPARTMENT OF HOUSING AND URBAN DEVELOPMENT (PARTS 0—99)

SUBTITLE B—REGULATIONS RELATING TO HOUSING AND URBAN DEVELOPMENT

- I Office of Assistant Secretary for Equal Opportunity, Department of Housing and Urban Development (Parts 100—199)
- II Office of Assistant Secretary for Housing-Federal Housing Commissioner, Department of Housing and Urban Development (Parts 200—299)
- III Government National Mortgage Association, Department of Housing and Urban Development (Parts 300—399)
- IV Office of Housing and Office of Multifamily Housing Assistance Restructuring, Department of Housing and Urban Development (Parts 400—499)

Title 24—Housing and Urban Development—Continued

Chap.

V   Office of Assistant Secretary for Community Planning and Development, Department of Housing and Urban Development (Parts 500—599)

VI   Office of Assistant Secretary for Community Planning and Development, Department of Housing and Urban Development (Parts 600—699) [Reserved]

VII Office of the Secretary, Department of Housing and Urban Development (Housing Assistance Programs and Public and Indian Housing Programs) (Parts 700—799)

VIII Office of the Assistant Secretary for Housing—Federal Housing Commissioner, Department of Housing and Urban Development (Section 8 Housing Assistance Programs, Section 202 Direct Loan Program, Section 202 Supportive Housing for the Elderly Program and Section 811 Supportive Housing for Persons With Disabilities Program) (Parts 800—899)

IX   Office of Assistant Secretary for Public and Indian Housing, Department of Housing and Urban Development (Parts 900—1699)

X   Office of Assistant Secretary for Housing—Federal Housing Commissioner, Department of Housing and Urban Development (Interstate Land Sales Registration Program) (Parts 1700—1799)

XII Office of Inspector General, Department of Housing and Urban Development (Parts 2000—2099)

XV   Emergency Mortgage Insurance and Loan Programs, Department of Housing and Urban Development (Parts 2700—2799)

XX   Office of Assistant Secretary for Housing—Federal Housing Commissioner, Department of Housing and Urban Development (Parts 3200—3899)

XXIV Board of Directors of the HOPE for Homeowners Program (Parts 4000—4099)

XXV Neighborhood Reinvestment Corporation (Parts 4100—4199)

Title 25—Indians

I   Bureau of Indian Affairs, Department of the Interior (Parts 1—299)

II   Indian Arts and Crafts Board, Department of the Interior (Parts 300—399)

III National Indian Gaming Commission, Department of the Interior (Parts 500—599)

IV   Office of Navajo and Hopi Indian Relocation (Parts 700—799)

V   Bureau of Indian Affairs, Department of the Interior, and Indian Health Service, Department of Health and Human Services (Part 900)

VI   Office of the Assistant Secretary-Indian Affairs, Department of the Interior (Parts 1000—1199)

VII Office of the Special Trustee for American Indians, Department of the Interior (Parts 1200—1299)

Title 26—Internal Revenue

Chap.

I Internal Revenue Service, Department of the Treasury (Parts 1—End)

Title 27—Alcohol, Tobacco Products and Firearms

I Alcohol and Tobacco Tax and Trade Bureau, Department of the Treasury (Parts 1—399)
II Bureau of Alcohol, Tobacco, Firearms, and Explosives, Department of Justice (Parts 400—699)

Title 28—Judicial Administration

I Department of Justice (Parts 0—299)
III Federal Prison Industries, Inc., Department of Justice (Parts 300—399)
V Bureau of Prisons, Department of Justice (Parts 500—599)
VI Offices of Independent Counsel, Department of Justice (Parts 600—699)
VII Office of Independent Counsel (Parts 700—799)
VIII Court Services and Offender Supervision Agency for the District of Columbia (Parts 800—899)
IX National Crime Prevention and Privacy Compact Council (Parts 900—999)
XI Department of Justice and Department of State (Parts 1100—1199)

Title 29—Labor

SUBTITLE A—OFFICE OF THE SECRETARY OF LABOR (PARTS 0—99)
SUBTITLE B—REGULATIONS RELATING TO LABOR

I National Labor Relations Board (Parts 100—199)
II Office of Labor-Management Standards, Department of Labor (Parts 200—299)
III National Railroad Adjustment Board (Parts 300—399)
IV Office of Labor-Management Standards, Department of Labor (Parts 400—499)
V Wage and Hour Division, Department of Labor (Parts 500—899)
IX Construction Industry Collective Bargaining Commission (Parts 900—999)
X National Mediation Board (Parts 1200—1299)
XII Federal Mediation and Conciliation Service (Parts 1400—1499)
XIV Equal Employment Opportunity Commission (Parts 1600—1699)
XVII Occupational Safety and Health Administration, Department of Labor (Parts 1900—1999)
XX Occupational Safety and Health Review Commission (Parts 2200—2499)
XXV Employee Benefits Security Administration, Department of Labor (Parts 2500—2599)

Title 29—Labor—Continued

Chap.
XXVII   Federal Mine Safety and Health Review Commission (Parts 2700—2799)
XL   Pension Benefit Guaranty Corporation (Parts 4000—4999)

Title 30—Mineral Resources

I   Mine Safety and Health Administration, Department of Labor (Parts 1—199)
II   Bureau of Safety and Environmental Enforcement, Department of the Interior (Parts 200—299)
IV   Geological Survey, Department of the Interior (Parts 400—499)
V   Bureau of Ocean Energy Management, Department of the Interior (Parts 500—599)
VII   Office of Surface Mining Reclamation and Enforcement, Department of the Interior (Parts 700—999)
XII   Office of Natural Resources Revenue, Department of the Interior (Parts 1200—1299)

Title 31—Money and Finance: Treasury

SUBTITLE A—OFFICE OF THE SECRETARY OF THE TREASURY (PARTS 0—50)

SUBTITLE B—REGULATIONS RELATING TO MONEY AND FINANCE

I   Monetary Offices, Department of the Treasury (Parts 51—199)
II   Fiscal Service, Department of the Treasury (Parts 200—399)
IV   Secret Service, Department of the Treasury (Parts 400—499)
V   Office of Foreign Assets Control, Department of the Treasury (Parts 500—599)
VI   Bureau of Engraving and Printing, Department of the Treasury (Parts 600—699)
VII   Federal Law Enforcement Training Center, Department of the Treasury (Parts 700—799)
VIII   Office of International Investment, Department of the Treasury (Parts 800—899)
IX   Federal Claims Collection Standards (Department of the Treasury—Department of Justice) (Parts 900—999)
X   Financial Crimes Enforcement Network, Department of the Treasury (Parts 1000—1099)

Title 32—National Defense

SUBTITLE A—DEPARTMENT OF DEFENSE

I   Office of the Secretary of Defense (Parts 1—399)
V   Department of the Army (Parts 400—699)
VI   Department of the Navy (Parts 700—799)
VII   Department of the Air Force (Parts 800—1099)

SUBTITLE B—OTHER REGULATIONS RELATING TO NATIONAL DEFENSE

Title 32—National Defense—Continued

Chap.
XII	Defense Logistics Agency (Parts 1200—1299)
XVI	Selective Service System (Parts 1600—1699)
XVII	Office of the Director of National Intelligence (Parts 1700—1799)
XVIII	National Counterintelligence Center (Parts 1800—1899)
XIX	Central Intelligence Agency (Parts 1900—1999)
XX	Information Security Oversight Office, National Archives and Records Administration (Parts 2000—2099)
XXI	National Security Council (Parts 2100—2199)
XXIV	Office of Science and Technology Policy (Parts 2400—2499)
XXVII	Office for Micronesian Status Negotiations (Parts 2700—2799)
XXVIII	Office of the Vice President of the United States (Parts 2800—2899)

Title 33—Navigation and Navigable Waters

I	Coast Guard, Department of Homeland Security (Parts 1—199)
II	Corps of Engineers, Department of the Army (Parts 200—399)
IV	Saint Lawrence Seaway Development Corporation, Department of Transportation (Parts 400—499)

Title 34—Education

SUBTITLE A—OFFICE OF THE SECRETARY, DEPARTMENT OF EDUCATION (PARTS 1—99)

SUBTITLE B—REGULATIONS OF THE OFFICES OF THE DEPARTMENT OF EDUCATION

I	Office for Civil Rights, Department of Education (Parts 100—199)
II	Office of Elementary and Secondary Education, Department of Education (Parts 200—299)
III	Office of Special Education and Rehabilitative Services, Department of Education (Parts 300—399)
IV	Office of Vocational and Adult Education, Department of Education (Parts 400—499)
V	Office of Bilingual Education and Minority Languages Affairs, Department of Education (Parts 500—599)
VI	Office of Postsecondary Education, Department of Education (Parts 600—699)
VII	Office of Educational Research and Improvement, Department of Education [Reserved]
XI	National Institute for Literacy (Parts 1100—1199)

SUBTITLE C—REGULATIONS RELATING TO EDUCATION

XII	National Council on Disability (Parts 1200—1299)

Title 35 [Reserved]

Title 36—Parks, Forests, and Public Property

I	National Park Service, Department of the Interior (Parts 1—199)

Title 36—Parks, Forests, and Public Property—Continued

Chap.
- II Forest Service, Department of Agriculture (Parts 200—299)
- III Corps of Engineers, Department of the Army (Parts 300—399)
- IV American Battle Monuments Commission (Parts 400—499)
- V Smithsonian Institution (Parts 500—599)
- VI [Reserved]
- VII Library of Congress (Parts 700—799)
- VIII Advisory Council on Historic Preservation (Parts 800—899)
- IX Pennsylvania Avenue Development Corporation (Parts 900—999)
- X Presidio Trust (Parts 1000—1099)
- XI Architectural and Transportation Barriers Compliance Board (Parts 1100—1199)
- XII National Archives and Records Administration (Parts 1200—1299)
- XV Oklahoma City National Memorial Trust (Parts 1500—1599)
- XVI Morris K. Udall Scholarship and Excellence in National Environmental Policy Foundation (Parts 1600—1699)

Title 37—Patents, Trademarks, and Copyrights

- I United States Patent and Trademark Office, Department of Commerce (Parts 1—199)
- II Copyright Office, Library of Congress (Parts 200—299)
- III Copyright Royalty Board, Library of Congress (Parts 300—399)
- IV Assistant Secretary for Technology Policy, Department of Commerce (Parts 400—499)
- V Under Secretary for Technology, Department of Commerce (Parts 500—599)

Title 38—Pensions, Bonuses, and Veterans' Relief

- I Department of Veterans Affairs (Parts 0—99)
- II Armed Forces Retirement Home (Parts 200—299)

Title 39—Postal Service

- I United States Postal Service (Parts 1—999)
- III Postal Regulatory Commission (Parts 3000—3099)

Title 40—Protection of Environment

- I Environmental Protection Agency (Parts 1—1099)
- IV Environmental Protection Agency and Department of Justice (Parts 1400—1499)
- V Council on Environmental Quality (Parts 1500—1599)
- VI Chemical Safety and Hazard Investigation Board (Parts 1600—1699)
- VII Environmental Protection Agency and Department of Defense; Uniform National Discharge Standards for Vessels of the Armed Forces (Parts 1700—1799)

Title 41—Public Contracts and Property Management

Chap.

SUBTITLE A—FEDERAL PROCUREMENT REGULATIONS SYSTEM [NOTE]

SUBTITLE B—OTHER PROVISIONS RELATING TO PUBLIC CONTRACTS

50	Public Contracts, Department of Labor (Parts 50–1—50–999)
51	Committee for Purchase From People Who Are Blind or Severely Disabled (Parts 51–1—51–99)
60	Office of Federal Contract Compliance Programs, Equal Employment Opportunity, Department of Labor (Parts 60–1—60–999)
61	Office of the Assistant Secretary for Veterans' Employment and Training Service, Department of Labor (Parts 61–1—61–999)
62—100	[Reserved]

SUBTITLE C—FEDERAL PROPERTY MANAGEMENT REGULATIONS SYSTEM

101	Federal Property Management Regulations (Parts 101–1—101–99)
102	Federal Management Regulation (Parts 102–1—102–299)
103—104	[Reserved]
105	General Services Administration (Parts 105–1—105–999)
109	Department of Energy Property Management Regulations (Parts 109–1—109–99)
114	Department of the Interior (Parts 114–1—114–99)
115	Environmental Protection Agency (Parts 115–1—115–99)
128	Department of Justice (Parts 128–1—128–99)
129—200	[Reserved]

SUBTITLE D—OTHER PROVISIONS RELATING TO PROPERTY MANAGEMENT [RESERVED]

SUBTITLE E—FEDERAL INFORMATION RESOURCES MANAGEMENT REGULATIONS SYSTEM [RESERVED]

SUBTITLE F—FEDERAL TRAVEL REGULATION SYSTEM

300	General (Parts 300–1—300–99)
301	Temporary Duty (TDY) Travel Allowances (Parts 301–1—301–99)
302	Relocation Allowances (Parts 302–1—302–99)
303	Payment of Expenses Connected with the Death of Certain Employees (Part 303–1—303–99)
304	Payment of Travel Expenses from a Non-Federal Source (Parts 304–1—304–99)

Title 42—Public Health

I	Public Health Service, Department of Health and Human Services (Parts 1—199)
IV	Centers for Medicare & Medicaid Services, Department of Health and Human Services (Parts 400—599)
V	Office of Inspector General-Health Care, Department of Health and Human Services (Parts 1000—1999)

Chap.

Title 43—Public Lands: Interior

SUBTITLE A—OFFICE OF THE SECRETARY OF THE INTERIOR (PARTS 1—199)

SUBTITLE B—REGULATIONS RELATING TO PUBLIC LANDS

I Bureau of Reclamation, Department of the Interior (Parts 200—599)
II Bureau of Land Management, Department of the Interior (Parts 1000—9999)
III Utah Reclamation Mitigation and Conservation Commission (Parts 10000—10099)

Title 44—Emergency Management and Assistance

I Federal Emergency Management Agency, Department of Homeland Security (Parts 0—399)
IV Department of Commerce and Department of Transportation (Parts 400—499)

Title 45—Public Welfare

SUBTITLE A—DEPARTMENT OF HEALTH AND HUMAN SERVICES (PARTS 1—199)

SUBTITLE B—REGULATIONS RELATING TO PUBLIC WELFARE

II Office of Family Assistance (Assistance Programs), Administration for Children and Families, Department of Health and Human Services (Parts 200—299)
III Office of Child Support Enforcement (Child Support Enforcement Program), Administration for Children and Families, Department of Health and Human Services (Parts 300—399)
IV Office of Refugee Resettlement, Administration for Children and Families, Department of Health and Human Services (Parts 400—499)
V Foreign Claims Settlement Commission of the United States, Department of Justice (Parts 500—599)
VI National Science Foundation (Parts 600—699)
VII Commission on Civil Rights (Parts 700—799)
VIII Office of Personnel Management (Parts 800—899) [Reserved]
X Office of Community Services, Administration for Children and Families, Department of Health and Human Services (Parts 1000—1099)
XI National Foundation on the Arts and the Humanities (Parts 1100—1199)
XII Corporation for National and Community Service (Parts 1200—1299)
XIII Office of Human Development Services, Department of Health and Human Services (Parts 1300—1399)
XVI Legal Services Corporation (Parts 1600—1699)
XVII National Commission on Libraries and Information Science (Parts 1700—1799)
XVIII Harry S. Truman Scholarship Foundation (Parts 1800—1899)
XXI Commission on Fine Arts (Parts 2100—2199)

Title 45—Public Welfare—Continued

Chap.
XXIII Arctic Research Commission (Part 2301)
XXIV   James Madison Memorial Fellowship Foundation (Parts 2400—2499)
XXV   Corporation for National and Community Service (Parts 2500—2599)

Title 46—Shipping

I   Coast Guard, Department of Homeland Security (Parts 1—199)
II   Maritime Administration, Department of Transportation (Parts 200—399)
III Coast Guard (Great Lakes Pilotage), Department of Homeland Security (Parts 400—499)
IV   Federal Maritime Commission (Parts 500—599)

Title 47—Telecommunication

I   Federal Communications Commission (Parts 0—199)
II   Office of Science and Technology Policy and National Security Council (Parts 200—299)
III National Telecommunications and Information Administration, Department of Commerce (Parts 300—399)
IV   National Telecommunications and Information Administration, Department of Commerce, and National Highway Traffic Safety Administration, Department of Transportation (Parts 400—499)

Title 48—Federal Acquisition Regulations System

1   Federal Acquisition Regulation (Parts 1—99)
2   Defense Acquisition Regulations System, Department of Defense (Parts 200—299)
3   Health and Human Services (Parts 300—399)
4   Department of Agriculture (Parts 400—499)
5   General Services Administration (Parts 500—599)
6   Department of State (Parts 600—699)
7   Agency for International Development (Parts 700—799)
8   Department of Veterans Affairs (Parts 800—899)
9   Department of Energy (Parts 900—999)
10 Department of the Treasury (Parts 1000—1099)
12 Department of Transportation (Parts 1200—1299)
13 Department of Commerce (Parts 1300—1399)
14 Department of the Interior (Parts 1400—1499)
15 Environmental Protection Agency (Parts 1500—1599)
16 Office of Personnel Management, Federal Employees Health Benefits Acquisition Regulation (Parts 1600—1699)
17 Office of Personnel Management (Parts 1700—1799)

Title 48—Federal Acquisition Regulations System—Continued

Chap.

18	National Aeronautics and Space Administration (Parts 1800—1899)
19	Broadcasting Board of Governors (Parts 1900—1999)
20	Nuclear Regulatory Commission (Parts 2000—2099)
21	Office of Personnel Management, Federal Employees Group Life Insurance Federal Acquisition Regulation (Parts 2100—2199)
23	Social Security Administration (Parts 2300—2399)
24	Department of Housing and Urban Development (Parts 2400—2499)
25	National Science Foundation (Parts 2500—2599)
28	Department of Justice (Parts 2800—2899)
29	Department of Labor (Parts 2900—2999)
30	Department of Homeland Security, Homeland Security Acquisition Regulation (HSAR) (Parts 3000—3099)
34	Department of Education Acquisition Regulation (Parts 3400—3499)
51	Department of the Army Acquisition Regulations (Parts 5100—5199)
52	Department of the Navy Acquisition Regulations (Parts 5200—5299)
53	Department of the Air Force Federal Acquisition Regulation Supplement [Reserved]
54	Defense Logistics Agency, Department of Defense (Parts 5400—5499)
57	African Development Foundation (Parts 5700—5799)
61	Civilian Board of Contract Appeals, General Services Administration (Parts 6100—6199)
63	Department of Transportation Board of Contract Appeals (Parts 6300—6399)
99	Cost Accounting Standards Board, Office of Federal Procurement Policy, Office of Management and Budget (Parts 9900—9999)

Title 49—Transportation

SUBTITLE A—OFFICE OF THE SECRETARY OF TRANSPORTATION (PARTS 1—99)

SUBTITLE B—OTHER REGULATIONS RELATING TO TRANSPORTATION

I	Pipeline and Hazardous Materials Safety Administration, Department of Transportation (Parts 100—199)
II	Federal Railroad Administration, Department of Transportation (Parts 200—299)
III	Federal Motor Carrier Safety Administration, Department of Transportation (Parts 300—399)
IV	Coast Guard, Department of Homeland Security (Parts 400—499)
V	National Highway Traffic Safety Administration, Department of Transportation (Parts 500—599)
VI	Federal Transit Administration, Department of Transportation (Parts 600—699)

Title 49—Transportation—Continued

Chap.

VII	National Railroad Passenger Corporation (AMTRAK) (Parts 700—799)
VIII	National Transportation Safety Board (Parts 800—999)
X	Surface Transportation Board, Department of Transportation (Parts 1000—1399)
XI	Research and Innovative Technology Administration, Department of Transportation [Reserved]
XII	Transportation Security Administration, Department of Homeland Security (Parts 1500—1699)

Title 50—Wildlife and Fisheries

I	United States Fish and Wildlife Service, Department of the Interior (Parts 1—199)
II	National Marine Fisheries Service, National Oceanic and Atmospheric Administration, Department of Commerce (Parts 200—299)
III	International Fishing and Related Activities (Parts 300—399)
IV	Joint Regulations (United States Fish and Wildlife Service, Department of the Interior and National Marine Fisheries Service, National Oceanic and Atmospheric Administration, Department of Commerce); Endangered Species Committee Regulations (Parts 400—499)
V	Marine Mammal Commission (Parts 500—599)
VI	Fishery Conservation and Management, National Oceanic and Atmospheric Administration, Department of Commerce (Parts 600—699)

CFR Index and Finding Aids

Subject/Agency Index

List of Agency Prepared Indexes

Parallel Tables of Statutory Authorities and Rules

List of CFR Titles, Chapters, Subchapters, and Parts

Alphabetical List of Agencies Appearing in the CFR

Alphabetical List of Agencies Appearing in the CFR
(Revised as of January 1, 2012)

Agency	CFR Title, Subtitle or Chapter
Administrative Committee of the Federal Register	1, I
Administrative Conference of the United States	1, III
Advisory Council on Historic Preservation	36, VIII
Advocacy and Outreach, Office of	7, XXV
African Development Foundation	22, XV
Federal Acquisition Regulation	48, 57
Agency for International Development	2, VII; 22, II
Federal Acquisition Regulation	48, 7
Agricultural Marketing Service	7, I, IX, X, XI
Agricultural Research Service	7, V
Agriculture Department	2, IV; 5, LXXIII
Advocacy and Outreach, Office of	7, XXV
Agricultural Marketing Service	7, I, IX, X, XI
Agricultural Research Service	7, V
Animal and Plant Health Inspection Service	7, III; 9, I
Chief Financial Officer, Office of	7, XXX
Commodity Credit Corporation	7, XIV
Economic Research Service	7, XXXVII
Energy Policy and New Uses, Office of	2, IX; 7, XXIX
Environmental Quality, Office of	7, XXXI
Farm Service Agency	7, VII, XVIII
Federal Acquisition Regulation	48, 4
Federal Crop Insurance Corporation	7, IV
Food and Nutrition Service	7, II
Food Safety and Inspection Service	9, III
Foreign Agricultural Service	7, XV
Forest Service	36, II
Grain Inspection, Packers and Stockyards Administration	7, VIII; 9, II
Information Resources Management, Office of	7, XXVII
Inspector General, Office of	7, XXVI
National Agricultural Library	7, XLI
National Agricultural Statistics Service	7, XXXVI
National Institute of Food and Agriculture	7, XXXIV
Natural Resources Conservation Service	7, VI
Operations, Office of	7, XXVIII
Procurement and Property Management, Office of	7, XXXII
Rural Business-Cooperative Service	7, XVIII, XLII, L
Rural Development Administration	7, XLII
Rural Housing Service	7, XVIII, XXXV, L
Rural Telephone Bank	7, XVI
Rural Utilities Service	7, XVII, XVIII, XLII, L
Secretary of Agriculture, Office of	7, Subtitle A
Transportation, Office of	7, XXXIII
World Agricultural Outlook Board	7, XXXVIII
Air Force Department	32, VII
Federal Acquisition Regulation Supplement	48, 53
Air Transportation Stabilization Board	14, VI
Alcohol and Tobacco Tax and Trade Bureau	27, I
Alcohol, Tobacco, Firearms, and Explosives, Bureau of	27, II
AMTRAK	49, VII
American Battle Monuments Commission	36, IV
American Indians, Office of the Special Trustee	25, VII
Animal and Plant Health Inspection Service	7, III; 9, I

1039

Agency	CFR Title, Subtitle or Chapter
Appalachian Regional Commission	5, IX
Architectural and Transportation Barriers Compliance Board	36, XI
Arctic Research Commission	45, XXIII
Armed Forces Retirement Home	5, XI
Army Department	32, V
Engineers, Corps of	33, II; 36, III
Federal Acquisition Regulation	48, 51
Bilingual Education and Minority Languages Affairs, Office of	34, V
Blind or Severely Disabled, Committee for Purchase from People Who Are	41, 51
Broadcasting Board of Governors	22, V
Federal Acquisition Regulation	48, 19
Bureau of Ocean Energy Management, Regulation, and Enforcement	30, II
Census Bureau	15, I
Centers for Medicare & Medicaid Services	42, IV
Central Intelligence Agency	32, XIX
Chemical Safety and Hazardous Investigation Board	40, VI
Chief Financial Officer, Office of	7, XXX
Child Support Enforcement, Office of	45, III
Children and Families, Administration for	45, II, III, IV, X
Civil Rights, Commission on	5, LXVIII; 45, VII
Civil Rights, Office for	34, I
Court Services and Offender Supervision Agency for the District of Columbia	5, LXX
Coast Guard	33, I; 46, I; 49, IV
Coast Guard (Great Lakes Pilotage)	46, III
Commerce Department	2, XIII; 44, IV; 50, VI
Census Bureau	15, I
Economic Affairs, Under Secretary	37, V
Economic Analysis, Bureau of	15, VIII
Economic Development Administration	13, III
Emergency Management and Assistance	44, IV
Federal Acquisition Regulation	48, 13
Foreign-Trade Zones Board	15, IV
Industry and Security, Bureau of	15, VII
International Trade Administration	15, III; 19, III
National Institute of Standards and Technology	15, II
National Marine Fisheries Service	50, II, IV
National Oceanic and Atmospheric Administration	15, IX; 50, II, III, IV, VI
National Telecommunications and Information Administration	15, XXIII; 47, III, IV
National Weather Service	15, IX
Patent and Trademark Office, United States	37, I
Productivity, Technology and Innovation, Assistant Secretary for	37, IV
Secretary of Commerce, Office of	15, Subtitle A
Technology, Under Secretary for	37, V
Technology Administration	15, XI
Technology Policy, Assistant Secretary for	37, IV
Commercial Space Transportation	14, III
Commodity Credit Corporation	7, XIV
Commodity Futures Trading Commission	5, XLI; 17, I
Community Planning and Development, Office of Assistant Secretary for	24, V, VI
Community Services, Office of	45, X
Comptroller of the Currency	12, I
Construction Industry Collective Bargaining Commission	29, IX
Consumer Financial Protection Bureau	12, X
Consumer Product Safety Commission	5, LXXI; 16, II
Copyright Office	37, II
Copyright Royalty Board	37, III
Corporation for National and Community Service	2, XXII; 45, XII, XXV
Cost Accounting Standards Board	48, 99
Council on Environmental Quality	40, V
Court Services and Offender Supervision Agency for the District of Columbia	5, LXX; 28, VIII

Agency	CFR Title, Subtitle or Chapter
Customs and Border Protection	19, I
Defense Contract Audit Agency	32, I
Defense Department	2, XI; 5, XXVI; 32, Subtitle A; 40, VII
Advanced Research Projects Agency	32, I
Air Force Department	32, VII
Army Department	32, V; 33, II; 36, III; 48, 51
Defense Acquisition Regulations System	48, 2
Defense Intelligence Agency	32, I
Defense Logistics Agency	32, I, XII; 48, 54
Engineers, Corps of	33, II; 36, III
National Imagery and Mapping Agency	32, I
Navy Department	32, VI; 48, 52
Secretary of Defense, Office of	2, XI; 32, I
Defense Contract Audit Agency	32, I
Defense Intelligence Agency	32, I
Defense Logistics Agency	32, XII; 48, 54
Defense Nuclear Facilities Safety Board	10, XVII
Delaware River Basin Commission	18, III
District of Columbia, Court Services and Offender Supervision Agency for the	5, LXX; 28, VIII
Drug Enforcement Administration	21, II
East-West Foreign Trade Board	15, XIII
Economic Affairs, Under Secretary	37, V
Economic Analysis, Bureau of	15, VIII
Economic Development Administration	13, III
Economic Research Service	7, XXXVII
Education, Department of	5, LIII
Bilingual Education and Minority Languages Affairs, Office of	34, V
Civil Rights, Office for	34, I
Educational Research and Improvement, Office of	34, VII
Elementary and Secondary Education, Office of	34, II
Federal Acquisition Regulation	48, 34
Postsecondary Education, Office of	34, VI
Secretary of Education, Office of	34, Subtitle A
Special Education and Rehabilitative Services, Office of	34, III
Vocational and Adult Education, Office of	34, IV
Educational Research and Improvement, Office of	34, VII
Election Assistance Commission	2, LVIII; 11, II
Elementary and Secondary Education, Office of	34, II
Emergency Oil and Gas Guaranteed Loan Board	13, V
Emergency Steel Guarantee Loan Board	13, IV
Employee Benefits Security Administration	29, XXV
Employees' Compensation Appeals Board	20, IV
Employees Loyalty Board	5, V
Employment and Training Administration	20, V
Employment Standards Administration	20, VI
Endangered Species Committee	50, IV
Energy, Department of	2, IX; 5, XXIII; 10, II, III, X
Federal Acquisition Regulation	48, 9
Federal Energy Regulatory Commission	5, XXIV; 18, I
Property Management Regulations	41, 109
Energy, Office of	7, XXIX
Engineers, Corps of	33, II; 36, III
Engraving and Printing, Bureau of	31, VI
Environmental Protection Agency	2, XV; 5, LIV; 40, I, IV, VII
Federal Acquisition Regulation	48, 15
Property Management Regulations	41, 115
Environmental Quality, Office of	7, XXXI
Equal Employment Opportunity Commission	5, LXII; 29, XIV
Equal Opportunity, Office of Assistant Secretary for	24, I
Executive Office of the President	3, I
Administration, Office of	5, XV

1041

Agency	CFR Title, Subtitle or Chapter
Environmental Quality, Council on	40, V
Management and Budget, Office of	2, Subtitle A; 5, III, LXXVII; 14, VI; 48, 99
National Drug Control Policy, Office of	21, III
National Security Council	32, XXI; 47, 2
Presidential Documents	3
Science and Technology Policy, Office of	32, XXIV; 47, II
Trade Representative, Office of the United States	15, XX
Export-Import Bank of the United States	2, XXXV; 5, LII; 12, IV
Family Assistance, Office of	45, II
Farm Credit Administration	5, XXXI; 12, VI
Farm Credit System Insurance Corporation	5, XXX; 12, XIV
Farm Service Agency	7, VII, XVIII
Federal Acquisition Regulation	48, 1
Federal Aviation Administration	14, I
Commercial Space Transportation	14, III
Federal Claims Collection Standards	31, IX
Federal Communications Commission	5, XXIX; 47, I
Federal Contract Compliance Programs, Office of	41, 60
Federal Crop Insurance Corporation	7, IV
Federal Deposit Insurance Corporation	5, XXII; 12, III
Federal Election Commission	5, XXXVII; 11, I
Federal Emergency Management Agency	44, I
Federal Employees Group Life Insurance Federal Acquisition Regulation	48, 21
Federal Employees Health Benefits Acquisition Regulation	48, 16
Federal Energy Regulatory Commission	5, XXIV; 18, I
Federal Financial Institutions Examination Council	12, XI
Federal Financing Bank	12, VIII
Federal Highway Administration	23, I, II
Federal Home Loan Mortgage Corporation	1, IV
Federal Housing Enterprise Oversight Office	12, XVII
Federal Housing Finance Agency	5, LXXX; 12, XII
Federal Housing Finance Board	12, IX
Federal Labor Relations Authority	5, XIV, XLIX; 22, XIV
Federal Law Enforcement Training Center	31, VII
Federal Management Regulation	41, 102
Federal Maritime Commission	46, IV
Federal Mediation and Conciliation Service	29, XII
Federal Mine Safety and Health Review Commission	5, LXXIV; 29, XXVII
Federal Motor Carrier Safety Administration	49, III
Federal Prison Industries, Inc.	28, III
Federal Procurement Policy Office	48, 99
Federal Property Management Regulations	41, 101
Federal Railroad Administration	49, II
Federal Register, Administrative Committee of	1, I
Federal Register, Office of	1, II
Federal Reserve System	12, II
Board of Governors	5, LVIII
Federal Retirement Thrift Investment Board	5, VI, LXXVI
Federal Service Impasses Panel	5, XIV
Federal Trade Commission	5, XLVII; 16, I
Federal Transit Administration	49, VI
Federal Travel Regulation System	41, Subtitle F
Financial Crimes Enforcement Network	31, X
Financial Research Office	12, XVI
Financial Stability Oversight Council	12, XIII
Fine Arts, Commission on	45, XXI
Fiscal Service	31, II
Fish and Wildlife Service, United States	50, I, IV
Food and Drug Administration	21, I
Food and Nutrition Service	7, II
Food Safety and Inspection Service	9, III
Foreign Agricultural Service	7, XV
Foreign Assets Control, Office of	31, V
Foreign Claims Settlement Commission of the United States	45, V
Foreign Service Grievance Board	22, IX

Agency	CFR Title, Subtitle or Chapter
Foreign Service Impasse Disputes Panel	22, XIV
Foreign Service Labor Relations Board	22, XIV
Foreign-Trade Zones Board	15, IV
Forest Service	36, II
General Services Administration	5, LVII; 41, 105
Contract Appeals, Board of	48, 61
Federal Acquisition Regulation	48, 5
Federal Management Regulation	41, 102
Federal Property Management Regulations	41, 101
Federal Travel Regulation System	41, Subtitle F
General	41, 300
Payment From a Non-Federal Source for Travel Expenses	41, 304
Payment of Expenses Connected With the Death of Certain Employees	41, 303
Relocation Allowances	41, 302
Temporary Duty (TDY) Travel Allowances	41, 301
Geological Survey	30, IV
Government Accountability Office	4, I
Government Ethics, Office of	5, XVI
Government National Mortgage Association	24, III
Grain Inspection, Packers and Stockyards Administration	7, VIII; 9, II
Harry S. Truman Scholarship Foundation	45, XVIII
Health and Human Services, Department of	2, III; 5, XLV; 45, Subtitle A,
Centers for Medicare & Medicaid Services	42, IV
Child Support Enforcement, Office of	45, III
Children and Families, Administration for	45, II, III, IV, X
Community Services, Office of	45, X
Family Assistance, Office of	45, II
Federal Acquisition Regulation	48, 3
Food and Drug Administration	21, I
Human Development Services, Office of	45, XIII
Indian Health Service	25, V
Inspector General (Health Care), Office of	42, V
Public Health Service	42, I
Refugee Resettlement, Office of	45, IV
Homeland Security, Department of	2, XXX; 6, I
Coast Guard	33, I; 46, I; 49, IV
Coast Guard (Great Lakes Pilotage)	46, III
Customs and Border Protection	19, I
Federal Emergency Management Agency	44, I
Human Resources Management and Labor Relations Systems	5, XCVII
Immigration and Customs Enforcement Bureau	19, IV
Immigration and Naturalization	8, I
Transportation Security Administration	49, XII
HOPE for Homeowners Program, Board of Directors of	24, XXIV
Housing and Urban Development, Department of	2, XXIV; 5, LXV; 24, Subtitle B
Community Planning and Development, Office of Assistant Secretary for	24, V, VI
Equal Opportunity, Office of Assistant Secretary for	24, I
Federal Acquisition Regulation	48, 24
Federal Housing Enterprise Oversight, Office of	12, XVII
Government National Mortgage Association	24, III
Housing—Federal Housing Commissioner, Office of Assistant Secretary for	24, II, VIII, X, XX
Housing, Office of, and Multifamily Housing Assistance Restructuring, Office of	24, IV
Inspector General, Office of	24, XII
Public and Indian Housing, Office of Assistant Secretary for	24, IX
Secretary, Office of	24, Subtitle A, VII
Housing—Federal Housing Commissioner, Office of Assistant Secretary for	24, II, VIII, X, XX
Housing, Office of, and Multifamily Housing Assistance Restructuring, Office of	24, IV
Human Development Services, Office of	45, XIII

Agency	CFR Title, Subtitle or Chapter
Immigration and Customs Enforcement Bureau	19, IV
Immigration and Naturalization	8, I
Immigration Review, Executive Office for	8, V
Independent Counsel, Office of	28, VII
Indian Affairs, Bureau of	25, I, V
Indian Affairs, Office of the Assistant Secretary	25, VI
Indian Arts and Crafts Board	25, II
Indian Health Service	25, V
Industry and Security, Bureau of	15, VII
Information Resources Management, Office of	7, XXVII
Information Security Oversight Office, National Archives and Records Administration	32, XX
Inspector General	
Agriculture Department	7, XXVI
Health and Human Services Department	42, V
Housing and Urban Development Department	24, XII, XV
Institute of Peace, United States	22, XVII
Inter-American Foundation	5, LXIII; 22, X
Interior Department	2, XIV
American Indians, Office of the Special Trustee	25, XVII
Bureau of Ocean Energy Management, Regulation, and Enforcement	30, II
Endangered Species Committee	50, IV
Federal Acquisition Regulation	48, 14
Federal Property Management Regulations System	41, 114
Fish and Wildlife Service, United States	50, I, IV
Geological Survey	30, IV
Indian Affairs, Bureau of	25, I, V
Indian Affairs, Office of the Assistant Secretary	25, VI
Indian Arts and Crafts Board	25, II
Land Management, Bureau of	43, II
National Indian Gaming Commission	25, III
National Park Service	36, I
Natural Resource Revenue, Office of	30, XII
Ocean Energy Management, Bureau of	30, V
Reclamation, Bureau of	43, I
Secretary of the Interior, Office of	2, XIV; 43, Subtitle A
Surface Mining Reclamation and Enforcement, Office of	30, VII
Internal Revenue Service	26, I
International Boundary and Water Commission, United States and Mexico, United States Section	22, XI
International Development, United States Agency for	22, II
Federal Acquisition Regulation	48, 7
International Development Cooperation Agency, United States	22, XII
International Joint Commission, United States and Canada	22, IV
International Organizations Employees Loyalty Board	5, V
International Trade Administration	15, III; 19, III
International Trade Commission, United States	19, II
Interstate Commerce Commission	5, XL
Investment Security, Office of	31, VIII
James Madison Memorial Fellowship Foundation	45, XXIV
Japan–United States Friendship Commission	22, XVI
Joint Board for the Enrollment of Actuaries	20, VIII
Justice Department	2, XXVIII; 5, XXVIII; 28, I, XI; 40, IV
Alcohol, Tobacco, Firearms, and Explosives, Bureau of	27, II
Drug Enforcement Administration	21, II
Federal Acquisition Regulation	48, 28
Federal Claims Collection Standards	31, IX
Federal Prison Industries, Inc.	28, III
Foreign Claims Settlement Commission of the United States	45, V
Immigration Review, Executive Office for	8, V
Offices of Independent Counsel	28, VI
Prisons, Bureau of	28, V
Property Management Regulations	41, 128

Agency	CFR Title, Subtitle or Chapter
Labor Department	5, XLII
Employee Benefits Security Administration	29, XXV
Employees' Compensation Appeals Board	20, IV
Employment and Training Administration	20, V
Employment Standards Administration	20, VI
Federal Acquisition Regulation	48, 29
Federal Contract Compliance Programs, Office of	41, 60
Federal Procurement Regulations System	41, 50
Labor-Management Standards, Office of	29, II, IV
Mine Safety and Health Administration	30, I
Occupational Safety and Health Administration	29, XVII
Office of Workers' Compensation Programs	20, VII
Public Contracts	41, 50
Secretary of Labor, Office of	29, Subtitle A
Veterans' Employment and Training Service, Office of the Assistant Secretary for	41, 61; 20, IX
Wage and Hour Division	29, V
Workers' Compensation Programs, Office of	20, I
Labor-Management Standards, Office of	29, II, IV
Land Management, Bureau of	43, II
Legal Services Corporation	45, XVI
Library of Congress	36, VII
Copyright Office	37, II
Copyright Royalty Board	37, III
Local Television Loan Guarantee Board	7, XX
Management and Budget, Office of	5, III, LXXVII; 14, VI; 48, 99
Marine Mammal Commission	50, V
Maritime Administration	46, II
Merit Systems Protection Board	5, II, LXIV
Micronesian Status Negotiations, Office for	32, XXVII
Millennium Challenge Corporation	22, XIII
Mine Safety and Health Administration	30, I
Minority Business Development Agency	15, XIV
Miscellaneous Agencies	1, IV
Monetary Offices	31, I
Morris K. Udall Scholarship and Excellence in National Environmental Policy Foundation	36, XVI
Museum and Library Services, Institute of	2, XXXI
National Aeronautics and Space Administration	2, XVIII; 5, LIX; 14, V
Federal Acquisition Regulation	48, 18
National Agricultural Library	7, XLI
National Agricultural Statistics Service	7, XXXVI
National and Community Service, Corporation for	2, XXII; 45, XII, XXV
National Archives and Records Administration	2, XXVI; 5, LXVI; 36, XII
Information Security Oversight Office	32, XX
National Capital Planning Commission	1, IV
National Commission for Employment Policy	1, IV
National Commission on Libraries and Information Science	45, XVII
National Council on Disability	34, XII
National Counterintelligence Center	32, XVIII
National Credit Union Administration	12, VII
National Crime Prevention and Privacy Compact Council	28, IX
National Drug Control Policy, Office of	21, III
National Endowment for the Arts	2, XXXII
National Endowment for the Humanities	2, XXXIII
National Foundation on the Arts and the Humanities	45, XI
National Highway Traffic Safety Administration	23, II, III; 47, VI; 49, V
National Imagery and Mapping Agency	32, I
National Indian Gaming Commission	25, III
National Institute for Literacy	34, XI
National Institute of Food and Agriculture	7, XXXIV
National Institute of Standards and Technology	15, II
National Intelligence, Office of Director of	32, XVII
National Labor Relations Board	5, LXI; 29, I
National Marine Fisheries Service	50, II, IV

1045

Agency	CFR Title, Subtitle or Chapter
National Mediation Board	29, X
National Oceanic and Atmospheric Administration	15, IX; 50, II, III, IV, VI
National Park Service	36, I
National Railroad Adjustment Board	29, III
National Railroad Passenger Corporation (AMTRAK)	49, VII
National Science Foundation	2, XXV; 5, XLIII; 45, VI
Federal Acquisition Regulation	48, 25
National Security Council	32, XXI
National Security Council and Office of Science and Technology Policy	47, II
National Telecommunications and Information Administration	15, XXIII; 47, III, IV
National Transportation Safety Board	49, VIII
Natural Resources Conservation Service	7, VI
Natural Resource Revenue, Office of	30, XII
Navajo and Hopi Indian Relocation, Office of	25, IV
Navy Department	32, VI
Federal Acquisition Regulation	48, 52
Neighborhood Reinvestment Corporation	24, XXV
Northeast Interstate Low-Level Radioactive Waste Commission	10, XVIII
Nuclear Regulatory Commission	2, XX; 5, XLVIII; 10, I
Federal Acquisition Regulation	48, 20
Occupational Safety and Health Administration	29, XVII
Occupational Safety and Health Review Commission	29, XX
Ocean Energy Management, Bureau of	30, V
Offices of Independent Counsel	28, VI
Office of Workers' Compensation Programs	20, VII
Oklahoma City National Memorial Trust	36, XV
Operations Office	7, XXVIII
Overseas Private Investment Corporation	5, XXXIII; 22, VII
Patent and Trademark Office, United States	37, I
Payment From a Non-Federal Source for Travel Expenses	41, 304
Payment of Expenses Connected With the Death of Certain Employees	41, 303
Peace Corps	2, XXXVII; 22, III
Pennsylvania Avenue Development Corporation	36, IX
Pension Benefit Guaranty Corporation	29, XL
Personnel Management, Office of	5, I, XXXV; 45, VIII
Human Resources Management and Labor Relations Systems, Department of Homeland Security	5, XCVII
Federal Acquisition Regulation	48, 17
Federal Employees Group Life Insurance Federal Acquisition Regulation	48, 21
Federal Employees Health Benefits Acquisition Regulation	48, 16
Pipeline and Hazardous Materials Safety Administration	49, I
Postal Regulatory Commission	5, XLVI; 39, III
Postal Service, United States	5, LX; 39, I
Postsecondary Education, Office of	34, VI
President's Commission on White House Fellowships	1, IV
Presidential Documents	3
Presidio Trust	36, X
Prisons, Bureau of	28, V
Procurement and Property Management, Office of	7, XXXII
Productivity, Technology and Innovation, Assistant Secretary	37, IV
Public Contracts, Department of Labor	41, 50
Public and Indian Housing, Office of Assistant Secretary for	24, IX
Public Health Service	42, I
Railroad Retirement Board	20, II
Reclamation, Bureau of	43, I
Recovery Accountability and Transparency Board	4, II
Refugee Resettlement, Office of	45, IV
Relocation Allowances	41, 302
Research and Innovative Technology Administration	49, XI
Rural Business-Cooperative Service	7, XVIII, XLII, L
Rural Development Administration	7, XLII

Agency	CFR Title, Subtitle or Chapter
Rural Housing Service	7, XVIII, XXXV, L
Rural Telephone Bank	7, XVI
Rural Utilities Service	7, XVII, XVIII, XLII, L
Saint Lawrence Seaway Development Corporation	33, IV
Science and Technology Policy, Office of	32, XXIV
Science and Technology Policy, Office of, and National Security Council	47, II
Secret Service	31, IV
Securities and Exchange Commission	5, XXXIV; 17, II
Selective Service System	32, XVI
Small Business Administration	2, XXVII; 13, I
Smithsonian Institution	36, V
Social Security Administration	2, XXIII; 20, III; 48, 23
Soldiers' and Airmen's Home, United States	5, XI
Special Counsel, Office of	5, VIII
Special Education and Rehabilitative Services, Office of	34, III
Special Inspector General for Iraq Reconstruction	5, LXXXVII
State Department	2, VI; 22, I; 28, XI
Federal Acquisition Regulation	48, 6
Surface Mining Reclamation and Enforcement, Office of	30, VII
Surface Transportation Board	49, X
Susquehanna River Basin Commission	18, VIII
Technology Administration	15, XI
Technology Policy, Assistant Secretary for	37, IV
Technology, Under Secretary for	37, V
Tennessee Valley Authority	5, LXIX; 18, XIII
Thrift Supervision Office, Department of the Treasury	12, V
Trade Representative, United States, Office of	15, XX
Transportation, Department of	2, XII; 5, L
Commercial Space Transportation	14, III
Contract Appeals, Board of	48, 63
Emergency Management and Assistance	44, IV
Federal Acquisition Regulation	48, 12
Federal Aviation Administration	14, I
Federal Highway Administration	23, I, II
Federal Motor Carrier Safety Administration	49, III
Federal Railroad Administration	49, II
Federal Transit Administration	49, VI
Maritime Administration	46, II
National Highway Traffic Safety Administration	23, II, III; 47, IV; 49, V
Pipeline and Hazardous Materials Safety Administration	49, I
Saint Lawrence Seaway Development Corporation	33, IV
Secretary of Transportation, Office of	14, II; 49, Subtitle A
Surface Transportation Board	49, X
Transportation Statistics Bureau	49, XI
Transportation, Office of	7, XXXIII
Transportation Security Administration	49, XII
Transportation Statistics Bureau	49, XI
Travel Allowances, Temporary Duty (TDY)	41, 301
Treasury Department	5, XXI; 12, XV; 17, IV; 31, IX
Alcohol and Tobacco Tax and Trade Bureau	27, I
Community Development Financial Institutions Fund	12, XVIII
Comptroller of the Currency	12, I
Customs and Border Protection	19, I
Engraving and Printing, Bureau of	31, VI
Federal Acquisition Regulation	48, 10
Federal Claims Collection Standards	31, IX
Federal Law Enforcement Training Center	31, VII
Financial Crimes Enforcement Network	31, X
Fiscal Service	31, II
Foreign Assets Control, Office of	31, V
Internal Revenue Service	26, I
Investment Security, Office of	31, VIII
Monetary Offices	31, I
Secret Service	31, IV
Secretary of the Treasury, Office of	31, Subtitle A

Agency	CFR Title, Subtitle or Chapter
Thrift Supervision, Office of	12, V
Truman, Harry S. Scholarship Foundation	45, XVIII
United States and Canada, International Joint Commission	22, IV
United States and Mexico, International Boundary and Water Commission, United States Section	22, XI
Utah Reclamation Mitigation and Conservation Commission	43, III
Veterans Affairs Department	2, VIII; 38, I
Federal Acquisition Regulation	48, 8
Veterans' Employment and Training Service, Office of the Assistant Secretary for	41, 61; 20, IX
Vice President of the United States, Office of	32, XXVIII
Vocational and Adult Education, Office of	34, IV
Wage and Hour Division	29, V
Water Resources Council	18, VI
Workers' Compensation Programs, Office of	20, I
World Agricultural Outlook Board	7, XXXVIII

List of CFR Sections Affected

All changes in this volume of the Code of Federal Regulations that were made by documents published in the FEDERAL REGISTER since January 1, 2001, are enumerated in the following list. Entries indicate the nature of the changes effected. Page numbers refer to FEDERAL REGISTER pages. The user should consult the entries for chapters and parts as well as sections for revisions.

For the period before January 1, 2001, see the "List of CFR Sections Affected, 1949–1963, 1964–1972, 1973–1985, and 1986–2000" published in 11 separate volumes.

2001

12 CFR

66 FR Page

Chapter VI

611.1135—611.1137 (Subpart I) Revised	16843
Regulation at 66 FR 16843 eff. 5-14-01	26785
613.3020 (c) added	28643
Regulation at 66 FR 28643 confirmed	36908
613.3030 (a)(1) and (2) amended	28643
Regulation at 66 FR 28643 confirmed	36908
615.5220 (a)(3) revised	16844
Regulation at 66 FR 16844 eff. 5-14-01	26785
615.5250 (c)(2) amended	16844
Regulation at 66 FR 16844 eff. 5-14-01	26785
620.2 (h)(1) and (2) revised	14301
Regulation at 66 FR 14301 confirmed	21064
620.4 (b) revised	14301
Regulation at 66 FR 14301 confirmed	21064
620.5 (a)(10) added	14301
Regulation at 66 FR 14301 confirmed	21064
650 Authority citation revised	19064
650.20—650.31 (Subpart B) Added	19065
Regulation at 66 FR 19064 eff. 5-23-01	28361

Chapter VII

700.1 Redesignated as 700.2; new 700.1 added; eff. 1-22-02	65624

12 CFR—Continued

66 FR Page

Chapter VII—Continued

700.2 Redesignated from 700.1; (h) and (j) removed; (e), (f), (g) and (i) redesignated as (g), (h), (i) and (e); new (f) and (j) added; eff. 1-22-02	65624
701.1 Revised; interim	15621
Revised; interim	65626
701.14 (b)(3)(ii) and (4)(ii) revised; eff. 1-22-02	65624
701.31 (d) introductory text, (1) and (2) revised	48206
701.33 (b)(2)(i) amended; eff. 1-22-02	65629
705.10 Regulation at 65 FR 80299 confirmed	20902
707 Compliance date lifted	48206
707.3 (a) revised; (g) added	33162
707.4 (a)(1) and (2)(i) revised	33163
707.6 (c) removed	33163
707.10 Added	33163
707 Appendix C amended	33163
709.0 Amended; interim	11230
Amended	40575
709.12 Added; interim	11230
Revised	40575
712.2 (d) revised; eff. 1-22-02	65624
712.3 (a) amended	40578
712.5 Amended	40578
712.7 Amended	40578
715 Authority citation revised	65624
715.2 (l) amended; eff. 1-22-02	65624
721 Revised	40857
722.3 (a)(1) amended; eff. 3-1-02	58662
723.4 Amended; eff. 1-22-02	65624
725.2 (o) revised; eff. 1-22-02	65624
742 Added; eff. 3-1-02	58662

1049

12 CFR—Continued

66 FR Page

Chapter VII—Continued
748 Heading and authority citation revised 8161
748.0 (b) revised 8161
748 Appendix A added 8161
749 Revised 40579
 Heading corrected 46307
790.2 (b)(13) heading revised; eff. 1–22–02 65624

2002

12 CFR

67 FR Page

Chapter VI
609 Added 16631
 Regulation at 67 FR 16631 eff. date confirmed 30772
611 Authority citation revised 17909
611.1200—611.1290 (Subpart P) Revised 17909
 Regulation at 67 FR 17909 eff. date confirmed 31938, 35895
614.4000 (d)(1) and (2) amended; (d)(3) added 1285
 Regulation at 67 FR 1285 eff. date confirmed 9581
614.4010 (e)(2) amended; (e)(3) added 1285
 Regulation at 67 FR 1285 eff. date confirmed 9581
614.4020 (b)(2) amended; (b)(3) added 1285
 Regulation at 67 FR 1285 eff. date confirmed 9581
614.4030 (b)(1) and (2) amended; (b)(3) added 1285
 Regulation at 67 FR 1285 eff. date confirmed 9581
614.4040 (b)(1) and (2) amended; (b)(3) added 1285
 Regulation at 67 FR 1285 eff. date confirmed 9581
614.4050 (c)(1) and (2) amended; (c)(3) added 1285
 Regulation at 67 FR 1285 eff. date confirmed 9581
614.4055 Added 1285
 Regulation at 67 FR 1285 eff. date confirmed 9581
614.4130 (a) amended 17917
 Regulation at 67 FR 17917 eff. date confirmed 31938
 Regulation at 67 FR 17917 eff. date confirmed 35895

12 CFR—Continued

67 FR Page

Chapter VI—Continued
614.4325 (a)(4) removed; (a)(5), (6) and (7) redesignated as (a)(4), (5) and (6); newly designated (a)(4) revised 1285
 Regulation at 67 FR 1285 eff. date confirmed 9581
614.4330 (a)(9) amended; (b) removed; (c) redesignated as (b) 1285
 Regulation at 67 FR 1285 eff. date confirmed 9581
614.4358 (b)(4)(i) removed; (b)(4)(ii) and (iii) redesignated as new (b)(4)(i) and (ii) 1285
 Regulation at 67 FR 1285 eff. date confirmed 9581
619.9195 Removed 1286
 Regulation at 67 FR 1286 eff. date confirmed 9581
620.1 (o) revised; (r) redesignated as (s); new (r) added 16633
 Regulation at 67 FR 16633 eff. date confirmed 30772
620.2 (b) introductory text revised; (d) through (i) redesignated as (e) through (j); (a), (b)(3)(i), (ii) and new (i)(3) amended; new (d) added 16633
 Regulation at 67 FR 16633 eff. date confirmed 30772
620.4 Heading, (a), (b)(1) and (2) amended 16633
 Regulation at 67 FR 16633 eff. date confirmed 30772
620.5 (a)(3) and (m)(2) amended 16633
 Regulation at 67 FR 16633 eff. date confirmed 30772
620.11 (b)(6) amended 16633
 Regulation at 67 FR 16633 eff. date confirmed 30772
620.15 Revised 16634
 Regulation at 67 FR 16634 eff. date confirmed 30772
620.17 (b)(4) amended 16634
 Regulation at 67 FR 16634 eff. date confirmed 30772
620.20 Heading and (a) amended 16634
 Regulation at 67 FR 16634 eff. date confirmed 30772
620.21 (c)(3), (d)(3)(i)(A), (B), (ii)(A) and (ii)(B) amended; (d)(5) revised 16634
 Regulation at 67 FR 16634 eff. date confirmed 30772
620.30 Amended 16634

List of CFR Sections Affected

12 CFR—Continued

67 FR Page

Chapter VI—Continued
Regulation at 67 FR 16634 eff. date confirmed...........................30772
620.40 Heading, (b) and (c) amended; (d) revised............................16634
Regulation at 67 FR 16634 eff. date confirmed...........................30772
622.61 Revised 68932

Chapter VII
701.1 Revised 20016
701.21 (c)(7)(ii)(C) revised.................7059
702.2 (i), (j) and (k) redesignated as (j), (k) and (l); (i) added; new (k)(1)(i) and new (iv) revised; (k)(2) amended..........................71087
702.101 (c) revised..........................12464
(b)(1) heading added; (b)(2), (c) heading and (1) revised; (b)(3) heading added 71087
702.102 (b) table revised 71087
702.103 (b) removed........................12464
(a) heading and (b) removed; (a), (1) and (2) redesignated as introductory text, (a) and (b) 71088
702.104 Introductory text amended; (h) Table 1 redesignated as Table 2..71088
702.105 Introductory text amended; (b) Table 2 redesignated as Table 3..71088
702.106 Introductory text amended; (h) Table 3 redesignated as Table 4..71088
702.107 (a) revised; (d) added; (d) Table 4 redesignated as Table 5; introductory text and (d) Table 5 amended................................71088
702.108 (a) and (b) redesignated as (b) and (c); new (a) added; heading and new (b) revised 71089
702.101—702.108 (Subpart A) Appendices A-F heading and Appendix C revised 71089
Appendix F redesignated as Appendix H; new Appendices F and G added...............................71090
Appendix H revised 71091
702.201 Revised 71091
702.202 (a)(1) heading and (b)(3) amended....................................71092
702.203 (a)(1) heading and (b)(3) amended....................................71092
702.204 (a)(1) heading, (b)(3), (c)(1)(iii) and (4) revised; (d) added..71092
702.205 (a)(1) and (c) amended 71092

12 CFR—Continued

67 FR Page

Chapter VII—Continued
702.206 (c)(1)(ii) and (iii) revised; (i) added......................................71092
702.302 (c) introductory text amended; (c) table and (d) revised..71092
702.303 Revised 71092
702.304 (a) revised..........................71093
702.305 (a) and (c)(2) revised; (c)(3) and (d) added..............................71093
702.306 (a) and (b)(2) revised; (h) added..71093
702.401 (c) revised..........................71093
702.403 (b) revised..........................71093
703.100 (c) amended 65651
704 Nomenclature change 65659
704.2 Amended; eff. in part 7-1-03...65651
704.3 (d) through (g) and (b) redesignated as (e) through (h) and (d); (c) removed; (b), (c) and (i) added; (a) heading, new (e) heading, (1) introductory text, (2), (3)(iii) and (f) revised 65652
(e)(3)(i), (ii), (g)(2)(v) and (3) amended 65659
704.4 (a) and (b) amended; (c) introductory text revised.............65654
704.5 (c)(6), (d)(3) and (6) removed; (d)(4) and (5) redesignated as (d)(3) and (4); (a)(1), (2), (c)(5), (d)(1), new (3), (e)(1), (3), (4), (f), (h)(2), (3) revised; (c)(4) and new (d)(4) amended 65654
704.6 (a) introductory text, (3), (4) and (b) through (e) revised..........65654
704.7 (c) through (g) removed; new (c) through (f) added; (h) redesignated as (g) 65655
704.8 (a)(2), (5) and (e) removed; (a)(3), (4), (6), (7), (f) and (g) redesignated as (a)(2), (3), (4), (5), (e) and (f); new (a)(2), (e), (f), (d)(1)(i), (ii), (iii) and (2) introductory text revised; new (a)(5) and (c) amended; new (a)(6) added..65655
704.10 Heading revised; (a) amended 65656
(a) introductory text, (b) and (c) amended 65659
704.11 (c), (d) and (e) redesignated as (f), (g) and (h); new (c), (d) and (e) added; (b) and nedw (g)(3) revised 65656
704.12 Revised 65656
704.13 Removed..............................65657

1051

12 CFR—Continued

67 FR Page

Chapter VII—Continued
704.14 (a) introductory text revised; (b), (c) and (d) redesignated as (c), (d) and (e); new (b) added...65657
704.15 (a) and (b) amended...............65659
704.18 (e)(1) amended......................65657
704.19 (b) revised; (c) removed........65657
704 Appendix A revised..................65657
  Appendix B revised.......................65658
722.3 (b)(2) amended 67102
741.3 (a) heading amended; (a)(2) removed; (a)(3) redesignated as (a)(2)..71094
741.6 (a) revised; (b) amended.........12464
747.2005 (b)(2) revised 71094
790.2 (b)(3) and (15) removed; (b)(4) through (14) and (16) redesignated as new (b)(3) through (14); new (b)(4), (7), (8), (9) and (11) amended; new (b)(13) revised...30773
792.50 (a) and (b) amended..............30774
792.51 (a) through (d) amended.......30774
792.54 (a) amended 30774
792.69 (a) amended..........................30774

2003
12 CFR

68 FR Page

Chapter VI
615.5201 (e) amended; (1)(8) added...18534
  Regulation at 68 FR 18534 eff. 6-5-03...33617
615.5210 (f)(2)(ii)(L) added; interim...15047
  Regulation at 68 FR 15047 confirmed...33347
615.5250 (c)(5) revised 18534
  Regulation at 68 FR 18534 eff. 6-5-03...33617
615.5301 (i)(2) amended; (i)(3) revised; (i)(4) through (7) redesignated as (i)(5) through (8); new (i)(4) and (j) added 18534
  Regulation at 68 FR 18534 eff. 6-5-03...33617

Chapter VII
Chapter VII Policy statement 31951
701.1 Revised; OMB number...........18340
701.19 Revised 23027
701.21 (c)(7)(ii)(C) revised 46441
701.22 (a)(4) and (5) revised; eff. 1-29-04..75111
702.106 (b) and (h) table revised 56547

12 CFR—Continued

68 FR Page

Chapter VII—Continued
702.101—702.108 (Subpart A) Appendices A, D and H revised 56548
703 Revised.....................................32960
704 Authority citation revised 56550
704.7 (e)(2) amended 56550
704.11 (b)(4) removed; (c) amended...56550
709 Policy statement 61735
709.13 Added 32356
712.5 (c) through (q) redesignated as (d) through (r); new (c) added...56551
723.1 (b)(3) amended; (c), (d) and (e) added 56551
723.3 (a) and (b) revised..................56551
723.5 Revised 56551
723.6 (c), (e) and (g) amended; (h) and (i) removed; (j), (l) and (m) redesignated as (h), (i) and (k) 56551
723.7 Revised 56551
723.8 Revised 56552
723.9 Removed 56552
723.10 Revised 56552
723.14 Removed 56552
723.15 Removed 56552
723.16 Revised 56552
723.21 Amended..............................56552
740 Revised 23382
741.11 Added 23030
742.4 Revised 32966
  (a) amended 56553
745.2 (e) and (f) added; eff. 1-29-04..75114
745.4 (c) revised; eff. 1-29-04............75114
745.9-1 (c) revised; eff. 1-29-04.........75114
745.9-2 (a) revised; eff. 1-29-04.........75114
745 Appendix amended; eff. 1-29-04..75114
748 Authority citation revised 25112
748.2 Heading and (b) revised 25112
791.8 (a) revised..............................31952
792.07 Revised 61737
792.08 (a) revised 61737
792.10 (f) added 61737
792.14 Amended..............................61737
792.28 Introductory text amended 61737

2004
12 CFR

69 FR Page

Chapter VI
609.910 (c) amended 10906
  Regulation at 69 FR 10906 eff. 4-19-04..21699

1052

List of CFR Sections Affected

12 CFR—Continued

69 FR Page

Chapter VI—Continued
609.930 (i) corrected........................42853
611.1223 (d)(6) amended.................10906
   Regulation at 69 FR 10906 eff. 4-19-04..21699
611.1290 Amended.........................10906
   Regulation at 69 FR 10906 eff. 4-19-04..21699
612 Heading revised........................10906
   Regulation at 69 FR 10906 eff. 4-19-04..21699
612.2130—612.2270 Designated as Subpart A; heading added.........10906
   Regulation at 69 FR 10906 eff. 4-19-04..21699
612.2300—612.2303 Designated as Subpart B; heading added..........10907
   Regulation at 69 FR 10907 eff. 4-19-04..21699
612.2300 Redesignated from 617.1; (a), (c) and (e) amended..............10907
   Regulation at 69 FR 10907 eff. 4-19-04..21699
612.2301 Redesignated from 617.2..10907
   Regulation at 69 FR 10907 eff. 4-19-04..21699
612.2302 Redesignated from 617.3..10907
   Regulation at 69 FR 10907 eff. 4-19-04..21699
612.2303 Redesignated from 617.4..10907
   Regulation at 69 FR 10907 eff. 4-19-04..21699
613.3100 (b)(2)(ii), (c)(1)(v) and (2) revised.......................................43514
   Regulation at 69 FR 43514 eff. 11-19-04..68767
613.3200 (a) revised; (b) introductory text, (c) introductory text and (1) amended........................43514
   Regulation at 69 FR 43514 eff. 11-19-04..68767
613.3300 (d) revised...........................43514
   Regulation at 69 FR 43514 eff. 11-19-04..68767
614 Authority citation revised......10906
Policy statement............................42853
614.4125 (a) amended....................43514
   Regulation at 69 FR 43514 eff. 11-19-04..68767
614.4165 Revised............................16470
   Regulation at 69 FR 16470 eff. date confirmed........................26763
614.4336 Removed.........................10906

12 CFR—Continued

69 FR Page

Chapter VI—Continued
   Regulation at 69 FR 10906 eff. 4-19-04..21699
614.4365—614.4368 (Subpart K) Removed.......................................16459
   Regulation at 69 FR 16459 eff. date confirmed........................26763
614.4440—614.4444 (Subpart L) Removed..10906
   Regulation at 69 FR 10906 eff. 4-19-04..21699
614.4514 Removed..........................10906
   Regulation at 69 FR 10906 eff. 4-19-04..21699
614.4515 Removed..........................10906
   Regulation at 69 FR 10906 eff. 4-19-04..21699
614.4516 Removed..........................10906
   Regulation at 69 FR 10906 eff. 4-19-04..21699
614.4517 Removed..........................10906
   Regulation at 69 FR 10906 eff. 4-19-04..21699
614.4518 Removed..........................10906
   Regulation at 69 FR 10906 eff. 4-19-04..21699
614.4519 Removed..........................10906
   Regulation at 69 FR 10906 eff. 4-19-04..21699
614.4520 Removed..........................10906
   Regulation at 69 FR 10906 eff. 4-19-04..21699
614.4521 Removed..........................10906
   Regulation at 69 FR 10906 eff. 4-19-04..21699
614.4522 Removed..........................10906
   Regulation at 69 FR 10906 eff. 4-19-04..21699
614.4540 (c) revised........................29862
   Regulation at 69 FR 29862 confirmed...44925
614.4550 Revised............................29863
   Regulation at 69 FR 29863 confirmed...44925
614.4560 (d) revised........................10906
   Regulation at 69 FR 10906 eff. 4-19-04..21699
(d) revised.....................................29863
   Regulation at 69 FR 29863 confirmed...44925
614.4590 (c) and (d) added.............29863
   Regulation at 69 FR 29863 confirmed...44925
614.4595 Added...............................29863
   Regulation at 69 FR 29863 confirmed...44925

12 CFR—Continued

Chapter VI—Continued

	69 FR Page
615.5210 (f)(2)(ii)(M), (iii)(C) and (iv)(E) added	29863
Regulation at 69 FR 29863 confirmed	44925
615.5280 (h) revised	10907
Regulation at 69 FR 10907 eff. 4-19-04	21699
615.5290 (a) and (b) revised	10907
Regulation at 69 FR 10907 eff. 4-19-04	21699
617 Removed; new 617 added	10907
Regulation at 69 FR 10907 eff. 4-19-04	21699
617.1 Redesignated as 612.2300	10907
Regulation at 69 FR 10907 eff. 4-19-04	21699
617.2 Redesignated as 612.2301	10907
Regulation at 69 FR 10907 eff. 4-19-04	21699
617.3 Redesignated as 612.2302	10907
Regulation at 69 FR 10907 eff. 4-19-04	21699
617.4 Redesignated as 612.2303	10907
Regulation at 69 FR 10907 eff. 4-19-04	21699
617.7000 Amended	16459
Regulation at 69 FR 16459 eff. date confirmed	26763
617.7100—617.7135 (Subpart B) Added	16459
Regulation at 69 FR 16459 eff. date confirmed	26763
617.7200 (Subpart C) Added	16459
Regulation at 69 16459 eff. date confirmed	26763
617.7300—617.7315 (Subpart D) Added	10908
Regulation at 69 FR 10908 eff. 4-19-04	21699
617.7500—617.7525 (Subpart F) Added	10908
Regulation at 69 FR 10908 eff. 4-19-04	21699
617.7600—617.7630 (Subpart G) Added	10908
Regulation at 69 FR 10908 eff. 4-19-04	21699
618.8000 (b) amended	43514
Regulation at 69 FR 43514 eff. 11-19-04	68767
618.8005 (a) and (c) amended	43515
Regulation at 69 FR 43514 eff. 11-19-04	68767
620.5 (n) added	16471
Regulation at 69 FR 16471 eff. date confirmed	26763

12 CFR—Continued

Chapter VI—Continued

	69 FR Page
630.20 (p) added	16471
Regulation at 69 FR 16471 eff. date confirmed	26763

Chapter VII

701.1 Amended	9200
701.14 (c), (d) and (e) removed; new (c) and (d) added; (f) redesignated as (e)	62562
701.20 Added	8547
701.21 (i)(4) revised	27828
701.36 Revised	58042
703.1 (b)(6) revised	27828
703.2 Amended	39831
703.4 (a) amended	27828
703.8 (b)(3) amended	39831
703.9 (d) amended	39831
703.14 (g)(4) and (13) introductory text revised	39831
703.16 (a) and (e) revised; (f) added	39832
703.19 (c) introductory text revised	39832
704.2 Amended	39832
704.5 (h)(1) and (4) revised; (h)(5) added	39832
704.8 (a)(4) revised	39833
705.3 (b) amended	45237
708a.4 (d) added	8550
709.1 (c) revised	27828
715.3 (a)(1) and (2) revised	27828
717 Added	69273
721.3 (l) revised	45238
723.3 Introductory text revised	62565
723.4 Revised	62565
723.7 (a) introductory text revised	62565
723.10 (h) revised	62565
723.20 (b) amended	27828
723.21 Amended	27828
724 Heading revised	45238
724.1 Heading revised; text amended	45238
724.2 Heading and introductory text revised	45239
725.18 (c) amended	27829
741.2 Existing text designated as (a); (b), (c) and (d) added	8547
Corrected	9926
741.221 Added	8548
742.4 (a) revised	58043
745.4 (e) revised; interim	8801
Regulation at 69 FR 8801 confirmed	45239
745 Appendix amended	8801
747.1001 (Subpart K) Revised	60080
748 Authority citation revised	69274

1054

List of CFR Sections Affected

12 CFR—Continued

69 FR Page

Chapter VII—Continued
748.0 (c) added 69274
748 Appendix A amended 69274
790.2 (a) and (c)(1) revised; (b)(6) amended 9201
795.1 (a) and (b) revised 12266

2005

12 CFR

70 FR Page

Chapter VI
600.1—600.4 (Subpart A) Revised (effective date pending) 69644
602.8 (a), (b) and (c) amended (effective date pending) 69645
603.340 (a) and (b) amended (effective date pending) 69645
604.435 (e) amended (effective date pending) 69645
606.670 (c) and (i) amended (effective date pending) 69645
607.2 (b) introductory text amended (effective date pending) 35348
Regulation at 70 FR 35348 confirmed 54471
611.1135 (f) revised (effective date pending) 53907
Regulation at 70 FR 53907 confirmed 67901
612.2165 (b)(12) and (13) revised; (b)(14) and (15) added (effective date pending) 53907
614.4351 (a) introductory text revised (effective date pending) 35348
(a)(3) added (effective date pending) 53907
Regulation at 70 FR 35348 confirmed 54471
Regulation at 70 FR 53907 confirmed 67901
615.5131 (a) amended; (b) removed; (c) through (m) redesignated as (b) through (l) (effective date pending) 51589
Regulation at 70 FR 51589 confirmed 62232
615.5132 Revised (effective date pending) 51589
Regulation at 70 FR 51589 confirmed 62232
615.5134 (a) and (c) revised; (d) added (effective date pending) 51590
Regulation at 70 FR 51590 confirmed 62232

12 CFR—Continued

70 FR Page

Chapter VI—Continued
615.5174 (a) amended (effective date pending) 51590
Regulation at 70 FR 51590 confirmed 62232
615.5175 Added (effective date pending) 53908
Regulation at 70 FR 53908 confirmed 67901
615.5200 Heading revised (effective date pending) 35348
Regulation at 70 FR 35348 confirmed 54471
615.5201 Revised (effective date pending) 35348
Amended (effective date pending) 53908
Regulation at 70 FR 35348 confirmed 54471
Regulation at 70 FR 53908 confirmed 67901
615.5206 Added (effective date pending) 35351
Regulation at 70 FR 35351 confirmed 54471
615.5207 Added (effective date pending) 35351
Regulation at 70 FR 35351 confirmed 54471
615.5208 Added (effective date pending) 35351
Regulation at 70 FR 35351 confirmed 54471
615.5209 Added (effective date pending) 35351
Regulation at 70 FR 35351 confirmed 54471
615.5210 Removed; new 615.5210 added (effective date pending) 35351
Regulation at 70 FR 35351 confirmed 54471
615.5211 Added (effective date pending) 35351
Regulation at 70 FR 35351 confirmed 54471
615.5212 Added (effective date pending) 35351
Regulation at 70 FR 35351 confirmed 54471
615.5230 (b)(1) revised (effective date pending) 53908
Regulation at 70 FR 53908 confirmed 67901
615.5240 Revised (effective date pending) 53908

1055

12 CFR—Continued

Chapter VI—Continued

	70 FR Page
Regulation at 70 FR 53908 confirmed	67901
615.5245 Added (effective date pending)	53908
Regulation at 70 FR 53908 confirmed in part	67901
615.5250 Revised (effective date pending)	53908
Regulation at 70 FR 53908 confirmed	67901
615.5255 Added (effective date pending)	53908
Regulation at 70 FR 53908 confirmed	67901
615.5260—615.5290 (Subpart J) Heading revised (effective date pending)	53909
Regulation at 70 FR 53909 confirmed	67901
615.5270 (c), (d) and (e) added (effective date pending)	53909
Regulation at 70 FR 53909 confirmed in part	67901
615.5295 Added (effective date pending)	53909
Regulation at 70 FR 53909 confirmed	67901
615.5301 (b)(3), (i)(2) and (8) revised (effective date pending)	35356
Regulation at 70 FR 35356 confirmed	54471
615.5330 (a)(2) and (b)(3) amended (effective date pending)	35356
Regulation at 70 FR 35356 confirmed	54471
617.7010 (a) amended; (b) and (c) revised	18968
Regulation at 70 FR 18968 eff. 5-26-05	31323
620.1 (j) amended (effective date pending)	35357
Regulation at 70 FR 35357 confirmed	54471
620.5 (j)(2) revised (effective date pending)	53909
Regulation at 70 FR 53909 confirmed	67901
620.40 Redesignated as 655.1 (effective date pending)	40643
Regulation at 70 FR 40643 confirmed	58293
621.20 Redesignated as 655.50 (effective date pending)	40643
Regulation at 70 FR 40643 confirmed	58293
622 Authority citation revised	12584

12 CFR—Continued

Chapter VI—Continued

	70 FR Page
622.52 (a) and (b) revised; (c) added	12584
622.53 Removed	12585
622.54 Removed	12585
622.55 (a) revised	12585
622.57 (a) amended	12585
622.58 Amended	12585
622.59 (b) amended	12585
622.60 revised	12585
622.61 revised	12585
627 Authority citation revised	55515
627.2726 Added (effective date pending)	55515
Regulation at 70 FR 55515 confirmed	70035
627.2780 (b) amended (effective date pending)	55515
Regulation at 70 FR 55515 confirmed	70035
650 Heading revised (effective date pending)	40650
Regulation at 70 FR 40650 confirmed	58293
650.1 Redesignated as 651.1; new 650.1 redesignated from 650.50 (effective date pending)	40650
Regulation at 70 FR 40650 confirmed	58293
650.2 Redesignated as 651.2 (effective date pending)	40650
Regulation at 70 FR 40650 confirmed	58293
650.3 Redesignated as 651.3 (effective date pending)	40650
Regulation at 70 FR 40650 confirmed	58293
650.4 Redesignated as 651.4 (effective date pending)	40650
Regulation at 70 FR 40650 confirmed	58293
650.5 Redesignated from 650.51 (effective date pending)	40650
Regulation at 70 FR 40650 confirmed	58293
650.10 Redesignated from 650.52 (effective date pending)	40650
Regulation at 70 FR 40650 confirmed	58293
650.15 Redesignated from 650.55 (effective date pending)	40650
Regulation at 70 FR 40650 confirmed	58293
650.20 Redesignated as 652.50; new 650.20 redesignated from 650.56 (effective date pending)	40650

List of CFR Sections Affected

12 CFR—Continued

70 FR Page

Chapter VI—Continued
Regulation at 70 FR 40650 confirmed...58293
650.21 Redesignated as 652.55 (effective date pending) 40650
Regulation at 70 FR 40650 confirmed...58293
650.22 Redesignated as 652.60 (effective date pending) 40650
Regulation at 70 FR 40650 confirmed...58293
650.23 Redesignated as 652.65 (effective date pending) 40650
Regulation at 70 FR 40650 confirmed...58293
650.24 Redesignated as 652.70 (effective date pending) 40650
Regulation at 70 FR 40650 confirmed...58293
650.25 Redesignated as 652.75; new 650.25 redesignated from 650.57 (effective date pending) 40650
Regulation at 70 FR 40650 confirmed...58293
650.26 Redesignated as 652.80 (effective date pending) 40650
Regulation at 70 FR 40650 confirmed...58293
650.27 Redesignated as 652.85 (effective date pending) 40650
Regulation at 70 FR 40650 confirmed...58293
650.28 Redesignated as 652.90 (effective date pending) 40650
Regulation at 70 FR 40650 confirmed...58293
650.29 Redesignated as 652.95 (effective date pending) 40650
Regulation at 70 FR 40650 confirmed...58293
650.30 Redesignated as 652.100; new 650.30 redesignated from 650.58 (effective date pending) 40650
Regulation at 70 FR 40650 confirmed...58293
650.31 Redesignated as 652.105 (effective date pending) 40650
Regulation at 70 FR 40650 confirmed...58293
650.35 Redesignated from 650.59 (effective date pending) 40650
Regulation at 70 FR 40650 confirmed...58293
650.40 Redesignated from 650.60 (effective date pending) 40650

12 CFR—Continued

70 FR Page

Chapter VI—Continued
Regulation at 70 FR 40650 confirmed...58293
650.45 Redesignated from 650.61 (effective date pending) 40650
Regulation at 70 FR 40650 confirmed...58293
650.20—650.45 (Subpart B) Appendix A redesignated as 652.50—652.105 (Subpart B) Appendix A (effective date pending) 40650
Regulation at 70 FR 40650 confirmed...58293
650.50 Redesignated as 650.1; new 650.50 redesignated from 650.62 (effective date pending) 40650
Regulation at 70 FR 40650 confirmed...58293
650.51 Redesignated as 650.5 (effective date pending) 40650
Regulation at 70 FR 40650 confirmed...58293
650.52 Redesignated as 650.10 (effective date pending) 40650
Regulation at 70 FR 40650 confirmed...58293
650.55 Redesignated as 650.15; new 650.55 redesignated from 650.63 (effective date pending) 40650
Regulation at 70 FR 40650 confirmed...58293
650.56 Redesignated as 650.20 (effective date pending) 40650
Regulation at 70 FR 40650 confirmed...58293
650.57 Redesignated as 650.25 (effective date pending) 40650
Regulation at 70 FR 40650 confirmed...58293
650.58 Redesignated as 650.30 (effective date pending) 40650
Regulation at 70 FR 40650 confirmed...58293
650.59 Redesignated as 650.35 (effective date pending) 40650
Regulation at 70 FR 40650 confirmed...58293
650.60 Redesignated as 650.40; new 650.60 redesignated from 650.64 (effective date pending) 40650
Regulation at 70 FR 40650 confirmed...58293
650.61 Redesignated as 650.45 (effective date pending) 40650
Regulation at 70 FR 40650 confirmed...58293

12 CFR—Continued

70 FR Page

Chapter VI—Continued
650.62 Redesignated as 650.50 (effective date pending) 40650
  Regulation at 70 FR 40650 confirmed 58293
650.63 Redesignated as 650.55 (effective date pending) 40650
  Regulation at 70 FR 40650 confirmed 58293
650.64 Redesignated as 650.60 (effective date pending) 40650
  Regulation at 70 FR 40650 confirmed 58293
650.65 Redesignated as 650.65 (effective date pending) 40650
  Regulation at 70 FR 40650 confirmed 58293
650.66 Redesignated as 650.70 (effective date pending) 40650
  Regulation at 70 FR 40650 confirmed 58293
650.67 Redesignated as 650.75 (effective date pending) 40650
  Regulation at 70 FR 40650 confirmed 58293
650.68 Redesignated as 650.80 (effective date pending) 40650
  Regulation at 70 FR 40650 confirmed 58293
650.70 Redesignated from 650.66 (effective date pending) 40650
  Regulation at 70 FR 40650 confirmed 58293
650.75 Redesignated from 650.67 (effective date pending) 40650
  (c) amended (effective date pending) 40651
  Regulation at 70 FR 40650 and 40651 confirmed 58293
650.80 Redesignated from 650.68 (effective date pending) 40650
  Regulation at 70 FR 40650 confirmed 58293
651 Heading and authority citation added (effective date pending) ... 40644
  Regulation at 70 FR 40644 confirmed 58293
651.1 Redesignated from 650.1 (effective date pending) 40650
  Regulation at 70 FR 40650 confirmed 58293
651.2 Redesignated from 650.2 (effective date pending) 40650
  Regulation at 70 FR 40650 confirmed 58293

12 CFR—Continued

70 FR Page

Chapter VI—Continued
651.3 Redesignated from 650.3 (effective date pending) 40650
  Regulation at 70 FR 40650 confirmed 58293
651.4 Redesignated from 650.4 (effective date pending) 40650
  Regulation at 70 FR 40650 confirmed 58293
652 Added (effective date pending) 40644
  Regulation at 70 FR 40644 confirmed 58293
652.50 Redesignated from 650.20 (effective date pending) 40650
  Regulation at 70 FR 40650 confirmed 58293
652.55 Redesignated from 650.21 (effective date pending) 40650
  Regulation at 70 FR 40650 confirmed 58293
652.60 Redesignated from 650.22 (effective date pending) 40650
  Regulation at 70 FR 40650 confirmed 58293
652.65 Redesignated from 650.23 (effective date pending) 40650
  Regulation at 70 FR 40650 confirmed 58293
652.70 Redesignated from 650.24 (effective date pending) 40650
  Regulation at 70 FR 40650 confirmed 58293
652.75 Redesignated from 650.25 (effective date pending) 40650
  Regulation at 70 FR 40650 confirmed 58293
652.80 Redesignated from 650.26 (effective date pending) 40650
  Regulation at 70 FR 40650 confirmed 58293
652.85 Redesignated from 650.27 (effective date pending) 40650
  Regulation at 70 FR 40650 confirmed 58293
652.90 Redesignated from 650.28 (effective date pending) 40650
  Regulation at 70 FR 40650 confirmed 58293
652.95 Redesignated from 650.29 (effective date pending) 40650
  Regulation at 70 FR 40650 confirmed 58293
652.100 Redesignated from 650.30 (effective date pending) 40650
  Regulation at 70 FR 40650 confirmed 58293

List of CFR Sections Affected

12 CFR—Continued
70 FR Page

Chapter VI—Continued
652.105 Redesignated from 650.31 (effective date pending) 40650
    Regulation at 70 FR 40650 confirmed 58293
652.50—652.105 (Subpart B) Appendix A redesignated from 650.20—650.31 (Subpart B) Appendix A (effective date pending) 40650
    Regulation at 70 FR 40650 confirmed 58293
655 Heading and authority citation added (effective date pending) 40643
    Regulation at 70 FR 40643 confirmed 58293
655.1 Redesignated from 620.40 (effective date pending) 40643
    Regulation at 70 FR 40643 confirmed 58293
655.50 Redesignated from 621.20 (effective date pending) 40643
    Regulation at 70 FR 40643 confirmed 58293

Chapter VII
701.21 (c)(7)(ii)(C) revised 3863
    (e), (f) and (g)(1) revised 8923
703.19 (c) amended 55517
707.2 (b) revised; interim 72898
707.6 (b)(3) revised; interim 72898
707.8 (a) revised; (f) added; interim 72898
707.11 Added; interim 72898
707 Appendix C amended; interim 72899
708a.4 (a) amended; (e) added 4009
708a.5 (b) redesignated as (b)(1) and amended; (b)(2) added 4009
708a.11 Added 4010
708b Revised 3288
712.3 (d)(2) revised 55228
713.4 (a) revised 61716
713.5 (a) and (b) revised 61716
713.6 (a)(1) revised; (c) added 61716
717 Authority citation revised 33993, 70692
717.1—717.3 (Subpart A) Revised; interim; eff. 3-7-06 33993
    Regulation at 70 FR 33993 eff. date delayed to 4-1-06 70664
    Revised; eff. 4-1-06 70692
717.30—717.32 (Subpart D) Added; interim; eff. 3-7-06 33993
    Regulation at 70 FR 33993 eff. date delayed to 4-1-06 70664
    Added; eff. 4-1-06 70692

12 CFR—Continued
70 FR Page

Chapter VII—Continued
    Correctly revised 75931
722 Policy statement 59987
723.7 (c)(1) revised; eff. 1-20-06 75722
723.16 (a) revised; eff. 1-20-06 75722
723.20 (c) added; eff. 1-20-06............. 75722
723.21 Amended; eff. 1-20-06............ 75722
741 Authority citation revised 75725
741.8 Revised; eff. 1-20-06 75725
741.201 (b) revised 61716
748.0 (b) revised 22778
748 Appendix B added 22778
790.2 (b) table, (4) and (11) amended; (b)(5)(i) and (ii) redesignated as (b)(5) and (15) 55517
791.4 (b)(1) amended 55517
796 Added 72703

2006

12 CFR
71 FR Page

Chapter VI
600.1—600.4 (Subpart A) Regulation at 70 FR 69644 confirmed 8938
602.8 Regulation at 70 FR 6965 confirmed 8938
603.340 Regulation at 70 FR 69645 confirmed 8938
603.345 Correctly amended (eff. date pending) 54900
603.350 Correctly amended (eff. date pending) 54900
604.435 Regulation at 70 FR 69645 confirmed 8938
605.500 Amended (eff. date pending) 54900
605.501 (b) amended (eff. date pending) 54900
605.502 (b) and (c) revised; (d), (e) and (i) amended (eff. date pending) 54900
606.670 Regulation at 70 FR 69645 confirmed 8938
608.807 Correctly amended (eff. date pending) 54900
611 Authority citation revised 5761, 44420, 65386
    Regulation at 71 FR 5761 confirmed 18168
611.210—611.220 (Subpart B) Added 5761
611.210 (a)(2) added; eff. 2-2-07 5761
    Regulation at 71 FR 5761; eff. 4-5-07 18168
611.220 (a)(2)(i) and (ii) added; eff. 2-2-07 5761

1059

12 CFR—Continued

71 FR Page

Chapter VI—Continued
Regulation at 71 FR 5761; eff. 4-5-07 18168
611.320 (b) and (e) revised 5761
Regulation at 71 FR 5761 confirmed..18168
611.325 Added; eff. 2-2-07 5762
Regulation at 71 FR 5762 eff. 4-5-07 18168
611.1030 Removed 5762
Regulation at 71 FR 5762 confirmed..18168
611.1124 (n) correctly amended (eff. date pending).....................54901
611.1135 (b) revised (eff. date pending) 65386
611.1200—611.1290 (Subpart P) Revised (eff. date pending) 44420
611.1223 (d)(9) revised 5762
Regulation at 71 FR 5762 confirmed..18168
611.1250 (a)(3) and (b)(4) amended (eff. date pending).....................76118
611.1255 (a)(3) and (b)(4) amended (eff. date pending).....................76118
612.2130 (a) amended; (d) removed; (e) through (u) redesignated as (d) through (t); (e) revised 5762
Regulation at 71 FR 5762 confirmed..18168
612.2150 (d) revised 5762
Regulation at 71 FR 5762 confirmed..18168
612.2155 (a) introductory text revised 5763
Regulation at 71 FR 5763 confirmed..18168
(d) revised (eff. date pending)........65386
612.2165 Regulation at 70 FR 59307 confirmed...................................25919
612.5245 Regulation at 70 FR 59308 confirmed in part......................25919
612.5270 Regulation at 70 FR 59309 confirmed in part......................25919
613.3100 (b)(1)(iii)(B) and (d)(1) revised (eff. date pending) 65386
614.4010 (d)(1) and (2) revised (eff. date pending)............................65387
614.4020 (a)(1) and (2) amended (eff. date pending).....................65387
614.4265 (c) removed; (d) through (h) redesignated as (c) through (g) (eff. date pending) 65387
614.4355 (a)(8) revised; (a)(9) amended (eff. date pending) 65387
614.4511 Removed 5763

12 CFR—Continued

71 FR Page

Chapter VI—Continued
Regulation at 71 FR 5763 confirmed..18168
614.4710 Removed (eff. date pending) 65387
615.5200 (b)(1) revised 5763
Regulation at 71 FR 5763 confirmed..18168
615.5230 (a)(1) introductory text, (2) introductory text, (3) introductory text and (b)(5) revised 5763
Regulation at 71 FR 5763 confirmed..18168
615.5550 Revised (eff. date pending) 65387
618.8310 (b) revised 5763
Regulation at 71 FR 5763 confirmed..18168
618.8430 Introductory text revised; (d) added 5763
Regulation at 71 FR 5763 confirmed..18168
618.8440 (b) introductory text and (2) revised.....................................5764
Regulation at 71 FR 5764 confirmed..18168
619 Authority citation revised........5764, 76118
Regulation at 71 FR 5764 confirmed..18168
619.9235 Added 5764
Regulation at 71 FR 5764 confirmed..18168
619.9270 Added (eff. date pending) 76119
619.9310 Added 5764
Regulation at 71 FR 5764 confirmed..18168
620 Authority citation revised 76119
620.1 (p) removed; (q), (r) and (s) redesignated as new (p), (q) and (r); (a) revised 5764
Regulation at 71 FR 5764 confirmed..18168
620.2 (b) and (c) removed; new (b) added; (d) through (j) redesignated as (c) through (i); (a) and new (c) revised (eff. date pending) 76119
620.3 Revised (eff. date pending) 76119
620.4 (a) amended (eff. date pending) 76119
620.5 (h)(3), (i)(1), (2) introductory text, (i) and (iii) revised; (m)(3) added 5764

List of CFR Sections Affected

12 CFR—Continued

71 FR Page

Chapter VI—Continued
Regulation at 71 FR 5764 confirmed...... 18168
Introductory text, (a) introductory text, (b), (c)(1), (f) introductory text, (g)(1)(iii)(A), (iv)(B), (E) and (m)(1) amended; (l) revised; (m)(2) removed; (m)(3) redesignated as (m)(2) (eff. date pending) 76119
620.10 (a) amended (eff. date pending) 76120
620.11 (d)(5) added; (d) introductory text and (e) revised...... 5765
Regulation at 71 FR 5765 confirmed...... 18168
620.20—620.21 (Subpart E) Heading revised 5765
Regulation at 71 FR 5765 confirmed...... 18168
620.20 Removed 5765
Regulation at 71 FR 5765 confirmed...... 18168
620.21 Introductory text, (c)(2) and (d) revised; eff. in part 2-2-07 5765
Regulation at 71 FR 5765 eff. in part 4-5-07 18168
620.30—620.31 (Subpart F) Revised 5766
Regulation at 71 FR 5766 confirmed...... 18168
620.30 (d)(2) revised (eff. date pending)...... 76120
621 Authority citation revised 76120
621.2 (i) removed; (j) redesignated as (i) (eff. date pending) 76120
621.4 (b) revised (eff. date pending) 76120
621.30—621.32 (Subpart E) Added (eff. date pending) 76120
624 Removed (eff. date pending) 76120
627.2785 (b) and (d) revised (eff. date pending)...... 76121
630.2 (c) revised (eff. date pending) 76121
630.3 (a), (f) and (h) revised (eff. date pending)...... 76121
630.4 (b) removed; (c) and (d) redesignated as (b) and (c); (a)(4), new (b)(4), (5) and (c) revised (eff. date pending) 76121
630.5 Revised (eff. date pending) 76121
630.6 Revised 5767

12 CFR—Continued

71 FR Page

Chapter VI—Continued
Regulation at 71 FR 5767 confirmed...... 18168
(a)(4)(ii) revised (eff. date pending)...... 76122
630.20 (h) heading, (2) and (l) introductory text revised 5767
Regulation at 71 FR 5767 confirmed...... 18168
(b)(3) and (m)(2)(iii) removed; (m)(2)(iv), (v) and (vi) redesignated as (m)(2)(iii), (iv) and (v); introductory text, (f) introductory text, (h)(1), (i), (k) and (l) introductory text revised (eff. date pending) 76122
630.40 (d) introductory text revised 5768
Regulation at 71 FR 5768 confirmed...... 18168
652.50—652.100 (Subpart B) Revised (eff. date pending) 77253
655.50 (c) amended (eff. date pending) 77262

Chapter VII
Chapter VII Policy statement 24551
701 Authority citation revised 42251, 62876
701.1 Revised 36670
701.21 (h) added 36666
(c)(7)(i) and (ii) revised 42251
(c)(4) and (f) amended; interim 62876
701.30 Added; interim 62876
701.34 Heading, (b), (c) and Appendix revised; (d) added 4238
703.1 (b)(2) revised; eff. 1-19-07 76124
703.2 Amended; eff. 1-19-07...... 76124
703.14 (h) added; eff. 1-19-07...... 76124
707.2 Regulation at 70 FR 72898 confirmed...... 24571
707.6 Regulation at 70 FR 72898 confirmed...... 24571
707.8 Regulation at 70 FR 72898 confirmed...... 24571
707.11 Regulation at 70 FR 72898 confirmed...... 24571
707 Regulation at 70 FR 72899 confirmed 24571
708a Revised; eff. 1-22-07...... 77167
740.4 (b) introductory text amended; (b)(2) revised; (f) added...... 67438
740.5 (c)(11) amended 67439
741.203 (c) added 36667
741.204 (c) amended; (d) added 4240
741.6 (a) revised 4034

1061

12 CFR—Continued

Chapter VII—Continued

	71 FR Page
742 Revised	4039
745 Authority citation revised	67440
745.1 (e) added; interim	14635
Regulation at 71 FR 14635 confirmed	56004
745.2 (d)(2) amended; interim	14635
Regulation at 71 FR 14635 confirmed	56004
745.3 (a), (2) and (b) amended; interim	14635
Regulation at 71 FR 14635 confirmed	56004
745.4 (b), (c), (e) and (f) amended; interim	14635
Regulation at 71 FR 14635 confirmed	56004
745.5 Amended; interim	14635
Regulation at 71 FR 14635 confirmed	56004
745.6 Amended; interim	14635
Regulation at 71 FR 14635 confirmed	56004
745.7 Added; interim	14635
Regulation at 71 FR 14635 confirmed	56004
745.8 Amended; interim	14636
Regulation at 71 FR 14636 confirmed	56004
745.9-1 Amended; interim	14636
Regulation at 71 FR 14636 confirmed	56004
745.9-2 Revised; interim	14636
Regulation at 71 FR 14636 confirmed	56004
745.9-3 Removed; interim	14636
Regulation at 71 FR 14636 confirmed	56004
745.10 Heading revised; text amended; interim	14636
Regulation at 71 FR 14636 confirmed	56004
745.203 (c) amended; interim	67440
745 Appendix amended; interim	14636
Regulation at 71 FR 14636 confirmed; Appendix amended	56004
747 Authority citation revised	67440
747.1 (c)(3) amended; interim	67440
747.202 (c) amended; interim	67440
747.303 Revised; interim	67440
747.304 Revised; interim	67441
748 Heading revised	62878
748.1 (c) revised	62878

2007

12 CFR

	72 FR Page
Chapter VI	
603.345 Regulation at 71 FR 54900 confirmed	3925
603.350 Regulation at 71 FR 54900 confirmed	3925
605.500 Regulation at 71 FR 54900 confirmed	3925
605.501 Regulation at 71 FR 54900 confirmed	3925
605.502 Regulation at 71 FR 54900 confirmed	3925
608.807 Regulation at 71 FR 54900 confirmed	3925
611 Regulation at 71 FR 44420 confirmed	1276
Regulation at 71 FR 65386 confirmed	5606
611.210 Regulation at 71 FR 18168 confirmed	16699
611.220 Regulation at 71 FR 18168 confirmed	16699
611.325 Regulation at 71 FR 18168 confirmed	16699
611.1124 Regulation at 71 FR 54901 confirmed	3925
611.1135 Regulation at 71 FR 65386 confirmed	5606
611.1200—611.1290 (Subpart P) Regulation at 71 FR 44420 confirmed	1276
611.1250 Regulation at 71 FR 76118 confirmed	7927
611.1255 Regulation at 71 FR 76118 confirmed	7927
612.2155 Regulation at 71 FR 65386 confirmed	5606
613.3100 Regulation at 71 FR 65386 confirmed	5606
614.4010 Regulation at 71 FR 65387 confirmed	5606
614.4020 Regulation at 71 FR 65387 confirmed	5606
614.4265 Regulation at 71 FR 65387 confirmed	5606
614.4355 Regulation at 71 FR 65387 confirmed	5606
614.4710 Regulation at 71 FR 65387 confirmed	5606
615.5550 Regulation at 71 FR 65387 confirmed	5606
619 Regulation at 71 FR 76118 confirmed	7927
619.9270 Regulation at 71 FR 76119 confirmed	7927

List of CFR Sections Affected

12 CFR—Continued

72 FR Page

Chapter VI—Continued
620 Regulation at 71 FR 76119 confirmed 7927
620.2 Regulation at 71 FR 76119 confirmed 7927
620.3 Regulation at 71 FR 76119 confirmed 7927
620.4 Regulation at 71 FR 76119 confirmed 7927
(a) revised; eff. date pending 68061
620.5 (i)(2)(i)(E) and (F) correctly added 4414
Regulation at 71 FR 76119 confirmed 7927
620.21 Regulation at 71 FR 18168 confirmed in part 16699
620.30 Regulation at 71 FR 76120 confirmed 7927
621 Regulation at 71 FR 76120 confirmed 7927
621.2 Regulation at 71 FR 76120 confirmed 7927
621.4 Regulation at 71 FR 76120 confirmed 7927
621.30—621.32 (Subpart E) Regulation at 71 FR 76120 confirmed 7927
624 Regulation at 71 FR 76120 confirmed 7927
627.2745 (i) added; eff. date pending 54527
Regulation at 72 FR 54527 confirmed 65655
627.2750 (j) added; eff. date pending 54527
(h) revised; eff. date pending 54529
Regulations at 72 FR 54527 and 54529 confirmed 65655
627.2752 (h) added; eff. date pending 54527
Regulation at 72 FR 54527 confirmed 65655
627.2755 (a) amended; eff. date pending 54529
Regulation at 72 FR 54529 confirmed 65655
627.2785 Regulation at 71 FR 76121 confirmed 7927
630.2 Regulation at 71 FR 76121 confirmed 7927
630.3 Regulation at 71 FR 76121 confirmed 7927
630.4 Regulation at 71 FR 76121 confirmed 7927
630.5 Regulation at 71 FR 76121 confirmed 7927

12 CFR—Continued

72 FR Page

Chapter VI—Continued
(d)(2) revised (eff. date pending) 64130
630.6 Regulation at 71 FR 76122 confirmed 7927
630.20 Regulation at 71 FR 76122 confirmed 7927
652.50—652.100 (Subpart B) Regulation at 71 FR 77253 confirmed 15812
655.50 Regulation at 71 FR 77262 confirmed 15812

Chapter VII
701 Authority citation revised 61500
701.2 Added 61500
701.3 Added 56253
701.21 (g)(6)(ii) amended 7928
(a) and (i)(1) introductory text amended 30246
701.23 (g) added 65442
701.33 (b)(2)(ii) amended; (c)(4) added... 30246
701.38 (b) added 30246
701 Appendix A added 61500
703.4 Amended 30246
707 Appendices B and C amended 30246
710.3 (a) introductory text amended 30246
711.3 (b) amended 58249
717 Authority citation revised 62981, 63768
717.1 Revised 62981
717.3 Introductory text revised 63768
717.20—717.28 (Subpart C) Added 62981
717.80—717.83 (Subpart I) Heading revised 63768
717.82 Added 63768
717.90—717.91 (Subpart J) Added 63768
717 Appendix C added 62989
Appendix J added 63769
722.3 (d) amended 30247
723.7 (a) introductory text amended 30247
742.4 (a)(3) amended 30247
745 Regulation at 71 FR 67440 confirmed 10595
745.203 Regulation at 71 FR 67440 confirmed 10595
747 Regulation at 71 FR 67440 confirmed 10595
747.1 Regulation at 71 FR 67440 confirmed 10595
747.202 Regulation at 71 FR 67440 confirmed 10595

1063

12 CFR—Continued

72 FR Page

Chapter VII—Continued
- 747.303 Regulation at 71 FR 67440 confirmed 10595
- 747.304 Regulation at 71 FR 67441 confirmed 10595
- 748.1 (b) amended 42273
- 749 Heading revised 42273
- 749.0 Revised 42273
- 749.1 Revised 42273
- 749.2 Revised 42273
- 749.3 Revised 42273
- 749.4 Revised 42273
- 749.5 Revised 42273
- 749 Appendix B added 42274

2008

12 CFR

73 FR Page

Chapter VI
- 613.3000 (a)(3) added (eff. date pending) 30475
  - Regulation at 73 FR 30475 confirmed 42517
- 613.3010 (a) revised; (c) and (d) added (eff. date pending) 30475
  - Regulation at 73 FR 30475 confirmed 42517
- 620.4 Regulation at 72 FR 68061 confirmed 8008
- 630.5 Regulation at 72 FR 64130 confirmed 7461
- 652.65 (b)(5) redesignated as (b)(6); new (b)(5) added (eff. date pending) 31940
  - Regulation at 73 FR 31940 confirmed 44137
- 652.85 (d) revised (eff. date pending) 31940
  - Regulation at 73 FR 31940 confirmed 44137
- 652.50—652.100 (Subpart B) Appendix A amended (eff. date pending) 31940
  - Regulation at 73 FR 31940 confirmed 44137

Chapter VII
- 700.2 Amended 30477
- 701.1 Revised; eff. 1–2–09 73398
- 701.34 (a) revised 71912
- 701 Appendix B added; eff. 1–2–09 73398
- 702.2 (f) revised 72691
- 704.2 Amended 72692
- 704.8 (a)(4) amended 30477
- 705.3 (a) revised 71913

12 CFR—Continued

73 FR Page

Chapter VII—Continued
- 705.5 (b)(1) introductory text amended 30477
- 707.8 (c)(5) revised 30477
- 708b.105 (b) amended 30477
- 708b.203 (e)(1) amended 30477
- 708b.301 (c) and (d)(5) amended 30477
- 708b.302 (c) and (d)(5) amended 30477
- 708b.303 (b) and (c)(5) amended 30477
- 711.2 (j) amended 30477
- 712.1 Amended; eff. 1–28–09 79311
- 712.2 (d)(3) added; eff. 1–28–09 79312
- 712.3 (b) amended; (d)(3) revised; eff. 1–28–09 79312
- 712.5 (a)(2), (3), (b)(9), (10), (c), (d), (f)(5), (6), (h)(2), (3), (j)(2), (3) and (n) amended; (a)(4), (b)(11), (f)(7), (h)(4), (j)(4), (5), (6), (s) and (t) added 79312
- 712.7 Removed 79312
- 712.10 Added 79312
- 713.4 (a) amended 30478
- 716.3 (b)(2)(iii) and (e)(2)(iii) amended 30478
- 721.3 (b) and (j) amended; (f) revised 62856
- 723.21 Amended 30478
- 740 Authority citation revised 56936
- 740.4 (b)(1) amended; interim 62858
- 740.5 (b) revised 56936
- 741.222 Added 79313
- 745.1 (e) revised; interim 62858
- 745.3 (a)(3) revised; interim 62858
- 745.4 Revised; interim 60620
- 745 Appendix amended 60622
- 760.7 Amended 30478
- 792.03 Introductory text and (c) amended 56937
- 792.04 (a) revised 56937
- 792.07 (a) amended; (b) revised 56937
- 792.08 Introductory text and (a) revised 56937
- 792.10 (b) amended 30478
  - (a), (b) and (e) amended 56937
- 792.11 (a)(6) introductory text amended 56937
- 792.15 (a) revised 56938
- 792.16 (a) amended 30478
- 792.17 Revised 56938
- 792.18 (b) amended 56938
- 792.19 (c)(1) revised 56938
- 792.27 (a)(1) through (4) revised 56938
- 792.28 Amended 30478
  - (a) amended; (c) revised 56938
- 792.50 (a) amended 30478
- 792.51 (b) amended 30478
- 792.52—792.69 (Subpart E) Nomenclature change 56938

List of CFR Sections Affected

12 CFR—Continued
73 FR Page

Chapter VII—Continued
792.53 (g), (h) and (i) added 56938
792.54 Revised 56938
792.55 (a)(1), (2), (3) and (c) revised 56939
792.57 (b) revised 56939
792.58 (a) revised; (b) amended 56939
792.59 (a) and (c) amended 56939
792.60 (j) revised 56939
792.61 (a) amended 56939
792.63 (a), (b)(1) and (4) revised 56939
792.66 (a) and (b)(2) revised; (b)(3) and (4) amended 56940
792.69 (a) revised 56940
797 Added 11341

2009

12 CFR
74 FR Page

Chapter VI
604.425 Revised (eff. date pending) 44727
  Regulation at 74 FR 44727 confirmed 55112
617.7130 (b) introductory text, (4) and (5) revised; (b)(6) added (eff. date pending) 67972
617.7135 (a)(2) revised; (b) redesignated as (c); new (b) added (eff. date pending) 67972
619 Authority citation revised 28599
  Regulation at 74 FR 28599 confirmed 40060
619.9270 (e) amended (eff. date pending) 28599
  Regulation at 74 FR 28599 confirmed 40060
620 Authority citation revised 28599
  Regulation at 74 FR 28599 confirmed 40060
620.3 (b)(3) revised (eff. date pending) 28599
  Regulation at 74 FR 28599 confirmed 40060
620.5 (a)(4), (10) introductory text, (g)(3)(i)(A), (h)(1) and (i)(1) introductory text revised; (a)(10)(iii), (iv), (e)(2), (f) heading, introductory text, (1)(iii) heading, (g) heading, introductory text, (1)(iv), (2)(ii), (vi), (j)(3)(ii), (l)(2) and (m)(1) amended; (a)(10)(v), (e)(4) and (f)(2) removed; (f)(3) and (4) redesignated as new (f)(2) and (3) (eff. date pending) 28599

12 CFR—Continued
74 FR Page

Chapter VI—Continued
  Regulation at 74 FR 28599 confirmed 40060
620.10 (a) revised (eff. date pending) 28600
  Regulation at 74 FR 28600 confirmed 40060
620.11 (b)(4) through (7) removed; (b)(8) redesignated as new (b)(4); (e) amended (eff. date pending) 28600
  Regulation at 74 FR 28600 confirmed 40060
620.21 Heading and (f) revised (eff. date pending) 28600
  Regulation at 74 FR 28600 confirmed 40060
621.2 (d) revised (eff. date pending) 28600
  Regulation at 74 FR 28600 confirmed 40060
621.5 (a) revised (eff. date pending) 28600
  Regulation at 74 FR 28600 confirmed 40060
621.12 (c) revised (eff. date pending) 28600
  Regulation at 74 FR 28600 confirmed 40060
622.61 Revised 2341

Chapter VII
701.6 (a) amended 29936
701.21 (f)(3) added; interim 29934
  Regulation at 74 FR 29934 confirmed 68370
701.36 (d) introductory text amended 13083
706 Revised; eff. 7-1-10 5575
707.1 (a) revised 36103
707.3 (a) revised; (g) removed 36104
707.4 (a)(1) and (2)(i) revised 36104
707.10 Removed 36104
707.11 Heading, (a), (b)(2)(x) and (xi) revised; (b)(2)(xii) and (c) added 36104
707 Appendix B amended 36104
707 Appendix C amended 36105
716.2 Revised 62955
716.6 Heading and (b) revised; (f) and (g) added; (g) removed eff. 1-1-12 62955
716.7 (i) added 62956
716 Appendix A redesignated as Appendix B; new Appendix A added 62956
  Appendix B amended; Appendix B removed eff. 1-1-12 62965

1065

12 CFR—Continued

74 FR Page

Chapter VII—Continued
717 Authority citation revised 31522
717.40—717.43 (Subpart E) Added eff. 7-1-10 31522
717.82 (a), (b), (c)(2)(i)(A), (d)(1) and (3) amended 22644
717.91 Heading revised 22644
717 Appendices C and J amended 22644
Appendix E added eff. 7-1-10 31524
740.1 (b) revised; (c) added 9348
740.4 (c) revised 9349
(b)(1) amended 55749
741.4 Revised; eff. 1-4-10 63279
741.6 (a) revised; (d) removed 35769
741 Appendix A added; eff. 1-4-10 63281
742.4 (a)(3) amended 13083
745.1 (e) revised 55749
745.3 (a)(3) revised 55749
745.4 Revised 55749
745.8 (b), (c) and (d) redesignated as (c), (d) and (e); new (b) added 55751
745 Appendix revised 55751
747.1001 (Subpart K) Revised 9351
748.1 (a) revised 35769
749 Appendix A amended 35769

2010

12 CFR

75 FR Page

Chapter VI
604.420 (i)(1) revised (eff. date pending) 35967
Regulation at 75 FR 35967 confirmed 59060
607.2 (j) amended (eff. date pending) 35968
Regulation at 75 FR 35968 confirmed 59060
610 Added 44700
Technical correction 51623
611 Authority citation revised 18740
Regulation at 75 FR 18740 confirmed 30687
611.100—611.110 (Subpart A) Added (eff. date pending) 18740
Regulation at 75 FR 18740 confirmed 30687
611.310 (b) revised; (e) and (f) added (eff. date pending) 18740
Regulation at 75 FR 18740 confirmed 30687
611.320 (a) and (d) amended; (c) and (e) revised; (f) added (eff. date pending) 18740

12 CFR—Continued

75 FR Page

Chapter VI—Continued
Regulation at 75 FR 18740 confirmed 30687
611.325 Revised (eff. date pending) 18741
Regulation at 75 FR 18741 confirmed 30687
611.326 Added (eff. date pending) 18741
Regulation at 75 FR 18741 confirmed 30687
611.330 Revised (eff. date pending) 18742
Regulation at 75 FR 18742 confirmed 30687
611.340 Revised (eff. date pending) 18742
Regulation at 75 FR 18742 confirmed 30687
611.350 Revised (eff. date pending) 18742
Regulation at 75 FR 18742 confirmed 30687
611.1210 (f) amended (eff. date pending) 18743
Regulation at 75 FR 18743 confirmed 30687
611.1240 (e) revised (eff. date pending) 18743
Regulation at 75 FR 18743 confirmed 30687
612.2300 (a) amended (eff. date pending) 35968
Regulation at 75 FR 35968 confirmed 59060
613.3300 (c)(1)(i)(B) amended (eff. date pending) 18743
Regulation at 75 FR 18743 confirmed 30687
614.4170 Redesignated from 614.4510 (eff. date pending) 35968
Regulation at 75 FR 35968 confirmed 59060
614.4175 Redesignated from 614.4513 (eff. date pending) 35968
Regulation at 75 FR 35968 confirmed 59060
614.4265 (d) amended (eff. date pending) 35968
Regulation at 75 FR 35968 confirmed 59060
614.4341 Removed 35968
Regulation at 75 FR 35968 confirmed 59060
614.4510—614.4513 (Subpart N) Removed (eff. date pending) 35968

List of CFR Sections Affected

12 CFR—Continued

75 FR Page

Chapter VI—Continued
Regulation at 75 FR 35968 confirmed 59060
614.4510 Redesignated as 614.4170 (eff. date pending) 35968
Regulation at 75 FR 35968 confirmed 59060
614.4512 Removed (eff. date pending) 35968
Regulation at 75 FR 35968 confirmed 59060
614.4513 Redesignated as 614.4175 (eff. date pending) 35968
Regulation at 75 FR 35968 confirmed 59060
615 Authority citation revised 18743
Regulation at 75 FR 18743 confirmed 30687
615.5030 (a) designation and (b) removed (eff. date pending) 35968
Regulation at 75 FR 35968 confirmed 59060
615.5230 (b) redesignated as (c); new (b) added; (a) and new (c)(1) revised; new (c)(5) removed (eff. date pending) 18743
Regulation at 75 FR 18743 confirmed 30687
615.5330 (a)(1) and (b)(1) amended (eff. date pending) 18744
Regulation at 75 FR 18744 confirmed 30687
615.5560 (Subpart R) Removed (eff. date pending) 35968
Regulation at 75 FR 35968 confirmed 59060
617.7130 Regulation at 74 FR 67972 confirmed 10411
617.7135 Regulation at 74 FR 67972 confirmed 10411
618.8320 (b)(4) amended (eff. date pending) 35968
Regulation at 75 FR 35968 confirmed 59060
619.9320 Added (eff. date pending) 18744
Regulation at 75 FR 18744 confirmed 30687
620 Authority citation revised 18744
Regulation at 75 FR 18744 confirmed 30687
620.1 (p) removed; (q) and (r) redesignated as new (p) and (q) (eff. date pending) 18744
Regulation at 75 FR 18744 confirmed 30687

12 CFR—Continued

75 FR Page

Chapter VI—Continued
620.5 (i)(2) introductory text amended (eff. date pending) 18744
Regulation at 75 FR 18744 confirmed 30687
620.20—620.21 (Subpart E) Heading revised (eff. date pending) 18744
Regulation at 75 FR 18744 confirmed 30687
620.20 Added (eff. date pending) 18744
Regulation at 75 FR 18744 confirmed 30687
620.21 Revised (eff. date pending) 18744
Regulation at 75 FR 18744 confirmed 30687
627.2705 (b) revised (eff. date pending) 35968
Regulation at 75 FR 35968 confirmed 59060
627.2735 (a) amended (eff. date pending) 35968
Regulation at 75 FR 35968 confirmed 59060
Chapter VII
701.1 Revised 36263
701.4 Added; eff. 1–27–11 81385
701.14 (b)(3)(i)(A), (B) and (C) amended 34620
701.21 (b)(1) introductory text, (c)(5), (8)(ii), (iii)(D), (d)(4) introductory text and (5)(iii) amended 34620
(c)(7)(iii) added 58289
701.33 (c)(5), (6) and (7) added; eff. 1–27–11 81386
701.34 (b)(7) introductory text amended; (b)(7)(i), (ii) and (d)(4) added; interim 7342
(a)(2) and (3) amended; interim 47172
(b)(7) and (c)(2) introductory text revised; (c)(2)(i) and (ii) introductory text added 57843
Regulation at 75 FR 47172 confirmed 80678
701.36 (d) introductory text and (1) revised 66297
701 Appendix A amended 34620
Appendix B amended 36263, 36265
Appendix A amended; eff. 1–27–11 81386
702.2 Heading and (g) amended 34620
702.103 Introductory text amended 34620

1067

12 CFR—Continued

75 FR Page

Chapter VII—Continued
702.104 (d) revised; interim 66300
702.105 (d) revised; eff. 10-20-11 64826
702.204 (b)(3) amended 34620
702.205 (a)(1) amended 34620
703.14 (b) revised; eff. 10-20-11 64826
704 Authority citation revised 64826
704.2 Revised; eff. 1-18-11 64826
    Revised; eff. 10-20-11 64829
    Amended; interim; eff. 1-18-11 71528
    Amended; interim; eff. 10-20-11
    71528
704.3 Revised; eff. 10-20-11 64833
704.4 Redesignated as 704.13 eff. 1-18-11; new 704.4 added eff. 10-20-11 64836
704.5 (d)(4) and (e) introductory text amended 34620
    Revised; eff. 1-18-11 64840
704.6 Revised; eff. 1-18-11 64841
    (b) revised; interim; eff. 1-18-11
    71528
704.7 (c) heading and (d) heading amended 34621
704.8 Revised; eff. 1-18-11 64842
704.9 Revised; eff. 1-18-11 64843
704.11 Revised; eff. 1-18-11 64843
704.13 Redesignated from 704.4; eff. 1-18-11 64836
704.14 (a) revised; eff. 1-18-11 64844
704.19 Revised; eff. 1-18-11 64844
704.20 Added; eff. 1-18-11 64845
704 Appendix A revised; eff. 1-18-11 64848
    Appendix B revised; eff. 1-18-11
    64851
    Appendix C added; eff. 1-18-11 64852
    Appendix A amended; interim; eff. 1-18-11 71528
706 Revised 6559
707.6 (b)(5) added; interim 47175
707.11 (a)(1)(i) revised; interim 47175
707 Appendices B and C amended; interim 47175
708a Authority citation revised 81386
    Heading revised; eff. 1-27-11 81386
708a.1 Amended; interim 80680
    Redesignated as 708a.101; eff. 1-27-11 81386
708a.2 Redesignated as 708a.102; eff. 1-27-11 81386
708a.3 Redesignated as 708a.103; eff. 1-27-11 81386
708a.4 Second (b)(4)(ii) redesignated as (b)(4)(iii) 34621

12 CFR—Continued

75 FR Page

Chapter VII—Continued
    Redesignated as 708a.104; eff. 1-27-11 81386
708a.5 Redesignated as 708a.105; eff. 1-27-11 81386
708a.6 Redesignated as 708a.106; eff. 1-27-11 81386
708a.7 Redesignated as 708a.107; eff. 1-27-11 81386
708a.8 Redesignated as 708a.108; eff. 1-27-11 81386
708a.9 Redesignated as 708a.109; eff. 1-27-11 81386
708a.10 Redesignated as 708a.110; eff. 1-27-11 81386
708a.11 Redesignated as 708a.111; eff. 1-27-11 81386
708a.12 Redesignated as 708a.112; eff. 1-27-11 81386
708a.13 Redesignated as 708a.113; eff. 1-27-11 81386
708a.101—708a.113 (Subpart A) Added; eff. 1-27-11 81386
708a.101 Redesignated from 708a.1; amended; eff. 1-27-11 81386
708a.102 Redesignated from 708a.2; eff. 1-27-11 81386
708a.103 Redesignated from 708a.3; eff. 1-27-11 81386
708a.104 Redesignated from 708a.4; eff. 1-27-11 81386
    (b)(4)(i) and (f)(2) amended; (c)(4) and (5) revised; (c)(6), (7) and (8) added; eff. 1-27-11 81387
708a.105 Redesignated from 708a.5; eff. 1-27-11 81386
708a.106 Redesignated from 708a.6; eff. 1-27-11 81386
708a.107 Redesignated from 708a.7; eff. 1-27-11 81386
    (a) revised; (c) added; eff. 1-27-11
    81387
708a.108 Redesignated from 708a.8; eff. 1-27-11 81386
708a.109 Redesignated from 708a.9; eff. 1-27-11 81386
708a.110 Redesignated from 708a.10; eff. 1-27-11 81386
708a.111 Redesignated from 708a.11; eff. 1-27-11 81386
708a.112 Redesignated from 708a.12; eff. 1-27-11 81386
708a.113 Redesignated from 708a.13; eff. 1-27-11 81386
    (e) added; eff. 1-27-11 81387
708a.301—708a.312 (Subpart C) Added; eff. 1-27-11 81387

List of CFR Sections Affected

12 CFR—Continued
75 FR Page

Chapter VII—Continued
708b.2 (h) through (k) redesignated as (i) through (l); new (h) added; interim 80680
   (a) through (k) designations removed; amended; eff. 1-27-11 81393
708b.103 (a)(5) revised; (a)(7) through (10) redesignated as (a)(8) through (11); NEW (a)(7) added; eff. 1-27-11 81394
708b.104 (a)(8) revised; eff. 1-27-11 81394
708b.106 (a)(2)(ii) revised; eff. 1-27-11 81394
708b.107 Heading amended; eff. 1-27-11 81394
708b.201 (c) revised; eff. 1-27-11 81394
708b.203 (d), (f) and (f) revised; eff. 1-27-11 81394
708b.206 (b) revised; eff. 1-27-11 81394
708b.302 Heading, (b) and (c) amended... 34621
709.4 (a) amended 34621
709.5 (b)(7) and (9) revised; eff. 1-18-11 64859
709.9 (f) introductory text amended 34621
711.2 (e) amended 34621
712.5 (c) amended 34621
715.5 (b) amended 34621
716.4 (f)(1) amended 34621
716.6 (e) heading amended 34621
717.3 (l) amended 34621
717.20 Heading amended................ 34621
717.25 (b)(1)(v) amended 34621
717.27 (c)(2) amended...................... 34621
721.3 (f) amended............................. 34621
722.2 (f)(2) amended......................... 34622
723.7 (b) amended 66298
740.4 (b) introductory text and (1) amended...................................... 53843
741 Technical correction............... 51623
741.8 (c) amended 34622
741.223 Added 44704
742.4 Heading amended 34622
   (a)(3) amended; (a)(4), (5) and (6) removed; (a)(7), (8) and (9) redesignated as new (a)(4), (5) and (6) 66298
745.1 (e) revised 53843
745.9-2 (a) amended 34622
745 Appendix amended 34622
747.7 (a) amended 34622
747.10 (c)(3) amended 34622
747.31 (a) amended 34622
747.39 (b)(2) amended 34622
747.40 (a) amended 34622

12 CFR—Continued
75 FR Page

Chapter VII—Continued
747.203 (a) amended 34622
747.207 Amended 34622
747.302 (a)(1) amended 34622
747.306 (a) and (b) amended 34622
747.602 (e) amended 34622
747.605 (c)(3) amended 34622
747.606 (a)(3)(ii) amended 34622
747.607 (a) amended 34622
747.611 Amended 34622
747.616 Amended 34622
747.803 (b)(1)(i) and (iv) amended 34622
747.901—747.905 (Subpart J) Heading revised 34623
747.902 Amended 34623
747.2003 (b)(4)(iii) amended............ 34623
747.3001—747.3006 (Subpart M) Added; eff. 10-20-11 64860
761 Added 44704
   Technical correction 51623
790.2 (b)(6), (13) and (c) amended; (b)(16) and (17) added 34623
791.4 (b)(1) amended 34623
791.5 (b)(2)(i) amended.................... 34623
791.8 (f) added.................................. 34623
791.12 (a)(1)(i) amended 34623
792.66 (b)(1) and (3) amended 34623
793.4 (b) introductory text added; (d) amended 34623
795 Removed................................... 34623

2011

12 CFR
76 FR Page

Chapter VI
Policy statement 54638
614.4070 (d) added (eff. date pending) 30250
   Regulation at 76 FR 30250 eff. date confirmed.......................... 42470
614.4325 (b) revised (eff. date pending) 30250
   Regulation at 76 FR 30250 eff. date confirmed.......................... 42470
614.4352 (a), (b)(1) and (2) amended; eff. 7-1-12 29997
614.4353 Amended; eff. 7-1-12 29997
614.4354 Removed; eff. 7-1-12.......... 29997
614.4356 Amended; eff. 7-1-12 29997
614.4362 Added; eff. 7-1-12 29997
651.1 (b) amended (eff. date pending) 23467
   Regulation at 76 FR 23467 eff. date confirmed..........................35966
652.5 Amended (eff. date pending) 23467

1069

12 CFR—Continued

76 FR Page

Chapter VI—Continued
Regulation at 76 FR 23467 eff. date confirmed............................35966
652.50 Amended (eff. date pending)..................................23467
Regulation at 76 FR 23467 eff. date confirmed............................35966
652.65 (b)(5) and (6) redesignated as (b)(6) and (7); new (b)(5) added; new (b)(6) and (d)(2) revised (eff. date pending)............23467
Regulation at 76 FR 23467 eff. date confirmed............................35966
652.50—652.100 (Subpart B) Appendix A amended (eff. date pending)..................................23468
Regulation at 76 FR 23468 eff. date confirmed............................35966

Chapter VII
Policy statement............................23871
700.2 Amended...............................60366
701.21 (h)(4)(iv) revised..................60366
701.30 (a) and (b) amended; interim..44763
Regulation at 76 FR 44763 confirmed.......................................73994
701.32 (c) amended...........................67587
701.34 (a)(3) amended......................36979
Amended...80227
702 Policy statement.....................16234
702.2 (f)(3) revised; (f)(4) added.......60367
704 Policy statement.....................10209
704.2 Regulation at 75 FR 71528 confirmed...................................16236
Amended...23867
Amended; eff. 1–23–12...................79533
704.6 Regulation at 75 FR 71528 confirmed...................................16236
(c)(3) and (f)(4) removed; (h) added; eff. 1–23–12........................79533
704.8 (f) and (g) amended; (j)(2)(ii) and (iii) revised; eff. 1–23–12.......79533
704.11 (g)(5) and (6) revised; (g)(7) added..23868
704.13 (c)(6) and (7) revised; (c)(8) added..23868
704.15 Revised................................23868
704.18 (e)(1) table revised; eff. 1–23–12..79533
704.19 (a) introductory text revised...23871

12 CFR—Continued

76 FR Page

Chapter VII—Continued
Heading revised; eff. 1–23–12..........79534
704.20 Removed.............................30517
704.21 Added; eff. 4–29–13................23871
704.22 Added..................................23871
704 Regulation at 75 FR 71528 confirmed...................................16236
Appendix A amended; eff. 1–23–12
....79534
705 Revised....................................67587
707.6 Regulation at 75 FR 47175 confirmed...................................3488
707.11 Regulation at 75 FR 47175 confirmed...................................3488
707 Regulation at 75 FR 47175 confirmed...................................3488
708a.1 Regulation at 75 FR 80680 confirmed...................................13505
708a.101 Amended..........................13505
708b.2 Regulation at 75 FR 80680 confirmed...................................13505
717.82 (c)(2)(i)(A) revised...............18365
717 Appendix J amended................18365
725.18 (c) amended..........................60367
738 Authority citation revised......54930
738.3 (b) amended...........................54930
738 Supplement No. 1 amended......54930
740 Authority citation revised......54930
740.1 (b) and (c) redesignated as (c) and (d); new (b) added................30523
740.5 (b) amended; (c)(1) removed; (c)(2) through (12) redesignated as new (c)(1) through (11); (a) and new (c)(7) and (8) revised..30523
740.7 (c)(1) amended......................54930
740 Supplement No. 1 amended......54931
741.4 (b) amended...........................60367
741.207 Amended.............................67591
741.224 Added.................................30517
745.1 (f) added.................................30253
745.14 Added...................................30253
745 Supplement No. 2 amended......54931
748 Authority citation revised......54931
748.1 (c)(2)(ii) and (iii) revised.......18366
748.2 (a) and (b) revised..................18366
748.9 (a)(1) amended........................54931
750 Added..30517
750.1 (e) amended; interim.............36980
Regulation at 76 FR 36980 confirmed.......................................73996